Scandinavian &
Baltic Europe
on a shoestring

Glenda Bendure
Graeme Cornwallis
Steve Fallon
Ned Friary
Markus Lehtipuu
Nicola Williams

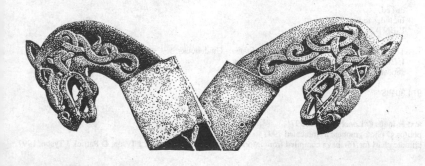

Scandinavian & Baltic Europe

3rd edition

Published by
   Lonely Planet Publications
   Head Office: PO Box 617, Hawthorn, Vic 3122, Australia
   Branches: 155 Filbert St, Suite 251, Oakland, CA 94607, USA
                  10 Barley Mow Passage, Chiswick, London W4 4PH, UK
                  71 bis rue du Cardinal Lemoine, 75005 Paris, France

Printed by
   SNP Printing Pte Ltd., Singapore

Photographs by
   Glenda Bendure (GB)   Ned Friary (NF)   Sulev Kalamäe (SK)   John Noble (JN)
   Paul Steele (PS)   Deanna Swaney (DS)   Eduards Voitkuns (EV)

   Front cover: lamp (DS)

First Published
   January 1993

This Edition
   February 1997

Although the authors and publisher have tried to make the information as
accurate as possible, they accept no responsibility for any loss, injury or
inconvenience sustained by any person using this book.

National Library of Australia Cataloguing in Publication Data

Scandinavian & Baltic Europe.

   3rd ed.
   Includes index.
   ISBN 0 86442 434 5.

   1. Scandinavia – Guidebooks. 2. Baltic States – Guidebooks.
   I. Bendure, Glenda. (Series : Lonely Planet on a
   shoestring).

914.80488

text & maps © Lonely Planet 1997
photos © photographers as indicated 1997
climate chart for Tórshavn compiled from information supplied by Patrick J Tyson, © Patrick J Tyson, 1997

Glenda Bendure

Glenda grew up in California's Mojave Desert and first travelled overseas as a high school AFS exchange student to India. She graduated from the University of California, Santa Cruz.

Ned Friary

Ned grew up near Boston, studied Social Thought & Political Economy at the University of Massachusetts in Amherst and upon graduating headed west.

Glenda and Ned, who wrote the Norway and Denmark chapters of this book, met in Santa Cruz. In 1978, with Lonely Planet's first book, *Across Asia on the Cheap*, in hand, they took the overland trail from Europe to Nepal. The next six years were spent exploring Asia and the Pacific, with a home base in Japan where Ned taught English and Glenda edited a monthly magazine. Their first book was Lonely Planet's *Micronesia – travel survival kit* and they have since authored LP's guides to *Denmark*, the *Eastern Caribbean*, *Hawaii* and *Honolulu*. Ned and Glenda live on Cape Cod in Massachusetts.

Graeme Cornwallis

Graeme updated the Faroe Islands and Iceland chapters of this book. Born and raised in Edinburgh, he later moved around Scotland before settling in Glasgow, which became a long-term base. While studying Astronomy at Glasgow University, Graeme developed a passionate interest in mountains and travel. Once he ascended all the mountains above 3000 feet in Britain and Ireland, Graeme travelled extensively in Scandinavia as well as many other parts of the world. In winter, he teaches Mathematics and Physics privately and he travels and writes in summer.

Steve Fallon

Steve worked on the introductory chapters. Born in Boston, Massachusetts, he says he can't remember a time when he was not obsessed with travel, other cultures and languages. As a teenager Steve worked an assortment of jobs to finance trips to Europe and South America, and he graduated from Georgetown University in 1975 with a Bachelor of Science in modern languages. The following year he taught English at the University of Silesia near Katowice, Poland. After he had worked for several years for a Gannett newspaper and obtained a master's degree in journalism, his fascination with the 'new' Asia took him to Hong Kong, where he lived and worked for 13 years for a variety of publications and was editor of *Business Traveller* magazine. In 1987 he put journalism on hold when he opened Wanderlust Books, Asia's only travel bookshop. Steve lived in Budapest for 2½ years from where he wrote *Hungary – travel survival kit* and *Slovenia – travel survival kit* before moving to London in 1994.

Markus Lehtipuu

Markus, a native of Finland, updated the Finland chapter and updated and rewrote much of the Sweden chapter. He left Finland at the age of 18 to work in Stockholm. Once there, he developed a passionate desire to travel. After travels in India, North Africa and Eastern Europe, he returned to Finland to study Economics. Since the early 1980s, Markus has spent a third of his time travelling and working in over 60 countries. He writes and publishes acclaimed guidebooks in Finnish and has authored *Finland – travel survival kit* for Lonely Planet. He speaks seven languages, and hopes to become fluent in Estonian soon.

Nicola Williams

Nicola, who updated the Baltic States, Kaliningrad and St Petersburg chapters of this book, caught 'the bug' in 1990 while travelling across Indonesia as an impoverished student. After three months bussing and boating it from Jakarta to East Timor, and back again, she returned to her native England to embark on a Master's degree at London's School of Oriental and African studies. Following a two-year stint as a journalist with the *North Wales Weekly News*, Nicola left the Wales of her childhood for Latvia. While bussing it round the Baltics as Features Editor for the English-language weekly *The Baltic Observer* Nicola stumbled upon the Lithuanian-based *In Your Pocket* Baltic and Russian city guides, of which she is now Editor-in-Chief.

From the Authors

Glenda Bendure & Ned Friary In Denmark, we'd like to thank Lillian Hess and Suzanna Paludan of the Danish Tourist Board; Christina Holm of Wonderful Copenhagen; Jeanett Geoffrey of Use It; and Jette Sandahl, curator of the Kvidemuseet in Århus.

In Norway, thanks to Harald Hansen of the Norwegian Tourist Board in New York; Asbjörn Gabrielsen in the Lofoten islands; Halfdan Haukeland of the Bergen Tourist Board; Karen Schimmel of the Bergen Line; Karoline Baltzersen of Oslo Promotion; Thea Martine Ottmann at the Oslo tourist office and Marius Revold of Use It ... and, of course, a hearty thanks to the numerous other helpful people we met along the way.

Graeme Cornwallis Graeme would like to thank Irene McLean (Glasgow), Penny Wilson (Glasgow), Ian Wilton (Dorset), Deanna Swaney (Alaska), Annika Joensen (Tóshavn), Oda Andreasen (Tóshavn), Ingigerð á Trøðni (Tóshavn), Harald Petersen (Klaksvík), the staff at the Tourist Information Centre in Reykjavík, Jón Illugasson (Mývatn) and Bergsveinn Ólafsson (Stafafell) for all their help.

Steve Fallon Special thanks to Michael Rothschild for keeping the fires burning (home and otherwise) over the past 20 years.

Markus Lehtipuu Special thanks to Jari Suvanto at the Swedish Tourist Office in Helsinki. Very warm thanks to Marie Persson at the Swedish State Railways, Ella Brehmer at Göteborg & Co and Birgitta Jansson at the Stockholm Information Service. Thanks also to the friendly Swedes who opened many doors.

In Finland, thanks go to Matkahuolto Oy in Helsinki, Eija Kare at VR Ltd Finnish Railways, Ulla Leppäkoski and Tarja Haili at Uudenmaan Liitto and Marja Haakana at the Finnish Youth Hostel Association. Special thanks to Russel Snyder and Johanna Rämö for support during the research and writing.

Nicola Williams Big thanks to Reine, Nomeda, Narimantas, Vikis, Anya, Rūta and all the In Your Pocket teams in Rīga and Vilnius; the two Neils, Nick Selby (& his doctor), Andrew Humphreys, Stephen Dewar, Steve Caron; Michael, Maureen, James, Tricia, Tarvo and Anu. Biggest thanks of all to Matthias Lüfkens for sharing his Baltic love.

This Book

The first edition of this book was researched by Glenda Bendure and Ned Friary (Denmark and Norway), John Noble (the Baltic states), Deanna Swaney (Iceland and the Faroe Islands) and Greg Videon (Finland and Sweden). The second edition was updated by Glenda and Ned, Andrew Humphreys (the Baltic states and Kaliningrad), Deanna, Markus Lehtipuu (Finland) and Greg (Sweden). The St Petersburg chapter in this edition was adapted from LP's *Russia, Ukraine & Belarus – travel survival kit.*

Scandinavian & Baltic Europe is part of LP's Europe shoestring series, which includes *Western Europe*, *Central Europe*, *Eastern Europe* and *Mediterranean Europe*. LP also publishes phrasebooks for these regions.

From the Publisher

This edition was edited and proofed by Lindsay Brown, Anne Mulvaney, Karin Riederer, Jane Fitzpatrick and Bethune Carmichael. Tony Fankhauser coordinated the maps and book design with help from Dorothy Natsikas, Lyndell Taylor and Tamsin Wilson. Thanks to Paul Hellander for the e-mail advice; to Vicky Wayland (LP UK) and Sacha Pearson (LP US) for comments on the introductory chapters; to Paul Clifton for the colour and back cover maps and to David Kemp and Simon Bracken for the cover. Special thanks to Dan Levin for technical wizardry.

Thanks

Thanks to the following travellers for writing to us about their travel experiences in Scandinavian and Baltic Europe (apologies if we've misspelt your name):

Mark & Tanya Allingham, Kerry Barker, Carol Bonchard, AnnMarie Critien, Caroline Dye, Froydis Erstad, Beverley Farmer, Seth Frankel, David Fuller, Margaret Garrett, Derek Griffis, E H M Harbers, Esther & John Horton, Richard Jones, Simon Kennedy, Debbie Kruse, Manda Leong, Michael Liddy, Alison Marten, James Murphy, Gudrun Rishede, Hugh Saffrey, Rob Scheffers, Simon Scott-Kemball, Irena Vrbova, Derek Weatherley, Chris White

Warning & Request

Things change – prices go up, schedules change, good places go bad and bad places go bankrupt – nothing stays the same. So, if you find things better or worse, recently opened or long since closed, please tell us and help make the next edition even more accurate and useful.

We value all of the feedback we receive from travellers. Julie Young coordinates a small team who read and acknowledge every letter, postcard and e-mail, and ensure that every morsel of information finds its way to the appropriate authors, editors and publishers.

Everyone who writes to us will find their name in the next edition of the appropriate guide and will also receive a free subscription to our quarterly newsletter, Planet Talk. The very best contributions will be rewarded with a free Lonely Planet guide.

Excerpts from your correspondence may appear in updates (which we add to the end pages of reprints); new editions of this guide; in our newsletter, Planet Talk; or in the Postcards section of our Web site – so please let us know if you don't want your letter published or your name acknowledged.

Contents

Map Legend

BOUNDARIES

.... International Boundary
.... Regional Boundary
.... Arctic/Antarctic Circle
_25°N_ .... Latitudes & Longitudes

ROUTES

.... Freeway
.... Highway
.... Major Road
.... Unsealed Road or Track
.... City Road
.... City Street
.... Railway
.... Metro Line
.... Underground Railway
.... Walking Track, Bicycle Track
.... Ferry Route
.... Cable Car or Chairlift

AREA FEATURES

.... Parks
.... Built-Up Area
.... Pedestrian Mall
.... Market
.... Cemetery
.... Reef
.... Beach or Desert
.... Glacier, Ice Cap

HYDROGRAPHIC FEATURES

.... Coastline
.... River, Creek
.... Intermittent River or Creek
.... Rapids, Waterfalls
.... Lake, Intermittent Lake
.... Canal
.... Swamp

SYMBOLS

✪ CAPITAL		National Capital
◉ Capital		Regional Capital
⬤ CITY		Major City
● City		City
● Town		Town
• Village		Village
■ ▼		Place to Stay, Place to Eat
☕ ☗		Cafe, Pub or Bar
✉ ☎		Post Office, Telephone
❶ ⑤		Tourist Information, Bank
⊖ ₽		Transport, Parking
⛪ ⬆		Museum, Youth Hostel
⛺ ⚑		Caravan Park, Camping Ground
⛪ ✚		Church, Cathedral
☪ ✡		Mosque, Synagogue
⊞ 卍		Buddhist Temple, Hindu Temple
✚ ★		Hospital, Police Station

◎ ☗		Embassy, Petrol Station
✈ ✝		Airport, Airfield
▭ ✿		Swimming Pool, Gardens
❖ 🐾		Shopping Centre, Zoo
⚘ ⛱		Winery or Vineyard, Picnic Site
← A25		One Way Street, Route Number
⛫ ♟		Stately Home, Monument
⛉ ▣		Castle, Tomb
⌒ ⌂		Cave, Hut or Chalet
▲ ❋		Mountain or Hill, Lookout
⛯ ⚓		Lighthouse, Shipwreck
)(◎		Pass, Spring
➴ ➘		Beach, Surf Beach
∴		Archaeological Site or Ruins
		Ancient or City Wall
		Cliff or Escarpment, Tunnel
ⓜ		Railway Station, Metro Station

Note: not all symbols displayed above appear in this book

Introduction

Scandinavia and the Baltic states encompass a huge area around the Baltic Sea and out into the frigid North Atlantic Ocean, offering the visitor rugged wilderness, safe travel, spectacular scenery and wonderful natural sights such as the aurora borealis and the midnight sun.

The countries covered in *Scandinavian & Baltic Europe on a shoestring* have everything from strikingly beautiful fjords, glaciers and mountains to the treeless arctic tundra. The cities range from cosmopolitan Copenhagen to the East-West blend of Helsinki, from modern Stockholm to the resurgent capitals of the Baltic states – Tallinn, Rīga and Vilnius with their lively arts and entertainment scenes – as well as St Petersburg, Russia's most European and enchanting city. Outdoor enthusiasts will get their fill of activities in Scandinavia from ski-touring in Norway or exploring the glaciers, hot springs, geysers and volcanoes of Iceland or bird-watching in the starkly beautiful Faroe Islands.

The range of attractions in the region is great. Norway has unspoiled fishing villages, rich historic sites including Viking ships and medieval stave churches; Denmark has Viking ruins and unspoiled islands; Sweden has impressive museums and national parks with many walking trails. Visitors to Finland can cruise around giant lakes and experience the Russian influence in the south and see reindeer in the north. The Baltic states have capital cities whose hearts are architectural delights, as well as interesting islands and coastal areas. St Petersburg is a treasure trove of architecture and culture.

Scandinavia and the Baltic states are vastly different regions and offer vivid contrasts: there are popular swimming beaches along the coast of Denmark, whereas Norway, Sweden and Finland all extend beyond the Arctic Circle. Sweden has in the past managed to combine socialist principles with some of the most successful capitalist enterprises on earth. The Baltic states and St Petersburg are once again hotbeds for local entrepreneurship after two generations of Soviet rule.

This book takes you through the Scandinavian and Baltic regions as well as St Petersburg and the intriguing Kaliningrad area, Russian territory reopened to foreign tourists in 1991, from predeparture preparations to packing your bag for the return home. There's information on how to get there and how to get around once you've arrived whether it's by ferry across the Baltic Sea or by bicycle along Danish cycling routes.

Scandinavia is famed for its high costs, but prices are more affordable than they have been for a long time. Several hard years of recession have brought real bargains to travellers and this book details the many ways of finding them – from staying in Denmark's *vandrerhjem* (hostels) to eating at Norway's *konditori* (bakeries). There are extensive recommendations about where to stay including backpacker hostels in the Baltic states and farmhouse accommodation in Iceland. Dining possibilities are also covered extensively, from Denmark's famed *smørrebrød* to traditional Icelandic dishes you'd probably rather not know about like *hakarl* (putrefied shark meat)

Scandinavia and the Baltic states offer travellers a real chance for adventure exploring natural and cultural frontiers. All you have to do is go.

Facts for the Visitor

There are those who say that much of Scandinavian and Baltic Europe is so well developed you don't have to plan a thing before your trip since anything can be arranged on the spot. As any experienced traveller knows, the problems you thought about at home often turn out to be irrelevant or will sort themselves out once you're on the move.

This is fine if you've decided to blow the massive inheritance sitting in your bank account, but if your financial status is somewhat more modest, a bit of prior knowledge and careful planning can make your hard-earned travel budget stretch further than you thought it would, an important consideration in pricey Scandinavia. You'll also want to make sure that the things you plan to see and do will be possible at the particular time of year when you'll be travelling.

PLANNING
When to Go

Any time can be the best time to visit Europe, depending on what you want to do. Summer offers the most pleasant climate for outdoor pursuits in the northern half of Europe. In general, the short summers in Scandinavia last from June to August and temperatures can get relatively hot; this is the best time for comfortable travelling is the region. Of course, everything will be crowded at the popular tourist destinations, but there are also surprises. In many Scandinavian cities, and especially in smaller towns, hotels cut their prices to less than half the ordinary winter ones, the supply of beds grows enormously as youth hostels, school dormitories, camping grounds and holiday villages open up. And naturally, the so-called right of common access (see Camping in the Accommodation section) is really only useful in summer, when camping in the woods would make any sense at all. Also, when it comes to entertainment, summer is certainly the best time to go, with festivals and other events taking place everywhere.

After August most tourists disappear, schools reopen and many summer activities wind down. September is a pleasant time to be in the region, but you most definitely get the impression it's already autumn. In the southern part of Sweden, spring is beautiful in early May.

If you want to enjoy concerts and beaches in Denmark, the best time of the year to visit is from late June to August. The shoulder seasons from May to June and from September until mid-October are less crowded, most sights are open and the weather is good.

Unless you're into winter sports such as skiing or you are in search of the aurora borealis, May to September is the best time to visit Norway: it's warmest then and the daylight hours are very long, even in Oslo and the south. Between late June (after midsummer) and mid-August is the best time for a visit to Finland (June to mid-August is the summer season): more hostels are open, the weather is at its best and there are fewer public holidays to disrupt your travel plans.

If you are keen on winter sports, you can find good accommodation deals in some Scandinavian cities during winter. In Iceland the tourist trade starts to slow down from mid-August, and by mid-September the main tourist attractions are inaccessible. Transport services are cut back during winter but there is skiing at Reykjavík and Akureyri. Tourist facilities in the Faroe Islands only operate from June to September.

If you're visiting the Baltic states, the annual Baltika folklore festival is held in mid-July. The climate is best in May, June and September. There's snow from mid-December to mid-March (as late as May in northern and central Scandinavia).

The Climate & When to Go sections in the individual country chapters explain what to expect and when to expect it, and the Climate Charts appendix in the back of the book will help you compare different destinations. As a rule, spring and autumn tend to be wetter and windier than summer and winter. The climate along the Norwegian coast is moderated by the warm Gulf Stream and is relatively wet all year.

What Kind of Trip?
Travelling Companions Travelling alone is not a problem in Scandinavia and the Baltic states; the region is well developed and safe.

If you decide to travel with others, keep in mind that travel can put relationships to the test like few other experiences can. Many a long-term friendship has collapsed under the strains of constant negotiations about where to stay and eat, what to see and where to go next. But many friendships have also become closer than ever before. You won't find out until you try, but make sure you agree on itineraries and routines beforehand and try to remain flexible about everything.

If travel is a good way of testing established friendships, it's also a great way of making new ones. Hostels and camping grounds are good places to meet fellow travellers, so even if you're travelling alone, you need never be lonely. Although in Scandinavia, not particularly known for its gregarious, extroverted people, you may have to work harder at making friends (fruitful in Norway and Finland, harder in Sweden, probably easiest in Denmark).

The Getting Around chapter has information on organised tours. The young, the elderly and the inexperienced tend to appreciate such tours because they take the daily hassles and uncertainties out of travel. Longer tours, however, can become experiments in social cohesion and friction can develop.

Move or Stay? 'If this is Saturday, it must be Stockholm.' Though often ridiculed, the mad dash that crams six countries into a month does have its merits. If you've never visited Scandinavia or the Baltic states before, you won't know which areas you'll like, and a quick 'scouting tour' will give an overview of the options. A rail pass that offers unlimited travel within a set period of time is the best way to do this.

But if you know where you want to go, or find a place you like, the best advice is to stay put for a while, discover some of the lesser known sights, perhaps make a few local friends and settle in. It's also cheaper in the long run.

Maps
Good maps are easy to come by once you're in Europe, but you might want to buy a few beforehand, especially if you're driving or cycling. The maps in this book will be a useful first reference when you arrive in a city.

You can't go wrong with Michelin maps, and because of their soft covers, they fold up easily so you can stick them in your pocket. Some people prefer the meticulously produced Freytag & Berndt, Kümmerly & Frey or Hallwag maps, which have been recommended for Scandinavian countries. Falk Plan city maps are very usable and detailed, and the Falk map of Scandinavia is good. In Scandinavia (notably Denmark), tourist offices are an excellent source for free maps.

The best road maps in Norway are Cappelens, while in Denmark Kort og Matrikels-tyrelsen's maps are recommended. In Finland, Karttakeskus sells excellent maps, especially the GT series, which is very useful. In Scandinavia, tourist office country maps can be excellent; they are free and up-to-date. See the Facts for the Visitor section of the Estonia chapter for recommended maps of the Baltic countries.

Online Services
The following web sites offer useful general information about European cities, transport systems, currencies etc:

Lonely Planet
  http://www.lonelyplanet.com. Lonely Planet's own web site is packed with information on Europe and other destinations, and is extensively hot-linked to other useful sites.

Tourist Offices
    http://www.mbnet.mb.ca/lucas/travel. Lists tourist offices at home and around the world for most countries.

Rail Information
    http://www.raileurope.com. Train fares and schedules on the most popular routes in Europe, including information on rail and youth passes.

Airline Information
    http://www.travelocity.com. What airlines fly where, when and for how much.

Currency Converters
    http://bin.gnn.com/cgi-bin/gnn/currency & http://pacific.commerce.ubc.ca/xr. Exchange rates of hundreds of currencies worldwide.

See the E-mail section under Post & Communications for some general advice on gaining access to the Internet while on the move in Europe.

What to Bring

Taking along as little as possible is the best policy. But although it's very easy to find almost anything you need along the way, most people travelling in this part of the world don't tend to buy things as they travel because of the high price of goods and value-added tax (VAT). Just be very selective as you pack and if you only think you *may* need an item or article of clothing, leave it out.

A backpack is still the most popular method of carrying gear as it is convenient, especially for walking. On the down side, a backpack doesn't offer too much protection for your valuables, the straps tend to get caught on things and some airlines may refuse to accept responsibility if the pack is damaged or tampered with.

Travelpacks, a combination backpack/shoulder bag, are very popular. The backpack straps zip away inside the pack when they are not needed, so you almost have the best of both worlds. Some packs have sophisticated shoulder-strap adjustment systems and can be used comfortably even on long hikes. Packs are always much easier to carry than a bag. Another alternative is a large, soft zip-bag with a wide shoulder strap so it can be carried with relative ease if necessary. Backpacks or travelpacks can be

made reasonably theft-proof with small padlocks. Forget suitcases altogether.

As for clothing, the climate will have a bearing on what you bring along. Remember that insulation works on the principle of trapped air, so several layers of thin clothing are warmer than a single thick one (and will be easier to dry, too). You'll also be much more flexible if the weather suddenly turns warm on you. Just be prepared for rain at any time of year. A minimum packing list could include:

- underwear, socks and swimming gear
- a pair of jeans and maybe a pair of shorts
- a few T-shirts and shirts
- a warm sweater
- a solid pair of walking shoes
- sandals or thongs for showers
- a coat or jacket
- a raincoat, waterproof jacket or umbrella
- a medical kit and sewing kit
- a padlock
- a Swiss Army knife
- soap and towel
- toothpaste, toothbrush and other toiletries

A padlock is useful to lock your bag to a luggage rack in a bus or train; it may also be needed to secure your hostel locker or for locking your room itself in some of the seedy, cheap hotels in Estonia, Latvia or Lithuania. A Swiss Army knife comes in handy for all sorts of things. (*Any* pocket knife is fine but make sure it includes such essentials as a bottle opener and strong corkscrew.) Soap, toothpaste and toilet paper are readily obtainable almost anywhere, as is paper in public toilets and those at camping grounds in Scandinavia. In Scandinavia, using toilets in public areas costs a sizeable chunk of change; plan visits carefully, use restaurant toilets discreetly and – boys – be on the lookout for trees. Tampons are available at pharmacies and supermarkets everywhere, including the Baltic states. Condoms, both locally made and imported, are widely available.

A tent and sleeping bag are vital if you want to save money by camping. Even if you're not camping, a sleeping bag is still very useful. It can double as a cushion on hard train-seats, a seat for long waits at bus or railway stations, and a bedspread in cold hotels (get one that can be used as a quilt). A sleeping bag will make it easier for you to take advantage of the free accommodation along trekking routes in Finland. A cheaper form of accommodation in the Faroe Islands is called 'sleeping-bag accommodation'.

A sleeping sheet with pillow cover (case) is necessary if you plan to stay in hostels. You may have to hire or purchase one if you don't bring your own. In any case, a sheet that fits into your sleeping bag is easier to wash than the bag itself. Make one yourself out of old sheets (include a built-in pillow cover), or buy one from your hostel association.

Other optional items include a compass, a torch (flashlight), an alarm clock, an adapter plug for electrical appliances (such as a cup or coil immersion heater to save on tea and coffee), a universal bath/sink plug (a film canister sometimes works), sunglasses, a few clothes pegs, and premoistened towelettes or a large cotton handkerchief that you can soak in fountains and use to cool off while touring cities in the warm summer months. During city sightseeing, a small daypack is better than a shoulder bag at deterring snatch thieves.

Finally, consider using plastic carry bags or garbage-bin liners inside your backpack to keep things separate but also dry if the pack gets soaked. Airlines do lose luggage from time to time, but you have a much better chance of it not being yours if it is tagged with your name and address *inside* the bag as well as outside; outside tags can always fall off or be removed.

Appearances & Conduct

Dress standards are fairly informal in northern Europe. By all means dress casually, but ensure sufficient body cover (trousers or a knee-length dress) if your sightseeing includes churches, monasteries or synagogues. Wearing shorts away from the beach, camp site or back garden is not very common among men in Europe. Some nightclubs and fancy restaurants may refuse entry to people wearing jeans, sneakers (trainers) or a tracksuit; men need only consider packing a tie if they plan on dining out at very up-market restaurants. In Estonia, Lithuania, and Latvia you can get away with wearing jeans (provided they're clean) and sneakers and, for men, no tie is needed in even the most select dining rooms.

Nude bathing is usually limited to restricted beach areas, but topless bathing among women is common in many parts of Scandinavia, particularly on the beaches of Denmark, where it can almost seem mandatory. However, women should be wary of topless bathing, especially in Finland where it is uncommon; the rule is, if nobody else seems to be doing it, don't you either.

Northern Europeans often shake hands and even kiss when they greet one another. Finns are the exception to this rule; they are happy to shake hands but they rarely kiss as a form of greeting. Depending on the country, you should get into the habit of shaking hands frequently. It is customary in many countries to greet the owner, bartender or shopkeeper when you enter a shop, quiet bar or café and to say goodbye when you leave.

The Top 10

There is so much to see in Scandinavian and Baltic Europe that compiling a top 10 is almost impossible. But we asked the authors of this book to list their personal highlights, and the results are as follows:

1. Geirangerfjord, Norway's western fjords
2. Frederiksborg Castle, Hillerød, Denmark
3. Mývatn, Iceland
4. Gamla Stan, Stockholm
5. Lofoten islands, north-west Norway
6. Bygdøy Viking Ship Museum, Oslo
7. Karelia and Saimaa lakes, Finland
8. The historic old towns of Tallinn (Estonia) and Vilnius (Lithuania)
9. The *Hurtigruten* coastal steamer trip from Bergen to Kirkenes, Norway
10. The Hermitage, St Petersburg

The Bottom 10

The writers were also asked to list the 10 worst sights and came up with the following:

1. Gröna Lund Tivoli, Stockholm
2. Santa Claus' house, Rovaniemi, Finland
3. The Little Mermaid, Copenhagen
4. Metro paintings, Stockholm
5. Cosy Danish cafés thick with cigar smoke
6. Seal clubbing display at Polar Museum, Tromsø, Norway
7. Legoland (Denmark) without kids
8. Blue Lagoon, Iceland
9. The Soviet-era suburbs of any sizeable town in Estonia, Latvia or Lithuania
10. Scandinavian tourists bingeing on duty-free booze

VISAS & DOCUMENTS
Passport
Your most important travel document is your passport, which should remain valid until well after your trip. If it's just about to expire, renew it before you go; having this done while travelling can be inconvenient and time-consuming. Some countries insist that your passport remain valid for a specified minimum period (usually three months but sometimes up to six months) after your visit. Even if they don't insist on this, expect questions from immigration officials if your passport is due to expire in a short time.

If you don't have a passport, you'll have to apply for one, which can be an involved process. A renewal or application can take anything from an hour to several months, depending on many factors, so don't leave it till the last minute (it can sometimes be speeded up with a good excuse, though this may attract a higher fee). Bureaucracy usually grinds faster if you do everything in person at the actual passport-issuing office rather than relying on the mail or agents. Check first what you need to bring with you: photos of a certain size, birth certificate, population register extract, signed statements, exact payment in cash etc.

Australian citizens can apply at a post office or the passport office in their state capital; Britons can get application forms from major post offices, and the passport is issued by the regional passport office; Canadians can apply at regional passport offices; New Zealanders can apply at any district office of the Department of Internal Affairs; US citizens must apply in person (but may usually renew by mail) at a US Passport Agency office or some courthouses and post offices.

Citizens of many European countries don't always need a valid passport to travel within the region; a national identity card may be sufficient. A citizen of the European Union (EU) travelling to another EU country will generally face the least problems. But if you want to take advantage of these options, check with your travel agent or the embassies of the countries you plan to visit.

Once you start travelling, carry your passport at all times and guard it carefully (see Photocopies below for extra security procedures). Some countries require residents and aliens alike to carry personal identification.

Visas
A visa is a stamp in your passport or a separate piece of paper permitting you to enter the country in question and stay for a specified period of time. There's a wide variety, including tourist, transit and business visas. Transit visas are usually cheaper than tourist or business visas, but they only allow a very short stay (one or two days) and can be difficult to extend. Often you can get the visa at the border or at the airport on arrival, but not for the Baltic states or Russia; check first with the embassies or consulates of the countries you plan to visit.

It's important to remember that visas have a 'use-by date', and you'll be refused entry after that period has elapsed. Also, visa requirements can change, and you should always check with the individual embassies or consulates or a reputable travel agent before travelling. If you plan to get your visas as you go along rather than arranging them all beforehand, carry spare passport photos.

Most readers of this book will have little to do with visas unless they're going to Russia or perhaps one of the Baltic states (see the accompanying Visa Requirements table and the relevant country chapters for more information). With a valid passport most travellers will be able to visit Scandinavian and Baltic countries for up to three (some-

Visas Requirements Country of Origin						
Aust	*Can*	*Ire*	*NZ*	*Sing*	*UK*	*USA*
Denmark (Faroe Is) –	–	–	–	–	–	–
Estonia –	–	–	–	✓	–	–
Finland –	–	–	–	–	–	–
Iceland –	–	–	–	–	–	–
Latvia ✓	✓	–	✓	✓	–	–
Lithuania –	–	–	✓	✓	–	–
Norway –	–	–	–	–	–	–
Russia ✓	✓	✓	✓	✓	✓	✓
Sweden –	–	–	–	–	–	–

✓ Tourist visa required

times even six) months, provided they have some sort of onward or return ticket and/or 'sufficient means of support' (money). Except at international airports, it's unlikely that immigration officials will give you and your passport more than a cursory glance – if one at all.

Many EU countries have abolished passport controls between their borders and an identity card should be sufficient, but it's always safest to carry your passport.

Photocopies
The hassles brought on by losing your passport can be considerably reduced if you have a record of its number and issue date, or even better, photocopies of the relevant data pages. A photocopy of your birth certificate can also be useful.

Also add the serial numbers of your travellers' cheques (cross them off as you cash them) and photocopies of your credit cards, airline ticket and other travel documents. Keep all this emergency material separate from your passport, cheques and cash, and leave extra copies with someone you can rely on back home. Add some emergency money, say US$50 in cash, to this separate stash. If you do lose your passport, notify the police immediately to get a statement, and contact your nearest consulate.

Travel Insurance
You should seriously consider taking out travel insurance. This not only covers you for medical expenses and luggage theft or loss but also for cancellation or delays in your travel arrangements. (You could fall seriously ill two days before departure, for example.) Cover depends on your insurance and type of airline ticket, so ask both your insurer and your ticket-issuing agency to explain where you stand. Ticket loss is also covered by travel insurance.

Buy travel insurance as early as possible. If you buy it the week before you fly, you may find, for instance, that you're not covered for delays to your flight caused by strikes or other industrial actions that may have been in force before you took out the insurance.

Paying for your airline ticket with a credit card often provides limited travel accident insurance, and you may be able to reclaim the payment if the operator doesn't deliver. In the UK, for instance, institutions issuing credit cards are required by law to reimburse consumers if a company goes into liquidation and the amount in contention is more than UK£100. Ask your credit card company what it's prepared to cover. See also Health Insurance in the Health section later.

International Driving Permit
Your local driver's licence will probably be acceptable for motoring in the region but play it safe by getting an IDP from your local automobile association before you leave –

you'll need a passport photo and a valid licence. They are usually inexpensive and valid for one year only. An IDP helps Europeans make sense of your unfamiliar local licence (make sure you take that with you, too) and can make life much simpler, especially when hiring cars and motorcycles.

Also ask your automobile association for a Letter of Introduction (Lettre de Recomandation). This entitles you to services offered by affiliated organisations in Europe, usually free of charge (touring maps and information, help with breakdowns, technical and legal advice etc). See the Getting Around chapter for more details on driving with your own vehicle.

Camping Card International
Your local automobile association also issues the Camping Card International, which is basically a camping ground ID. These cards are also available from your local camping federation, and sometimes on the spot at camping grounds. They incorporate third-party insurance for damage you may cause, and many camping grounds offer a small discount if you sign in with one.

Hostelling Card
A hostelling card is useful for those staying at hostels. It may not be mandatory in Scandinavia but a Hostelling International (HI) card will mean a sizeable discount every time you check in. Some hostels will issue one on the spot or after a few stays, though this might cost a bit more than getting it in your home country. See Hostels in the later Accommodation section for more details.

Student & Youth Cards
The most useful of these is the International Student Identity Card (ISIC), a plastic ID-style card with your photograph, which provides discounts on many forms of transport (including airlines and local public transport), reduced or free admission to museums and sights, and cheap meals in some student restaurants – a worthwhile way of cutting costs in expensive Scandinavia.

There is a worldwide industry in fake student cards, and many places now stipulate a maximum age for student discounts or, more simply, they've substituted a 'youth discount' for a 'student discount'. If you're aged under 26 but not a student, you can apply for a GO25 card issued by the Federation of International Youth Travel Organisations (FIYTO), or the Euro<26 card, which goes under various names in different countries. All these cards are available through student unions, hostelling organisations or youth-oriented travel agencies. They don't automatically entitle you to discounts, and some companies and institutions refuse to recognise them altogether, but you won't find out until you flash the card.

Senior Cards
Museums and other sights, public swimming pools and spas and transport companies frequently offer discounts to retired people/OAPs/those over 60 (sometimes slightly younger for women). Make sure you bring proof of age; the ever proper, always polite Scandinavian ticket-taker is not going to believe you're a day over 39.

For a small fee, European nationals aged over 60 can get a Rail Europe Senior Card as an add-on to their national rail senior pass. It entitles the holder to reduced fares in some European countries, and percentage savings vary according to the route. See Cheap Tickets under Train in the introductory Getting Around chapter. See Rail Passes in the same section for details on the ScanRail 55+ pass.

International Health Certificate
You'll need this yellow booklet only if you're coming to the region from certain parts of Asia, Africa and South America, where outbreaks of such diseases as yellow fever have been reported. See Immunisations in the Health section for more information on jabs.

CUSTOMS
Throughout most of Scandinavia, the usual allowances on tobacco (eg 200 cigarettes), alcohol (two litres of wine, one of spirits) and

A	B	D
C		E
F		
G	H	

A Chalk cliffs, Møns Klint, Den (NF)
B Tilsandede Kirke, Skagen, Den (GB)
C Alexandr Nevsky Cathedral, Tallinn, Est (SK)
D Estonian Boy (SK)
E Farmhouse door, Streymoy, Far (DS)
F Sibelius Monument, Helsinki, Fin (PS)
G Graffiti in subway, Reykjavík, Ice (DS)
H Uspensky Cathedral, Helsinki, Fin (PS)

A	B
C	D
	E
F	G
	H

A Street market, Kal (JN)

B Tower & bathhouse, Svetlogorsk, Kal (JN)

C Meistaru iela, Rīga, Lat (EV)

D Hill of Crosses, Šiauliai, Lith (JN)

E Reindeer, Nor (PS)

F Geirangerfjord, Nor (PS)

G Midnight Sun, Lappland, Swe (PS)

H Stockholm, Swe (PS)

perfume (50g) apply to *duty-free* goods purchased at the airport or on ferries. Do not confuse these with *duty-paid* items (including alcohol and tobacco) bought at normal shops and supermarkets in one EU country and brought into another EU country, where certain goods might be more expensive. Then the allowances are more than generous: 800 cigarettes; 10/90 litres of spirits/wine; unlimited quantities of perfume.

Customs inspections among EU countries have all but ceased. They can be quite thorough, though, between liberal Denmark and more conservative Sweden. At most border crossings and airports elsewhere they are pretty cursory, but not always.

MONEY
Costs
First, a general disclaimer about all those prices that we list so faithfully throughout this book: they're likely to change, probably upwards, but if last season was particularly slow they just might come down. Nevertheless, relative price levels should stay fairly constant – if hotel A costs twice as much as hotel B, it's likely to stay that way.

Scandinavia is expensive, even by European standards. Nevertheless, it is possible to travel in the region without spending a fortune.

One secret is cheap accommodation. There's a highly developed network of camping grounds, some of them quite luxurious, and they're great places to meet people. The hostel network, too, is well developed, and used equally by all age groups. Except for Estonia, camping and hostels are not so well developed, but hotels can be quite cheap.

Other money-saving strategies include using a student card, which offers worthwhile discounts (see the Visas & Documents section); various rail and public transport passes (see the Getting Around chapter); and applying for consumer tax rebates on purchases (see the following Taxes & Refunds section and the Facts for the Visitor sections of the individual countries). Avoiding alcohol in most of the Scandinavian countries is probably the best money-saving strategy of all. For the most part you can afford to drink your fill in the Baltic states and Russia.

Including transport, but not private motorised transport, your daily expenses could be around US$40 a day if you're on a rock-bottom budget. This means camping or staying in hostels, eating economically and using a transport pass. In Estonia, Latvia and Lithuania using rock-bottom priced hotels you might get by on US$25 a day.

Travelling on a moderate budget you should be able to manage on US$60 to US$80 a day. This would allow you to stay at cheap hotels, guesthouses or B&Bs. You could afford meals in economical restaurants and maybe even one or two beers!

Cash
Nothing beats cash for convenience... or risk. If you lose it, it's gone forever and very few travel insurers will come to your rescue. Those that will, limit the amount paid out to about US$300.

It's still a good idea, though, to bring some local currency in cash, if only to tide you over until you get to an exchange facility or find an automatic teller machine (ATM). The equivalent of, say, US$100 should usually be enough. Some extra cash in an easily exchanged currency (eg US dollars or Deutschmarks) is also a good idea. Remember that banks will always accept paper money but very rarely coins in foreign currencies, so you might want to spend (or donate) your local coins before you cross a border.

Travellers' Cheques
The main idea of carrying travellers' cheques rather than cash is the protection they offer from theft, though they are losing their popularity as more travellers – including those on tight budgets – deposit their money in their bank at home and withdraw it as they go along through ATMs. American Express, Visa and Thomas Cook cheques are widely accepted and have efficient replacement policies for lost and stolen cheques.

A limited amount of travellers' cheques may be useful in the Baltic states though it can still be difficult to find places to exchange them and commissions are often high. American Express and Thomas Cook seem to be the best choices as they have a couple of offices in the Baltic states where you can get replacement cheques.

Keeping a record of the cheque numbers and those you have used is vital when it comes to replacing lost travellers' cheques. You should keep this separate from the cheques themselves. Cheques are available in various currencies, but ones denominated in US dollars and Deutschmarks are the easiest to cash. Still, you might not be comfortable using a currency you're not familiar with and watching it converted into still another (for example an Australian cashing Deutschmark cheques into Finnish markka) is confusing and risky

When you change cheques, don't look at just the exchange rate; ask about fees and commissions as well. There may be a per-cheque service fee, a flat transaction fee, or a percentage of the total amount irrespective of the number of cheques. Some banks charge fees to cash cheques and not cash; others do the reverse. But in most European countries these days, the exchange rate for travellers' cheques is slightly better than the exchange rate for cash.

Plastic Cards & ATMs

A credit card can be an ideal travelling companion. If you're not familiar with credit, credit/debit, debit and charge cards, ask your bank to explain the workings and relative merits of each. Make sure you know what to do in case of theft (telephone hotline numbers).

With a credit card you can put big expenses like airline tickets on your account and save carrying so much cash and so many travellers' cheques around with you. Another major advantage is that they allow you to withdraw cash at selected banks or to draw money from ATMs.

ATMs linked up internationally will give you instant cash as soon as you punch in your personal identification number (PIN). Cirrus is accepted throughout Norway and Iceland, and is slowly appearing in Sweden and Denmark though not yet in Finland or the Baltic States. Remember that ATMs aren't completely fail-safe. If an ATM swallows your card abroad it can be a major headache. You should also ask which ATMs abroad will accept your particular card. Note that many ATMs in Europe won't accept PIN numbers of more than four digits.

Cash cards, which you use at home to withdraw money directly from your bank account, are also widely linked internationally – ask your bank at home for advice. Withdrawals may incur a small transaction fee.

If you use a credit card to get money from an ATM, you pay interest on the money from the moment you get it. You can get around that by leaving the card in credit when you depart or by having somebody at home pay money into the card account from time to time. On the plus side, you don't pay commission charges to exchange money and the exchange rate is usually at a better interbank rate than that offered for travellers' cheques or cash exchanges. Bear in mind that if you use a credit card for purchases, exchange rates may have changed by the time your bill is processed, which can work out to your advantage or disadvantage. Credit cards are very popular in Scandinavia; Visa is the most common one followed by MasterCard.

Credit and charge cards are widely accepted at hotels and restaurants in the Baltic states, especially at the upper end of the market. There are now several Visa ATMs and Diners Club, MasterCard and American Express are also available.

Charge cards like American Express and Diners Club have offices in most countries, and they can generally replace a lost card within 24 hours. That's because they treat you as a customer of the company rather than of the bank that issued the card. In theory, the credit they offer is unlimited and they don't charge interest on outstanding accounts, but they do charge fees for joining and annual membership, and payment is due in full within a few weeks of the account statement date. Charge cards may also be hooked up to ATM networks.

Credit and credit/debit cards like Visa and MasterCard are more widely accepted because they tend to charge merchants lower commissions. Their major drawback is that they have a credit limit based on your regular income, and this limit can stop you in your tracks if you are charging major expenses like long-term car rental or long-distance airline tickets and travelling extensively. You can get around this by leaving your card in credit when you leave home. Other drawbacks are that interest is charged on outstanding accounts, either immediately or after a set period (always immediately on cash advances) and that the card can be very difficult to replace if lost abroad.

If you choose to rely on plastic, go for two different cards – a Visa or MasterCard, for instance, with an American Express or Diners Club backup. Better still is a combination of credit card and travellers' cheques so you have something to fall back on if an ATM swallows your card or the banks in the area won't accept it for some inexplicable reason.

A word of warning: though it is not common in this region, fraudulent shopkeepers have been known quickly to make several charge-slip imprints with customers' credit cards when they're not looking; they then simply copy the signature from the authorised slip. Try not to let your card out of your sight, and always check your statements carefully.

International Transfers

If you run out of money, need more and your card won't work in the ATM, you can instruct your bank back home to send you a draft. Make sure you specify the city, the bank and the branch to which you want your money directed, or ask your home bank to tell you where a suitable one is, and ensure you get the details correct.

The whole procedure will be easier if you've authorised someone back home to access your account. Also, a transfer to a tiny bank in a remote village in Lapland is obviously going to be more difficult than to the head office in Helsinki. If you have the choice, find a large bank and ask for the international division.

Money sent by telegraphic transfer (there will be costs involved, typically from US$40) should reach you within a week; by mail, allow at least two weeks. When it arrives, it will most likely be converted into local currency – you can take it in cash or buy travellers' cheques.

You can also transfer money faster through American Express or Thomas Cook; the former charges US$40 for amounts up to US$300 and US$70 for amounts over US$500. Western Union Money Transfers can be collected from banks throughout Scandinavian Europe.

Guaranteed Cheques

Guaranteed personal cheques are another way of carrying money or obtaining cash, though they are still not very common in Scandinavia. The most popular of these is the Eurocheque. To get Eurocheques and the required guarantee card, you need a European bank account; depending on the bank, it takes at least two weeks to apply for the cheques.

Currency Exchange

Most currencies can be easily exchanged but US dollars and Deutschmarks followed by pounds sterling and Swiss and French francs are the best to carry. You may well decide, however, that other currencies suit your purposes better. You lose out through commissions and customer exchange rates every time you change money, so if you only visit Finland, for example, you may be better off buying some markkaa straight away if your bank at home can provide them.

All Scandinavian currencies are fully convertible; the currencies of the three Baltic states – Estonian kroons, Latvian lats and Lithuanian litas – are stable but at various stages of convertibility. See the Money section in the relevant country chapters for further details.

Unlike in the rest of Europe, travellers should avoid banks in Scandinavia in favour of *bureaux de change*, such as the Swedish operator Forex, which usually offer better rates and charge smaller fees or commissions than banks. They usually also keep better hours than the banks, which are closed at weekends and on public holidays (see the individual country chapters for lists). However, most airports, central railway stations, some fancy hotels and many border posts have banking facilities outside working hours. Post offices often provide banking services too; they tend to be open longer hours, and outnumber banks in more remote places.

If you visit several countries, the constant currency conversions can drive you up the wall. Buy a cheap pocket calculator, cut out the list of exchange rates from a newspaper, and stick it to the back of the calculator for easy reference.

Tipping

For the most part in Scandinavia, it's common for a service charge to be added to restaurant bills, in which case no tipping is necessary. In other cases, simply rounding up the bill is sufficient. See the individual country chapters for more details.

Taxes & Refunds

A kind of sales tax called value-added tax (VAT) applies to most goods and services throughout most of Scandinavia. Visitors usually can claim back the VAT on purchases that are being taken out of the country. Remember, though, that those people actually residing in an EU country are not entitled to a refund on VAT paid on goods bought in another EU country (eg a Briton returning home with goods from Finland, Sweden or Denmark). The procedure on making the claim is usually pretty straightforward, and there will be minimum-purchase amounts imposed (as low as 300 kr in Norway). For guidance, see the relevant country chapter.

POST & COMMUNICATIONS
Post

Air mail typically takes about a week to North American or Australasian destinations. Postage costs do vary from country to country, but postal services are very efficient in Scandinavian countries.

You can collect mail from post office poste-restante sections. Ask people writing to you to print your name clearly and underline your surname and write it in capital letters. When collecting mail you may need your passport for identification. If an expected letter is not waiting for you, ask to check under your given name as letters do get misfiled. Unless the sender specifies otherwise, mail will always be sent to the city's main post office.

You can also have mail (but not parcels) sent to you at American Express offices so long as you have an American Express card or travellers' cheques. When you buy American Express travellers' cheques you can ask for a booklet listing all their office addresses worldwide.

Telephone

You can ring abroad from almost any phone box in Scandinavia nowadays. Public telephones accepting stored-value phonecards, available from post offices, telephone centres, newsstands or retail outlets, are not only the norm, in some places, coin-operated phones are almost impossible to find. The card solves the problem of finding the correct coins for calls (or lots of correct coins for international calls).

Without a phonecard, you can ring from a booth inside a post office or telephone centre and settle your bill at the counter. Reverse-charge (collect) calls are usually possible, and communicating with the local operator in English should not be much of a problem in Scandinavia. From some countries you can avoid the local operator, and dial direct to your home operator. See the Telephones appendix in the back of this book for information on international dialling, local phones, costs, country codes and 'home direct' services.

Fax & Telegraph

You can send faxes and telegrams from most main post offices.

E-mail

Maintaining your Internet connectivity while you are on the road in Europe can be done with a little planning and forethought. All European countries are now connected to the Internet and finding access is becoming easier. You have a few options. You can take your laptop PC and modem and dial your home country service provider, or take out a local account in the region you will be visiting most (there are kits to help you cope with local telephone plugs). For more information, have a look at Lonely Planet's site at http://www.lonelyplanet.com.

Internet cafés, where you can buy online time and have a coffee are springing up all over Europe. Check http://www.cyberiacafe .net/cyberia/guide/ccafe.htm for the latest list. Failing that, make friends with local students and ask if you can sneak time on a university, or even private machine. Before leaving home, contact your service provider to see if they can offer any specific advice about the countries you intend to visit.

NEWSPAPERS & MAGAZINES

If you want to keep up with the news in English, you can get the excellent *International Herald Tribune*, the European edition of the *Wall Street Journal* or the colourful but very superficial *USA Today* in large towns in Scandinavia. The British *Guardian* and *Financial Times* are also widely available. Other UK papers are often on sale but are expensive and likely to be a day or so behind. Western newspapers are available on the same day or a day late in major cities of the Baltic states. In the news-magazine category *Time*, *Newsweek* and the *Economist* are widely available in Scandinavia and the Baltic states.

RADIO & TV

In Scandinavia, the BBC World Service can be found on medium wave at 648 kHz, on short wave at 6195, 9410, 12095 and 15575 kHz, and on long wave at 198 kHz; the appropriate frequency depends on where you are and the time of day. The Voice of America (VOA) can usually be found on short wave at 15205 kHz. There are also numerous English-language broadcasts (and even BBC World Service and VOA repeat broadcasts) on local AM radio stations.

Cable and satellite TV have spread across Europe with much more gusto than radio but networks like Sky TV and CNN are usually only found in expensive hotels.

VIDEO SYSTEMS

If you want to record or buy video tapes to play back home, you won't get a picture if the image registration systems are different. Most of Europe uses PAL (France and Poland uses SECAM), which is incompatible with the North American and Japanese NTSC system. Australia uses PAL.

PHOTOGRAPHY

Scandinavia and the Baltic states are extremely photogenic, but where you'll be travelling and the climate will dictate what film to take or buy locally. In certain parts of the region in the autumn, when the sky can often be overcast, photographers should bring high-speed film (eg 200 or 400 ASA). In sunny weather (or under a blanket of snow) slower film is the answer.

Film and camera equipment is available everywhere in Scandinavia, but obviously shops in the larger cities and towns have a wider selection.

ELECTRICITY

Voltage & Cycle

Most of the region runs on 220V, 50 Hz AC. Check the voltage and cycle (usually 50 Hz) used in your home country. Most appliances that are set up for 220V will handle 240V quite happily without modifications (and vice versa); the same goes for 110V and 125V combinations. It's always preferable to adjust your appliance to the exact voltage if you can (some modern battery chargers and radios will do this automatically). Just don't mix 110/125V and 220/240V without a transformer (which will be built into an adjustable appliance).

Several countries outside Europe (such as the USA and Canada) have 60 Hz AC, which will affect the speed of electric motors even after the voltage has been adjusted to European values, so CD and tape players (where motor speed is all-important) will be useless. But things like electric razors, hair dryers, irons and radios will be fine.

Plugs & Sockets

The standard here is the so-called europlug with two round pins, though in some parts of the Baltic states sockets take only the thinner pinned Russian plugs. Adapters are available from most supermarkets. Many europlugs and some sockets don't have provision for earth since most local home appliances are double-insulated; when provided, earth usually consists of two contact points along the edge.

HEALTH

Scandinavia is a very healthy place in which to travel. Though health risks are slightly higher in the Baltic states and Russia, there's still little to worry about. Your main risks are likely to be viral infections in winter, sunburn and insect bites in summer, and foot blisters and upset stomach from overeating or drinking any time.

A healthy trip depends on your predeparture preparations and fitness, your day-to-day health care while travelling, and how you handle any medical problem or emergency that does develop. If you're reasonably fit, the only things you should organise before departure are a visit to your dentist to get your teeth in order, and travel insurance with good medical cover (see the following section). To put your mind at ease, you might also ensure that your normal childhood vaccines (against measles, mumps, rubella, diphtheria, tetanus and polio) are up to date and/or you are still showing immunity.

Predeparture Preparations

Health Insurance A travel insurance policy to cover theft, personal liability, loss and medical problems is strongly recommended. There is a wide variety of policies available and your travel agent will have recommendations. The international travel policies handled by STA Travel or other student travel organisations are usually good value. Check the small print:

• Some policies specifically exclude 'dangerous activities' such as motorcycling, skiing, mountaineering, scuba diving or even hiking.
• A policy that pays doctors or hospitals directly may be preferable to one where you pay on the spot and claim later. If you have to claim later, make sure you keep all documentation. Some policies ask you to call back (reverse charges) to a centre in your home country where an immediate assessment of your problem can be made.
• Check if the policy covers ambulances and an emergency flight home. If you have to stretch out you will need two seats and somebody has to pay for them!

EU citizens are covered for emergency medical treatment in all EU countries on presentation of an E111 form. Enquire about these at your national health service or travel agent well in advance; in some countries post offices have them. Similar reciprocal arrangements exist between individual countries; see the individual chapters for details. Australian Medicare covers emergency treatment in a half-dozen European countries, including Finland and Sweden. You may still have to pay on the spot, but you'll be able to reclaim these expenses at home. Travel insurance is still advisable, however, because of the flexibility it offers as to where and how you're treated, as well as covering expenses for ambulance and repatriation.

Medical Kit A small, straightforward medical kit is a good thing to carry. A possible list includes:

• aspirin or paracetamol – for pain or fever
• antihistamine (such as Benadryl) – useful as a decongestant for colds, allergies, to ease the itch from insect bites or stings, or to help prevent motion sickness
• kaolin preparation (eg Pepto-Bismol), Imodium or Lomotil – for possible stomach upsets

- antiseptic, such as Betadine, and antibiotic powder or similar 'dry' spray – for cuts and grazes
- calamine lotion – to ease irritation from insect bites or stings
- bandages and Band-aids – for minor injuries
- scissors, tweezers and a thermometer (note that mercury thermometers are prohibited by airlines)
- insect repellent, sunblock cream, lip balm and possibly water-purification tablets

Health Preparations If you wear glasses, take a spare pair as well as your prescription. You'd have no problem getting new spectacles made up quickly and competently in Scandinavia but you'd pay for the privilege. Wearers of contact lenses should bring generous supplies of cleaning fluids and wetting solutions when travelling in the Baltic states and Kaliningrad as they are still difficult to find there.

If you need a particular medication, take an adequate supply, as it may not always be available quickly. The same applies for your oral contraceptive. Take the prescription, or better still, part of the packaging showing the generic rather than the brand name (which may not be locally available), as it will make getting replacements easier.

It's a good idea to have a legible prescription to show that you legally use the medication – it's surprising how often over-the-counter drugs from one place are illegal without a prescription (eg Benadryl in Norway) or even banned in another. If you're carrying a syringe for some reason, have a note from your doctor to explain why you're doing so.

A Medic Alert tag is a good idea if your medical condition is not always easily recognisable (heart trouble, diabetes, asthma, allergic reactions to antibiotics etc).

Immunisations Jabs are not necessary for travel in the region (including the Baltic states), but they may be an entry requirement if you're coming from an infected area – yellow fever is the most likely requirement. If you're going to Europe with stopovers in Asia, Africa or Latin America, check with your travel agent or with the embassies of the countries you plan to visit.

There are, however, a few routine vaccinations that are recommended whether you're travelling or not, and this Health section assumes that you've had them: polio (usually administered during childhood), tetanus and diphtheria (usually administered together during childhood, with a booster shot every 10 years), and sometimes measles. See your physician or nearest health agency about these.

All vaccinations should be recorded on an International Health Certificate (see Visas & Documents). Don't leave this till the last minute, as the vaccinations may have to be spread out a bit.

Basic Rules
Water Tap water is always safe to drink in Scandinavia, but may be dubious in the Baltic states, where it is an unpalatable orange colour in some areas. Some Baltic nationals boil tap water before drinking it; others don't. Never drink tap water in Kaliningrad or St Petersburg. It's a matter of taking local advice in each place you visit and exercising care: even if locals can drink the stuff happily, you might not be able to since you won't have built up any immunity to whatever organisms it might contain. If in doubt, stick to mineral water (widely available and cheap), tea etc, or boil the tap water (an electric water-heating element is a useful item of luggage for this reason).

Always be wary of drinking natural water. The burbling stream may look crystal clear and very inviting, but before drinking from it you want to be absolutely sure there are no people or cattle upstream; take particular care in Iceland, the Faroe Islands, and the Baltic states. Run-off from fertilised fields is also a concern.

If you are planning extended hikes where you have to rely on natural water, it may be useful to know about water purification. The simplest way to do this is to boil water thoroughly. Technically this means boiling for 10 minutes, something which happens very rarely.

Simple filtering will not remove all dangerous organisms, so if you cannot boil water it should be treated chemically. Chlorine tablets (Puritabs, Steritabs or other brand names) will kill many but not all pathogens. Iodine in tincture form or tablets (such as Potable Aqua) can also be used. Four drops of tincture of iodine per litre of clear water is the recommended dosage (too much iodine can be harmful); the treated water should be left to stand for 30 minutes before drinking. Iodine loses its effectiveness if exposed to air or damp, so keep it in a tightly sealed container. Flavoured powder will disguise the taste of treated water and is a good idea if you are travelling with children.

Food Stomach upsets are a more likely travel-health risk in the Baltic states and Russia than in Scandinavia, but most of these upsets will be relatively minor.

Salads and fruit should be safe. Ice cream is usually OK, but be wary of ice cream that has melted and been refrozen. Take great care with fish or shellfish (for instance, cooked mussels that haven't opened properly can be dangerous), and avoid undercooked meat.

If a place looks clean and well run and if the vendor also looks clean and healthy, then the food is probably safe. In general, places that are packed with travellers or locals will be fine. Be careful with food that has been cooked and left to go cold.

Mushroom-picking is a favourite pastime in this part of the world as autumn approaches, but make sure you don't eat any mushrooms that haven't been positively identified as safe.

Nutrition If you don't vary your diet, and are travelling hard and fast and therefore missing meals, or you simply lose your appetite, you can soon start to lose weight and place your health at risk, just as you could at home.

If you rely on fast foods, you'll get plenty of fats and carbohydrates but little else. Remember that overcooked food loses much of its nutritional value. If your diet isn't well balanced, it's a good idea to take vitamin and iron pills (women lose a lot of iron through menstruation). Fruit and vegetables are good sources of vitamin, but are also very expensive in Scandinavia where they're not often served in large quantities; taking vitamin supplements may be a good idea.

In hot weather (and Scandinavia can get very warm in summer) make sure you drink enough fluids – don't rely on feeling thirsty to indicate when you should drink. Not needing to urinate or very dark-yellow (or strong-smelling) urine is a danger sign. Carry a water bottle on long trips. Excessive sweating can lead to loss of salt and therefore muscle cramps. Salt tablets are not a good idea as a preventative, but in places where salt is not used much, adding salt to food can help.

Medical Problems & Treatment

Local pharmacies or neighbourhood medical centres are good places to visit if you have a small medical problem and can explain what it is. Hospital casualty wards will help if it's more serious, and will tell you if it's not. Major hospitals and emergency numbers are indicated on the maps in this book or mentioned in the text. Tourist offices and hotels can put you on to a doctor or dentist; your embassy will probably know one who speaks your language.

In an emergency while travelling in the Baltic states, seek help initially at your hotel or hostel. The bigger hotels may have a doctor on call. There are a few expensive medical and dental services aimed primarily at foreigners. They often advertise in the top hotels.

Sunburn You can get sunburned surprisingly quickly, even through cloud, anywhere on water, ice, snow or sand. Use a sunscreen and take extra care to cover areas that don't normally see sun – eg your feet. A hat provides added protection, and it may be a good idea to use zinc cream or some other barrier cream for your nose and lips. Calamine lotion is good for mild sunburn.

Remember that too much sunlight can damage your eyes, whether it's direct or reflected (glare). If your plans include being near water, ice, snow or sand, then good sunglasses are doubly important. Make sure they're treated to absorb ultraviolet radiation – if not, they'll actually do more harm than good by dilating your pupils and making it easier for ultraviolet light to damage the retina.

Hypothermia Too much cold is just as dangerous as too much heat, particularly if it leads to hypothermia. Cold combined with wind and moisture (ie soaking rain) is particularly risky. If you are hiking at high altitudes or in a cool, wet environment, be prepared.

Hypothermia occurs when the body loses heat faster than it can produce it and the core temperature of the body falls. It is surprisingly easy to progress from very cold to dangerously cold through a combination of wind, wet clothing, fatigue and hunger, even if the air temperature is above freezing. It is best to dress in layers – silk, wool and some of the new artificial fibres are all good insulating materials. A hat is important, as a lot of heat is lost through the head. A strong, waterproof outer layer is essential. Carry basic supplies, including food that contains simple sugars to generate heat quickly, and lots of fluid to drink.

Symptoms of hypothermia are exhaustion, numb skin (particularly toes and fingers), shivering, slurred speech, irrational or violent behaviour, lethargy, stumbling, dizzy spells, muscle cramps and violent bursts of energy. Irrationality may take the form of sufferers claiming they are warm and trying to take off their clothes.

To treat hypothermia, first get the person out of the wind and/or rain, remove their clothing if it's wet and replace it with dry, warm clothing. Give them hot, nonalcoholic liquids and some high-kilojoule (high-calorie), easily digestible food. Do not rub victims' skin; place them near a fire or, if possible, in a warm (not hot) bath. This should be enough for the early stages of hypothermia. The early recognition and treatment of mild hypothermia is the only

---

Vital Signs
The normal body temperature for an adult human being is 98.6˚F or 37˚C; more than 2˚C (4˚F) higher than that is a 'high' fever. A normal adult pulse rate is 60 to 100 per minute (children 80 to 100, babies 100 to 140). You should know how to take a temperature and a pulse rate. As a general rule, the pulse increases about 20 beats per minute for each ˚C (2˚F) rise in body temperature.

The respiration rate is also an indicator of illness. Count the number of breaths per minute: between 12 and 20 is normal for adults and older children (up to 30 for younger children, 40 for babies). People with a high fever or serious respiratory illness (like pneumonia) breathe more quickly than normal. More than 40 shallow breaths a minute could indicate pneumonia. ■

---

way to prevent severe hypothermia, which is a critical condition.

Motion Sickness Eating lightly before and during a trip will reduce the chances of motion sickness. If you are prone to the syndrome, try to find a place that minimises disturbance – near the wing on an aircraft, close to midships on boats, near the centre on buses. Fresh air and a steady reference point like the horizon usually help, whereas reading or cigarette smoke exacerbate the problem. Commercial antimotion-sickness preparations, which can cause drowsiness, have to be taken before the trip commences – when you're feeling sick, it's already too late. Ginger is a natural preventative and is available in capsule form.

Jet Lag Jet lag is experienced when a person travels by air across more than three time zones (each time zone usually represents a one-hour time difference). It occurs because many of the functions of the human body (such as temperature, pulse rate and the emptying of the bladder and bowels) are regulated by internal 24-hour cycles called circadian rhythms. When we travel long distances rapidly, our bodies take time to adjust to the 'new time' of our destination, and we may experience fatigue, disorientation, insomnia, anxiety, impaired concentration and loss of appetite. These effects will usually be gone within three days of arrival, but there are ways of minimising the impact of jet lag:

- Rest for a couple of days prior to departure; try to avoid late nights, too many bon voyage parties, and last-minute dashes for travellers' cheques, visas etc.
- Try to select flight schedules that minimise sleep deprivation; arriving late in the day means you can go to sleep soon after you arrive. For very long flights, try to organise a stopover.
- Avoid excessive eating (which bloats the stomach) and alcohol (which causes dehydration) during the flight. Instead, drink plenty of noncarbonated, nonalcoholic drinks such as fruit juice or mineral water.
- Avoid smoking, as this reduces the amount of oxygen in the aircraft cabin even further and causes greater fatigue.
- Make yourself comfortable by wearing loose-fitting clothes and perhaps bringing an eye mask and ear plugs to help you sleep.

Diarrhoea A change of water, food or climate can all cause the runs; diarrhoea caused by contaminated food or water is more serious. Despite all your precautions, you may still have a bout of mild travellers' diarrhoea, but a few rushed toilet trips with no other symptoms is not indicative of a serious problem.

Moderate diarrhoea, involving a half-dozen loose movements in a day, is more of a nuisance. Dehydration is the main danger with any diarrhoea, particularly for children, so fluid replenishment is the number one treatment. Weak black tea with a little sugar, soda water, or soft drinks allowed to go flat and diluted 50% with water are all good.

With any diarrhoea more severe than this, go straight to the casualty ward of the nearest hospital and have yourself checked. You may need a rehydrating solution to replace minerals and salts. Stick to a bland diet as you recover.

If you're going to Iceland and the Faroes and are likely to go trekking, you'll want to know about *Giardia lamblia* (an intestinal parasite which causes giardiasis, commonly known as giardia or 'beaver fever').

The parasite causing this intestinal disorder is present in contaminated water. The symptoms are stomach cramps, nausea, a bloated stomach, watery, foul-smelling diarrhoea and frequent gas. Giardiasis can appear several weeks after you have been exposed to the parasite. The symptoms may disappear for a few days and then return; this can go on for several weeks. Tinidazole, known as Fasigyn, or metronidazole (Flagyl) are the recommended drugs for treatment. Either can be used in a single treatment dose.

Viral Gastroenteritis This is caused not by bacteria but, as the name suggests, by a virus. It is characterised by stomach cramps, diarrhoea, and sometimes by vomiting and/or a slight fever. All you can do is rest and drink lots of fluids.

Hepatitis B This disease is spread through contact with infected blood, blood products or bodily fluids, for example through sexual contact, unsterilised needles and blood transfusions. Other risk situations include tattooing and body-piercing. The symptoms are fever, chills, headache and fatigue followed by vomiting, abdominal pain, dark urine and jaundiced skin. Hepatitis B can lead to irreparable liver damage, even liver cancer. There is no treatment (except rest, drinking lots of fluids and eating lightly) but an effective prophylactic vaccine is readily available in most countries.

Rabies Rabies, caused by a bite or scratch by an infected mammal, is found throughout Europe, and the risk has increased since the physical and political barriers were removed between the East and West in 1989. Dogs are a noted carrier, but cats, foxes and bats can also be infected. Any bite, scratch or even lick from a warm-blooded, furry animal should be cleaned immediately and thoroughly. Scrub with soap and running water, and then clean with an alcohol solution. If there is any possibility that the animal is infected, particularly if it froths at the mouth and behaves strangely, medical help should be sought immediately. Even if it is not rabid, all bites should be treated seriously as they can become infected or can result in tetanus.

A rabies vaccination is available and should be considered if you are in a high-risk category – eg if you intend to explore caves (bat bites can be dangerous), work with animals, or travel so far off the beaten track that medical help is more than two days away.

Tuberculosis (TB) Although this disease is widespread in many developing countries and used to be a scourge in Europe, it is not a serious risk to healthy travellers. Young children are more susceptible than adults and vaccination is a sensible precaution for children under 12 travelling in endemic areas. TB is commonly spread by coughing (droplet infection), or by eating or drinking unpasteurised dairy products from infected cows. Milk that has been boiled is safe to drink; the souring of milk to make yoghurt or cheese also kills the bacilli.

Sexually Transmitted Diseases Sexual contact with an infected partner spreads what are now commonly called STDs. Abstinence is the only 100% preventative, but the proper use of condoms can be almost as effective. Gonorrhoea and syphilis are the most common of these diseases: sores, blisters or rashes around the genitals, discharges, or pain when urinating are common symptoms. Symptoms may be less marked or not observed at all in women. Syphilis symptoms eventually disappear completely, but the disease continues and can cause severe problems in later years. The treatment of gonorrhoea and syphilis is by antibiotics. STD clinics are widespread in Scandinavian and Baltic Europe. Don't be shy about visiting them if you think you may have contracted something; they are there to help and have seen it all before.

There are numerous other STDs – effective treatment is available for most – but as yet there is no cure for herpes or HIV/AIDS. HIV, the 'human immunodeficiency virus', may develop into AIDS (acquired immune deficiency syndrome). Apart from absti-

nence, the most effective preventive is always to practise safe sex using condoms. It is impossible to detect the HIV-positive status of an otherwise healthy-looking person without a blood test.

HIV/AIDS can also be spread through infected blood transfusions or by dirty needles – vaccinations, acupuncture, tattooing and body-piercing can potentially be as dangerous as intravenous drug use if the equipment is not sterile. HIV *cannot* be transmitted by shaking hands, kissing, cuddling, fondling, sneezing or sharing eating or drinking utensils. Toilet seats, swimming pools and mosquito bites cannot spread AIDS.

Cuts, Bites & Stings Treat any cut with an antiseptic solution such as Betadine. Where possible avoid bandages and Band-aids, which can keep wounds wet.

Bee and wasp stings are usually more painful than dangerous. Calamine lotion will give relief and ice packs will reduce the pain and swelling. There are some spiders with dangerous bites (rare in Europe) but anti-venenes are usually available. Midges, small blood-sucking flies related to mosquitoes, are common in arctic regions during summer. One health-threatening pest indigenous to parts of the Baltic states (especially Latvia) is the forest tick, which burrows under the skin causing inflammation and even encephalitis. Consider getting a meningo-encephalitis vaccination if you plan to do extensive hiking and camping there between May and September.

Mosquitoes, as well as being a nuisance, can almost drive you insane during the summer months in northern Europe – Finland, with its many lakes, is particularly notorious. Mid-summer is the worst period, and hikers will have to cover exposed skin and may even need special mosquito hats with netting to screen their faces. Seek local advice, as regular mosquito repellents and coils are hardly effective against the ravenous hordes that home in on you 24 hours a day. A mosquito-proof tent is essential at night. Fortunately, mosquito-borne diseases such as malaria are unknown in this part of the world, and the main risks are mental (people have been driven literally insane by the incessant buzzing and itching).

Most people get used to mosquito bites after a few days as their bodies adjust and the itching and swelling become less severe. An antihistamine cream should help alleviate the symptoms.

All lice cause itching and discomfort. They make themselves at home in your hair (head lice), your clothing (body lice) or in your pubic hair (crabs). You catch lice through direct contact with infected people or by sharing combs, clothing and the like. Powder or shampoo treatment will kill the lice, and infected clothing should then be washed in very hot water.

Snakes tend to keep a very low profile in Scandinavia, but to minimise your chances of being bitten always wear boots, socks and long trousers when walking through undergrowth or rocky areas where snakes may be present. Tramp heavily and they'll usually slither away before you come near. Don't put your hands into holes and crevices, and be careful when collecting firewood.

Snake bites do not cause instantaneous death and antivenenes are usually available. Keep the victim calm and still, wrap the bitten limb tightly, as you would for a sprained ankle, attach a splint to immobilise it and seek medical help. If possible keep the dead snake for identification, but don't attempt to catch the snake if there is even a remote possibility of being bitten again. Tourniquets and sucking out the poison are now comprehensively discredited.

Women's Health

Some women experience an irregular menstrual cycle when travelling because of the upset in routine. Don't forget to take time zones into account if you're on the pill. If you run into intestinal problems, the pill may not be absorbed. Ask your physician about these matters.

Poor diet, lowered resistance through the use of antibiotics for stomach upsets, and even contraceptive pills, can lead to vaginal infections when travelling in hot climates. Maintaining good personal hygiene, and wearing skirts or loose-fitting trousers and cotton underwear will help to prevent infections.

Yeast infections (thrush), characterised by a rash, itch and discharge, can be treated with a vinegar or even lemon-juice douche or with yoghurt. Nystatin suppositories are the usual medical prescription. Trichomonas is a more serious infection; symptoms are a discharge and a burning sensation when urinating, and if a vinegar-water douche is not effective, medical attention should be sought. Metronidazole (Flagyl) is the prescribed drug. In both cases, male sexual partners must also be treated.

WOMEN TRAVELLERS

Scandinavia is one of the safest places to travel in all of Europe. Women often travel alone or in pairs around the region, which should pose no problems, but women do tend to attract more unwanted attention than men, and common sense is the best guide to dealing with potentially dangerous situations like hitchhiking, walking alone at night etc.

In Estonia, Latvia and Lithuania, prostitution is still rife at some tourist hotels (rarer in the new ones run by Western companies): a woman sitting alone in a lobby, corridor or café might be propositioned.

Recommended reading is the *Handbook for Women Travellers* by M & G Moss, published by Judy Piatkus Publishers (London).

GAY & LESBIAN TRAVELLERS

Gays and lesbians should get in touch with their national organisation for more detailed information about Scandinavia and the Baltic states. This book lists contact addresses and gay and lesbian venues in some of the individual country chapters, but your organisation should be able to give you more information. The *Spartacus International Gay Guide*, published by Bruno Gmünder Verlag (Berlin), is a good international directory of gay entertainment venues, but it's best used in conjunction with more up-to-date listings in local papers; as elsewhere, gay venues in the region can change with the speed of summer lightning. *Places for Women* (Ferrari Publications) is the best international guide for lesbians.

DISABLED TRAVELLERS

Scandinavia leads the world in terms of facilities for disabled people. For instance, by law every new restaurant in Finland must have a special toilet for the handicapped. There are wheelchair ramps to practically all public buildings and most department shops, shopping centres and many private shops and some train carriages are fitted with special lifts for wheelchairs. Some city buses are also accessible by wheelchair.

If you have a physical disability, get in touch with your national support organisation (preferably the 'travel officer' if there is one) and ask about the countries you plan to visit. They often have complete libraries devoted to travel, and they can put you in touch with travel agents who specialise in tours for the disabled.

The British-based Royal Association for Disability & Rehabilitation (RADAR) publishes a useful guide titled *Holidays & Travel Abroad: A Guide for Disabled People* (UK£5), which gives a good overview of facilities available to disabled travellers in Europe (in even-numbered years) and farther afield (in odd-numbered years). Contact RADAR (☎ 0171-250 3222) at 12 City Forum, 250 City Rd, London EC1V 8AF.

SENIOR TRAVELLERS

Senior citizens are entitled to many discounts in Scandinavia on public transport, museum admission fees etc, provided they show proof of their age. In some cases they might need a special pass. The minimum qualifying age is generally 60 or 65.

In your home country, a lower age may already entitle you to all sorts of interesting travel packages and discounts (on car hire, for instance) through organisations and travel agents that cater for senior travellers. Start hunting at your local senior citizens advice bureau.

TRAVEL WITH CHILDREN

Successful travel with young children requires planning and effort. Don't try to overdo things; even for adults, packing too much into the time available can cause problems. And make sure the activities include the kids as well – balance that day at Copenhagen's Nationalmuseet with a day at Legoland. Include your children in the trip planning; if they've helped to work out where you will be going, they will be much more interested when they get there. Lonely Planet's *Travel with Children* by Maureen Wheeler is a good source of information.

Most of Scandinavia is very child-friendly. There are numerous public parks for kids, and commercial facilities are numerous. Domestic tourism is largely dictated by children's needs: theme parks, water parks and so on. Many museums, such as the national ones in Stockholm, invariably have a children's section with toys and activities. The Musikmuseet in that city, for instance, has 'hands-on' musical instruments in its permanent collection.

Car-rental firms have children's safety seats for hire at a nominal cost, but it is essential that you book them in advance. The same goes for highchairs and cots (cribs); they're standard in many restaurants and hotels, but numbers may be limited. The choice of baby food, infant formulas, soy and cow's milk, disposable nappies (diapers) and the like can be as great in the supermarkets of most Scandinavian countries as it is back home, but not so great in the Baltic states. Remember, though, that opening hours may be quite different. Run out of nappies at lunchtime on Saturday in Stockholm and you're facing a very long and messy weekend.

DANGERS & ANNOYANCES

Scandinavia (but, less so, the Baltic states) is generally a very safe, non-threatening region to travel in but there are other potential risks to consider. Rural Iceland and many areas of Norway, as well as the Swedish and Finnish countryside are areas where you can easily get lost. There are few people around, and if you injure yourself and can't get away, the cold climate might even kill you. Because there are so few people, you will have to accept eccentric people in more remote places as they are: sometimes extremely frustrated (even aggressive) and suspicious of outsiders. The gloom that winter brings may lead to unpredictable behaviour and alcohol abuse.

So-called neo-Nazis are emerging throughout the Scandinavian region and are a potential danger to unwary travellers.

Whatever you do, don't leave friends and relatives back home worrying about how to get in touch with you in case of emergency. Work out a list of places where they can contact you or, best of all, phone home now and then.

Theft

As a traveller, you're often fairly vulnerable and when you do lose things it can be a real hassle. Theft is more of a problem in the Baltic states than in Scandinavian countries and it's not just other travellers you have to be wary of. The most important things to guard are your passport, other documents, tickets and money – in that order. It's always best to carry these next to your skin or in a sturdy leather pouch on your belt. Train station lockers or luggage storage counters are useful places to store your luggage (but not valuables) while you get your bearings in a new town. Be very suspicious about people who offer to help you operate your locker. Carry your own padlock for hostel lockers.

Be careful even in hotels; don't leave valuables lying around in your room. Parked cars are prime targets for petty criminals in most cities, and cars with foreign number plates and/or rental agency stickers are particularly targeted, especially in the Baltic states. If possible, remove the stickers (or cover them with local football club stickers or something similar), leave a local newspaper on the seat and generally try to make it look like a local car. Don't ever leave valuables in the car, and remove all luggage overnight.

In case of theft or loss, always report the incident to the police and ask for a statement, or your travel insurance won't pay up.

Drugs

Always treat drugs with a great deal of caution. There is a fair bit of dope available in the region, sometimes quite openly, but that doesn't mean it's legal. Even a little harmless hashish can cause a great deal of trouble.

Don't bother bringing drugs home with you. With 'suspect' stamps in your passport (including Copenhagen airport) energetic customs officials could well decide to take a closer look.

ACTIVITIES

Scandinavia and the Baltic states offer countless opportunities to indulge in more active pursuits than sightseeing. The varied geography and climate supports the full range of outdoor sports: windsurfing, skiing, fishing, hiking and mountaineering, boating and cycling. For more local information, see the individual country chapters.

Windsurfing

Though this sport is not as popular as it was a decade ago, the beaches of Denmark continue to attract crowds of windsurfers in summer. Wetsuits enable the keener windsurfers to continue their sport throughout the colder months. Sailboards can be rented in some tourist centres, and courses are sometimes on offer for beginners.

Skiing

Scandinavia is famous for winter sports and snow skiing is a popular activity. Skiing in Scandinavia is usually cross-country (also known as 'nordic skiing'), with some of the world's best trails. Alpine or downhill skiing is quite expensive due to the costs of ski lifts, accommodation and the après-ski drinking sessions.

Sweden and Norway have the highest slopes, but the Finnish ones are equally popular and well equipped. Åre in Sweden is probably the single best area for Alpine skiing. Top resorts in Norway are Geilo and

Lillehammer and telemark skiing is popular there.

Downhill skiing is always easier to arrange in Scandinavia as rentals can be organised easily. For cross-country skiing, travellers will have to either rely on friendly locals to lend their equipment, or plan on buying the skis, poles and boots. (Flea markets are the cheapest places to look.)

Skiing – especially the cross-country variety – should only be attempted after studying the trails/tracks (wilderness trails are identified by colour codes on maps and signposts) and making sure that your clothing is appropriate and your small daypack has food, extra clothing and emergency supplies, such as matches and something to burn. Skiers should be extra careful about darkness. In Scandinavia, days are very short in winter, and during December and January there is no daylight in the extreme north.

The skiing season generally lasts from early December to April. Snow conditions can vary greatly from one year to another and from region to region, but January and February tend to be the best (and busiest) months. Snow cannons for producing artificial snow are common. Practically all towns and villages illuminate some skiing tracks.

Hiking

Keen hikers can spend a lifetime exploring the region's many exciting trails. There are national parks, nature reserves, and other interesting areas that may qualify as a trekker's paradise, depending on your preferences. You can hike on well-marked trails (some with duration indicators), and accommodation is available along the way. Be sure to bring food along with you though.

The 'right of common access' is a law in Sweden, Norway, Finland and Iceland allowing everyone to walk anywhere he or she likes. Naturally, there are certain rules of conduct to follow. Huge national routes like Kungsleden in Sweden and the UKK route in Finland are popular, as are the provincial or regional routes spanning hundreds of km and the tracks in national parks. Local and regional tourist offices distribute free maps

for shorter routes and sell excellent trekking maps for the national parks.

Cycling

Along with hiking, cycling is the best way to really get close to the scenery and the people, keeping yourself fit in the process. It's also a good way to get around the cities.

Popular cycling areas include much of Denmark, greater Oslo, the islands of Gotland in Sweden and Åland in Finland. Be wary of western Norway, as beautiful as it is: there are tunnels galore (one is five km long), the serpentine roads to/from mountain tops are killers and, unless you want to pedal an extra 50 km around a fjord, you'll have to take an expensive ferry.

If you come from outside Europe, you can often bring your bicycle along on the plane for a surprisingly reasonable fee. Alternatively, this book lists places where you can rent one (make sure it has plenty of gears if you plan anything serious). The minimum rental period in Scandinavia is usually one day.

See the Getting Around chapter and the individual country chapters for more information on bicycle touring, and for rental agencies and tips on places to visit.

Boating

The many lakes, rivers and diverse coastlines in Scandinavia and the Baltic states offer a variety of boating options unmatched anywhere in the world. You can ride the rapids in a canoe in Finland or, during winter, take a trip on a Bothnian icebreaker; charter a yacht or hire a rowing boat or cruise the fjords or peaceful Lake Mjøsa in Norway; cruise from Helsinki to Tallinn in Estonia or to St Petersburg in Russia – the possibilities are endless. The country chapters have more details.

COURSES

Apart from learning new physical skills by doing something like a downhill skiing course in Norway or windsurfing in Denmark, you can enrich your mind in a variety of structured courses on anything from language to alternative medicine. Language courses are often available to foreigners through universities, folk high schools or private institutions, and are justifiably popular since the best way to learn a language is in the country where it's spoken. But you can also take courses in art, literature, architecture, drama, music, cooking, alternative energy, photography and organic farming, among other things. The individual country chapters in this book give pointers on where to start looking. In general, the best sources of information are the cultural institutes, tourist offices and embassies of Scandinavian countries aboard. Student exchange organisations, student travel agencies, and organisations like the YMCA/YWCA and HI can also put you on the right track. Ask about special holiday packages that include a course.

In the Baltic states, Tartu and Vilnius universities are among the institutes offering language and cultural courses in summer.

WORK

Officially, a citizen of the European Union (EU) is allowed to work in other EU countries. The paperwork isn't always straightforward for longer term employment, however. Other country/ nationality combinations require special work permits that can be almost impossible to arrange, especially for temporary work.

That doesn't prevent enterprising travellers from topping up their funds occasionally, and not always illegally. Your national student-exchange organisation may be able to arrange temporary work permits to several countries through special programmes. For more details on working in Scandinavia, see Work in the Facts for the Visitor sections of the individual country chapters.

If you have a parent or grandparent who was born in an EU country, you may have certain rights you never knew about. Get in touch with that country's embassy and ask about dual citizenship and work permits – if you are eligible for citizenship, also ask about any obligations, such as military service, taxation and having to relinquish your first passport. Not all countries allow dual citizenship, so a work permit may be all you can get. Ireland is particularly easygoing about granting citizenship to people with Irish ancestry, and with an Irish passport, the EU is your oyster.

If you do find a temporary job, the pay may be less than that offered to locals, though this is not always the case in Scandinavia. Teaching English can pay well, but such work is hard to come by. Other typical tourist jobs (such as working in a restaurant, resort hotel or fish-processing plant) may come with board and lodging and the pay is little more than pocket money, but you'll have a good time partying with other travellers.

Work Your Way Around the World by Susan Griffith gives good, practical advice on a wide range of issues. The same publisher, Vacation Work, has many other useful titles, including *The Au Pair and Nanny's Guide to Working Abroad* by Susan Griffith & Sharon Legg.

If you play an instrument or have other artistic talents, you could try busking (street entertainment). It's fairly common in many major cities. In Finland you'll need to get a busking permit, which is available from the police, although not everybody actually has the permit. In Copenhagen acoustic music is allowed without a permit in pedestrian streets and squares between 4 and 8 pm on weekdays and noon to 5 pm at the weekend. Most other Scandinavian countries require municipal permits that can be hard to obtain. Talk to other buskers first.

Selling goods on the street is generally frowned upon and can be tantamount to vagrancy, apart from at flea markets. It's also a hard way to make money if you're not selling something special.

ACCOMMODATION

The cheapest places to stay are camping grounds, followed by hostels and student accommodation. Cheap hotels are virtually unknown in most of the northern half of Europe, but guesthouses, pensions, private rooms and B&Bs sometimes present good value. (See the Accommodation sections of the Estonia, Latvia and Lithuania chapters for specific details of accommodation in the Baltic states, where the situation is different.) Self-catering flats and cottages are worth considering if you're with a group, especially if you plan to stay somewhere for a while.

See the Facts for the Visitor sections in the country chapters for an overview of the local accommodation options. During peak holiday periods, accommodation can be hard to find, and unless you're camping, it's advisable to book ahead. Even camping grounds can fill up, especially popular big-city ones.

Reservations

If you arrive in a country by train, there is often a hotel-booking desk at the railway station. Tourist offices in cities and towns often have extensive lists of accommodation, and the more helpful ones will go out of their way to find you something suitable. In most countries there is a small fee for this service, but if accommodation is tight, it can save you a lot of running around. This is also an easy way to get around any language problems. Agencies offering private rooms can be good value. Staying with a local family doesn't always mean that you'll lack privacy, but you'll probably have less freedom than in a hotel.

Camping

Camping is immensely popular in most of the region (Estonia, Latvia and Lithuania are the exceptions) and is the cheapest form of accommodation. There's usually a charge per tent or site, per vehicle and per person. National tourist offices should have booklets or brochures listing camp sites all over their country. See the previous Documents section for information on the Camping Card International.

Although some camping grounds are commendably close to city centres, in most cases they will be some distance out from the centre, especially in larger cities. For this reason camping is most popular among people with their own vehicles. If you're on foot the money you save by camping can quickly be outweighed by the money you spend on commuting to and from a town centre. Unless the camping ground rents bungalows or small cabins on site (common in Scandinavia), you'll also need a tent, sleeping bag, cooking equipment and other bits and pieces – easier to cart around if you have a vehicle.

Camping other than in designated camping grounds is not always as straightforward as you'd think. Often it is illegal without permission from the local authorities (the police or local council office) or from landowners (don't be shy about asking, since you may be pleasantly surprised by their response).

In some countries (eg Denmark) free camping is illegal on all but private land. This doesn't prevent hikers from occasionally pitching their tent for the night, and they'll usually get away with it if they keep a low profile (don't disturb the locals, don't build a fire and don't leave rubbish).

The right of common access applies to all forests and wilderness areas in Sweden, Norway, Finland and Iceland. Camping for the night is always legal within the framework of these regulations but there are restrictions, and tourist offices usually stock the official publication of these in English. See the Facts for the Visitor sections of the relevant country chapters for additional information.

Hostels

Hostels offer the cheapest roof over your head in Scandinavia, and you don't have to be a youngster to use them. Most hostels are part of the national YHA (Youth Hostel Association), which is affiliated with Hostelling International (HI) in order to attract a wider clientele and move away from the emphasis on 'youth'.

Technically you're supposed to be a YHA or HI member to use affiliated hostels, but in practice most are open to anyone. You may have to pay a bit extra without a card but this may be set against future membership. Stay enough nights as a nonmember and you're automatically a member.

In Scandinavian countries, the hostels are geared for budget travellers of all ages, including families with kids, and have both dorms and private rooms. These hostels usually serve breakfast and/or have a group kitchen.

To join HI ask at any hostel or contact your local or national hostelling office. The offices for the Scandinavian and Baltic countries are included in the country chapters. The offices in English-speaking countries are as follows:

Australia
Australian Youth Hostels Association, Level 3, 10 Mallett St, Camperdown, NSW 2050 (☎ 02-9565 1699)

Canada
Hostelling International Canada, 1600 James Naismith Drive, Suite 608, Gloucester, Ontario K1B 5N4 (☎ 613-237 7884)

England & Wales
Youth Hostels Association, Trevelyan House, 8 St Stephen's Hill, St Albans, Herts AL1 2DY (☎ 01727-855215)

Ireland
An Óige, 61 Mountjoy St, Dublin 7 (☎ 01-830 4555)

New Zealand
Youth Hostels Association of New Zealand, PO Box 436, 173 Gloucester St, Christchurch 1 (☎ 03-379 9970)

Northern Ireland
Youth Hostel Association of Northern Ireland (YHANI), 22-32 Donegall Rd, Belfast BT12 5JN (☎ 01232-324733)

Scotland
Scottish Youth Hostels Association, 7 Glebe Crescent, Stirling FK8 2JA (☎ 01786-451181)

South Africa
Hostel Association of South Africa, 101 Boston House, 46 Strand St, Cape Town 8001 (☎ 021-419 1853)

USA
Hostelling International/American Youth Hostels, 733 15th St NW, Suite 840, Washington DC 20005 (☎ 202-783 6161)

At a hostel, you get a bed for the night, plus use of communal facilities which often include a kitchen where you can prepare your own meals. You are usually required to have a sleeping sheet – simply using your sleeping bag is not permitted. If you don't have your own approved sleeping sheet, you can usually hire or buy one.

Hostels vary widely in character, but increasingly, hostels are open longer hours, curfews are disappearing and 'wardens' with a sergeant-major mentality are an endangered species. Also the trend has been towards smaller dormitories with just four to six beds.

There are many hostel guides available, including the HI's *Europe* guide. Some hostels accept reservations by phone or fax but usually not during peak periods; they'll often book the next one you're headed to for a small fee. You can also book hostels through national hostel offices. Popular hostels in capital cities can be heavily booked in summer and limits may even be placed on how many nights you can stay.

There is only a handful of hostels in the Baltic states. For further information see the Facts for the Visitor sections in the country chapters.

Student Accommodation

Some universities and colleges rent out student accommodation from June to mid-August; in Finland this kind of accommodation is usually affiliated with the national YHA. These will often be single or double rooms and cooking facilities may be available. Enquire directly at the college or university, at student information services or at local tourist offices.

B&Bs, Guesthouses & Hotels

There's a huge range of accommodation above the hostel level. B&Bs, where you get a room and breakfast in a private home, can often be the real bargains in this field in some countries. Private accommodation may go under the name of pensions, guesthouses and so on. In Norway, for example, there are plenty of private guesthouses along main roads, and they are indeed cheaper than hotels. In Finland, most towns have guesthouses near the train station; an overnight stay usually costs at least twice as much as at a hostel, but will still be cheaper than at a hotel.

Above this level are hotels, which are always much more expensive than B&Bs and guesthouses; in cities luxury five-star hotels have five-star prices. Although categorisation varies from country to country, the hotels recommended in this book will usually range from no stars to one or two stars.

Check your hotel room and the bathroom before you agree to take it, and make sure you know what it's going to cost – discounts are often available for longer stays. Also ask about breakfast: it's sometimes included but at other times you may be required to have it and to pay extra for it (which can be a real rip-off).

If you think a hotel is too expensive, ask if they have anything cheaper, which is sometimes the case. If you are with a group or plan to stay for a reasonable length of time, it's always worth trying to negotiate a special rate.

FOOD

The Facts for the Visitor sections in the individual country chapters contain details of local cuisine, and there are many suggestions on places to eat in the chapters themselves. As a rule, Scandinavian food is rather bland, and some travellers might want to carry along a small collection of spices and condiments (ground pepper, chilli etc) to liven up some dishes.

Restaurant prices vary enormously. In Scandinavia the cheapest places for a decent meal are often the self-service restaurants in department stores. Official student mensas

or cafeterias are also cheap, and though the food tends to be unexciting it's of better quality than at mensas elsewhere in Europe. Without a university card, you probably won't get the student discount, but you'll be allowed to eat there and prices are still low. Kiosks also sell cheap snacks that can be as much a part of the national cuisine as more complex dishes.

Self-catering (buying your ingredients at a shop, market or supermarket and preparing your own meals) can be a cheap and wholesome way of eating. Most campers and hostellers will end up preparing at least some of their meals (Camping Gaz replacement canisters are widely available), and hostels and student accommodation often have cooking facilities. Even if you don't cook, a lunch in a park with some crisp bread, local cheese and slivers of smoked fish or salami can be one of the recurring highlights of your trip. It also makes a nice change from budget-restaurant food.

Vegetarians are fairly well catered for in Scandinavian cities, less so in towns and in the Baltic states and Russia. Tourist offices can supply lists of vegetarian restaurants, and some are recommended in this book. Many standard restaurants have one or two vegetarian dishes, or at least a few items on the menu that don't contain meat. Restaurants open at lunch often have a salad bar, and pizzerias are good bets for the green stuff. Some restaurants will prepare special diets if approached about this in advance, and you can always ask the waiter to talk with the cook on your behalf. If all else fails, you'll have to put together your own meals from ingredients bought in shops and markets.

Getting There & Away

Step one is to get to Europe and, in these days of severe competition among airlines, there are plenty of opportunities to find cheap tickets to a variety of 'gateway' cities including London, Athens, Frankfurt, Berlin or even Copenhagen, which has one of the busiest airports in Europe, Oslo and Stockholm.

Forget ships, unless by 'ships' you mean the many ferry services operating in the Baltic and North seas and in the Atlantic Ocean between Iceland and the Faroe Islands and the UK or Denmark. Only a handful of ships still carry passengers across the Atlantic; they don't sail often and are very expensive even compared with full-fare air tickets. See the Sea section at the end of this chapter for details.

Some travellers still arrive in Scandinavia or the Baltic states overland through what used to be the Soviet Union: Russia has borders with Norway, Finland, Estonia and Latvia; Belarus borders Lithuania and Latvia. The trans-Siberian and Mongolian express trains could well begin to carry more people to and from Europe as Russia opens up to tourism. See the Land section later in this chapter for more information.

AIR

Remember always to reconfirm your onward or return bookings by the specified time – at least 72 hours before departure on international flights. Otherwise there's a real risk that you'll turn up at the airport only to find that you've missed your flight because it was rescheduled, or that you've been reclassified as a 'no show' and 'bumped' (see the Air Travel Glossary later in this chapter).

Buying Tickets

Your plane ticket will probably be the single most expensive item in your travel budget, and it's worth taking some time to research the current state of the market. Start early: some of the cheapest tickets have to be bought well in advance, and some popular flights sell out early. Have a talk to recent travellers, look at the ads in newspapers and magazines, and watch for special offers. Don't forget to check the press of the ethnic group whose country you plan to visit.

Cheap tickets are available in two distinct categories: official and unofficial. Official ones have a variety of names including advance purchase tickets, advance purchase excursion (Apex) fares, super-Apex and simply budget fares.

Unofficial tickets are simply discounted tickets that the airlines release through selected travel agents and are usually not sold by the airline offices themselves. Airlines can, however, supply information on routes and timetables and make bookings; their low-season, student and senior citizens' fares can be competitive. Also, normal, full-fare airline tickets sometimes include one or more side trips in Europe free of charge, which can make them good value.

Return (round-trip) tickets usually work out cheaper than two one-way fares – often *much* cheaper. Be aware that immigration officials may ask to see return or onward tickets, and that if you can't show either, you might have to provide proof of 'sufficient means of support', which means you have to show a lot of money or, in some cases, valid credit cards.

Round-the-world (RTW) tickets are often real bargains, and can work out to be no more expensive or even cheaper than an ordinary return ticket. The official airline RTW tickets are usually put together by a combination of two or more airlines, and permit you to fly anywhere you want on their route systems so long as you don't backtrack. Other restrictions are that you (usually) must book the first sector in advance and cancellation penalties then apply. There may be restrictions on how many stops (or miles) you are permitted, and usually the tickets are valid for 90 days up to a year. Prices start at about

UK£1000/US$1500, depending on the season and length of validity. An alternative type of RTW ticket is one put together by a travel agent using a combination of discounted tickets. These can be much cheaper than the official ones but usually carry a lot of restrictions.

Generally, you can find discounted tickets at prices as low as, or lower than, advance purchase or budget tickets. Phone around the travel agencies for bargains. You may discover that those impossibly cheap flights are 'fully booked, but we have another one that costs a bit more...' Or that the flight is on an airline notorious for its poor safety standards and leaves you in the world's least favourite airport in mid-journey for 14 hours – where you're confined to the transit lounge because you don't have a visa. Or the agent claims to have the last two seats available for that country for the whole of August, which he will hold for you for a maximum of two hours as long as you come in and pay cash. Don't panic – keep ringing around.

If you are travelling from the USA and South-East Asia, or you are trying to get to Scandinavia from the UK, you will probably find that the cheapest flights are being advertised by obscure agencies whose names probably haven't even reached the telephone directory. Many such firms are honest and solvent, but there are a few rogues who will take your money and disappear – only to reopen elsewhere a month or two later under a new name.

If you feel suspicious about a firm, don't give them all the money at once – leave a deposit of 20% or so and pay the balance when you get the ticket. If they insist on cash in advance, go somewhere else or be prepared to take a very big risk. And once you have the ticket, ring the airline to confirm that you are actually booked onto the flight.

You may decide to pay more than the rock-bottom fare by opting for the safety of a better-known travel agent. Firms such as STA Travel, which has offices worldwide, Council Travel in the USA and elsewhere or Travel CUTS in Canada offer good prices to most destinations, and won't disappear overnight leaving you clutching a receipt for a nonexistent ticket.

Use the fares quoted in this book as a guide only. They are approximate and based on the rates advertised by travel agents at the time of research. Most are likely to have changed by the time you read this.

Travellers with Special Needs

If you have special needs of any sort – you're vegetarian or require a special diet, you're travelling in a wheelchair, taking the baby, terrified of flying, whatever – let the airline people know as soon as possible so that they can make the necessary arrangements. Remind them when you reconfirm your booking (at least 72 hours before departure) and again when you check in at the airport. It may also be worth ringing around the airlines before you make your booking to find out how they can handle your particular requirements.

Children aged under two travel for 10% of the full fare (or free on some airlines) as long as they don't occupy a seat. They don't get a baggage allowance in this case. 'Skycots', baby food and nappies (diapers) should be provided by the airline if requested in advance. Children aged between two and 12 can usually occupy a seat for half to two-thirds of the full fare. They do get a standard baggage allowance.

The USA

The North Atlantic is the world's busiest long-haul air corridor, and the flight options are bewildering. Larger newspapers such as the *New York Times*, the *Chicago Tribune*, the *San Francisco Chronicle* and the *Los Angeles Times* all produce weekly travel sections in which you'll find any number of travel agents' adverts for air fares to Europe.

You should be able to fly return from New York or Boston to Copenhagen, Oslo or Stockholm for around US$600 in the low season and US$800 in the high season. With most tickets you can usually travel 'open jaws', allowing you to land in one city (Copenhagen, for example) and return from another (such as Oslo) at no extra cost.

Air Travel Glossary

Apex Tickets Apex stands for Advance Purchase Excursion fare. These tickets are usually between 30% and 40% cheaper than the full economy fare, but there are restrictions. You must purchase the ticket at least 21 days in advance (sometimes more) and must be away for a minimum period (normally 14 days) and return within a maximum period (90 or 180 days). Stopovers are not allowed, and if you have to change your dates of travel or destination, there will be extra charges to pay. These tickets are not fully refundable – if you have to cancel your trip, the refund is often considerably less than what you paid for the ticket. Take out travel insurance to cover yourself in case you have to cancel your trip unexpectedly – for example, due to illness.

Baggage Allowance This will be written on your ticket; you are usually allowed one 20-kg item to go in the hold, plus one item of hand luggage. Some airlines which fly transpacific and transatlantic routes allow for two pieces of luggage (there are limits on their dimensions and weight).

Bucket Shops At certain times of the year and/or on certain routes, many airlines fly with empty seats. This isn't profitable and it's more cost-effective for them to fly full, even if that means having to sell a certain number of drastically discounted tickets. They do this by off-loading them onto bucket shops (UK) or consolidators (USA), travel agents who specialise in discounted fares. The agents, in turn, sell them to the public at reduced prices. These tickets are often the cheapest you'll find, but you can't purchase them directly from the airlines. Availability varies widely, so you'll not only have to be flexible in your travel plans, you'll also have to be quick off the mark as soon as an advertisement appears in the press.

Bucket-shop agents advertise in newspapers and magazines and there's a lot of competition – especially in places like Amsterdam and London which are crawling with them – so it's a good idea to telephone first to ascertain availability before rushing from shop to shop. Naturally, they'll advertise the cheapest available tickets, but by the time you get there, these may be sold out and you may be looking at something slightly more expensive.

Bumped Just because you have a confirmed seat doesn't mean you're going to get on the plane – see Overbooking.

Cancellation Penalties If you have to cancel or change an Apex or other discount ticket, there may be heavy penalties involved; insurance can sometimes be taken out against these penalties. Some airlines impose penalties on regular tickets as well, particularly against 'no show' passengers.

Check In Airlines ask you to check in a certain time ahead of the flight departure (usually two hours on international flights). If you fail to check in on time and the flight is overbooked, the airline can cancel your booking and give your seat to somebody else.

Confirmation Having a ticket written out with the flight and date on it doesn't mean you have a seat until the agent has confirmed with the airline that your status is 'OK'. Prior to this confirmation, your status is 'on request'.

Courier Fares Businesses often need to send their urgent documents or freight securely and quickly. They do it through courier companies. These companies hire people to accompany the package through customs and, in return, offer a discount ticket which is sometimes a phenomenal bargain. In effect, what the courier companies do is ship their freight as your luggage on the regular commercial flights. This is a legitimate operation – all freight is completely legal. There are two shortcomings, however: the short turnaround time of the ticket, usually not longer than a month; and the limitation on your luggage allowance. You may be required to surrender all your baggage allowance for the use of the courier company, and be only allowed to take carry-on luggage.

Discounted Tickets There are two types of discounted fares – officially discounted (such as Apex – see Promotional Fares) and unofficially discounted (see Bucket Shops). The latter can save you more than money – you may be able to pay Apex prices without the associated Apex advance booking and other requirements. The lowest prices often impose drawbacks, such as flying with unpopular airlines, inconvenient schedules, or unpleasant routes and connections.

Economy Class Tickets Economy-class tickets are usually not the cheapest way to go, though they do give you maximum flexibility and they are valid for 12 months. If you don't use them, most are fully refundable, as are unused sectors of a multiple ticket.

Full Fares Airlines traditionally offer first class (coded F), business class (coded J) and economy class (coded Y) tickets. These days there are so many promotional and discounted fares available that few passengers pay full fare.

Lost Tickets If you lose your airline ticket, an airline will usually treat it like a travellers' cheque and, after inquiries, issue you with a replacement. Legally, however, an airline is entitled to treat it like cash, so if you lose a ticket, it could be forever. Take good care of your tickets.

MCO An MCO (Miscellaneous Charges Order) is a voucher for a value of a given amount, which resembles an airline ticket and can be used to pay for a specific flight with any IATA (International Air Transport Association) airline. MCOs, which are more flexible than a regular ticket, may satisfy the irritating onward ticket requirement, but some countries are now reluctant to accept them. MCOs are fully refundable if unused.

No Shows No shows are passengers who fail to show up for their flight for whatever reason. Full-fare no shows are sometimes entitled to travel on a later flight. The rest of us are penalised (see Cancellation Penalties).

Open Jaw Tickets These are return tickets which allow you to fly to one place but return from another, and travel between the two 'jaws' by any means of transport at your own expense. If available, this can save you backtracking to your arrival point.

Overbooking Airlines hate to fly with empty seats, and since every flight has some passengers who fail to show up (see No Shows), they often book more passengers than they have seats available. Usually the excess passengers balance those who fail to show up, but occasionally somebody gets bumped. If this happens, guess who it is most likely to be? The passengers who check in late.

Promotional Fares These are officially discounted fares, such as Apex fares, which are available from travel agents or direct from the airline.

Reconfirmation You must contact the airline at least 72 hours prior to departure to 'reconfirm' that you intend to be on the flight. If you don't do this, the airline can delete your name from the passenger list and you could lose your seat.

Restrictions Discounted tickets often have various restrictions on them, such as necessity of advance purchase, limitations on the minimum and maximum period you must be away, restrictions on breaking the journey or changing the booking or route etc.

Round-the-World Tickets These tickets have become very popular in the last few years; basically, there are two types – airline tickets and agent tickets. An airline RTW ticket is issued by two or more airlines that have joined together to market a ticket which takes you around the world on their combined routes. It permits you to fly pretty well anywhere you choose using their combined routes as long as you don't backtrack, ie keep moving in approximately the same direction east or west. Other restrictions are that you (usually) must book the first sector in advance and cancellation penalties then apply. There may be restrictions on how many stopovers you are permitted. The RTW tickets are usually valid for 90 days up to a year.

The other type of RTW ticket, the agent ticket, is a combination of cheap fares strung together by an enterprising travel agent. These may be cheaper than airline RTW tickets, but the choice of routes will be limited.

Standby This is a discounted ticket where you only fly if there is a seat free at the last moment. Standby fares are usually only available directly at the airport, but sometimes may also be handled by an airline's city office. To give yourself the best possible chance of getting on the flight you want, get there early and have your name placed on the waiting list. It's first come, first served.

Student Discounts Some airlines offer student-card holders 15% to 25% discounts on their tickets. The same often applies to anyone under the age of 26. These discounts are generally only available on ordinary economy-class fares. You wouldn't get one, for instance, on an Apex or an RTW ticket, since these are already discounted.

Tickets Out An entry requirement for many countries is that you have an onward or return ticket, in other words, a ticket out of the country. If you're not sure what you intend to do next, the easiest solution is to buy the cheapest onward ticket to a neighbouring country or a ticket from a reliable airline which can later be refunded if you do not use it.

Transferred Tickets Airline tickets cannot be transferred from one person to another. Travellers sometimes try to sell the return half of their ticket, but officials can ask you to prove that you are the person named on the ticket. This may not be checked on domestic flights, but on international flights, tickets are usually compared with passports.

Travel Periods Some officially discounted fares, Apex fares in particular, vary with the time of year. There is often a low (off-peak) season and a high (peak) season. Sometimes there's an intermediate or shoulder season as well. At peak times, when everyone wants to fly, both officially and unofficially discounted fares will be higher, or there may simply be no discounted tickets available. Usually the fare depends on your outward flight – if you depart in the high season and return in the low season, you pay the high-season fare. ■

Icelandair (☎ 800-223-5500) has expanded its routes and now flies from New York, Boston, Baltimore, Fort Lauderdale and Orlando via Reykjavík to Oslo, Stockholm and Copenhagen. It can offer some of the best deals, and on all of its transatlantic flights it allows a free stopover in Reykjavík – making it an great way to spend a few days in Iceland.

On the other hand, if you're planning on flying within Scandinavian and Baltic Europe, SAS (☎ 800-221-2350) has some interesting air passes available to passengers who fly on their transatlantic flights (see Air in the Getting Around chapter).

Airhitch (☎ 212-864-2000 in New York, 310-394-0550 in Los Angeles) specialises in stand-by tickets and can often get travellers to Europe one way from US$169/$269/$229 from the East Coast/West Coast/elsewhere in the USA.

Another option is a courier flight, where you accompany a parcel or freight to be picked up at the other end. The drawbacks are that your stay may be limited to one or two weeks, your luggage is usually restricted to carry-on items (the freight you carry comes out of your luggage allowance), and you may have to be a resident and apply for an interview before they'll take you on. It's best to make your initial contact with the courier services a few months before you plan to travel.

Find out more about courier flights from Discount Travel International in New York (☎ 212-362-3636), Now Voyager in New York (☎ 212-431-1616) and Way to Go in Los Angeles (☎ 213-466-1126). They all work slightly differently. Now Voyager, for example, charges a $50 annual registration fee, after which most flights to Europe (including some to Copenhagen) cost US$199 return and allow a stay of seven days. When they're in a bind they do occasionally have great last-minute specials as low as US$99 return.

The *Travel Unlimited* newsletter, PO Box 1058, Allston, MA 02134 publishes details of the cheapest airfares and courier possibilities for destinations all over the world from the USA and other countries, including the UK. It's a treasure trove of information. A single monthly issue costs US$5 and a year's subscription costs US$25 (US$35 abroad).

Canada

Travel CUTS has offices in all major Canadian cities. Scan the budget travel agents' ads in the *Toronto Globe & Mail*, *Toronto Star* and *Vancouver Province*.

See the previous USA section for general information on courier flights. For those originating in Canada, contact FB on Board Courier Services (☎ 905-612 8095 in Toronto, ☎ 604-278 1266 in Vancouver). A courier return flight to London will cost from about C$350 from Toronto or Montreal, C$570 from Vancouver, depending on the season. Airhitch (see the USA section) has stand-by fares to Europe from Toronto, Montreal and Vancouver.

Icelandair (see the USA section) now has low-cost seasonal flights from Halifax in Nova Scotia to Oslo, Stockholm and Copenhagen via Reykjavík.

Australia

STA Travel and Flight Centres International are major dealers in cheap airfares. Check the travel agents' ads in the Yellow Pages and ring around.

The Saturday travel sections of the *Sydney Morning Herald* and Melbourne's *Age* newspapers have many ads offering cheap fares to Europe, but don't be surprised if they happen to be 'sold out' when you contact the agents: they're usually low-season fares on obscure airlines with conditions attached. With Australia's large and well-organised ethnic populations, it pays to check special deals in the ethnic press.

Discounted return fares on mainstream airlines through a reputable agent like STA Travel cost between A$1500 (low season) and A$2500 (high season). Flights to/from Perth are a couple of hundred dollars cheaper. Lauda Air flies from Sydney via Singapore to Vienna in the heart of Central Europe.

New Zealand

As in Australia, STA Travel and Flight Centres International are popular travel agencies. Not surprisingly, the cheapest fares to Europe are routed through the USA, and a RTW ticket can be cheaper than an advance purchase return ticket.

Africa

Nairobi is probably the best place in Africa to buy tickets to Europe, thanks to the strong competition between its many bucket shops. Several West African countries such as Burkina Faso and The Gambia offer cheap charter flights to France, and charter fares from Morocco can be incredibly cheap if you're lucky enough to find a seat. From South Africa, Air Namibia has particularly cheap return youth fares to London but they are expected to rise shortly following the devaluation of the rand. Students' Travel (☎ 011-716 3945) in Johannesburg, and the Africa Travel Centre (☎ 021-235 555) in Cape Town are worth trying for cheap tickets.

Asia

Hong Kong is still the discount plane-ticket capital of Asia, and its bucket shops offer some great bargains. But be careful: not all are reliable. Ask the advice of other travellers before buying tickets. Many of the cheapest fares from South-East Asia to Europe are offered by Eastern European carriers (eg LOT or Aeroflot). Lauda Air flies direct to Vienna from Hong Kong via Bangkok. STA Travel has branches in Tokyo, Singapore, Bangkok and Kuala Lumpur.

To/from India, the cheapest flights tend to be with Eastern European carriers or certain Middle Eastern airlines like Syrian Arab Airlines. Mumbai (Bombay) is India's air transport hub, with many transit options to/from South-East Asia, but tickets are slightly cheaper in Delhi.

From the UK

If you're looking for a cheap way into or out of Scandinavia, London is Europe's major centre for discounted fares. You can fly from London to Copenhagen for between UK£94

and £161, to Stockholm for UK£170 to £186, to Rīga for UK£287 to £317, and to Tallinn for UK£251.

You can often find airfares from London that either match or beat surface alternatives in terms of cost. A restricted return (valid for one month maximum) from London to Copenhagen, for example, is available through discount travel agents for less than UK£100. By comparison, a two-month return by rail between the same cities costs UK£228. Getting between airports and city centres is not a problem in Scandinavia thanks to good transport networks.

If you are travelling alone, courier flights are a possibility. You get cheap passage in return for accompanying a package or documents through customs and delivering it to a representative at the destination airport. EU integration and electronic communications means there's increasingly less call for couriers, but you might find something. British Airways, for example, offers courier flights through the Travel Shop (☎ 0181-564 7009) in London. People taking flights from Britain pay an Air Passenger Duty; those flying to countries in the EU pay £5; those flying beyond it, £10. This may or may not be quoted in the price of your ticket; check with your travel agent. At present, there is no departure tax if you depart by sea or via the Channel Tunnel.

Following are the addresses of some of the best agencies to contact for discounted airfares in London:

Trailfinders
    198 Kensington High St, London W8 (☎ 0171-938 3232); tube: High St Kensington
STA Travel
    86 Old Brompton Rd, London SW7 3LQ (☎ 0171-581 4132); tube: South Kensington
Campus Travel
    52 Grosvenor Gardens, London SW1W OAG (☎ 0171-730 8832); tube: Victoria
Council Travel
    28A Poland St, London W1V 3DB (☎ 0171-287 3337); tube: Oxford Circus

The entertainment listings magazine *Time Out*, the Sunday papers, the *Exchange &*

Mart and *Evening Standard* carry ads for cheap fares. Also look out for the free magazines and newspapers widely available in London, especially *TNT* and *Southern Cross*. You can often pick them up outside the main train and tube stations.

Make sure the agent is a member of some sort of traveller-protection scheme, such as that offered by the Association of British Travel Agents (ABTA). If you have paid for your flight to an ABTA-registered agent who subsequently goes out of business, ABTA will guarantee a refund or an alternative. Unregistered bucket shops are riskier but sometimes cheaper.

From Continental Europe

Though London is the travel discount capital of Europe, there are several other cities in the region where you'll find a wide range of good deals, particularly Amsterdam and Athens.

Berlin is becoming Scandinavian and Baltic Europe's new air hub including flights to/from Moscow, and it's worth looking there for airfare bargains. One reliable agency for cheap tickets is Kilroy Travels (☎ 030-310 0040), Hardenbergstrasse 9, 10623 Berlin.

From Germany Lufthansa has regular connections with the Baltic states, Belarus, Ukraine, Moscow and St Petersburg – a return Frankfurt-Minsk fare, for instance, can be had from DM1037. For other information on cheap flights from Germany, check with travel agencies. Individuals offering plane tickets they no longer require, at very cheap prices, advertise in the *Urlaub & Reisen (biete)* section of major city newspapers.

Many travel agents in Europe have ties with STA Travel, where cheap tickets can be purchased, and STA tickets can often be altered free of charge the first time around. Outlets in important transport hubs include: CTS Voyages (☎ 01 43 25 00 76), 20 Rue des Carmes, 75005 Paris; SRID Reisen (☎ 069-70 30 35), Bockenheimer Landstrasse 133, 60325 Frankfurt; and International Student & Youth Travel Service (☎ 01-322 1267), Nikis 11, 10557 Athens.

LAND
Bus

If you're already in Europe and you don't have a rail pass, it's generally cheaper to get to Scandinavian and Baltic Europe by bus than it is by train or plane. Long bus rides can be tedious, so bring along a good book. On the plus side, some of the coaches are quite luxurious with WC, air-con, stewards and snack bar.

Small bus companies come along occasionally with cut rates, although most of them don't remain in business for more than a year or two. Ask around at student and discount travel agencies for the latest information.

Eurolines, one of the biggest and best-established express bus services, connects Scandinavia with the rest of Europe. Most of the buses operate daily (or near-daily) in summer and between two and five days a week in winter. Eurolines' representatives in Europe include:

Eurolines Nederland, Rokin 10, Amsterdam (☎ 020-627 5151)
Bayern Express, Central Coachstation am Funkturm, Masurenallee 4, Berlin (☎ 030-301 2028)
Eurolines Belgium, Place de Brouckère 50, Brussels (☎ 02-217 0025)
Eurolines Denmark, Reventlowsgade 8, Copenhagen (☎ 33 25 10 44)
Deutsche Touring, Mannheimerstrasse 4, Frankfurt (☎ 069-23 07 35)
Eurolines Sweden, Kyrkogatan 40, 411 15 Gothenburg (☎ 31-10 02 40)
Matkakeskus Resecenter, Georgsgatan 23A, Helsinki (☎ 0-68 09 01)
Eurolines, 52 Grosvenor Gardens, London SW1W 0AU (☎ 0990-143219 or 01582-404511)
Eurolines/Nor-Way Bussekspress, Karl Johans gate 2, 0154 Oslo (☎ 22 17 52 90)
Eurolines France, 28 Avenue du Général de Gaulle, 75020 Paris (☎ 01 49 72 51 51)
Eurolines Czech Republic, Opletalova 37, Prague 1(☎ 02-2421 3420)
Eurolines Italy, Circonvallazione Nonentana 574, Lato Stazione Tiburtina, Rome (☎ 06-44 23 39 28)
Eurolines Austria (☎ 0222-712 0453), Autobusbahnhof Wien-Mitte, Landstrasser Hauptstrasse 1/b, 1030 Vienna

These offices may have information on other companies and deals. Advance reservations and ticket purchases may be necessary on international buses; either call the bus companies directly or enquire at a travel agency.

Sample one-way Eurolines fares from Copenhagen are 395 Dkr to Stockholm, 470 Dkr to Prague, 595 Dkr to Paris and 675 Dkr to London. There's a discount of around 10% for those aged under 26 or over 60 years. Return fares are about 20% less than two one-way fares.

Eurolines has 10 circular Explorer routes, always starting and ending in London. The one taking in Amsterdam, Copenhagen and Paris costs UK£125; Copenhagen, Gothenburg and Hamburg is UK£132. There are regular services to Scandinavia from the Netherlands – from Amsterdam to Copenhagen takes 12 hours and costs f115.

Eurolines also offers passes, but they're neither as extensive nor as flexible as rail passes (see Train in the Getting Around chapter). They cover 18 European cities as far apart as London, Barcelona, Rome, Budapest and Copenhagen, and cost UK£229 for 30 days (UK£199 for students/senior citizens) or UK£279 for 60 days (UK£249). The passes may be cheaper off-season.

Most buses to the Baltic states start from Poland, so you may find it easier when heading for the Baltics to start with a bus to Warsaw, which is reached by many services. Buses from Warsaw to the Baltics can get heavily booked, however, so be prepared to take a train or fly if necessary. Also check up on likely delays at road borders before committing yourself to a bus.

Train
The UK Going by train from the UK to Scandinavia can be more expensive than flying. From London a return 2nd-class train ticket will cost UK£228 to Copenhagen, UK£281 to Stockholm and UK£367 to Oslo. The lowest equivalent airfares are UK£94/£170/£202.

Central Europe Hamburg is the Central European gateway for Scandinavia and Warsaw for the Baltic states. From Hamburg,

there are several direct trains daily to Copenhagen and a few to Stockholm. The train from Hamburg to Copenhagen travels for an hour by ferry, which is included in the ticket price. It also goes by ferry from Denmark to Sweden, but takes only 15 or 20 minutes.

From Warsaw, you can take a Polish train to the appropriate port for a ferry to Sweden, or take a train to Lithuania. From Berlin, there are trains to Hamburg, Warsaw and the ports with connecting ferries to Sweden.

A good train deal to know about is the Sparpreis fare which allows a round trip anywhere in Germany within one month for DM199 (an accompanying person pays just DM99). This ticket can be purchased at any German train station and unlimited stopovers along the direct route are allowed, but you are not allowed to complete the return trip within a single Monday-to-Friday period. From northern Germany, you can easily make your way to Denmark and the rest of Scandinavia.

Asia To/from central and eastern Asia, a train can work out at about the same price as flying, depending on how much time and money you spend along the way, and it can be a lot more fun. There are three routes to /from Moscow across Siberia: the trans-Siberian to/from Vladivostok, and the trans-Mongolian and trans-Manchurian, both to/from Beijing. There's a fourth route south from Moscow and across Kazakstan, following part of the old Silk Road to Beijing. Prices can vary enormously, depending on where you buy the ticket and what is included – the prices quoted here are a rough indication only. For connections from Moscow to St Petersburg see Getting There & Away in the St Petersburg chapter.

The trans-Siberian takes just under seven days from Moscow via Khabarovsk to Vladivostok, from where there is a boat to Niigata in Japan from May to October. Otherwise you can fly to Niigata as well as to Seattle and Anchorage, Alaska, in the USA. The complete journey from Moscow to Niigata costs from about US$600 per person for a 2nd-class sleeper in a four-berth cabin.

The trans-Mongolian passes through Mongolia to Beijing and takes about 5½ days. A 2nd-class sleeper in a four-berth compartment would cost around US$265 if purchased in Moscow or Beijing. If you want to stop off along the way or spend some time in Moscow, you'll need 'visa support' – a letter from a travel agent confirming that they're making your travel/accommodation bookings as required in Russia or Mongolia. Locally based companies that do all-inclusive packages (with visa support) include the Travellers Guest House (☎ 095-971 4059; fax 280 9786) in Moscow; and Monkey Business (☎ 2723 1376; fax 2723 6653) in Hong Kong, with an information centre in Beijing. There are a number of other budget operators.

The trans-Manchurian passes through Manchuria to Beijing and takes 6½ days, costing about US$225.

A trans-Central Asia route runs from Moscow to Almaty in Kazakhstan, crosses the border on the new line to Ürümqi (northwestern China), and follows part of the old Silk Road to Beijing. At present you can't buy through tickets. Moscow to Ürümqi in 2nd class costs about US$160 and takes five or more days, depending on connections.

The *Trans-Siberian Handbook* (Trailblazer) by Bryn Thomas is a comprehensive guide to the route, and Lonely Planet's *Russia, Ukraine & Belarus* has a separate chapter on trans-Siberian travel.

Car & Motorcycle

Travelling by private transport beyond Europe requires plenty of paperwork and other preparations. A detailed description is beyond the scope of this book, but the Getting Around chapter tells you what's required within Scandinavian and Baltic Europe.

Cycling

Cycling is a cheap, convenient, healthy, environmentally sound and above all enjoyable way of travelling. One note of caution:

before you leave home, go over your bike with a fine-toothed comb and fill your repair kit with every imaginable spare. As with cars and motorbikes, you may not be able to find that crucial gizmo for your machine in the Baltic states – or be able to pay for it in Scandinavia.

Bicycles can travel by air. You can take them to pieces and put them in a bike bag or box, but it's much easier to simply wheel your machine to the check-in desk, where it should be treated as a piece of baggage. You may have to remove the pedals and turn the handlebars sideways so that it takes up less space in the aircraft's hold; check all this with the airline well in advance, preferably before you pay for your ticket. See also the introductory Getting Around chapter and the Getting Around sections of the individual country chapters.

Hitching & Ride Services

Several European organisations can help you find a ride to/from the Scandinavian or Baltic countries. Besides hitchhiking, the cheapest way to get to northern Europe from elsewhere in Europe is as a paying passenger in a private car.

If you are leaving from Germany, or travelling within that country, such rides are arranged by Mitfahrzentrale agencies in many German cities. You pay a reservation fee to the agency and your share of petrol to the driver. The local tourist information office will be able to direct you to several such agencies, or you can check the entry 'Mitfahrzentralen' in the Yellow Pages phone book.

There are organisations offering ride services in a number of other European countries, including France (Allostop Provoya ☎ 01 42 46 00 66; 84 Passage Brady, Paris, 10e; metro Château d'Eau and Auto-Passage ☎ 01 45 85 52 53; 189 Ave de Choisy, Paris, 13e; metro Place d'Italie) and Hungary (Kenguru ☎ 1-266 5857; VIII Kőfaragó út 15 Budapest)

For more details of local conditions and laws, see the individual country chapters.

SEA
Boat Companies
The following are the reservation numbers for the larger ferry companies operating in Scandinavia.

Scandinavian Seaways Known also as DFDS, Scandinavian Seaways runs ferries from Copenhagen to Oslo via Helsingborg, Sweden; from Esbjerg to Harwich, UK; and from Hamburg, Germany, to Harwich and Newcastle.

Booking agents include:

Denmark
Scandinavian Seaways, Sankt Annæ Plads 30, 1295 Copenhagen (☎ 33 42 30 00 in Copenhagen, ☎ 79 17 79 17 in Esbjerg)

Germany
Scandinavian Seaways, DFDS, Van-der-Smissen-Strasse 4, 22 767 Hamburg 50 (☎ 040-38 9 03 71)

Norway
Scandinavian Seaways, Utstikker II Vippetangen, Oslo (☎ 22 41 90 90)

Sweden
Scandinavian Seaways, Birger Jarlsgatan 6, 114 34 Stockholm (☎ 08-679 8880 in Stockholm, ☎ 042-24 10 00 in Helsingborg)

UK
Scandinavian Seaways, 15 Hanover St, London W1R 9HG (☎ 0171-409 6060 in London, ☎ 0125-524 4370 in Harwich, ☎ 0191-293 6262 in Newcastle)

USA
DFDS Seaways, Cypress Creek Business Park, 6555 NW 9th Avenue, Suite 207, Fort Lauderdale, FL 33309 (☎ 800-533 3755)

Stena Line Stena operates ferries from Frederikshavn, Denmark, to Oslo and Moss in Norway and Gothenburg in Sweden, as well as from Gothenburg to Kiel, Germany.

Booking agents include:

Denmark
Stena Line, Stenaterminalen, 9900 Frederikshavn (☎ 96 20 02 00)

Germany
Stena Line, Schwedenkai, 2300 Kiel 1 (☎ 0431-90 90)

Norway
Stena Line, Jernbanetorget 2, 0154 Oslo (☎ 22 41 22 10 in Oslo, ☎ 69 25 75 00 in Moss)

Sweden
Stena Line, 405 16 Gothenburg (☎ 031-85 80 00)

UK
Stena Sealink Line, Charter House, Park Street, Ashford, Kent TN24 8EX (☎ 01233-647022)

Color Line The Color Line operates ferries between Hirtshals, Denmark, to Oslo and Kristiansand, Norway; from Oslo to Kiel, Germany; and from Bergen, Norway, to Newcastle, UK.

Booking agents include:

Denmark
Color Line, Fergeterminalen, Postboks 30, 9850 Hirtshals (☎ 99 56 19 66)

France
Color Line, c/o Scanditours, 36 rue Tronchet, 75009 Paris (☎ 01 45 61 65 00)

Germany
Color Line GmbH, Postfach 2646, 24025 Kiel (☎ 0431-97 41 10)

Norway
Color Line, Postboks 1422 Vika, 0115 Oslo (☎ 22 94 44 00 in Oslo, ☎ 38 07 88 00 in Kristiansand, ☎ 55 54 86 00 in Bergen)

UK
Color Line, Tyne Commission Quay, North Shields NE29 6EA (☎ 0191-296 1313)

USA
Bergen Line, 405 Fifth Avenue, New York, NY 10017 (☎ 212-319 1300)

P&O Scottish Ferries P&O operates a ferry from Aberdeen, Scotland, to Bergen, Norway, via Lerwick in the Shetland Islands.

Booking agents include:

Norway
Color Lines, Skuteviksboder 1, Postboks 4098, 5023 Bergen (☎ 55 54 86 60)

UK
P&O Scottish Ferries, PO Box 5, Jamiesons Quay, Aberdeen AB9 8DL (☎ 01224-572615)

Silja Line The Silja Line has ferries from Helsinki to Travemünde and Stockholm, and various other routes between Finland and Sweden. The head office is: Silja Line (☎ 0-180 4413), Mannerheimintie 2, PB 880, 00101 Helsinki.

See the individual Getting There & Away sections of the country chapters for information about boat-trains or rail/ferry links within Scandinavian and Baltic Europe. See also the following Getting Around chapter for details of rail passes and their validity on state-owned and other ferries.

Germany

Hamburg is 20 hours by car ferry from the East Anglian port of Harwich. Timetables vary according to the time of year, and may be affected by extremes in the weather, but sailings are at least twice weekly in either direction.

The busy train, car and passenger ferry from Puttgarden to Rødbyhavn (the quickest way to Copenhagen) runs every half-hour round the clock and takes an hour.

From Kiel there are ferries to a number of Scandinavian and Baltic ports, including Gothenburg (Sweden), Bagenkop (Denmark), Oslo (Norway) and Klaipéda (Lithuania). In eastern Germany, there are five large ferries daily in each direction all year round between Trelleborg (just south of Malmö in Sweden), and Sassnitz near Stralsund. From April to October, ferries also run several times a week between the Danish island of Bornholm and Sassnitz.

Coming from Berlin there are two car-ferry trains a day between Berlin-Zoo Station and Copenhagen via Rostock. These trains connect with the international ferry service from Warnemünde (Germany) to Gedser (Denmark). The ferry terminal is a few minutes walk from Warnemünde railway station, and the crossing takes only two hours. There is at least one ferry departure every day from Rostock to Trelleborg, Sweden. See also the relevant Getting There & Away sections in the individual country chapters.

The UK

There are ferry services between Newcastle in the UK and Esbjerg (Denmark). The ferry *Smyril* sails weekly from Aberdeen in Scotland to Tórshavn in the Faroe Islands.

One of the most interesting Scandinavian travel possibilities is the summer-only link between the Shetlands, Norway, the Faroes,

Iceland, and Denmark. The agent is P&O, but the operator is the Smyril Line.

From Newcastle, Color Line operates ferries all year to Stavanger and Bergen in Norway. Scandinavian Seaways has ferries from Harwich to Esbjerg in Denmark.

P&O also runs two ferries a day from Felixstowe to Zeebrugge in Belgium from where you can travel by bus or train to Scandinavia or the Baltic states. The shortest cross-Channel routes (from Dover to Calais or from Folkestone to Boulogne) are the busiest, though the Eurostar passenger train and Le Shuttle car and lorry train connecting the UK and France are taking a lot of their business these days.

There are cargo ships from the UK to Baltic ports but agents say they don't take passengers. See the relevant Getting There & Away sections in the individual country chapters for fares and more travel details.

Sealink runs two ferries a day from Harwich to the Hook of Holland in the Netherlands from where you can head north by land. Otherwise you can catch a Scandinavian Seaways ferry to either Kristiansand (Norway) or Gothenburg (Sweden).

Transatlantic Passenger Ships & Freighters

Regular, long-distance passenger ships disappeared with the advent of cheap air travel and were replaced by a small number of luxury cruise ships. Cunard's *Queen Elizabeth 2* sails between New York and Southampton 20 times a year; the trip takes six nights each way and costs around UK£1500 for the return trip, though there are also one-way and 'fly one-way' deals. Your travel agent will have more details. The standard reference for passenger ships is the *OAG Cruise & Ferry Guide* published by the UK-based Reed Travel Group (01582-600111), Church St, Dunstable, Bedfordshire LU5 4HB.

A more adventurous (though not necessarily cheaper) alternative is as a paying passenger on a freighter. Freighters are far more numerous than cruise ships, and there are many more routes from which to choose.

With a bit of homework, you'll be able to sail between Europe and just about anywhere else in the world, with stopovers at exotic ports that you may never have heard of. Again, the *OAG Cruise & Ferry Guide* is the most comprehensive source of information, though *Travel by Cruise Ship* (Cadogan, London) is also a good source.

Passenger freighters typically carry six to 12 passengers (more than 12 would require a doctor on board) and, though less luxurious than dedicated cruise ships, give you a real taste of life at sea. Schedules tend to be flexible and costs vary, but seem to hover around US$100 a day; vehicles can often be included for an additional fee.

DEPARTURE TAXES

Some countries charge you a fee for the privilege of leaving from their airports. Some also charge port fees when you're leaving by ship. Such fees are often included in the price of your ticket, but it pays to check this when purchasing your ticket. If not, you'll have to have the fee ready when you leave – usually in local currency. Details are given at the end of the Getting There & Away section in the relevant country chapters.

WARNING

This chapter is particularly vulnerable to change – prices for international travel are volatile, routes are introduced and cancelled, schedules change, special deals come and go, and rules and visa requirements are amended. Airlines seem to take a perverse pleasure in making price structures and regulations as complicated as possible; you should check directly with the airline or travel agent to make sure you understand how a fare (and ticket you may buy) works. In addition, the travel industry is highly competitive and there are many schemes and bonuses. The upshot of this is that you should get opinions, quotes and advice from as many airlines and travel agents as possible before you part with your hard-earned cash. The details given in this chapter should be regarded as pointers and are not a substitute for your own careful, up-to-date research.

Getting Around

Getting around in Scandinavia is a hassle-free experience; public transport services are efficient with great connections. Travelling around the Baltic states will not be quite so straightforward, however.

If you're having trouble communicating in the Baltic states, where few ticket clerks speak foreign languages, you can simplify ticket-buying by writing your requirements on a slip of paper, using the 24-hour clock for departure times and Roman numerals for the month in the date. If you want a ticket on the 3.45 pm departure to Vilnius on 24 July, for example, write: 15.45 Vilnius 24/VII.

Another problem in Estonia, Latvia and Lithuania is knowing which ticket window to go to. Some windows are reserved for same-day tickets, others for advance bookings, and still others for some arcane purposes. So don't be put off if the first clerk you deal with shouts brusquely at you and turns away.

AIR

In 1997, as part of the EU's 'open skies' policy, national airlines will no longer have to include a domestic airport in their routes and can fly directly from one EU city to another. Pundits forecast increased competition and lower prices but there are problems, such as finding additional take-off slots at oversubscribed airports. But look out for the new breed of small airlines, such as the UK-based EasyJet, which sell budget tickets directly to the customer. In any case, such deregulation will only affect Denmark, Sweden and Finland at this point, the only EU members in Scandinavian and Baltic Europe.

Refer to the Air Travel Glossary in the Getting There & Away chapter for information on types of air tickets. London is a good centre for picking up inexpensive, restricted-validity tickets through bucket shops. Amsterdam and Athens are other good places for tickets in Europe. The different classes of cheap air tickets are also available on routes within Scandinavian and Baltic countries.

For longer journeys, you can sometimes find airfares that beat on-the-ground alternatives in terms of cost. Getting between airports and city centres is rarely a problem in Scandinavia and the Baltic states thanks to good bus services.

Air travel is best viewed as a means to get you to the starting point of your itinerary rather than as your main means of travel, as it lacks the flexibility of ground transport. Also, if you use aeroplanes for relatively short hops it gets expensive, particularly as special deals are rarely available on internal flights. In Russia, foreigners pay several times more for internal flights than locals.

Open jaw returns, by which you can travel into one city and out of another, are worth considering, though they usually work out more expensive than straightforward returns (see the Getting There & Away chapter).

Visitors who fly SAS to Scandinavia from Continental Europe, North America or Asia can purchase tickets on a Visit Scandinavia Air Pass which allows one-way travel on direct flights between any two Scandinavian cities serviced by SAS for US$80 to US$110. You can buy from one to six tickets; they must be purchased in advance before arriving in Scandinavia and in conjunction with a return SAS international ticket.

A similar deal applies with the SAS Visit Europe and Visit Baltic Air Passes. You can buy from three to eight Visit Europe Air Passes, valid for a one-way flight on any of a number of routes within Europe, for US$120 each. You can also buy two to four Visit Baltic Air Passes, valid for a one-way flight between Scandinavian and Baltic countries for US$110 each.

BUS
International Buses
Bus travel tends to take second place to

getting around by train in most of Europe, though when it comes to Estonia, Latvia and Lithuania it's at least as efficient and much cheaper (almost half the price, in fact) than the train. In Scandinavia, the bus also has the edge in terms of cost but is generally slower and less comfortable. Eurolines offers a variety of city 'loops'; see the Getting There & Away chapter for more details.

On ordinary return trips, Eurolines youth fares cost around 10% less than the ordinary adult fare. Onward or return journeys must be reserved prior to departure for all tickets. See the individual country chapters for details.

National Buses

Buses provide a viable alternative to the rail network in Scandinavian countries. Again, compared to trains they are usually cheaper (though not in Finland) and slightly slower. Bus travel tends to be best for shorter hops such as getting round cities and reaching remote rural villages.

Buses are often the only option in regions where rail tracks fear to tread; these buses often connect with train services. Advance reservations are rarely necessary. Many city buses operate on a pay-in-advance system and you cancel your own ticket on boarding. In the Baltic states buses are generally more frequent, quicker, and much cheaper than trains. See the individual country chapters for details.

TRAIN

Trains are a popular way of getting around: they are good meeting places and in Scandinavia are comfortable, frequent, and generally on time. Also in the Scandinavian countries, European rail passes make travel affordable. Supplements and reservation costs are not covered by passes, and pass holders must always carry their passport on the train for identification purposes.

If you plan to travel extensively by train, it might be worth getting hold of the *Thomas Cook European Timetable*, which gives a complete listing of train schedules and indicates where supplements apply or where reservations are necessary. It is updated monthly and is available from Thomas Cook outlets in the UK and Australia, in the USA from Forsyth Travel Library (☎ 800-367 7984), 9154 West 57th St, PO Box 2975, Shawnee Mission, Kansas 66201-1375. If you are planning to do a lot of train travel in one or a handful of countries – Norway, say, or the three Baltic states – it might be worthwhile getting hold of the national rail timetable(s) published by the state railroad(s).

Oslo, Stockholm, Helsinki and Copenhagen are all important hubs for international rail connections. See the relevant city sections for details and budget ticket agents.

Express Trains

Fast trains, or ones that make few stops, are usually identified by the symbols EC (Eurocity) or IC (Intercity) though there are national variations; in Finland they are called EP and IC trains. Supplements usually apply on fast trains, and it is a good idea (sometimes obligatory) to make seat reservations at peak times and on certain lines.

In Estonia, Latvia and Lithuania there are no fast trains. The few that are classed 'quick' (Russian: *skoryy*) are just a bit slower than the others *passazhirskiy* or *dizel*. To make up for this, trains (like buses) in these countries are fairly cheap. The 440-km trip from Tallinn to Rīga may take 7½ hours but it'll only cost US$28 in a four-bunk couchette if you buy the ticket yourself from the station. (You might be asked to pay a couple of dollars extra for bedding once on board.)

Overnight Trains

Overnight trains will usually offer a choice of couchette or sleeper if you don't fancy sleeping in your seat with somebody else's head on your shoulder. Again, reservations are advisable and in Scandinavia are often necessary as sleeping options are allocated on a first-come, first-served basis.

Couchettes are bunks numbering four (1st class) or six (2nd class) per compartment and are comfortable enough, if lacking a bit in privacy. A bunk costs around US$25 for most

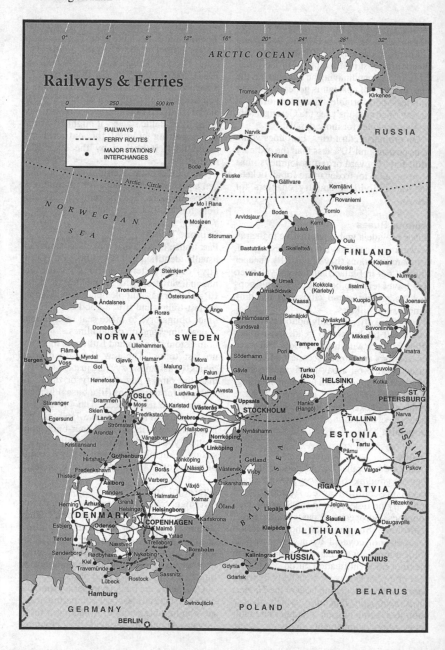

Railways & Ferries

international trains irrespective of the length of the journey except between Estonia, Latvia and Lithuania.

In Russian, the 'international' language still used most commonly on Baltic trains, a four-bunk couchette is called *kupeynyy* (compartmentalised) and regarded as 2nd-class. Third class is *platskartnyy* (reserved place), which is six bunks partitioned, but not closed, off from each other. Kupeynyy and platskartnyy together make up 'hard-class' *(zhyostkiy)*. *Obshchiy* or 'general class' is unreserved bench-type seating.

Sleepers are the most comfortable option, offering beds for one or two passengers in 1st class, and two or three passengers in 2nd class. All sleepers in Norway, for example, are either for one person (1st class only) or two to three people (2nd class); there are no couchettes as previously described, but the three-person 2nd-class compartments function the same way. An individual traveller can book a bed in one (100 Nkr), in which case they'll be booked into a compartment with two other people of the same sex. Denmark has six-person compartments (60 Dkr), as well as single and double cabins. Charges vary depending upon the journey but they tend to be significantly more expensive than couchettes. Couchettes (but not sleepers) are available on trains within Estonia, Latvia and Lithuania but sleepers may be available on trains to/from Moscow, St Petersburg, Warsaw or Berlin. In Russian, a sleeper is a *spalnyy vagon (SV)* also known as *myngkiy* ('soft class').

Most long-distance trains, except those in the Baltic states, have a dining car or an attendant who wheels a drink-and-snack-laden trolley through carriages, but prices tend to be steep. On overnight trains in the Baltic states be prepared to bake or freeze depending on whether the heating is on or not.

Rail Passes

Eurail In Scandinavia, the Scanrail pass (see the following) is generally a better deal than the Eurail pass, so this information will only be of interest to travellers visiting other parts of Europe too.

Eurail passes can only be bought by residents of non-European countries, and are supposed to be purchased before arriving in Europe. However, Eurail passes can be purchased within Europe as long as your passport proves you've been there for less than six months, but the outlets where you can do this are limited, and the passes will be more expensive than getting them outside Europe. For example, Copenhagen is the only city in Denmark and Oslo is the only place in Norway where you can buy Eurail passes (at the international ticket counters at the main train stations). In London, the Rail Shop (☎ 0990-300003) at 179 Piccadilly is another such outlet.

If you've lived in Europe for more than six months, you are eligible for an Inter-Rail pass, which is a better buy.

Eurail passes are valid for unlimited travel on national railways and some private lines in Austria, Belgium, Denmark, Finland, France (including Monaco), Germany, Greece, Hungary, Ireland, Italy, Luxembourg, the Netherlands, Norway, Portugal, Spain, Sweden and Switzerland (including Liechtenstein). The passes do *not* cover the UK or the Baltic states.

Eurail is also valid for some ferries between Ireland and France (but not between the UK and France), between Italy and Greece, and from Sweden to Finland, Denmark or Germany. Reductions are given on some other ferry routes and on steamer services in various countries.

Eurail passes offer reasonable value to people aged under 26. A Youthpass is valid for unlimited 2nd-class travel for 15 days (US$418), one month (US$598) or two months (US$798). The Youth Flexipass, also for 2nd class, is valid for freely chosen days within a two-month period: 10 days for US$438 or 15 days for US$588. Overnight journeys commencing after 7 pm count as the following day's travel. The traveller must fill out in ink the relevant box in the calendar before starting a day's travel; not validating the pass in this way earns a fine of US$50.

Tampering with the pass (eg using an erasable pen and later rubbing out earlier days) costs the perpetrator the full fare plus US$100.

For those aged over 26, a Flexipass (available in 1st class only) costs US$616 or US$812 for 10 or 15 freely chosen days within two months. The standard Eurail pass has five versions, costing from US$522 for 15 days unlimited travel up to US$1468 for three months. Two or more people travelling together (minimum three people between April and September) can get good discounts on a Saverpass, which works like the standard Eurail pass. A 15-day Saverpass costs US$452. Eurail passes for children are also available.

Inter-Rail Inter-Rail passes are available to European residents of six-months standing (passport identification is required). Terms and conditions vary slightly from country to country, but in the country of origin there is only a discount of around 50% on normal fares.

Travellers over 26 can get the Inter-Rail 26+, valid for unlimited rail travel in Austria, Bulgaria, Croatia, Czech Republic, Denmark, Finland, Germany, Greece, Hungary, Luxembourg, Netherlands, Norway, Poland, Romania, Ireland, Slovakia, Slovenia, Sweden, Turkey and Yugoslavia. The pass also gives free travel on shipping routes from the Italian port of Brindisi to Patras in Greece, as well as 30 to 50% discounts on various other ferry routes (more than covered by Eurail) and certain river and lake services. A 15-day pass costs UK£215 and one month costs UK£275.

The Inter-Rail pass for those under 26 is split into zones. Zone A is Ireland; B is Sweden, Norway and Finland; C is Denmark, Germany, Switzerland and Austria; D is the Czech Republic, Slovakia, Poland, Hungary, Bulgaria, Romania and Croatia; E is France, Belgium, Netherlands and Luxembourg; F is Spain, Portugal and Morocco; G is Italy, Greece, Turkey and Slovenia. The price for any one zone is UK£185 for 15 days. Multi-zone passes are better value and

are valid for one month: two zones is UK£220, three zones is UK£245, and all zones is UK£275.

The Baltic states are expected to join the Inter-Rail system at some future date. Check for the latest information if considering buying a pass.

Euro Domino There is a Euro Domino pass (called a Freedom pass in Britain) for each of the countries covered in the zonal Inter-Rail pass, except for Croatia and Romania. Adults (travelling 1st or 2nd class) and youths under 26 can choose from three, five, or 10 days validity within one month. Examples of adult/youth prices for 10 days in 2nd class are UK£179/£129 for Sweden, UK£119/£89 for Denmark, and UK£189/£149 for Norway.

Scanrail This is a flexible rail pass covering travel in Denmark, Norway, Sweden and Finland.

There are three versions. For travel on any five days within a 15-day period, the pass costs US$222/$176 for 1st/2nd-class travel (US$167/$132 for travellers under age 26). For travel on any 10 days within a one-month period, the pass costs US$346/$278 for 1st /2nd class (US$260/$209 for those under 26). For a pass allowing unlimited travel during 30 consecutive days, the cost is US$504/$404 for 1st/2nd class (US$378/$303 for those under 26).

If you're age 55 or over, then you're eligible for the Scanrail 55+ pass, which will allow 1st/2nd-class travel over five days in a 15-day period for US$193/$153, 10 days in a one-month period for US$301/$242 and one month for US$438/$351.

To get the Scanrail passes at these prices, they must be purchased before you arrive in Scandinavia. Scanrail passes can also be purchased in Scandinavia, but they'll cost roughly 10% to 20% more, depending on exchange rates.

Scanrail passes are valid on trains run by state railways in Denmark (DSB), Finland (VR), Norway (NSB) and Sweden (SJ), except the SL (Stockholm Local). The pass also includes free travel on the NSB-bus (Trondheim-Storlien), buses between Luleå/Boden and Haparanda, as well as Helsingør-Helsingborg (ScandLines), Rødbyhavn-Puttgarden (DSB) and Trelleborg-Sassnitz (SJ/DB) boat services and DSB domestic ferry lines (Denmark).

There's a 50% discount if you're travelling on the following services:

Esbjerg-Harwich	(DFDS)
Copenhagen-Rønne	(Bornholmstrafikken)
Rønne-Ystad	(Bornholmstrafikken)
Copenhagen-Oslo	(DFDS)
Hjørring-Hirtshals	(train)
Frederikshavn-Oslo	(Stena Line)
Frederikshavn-Gothenburg	(Stena Line)
Frederikshavn-Moss	(Stena Line)
Frederikshavn-Larvik	(Larvik Line)
Frederikshavn-Skagen	(train)
Hirtshals-Kristiansand	(Color Line)
Stockholm-Helsinki	(Viking or Silja Line)
Stockholm-Turku	(Viking or Silja Line)
Umeå/Sundsvall-Vasa	(Silja Line)
Travemünde-Helsinka	(Silja Line)
Travemünde-Trelleborg	(TT Line)
Stavanger-Bergen	(Flaggruten)
Sandefjord-Strøstad	(Scandi Line)
Nynäshamn-Visby	(Gotlandslinien)
Oskarshamn-Visby	(Gotlandslinien)
Mora-Gällivare	(train)

There's also a 50% discount on most of Norway's northern express buses (Bodø-Fauske-Narvik-Tromsø-Alta-Kirkenes), on the Lofotbus (Narvik-Harstad-Andenes-Svolvær-Leknes-Å) and on some other Norway buses. A few other boats offer a discount of 20% or 25%.

Cheap Tickets

European rail passes are only worth buying if you plan to do a reasonable amount of inter-country travelling within a short space of time. Some people tend to overdo it and spend every night they can on the train, and end up too tired to enjoy the sightseeing.

When weighing up options, consider the cost of other cheap ticket deals. Travellers aged under 26 can pick up BIJ (Billet International de Jeunesse) tickets, which sometimes cut international fares by up to about 30%. Unfortunately, you can't always bank on a substantial reduction.

Various agents issue BIJ tickets in Europe, eg Campus Travel (☎ 0171-730 3402), 52 Grosvenor Gardens, London SW1 0AG, which also sells Eurotrain tickets for people aged under 26. Eurotrain options include circular Explorer tickets, allowing a different route for the return trip. British Rail International (☎ 0171-834 2345) and Wasteels (☎ 0171-834 7066) also sell BIJ tickets.

Though Estonia, Latvia and Lithuania are outside the Eurail and Inter-Rail networks, Eurotrain, Campus and Council travel offices in the UK sell a Baltic rail pass giving unlimited train travel in these three countries costing US$31/$42/$58 for one/two/three weeks. Only student and teacher card-holders and those aged under 26 are eligible.

For a small fee, European residents aged over 60 can get a Rail Europe Senior Card as an add-on to their national rail senior pass. It entitles the holder to reduced European fares and the percentage saving varies according to the route.

CAR & MOTORCYCLE

Travelling with your own vehicle is the best way to get to remote places and it gives you the most flexibility. Unfortunately, the independence you enjoy does tend to insulate you from the local people. Also, cars are usually inconvenient in city centres where it is generally worth ditching your vehicle and relying on public transport.

A useful general reference on motoring in Europe is Eric Bredesen's *Moto Europa* (Seren Publishing). It's updated annually, and contains information on rental, purchase, documents, tax and road rules (and even a small section on the Baltic states). It can be ordered from US and Canadian bookshops (US$24.95) or directly from Seren Publishing (☎ 800-EUROPA-8 or 319-583 1068 from abroad) at PO Box 1212, Dubuque, Iowa 52004 (add US$3 for shipping).

Paperwork & Preparations

Proof of ownership of a private vehicle

should always be carried (Vehicle Registration Document for British-registered cars) when touring Europe. An EU driving licence is acceptable for driving throughout Scandinavia as generally are North American and Australian ones. But to be on the safe side – or if you have any other type of licence – you should obtain an International Driving Permit (IDP) from your motoring organisation (see Visas & Documents in the Facts for the Visitor chapter).

The Estonian and Latvian tourist boards say that an IDP is required of all Western tourists driving in their countries; the same can be assumed for Lithuania. You will need to take along your home-country licence too, as without it your IDP is worthless.

Third-party motor insurance is a minimum requirement in most of Europe but is still not compulsory in Estonia, Latvia or Lithuania, so it's highly advisable to take out a comprehensive policy if you're driving in the Baltic states. If you have difficulty getting cover for travel in these countries by mainstream motor insurers, try Black Sea & Baltic General Insurance (☎ 0171-709 9202), 65 Fenchurch St, London EC3M 4EY.

Most UK motor insurance policies automatically provide third-party cover for EU countries and some others. Get your insurer to issue a Green Card (which may cost extra), an internationally recognised proof of insurance, and check that it lists all the countries you intend to visit. You'll need this in the event of an accident outside the country where the vehicle is insured. Also ask your insurer for a European Accident Statement form, which can simplify things if worse comes to worst. Never sign statements you can't read or understand – insist on a written translation and only sign it if it's acceptable.

If you want to insure a vehicle you've just purchased (see the following Purchase section) and have a good insurance record, you might be eligible for considerable discounts if you can show a letter to this effect from your insurance company back home.

A European breakdown assistance policy, such as the AA Five Star Service or the RAC Eurocover Motoring Assistance, is a good investment. Expect to pay about UK£46 for 14 days cover with a small discount for association members. Ask your motoring organisation for details about free and reciprocal services offered by affiliated organisations around Europe.

Every vehicle travelling across an international border should display a sticker showing its country of registration (see the International Country Abbreviations appendix). A warning triangle, to be used in the event of breakdown, is compulsory almost everywhere. Recommended accessories are a first-aid kit, a spare bulb kit, and a fire extinguisher. In the UK contact the RAC (☎ 0800-550055) or the AA (☎ 0990-500600) for more information.

Road Rules

You drive on the right in all the northern European countries. Vehicles brought over from the UK or Ireland should have their headlights adjusted to avoid blinding oncoming traffic at night (a simple solution on older headlight lenses is to cover up the triangular section of the lens with tape). Priority is usually given to traffic approaching from the right. The British RAC publishes an annual *European Motoring Guide*, which gives an excellent summary of regulations in each country, including parking rules. Motoring organisations in other countries may have similar publications.

Take care with speed limits as they vary from country to country. Many driving infringements are subject to an on-the-spot fine; Denmark has on-the-spot fines for all offences. You should be given a receipt – always insist on this, particularly in the Baltic States and Russia.

Scandinavian countries are particularly strict with drink-driving regulations and the permissable blood-alcohol concentration (BAC) varies from 0.02% in Sweden to 0.08% in Denmark (see the Getting Around sections in the individual country chapters for details). In the Baltic states, the BAC limit when driving is *zero* so don't drive after drinking at all.

Roads

Conditions and types of roads vary across Europe, but it is possible to make some generalisations. The fastest routes are four or six-lane dual carriageways, ie two or three lanes either side. These tend to skirt cities and plough though the countryside in straight lines, often avoiding the most scenic bits. Motorways and other primary routes are universally in good condition.

Road surfaces on minor routes are not so reliable in some countries although normally they will be more than adequate. These roads are narrower and progress is generally much slower. To compensate you can expect much better scenery and plenty of interesting villages along the way.

Motorways are being built in Sweden; the Stockholm-Helsingborg stretch should be completed by now. Finland and Norway have few motorways, but the rate of surfacing country roads is accelerating. Norway has some particularly hair-raising roads: there are serpentine ones that climb from sea level to 1000 metres in what on a map seems to be no distance at all. These roads will consume plenty of petrol and will strain your car's engine. Coming down, it's going to strain the brakes and your nerves.

In Norway you must pay tolls for some tunnels, bridges and roads and practically all ferries crossing fjords. Roads, tunnels, bridges and ferries in Finland are always free, though Sweden may introduce tolls on some roads soon.

When driving in Scandinavia in winter, snow tyres are compulsory – the tyre chains common in the Alps are strictly forbidden here.

Main roads in the Baltic states are good enough. They may have a few more bumps and potholes than those in Scandinavia, but they also have less traffic.

Rental

Renting a car is very expensive within Scandinavian countries (see the individual country chapters for details). The variety of special deals and terms and conditions attached to renting a car can be mind-boggling. However, there are a few pointers that can help you through the morass. The big international firms – Hertz, Avis, Budget Car, Eurodollar, and Europe's largest rental agency, Europcar – will give you reliable service and a good standard of vehicle. Usually you will have the (sometimes chargeable) option of returning the car to a different outlet at the end of the rental period.

Unfortunately, if you walk into an office and ask for a car on the spot, you will pay over the odds, even allowing for special weekend deals. If you want to rent a car and haven't prebooked, look for national or local firms, which can often undercut the big companies substantially.

Prebooked and prepaid rates are always cheaper, and there are fly/drive combinations and other programmes that are worth looking into (eg SAS often offers cheaper car rentals to its international passengers). The Scanrail 'n' Drive programme gives you a five-day rail pass and a car for three days to be used within 15 days. Prices start at US$325 for an adult on 2nd-class trains and an economy car (US$498 for two adults) with an option of retaining the car for US$55 extra per day.

Holiday Autos (☎ 909-949 1737), 1425 W Foothill Blvd, Upland, California 91786, has good rates for Europe, for which you need to prebook; it has offices in the UK (☎ 0990-300400) and other European countries. Ask in advance if you can drive a rented car across borders or into the Baltic states.

No matter where you rent, make sure you understand what is included in the price (unlimited or paid km, tax, injury insurance, collision damage waiver etc) and what your liabilities are. Always take the collision damage waiver, though you can probably skip the injury insurance if you and your passengers have decent travel insurance.

The minimum rental age is usually 21 or even 23, and you'll probably need a credit card (or a mountain of cash for the deposit). Note that prices at airport rental offices are usually higher than at branches in the city centre.

It is possible to rent cars in Estonia, Latvia

and Lithuania. Some Finnish or Swedish car-hire firms will apparently let you take their cars to the Baltic states, which is well-worth investigating. When renting a car on the spot in the Baltic states, pay special attention to the insurance provisions. You may be able to limit your liability by paying extra.

Motorcycle and moped rental is common in some countries, but it is all too common to see inexperienced riders leap on bikes and very quickly fall off them again. Take care!

Purchase

The purchase of vehicles in some European countries is illegal for nonresidents of that country. Britain is probably the best place to buy second-hand cars: prices are good and, whether buying privately or from a dealer, the absence of language difficulties will help you establish exactly what you are getting and what guarantees you can expect in the event of a breakdown. Amsterdam is not a bad place to buy second-hand either.

Bear in mind that you will be getting a car with the steering wheel on the right in Britain. If you want left-hand drive and can afford to buy new, prices are reasonable in the Netherlands (without tax), in France and Germany (with tax), and in Belgium and Luxembourg (regardless of tax). Cars are very expensive in Finland but somewhat cheaper in Sweden. Paperwork can be tricky wherever you buy, insurance expensive and many countries have compulsory roadworthiness checks on older vehicles.

Leasing

Leasing a vehicle has none of the hassles of purchasing and can work out considerably cheaper than hiring over longer periods. The Renault Eurodrive Scheme provides new cars for non-EU residents for a period of between 17 days and six months. Under this scheme, a Renault Clio 1.2 for 30 days, for example, would cost 4688FF (US$938), including insurance and roadside assistance. Unfortunately, the closest Renault pick-up point to Scandinavia is Amsterdam. Peugeot's European Self-Drive programme is slightly more expensive.

Camper Van

A popular way to tour Europe is for three or four people to band together to buy or rent a camper van. London is the usual embarkation point. Look at the advertisements in London's free magazine *TNT* if you wish to form or join a group. *TNT* is also a good source for purchasing a van, as is the *Loot* newspaper and the Van Market in Market Rd, London N7 (near the Caledonian Rd tube station), where private vendors congregate on a daily basis. Some second-hand dealers offer a 'buy-back' scheme for when you return from Europe, but buying and re-selling privately should be more advantageous if you have the time.

Camper vans usually feature a fixed high-top or elevating roof and two to five bunk beds. Apart from the essential camping gas cooker, professional conversions may include a sink, fridge and built-in cupboards. You will need to spend from at least UK£1500 (US$2325) for something reliable enough to get you around Europe. An eternal favourite for budget travellers is the VW Kombi; they aren't made any more but the old ones seem to go on forever, and getting spare parts isn't a problem. Once on the road you should be able to keep budgets lower than backpackers using trains, but don't forget to set some money aside for emergency repairs.

The main advantage of going by camper van is flexibility: with transport, eating and sleeping requirements all taken care of in one unit, you are tied to nobody's timetable but your own.

A disadvantage of camper vans is that you are in a confined space for much of the time. Four adults in a small van can soon get on each other's nerves, particularly if the group has been formed at short notice. Tensions can be minimised if you agree on daily routines and itineraries before setting off.

Other disadvantages are that they're not very manoeuvrable around town, and you'll often have to leave your gear unattended inside (many people bolt extra locks onto the van). They're also expensive to buy in spring and hard to sell in autumn. As an alternative, consider a car and tent. Remember, too, that by travelling, sleeping and even eating in the self-contained little 'world' of a van, you'll be missing a lot of the outside.

Motorcycle Touring

Europe is excellent for motorcycle touring, with good-quality winding roads, stunning scenery, and an active motorcycling scene. Just make sure your wet-weather gear is up to scratch. The best time for motorcycle touring is from May or June to August or September.

The wearing of crash helmets by both rider and passenger is compulsory in Europe. Using headlights during the day is recommended and is compulsory in some parts of Scandinavia.

On ferries, motorcyclists rarely have to book ahead as they can generally be squeezed in. Take note of local custom about parking motorcycles on pavements (sidewalks). Though this is illegal in some countries, the police usually turn a blind eye so long as the vehicle doesn't obstruct pedestrians.

Anyone considering a motorcycle tour from Britain might benefit from joining the International Motorcyclists Tour Club (UK£19 per annum plus UK£3 joining fee). It organises European (and worldwide) biking jaunts, and members regularly meet to swap information. Contact James Clegg (☎ 01489-664868), Membership Secretary, 238 Nettham Rd, Netherton, Huddersfield, HD4 7HL.

Fuel

Fuel is very expensive in Scandinavia due to heavy taxation. All types of petrol, including unleaded 95 octane, are now widely available throughout the Baltic states. For unleaded petrol, look for the pump with green markings and the word *Bleifrei*, German for 'unleaded'. Diesel is usually significantly cheaper than petrol.

BICYCLE

If you want to bring your own bicycle to Europe, you should be able to take it along with you on the plane relatively easily (see the earlier Getting There & Away chapter for details).

A tour of Europe by bike may seem a daunting prospect, but one organisation that can help in the UK is the Cyclists' Touring Club (CTC; ☎ 01483-417 217), Cotterell House, 69 Meadrow, Godalming, Surrey GU7 3HS. It can supply information to members on cycling conditions in Europe, including Scandinavia, as well as detailed routes, itineraries, maps and cheap specialised insurance. Membership costs UK£25 per annum, UK£12.50 for students and people under 18, or UK£16.50 for senior citizens.

Europe by Bike, by Karen & Terry Whitehall, a paperback available in the USA or selected outlets in the UK, is a little out of date but has good descriptions of 18 cycling tours of up to 19 days duration.

A primary consideration on a cycling tour is to travel light, but you should take a few tools and spare parts, including a puncture repair kit and an extra inner tube. Panniers are essential to balance your possessions on either side of the bike frame. A bike helmet is also a very good idea. Take a good lock and always use it when you leave your bike unattended; theft is not uncommon in places like Helsinki and Copenhagen.

Seasoned cyclists can average 80 km a day, but there's no point in overdoing it. The slower you travel, the more local people you are likely to meet. If you get weary of pedalling or simply want to skip a boring section, you can put your feet up on the train. On slower trains, bikes can usually be transported as luggage, subject to a small fee. Fast trains can rarely accommodate bikes: they need to be sent as registered luggage and may end up on a different train from the one you take.

For more information on cycling, see Activities in the Facts for the Visitor chapter and in the individual country chapters.

Rental

It is easy to hire bikes throughout Scandinavia on a half-day, daily or weekly basis, and sometimes it is possible to return the machine at a different outlet so you don't have to double back. Some train stations have bike-rental counters; see the country chapters for details.

Purchase

For major cycling tours, it's best to have a bike you're familiar with, so consider bringing your own rather than buying on arrival. There are plenty of places to buy in Scandinavia, but you'll need a specialist bicycle shop for a machine capable of withstanding European touring, as well as lots of cash. CTC can provide a leaflet on purchasing.

HITCHING

Hitching is never entirely safe in any country in the world, and we don't recommend it. Travellers who decide to hitch should understand that they are taking a small but potentially serious risk. People who do choose to hitch will be safer if they travel in pairs and let someone know where they are planning to go.

Also, hitching is neither popular nor particularly rewarding in most of Scandinavia. Finns are wary of Russian criminals and Swedes worry about strangers dirtying their Volvos.

That said, with a bit of luck hitchers can end up making good time in some areas, but obviously your plans need to be flexible in case a trick of the light makes you appear invisible to passing motorists. A man and woman travelling together is probably the best combination. Two or more men must expect some delays; two women together will make good time and should be relatively safe. A woman hitching on her own is always taking a risk – even in safe Scandinavia.

Don't try to hitch from city centres: take public transport to suburban exit routes. Hitching is usually illegal on motorways – stand on the slip roads (entrance ramps). Look presentable and cheerful and make a cardboard sign indicating your intended destination in the local language. Never hitch where drivers can't stop in good time or without causing an obstruction.

It is sometimes possible to arrange a lift in advance: scan student notice boards in colleges or contact car-sharing agencies (see the Getting There & Away chapter).

BOAT

Ferry

You can't really cover Scandinavia without extensive use of ferries. Denmark consists mostly of islands, Sweden is separated by a strait from Denmark and you need to catch a ferry for a direct Denmark-Norway connection. The same applies to Finland-Estonia connections and Sweden-Finland ones (unless you want to travel to the extreme north just to avoid the ferry.)

Ferries are usually good value. Tickets are very cheap on competitive routes (especially when supply exceeds demand) and there's always the duty-free prices on food and alcohol to consider. Transporting cars can be expensive but bicycles are usually transported free.

Avoid weekend ferries (especially on Friday nights) due to the excessive noise and drinking and the higher prices. Teenage travellers may be banned altogether on some Friday night departures.

There are several different ferry companies competing on all the main ferry routes. The resulting service is comprehensive but complicated.

Stena Line is the largest ferry company in the world and services British, Irish and Scandinavian routes. Rail-pass holders are entitled to discounts or free travel on some of the routes.

The already dense traffic in the Baltic Sea between Scandinavia and Germany and Poland has been swelled by new services to the Baltic states, and the emergence of a few Baltic circle cruises in summer. Food is often expensive on ferries so it is worth bringing your own when possible. It is also worth knowing that if you take your vehicle on board you are usually denied access to it during the voyage.

For further information about ferry options between the destinations in this book, see the Getting There & Away sections of the individual country chapters.

Steamers

Scandinavia's main lakes and rivers are serviced by steamers in the summer months. In general, consider extended boat trips as relaxing and scenic excursions; if you view them merely as a functional means of transport, they can be very expensive.

Stockholm has probably the biggest fleet of steamships in Scandinavia, and sailing on at least one is a must. Most sail east to the Stockholm archipelago, a maze of 14,000 islands and islets, and west to historic Lake Mälaren, home base of the Swedish Vikings a millennium ago. The Göta Canal is the longest water route in Sweden.

In Finland, steamships ply Lakes Saimaa, Päijänne and Näsijärvi. There are also diesel-engined boats that are a bit faster and noisier but equally attractive.

TAXI

Taxis in Scandinavia are an avoidable and ill-affordable luxury. Taxis are metered and rates are high (watch your savings ebb away) unless you share the fare; there are also supplements (depending on the country) for things like the time of day, the location from which you were picked up, and the presence in the cab of extra people.

Good bus, rail and, in Scandinavia, underground railway networks make the taking of taxis all but unnecessary, but if you need one in a hurry they can usually be found idling near train stations and in front of expensive hotels. By contrast, lower fares in Estonia, Latvia and Lithuania make taxis a viable transport option.

ORGANISED TOURS

A package tour of Scandinavian and Baltic Europe is really worth considering only if your time is very limited or you have a special interest such as canoeing, bird-watching, bicycling, rock climbing etc. But tailor-made tours abound; see your travel agent or look under special interests headings in the small ads (classifieds) in newspaper travel pages. Specialists in Britain include Ramblers Holidays (☎ 01707-331133 for walkers, and Arctic Experience Discover the World (☎ 016977-48361) for wilderness and wildlife holidays. A UK company specialising in travel to the Baltic states is Regent Holidays (☎ 0117-921 1711), 15 John St, Bristol BS1 2HR.

Young revellers can party on Europe-wide bus tours. An outfit called Tracks offers budget coach/camping tours for under US$40 per day, plus food fund. It has a London office (☎ 0171-937 3028) and is represented in Australia and New Zealand by Adventure World; in North America, call ☎ 800-233 6046. Contiki (☎ 0181-290 6422) and Top Deck (☎ 0171-370 4555) offer camping or hotel-based bus tours, also for the 18 to 35 age group. The latter's 12-day 'Taste of Europe' tour costs UK£299 plus food fund. Both have offices or representatives in North America, Australasia and South Africa.

For people aged over 50, Saga Holidays (☎ 0800-300500), Saga Building, Middelburg Square, Folkestone, Kent CT20 1AZ, UK, offers holidays ranging from cheap coach tours to luxury cruises (and has cheap travel insurance). Saga also operates in the USA as Saga International Holidays (☎ 617-262 2262), 222 Berkeley St, Boston, Massachusetts 02116, and in Australia as Saga Holidays Australasia (☎ 02-9957 5660), Level One, 110 Pacific Highway, North Sydney, NSW 2060.

National tourist offices in most countries offer organised trips to points of interest. These may range from one-hour city tours to several-day circular excursions. They often work out more expensive than going it alone, but are sometimes worth it if you are pressed for time. A short city tour will give you a quick overview of the place and can be a good way to begin your visit.

Denmark

The smallest and southernmost of the Scandinavian countries, Denmark (Danmark) is an interesting mix of lively cities and pastoral farmland. The country abounds with medieval churches, Renaissance castles and tidy 18th-century fishing villages. Copenhagen, Scandinavia's largest and most cosmopolitan capital, has renowned museums and a spirited music scene.

Denmark's historic treasures include 2000-year-old 'bog people', Neolithic dolmens and Viking ruins. Denmark has wonderful white sand beaches, Scandinavia's warmest waters and scores of unspoiled islands to explore.

Despite gentle hills here and there, Denmark is largely flat, which combined with an extensive network of cycle routes, makes it a great place to explore by bike.

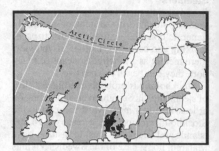

Facts about the Country

HISTORY

Although there were agricultural villages in the region in the Stone and Bronze Ages, present-day Denmark traces its linguistic and cultural roots to the arrival of the Danes, a tribe that is thought to have migrated south from Sweden around 500 AD.

In the late 9th century, warriors led by the Viking chieftain Hardegon conquered the Jutland peninsula. The Danish monarchy, which is Europe's oldest, dates back to Hardegon's son, Gorm the Old, who established his reign in the early 10th century. Gorm's son, Harald Bluetooth, completed the conquest of Denmark and spearheaded the conversion of the Danes to Christianity. Succeeding Danish kings went on to invade England and conquer most of the Baltic region.

In 1397 the Danish queen, Margrethe I, established a union between Denmark, Norway and Sweden to counter the influence of the powerful Hanseatic League which had come to dominate the region's trade. Sweden withdrew from the union in 1523 and over the next few hundred years Denmark and Sweden had numerous border skirmishes and a few fully fledged wars, largely over control of the Baltic Sea. Norway remained under Danish rule until 1814.

In the 16th century the Reformation swept through the country amidst church burnings and civil warfare. The fighting ended in 1536 with the ousting of the powerful Catholic church and the establishment of a Danish Lutheran church headed by the monarchy.

Denmark's golden age was under Christian IV (1588-1648), with Renaissance cities, castles and fortresses flourishing throughout his kingdom. A wealthy upper class prospered during his reign and many of Denmark's most lavish mansions and palaces were built during that period. In 1625 Christian IV, hoping to neutralise Swedish expansion, entered a protracted struggle known as the Thirty Years' War. The Swedes triumphed and in 1658 Denmark lost Skåne and its other territories on the Swedish mainland.

Literature, the arts, philosophy and populist ideas flourished in the 1830s, and Europe's 'Year of Revolutions' in 1848 helped inspire a democratic movement in

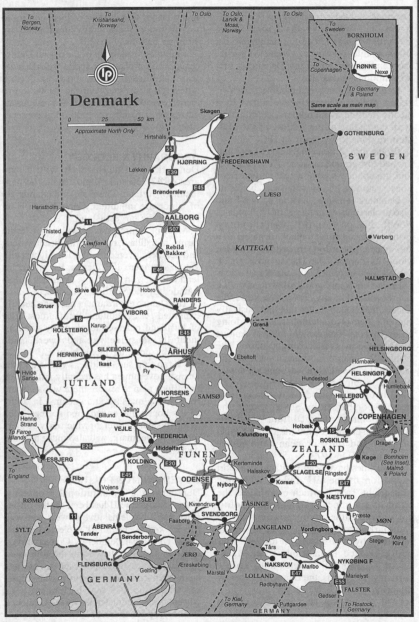

Denmark

0   25   50 km
Approximate North Only

To Bergen, Norway
To Kristiansand, Norway
To Oslo
To Oslo, Larvik & Moss, Norway
To Oslo

BORNHOLM
To Sweden
To Copenhagen
RØNNE Nexø
To Germany & Poland
Same scale as main map

GOTHENBURG
SWEDEN

Skagen
Hirtshals
HJØRRING
Løkken
Brønderslev
FREDERIKSHAVN
LÆSØ
AALBORG
Hanstholm
Thisted
Limfjord
Rebild Bakker
KATTEGAT
Varberg
Skive
Hobro
RANDERS
HALMSTAD
Struer
VIBORG
Karup
HOLSTEBRO
Grenå
HERNING
SILKEBORG
Ikast
ÅRHUS
HELSINGBORG
Hvide Sande
Ry
Ebeltoft
Hornbæk
HELSINGØR
JUTLAND
Humlebæk
Hundested
HILLERØD
HORSENS
SAMSØ
Billund
Jelling
VEJLE
Holbæk
COPENHAGEN
Henne Strand
To Faroe Islands
FREDERICIA
Kalundborg
ROSKILDE
Dragør
Middelfart
FUNEN
ZEALAND
To Bornholm (See Inset), Malmö & Poland
ESBJERG
KOLDING
Kerteminde
Køge
To England
ODENSE
Halsskov
E20
Ribe
Nyborg
SLAGELSE Ringsted
RØMØ
Vojens
Korsør
HADERSLEV
Kvændrup
TÅSINGE
NÆSTVED
SVENDBORG
SYLT
ÅBENRÅ
Faaborg
LANGELAND
Vordingborg
MØN
Tønder
Sønderborg
Søby
Præstø
ÆRØ
Stege
Møns Klint
FLENSBURG
Ærøskøbing
Tårs
NYKØBING F
Gelting
Marstal
NAKSKOV Maribo
GERMANY
LOLLAND
Marielyst
Rødbyhavn
FALSTER
Gedser
To Kiel, Germany
Puttgarden
To Rostock, Germany
GERMANY

Denmark that led to the adoption of a constitution on 5 June 1849. As a result, King Frederik VII was forced to relinquish most of his political power to an elected parliament and in doing so became Denmark's first constitutional monarch.

Denmark's involvement in a series of failed military campaigns resulted in a steady decline of its borders, culminating with the ceding of the Schleswig and Holstein regions to Germany in 1864.

By the turn of the century, large landowners had lost ground to farmers' cooperatives and the country's government shifted from conservative to liberal with a socialist bent.

Denmark remained neutral in WWI and also declared its neutrality at the outbreak of WWII. Still, on 9 April 1940 an unfortified Denmark faced either a quick surrender or a full-scale invasion by German troops massed along its border. The Danish government settled for the former, in return for an assurance that the Nazis would allow the Danes a degree of autonomy. For three years the Danes managed to walk a thin line, basically running their own internal affairs but doing so under Nazi supervision, until in August 1943 the Germans took outright control. The Danish Resistance movement mushroomed and 7000 Jewish Danes were quickly smuggled into neutral Sweden.

Although the island of Bornholm was heavily bombarded by Soviet forces, the rest of Denmark emerged from WWII relatively unscathed. Denmark joined NATO in 1949 and the European Community (now the EU) in 1973.

The Danes have been hesitant to support expansion of the EU. Indeed when the Maastricht Treaty, which established the terms of a European economic and political union, came up for ratification in Denmark in June 1992, Danish voters rejected it by a margin of 51% to 49%. After being granted exemptions from Maastricht's common defence and single currency provisions, the Danes, by a narrow majority, voted to accept the treaty in a second referendum held in 1993. Danish support for the EU continues to be tepid as many Danes fear the loss of local control to a European bureaucracy dominated by stronger nations.

Under the leadership of the Social Democrats, a comprehensive social welfare state was established in the postwar period. Although a tax revolt in the 1980s led to some revisions, Denmark still provides its citizens with extensive cradle-to-grave securities.

GEOGRAPHY & ECOLOGY

Denmark is a small country with a land area of 42,930 sq km, mostly on the peninsula of Jutland. There are 406 islands, 90 of which are inhabited. Copenhagen is on Zealand, the largest island.

Most of Denmark is a lowland of fertile farms, marshland, rolling hills, beech woods and heather-covered moors. The highest elevation is a mere 173 metres. Except for its land border with Germany, Denmark is surrounded by the North and Baltic seas.

The Danish environment has been heavily exploited for agriculture. With almost 20% of farmland near sea level, many environmentally sensitive wetlands were made arable by draining them. New EU quotas make farming such land less viable and the Danish government has recently initiated an ambitious plan to restore these wetlands and re-establish marshes and streams. In doing so it's hoped that endangered species, such as the freshwater otter, of which only 50 pairs remain in Denmark, will also make a comeback.

GOVERNMENT & POLITICS

Denmark is a constitutional monarchy. Queen Margrethe II has been on the throne since 1972 but legislative powers rest with the *Folketing*, Denmark's elected parliament. The Social Democrats, Conservatives, Liberals and Socialists form the four main political parties, though in recent times there have been close to a dozen parties represented in the 179-seat parliament. The current prime minister is Social Democrat Poul Nyrup Rasmussen.

ECONOMY
Denmark has one of the world's highest per capita GNPs and a high standard of living. It's the world's leading exporter of canned meat and boasts the EU's largest fish catches. Other important exports include butter, cheese, beer, furniture, electronics, silverware and porcelain.

POPULATION & PEOPLE
Denmark's population is about 5.2 million, with 70% living in urban areas. The four largest cities are Copenhagen (1.4 million), Århus (265,000), Odense (173,000) and Aalborg (155,000).

Foreign nationals account for 3% of Denmark's population, and 8% of Copenhagen's population. About 40% come from Western European countries but there are also Turkish, Pakistani, Somalian and Ethiopian communities.

ARTS
Famed Danish writers include Hans Christian Andersen, whose fairy tales have been translated into more languages than any other book except the Bible; religious philosopher Søren Kierkegaard, whose writings were a forerunner of existentialism; and Karen Blixen, who penned *Out of Africa*.

Blixen also wrote *Babette's Feast*, whose movie adaptation by Danish film director Gabriel Axel won the Academy Award for Best Foreign Film in 1988. The following year director Bille August won an Academy Award as well as the Cannes Film Festival's Palme d'Or for *Pelle the Conqueror*, adapted from the novel by Danish author Martin Andersen Nexø. In 1996 Bille August produced a film adaptation of *Smilla's Sense of Snow* (published outside the USA as *Miss Smilla's Feeling for Snow*), a suspense mystery by Denmark's foremost contemporary author, Peter Høeg.

The Royal Danish Ballet, which performs in Copenhagen's Royal Theatre from autumn to spring, is regarded as northern Europe's finest. The Royal Theatre is also the venue for the Royal Orchestra, Royal Opera and various theatrical performances.

On a different front, Denmark is a leader in industrial design, with a style marked by cool, clean lines applied to everything from architecture to furniture and silverwork. Denmark has produced a number of leading contemporary architects including Jørn Utzon who designed the Sydney Opera House in Australia.

CULTURE
Danes pride themselves on being thoroughly modern, and the wearing of folk costumes, the celebration of traditional festivals and the clinging to old-fashioned customs is less prevalent in Denmark than elsewhere in Scandinavia. There are, of course, traditional aspects of the Danish lifestyle that aren't immediately apparent at first glance.

Perhaps nothing captures the Danish perspective more than the concept of *hygge* which, roughly translated, means cosy and snug. It implies shutting out the turmoil and troubles of the outside world and striving instead for a warm intimate mood. Hygge affects how Danes approach many aspects of their personal lives, from designing their homes to a fondness for small cafés and pubs. There's no greater compliment that a Dane can give their host than to thank them for a cosy evening.

Visitors will find Danes to be relaxed, casual and not given to extremes. They are tolerant of different lifestyles; in 1989 Denmark became the first European nation to legalise same-sex marriages. The national sport is soccer, while cycling, rowing, sailing and windsurfing are popular pastimes.

RELIGION
More than 90% of Danes belong to the state-supported National Church of Denmark, an Evangelical Lutheran denomination, though fewer than 5% are regular church-goers.

LANGUAGE
The Danish language belongs, together with Swedish, Norwegian, Icelandic and Faroese, to the northern branch of the Germanic language group. Consequently, written Danish bears a strong resemblance to these languages.

Spoken Danish on the other hand has evolved in a different direction, introducing sounds and pronunciation not found elsewhere.

Grammatically it has the same general rules and syntax as the other Germanic languages of Scandinavia. The nouns have two genders: masculine, *en*, and neuter, *et*. Definite articles are suffixed to the noun: *-en* and *-et* for singular nouns, and *-ne* (indefinite) and *-ene* (definite) for plural nouns regardless of gender.

Danish has a polite form of address, using the personal pronouns *De* and *Dem*. The translations in this chapter are mostly in the familiar form using *du* and *deg*, except where it is appropriate and/or wise to use the formal form. In general, use the formal form when speaking to senior citizens and officials, and the familiar form the rest of the time.

Danish is a minor language and most Danes speak English. However, an effort to at least learn the basics, such as memorising the words for 'thank you', 'goodbye', 'hello' and 'I'm sorry', will be appreciated. With an increased command of the language, you will be rewarded by gaining a greater insight into Denmark and the Danes.

See the Language Guide at the back of the book for pronunciation guidelines and useful words and phrases.

Facts for the Visitor

PLANNING
Climate & When to Go
Considering its northern latitude, Denmark has a fairly mild climate. May and June can be a delightful time to visit: the countryside is a rich green accented with fields of yellow rapeseed flowers, the weather is generally warm and comfortable, and you'll beat the rush of summer tourists. While autumn can also be pleasant, it's not nearly as scenic – the rural landscape has largely turned to brown and the air quality suffers as many Danish farmers burn crop waste in the fields.

July and August is the peak tourist season

and the time for open-air concerts, lots of street activity and basking on the beach. Other bonuses for travellers during midsummer are longer opening hours at museums and other sightseeing attractions and potential savings on accommodation, as some hotels drop their rates.

Books
These books provide useful information:

Lonely Planet's *Denmark – a travel survival kit* by Glenda Bendure & Ned Friary is the most extensive all-around guidebook available.
Denmark: A Modern History by W Glyn Jones gives a comprehensive account of contemporary Danish society.
Facts About Denmark (Ministry of Foreign Affairs) provides a concise readable history, with statistics and cultural background.
Camping Danmark, published annually by the Danish Camping Board (Campingrådet), has detailed information on all camping grounds in Denmark.

Maps
Most tourist offices have fairly good city and regional maps that they distribute free. If you're renting a car, you can usually pick up a suitable Denmark road map free from the rental agency. The most detailed road map of Denmark is published by Kort-og Matrikelstyrelsen in a handy atlas format (1:200,000) and can be bought in Danish bookshops for 95 kr.

Online Services
Useful web sites are the Danish Tourist Board at www.deninfo.com and the Danish foreign ministry at www.denmark.org; the latter accesses the tourist board site, plus a wealth of other information, including updated weather and exchange rates.

What to Bring
If you visit Denmark during the warm season you can travel light. Unless you plan on fine dining there's little need to bring dressy clothing. If you're using hostels, bringing your own sleeping sheet will save a lot of money.

SUGGESTED ITINERARIES

Depending on the length of your stay you might like to see and do the following:

Two days

    Copenhagen – get a Copenhagen Card and explore the city

One week

    Copenhagen, North Zealand's castles and beaches, Roskilde, Køge and Ærø

Two weeks

    Sights listed above plus Odense, Århus, Skagen, Ribe and other Jutland sights of interest (or Bornholm)

One month

    As above plus Bornholm, south Funen (including the islands of Tåsinge and Langeland), Møn and Falster

Two months

    As above but at a slower pace, possibly much of it by bicycle

HIGHLIGHTS
Castles

Denmark has castles aplenty, some with lofty turrets and towers, some with dungeons and others just misnamed manor houses. The most strikingly set is Egeskov Castle, surrounded by a moat and formal gardens in the Funen countryside. For the most elaborately decorated Renaissance interior, Frederiksborg Castle in Hillerød is unequalled. In Copenhagen the king of castles is Rosenborg, where the dazzling crown jewels are on display.

Historic Towns

Half-timbered houses (with a timber frame and interstices filled in with brick or plaster), cobblestone streets and ancient churches are thick on the ground in Denmark, but a few places are singularly unique. Ribe, the oldest town in Denmark, has an exquisite historic centre encircling a 12th-century cathedral.

The tiny fortress island of Christiansø, off Bornholm, retains its ramparts and 17th-century buildings, with almost no trace of the 20th century. And Ærøskøbing on Ærø has a town centre of 18th-century houses that's arguably the most picturesque in Denmark.

Museums

Denmark has several open-air folk museums with period buildings. The most impressive is Den Gamle By in Århus, which is set up as a provincial town, while the folk museum in Odense has the most engaging natural setting.

The best preserved bog people – intact Iron Age bodies found preserved in peat bogs – are at the Silkeborg Museum in Silkeborg and the Moesgård Prehistoric Museum in Århus. In Zealand, top art museums are Ny Carlsberg Glyptotek in Copenhagen and Louisiana in Humlebæk.

Viking Sites

The Danish countryside holds a number of Viking sites, including Viking fortresses dating back to approximately 980 AD. Their circular earthen-work walls remain intact and surround the faint remains of house sites where timbered stave-style structures once stood. Best preserved are the Trelleborg fortress in southern Zealand, seven km outside Slagelse, and the Fyrkat fortress in Jutland, three km outside Hobro; both have reconstructed Viking houses.

There are Viking ships on display at the Viking Ship Museum in Roskilde and the Bangsbo Museum in Frederikshavn. The impressive Lindholm Høje, outside Aalborg, contains the largest plot of Viking and Iron Age graves in Scandinavia.

In summer, Viking festivals and open-air Viking plays can be found at several locations, including Frederikssund in Zealand and the Fyrkat fortress and Ribe Vikingecenter in Jutland.

TOURIST OFFICES
Local Tourist Offices

Brochures about all parts of Denmark are available at the main tourist office: Danish Tourist Board, Bernstorffsgade 1, 1577 Copenhagen V. Virtually every good-sized town in Denmark has a local tourist office, most often found in the town hall (*rådhus*) or elsewhere on the central square (*torvet*).

Tourist Offices Abroad

Danish tourist offices abroad include:

Canada
> Danish Tourist Board,
> PO Box 636, Mississauga, Ontario L5M 2C2
> (☎ 905-820 8984)

Germany
> Dänisches Fremdenverkehrsamt,
> Glockengiesserwall 2, Postfach 101329,
> 20008 Hamburg (☎ 040-32 78 03)

Norway
> Danmarks Turistkontor,
> Tollbugaten 27, Postboks 406 Sentrum, 0103
> Oslo (☎ 22 41 17 76)

Sweden
> Danska Turistbyrån, Biblioteksgatan 25,
> Box 5524, 114 85 Stockholm (☎ 08-611 72 22)

UK
> Danish Tourist Board, 55 Sloane St,
> London SW1X 9SY (☎ 0171-259 5959)

USA
> Danish Tourist Board, 655 Third Ave,
> New York, NY 10017 (☎ 212-949 2333)

VISAS & DOCUMENTS

Visas

Citizens of the USA, Canada, Australia and
New Zealand need a valid passport to enter
Denmark, but don't need a visa for stays of
less than three months.

Documents

A Hostelling International (HI) card will get
you lower hostel rates and showing a student
identity card will often get you a discount on
museum fees.

EMBASSIES

Danish Embassies Abroad

Australia
> Royal Danish Embassy, 15 Hunter St,
> Yarralumla, ACT 2600 (☎ 06-273 2195)

Canada
> Royal Danish Embassy, 85 Range Road, Apt 702,
> Ottawa, Ontario K1N 8J6 (☎ 613-234 0704)

Germany
> Königliche Dänische Botschaft, Pfälzer Strasse
> 14, 53032 Bonn (☎ 228-729 910)

New Zealand
> Contact the embassy in Australia

UK
> Royal Danish Embassy, 55 Sloane St,
> London SW1X 9SR (☎ 0171-333 0200)

USA
> Royal Danish Embassy, 3200 Whitehaven St
> NW, Washington DC 20008 (☎ 202-234 4300)

Foreign Embassies in Denmark

Australia
> Kristianiagade 21, Copenhagen (☎ 35 26 22 44)

Canada
> Kristen Bernikows Gade 1, Copenhagen
> (☎ 33 12 22 99)

Germany
> Stockholmsgade 57, Copenhagen
> (☎ 35 26 16 22)

New Zealand
> Contact the British embassy

UK
> Kastelsvej 40, Copenhagen (☎ 35 26 46 00)

USA
> Dag Hammarskjölds Allé 24, Copenhagen
> (☎ 31 42 31 44)

CUSTOMS

One litre of hard liquor or two litres of wine,
and 200 cigarettes, can be brought into
Denmark duty free.

MONEY

All common travellers' cheques are accepted
in Denmark. Bring travellers' cheques in
higher denominations as bank fees for
changing money are a hefty 20 kr per cheque
with a 40 kr minimum. Cash transactions are
charged a 25 kr fee for any size transaction.
Travellers' cheques command a better
exchange rate than cash by about 1%.

Post offices also exchange foreign currency (cash only) at comparable rates – the
main benefit for travellers being Saturday
morning opening hours. Most major banks
have automatic teller machines (ATMs),
many of them accessible outside normal
banking hours, that give cash advances on
Visa, MasterCard and Cirrus bank cards.

Visa, Eurocard, MasterCard, American
Express and Diners Club credit cards are
widely accepted throughout Denmark.

Currency

The Danish krone is most often written as
DKK in international money markets, Dkr in
northern Europe and kr within Denmark.

The krone is divided into 100 øre; there are 25 øre, 50 øre, one krone, two kroner, five kroner, 10 kroner and 20-kroner coins. Notes come in 50, 100, 500 and 1000-kroner denominations.

Exchange Rates
The following currencies convert at these approximate rates:

Australia	A$1 =	4.63 Dkr
Canada	C$1 =	4.30 Dkr
France	1FF =	1.14 Dkr
Germany	DM1 =	3.84 Dkr
Japan	¥100 =	5.41 Dkr
New Zealand	NZ$1 =	4.09 Dkr
Norway	1 Nkr =	0.90 Dkr
Sweden	1 Skr =	0.88 Dkr
UK	UK£1 =	9.15 Dkr
USA	US$1 =	5.86 Dkr

Costs
Costs in Denmark are not exorbitant, at least by Scandinavian standards, but nothing's cheap either – partly due to the 25% value-added tax (VAT), called *moms* in Danish, included in every price.

Your costs will depend on how you travel. In terms of basic expenses, if you camp or stay in hostels and prepare your own meals you might get by on 150 kr a day. If you stay in modest hotels and eat at inexpensive restaurants, expect to spend about 400 kr a day if you're doubling up, 500 kr if you're travelling alone.

To this you need to add local transport, museum admission fees, entertainment and incidentals. Long-distance transport is reasonably priced and it helps that Denmark is small – the most expensive train ticket possible between two points costs just 237 kr.

Tipping & Bargaining
Restaurant bills and taxi fares include service charges in the quoted prices. Although further tipping is unnecessary, rounding up the bill is not uncommon. Bargaining is not a common practice in Denmark.

Consumer Taxes
Foreign visitors who are not EU citizens can get a refund on the 25% VAT, less a handling fee, for goods costing more than 300 kr purchased at stores participating in the Tax-Free plan. Present the tax-refund 'cheque' to the refund window at your departure point.

POST & COMMUNICATIONS
Most post offices are open either from 9 am to 5.30 pm or from 10 am to 5 pm on weekdays and to noon on Saturday. You can receive mail poste restante at any post office in Denmark. It costs 3.75 kr to mail a postcard or letter weighing up to 20g to Western Europe, 5 kr to other countries. International mail sent from Copenhagen is usually out of the country in 24 hours.

It costs 2 kr minimum to make a local call at coin phones and you must dial all eight numbers. You get twice as much calling time for your money on domestic calls made between 7.30 pm and 8 am daily and all day on Sunday.

If you're going to be making many calls, consider buying a plastic *telekort* phonecard, which is used in card phones that are found in busier public places side by side with coin phones. The card can be bought at post offices and kiosks.

The country code for calling Denmark from abroad is ☎ 45. To make international calls from Denmark dial ☎ 00 and then the country code for the country you're calling. There are no area codes within Denmark.

Faxes and telegrams can be sent from public telephone offices, commonly found beside larger post offices.

NEWSPAPERS & MAGAZINES
Denmark has 48 daily newspapers, the largest of which is *Politiken*. None are in English but the *International Herald Tribune* and other English-language newspapers and magazines are readily available at train station kiosks in larger towns.

RADIO & TV
You can listen to the news in English at 8.30 am Monday to Friday on Radio Denmark

(93.8 FM in Copenhagen, 92.9 FM in Århus). The BBC World Service is broadcast in Denmark at 6195 and 9410 kHz. British and US programmes are common on Danish TV and are usually in English with Danish subtitles.

PHOTOGRAPHY & VIDEO
Print and slide films are readily available in major cities. A 24-exposure roll of Kodacolor Gold 100 will cost about 50 kr to buy, 100 kr to develop and print. A 36-exposure roll of Kodachrome 64 with processing costs about 110 kr.

If you purchase videos in Denmark, make sure they're compatible with your home system. Denmark uses PAL, which is incompatible with the North American NTSC system.

TIME
Time in Denmark is normally one hour ahead of GMT/UTC, the same as in neighbouring European countries. When it's noon in Denmark, it's 11 am in London, 6 am in New York and Toronto, 3 am in San Francisco, 9 pm in Sydney and 11 pm in Auckland.

Clocks are moved forward one hour for daylight-saving time from late March to October. Denmark uses the 24-hour clock and all timetables and business hours are posted accordingly.

ELECTRICITY
The electric current is 220V, 50 Hz, and plugs have two round pins.

WEIGHTS & MEASURES
Denmark uses the metric system. Fruit is often sold by the piece *(stykke)*, abbreviated 'stk'. Decimals are indicated by commas and thousands by points.

LAUNDRY
Laundrettes *(møntvaskeri)* are much easier to find in Denmark than in other Scandinavian countries. Not only can you find them in larger cities and towns, but hostels and camping grounds often have coin-operated

machines as well. The cost to wash and dry a load of clothes is generally around 40 kr.

TOILETS
No surprises here – toilets in Denmark are western-style and reasonably easy to find in public places.

HEALTH
No unusual precautions are needed. Visitors whose countries have reciprocal agreements with Denmark are covered by the national health insurance programme. All visitors, however, receive free hospital treatment in the event of a sudden illness or accident. For medical emergencies dial ☎ 112, for non-emergency medical and dental needs your hotel or the nearest pharmacy *(apotek)* can make a referral. For more health information, see the Facts for the Visitor chapter at the front of this book.

WOMEN TRAVELLERS
KVINFO, the Danish Centre for Information on Women and Gender (☎ 33 13 50 88), Nyhavn 22, 1051 Copenhagen K, has information on feminist issues, whereas Kvindehuset (☎ 33 14 28 04), at Gothersgade 37 in Copenhagen, is a help centre and meeting place for women. Dial ☎ 112 for rape crisis or other emergencies.

GAY & LESBIAN TRAVELLERS
Denmark is a popular destination for gay and lesbian travellers. Copenhagen in particular has an active, open gay community and lots of nightlife options.

Landsforeningen for Bøsser og Lesbiske, or LBL (☎ 33 13 19 48), the national organisation for gay men and lesbians, is at Teglgårdstræde 13 in Copenhagen.

DISABLED TRAVELLERS
Overall, Denmark is user-friendly to the disabled. The Danish Tourist Board publishes *Access in Denmark – a Travel Guide for the Disabled*, an English-language booklet with information on accommodation, transportation and sightseeing options for disabled travellers.

SENIOR TRAVELLERS

Senior citizens are given discounts at most museums by showing proof of age. Transportation is often discounted for seniors; the DSB railway system, for example, gives a 25 to 50% discount to those aged 65 and older.

DANGERS & ANNOYANCES

Denmark is by and large a safe country and travelling presents no unusual dangers. Nevertheless, be careful with your belongings, particularly in busy places such as Copenhagen's Central Station. In cities, you'll need to quickly become accustomed to the busy cycle lanes between vehicle roads and the pedestrian pavement, as these lanes are easy to step into accidentally.

BUSINESS HOURS

Office hours are generally from 9 am to 4 pm Monday to Friday. Most banks are open from 9.30 am to 4 pm weekdays and to 6 pm on Thursday, though banks at international ports and at Copenhagen's Central Station are open longer hours and on weekends. Most stores are open to 5.30 pm weekdays and to 2 pm on Saturday.

PUBLIC HOLIDAYS & SPECIAL EVENTS

Summer holidays for schoolchildren begin around 20 June and end around 10 August. Many Danes go on holiday during the first three weeks of July. Public holidays observed in Denmark are:

1 January, *New Year's Day*
Thursday before Easter, *Maundy Thursday*
Good Friday
Easter Day
Easter Monday
Fourth Friday after Easter, *Common Prayer Day*
Fifth Thursday after Easter, *Ascension Day*
Seventh Sunday after Easter, *Whit Sunday*
Eighth Monday after Easter,*Whit Monday*
5 June, *Constitution Day*
24 December (from noon), *Christmas Eve*
25 December, *Christmas Day*
26 December, *Boxing Day*

Beginning with Midsummer's Eve bonfires in late June, Denmark buzzes with outdoor activity throughout the summer. The main attractions are the hundred-plus music festivals which run almost nonstop, covering a broad spectrum of music that includes not only jazz, rock and blues but also gospel, Irish, classical, country, Cajun, ballads and much more.

The acclaimed 10-day Copenhagen Jazz Festival is held in early July, with outdoor concerts and numerous performances in clubs around the city. Roskilde has a grand Woodstock-style rock festival with big international names, held the last weekend of June; a single admission fee includes tent space and entry to all concerts.

There are folk festivals in Skagen near the end of June and in Tønder in late August. The nine-day Århus Festival in early September features an array of music and multi-cultural events. For a booklet with details on music festivals nationwide, contact Dansk Musik Informations Center (☎ 33 11 20 66), Gråbrødretorv 16, 1154 Copenhagen K.

ACTIVITIES

Cycling

Denmark is a bicycle-friendly country, with thousands of km of established cycling routes. Those around Bornholm and Ærø, as well as the 440-km-long Old Military Road (Hærvejen) through central Jutland, are among the most popular.

The Danish cycling federation, Dansk Cyklist Forbund (☎ 33 32 31 21), Rømersgade 7, 1362 Copenhagen K, publishes *Cykelferiekort* (49 kr), a cycling map of the entire country, as well as more detailed regional cycling maps. It also publishes *Overnatning i det fri* (80 kr), which lists hundreds of farmers who provide cyclists with a place to pitch a tent for only 12 kr a night. Maps can be purchased in advance from the address above or from tourist offices and bookshops upon arrival. Tourist offices can provide information on packaged cycling holidays.

Hiking

While Denmark does not have substantial forests, there are numerous small tracts of woodlands crisscrossed by a few km of walking trails. Skov og Naturstyrelsen (Forest & Nature Bureau) produces brochures with sketch maps that show trails in nearly 100 such areas. The brochures can be picked up free at public libraries and some tourist offices.

The coast in Denmark is public domain and in many areas there are nice walking tracks along the shoreline.

COURSES

Scandinavia's unique *folkehøjskole*, literally 'folk high school' (the 'high' meaning institute of higher learning), provides a liberal education within a communal living environment. Folk high schools got their start in Denmark, inspired by philosopher Nikolai Grundtvig's concept of 'enlightenment for life'. The curriculum varies among schools but includes such things as drama, Danish culture, peace studies and organic farming. People aged 19 and older can enrol; there are no entrance exams and no degrees. For a catalogue of the nearly 100 schools, contact Højskolernes Sekretariat (☎ 33 13 98 22), Nytorv 7, 1450 Copenhagen K.

While most folk high schools teach in Danish only, at the International People's College (☎ 49 21 33 61), Montebello Allé 1, 3000 Helsingør, students and teachers come from around the world and instruction is in English. Eight-week courses cost 12,500 kr including meals, accommodation, tuition and outings.

WORK

Denmark has high unemployment and the job situation is bleak for those who are not Danes, doubly so for those who don't speak Danish. In terms of work, foreigners are divided into three categories.

Citizens of other Scandinavian countries have the right to reside and work in Denmark without restrictions.

Citizens of EU countries are entitled to look for work in Denmark and it's fairly straightforward to get a work and residency permit if you find work. The main prerequisite is that your job provide an income high enough to cover your living expenses.

Citizens of other countries are required to get a work permit before entering Denmark. This requires first securing a job offer and then applying for a work and residency permit while you're still in your home country. You can enter Denmark only after the permit has been granted. Currently these permits are extraordinarily rare for anyone without a specialised skill.

ACCOMMODATION
Camping & Cabins

Denmark's 529 camping grounds charge from 32 to 45 kr per person to pitch a tent. Places with the simplest facilities have the cheapest rates. A camping pass is required (24 kr for the season) and can be picked up at any camping ground.

Many camping grounds rent cabins that sleep four to six people and cost from 200 to 450 kr a day. Though cabins often have cooking facilities, bedding is rarely provided so you'll need your own sleeping bag.

Camping is restricted to camping grounds, or on private land with the owner's permission. While it may seem tempting, camping in a car along the beach or in a parking lot is prohibited and can result in an immediate fine. Most maps show camping grounds and the tourist office provides a brochure listing the locations of camping grounds throughout Denmark.

Hostels

Most of Denmark's 102 HI hostels, called *vandrerhjem* in Danish, have private rooms in addition to dormitory rooms, making hostels an affordable alternative to hotels. Depending on the category of the hostel, dorm beds cost from 59 to 85 kr, while private rooms range from 125 to 225 kr for singles, 150 to 250 kr for doubles, plus about 50 kr for each additional person.

Blankets and pillows are provided at all hostels but if you don't bring your own sheets you'll have to hire them for around 35 kr. Sleeping bags are not allowed.

Travellers without an international hostel card can buy one in Denmark for 125 kr or pay 25 kr extra a night. During the summer, hostels can book out in advance; it's always a good idea to call ahead for reservations. Outside Copenhagen, check-in is generally between 4 and 9 pm, and the reception office is usually closed (and the phone not answered) between noon and 4 pm.

In spring and autumn, hostels can get crowded with children on school outings and many hostels require advance reservations from 1 September to 15 May. Most Danish hostels close in winter for any time from a few weeks to several months.

You can pick up a free 185-page hostel guide from tourist offices giving information on each hostel, including such matters as which have laundry facilities, bicycle rentals and wheelchair-accessible rooms.

All Danish hostels provide an all-you-can-eat breakfast for 40 kr or less and many also provide dinner (60 kr maximum). Except for the Bellahøj hostel in Copenhagen, hostels also have guest kitchens with pots and pans where you can cook your own food.

The national HI office is: Danmarks Vandrerhjem (☎ 31 31 36 12), Vesterbrogade 39, 1620 Copenhagen V.

Hotels

Hotels are found in the centre of all major towns, with the lower end averaging around 325/450 kr for singles/doubles. Although the cheapest places tend to be spartan, they're rarely seedy or unsafe. *Kro*, a name that implies country inn but is more commonly the Danish version of a motel, is a type of accommodation common along motorways near the outskirts of town; they are generally cheaper than hotels by about a third. Both hotels and kros usually include an all-you-can-eat breakfast which varies from a simple meal of bread, cheese and coffee to a generous buffet.

Rates listed in this chapter include all taxes and, unless otherwise noted, are for rooms with shared baths accessed from the hall. Although it varies greatly, many hotels charge about 100 kr more for a room with its own toilet and shower. Some hotels offer discount schemes in summer, when business travel is light, and on weekends all year round.

The Danish Tourist Board's free *Hotels Denmark* booklet, published annually, lists hotels and kros around the country and explains the discounts available.

Rooms in Private Homes

Many tourist offices book rooms in private homes for a small fee, or provide a free list of the rooms so travellers can phone on their own. Rates vary widely, but average about 150/250 kr for singles/doubles. Dansk Bed & Breakfast (☎ 39 61 04 05), Postbox 53, 2900 Hellerup, publishes a free booklet listing 400 homes throughout Denmark offering private rooms at similar rates.

If you'd like to be in the country, Horsens Turistbureau (☎ 75 62 38 22), Søndergade 26, 8700 Horsens, books stays on farms throughout Denmark for 175 kr a person a day (half-price for children under 12 years), with a three-night minimum. They also book self-contained flats for 2100 kr a week for up to six people. If you're cycling or driving around Denmark on your own, you'll come across farmhouses displaying 'room' (*værelse*) signs.

FOOD

Nothing epitomises Danish food more than *smørrebrød* (literally 'buttered bread'), an open-faced sandwich that ranges from very basic fare to elaborate sculpture-like creations. Typically it's a slice of rye bread topped with either roast beef, tiny shrimps, roast pork or fish fillet and finished off with a variety of garnishes. Though it's served in many restaurants at lunchtime, it's cheapest at bakeries or at specialised smørrebrød takeaway shops found near train stations and office buildings.

The rich pastry known worldwide as 'Danish' is called *wienerbrød* in Denmark, and nearly every second street corner has a bakery with mouthwatering varieties. For a cheap munch, stop at one of the ubiquitous *pølsemandens*, the wheeled carts which sell a variety of frankfurters for around 15 kr.

The cheapest restaurant food is generally

pizza and pasta; you can eat your fill for about 40 kr at lunch, 60 kr at dinner. Danish food, which relies heavily on fish, meat and potatoes, generally costs double that. *Dagens ret*, which means daily special, is usually the best deal on the menu, while the *børn* menu is for children.

Typical Danish dishes include *frikadeller*, ground-pork meatballs; *kogt torsk*, poached cod in mustard sauce; *flæskesteg*, roast pork with crackling; *hvid labskovs*, beef and potato stew; and *hakkebøf*, a ground-beef burger with fried onions. Then there's the *koldt bord*, a buffet-style spread of cold foods, including herring dishes, salads, cold cuts, smoked fish and cheeses.

Larger cities usually have restaurants featuring vegetarian dishes, cafés commonly serve a variety of salads, and vegetarians can often find something suitable at the smørrebrød counter.

DRINKS

Denmark's Carlsberg and Tuborg breweries both produce excellent beers. The most popular spirit in Denmark is caraway-spiced Aalborg aquavit; it's drunk straight down as a shot, followed by a chaser of beer. Beer *(øl)*, wine *(vin)* and spirits can be purchased at grocery stores during normal shopping hours and prices are quite reasonable compared to those in other Scandinavian countries. The minimum legal age for purchasing all alcoholic beverages is 18 years.

ENTERTAINMENT

Denmark's cities have some of the most active nightlife in Europe, with live music wafting through side-street cafés, especially in the university cities of Copenhagen, Århus and Odense. Little begins before 10 pm or ends before 3 am. Most towns have movie theatres showing first-run English-language films (from 35 to 50 kr), subtitled in Danish.

THINGS TO BUY

Silverwork, ceramics and handblown glass – all in the sleek style that typifies Danish design – are popular though not inexpensive purchases. Amber, which washes up on Jutland's west coast beaches, makes lovely jewellery and prices are reasonable.

Getting There & Away

AIR

Scandinavian Airlines (SAS) is the largest carrier serving Denmark. Other airlines flying into Copenhagen include Aer Lingus, Air France, Alitalia, Austrian Airlines, British Airways, British Midland, Delta, Egypt Air, El Al, Finnair, Iberia, Icelandair, KLM, LOT, Lufthansa, Maersk Air, Olympic Airways, TAP Air Portugal, Sabena, Swissair, Varig and Turkish Airlines.

BUS & TRAIN
Germany

The E45 is the main route between Germany and Denmark's Jutland peninsula. Three railway lines link the two countries; 2nd-class trains from Copenhagen to Frankfurt cost 940 kr (855 kr for those under 26 years). Eurolines (☎ 33 25 10 44) operates year-round buses from Copenhagen to Berlin (245 kr) and Frankfurt (595 kr).

Norway

Trains operate daily between Copenhagen and Oslo; the 2nd-class rail fare between the two (via Sweden) is 550 kr (485 kr for those aged under 26). There is also a bus service a few times a week between Oslo and Copenhagen (430 kr).

Sweden

Trains run many times a day between Denmark and Sweden via the ferries shuttling between Helsingør and Helsingborg. The 2nd-class rail fare from Copenhagen is 255 kr to Gothenburg and 455 kr (395 kr under 26) to Stockholm.

There are numerous buses between Copenhagen and Sweden, including Eurolines (☎ 33 25 10 44) buses to Gothenburg (210 kr) and Stockholm (395 kr).

SEA

Germany

The frequent Rødbyhavn-Puttgarden ferry takes one hour and is included in rail tickets for those travelling by train; otherwise, the cost for a car with passengers is 315 kr.

Other ferries run from Rømø to Sylt (one hour, 32 kr), Faaborg to Gelting (two hours, 30 kr), Langeland to Kiel (2½ hours, 36 kr), Rønne to Sassnitz (four hours, 120 kr), Rønne to Neu Mukran (3½ hours, 100 kr) and Gedser to Rostock (two hours, 20 kr). These are passenger fares for midsummer travel; some ferries lower their fares in the off season. See also the relevant Getting There & Away sections.

Iceland & the Faroe Islands

The Smyril Line (☎ 33 11 22 55) runs weekly ferries from Esbjerg to Tórshavn (Faroe Islands) and Seyðisfjörður (Iceland) from early June to the end of August. The boat leaves Esbjerg on Saturday at 10 pm, arriving in Tórshavn on Monday at 10 am. Visitors then have a two-day layover in the Faroe Islands (while the boat makes a run to Bergen, Norway), departing from Tórshavn at 3 pm Wednesday and arriving in Seyðisfjörður at 7 am Thursday. The return boat departs from Seyðisfjörður at 11 am Thursday, arriving in Tórshavn at 6 am Friday and in Esbjerg at 7 pm Saturday.

The cheapest fares are for a couchette, which costs 880 kr to Tórshavn and 1390 kr to Seyðisfjörður for the first three and last four sailings of the season and 1260/1980 kr to Tórshavn/Seyðisfjörður in midsummer. Four-person cabins are 90 kr more, while two-person cabins cost 1470/2100 kr a person in the low/high season to Tórshavn, 2380/3400 kr to Seyðisfjörður. There's a 25% discount for students aged under 26 and travellers over 60. You can bring a bicycle along for 80 kr more, a motorcycle for about 500 kr and a car for about 85% of the passenger fare.

Norway

A daily overnight ferry operates between Copenhagen and Oslo. Ferries also run from Hirtshals to both Kristiansand and Oslo; from Hanstholm to Bergen; and from Frederikshavn to Oslo, Moss and Larvik. In addition, there's a catamaran service between Skagen and Larvik. For more details see the relevant Getting There & Away sections.

Poland

The Polish Baltic Shipping Co (☎ 33 11 46 45) operates ferries to Swinoujscie from both Copenhagen (10 hours, 315 kr) and Rønne (5½ hours, 170 kr).

Sweden

The cheapest ferry to Sweden is the shuttle between Helsingør and Helsingborg (25 minutes, 19 kr one way, 28 kr return); if you're travelling by train it's included in your rail ticket. Ferries leave opposite the Helsingør train station every 20 minutes during the day and once an hour through the night. Passage for a motorcycle and up to two riders costs 105 kr; a car with up to five people costs 305 kr.

Other ferries go from Dragør to Limhamn (one hour, 33 kr), Frederikshavn to Gothenburg (3¼ hours, 90 kr), Rønne to Ystad (2½ hours, 110 kr) and Grenå to Halmstad or Varberg (4¼ hours, 90 kr). There are also hydrofoils from Copenhagen to Malmö which leave frequently, take 45 minutes and cost 87 kr, and from Frederikshavn to Gothenburg, which leave a few times a day, take 1¾ hours and cost 84 kr. See also the relevant Getting There & Away sections in this chapter.

UK

Scandinavian Seaways sails from Esbjerg (☎ 79 17 79 17) to Harwich (☎ 01255-244 370) at least three times a week at 6 pm all year round. It takes about 20 hours and costs from 830 kr in summer, half that in winter.

LEAVING DENMARK

There are no departure taxes when leaving Denmark.

Getting Around

AIR

Most of Denmark's domestic air routes are operated by Maersk Air (☎ 32 31 45 45), which connects Copenhagen with Billund, Esbjerg, Odense, Rønne and Vojens. The regular one-way fare from Copenhagen is 620 kr to Odense and Rønne, and from 700 to 730 kr to the other destinations. The regular return fare is double. If you purchase your ticket a week in advance and stay over a Saturday night, you can get a return *minipris* ticket for about the same price as a one-way fare.

SAS (☎ 70 10 30 00) links Copenhagen with Aalborg and Århus, both about a dozen times a day. The one-way fare is 625 kr, while the return fare, with a seven-day advance purchase, is 650 kr.

There are discounts for travellers aged under 21 and over 65 and for family members travelling together.

BUS

All large cities and towns have a local bus system and most places are also served by regional buses, many of which connect with trains. There are also a few long-distance bus routes, including from Copenhagen to Aalborg or Århus. Travelling by bus on long-distance routes is about 25% cheaper than travel by train.

TRAIN

With the exception of a few short private lines, the Danish State Railways (DSB) runs all train services in Denmark.

There are two types of long-distance trains and ticket prices are the same on both. The sleek intercity (IC) trains have ultra-modern comforts in both 1st and 2nd-class carriages. While IC trains generally require reservations, they aren't needed if you board an IC train after 8 pm or on any IC trains between Aalborg and Frederikshavn. Inter-regional (IR) trains are older, a bit slower, and don't require reservations except for a few

weekend IR trains that go on the ferry between Zealand and Funen. While you'll usually be fine taking your chances on IR trains, you might want to consider reservations during rush hour to be assured of a seat. Regardless of distance, reservation fees are 30 kr (60 kr for 1st class) for IC trains and 20 kr for IR trains. Rail passes don't cover reservation fees.

Sleepers are available on overnight trains between Copenhagen and Frederikshavn or Esbjerg. The cost per person is 65 kr in a six-person compartment, 160 kr in a two-person cabin, or 300 kr in a private 1st-class cabin, all in addition to the usual train fare.

In general, travelling in 2nd class is quite comfortable and there's no need to pay the 50% surcharge for 1st-class travel. Second-class fares work out to about 1 kr per km. Three or more adults travelling together are entitled to either a 20% discount or to travel 1st class for 2nd-class fares. People aged 65 and older are entitled to a 25% discount on Friday and Sunday and a 50% discount on other days. Children under four, and one child aged four to 11, travel free with an adult; additional children pay half fare.

ScanRail, Eurail and other rail passes are valid on DSB ferries and trains, but not on the private lines. For rail pass information, see the Getting Around chapter.

CAR & MOTORCYCLE

Denmark is a pleasant country for touring by car. Roads are in good condition, almost invariably well signposted and overall traffic is surprisingly manageable, even in major cities including Copenhagen (rush hours excepted).

Access to and from motorways is made easy in Denmark as roads leading out of city and town centres are sensibly named after the main city to which they're routed. For instance, the road leading out of Odense to Faaborg is Faaborgvej, the road leading to Nyborg is Nyborgvej, and so on.

Denmark's extensive network of ferries carries motor vehicles for reasonable rates. Though fares vary, as a rule of thumb, domestic fares for cars average three times the passenger rate. The motoring organisation FDM distributes a handy timetable listing fares and phone numbers for all car ferries serving Denmark; it's always a good idea for drivers to call ahead and make a reservation.

One litre of unleaded petrol costs about 6.5 kr, a litre of super petrol costs about 6.7 kr and a litre of a diesel fuel costs about 5.1 kr. You'll find the best prices at stations along motorways and at the unstaffed OK Benzin chain, which has self-serve pumps that accept 100 kr notes.

Denmark's main motoring organisation, Forenede Danske Motorejere, or FDM (☎ 45 93 08 00), is headquartered at Firskovvej 32, 2800 Lyngby.

Road Rules

In Denmark you drive on the right-hand side of the road, seat belt use is mandatory (provided the car is fitted with seat belts) and all drivers are required to carry a warning triangle. Speed limits range from 50 km/h in towns to 110 km/h on expressways. Cars and motorcycles must have dipped headlights on at all times. It's a good idea for visitors to carry a Green Card (see Paperwork & Preparations in the Getting Around chapter).

The authorities are very strict about drink driving. It's illegal to drive with a blood alcohol concentration of 0.08% or greater, and driving under the influence will subject drivers to stiff penalties and a possible prison sentence.

Car Rental

You'll generally get the best deal by booking through an international rental agency before you arrive in Denmark. Otherwise rates for the cheapest cars, including VAT, insurance and unlimited km, begin at about 620 kr a day, or 470 kr a day on rentals of two days or more. Some companies offer a special weekend rate that allows you to keep the car from Friday afternoon to Monday morning and includes unlimited km, VAT and insurance for around 1000 kr. The largest companies – Avis, Hertz and Europcar

(National) – have offices throughout Denmark.

Parking

To park in the street in city centres you usually have to buy a ticket from a pavement machine (billetautomat). The billetautomat has an LCD read-out showing the current time and as you insert coins the time advances. Put in enough money to advance the read-out to the time you desire and then push the button to eject the ticket from the machine. Place the ticket, which shows the exact time you've paid for, face up inside the windscreen. The cost is generally from 4 to 16 kr an hour. Unless otherwise posted, street parking is usually free from 6 pm to 8 am, after 2 pm on Saturday and all day on Sunday.

In smaller towns, which are delightfully free of coin-hungry billetautomats, street parking is free within the time limits posted. You will, however, need a windscreen parking disk (free from tourist offices and petrol stations) which you set at the time you park. *Parkering forbudt* means 'no parking'.

BICYCLE

Cycling is a practical way to get around Denmark. There are extensive bike paths linking towns throughout the country and bike lanes along the streets of most city centres.

You can rent bikes in most towns from 35 to 60 kr a day, plus a deposit of around 250 kr. Bikes can be taken on ferries and most trains for a modest cost; ask DSB for the pamphlet *Bikes and Trains in Denmark*. See also Cycling under Activities in Denmark's Facts for the Visitor section.

HITCHING

Hitching in Denmark is quite rare, generally not very good, and illegal on motorways.

BOAT

An extensive network of ferries links Denmark's main islands as well as most of the smaller populated ones. Generally where there's not a bridge, there's a ferry. Specific ferry information is given under the relevant destination sections.

LOCAL TRANSPORT

All cities and towns of any size in Denmark are served by local buses. As a rule, the main local bus terminal is adjacent to the train station or ferry depot. For more details, see the relevant destination sections.

Taxi

Taxi stands can be found at train stations and major shopping areas throughout Denmark. The fare is typically 20 kr at flagfall and from 8 to 10 kr per km with the higher rates prevailing after 6 pm and on weekends. If you call for a taxi, the meter isn't started until you're picked up.

ORGANISED TOURS

Denmark is so small and public transport systems so extensive that organised tours are limited. DSB (☎ 33 14 17 01) does offer one-day self-guided tours from Copenhagen to the Louisiana art museum (87 kr) and to Legoland (550 kr for an adult and one child). There's also a circular tour around the Øresund (125 kr) that goes from Copenhagen to Malmö, Sweden, north to Helsingborg and back to Copenhagen via North Zealand. Some local tourist offices offer walking tours of their towns, and occasionally provide more extensive city tours.

Copenhagen

Copenhagen (Danish: København) is Scandinavia's largest and liveliest city, with a population of 1.4 million. Founded in 1167, it became the capital of Denmark in the early 15th century. Copenhagen is largely a low-rise city, with block after block of historic six-storey buildings. Church steeples add a nice punctuation to the skyline and only a couple of modern hotels burst up to mar the scene.

The city has an active nightlife which rolls into the early hours of the morning, and for

sightseers there's a treasure trove of museums, castles and old churches to explore.

For a big city, Copenhagen is easy to get around. The central area is largely reserved for foot traffic, while the main roads have cycle lanes for those who prefer to move at a faster pace.

Orientation

The train station, Central Station (Danish: Hovedbanegården or København H), is flanked on the west by the main hotel zone and on the east by Tivoli amusement park. At the northern corner of Tivoli is Rådhuspladsen, the central city square and the main bus transit point.

Strøget, 'the world's longest pedestrian mall', runs through the city centre between Rådhuspladsen and Kongens Nytorv, at the head of the Nyhavn canal. Strøget is made up of five continuous streets: Frederiksberggade, Nygade, Vimmelskaftet, Amagertorv and Østergade. Other pedestrian streets run north from Strøget in a triangular pattern to the Latin Quarter, a popular student haunt.

Information

Tourist Offices The Danish Tourist Board (☎ 33 11 13 25), at Bernstorffsgade 1, just north of the train station, distributes the informative *Copenhagen This Week* and brochures for all Denmark. It's open from 9 am to 9 pm daily from May to mid-September, to 5 pm weekdays and 2 pm on Saturday the rest of the year.

Use It (☎ 33 15 65 18), Rådhusstræde 13, is a terrific alternative information centre catering to young budget travellers but open to all. They book rooms, store luggage, hold mail, provide information on everything from hitching to nightlife, and have excellent city maps and a useful general guide *Playtime* – all free of charge. It's open from 9 am to 7 pm daily from June to September, from 10 am to 4 pm weekdays at other times.

Copenhagen Card The Copenhagen Card allows unlimited travel on buses and trains around Copenhagen and North Zealand and free admission to virtually all of the region's museums and attractions. The card costs 140/230/295 kr (half-price for children aged from five to 11 years) for one/two/three days and is sold at Central Station, the tourist office and some hotels. If you want to rush through a lot of sights in a few days this card can be a bargain but for a more leisurely exploration of select places it may work out better to pay individual admissions and use one of the transport passes (see the Getting Around section for Copenhagen).

Money American Express (☎ 33 12 23 01), on Strøget at Amagertorv 18, cashes travellers' cheques free of commission and notes for 15 kr. It's open from 9 am to 5 pm weekdays, until noon (2 pm in summer) on Saturday.

Banks, all of which charge transaction fees, are found on nearly every second corner in the city centre. The bank at Central Station is open from 7 am to 9 pm daily. The airport bank is open from 6.30 am to 10 pm daily.

Post & Communications Pick up poste-restante mail at the main post office, Tiet-gensgade 37, from 10 am to 6 pm weekdays, to 1 pm on Saturday. The post office in Central Station is open from 8 am to 10 pm weekdays, 9 am to 4 pm on Saturday, 10 am to 5 pm on Sunday.

You can make international phone calls and send faxes and telegrams from 8 am to 10 pm weekdays, 9 am to 9 pm weekends, at the Telecom Center above the Central Station post office.

Babel (☎ 33 33 93 38), a café at Frederiks-borggade 33, has Internet access for 30 kr.

Travel Agencies Kilroy Travels (☎ 33 11 00 44), Skindergade 28, specialises in student travel, while the nearby American Express office handles general travel.

Bookshops GAD on Strøget at Vimmel-skaftet 32, and Boghallen at Rådhuspladsen 37, both have good selections of English-language books, travel guides and maps. Pick up foreign newspapers at Central Station or the 7-Eleven store opposite Rådhuspladsen.

Laundry Laundrettes (look for the word *møntvask*) are not terribly difficult to find around the city. Near Nyhavn, there's one at Herluf Trolles gade 19, open from 6 am to 10 pm daily.

Emergency Dial ☎ 112 for police or an ambulance. Several city hospitals have 24-hour emergency wards; the most central is Rigshospitalet (☎ 35 45 35 45), Blegdams-vej 9. Private doctor visits (☎ 33 93 63 00 for referrals) usually cost from 250 to 350 kr. There's a 24-hour pharmacy, Steno Apotek, at Vesterbrogade 6 opposite Central Station.

Things to See
No trip to Copenhagen is complete without a visit to Tivoli and a stroll down Strøget. The most outstanding museums are Ny Carlsberg Glyptotek and Nationalmuseet.

Walking Tour Taking a half-day's walk from the Rådhus (city hall) to the Little Mermaid is a good way to get oriented and take in some of the city's central sights.

The **Rådhus** building itself is worth a glance. You can take a free look at the theatre-like interior or, for 10 kr, walk 300 steps to the top of its tower weekdays at 10 am, noon and 2 pm.

From the Rådhus walk down Strøget, which after a couple of blocks cuts between two squares, Gammel Torv and Nytorv. The water fountain at **Gammel Torv** marks what was once the old city's central market. Pedlars still sell jewellery, flowers and fruit, and the square is one of Copenhagen's most popular hang-outs.

At the end of the Strøget mall you'll reach Kongens Nytorv, a square circled by gracious old buildings including the **Royal Theatre**, home to the Royal Danish Ballet, and **Charlottenborg**, a 17th-century Dutch baroque palace that houses the Royal Academy of Arts. The academy's rear building has changing exhibits of contemporary art and is open from 10 am to 5 pm daily, usually charging a fee of 20 kr.

On the east side of Kongens Nytorv is picturesque **Nyhavn** canal, dug 300 years

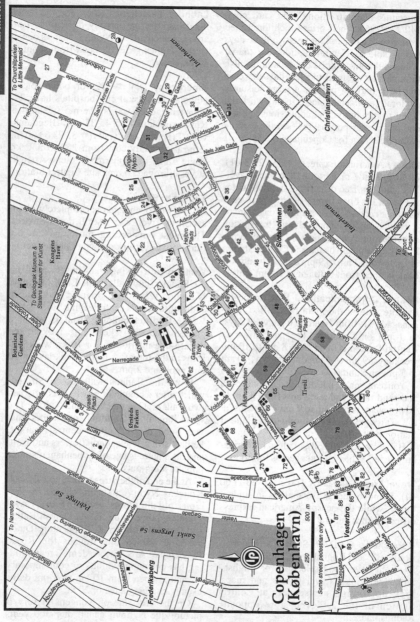

Copenhagen
(København)

PLACES TO STAY

1 Cab-Inn Scandinavia
4 Hotel Jørgensen
25 Hotel d'Angleterre
30 Sømandshjemmet Bethel
33 Hotel Maritime
76 Missionshotellet Nebo
81 Turisthotellet
82 Absalon Hotel
83 Hotel du Nord
84 Hotel Centrum
85 Selandia Hotel
86 Hotel Hebron
90 City Public Hostel

PLACES TO EAT

5 Govindas
6 Hellas
7 Klaptræet
8 Nacho's Cantina
10 Ankara
15 Det Lille Apotek
16 Peder Oxe & Jensen's Bøfhus
17 Pasta Basta
22 Café Sommersko
23 Grocery Store
24 Bakery
26 Nyhavns Færgekro
34 Restaurant Shezan
50 RizRaz
51 Restaurant Gråbrødre
52 Café de Paris &
   Restaurant Eastern
53 Café Sorgenfri
55 Restaurant Shanghai
60 Peppe's Pizza
61 Burger King
62 Atlas Bar & Flyvefisken
63 Shawarma Grill House
67 Scala(Food Hall)
69 Hard Rock Cafe
79 Fruit Stand
87 Restaurant Koh-I-Noor
88 Indus Restaurant
89 Merhaba

OTHER

2 Café Babooshka
3 Dansk Cyklist Forbund (Cycling
  Federation)

9 Rosenborg Slot (Castle)
11 Library
12 University Library
13 Vor Frue Kirke (Cathedral)
14 Kilroy Travels
18 Rundetårn (Tower)
19 American Express
20 Copenhagen Jazz House
21 Den Danske Bank
27 Amalienborg Palace
28 Boats to Oslo & Bornholm
29 Laundrette
31 Charlottenborg Palace
32 Royal Theatre
35 Hydrofoils to Malmö
36 Christiana
37 Vor Frelsers Kirke (Church)
38 Netto Bådene Boats
39 Royal Library
40 Tøjhusmuseet (Royal
   Arsenal)
41 Folketing (Parliament)
42 Royal Reception
   Chambers
43 Ruins of Absalon's Fortress
44 Thorvaldsens Museum
45 Teatermuseet
46 Christiansborg Palace
47 Museum of Royal Coaches
48 Nationalmuseet
49 Use It (Information Service)
54 GAD Bookshop
56 Mojo (Nightspot)
57 Sabor Latino (Nightspot)
58 Ny Carlsberg Glyptotek (Art Museum)
59 Rådhus (City Hall)
64 Boghallen Bookshop
65 Louis Tussaud's Wax Museum
66 Rådhusarkaden Shopping Centre
68 Cool Bikes (Scooter
   Rental)
70 Tourist Office
71 SAS Ticket Office
72 Steno Apotek (Pharmacy)
73 Hertz Car Rental
74 Petrol Station
75 Danwheel
77 Eurolines Office
78 Central Station
80 Main Post Office

ago to allow traders to bring their wares into the heart of the city. Long a haunt for sailors and writers, including Hans Christian Andersen, Nyhavn is nowadays half-salty, half-gentrified, with a line of trendy pavement cafés and restored gabled townhouses.

From the north side of Nyhavn, head north on Toldbodgade, turn right on Sankt Annæ Plads and then turn left to continue walking north along the waterfront. When you reach the fountain, turn inland to get to the **Amalienborg Palace**, home of the royal family since 1794. The palace's four nearly identical Rococo mansions surround a central square that's the scene of a ceremonious noontime changing of the guard. The interior of the north-west mansion, which features royal memorabilia and the study rooms of three kings, can be viewed for 40 kr from 10 am to 5 pm daily.

Continue north on Amaliegade to Churchillparken, where you'll find **Friheds-museet**, which depicts the history of Danish Resistance against Nazi occupation. The museum is free and open from 10 am to 4 pm Tuesday to Saturday, to 5 pm on Sunday.

Taking a 10-minute walk up past the immense **Gefion Fountain** and through the park will lead you to the statue of the famed **Little Mermaid** (Den Lille Havfrue), a diminutive bronze with an industrial harbour backdrop that tends to disappoint all but the most steadfast Hans Christian Andersen fans.

From the Little Mermaid continue on the road inland (west). In just a few minutes you'll reach steps leading down to a wooden bridge that crosses a moat into an interesting 17th-century citadel called the **Kastellet**. It's a short walk south through the Kastellet, where a second bridge spans the moat and leads back into Churchillparken. From the park, turn right onto Esplanaden to Store Kongensgade, where you can catch bus No 1 or 6 back to the Rådhus.

Latin Quarter With its cafés and second-hand bookshops, the area north of Strøget surrounding the university is a good place for ambling around.

Ascend the stairs of the **University Library** (enter from Fiolstræde) to see one quirky remnant of the 1807 British bombardment of Copenhagen: a cannonball in five fragments and the target it hit, a book titled *Defensor Pacis* (Defender of Peace).

Opposite the university is **Vor Frue Kirke**, Copenhagen's neoclassical cathedral. With its high vaulted ceilings and columns it seems as much museum as church – all quite apropos as it's also the display for the most acclaimed works of Bertel Thorvaldsen, his statues of Christ and the 12 apostles. The cathedral is open from 9 am to 5 pm Monday to Saturday and entry is free.

At the north side of the Latin Quarter is **Kultorvet**, a lively square where on sunny days you'll almost surely find impromptu street entertainment, as well as beer gardens, flower stalls and produce stands.

Rundetårn The Round Tower, at Køb-magergade 52, is the best vantage point for viewing the old city's red-tiled rooftops and abundant church spires. Built by Christian IV in 1642 as an astronomical observatory, it still offers occasional astronomy programmes. Halfway up the 209-metre spiral walkway is a hall with interesting changing exhibits. The tower is open daily from 10 am to 8 pm in summer (on Sunday from noon), to 5 pm in winter. Admission is 15 kr.

Rosenborg Slot This 17th-century castle, built by Christian IV in Dutch Renaissance style, is a repository of regalia. The main attraction is the dazzling collection of crown jewels which includes Christian IV's crown, the jewel-studded sword of Christian III and Queen Margrethe II's emeralds and pearls. It's open daily from 10 am to 4 pm from 1 June to 31 August, from 11 am to 3 pm in spring and autumn. Admission costs 40 kr.

Gardens The green stretch of gardens along Øster Voldgade offers a refuge from the city traffic. **Kongens Have**, the large public park behind Rosenborg Slot, is a popular picnic spot and the site of a free marionette theatre on summer afternoons.

The **Botanical Gardens** on the west side of Rosenborg Slot have fragrant trails amidst arbours, terraces and ponds, open free from 8.30 am to 6 pm daily. Also in the grounds is the **Palmehus**, a large walk-through glasshouse with tropical plants, open from 10 am to 3 pm. One entrance to the gardens is at the intersection of Gothersgade and Voldgade and the other is off Øster Farimagsgade.

Statens Museum for Kunst Denmark's national gallery, Statens Museum for Kunst, at Sølvgade 48, contains a good fine-arts collection by 19th-century Danish masters, such as Jens Juel and CW Eckersberg, and works by European artists including Matisse, Picasso and Munch. Hours are from 10 am to 4.30 pm (to 9 pm on Wednesday); it's closed on Monday. Admission is 20 kr.

Slotsholmen On an island separated from the city centre by a moat-like canal, Slotsholmen is the site of **Christiansborg Palace** and the seat of Denmark's national government. Of the numerous sites to explore, grandest is the **Royal Reception Chambers**, the ornate Renaissance hall where the queen entertains heads of state. Tours with commentary in English (30 kr) are at 11 am and 3 pm (also 1 pm in midsummer) Tuesday to Sunday.

The **Ruins of Absalon's Fortress**, the excavated foundations of the original castle built by Bishop Absalon in 1167, are in the basement below the present palace tower and can be explored for 20 kr from 9.30 am to 3.30 pm daily (closed Saturday and Monday from October to April).

During summer when the **Folketing** (Parliament) is in recess, free tours of the assembly chambers are given hourly in Danish from 10 am to 4 pm daily except Saturday.

Thorvaldsens Museum (enter from Vindebrogade) features grand statues by the famed Danish sculptor who was heavily influenced by Greek and Roman mythology. It's open from 10 am to 5 pm Tuesday to Sunday year round and entry is free.

The **Royal Library**, which dates from the 17th century and has lovely flower gardens at the front, is open to 7 pm Monday to Saturday. Hans Christian Andersen applied for work here in 1834 'to be freed from the heavy burden of having to write in order to live'. His unsuccessful application and many of his original manuscripts are now part of the archives.

Next door at **Tøjhusmuseet**, the royal arsenal built in 1600, there's an impressive collection of hand weapons and old armour and a huge hall filled with historic cannons. Hours are from 10 am to 4 pm Tuesday to Sunday year round. Admission costs 20 kr.

At the **Museum of Royal Coaches** the coaches used for regal events can be viewed

from 2 to 4 pm on weekends for 10 kr. The **Teatermuseet**, which houses the royal stage, dates from 1766 and has exhibits on Danish theatre history. It's open from 2 to 4 pm on Wednesday and noon to 4 pm on Saturday and Sunday. Admission costs 20 kr.

Nationalmuseet The National Museum, at Ny Vestergade 10, holds the world's most extensive collection of Danish artefacts from the Palaeolithic period to the 19th century. Highlights include Viking weaponry, church booty and other treasure hoards and an exceptional collection of Bronze Age lurs and millennium-old rune stones. There's also a noteworthy coin collection, Egyptian mummies and Grecian urns. The museum is open from 10 am to 5 pm Tuesday to Sunday. Admission costs 30 kr.

Christianshavn Christianshavn was established by King Christian IV in the early 1600s as a commercial centre and military buffer for the expanding city of Copenhagen. Still surrounded by ramparts and cut by canals, Christianshavn today is a mix of renovated period warehouses and newer apartment buildings.

In 1971 an abandoned military camp on the east side of Christianshavn was taken over by squatters who proclaimed it the 'free state' of **Christiania**, subject to their own laws. Bowing to public pressure the government eventually agreed to allow Christiania to continue as a 'social experiment' in communal living. About 1000 people settled into Christiania, starting their own collective businesses, schools and recycling programme.

Along with progressive happenings, Christiania also became a magnet for runaways and junkies. Hard drugs have since been outlawed. Visitors are welcome to stroll through car-free Christiania, though large dogs may intimidate some free spirits. Photography is frowned upon, and outright forbidden on Pusherstreet where hashish is openly (though not legally) smoked and sold. If you want to learn more about Christiania, guided tours (☎ 31 57 96 70) are given at 3 pm daily in summer for 20 kr.

A few minutes walk from Christiania is the 17th-century **Vor Frelsers Kirke**, on Sankt Annæ Gade, which has an elaborately carved pipe organ and a baroque altar with cherubs and angels. For a panoramic city view, make the dizzying 400-step ascent up the church's 95-metre spiral tower – the last 160 steps run along the outside rim, narrowing to the point where they literally disappear at the top. Entrance is free to the church and 20 kr to the tower.

To get to Christianshavn, walk over the bridge from the north-east side of Slotsholmen or take bus No 8 from Rådhuspladsen.

Tivoli Right in the heart of the city, Tivoli, Copenhagen's century-old amusement park, is a mishmash of gardens, food pavilions, amusement rides, carnival games and stage shows that can be surprisingly tantalising, particularly in the evening. Fireworks light up the skies at 11.45 pm on Wednesday and Saturday. It's open 1 May to mid-September from 11 am to midnight daily. Admission is 44 kr (30 kr on Sunday, 20 kr after 9.30 pm every day).

Ny Carlsberg Glyptotek This museum, housed in a grand period building on HC Andersens Boulevard near Tivoli, has an exceptional collection of Greek, Egyptian, Etruscan and Roman sculpture, paintings by Gauguin, Monet and Van Gogh and a complete set of Degas bronzes. From 1 May to 31 August it's open Tuesday to Sunday from 10 am to 4 pm; the rest of the year it's open from noon to 3 pm Tuesday to Saturday and 10 am to 4 pm on Sunday. Admission is free on Wednesday and Sunday, 15 kr other days.

Louis Tussaud's Wax Museum At HC Andersens Boulevard 22, these wax figure exhibits have an emphasis on great Danes. It's open from 10 am to 11 pm, to 6 pm in winter. Admission is a hefty 48 kr.

Zoo The Copenhagen Zoo, in the Frederiksberg area, has the standard collection of caged creatures, including elephants, lions, gorillas and polar bears. Bus No 28 stops outside the gate. It's open daily year round from 9 am to either 5 or 6 pm. Admission is 55 kr.

Other Museums It could take weeks to fully explore all of Copenhagen's museums, which cover practically every special interest including Danish architecture, decorative art, erotica, working-class cultural history, geology, medical sciences, Copenhagen city history, tobacco & pipes, post & telegraph, shipbuilding, Danish naval history, European musical instruments, the drawings of humourist Storm P and the silver designs of Georg Jensen. Copenhagen also has a planetarium and a tourable Soviet submarine. *Copenhagen This Week* has a complete list with addresses, hours and admission fees.

Dragør If Copenhagen begins to feel crowded, consider an afternoon excursion to Dragør, a quiet maritime town on the island of Amager, a few km south of the airport. In the early 1550s King Christian II allowed Dutch farmers to settle in Amager to provide his court with flowers and produce, and Dragør still retains a bit of Dutch flavour.

Along the waterfront are fish shops, smokehouses, a sizeable fishing fleet and the Dragør Museum (20 kr), a half-timbered house holding ship models and period furnishings. The winding cobblestone streets leading up from the harbour are lined with the thatch-roofed, mustard-coloured houses that comprise the old town. Take bus No 30 or 33 (15 kr) from Rådhuspladsen, a 35-minute ride.

Klampenborg Only 20 minutes from Central Station on the S-train's line C, Klampenborg is a favourite spot for people from Copenhagen on family outings.

A 10-minute walk west from Klampenborg station is **Bakken**, the world's oldest amusement park. A blue-collar version of Tivoli, it's a honky-tonk carnival of bumper cars, slot machines and beer halls. It's open from 2 pm to midnight daily from late March to late August. Entry is free.

Bakken is at the southern edge of **Dyrehave**, an expansive woodland of beech trees and meadows crossed with walking and cycling trails. Dyrehave was established as a royal hunting ground in 1669 and has evolved into the capital's most popular picnicking area. At its centre, two km north of Bakken, is the old manor house **Eremitagen**, a good vantage point for spotting herds of deer.

A couple of hundred metres east of Klampenborg station is **Bellevue beach**, a sandy strand that gets packed with sunbathers in summer.

Frilandsmuseet Frilandsmuseet is a sprawling open-air museum of old countryside dwellings, workshops and barns in the town of Lyngby. The museum, at Kongevejen 100, is a 10-minute walk from Sorgenfri station which is 25 minutes from Central Station on the S-train's line B. Opening hours are from 10 am to 5 pm from April to September, to 4 pm in October; closed Monday and in winter. Admission is 30 kr.

Louisiana Museum of Modern Art Louisiana, Denmark's foremost modern art museum, is on a seaside knoll in a strikingly modernistic building with sculpture-laden grounds. In addition to the permanent collection, the museum has top-notch changing exhibits. It's a fascinating place to visit even if you're not passionate about modern art. The museum is a 10-minute walk north on Strandvej from Humlebæk station, a 35-minute train ride from Copenhagen. It's open daily from 10 am to 5 pm (to 10 pm on Wednesday). Admission costs 48 kr.

Organised Tours
Brewery Visits Carlsberg Brewery at Elephant Gate, Ny Carlsbergvej 140 (take bus No 6 westbound), has free tours at 11 am and 2 pm weekdays that are capped with a brew sampling.

Sightseeing Bus From mid-June to September the city operates a sightseeing bus

which runs every 20 minutes between 10 am and 5 pm. It takes a circular route from the Rådhus, stopping at Vor Frue Kirke, the Royal Theatre, Amalienborg Palace, the Little Mermaid, Rosenborg Slot, Slotsholmen, the National Museum and more. You can get on and off as often as you want within 24 hours for 20 kr.

Canal Tours For a different angle on the city, hop onto one of the hour-long boat tours that wind through Copenhagen's canals from April to September. Though most passengers are usually Danes, multilingual guides give a lively commentary in English as well. The biggest company, Canal Tours Copenhagen, leaves from the head of Nyhavn and charges 40 kr, but the best deal is with Netto-Bådene, whose guided tour includes Nyhavn, the Little Mermaid, Christianshavn and the Christiansborg Slot canals for only 20 kr. Netto-Bådene boats leave from Holmens Kirke, opposite the stock exchange, a few times an hour between 10 am and 5 pm.

Canal boats also make a fine traffic-free alternative for getting to some of Copenhagen's waterfront sites, including the Little Mermaid and Christianshavn. Canal Tours Copenhagen charges 35 kr for a one-day pass on its 'water bus' from 1 May to 15 September. The boats leave Nyhavn every 30 minutes from 10.15 am to 4.45 pm (to 6.30 pm in midsummer) and make eight stops, allowing you to get on and off as you like.

Special Events
The Copenhagen Jazz Festival is the biggest event of the year, with 10 days of music in early July. The festival presents a wide range of Danish and international jazz, blues and fusion music. It's a cornucopia of more than 400 indoor and outdoor concerts, with music wafting out of practically every public square, park, pub and café from Strøget to Tivoli. For information, contact the festival office (☎ 33 93 20 13).

Places to Stay
The *værelseanvisning* counter at the tourist office, at Bernstorffsgade 1, books rooms in

private homes for around 150/250 kr for singles/doubles. It also books unfilled hotel rooms, often at discounted rates; expect a double room without bath to cost around 425 kr (with bath 575 kr) at many of the hotels listed in this section. However, discounts are based on supply and demand and so are not always available during busy periods. The counter is open from 9 am to midnight daily from mid-April to mid-September and from 9 am to 5 pm Monday to Friday and 9 am to 2 pm on Saturday the rest of the year. The booking fee is 15 kr per person.

Use It, Rådhusstræde 13, books private rooms for about 150/200 kr (no booking fee), keeps tabs on which hostel beds are available, and is a good source of information for subletting student housing and other long-term accommodation.

Camping *Bellahøj-Camping* (☎ 31 10 11 50), near the Bellahøj hostel about five km west of the city centre, is open from 1 June to 31 August and costs 45 kr per person. From Rådhuspladsen take bus No 2 to the Bellahøj stop.

Absalon Camping (☎ 31 41 06 00), which is open all year round also costs 45 kr per person. It is nine km west of the city centre at Korsdalsvej 132 near Brøndbyøster station on the S-train's line B.

Hostels Copenhagen has two HI hostels, each about five km from the city centre. The Bellahøj hostel is open from 1 March to 15 January, while the Amager hostel operates from 15 January to 30 November. Both have laundry facilities, but only the Amager hostel has a guest kitchen. They often fill early in the summer so it's best to call ahead for reservations.

The more conveniently located *Bellahøj Vandrerhjem* (☎ 31 28 97 15), Herbergvejen 8, has 299 dorm beds (70 kr), 14 family rooms and 24-hour reception. From Rådhuspladsen you can take bus No 2-Brønshøj and get off at Fuglsangs Allé.

The newer *Copenhagen Vandrerhjem Amager* (☎ 32 52 29 08), in Amager just off the E20 and south of the city centre, is

Europe's largest hostel with 528 beds (70 kr) in cell-like two-bed and five-bed rooms. Check-in time is from 1 pm. From Central Station take bus No 16-Vigerslev, change at Mozarts Plads to bus No 37-Holmens Bro and get off at Vejlands Allé. Until 6 pm weekdays bus No 46 runs from Central Station directly to the hostel.

Even when the HI hostels are full you can nearly always find a bed at one of the city-sponsored hostels. Though they tend to be more of a crash-pad scene, they're also more central.

City Public Hostel (☎ 31 31 20 70) at Absalonsgade 8 sleeps 200 people. There's one 72-bed dorm but the other rooms average around 12 beds each. From Central Station, walk west 10 minutes along Vesterbrogade. It's open from early May to late August, has 24-hour reception and costs 100 kr. Use your own sleeping bag or hire a bedsheet (30 kr).

The city-run 300-bed *Sleep-In* (☎ 35 26 50 59), Blegdamsvej 132A, is in the Østerbro area, a few km north of the centre. Occupying a sports centre hall that's curtained off into two to six-bed 'rooms', this well-managed operation is open from 1 July to 31 August and costs 100 kr with breakfast. Use your own sleeping bag or hire bedsheets and blankets for 30 kr. Reception is open 24 hours; there's a group kitchen and free lockers. From Rådhuspladsen take bus No 1-Ordrup, No 6-Klampenborg or No 14 to Trianglen and walk 300 metres south on Bledgdamsvej.

The *YMCA Interpoint* (☎ 31 31 15 74) at Valdemarsgade 15 is open from early July to mid-August. There are only 28 dorm beds (70 kr) in all, so it fills early; call ahead for reservations. Bedsheets (20 kr) and breakfast (25 kr) are available. Reception hours are from 8 am to noon, 2.30 to 6 pm and 7 pm to 12.30 am. It's a 15-minute walk from Central Station (take Vesterbrogade west to Valdemarsgade), or take bus No 6 or 16.

In addition there are occasionally a couple of small private hostel-like operations run by youth groups – for the latest, check with the tourist office or Use It.

Hotels – Around Central Station Copenhagen's main sleeping quarter (and red-light district) is along the west side of Central Station where rows of six-storey turn-of-the-century buildings house one hotel after the other. Rates given are for singles/doubles without private baths; rooms with private bath average 50% more.

The area's cheapest hotel, *Turisthotellet* (☎ 31 22 98 39), Reverdilsgade 5, has small well-worn rooms that are quite basic but suitable for the price of 200/300 kr, a simple breakfast included.

Missionshotellet Nebo (☎ 31 21 12 17), Istedgade 6, is only a stone's throw from the station. While the rooms are small and a bit drab, the common spaces are pleasant and the shared showers are large and clean. Rates are 340/520 kr.

A cut above others in this price range is *Hotel Hebron* (☎ 31 31 69 06), Helgolandsgade 4, a quiet hotel with nicely renovated rooms for 390/500 kr.

The *Selandia Hotel* (☎ 31 31 46 10), Helgolandsgade 12, has adequate rooms and a few agreeable touches, including a luggage room. Rates are 390/540 kr.

The *Hotel Centrum* (☎ 31 31 31 11), Helgolandsgade 14, has clean, straightforward rooms for 350/570 kr. When the hotel's not busy the rates are negotiable – making this a good place to look for a last-minute deal.

Hotel du Nord (☎ 31 31 77 50), Colbjørnsensgade 14, is a small tidy hotel with comfortable rooms for 400/600 kr – when it's slow they'll drop the doubles rate to 500 kr. Courtyard rooms are quieter than streetside ones.

At the *Absalon Hotel* (☎ 31 24 22 11), Helgolandsgade 15, the cheaper rooms (400/500 kr) are faded, but the hotel is easy to book through the tourist office's room booking service at discounted rates.

Hotels – Elsewhere in Copenhagen There are two moderately priced hotels in Nyhavn. *Hotel Maritime* (☎ 33 13 48 82), Peder Skramsgade 19, has small, clean rooms with TV and private baths; although listed prices

are higher, the manager will generally let the rooms go for 450/585 kr. If you prefer not to bargain, go straight to *Sømandshjemmet Bethel* (☎ 33 13 03 70), Nyhavn 22, which has good-sized rooms, private baths and unbeatable views of Nyhavn harbour for 395/595 kr. Ask for a corner room.

The modern *Cab-Inn Scandinavia* (☎ 35 36 11 11), Vodroffsvej 57, has 201 sleekly compact rooms that resemble cabins in a cruise ship. Though small, they're quite comfortable, with amenities like remote-control TV, phones, air-con and private bathrooms. Rates are 395/495 kr. As it's a popular place, reservations are suggested; if it's full its sister hotel, *Cab-Inn Copenhagen* (☎ 31 21 04 00) at Danasvej 32, charges the same rates and is just a few blocks away.

The *Hotel Jørgensen* (☎ 33 13 81 86), at Rømersgade 11 near Nørreport station, is popular with gay travellers. Room rates start at 380/480 kr. In summer it also has dorm beds for 100 kr, breakfast included.

Copenhagen also has many expensive upmarket hotels, all listed in the annual *Hotels Denmark* booklet available from the tourist office. Visiting celebrities generally opt for the *Hotel d'Angleterre* (☎ 33 12 00 95), Kongens Nytorv 34, which has chandeliers, marble floors and a history dating back to the 17th century. Rates begin at 1850/2050 kr.

Places to Eat

Around Central Station Central Station has a supermarket open daily from 8 am to midnight, a bakery with good breads and pastries and fast-food eateries including a *McDonald's*. Of the DSB restaurants in the station, cheapest is *Spise Hjørnet*, open from 6.30 am to 10 pm, which serves up a filling if unexciting weekday special for 37 kr. You'll find a pavement fruit stand outside the station on the corner opposite the main post office.

Hard Rock Cafe, Vesterbrogade 3, near the tourist office, has burgers, barbecued ribs and a décor of rock memorabilia.

Hercegovina, inside Tivoli, is a fun place for a splurge. After 9 pm a buffet of barbecued meats and other Bosnia-Hercegovinian specialities with wine costs 99 kr. Dine on the balcony and you can watch Tivoli's pantomime ballet perform below!

Scala, on Vesterbrogade opposite Tivoli, is a multi-storied building full of fast-food eateries, restaurants, bakeries and a cinema. Good bets include *Matahari*, with wok-cooked dishes for around 50 kr, and *Th Sørenson*, with smørrebrød sandwiches for 25 kr. Even if you're not hungry, it's worth taking a look at the smørrebrød case just to see what can be done with a lowly slice of bread.

Rådhusarkaden, an indoor shopping centre on Vesterbrogade near Rådhus, has an *Irma* grocery store and the *Conditori Hans Christian Andersen* which has good sandwiches, pastries and coffee.

Indus Restaurant, Istedgade 25, serves Pakistani food from 11.30 am to 11.30 pm daily. Vegetarian dishes with rice cost 50 kr, curries 60 kr. There's another inexpensive Pakistani restaurant on the opposite corner.

Restaurant Koh-I-Noor, Vesterbrogade 33, has candlelight dining and a good Indian buffet that includes curried lamb, beef and chicken dishes, nan, lentils, rice and salad for 79 kr from 5 to 10.30 pm nightly.

Merhaba, a Turkish restaurant at Vesterbrogade 39, has good-value specials, including a three-course meal for 49 kr from noon to 3 pm, 69 kr at dinner. You can choose from several options, including a tasty dolma starter and shish kebab as a main dish.

Strøget & Around Strøget has an abundance of cheap eateries including hot-dog, hamburger and ice-cream stands and numerous hole-in-the-wall kebab joints selling felafels and kebabs for around 25 kr. The best is *Shawarma Grill House* at the west end of Strøget, a two-minute walk from Rådhuspladsen. It's a friendly spot open from 11 am to 11 pm daily, with a sit-down counter at ground level and a dining room upstairs.

For night owls the pleasant and popular *Pasta Basta*, Valkendorfsgade 22, is open to 3 am (to 5 am weekends) and has a self-service table of cold pasta dishes and salads for 69 kr.

Best of the area's numerous pizzerias is *Peppe's Pizza*, Rådhuspladsen 57, which offers a pizza and salad buffet from noon to 4 pm daily for 39 kr and has a nice basement setting. For a reasonable dinnertime deal (39 kr) head to *Café de Paris*, Vimmelskaftet 39, which also has all-you-can-eat pizza and salad.

Restaurant Eastern, in the same complex as Café de Paris, offers a buffet of Indian and Pakistani dishes from 11 am to 4 pm for 49 kr and a three-course dinner for 98 kr.

At *RizRaz*, just south of Strøget at Kompagnistræde 20, you can feast on a superb Mediterranean-style vegetarian buffet including salads, felafels and pizza for 39 kr daily from 11.30 am to 5 pm, 59 kr at 11.30 pm.

Restaurant Gråbrødre, Kompagnistræde 18, is a friendly café with good food, including a fried salmon special for just 36 kr until 5.30 pm, 59 kr at dinner.

Café Sorgenfri, Brolæggerstræde 8, is a smoky corner pub with good reasonably priced Danish food. Cold items average 40 kr, hot dishes about 60 kr. The roast pork is a speciality and a full plate of traditional Danish foods costs 98 kr. It's open from 11 am to 9 pm.

For fine dining there's *Peder Oxe* at Gråbrødre Torv, just north of Strøget, which is housed in a traditional building with an engaging ambience. It's open from 11.30 am to 10.30 pm and specialises in meat dishes, served with a salad buffet, for 70 to 150 kr.

There's also a nice atmosphere at *Jensen's Bøfhus* in another period house fronting Gråbrødre Torv. It has a good lunch deal of a steak and baked potato served from 11 am to 4 pm for 39 kr. At dinner there's a tasty chicken dish that includes a salad buffet for 89 kr.

Restaurant Shanghai has a good balcony view of Gammel Torv and a variety of lunch dishes for 46 kr (from 11 am to 3 pm), as well as three-course meals for 99 kr that are served until 10 pm.

In & Around the Latin Quarter *Hellas*, Fiolstræde 21, has a lunch buffet of Greek salads and hot dishes for just 32 kr from noon to 4 pm and a dinner buffet for 78 kr.

Ankara, at Krystalgade 8, has a good Turkish buffet of salads, hummus, rice and various hot and cold dishes for 49 kr until 4 pm, 59 kr from 4 pm to midnight.

Klaptræet, a 2nd-floor café at Kultorvet 13, is a student haunt with a nice view of the square and simple sandwiches and salads for around 35 kr. It's open daily from 10 am to the wee hours of the morning. *Nacho's Cantina*, Kultorvet 14, has various Mexican plates for around 90 kr and lunch specials for half that price.

Det Lille Apotek, Store Kannikestræde 15, serves Danish lunch plates that include pickled herring, fish fillet and open-faced sandwiches for 59 to 125 kr and a three-course dinner for 148 kr.

Café Sommersko, Kronprinsensgade 6, draws a high-energy university crowd and has 50 different beers and a menu of salads, sandwiches and hot dishes (65 kr) like shrimp rissoto, Greek moussaka and chicken curry. It's open from 9 am to 1 am daily.

Elsewhere in Copenhagen For a thoroughly Danish experience, try the herring buffet at *Nyhavns Færgekro*, an atmospheric restaurant on the canal at Nyhavn 5. There are 10 different kinds of herring including baked, marinated and rollmops, with condiments to sprinkle on top and boiled potatoes to round out the meal. The all-you-can-eat buffet costs 68 kr and is available from 11.30 am to 4 pm daily. If you're not a herring lover, there are salads and smørrebrød for 35 to 55 kr.

Restaurant Shezan, Havnegade 3, serves moderately priced Pakistani meat and vegetarian dishes from 11 am to 11 pm daily.

You can also get good vegetarian food at *Govindas*, Nørre Farimagsgade 82, south of the Botanical Gardens, where Hare Krishna members serve up an all-you-can-eat meal for a mere 40 kr.

More up-market is *Atlas Bar*, Larsbjørnsstræde 18, which has vegetarian meals for around 60 kr at lunch, 100 kr at dinner.

Upstairs is *Flyvefisken*, a good Thai dinner restaurant with moderate prices.

The main city produce market is at Israels Plads, a few minutes walk west of Nørreport station. Stalls are set up from Monday to Friday to 5 pm and on Saturday, when it doubles as a flea market, to 2 pm.

Entertainment
Copenhagen is a 24-hour party city. For free entertainment simply stroll along Strøget, especially between Nytorv and Højbro Plads, which is a bit like an impromptu three-ring circus of musicians, magicians, jugglers and other street performers.

Throughout the summer, numerous free concerts are held in city parks and squares. Fælledparken, at the north part of Copenhagen, features big-name Danish bands on weekends from May to August. Also popular are the rock and jazz concerts sponsored by the city breweries on weekends from June to August at Femøren on the coast of Amager.

Copenhagen has scores of backstreet cafés with live music. Entry is generally free on weeknights, while there's usually a cover charge averaging 40 kr on weekends.

The westside Nørrebro area has a number of good entertainment spots, most notably *Rust*, Guldbergsgade 8, which attracts a college-age crowd with trendy rock bands, and *Bananrepublikken*, Nørrebrogade 13, a friendly spot with a mixed-age crowd and salsa, calypso and other international music.

Copenhagen Jazz House, Niels Hemmingsens gade 10, is the city's leading jazz spot, with top Danish musicians and occasional international names. *Mojo*, Løngangstræde 21, is a hot spot for blues, with entertainment nightly. A popular venue for Latin music is *Sabor Latino*, Løngangstræde 39. *Loppen* in Christiania has live rock, reggae or jazz music Wednesday to Saturday nights.

There are numerous cinemas showing first-release movies along Vesterbrogade between Central Station and Rådhuspladsen.

Gay & Lesbian Scene Copenhagen has more than a dozen gay bars and clubs. Popular meeting places include *Sebastian*, a café at Hyskenstræde 10 for both men and women; *Cosy Bar*, Studiestræde 24, which attracts mostly men; and, for women, *Café Babooshka* at Turensensgade 6.

Things to Buy

Copenhagen's main shopping street is Strøget where you can find speciality shops selling top-quality amber and Danish silver, china and glass. Two big up-market department stores, Magasin and Illum, are also located in the Strøget area.

Getting There & Away

Air Copenhagen's modern international airport is in Kastrup, 10 km south-east of the city centre. Most airline offices are north of Central Station near the intersection of Vester Farimagsgade and Vesterbrogade. The SAS ticket office (☎ 70 10 20 00), in the SAS Royal Hotel, is open weekdays to 5.30 pm.

Bus Buses to the Swedish cities of Halmsted and Kristianstad leave from Kastrup airport, while those to Ysted, Malmö and Bornholm leave from Bernstorffsgade in front of Central Station. Reservations for other international buses, which also leave from Bernstorffsgade, can be made at Eurolines (☎ 33 25 10 44) at Reventlowsgade 8.

Train All long-distance trains arrive and depart from Central Station, a huge complex with eateries and numerous services. There are lockers in the lower level near the Reventlowsgade exit and public showers at the underground toilets opposite the police office.

Car & Motorcycle The main highways into Copenhagen are the E20 from Jutland and Funen, and the E47 from Helsingør and Sweden. If you're coming from the north on the E47, exit onto Lyngbyvej (route 19) and continue south to get into the heart of the city.

Car Rental In addition to airport booths, the following agencies have branches in central Copenhagen:

Avis, Kampmannsgade 1 (☎ 33 15 22 99)
Hertz, Ved Vesterport 3 (☎ 33 12 77 00)
Europcar, Gammel Kongevej 13 (☎ 33 55 99 00)

Hitching Hitching is seldom rewarding but if you want to try your luck it's best to start outside the city centre. For rides north, take bus No 1 to Vibenhus Runddel. If you're heading towards Funen, take the S-train's line A to Ellebjerg. Use It has a free message board that attempts to link up drivers and riders.

Boat The Oslo ferry departs from Copenhagen at 5 pm daily and the Bornholm ferry departs at 11.30 pm nightly. Both leave from Kvæsthusbroen, north of Nyhavn; take bus No 28. Boats to Malmö leave from Havnegade, south of Nyhavn; take bus No 27. See also the Denmark Getting There & Away section.

Getting Around

To/From the Airport The airport is 15 minutes and about 125 kr from the city centre by taxi. The SAS airport bus makes frequent, though sometimes packed, runs from Central Station for 35 kr. If your baggage is light, you could also take local bus No 32 or 250 (15 kr) which runs frequently between Rådhuspladsen and the airport terminal.

Local Transport Copenhagen has an extensive public transit system consisting of a metro rail network called S-train, whose 10 lines pass through Central Station (København H), and a vast bus system, whose main terminus is nearby at Rådhuspladsen.

Buses and trains use a common fare system based on the number of zones you pass through. The basic fare of 10 kr for up to two zones covers most city runs and allows transfers between buses and trains on a single ticket as long as they're made within an hour. Third and subsequent zones cost 5 kr more with a maximum fare of 35 kr for travel throughout North Zealand. There's also a 24-hour pass allowing unlimited travel in all zones for 65 kr and a 72-hour one for 150 kr.

On buses, fares are paid to the driver when you board, while on S-trains tickets are purchased at the station and then punched in the yellow timeclock on the platform.

Trains and buses run from about 5 am to 12.30 am, though buses continue to run through the night (and charge double fare) on a few main routes. For information on trains call ☎ 33 14 17 01, for buses call ☎ 36 45 45 45.

Taxi Taxis with signs saying *'fri'* can be flagged down or you can call ☎ 31 35 35 35. The cost is 20 kr at flagfall plus about 8 kr per km (10 kr between 6 pm and 6 am and on weekends). Most taxis accept credit cards.

Car & Motorcycle With the exception of the weekday-morning rush hour, when traffic can bottleneck coming into the city (and vice versa around 5 pm), traffic is usually manageable. Getting around by car is not problematic other than for the usual challenges of finding a parking space in the most popular places. To explore sights in the centre of the city, you're best off on foot or using public transport, but a car is convenient for reaching suburban sights.

For kerbside parking, buy a ticket from a streetside billetautomat and place it inside the windscreen. Search out a blue or green zone where parking costs 5 to 9 kr an hour; in red zones it's a steep 20 kr. Parking fees must be paid from 8 am to 6 pm weekdays in all zones and also from 8 am to 2 pm on Saturday in red and yellow zones. Overnight kerbside parking is generally free and finding a space is not usually a problem. There's a central, reasonably priced underground parking garage on the north side of Scala; enter via Jernbanegade.

Bicycle & Scooter Københavns Cykler, outside Central Station at Reventlowsgade 11, rents bicycles for 50 kr a day. For cheaper prices (35 kr a day) walk a few blocks northwest to Danwheel at Colbjørnsensgade 3.

If you just want to ride in the city centre, look for a City Bike, a free-use bicycle that has solid spokeless wheels painted with sponsor logos. There are 120 City Bike racks scattered throughout central Copenhagen. If you're lucky enough to find one with a bike, deposit a 20 kr coin in the stand to release the bike. You can return the bicycle into any rack to get your 20 kr coin back.

Except during weekday rush hours, you can carry bikes on S-trains for 11 kr. If you're travelling with a bike be careful, as expensive bikes are theft targets on Copenhagen streets.

Cool Bikes (☎ 33 16 15 12), at Studiestræde 57, rents Suzuki scooters for 250 kr a day.

Around Zealand

There are a number of places around Zealand (Danish: Sjælland) that make for interesting excursions from Copenhagen. Northern Zealand has sandy beaches and grand castles, while a trip to the southern islands of Møn and Falster will take you further off the beaten path.

NORTH ZEALAND
Considering its proximity to Copenhagen, the northern part of Zealand is surprisingly rural, with small farms, wheat fields and beech woodlands. It also has fine beaches and some notable historic sights.

One of the most popular day trips from Copenhagen is a loop tour taking in Frederiksborg Castle in Hillerød and Kronborg Castle in Helsingør, with a stop at Fredensborg Palace in between. With an early start you might even have time to continue on to one of the north shore beaches before making your way back to the city.

If you're driving between Helsingør and Copenhagen ignore the motorway and take the coastal road, Strandvej (route 152), which is far more scenic.

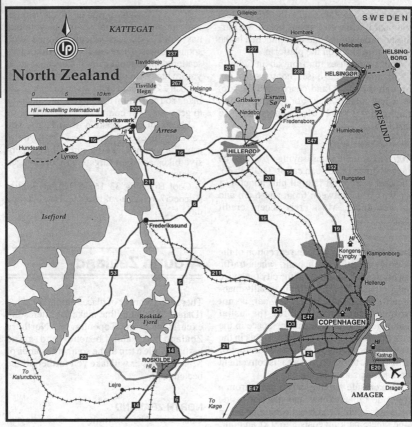

KATTEGAT

SWEDEN

North Zealand

0   5   10 km

HI = Hostelling International

Gilleleje

Hornbæk

Hellebæk

HELSING-BORG

Tisvildeleje

237

227

235

HI

251

HELSINGØR

Tisvilde Hegn

267

Helsinge

Gribskov

Esrum Sø

HI

ØRESUND

205

Frederiksværk

HI

Arresø

Nødebo

Fredensborg

6

Humlebæk

Hundested

16

HILLERØD

E47

Lynæs

16

Isefjord

211

201

19

152

Rungsted

6

16

19

HI

Frederikssund

Kongens Lyngby

Klampenborg

53

211

Hellerup

6

O4

E47

HI

O3

COPENHAGEN

Roskilde Fjord

14

21

HI

Kastrup

ROSKILDE

HI

23

To Kalundborg

Lejre

E47

To Køge

14

6

E20

Dragør

AMAGER

Frederiksborg Castle

Hillerød, 30 km north of Copenhagen, is the site of Frederiksborg Slot, a Dutch Renaissance castle spread across three islands. The oldest part of the castle dates from Frederik II's time, though most of the present structure was built by his son Christian IV in the early 1600s. After parts of the castle were ravaged by fire in 1859, Carlsberg beer baron JC Jacobsen spearheaded a drive to restore the castle and make it a national museum.

The sprawling castle has a magnificent interior with gilded ceilings, wall-sized tapestries, royal paintings and antiques. The richly embellished Knights Hall (Riddershalen) and the coronation chapel where Danish monarchs were crowned between 1671 and 1840 (and where Prince Joachim was married in 1995) are alone worth the 30 kr admission fee. It's open daily from 10 am to 5 pm from May to September, to 3 or 4 pm from October to April.

Getting There & Away The S-train (A & E lines) runs every 10 minutes from Copenhagen to Hillerød (35 kr), a 40-minute ride. From Hillerød station follow the signs to Torvet and then continue along Slotsgade to the castle, a 15-minute walk in all, or grab bus No 701 which can drop you at the gate.

Fredensborg Palace

Fredensborg, the royal family's residence during part of summer, is an 18th-century Italianate mansion in the midst of formal gardens. Although the palace is not a must-see sight, if the queen is in residence you might want to stop to catch the changing of the guard that takes place just before noon.

The palace's wooded grounds, on the edge of Denmark's second largest lake, make for serene walks and are open to the public all year round. The palace interior can only be visited during July (from 1 to 5 pm, 10 kr).

Getting There & Away Fredensborg is midway along the railway line between Hillerød and Helsingør. Go left out of Fredensborg station and turn right onto the main road which runs through town to the palace, a km away.

Helsingør (Elsinore)

Helsingør is a busy port town, with ferries shuttling across the Øresund strait to and from Sweden 24 hours a day. The tourist office (☎ 49 21 13 33), Havnepladsen 3, is opposite the train station.

Things to See & Do Helsingør's top sight is **Kronborg Castle**, made famous as the Elsinore Castle in Shakespeare's *Hamlet*. Actually, Kronborg's primary function was not as a royal residence but rather as a grandiose tollhouse, wresting taxes from ships passing through the narrow Øresund for more than 400 years. The castle is open from 10.30 am to 5 pm in summer, from 11 am to 3 pm in winter. You can cross the moat and walk around the courtyard for free; tour the chapel, dungeons and royal quarters for 30 kr or get a combined ticket that includes the Danish Maritime Museum for 45 kr.

The castle is on the north side of the harbour; the best way to get there is to walk past the tourist office up Brostræde and along Sanct Anna Gade. This route will take you through the **medieval quarter** and past the

old cathedral, **Sanct Olai Kirke**; the **city history museum**; and **Karmeliterklostret**, one of Scandinavia's best preserved medieval monasteries.

Places ,to Stay & Eat *Helsingør Hostel* (☎ 49 21 16 40), Nordre Strandvej 24, is two km north-west of the centre at an old coastal manor house. The 200-bed hostel is open from 1 February to 1 December; dorm beds cost 74 kr. The beachside *Helsingør Camping* (☎ 49 21 58 56), Campingvej 1, is east of the hostel.

The tourist office books rooms in private homes for 150/300 kr for singles/doubles, plus a 25 kr booking fee. The cheapest in-town hotel is *Hotel Skandia* (☎ 49 21 09 02), Bramstræde 1, with large, clean rooms for 300/500 kr.

Kammercaféen, in the old customs house behind the tourist office, has reasonably priced sandwiches. Or head for Axeltorv square, four blocks north-west of the train station, which has beer gardens and numerous places to eat.

Getting There & Away Trains from Hillerød (30 minutes, 30 kr) run at least once hourly. Trains from Copenhagen run a few times hourly (55 minutes, 35 kr). For information on ferries to Helsingborg (25 minutes, 19 kr) see Denmark, Getting There & Away.

Zealand's North Coast

The north coast of Zealand has a handful of small maritime towns which date back to the 1500s. Along their backstreets you'll find half-timbered thatch-roofed houses and tidy flower gardens. Although the towns have only a few thousand winter residents, in summer the population swells with throngs of swimmers, sunbathers and windsurfers.

Hornbæk has the best beach on the north coast, a vast expanse of soft white sand that runs the entire length of the town. From the train station, it's a five-minute walk directly down Havnevej to the harbour. Climb the dunes to the left and you're on the beach. The library at Vester Stejlebakke 2A doubles as the tourist office (☎ 49 70 47 47).

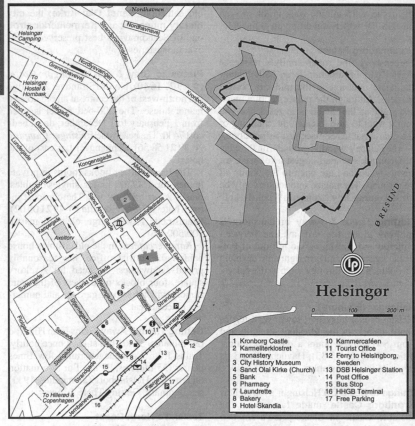

Ø RESUND

Helsingør

0   100   200 m

1	Kronborg Castle	10 Kammercaféen
2	Karmeliterklostret	11 Tourist Office
	monastery	12 Ferry to Helsingborg,
3	City History Museum	Sweden
4	Sanct Olai Kirke (Church)	13 DSB Helsingør Station
5	Bank	14 Post Office
6	Pharmacy	15 Bus Stop
7	Laundrette	16 HHGB Terminal
8	Bakery	17 Free Parking
9	Hotel Skandia	

Zealand's northernmost town, **Gilleleje**, has the island's largest fishing port, dockside fish markets and a smokehouse with cheap takeaway fish. The tourist office (☎ 48 30 01 74) is in the centre at Hovedgade 6.

Tisvildeleje is a pleasant little seaside village with a broad stretch of sandy beach backed by low dunes. At the back of the beach is **Tisvilde Hegn**, a windswept forest of twisted trees and heather-covered hills with good walking paths. The tourist office (☎ 42 30 74 51), at Banevej 8, is in the train station.

Places to Stay There are camping grounds at Hornbæk and Gilleleje. There's a modern, cheery, 272-bed *hostel* (☎ 42 30 98 50) 10 minutes walk from the beach at Bygmarken 30 in Tisvildeleje. It's open year round and dorms cost 85 kr, doubles 275 kr. The tourist office in Gilleleje books double rooms in private homes for about 200 kr and there are 'room for rent' signs along the beach road in Hornbæk.

Getting There & Away Trains from Hillerød run to Gilleleje and to Tisvildeleje (25 kr), but there's no rail link between the two. Trains from Helsingør go to Hornbæk (15 kr) and on to Gilleleje (30 kr) twice an hour on weekdays and once hourly on weekends. The north coast towns are also linked by bus. Bus No 347 from Helsingør station to Hornbæk leaves at 16 minutes past the hour (every second hour on weekends) and takes 30 minutes.

ROSKILDE

Roskilde, Denmark's first capital, was a thriving trade centre throughout the Middle Ages. It was also the site of Zealand's first Christian church, which was built by Viking king Harald Bluetooth in 980 AD. As Roskilde was the centre of Danish Catholicism, its population shrank radically after the Reformation. Today it's a likeable, low-profile town.

You can easily walk to the main sights. The cathedral is on Torvet, 10 minutes northwest of the train station: cut diagonally across the old churchyard and go left along Algade. The harbourside Viking ship museum is north of the cathedral, a pleasant 15-minute stroll through city parks.

Northern Europe's largest music festival rocks Roskilde each summer, usually during the last weekend in June. The Roskilde tourist office (☎ 46 35 27 00) is at Gullandsstræde 15.

Things to See

Roskilde Domkirke Although most of Roskilde's medieval buildings have vanished in fires over the centuries, the imposing cathedral still dominates the city centre. Started in 1170 by Bishop Absalon, the Roskilde Domkirke has been rebuilt and added onto so many times that it represents a millennium of Danish church architectural styles.

The cathedral has tall spires, a splendid interior and the crypts of 37 Danish kings and queens. Some of the crypts are lavishly embellished and guarded by marble statues of knights and women in mourning, while others are simple unadorned coffins. There's something quite awesome about being able to stand next to the bones of so many of Scandinavia's most powerful historical

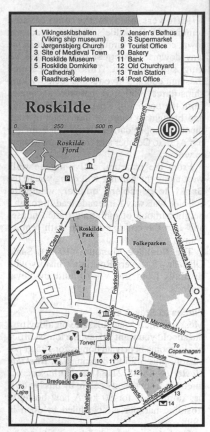

1	Vikingeskibshallen (Viking ship museum)	7	Jensen's Bøfhus
2	Jørgensbjerg Church	8	S Supermarket
3	Site of Medieval Town	9	Tourist Office
4	Roskilde Museum	10	Bakery
5	Roskilde Domkirke (Cathedral)	11	Bank
6	Raadhus-Kælderen	12	Old Churchyard
		13	Train Station
		14	Post Office

Roskilde

figures. Take note also of the 16th-century clock above the entrance, where a tiny St George on horseback marks the hour by slaying a yelping dragon.

From May to August, the cathedral (6 kr) is open from 9 am to 4.45 pm on weekdays, 9 am to noon on Saturday, 12.30 to 4.45 pm on Sunday. Off-season hours are shorter. The cathedral sometimes closes for weddings and funerals; check in advance by calling the tourist office.

Other City Sights From the north side of the cathedral, you can walk across a field where wildflowers blanket the unexcavated remains of Roskilde's original medieval town, continuing through a green belt all the way down to **Vikingeskibshallen**, the Viking ship museum. This well-presented museum contains five reconstructed Viking ships (circa 1000 AD) that were excavated from the bottom of Roskilde Fjord in 1962 and brought to shore in thousands of fragments. It's open daily (30 kr) from 9 am to 5 pm April to October and from 10 am to 4 pm in winter.

From the museum, a five-minute walk west along the harbour will bring you to the **Sankt Jørgensbjerg quarter**, where the cobbled walkway Kirkegade leads through a neighbourhood of old straw-roofed houses and into the courtyard of an 11th-century church.

The **Roskilde Museum** (10 kr), Sankt Olsgade 15, covers Roskilde's history with displays from the Viking and medieval periods.

Places to Stay & Eat

Most travellers visit Roskilde on a day trip, but should you want to stay, the tourist office books rooms in private homes for 125 kr per person, plus a 25 kr booking fee. *Roskilde Hostel* (☎ 46 35 21 84) at Hørhusene 61, three km from the city centre by bus No 601, has dorm beds for 80 kr. A new hostel at Roskilde harbour is scheduled to open in 1998.

The bakery at Algade 6 has good pastries and sandwiches. On Skomagergade there's a *Jensen's Bøfhus* with inexpensive steak lunches. For a treat, the atmospheric *Raadhus-Kælderen* in the old town hall (circa 1430) has a nice fish lunch for 58 kr from 11 am to 5 pm and a three-course dinner for 198 kr.

Getting There & Away

Trains from Copenhagen to Roskilde are frequent (25 minutes, 37 kr). If you're continuing to Odense the same day you can stop over for free. There are lockers at the train station. From Copenhagen by car, route 21 leads to Roskilde; upon approaching the city,

exit onto route 156, which leads into the centre.

KØGE

Køge, 42 km south of Copenhagen, was an important trading city in the Middle Ages and retains an engaging centre of historic buildings that makes for good strolling. The tourist office (☎ 53 65 58 00), at Vestergade 1, has a free booklet that describes 30 of these buildings, all of which are nearby in the narrow streets radiating out from Torvet. Among them are the oldest known (1527) half-timbered building in Denmark, at Kirkestræde 20; the town's historic museum (10 kr) in a lovely, listing building dating from 1610, at Nørregade 4; and a building at Brogade 23 decorated with cherubs carved by the famed 17th-century artist Abel Schrøder.

Places to Stay & Eat

The *Køge Hostel* (☎ 53 65 14 74), two km north-west of the centre at Vamdrupvej 1, has dorm beds for 69 kr and double rooms for 200 kr. The tourist office can book rooms in private homes for 150 kr per person, plus a 25 kr booking fee.

Torve Konditori is a good bakery at the north side of Torvet; there's an inexpensive café above the bakery and a fast-food eatery next door. At the south side of Torvet you'll find a good fruit stand.

Getting There & Away

Køge, at the end of the E line, is the southernmost point of greater Copenhagen's S-train network. Trains from Copenhagen run three times an hour, take 38 minutes and cost 35 kr.

TRELLEBORG

Trelleborg, in the countryside of southern Zealand, is the best preserved of Denmark's four Viking ring fortresses.

The earthen-walled fortress, which dates to 980 AD, has two compounds, the inner of which is cut with gates at the four points of the compass. The gates are linked by streets, one east-west, the other north-south, which divide the inner ward into four symmetrical quadrants. In Viking times, each quadrant contained four long elliptical buildings that surrounded a courtyard. Each of the 16 buildings, which served as barracks, was exactly 100 Roman feet long.

You can walk up onto the grassy circular rampart and readily grasp the fortress' precise geometric design. Cement blocks have been placed to show the outlines of the house foundations and there are a few interpretive plaques that point out burial mounds and other features. Grazing free-range sheep wandering from the surrounding farmland imbue a timeless aura to the scene.

At Trelleborg's entrance is a reconstructed Viking house, built in stave style, using rough oak timbers erected above mud floors. A museum displays items excavated from the fortress grounds and a 20-minute video on Trelleborg's history plays in Danish, English and German. There are usually a few costumed interpreters cooking over a fire or giving archery demonstrations to Danish schoolchildren, but the highlight is just strolling the grounds.

Trelleborg, on Trelleborg Allé, seven km west of Slagelse, is open from 10 am to 5 pm daily. Admission is 30 kr.

Getting There & Away

To get there, take the train to Slagelse (33 minutes, 44 kr from Roskilde) and then either catch the infrequent bus No 312 to Trelleborg (12 minutes, 10 kr), grab a taxi or – best yet – rent a bicycle at the Slagelse tourist office.

MØN, FALSTER & LOLLAND

The three main islands south of Zealand – Møn, Falster and Lolland – are all connected with Zealand by bridges. Møn is known for its spectacular white chalk sea cliffs and Falster has fine white sand beaches. Lolland, the largest and least interesting island, has a handful of scattered sights that are only worth exploring if you have your own transport. All three islands are predominantly rural and, except for Møn's rolling hills, the terrain is largely flat and monotonous.

Møn

Stege, the main town on Møn, has a church with unique medieval frescos and is the site of the Møn tourist office (☎ 55 81 44 11), Storegade 2, which distributes information on the entire island. The island's main lure, however, is the white cliffs of Møns Klint on the east coast.

With time on your hands, Møn would be a fine island to explore more thoroughly. The scenery is rustic, the pace slow, and there are good beaches, prehistoric passage graves and medieval churches with outstanding frescos, but the island lacks a rail system and the bus service is sketchy.

Møns Klint The chalk cliffs at Møns Klint were created 5000 years ago when the calcareous deposits from eons of seashells were uplifted from the ocean floor. The gleaming white cliffs rise sharply 128 metres above an azure sea, presenting one of the most striking landscapes in Denmark.

Møns Klint is a popular destination for Danish tourists. The park contains a cafeteria, souvenir shops and picnic grounds in the woods above the cliffs, but none of this detracts from the cliffs themselves.

You can walk down the cliffs to the beach and back up again in about 30 minutes, or go along the shoreline in either direction and then loop back up through a thick forest of beech trees for a longer walk. Either way, start on the path directly below the cafeteria – it's a quick route to the most scenic stretch of the cliffs.

Places to Stay & Eat *Møns Klint Hostel* (☎ 55 81 20 30), in a former lakeside hotel three km from the cliffs, is open from 1 May to 1 October with beds for 70 kr. *Camping Møns Klint* (☎ 55 81 20 25), opposite the hostel, is open from 1 April to 1 November.

Hotel Store Klint (☎ 55 81 90 08), a small hotel at the cliffs, has 500 kr doubles. You can get meals at the cafeterias at the cliffs and camping ground, or pick up supplies in Stege.

Getting There & Away From Copenhagen take the train to Vordingborg (1½ hours, 81 kr) from where it's a 45-minute (36 kr) bus ride to Stege. From late June to mid-August, buses make the 45-minute run (24 kr) from Stege to Møns Klint six times a day weekdays, four times on weekends. The bus stops at the camping ground en route.

Falster

The east coast of Falster is lined with white sandy beaches that are a magnet for German and Danish holiday-makers.

The most glorious stretch is at **Marielyst**, a lively beach resort. Although Marielyst draws crowds in summer, the beach runs on for many km and there's easy access to its entire length so you'll never need to feel crowded. A bike trail runs on top of the dunes the whole way, which makes it easy to get around even if you're staying at one of the camping grounds a few km out of the town centre. Bikes can be rented for around 35 kr at several places including the Statoil Servicenter.

Places to Stay Marielyst's most central camping ground is *Smedegårdens* (☎ 54 13 66 17), right in town two minutes from the beach, open from May to mid-September.

The Marielyst tourist office (☎ 54 13 62 98), at Marielyst Strandvej 54, is open from 9 am to 5 pm Monday to Saturday and maintains a list of rooms in private homes for 150/230 kr singles/doubles.

The nearest *hostel* (☎ 54 85 66 99) is in Nykøbing, one km east of the train station, opposite the zoo.

Places to Eat Marielyst is filled with cafés, hot-dog stands and ice-cream shops. A good alternative to junk food is *Schous Kød*, 200 metres down Bøtøvej, which sells inexpensive cod cakes, fish and chips and deli takeaway foods; there's a fruit and vegetable stand next door. You'll find a good bakery, open daily from 7 am to 5 pm, just west of the tourist office.

Getting There & Away Trains leave Copenhagen hourly for Gedser at the southern tip of Falster, stopping in Nykøbing (two hours,

98 kr) from where it's a 25-minute (18 kr) bus ride to Marielyst. If you prefer to pedal the final leg to Marielyst, DSB rents bikes at the Nykøbing train station. There are daily ferries from Gedser to Rostock, Germany; the trip takes two hours and costs 20 kr per person, 160/290 kr for a motorcycle/car with passengers.

Bornholm

Bornholm, 200 km east of Copenhagen, is a delightful slow-paced island that makes for a nice getaway. The centre of the island is a mixture of wheat fields and forests, the coast is dotted with small fishing villages, and there's a scattering of half-timbered houses throughout. The northern part of Bornholm has sea cliffs and a rocky shoreline, while the south coast has long stretches of powdery white sands.

Unique among Bornholm's sights are its four 12th-century round churches, with two-metre-thick whitewashed walls and black conical roofs. Each was designed not only as a place of worship but also as a fortress against enemy attacks, with an upper storey that served as a shooting gallery. All four churches are still used for Sunday services and are otherwise open to visitors from Monday to Saturday.

Be sure to try Bornholm's smoked herring, *bornholmers*, and Christiansø's spiced herring, considered the best in Denmark.

Getting There & Away

Bornholmstrafikken (☎ 33 13 18 66) operates a ferry between Copenhagen and Rønne which leaves at 11.30 pm daily (in both directions), takes seven hours and costs 179 kr. Add 62 kr for a dorm bunk, 296 kr for a double cabin, or spread out your sleeping bag in the lounge for free. It costs 52 kr to take along a bicycle, 192 kr for a motorcycle and 389 kr for a car. In midsummer there's also a day ferry, except on Wednesday, that leaves

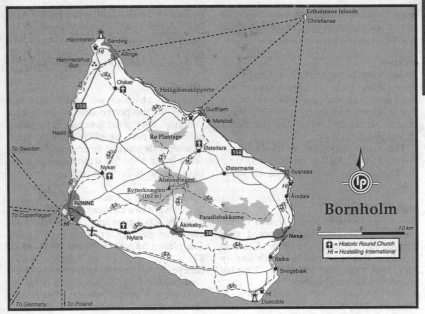

Bornholm

= Historic Round Church
HI = Hostelling International

Copenhagen at 8.30 am and returns from Rønne at 3.30 pm.

Bornholmstrafikken also operates at least two ferries a day to Rønne from Ystad, Sweden (2½ hours, 110 kr one-way or same day return) and near daily in summer from Neu Mukran, Germany (3½ hours, 100 kr).

Pilen (☎ 33 32 12 60) provides transport from Copenhagen to Bornholm via its hydrofoil to Malmö (Sweden), followed by bus and ferry connections to Rønne. The whole package takes about five hours and leaves a few times a day, with the first departure at 9 am. The cost is 169 kr.

Another option is bus No 866 (☎ 44 68 44 00) which goes from Copenhagen's Central Station to Ystad, where it connects with a ferry to Rønne. The bus leaves Copenhagen at 8.25 am and 4.10 pm daily, takes 5½ hours and costs 160 kr. There are also ferries to Bornholm from Swinoujście (Poland) and Sassnitz (Germany). For details see Denmark, Getting There & Away.

Getting Around

Bus Bornholms Amts Trafikselskab (BAT) operates a good, inexpensive bus service around the island. Fares are based on a zone system and cost 8 kr per zone, with the maximum fare set at 10 zones. Save money by buying a 'RaBATkort' from the bus driver for 60 kr, which is good for 10 zones of travel and can be used for multiple rides and by more than one person. There are also day/week passes for 100/350 kr. Buses operate all year, but schedules are less frequent in winter.

In summer, bus No 7 leaves from the Rønne ferry terminal every two hours from 8 am to 6 pm and goes anticlockwise around the island, stopping at Dueodde beach and all major coastal villages before terminating at Hammershus. Other buses make direct runs from Rønne to Nexø, Svaneke, Gudhjem and Sandvig.

Bicycle Cycling is a great way to get around, as Bornholm is crisscrossed with bike trails, many built over former rail routes. Bicycles can be rented around the island for about 50 kr a day.

RØNNE

Rønne (population 15,000) is Bornholm's largest town. There are a few museums and older neighbourhoods you could explore, but Rønne is more of a watering hole and shopping locale for Swedes on day trips than a sightseeing destination.

The tourist office (☎ 56 95 95 00) at Nordre Kystvej 3, a few minutes walk from the harbour, has information on all Bornholm.

Things to See

The attractive round church **Nylars Rundkirke**, built in 1150 and decorated with 13th-century frescos, is only a 15-minute ride from Rønne on bus No 6. It's usually open until 5 pm from Monday to Saturday and there's no admission fee.

Places to Stay & Eat

The 160-bed *Rønne Hostel* (☎ 56 95 13 40) at Arsenalvej 12, about a km south of the centre, is open from 1 March to 1 November; dorm beds cost 80 kr. The tourist office books private rooms for 150 kr a person.

Rothes Konditori, opposite the central bus stop on Snellemark, has inexpensive sandwiches and there are many fast-food eateries at nearby Store Torv. For a classier setting with reasonable prices, check the daily special at *Strøgets Spisehus*, Store Torvegade 39.

DUEODDE

Dueodde is a vast stretch of white sand beach backed by woodlands and dunes. There's no village, just a bus stop with a single hotel, a moderately priced restaurant and a couple of kiosks selling ice cream and hot dogs. Dueodde is a true beach-bum hang-out. The only 'sight' is a lighthouse (4 kr), a short walk west along the beach.

Places to Stay & Eat

The beachside *Dueodde Hostel & Camp-*

ground (☎ 56 48 81 19), open from 1 April to 1 October, is a 10-minute walk east of the bus stop. It's cheapest to bring your own food supplies, but you can get meals at the hostel or the beachside *Dueodde Badehotel*.

SVANEKE

Svaneke is a harbourfront town that has won awards for the preservation of its historic buildings. One of the better areas for period buildings is near the village church, a few minutes walk south of the centre. The tourist office (☎ 56 49 63 50) at Storegade 24 is two blocks north of Torv, the central square.

Places to Stay & Eat

Svaneke has two camping grounds: one in a meadow 400 metres south of the hostel and another on the coast at the north side of town. The pleasant *Svaneke Hostel* (☎ 56 49 62 42) is a km south of the centre, at Reberbanevej 5, and has 100 kr dorms and 250 kr doubles.

There's a pizza parlour, bakery and grocery store at Torv and more expensive restaurants along the harbour.

GUDHJEM

Gudhjem is a pretty seaside village with half-timbered houses and sloping streets. The harbour was one of the settings for Bornholm novelist Martin Andersen Nexø's Oscar-winning film *Pelle the Conqueror*. The tourist office (☎ 56 48 52 10) is at Åbogade 7, a block inland of the harbour.

Things to See & Do

At the dockside **Glasrøgeri** you can watch glass being hand blown. Stroll the footpath running south-east from the harbour for a pleasant coastal view. Gudhjem's shoreline is rocky, though sunbathers will find a small sandy beach at Melsted, one km east. A bike path leads inland four km south from Gudhjem to **Østerlars Rundkirke**, the most impressive of the island's round churches; bus Nos 3 and 9 also go by the church.

Places to Stay & Eat

The nearest camping ground is *Sletten*

Camping (☎ 56 48 50 71), a 15-minute walk south of the village. The *Gudhjem Hostel* (☎ 56 48 50 35), at the harbourside bus stop and open year round, has 80 kr dorms and books rooms in private homes. The family-run *Therns Hotel* (☎ 56 48 50 99), a short walk from the waterfront at Brøddegade 31, has pleasant rooms for 425/550 kr singles/doubles.

The hostel serves up lunch and dinner at reasonable prices. *Gudhjem Røgeri*, a water-front smokehouse, sells fish and salads deli-style, has a 68 kr fish buffet and doubles as a nightspot featuring live folk music. *Pub McArthur*, Brøddegade 20, also has moderately priced buffet meals.

SANDVIG

Sandvig, a quiet village of attractive older houses, has a nice sandy beach right in town. Three km south is Bornholm's best known sight, **Hammershus Slot**. These impressive 13th-century castle ruins, dramatically perched on top of a sea cliff, are the largest in Scandinavia. There's an hourly bus to the ruins, but the best way to get there from Sandvig is via footpaths through the heather-covered hills of Hammeren – a wonderful hour-long hike. The trail begins down by the camping ground.

Places to Stay & Eat

Sandvig Familie Camping (☎ 56 48 04 47) is near the beach on the north side of town. *Sandvig Hostel* (☎ 56 48 03 62), open from 1 June to 1 October, is midway between Hammershus Slot and Sandvig; dorm beds cost 80 kr, double rooms 300 kr. There are also moderately priced pensions in the village. There's a cafeteria by the beach and restaurants near the camping ground.

CHRISTIANSØ

Tiny Christiansø is a charmingly preserved 17th-century fortress island an hour's sail north-east of Bornholm. A seasonal fishing hamlet since the Middle Ages, Christiansø fell briefly into Swedish hands in 1658, after which Christian V decided to turn the island into an invincible naval fortress. Bastions and barracks were built; a church, school and prison followed.

By the 1850s the island was no longer needed as a forward base against Sweden and the navy withdrew. Soldiers who wanted to stay on as fishermen were allowed to live as free tenants in the old cottages. Their offspring, and a few latter-day fisherfolk and artists, currently comprise Christiansø's 140 residents. The entire island is an unspoiled reserve – there are no cats or dogs, no cars, and no modern buildings.

Christiansø is connected to a smaller island, Frederiksø, by a footbridge.

Things to See & Do

You'll find a **local history museum** in Frederiksø's tower and a great 360-degree view from Christiansø **lighthouse**. Otherwise the main activity is walking the footpaths along the fortified walls and batteries that skirt the island. There are skerries with nesting sea birds and a secluded swimming cove on Christiansø's east side.

Places to Stay & Eat

Christiansø Gæstgiveriet (☎ 56 46 20 15), the island's only inn, has a few rooms with shared bath for 400 kr including breakfast. Camping (30 34 96 05) is allowed in a small field at the Duchess Battery from June to August. There's a restaurant at the inn, a small food store and a snack shop.

Getting There & Away

Boats sail to Christiansø from Allinge and Gudhjem daily from early May to mid-September, while the mailboat from Svaneke makes the trip all year round. All boats charge 125 kr return on a day trip, 200 kr open return.

Funen

Funen (Danish: Fyn) is Denmark's garden island. It's largely rural and green, with rolling woodlands, pastures, wheat fields and lots of old farmhouses. During May, the landscape is ablaze with solid patches of yellow rapeseed flowers.

The main railway line from Copenhagen runs straight through Odense, Funen's main city, and westward to Jutland, but it would be a shame to zip through without stopping to explore some of the unspoiled islands in the South Funen archipelago. Svendborg and Faaborg are the main jumping-off points to Ærø, the most popular island.

Store Bælt (Great Belt), the channel that separates Zealand and Funen, can only be crossed by boat. The IC trains roll right onto rail ferries, whereas on most IR trains you walk onto the ferry and then off onto a waiting train upon reaching the other side of the channel.

A massive project is underway to build both a 20-km vehicle bridge and an undersea railroad tunnel which will eventually link the islands at Korsør and Nyborg, two industrial ports. In the meantime automobiles must travel between the two ports via a ferry. The ferry operated by Vognmandsruten (☎ 53 57 02 04) has the cheapest fares, runs about 20 times a day, takes 70 minutes and charges 120 kr for a motorcycle and 245 kr for a car, passengers included.

ODENSE

Denmark's third largest city makes much ado about being the birthplace of Hans Christian Andersen though in actuality, after a fairly unhappy childhood, Hans got out of Odense as fast as he could. Nonetheless, Odense is an affable university city with lots of bike lanes and pedestrian streets, an interesting cathedral and a number of worthy museums.

Orientation & Information

The tourist office (☎ 66 12 75 20), at Rådhus, is a 15-minute walk from the train station. It's open from 9 am to 7 pm (on Sunday from 11 am) daily in summer, and from 9.30 am to 4.30 pm weekdays and 10 am to 1 pm Saturday in the off season.

The cathedral is on Klosterbakken, two minutes from the tourist office, and most other city sights are within walking distance. The public library is at the train station.

Things to See

The east side of the city centre has some of Odense's oldest buildings. You can make a pleasant loop from the centre by strolling down Nedergade, a cobblestone street with leaning half-timbered houses and antique shops, and returning via Overgade. En route you'll pass **Vor Frue Kirke**, Odense's oldest church, which dates back to the 13th century and is open from 10 am to 3 pm Monday to Saturday.

Around the corner, **Møntergården**, a city museum at Overgade 48, has displays of Odense's history dating back to the Viking Age and a number of 16th and 17th-century half-timbered houses that can be walked through. It's open daily from 10 am to 4 pm; admission is 15 kr.

HC Andersen Museums The **HC Andersens Hus**, at Hans Jensens Stræde 39, depicts Andersen's life story through his memorabilia and books, though the presentation doesn't quite match up to the author's rich imagination. It's open daily, from 9 am to 6 pm from 1 June to 31 August and from 10 am to 4 pm the rest of the year. Admission costs 25 kr for adults and 15 kr for children.

At Munkemøllestræde 3, **HC Andersens Barndomshjem** has a couple of rooms of exhibits in the small house where Hans grew up. It's open daily from 10 am to 5 pm June to August and from 11 am to 3 pm September to May. Admission costs 5 kr.

Sankt Knuds Kirke Odense's 13th-century Gothic cathedral has an ornate gilded altar dating from 1520, but the cathedral's real intrigue lies in the basement where you'll find a glass case containing the 900-year-old skeleton of King Knud II.

A few metres west of the coffin, stairs lead down to the remains of St Alban's church. In 1086 Knud II fled into St Alban's and was killed at the altar by farmers in a tax revolt. Though less than saintly, in 1101 Knud was canonised Knud the Holy by the pope in a

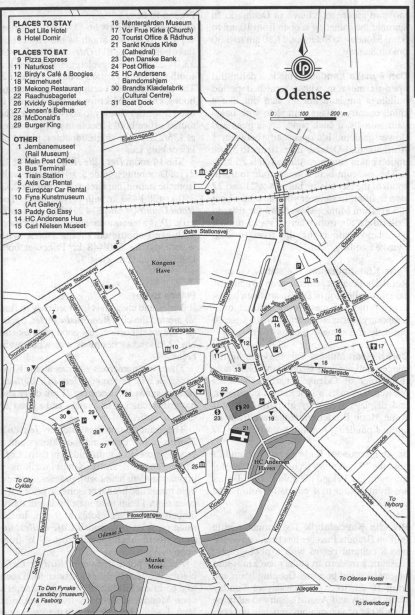

Odense

PLACES TO STAY
6 Det Lille Hotel
8 Hotel Domir

PLACES TO EAT
9 Pizza Express
11 Naturkost
12 Birdy's Café & Boogies
18 Kærnehuset
19 Mekong Restaurant
22 Raadhusbageriet
26 Kvickly Supermarket
27 Jensen's Bøfhus
28 McDonald's
29 Burger King

OTHER
1 Jernbanemuseet
(Rail Museum)
2 Main Post Office
3 Bus Terminal
4 Train Station
5 Avis Car Rental
7 Europcar Car Rental
10 Fyns Kunstmuseum
(Art Gallery)
13 Paddy Go Easy
14 HC Andersens Hus
15 Carl Nielsen Museet

16 Møntergården Museum
17 Vor Frue Kirke (Church)
20 Tourist Office & Rådhus
21 Sankt Knuds Kirke
(Cathedral)
23 Den Danske Bank
24 Post Office
25 HC Andersens
Barndomshjem
30 Brandts Klædefabrik
(Cultural Centre)
31 Boat Dock

0   100   200 m

Eiskovsgade

Dannebrogsgade

Thomas B Thriges Gade

Kochgade

Søndergade

Østre Stationsvej

Østergade

Kongens
Have

Vestre Stationsvej

Hans Tausensgade

Nørregade

Nørregade

Claus Bergs Gade

Hans Jensens Stræde

Hans Mule Gade

Sortebrødre

Claus Bergs Gade

Bangs Boder

15

14

Klostervej

Kløvergej

Vindegade

Vindegade

Slotsgade

Gravene

11

10

12

Thomas B Thriges Gade

Overgade

13

18

Nedergade

Frue Kirkestræde

Konventgade

26

Slotsgade

Sct Gertrude Stræde

24

Stat stræde

22

Overgade

Paaske stræde

Dronnir gensgade

Brandts Passage

30

29

28

27

Pantheonsgade

Vindenegade

Vestergade

Klareregade

23

20

19

Tvergade

Albanigade

To City
Cykler

Klareregade

25

HC Andersen
Haven

21

Klosterbakken

Kronprinsensgade

Hunderupvej

To Nyborg

Filosofgangen

Sdr.

Søndre
Boulevard

31

Odense Å

Munke
Mose

To Odense Hostel

To Den Fynske
Landsby (museum)
& Faaborg

Allegade

To Svendborg

move to secure the church in Denmark. In summer the cathedral is open from 10 am to 5 pm Monday to Saturday, 11.30 am to 3.30 pm on Sunday.

Den Fynske Landsby This is a delightful open-air museum whose furnished period buildings are authentically laid out like a small country village, complete with barnyard animals, a duck pond, apple trees and flower gardens. It's open daily between 1 April and mid-October from 10 am to 5 pm, until 7 pm in summer. Admission is 25 kr.

The museum is in a green zone four km south of the city centre; buses Nos 21 and 22 stop in front. In summer you can take a boat (26 kr) from Munke Mose down the river to Erik Bøghs Sti, from where it's a 15-minute woodland walk along the river to Den Fynske Landsby.

Fyns Kunstmuseum The stately Graeco-Roman building at Jernbanegade 13 contains a quality collection of Danish art, from paintings of the old masters to abstract contemporary works. It's open from 10 am to 4 pm daily and admission costs 15 kr.

Carl Nielsen Museet This museum, in the concert hall at Claus Bergs Gade 11, details the career of Odense's native son Carl Nielsen, Denmark's best known composer, and displays works by his wife, sculptor Anne Marie Brodersen. Hours are from 10 am to 4 pm daily. Admission costs 15 kr.

Jernbanemuseet Railway buffs shouldn't miss the 19th-century locomotives at the rail museum, just behind the train station. Hours are from 10 am to 4 pm daily. Admission costs 20 kr.

Brandts Klædefabrik The former textile mill on Brandts Passage has been converted into a cultural centre with a photography museum, a modern art gallery and a museum of graphics and printing. Opening hours are from 10 am to 5 pm Tuesday to Sunday (daily in July and August). Entry to all three costs 40 kr or you can buy separate tickets.

Places to Stay

Odense Camping (☎ 66 11 47 02), Odensevej 102, is 3.5 km south of the city centre (take bus No 41 or 81). *Odense Hostel* (☎ 66 13 04 25) is at Kragsbjergvej 121, two km south-east of the centre via bus No 61 or 62. The 168-bed hostel occupies a former manor house, changes 65 kr for a dorm bed and is open from 15 February to 30 November. The tourist office books rooms in private homes at 175/250 kr for singles/doubles, plus a 25 kr booking fee.

The 14-room *Det Lille Hotel* (☎ 66 12 28 21) at Dronningensgade 5, a 10-minute walk from the station, has adequate rooms for 220/350 kr (280/450 kr with private bath). The *Hotel Domir* (☎ 66 12 14 27), Hans Tausensgade 19, is a recommendable mid-sized hotel with well-appointed rooms (some with waterbeds) for 360/448 kr. Prices at both hotels include breakfast.

Places to Eat

Bakeries and cheap fast food are easy to find all around the city. *Raadhusbageriet*, opposite the tourist office, has good pastries and big 22 kr sandwiches made with wholegrain bread.

There are numerous eateries along Kongensgade and Vestergade. *Jensen's Bøfhus*, Kongensgade 10, is open to 11 pm daily and has grilled chicken and steaks and a good 29 kr salad buffet.

The train station has another *Jensen's Bøfhus*, a few cafés and food kiosks and a grocery store open until midnight daily. *Café Biografen* at Brandts Klædefabrik is a popular student haunt with pastries, coffees, light meals and beer at reasonable prices. It's open from 11 am to at least midnight daily, though the kitchen closes at 9 pm. In the same complex is *Brandt's Café & Restaurant*, where lunch specials cost 49 kr from noon to 3 pm.

Another popular spot is *Birdy's Café*, Nørregade 21, which has Mexican food such as a 65 kr enchilada with rice and salad; it's open Monday to Saturday from 4 pm to at least 1 am. *Mekong*, at Albanitorv 3, has moderately priced Vietnamese food and is open for dinner nightly.

Pizza Express, Vindegade 73, has a variety of 37 kr pizzas for takeaway only and is open from 3 pm to at least 11 pm daily. *Kvickly*, a supermarket on Slotsgade, has a bakery and a cafeteria with hot dishes for 45 kr and good smørrebrød sandwiches.

There's a well-stocked health-food store, *Naturkost*, at Gravene 8. *Kærnehuset*, a homy vegetarian restaurant at Nedergade 6, offers a 35 kr main course at 6 pm Tuesday to Friday.

Entertainment
Boogies, a dance spot at Nørregade 21, is a popular student hang-out. The outdoor amphitheatre at *Brandts Klædefabrik* is a venue for free summer weekend concerts and *Café Biografen* screens first-run movies for 45 kr. *Paddy Go Easy*, a pub on Nørregade, has live Irish music on weekends. The outdoor cafés on Vintapperstræde are good for a quiet evening drink. *Café Frederik*, Brogade 3, is a popular gay meeting place.

Getting There & Away
Odense is on the main railway line between Copenhagen (2½ hours, 146 kr) and Århus (1¾ hours, 122 kr). Buses leave from the rear of the train station. Odense is just north of the E20; access from the highway is clearly marked. Route 43 connects Odense with Faaborg, while route 9 connects Odense with Svendborg.

Car Rental Avis (☎ 66 14 39 99) is at Østre Stationsvej 37 and Europcar (☎ 66 14 15 44) is at Kongensgade 69.

Getting Around
In Odense you board city buses at the back and pay the driver (10 kr) when you get off. You can buy a 24-hour bus pass at the train station or tourist office for 25 kr, or buy an 'adventure pass' that allows free bus travel and museum admissions – a bargain at 50 kr for one day, 90 kr for two.

Outside rush hour, driving in Odense is not difficult, though many of the central sights are on pedestrian streets, so it's best to park your car and explore on foot. Near the city centre, parking is largely metered, with a fee of 5 kr an hour from 9 am to 5 pm weekdays and to noon on Saturday; outside those hours it's free. There are parking lots near the west side of Rådhus and around Brandts Passage.

Bicycles rent for 45 kr a day at City Cykler (☎ 66 12 97 93), Vesterbro 27, west of the city centre.

EGESKOV CASTLE
Egeskov Castle is a gem of a Renaissance castle, complete with moat and drawbridge. Egeskov, literally 'oak forest', was built in 1554 in the middle of a small lake on top of a foundation of thousands of upright oak trunks. The expansive grounds include century-old privet hedges, free-roaming peacocks, topiary and English gardens.

However, not all is formal – laugh your way through the a-maze-ing bamboo grass labyrinth, dreamed up by the contemporary Danish poet-artist Piet Hein.

The castle is open daily from May to September from 10 am to 5 pm, the grounds from 9 am to 6 pm in summer. Admission to the grounds and an antique car museum is 55 kr. The castle is most impressive from the outside – the interior is largely Victorian furnishings, guns, and hunting trophies of rare beasts, and costs 45 kr extra.

Getting There & Away
Egeskov Castle is two km west of Kværndrup on route 8. From Odense take the Svendborg-bound train to Kværndrup station (38 kr) and continue on foot or by taxi, or take bus No 801 to Kværndrup Bibliotek, where you can catch bus No 920, which stops at the castle on its way between Faaborg and Nyborg.

FAABORG
In the 17th century, Faaborg was a bustling harbour town with one of Denmark's largest fleets. Home to only 6000 people today, Faaborg retains many vestiges of that earlier era and its picturesque cobblestone streets and leaning half-timbered houses make for

delightful walking. Pick up a walking-tour map at the tourist office (☎ 62 61 07 07), Havnegade 2.

Things to See & Do

Faaborg has two fine museums: **Den Gamle Gaard**, at Holkegade 1, an old merchant's house with period furnishings; and **Faaborg Museum**, a former winery at Grønnegade 75 which contains Denmark's best collection of Funen art. Den Gamle Gaard is open daily from mid-May to mid-September from 10.30 am to 4.30 pm and admission costs 20 kr. The Faaborg Museum is open daily, from 10 am to 5 pm in summer, and admission costs 25 kr.

If you have more time, the countryside north of Faaborg is worth exploring, as are the small rural islands of Avernakø, Lyø and Bjørnø. Bikes can be rented at the hostel.

Places to Stay & Eat

Holms Camping (☎ 62 61 03 99) is on route 43, one km north of the town centre. The tourist office has a list of rooms in private homes for 125 to 185 kr per person. The 79-bed *Faaborg Hostel* (☎ 62 61 12 03), in a half-timbered building at Grønnegade 71, opposite Faaborg Museum, has 75 kr beds. *Hotel Strandgade* (☎ 62 61 20 12), near Torvet at Strandgade 2, has pleasant rooms with bath from 325/450 kr for singles/ doubles.

The cheapest eateries on Torvet are *Hæstrups Konditori & Café*, which opens early and has good bakery items, and *Harlem Pizza*, which has good pizza, pitta-bread sandwiches and late hours. For an inexpensive local meal, go down to the harbourside *Det Gamle Røgeri* and pick up some smoked fish.

Getting There & Away

Faaborg has no rail service. Bus Nos 961 and 962 from Odense take an hour, cost 42 kr and run at least hourly. Getting to Faaborg by car is straightforward; from the north, simply follow route 43, which is called Odensevej as it enters the town.

There are numerous daily ferries to the nearby islands of Avernakø and Lyø (50 kr

return, bicycle 15 kr) and a passenger boat to Bjørnø. Ferries leave Faaborg daily for Ærø and for Gelting in Germany.

SVENDBORG

South Funen's largest municipality and a transit point for travel between Odense and Ærø, Svendborg itself is a rather ordinary town and there's not much reason to linger. The railway and bus station are two blocks north-west of the dock.

More appealing is the island of **Tåsinge**, just over the bridge from Svendborg, with its charming harbourside village of Troense and the nearby 17th-century castle **Valdemars Slot**, whose grounds and white sand beach are open free 24 hours a day. Visitors can tour the castle's lavish interior for 45 kr. In addition to the public bus, the MS *Helge* ferry carries passengers from Svendborg to Troense and Valdemars Slot every few hours in summer.

Places to Stay & Eat

The *Svendborg Hostel* (☎ 62 21 66 99), in a renovated 19th-century iron foundry at Vestergade 45 in the town centre, has 85 kr beds. *Hotel Ærø* (☎ 62 21 07 60), opposite the Ærø ferry dock, has 13 straightforward but clean rooms at 250/400 kr for singles/ doubles. There are four camping grounds on Tåsinge.

There's a *DSB restaurant* at the train station and a number of inexpensive eateries along Gerritsgade in the town centre.

Getting There & Away

Trains leave Odense for Svendborg at 15 minutes past the hour, cost 44 kr and take one hour. Ferries to Ærøskøbing depart five times a day, the last at 10.30 pm in summer.

LANGELAND

The long, narrow island of Langeland, connected by bridge to Funen via Tåsinge, has good beaches, cycling and bird-watching. You can pick up information on the entire island from the Langelands Turistbureau (☎ 62 51 35 05), Torvet 5, Rudkøbing.

Things to See & Do

For beaches head for **Ristinge**; for bird-watching there's a sighting tower at **Tryggelev Nor** and a sanctuary at **Gulstav Bog** at the island's southern tip.

Langeland's top sight is the salmon-coloured **medieval castle** at Tranekær, scenically set above a lake with swans and herons. The castle is the private residence of a count, but the park-like grounds, enlivened with environmental art, are open to the public (15 kr).

Places to Stay & Eat

There are nine camping grounds scattered around the island, including one at Langeland's only *hostel* (☎ 62 51 18 30), at Engdraget 11 in Rudkøbing. *Hotel Skandinavien* (☎ 62 51 14 95), Brogade 13, a five-minute walk from the Rudkøbing ferry dock, has simple rooms above a restaurant for 235/410 kr for singles/doubles. For someplace up-market, the modern *Hotel Rudkøbing Skudehavn* (☎ 62 51 46 00) has a fine setting on the yacht harbour, an indoor pool, a seaview restaurant and comfortable rooms for 535/695 kr.

Getting There & Away

Buses make the 25-minute run from Svendborg to Rudkøbing at least hourly; most connect onwards to Tranekær. There are numerous daily ferries from Rudkøbing to Marstal in Ærø; hourly ferries from Spodsbjerg to Tårs in Lolland (50 kr); and thrice-daily boats from Bagenkop to Kiel, Germany (27 kr).

ÆRØ

Well off the beaten track, Ærø is an idyllic island with small fishing villages, rolling hills and patchwork farms. It's a great place to tour by bicycle – the country roads are enhanced by thatched houses and old windmills, and the island has ancient passage graves and dolmens to explore.

Ærø has three main towns: Ærøskøbing, Marstal and Søby. The Ærøskøbing tourist office (☎ 62 52 13 00) is at Torvet in the town centre; the Marstal tourist office (☎ 62 53 19 60)

is at Havnegade 5, a few minutes walk south of the harbour.

Things to See & Do

Ærøskøbing A prosperous merchants' town in the late 1600s, Ærøskøbing has been preserved in its entirety. Its narrow cobblestone streets are tightly lined with 17th and 18th-century houses, many of them gently listing half-timbered affairs with handblown glass windows, decorative doorways and street-side hollyhocks.

In keeping with the town's nature, sights are low-key. The main attraction is **Flaskeskibssamlingen**, at Smedegade 22, where Bottle Peter's lifetime work of 1700 ships-in-a-bottle and other local folk art are displayed in the former poorhouse. It's open (15 kr) daily from 10 am to 5 pm. There are also two **local history museums** stuffed with antiques and period furnishings.

Søby This town has a shipyard, which is the island's biggest employer, a sizeable fishing fleet and a popular yacht harbour. Five km beyond Søby, at Ærø's northern tip, there's a pebble beach with clear water and a stone **lighthouse** with a view.

Marstal On the south-eastern end of the island, Marstal is Ærø's most modern-looking town though it too has a nautical character with a **maritime museum** (25 kr), shipyard and yacht harbour, and a reasonably good beach on the south side of town.

Store Rise This village is the site of **Tingstedet**, a Neolithic Age passage grave in a field behind an attractive **12th-century church**. A few km to the south is **Risemark Strand**, the best of Ærø's few sandy beaches.

Places to Stay

There are camping grounds at Søby, Ærøskøbing and Marstal. The tourist offices distribute an island-wide list of private rooms costing 110 to 150 kr per person.

There's a *hostel* (☎ 62 52 10 44) in Ærøskøbing, a km from town on the road to Marstal, open from 1 April to 30 September, and another in Marstal centre (☎ 62 53 10 64), Færgestræde 29, open from 1 May to 1 September. Both charge 74 kr for a dorm bed.

In Ærøskøbing, the cosy *Det Lille Hotel* (☎ 62 52 23 00), Smedegade 33, and the historic *Hotel Ærøhus* (☎ 62 52 10 03), Vestergade 38, have nice rooms from 260/ 400 kr for singles/doubles. In Marstal, *Hotel Marstal* (☎ 62 53 13 52) at Dronningestræde 1A, near the harbour, has 10 rooms for 250/ 350 kr.

Places to Eat

All three towns have bakeries, restaurants and food stores. In Ærøskøbing on Vestergade, 100 metres from the ferry dock, there's a fast-food café, a small grocery store and some moderately priced restaurants. *Det Lille Hotel* has good meals from about 60 kr.

At Marstal's harbour, there's a small food store and a grill with inexpensive sandwiches. For something more substantial, *Hotel Marstal* has a two-course daily special for 75 kr.

Getting There & Away

There are year-round car ferries to Søby from Faaborg, to Ærøskøbing from Svendborg and to Marstal from Rudkøbing. All run about five times a day, take about an hour and charge 50 kr a person, 18 kr for a bike, 135 kr for a car. If you have a car it's a good idea to make reservations (☎ 62 52 40 00), particularly on weekends and in midsummer.

There's also a ferry (☎ 62 58 17 17) between Søby and Mommark that runs a few times daily from spring to autumn at comparable fares.

Getting Around

Bus No 990 runs from Søby to Marstal via Ærøskøbing hourly on weekdays, half as frequently on weekends. A pass for unlimited one-day travel costs 46 kr.

You can rent bikes for 40 kr a day at the hostel and camping ground in Ærøskøbing, Nørremark Cykelforretning at Møllevejen 77 in Marstal, and Søby Cykelforretning at Langebro 4 in Søby. The tourist office sells a 15 kr cycling map.

Jutland

The Jutland (Jylland) peninsula, the only part of Denmark connected to the European mainland, was originally settled by the Jutes, a Germanic tribe whose forays included invading England in the 5th century. Jutland's southern boundary has been a fluid one, last drawn in 1920 when Germany relinquished its holdings in Sønderjylland.

Jutland's west coast has endless stretches of windswept sandy beaches, often a good km wide and packed down hard enough to drive cars on. Most of the main cities, including Århus and Aalborg, are along the more sheltered east coast.

The northern end of Jutland is largely sand dunes and heathland, while southern Jutland is dominated by moors and marshes. Although parts of the interior are forested, most of Jutland is level farmland whose fields are a brilliant green in spring and a monotonous brown in autumn.

ÅRHUS

On the middle of Jutland's east coast, Århus has been an important trade centre and seaport since Viking times. Today it is Denmark's second largest city, with just over a quarter of a million residents.

The cultural heart of Jutland, Århus is a lively university city with more than 40,000 students. It has one of Denmark's best music and entertainment scenes, a well-preserved historic quarter and plenty to see and do, ranging from good museums and old churches in the centre to woodland trails and beaches along the city's outskirts.

Orientation

Århus is fairly compact and easy to get around. The train station is on the south side of the city centre. The pedestrian shopping streets of Søndergade and Sankt Clements Torv lead to the cathedral in the heart of the old city.

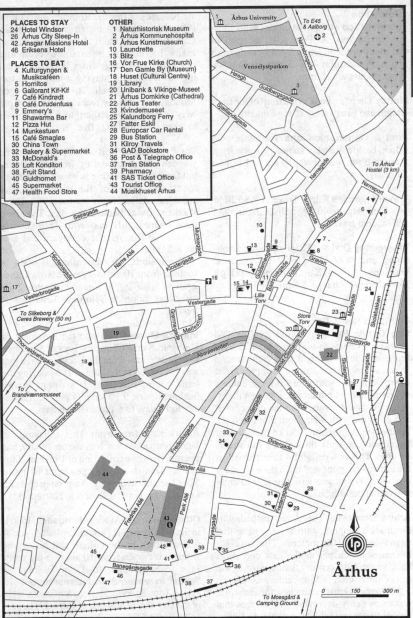

PLACES TO STAY
24 Hotel Windsor
26 Århus City Sleep-In
42 Ansgar Missions Hotel
46 Eriksens Hotel

PLACES TO EAT
4 Kulturgyngen & Musikcaféen
5 Hornitos
6 Gallorant Kif-Kif
7 Café Kindrødt
8 Café Drudenfuss
9 Emmery's
11 Shawarma Bar
12 Pizza Hut
14 Munkestuen
15 Café Smagløs
30 China Town
32 Bakery & Supermarket
33 McDonald's
35 Loft Konditori
38 Fruit Stand
40 Guldhornet
45 Supermarket
47 Health Food Store

OTHER
1 Naturhistorisk Museum
2 Århus Kommunehospital
3 Århus Kunstmuseum
10 Laundrette
13 Blitz
16 Vor Frue Kirke (Church)
17 Den Gamle By (Museum)
18 Huset (Cultural Centre)
19 Library
20 Unibank & Vikinge-Museet
21 Århus Domkirke (Cathedral)
22 Århus Teater
23 Kvindemuseet
25 Kalundborg Ferry
27 Fatter Eskil
28 Europcar Car Rental
29 Bus Station
31 Kilroy Travels
34 GAD Bookstore
36 Post & Telegraph Office
37 Train Station
39 Pharmacy
41 SAS Ticket Office
43 Tourist Office
44 Musikhuset Århus

Århus University
To E45 & Aalborg
Vennelystparken
To Århus Hostel (3 km)
To Silkeborg & Ceres Brewery (50 m)
To Brandværnsmuseet
Lille Torv
Store Torv
Skt Clemens Torv
Vestergade
Aboulevarden
Sønder Allé
To Moesgård & Camping Ground

Århus

0   150   300 m

Information

Tourist Office The tourist office (☎ 86 12 16 00), in Rådhus on Park Allé, is open in summer from 9.30 am to 6 pm weekdays, to 5 pm on Saturday and 3 pm on Sunday. Winter hours are shorter.

Money There's a bank at the front of the train station and many more along Søndergade.

Post & Communications The main post office, beside the train station, is open from 9 am to 6 pm weekdays, 10 am to 1 pm on Saturday.

Travel Agencies Kilroy Travels (☎ 86 20 11 44), Fredensgade 40, specialises in discount and student travel.

Emergency Dial ☎ 112 for police or ambulance and ☎ 86 20 10 22 for medical services. Århus Kommunehospital on Nørrebrogade has a 24-hour emergency ward.

Things to See & Do

Den Gamle By Den Gamle By (the Old Town) is a fine open-air museum of 75 half-timbered houses brought here from around Denmark and reconstructed as a provincial town, complete with a functioning bakery, silversmith, bookbinder etc. It is on Viborgvej, a 20-minute walk from the city centre, and open daily all year, from 9 am to 6 pm in summer. Admission is 50 kr, though after hours you can walk through the old streets for free. This is a delightful time to visit as the crowds are gone and the light is ideal for photography, but you won't be able to enter individual buildings.

Århus Domkirke The Århus cathedral is Denmark's longest, with a lofty nave that spans nearly 100 metres. The original Romanesque chapel at the east end dates back to the 12th century, while most of the rest of the church is 15th-century Gothic.

Like other Danish churches, the cathedral was once richly decorated with frescos that served to convey biblical parables to illiterate peasants. After the Reformation, church authorities who felt the frescos represented Catholicism had them all whitewashed, but many have now been uncovered and restored. They range from fairy-tale paintings of St George slaying a dragon to tormented scenes of hell. The church is open Monday to Saturday from 9.30 am to 4 pm May to September, 10 am to 3 pm October to April. Admission is free.

Vor Frue Kirke This church has a carved wooden altarpiece dating from the 1530s, but far more interesting is what's in its basement: the crypt of the city's original cathedral, dating from around 1060. Enter via the stairway beneath the altar. To enter a third chapel, this one with 16th-century frescos, go through the courtyard and take the left door.

The church, off Vestergade, is open in summer from 10 am to 4 pm weekdays, until 2 pm on Saturday; in winter it closes at 2 pm weekdays, noon on Saturday. Admission is free.

Vikinge-Museet Pop into the basement of Unibank, Sankt Clements Torv 6, for a free look at artefacts from the Viking village that was excavated at this site in 1964 during the bank's construction. It's open during banking hours: 9.30 am to 4 pm from Monday to Friday, to 6 pm on Thursday.

Århus Kunstmuseum This museum, at Vennelystparken south of the university, has a comprehensive collection of 19th and 20th-century Danish art. It's open from 10 am to 5 pm Tuesday to Sunday. Admission costs 25 kr. Take bus No 1, 2, 3 or 6 to Nørreport.

Other Museums At **Kvindemuseet** (15 kr), in the old city hall at Domkirkeplads 5, you'll find exhibits on the culture and history of women; it's open from 10 am to 5 pm daily June to September, to 4 pm Tuesday to Sunday in winter. **Brandværnsmuseet** (40 kr), at Tomsagervej 25, four km south-west of the city centre, has one of Europe's largest collection of fire engines. The university's

Naturhistorisk Museum (25 kr) displays stuffed creatures from around the world.

Moesgård The Moesgård woods, five km south of the city centre, make for an absorbing half-day outing. The main focal point is the **Moesgård Prehistoric Museum** with quality displays from the Stone Age to the Viking Age, including a roomful of rune stones. The most unique exhibit is the 2000-year-old Grauballe man, found preserved in a nearby bog in 1952. The dehydrated, leathery body is amazingly intact, right down to its red hair and fingernails. The museum is open from 10 am to 5 pm daily from April to September, and to 4 pm Tuesday to Sunday from October to March. Admission is 30 kr.

An enjoyable trail dubbed the **prehistoric trackway** leads from behind the museum through fields of grazing sheep and beech woods down to Århus' best sandy beach. The trail, marked by red-dotted stones, passes reconstructed historic sights including a dolmen, burial cists and an Iron Age house. Pick up a trail-guide booklet at the museum. You can walk one way and catch a bus from the beach back to town, or do the trail both ways as a five-km loop. Bus No 6 from Århus train station terminates at the museum, and bus No 19 at Moesgård beach; both buses run twice an hour.

Organised Tours

Ceres Brewery In summer there are tours of the Ceres Brewery on Wednesday. Passes (5 kr) are distributed at the tourist office, but tours may be booked out for days.

Sightseeing Tour A guided two-hour bus tour leaves from the tourist office at 10 am daily from late June to the end of August, giving a glimpse of the main city sights. The 45 kr tour is a good deal as it includes entry into Den Gamle By and also leaves you with a 24-hour public bus pass.

Places to Stay

Camping The nearest camping ground, *Blommehaven* (☎ 86 27 02 07), has a nice seaside setting in the Marselisborg woods,

six km south of Århus on bus No 19 or 6. It's open from April to mid-September.

Hostel & Rooms *Århus Hostel* (☎ 86 16 72 98), Marienlundsvej 10, is in a renovated 1850s dance hall at the edge of the Risskov woods, four km north of the city centre, reached by bus No 6 or 9. It's open from late January to late December and charges 70 kr a bed. The tourist office books rooms in private homes for 150/250 kr singles/doubles, plus a 25 kr booking fee.

The friendly *Århus City Sleep-In* (☎ 86 19 20 55), conveniently located in a former mariners' hotel at Havnegade 53, has dorm beds for 75 kr and comfy double rooms for 180 kr (240 kr with private shower). Breakfast costs 25 kr, sheets can be hired for 30 kr and reception is open 24 hours. There's a TV and pool room, a guest kitchen and free lockers.

Hotels *Eriksens Hotel* (☎ 86 13 62 96), Banegårdsgade 6, is a straightforward family-run hotel a few minutes from the train station with singles/doubles for 315/460 kr.

Hotel Windsor (☎ 86 12 23 00), near the harbour at Skolebakken 17, has tidy rooms with phones and washbasins at 350/485 kr.

For someplace more up-market, there's *Ansgar Missions Hotel* (☎ 86 12 41 22) at Banegårdsplads 14. Rates are 330 kr for a single room with shared bath, from 455/590 kr for singles/doubles with private bath. For 100 kr more there are courtyard rooms in the rear with pleasantly old fashioned décor and deep bathtubs.

Places to Eat

The narrow streets of the old quarter north of the cathedral are thick with cafés serving Danish and ethnic foods at moderate prices.

The countercultural *Kulturgyngen* at Mejlgade 53, open from 11 am to 5 pm and 6 to 9 pm except Sunday, serves healthy food, offering one vegetarian and one fish or meat dinner nightly for 40 to 50 kr; lunch specials of salad and a hot dish cost 28 kr.

Nearby, the cosy *Gallorant Kif-Kif*, Mejlgade 41, is open nightly and has good Greek dishes served with salad and hummus for around 70 kr. *Hornitos*, at the end of the courtyard at Mejlgade 46B, has authentic Chilean empanadas (meat pies) for takeaway (25 kr) and is open from 11.30 am to 9 pm Monday to Saturday.

Café Drudenfuss, on the corner of Graven and Studsgade, is a popular meeting place with inexpensive sandwiches and drinks, while *Café Kindrødt* at Studsgade 8 has candlelight dining with salads, empanadas and pastas for under 50 kr. For a treat, stop by *Emmery's*, Guldsmedgade 24, a fashionable konditori with delicious breads, pastries and sandwiches.

Munkestuen, at Klostertorv 5, is a hole-in-the-wall serving home-style Danish food at honest prices, including a daily lunch for 40 kr, dinner for 70 kr. If it's full, the next-door *Café Smagløs* is a pleasant spot with sandwiches and 40 kr lasagne. Other nearby options are the *Shawarma Bar*, which has filling Turkish sandwiches for 25 kr, and a branch of the American-chain *Pizza Hut*.

The train station has a small supermarket open to midnight, a fruit stand out the front and a good bakery, *Loft Konditori*, across the street. A two-minute walk from the station is *Guldhornet*, a streetside solarium restaurant at the Ritz Hotel with a typical Danish lunch that includes smoked herring and roast beef for 50 kr.

China Town, at Fredensgade 46 opposite the bus station, has 10 daily lunch specials until 4 pm for under 50 kr. It's open from noon to 11 pm daily.

Entertainment

Much of Århus' vibrant music scene is centred around backstreet cafés – cover charges are typically from 20 to 60 kr. *Blitz*, Klostergade 34, attracts the youngest crowd and has good dance music. *Fatter Eskil*, Skolegade 25, usually features jazz or blues. *Musikcaféen* and the adjacent *Gyngen*, Mejlgade 53, offer an alternative scene with rock, reggae, jazz and Latin American music.

There's usually something happening at *Huset*, Vester Allé 15, a good-energy cultural centre with rock, jazz and folk concerts. The main gay and lesbian hang-out is the *Pan Club*, a café and disco at Jægergårdsgade 42, south of the train station.

The city concert hall, *Musikhuset Århus*, presents dance, opera and concerts by international performers. The nine-day Århus Festival in early September turns the city into a stage for nonstop revelry with jazz, rock, classical music, theatre and dance.

The free publications *Ugen Ud* and *What's On in Århus* list current happenings in detail.

Getting There & Away

Air The airport, in Tirstrup 44 km north-east of Århus, has direct flights from Copenhagen and London. The airport bus to Århus train station costs 50 kr.

Bus Express buses (☎ 86 78 48 88) run a few times daily between Århus and Copenhagen's Valby station via a channel crossing at Ebeltoft. They take 4½ hours and cost 150 kr.

Train Trains to Århus, via Odense, leave Copenhagen hourly from early morning to around 8 pm (4½ hours, 207 kr) and there's a night train at 11.30 pm.

Car & Motorcycle The main highways to Århus are the E45 from the north and south and route 15 from the west. The E45 curves around the western edge of the city as a ring road. There are a number of turn-offs from the ring road into the city, including Åhavevej from the south and Randersvej from the north.

Car Rental Cars can be rented from Europcar (☎ 86 13 23 33), Sønder Allé 35, or Hertz (☎ 86 19 18 12), Silkeborgvej 4.

Boat DSB car ferries (☎ 86 18 17 88) sail three to six times a day between Århus and Kalundborg. They take 3¼ hours and cost 245 kr for a car (180 kr for a motorcycle) and driver, 75 kr for each extra passenger.

Getting Around

Bus Most in-town buses stop in front of the train station or around the corner on Park

Allé. City bus tickets are bought from a machine in the back of the bus for 13 kr and are good for unlimited rides within the time period stamped on the ticket, which is about two hours.

You can also buy a 24-hour pass at newsstands for bus travel in Århus county (75 kr) or in Århus municipality alone (45 kr). Or buy a two-day 'Århus Pass' (110 kr) that includes both the bus and entry into Århus museums.

Car & Motorcycle A car is convenient for getting to sights such as Moesgård on the city outskirts, though the city centre is best explored on foot.

Århus has numerous billetautomats (parking meters) along its streets. Parking generally costs 1 kr per seven minutes, with a three-hour maximum, between 8 am and 6 pm from Monday to Thursday, to 8 pm on Friday and to 2 pm on Saturday. Outside those hours you can park free of charge.

Bicycle Århus City Sleep-In rents bicycles for 50 kr a day.

JELLING

Jelling is a sleepy rural town with one of Denmark's most important historic sites – the **Jelling church**. Inside the small whitewashed church are 12th-century **frescos** and outside the door are two **rune stones**.

The smaller stone was erected in the early 900s by King Gorm the Old, Denmark's first king, in honour of his wife. The larger one, raised by Harald Bluetooth and dubbed 'Denmark's baptismal certificate', is adorned with the oldest representation of Christ found in Scandinavia and reads:

Harald king bade this be ordained for Gorm his father and Thyra his mother, the Harald who won for himself all Denmark and Norway and made the Danes Christians.

Two huge **burial mounds** flank the church; the one on the north side is speculated to be King Gorm's and the other, his wife's.

Jelling makes a good two-hour side trip off the Odense-Århus run. Change trains at Vejle for the 15-minute ride to Jelling (19 kr). The church is 100 metres straight up Stationsvej from the Jelling train station.

THE LAKE DISTRICT

The Danish Lake District, the closest thing Denmark has to hill country, is a popular 'active holiday' spot for Danes, with good canoeing, biking and hiking. The scenery is pretty, but placid and pastoral rather than stunning. The district contains the Gudenå, Denmark's longest river; Mossø, Jutland's largest lake; and Yding Skovhøj, Denmark's highest point – none of which are terribly long, large or high!

Silkeborg

Silkeborg, the Lake District's biggest town, has a rather bland and modern town centre though it's bordered by green areas and waterways. The tourist office (☎ 86 82 19 11) is near the harbour at Åhavevej 2A.

Things to See & Do The main attraction at the **Silkeborg Museum**, a respectable cultural history museum on Hovedgårdsvej, is the Tollund Man, who was executed in 200 BC and whose leather-like body, complete with the rope still around his neck, was discovered in a nearby bog in 1950. The face is so well preserved you can count the wrinkles in his forehead. Museum hours are from 10 am to 5 pm daily from May to mid-October, from noon to 4 pm on Wednesday, Saturday and Sunday in winter. Admission costs 20 kr.

Silkeborg Kunstmuseum on Gudenåvej, one km south of the town centre, features the works of native son Asger Jorn and other modern artists. Hours are from 10 am to 5 pm, closed Monday. Admission costs 30 kr.

To get to **Nordskoven**, a beech forest with hiking and bike trails, simply walk over the old railway bridge down by the hostel. You can rent mountain bikes at Cykel-Klubben (☎ 86 82 26 33), Frederiksberggade 1, and canoes and rowing boats at Slusekiosken (☎ 86 80 08 93) at the harbour.

Places to Stay & Eat *Indelukkets Camping* (☎ 86 82 22 01), Vejlsøvej 7, is one km south of the art museum. *Silkeborg Hostel* (☎ 86 82 36 42) has a scenic riverbank location at Åhavevej 55, a 10-minute walk east of the train station. It's open from 1 March to 1 December, with dorm beds from 70 kr and double rooms from 280 kr. The tourist office has a list of rooms in private homes from 120/200 kr for singles/doubles. For a 20 kr fee the office will call to book a room, or pick up the list and call on your own.

There's a health-food store and several drinking spots and restaurants on Nygade, including a café with vegetarian dishes at Nygade 18 and a pizzeria at Nygade 34. *Føtex* supermarket at Torvet has a bakery and a cafeteria with good-value specials – you can get a solid meal for 30 kr.

Getting There & Away Hourly trains connect Silkeborg with Skanderborg (30 minutes, 32 kr) and Århus (45 minutes, 50 kr) via Ry.

Ry

A smaller town in a more rural setting than Silkeborg, Ry is a good place from which to base your exploration of the Lake District. The helpful tourist office (☎ 86 89 34 22), in the train station at Klostervej 3, is open from 9 am to 4.30 pm Monday to Saturday.

Things to See & Do The Lake District's most visited spot is the whimsically named **Himmelbjerget** (Sky Mountain) which, at just 147 metres, is one of Denmark's highest hills. It can be reached via a pleasant six-km hike from Ry, or by bus or boat. From the hill-top **tower** (5 kr) there's a fine 360-degree view of the lakes and surrounding countryside.

Another good half-day outing is to cycle from Ry to **Boes**, a tiny hamlet with picturesque thatch-roofed houses and bounteous flower gardens. From there continue across the Danish countryside to **Øm Kloster**, the ruins of a medieval monastery (open from 10 am to 4 pm, closed Monday; 25 kr), where glass-topped tombs reveal the 750-year-old

bones of Bishop Elafsen of Århus and many of his abbots. The whole trip from Ry and back is 18 km.

Ry Cykel, Skanderborgvej 19, rents bikes for 48 kr a day. If you want to explore the lakes in the district, Ry Kanofart, Kyhnsvej 20, rents canoes for 50 kr an hour.

Places to Stay & Eat The lakeside *Sønder Ege Camping* (☎ 86 89 13 75), Søkildevej 65, is a km north of town. *Ry Hostel* (☎ 86 89 14 07) is on the same bathing lake at Randersvej 88. To get there from the train station cross the tracks, turn left and go 2.5 km; or take the infrequent bus No 104. Dorm beds cost 75 kr, double rooms 150 kr. The tourist office books private rooms for 125 to 150 kr a person.

The best place in town to eat is *Alberto*, Randersvej 1, a popular spot serving tasty vegetarian food and chicken or lamb dishes with salad for around 50 kr. The butcher shop opposite the train station has inexpensive takeaway sandwiches and there's a bakery next door.

Getting There & Away Hourly trains connect Ry with Silkeborg (20 minutes, 25 kr) and Århus (30 minutes, 38 kr).

AALBORG

Jutland's second largest city, Aalborg is an industrial and trade centre, well known to bar hoppers as the leading producer of aquavit. Linked by bridge and tunnel, Aalborg spreads across both sides of the Limfjord, the long body of water that cuts Jutland in two.

Although it's skipped over by most travellers, Aalborg has a few worthwhile sites, the paramount attraction being Lindholm Høje, Denmark's largest Viking burial ground.

Orientation & Information

The town centre is a 10-minute walk from the railway and bus stations, north down Boulevarden. The tourist office (☎ 98 12 60 22), at Østerågade 8, is open from 9 am to 5 pm Monday to Saturday, with slightly shorter hours in winter.

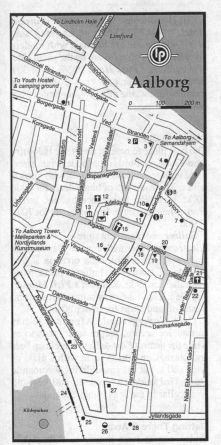

Aalborg

0   100   200 m

PLACES TO STAY
23   Prinsens Hotel
27   Park Hotel

PLACES TO EAT
3   Romeo & Julie
5   Burger King
16   Brugsen Supermarket
17   Bakery
18   Skibsted's Fish Market
19   Café Underground
20   Fast & Easy

OTHER
1   Laundrette
2   Parking Garage
4   Jørgen Olufsens House
6   Aalborghus Slot (Castle)
7   Salling Department Store
8   Bank
9   Tourist Office
10   Jens Bangs Stenhus
11   Old Town Hall
12   Monastery of the Holy Ghost
13   Aalborg Historiske Museum
14   Post Office
15   Budolfi Domkirke (Cathedral)
21   Vor Frue Kirke (Church)
22   Danes Worldwide Archives
24   Train Station
25   Avis Car Rental
26   Bus Station
28   Europcar Car Rental

Danes Worldwide Archives (☎ 98 12 57 93), behind Vor Frue Kirke (Postboks 1731, 9100 Aalborg), helps foreigners of Danish descent trace their roots.

Things to See
Old Town The whitewashed **Buldolfi Domkirke** marks the centre of the old town, and has colourful frescos in the foyer. On the cathedral's east side is the **Aalborg Historiske Museum** with interesting excavated artefacts, the requisite Renaissance furnishings and a collection of antique coins. It's open from 10 am to 5 pm Tuesday to Sunday. Admission is 10 kr.

The alley between the museum and church leads to the rambling **Monastery of the Holy Ghost**, which dates back to 1431; the tourist office arranges guided tours (25 kr). Northeast of the cathedral on Østerågade are three noteworthy historic buildings: the **old town hall** (circa 1762), the five-storey **Jens Bangs Stenhus** (circa 1624) and **Jørgen Olufsens House** (circa 1616).

In addition, the half-timbered neighbourhoods around **Vor Frue Kirke** are worth a stroll, particularly the cobbled Hjelmerstald. **Aalborghus Slot**, near the waterfront, is more administrative office than castle, but there's a small dungeon you can enter for free.

Nordjyllands Kunstmuseum This regional art museum, at Kong Christian Allé 50 in a marble building designed by Finnish architect Alvar Aalto, has a fine collection of Danish modern art. It's open from 10 am to 5 pm daily in summer and from Tuesday to Sunday the rest of the year. Admission is 20 kr.

To get there, take the tunnel beneath the train station which emerges into Kildeparken, a green space with statues and water fountains. Go directly through the park, cross Vesterbro and continue through a wooded area to the museum, a 10-minute walk in all.

Aalborg Tower The hill behind the art museum has an ungainly tower offering a panoramic view of the city's steeples and smokestacks (15 kr). The tower sits on the edge of an expansive wooded area, **Mølleparken**, which has walking trails, views and a zoo.

Lindholm Høje On a hill-top pasture overlooking the city, Lindholm Høje is the site of 682 graves from the Iron Age and Viking Age. Many of the **Viking graves** are marked by stones placed in an oval ship shape, with two larger end stones as stem and stern. It's an intriguing place to walk, as there's something almost spiritual about the site. Open free from dawn to dusk, it's 15 minutes from Aalborg on bus No 6. Cross the fence 50 metres beyond the bus stop and you're in the burial field.

A museum (20 kr) depicting the site's history is at the opposite side of the field. The museum is open from 10 am to 5 pm from Easter to October and to 4 pm daily except Monday in winter.

Places to Stay

Aalborg Hostel (☎ 98 11 60 44), at Skydebanevej 50 at the marina four km west of the centre, has dorm beds for 85 kr and an adjacent camping ground with cabins. It's reached by bus No 8. The tourist office books rooms in private homes.

Aalborg Sømandshjem (☎ 98 12 19 00), about a km east of the centre at Østerbro 27, has straightforward rooms from 275/475 kr

for singles/doubles. Rooms at the *Prinsens Hotel* (☎ 98 13 37 33), Prinsensgade 14, start at 395/490 kr and are pleasant with modern amenities, though most are on the small side. The traditional *Park Hotel* (☎ 98 12 31 33), Boulevarden 41, has very comfortable rooms with soaking tubs, TVs and rates from 600/710 kr.

Places to Eat

The best place to head at mealtime is Jomfru Ane Gade, a boisterous pedestrian street lined with restaurants and cafés with outside tables. There are lots of lunch deals for 30 to 50 kr, including a few nice buffets, and at dinner there are three-course meals for 70 to 100 kr.

Salling, a department store on Nytorv, has a basement supermarket with a good deli. *Romeo & Julie*, a pleasant pizzeria at Ved Stranden 5, has a lunch buffet of pizza, pasta and salad for 59 kr. *Skibsted's Fish Market*, Algade 23, has takeaway salmonburgers and fresh fish and chips for under 20 kr.

Café Underground, Algade 21, has natural ice cream, crêpes and sandwiches while the nearby *Fast & Easy* has cheap beer and pizza. Cap off the night with a glass of wine (20 kr) at the smoulderingly romantic *Duus Vinkjælder*, a candle-lit 300-year-old wine cellar in the Jens Bangs Stenhus.

Getting There & Away

Trains run at least hourly to Århus (1½ hours, 98 kr) and every two hours to Frederikshavn (one hour, 56 kr). Express buses (☎ 70 10 00 30) run daily to Copenhagen (six hours, 180 kr).

The E45 bypasses the city centre, tunnelling under the Limfjord, whereas the connecting route 180 leads into the centre. To get to Lindholm Høje or points north from Aalborg centre, take route 180 (Vesterbro) which crosses the Limfjord by bridge.

Car Rental Avis (☎ 98 13 30 99) is at the train station. Europcar (☎ 98 13 23 55) is nearby at Jyllandsgade 4.

Getting Around

City buses leave from Østerågade and Nytorv, near Burger King. The bus fare is 11 kr to any place in greater Aalborg.

Other than for a few one-way streets that may have you driving in circles, Aalborg is easy to get around by car. There's free street parking along many side streets, as well as metered parking in the centre. If you're unable to find a parking space, there's a large parking garage at Ved Stranden 11.

REBILD BAKKER

If you're ready for a break in the countryside, Rebild Bakker National Park is a good destination. Founded in 1912 by Danish-Americans, it's best known for its US-style 4 July celebration, the largest held outside the USA.

Although there's a Lincoln log cabin and a few souvenir shops near the centre, the rest of the park is an unspoiled area of rolling hills and heathland. A four-km trail begins in a sheep meadow opposite the Lincoln cabin, and numerous other trails crisscross the park and the adjacent Rold Skov, Denmark's largest forest.

Places to Stay & Eat

The thatch-roofed *Rebild Hostel* (☎ 98 39 13 40), next to the park entrance, has beds for 80 kr. *Safari Camping* (☎ 98 39 11 10) is nearby at Rebildvej 17. You can take meals at the hostel or the park cafeterias.

Getting There & Away

From Aalborg, Århus-bound trains stop in Skørping (16 minutes, 25 kr), from where it's three km to Rebild. Bus No 104 runs between Aalborg and Rebild (45 minutes, 40 kr) via Skørping 12 times daily on weekdays, four times daily on weekends.

FREDERIKSHAVN

Frederikshavn is a major ferry town with a busy industrial port. There are a couple of local museums, but overall the town has no particular appeal and most travellers just pass right through. If you're waiting for a train, you might want to climb the nearby whitewashed **gun tower** (10 kr), a remnant of the 17th-century citadel that once protected the port.

An overhead walkway leads from the ferry terminal to the tourist office (☎ 98 42 32 66) at Brotorvet 1. The train station and adjacent bus terminal are a 10-minute walk to the north.

Bangsbo Museum

Bangsbomuseet, three km south of Frederikshavn centre, is an old country estate with a mishmash of exhibits. The manor house holds local history displays, Victorian furniture, antique dolls and a peculiar collection of ornaments woven from human hair.

The farm buildings have ship figureheads, military paraphernalia and exhibits on the Danish resistance to German occupation. The most intriguing exhibit is the Ellingå ship, the reconstructed remains of a 12th-century Viking-style merchant ship that was dug up from a nearby stream bed. The museum (20 kr) is open from 10 am to 5 pm daily. Bus Nos 1 and 2 stop near the entrance to the estate, from where it's an enjoyable 500-metre walk through the woods to the museum.

Places to Stay & Eat

Frederikshavn Hostel (☎ 98 42 14 75), Buhlsvej 6, two km north of the ferry terminal, is open from February to mid-December with dorms (53 kr) and double rooms (160 kr). The central *Sømandshjemmet* (☎ 98 42 09 77), Tordenskjoldsgade 15B, has cheery rooms with TV for 285/435 kr singles/doubles.

Damsgaard Supermarked on Havnegade behind the tourist office has a cafeteria open at breakfast and lunch. Other nearby eateries include pizzerias on Danmarksgade and Søndergade, a block to the north. If you're catching a ferry, the *Havne Super*, a supermarket at the harbour, has long hours and a bistro-style restaurant – consider picking up food provisions if you're going on to pricey Norway.

Getting There & Away

Bus & Train Frederikshavn is the northern terminus of the DSB rail line. Trains run about hourly south to Aalborg (56 kr) and on to Copenhagen (231 kr). Nordjyllands Trafikselskab (NT) has both a train (40 minutes) and bus service (one hour) north to Skagen (33 kr). NT sells a clip-ticket *(klippekort)* for 74 kr that's good for 110 kr worth of travel; several people can clip the same card.

Boat The Stena Line (☎ 96 20 02 00) runs ferries from Frederikshavn to Gothenburg, Sweden, four to eight times daily (3¼ hours, 90 kr); and to Oslo, Norway, daily in summer, almost daily in winter (nine hours, from 190 to 410 kr).

The Larvik Line (☎ 99 20 40 60) has daily ferries to Larvik, Norway. It takes six hours and costs from 220 to 350 kr, depending upon the season and day of the week. The cost to take a car on the ferries is roughly double the passenger fare.

SeaCat (☎ 98 42 83 00) operates a fast (1¾ hours) catamaran to Gothenburg, Sweden, five times daily in summer, three times in winter; the cost is 84 kr per person, 670 kr for a car with up to five people. There's also a twice-daily summertime catamaran service between Frederikshavn and Langesund, Norway.

SKAGEN

A fishing port for centuries, Skagen's luminous heath-and-dune landscape was discovered in the mid-1800s by artists and in more recent times by summering urbanites.

The town's older neighbourhoods are filled with distinctive yellow-washed houses, each roofed with red tiles edged with white lines. Skagen is half arty, half touristy, with a mix of galleries, souvenir shops and ice-cream parlours. The peninsula is lined with fine beaches, including a sandy stretch on the east end of Østre Strandvej, a 15-minute walk from the town centre.

Orientation & Information

Sankt Laurentii Vej, Skagen's main street, runs almost the entire length of this long thin town, never more than five minutes from the waterfront. The tourist office (☎ 98 44 13 77), in the train/bus station at Sankt Laurentii Vej 22, is open from 9 am to 7 pm daily in summer.

Things to See & Do

Grenen Denmark's northernmost point is the long curving sweep of sand at Grenen, three km north-east of Skagen. From the end of route 40 it's a 30-minute walk out along this vast beach to its narrow tip where the waters of Kattegat and Skagerrak clash and you can put one foot in each sea.

Skagens Museum This notable museum, Brøndumsvej 4, displays the paintings of PS Krøyer, Michael & Anna Ancher and other artists who flocked to Skagen between 1830 and 1930 to 'paint the light'. Opening hours are from 10 am to 5 or 6 pm daily from May to September, with shorter hours in the off season. Admission costs 30 kr.

Skagen Fortidsminder Evocatively presented, this open-air museum depicts Skagen's maritime history and includes the homes of fisherfolk and a picturesque old windmill. It's a 15-minute walk from the train station, west down Sankt Laurentii Vej, then south on Vesterled. Hours are 10 am to 5 pm daily from May to September, weekdays to 4 pm in March, April, October and November. Admission costs 25 kr.

Tilsandede Kirke This whitewashed medieval church tower still rises up above the sand dunes that buried the church and surrounding farms in the late 1700s. The tower, in a nature reserve, is five km south of Skagen and well signposted from route 40. By bike, take Gammel Landevej from Skagen. The tower interior (7 kr) is open from 11 am to 5 pm from 1 June to 31 August.

Råbjerg Mile Denmark's largest expanse of shifting dunes, these undulating 40-metre hills are almost large enough to disappear in and good fun to explore. Råbjerg Mile is 16 km south of Skagen, off route 40 on the road to Kandestederne. In summer, bus No 99 runs six times a day from Skagen station (25 minutes, 16.50 kr).

Places to Stay

There are two summer camping grounds 1.5 km north-east of Skagen centre. The best is *Grenen Camping* (☎ 98 44 25 46), which has a fine seaside location, some semi-private tent sites and pleasant four-bunk huts at reasonable rates.

The 100-bed *Skagen Hostel* (☎ 98 44 22 00) at Rolighedsvej 2, a km west of the centre, has dorm beds for 70 kr. The tourist office books private rooms for 150/300 kr singles/doubles, plus a 25 kr booking fee.

The following places all have bright, cosy rooms: *Skagen Sømandshjem* (☎ 98 44 25 88), near the harbour at Østre Strandvej 2 (260/490 kr); the 12-room *Marienlund Badepension* (☎ 98 44 13 20), at Fabriciusvej 8 on the older west side of town near Fortidsminder (250/450 kr); and *Clausens Hotel* (☎ 98 45 01 66), across from the train station (395/500 kr). All prices include breakfast and are for rooms with shared bathrooms.

Places to Eat

Moderately priced restaurants are few. There are a couple of pizzerias and a kebab shop on Havnevej and the nearby *Sømandshjem Hotel* has an inexpensive cafeteria. For more atmosphere, the *Pakhuset Fiskerestaurant* on the harbour has long hours and good Danish fish dishes at reasonable prices. There are bakeries on Sankt Laurentii Vej, the best being *Krages Bageri* at No 104, and there's a grocery store two minutes walk west of the tourist office.

Getting There & Away

Either a bus or a train leaves Skagen station for Frederikshavn (33 kr) about once an hour. The seasonal Skagerakkeren bus (No 99) runs seven times daily between Hirtshals and Skagen (1½ hours, 28 kr) from mid-June to mid-August.

Getting Around

Cycling is the best option for getting around. Both camping grounds rent bicycles, as does the cycle stand at the west side of the train station (60 kr a day). In summer, buses run from Skagen station to Grenen hourly (11 kr). Taxis, available at the train station, charge about 35 kr to Grenen.

HIRTSHALS

Hirtshals gets its character from its commercial fishing harbour and ferry terminal. The main street is lined with supermarkets catering to Norwegian shoppers who pile off the ferries to load up with relatively cheap Danish meats and groceries. The tourist office (☎ 98 94 22 20) is at Nørregade 40.

Though it's not a town that invites lingering, at least the hostel and camping ground are on the more scenic western side, where there are coastal cliffs and a lighthouse. If you want beaches and dunes, there's a lovely unspoiled stretch at **Tornby Strand**, five km to the south.

Places to Stay & Eat

Hirtshals Hostel (☎ 98 94 12 48) at Kystvejen 53, a km west of the train station, is open from March to November and has beds for 65 kr. *Hirtshals Camping* (☎ 98 94 25 35) is nearby at Kystvejen 6. There are cafés and a bakery at the north end of Hjørringgade.

In Tornby Strand, *Munch Badepension* (☎ 98 97 71 15), right on the beach at the end of Tornby Strandvej, has a handful of rustic double rooms with dune views for 275 kr, a food store and a restaurant.

Getting There & Away

Train Hirtshals' main train station is 500 metres south of the ferry terminal, but trains connecting with ferry services terminate at the harbour. The railway, which is operated by a private company, connects Hirtshals with Hjørring (16.50 kr), 20 minutes to the south. Trains run at least hourly, with the last departure from Hjørring to Hirtshals at 10.43 pm. From Hjørring you can take a DSB train to Aalborg (38 kr) or Frederikshavn (32 kr).

DENMARK

From mid-June to mid-August there's a bus from Hirtshals station to Hjørring (16.50 kr) which stops en route at Tornby Strand six times a day.

Boat Color Line (☎ 99 56 19 77) runs year-round ferries to the Norwegian ports of Oslo (at 10 am daily in summer, 8½ hours, 141 to 189 kr) and Kristiansand (four times daily in summer, 4¼ hours, from 130 to 340 kr). There's no Monday sailing to Oslo from mid-August to mid-June.

ESBJERG

Esbjerg was established as a port in 1868 following the loss of the Schleswig and Holstein regions to Germany. It's now Denmark's fifth largest city, the centre of Denmark's North Sea oil activities and the country's largest fishing harbour. Although it has its fair share of turn-of-the-century buildings, Esbjerg lacks the intrigue found in the medieval quarters of other Danish cities

and isn't on the itinerary of most travellers unless they're heading to or from the UK.

Orientation & Information

Torvet, the city square where Skolegade and Torvegade intersect, is bordered by cafés, a bank, the post office and the tourist office. The tourist office (☎ 75 12 55 99), Skolegade 33, is open from 9 am to 5 pm Monday to Saturday. The train and bus stations are about 300 metres east of Torvet, the ferry terminal is one km south. Trains that meet the ferries continue down to the harbour.

Things to See & Do

Fiskeri og Søfartsmuseet at Tarphagevej, four km north-west of the centre, has an aquarium with 50 species of fish, an outdoor seal pool and various fisheries exhibits. It's open from 10 am to 8 pm in summer and costs 45 kr (20 kr children). Take bus No 3 or 6.

There are also a few local museums that could be explored if you're waiting for a ferry: **Esbjerg Kunstmuseum** has Danish modern art; **Esbjerg Museum**, history and amber collections; and **Bogtrykmuseet**, a 19th-century printing operation.

Places to Stay

Esbjerg Hostel (☎ 75 12 42 58), in a former folk high school at Gammel Vardevej 80,

Esbjerg

0   250   500 m

1	Esbjerg Museum
2	Library
3	Bus Station
4	Train Station
5	Park Hotel
6	Tourist Office
7	Hotel Ansgar
8	Post Office
9	Bank
10	Peking Grill
11	McDonald's
12	Midt-I (Shopping Centre)
13	Torvet
14	Flannigan's
15	Cab-Inn Hotel
16	Café Bageriet
17	Bogtrykmuseet (Printing Museum)
18	Esbjerg Kunstmuseum
19	Ferries to England & the Faroe Islands

three km north-west of the city centre (bus No 4), has dorm beds for 80 kr. The tourist office books private rooms for 125 to 150 kr a person. The nearest camping ground, *Ådalens Camping* (☎ 75 15 88 22) at Gudenåvej 20, is five km north of the city via bus No 2.

The *Park Hotel* (☎ 75 12 08 68), Torvegade 31, has small, simple rooms at 300/520 kr for singles/doubles, without breakfast. Much nicer is the *Hotel Ansgar* (☎ 75 12 82 44), Skolegade 36, which has comfortable rooms from 350/570 kr, including a good breakfast. *Cab-Inn Hotel* (☎ 75 18 16 00), Skolegade 14, has renovated rooms with private baths for 395/495 kr.

Places to Eat
Restaurants, cafeterias and grocery stores can be found east of Torvet on Kongensgade. *Café Bageriet*, at Kongensgade 7, is a good place to get cheap coffee and pastries if you're stumbling off an early-morning train. *Midt-I* shopping centre, on Kongensgade and Torvet, has a bakery and cafeteria. *Flannigan's* on Torvet has moderately priced food, a nice pub-like interior and summertime pavement tables. *Peking Grill*, next to *McDonald's*, has takeaway Chinese meals for around 35 kr. *Biblioteks Caféen*, the cafeteria in the public library at Nørregade 19, has inexpensive food, including good salads.

Getting There & Away
Trains between Esbjerg and Copenhagen (five hours, 207 kr) run about hourly during the day; an overnight sleeper train departs around midnight.

If you're driving into Esbjerg from the east, the E20 leads into the city centre. If you're coming from the south, route 24 merges with the E20 on the city outskirts. From the north, route 12 makes a beeline into the city, ending at the harbour.

For details of ferry services to the UK and the Faroe Islands see Denmark, Getting There & Away.

Getting Around
Most city buses (11 kr) can be boarded at the north side of the train station. There's free parking with no time limit in the parking lot on Nørregade east of the library.

LEGOLAND
At Legoland (☎ 75 33 13 33), a popular theme park in the town of **Billund**, 30 million plastic blocks have been arranged into a world of miniature cities, Lego pirates, safari animals and amusement rides. While it will no doubt seem like a mecca for kids who have grown up with Lego blocks, most adults won't find it nearly as riveting.

It's open from 10 am to 8 pm (9 pm in midsummer) from April to late September. Admission is 110 kr for adults, 100 kr for children aged 3 to 13. Admission is free once the rides stop, which is two hours before closing. There's a frequent 25-minute bus from Vejle to Legoland, as well as an express bus package from Esbjerg (160 kr adults, 125 kr children, admission included).

RIBE
Ribe, the oldest town in Scandinavia, dates back to 869 AD and was an important medieval trading centre. With its crooked cobblestone streets and half-timbered 16th-century houses, it's like stepping into a living history museum. The entire old town is a preservation zone, with more than 100 buildings in the National Trust.

Ribe is a tightly clustered place, easy to explore. Almost everything, including the hostel and train station, is within a 10-minute walk of Torvet, the town square dominated by a huge Romanesque cathedral. The tourist office (☎ 75 42 15 00) is at Torvet.

Things to See & Do
You can climb the **cathedral steeple** (7 kr) for a towering view of the countryside. For a nice stroll, the streets radiating out from Torvet are all picturesque, especially Puggårdsgade.

Ribes Vikinger (30 kr), opposite the train station, has displays of Ribe's Viking history, whereas **Ribe Vikingecenter** (30 kr) at

Lustrupvej 4, three km south of the centre, is a recreated Viking village open in summer. **Ribe Kunstmuseum** (20 kr), Sct Nicolajgade 10, has a good collection of 19th-century Danish art, and there are a couple of local history museums, including one at the old town hall (5 kr) that displays the now-retired executioner's axe.

A costumed **night watchman** makes the rounds from Torvet at 8 and 10 pm during the tourist season and you can follow him as he sings his way through the old streets – touristy but fun and free.

Places to Stay & Eat

The friendly 152-bed *Ribe Hostel* (☎ 75 42 06 20), Sct Pedersgade 16, has dorm beds from 80 kr, double rooms from 225 kr. The tourist office has a list of private rooms from 125/200 kr for singles/doubles. Three in-town taverns rent 2nd-storey rooms for 200/400 kr for singles/doubles with breakfast: *Weis Stue* at Torvet, *Backhaus* at Grydergade 12 and *Hotel Sønderjylland* at Sønderportsgade 22.

Weis Stue, a leaning half-timbered tavern with wooden-plank tables, has traditional Danish meals from 65 kr at lunch, 100 kr at dinner. *Firenze*, at Skolegade 6, has good pizza and pasta from 50 kr.

Getting There & Away

Trains from Esbjerg to Ribe take 40 minutes and cost 32 kr.

RØMØ

The island of Rømø lies off the coast midway between the historic towns of Ribe and Tønder and is a mere 30-minute drive from either. It's connected to the Jutland mainland by a 10-km causeway that passes over a scenic marshland with grazing sheep and wading waterbirds.

Rømø is a windsurfing haven whose western side is lined with expansive sandy beaches that attract scores of German tourists. Despite the caravan parking lots, most of Rømø is a rural scene with thatch-roofed houses, open spaces and the scent of the sea heavy in the air.

The tourist office (☎ 74 75 51 30), open from 9 am to 5 pm (to 4 pm on Sunday), is at Havnebyvej 30 on the east side of the island, a km south of the bridge.

Things to See & Do

The inland section of this flat island has **trails** through heathered moors and wooded areas which offer quiet hiking. There's an **old church** with unique Greenlandic gravestones on the main road in Kirkeby and a small **sea captain's museum** on the northwest side of the island.

Places to Stay & Eat

Kommandørgårdens Camping (☎ 74 75 51 22) is on Havnebyvej 201 near the hostel and *Lakolk Camping* (☎ 74 75 52 28) is on the west coast beach at Lakolk. The 91-bed *Rømø Hostel* (☎ 74 75 51 88), on the southeastern side of Rømø near Havneby, is in a delightful traditional building with a thatched roof. It's open from 15 March to 1 November and has dorm beds for 70 kr and doubles from 210 kr.

Rømø Røgeri in Havneby, close to the harbour, sells smoked herring and cooked shrimp by the kilo and has a small café with reasonably priced fish dishes. There are grocery stores and a bakery within walking distance of the hostel and many places to eat near the beach at Lakolk.

Getting There & Away

Rømø is 14 km west of the town of Skærbæk and route 11. Buses run from Skærbæk to Havneby (35 minutes, 10 kr) numerous times a day. From Skærbæk there's train service to Ribe, Tønder and Esbjerg about once an hour. Car ferries connect Havneby with Germany's island of Sylt (one hour, 32 kr) about six times a day.

Getting Around

Rømø is a good place for cycling; bicycles can be rented in several places, including Kommandørgårdens Camping. In summer a limited bus service (10 kr) connects villages on the island.

TØNDER

Tønder is another historic southern town that
retains a few curving cobblestone streets
with half-timbered houses. Its high point is
during the last weekend of August when the
Tønder Festival (☎ 74 72 46 10), one of
Denmark's largest, brings a multitude of
international and Danish folk musicians to
town. The tourist office (☎ 74 72 12 20) is at
Torvet 1.

Things to See & Do

Town Sights The **Tønder Museum** has
regional history exhibits including a collection of Tønder lace, once considered among
the world's finest. The adjacent **South
Jutland Art Museum** features Danish surre-
alist and modern art. Both are at Kongevej
55, a 10-minute walk east of the station, and
are open from 10 am to 5 pm April to September, 2 to 5 pm in winter, closed on Monday. Admission is 15 kr.

The 16th-century **Tønder church** on
Torvet has a notable interior of ornate woodwork and paintings.

Møgeltønder Slotsgade, the main street of
this fetching village, is cobblestoned and
lined with period houses sporting thatched
roofs and colourful wooden doors. At one
end of Slotsgade is the private castle of
Prince Joachim and a small public park,
while at the other end is a 12th-century
church with one of the most lavish interiors
in Denmark.

Bus No 66 (10 minutes, 10 kr) connects
Tønder (four km west via route 419) with
Møgeltønder, about hourly on weekdays,
less frequently on weekends.

Places to Stay

Tønder Hostel (☎ 74 72 35 00), Sønderport
4, on the east side of the centre, a 15-minute
walk from the train station, has bicycle
rentals and sports facilities. Rooms are comfortable; dorm beds cost 80 kr and singles/
doubles with private bath cost 175/240 kr.
The tourist office has a list of private rooms
for around 140/200 kr. **Tønder Camping**
(☎ 74 72 18 49) is just beyond the hostel at
Holmevej 2.

Places to Eat

Choices are limited and many people simply
drive south to Germany where food is
cheaper. **Torve Bistroen** on Torvet has vegetarian omelettes and light eats for around 50
kr. A short walk east is **Pizzeria Italiano** at
Østergade 40, which has good pizza and
pasta dishes from 60 kr. There's a market
selling fruit and cheese at Torvet on Tuesday
and Friday mornings.

Getting There & Away

Tønder is on route 11, four km north of the
German border. Trains run hourly on weekdays and slightly less frequently on
weekends from Ribe (50 minutes, 44 kr) and
Esbjerg (1½ hours, 63 kr).

Estonia

Estonia (Eesti) is just 80 km over the Gulf of Finland from Helsinki but socially and economically creeping closer week by week. Only fully independent since August 1991, Estonia's transition from Soviet socialist republic to Western-style economy has been little short of miraculous. There are still certain problems with much of what the West would take for granted (hot water is sometimes optional and finding somewhere to stay can be difficult) but things are far less problematic than they were just a few years ago.

Estonia is the most northerly of the three Baltic states and the most Scandinavian in atmosphere. Ethnically the Estonians and Finns are cousins, and it is partly the close links between the two that enabled Estonia to make the transition to capitalism and independence a lot more quickly and painlessly than its Baltic siblings. This makes visiting Estonia perhaps less of a shock to a Westerner and a good starting point for a trip through the Baltic states.

Estonia's German past lingers and is particularly evident in Tallinn's medieval Old Town, which is a high point of any visit to the Baltic region. Tallinn is the hub of Estonian life but Tartu (the second largest city), the coastal town of Pärnu, and the island of Saaremaa are also appealing destinations.

Facts about the Country

HISTORY
German Crusades

Estonia's pagan clans encountered Scandinavians pushing east and Slavs pushing west in the 8th to 12th centuries AD. However, they were little influenced from outside until the 12th century, when German traders and missionaries were followed by knights unleashed by Pope Celestinus III's 1193 call for a crusade against the northern heathens. In

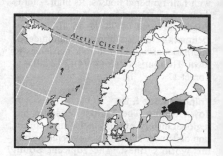

1202 the Bishop of Rīga established the Knights of the Sword (also known as the Livonian Order), whose white cloaks were emblazoned with blood-red swords and crosses, to convert the region by conquest. Within about 25 years this 'unwholesome' brood had subjugated what is now Latvia and the southern half of Estonia. Northern Estonia fell to Denmark.

The Knights of the Sword were later subordinated to a second band of German crusaders, the Teutonic Order, which by 1290 ruled the eastern Baltic area as far north as southern Estonia, and most of the Estonian islands. In 1346 Denmark sold northern Estonia to the knights, sealing Estonia's subordination to German nobility until the early 20th century. This ruling class tightened its hold through military, religious and commercial might. Hanseatic towns like Tallinn, Tartu, Pärnu and Narva – on the routes between Russia and the West – often prospered, but the indigenous peoples in the countryside were forced into serfdom.

Swedish & Russian Rule

Sweden, a rising power, took northern Estonia between 1559 and 1564 and southern Estonia in the 1620s, consolidating Estonian Protestantism, which had taken root with the Reformation in the early 16th century. Some Estonians now look back on

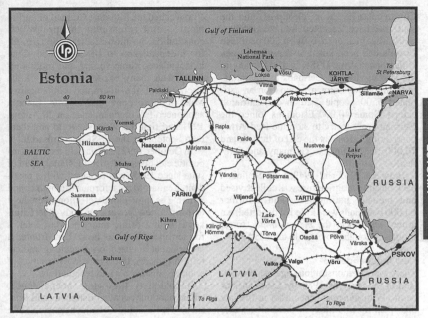

ESTONIA

the Swedish era as a pre-Russian golden age but, although the Swedes tried to establish universal education, the frequent wars were devastating. Under Peter the Great, Russia smashed Swedish power in the Great Northern War (1700-21), and Estonia became part of the Russian empire.

Repressive government from Moscow and economic control by German landowners and burghers encouraged national self-awareness among native Estonians. Serfs were freed in the 19th century, and improved education and broader land ownership promoted native culture and welfare.

Independence

Russia's Soviet government, eager to get out of WWI, abandoned the Baltic region to Germany with the Treaty of Brest-Litovsk in March 1918. Estonian nationalists had declared independence on 24 February, and the declaration was repeated after the German surrender in November. The Bolsheviks

then tried to win the Baltic states back but were beaten by local opposition and outside military intervention – in Estonia's case, a British fleet and volunteer forces from Scandinavia.

Damaged by the war and hampered by the disruption of trade with Russia and the world slump, independent Estonia suffered dire economic problems. In 1933 the anti-communist, antiparliamentary 'vaps' movement won a constitutional referendum. But Prime Minister Konstantin Päts outflanked it in a bloodless coup and took over as a moderate, relatively benevolent dictator.

Soviet Rule & WWII

The Molotov-Ribbentrop Pact of 23 August 1939, by which Nazi Germany and the USSR agreed on mutual nonaggression, secretly divided Eastern Europe into German and Soviet spheres of influence. The Baltic states ended up in the Soviet sphere and by August 1940 they were under occupation,

Communists had won 'elections', and the states had been 'accepted' into the USSR.

Within a year or so, over 10,000 people in Estonia had been killed or deported. When Hitler invaded the USSR in 1941, many in the Baltics saw the Germans as liberators, but during the German occupation an estimated 5500 people died in concentration camps. Some 40,000 Estonians joined the German army to try to stop the Red Army conquering Estonia at the end of the war and 70,000 fled, mainly to Germany and Sweden.

Between 1945 and 1949, with Stalinism back on course, agriculture was collectivised and industry nationalised, and a further 60,000 Estonians were killed or deported. An armed resistance, the *metsavennad* (forest brothers), fought Soviet rule until 1953.

New Independence

There were demonstrations against 'Sovietisation' as early as 1980 by Estonian students. With *glasnost* (openness) in the late 80s, pent-up bitterness in the Baltic states was released and national feeling surged. By 1988 a reformist popular front had been formed in each republic to press for democratic change, virtually in alliance with the local Communist parties. Estonia's popular front, claiming 300,000 members, at its first congress in October 1988 called for autonomy, democracy and cuts in Russian immigration.

Like Latvia and Lithuania, Estonia paid lip service to *perestroika* (restructuring) while dismantling Soviet institutions. On 23 August 1989, the 50th anniversary of the Molotov-Ribbentrop Pact, an estimated two million people formed a human chain across all three republics, many of them calling for secession from the USSR. In November, Moscow granted the republics economic autonomy.

In 1990 attention focused on Lithuania as it declared itself independent, then suffered intimidation and economic blockade. Estonia followed a similar path but more cautiously. In the spring, nationalists won a big majority in the Estonian Supreme Soviet

– now called the Supreme Council or parliament – and reinstated the pre-WWII constitution, but allowed a 'transition period' for independence to be negotiated. That independence came sooner and more suddenly than many expected as part of the aftermath of the attempted coup against Mikhail Gorbachev in Moscow. Estonia announced full independence on 20 August 1991 and first the Western world and then, on 6 September, the USSR recognised it.

In October 1992 Estonia held its first democratic elections and Arnold Rüütel, head of state since 1983, was replaced with a president, Lennart Meri, a former film maker and writer. The same month, elections were held to form a new governing body (the Riigikogu) with a prime minister, Mart Laar, a former historian, at its head. Laar fronted a government focused on launching radical reform policies, but wracked by a series of scandals, dismissals and resignations.

Immediately following independence, ethnic relations between Estonians and Russians were a source of much tension. The several thousand Russian troops which remained based on Estonian territory following the demise of the Soviet empire, added further fuel to the fire. However, under international pressure, the last Russian military personnel departed from Estonian soil on 31 August 1994.

In September 1994, just two days before the *Estonia* ferry disaster, Mart Laar was sunk by a vote of no-confidence. Andres Tarand, a member of the Moderates was appointed interim prime minister until the next general election. In March 1995 a new centre-left government headed by Prime Minister Tiit Vahi was formed. Six months later, however, Vahi's government collapsed, following the 'Estonian Watergate' scandal during which it emerged that Interior Minister Edgar Savisaar had been involved in tapping top politicians' telephones during talks on forming the new government. Vahi stepped down on 11 October, only to be renominated as prime minister days later by President Meri.

Following the Riigikogu's failure to elect

a new president in three rounds of voting in August 1996, an electoral college composed of the 101 parliamentary deputies and 273 representatives of local governments converged on 20 September and elected Lennart Meri over arch-rival and communist-era predecessor Arnold Rüütel.

GEOGRAPHY & ECOLOGY
With an area of 45,200 sq km, Estonia is the smallest of the Baltic states but it is still bigger than Denmark. It's mainly low-lying, with extensive bogs and marshes, but rises slightly in the eastern half. Suur Munamägi (318 metres) in the south-east near Võru is the highest point in any of the Baltic states. Nearly 40% of the land is forested, mainly with pine along the coasts and mixed forests inland.

Estonia's 3794-km coast is heavily indented. Offshore there are over 800 islands, the biggest being Saaremaa and Hiiumaa to the west. Inland, there are over 1400 lakes, and Lake Peipsi (3548 sq km) on Estonia's border with Russia, is the fourth largest in Europe (though its maximum depth is only 15 metres).

The Baltic Sea is extremely polluted. In 1993 the Estonian beach resort of Pärnu was given the all clear after several years of being closed to swimmers, and there are still many resorts where swimming is not recommended. After 1945 the Soviet Union pushed to industrialise the Baltic states and huge chemical plants were established, resulting in some of the most polluted towns in the USSR. Since independence, 'clean-up' attempts have been made although Estonia is the only Baltic state to show any real interest in green issues. In 1995 the Kodukant Ecotourism Initiative was set up in an attempt to encourage low impact tourism.

GOVERNMENT & POLITICS
Estonia is an independent republic with its own constitution and governing body, the Riigikogu. The head of state is the president but the duties of the office are mainly ceremonial and the Riigikogu, a 101-seat

parliament elected every four years, is led by the prime minister. The parliament is composed of numerous parties and factions with the majority of seats held by the Konderakond-Maarahua Uhendus (KMU; Coalition Party-Country People's Party Union) centrist alliance.

The coalition government, shaky as it is, totally embraces free-market economics and enjoys considerable popular support, including amongst the Russian population whose flair for entrepreneurial activity enables them to best exploit the current opportunities.

Noncitizens can vote in local government elections providing they have legal residency (in the 1992 elections most of Estonia's Russian population was excluded from voting). They can also apply for citizenship, and must pass history and Estonian language tests to become Estonian citizens.

ECONOMY
During Soviet rule Estonia was transformed from an agrarian based economy to an industrial one subservient to Moscow. With the onset of independence, people were hit badly by the loss of the large Soviet market, and the end of subsidies, cheap fuel and other supplies from Russia. There was spiralling inflation, shortages and unemployment. The cost of living increased tenfold in the year to March 1992. With the introduction of the kroon in June 1992 – making Estonia the first ex-Soviet republic to break free of the rouble – the country began a programme of stabilisation.

The effects are now evident, and the Western media every now and again runs a story on the 'Estonian economic miracle'. Estonia enjoys the strongest economy of the three Baltic states and is the most attractive market in the post-communist world for Western importers and investors. In 1995 foreign investment in Estonia stood at US$275 million, and by mid-1996 Estonian companies were beginning to expand into Latvia and Lithuania. Privatisation continues at a rapid pace while economic ties with the West have strengthened to the point that

ESTONIA

Estonia is no longer dependent on Russia. Finland is now Estonia's biggest trading partner.

Estonia's natural resources include oil shale, peat and large tracts of forest supporting timber and paper industries. In mid-1996 inflation in Estonia stood at 30%.

POPULATION & PEOPLE

Estonia's population is 1.5 million, 65% of which is Estonian, 30% Russian, 3% Ukrainian and just under 2% Belarusian. In 1934, 88% of the population was native Estonian. Russian speakers are concentrated in Tallinn, where they form just over 50% of the population, and in the industrial north-east, where they account for up to 94%.

Estonians are a Finno-Ugric people, part of an ethno-linguistic group which is scattered across Siberia and along the Volga River. Their ancestors reached Estonia from the east between 2500 and 2000 BC. They're related closely to the Finns, and more distantly to the Sami or Lapps and Hungarians, but not to the Latvians and Lithuanians, who are Indo-European.

ARTS

Until the mid-19th century Estonian culture existed only in the form of peasant, oral folk tales and chanted verses. Hundreds of these were collected to form the national epic poem *Kalevipoeg* (The Son of Kalev) written by Friedrich Reinhold Kreutzwald between 1857 and 1861. *Kalevipoeg*, inspired by Finland's *Kalevala*, a similar epic written a few decades earlier, relates the adventures of the mythical Estonian hero of the title. It ends with his death and his land's conquest by foreigners but also with the idea that he would return to restore freedom. The epic became an inspiration to patriotism and played a large role in fostering the national awakening of the 19th century which in turn led to the development of a new urbanised national culture embracing literature and the visual arts.

By the time of the first period of independence, Estonia had its own 'great' writer, AH Tammsaare who wrote the monumental *Tõde ja õigus* (Truth and Justice) between 1926 and 1933, and a world-class artist, Eduard Viiralt who produced fantastic and grotesque graphics from his studio in Paris between 1928 and 1935.

The artistic life of Estonia was almost snuffed out during the Soviet occupation, but following the Khrushchev thaw of the 1960s, nationalist themes re-emerged in the arts, particularly in poetry. Poets became figures of enormous spiritual stature, particularly Jaan Kross (*The Czar's Madman* and *Professor Marten's Departure*, both published in English-language editions by Harvill Collins), Jaan Kaplinski (*The Same Sea in Us All* and *The Wandering Border*, also published by Harvill Collins), and Paul-Eerik Rummo, whose play *Four Kings' Day* was banned for some time under the Soviets. Kross and Kaplinski were both rumoured to be candidates for the 1991 Nobel Prize for literature, and Rummo was the minister of culture for a time.

In music, Veljo Tormis revived the ancient form of runic chanting to mesmerising effect, although Estonia's most famous and internationally recorded composer, Arvo Pärt, emigrated to Berlin in 1980 because he felt he could no longer work within the system.

CULTURE

The Estonians are a rural people said to be happiest when their nearest neighbours are no closer than a km or two distant. Most people in Tallinn, if they don't actually own a country cottage in some isolated spot, at least have access to one which they retire to for as much of the summer as possible.

The attachment to the land is strong and a favourite Estonian pastime is to go berry or mushroom picking, depending on the time of year. An urban echo of this is that Estonians have a habit of taking flowers whenever they go visiting or attend any kind of celebration. You will see flower kiosks and stalls in every town.

It helps if you are able to say a few words

in the local language (even if most of the time the reply is in English). Most Estonians speak Russian but view it as the language of occupation. If you speak Russian try some other language first. Finnish-speakers might find they get a better res-ponse speaking English. Tallinn and Tartu particularly have rapidly become dubbed 'suburbs of Helsinki', much to the annoyance of many Estonians.

RELIGION

Under Soviet rule religious practices were discouraged (a church wedding could cost students their place at university), but then again Estonia has always been possibly the most secular country in Europe. From 1987 to 1990 there was a surge of interest in religion as the state Lutheran Church allied itself to the independence cause and baptisms rose tenfold, but that enthusiasm has since waned. Since independence the Russian Orthodox Church, largely made up Russians, has grown.

LANGUAGE

Like Finnish, Estonian is a Finno-Ugric language, part of the Ural-Altaic language family, which sets it apart from Russian, Latvian and Lithuanian, which are in the Indo-European family.

English is well on its way to becoming the lingua franca of the Baltic states and many Estonians, especially the younger generations, speak some. With older people, German is often of more use. Finnish and Estonian are related closely enough for their speakers to make some sense of each other.

Russian is also of use, particularly if you're travelling through more than one of the three Baltic states. While few of the many Russians in Estonia speak much Estonian, nearly all Estonians speak some Russian, but take note of the warning in the Culture section above.

See the Language Guide at the back of the book for pronunciation guidelines and useful words and phrases.

Facts for the Visitor

PLANNING
Climate & When to Go

From May to September daytime maximum temperatures are usually between 14°C and 22°C. July and August, the warmest months, are also the wettest, with days of persistent showers. May, June and September are more comfortable. Mid to late June is also favoured by 'white nights', when there is virtual 24-hour daylight.

April and October have cold, sharp, wintry days, as well as mild spring-like or autumnal ones. There's usually snow on the ground from January to late March.

Temperatures in the east average 2°C colder than on the coast; the uplands have around 700 mm of precipitation annually, against 500 mm on the coast. Coastal waters average 18°C in summer.

Books

For anyone interested in a comprehensive but extremely readable survey of the region, past and present, then no book can be more thoroughly recommended than *The Baltic Revolution* by Anatol Lieven. The author spent the early 1990s as the Baltic states correspondent for the London *Times* and his book is shot through with insight and startling information (such as the phrase 'Going to Rīga' is a Lithuanian colloquialism meaning 'to vomit').

Lonely Planet's *Baltic States & Kaliningrad – a travel survival kit* contains 438 pages of practical and invaluable information, and over 80 maps. There is also the intriguing *People to People – The Baltic Republics*, part of a series of books (at the moment limited to Eastern Europe) which simply lists the names, addresses and a few personal details of people who would like to meet and get to know visitors from the West. There are over a thousand potential contacts listed in the book, some of whom are prepared to offer accommodation.

ESTONIA

Maps

There is an excellent locally produced 1:1,000,000 motoring map, *Via Baltica – Baltic States Road Map*, with coverage from Helsinki to Warsaw, published by the Briedis company of Vilnius. This should be sufficient for most purposes and is widely available at bookshops, hotels and tourist offices. You can also find good quality maps of the Baltics in the West.

Online Services

Web sites worth logging onto include the *Estonia Country Guide* (http://sun.nlib.ee/ESTCG) and *Travel World – About Estonia* (http://www.theworld.com/travel/PLACES/Estonia).

What to Bring

Even in summer bring a warm pullover because the evenings can occasionally be quite chilly. However, bring your shorts too, because the next day could be gloriously warm. A light waterproof coat or an umbrella is also essential. Between September and May you will need a warm jacket and trousers and during winter (December to March) you will also need thermal underwear, a thick coat, a scarf, gloves and a woollen hat; this clothing is not optional, as you need it to deal with constant subzero temperatures, sometimes as low as -25°C.

Everything you will need is easily available in Estonia's urban centres including basic Western medication products such as aspirin, cough medicines etc. In summer bring mosquito repellent or coils. If you are going to be staying in cheap hotels bring a towel and soap.

SUGGESTED ITINERARIES

The following are some suggestions:

Two days
　Tallinn and on the second day Tartu, Pärnu or Lahemaa National Park
One week
　Two days in Tallinn, a full-day trip to Pärnu, down to Tartu spending the night in south-eastern Estonia, and a night or two on Saaremaa

HIGHLIGHTS

Tallinn's Old Town with its winding cobbled streets and gingerbread façades is a definite high point of any trip to Estonia. The city's numerous lively bars and inexpensive clubs, open virtually round the clock (especially during summer), make for many memorable evenings. The locals rave about the island of Saaremaa, a place which represents for them everything that is best about Estonia – solitude and the land.

TOURIST OFFICES

To date, the Baltic states have not opened any tourist information offices in other countries but Estonia has three representatives abroad:

Canada
　Orav Travel, 5650 Yonge St, North York, Ontario M2M 4G3 (☎ 416-221 4164; fax 416-221 6789)
Finland
　Estonian Tourist Information, Merimiehenkatu 29, 00150 Helsinki (☎ 09-630 522; fax 09-637 887)
Germany
　Estonian Tourist Information, Woldsenstrasse 36, 25813 Husum (☎ 048-413 004; fax 048-412 109)

Baltic embassies and consulates are often happy enough to answer questions relating to tourism and travel and Baltic-specialist travel agencies in Western countries are also useful sources of information (see Getting There & Away in this chapter).

There are tourist information centres all over Estonia, including Tallinn city office (☎ 6313 940); Tallinn harbour office (☎ 6318 321); in Tartu (☎ 432 141); in Narva (☎ 60 186) and in Pärnu (☎ 40 639). See individual city sections for addresses. The Estonian Tourist Board (☎ 6411 420; fax 6411 432, e-mail tallinn@tourism.uninet.ee) at Pikk 71, Tallinn, is also extremely helpful.

VISAS & DOCUMENTS

Visas

Who Needs Visas? Visa regulations are constantly changing and a check with your local Estonian consulate or embassy is the first step. Estonia has a growing list of nationalities that don't need visas to enter the country, just a valid passport. Currently this applies to:

Andorra, Australia, Bulgaria, Canada, the Czech Republic, Denmark, Hungary, Ireland, Japan, Latvia, Liechtenstein, Lithuania, Monaco, New Zealand, Poland, San Marino, Slovakia, the UK, the USA and the Vatican City

Citizens of the following countries can obtain a three-day transit visa or a single-entry visa at Estonian land borders and other points of entry into Estonia:

Austria, Belgium, Finland, France, Germany, Israel, Italy, Korea, Luxembourg, Malta, Netherlands, Norway, Portugal, South Africa, Spain, Sweden, Switzerland

The Common Visa Regime The Baltic states established a 'common visa space' in 1992, meaning that a visa for one country is good for the other two. So, if you want to travel around all three states for, say, a total of three weeks, all you need is one three-week visa for Estonia, Latvia or Lithuania. Estonia, however, has backtracked on this to a certain extent because it only recognises Latvian and Lithuanian visas for the holders of some 32 countries. Citizens of other countries – mainly those in Africa, South America, Asia and the former USSR – need a separate Estonian visa even if they have a Latvian or Lithuanian one.

Types of Visa All the Baltic states issue three main types of visa: transit, single-entry and multiple-entry.

Transit These visas are valid for up to three days. Single-entry transit visas cost US$10. Transit visas issued at Estonian borders cost US$20 – twice as much as those obtained from an embassy.

Single-Entry These visas are usually valid for periods of up to six months. Single-entry visas cost upwards of US$20. Single-entry visas issued at Estonian borders cost US$40.

Because of the Baltic's common visa regime, a single-entry visa for Estonia allows you to travel back and forth over the Estonian-Latvian and Latvian-Lithuanian borders as many times as you like within the period of its validity, provided you don't leave the common visa space during that time. Not all border officials seem to understand this detail. If you are coerced into paying additional fees take down the details and report the incident to the National Migration Board (see Visa Extensions).

Multiple-Entry These are issued for various periods of up to 12 months. They cost between US$50 and US$120.

Applying for Visas You can get visas at Estonian, Latvian and Lithuanian embassies and consulates in most countries.

Embassies and consulates usually process visa applications in a few days at the most. The Lithuanian embassy in Warsaw reportedly issues visas in one day. The busy Baltic state embassies in Helsinki and Stockholm all have 'immediate processing' services at about double the usual cost.

When applying for a visa you normally need to supply your passport (which should expire at least two months after your planned departure from the country in question), a completed application form and at least one photo, sometimes two. Invitations are not required.

Visa Extensions Once in the Baltics you can extend a visa. In Estonia go to the National Immigration Board (☎ 2-664 442) at Lai 38/40, Tallinn . In Latvia go to the visa office (☎ 2-7219 118, 7219 834) at Raiņa bulvāris 5, Rīga – you must apply at least three days before the expiry of your existing visa. In Lithuania go to the immigration office at Saltoniškių 19, Vilnius (☎ 22-725 864, 725 853, 659 847) or at Verkių 3, Vilnius (☎ 22-756 453).

Documents

Make sure your passport extends at least two months after the end of your Baltic travels as this may be a requirement for certain visas.

ESTONIA

If you are planning to drive to or in the region an International Driving Permit (IDP) will be useful, though if you don't have one your own licence (if from a European country) will suffice. Licences which do not bear a photograph of the holder (such as British ones) have been known to upset traffic police: try to get an IDP before you arrive. You will also need your vehicle's registration document, and in Estonia accident insurance is compulsory.

Student and youth cards can certainly cut the cost of getting there and are becoming increasingly useful within the Baltics States too.

EMBASSIES
Estonian Embassies Abroad

Australia
   Consulate, 86 Louisa Road, Birchgrove, NSW 2041 (☎ 02-9810 7468)
Canada
   Consulate, 958 Broadview Avenue, Toronto, Ontario, M4K 2R6 (☎ 416-461 0764)
Finland
   Embassy, kasarmikatu 28, Helsinki (☎ 09-179 719)
Germany
   Embassy, Fritz-Schäffer Strasse 22, 53113 Bonn (☎ 228-914 790)
Latvia
   Embassy, Skolas 13, Rīga (☎ 7820 460, 7226 845)
Lithuania
   Embassy, Tilto 29, Vilnius (☎ 2-622 030, 220 486)
Russia
   Embassy, Malo Kislovski 5, 103009 Moscow (☎ 095-2905 013, 2903 178)
Sweden
   Embassy, Storgatan 38, 1 tr, Stockholm 10440 (☎ 08-665 6550, 661 9980)
UK
   Embassy, 16 Hyde Park Gate, London SW7 5DG (☎ 0171-589 3428)
USA
   Embassy, 2131 Massachusetts Avenue, NW, Washington DC 20008 (☎ 202-588 0101)
   Consulate, 630 5th Avenue, Suite 2415, New York, NY 10111 (☎ 212-247 7634, 247 1450)

Foreign Embassies in Estonia

Canada
   Toomkooli 13, Tallinn (☎ 6313 570)

Finland
   Liivalaia 12, Tallinn (☎ 6311 445, 6314 444)
Germany
   Rävala puiestee 9, 7th floor, Tallinn (☎ 6313 970, 6313 976)
Latvia
   Tõnismägi 10, Tallinn (☎ 6461 313, 6461 310)
Lithuania
   Uus tn 15, Tallinn (☎ 6314 030)
Russia
   Hobuse 3, Tallinn (☎ 443 014)
Sweden
   Pikk 28, Tallinn (☎ 6405 600, 6405 640)
UK
   Kentmanni 20, 2nd floor, Tallinn (☎ 6313 462, 6313 463)
USA
   Kentmanni 20, Tallinn (☎ 6312 021/3/4)

CUSTOMS

You'll be charged tax from 30% to 100% of the retail price for taking out of Estonia more than one litre of spirits, one litre of wine or 10 litres of beer, 200 cigarettes, 20 cigars or 250 grams of tobacco. Latvia and Lithuania have similar restrictions, though in Lithuania the wine allowance is two litres, and in Latvia the overall volume of alcohol permitted in or out is just one litre. None of the Baltic states allows you to bring in any firearms, ammunition, drugs or dangerous chemical substances. Latvia and Lithuania also prohibit the import and export of pornography.

In Estonia and Latvia works of art or of cultural significance (including antique books) that date from before 1945, but are less than 100 years old, are subject to a 50% customs duty; those older than 100 years attract 100% duty. They may only leave with written permission from the relevant Ministry of Culture: in Rīga at Pils 22 (☎ 2-7214 100); and in Tallinn at Sakala 14 (☎ 2-448 501). For some bizarre reason, Lithuania applies slightly different rules (see the Facts for the Visitor section in the Lithuania chapter).

MONEY

Prior to independence the Baltic states used the Russian rouble, but since 1992, beginning with Estonia, each country has introduced its own currency, largely to escape the raging inflation that went with the Russian rouble.

The best currencies to bring into the Baltics are US dollars or Deutschmarks, though most Western currencies are perfectly acceptable (especially Finnish marks and Swedish krona in Estonia). Unless you are going to Kaliningrad, Polish złoty, Russian roubles and other Eastern European money is useless.

A limited amount of travellers' cheques may be useful though it can still be difficult to find places to exchange them and commissions are often high. American Express and Thomas Cook seem to be the best choices as they have a couple of offices in the Baltic states where you can get replacement cheques.

Crédit cards are widely accepted, especially at the upper end of the market. Master-Card, Diners Club and American Express all crop up. A Visa card is particularly useful as there are now a fair number of Visa automatic teller machines (ATMs) in the Baltics (see Money in the Tallinn, Rīga and Vilnius sections for further details).

Within the Baltics it is easy to change one Baltic currency into another although rates are not always as favourable as with other currencies, eg US dollars.

Currency

Estonia introduced its own currency, the kroon (pronounced 'krohn' and abbreviated to EEK), in June 1992. The kroon is Estonia's only legal tender and it is a criminal offence to buy or sell in any other currency (roubles and dollars included). Since its introduction the kroon, a 'hard' (freely convertible) currency, has held close to its initial rate of eight kroons to one Deutschmark, making it a stable currency by any standards.

The kroon comes in one, two, five, 10, 25, 50, 100 and 500 EEK denomination notes. One kroon is divided into 100 sents, and there are coins of five, 20 and 50 sents and, less commonly, 1 EEK.

Exchange Rates

The following currencies convert at these approximate rates:

Australia	A$1	=	9.41 EEK
Canada	C$1	=	8.70 EEK
Finland	1 Fmk	=	2.64 EEK
Germany	DM1	=	8.10 EEK
Sweden	1 SKr	=	1.79 EEK
UK	UK£1	=	18.58 EEK
USA	US$1	=	11.87 EEK

Costs

Despite their status as ex-Soviet republics there are unfortunately few bargains to be had in the Baltic states. Latvia is the most expensive, with prices comparable to those of Scandinavia. Accommodation is expensive and will be your biggest cost (see Accommodation later in this section), especially in Estonia. After that will come food – allow perhaps 60 to 100 EEK per day, depending on how frugal you want to be. Goods in the shops vary from Helsinki-priced (which means some of the most expensive in Western Europe) to cheap, but then that usually applies to the quality too. Eating out in Lithuania is still ridiculously cheap and by far the cheapest of the Baltics. Overland travel in all three, however, is still very affordable.

Tipping & Bargaining

Tipping is not traditional in the Baltics, but nobody is going to complain if you leave 10% or so on top of the bill. Outside of flea markets bargaining is uncommon.

POST & COMMUNICATIONS
Post

Mail service in and out of Estonia isn't too bad: expect letters or postcards to take about four days to Western Europe or up to 10 days to North America. Air-mail rates for letters/postcards weighing up to 20 grams are 3.20/4 EEK to European countries, and 3.60/4.50 EEK to the USA, Canada and Australia. Stamps can only be bought at post offices, tourist information offices and hotels. There is a poste restante bureau at the main post

ESTONIA

office, Narva maantee 1, Tallinn EE0001. They keep mail for one month.

Telephone

To call other cities in Estonia or in the former Soviet Union, simply dial ☎ 8, followed by the area code and telephone number. Area codes from Estonian phones include Tallinn ☎ 2, Tartu ☎ 27, Pärnu ☎ 244, Kuresaare ☎ 245, Saaremaa ☎ 245, Haapsalu ☎ 247, Narva ☎ 235, Rakvere ☎ 232, Vilnius ☎ 0122, Rīga ☎ 013, Kaliningrad ☎ 0112, St Petersburg ☎ 812 and Moscow ☎ 095. If the number you are calling in Rīga is analogue the area code is ☎ 0132 (see the Rīga section in the Latvia chapter).

To make an international call dial ☎ 8-00 followed by the country code, area code and telephone number (if 0 is the first digit in the area code, omit it, eg for the telephone code 0171 just dial 171). Tariffs per minute are: to Europe 11 EEK, the USA and Canada 24 EEK and Australia 30 EEK.

The country code for calling Estonia from abroad is ☎ 372, which is followed by the international area code which you can work out by dropping the first 2 from the area code used from Estonian phones, eg no area code for Tallinn, Tartu 7, and so on.

Public telephones accept chip cards costing 30, 50 or 100 EEK which are available at post offices, hotels and most kiosks.

To call AT & T USA-direct dial ☎ 8-00 8001 001.

Analogue Phones Analogue numbers have only six digits. To call an old analogue phone from a digital line or from abroad simply dial ☎ 2 before the six-digit number. The only difference with long-distance and international calls from an analogue phone is that you have to wait for a long dialling tone after dialling 8.

Fax, Telegraph & E-mail

There is a fax service at the main post office in Tallinn costing 29 EEK per sheet to Europe, 40 EEK to the USA and 45 EEK to Australia. Faxes can also be sent from the service bureaus at the Viru, Palace and Olümpia hotels but their rates are substantially more expensive.

Telegrams can be sent from any telegraph (*telegraaf*) office, often the same place as post offices, and cost 2.50 EEK a word to Western Europe, 5 EEK elsewhere. Outgoing and incoming telegrams rarely take more than 24 hours.

For Internet access contact Estpak Daea (☎ 6322 662; fax 6323 070) at Koorti 15, Tallinn. If you subscribe to SprintNet, CompuServe or MCIMail you can access your account in Tallinn (☎ 6312 286).

NEWSPAPERS & MAGAZINES

The Rīga-based weekly *Baltic Times* is an authoritative English-language digest of Baltic news and information, not particularly strong on Estonian news but still a worthwhile read. The bimonthly Tallinn-based *City Paper* – a news magazine and Baltic city guide rolled into one – contains some fine analytical pieces on Baltic politics as well as hotel, restaurant and bar listings for Estonia's hot spots. Both publications are available at hotels and newsstands for a few EEK. Distributed free in some hotels and ferries, the glossy city guide *Tallinn This Week* is packed with somewhat outdated, but still useful, information about Tallinn and Estonia.

An impressive selection of Western newspapers and magazines are sold at Tallinn's Viru and Olümpia hotels. By far the best bet for English and Finnish-language glossy magazines is the Finnish supermarket, Stockmann, close to the Hotel Olümpia at Liivalaia 51.

RADIO & TV

Along the north coast of Estonia it's possible to pick up four Finnish TV channels which broadcast a lot of English-language programmes. See the local press for schedules. Almost all hotels have Satellite TV offering an onslaught of European programmes.

State-run Eesti Raadio broadcasts 10 minutes of news in English from Monday to Friday at 6.20 pm local time, and the *Estonia Today* magazine programme, also in English, on Monday and Thursday from 11.30

pm until midnight local time. Its frequencies are 103.5 mHz on FM and 5.925 mHz on short wave. The BBC World Service can be picked up on 100.3 FM.

PHOTOGRAPHY & VIDEO
Western print film including Kodak, Agfa and Fuji is easily available in towns and cities from specialist shops and some hotels. There are also quick print-processing outlets. However, you'll find prices for film and processing are likely to be higher than at home. Even in summer, sunlight can be at a premium in the Baltic states, so make use of whatever you get and bring some fast film, ASA 400 or more. Bring your own video tapes with you for your camcorder.

TIME
Estonian, Latvian and Lithuanian time is GMT/UTC plus two hours, except from the last Sunday in March to the last Saturday in September when daylight saving is in force and it's GMT/UTC plus three hours. The 24-hour clock is in common use.

ELECTRICITY
The Baltic states run on 220V, 50 Hz AC. Most appliances that are set up for 240V will handle this supply happily. Sockets require a European plug with two round pins. Some sockets are still only compatible with the thinner pin Russian plugs in which case you have no choice but shop for an adapter locally. Large supermarkets sometimes sell them. Otherwise, try to bring all adapters, leads and plugs with you as they can be hard to come by in the Baltics.

WEIGHTS & MEASURES
All the Baltic states use the metric system, sometimes to amusing excess in some Soviet-style restaurants where menus still spell out the price of bread, meat and fish per 10g. More common is the practice of serving drinks by weight: a standard shot of spirits is 50g and a glass of wine is 200g.

LAUNDRY
The better hotels offer laundry services, oth-erwise you will find that there are laundrettes *(pesumaja)* in most towns and cities. In Tallinn there are two close to the city centre (see the Tallinn section for details).

TOILETS
Public toilets in Tallinn are well-signposted, clean and a sheer pleasure to use compared to the vile, stinking black holes you will generally encounter elsewhere in the Baltics. Regardless of their lack of cleanliness, you are obliged to pay a small fee in exchange for a few sheets of exceedingly rough toilet paper or squares of newspaper. Bring your own toilet paper and be prepared to squat. If a bin or basket is placed in the cubicle, put toilet paper in there.

Smelly public toilets can be found at every bus and train station in the Baltics. As a Westerner, you can quite easily stroll into any large hotel in the major cities and use their toilets without upsetting the staff too much. Alternatively, do what everyone else does and pop into the nearest McDonald's.

The letter M marks a men's toilet in Estonian and Russian, V in Latvian and Lithuanian. N indicates a women's toilet in Estonian, S in Latvian, M in Lithuanian and Ж in Russian. Some toilets sport an upside down triangle for men and a triangle the right way up for women.

HEALTH
A small, basic medical kit is a wise thing to carry, especially if you're going off the beaten track, as you cannot rely on availability in rural areas. In major towns and cities however, Western medicines, tampons and insect repellent are readily available. Contraceptives are likewise available although it is probably safer to bring condoms with you from the West. No immunisations are needed for any of the Baltic states, except in Latvia where it is advisable to get a vaccine against tick-borne encephalitis (see Facts for the Visitor in the Latvia chapter). In all three Baltics, you must have an AIDS test before you can be issued a residence permit, which you need if you plan to stay longer than three months.

ESTONIA

In an emergency seek your hotel's help first; the bigger hotels may have doctors on call. Your embassy should be able to recommend a doctor or hospital, but if things are serious be prepared to fly out. Emergency care is not free in Estonia so it is a good idea to have medical insurance. Pharmacies are open from 8 am to 7 pm and every town has at least one all-night pharmacy.

Tap water in Estonia is clean and drinkable. There are problems with polluted sea water along the Baltic coast, and swimming was not recommended for several years at the Estonian resorts of Pärnu and Haapsalu. Many of the inland lakes are cleaner than the Baltic Sea but we suggest you still take local advice about swimming anywhere.

WOMEN TRAVELLERS

Western women are likely to find less aggravation from men in the Baltics than at home although unaccompanied women may want to avoid a few of the sleazier bars and beer cellars. In some tourist hotels prostitution is a fact of life, and a woman sitting alone in a lobby, corridor or café might be propositioned.

GAY & LESBIAN TRAVELLERS

Estonia is not particularly tolerant as far as homosexuality goes. One friend of ours was severely harassed on the street just because he was wearing a shiny shirt, which his aggressor told him meant he was gay. In Tallinn, an underground gay and lesbian scene does exist, however. For information contact the Estonian Lesbian Union (e-mail elvell@saturn.zzz.ee).

DISABLED TRAVELLERS

With their cobbled streets, rickety pavements and old buildings the Baltics are completely nonuser-friendly for disabled travellers. You could contact the Baltic Association of Rehabilitation of Disabled Persons at the University Department of Special Education (☎ 270 071; fax 935 041), Tiigi 78, EE2484 Tartu.

DANGERS & ANNOYANCES

Theft from hotel rooms is a danger in all the Baltic states, but more significantly in cheap hotels. Using your own padlock can be a help. Keep valuables with you or in a hotel safe.

Most of the surly, rude, obstructive goblins employed in service industries in the Soviet era have miraculously changed character now that pleasing the customer has become worthwhile, but there are still one or two hangovers from the bad old days. When you encounter them, all you can do is grit your teeth and quietly persist.

Drunks on the streets and in hotels can be a nuisance in the evenings, especially at weekends. Steer clear and don't get involved. Street crime has also become an unfortunate fact of contemporary Baltic life and it is wise to avoid walking alone along darkened routes, even during early evening.

BUSINESS HOURS

Most shops in the Baltic states are open from 9 or 10 am to 6 pm Monday to Friday, to 3 or 4 pm Saturday, closed Sunday. Restaurants usually open from 11 am to around midnight.

Museums are open varying hours but nearly always between 11 am and 4 pm. They are usually closed Monday and/or Tuesday. Normal office hours are from 9 am to 5 pm. Offices and shops tend to stretch a one-day public holiday to two or even three days.

PUBLIC HOLIDAYS & SPECIAL EVENTS

National holidays are:

1 January, *New Year's Day*
24 February, *Independence Day* (anniversary of the 1918 declaration)
Good Friday
23 June, *Victory Day* (anniversary of Battle of Võnnu, 1919)
24 June, *Jaanipäev* (taken together with Victory Day this usually becomes an excuse for a week-long holiday)
26 December, *Boxing Day*

The biggest occasion of the year is the night of June 23, *Jaanipäev* (St John's Eve), which despite its Christian tag is a celebration of the pagan Midsummer's Night. Jaanipäev is best experienced out in the country where huge bonfires are lit and the parties run through the night.

Estonia also has a busy calendar of festivals encompassing music, art, folk culture and more. Two regular events stand out. One is the Baltika international folk festival (usually mid-July), which is a week of music, dance, exhibitions and parades focusing on Baltic and other folk traditions. The festival takes place in each Baltic capital in turn and is next due in Tallinn in 1998. The All-Estonian Song Festival, which climaxes with a choir of up to 30,000 people singing traditional Estonian songs on a vast open-air stage to an audience of 100,000, is held every five years, next in Tallinn in 1999.

Smaller annual festivals include: in June, the Tallinn Old Town Days; in late June, Pärnu's international music and theatre festival FiESTa; in early July, Tallinn Rock Summer, the biggest rock-music festival in Eastern Europe attracting crowds of 20,000; and in early August, the international organ music festival with concerts throughout Estonia.

ACTIVITIES
Cycling
Bicycle tours of Estonia, including farmhouse accommodation, are offered by AS Velo Ltd (☎ 6313 399; fax 472 867) at Sakala 11c, Tallinn. For bicycle rental try The Barn (☎ 443 465) at Väike-Karja 1, Tallinn, which hires bikes for 100 EEK a day, or Pirita Velodroom (☎ 239 148), which offers a day's rental for a bargain 30 EEK. The bicycle rental outlet in Tallinn at Tartu 73 offers a three-day deal for 75 EEK. See also Bicycle in the Getting Around section.

Sailing
Existing harbour facilities are being upgraded and there are ports at Nasva (☎ 245-75 140) on the island of Saaremaa, and at Lehtma (☎ 246-49 214) on the island of Hiiumaa. Yachts, skippered or unskippered, can be hired by the hour, week or day from the Olympic Yachting Centre (☎ 238 033), which operates out of the Pirita marina at Regati puiestee 1, Tallinn.

Winter Sports
Skiing (mainly cross-country) is extremely popular but there is little, if anything, on an organised basis for foreign visitors. The main skiing centre is Otepää in south-east Estonia where there are now several skiing centres that hire out equipment.

Sauna
The sauna is an Estonian institution that is relaxing, cleansing and on occasion comes close to being a religious experience. Most hotels have saunas: for the most luxurious experience, make a reservation at Tallinn's Hotel Olümpia (☎ 6315 333) where they have two saunas on the 26th floor with fantastic views from the plunge pool out over the Old Town to the islands in the bay. The saunas cost 200 EEK for one hour and fit eight to 10 people. Public saunas in town charge about 80 EEK per hour.

WORK
Unless you speak Estonian there is little temporary work for visitors, and even then you will have to work hard to convince your prospective employer that you can do something for them that a native Estonian couldn't. Most Westerners working here have been posted by companies back home.

The main possibilities lie with teaching English, a language which is in great demand throughout the Baltics. However, these *are* times of change and opportunity, and there is some scope for those with entrepreneurial ability who want to stay awhile and carve themselves a new niche – though, in Western terms, nobody can expect to get rich doing so.

The process of obtaining a work permit is arduous, not only involving official documentation from an Estonian company or organisation but a certificate of proof of accommodation from the city council (to be obtained by your landlord), and a medical examination which includes an AIDS test.

Contact the National Immigration Board (see Visas & Documents earlier in this section) for further details.

ACCOMMODATION

The Estonian Tourist Board (☎ 6411 420; fax 6411 432; e-mail tallinn@tourism .uninet.ee), Pikk 71, EE0001 Tallinn, has lists of hotels, camping grounds, motels and guesthouses throughout Estonia, as does the Tallinn tourist information centre (☎ & fax 6313 940), Raekoja plats 18, EE0001 Tallinn.

It's worth trying to book ahead wherever you plan to stay as vacancies, particularly during summer, can be scarce. Agents in other countries as well as in Tallinn itself can make bookings for you but they work mainly with the more expensive hotels and may charge a commission. See the Getting There & Away section for contact details.

Camping

There are a few tent-only camping grounds (*kämpingud*) and some that allow you to pitch a tent, but most camping grounds consist mainly of permanent wooden cabins, or even occasionally brick bungalows. Showers and toilets are usually communal. Camping grounds are usually open from June to August, and sometimes during part of May and September.

Hostels & Colleges

The Estonian Youth Hostel Association (Eesti Puhkemajade Organisatsioon) has 12 hostels in Estonia: three in Tallinn, two in Maardu (north-east), two in Harju county (north-west), one in Tõrva (south), one in Otepää and three in Pärnu. Most have from 15 to 40 places; some are open only a few months a year. Accommodation is mainly in small two to four-bed rooms (sheets are usually provided) with prices between 60 and 160 EEK a person.

Some hostels have cooking facilities, some supply meals, and some do neither. Hostel cards are not needed but they will get you a discount of between 15% and 30%, depending on the hostel. Advance bookings

are recommended for the Tallinn hostels and are made through the head office (☎ & fax 6461 595) at Tatari 39-310, Tallinn (open weekdays from 10 am to 5 pm).

The Estonian Youth Hostel Association cooperates with the Finnish Youth Hostel Association (SRM; ☎ 358-0 694 0377; fax 358-0 693 1349), Yrönkatu 38B, SF-00100 Helsinki, and Eurohostel (☎ 358-0 66 4452; fax 358-0 65 5044), Linnankatu 9, SF-00160 Helsinki.

Student rooms are another accommodation possibility, for around 60 to 200 EEK a person. Booking ahead is particularly advisable (see Places to Stay in Tartu).

Private Homes & Flats

There are a number of homestay organisations which will rent you a room in a private home, an excellent way to see more of what local life is really like. The following organisations are a good place to start:

CDS Reisid, Raekoja plats 17, EE0001, Tallinn (☎ 445 262; fax 6313 666; e-mail cds@zen .estpak.ee) – B&B with English-speaking families throughout Estonia, also Vilnius and Rīga, 295/445 EEK a single/double.

Family Hotel Service, Mere puiestee 6, Tallinn (☎ & fax 441 187) – rooms in flats throughout Estonia and St Petersburg from 198 to 460 EEK per person per night; also a few unoccupied flats.

Bed & Breakfast Rasastra Ltd, Sadama 11, EE0001, Tallinn (☎ & fax 602 091) – B&B in family homes and separate apartments throughout Estonia, Latvia, Lithuania and St Petersburg from US$15 per person a night.

Farmstays

The Estonian Farmers Union (ETKL; ☎ 683 410; fax 6311 045) at Liivalaia 12, Tallinn EE0106, runs a network of B&B accommodation based around 28 farms in rural and not-so-rural Estonia. Farms offer single or double rooms, private or shared bathroom facilities, in some cases a sauna, and meals on request, as well as a mind-boggling choice of activities including horse riding, hunting, fishing, boating, surfing, hiking, golfing and swimming. Prices start at around 300 EEK per night. Bookings are made through the head office.

Hotels

Hotel accommodation, especially in the mid and upper ranges, is extremely scarce in Estonia and Lithuania and must be booked in advance for the summer months. In Latvia, mid-range and expensive rooms are readily available year-round; however, there is a distinct shortage of low-budget accommodation.

Hotels – bottom end These are generally lower-grade old Soviet hotels with bare, dowdy, but usually tolerably clean rooms. Some have a shower and basin and a private toilet; in others you share smelly facilities with other rooms. Often the staff speak no English.

Hotels – middle & top end These are the better ex-Soviet hotels (usually former Intourist establishments) plus some new places (including some motels) built and at least partly run by Western companies. Prices for single/double rooms range from 500/750 EEK up to three or four times that. In all, the rooms are comfortable, and have private bathrooms.

FOOD

There are numerous decent restaurants in all three Baltic capitals, and a few in most other sizeable towns. There are many good cafés, too. You can also usually supply yourself with basic foods without much trouble: bread is easy to get from bakeries for around 5 EEK a loaf, and fruit and vegetables are readily available at the growing number of supermarkets. Freshly-baked cakes, breads and pastries can be picked up for dirt-cheap prices everywhere.

Most restaurants are completely Western in terms of the fare they offer and the service they provide. A few Soviet hangovers still lurk though, where you'll be offered a choice from a few starters, a couple of soups – one of which will almost always be *seljanka*, a rich meaty broth – and two or three meat courses (which come with a few vegetables).

Vegetarians may find life difficult, but a growing number of restaurants are recognising their existence and including at least one *taimetoit* (vegetarian dish) on the menu. Estonian specialities tend to be in the fishy realm, with smoked trout *(forrell)*, traditionally served with fried bread, being one of the best.

bread/white bread	*leib/sai*
starters	*eelroad*
salad	*salat*
soup	*supp*
meat	*liha*
beef	*looma*, pronounced 'LOH-ma'
pork	*sea*, pronounced 'SEE-ah'
chicken	*kana*
fish	*kala*
vegetables	*köögivili*
fruit	*puuvili*
cheese	*juust*
ice cream	*jäätis*
the bill	*arve*

DRINKS

Beer *(õlu)* is the favourite alcoholic drink in Estonia and the local product is much in evidence. Foremost is the Saku brewery's excellent range of medium strength, light beers, sold for around 10 EEK a bottle, and in restaurants and bars for around 25 EEK. Vodka *(viin)* and brandy *(konjak)*, legacies of Soviet times, are also still popular and sold in bars and restaurants by weight: a normal shot (bigger than the average Western measure) is 50g. Estonia also has its own liqueurs, most notoriously Vana Tallinn (Old Tallinn), a sickly-sweet syrup with a hard-hitting punch. Some Estonian cafés and bars serve *hõõgvein* (mulled wine), a warming local speciality.

ENTERTAINMENT

The three Baltic capitals are becoming increasingly happening places with every month that passes; while the university cities of Kaunas and Tartu, and the summer resorts of Pärnu, Jūrmala and Palanga, are more than active enough to satisfy the western traveller. In fact, the nightlife has developed so much

ESTONIA

in recent years that nostalgic theme bars and clubs recapturing the Soviet experience of just five years ago are beginning to sprout in the major cities. Rīga is considered the Baltic's clubbing (and casino) capital, Tallinn is the place to drink, whereas it is in Vilnius that the heart of fun theme bars and low-key dance parties is said to lie.

Classical music, opera and ballet feature strongly in all three cities with festivals of music, dance and theatre being an integral part of the entertainment and arts calendar. See the individual city sections for more details.

Getting There & Away

There are daily flights and numerous daily ferries between Helsinki and Tallinn. But Helsinki can be a relatively expensive place to reach, so consider the other options: direct flights to Estonia from several other countries; a ferry from Sweden; or the Baltic corridor through Lithuania and Latvia. Estonia also has direct connections with Warsaw, Moscow and Minsk. For any travel to or through parts of the CIS such as Russia, Belarus or Kaliningrad, look into the visa situation well in advance.

TRAVEL AGENCIES

Travel-industry professionals can help smooth your path with bookings (including cheap flights), accommodation assistance, visa information, and so on. The following is a wide-ranging selection of agents specialising to some degree in travel to the Baltic states. Some are tour operators as well. Consulates and embassies, and emigré organisations may also be able to help with information on charter flights or other economical ways of getting to the Baltic states.

Australia
   Gateway Travel, 48 The Boulevard, Strathfield, Sydney 2135, NSW (☎ 02-9745 3333; fax 02-9745 3237)

   Eastern Europe Travel Bureau, 75 King St, Sydney 2000, NSW (☎ 02-9262 1144; fax 02-9262 4479/3857)
Canada
   Acropolis & Baltic Travel, 1125 King St, East Hamilton, L8M 1E5 (☎ 905-545 2455; fax 905-545 3765)
   Canadian Gateway, 7000 Bathurst St, Toronto, Ontario L4J 7LI (☎ 800-668 8401; fax 416-660 7004)
Finland
   Estum, Vuorimiehenkatu 23A, Helsinki (☎ 09-62 92 99)
   Finnsov Tours, Eerinkatu 3, 00100 Helsinki (☎ 09-694 2011; fax 09-694 5534)
   Kilroy travels, Kaivokatu 10d, 00100 Helsinki (☎ 09-680 7811)
Germany
   KL Reisen, Raimundstrasse 157, D-6000, Frankfurt 1 (☎ 069-563 047; fax 069-561 045)
   Lernidee Reisen, Dudenstrasse 78, W-1000 Berline 61 (☎ 030-786 5056; fax 030-786 5596)
   Greif Reisen, Universitätsstrasse 2, 5810 Witten-Heven (☎ 0230-22 40 44)
   Reisebüro Alainis, Revalweg 4, 8940 Memmingen (☎ 08331-35 82)
Sweden
   Estlandsresor, Runebergsgatan 3, S-216 11 Malmö (☎ 040-15 22 66)
   Nordisk Reseservice, Engelbrektsgatan 18, S-10041 Stockholm (☎ 08-791 50 55)
UK
   Alpha-Omega Travel, Borodin House, Beaconsfield Centre, Garforth, Leeds LS25 1QH (☎ 0113-286 2121; fax 0113-286 4964)
   Explore Worldwide, 1 Frederick St, Aldershot, Hants GU11 1LQ (☎ 0125-231 9448; fax 0125-234 3170)
   Progressive Tours, 12 Porchester Place, London W2 2BS (☎ 0171-262 1676; fax 0171-724 6941)
   Regent Holidays, 15 John St, Bristol BS1 2HR (☎ 0117-921 1711; fax 0117-925 4866)
   ScanTours, 21-24 Cockspur St, 4th floor, Trafalgar Square, London SW1Y 5BW (☎ 0171-839 2927; fax 0171-839 4327)
USA
   Adventure Centre, 1311 63rd St, Suite 200, Emeryville, CA 94608 (☎ 800-227 8747; fax 510-654 1879)
   Baltic-American Holidays, 501, 5th Avenue, Suite 1605, New York, NY 10017 (☎ 212-972 0200)
   Baltic Tours, 77 Oak St, Suite 4, Newton, MA 02164 (☎ 617-965 8080)
   Intourist, 630 Fifth Avenue, Suite 868, New York, NY 10111 (☎ 212-757 3884; fax 212-459 0031)
   GT International, 9525 South 79th Avenue, Hickory Hills, Il 60457-2259 (☎ 708-430 7272)

STA Travel, 3730 Walnut St, Philadelphia PA 191 04 (☎ 215-382 2928; fax 215-382 4716) Worldwide Visas, Washington DC (☎ 800-692 0203; e-mail visas@imssys.imssys.com)

AIR
Routes

Western airlines and the national airline Estonian Air, which took to the air in former Aeroflot planes in 1992, operate in and out of Tallinn. Estonian Air flies to/from: Helsinki twice daily; Moscow, Minsk and Hamburg three times weekly; Vilnius and Amsterdam daily; Stockholm nine times weekly; Copenhagen twice weekly; and Frankfurt and Kiev three times weekly. Estonian Air is the only Baltic airline which still has two-tier prices.

Helsinki, Stockholm, and Frankfurt are also served with equal or greater frequency by Finnair, SAS and Lufthansa, respectively. The Western airlines offer worldwide connections via their hubs (Helsinki for Finnair etc). Also see the Latvia and Lithuania chapters for direct routes to Rīga and Vilnius, from where a bus or train can cheaply and easily be taken to Tallinn. See also Travel Between the Baltics later in this section.

Fares

Sometimes the cheapest fares are sold by 'general sales agents' – travel agents (often Baltic specialists) appointed by an airline to sell reduced-price tickets on certain routes – so it's worth asking an airline's reservations department whether there are any such agents.

In summer 1996 the cheapest flights from England to Tallinn were UK£226 with Lufthansa and around UK£246 with Estonian Air, SAS and Finnair. From Germany, Estonian Air and Lufthansa fly for similar fares, starting at around DM700 return. From Canada, KLM were offering the best prices at about US$850 for a return trip, which drops to US$550 out of season. Another option is to fly to Helsinki, Stockholm or Warsaw and complete your journey by sea or land. To fly Helsinki-Tallinn-Helsinki costs a minimum of US$86 with Finnair (if you

are under 25 years) or there's a US$108 'Apex' return, valid if you stay in Helsinki overnight on a Sunday. Estonian Air prices are similar.

Charter Flights Individuals can often buy seats on charter flights, or in block bookings on scheduled flights, from tour companies or with groups of emigrés returning to visit Estonia. Specialist travel agents and Estonian embassies are places to start asking. For charters from Germany contact Greif Reisen (see Travel Agencies above).

LAND
Bus

Europe Buses are the cheapest but least comfortable way of reaching the Baltic states. The Estonian bus company Mootorreise (☎ 6410 100; fax 6410 101) Lastekodu 46, EE0001 Tallinn, in cooperation with Eurolines, runs direct buses daily to Tallinn from Oslo, Stockholm, Frankfurt, Berlin, Munich and Stuttgart. One bus leaves Stuttgart at 7 am, departs from Berlin at 7.10 pm and arrives in Tallinn the following day at 10 pm, passing through Kaunas, Rīga and Pärnu on the way. Another bus leaves Munich at 9.30 am and arrives in Berlin in time for passengers to catch the Stuttgart bus. The Mootorreise booking agent in Germany is Deutsche Touring (☎ 030-252 34), Mausurenallee 4-6, Berlin.

The Tallinn Bus Company (*Tallinna Autobussikoondise*; ☎ 532 065, 532 063; fax 532 277), Kadaka tee 62a, EE0026 Tallinn, operates a bus twice weekly between Kiel and Tallinn, passing through Hamburg, Berlin, Rīga, and Pärnu. Tickets can be booked in Germany through Autokraft GmbH (☎ 0431 666 311), Von der Tann Strasse, 2300 Kiel 1.

In Tallinn tickets for both buses can be bought from the bus ticket office at Pärnu maantee 24 or from the international ticket booth marked *Ekspress Ja Kirbussilinide Kassa* on the right as you enter the main bus station.

Russia Buses leave Tallinn for St Petersburg daily at 7.30 am and 4 pm, arriving eight hours later. Tickets cost 122 EEK. There is also one bus daily from Tallinn to Kaliningrad. The bus departs from the main bus station in Tallinn each evening at 7.45 pm and a ticket costs 218 EEK.

Train
Poland You can reach the Baltics from most places in Western Europe with just a single change in Warsaw to the daily *Baltic Express*. The route is Warsaw-Šeštokai-Kaunas-Rīga-Valga-Tartu-Tallinn, and the trip takes 22 hours, which includes a transfer of trains at Šeštokai due to the different gauges. Departures at either end are in the afternoon and a one-way ticket is 624 EEK for a place in a four-berth coupe.

Russia Between St Petersburg and Tallinn there is one overnight train each way, taking nine hours for a fare of 176 EEK. From Moscow there is one train daily (leaving from the St Petersburg station) via Narva, taking from 17 hours for 437 EEK.

Car & Motorcycle
See the Getting Around chapter at the beginning of this book for general comments on driving and riding in the Baltic states. From Finland it's easier to put your vehicle on a Helsinki-Tallinn ferry than to drive round via St Petersburg with possible border delays and visa requirements. From Western Europe you can put your vehicle on a ferry from Kiel to Klaipėda (see Getting There & Away in the Lithuania chapter) which though expensive may be worth considering rather than braving the Polish-Lithuanian borders at Lazdijai or Kalvarija; this is the Baltics' only direct land link with Western Europe and you can be bogged down here for anything between one and 10 days. Check beforehand with a Polish embassy for the current situation if you are thinking of travelling to the Baltic states via this route.

SEA
Finland
The *Georg Ots*, *Vana Tallinn* and *Tallink* are all ferries run by the Finnish-Estonian joint

venture Tallink. All three sail from either Tallinn or Helsinki and make the return journey each day. One-way deck fares cost 225 EEK (students 175 EEK); a berth in a cabin costs 325 EEK. They take cars for 375 EEK, motorbikes for 125 EEK and minibuses for 750 EEK. Cabins can be occupied overnight in Helsinki before or after a crossing for 300 EEK. For booking in Estonia go to the Tallink office (☎ 6409 808, 6409 877) at Roosikrantsi 17; in Helsinki the booking office (☎ 09-2282 211; fax 09-635 337) is at Eteläranta 14. These ferries generally make the crossing in four hours.

Two further ferries, the *Silja Festival I & II*, also taking four hours, sail between Tallinn and Helsinki, leaving Tallinn at midnight and 3.30 pm. A one-way ticket on deck costs 380 EEK, and a cabin costs from 400 to 1350 EEK. Tickets can be booked direct through the Silija Line harbour office (☎ 6318 623) or through Baltic Tours (☎ 6318 331, 6313 255) at Aia 18 in Tallinn.

The *Laura* and *Liisa* are hydrofoils, also run by Tallink, which make six crossings each way daily from June to September. A one-way trip costs 250 EEK and takes two hours. For bookings contact Tallink (see details above).

Viking Express is a sleek, 450-seat jet catamaran operated by Viking Line (☎ 6318 193/6), Terminal C, Reisisadam, Tallinn; Makasiini Terminal (☎ 09-1235 432), Catamaran Harbour, Helsinki. It sails from Helsinki to Tallinn and back six times a day in summer and three times a day in winter, taking 1¾ hours each way. A one-way crossing costs around 340 EEK.

Other Countries
From Germany there is the twice-weekly Tallink-Hansaway service, departing from Travemünde and arriving in Tallinn 1½ days later. A berth in a cabin for four costs from 1600 EEK, a double cabin costs 2862 EEK and a budget couchette (only available in summer) costs 1215 EEK. Bookings are through the Tallink offices (see Finland above) or through Baltic Tours' city office

(☎ 440 760, 446 331) at Aia 18, and the port office (☎ 6318 331) at Sadama 25.

The two Estline ferries *Regina Baltica* and *Mare Balticum* sail daily between Tallinn and Stockholm in the summer. In winter just one of them sails each day. The trip takes around 13 hours. A one-way ticket costs 640 EEK, with a 160 EEK reduction for students. A berth in a two-bed/four-bed cabin costs an extra 400/200 EEK. A car costs 576 EEK. Tickets should be booked in advance through the Estline city office (☎ 666 579) at Aia 5a, at the Estline harbour office, which, at the time of writing, was expected to open shortly, or at the Estline terminal in the Frihamnen (Free Harbour) in Stockholm (☎ 08-667 0001).

ORGANISED TOURS

Regent Holidays (☎ 0117-921 1711; fax 0117-925 4866), 15 John St, Bristol BS1 2HR, UK, plans tours typically costing around UK£995 for 12 nights in the three Baltic states including visits to Saaremaa, Cēsis and Nida. It's also a good firm to contact for one-off special-interest tours.

The UK-based art-tour specialist Martin Randall Ltd (☎ 0181-742 3355; fax 0181-742 1066), 10 Barley Mow Passage, London W4 4PH, offers one-week northern capital tours encompassing Tallinn, Rīga and Helsinki for UK£1290. Architectural buffs should look no further than specialists ACE (☎ 01223-835 055; fax 01223-837 394), Babraham, Cambridge CB2 4AP, UK, who offer a one-week architectural tour of Estonia for UK£795 and plan a similar tour of Lithuania in 1997.

Intourist, the Russian state travel company, still does Baltics tours. Contact its many branches in capital and major cities worldwide.

TRAVEL BETWEEN THE BALTICS

One would assume, given that distances between the Baltic capitals are not too great, it should be fairly painless to travel, say, from Tallinn to Vilnius, or vice versa. This, however, is not the case. Train and bus services have been cut recently, meaning inter-Baltic buses are generally packed full, ensuring little sleep, and flights are prohibitively expensive.

The train and bus connections between the three Baltic capitals are listed below but there are other possibilities, for instance buses between Kaunas in Lithuania and Tallinn, and trains between Valmiera in Latvia and Tartu in Estonia – check the Getting There & Away sections of particular towns for more details.

Air

Estonian Air flies daily from Tallinn to Vilnius and back. Schedules change frequently but what are unlikely to alter much are the extortionate fares: an incredible US$600 return (Baltic citizens only pay a third of the 'foreigner' price). Air Baltic has flights linking all three Baltic cities. It has five flights weekly from Tallinn to Rīga and four flights weekly from Vilnius to Rīga. Round-trip fares start at US$215.

Bus

On Estonian bus tickets seat is *koht*; on Latvian and Lithuanian tickets, *vieta*. Bus services within the Baltics include:

Vilnius to Rīga – six buses daily (8 am, 9.45 am, 12.40 pm, 5.10 pm, 9.45 pm, 12.30 am) taking 5½ hours for US$5

Vilnius to Tallinn – three buses daily (8 am, 9.45 am, 9.45 pm) taking 12 hours for US$10

Rīga to Vilnius – four buses daily (8.10 am, 11.00 am, 12.20 pm, 3.20 am) taking 5½ hours for US$6. A speed bus which takes just four hours leaves daily at 5.40 pm

Rīga to Tallinn – five buses daily (7.20 am, 11.50 am, 1 pm, 5.10 pm, 3.30 pm) taking six hours for US$6

Tallinn to Vilnius – one overnight service leaving at 9.30 pm and arriving 12 hours later for US$15

Tallinn to Rīga – seven buses run daily (7 am, 9.40 am, 12.30 pm, 3 pm, 7.45 pm, 9.30 pm and 11.40 pm) taking six hours for US$9

Train

The most pleasant way of travelling the Baltic states is to take the overnight trains, such as the Rīga-Vilnius service which, though slower and bumpier than buses, are more comfortable and generally allow for a pleasant night's sleep.

For overnight travel you need to buy a *kupe* (coupe) class ticket which will give you a place in a four-berth compartment. Train tickets issued in the Baltic states are similar to those issued under the Soviet system. The date and departure time of your train will be on the top line, the second and third items, respectively, after the train number. Your carriage number is next to the time, followed by a letter denoting class (K = coupe). Your berth number (МЕСТА, the Russian for seat) is on the third line.

Carriage doors open 20 minutes or so before departure and trains usually leave on time. Soon after leaving the conductor will collect your ticket and for around the equivalent of US$1 you can hire sheets and blankets. The toilet is locked about 15 minutes before the train reaches a border crossing and not unlocked for a good 15 minutes after the crossing has been passed. Services include:

From Vilnius to Rīga trains depart at 2.27 am, 4 pm and 11.20 pm. The journey takes approximately seven hours and costs US$16.30 for a coupe class ticket
From Rīga to Vilnius the one overnight service departs at 11.15 pm and arrives 6.26 am the next day. A berth in a coupe costs US$16
From Tallinn to Rīga there are two trains (6.30 am and 11.30 pm), both taking eight or nine hours and costing US$12
From Rīga to Tallinn two trains (5.46 am and 10.30 pm) run, costing US$12

There is also the *Baltic Express* service leaving Tallinn each day at 5.45 pm and passing through Tartu, Valga, Rīga (arriving 12.25 am), Joniškis, Gubernija, Šiauliai (arriving 3.12 am), Radviliskis and Kaunas (arriving 5.50 am) before going on to Šeštokai where it connects with a Warsaw train. Heading north the *Baltic Express* leaves Kaunas at 12.09 am and goes as far as Tartu, where it arrives at 9.28 am.

LEAVING ESTONIA

There are no departure taxes to be paid and

no other formalities to be completed before leaving.

Getting Around

AIR

There are no domestic flights within Estonia or Latvia. For domestic flights within Lithuania see the Getting There & Away section in the Lithuania chapter.

BUS

Long-distance buses serve all major Baltic states towns. Buses are generally cheaper, more frequent and definitely faster than the train, though make sure you get an *ekspress* or *kiir* (fast). From Vilnius to Kaunas for instance, there are 20 buses a day compared with just a handful of trains. One drawback is that the buses have no toilet facilities but drivers are prepared to stop by the roadside.

TRAIN

In Estonia the most frequent train services, which are a bit more expensive than bus services, are on suburban routes to places of limited interest around Tallinn. Elsewhere, trains are slower and rarer than buses. In Latvia a good network of suburban (*piepilsetas*) trains provides the best transport option for many places within about 50 km of Rīga, but on longer routes rail services are generally poorer than bus services.

CAR & MOTORCYCLE

Having a car at your disposal is by far the best way to travel around the Baltics. One of the rare benefits of the Soviet occupation – and Moscow's penchant for tanks – is that the major routes connecting urban centres are well defined and in good condition. Western-quality leaded and unleaded petrol is available at 24-hour Shell, Neste, Statoil and Texaco petrol stations found at strategic points in all the major Baltic cities and highways.

Car repair is something of a headache with spare parts often hard to come by, but local mechanics are nothing if not inventive. As car ownership is far less common than in Western countries, parking is not a problem. Your biggest headache is likely to be security as car theft, and theft from cars, is rife. Park in well-lit places, come with an alarm fitted to your car and use a steering lock.

See the Getting Around chapter at the beginning of this book for information on driving and riding in the Baltics. See the Tallinn, Rīga and Vilnius Getting There & Away sections for information on car rentals and repairs.

BICYCLE
The Baltic states are predominantly flat, with good roads and light traffic, and distances between urban centres are relatively small, which makes cycling the ideal way of getting around. However, bike rental is limited (see Activities in Facts for the Visitor in this chapter) so bring your own two wheels.

HITCHING
Hitching is an accepted, and increasingly common, way of getting around.

LOCAL TRANSPORT
Baltic cities and towns have good networks of buses, trolleybuses and trams usually running from 6 am to midnight. You pay for your ride by punching a ticket in one of the ticket-punches fixed inside the vehicle. In Estonia tickets (piletid) are sold from street kiosks displaying them in the window or can be purchased from the driver. Buy five or 10 at once. Ten-day passes costing 60 EEK as well as 20 and 30-day passes (kuupilet) can also be bought from the same kiosks. Ticket inspection is rare but on-the-spot fines are levied.

In Lithuania there is no tram system.

Taxi
Taxis are supposed to cost a minimum of 4 EEK a km in Estonia or 0.20 lati a km in Latvia, which makes them prohibitively expensive for long-distance journeys. Taxis in Estonia (forget the Ladas – they're all snazzy Western-made cars in Estonia) are by far the most efficient of all three Baltics. Taxi stands are marked takso.

ORGANISED TOURS
The Kodukant Ecotourism Initiative (e-mail ecotour@jsoft.fido.ee), Saarisso, EE3482 Jõesuu, Pärnu, Estonia, which receives funding from the Swedish Environmental Protection Agency, organises cultural and nature tours based on low-impact tourism to protected areas around Estonia. Areas they tour include the bird lovers' paradises of Matsalu Nature Reserve and Käina Bay, Karula National Park in southern Estonia and the Hiiumaa Islets Landscape Reserve. It also arranges special interest tours such as bird-watching, horse riding, skiing etc. Tour bookings can be made through Haapsalu Travel Service (☎ 47-450 37; fax 47-443 35), Karja 7, EE3170 Haapsalu, or Mere Travel Bureau (☎ 51-250 100; fax 45-544 61; e-mail lii@evk.oesel.ee), Pikk 60, EE3300 Kuressaare.

CDS Reisid Travel Agency (☎ 445 262; fax 6313 666; e-mail cds@zen.estpak.ee), Raekoja plats 17, Tallinn, organises 1½-hour walking tours of Tallinn between May and September, costing 45 EEK and starting at 2 pm from its office. It also arranges a variety of day trips including one to Paldiski, the former closed Soviet military base and submarine training school, 50 km west of Tallinn. The base was opened for the first time since WWII in 1994, following the shut-down of the nuclear submarine station in 1992 and the withdrawal of Russian troops.

Viru Tour (☎ 6563 006; fax 6563 000) offers an impressive range of one, two, three, four and six-day tours around Estonia as well as short medieval or panoramic tours of Tallinn.

Tallinn

Tallinn (population 442,000) fronts a bay on the Gulf of Finland and is dominated by Toompea, the hill over which it has tumbled

ESTONIA

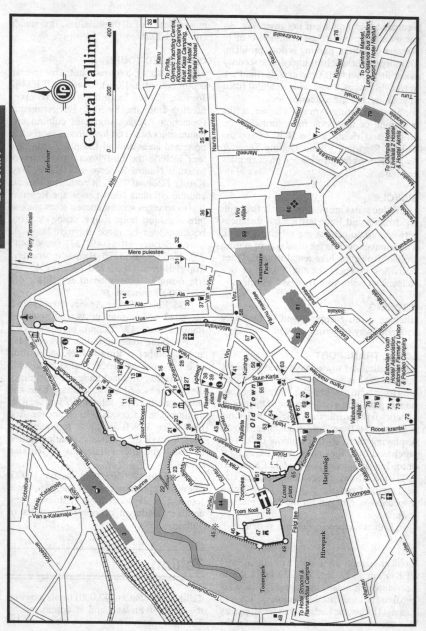

Central Tallinn

0   200   400 m

Harbour

To Ferry Terminals

To Pirita,
Olympic Yachting Centre,
Kloostrimetsa Camping,
Must Kass Camping,
Mahtra Hostel &
Vikerlase Hostel

To Central Market,
Long-Distance Bus Station,
Airport & Hotel Neptun

To Olümpia Hotel,
Hotell Peoleo
& Hostel Akmis

To Estonian Youth
Hostels Association,
Estonian Farmer's Union
& Peoleo Camping

To Hotel Stroomi &
Ramandisa Camping

Old Town

ESTONIA

PLACES TO STAY		OTHER		37	Bel Air
33	Dorell	3	Train Station	39	CDS Reisid Travel
35	Central Hotel	4	Local Bus Station		Agency
43	Hotel Eeslitall &	5	Great Coast Gate, Fat	40	Tourist Information
	Restaurant		Margaret Bastion &		Centre
48	Hotel Tallinn		Sea Museum	42	Town Hall
56	The Barn	6	Estonia Ferry Disaster	44	Toom Kirik
59	Hotel Viru		Memorial	45	Lookout Point
76	Hotel Palace	7	Estonian Tourist Board	47	Toompea Castle &
78	Hotel Kungla	8	Oleviste Church		Parliament
		10	Diesel Boots	49	Pikk Hermann
PLACES TO EAT		11	Applied Art Museum	50	Alexandr Nevsky
1	Peetri Pizza	12	Tehas N° 43		Cathedral
2	Wagon Iits	13	Hell Hunt	51	Von Krahl Theatre Bar
9	Teater	14	Baltic Tours	52	Niguliste Church
20	Peetri Pizza	15	City Museum	55	Nimeta Baar
26	Grill Mexicana	16	Brotherhood of	58	Viru Gate
28	Controvento		Blackheads & St	60	Kaubamaja
31	Paan		Olaus' Guild		(Department Store)
34	Primavera	17	Russian Embassy	61	Estonia Theatre &
38	Maharaja Restaurant	18	Drakon Gallery &		Concert Hall
41	Gnoom Grill		Maiasmokk	62	Estonia Drama Theatre
46	Toomkooli	19	History Museum	64	Estravel
53	Wana Tunnel	21	Puppet Theatre	66	George Brownes
54	Hõbe Kass	22	Patkuli Trepp (Steps)	68	Kiek-in-de-Kök Tower
57	Mamma Mia	23	Lookout Point	71	Kaarli Kirik Church
63	Vesi Veski	24	Lookout Point	72	Tallink Office
65	Neitsitorn	25	Pikk Jalg Gate Tower	73	Bus Ticket Office
67	Pizza Americana	27	Holy Spirit Church	75	Max Marine
69	Metropole	29	Dominican Monastery	79	Stockmann
70	Wiiralti	30	Estline City Office		(Supermarket)
74	Peetri Pizza	32	Family Hotel Service		
77	Ervin's Mexican Kitchen	36	Main Post Office		

since the Middle Ages. The aura of the 14th and 15th centuries survives intact in central Tallinn's jumble of medieval walls and turrets, spires and winding cobbled streets; the area has been judiciously restored and it's fascinating to explore. Tallinn is also a national capital, with government buildings, a university, entertainment, and modern styles on its streets. Finns flock over from Helsinki at weekends, more often than not for a cheap shopping spree.

Tallinn is on a similar latitude to St Petersburg and shares that city's summer 'white nights' and short, dark winter days.

History
The Danes set a up castle and a bishop on Toompea (pronounced 'TOM-pe-ah') in 1219. German traders arrived and Tallinn joined the Hanseatic League in 1285, becoming a link between Novgorod, Pskov and

the West. Exports included furs, leather and seal fat.

By the mid-14th century, after the Danes had sold northern Estonia to the German knights, Tallinn was a major Hanseatic town with about 4000 residents. The merchants and artisans in the lower town built a fortified wall to separate themselves from the bishop and knights on Toompea. Many of Tallinn's characteristic German-style buildings were constructed at this time. The city's German name, Revel or Reval, coexisted for centuries with the local name, Tallinn.

The prosperity faded in the 16th century as Swedes, Russians, Poles and Lithuanians fought over the Baltic region. Sweden held Tallinn from 1561 to 1710, then Russia took over. The city grew in the 19th century and by WWI had shipyards and a population of 150,000. In 1944 thousands of buildings were destroyed by Soviet bombing. After

WWII industry was developed and Tallinn expanded quickly, much of the population growth owing to immigration from outside Estonia. Only around half Tallinn's population today is Estonian.

Orientation

Tallinn spreads south from Tallinn Bay, which lies between two promontories jutting north into the Gulf of Finland. The city centre (or the Old Town), just south of the bay, is essentially two parts: Toompea (the upper town) and the lower town.

Toompea is the hill on which Tallinn has always been centred, covered in old cobbled streets and protected on the north, south and west by steep slopes. The lower town, also medieval, spreads round the eastern foot of Toompea, still surrounded by much of its 2.5-km defensive wall. Its centre is Raekoja plats (Town Hall Square). Around the Old Town is a belt of green parks which follows the line of the city's original moat defences. On this green belt are a number of places useful for orientation: Vabaduse väljak, the centre of the city today; the train station (Balti jaam), north-west of the Old Town, and the tall slab of the Hotel Viru, just outside the eastern edge of the Old Town, a major landmark.

Information

Tourist Offices There is an excellent tourist information centre (☎ 2-6313 940; fax 2-6313 941) at Raekoja plats 18 offering a range of services.

An equally useful tourist office is at Tallinn harbour (☎ 2-6318 321) at Sadama 25. The Estonian Tourist Board (☎ 2-6411 420; fax 2-6411 432; e-mail tallinn @tourism.unient .ee) is at Pikk 71.

Ekspress hotline (☎ 2-6313 222) is a free phone information service (in English) offering advice on anything and everything.

Money There are exchange counters just about everywhere you turn: in the airport, the sea passenger terminal, the train station, the main post office and at all banks and major hotels. The currency exchange bureau inside the Hotel Viru opens from 8 am to 8 pm, as does the exchange in the Old Town at Viru 20, which also gives cash advance on Visa.

There is a 24-hour currency exchange inside the Hotel Olümpia. Close by at Liivalaia 51 is *Hansapank* which accepts every currency under the sun as well as most credit cards. Branches of Hansapank (Aia 1) and Tallinna Bank (Pärnu maantee 10) will also issue cash on Visa, MasterCard, Eurocard and Diners Club. Cash can also be drawn on Visa at the ATM in the foyer of the Hotel Viru and the foyer of the Hansapank at Liivalaia 12.

Travellers' cheques can be cashed at the Viru and Olümpia hotels' service bureaus. As the official agents for American Express, Estravel (☎ 2-6266 206; fax 2-6266 262; e-mail sales@estravel.ee) at Suur-Karja 15 can replace lost American Express travellers' cheques or cards.

Post & Communications The main post office is at Narva maantee 1 on the north side of Viru väljak. Telegrams and faxes can only be sent from window No 45 on the 2nd floor. Public card phones from which international calls can be made are all over town and at the post office. The international phones in the foyers of the Olümpia and Viru hotels only accept chip cards available from the hotel reception. These cards cannot be used in any other phones.

The telephone area code for Tallinn is 2 (no area code when calling from abroad).

Travel Agencies The travel agency Carol (☎ 454 900; fax 6313 918), at Lembitu 4, is a good source of information for budget travellers. Another leading travel and tour company is Estravel, which has branches at Suur-Karja 15 (☎ 6266 206), Liivalaia 12 (☎ 6461 461) and Narva maantee 9a (☎ 6302 202). Estonian Holidays (☎ 6301 930; fax 6301 900; e-mail holidays@holi days.ee) in the Hotel Viru at Viru Välijak 4 and at Pärnu maantee 12 (☎ 6314 109) offers some good budget deals as does the much-recommended CDS Reisid (☎ 445 262; fax 6313 666; e-mail cds@zen.estpak.ee) next to the tourist information centre at Raekoja plats 17.

Bookshops Viruvärava Raamatukauplus at Viru 23 stocks a fine choice of Western books and Baltic maps, including the 1:25,000 *Tallinn City Plan*, published in 1996 with a street index and keys in Estonian, Russian, English and German. It costs 35 EEK. The 1:500,000 *Estonia Road Map* is also worth picking up while you are here. Kuper at Harju 1 has a large range of locally produced guides and maps of various parts of Estonia. ARP at Voorimehe 9 has a small selection of second-hand English books.

Laundry There are two laundrettes close to the city centre, at Pärnu maantee 48 (opposite the Kosmos cinema) and at Liivalaia 26. Cost per machine (which takes a five-kg load) is around 50 EEK. Service wash is available for an extra charge.

Left Luggage There's a left-luggage room *(pakihoid)* at the main ferry terminal, another at the bus station by the main street entrance (called *käsipakkide hoiurruum*), and one at the train station.

Medical & Emergency Services There's a hospital with emergency medical services at Sütiste tee 19 in Mustamäe, a south-western suburb (☎ 525 652; open 24 hours, seven days a week), and at Ravi 18 (☎ 661 234), near the Hotel Olümpia (weekdays from 9 am to 6 pm). An Estonian-Finnish Medical Centre (☎ 238 376) is at Regati 1. Baltic Medical Partners (☎ 6311 222) is a Western-standard dental practice at Toompuiestee 4. The pharmacies at Pärnu maantee 10, Vene 1 and Rävala puiestee 7 sell Western medicines. To call an ambulance dial ☎ 003. The operators do not speak English.

Things to See
Walking Tour A good place to start exploring old Tallinn is the twin towers of the **Viru Gate**, once the easternmost of the six entrances in the lower town walls. From the gate continue along Viru to the corner of

Vene, surrounded by tall 15th to 17th-century houses and warehouses, then into **Raekoja plats**, the heart of the lower town. From here you can climb Pikk jalg to **Toompea**, or walk north up Pikk to Fat Margaret, the northern bastion of the lower town, and return south along Lai or Laboratooriumi.

Raekoja Plats & Around Wide Raekoja plats (Town Hall Square) has been the centre of Tallinn life since markets began here probably in the 11th century (the last was held in 1896). It's dominated by the only surviving Gothic **town hall** (1371-1404) in northern Europe, the seat of medieval power in the lower town. Its spire is 17th century but Vana Toomas (Old Thomas), the warrior-and-flag weather vane at its top, has guarded Tallinn since 1530. Tours of the town hall are available on request and highlights include the intricately painted main chamber and the guest book with its signatures of Gorbachev, Dan Quayle and the Dalai Lama.

The **Raeapteek** (Town Council Pharmacy) on the north side of Raekoja plats is another ancient Tallinn institution: there's been a pharmacy or apothecary's shop here since at least 1422, though the present façade is 17th century. An arch beside it leads into short, narrow Saia käik (White Bread Passage), at the far end of which is the 14th-century Gothic **Holy Spirit Church** (Pühavaimu Kirik), used by Lutherans. Its clock is the oldest in Tallinn, with carvings from 1684 and a tower bell cast in 1433. Inside is a 1483 wooden altarpiece. A medieval merchant's home at Vene 17, on the corner of Pühavaimu, houses the **City Museum** (Linnamuuseum), devoted mainly to Tallinn in the 18th and 19th centuries (open daily except Tuesday).

Also on Vene (Estonian for 'Russian', so named for the number of Russian merchants who used to inhabit this street), look for an 1844 Catholic church set back from the street with the inscription *Hic Vere Est Domus Dei*. A door in the courtyard leads into the **Dominican Monastery** (Dominiiklaste Klooster), founded in 1246, which was home base for the Scandinavian monks who played a big role in converting Estonia to Christianity and starting education in Tallinn. Once wealthy, it was plundered during the Reformation in 1524 and burnt in 1531, but the cloister and surrounding rooms are rich in 15th to 17th-century stonecarving. The monastery is open in summer only, daily except Monday.

A minute's walk south of Raekoja plats, **Niguliste Church** has an early Gothic north doorway, but is mostly 15th century. It is now used for organ recitals and as a museum of medieval church art. It's open Wednesday from 2 to 6 pm, Thursday to Sunday 11 am to 6 pm, unless there's a concert on.

At the foot of the slope below the Niguliste is the carefully exposed wreckage of the buildings that stood here before the Soviet bombing of Tallinn on the night of 9 March 1944. A sign facing Harju details the damage done that night.

Toompea The best approach to Toompea is through the red-roofed 1380 **gate tower** at the west end of Pikk in the lower town, and up Pikk jalg (Long Leg). The 19th-century Russian Orthodox **Alexandr Nevsky Cathedral** dominates Lossi plats at the top of Pikk jalg. Estonia's governing body meets in the pink, classical-style **Parliament building** at the western end of Lossi plats. The Parliament building is an 18th-century addition to **Toompea Castle**, Estonia's traditional seat of power. Nothing remains of the original 1219 Danish castle. However, still standing are three of the four corner towers of its successor, the Knights of the Sword's Castle. The finest of these towers is the 14th-century **Pikk Hermann** (Tall Hermann) at the south-west corner. Sixteenth-century shell scars are visible on its walls.

The Lutheran **Toom Kirik** (Dome Church), at the north end of Toom-Kooli, dates mostly from the 15th and 17th centuries but the tower dates from 1779. Inside are many fine carved tombs. One of those on the right as you approach the altar bears life-size figures of the 16th-century Swedish commander Pontus de la Gardie and his wife. The Swedish siege of Narva, where de la Gardie

died, is depicted on the side of their sarcophagus.

The marble Greek temple-style sarcophagus belongs to Admiral Samuel Greigh, an 18th-century Scot who joined the Russian navy and became a hero of Russo-Turkish sea battles.

Across from the Dome Church, at Kiriku plats 1, is an 18th-century noble's house, now home to the **Estonian Art Museum** (Kunstimuuseum), open Wednesday to Monday from 11 am to 6 pm.

A path leads down from Lossi plats through a hole in the walls to an open space where, in summer, artists paint portraits. One of the towers here, the **Virgin's Tower** (Neitsitorn), has been turned into a popular café, with good views (see Places to Eat).

Nearby **Kiek-in-de-Kök**, a tall tower built in about 1475, is a museum with several floors of maps, weapons and models of old Tallinn, which also doubles as a photographic gallery. Its name is Low German for 'Peep into the Kitchen' – from the upper floors a watch could be kept over the entire lower town, even the kitchens, and the views are still great. It's open daily except Monday.

Lower Town North Pikk, running north from Raekoja plats to the **Great Coast Gate** – the medieval exit to Tallinn port – is lined with the houses of medieval merchants and gentry, many of them built in the 15th century. Also here are the buildings of several old Tallinn guilds. Pikk 17 is the 1440 building of the Great Guild, to which the most important merchants belonged. Today it houses the **History Museum** (Ajaloomuuseum) featuring Estonian history up to the mid-19th century, with labelling in English. It's open daily except Wednesday from 11 am to 6 pm.

Across from the museum is **Maiasmokk** (Sweet Tooth), a café that has existed in almost its present state since Estonia's first period of independence. Next door, at Pikk 18, is the **Drakon gallery** with its fantastically sculpted façade of dragons and semi-nude maidens, built in 1911 by a merchant who had spent time in the East.

Pikk 20, with statues of Martin Luther and St Canutus, dates only from the 1860s, but the site had already housed **St Canutus' Guild** for several centuries. Its members were mainly German master artisans.

Pikk 24 and 26 are the adjoining buildings of the **Brotherhood of Blackheads** and **St Olaus' Guild**. The Blackheads were unmarried, mainly foreign merchants who took their name from their patron saint, Mauritius. His head is between two lions on the building's façade (dating from 1597).

Further north on Pikk, immediately beyond the four-storey beige block that used to house the headquarters of the KGB, the tower of **Oleviste Church** is a chief Tallinn landmark. The church is dedicated to the 11th-century King Olav II of Norway but linked in local lore with another Olav (Olaf), the church's legendary architect, who fell to his death from the 120-metre tower. It's said a toad and snake then crawled out of his mouth. The incident is recalled in one of the carvings on the eastern wall of the 16th-century Chapel of Our Lady adjoining the church. Most of the church was rebuilt to resemble something close to its original Gothic appearance after a fire in the 1820s.

The Great Coast Gate is joined to **Fat Margaret** (Paks Margareeta), the rotund 16th-century bastion which protected this entrance to the Old Town. Its walls are more than four metres thick at the base. Inside is the **Sea Museum** (Meremuuseum), open daily except Monday and Tuesday from 10 am to 6 pm. There are great views from the platform on the roof.

In the grounds stands a white cross erected in 1995 in memory to the victims of the *Estonia* ferry disaster, now considered Europe's worst peacetime maritime tragedy. More than 900 people died when the popular Estline ferry sank en route between Stockholm and Tallinn.

While Pikk was a street of traders, **Lai**, running roughly parallel, was the street of artisans. Testament to this is the **Applied Art Museum** (Tarbekunstimuuseum), in a 17th-century granary at No 17, with excellent ceramics, glass, rugs, metalwork and leather-work. It's open daily except Tuesday from 11 am to 6 pm.

Suur-Kloostri leads past the former **St Michael's Convent** to the longest-standing stretch of the **Lower Town Wall**, with nine towers marching back along Laboratooriumi to the north end of Lai.

Kadriorg To reach the pleasant, wooded **Kadriorg Park** with its pretty wooden houses, two km east of the Old Town along Narva maantee, take tram No 1 or 3, or bus No 1 from Pärnu maantee in front of Tammsaare Park, to the Kohvik (café) Kadriorg. The park itself, and the 1718-36 **Kadriorg Palace** (Kadrioru Loss) in the park at Weizenbergi tee 37, were designed for the Russian tsar Peter the Great by the Italian Niccolo Michetti, soon after Peter's conquest of Estonia in the Great Northern War. The palace is now the residence of the president of Estonia.

Maarjamäe & Pirita One km north of Kadriorg, at Pirita tee 56, **Maarjamäe Palace** (Maarjamäe Loss) contains the mid-19th century onwards section of the Estonia History Museum, open from Wednesday to Sunday.

Some 1.5 km beyond Maarjamäe, just before Pirita tee crosses the Pirita River, a side road leads down to Pirita Yacht Club and the **Olympic Yachting Centre** at the mouth of the river, the base for the 1980 Olympic sailing events. International regattas are still held here. In summer you can rent rowing boats and pedalos beside the bridge where Pirita tee crosses the river. North of the bridge are a beach backed by pine woods, and the 15th-century Swedish **Convent of St Birgitta**, ruined by war in 1577 (open daily except Monday). Bus Nos 1, 8 and 34 run between the city centre and Pirita, stopping at Kohvik Kadriorg en route.

Along Paldiski Maantee Paldiski maantee leads west out of town from the Hotel Tallinn. A large, informal **bazaar** with many imported goods is held on Saturday and Sunday mornings at Mustjõe, three km out on the north side of the road. About one km further, Vabaõhumuuseumi tee branches right to **Rocca al Mare**, another 1.5 km away, where wooden buildings from 18th and 19th-century rural Estonia have been assembled in the **Estonian Village Museum**. You can walk in the woods or down to the sea. The museum is open daily from 10 am to 7 pm from June to September, and from 10 am to 5 pm between October and May. On Saturday and Sunday mornings there are folk song and dance shows. Bus No 21 from the train station, and bus No 45 from Vabaduse väljak, go to the bazaar and Rocca al Mare.

Places to Stay

Camping Top camp sites include *Peoleo* (☎ 771 601; fax 771 463), 10 km from Tallinn at Pärnu maantee 555. It has 50 parking places, a great deal more tent spaces and saunas, showers and a small catering service. *Kloostrimetsa*, slightly out of Tallinn at Kloostrimetsa maantee 6, also comes highly recommended. *Must Kass Camping* (☎ 723 881) is 29 km from Tallinn on the road to St Petersburg at St Peterburi maantee, and *Rannamõisa* (☎ 716 332), eight km from Tallinn on the road to Haapsalu at Rannamõisa, has 132 places. Take bus No 108 or 126 from beside Tallinn train station

Hostels At present there are three hostels in Tallinn operated by the Estonian Youth Hostel Association (see Accommodation in the Facts for the Visitor section). The *Vikerlase* (☎ 6327 781; fax 6327 715), at Vikerlase 15, in the unappealing suburb of Lasnamäe has 15 or so basic two to three-bed 'family' rooms with showers and toilets shared between three rooms for 105 EEK per person. HI members get a 10 EEK discount. To get there take bus No 35 from outside the Tallinna food store at Narva maantee 2 and get off 10 minutes later at the Pikri stop; cross the road and walk down Pikri, turning left onto Vikerlase at the end.

To reach the *Mahtra* (☎ 218 828), a further 10-minute journey by bus No 35, get off at the third stop after Pikri, at Mahtra 44

where the hostel is. Beds here cost 100 EEK a night unless you have a HI card in which case you pay just 60 EEK.

The *Merevaik* (☎ 529 604) is a similar establishment with the addition of a common room and kitchens for self-catering. The overnight fee is 100 EEK. Take trolleybus No 2 or 3 from diagonally opposite the Hotel Palace and get off at the Linnu tee stop. The hostel is 100 metres along the street at Sõpruse puiestee 182.

Privately run is the central *Liivalaia 2 Hostel* (☎ 446 143, 6461 130) at Liivalaia 2. Beds in shared rooms cost 90 EEK a night. Take tram No 3 or 4 to the Kino Kosmos stop. Close by is *Hostel Akmis* (☎ 454 964), also privately run, at Lauteri 3. Prices start at 70 EEK.

The Barn (☎ 443 465) has a dream location 30 seconds walk from Raekoja plats. Prices have gone up, however, since it moved to its new location at Väike-Karja 1 in mid-1996 (don't be put off by the nonstop striptease sign outside for the next-door bar; it's not that seedy). Rooms with three or five bunk-beds cost 160/150 EEK with/without bedding. A private double/family room costs 400/700 EEK. Breakfast costs an extra 25 EEK; a cheaper bet is to pop into the Balti Sepik bakery a few doors down at Suur-Karja 5 where excellent breads and pastries, still warm, are sold.

Private Homes See Accommodation in the Facts for the Visitor section of this chapter.

Hotels – bottom end The drab 50-room *Hotel Neptun* (☎ 215 431) at Asunduse 15, 2.5 km south-east of the centre, has clean singles and doubles with bath for 150/240 EEK. Bus No 39 goes there from the corner of Tartu maantee and Pronksi. Much closer to the centre is the *Dorell* (☎ 585 414) at Karu 39 (take tram No 1 or 3 from the Viru stop to the Kreutzwaldi stop, walk back 10 metres and go through the arch on your right), which offers 17 sparse double rooms with shared toilets for 200 EEK a night.

Cheaper, but a fair way from the centre, is *Bris* (☎ 601 390) at Tööstuse 50. Singles start at 100 EEK a night. Also good value is the *EHI Hotel* (☎ 521 615) at Sütiste tee 21 in the suburb of Mustamäe, which has 32 comfortable rooms with shared showers for 170 EEK, and with private bath for 400 EEK. Take bus No 17 or 17a from Vabaduse väljak.

Hotels – middle One of the best hotels in this range is the *Hotel Eeslitall* (☎ 6313 755) in the Old Town and a minute's walk from Raekoja plats, at Dunkri 4. Below is the popular Eeslitall restaurant, giving guests the chance to pop downstairs to the great courtyard for breakfast in the sun. Singles/doubles cost 350/485 EEK.

The large Soviet-style *Hotel Kungla* (☎ 6305 325) at the junction of Gonsiori and Kreutzwaldi claims to have a three-star rating and offers small, single/doubles with en-suite bathrooms for 380/490 EEK. Similarly Soviet is the *Hotel Tallinn* (☎ 6264 111) at Toompuieste 27, just to the west of Toompea, with gloomy singles/doubles at 450/600 EEK, but offering an abundance of services.

Out of the centre, but a better deal, is the *Hotel Stroomi* (☎ 6304 200) at Tšaikovski 11 in the suburb of Pelguranna, five km north-west of Vabaduse väljak by bus No 40. The 150 clean rooms with cable TV and showers start at 315 EEK and rise to 1290 EEK.

A more up-market option is the two-storey *Hotel Pirita* (☎ 6398 600) on the seafront at Regati puiestee 1 by the Olympic Yachting Centre, just south of the Pirita River. Singles/doubles cost 600/800 EEK. Bus No 8 from the train station and Nos 1 and 34 from Narva maantee, 400 metres east of the Hotel Viru, all stop on Pirita tee, a minute's walk from the Pirita.

Hotels – top end Tallinn's top hotel is the 91-room *Hotel Palace* (☎ 6407 300; fax 6407 299) at Vabaduse väljak 3, renovated to 'international four-star standards' by Scandinavian companies in 1989. The elegant, if not huge, rooms cost 2200/2800 EEK singles/doubles, but at weekends drop to 1400/2000 EEK. In Helsinki you can book

through Arctia Hotel Partners (☎ 09-696 901; fax 09-698 958).

Favoured for its 24-hour currency exchange, Café Boulevard and 95 EEK breakfast popular with people arriving in Tallinn early in the morning, is the *Hotel Oliimpia* (☎ 6315 333; fax 6315 675; e-mail hotell@olympia.ee), 700 metres south of the Old Town at Liivalaia 33. Singles/doubles start at 1300/1600 EEK.

Ugly from the outside but more attractive inside is the ever-popular, former Intourist flagship *Hotel Viru* (☎ 6301 311) at Viru väljak 4, always packed with guests of Scandinavian descent. Singles/doubles start at 1040/1360 EEK. Open since 1850, the exclusive *Hotel Rataskaevu* (☎ 442 939; fax 443 688), Rataskaevu 7, was formerly a closed hotel, and even today guests have to wait for the doorman to unlock the door. The décor is fascinating though and worth the 970/1180 EEK if you've got the cash.

The cheapest of the most expensive is the fairly new and very friendly *Central Hotel* (☎ 438 858) at Narva maantee 7. Singles/doubles cost 800/990 EEK

Places to Eat
For most of the restaurants given below it is advisable to make a reservation, especially at weekends.

Restaurants One of the first Western-style restaurants to open in Tallinn, and still unrivalled, is the *Maharaja Restaurant* at Raekoja plats 13, open from noon to 5 pm and 7 pm to 2 am. The Indian dishes they serve are authentic and worth the 250 to 300 EEK per head you'll end up paying.

Spaghetti lovers should head straight for the Baltic's best Italian restaurant, *Controvento*, tucked down an alleyway in the Old Town off Vene 12. The salads are heavenly, the carbonara authentically creamy, and the décor inside the old granary a sheer delight. Main dishes start at 60 EEK. It's open daily from 12.30 pm to 2.30 pm and 6.30 to 10.30 pm. Less refined and cheaper pasta is dished up at the Italian-inspired *Primavera*, next to the Central Hotel at Narva maantee 7.

ESTONIA

Just off Raekoja plats, at Dunkri 4, is *Eeslitall*, a fairly calm, laid-back place with a good cellar bar and an enjoyable courtyard round the back. It is open until 1 am. The old favourite *Toomkooli*, up on Toompae at Toom-Kooli 13, remains as popular as ever for its fantastic views of the city.

At Lai 23 in the cellar is the *Teater* restaurant serving mammoth portions of jambalaya, gumbo and filling daily specials for 67 EEK.

Paan, close to the Viru Hotel at Mere puiestee 5 is a must for late-night eaters. With just 28 seats this exclusive bistro serves mouth-watering French-inspired fare and is the only place in town open daily from noon until 6 am. *Ervin's Mexican Kitchen* at Tartu maantee 50 has Tex Mex dishes as well as lots of tequila, beer and flamenco dancers (open weekdays from noon to 11 pm and on weekends from noon to 3 am).

Pirita, at Merivälja 5, boasting fine sea views, has a special vegetarian menu, as does the less formal *Baar Vegan* in the Old Town at Uus 22. For dinner in a medieval water tunnel, try *Wana Tunnel* inside the Tallinn Business Centre at Harju 6 (open 1 pm to midnight). A step back in time to Tallinn's Soviet delights can be taken at the *Gnoom* grill, near Raekoja plats at Viru 2. It has a fine spacious 15th-century stone interior but the menu is overpriced and uninspired, and the service lousy from the time it opens at noon to when it closes at midnight.

Cafés In the Old Town at Harju 9 the popular *Hõbe Kass* (Silver Cat) café has a limited selection of good, inexpensive hot food including sardelid (spicy sausage) and omelettes for 16 EEK. *Vesi Veski* at Suur-Karja 17/19 has no hot food but lots of savoury pastries and home-made cakes. For the best Danishes in town make your way to the nearby *Wiiralti* café at Vabaduse väljak 10, buzzing with life from 8 am to 8 pm.

Once that closes, try the recently refurbished *Metropole* complex just a few doors down on Vabaduse väljak. Open from 8 am to 6 am, this establishment has rapidly become an early-morning hang-out for

Tallinn's night-clubbing scene and is a great meeting place.

For fun on a different level, sample a quick lunch at *Wagon lits*, across from the train station at Kopli 2 (open 8 am to 10 pm). It's decked out with seeming bits of trash from the old Soviet railways, while the steel stools have brakes as seats. For Italian ice cream go to *Mamma Mia* at Müürivahe 52 which opens daily from 10 am to 10 pm.

Fat Margaret's is well worth the hike up Pikk maantee to the Old Town limits. This maritime coffee and light snacks place inside a 16th-century bastion has a great wooden interior and terrace offering panoramic views of the city.

On Toompea, the *Neitsitorn*, in one of the old towers of the city wall, serves good höögvein (mulled wine), coffee and snacks from 11 am to 10 pm and the views are great.

Fast Food *Peetri Pizza* has numerous outlets doling out a variety of thin-crust one-person pizzas for 25 EEK. Locations include Pärnu maantee 22 (takeaway only, open from 11 am until 2 am); Lai 4 in the Old Town (takeaway only, open from 10 am to 9 pm); Liivalaia 40, by the Hotel Olümpia (11 am to 10 pm); and Kopli 2c, behind the train station (open from 11 am until 10 pm).

The newer *Pizza Americana* outlets at Müürivahe 2 and Pikk 1-3 dish up deep-pan pizzas with far superior toppings for similar prices. Adjoining the Pikk street branch is *Grill Mexicana*, owned by the same team and serving very satisfying nachos, tortillas and other Mexican specialities for around 45 to 60 EEK.

McDonald's, at Viru 24 and Sopruse 200b (both open daily from 8 am to midnight) is impossible to miss.

Self-Catering A good source of basic foodstuffs and fresh fruit and vegetables is the *kaubahall* (shopping hall) on Aia, near the Viru gates. Unbeatable for its imported products is the Finnish-run Stockmann supermarket, close to the Hotel Olümpia, at Liivalaia 53 (open weekdays from 10 am to 9 pm and on weekends from 10 am to 8 pm).

Also close to the Olümpia is Tallinn's central market at Puru põik 2. It's open every day from early morning until 4 pm and on Sunday until 1 pm. There is a 24-hour store, *Roosa Krants*, at Pärnu maantee 36.

Entertainment

Flyers for warehouse groove all-nighters, and large multilingual posters listing what's on where are plastered up at every major street corner in the Old Town, including the corner of Kullassepa and Niguliste. The *Baltic Times* and *Tallinn This Week* also run entertainment listings.

Bars & Clubs The top bar in town is *Nimeta Baar* (the bar with no name) in the Old Town at Suur-Karja 4/6. Under Scottish management, this place is packed every night, and not just with foreign clientele. The guest book alone makes interesting reading. It's open daily from 11 am to 3 am.

Another favoured bar is *Tehas N° 43* (Factory N° 43) at Pikk 43. The oldest drinking establishment in Tallinn, dating back to 1807, this bar was formerly a beer factory run by British beer trader Albert le Coq until it was shut down during the 1940 Soviet occupation. It's open weekdays from 9 am to 2 am and on weekends until 4 am.

A few doors down at Pikk 39 is *Hell Hunt* (Gentle Wolf), an Irish pub with live music most nights entertaining a dwindling crowd. *George Brownes* is another, more self-conscious, Irish pub at Harju 6. For a touch of the American life, head for *Diesel Boots* at Lai 23. The *Von Krahl Theatre Bar* at Rataskaevu 10 is great if you don't mind sweating a little, though from late May to September it has a terrace bar to take off some of the heat. Again, it's open until the early hours.

Clubs include *Bel Air* opposite the Viru Hotel at Vana-Viru 14. It often has excellent live bands playing although the admission can be pricey, especially at weekends when it is open until 4 am. *Piraat*, slightly out of town at Regati 1, and *Max Marine* at Pärnu maantee 19 are large, Western-style nightclubs with all the trimmings.

For a sedate glass of wine amidst Italian-inspired furnishings, and overlooking the best view of Tallinn you will ever find, head straight for the *Veinide Pöönine* (wine attic) on the 22nd floor of the Viru Hotel. This European-style 'enoteca' sells excellent wines by the glass or bottle at retail price. At the time of writing a small but select menu was being drawn up.

Theatre, Ballet & Opera *The Estonia Theatre*, at Estonia puiestee 4, stages a range of classical operas and ballets in repertory, and the *Estonia Concert Hall* (Kontsertisaal) next door has concerts every night of the week. Both box offices are open daily except Sunday from 1 to 7 pm and tickets generally cost from 10 to 25 EEK. There are regular organ concerts in *Niguliste Church*, the *House of the Brotherhood of Blackheads* and various recitals in the *Town Hall* (Raekoda); tickets are sold at the church and at the Estonia Concert Hall. During the summer there are also numerous open-air concerts around town.

Of particular interest is the *Puppet Theatre* (Nukuteater), at Lai 1, which keeps alive a tradition lost to most of Western Europe. The performances, while primarily aimed at children, are so beautifully produced they can't fail to enchant more mature sensibilities.

Getting There & Away

Air For information on flights in and out of Tallinn see the Getting There & Away section earlier in this chapter. Some travel agencies in town are able to obtain flights cheaper than the airlines. Airline offices in Tallinn include:

Estonian Air
   Vabaduse väljak 10 (☎ 446 382, 6313 303)
Finnair
   Liivalaia 14 (☎ 6311 455)
Lufthansa
   Mündi 2 (☎ 448 862)
LOT
   Lembitu 14-11 (☎ 661 838)
SAS
   Roosikrantsi 17 (☎ 6312 240)

Bus Buses to places within 40 km or so of Tallinn, and some Pärnu services, go from the local bus station beside the train station, but most services use the long-distance bus station *(Autobussijaam)* two km out of the centre along Tartu maantee – take tram No 2 east from Tammsaare Park or tram No 4 south from Mere puiestee.

For bus information and advance tickets, go to the ticket office at Pärnu maantee 24, down the street from the Hotel Palace, just beyond Peetri Pizza (open weekdays from 9 am to 5 pm). Alternatively, go to the long-distance bus station itself where the staff speak some English. There's a big, easily understood timetable here, an information desk, and an international booking ticket window on the right as you enter the main building.

For information on buses to places outside Estonia see the Getting There & Away section earlier in this chapter. Domestic services include:

Haapsalu – 100 km, 2½ hours, 10 buses daily, 32 EEK
Kärdla – 160 km, five hours, seven buses daily, 70 EEK
Kuressaare – 220 km, 4½ hours, 10 buses daily, 90 EEK
Narva – 210 km, four hours, seven buses daily, 70 EEK
Pärnu – 130 km, 2½ hours, more than 20 buses daily, 46 EEK
Tartu – 190 km, three hours, more than 20 buses daily, 66 EEK
Viljandi – 160 km, 2½ hours, 14 buses daily, 54 EEK

Train Tallinn's Baltic station *(Balti jaam)* is on the north-west edge of the Old Town at Toompuiestee 35 – a short walk from Raekoja plats, or a ride of three stops on tram No 1 or 2 north from the Viru Hotel. There are two ticket halls: one, as you're facing the station, to the left for longer-distance trains including to Tartu, Narva and places outside Estonia (signposted *eelmüügi kassad*), and another for 'suburban' trains, which includes some going as far as Viljandi.

For information about trains to places outside Estonia see the Getting There & Away section earlier in this chapter. Services

within Estonia include three daily to Tartu (three to four hours, 67 EEK), two daily to Pärnu (three to four hours, 39 EEK), two daily to Narva (from 3¼ to 4¼ hours, 58 EEK), and three daily to Viljandi (2½ hours, 48 EEK).

Car & Motorcycle There are 24-hour petrol stations belonging to Neste, Statoil and Shell at strategic spots within the city and along major roads leading to and from Tallinn. The Pärnu maantee Neste has a car repair service. Mazda and Citroen car showrooms and workshops are at Pärnu maantee 67a.

Car Rental Europcar at Mere puiestee 6 (☎ 441 637, 449 196) and at Tallinn airport (☎ 219 031) rents self-drive cars from US $110 a day with unlimited km. Avis (☎ 6388 222),which also has an office at Tallinn airport, offers one-way rentals between the three Baltics from US$150, as does Hertz (☎ 6388 923), at Tartu maantee, whose prices also start around the US$150 mark. Probably the best value in town is Eurodollar (☎ 6301 526, 6388 071), which has offices at the airport and in the Hotel Viru. A Seat Ibiza costs US$70 a day and a Nissan Sunny US$99 including unlimited mileage.

Boat See the Getting There & Away section earlier in this chapter for information on the many ferries and cruises between Tallinn and Helsinki, Stockholm and Germany. Tallinn's sea passenger terminal is at the end of Sadama, about a km north-east of the Old Town. Tram Nos 1 and 2 and bus Nos 3, 4 and 8 go to the Linnahall stop (by the Statoil petrol station), five minutes walk from the terminal. A shuttle bus costing 25 EEK runs every 15 minutes between the terminal and the Viru, Palace and Olümpia hotels.

Getting Around
To/From the Airport Tallinn airport is on the Tartu road three km from the centre. Bus No 22 runs every 20 minutes from the train station, via Vabaduse väljak and Estonia puiestee (stops along Narva maantee, on the corner opposite the Estonia Theatre), up to

the airport forecourt. There is also an additional summer airport bus (No 90) that runs every 30 minutes calling at the Palace, Viru, Olümpia, Kungla and Tallinn hotels.

Local Transport The train station and many hotels are an easy walk from the city centre. Buses and trams will take you everywhere else. See also Local Transport in the Getting Around section earlier in this chapter.

North-East Estonia

You travel across north-eastern Estonia if you are approaching Tallinn from St Petersburg. The border town of Narva, except for one or two historical ruins, is not of much interest and the area to the west is blighted by pollution from the heavy industry, which developed here during Soviet times. The towns in this north-eastern corner have a predominantly Russian-speaking population.

Closer to Tallinn, the attractive landscape around the towns of Viitna and Võsu remains unspoilt and is preserved as a national park.

LAHEMAA NATIONAL PARK
A rocky stretch of the north coast with numerous peninsulas and bays, plus 644 sq km of hinterland with 14 lakes, eight rivers and numerous waterfalls, forms Estonia's national park *(rahvuspark)*, Lahemaa, 70 km east of Tallinn. The landscape is 30% cultivated, 65% forest or heath, and 5% bog. Roads crisscross the park from the Tallinn-Narva highway and several parts of the park are accessible by bus.

Information
Lahemaa National Park Visitors' Centre (☎ 232-34 196) is in a converted wagon-house and stable in Palmse, nine km north of Viitna in the south-eastern part of the park.

Things to See
The park has several nature trails winding through it. The small coastal towns of **Võsu**

and **Loksa** are popular seaside spots in summer and many old wooden buildings still stand in the 400-year-old fishing village of **Altja**. There are also **prehistoric stone barrows** (tombs) at Kahala, Palmse and Vihula, and a **boulder field** on the Käsmu Peninsula.

The showpiece of Lahemaa is **Palmse Manor** and Park, nine km north of Viitna. The existing building is a restored version of the 18th-century Baroque house that belonged to the Baltic-German Von der Pahlen family. It is open as a museum from 10 am to 3 pm daily except Monday.

Places to Stay
The Lahemaa National Park Visitors' Centre (see Information) arranges accommodation to suit every budget including divine singles/doubles at *Palmse Manor* (☎ 232-34 167) for 450/700 EEK. The *Viitna Motel* (☎ 232-93 651), in Viitna among trees beside a lake, which is suitable for swimming, has beds for 36 people. Singles/doubles cost 100/150 EEK. More humble is the *Ojaäärse Holiday Centre* (☎ 232-34 108), near Palmse Manor, which has bunk rooms for 55 EEK per person.

The *Mere* hotel (☎ 232-99 179), a large, unlovely Soviet-era building at Mere 21 on Võsu's main street, has reasonable rooms with private bathroom for 250 EEK per person. The *Lepispea* camp site (☎ 232-99 199) in Võsu has 50 places.

Getting There & Away
There are buses from Tallinn to Viitna (take one of the nine daily buses for Rakvere), Käsmu, Võsu, Loksa, Leesi, Pärispea and elsewhere in the park. It is quite possible to make a day trip from Tallinn.

NARVA
Estonia's easternmost town (population 84,000) is separated only by the Narva River from Ivangorod in Russia and is almost entirely peopled by Russians. Narva was a Hanseatic League trading point by 1171. Later it became embroiled in Russia's border disputes with the German knights and Sweden. Ivan III of Muscovy founded Ivangorod

in 1492 and the large castle still stands. Narva was almost completely destroyed in WWII.

Today the Narva region is blighted by phosphorite and oil-shale industries. It also suffers the highest unemployment rate in the country and is a centre of Russian political discontent. The tourist information office is at Puškini 13 (☎ 235-60 186; fax 235-60 184).

The telephone code for Narva is ☎ 235.

Things to See
Restored after being damaged in WWII, **Narva Castle** guarding the road bridge (the 'Friendship Bridge') over the river dates from Danish rule in the 13th century. It houses the **town museum**, open Saturday to Tuesday from 10 am to 6 pm. The Baroque **town hall** (1668-71) on Raekoja väljak, north of the bridge, is also restored.

Places to Stay & Eat
The *Hotel Vanalinn* (☎ 22 486), at Koidula 6 just north of the castle, is one of the best things about Narva. There are 28 rooms, all with private bathroom. Singles/doubles are 400/600 EEK. The 160-bed Soviet-style *Hotel Narva* (☎ 22 700), at Puškini 6 just south of the castle, charges similar prices but is not nearly as good value.

There are a few restaurants and cafés on Puškini and Peterburi in the centre, the best of which is the *German Pub* (☎ 31 548) at Puškini 10, which closes at 2 am. *Café Roldis* at Puškini 6 is the place to go for light snacks. The most expensive is *Rondeel* at Peterburi 2, inside the fortified wall of Narva Castle.

Getting There & Away
Narva is 210 km east of Tallinn on the road and railway to St Petersburg, just 140 km away. From Tallinn there are at least seven buses and two trains daily. The bus and train stations are together at Vaksali 2 opposite the Russian Orthodox Voskrenesky Cathedral. Walk north up Puškini to the castle (half a km) and the centre.

South-East Estonia

The focus of south-east Estonia is the historic university town of Tartu, Estonia's second 'city'. Beyond Tartu is an attractive region of gentle hills and lakes.

TARTU
Tartu (population 115,000), formerly known as Dorpat, is 190 km south-east of Tallinn on the Emajõgi River, which flows into Lake Peipsi. Tartu was the cradle of the 19th-century Estonian nationalist revival and lays claim to being the spiritual capital of the country. It managed to escape Sovietisation to a greater degree than Tallinn and retains a sleepy pastoral air. The town is notable for its university, with over 7600 students, and its classical architecture stemming from a comprehensive rebuilding after most of the town burnt down in 1775.

History
There was an Estonian stronghold on Toomemägi Hill around the 6th century. In 1030, Yaroslav the Wise of Kiev is said to have founded a settlement here called Yuriev. By the early 13th century the Knights of the Sword were in control, placing a bishop, castle and cathedral on Toomemägi Hill. The town that grew up between the hill and the river became a member of the Hanseatic League. In the 16th and 17th centuries Tartu suffered repeated attacks and changes of ownership as Russia, Sweden and Poland-Lithuania all vied for control.

The university, founded in 1632 during Swedish rule to train Protestant clergy and government officials, closed in about 1700 but reopened in 1802, and developed into a foremost 19th-century seat of learning. The first Estonian Song Festival was held in Tartu in 1869. In 1920 the treaty recognising Estonian independence was signed here by the Soviets. Later, during the Soviet occupation, Westerners were not allowed to stay overnight because of the supposed security risk it presented to a nearby military airfield.

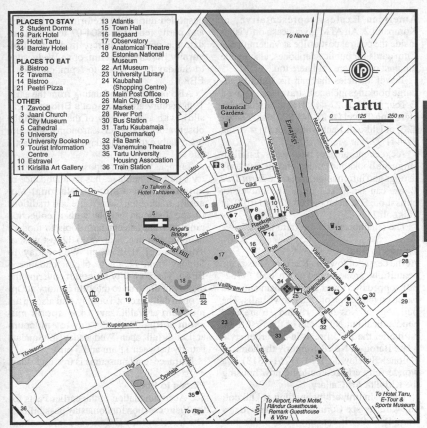

PLACES TO STAY	13 Atlantis
2 Student Dorms	15 Town Hall
19 Park Hotel	16 Illegaard
29 Hotel Tartu	17 Observatory
34 Barclay Hotel	18 Anatomical Theatre
	20 Estonian National
PLACES TO EAT	Museum
8 Bistroo	22 Art Museum
12 Taverna	23 University Library
14 Bistroo	24 Kaubahall
21 Peetri Pizza	(Shopping Centre)
	25 Main Post Office
OTHER	26 Main City Bus Stop
1 Zavood	27 Market
3 Jaani Church	28 River Port
4 City Museum	30 Bus Station
5 Cathedral	31 Tartu Kaubamaja
6 University	(Supermarket)
7 University Bookshop	32 Hia Bank
9 Tourist Information	33 Vanemuine Theatre
Centre	35 Tartu University
10 Estravel	Housing Association
11 Kirisilla Art Gallery	36 Train Station

Tartu

ESTONIA

In 1993 the Estonian Supreme Court was re-established in Tartu.

Orientation

Toomemägi Hill and the area of older buildings between it and the Emajõgi River are the focus of Tartu. At the heart of this older area are Raekoja plats (Town Hall Square) and the street Ülikooli, which runs across the west end of the square. This is also the main shopping area.

Information

Tartu tourist information centre is at Raekoja plats 14 (☎ & fax 27-432 141). The English-speaking Express Hotline (☎ 27-487 222) in Tartu is also well worth calling.

Places to change cash include the Tartu Kaubamaja supermarket close to the bus station at Riia 2, and Hia Bank next door, which also accepts travellers' cheques. Other banks accepting travellers' cheques include Eesti Ühis Bank at Ülikooli 1 and Hansapank inside another supermarket at Tehase 16.

Lost American Express cards and travellers' cheques can be replaced at Estravel (☎ 27-447 979, 447 974; fax 27-447 977; e-mail ann@estravel.ee), the official

American Express representative, at Kompanii 2. An ATM giving cash on Visa is inside the central post office at Vanemuise 7. Chip cards for public telephones, also inside the post office, are sold here too.

Travel agencies that can fix tours or arrange bookings include Estravel (see above), E-Tour (☎ & fax 27-441 716) at Ülikooli 10, Hermann Travel (☎ 27-441 222; fax 27-441 425) at Ülikooli 1 and Minimatkad (☎ & fax 27-441 727) at Munga 18.

A excellent range of local maps, English-language books and guides, and the quarterly listings and information magazine *Tartu This Week*, can be picked up at the university bookshop, Raamatupood (☎ 27-441 102), at Ülikooli 11.

The telephone code for Tartu is ☎ 27.

Things to See

At the centre of town on Raekoja Plats is the beautifully proportioned **town hall** (1782-89), topped by a tower and weather vane, and based on the design of Dutch town halls. The buildings at Nos 6, 8, 12 and 16 are also neoclassical but No 2, one of the first to be built after the 1775 fire, is in an earlier style – late Baroque. No 18, formerly the home of Colonel Barclay de Tolly (1761-1818) is a wonderfully crooked building now housing the **Kirisilla Art Gallery**.

The main **university** building at Ülikooli 18, with its six Corinthian columns, dates from 1803-09. It contains Tartu's classical art museum. Further north, the Gothic brick **Jaani Kirik** (St John's Church), founded in 1330 but ruined in 1944, is being restored as a museum. It has rare **terracotta sculptures** around the main portal. The **Botanical Gardens**, founded in 1803 on the corner of Lai and Vabaduse puiestee, is home to 6500 different species of plants, including a large collection of palm trees housed in the 26-metre-high glasshouse. It is open daily from 9 am to 5 pm between May and September.

Rising to the west of Raekoja plats is Toomemägi Hill, landscaped in the manner of a 19th-century English-style park. The 13th-century Gothic **cathedral** (Toomkirik) at the top was rebuilt in the 15th century,

despoiled during the Reformation in 1525, and partly rebuilt in 1804-07 to accommodate the university library (today the **University History Museum**, open Wednesday to Sunday from 11 am to 5 pm, entrance 2 EEK).

Also on the hill and dating from the early 19th century are the **Angel's Bridge** (Inglisild), with a good view of the city, and the observatory (now an astronomy museum open daily except Tuesday) on the old castle site.

Tartu, as the major repository of the country's cultural heritage, has an abundance of museums. The **Estonian National Museum**, tracing the history, life and traditions of the Estonian people with a collection ranging from ancient farm tools to modern national costume, is at Veski 32 just west of Toomemägi Hill, open Wednesday to Sunday from 11 am to 6 pm (entrance 6 EEK). There's a **City Museum** covering the history of Tartu up to the 19th century at Oru 2, open daily except Tuesday, and also an **art museum** at Vallikraavi 14, a **sports museum** at Riia 27a, and a tiny **toy museum** at Lai 1 (all open Wednesday to Sunday, usually between 11 am and 5 pm).

Entrance to all museums is free on Friday.

Places to Stay

See Accommodation in the earlier Facts for the Visitor section for homestay possibilities. The travel agency E-Tour (see Information) can also arrange family accommodation for around 170/300 EEK for singles/doubles.

For accommodation in student dorms at Narva 27, try *Tartu University Housing Association* at Pepleri 14. It offers basic accommodation with no hot water for around 50 EEK. If the university housing director is not in his office it is worth trying the hostels direct. Just walk in and ask nicely if there is a room available. You will probably be told to go to the housing association office, but you may be able persuade the staff to give you a room.

Hotels – bottom end The *Hotel Tarim* (☎ 475 433; fax 473 357) at Rahu 8, 2.5 km south of the centre, has 60 beds at 250/320 EEK for singles/doubles with private kitchen and bathroom. Take bus No 4 from the bus stop on Riia and get off by the cemetery gates on Võru, just after you cross the railway; walk south and turn left onto Rahu. Also in the vicinity of the Tarim is another cheap alternative, the *Rändur Guesthouse* (☎ 475 691, 471 713) at Vasara 25, which has 20 singles/doubles starting at 50/70 EEK.

Just under one km north-west of the centre is the *Hotel Tähtvere* (☎ 421 708) at Laulupeo 19. Singles/doubles start at 100/ 200 EEK with shower, toilet and TV. There is also a sauna and tennis court on the premises.

Also good value is the *Rehe Motel* (☎ 412 234; fax 412 355) five km from the centre on the road to Võru. Singles/doubles/triples cost 250/380/540 EEK.

Hotels – middle & top end The *Park Hotel* (☎ 433 663; fax 434 382), in a beautiful woodland setting at Vallikraavi 23, has overpriced singles/doubles from 200/500 EEK. Smaller and more cosy is the *Remark Guesthouse* (☎ 477 744, 477 420) at Tähe 94. Prices for their nine beds start at 400 EEK.

Directly opposite the bus station in a drab Soviet block in desperate need of a paint is *Hotel Tartu* (☎ & fax 432 091). Singles/ doubles/triples without private shower cost 350/600/740 EEK. Singles/ doubles with shower start at 550/800 EEK.

Top hotels include the stylish *Hotel Taru* (☎ 441 177; fax 474 095) at Rebase 9, which is run by Tallinn's Hotel Palace team with prices set accordingly at 960/1240 EEK. Cheaper and more exclusive is the *Barclay Hotel* (☎ 447 100; fax 447 101) at Ülikooli 8. The building, formerly a Soviet army headquarters, dates to 1912. The extravagantly furnished singles/doubles start at 900/ 1080 EEK. Apparently the luxury suite used to be Dzhokhar Dudayev's (Chechen rebel leader) office.

Places to Eat
For quick, cheap eating try the two *student canteens* at Tähe 4 and Narva 27, both open 9 am to 3 pm. Here you can have a plate of potatoes, vegetables and mystery meat for around 12 EEK. Still cheap but far superior is the *Old Student Café* on the 2nd floor of the main university building at Ülikooli 18. Housed in the original part of the university dating to 1632, this old-world café with worn wooden floors and a homely smell of baking, is a must. Omelettes cost 7 EEK, seljanka 9 EEK and the best cakes in town, 1 to 3 EEK.

Cheap, uninspiring Estonian 'fast food' such as šnitsel, kooreklops (meat in white sauce) and kotlett (meat cutlet) all with fries for 20 EEK can be eaten sitting down at the *Bistroo*, which has outlets at Raekoja plats 9 and Rüütli 4 (both open 7 am to 10 pm). A *Peetri Pizza* outlet is at Tiigi 11 and *McDonald's* is opposite the bus station. Italian food is served at Raekoja plats 20, at the smart and formal *Taverna* where pasta costs 40 EEK, main dishes from 60 EEK. Vegetarian dishes are also included on its wide menu.

Entertainment
In a class of its own stands *Illegaard* at Ülikooli 5. Also an art gallery, this cellar bar-cum-café is the place to be seen, so much so that after 5 pm it becomes a members-only club (a year's membership costs 200/400 EEK for Estonians/foreigners). The place to hang out at night is the *Zavood* (Factory) at Lai 30, a fun bar open daily from 4 pm to 2 am. Overlooking the river Emajõgi at Narva boulevard 2 is the *Atlantis* nightclub, open Sunday to Thursday from 9 pm to 3 am and on Friday and Saturday from 9 pm to 4 am.

Getting There & Away
More than 20 buses a day run to/from Tallinn, taking between 2½ and 3½ hours depending on the service, and costing 66 EEK. There are also three trains daily, taking from three to four hours for 67 EEK in unreserved seating.

OTEPÄÄ
The small hilltop town of Otepää, 44 km south of Tartu, is the centre of a pretty area much loved by the Estonians for its hills and lakes, and often referred to jokingly as the

ESTONIA

'Estonian alps'. It is an excellent place to enjoy the Estonian countryside. In winter Otepää also becomes a popular skiing centre.

Orientation & Information

The centre of town is the triangular main 'square', Lipuväljak, with the bus station just off its east corner. The tourist information office is at Lipuväljak 13 (☎ 27-655 364; fax 27-661 214). The post office, bank and main food shop are beside the bus station. Staff at the Otepää Travel Agency (☎ 27-654 060; fax 27-661 229) at Lipuväljak 11 are efficient and friendly.

The telephone code for Otepää is ☎ 27.

Things to See & Do

Otepää's pretty little 17th-century **church** is on a small hilltop about 400 metres north-east of the bus station. It was in this church in 1884 that the Estonian Students' Society consecrated its new blue, black and white flag, which later became the flag of independent Estonia. The tree-covered hill south of the church is the **Linnamägi** (Castle Hill), a major stronghold from the 10th to 12th centuries. There are traces of fortifications on top and good views all round. The best views to be had, however, are along the shores of the 3.5-km-long **Pühajärv** (Holy Lake) on the south-west edge of the town. The lake was blessed by the Dalai Lama when he visited Tartu in 1992 and there is a monument to him on the east shore. Otepää is home to many rare species of birds including the black stork, osprey and the white-backed woodpecker.

Places to Stay

The *Hundisoo Motel* (☎ 55 238; fax 244-40 230), run by the Estonian Youth Hostel Association at Kastolatsi tee 3, 1.5 km from the town centre, has 25 beds for 50 EEK per night and there are showers and a sauna. The *Tamme* guesthouse (☎ 55 237), two km south-east of the centre also has quite reasonable rooms with their own shower and toilet for 100 EEK per person.

Getting There & Away

To and from Tartu there are five or six direct buses and three or four route taxis daily. Buses take just over an hour and cost around 16 EEK, taxis take 45 minutes and cost about 32 EEK. There's a daily Tallinn-Otepää bus (via Tartu) which takes about 4½ hours. Other places served by bus to/from Otepää include Pärnu, Sangaste, Valga, Viljandi and Võru.

AROUND OTEPÄÄ

About 25 km from Otepää is one of the most unusual places in Estonia, **Sangaste Castle** (Sangaste Loss; ☎ 27-91 343), a fairy-tale brick castle. Erected in Tudor-cum-Gothic style between 1874 and 1881, the place is said to be modelled on Britain's Windsor Castle. Sangaste sits in parkland close by a river and it's possible to hire boats and bicycles. The castle also operates as a hotel with double, triple and four-person rooms available at 150 EEK per person (with breakfast included). There are buses between Otepää and Sangaste twice a day.

VÕRU

Võru, 64 km south of Tartu, is a small, ordinary town, but a good base for visiting some interesting points in Estonia's far south-east, such as Suur Munamägi (the highest point in the Baltics) or the castle at Vahtseliina (see Around Võru).

Orientation & Information

Võru lies on the eastern shore of Lake Tamula. The main streets, both running parallel to the shore, are Jüri and, closer to the lake, Kreutzwaldi. The central square, on Jüri, is dominated by the Lutheran church. The bus station is half a km east of this along Tartu tänav.

The tourist information centre is at Tartu 31 (☎ 27-821 881). You can exchange money at the Kubija and Hermes hotels (see Places to Stay).

Võru's telephone code is ☎ 27.

Things to See & Do

Võru's main claim to fame is that it was the home of Friedrich Reinhold Kreutzwald, regarded as the father of Estonian literature – if not culture – for his verse epic *Kalevipoeg*. His home at Kreutzwaldi 31, an 18th-century wooden building, now houses the **Kreutzwald Memorial Museum**, open Wednesday to Monday from 11 am to 6 pm. Võru also has a **local history museum** at Kreutzwaldi 16.

People staying at the Kubija Hotel (see Places to Stay) can also rent bicycles or canoes. Just north of the town on the bank of the Võhandu River are the ruins of the **Kirumpää fortress**, founded by the Germans in 1322. **Verijärv** (Blood Lake), four km south-east of the Vastseliina and Pskov road is a fine steep-sided lake.

Places to Stay

The *Võru Farmers' Union* at Liiva 11 offers rooms in farms in the Võru region from May to August.

Hermes Hotel (☎ 821 326) is at Jüri 32a in the town centre. Another option is the *Kubija Hotel* (☎ 831 581; fax 842 498), which has 70 rooms in a reasonable Soviet-era building and 13 summer cabins near a small lake. Singles/doubles in the hotel cost 440/480 EEK, and summer cabins cost 200 EEK per person for four persons sharing and 280 EEK if there is less then four sharing. Take bus No 1 or 5 going south on Kreutzwaldi and get off at the Kubija stop.

Getting There & Away

There are several daily buses to/from Tartu taking 1½ hours, six daily from Tallinn taking 4½ hours plus two to/from Otepää and Pärnu (four to 4½ hours).

AROUND VÕRU

Seventeen km south of Võru, is **Suur Munamägi** (literally Great Egg Hill), the highest peak in the Baltic states at 318 metres. It is topped by a 29-metre-high observation tower which commands views of up to 50 km – to the towers of Pskov in Russia – in good weather. The tower has quite strange opening hours but if you turn up any day from May to September, between 10 am and 6 pm, you should be okay. To get there take a bus from Võru to Hanja or Ruusmäe.

Although all that's left of **Vastseliina Castle** is a couple of towers, a length of wall, a ditch and some ramparts, their dramatic perch and remoteness make them evocative of a past age. The surrounding countryside with its sandstone cliffs and river valleys is a protected landscape reserve and quite enchanting. Vahtseliina Castle is on the eastern edge of the village of Vahtseliina (pronounced 'Vochtselina') which is, rather confusingly, five km east of the small town of Vastseliina, to which there are several buses daily from Võru.

South-West Estonia

South-west Estonia is a predominantly flat, densely forested region with two main towns as its focus. Viljandi (population 24,000), 160 km south of Tallinn, is quite a pretty place which benefits greatly from a lakeside setting. To the north of the town are the ruins of what was once the largest castle in the Baltics spread over three hills. Pärnu lies roughly at the midpoint on the main Tallinn-Rīga road and is worth a day's stop if you have the time.

PÄRNU

Pärnu ('PAIR-nu', population 52,000), 130 km south of Tallinn on the road to Rīga, is Estonia's leading seaside resort. Out of season it's a little quiet and forlorn but between June and August it's lively and extremely pleasant with some good places to stay, wide leafy streets and white sandy beaches.

History

In the 13th century the Knights of the Sword built a fort at Pärnu, on what was then their border with Estonia to the north. It became a Hanseatic port in the 14th century and flourished in the 17th century under Swedish rule.

From 1838 the town grew as a resort, with mud baths proving a draw, as well as the

ESTONIA

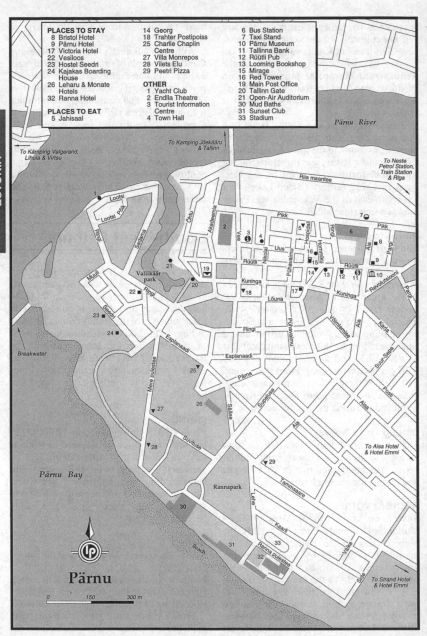

PLACES TO STAY
8 Bristol Hotel
9 Pärnu Hotel
17 Victoria Hotel
22 Vesiloos
23 Hostel Seedri
24 Kajakas Boarding House
26 Leharu & Monate Hotels
32 Ranna Hotel

PLACES TO EAT
5 Jahisaal

14 Georg
18 Trahter Postipoiss
25 Charlie Chaplin Centre
27 Villa Monrepos
28 Vilets Elu
29 Peetri Pizza

OTHER
1 Yacht Club
2 Endlla Theatre
3 Tourist Information Centre
4 Town Hall

6 Bus Station
7 Taxi Stand
10 Pärnu Museum
11 Tallinna Bank
12 Rüütli Pub
13 Looming Bookshop
15 Mirage
16 Red Tower
19 Main Post Office
20 Tallinn Gate
21 Open-Air Auditorium
30 Mud Baths
31 Sunset Club
33 Stadium

Pärnu River

To Kämping Valgerand,
Lihula & Virtsu

To Kamping Jõekääru
& Tallinn

To Neste
Petrol Station,
Train Station
& Riga

Riia maantee

Pikk

Pikk

Õhtu

Akadeemia

Vee

Hospidali

Aia

Pargi

Uus

Nikolai

Rüütli

Puhavaimu

Hommiku

Rüütli

Lootsi

Lootsi Põik

Sadama

Vallikäär
park

Muuli

Ringi

Seedri

Kuninga

Lõuna

Kuninga

Revolutsiooni

Breakwater

Ringi

Pargi

Esplanaadi

Esplanaadi

Mere puiestee

Pärna

Supeluse

Ala

Aia

Karja

Suur-Sepa

Posti

Ala

Säkse

Puhavaimu

Võitlemise

To Aisa Hotel
& Hotel Emmi

Suvituse

Pärnu Bay

Rannapark

Tammsaare

Lehe

Kaarli

Ranna puiestee

Valke

Side

To Strand Hotel
& Hotel Emmi

Beach

Pärnu

0   150   300 m

beach and relatively good weather. During the 1930s Pärnu was attracting holidaying Finns and Swedes. In the Soviet era all the guesthouses, hotels and villas were turned into sanatoriums providing treatments and cures for visitors from all over the Soviet Union but since independence they have been turned back into hotels.

Orientation

Pärnu lies either side of the estuary of the Pärnu River which empties into Pärnu Bay. The southern part of town is the centre. The main shopping street and heart of the old town is Rüütli, 100 metres south of the bus station, with the Hotel Pärnu at one end and Vallikäär park at the other. Running southward the streets get wider and greener before terminating (after about 1.5 km) at Ranna puiestee and the beach.

Information

There is an excellent tourist information centre (☎ 244-40 639; fax 244-45 633) at Munga 2. The English-speaking Express Hotline (☎ 244-36 222) is a valuable information source too.

The branch of Tallinna Bank at Rüütli 55 will exchange travellers' cheques and give a cash advance on Visa, Diners Club, Eurocard and MasterCard. The main post office, open from 8 am to 7 pm weekdays and 9 am to 3 pm Saturday, is at Akadeemia 7.

Local maps can be picked up at the Looming bookshop at Rüütli 41 or at the tourist information centre.

The telephone code for Pärnu is ☎ 244.

Things to See & Do

Town Centre The **Red Tower** (Punane Torn) on Hommiku is the oldest building in Pärnu, probably originally built by the Knights of the Sword. The ground floor is now a small museum and the upper floor an arts shop. It's open Tuesday to Saturday from noon to 5 pm. Two blocks west, on Pühavaimu, is a fine pair of large **17th-century houses**, and at Rüütli 21 there is a house of a similar age with a shoe hanging from its eaves said to

have been lost by Sweden's King Carl XII in this street in 1700.

Parts of the 17th-century Swedish moat and ramparts survive in Vallikäär park, including the tunnel-like **Tallinn Gate** (Tallinna Värav) at the west end of Rüütli. A display of local history is included in the **Pärnu Museum** on the corner of Rüütli and Aia, open Wednesday to Sunday from 11 am to 5 pm.

Resort Area The wide, white-sand beach just south of Ranna puiestee is surprisingly beautiful. The 1920 to 1930s buildings that edge the beach, and now serve as cafés and restaurants, are also extremely tasteful. The eye-catching 1927 neoclassical structure at the sea end of Supeluse at Ranna 1 is the still-functioning **mud baths** (☎ 42 461). It is possible to walk west along the coast from here out to the two-km stone breakwater which stretches out into the mouth of the river, but beware of the tides.

Places to Stay

Camping There are three camping grounds around Pärnu all of which have cabins but possibly space for tents too. *Kämping Jõekääru* (☎ 41 121) is in Sauga, 10 km north of Pärnu. *Kämping Valgerand* (☎ 64 231), approved by the Estonian Youth Hostel Association, is 10 km west of Pärnu in a wooded strip beside the sea. *Resort Village Green* (☎ 43 776) at Suure-Jõe is the most exclusive.

Hostels Some of the cheapest beds in town are at the *Kajakas* boarding house (☎ 43 098; fax 42 181) at Seedri 2, and the neighbouring *Hostel Seedri* (☎ 43 350; fax 43 963) run by the Estonian Youth Hostel Association at Seedri 4. They are out in a green part of town backing onto the sea, and about a km from the bus station. The hostel has 86 beds costing 85 EEK a night. It also offers water sports and bicycle rental.

More up-market is the *Vesiloos* (☎ 43 534; fax 43 963), also run by the hostel organisation, three km from the centre at Esplanadi

42a. It has 35 beds costing 205 EEK a night and it, too, rent out bicycles.

Hotels – middle The twin set of ugly concrete-block hotels 500 metres from the beach at Sääse 7, the *Leharu* (☎ 45 895; fax 40 064) and *Monate* (☎ 41 472; fax 44 656), are both far more appealing than the exterior suggests. Prices for both are 250/260 EEK for singles/doubles.

Two km east of the centre at Laine 2 is the small and modern *Hotel Emmi* (☎ 22 043; fax 45 472) with singles/doubles at 285/355 EEK. The rooms are comfortable, a good size and have their own bathrooms. To reach the Emmi take bus No 7, 19 or 21 from the Sidesõlm stop at the post office and get off at U Haigla which is just a couple of minutes walk from the hotel. At Tammsaare 27D in the same part of town is the 60-room *Strand Hotel* (☎ 24 243; fax 24 276) with renovated singles/doubles at 495/695 EEK and a wildly popular nightclub.

The *Pärnu Hotel* (☎ 78 911) at Rüütli 44 is a rather depressing Soviet-era construction which has been massively renovated. Singles/doubles cost 490/650 EEK.

Hotels – top end The *Victoria Hotel* (☎ 43 112; fax 43 415), in the centre at Kuninga 25, is the best hotel in Pärnu and amongst the top few in the Baltics. The rooms are extremely comfortable and tasteful with all conveniences. Also run by the Victoria is the appealing *Bristol* (☎ 31 455), right next door to the Pärnu Hotel. Singles/doubles cost 750/990 EEK at both.

The elegant 1930s *Ranna* (☎ 45 312) on the seafront, beautifully restored, is run by the team who runs the prestigious Palace Hotel in Tallinn. Singles/doubles cost 1050/1350 EEK. Even if you are not staying here it's worth coming by just to enjoy the expensive but delicious terrace restaurant and cheaper beer garden backing on to the beach.

Places to Eat
A block west from the bus station is the *Georg* at Rüütli 43, a smart and clean cafeteria offering soups and salads for 8 EEK and

hot dishes such as the ubiquitous viinerid (sausage) and šnitsel (hamburger) for around 25 EEK. Opposite at Rüütli 44, inside the Pärnu Hotel, is the perfectly acceptable but not particularly exciting *Embecke* restaurant.

The *Trahter Postipoiss* at Vee 12 is a 19th-century post office turned into a tavern-restaurant with a limited menu of meat and veg dishes (open daily 11 am to midnight). The bar-cum-restaurant *Jahisaal* (Hunter's Hall) at Hospidall 6 serves a variety of game dishes as well as a wide range of beers. It's open daily from noon to 1 am.

Close to the Leharu and Monate hotels at Mere 14 is the *Villa Monrepos*, a cosy restaurant overlooking the sea, serving excellent value food that draws in the locals. In the beach area, at Tammsaare tee 6, is *Peetri Pizza* with outdoor terrace seating and a takeaway service – open 7.30 am to 11 pm.

For a funky, very stylish art café-cum-gallery look no further than *Vilets Elu* (Hard Life) at Mere 22. It opens daily from 10 am to 2 am and is well worth a visit. At Esplanadi 10, in what was once Communist Party headquarters, is the *Charlie Chaplin Centre*, a cinema, bookshop and coffee shop.

Entertainment
Pärnu's night scene rocks, the highlight of it being the newly opened and very flashy *Sunset Club* which spills out onto the beach at Ranna 3. It does not close until at least 5 am on Friday and Saturday. Other clubs, less hip, include *Mirage* at Rüütli 40 and *Venus* inside the Pärnu Hotel. Opposite is the *Rüütli Pub* which pertains to be Irish. There's a wild cocktail bar in the Strand Hotel.

Getting There & Away
Pärnu is 2½ hours by bus from Tallinn. There are more than 20 buses daily, departing in Tallinn mostly from the bus station on Tartu maantee, but also from beside the train station. The fare is 46 EEK. In Pärnu the ticket office, open from 4.45 am to 9 pm, is in a wooden building on Ringi, across from the bus station.

KIHNU & RUHNU

Six-km-long Kihnu island (population 550), in the Gulf of Riga 40 km south-west of Pärnu, is almost a living museum of Estonian culture, and an anthropologist's delight. Many of the island's women still wear traditional colourful striped skirts and singing is still used as a form of communication.

Ruhnu island, a little smaller than Kihnu, is 100 km south-west of Pärnu and nearer to the Latvian than the Estonian mainland. For several centuries the island had a mainly Swedish population of 200 or 300 but most of them left, abandoning their homes on 6 August 1944 to escape the advancing Red Army.

Getting There & Away

Reiser Travel Agency (☎ 44 556; fax 44 566) at Rüütli 29 offers boat excursions from Pärnu to Kihnu and Ruhnu.

West Estonia & The Islands

The main town in the region is **Haapsalu** (population 15,000) with a fine castle and cathedral, a marvellous old train station built for the visit of Tsar Nicholas II in 1905, and the Tchaikovsky bench, a memorial to the composer who used to spend summer here. However, the main draw of the region is the islands of Saaremaa and Hiiumaa, which with their windmills, juniper groves, old-fashioned rural pace and coastal vistas stretching gently away into infinity, are close to the Estonian ideal of an earthly paradise.

SAAREMAA

Soviet industry and immigration barely touched the country's biggest offshore island, Saaremaa (literally 'Island land'), and it retains the appearance of agricultural pre-WWII Estonia. Though Saaremaa has long been a popular local holiday retreat, during the Soviet era it was closed to foreigners, and even mainland Estonians needed an invitation to visit because of the presence of an early-warning radar system and rocket base.

Orientation

To reach Saaremaa you have to first cross Muhu, the small island where the ferry from the mainland docks and which is connected to the eastern edge of Saaremaa by a 2.5-km causeway. About 70 km from Muhu, is the capital of Saaremaa, Kuressaare (population 17,000), which lies on the south coast of the island. Kuressaare is the transport hub of the island and a natural base for visitors.

Information

Kuressaare tourist information office is at Tallinna 2 (☎ 245-55 120; fax 245-54 267). You can change money at the bus station in Kuressaare or at Hansapank at Kohtu 1 or Hoiupank at Losini 11. The post office is west of the bus station at Torni 1, north of the main street Tallinna, where it widens into the town square.

Mardi Ltd (☎ 245-54 875; fax 245-56 241) at Tallinna 4, Baltic Tours (☎ 245-55 480) at Tallinna 1 and Saaremaa Travel Agency (☎ 245-55 079; fax 245-54 035) are three friendly travel agencies which can fix you up with a variety of accommodation, tours and other services.

The telephone code for Saaremaa is ☎ 245.

Things to See

The yellow **town hall** in the main Old Town square dates back to 1654. Opposite stands the baroque **Weighing House** built in 1663. To the left is a converted 18th-century firehouse which is now the tourist information centre.

The island's most distinctive landmark is the restored **Bishop's Castle** (1338-80) at the south end of the town, an impressive if ugly structure. An exploration of its interior, however, is fun. It houses the **Saaremaa Regional Museum**, open from 11 am to 7 pm, Wednesday to Sunday. At Angla, in the east of the island 40 km from Kuressaare on the main road to the north coast, is the biggest and most photogenic grouping of

ESTONIA

windmills – five of them lined along the roadside. Two km away, along the road opposite the windmills, is **Karja church**, the island's most evocative 13th to 14th-century German Gothic church. Other good examples of this architecture in the area include the churches at **Pöide** and **Valjala**, and, 12 km north of Kuressaare, at **Kaarma**. At Valjala there are also the remains of a 12th to 13th-century fortress of the native Saaremaa people.

The highlight of Saaremaa is **Lake Kaali**, 18 km from Kuressaare on the road to the harbour, signposted 'Kaali'. This magnificent, haunting lake was formed 2700 years ago after a meteorite fell. The water-filled crater today remains a source of mystery and much pride for the islanders, who relish relating exaggerated tales of Lake Kaali's spectacular beginnings.

Places to Stay
Kuressaare The tourist information centre (see Information) can fix you up with accommodation in private flats in town for 100 EEK per person.

The *Hotel Lossi* (☎ 54 443), an old building at Lossi 27 just in front of the castle, has clean singles/doubles at 220/440 EEK. The *Panga Pansionaat* (☎ 57 989), at the back of the bank building at Tallinna 27, has good clean rooms with spotless shared showers and toilets for 400 EEK.

Out of Town The *Nasva Jachtklubi Hotel* (☎ 75 100), six km west of Kuressaare in the village of Nasva has idyllic sea-view rooms for 200/300 EEK. The Nasva Yacht Club (☎ 75 140, 75 171) also rents out boats.

The *Saare Maakonna Koduturismi Ühendus* (Saaremaa Guest House Association; ☎ 77 269; fax 53 331), run from a home in Saia, on the Aste road 10 km north of Kuressaare, offers rooms in private homes around Saaremaa for 150 to 200 EEK per person. The *Tahula Motel* (☎ 57 490, 57 410), on the Kuivastu-Tallinn road 10 km from Kuressaare, is an excellent, modern

place with friendly staff and 41 beds. Clean rooms with private bath are 420/490 EEK.

Kämping Mändjala (☎ 55 079, 75 193; fax 54 035) is open June, July and August in woods behind a sandy beach 10 km along the coast road west of Kuressaare. Accommodation is in two-person cabins costing 240 EEK for two. Students can get a bed for the night for 45 EEK without linen. Buses from Kuressaare to Torgu or Sääre (three a day) go to the Mändjala bus stop, about half a km beyond the site. The beach-side *Hotel Männikäbi* (☎ 24 575; fax 54 772) which lies about 10 km along the coast road, west of Kuressaare, has spacious double rooms with private bath and TV for 620 EEK.

Places To Eat
Kuurort at Kastini 20 is one of the best restaurants in Kuressaare although you pay a price for it. More central and very popular is *Vanakinna* at Kauba 8 serving European cuisine. Opposite is *Lonkav Konn* (The Limping Frog), Kuressaare's Irish pub offering pub grub and live music at weekends.

Café Hansa, inside an art gallery at Tallinna 9, is small, cosy and serves delicious muffins. The *Café Kuursaal* (Cure Hall) inside a former turn-of-the-century health resort at Pargi 2 in a park opposite the Bishop's Castle opens Sunday to Thursday from noon to 9 pm and on Friday and Saturday from noon to 11 pm. Unfortunately the food is not quite as impressive as the setting.

The central market in Kuressaare, offering a fine array of fresh produce and Estonian handicrafts is just of the town hall square in the Old Town.

Getting There & Away
A vehicle ferry runs several times daily from Virtsu on the mainland across the seven-km strait to Muhu island, which is joined by a causeway to Saaremaa. Ten buses daily travel each way between Tallinn and Kuressaare (4½ hours, 90 EEK) and the ferry crossing is included in the trip.

Faroe Islands

The 18 Faroe Islands (Føroyar) form an independent nation within the Kingdom of Denmark. Here the forces of nature, the old Norse culture and today's technology combine to create a slice of modern Europe superimposed on a stunning natural and traditional backdrop.

Visitors aren't usually prepared for the beauty of the landscape and, apart from news about the traditional *grindadráp* (pilot whale slaughters), these North Atlantic islands receive very little press.

Facts about the Country

HISTORY

The first Norse settlers, who were primarily farmers and pastoralists, arrived in the uninhabited Faroes in the early 9th century from southern Norway and the Orkneys.

From early on the administration of these islands lay in the hands of a parliamentary body known as the Alting. In 1380 parliamentary procedures ceased, the Alting became simply a royal court and the legislative body was renamed Løgting. With the Kalmar Union of 1397, in which Norway, Sweden and Denmark merged politically, the Faroes became a Danish province. In 1535 Denmark imposed the religious influences of the Protestant Lutheran church.

During the 19th century Denmark increasingly dominated the Faroes and in 1849 the Danish Rigsdag (parliament) officially incorporated the islands into Denmark. During WWII, the British occupied the islands in order to secure the strategic North Atlantic shipping lanes and prevent German occupation.

On 23 March 1948 the *Act on Faroese Home Rule* was passed and the Faroes' official status was changed from 'county of Denmark' to 'self-governing community within the Kingdom of Denmark'. When Denmark joined the EEC (now EU), the Faroes refused to follow because of the hot issue of fishing rights. Despite the Faroese claim to a 200-mile fisheries exclusion limit, stocks dwindled as a result of overfishing. After years of high spending by the Faroese government, the economy went into serious recession in the early 1990s; unemployment peaked at 26% and, with emigration, the population decreased by 9%.

GEOGRAPHY & ECOLOGY

The mountainous Faroe Islands, located 400 km from Iceland and 280 km from Scotland, cover 1399 sq km. Coastal cliffs provide nesting sites for large numbers of sea birds such as puffins, fulmars and kittiwakes, while inland you'll find great skuas, ducks and many species of wading birds. Land mammals are mainly cattle and sheep. Trees are virtually nonexistent, partly due to large numbers of sheep; however, the classic image of the islands is of bare grassy hillsides soaring out of the sea.

GOVERNMENT & POLITICS

Currently, a coalition of Unionists, Conservatives, Liberals and Trade Unionists is in power, with the Unionist Edmund Joensen as prime minister. There's a long tradition of coalition governments in the Faroes. Some governments, including the current one,

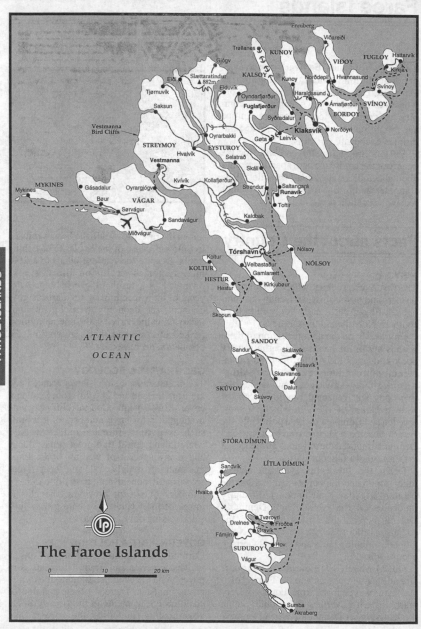

The Faroe Islands

0   10   20 km

have been formed by coalitions of right and left in preference to the other stronger division, home rule or union.

ECONOMY

The economy, based almost entirely upon fishing and fish processing, is recovering from the recent recession. Cod fisheries are doing well owing to a resurgence in stocks. Preliminary drilling for oil commenced in 1996 on Suðuroy. In mid-1996 the unemployment rate was 10%, and inflation was 2%. In 1994 the GNP stood at 4965 million Danish kroner.

POPULATION & PEOPLE

About 43,000 people live in the Faroes: 14,000 of them in the capital, Tórshavn, and 5000 more in Klaksvík. While on first appearances the Faroese may seem somewhat reserved, on getting to know them you'll discover the friendliest and most hospitable people in the North Atlantic region.

Every summer there are local festivals where you'll see the traditional Faroese chain dance. The largest festival takes place in Tórshavn on Ólavsøka (Faroese National Day).

LANGUAGE

Faroese is a Germanic language derived from old Norse, closely related to Icelandic and some Norwegian dialects.

In 1890 a standard written version of Faroese, Føroyskt, was made official and given equal status with Danish in public and government affairs.

See the Language Guide at the end of the book for some useful words and phrases.

Facts for the Visitor

PLANNING
Climate & When to Go

The best season to visit is from June to August. Rain in one form or another can be expected 280 days of the year. Fortunately,

weather is somewhat localised. Tune to Útvarp Føroya radio (89.8 MHz FM, 531 kHz MW) for weather information in English, on weekdays at 8.45 am. For information on what to bring, see the Iceland chapter.

Books & Maps

For more detailed background and practical information, consult the Lonely Planet guide *Iceland, Greenland & the Faroe Islands – travel survival kit*. Another background text is *The Faroe Islands* by Liv Kjørsvik Schei and Gunnie Moberg (John Murray, London, 1991).

A handy booklet of topographic maps covering the Faroes (Danish: Færøerne) on a scale of 1:100,000 is available at tourist offices and bookshops in the Faroes for Dkr115, or directly from the publishers Kort og Matrikelstyrelsen (☎ 45-35 87 50 50; fax 45-35 87 50 51), Rentemestervej 8, DK-2400 Copenhagen, Denmark. The islands are also mapped at a scale of 1:20,000 (Dkr70).

Online Services

There's lots of tourist and general information on the Faroese University Internet home page (http://www.sleipnir.fo/).

HIGHLIGHTS & SUGGESTED ITINERARIES

Depending on the length of your stay you might like to include these highlights:

Two days
    Tórshavn and a tour of the Vestmanna bird cliffs or a visit to a village such as Gjógv, Kirkjubøur, Oyndarfjørður or Tjørnuvík
One week
    As above plus Klaksvík, the islands of Viðoy (for the tough walk to the Enniberg cliffs, the highest sheer cliff face in Europe), and Kalsoy
Two weeks
    As above plus the islands of Vágar and Mykines

TOURIST OFFICES

For local tourist offices see Organised Tours in the Getting Around section of this chapter and under Tórshavn, Information. Representatives abroad include:

Denmark
  Færøernes Repræsentationskontor, Højbroplads 7, DK-1200 Copenhagen K (☎ 33 14 08 66)
  Danish Tourist Board, Vesterbrogade 6D, DK-1620 Copenhagen V (☎ 33 11 14 15)
UK
  Faroese Commercial Attaché, 150 Market St, Aberdeen, AB1 2PP, Scotland (☎ 1224-592777)
USA
  Danish Tourist Board, 655 Third Avenue, 18th Floor, New York, NY 10017 (☎ 212-949 2333)

VISAS, EMBASSIES & DOCUMENTS
Visas & Embassies
Citizens of Western European countries, the USA, Canada, Australia and New Zealand need only a valid passport to visit the Faroes for up to three months. The Faroes are represented abroad by Danish embassies.

Documents
To drive in the Faroes, you'll need a full driving licence and proof of insurance (eg a Green Card) from your insurance company.

Holders of student identity cards will get discounts on bus and ferry fares and at camping grounds.

CUSTOMS
Visitors over 18 years of age may import 200 cigarettes, 50 cigars or 250g of tobacco, a litre of wine (up to 22%), a litre of spirits (from 22% to 60% proof), and two litres of beer (less than 5.8%, and in long-necked bottles only). Two additional litres of spirits may be imported upon payment of duties. Confectionery is limited to three kg per person. Nonrecyclable containers are forbidden and animals may not be brought in.

MONEY
Although the Faroes issue their own currency, the Faroese króna (Fkr) is tied to the Danish krone (Dkr) and the two are used interchangeably throughout the Kingdom of Denmark. Foreign currency may be exchanged at any Faroese bank from Monday to Friday between 9 am and 4 pm and Thursday until 6 pm. The exchange bank at Vágar airport is open from 10 am to 2 pm and for arriving or departing international flights.

Often a small commission is charged for exchange services. Outside banking hours, hotels usually exchange money as do tourist information offices and travel agencies. All brands of travellers' cheques and major currencies are accepted. Postal cheques may be exchanged at post offices in larger towns.

Costs
The minimum price of a single hotel room is about Dkr500, but there are also guesthouses, youth hostels and camping grounds offering more economical options. Eating out, supermarket food and bus travel are expensive compared to most other Western European countries. Tipping is not required. There is a 25% value-added tax included in all quoted prices.

Currency
One króna is equal to 100 øre. Notes come in denominations of 50, 100, 500 and 1000 krónur; the Danish coins in use include 25 and 50 øre, one króna and two, five, 10 and 20 krónur.

Currency Exchange
See the Denmark chapter for the Danish krone's rates.

POST & COMMUNICATIONS
The postal service, Postverk Føroya, has offices in most towns and villages. Village post offices often close for a one to three-hour lunch break. The central post office in Tórshavn is open Monday to Friday only, from 9 am to 5 pm. Poste restante is reliable.

Make international telephone calls and send faxes from the telephone office (Tinghúsvegur 3, Tórshavn), open daily from 8 am to 9 pm. The public fax number there is 16498. Telephone cards with denominations of Dkr20, 50 and 100 are available. From public phones, local calls cost Dkr2 for up to five minutes.

The Faroes' international country code is ☎ 298. To dial out of the Faroes, you must dial ☎ 009 then the destination country code, area or city code and phone number (to ring Denmark, use 0 rather than 009).

TIME

From 25 October to 24 March, local time in the Faroes is GMT/UTC, the same time as London, but five hours ahead of New York, eight hours ahead of Los Angeles and 11 hours behind Sydney. The rest of the year, they're on GMT plus one hour.

ELECTRICITY

Electricity is at 220V, 50 Hz. Most plugs have two round pins, but some have three.

WEIGHTS & MEASURES

The metric system is used in the Faroes.

WOMEN TRAVELLERS

Women will have no special problems in the Faroe Islands.

GAY & LESBIAN TRAVELLERS

Although homosexuality is legal in the Kingdom of Denmark, be aware that there are strong religious traditions in the Faroes so, to avoid upsetting local people, be discreet.

DISABLED TRAVELLERS

Most public transport in the Faroes can take at least one passenger in a wheelchair. Some hotels and hostels have wheelchair access. For further details, contact the Faroese Association for the Handicapped (☎ 17373), Íslandsvegur 10c, FR-100 Tórshavn.

BUSINESS HOURS

Shops are generally open Monday to Friday from 9 am to 5.30 pm, and Saturday from 9 am to noon. For banks and post offices, see Money and Post & Communications, respectively.

PUBLIC HOLIDAYS & SPECIAL EVENTS

The Faroese observe the following holidays:

1 January, *New Year's Day*
6 January, *Epiphany*
March, *Gregorius' Day*
Maundy Thursday, Good Friday, Easter Sunday, Easter Monday
25 April, *Flag Day*
1 May, *Labour Day*
11 May, *Common Prayers Day*
May, *Ascension Day*
June, *Whitsunday, Whitmonday*
5 June, *Constitution Day*
28 & 29 July, *Ólavsøka (Faroese National Day and Festival)*
1 November, *All Saints' Day*
24 December, *Christmas Eve*
25 December, *Christmas Day*
26 December, *Boxing Day*
31 December (afternoon only), *New Year's Eve*

ACTIVITIES

Activities in the Faroe Islands include birdwatching (particularly on the Mykines and Vestmanna cliffs), fishing and hiking. Most hiking trails on the main islands are marked on the 1:100,000 map; more adventurous hikers may wish to climb the highest peak, Slættaratindur (882 metres), from Eiði.

WORK

Because of high unemployment in the Faroes, foreigners have little chance of finding paid work.

ACCOMMODATION

Those with webbed feet can try camping! You'll find camping grounds in Tórshavn on Streymoy and Eiði on Eysturoy. A new one in Klaksvík on Borðoy may be open from 1997. Most hostels allow camping on their land. With permission, wilderness camping is possible.

There are also several *gistiheimilið* (guesthouses) and *ferðamannaheim* (youth hostels) belonging to the Danish Youth Hostels Association (HI), the YMCA and other associations. Average hostel rates are Dkr90/95 for members/nonmembers. There are hostels in Tórshavn (☎ 18900; fax 15707) and Vestmanna (☎ 24610) on Streymoy; on Nólsoy (☎ 27025); Selatrað (☎ 48950), Fuglafjørður (☎ 44860 or 44437), Elduvík (☎ 44944), Gjógv (☎ 23175; fax 23505) and Oyndarfjørður (☎ 44522; fax 44570) on Eysturoy; Sandavágur (☎ 33465; fax 32901) on Vágar; on Mykines (☎ 18432); Øravík (☎ 71302) and Vágur (☎ 73060) on Suðuroy; Klaksvík (☎ 55403) on Borðoy; and on Svínoy (☎ 51105).

The average cost of a double hotel room is about Dkr700. Alternatively, there are *sjómansheimið* (seamen's homes) in Tórshavn, Runavík and Klaksvík, which were established by the Danish Lutheran church as safe lodging for sailors and fishermen. Strict Christianity is enforced – no carousing – and there are formal prayers every morning. They have cafeterias that serve breakfast, lunch, pizzas and *smørrebrød* (open sandwiches) all day, as well as meals for several hours in the evening. Double rooms cost from Dkr370 to Dkr420 without bath.

FOOD & DRINKS

Supermarkets are found in all towns and all but the smallest villages. Snacks such as burgers and chips are available at grill-bars and cafeterias in most towns and villages and at some petrol stations. There are relatively few restaurants and cafeterias that serve full meals. These meals usually consist of meat-and-two-veg, but finer restaurants have fish and Faroese specialities such as lamb and puffin. Traditional foods served at special events include horse and offal sausage, birds' eggs, sheep heads and whale meat. Alcohol is available from state alcohol stores, local brewery outlets and a few licenced bars, clubs and restaurants.

Getting There & Away

AIR

The Faroes international airport on Vágar is a bus ride, ferry ride and another bus ride from Tórshavn. Through buses to the airport run twice daily (once daily at weekends), leaving Tórshavn three hours before flight departures. For information and bookings, contact the tourist office or phone ☎ 12626.

Icelandair flies to the Faroes from Glasgow (May to September, once weekly) and Reykjavík (two or three times weekly).

Another option is to fly Maersk or Atlantic Airways, which have daily flights between Copenhagen and Vágar. During the summer, they fly from Billund or Århus (Denmark) and return, once or twice weekly.

The discounted Icelandair Apex fare for Glasgow to Vágar return is UK£198. Copenhagen to Vágar return is Dkr2670 with Maersk and Dkr2550 with Atlantic Airways. For these tickets, you must stay one Saturday night and the maximum stay is one month. The nondiscounted return fares are UK£398 with Icelandair, and Dkr4080 with both Maersk and Atlantic Airways. If you're staying for only one weekend, the fare is just Dkr2085 return with Maersk and Dkr1995 with Atlantic Airways. Special fares are available for students, over-65s and groups.

SEA

Smyril Line's *Norrøna* operates from early June to early September. It sails from Esbjerg in Denmark on Saturday evening and arrives in Tórshavn on Monday morning.

Iceland-bound passengers must disembark while the ship continues to Bergen, Norway. After returning to Tórshavn on Wednesday, it collects Iceland passengers and sails overnight to Seyðisfjörður. It returns to Tórshavn on Friday morning, and continues to Esbjerg for another circuit. See also the introductory Getting There & Away chapter.

For more time in the Faroes, Iceland-bound passengers have to break the journey and pay for two sectors. The one-way high season deck fare from Esbjerg to Tórshavn (including a couchette) is Dkr1260, with 25% discount for student card-holders. Transporting vehicles up to five metres long costs Dkr1000. Above deck class, there are three classes of cabins and a luxury suite. The ship also has a bar, cafeteria, restaurant, disco, casino and duty-free shops.

For further information, contact Smyril Line (☎ 15900; fax 15707), J Broncksgøta 37, Postbox 370, FR-110 Tórshavn, Faroe Islands. In the UK, contact P&O Scottish Ferries (☎ 1224-572615; fax 1224-574411), PO Box 5, Jamieson's Quay, Aberdeen, AB9 8DL, Scotland.

Those coming from the UK can take Strandfaraskip Landsins' ferry *Smyril*, which sails twice weekly between 14 June and 18 August (once weekly at other times) from Aberdeen (Scotland) to Tórshavn. In summer it departs from Aberdeen on Thursday at 10 am and Sunday at 5 pm, arriving in Tórshavn on Friday and Monday, respectively.

The one-way deck class fare is Dkr600 in the high season, with 25% discount for student card-holders; for a cabin, you'll pay from Dkr1100 to Dkr1500. Transport of vehicles up to five metres long costs Dkr600. For information contact Strandfaraskip Landsins (☎ 14550; fax 18140), Yviri við Strond 4, Postbox 88, FR-110 Tórshavn, Faroe Islands. The UK agent is P&O Ferries.

Getting Around

Remember that the weather has the final say on whether transport services will actually run.

AIR

The Faroes have only one airport, the international terminal on Vágar, so inter-island air travel is by helicopter (*tyrlan*, pronounced 'TOOR-lan'). Several times a week, helicopters connect Vágar airport with Tórshavn, Klaksvík, Skúvoy, Froðba and Stóra Dímun. There are also routes from Vágar airport to Mykines and Gásadalur and from Klaksvík to Svínoy and Fugloy. The flights to Mykines are popular, so book early.

Helicopter services are operated by Atlantic Airways (☎ 33410; fax 33380), Vágar Airport, FR-380 Sørvágur. The Tórshavn heliport is 500 metres north of the camping ground. A helicopter flight from Tórshavn to Klaksvík will cost Dkr215; from Tórshavn to Skúvoy or Stóra Dímun Dkr130; from Vágar to Mykines or Gásadalur Dkr145; and from Klaksvík to Svínoy and Fugloy Dkr110.

BUS

The Bygdaleiðir long-distance bus service is excellent. It follows a strict and convenient schedule and, when combined with the ferry services, links virtually every corner of the country, including some fairly remote outposts. The bus timetable and map *Ferða-ætlan* is issued annually (Dkr20). Bus fares are steep but visitors can minimise costs by purchasing the SL Visitor Travelcard for Dkr385/600/900 for four/seven/14 days of unlimited travel on all buses and inter-island ferries (50% child discount, 7 to 13 years). Passes are available from the tourist information desk at the airport or the Farstøðin (harbour) transport terminal in Tórshavn.

CAR & MOTORCYCLE

There are few unsurfaced roads and most islands are connected to Tórshavn by car ferry. The greatest hazards are fog, sheep and precipitous drop-offs. Some of the numerous tunnels, especially those in the north-eastern islands, are wide enough for only one vehicle to pass through but there are bays every few hundred metres. If they are marked 'V', you have to pull in and allow the other car to pass. If they are marked 'M', the other car has to give way.

Be extremely alert in thick fog; motorists must take financial responsibility for anything they hit. The speed limit on open highways is 80 km/h, and 50 km/h through villages. Seat belt use is compulsory. In Tórshavn, you must place a parking disc (set at the time you parked your car) in the front window. These discs are available free from tourist offices and banks. Legal parking spaces are marked with a P followed by a number and the word '*tíma*', which indicates the maximum permitted parking time.

Rental agencies tack on a Collision Damage Waiver (CDW) but, with your own vehicle, you'll need either proof of third party insurance (eg a Green Card) or to be prepared to purchase it from the customs department upon entering the country.

Car Rental

You must be at least 18 years old to rent a car. It's expensive but there's no per km charge and the daily rate decreases the longer you keep the car. For a sedan, the first six

FAROE ISLANDS

days will cost from Dkr440 per day, whereas weekly rental starts at Dkr2464. A deposit of about Dkr1200 may be required against liability; the 25% VAT and petrol are not included. Car rental outlets include:

Avis Bílutleigan, Vágar Airport, FR-380 Sørvágur (☎ 32765; fax 33155)
Avis Føroyar v/Johs Berg, Staravegur 1, FR-110 Tórshavn (☎ 13535; fax 17735)
Eyðbjørn Hansen, Varðagøta 75, FR-100 Tórshavn (☎ 13375; fax 11495)
Hertz, Svend Aage Ellefsen, FR-360 Sandavágur (☎ 32583)

BICYCLE

Although there are lots of steep hills, tunnels, wind and rain, the Faroes are not too bad for cycling because all highways are surfaced. Don't take Faroese cycling too lightly though; warm, windproof and waterproof clothing is essential. If the weather gets too wretched, remember that buses accept bicycles as luggage for Dkr10 per ride.

The biggest obstacles for cyclists are the road tunnels, which are best avoided (especially Kollafjørður-Kaldbaksfjørður and Oyrarbakki-Vesturdalur); toxic gases can be trapped in the more congested tunnels. You'll need a good bicycle light both front and back, visible from several km away. Hills are steep, highways are wet and dropoffs severe, so check your brakes carefully.

Bicycle hire is available from Erling Midjord (☎ 16756), Hetlandsvegur 8, Tórshavn (Dkr80 per day) and John W Thomsen (☎ 55858), Nólsoyar Pálsgøta, Klaksvík (Dkr50 per day; discount for further days).

BOAT

All islands except Koltur and the Dímuns are connected by ferry or the bus system. Some ferries take vehicles and others only carry passengers. Children (7 to 13 years), students and people over 65 receive 14% to 50% discounts. Some ferry trips, especially those to Mykines, Svínoy and Fugloy, are through open seas in small boats and are frequently cancelled because of the weather. Keep plans as flexible as possible.

ORGANISED TOURS

Tours and bookings are available from the following organisations:

Atlantic Adventure, í Grønulág 2, FR-100 Tórshavn (☎ 17059; fax 17108) – a wide variety of packages, including guided mountain hikes and fishing trips
Kunningarstovan, Niels Finsensgøta 13, FR-100 Tórshavn (☎ 15788; fax 16831) – trips to the storm petrel colony on Nólsoy Island; hiking trips on Streymoy, Eysturoy and Sandoy; sea angling
Norðoya Kunningarstova, Nólsoyar Pálsgøta, FR-700 Klaksvík (☎ 56939; fax 56586) – hiking on the northern islands, including the Enniberg cliffs; sightseeing around Kalsoy by boat; sea angling
Kunningarstovan Suðuroy, FR-800 Tvøroyri (☎ 72480; fax 72380) – guided hikes on Suðuroy, sailing, fishing and diving
Gunnar Skúvadal, FR-350 Vestmanna (☎ 24305; fax 24292) – exceptionally friendly boat tours to the Vestmanna bird cliffs
Palli Lamhauge, FR-350 Vestmanna (☎ 24155; fax 24383) – boat tours to the Vestmanna bird cliffs and Eiði
Óðin, Postbox 1371, FR-110 Tórshavn (☎ 12499; fax 19124) – charters and tours between Tórshavn and Nólsoy, Hestur and Koltur
Strandfaraskip Landsins, Postbox 88, FR-110 (Yviri við Strod 4) Tórshavn (☎ 16660; fax 16000) – bus, boat and fishing day trips
Tora Tourist Traffic, Postbox 3012, FR-110 (Niels Finsengøta 21)Tórshavn (☎ 15505; fax 15667) – mainly day tours by bus

Tórshavn

The capital and largest community of the Faroes, Tórshavn, has a relaxed atmosphere and enjoys picturesque charm. A stroll around Tinganes, the small peninsular headland where the town began nearly a thousand years ago, will endear this quiet and rainy little place to most visitors.

Orientation

Tórshavn is easy to walk around. The older section surrounds the two harbours, which are separated by the historical Tinganes peninsula. The eastern harbour is the ferry terminal and the western harbour is for commerce.

Uphill from the harbours, there's a modern centre with most shops, restaurants and services, including the SMS indoor shopping mall on RC Effersøesgøta.

Information

Tourist Office The Faroe Islands Tourist Board (Postbox 118, FR-110 Tórshavn; ☎ 16055; fax 10858), is on Gongin (Tinganes), and the Kunningarstovan city tourist office (☎ 15788; fax 16831) is at Niels Finsensgøta 13. They're open Monday to Friday from 8 am to 5 pm, and Saturday from 2 to 5 pm and 9 am to 2 pm, respectively. The tourist board is also open on Sunday from 2 to 5 pm. Both offices distribute the useful free publication, *Around the Faroe Islands*, with details on sights and tourist facilities around the country.

Money Tórshavn's banks are open on weekdays from 9 am to 4 pm (late closing on Thursday at 6 pm); all handle foreign exchange. Outside normal banking hours, the tourist office will exchange money. After hours, try the Hotel Hafnia, which will charge a higher commission but it's open evenings and Sunday. Visa, Plus, Eurocard, MasterCard, Cirrus and JCB are accepted by the Føroya Banki ATM at Niels Finsensgøta 15.

Post & Communications The central post office, on Vaglið (the town square) and behind the Ráðhús (town hall), is open Monday to Friday from 9 am to 5 pm. Philatelic services are also available there. Purchase telephone cards, send or receive faxes and make international calls at the telephone office, Tinghúsvegur 3.

Bookshops The best place to find foreign language publications is HN Jacobsens Bókahandil (☎ 11036), on Vaglið. Other bookshops in Tórshavn stock some English and German titles.

Laundry The Myntvask automatic laundrette on J Broncksgøta is open from 6 am to 9 pm Monday to Saturday and 3 to 9 pm on Sunday. If you'd rather have someone else do your laundry, try Seytjan on Áarvegur 12, open Monday to Friday from 9 am to 5.30 pm, and Saturday from 9 am to 2 pm.

Medical & Emergency Services There's a casualty service at the hospital (☎ 13540) on JC Svabosgøta. Call ☎ 000 for police, ambulance or the fire service.

Things to See

Until the early 1900s, Tórshavn didn't extend beyond the Tinganes peninsula. The narrow Gongin, still lined with some lovely 19th-century wooden houses, was the main street.

Probably dating from the 15th century, **Munkastovan** had a religious role as a lodging house for monks. The 16th-century **Leigubúðin** was the king's storehouse. When most of the old buildings on Tinganes burnt down in 1673 this and Munkastovan were spared. **Reynargarður**, once a vicarage, was constructed in 1630 and it's an excellent example of 17th-century Faroese architecture. **Skansapakkhúsi**, at the southern end of Tinganes, was built in 1750 for artillery storage. The stone **Myrkastovan** (Dark house), dating from 1693, was a guard house.

The fort **Skansin**, now in ruins, on the edge of the eastern harbour, was ostensibly constructed to keep pirates and smugglers from upsetting the local monopoly trade. It affords a great view of the harbour.

The Faroese Museum of Art, **Listaskálin**, north of Viðarlund Park, has works by Faroese artists. It's open between 3 June and 1 September on weekdays from 11 am to 5 pm, and Saturday and Sunday, 2 to 6 pm (Dkr20).

The new historical museum **Fornminnisavn**, at Hoyvík (two km north of the city centre), contains religious and maritime artefacts, boats, early art, and practical household and farming implements from the Viking Age and the medieval period to modern times. It's open on weekdays from 10 am to 4 pm and on weekends from 1 to 5 pm, and it's well worth a visit. Admission costs Dkr20. Red buses 3 and 4 pass near the

FAROE ISLANDS

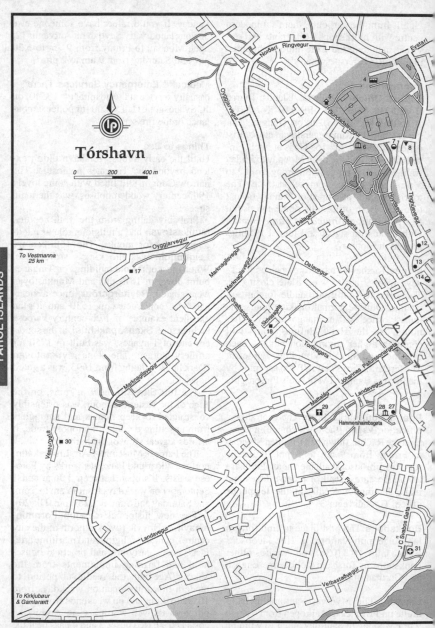

Tórshavn

0   200   400 m

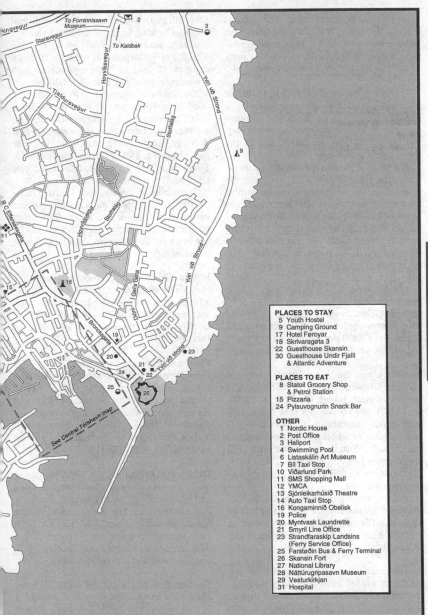

PLACES TO STAY
5 Youth Hostel
9 Camping Ground
17 Hotel Føroyar
18 Skrivaragøta 3
22 Guesthouse Skansin
30 Guesthouse Undir Fjalli
   & Atlantic Adventure

PLACES TO EAT
8 Statoil Grocery Shop
   & Petrol Station
15 Pizzaria
24 Pylsuvognurin Snack Bar

OTHER
1 Nordic House
2 Post Office
3 Heliport
4 Swimming Pool
6 Listaskálin Art Museum
7 Bil Taxi Stop
10 Viðarlund Park
11 SMS Shopping Mall
12 YMCA
13 Sjónleikarhúsið Theatre
14 Auto Taxi Stop
16 Kongaminnið Obelisk
19 Police
20 Myntvask Laundrette
21 Smyril Line Office
23 Strandfaraskip Landsins
   (Ferry Service Office)
25 Farstøðin Bus & Ferry Terminal
26 Skansin Fort
27 National Library
28 Náttúrugripasavn Museum
29 Vesturkirkjan
31 Hospital

museum, on Hvítanesvegur. The natural history museum **Náttúrugripasavn**, on Debesartrøð, just off VU Hammershaimbsgøta is open in summer on weekdays from 11 am to 4 pm and on weekends from 3 to 5 pm (Dkr20).

The rather low-profile **Smiðjan í Lítluvík** gallery is housed in an old iron forge on Grím Kambansgøta, not far from the western harbour. It has no set opening hours, but visiting exhibitions are advertised at the Kunningarstovan tourist office.

The **Niels R Finsen Memorial** commemorates the Faroese physician who won the Nobel Prize for medicine around the turn of the century and who is now considered the father of radiology. As a child, he carved his initials into a rock in what is now a tiny city park. A plaque reads 'On this rock Niels R Finsen carved his name as a youth. His achievement has etched it into the hearts of all'.

Places to Stay

Camping The camping ground (☎ 17661) is 1500 metres north along the coast from the centre. For Dkr40 per person you can camp and use the kitchen and bathroom facilities.

Hostels Up in the valley Gundadalur, just over one kilometre from central Tórshavn, is the official youth hostel, *Tórshavn* (☎ 18900; fax 15707), open between 5 June and 6 September. Accommodation is in two to eight-bed dormitories set off by partitions inside a sports hall. Hostelling International (HI) members/nonmembers pay Dkr85/95. Breakfast costs Dkr35 extra. Cooking facilities are available.

In the centre, near Vaglið square, is *Tórshavnar Sjómansheim* (☎ 13515; fax 13286), at Tórsgøta 4, where singles/doubles without bath cost Dkr275/395, including breakfast.

Guesthouses A local couple at Skrivaragøta 3 (☎ 11686) have dormitory sleeping-bag accommodation for Dkr80 per person, with discounts available for groups of over 10 people. Single/double rooms cost Dkr180/280. Breakfast is an additional Dkr40. Cooking facilities are available.

Guesthouse Undir Fjalli (☎ 17059; fax 17108), at Vesturgøta 15, operates from 28 June to 10 August. Singles/doubles with shower and breakfast cost Dkr360/430.

Guesthouse Skansin (☎ 12242; fax 10657), at Jekaragøta 8, near the harbour, offers clean rooms for Dkr360/490, including breakfast. Less expensive is *Bládýpi Bed & Breakfast* (☎ 11951; fax 19451) in a nice part of town at Dokta Jacobsensgøta 14-16. Singles/doubles with shared facilities cost Dkr210/320, including breakfast.

The tourist offices and Tora Tourist Traffic (☎ 15505; fax 15667) on Niels Finsensgøta keep lists of families with rooms for tourists (singles/doubles average Dkr280/430). Staff can book similar accommodation elsewhere in the islands.

Hotels The more economical of Tórshavn's two hotels is *Hotel Hafnia* (☎ 11270; fax 15250), at Áarvegur 4-10, near the harbour. Singles/doubles with private bath begin at Dkr670/830. Extra beds are available for Dkr155.

Places to Eat

Fine Dining At the *Hotel Hafnia* you'll find a huge buffet breakfast for Dkr60. Two-course lunches cost about Dkr220 and Faroese specialities (including roast puffin) cost from Dkr65 to Dkr170. Alternatively, there's *Rio Bravo* at Tórsgøta 11, with an emphasis on steaks (Dkr160).

Cafeterias *Perlan* in the SMS shopping mall serves a variety of smørrebrød, desserts and hot snacks or a daily special for fairly reasonable prices. The special is Dkr39. The *Sjómansheimið* cafeteria (in the Tórshavn Sjómansheim) is open from 7 am to 9.30 pm with continental breakfasts, lunches, à la carte, smørrebrød and set specials.

Snacks The nicest but far from cheapest place for a snack is the cosy *Kondittaríið* at Niels Finsensgøta 11. For hot dogs, burgers and chips, try the *Pylsuvognurin* opposite

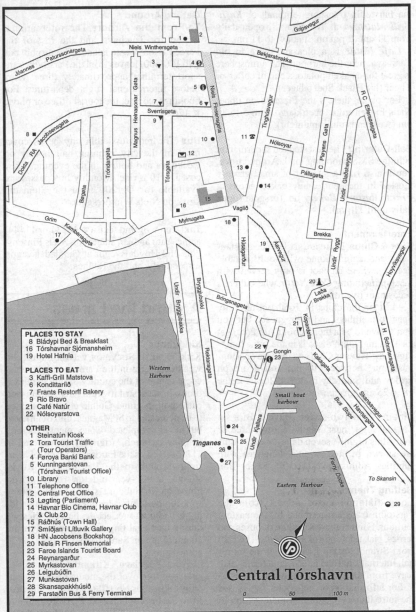

FAROE ISLANDS

PLACES TO STAY
8 Bládypi Bed & Breakfast
16 Tórshavnar Sjómansheim
19 Hotel Hafnia

PLACES TO EAT
3 Kaffi-Grill Matstova
6 Kondittaríð
7 Frants Restorff Bakery
9 Rio Bravo
21 Café Natúr
22 Nólsoyarstova

OTHER
1 Steinatún Kiosk
2 Tora Tourist Traffic
  (Tour Operators)
4 Føroya Banki Bank
5 Kunningarstovan
  (Tórshavn Tourist Office)
10 Library
11 Telephone Office
12 Central Post Office
13 Løgting (Parliament)
14 Havnar Bio Cinema, Havnar Club
   & Club 20
15 Ráðhús (Town Hall)
16 Smíðjan í Lítluvík Gallery
18 HN Jacobsens Bookshop
20 Niels R Finsen Memorial
23 Faroe Islands Tourist Board
24 Reynargarður
25 Myrkastovan
26 Leigubúðin
27 Munkastovan
28 Skansapakkhúsið
29 Farstøðin Bus & Ferry Terminal

Western Harbour

Small boat harbour

Tinganes

Eastern Harbour

To Skansin

Central Tórshavn

0   50   100 m

the Farstøðin transport terminal, or **Kaffi-Grill Matstova** at Tórsgøta 17, open daily from 11 am (2 pm on Sunday) to 11 pm.

Café Natúr is a pleasant place in old Tórshavn, near the harbour. The atmosphere is great for a baked potato, a cup of coffee or a beer (try Black Sheep lager).

For pizza, there's the *Pizzaria* on upper Niels Finsensgøta, open daily from 5 to 11 pm (weekends until midnight).

Self-Catering The best stocked supermarket is in the SMS shopping mall. Around town, you'll also find a number of small grocery kiosks. In the centre, buy baked goods at *Frants Restorff Bakery* on Tórsgøta (open daily until 11 pm).

Entertainment
Bars & Clubs There are six licenced restaurants and cafés (some with only a table licence, where alcohol is only served with meals), including *Café Natúr* where there's occasional live music.

Most of the clubs in Tórshavn are only open to members and their guests, but you don't have to be a member of *Club 20* to get in. This nightclub/disco is in the same building as the Havnar Club and cinema on Tinghúsvegur; between 10 pm and 4 am on Friday and Saturday it attracts locals in the 18 to 25 age group.

Cinema The two-screen Havnar Bio, on Tinghúsvegur near Vaglið, shows three or four films nightly, seven days a week. Films are shown in their original language with subtitles. Admission is Dkr50 or 55 per film.

Getting There & Away
Long-distance buses depart from the Farstøðin transport terminal by the eastern harbour. For a concise schedule of buses and ferries, pick up a copy of *Ferðaætlan* (Dkr20) from Strandfaraskip Landsins at the terminal. International and inter-island ferries also leave from the Farstøðin terminal.

For information on helicopter flights, see the introductory Getting Around section in this chapter.

Getting Around
To/From the Airport The international airport for Tórshavn and the rest of the Faroes is on Vágar island. The airport bus (No 100/300) leaves from the Farstøðin transport terminal approximately three hours before international flight departures. For bookings, contact the tourist office or phone ☎ 12626.

Bus The red Bussleiðin city buses cover most of the city, running half hourly on weekdays and hourly in the evening. They cost Dkr10 a ride. Monthly bus passes are available for Dkr200 from the Steinatún kiosk on Niels Winthersgøta.

Taxi You will find taxis (☎ 11234 or 11444) at the Auto and Bíl stands, on Niels Finsensgøta and Hoydalsvegur at Gundadalsvegur, respectively, and the Ráðhús.

Around the Faroes

Kirkjubøur
Kirkjubøur, on Streymoy, was the largest and wealthiest farm in the Faroes, and the episcopal centre of the country during medieval times. Its most striking ruin is the 'unfinished cathedral', a grand Gothic church intended to be dedicated to St Magnus, Earl of Orkney, but never completed. Consequently, nearby St Olav's church, originally constructed in 1111, served as the Faroes' ecumenical heart right through to the Reformation. Roykstovan, a 900-year-old turf-roofed farmhouse at Kirkjubøur, is a large two-storey split-log building. The interior of the building is laid out to reflect the Faroese lifestyle during medieval times. It's open daily from 10 am (2 pm on Sunday) to 5.30 pm (Dkr20 admission).

From Tórshavn, Kirkjubøur is reached either on foot over the mountain (eight km) or by taking bus No 101 (Dkr20, 30 minutes) from the Farstøðin Bus & Ferry Terminal to Gamlarætt and walking two km from there.

Vestmanna Bird Cliffs

The magnificent boat tours (see Organised Tours under the Getting Around section in this chapter) to the wild Vestmanna bird cliffs of north-western Streymoy are probably the highlight of the Faroe Islands. When the weather's fine, you sail from Vestmanna up the west coast of Streymoy to towering cliffs and sea stacks that teem with fulmars, kittiwakes, guillemots, razorbills and, occasionally, puffins. If the sea is calm, the boats pass through some beautiful sea caves beneath the cliffs.

To reach Vestmanna, take bus No 100 (Dkr40, 50 minutes) from the Farstøðin Bus & Ferry Terminal in Tórshavn.

Gjógv

The quiet village of Gjógv in the north of Eysturoy is one of the most picturesque in the Faroes. It's named after its harbour, which is an unusual sea-filled gorge. In Gjógv there's a pleasant *youth hostel* that is a good base if you want to climb the 882-metre Slættaratindur, the Faroes' highest peak. There's also a great walk to the Búgvin cliffs and sea stack.

To reach Gjógv from Tórshavn, take bus No 400 to Oyrarbakki then connect with bus No 205, which runs twice on weekdays, once on Saturday. The fare is Dkr50 and the trip takes two hours.

Klaksvík

Klaksvík, on the island of Borðoy, is the Faroes' second town. Like most Faroese towns, its economy is based on fishing and fish processing. Its most interesting site is the church Christianskirkja which has a baptismal font that is a 4000-year-old sacrificial bowl from a pagan temple in Denmark. Also of interest is the Norðoya Fornminnasavn (North Islands Museum), which is open daily from 2 to 4 pm (Dkr20).

Buses from Tórshavn connect with ferries to Klaksvík nine times on weekdays, five times on Saturday and six times on Sunday. The journey takes just over two hours and costs Dkr80.

Kalsoy

Kalsoy is an enigmatic island that ferry-bound travellers pass on their way to Klaksvík. Its four tiny villages are connected by a partly unsurfaced road that spends half its length in dark and wet tunnels. A bus takes you to Trøllanes, from where you should take the two-hour return walk to the Kollur lighthouse – it's well worth the effort. The bus (Dkr20) connects at Húsar with the two or three-times-daily ferry (Dkr30) from Klaksvík.

Viðareiði

The Faroes' northernmost village, Viðareiði, occupies a windy pass near the northern end of Viðoy island. Looking west from the village, the view to the headlands of northern Borðoy, Kunoy and Kalsoy is spectacular. The main attraction is the stiff walk up to the 750-metre Enniberg headland, the highest sheer cliff face in Europe. On weekdays, bus No 500 makes seven daily runs between Klaksvík and Viðareiði. On Saturday there are three runs, and on Sunday there are two.

Mykines

Most visitors agree that Mykines, the westernmost of the islands, is the jewel of the Faroes. Lying up 135 steps from the ferry landing site, Mykines' single village is magical, with earthen streets and bright turf-roofed houses.

Most visitors make a point of visiting Lundaland (land of puffins) on the islet of Mykineshólmur, which is connected to Mykines by a footbridge over a 35-metre gorge. The lighthouse on the islet's westernmost cape has a magnificent location, and it's surrounded by some of the world's most densely populated bird colonies.

For longer stays, there's a small guesthouse/snack bar, *Kristianshús* (☎ 18432), which charges Dkr195 per person, including breakfast, or just Dkr100 for a dormitory bed. Access to the island is by weather-dependent ferry service (daily in summer) from Sørvágur (Vágar island), or by helicopter from the international airport.

FAROE ISLANDS

Finland

Finland (Suomi) is a large country with friendly people, pristine nature and an interesting culture. It is usually considered a Scandinavian country, a categorisation based on geographical proximity that ignores Finland's unique character. Finland has shared almost 700 years of history with Sweden, but the Russian tradition has also been a strong influence in the very east.

The Finns have one of the longest traceable tenancies and have stubbornly resisted servitude or eviction. But the blooming of Finnish nationalism was late and delicate.

Summer is the best season, and north of Rovaniemi there are chances to see the midnight sun. Experiencing Lapland could introduce you to the Sami people and their culture.

Should you wish to brave the Finnish winter then go north during the eerie 'blue light' season and take a cruise on a Bothnian icebreaker.

Facts about the Country

HISTORY

Finland has traces of human settlement dating back almost 10,000 years. The Finns' ancestors seem to have dominated half of northern Russia before arriving on the north of the Baltic coast before the Christian era.

They established themselves in the forests, driving the nomadic Sami people to the north. The awakening of an early pre-Christian Finnish society is visible from the remains of hill-top fortresses, which are found in South Häme, and in Karelia on the shores of Lake Ladoga.

By the end of the Viking Age, Swedish traders had extended their interests to Ladoga and throughout the Baltic region. The growth of central power in Sweden and in Russian Novgorod anticipated Finland's fate as a marchland in play between the two countries.

In 1155 the Swedes made Finland a province, but in 1240 Alexander Nevsky defeated the Swedes, beginning a strong Orthodox tradition in the east. The Treaty of Nöteborg in 1323 delivered East Karelia to Novgorod.

In the 1520s the Reformation came to Swedish Finland which grew to include Lapland, North Karelia and the western shore of Ladoga. But Gustav II Adolf began to Swedify his Finnish subjects, starting with the establishment of the first university in the capital Turku. His heavy-handedness began to split the country along religious lines and most followers of the Orthodox faith fled to Russia. Famine killed a third of all Finns and so brought a weaker Finland into the 18th century and an age of wars with Russia.

Russia took Ladoga and Vyborg (Finnish: Viipuri) and, in 1809, the whole country. But Finland gained greater autonomy as a Grand Duchy with its Swedish laws, Lutheran Church and Finnish Senate. In 1812 the capital moved to Helsinki. Nationalism began to surge, although the first prominent Finns bore Swedish names. This suited the tsars until the 1880s, when a firmer policy appeared to dismantle and Russify the Finnish state.

From the end of WWI Finnish activists began to break Russian control and introduce reforms. Independence was declared in December 1917 under a bilateral coalition, but the divisions between socialists and

Finland

FINLAND

conservatives, after a bloody civil war, forced out the socialists and more moderate social democrats took their place.

The question of Åland's status soured relations with Sweden. Åland (Finnish: Ahvenanmaa) maintained its Swedish culture but submitted to Finnish sovereignty in 1921.

Further anti-communist violence broke out early in the 1930s and relations with the Soviet Union remained uneasy after the 1932 non-aggression pact. Finland sought neutrality and formalised a commitment to Scandinavian solidarity, but it was probably Soviet concern about its security in the north-west that led to demands for Karelian territory and the Winter War in 1939.

Finnish defiance of the Soviet Union ended after months of fighting and Finland again lost part of Karelia and some nearby islands. Almost half a million people had to be resettled to the west. The Finnish predicament prompted concrete aid only from Germany, and Finland resumed hostilities late in 1941 (the Continuation War).

By September 1944, growing Soviet strength forced another armistice, the terms of which meant Finns turning to fight entrenched German forces in Lapland until the general peace. This was the last of more than 40 wars with Russia. It cost Finland almost 100,000 lives and heavy reparations.

Under President Paasikivi, Finland took a new line in its Soviet relations and signed a new treaty. Finland was to recognise Soviet security concerns and agree to Soviet aid in defending the frontier. This developed further during the 25 years of Urho Kekkonen's presidency and Finland was able to craft an independent view of East-West relations.

Thus Finland was put in the forefront of international dialogue, and this brought the security to develop its economy and welfare and its Scandinavian links through the Nordic Council. The several Helsinki conferences and accords were significant until the downfall of the Soviet Union. Since then, Finland has tried to solve its worst post-war recession and an endless number of bankruptcies, reforms and dire inconveniences. In 1995 Finland joined the EU, giving this oft-forgotten country new opportunities.

GEOGRAPHY & ECOLOGY

Finland is Europe's seventh-biggest country. It is an uneven lowland apart from the northern tip of the Scandinavian spine. The postglacial lakes are the country's dominant feature. Forests cover two-thirds of Finland and the Arctic Zone covers one-third. Altogether there are 180,000 lakes, and winding ridges separating the lakes are common.

Finland boasts over 30 national parks and some of the last wilderness areas in Europe although pulp factories, clear felling and acid rain (in north-east Lapland – legacy of Soviet-era industries across the border) threaten the environment.

GOVERNMENT & POLITICS

Finland is a presidential republic and a prime minister is elected every four years by the assembly of 200 members.

The president, chosen by the people, has a six-year term and, in council with the prime minister and cabinet, forms the executive government. Mr Martti Ahtisaari was elected in 1994 (for further information see the president's home page: http://www.tpk.fi/). The parliament is elected by proportional representation over 14 national districts. There are 12 provincial administrations, the *lääni*, and more than 450 *kunta* or municipalities.

The exception to this structure is Åland, which has a small local parliament and a high degree of autonomy. It also sends one member of parliament to Helsinki.

ECONOMY

Most businesses in Finland are privately owned but government spending constituted over 63% of GDP in 1993. Finland's economy has stagnated during the 1990s.

Finland borrows heavily to finance a welfare system that allows some Finns to earn a similar amount of money either through working or remaining on the dole. During the 1990s unemployment has remained above 16% and some statistics claim that Finland's tax rate is the highest in the world – 95% of the price of a bottle of vodka goes to the government.

Industry only developed fully after WWII but delivered sustained growth of about 4% annually until about a decade ago. The metals and engineering sector dominate foreign earnings: cruise ships and mobile phones are two examples.

For the traveller, general costs are lower than they have been for decades and five-star comforts are almost cheap compared to many European countries. A general value-added tax is set at 12% or 22% depending on the item purchased.

POPULATION & PEOPLE

Finland has a population of 5,200,000 people, more than half of whom live in the south and south-west. Finland is the third most sparsely populated country in Europe with 16 people per sq km. There are approximately 300,000 Swedish-speaking Finns, and more than 4000 Sami people, living mostly in the deep north, and a similar number of Romany people (Gypsies) in the south.

The Sami population in Finland consists of three distinctive groups, each speaking their own dialect. The Scandinavian Sami region has its own flag, and many Samis look across the border at the more developed Sami community in Norway for a deeper cultural identity.

In the west of Finland there are Swedish-speaking towns and fishing communities along the coast and on the Åland islands.

ARTS

The author of the Moominland stories, Tove Jansson, probably has the highest international profile among contemporary Finns although you cannot escape the design work of the late Alvar Aalto in public buildings and furniture. One of the very greatest of modern composers, Jean Sibelius, was a Finn at the forefront of national aspirations.

Sibelius and the nationalistic painter Akseli Gallen-Kallela fell under the spell of Karelianism, a movement going back to the folk songs collected to form the national epic, the *Kalevala*, by Elias Lönnrot in the 1830s. That compilation permeated the national consciousness and developed with the literary language of the 19th century to form a bridge between liberal and Karelian folk traditions. But the greatest of Finnish writers, Aleksis Kivi, worked in a late-Romantic framework.

Great Finnish authors, including Mika Waltari and Väinö Linna, have been translated by Finnish and American publishers. *Contemporary Finnish Poetry* by Herbert Lomas highlights the best poets, and *A Way to Measure Time* (Finnish Literature Society) contains contemporary Finnish literature by over 50 authors. For an excellent introduction to Finnish cinema, see *A Couple of Finns and Some Donald Ducks* (VAPK, 1991) by Roger Connah, though this is a government publication and perhaps slightly biased.

CULTURE

The image of a log cabin with a sauna by a forest lake captures the spirit of Finnish culture: independence, endurance *(sisu* or 'guts'), a love of open space and a capacity for reflection. The music of Sibelius reveals a mysticism that cannot be explained unless it's speaking through the *Kalevala* or through the stark simplicity of modern Finnish design. Perhaps the great Finnish distance runners sum up the society best by their very resilience.

A crude division of population into western and eastern Finns will help to differentiate certain aspects of the culture.

RELIGION

About 90% of Finns are Evangelical Lutherans and only 50,000 or so are now Orthodox. Minority churches, including the Roman Catholic Church, make up only a few per cent.

LANGUAGE

Finnish is a Uralic language and belongs to the Finno-Ugric group. Finnish is closely related to Estonian and had common origins with Samoyed and languages spoken in the

FINLAND

Volga basin. The most widely spoken of the Finno-Ugric languages is Hungarian, but similarities with Finnish are few.

Finnish is spoken by some five million people in Finland, Sweden, Norway and Russian Karelia. The country is known as *Suomi*, and the language as *suomi*. It is not a Scandinavian language, nor is it related to Indo-European languages. There are, however, many words on loan from Baltic, Slavic and Germanic languages, and many words are derived from English.

Staff at most tourist offices and hotels will speak fluent English but bus drivers and staff at guesthouses, some hostels and restaurants won't. Finnish is by no means an easy language to master but it is easy to read out loud, and mistakes made by visitors are usually disregarded.

Swedish is spoken on Åland, as well as on the coast near Helsinki, Turku and Vaasa, and all Finns learn Swedish at school. Some local dialects are very difficult to understand, but usually your Swedish lessons will bear fruit.

See the Language Guide at the back of the book for pronunciation guidelines and useful words and phrases.

Facts for the Visitor

PLANNING
Climate & When to Go
Finland enjoys four seasons that differ enormously: from continuing darkness in Arctic winter to a two-month 'day' in northern Lapland's summer. The tourist season is from early June to the end of August, although in Lapland the mosquitoes are annoying in July – autumn *(ruska)* colours appear in September there. Snow remains in Lapland until late May and may reappear by late September.

Don't underestimate the Finnish summer – natural attractions are superb, temperatures are high and almost all attractions, hostels and camping grounds are open. It never gets dark – you can walk any time, anywhere, and even camp almost anywhere. In autumn, winter and spring, travelling should be restricted and better planned.

Books & Maps
Lonely Planet's *Finland – travel survival kit* is the most comprehensive English-language guidebook ever published on Finland. There are several guidebooks on Helsinki, including *Helsinki an Architectural Guide* (Otava, 1990) and *Helsinki Urban Guide* by Helsinki City Planning Department (1994).

For history, see the hardback *A History of Finland* (1996, WSOY) by E Jutikkala & K Pirinen, or the paperback *A Brief History of Finland* (Otava 1994) by Matti Klinge.

There are several books on sauna – a technical introduction is *Finnish Sauna* by the Building Information Institute (1995).

Good maps on Finland include the GT brand series in 1:200,000 (cheapest in book form) and trekking maps from 1:50,000 to 1:100,000. Look for 1:20,000 maps in libraries throughout Finland (and a photo-copy machine nearby!).

Online Services
Finland has more Internet home pages per capita than any other country, so use the WWW before leaving home. For natural attractions and wilderness cottage rentals, check http://www.metsa.fi/, or e-mail tikankontti@metsa.fi for further information. See also http://www.travel.fi.

What to Bring
Bring what you can from home to avoid the high retail prices of Finnish shops. Small refill packs (for washing powder, spices, cosmetics) save money and space. Even in summer you should have warm clothes and a waterproof and windproof jacket. Sheets are essential for hostelling. Budget travellers should consider a sleeping bag, a tent and the regular trekking kit.

SUGGESTED ITINERARIES
Depending on the length of your stay you might like to see and do the following things:

Two days
Helsinki: National museum and/or the Ateneum plus a stroll down the Pohjoisesplanadi to the market, and a boat trip to Suomenlinna; second day make a trip to Porvoo

One week
After a few days in Helsinki, you can do a loop reaching even Lapland, but better is the eastern route via Joensuu, Savonlinna and Kuopio

Two weeks
A triangle from Helsinki to Turku to Tampere to Hämeenlinna and back to Helsinki, the eastern route and several days in Lapland or Åland

One month
You can cover practically all major regions, and include a bicycle tour in Åland, a short trek in Lapland or North Karelia and visits to all major towns

Two months
Any extra time allocated for Finland should be spent exploring nature, either in Lapland, the Lakeland or North Karelia

HIGHLIGHTS

The best things in Finland are free: friendly people outside big cities, the 24-hour daylight in summer, architecture and pristine nature.

Islands

Apart from the main Åland Island itself, Kökar and Kumlinge typify the colourful archipelago culture of the Åland islands group. Similar old fishing communities are to be found outside Kotka (Haapasaari), Kalajoki (Maakalla) and Oulu (Hailuoto). The fortress and museums of Suomenlinna, 20 minutes by ferry from Helsinki are more accessible.

Museums & Galleries

Ateneum and the grottoes of the big Retretti complex at Punkaharju are the best art venues but you should begin with the collections of the National Museum. The open-air museums at Seurasaari near Helsinki and Pielisen museo at Lieksa in North Karelia are two of the best in the country. Regional museums in Pori, Oulu, Tornio and Vaasa are also interesting. For experiencing the northern culture, Arktikum in Rovaniemi and Saamelaismuseo in Inari are top class.

Castles

Olavinlinna at Savonlinna is the mightiest and best preserved of the northern medieval castles and is superbly set between two lakes. Only a little less imposing are the castles of Turku and Hämeenlinna, each with extensive museums.

Historic Towns

Turku is the oldest town in Finland, with the small wooden Luostarinmäki area remaining. Porvoo, Rauma and Naantali date from the 15th century, and all three have a medieval church and old town quarters.

Churches

There are approximately 70 medieval greystone churches in Finland, including Finland's oldest on Åland and the four most historical ones in Turku, Naantali, Nousiainen and Mynämäki. There are old paintings in the churches of Kalanti (near Turku), Parainen, Taivassalo and Rymättylä. There are also historically important churches in Isokyrö (near Vaasa), Hattula (near Hämeenlinna) and Porvoo.

The Keminmaa Church near Kemi displays a mummified corpse of a 16th-century Lutheran clergyman. The most significant wooden churches from the 17th and 18th century are those in Petäjävesi, Keuruu (near Jyväskylä) and Sodankylä. Fine paintings are to be found in the churches of Paltaniemi (near Kajaani) and Tornio. The largest church in Finland is in Kerimäki and has 3300 seats. The Tampere Cathedral is the most noteworthy example of national romantic edifices.

TOURIST OFFICES

Every town has a tourist office with good brochures and free maps covering most of the country. The main tourist information centre is run by the Finnish Tourist Board (Matkailun edistämiskeskus or MEK; ☎ 403 011) in Helsinki at Unionkatu 26, (Box 249, 00131) Helsinki.

FINLAND

Tourist Offices Abroad
Australia
   Finnish Tourist Board, Level 14, 33 Berry Street, North Sydney, NSW 2060 (☎ 02-9959 1982; fax 02-9959 1996)
Denmark
   Finlands Turistbureau, Vester Farimagsgade 3, 1606 Copenhagen V (☎ 3313 1362)
Estonia
   Soome turismi arenduskeskus, Pikk 71, EE-0001, Tallinn (☎ 2-631 3990)
Norway
   Finlands Turistkontor, Lille Grensen 7, 0159 Oslo 1 (☎ 2241 1070)
Sweden
   Finska Turistbyrån, Kungsgatan 4A, 11143 Stockholm (☎ 08-207 570; fax 08-249 594)
UK
   Finnish Tourist Board, 30-35 Pall Mall, London SW1Y 5LP (☎ 0171-839 4048; fax 0171-321 0696)
USA
   Finnish Tourist Board, 655 Third Avenue, New York, NY 10017 (☎ 212-370 5540; fax 212-983 5260)

VISAS & DOCUMENTS
Always bring a passport. Citizens of the EU countries, Norway and Iceland can, however, come and go without one. Most Western nationals don't need a tourist visa for stays of less than three months. Visas for Russia take two weeks to process in Helsinki, so you may want to get one before leaving home.

Alien's Permit Affairs (☎ 1891) at Punanotkonkatu 2, 00130 Helsinki, deals with work permits.

EMBASSIES
Finnish Embassies Abroad
Australia
   10 Darwin Avenue, Yarralumla 2600 ACT Australia (☎ 06-273 3800)
Canada
   Suite 850, 55 Metcalfe Street, Ottawa K1P 6L5, (☎ 613-236 2389)
Denmark
   Sankt Annae Plads 24, 1250 Copenhagen K, (☎ 3313 4214)
Estonia
   Liivalaia 12, EE0001 Tallinn, (☎ 2-311 444)
Germany
   Friesdorferstrasse 1, 5300 Bonn 2, (☎ 0 228-382 980)
Norway
   Thomas Heftyes gate 1, 0244 Oslo (☎ 2243 0400)

Russia
   Kropotkinskij Pereulok 15/17, 119034 Moskva G-34 (☎ 095-246 4027)
Sweden
   Jakobsgatan 6, 6tr, 111 52 Stockholm, (☎ 08-676 6700)
UK
   38 Chesham Place, London SW1X 8HW, (☎ 0171-838 6200)
USA
   3301 Massachusetts Ave NW, Washington DC 20008 (☎ 202-298 5800)

Foreign Embassies in Finland
Australia
   Consulate, Museokatu 25B, Helsinki (☎ 447 233)
Canada
   Pohjoisesplanadi 25B, Helsinki (☎ 171 141)
Denmark
   Keskuskatu 1A, Helsinki (☎ 171 511)
Estonia
   Kasarmikatu 28, Helsinki (☎ 622 0288)
Latvia
   Armfeltintie 10, Helsinki (☎ 476 4720)
Lithuania
   Rauhankatu 13 A, Helsinki (☎ 608 210)
Norway
   Rehbinderintie 17, Helsinki (☎ 171 234)
Poland
   Armas Lindgrenintie 21, Helsinki (☎ 684 8077)
Russia
   Tehtaankatu 1B, Helsinki (☎ 661 876)
Sweden
   Pohjoisesplanadi 7B, Helsinki (☎ 651 255)
UK
   Itäinen Puistotie 17, Helsinki (☎ 661 293)
USA
   Itäinen Puistotie 14A, Helsinki (☎ 171 931)

CUSTOMS
Travellers should encounter few problems with Finnish customs. You can bring currency and gifts up to the value of 1100 mk into Finland without declaration. You can bring 15 litres of beer, five litres of wine and one litre of strong alcohol (new, more generous limits will apply from 1 January 1997). Check current rules on the international ferry or at the border post.

MONEY
Currency
The markka (plural markkaa), or 'mark' in Swedish, is abbreviated as mk. Notes come

in 20, 50, 100, 500 and 1000-mk denominations and coins in one, five and 10 markkaa and 50 and 10 penniä. All banknotes issued until 1980 (and 1, 5 and 20-penniä coins), are now annulled, and can be changed only at Suomen Pankki (Finland's Bank) offices until 31 December 2003.

The Swedish krona (including coins) is accepted on Åland and in western Lapland, and the Norwegian krona can be used in areas near the Norwegian border in northern Lapland.

Exchange Rates
The markka may be pegged to the main EU currencies by the time you reach Finland. The following currencies convert at these approximate rates:

Australia	A$1	=	3.61 Fmk
Canada	C$1	=	3.35 Fmk
Estonia	1 Ekr	=	0.38 Fmk
Germany	DM1	=	2.99 Fmk
New Zealand	NZ$1	=	3.19 Fmk
Norway	1 Nkr	=	0.70 Fmk
Sweden	1 Skr	=	0.69 Fmk
UK	UK£1	=	7.13 Fmk
USA	US$1	=	4.56 Fmk

Costs
Finland is cheaper than Sweden and Norway but budget travellers should be careful at train and bus station kiosks and restaurants. Free things are numerous, including public libraries and many wilderness huts. A lunch package in a cheap restaurant starts at 30 mk. Alcohol is dear but a bottle of light beer in supermarkets costs just 3 mk. Trains are cheaper than buses, unlike in Sweden. Petrol is expensive but there are no extra charges (such as road tolls or ferry charges) for car travel.

Ask at tourist offices about package and discount cards such as the Helsinki Card.

Changing Money
Finland has just three national banks, and they have similar rates and charges (20 mk per cash transaction). Cheaper are independent exchange facilities such as Forex, but they will not be found in small towns. Travellers' Cheques are expensive to change, usually at 40 mk per transaction. Finnish ATMs only accept foreign bank cards with Visa or Plus symbols. Credit cards are widely accepted. Visa and Eurocard-MasterCard are the main cards accepted by banks, but American Express, Diner's Club and Access are common in hotels and restaurants. Banks are open from 9 am to 4.15 pm weekdays.

Tipping & Bargaining
Tipping is generally not necessary anywhere. In small specialist shops and small guesthouses you can reduce the price by 10% to 20% if you are friendly towards the owner. Flea markets are excellent places for bargaining, especially for used clothes.

Consumer Taxes
The VAT of 22% can be deducted if you post goods from the point of sale. Alternatively, at stores showing the 'Tax Free for Tourists' sign you can buy items priced over 200 mk at discounts of 12% to 16% if you show your tax-free cheque and sealed goods at the refund window at customs posts to claim the refund. A brochure (with a list of collection points) is available from Europe Tax-Free Shopping (☎ 6132 9600), Salomonkatu 17A, 00100 Helsinki.

POST & COMMUNICATIONS
Post offices are generally open from 9 am to 5 pm weekdays, but stamps can be bought at stations and newspaper shops. Postcards and letters weighing up to 20g cost 3.20 mk to EU countries, 2.70 mk to other countries in Europe, and 3.40 mk elsewhere (air-mail or *lentoposti*). There is poste restante at the main post offices in cities.

Telephone
Most public phones accept coins but the number that only accept national Tele cards (30, 50 or 100 mk) is increasing. After a telephone number reform, Finland now has 13 area codes each starting with a zero –

FINLAND

beware of old listings with old numbers. For enquiries dial ☎ 118.

You could make a short local call for 1 mk but expect to pay at least 2 mk. Calls between 10 pm and 8 am are cheaper; remember this when calling internationally. Daytime tariffs are 1 to 1.65 mk a minute to Sweden, 3 to 3.40 mk to the UK, 4.40 to 5.20 mk to the USA and 4.50 to 5.40 mk to Australia. Prefix 994 currently gives the lowest rates (4 mk a minute in the night to Australia).

Fax, Telegraph & E-mail
Go to post offices for fax and telegraph services, or enquire at your hotel or hostel – domestic faxes cost 5 to 10 mk and international faxes up to 25 mk depending on the destination.

Using the Internet free of charge is possible in many public libraries and normally you can send e-mail – but you can't receive it.

NEWSPAPERS & MAGAZINES
No local dailies in English are available. *Keltainen pörssi* and *Palsta* are the best sources for ads for used vehicles and other bargains.

You will find imported English-language magazines and newspapers at railway stations, R-kioski newsagents and at Suomalainen and Akateeminen bookshops.

RADIO & TV
Finnish radio stations use FM frequencies throughout the country. Radio Finland and national radio YLE-3 (and in Helsinki FM 103.7MHz) broadcast several BBC and Voice of America reports as well as local programmes. There are two national television networks and MTV and the cable-PTV commercial stations.

PHOTOGRAPHY & VIDEO
Go to large supermarkets and look for bargains, or visit Hertell on Tuomiokirkonkatu in Tampere and buy in bulk. Standard 24-shot rolls of film cost about 22 mk and slide film costs about 40 mk or more.

TIME
Finland is two hours ahead of GMT/UTC and summer time applies from April to the end of September. At noon in Finland it is 10 am in London, 5 am in New York, 2 am in San Francisco, 5 am in Toronto, 8 pm in Sydney, 10 pm in Auckland, 11 am in Stockholm, Copenhagen and Oslo and 1 pm in Moscow and St Petersburg.

ELECTRICITY
The electric current is 220V AC, 50 Hz, and plugs are of the standard European type with two round pins which require no switch.

WEIGHTS & MEASURES
Finland uses the metric system. Decimals are indicated by commas.

LAUNDRY
There are few laundrettes. The traveller's best options are hostels with washing machines, and the many camping grounds.

TOILETS
The world's most expensive pee is to be had in Finnish bus stations – over one US dollar. Other public toilets also charge, so it's not rare for men to urinate in the street. However, by law, all restaurants and cafés must have a public toilet and it must be accessible to a person using a wheelchair. Many department stores also have free toilets.

HEALTH
Pharmacies *(apteekki)* provide medicines and advice and some are open 24 hours a day in cities. Duty public hospitals, for emergencies and first aid, charge 67 mk for outpatients and 87 mk a day for ward beds (everywhere in Finland, dial ☎ 112 for emergencies, ☎ 10023 for an emergency doctor). Surgery and private care can be expensive, so take out the highest level of insurance cover.

The AIDS Information & Support Centre (☎ 665 081) is at Linnankatu 2B in Helsinki.

WOMEN TRAVELLERS
The only likely annoyance is harassment by drunken men. Ignore them, and avoid

neighbourhood pubs in the evening. Unioni (☎ 643 158) is the national feminist organisation at Bulevardi 11A, Helsinki.

GAY & LESBIAN TRAVELLERS

Finland has not yet accepted marriage registration between persons of the same sex, unlike all other Scandinavian countries. In other respects, Finland is almost as tolerant as other Nordic countries.

Current information can be obtained from SETA (Seksuaalinen tasavertaisuus; ☎ 135 8302 or e-mail toimisto@seta.fi), the organisation for gay and lesbian equality, at Oikokatu 3, Helsinki.

DISABLED TRAVELLERS

By law, most public and private institutions must provide ramps, elevators and special toilets for disabled persons making Finland one of the easiest countries to negotiate. Even some fishing spots can be reached.

TRAVEL WITH CHILDREN

Families with children should visit Finland: most hostels have family rooms, supermarkets stock everything your children need and many trains have special children's carriages. If in doubt, ask around – special needs can usually be met.

DANGERS & ANNOYANCES

Violence has been on the increase during the 1990s and mostly occurs in association with intoxicated local males. Foreign males of dark complexion run the highest risk of street harassment.

Weather extremes in Lapland can cause unexpected danger at any time of the year. Excess cold kills lone trekkers almost every winter in the wilderness, and cold rain can also be a problem in summer.

June and July are the worst months for mosquitoes in Lapland. Insect repellent or hat nets are essential.

Wolves are not common but are most likely to be seen in winter. Bears avoid people but females with cubs may attack a person if threatened.

LEGAL MATTERS

Traffic laws are strict as are drug laws. However, police usually treat bonafide tourists politely in less serious situations. Fishing without a permit is illegal.

BUSINESS HOURS

Shops and post offices are generally open from 9 am to 5 pm weekdays, and to 1 pm on Saturday. Many supermarkets and Helsinki department stores open until 7 or 8 pm, although on holiday eves they shut at 6 pm. Town markets begin about 7 am weekdays and Saturday and continue until 2 pm.

PUBLIC HOLIDAYS & SPECIAL EVENTS

Finland closes down twice a year: around Christmas (sometimes including the New Year) and during the Midsummer weekend at the end of June. Plan ahead and avoid travelling during those times. The public holidays are:

1 January, *New Year's Day*
6 January (usually), *Epiphany*
Good Friday
30 April & 1 May, *May Day Eve & May Day*
May, *Ascension Day*
Late in May or early in June, *Whit Sunday*
Third weekend in June, *Juhannus (Midsummer's Day) & Midsummer's Eve*
6 December, *Independence Day*
24 December, *Christmas Eve*
25 December, *Christmas Day*
26 December, *Boxing Day*

Finland Festivals coordinates some 55 annual feature events and produces guides which are available from tourist offices. The foremost events are the Pori Jazz Festival, and the Savonlinna Opera Festival at Olavinlinna Castle in July. Some of the best festivals are the most remote ones: chamber music in Kuhmo, or folk music in Kaustinen. A few smaller communities arrange some of the weirdest events imaginable (eg national championships in wife-carrying in Sonkajärvi). Check http://www.festivals.fi/ffhomefi.htm.

FINLAND

ACTIVITIES

Boating

Boating can be enjoyed on both sea and lake. The prime sailing region, the Turku Archipelago, is demanding to navigate. The south and south-west coast are best equipped for visiting craft and there are coastguard stations in Helsinki, Turku and Vaasa. The rescue channel is VHF 16.

Hire of small motorboats and sailing boats starts at about 1200 mk per week. For information write to the navigation authority Merenkulkuhallitus (☎ 180 81), Vuorimiehenkatu 1, 00140 Helsinki.

Canoeing

Canoeing is best on lakes and rivers in summer. Only the experienced should try the sea. Packages are offered by tourist offices and the Finnish Canoe Association (☎ 494 965) at the Olympic Stadium in Helsinki. There are wilder rapids in Lapland and North Karelia. Canoe and kayak hire is possible in most towns. Prices start at around 100 mk a day or 500 mk a week, but you will have to arrange the transport.

Fishing

To fish you need an annual fishing licence (except if you are under 18 years of age), which is available at post offices for 80 mk. Northern Lapland requires a separate regional licence.

Most fishing spots are owned privately or by local or national authorities. So as well as the above licences you need a local permit for the day or week (available at varying rates from municipal or forestry authorities or from whoever owns the waters – tourist offices have information). Salmon and trout cannot be fished in May. Check local rules before you cast out. It is customary to catch only the fish you need.

Hiking

Hiking or trekking is best from June (May in the south) to September. Wilderness huts line the northern trails and can be used (and must be shared). According to the law, a principle of common access to nature applies, so you are generally allowed to hike in any forested or wilderness area, and camp for a night anywhere outside inhabited, privately owned areas.

For your own security, keep to marked trails, lodge plans with tourist offices or trekking centres before you leave, and camp only at official sites. Burn your rubbish or leave it in proper bins. Light fires only at camp sites or with the landowner's permission.

Unprotected wildflowers, berries and mushrooms are usually free for picking (check on any local prohibitions) but do not experiment – some berries and mushrooms are poisonous.

Close-fitting waterproof boots and an anorak are essential. If you are an inexperienced hiker, use developed hiking areas such as Ruunaa in Karelia or try a national park *(Kansallispuisto)*. Organised tours are available, and routes such as Karhunkierros and the Lemmenjoki are very scenic. The huts in Lapland are free, but some are locked and you must get keys from nearby trekking centres.

Sauna

The sauna symbolises the Finnish predilection for freedom and introspection. It is a physical and emotional cleansing experience that reveals much about people, hence an invitation to enjoy a sauna is personal and most hospitable. The traditional sauna is a wooden room with benches and a properly stoked wooden stove, but saunas at hotels, camping grounds and in homes tend to have more modern heating. Temperatures from 80°C to 100°C are common. Lightly switching the body with birch twigs increases perspiration and then a cold swim or wash and scrub (fanatics roll in snow in winter) completes the refreshment. Public saunas will cost about 50 mk, so go to a swimming pool that has one for around 15 mk. The most comfortable is the traditional *savusauna*. See Helsinki for urban options.

Skiing

Nordic skiing is popular and there are cross-country trails (some lit) of varying difficulty.

Downhill skiers go to Lapland, or to resorts such as Koli in North Karelia or Ruka in Kuusamo. Expect to pay 70 mk a day to hire cross-country gear, but around 100 mk for downhill gear.

The season runs from October (in the south from December) to April and, although daylight is limited before Christmas, you can ski in nocturnal twilight in Lapland from late October.

WORK

There is very little work open to foreigners due to high local unemployment. Students can apply for limited summer employment. Au pair arrangements are possible for up to 18 months.

ACCOMMODATION

If you want the best rates on hotels, come to town on Friday, this gives you two or three nights at holiday rates (check when booking). Summer rates are lower, but seasons vary by region.

Finncheques allow discounted accommodation in a designated hotel for 170 mk per person. They and are valid (and obtained) at about half of Finland's hotels from June to August (in some places you will pay an extra 50 mk).

Holiday cabins can be booked through regional tourist offices, generally for 1200 mk a week or more for four people. For listings on the mainland and booking information, write to Lomarengas, Malminkaari 23C, 00700 Helsinki.

The 160 SRM hostels and summer hotels are cheap (about half are open all year). The free publication *Hostellit* gives a full listing with details.

Camp sites cost from 35 to 80 mk, but if you have no International Camping Card (90 mk) buy a National Card for 15 mk. Ask for an annual budget accommodation guide at tourist offices.

FOOD

Restaurant meals are expensive, but lunch is usually served between 11 am and 2 pm, and a 35 mk package often includes salad, bread,

milk and even coffee. The *grilli* is the usual venue for takeaways. Finnish cuisine is not easy to find: a *seisova pöytä* (smorgasbord) includes soups and fish and can be had for 40 to 60 mk in restaurants. Helsinki is famous for Russian food, but high prices go with this reputation. Simpler fare are Karelian pastries, mostly costing under 10 mk.

Useful discount food chains include Eurospar, Rabatti, Ruokavarasto, Siwa and Alepa. *Tarjous* means special price. When buying milk products, note that *rasvaton maito* is fat-free; *kevyt maito* is low-fat; and *kulutus maito* is conventional milk.

DRINKS

Strong beers, wines and spirits are sold by the state network, aptly named Alko (open from 10 am to 5 pm, and often only until 2 pm Saturday). Alcohol stronger than one-fifth by volume is not sold to those under 20 years of age. For beer and wine purchases the age limit is 18. Group III ales (second rank in strength), however, can often be bought in supermarkets. Wines rarely cost less than 30 mk, though the popular and drinkable ones can be bought for less than 60 mk a bottle.

ENTERTAINMENT

Live music is the best option as theatre performances are either in Finnish or otherwise incomprehensible. Cinema tickets will cost from 40 mk (films classified K are restricted to people over 16 or 18 years of age, films classified S are for general audiences). Foreign films are in their original language and have subtitles in Finnish. Discos charge from 20 mk at the door, nightclubs up to 60 mk (the usual age limit is 18 or 20 years, sometimes 24).

Football (soccer) and athletics are popular in summer, ice hockey and skiing in winter. *Pesäpallo* is the Finnish version of baseball, and is a popular spectator sport.

THINGS TO BUY

Finland has become an attractive country for any kind of shopping due to the cheap markka, low inflation and domestic discounts. Handicrafts made of domestic raw

FINLAND

materials are especially interesting. Flea markets are booming. It is certainly worth keeping your eyes open for bargains.

Duodji are authentic handicrafts produced according to Sami traditions. A genuine item, which can be expensive, should carry a round, coloured 'Duodji' token. The range of items in bone, hide, wood and metals includes jewellery, clothing and the knives characteristic to the Sami communities.

Getting There & Away

AIR

You can often find cheap flights to Helsinki from Asia or America – bucket shops will sell a flight to Helsinki at the standard 'Europe rate'. Finland is not a bad place to start a northern European tour; look for a cheap return flight, from say London or Athens.

Finnair and SAS have 12 flights per day between Helsinki and Stockholm (Finnish: Tukholma), and you can fly daily to Helsinki from Gothenburg, Copenhagen (Finnish: Kööpenhamina) and Oslo, or from Stockholm to Turku and Tampere.

Finnair flies to Moscow, St Petersburg (Finnish: Pietari) Murmansk, Petrozavodsk as well as Tallinn, Kiev, Rīga and Vilnius. Services extend to most European cities. Finnair flies daily from New York to Helsinki nonstop.

Discount flights are available to and from Finland for holders of Go 25 or ISIC (International Student Identity Card) cards from student travel agents. In Finland, contact Kilroy travels in Helsinki, Turku, Tampere and Oulu.

LAND
Sweden

There are six crossings from northern Sweden to northern Finland across the rivers Tornionjoki (Swedish: Torneälv) and Muonionjoki. Some of the crossings are far from the towns or the main road, especially on the Swedish side.

From southern Sweden or Narvik (Norway), there are trains to Boden and further buses (train passes are valid) to the Swedish town of Haparanda, from where you can easily walk (or take another bus) to the Finnish town of Tornio. From Tornio, you will have to pay for the bus ride to the nearest train station, in Kemi, but train passes are valid on most buses.

From Övertorneå, a beautiful bridge links Sweden to Aavasaksa, a tourist centre below Aavasaksa hill.

From the small Swedish settlement of Pello, several km from road No 400, there is a bridge to the larger Finnish centre of Pello.

From the Swedish township of Pajala further north, there is a narrow road (about 30 km long) which makes the crossing just south of Kolari.

From Muodoslompolo, it is 13 km to the bridge, which is just 2 km south of Muonio.

Karesuando is the northernmost town in Sweden and the end of road No 400, with direct access to the Finnish Karesuvanto on road No 21.

Norway

There are six border crossings along roads plus a few legal crossings along wilderness tracks. Finnish buses run between Rovaniemi and the Norwegian border post, and some buses continue on to the first Norwegian town, which is usually on a Norwegian bus route. Free timetables (ask bus drivers or at stations) usually list these connections. With a car, crossing is often simple, although a brief check takes place occasionally.

The north-western route takes you through beautiful scenery to Skibotn in Norway via Kilpisjärvi. Some buses run from Rovaniemi all the way to Skibotn. The border station is on the Finnish side.

To reach Alta from Hetta (aka Enontekiö) take the road north to Kautokeino. Some buses will take you from Hetta to Kautokeino, which is connected to Alta and Karasjok by Norwegian companies.

The main Nordkapp route goes from Rovaniemi via Inari and Kaamanen to Karigasniemi and across the border to

Karasjok and Lakselv. Many buses run from Ivalo to Karasjok. The border station is on the Finnish side.

There is a bridge into Norway at Utsjoki over the Teno River. There is nothing on the Norwegian side here, but Norwegian buses run on this road.

The road from the northernmost point of Finland, at Nuorgam, will take you to Tana Bru, with further connections to various parts of Finnmark. Buses take you to the border, four km from Nuorgam.

To reach Kirkenes from Finland, cross the border at Näätämö, to reach Neiden, 10 km away, which has bus connections to Kirkenes and to other centres in Finnmark. You may have to hitchhike from Näätämö to Neiden.

Russia

New border posts are being opened, but some are open exclusively for trade or to Russians and Finns.

Along the heavily travelled Helsinki-Vyborg-St Petersburg corridor there are one rail and two road crossings. The rail crossing is at Vainikkala (Russian side, Luzhayka). Highways cross at the Finnish border posts of Nuijamaa (Russian side, Brusnichnoe) and Vaalimaa (Russian side, Torfyanovka), just north of Vainikkala.

Further north, groups and individuals may be able to drive from Joensuu to the Finnish post of Niirala (Russian side, Vyartsilya) and 500 km on to Petrozavodsk. In Kainuu, there is an open border from Vartius to the mining town of Kostomuksha (Finnish: Kostamus). From Salla, there is a road across the border to Alakurtti, and from Ivalo, a road goes to Murmansk via the Finnish border post of Raja-Jooseppi.

If you drive, you'll need an international licence and certificate of registration, passport and visa and insurance. The Ingosstrakh, Salomonkatu 5C, 00100 Helsinki, (☎ 694 0511), is the only Russian insurer in Helsinki. It will cover you in Russia but not in other republics.

Train There is a Moscow sleeper running daily to and from Helsinki. There are also two daily St Petersburg services. You can buy Russian rail tickets in Helsinki (all the way to the Chinese border), at the special ticket office in the central station.

Bus There are bus connections from Helsinki to St Petersburg, and the visa rule applies. Check current timetables at either end.

There are also post buses on routes from Joensuu to Sortavala (130 mk) and to Petrozavodsk (Finnish: Petroskoi, 290 mk) and from Rovaniemi to Ivalo to Murmansk. From Ivalo to Murmansk costs 240 mk, and there are services from Monday to Friday subject to road conditions. To qualify to travel, you need a passport and a visa and you need to pay for this journey beforehand at a post office.

Tours There are a number of companies in Helsinki offering tours to St Petersburg and other Russian towns.

Regional tour centres for visits to Russia include Lappeenranta, Joensuu and Kuhmo, where local travel agents book tours across the border to several Russian Karelian communities. These tours take a few days and require a visa.

SEA

The Baltic ferries are some of the most impressive seagoing craft and have been compared to hotels and shopping plazas. You can pay a basic fee and find a seat or hire a cabin – taking a car is easy but you should book when travelling in July. On some routes services only run in summer or from March to December. Many ferries offer 50% discounts for holders of Eurail, Scanrail and Inter-Rail passes. Some services offer pensioner reductions and discounts for ISIC and GO 25 card-holders.

Sweden

The Stockholm to Helsinki, Stockholm to Turku and Kapellskär to Mariehamn runs are covered by Silja Line and Viking Line. Cabins are not compulsory on Viking Line as they are on Silja Line. Be warned, though, that Friday night departures on Viking Line in the low season are considerably more expensive than departures on other nights of the week. Birka Cruises and Ånedin-Line link Mariehamn and Stockholm, and Eckerö Linjen sails from Grisslehamn north of Stockholm to Eckerö in Åland for a very reasonable price.

In summer, Silja Line also sails from Vaasa (Finland) to Umeå and Sundsvall (Sweden) and from Pietarsaari (also known as Jakobstad) to Umeå and Skellefteå. At the time of writing Silja Line's Vaasa to Sundsvall service was suspended, but there were noises of a new catamaran service (not Silja Line) starting up in 1997 for this route.

Estonia

The Helsinki to Tallinn sea route has been the fastest growing service in the world in the 1990s. At the time of writing, there were five companies covering the 80-km trip between Helsinki and Tallinn. In winter there are fewer departures, and the traffic is also slower due to the ice. Car ferries cross in three to four hours whereas catamarans do it in under two hours.

Car ferries (except Silja Line) depart from Länsisatama in Helsinki, and include three Tallink ferries (90 mk one way) and MS *Apollo* of Eestin Linjat (100 mk). Silja Line departs from the main harbour and charges 140 mk. Viking Line runs one or two catamarans that take one hour 45 minutes and cost 160 mk. Tallink has two smaller hydrofoils for 100 mk per passenger.

There are occasional discounts and return packages. Tickets are now available at the harbour until the departure, but it is advisable to book several hours before in summer.

Germany

Silja Line runs its *Finnjet* service from Travemünde to Helsinki (22 hours or more) and there is a bus link between Helsinki and Hamburg. The Finnlines' *Poseidon* sails from Lübeck to the cargo harbour near Sönäinen in Helsinki, and there are container ships that take passengers.

Russia

There is demand for direct sea routes between Finland and Russia, but at the time of writing there was no service operating.

The impressive Saimaa Canal runs from Vyborg to Lappeenranta, takes private boats and has cruises from Kotka in summer. The canal is almost entirely on Russian territory but is run by Finns.

LEAVING FINLAND

There are no departure taxes.

To Sweden & Norway

There is no fuss involved, often no control and only occasional checks. However, those travellers who look noticeably foreign may have their passports checked.

To Estonia

Passports (and visas for some nationals) are necessary and they are always checked.

To Russia

There is more red tape at Russian borders, but you shouldn't meet problems if your passport and visa are in order. Check ahead whether your intended border crossing is legal for your nationality (some are only open to Finns and Russians).

Getting Around

The comprehensive travel guide *Suomen Kulkuneuvot* (known as *Turisti*) costs 95 mk at kiosks and bus stations and gives full listings of timetables and connections. It is issued three times a year.

AIR

Finnair, Finnaviation and Karair fly domestic but not especially cheap services between big centres and to Lapland. From Helsinki to Rovaniemi costs 720 mk. But advance-purchase return tickets give 50% discounts, and summer deals are cheaper still. A holiday ticket for 15 days costs US$425, and is available from Finnair offices and travel agents.

Children aged under 12 years pay half price. Buses connect with most airports. Check also http://www.finnair.fi/.

BUS

Buses are the principal carriers outside the railway network – just hail the coach at a bus stop and pay your fare to the driver. A 500-km journey costs 250 mk. You can arrange discounts if you book (there are 30% savings with GO 25 cards). There is little traffic during Juhannus (Midsummer) and restricted services operate on Saturday and public holidays.

Oy Matkahuolto Ab coordinates long-distance and express buses and maintains bus stations with cafeterias. National timetables are available from it and at tourist offices, or at http://www.okanecom.fi/ExpressBus/.

Children, families, groups and old people receive discounts. Holiday tickets valid for two weeks and 1000 km cost 340 mk (distributed like notes for 250, 100, 50, and 10 km, so you must juggle them to suit journeys as there are no refunds).

Regional private operators and postbuses comprise the national network and charge similar rates. No route numbers are shown, so find the numbered berth for your destination at the bus station or see the destination on the bus.

TRAIN

Finnish trains are cheaper than those in Sweden and Norway, and there are good discount passes available. On some routes, buses accept train passes. Trains offer economical comfort on long-distance journeys and frequent intercity services. Rovaniemi is the main northern rail terminus.

VR Ltd Finnish Railways has its own travel bureau at main stations and can advise on all tickets. Special package tickets include one-month Finnrail passes for 10, five and three travel days (2nd class costs 995, 730 and 540 mk) and Eurail, Inter-Rail and Scanrail passes apply.

There is a 30% discount for holders of Rail Europ S cards. Children under 17 pay half-fare, accompanied children aged under six

pay nothing (and have no seat). Return tickets are valid for a month. Seat bookings are compulsory on Intercity and Pendolino expresses (25 mk). The normal reservation charge is 15 mk, but you can avoid compulsory surcharges on all routes – just wait for the next train.

There are two and three-bed sleepers (costing from 60 mk per bed) running on long routes. There are special car-carriers to northern destinations.

Look for the excellent summer passes. In 1996, a seven-day unlimited train pass with two hotel vouchers cost 888 mk, and better yet, regional one-month passes cost less than 200 mk (with some restrictions). Check at the train station on arrival for current offers.

CAR & MOTORCYCLE

The highway and freeway network is good between centres, although in the forests you can find unsurfaced roads or dirt tracks. There are many rest areas. Petrol prices vary, so shop around – Lapland has no good deals. Motorcyclists shouldn't have any troubles, although frequent rain can be a bit unpleasant at times.

Beware of elk and reindeer, which do not respond to motor horns. Police must by law be notified about accidents involving elks and reindeer. Report the accident, as only if you *don't* might there be legal trouble. To take meat is illegal (elk hunting is possible only if you have a permit).

It is compulsory to carry studded or mud-snow tyres (coded MS) from November to March. Studded tyres can be hired at Isko stores from 650 mk for up to two weeks.

Autoliitto (☎ 774 761) is the national motoring organisation, Kansakoulukatu 10, 00100 Helsinki.

Road Rules

No international licence is needed to drive in Finland. The speed limits are 50 km/h in built-up areas (note the yellow signs with a town silhouette) and from 80 to 100 km/h on highways (up to 120 km/h on motorways). Traffic keeps to the right and you must use headlights always when driving on the open

FINLAND

road. Wearing seat belts is obligatory in all seats. The blood alcohol limit is 0.05%.

Foreign cars must display their nationality and visitors must be fully insured (bring a Green Card if you have one). Accidents must be reported to the Motor Insurers' Bureau (☎ 192 51), Bulevardi 28, 00120 Helsinki.

Car Rental
The smallest car costs about 180 mk per day and 2 mk per km. Weekly packages start at about 1800 mk all up, 750 mk for a weekend. A modest middle-sized sedan can cost up to 220 mk per day and 2.5 mk per km.

Purchase
Small 10-year-old sedans and old vans can cost less than 10,000 mk, but those costing less than 5000 mk should have been recently inspected (katsastettu).

BICYCLE
Daily hire at about 50 mk is common and there are weekly rates. SRM offers a cycling & hostel package that takes in the flat south and lakes. New bicycles range from 1000 mk, but good second-hand models may only cost 500 mk or less.

HITCHING
Hitching in Finland is certainly easier than in Sweden, especially if you try it outside the biggest cities and look clean.

BOAT
Lake and river ferries operate over the summer period. Tampere, Lahti, Jyväskylä, Savonlinna, Kuopio and Lappeenranta are the main centres – a cruise leg is a pleasant and lazy travel variation.

All ferries that cross the straits, and many of those that run between the islands along the coast, are free. See Åland for specific information.

LOCAL TRANSPORT
The only tram and metro networks are in Helsinki. Otherwise, there are city bus services and networks in Helsinki, Turku and Tampere and local buses in other cities.

Taxi
Taxi is an expensive travel option at 19 mk for flagfall (up to 29 mk at night and on Sunday) and about 120 mk for a trip from Helsinki to Vantaa airport. You can hail a cab on the street, but it's easier to pick one up at the airport or the station.

ORGANISED TOURS
Theoretically, there is a great variety of tours in most Finnish towns. But there are not always people to go – don't believe every printed word in pamphlets. Ask first, and look for the weekly programme at the tourist office. Some tours in places like Lieksa or Kuusamo can be the cheapest or the only way to visit isolated attractions.

Helsinki

Helsinki is a small and intimate city (population 530,000); lively but not bustling. Its size makes it easy to walk around and cafés, markets and the nearby islands are its summer delights.

The capital did not come to Helsinki (Swedish: Helsingfors) until 1812. The first town was founded in the Vantaa area in 1550. It was later moved and the fortress on Suomenlinna was begun by the Swedes in 1748. It became the seat of the Russian Grand Duchy after falling to the tsar in 1808 when much of the town was wrecked. The monumental buildings of Senaatintori were designed by CL Engel, who had earlier worked in St Petersburg. Among its free attractions, Helsinki today has a superb collection of architecture and nice parks.

Orientation
Helsinki occupies a peninsula and there are links by bridge and ferry with the nearby islands. There are three other towns nearby, Espoo and the enclosed Kauniainen to the east and Vantaa, with the international airport, to the north.

The city centre surrounds the main harbour Eteläsatama and the market square

Kauppatori and the ferry terminals lie either side. The main street axes are the twin shopping avenues Pohjoisesplanadi and Eteläesplanadi and Mannerheimintie.

Information

Apart from the tourist-office publications there are free tourist brochures such as *Helsinki This Week* and the *City in English*. The youth information centre Kompassi, on the lower level of the Asematunneli subway from the main station, is open on Monday to Friday (there are some useful travel books there).

Tourist Offices The main tourist office of MEK, the Finnish tourist board, is at Eteläesplanadi 4 and has brochures on most of the country.

The City Tourist Office (☎ 169 3757) is opposite at Pohjoisesplanadi 19 and is open weekdays from 8.30 am to 4 pm, from mid-May to September 8.30 am to 6 pm and Saturday from 8.30 am to 1 pm. It is the best centre for current information and for buying a Helsinki Card.

Jugendsali, next to the tourist office, has regular exhibitions, information and literature on cultural themes.

Helsinki Card This pass gives free urban travel, entry to over 50 attractions in Helsinki and the satellite cities and some discounts (one day costs 105 mk, two days 135 mk, three days 165 mk). The card is worthwhile if you take the free sightseeing tour and are keen to visit the main attractions.

Money Forex, at the train station, offers the best rates and is open daily from 8 am to 9 pm. There is no commission for reconversion. There are also other branches and other companies. Banks are open weekdays from 9.15 am to 4.15 pm. At the airport the counter is open daily from 6.30 am to 11 pm, although a machine operates 24 hours. Ferry terminals also change money on weekends.

American Express (☎ 628 788) is at Mikonkatu 2D, Western Union is at the Stockmann Department Store, 7th floor.

Post & Communications The main post office is at Mannerheimintie 11 and is open from 9 am to 5 pm weekdays. The Tele (the national telephone company) is in the same building as poste restante (door F), which is open until 9 pm weekdays and Sunday, 6 pm on Saturday. There is also a telegram counter. The telephone code for Helsinki is 09.

Nettikahvila, in the Vanha building on Mannerheimintie, has almost 10 computers that can be used free of charge on weekdays from noon to 7 pm. Public libraries have one or two terminals that must be reserved but are also free.

Travel Agencies The budget agency Kilroy travels (☎ 680 7811) is at Kaivokatu 10 C. The Finnish Travel Association (☎ 170 868) at Mikonkatu 25 is the central Finncheque agent. Ageba Oy (☎ 615 0155), the organiser of package and city sightseeing tours, will be found at main ferry terminals. A few agencies near the Olympia ferry terminal arrange Russian and other visas.

Bookshops The premier bookshop is Akateeminen Kirjakauppa at Pohjoisesplanadi 39 and it boasts stock in 40 lan- guages. Next best is Suomalainen Kirjakauppa, Aleksanterinkatu 23, which has paperbacks and international periodicals. For maps and official publications, try Edita at Eteläesplanadi 4. The American Bookshop at Museokatu 3 has cheapish books in English, including guidebooks.

Medical & Emergency Services The police have stations at Helsinki's main train and bus stations (in emergencies dial ☎ 10022). For other emergencies dial ☎ 112. English speakers should use the university's central hospital at Haartmaninkatu 4 or the first-aid centre at Töölönkatu 40. The 24-hour pharmacy is at Mannerheimintie 96.

Private doctors are listed in the yellow pages of the telephone directory under *Lääkärikeskuksia*. For sea rescue dial ☎ 112 or 667 766. There is a police lost-property office at the police building, 7th floor, Päijänteentie 12.

FINLAND

FINLAND

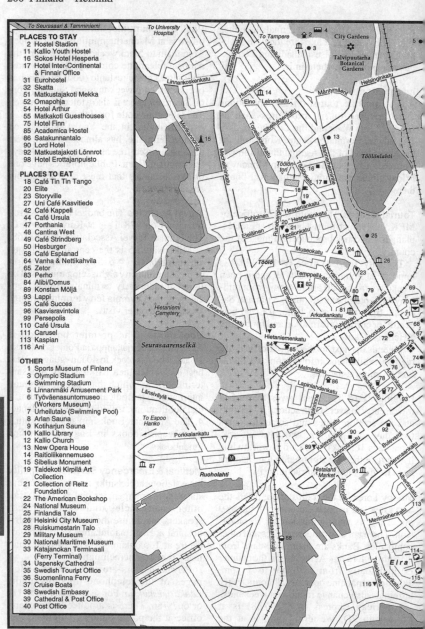

To Seurasaari & Tamminiemi

PLACES TO STAY
2 Hostel Stadion
11 Kallio Youth Hostel
16 Sokos Hotel Hesperia
17 Hotel Inter-Continental
& Finnair Office
31 Eurohostel
32 Skatta
51 Matkustajakoti Mekka
52 Omapohja
54 Hotel Arthur
55 Matkakoti Guesthouses
75 Hotel Finn
85 Academica Hostel
86 Satakunnantalo
90 Lord Hotel
92 Matkustajakoti Lönnrot
98 Hotel Erottajanpuisto

PLACES TO EAT
18 Café Tin Tin Tango
20 Elite
23 Storyville
27 Uni Café Kasvitiede
42 Café Kappeli
44 Café Ursula
47 Porthania
48 Cantina West
49 Café Strindberg
50 Hesburger
58 Café Esplanad
64 Vanha & Nettikahvila
65 Zetor
83 Perho
84 Alibi/Domus
89 Konstan Möljä
93 Lappi
95 Café Succes
96 Kasvisravintola
99 Persepolis
110 Café Ursula
111 Carusel
113 Kaspian
116 Ani

OTHER
1 Sports Museum of Finland
3 Olympic Stadium
4 Swimming Stadium
5 Linnanmäki Amusement Park
6 Työväenasuntomuseo
(Workers Museum)
7 Urheilutalo (Swimming Pool)
8 Arlan Sauna
9 Kotiharjun Sauna
10 Kallio Library
12 Kallio Church
13 New Opera House
14 Raitioliikennemuseo
15 Sibelius Monument
19 Taidekoti Kirpilä Art
Collection
21 Collection of Reitz
Foundation
22 The American Bookshop
24 National Museum
25 Finlandia Talo
26 Helsinki City Museum
28 Ruiskumestarin Talo
29 Military Museum
30 National Maritime Museum
33 Katajanokan Terminaali
(Ferry Terminal)
34 Uspensky Cathedral
35 Swedish Tourist Office
36 Suomenlinna Ferry
37 Cruise Boats
38 Swedish Embassy
39 Cathedral & Post Office
40 Post Office

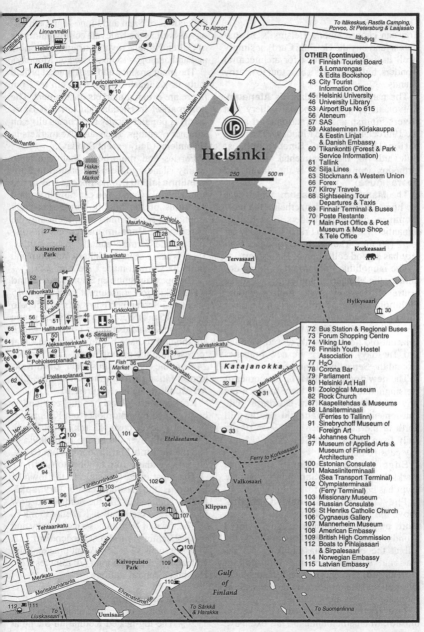

To Linnanmäki
To Airport
To Itäkeskus, Rastila Camping, Porvoo, St Petersburg & Laajasalo
Itäväylä
Helsingkatu
Kallio
Agricolankatu
Hämeentie
Eläinanmantie
Haka-niemi Market

Helsinki

0   250   500 m

OTHER (continued)
41 Finnish Tourist Board
   & Lomarengas
   & Edita Bookshop
43 City Tourist
   Information Office
45 Helsinki University
46 University Library
53 Airport Bus No 615
56 Ateneum
57 SAS
59 Akateeminen Kirjakauppa
   & Eestin Linjat
   & Danish Embassy
60 Tikankontti (Forest & Park
   Service Information)
61 Tallink
62 Silja Lines
63 Stockmann & Western Union
66 Forex
67 Kilroy Travels
68 Sightseeing Tour
   Departures & Taxis
69 Finnair Terminal & Buses
70 Poste Restante
71 Main Post Office & Post
   Museum & Map Shop
   & Tele Office

Maurinkatu
Pohjoisranta
Liisankatu
Kaisaniemi Park
Siltasaarenkatu
Unioninkatu
Kaisaniemenkatu
Fabianinkatu
Meritullinkatu
Kirkkokatu
Tervasaari
Korkeasaari
Hylkysaari
Vilhonkatu
Mikonkatu
Keskuskatu
Senäätin-tori
Hallituskatu
Aleksanterinkatu
Pohjoisesplanadi
Etätäesplanadi
Korkeavuorenkatu
Fredrikinkatu
Iso-roobertinkatu
Kasarmikatu
Fish Market
Laivastokatu
Kanavakatu
Merikasarminkatu
Katajanokka
Etätäsatama
Ferry to Korkeasaari
Valkosaari
Ratakatu
Tähtitorninkatu
Klippan
Tehtaankatu
Neitsytpolku
Puistokatu
Laivurinkatu
Harakatu
Kaivopuisto Park
Merikatu
Merisatamaranta
Elverströmintie
Gulf of Finland
To Liuskasaari
To Säräkä & Harakka
Uunisaari
To Suomenlinna

72 Bus Station & Regional Buses
73 Forum Shopping Centre
74 Viking Line
76 Finnish Youth Hostel
   Association
77 H2O
78 Corona Bar
79 Parliament
80 Helsinki Art Hall
81 Zoological Museum
82 Rock Church
87 Kaapelitehdas & Museums
88 Länsiterminaali
   (Ferries to Tallinn)
91 Sinebrychoff Museum of
   Foreign Art
92 Johannes Church
97 Museum of Applied Arts &
   Museum of Finnish
   Architecture
100 Estonian Consulate
101 Makasiiniterminaali
   (Sea Transport Terminal)
102 Olympiaterminaali
   (Ferry Terminal)
103 Missionary Museum
104 Russian Consulate
105 St Henriks Catholic Church
106 Cygnaeus Gallery
107 Mannerheim Museum
108 American Embassy
109 British High Commission
112 Boats to Pihlajasaari
   & Sirpalesaari
114 Norwegian Embassy
115 Latvian Embassy

FINLAND

Things to See

You can choose among Helsinki's 30 museums (and buy the Helsinki Card) or simply stroll in the parks or look for architectural wonders, but don't miss a boat tour to nearby islands.

The national art foundation's **Ateneum**, Kaivokatu 2, is the principal gallery and covers Finnish and international art since the 19th century (closed Monday). The international art museum, **Sinebrychoff**, at Bulevardi 40, has Continental works and Orthodox icons (nearby is the quaint **old opera house**).

The **Mannerheim Museum**, which was the home of General Mannerheim, the most prominent of Finnish leaders, is at Kalliolinnantie 14 and is open Friday to Sunday for tours (30 mk). The nearby **Cygnaeus Gallery** has a good collection of Finnish art.

The monolithic **Parliament** building dominates the Mannerheimintie entrance to the centre of Helsinki. Alvar Aalto's angular **Finlandia talo** (concert hall) is on the other side of the road, to the west of the railway, by the lake. The **City Museum** is in an adjacent old house (15 mk, closed Monday and Tuesday), but there are new branches around the Senaatintori square.

The **new opera house** is on the corner of Helsinginkatu, turn right there to reach the tiny and manicured **City Gardens**. The amusement park **Linnanmäki** on the hill north of the lake is open until 9 or 10 pm daily from late April to September (15 mk, day pass 70 mk).

Engel's sparse **Lutheran Cathedral** marks the main square **Senaatintori** and the crypt has been opened for exhibitions.

The Orthodox **Uspensky Cathedral** above the harbour at Kanavakatu 1 is even more magnificent, inside and out (closed Monday). The style of **Kallion kirkko** on the hill at the end of Siltasaarenkatu defines National Romanticism and **Temppeliaukion kirkko**, hewn into rock on Temppelikatu, symbolises the modern meanderings of Finnish religious architecture.

The **National Museum** (Kansallismuseo), Mannerheimintie 34, has extensive collections of Sami and Finno-Ugric ethnology as well as the Kalevala ceiling paintings of Gallen-Kallela, royal portraiture, interiors and archaeology (15 mk, closed on Monday).

The main produce and craft market is held daily in Kauppatori from 6.30 am to 2 pm (there are evening markets in summer). The **flea market** in Hietalahden tori (off Bulevardi) is popular locally and comes alive on summer evenings. There are also markets in Hakaniemi (daily except Sunday).

Ferries and motorboats that shuttle to nearby islands, go from Kauppatori to **Suomenlinna Island** (from 9 mk one way or use your Helsinki Card). You can ramble around the ruins of the mighty fortress or look around the several museums, including the **Ehrensvärd Museum** that covers the history of the fortress and its many battles. There is also a separate **Military Museum** and the 1930s German-made U-boat *Vesikko*.

The open-air centre on **Seurasaari Island** is Helsinki's folk museum. It's open from 15 May to 15 September, entry is free except to houses (15 mk). Seurasaari is also the venue for Helsinki's Midsummer bonfires, which are thought to have begun as a pagan ritual representing the midnight sun. Take bus No 24 from the central train station. **Urho Kekkonen Museum Tamminiemi** and the **City Art Museum** are near Seurasaari.

Korkeasaari Island has the **zoo** and is best reached by motorboat from Kauppatori (a return ticket costs 13 mk, plus 20 mk entry). Walk over the bridge to Hylkysaari and the **National Maritime Museum** (6 mk, closed weekdays from October to April).

The most important sight in the town of **Espoo** is the pastiche castle **Tarvaspää**, Gallen-Kallelantie 27, the studio and now museum of Akseli Gallen-Kallela (35 mk).

The town of **Vantaa** has a technology and science centre **Heureka** at Tiedepuisto 1. A visit is expensive at 55 mk but practical and educational. Take the train (20 minutes from Helsinki's central station).

Sauna & Swimming

Helsinki boasts two public saunas from the 1920s. The log-heated Kotiharjun Sauna at

Harjutorintie 1 charges 30 mk per session, and is open from Tuesday to Friday from 2 to 8 pm and on Saturday from 1 to 6 pm. More basic is Arlan Sauna at Kaarlenkatu 15 that costs 25 mk and is open from Thursday to Friday from 1 to 6.30 pm, from 11 am to 4.30 pm on Saturday. These two saunas are remaining relics and include cupping (bloodletting) and traditional massage services, and use of a *vasta* (birch twigs) is allowed.

The public sauna and pool on Yrjönkatu is closed in summer, but go to Urheilutalo at Helsinginkatu 25 with a large pool and saunas for 20 mk per person. The open-air Swimming Stadium near the Olympic Stadium is open daily from mid-May to early September, has a café and four saunas and charges just 10 mk.

Something special is Café Tin Tin Tango (☎ 2709 0972), at Töölöntorinkatu 7, which books an electric sauna for up to six people for 100 mk per hour, and has laundry facilities and a bar.

Organised Tours

Ageba coach tours range from 1½-hour tours (60 mk) to 2½-hour lunch tours (from 95 mk). Several companies operate island cruises for around 50 mk from the market. There are also popular city walks, organised by Guide Booking Centre (☎ 601 966). These are free to Helsinki Card holders.

Places to Stay

Camping *Rastila Camping* (☎ 316 551), on Vuosaari near the bridge, is open all year round. It charges 50 mk per head or 80 mk per group. Basic cottages cost from 265 to 320 mk. Take bus No 90 or 96 from Itäkeskus.

Free camping is allowed on the island of Pihlajasaari on weekends (return 20 mk from the end of Laivurinkatu), and also in the Keskuspuisto Park any time, but you are advised to be extremely discreet to avoid harassment!

Hostels The clean and popular *Kallio Youth Hostel* (☎ 7099 2590), Porthaninkatu 2, has 30 dormitory beds from 1 June to 31 August

for 50 mk each. There is a laundry (10 mk), a kitchen with a TV, plus good information upstairs at the Light House Centre. Take the metro to Hakaniemi station (the northern exit), or tram No 1, 2 or 3B.

The traditional *Hostel Stadion* (☎ 496 071) at the 1952 Olympic Stadium has 130 beds in 20 rooms, with dorm beds from 50 mk and singles/doubles at 115/140 mk. It is open until 2 am. A buffet breakfast costs 25 mk, and there is a well-equipped kitchen, two TV rooms and a 15 mk laundry. The place is currently run by Ms Leena Rautavaara, daughter of the Finnish javelin gold medallist of the 1948 Games. Take tram No 3T or 7A, or walk.

Hostel Academica (☎ 402 0206) is a central hostel and summer hotel at Hietaniemenkatu 14 with beds from 75 mk, including morning sauna and swimming.

The central hostel *Erottajanpuisto* (☎ 642 169), Uudenmaankatu 9, has stylish large rooms at approximately 100 mk for HI members.

The large *Eurohostel* (☎ 664 452), Linnankatu 9 near the Viking Line terminal, has beds for 100 mk for HI members and perhaps the best array of services among Helsinki hostels.

Satakuntatalo (☎ 695 851), Lapinrinne 1, which is open from June to August, has dorm beds at 50 mk, and an inexpensive student restaurant.

Guesthouses The best is *Omapohja* (☎ 666 211) near the train station. There are 15 spotlessly clean singles/doubles, from 195/260 mk. There are three *Matkakoti* guesthouses at Vilhonkatu 6. The upper floors are mostly used by short-term visitors, but *Paalupaikka* (☎ 630 260) on the second floor has dorm beds for 80 mk and singles/doubles from 185/240 mk. *Matkustajakoti Mekka* at Vuorikatu 8B and *Matkustajakoti Lönnrot* at Lönnrotinkatu 16 are similar options in this category.

Hotels There are plenty of hotels in Helsinki, and the current prices are available at the Hotel-booking Centre (☎ 171 133) in the

FINLAND

central station, open in summer from 9 am to 7 pm weekdays and Saturday, and 10 am to 6 pm Sunday. In winter it is open from 9 am to 5 pm weekdays only. The booking charge is 12 mk for hotel rooms, but the rates are often cheaper through the booking centre.

Cheap hotels in the centre include *Arthur*, *Finn* and *Skatta*. Stylish hotels include *Torni*, *Klaus Kurki* and the Art-Nouveau *Lord Hotel*.

Places to Eat

There are plenty of hamburger restaurants, kebab joints and grills in Helsinki. There are several budget restaurants on the ground level of the Forum shopping centre.

Helsinki University has several student *cafeterias* around the city, including *Porthania*, *Taukotupa* and *Uni Café Kasvitiede*. *Alibi* in the Domus building is also pleasant. Nearby, students in a catering college practise at *Perho*, serving good meals at reasonable prices.

For the pick of Finnish cuisine try *Konstan Möljä* at Hietalahdenkatu 14 near the flea market, or *Lappi* at Annankatu 22, with genuine Lappish specialities and reasonable lunch prices. The very central *Zetor* at Kaivopiha is the most Finnish of all Finnish restaurants. *Kasvisravintola* at Korkeavuorenkatu 3 is a good vegetarian restaurant.

Kaspian at Albertinkatu 7 offers a Persian buffet at 38 mk, *Ani* at Telakkakatu 2 is Armenian-Turkish with similar rates. *Cantina West* at Kasarmikatu 23 is a Mexican restaurant and bar.

There are a number of good cafés around Esplanadi park. *Café Esplanad* at Pohjoisesplanadi 37 is a shoestring haven with huge wheat buns, whereas the nearby two-storey *Café Strindberg* at Pohjoisesplanadi 33 is more sophisticated. There are light meals plus a small brewery at *Café Kappeli*, Eteläesplanadi 1. *Café Ursula*, by the water at Kaivopuisto, is best in summer, and has a branch on Pohjoisesplanadi.

Entertainment

Theatre tickets cost from 80 mk, but are usually more expensive. The theatres are closed in July, when the outdoor summer theatres are popular. Expect to pay 40 mk or more at the cinema. For events, concerts and performances, see *Helsinki This Week*, enquire at the tourist office, or book at Lippupalvelu or Tiketti.

Corona Bar at Eerikinkatu 11 is famous for its billiard tables. Opposite, *H2O* is the most popular gay bar in town. There are jazz clubs in Helsinki, including *Storyville* at Museokatu 8.

Sports events in Helsinki are numerous. There is athletics in the 1952 Olympic Stadium and ice hocky in the new indoor arena.

Getting There & Away

You can get to Helsinki from anywhere in Europe by air and from Tallinn, Travemünde or Stockholm by sea.

Air Finnair flies to most large towns and to Lapland, generally at least once a day but several times on such routes as Turku, Tampere, Kuopio and Oulu. The airline has an office at Asema-aukio near the train station.

Bus Buy your long-distance and express bus tickets at the main bus station off Mannerheimintie (open from 7.30 am to 7 pm weekdays, 7.30 am to 3.30 pm Saturday and noon to 5.30 pm Sunday), or on the bus itself.

Train There is an information booth in the front hall of the main train station, which is linked with the metro by Asematunneli. A VR travel agency is in the main ticket hall (open daily) and staff can answer all queries on national services. There is a Eurail counter, an international ticket counter and a separate office for buying tickets to Russia.

Regular express trains run daily to Turku, Tampere, Lahti and Lappeenranta and there's a choice of day and overnight trains to Oulu, Rovaniemi and Joensuu. There are also daily trains to St Petersburg and Moscow. Luggage lockers cost 10 mk.

Boat See also the Getting There & Away section of this chapter. International boats depart from four terminals. Ferry tickets can be bought at terminals, ferry companies and the main train station. It is not necessary to book tickets to all destinations unless it is the high season (late June onwards). Silja Lines' office (☎ 9800-74552) is at Mannerheimintie 2 and the Olympia terminal. Viking Line's office (☎ 123 577) is at Mannerheimintie 14 and in the Katajanokka terminal and Makasiiniterminaali. Tickets for the Tallink Express and Tallink car ferries (☎ 2282 1211) can be bought at Erottajankatu 19 or at the terminals. Eestin Linjat (☎ 228 8544) is at Keskuskatu 1 and departs from Länsisatama.

Getting Around

Single journeys on buses, trams, the metro, Suomenlinna ferries and local trains within Helsinki's HKL network cost 9 mk for adults, 4 mk for children. The ticket is valid for one hour from the time of purchase (the ticket will be stamped). Regional single tickets within Espoo, Vantaa, and Helsinki are 15 mk. A Helsinki Card gives you free travel anywhere within Helsinki. HKL information and sales offices are open weekdays in Asematunneli and at Hakaniemi Metro station. Route maps and timetables are free. You can buy single tickets from the driver or ticket machines. Tourist tickets are available at 25 mk for 24 hours, 50 mk for three days and 75 mk for five days; 10-trip tickets cost 75 mk.

To/From the Airport Bus No 615 runs to Rautatientori (15 mk). Finnair buses depart from Asema-aukio, next to the main train station, every 20 minutes from 5 am to midnight (24 mk). There are also shared taxis at 60 mk per person, otherwise the fare is 120 mk.

Bus There are free bus maps available at HKL offices. Most city and local buses depart from the bus station and outside the train station.

Train Regional trains run through Espoo and Kauniainen (towards Turku) and Vantaa (towards Tampere and Lahti). Train travel within Helsinki costs 9 mk per ride.

Tram This is the simple way of getting around Helsinki. Validate your ticket after buying it from the driver – a single ticket costs less than the regular one-hour HKL ticket.

Underground The city metro station Rautatientori is linked with the central station by Asematunneli. Services run from about 6 am to 11.30 pm every day. The line extends to Ruoholahti in the western part of the city and north-east to Mellunmäki.

Bicycle Cycling is practical in Helsinki with well-marked and good-quality bicycle paths. You can rent bicycles at the Kallio Youth Hostel (see Places to Stay). There is also a rental centre on the lake behind Finlandia talo in summer.

Boat The main visitors' harbour (☎ 636 047) is on Valkosaari Island at the entrance to Eteläsatama (60 mk a night).

Åland

The Åland islands (Finnish: Ahvenanmaa) are unique, autonomous islands, with their own flag and culture. The fierce local pride is channelled through careful protection of nature and historical and cultural heritage, and legislation by the *lagtinget*. Several dialects of Swedish are spoken, and few Ålanders speak Finnish. This situation goes back to a League of Nations' decision in 1921, after a Swedish-Finnish dispute over sovereignty came to a head. Åland took its own flag in 1954 and has issued stamps since 1984.

The islands are popular for cycling and camping and cabin holidays. There are medieval parish churches, ruins and fishing villages. The islands are popular for the Midsummer weekend celebrations. Nature is prized and a more restricted outdoor code

FINLAND

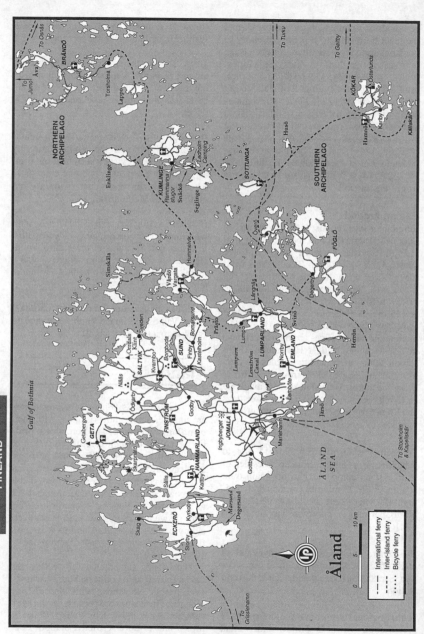

Åland

FINLAND

operates in Åland. Fishing waters are separately licensed and you should ask about appropriate fishing permits at tourist offices.

The centre of Åland is Mariehamn, a port with two harbours, in the south of the main island group. You can take your wheels almost anywhere around the islands using the bridges or the network of car and bicycle ferries.

History
The first settlers set foot on Åland 6000 years ago, near Orrdals klint where a 'prehistoric trail' has been set up. More than a hundred Bronze and Iron Age cemeteries have been discovered, and they are clearly signposted *fornminne*. Of the six Viking Age fortresses, those in Saltvik (Borgboda and Nääs) are particularly worth a visit. Medieval churches date from the 12th to 15th century, and the ones in Finström, Kumlinge, Lemland, Saltvik and Sund are not to be missed, although Hammarland, Eckerö and Jomala's churches are older.

Kastelholm castle, which was established in the 14th century is worth a visit, but the impressive Russian fortifications of Bomarsund from the 1830s were destroyed during the Crimean War.

Information
The main tourist office is Ålands Turistinformation (☎ 24000), Storagatan 8, Mariehamn. For information about cabins all over Åland write to Ålandsresor (on Torggatan) at Box 62, 22101 Mariehamn.

Finnish markka and Swedish krona can be used on Åland.

To call Sweden use the prefix 81, and for other countries 82 or 990. For emergencies call ☎ 112, for police ☎ 10023, and for medical service ☎ 10022.

The telephone code for the islands is ☎ 018.

Getting There & Away
Air Finnair has an office at Skarpansvägen 24 in Mariehamn and offers three or four flights daily from Helsinki via Turku and twice daily from Stockholm.

Boat Viking Line is at Storagatan 2, Silja Line is at Norragatan 2, Eckerö Linjen is at Torggatan 2 and Birka Line is at Östra Esplanadsgatan 7.

Viking and Silja lines have daily ferries to Mariehamn from Turku and Naantali as part of their links with Stockholm: you can stop-off 'between' countries.

Birka Line also sails from Stockholm, Eckerö Linjen sails from Grisslehamn (north of Stockholm) to Eckerö, and Viking sails from Kapellskär (north of Stockholm). From Grisslehamn to Eckerö is the cheapest route.

Free travel for pedestrians and cyclists on the archipelago ferries all the way to mainland Åland is possible via south-eastern harbours at Korppoo (southern route, from Galtby) or Kustavi (northern route, from Osnäs), but only if you break your journey to stay on one or more islands. Travelling nonstop costs 50 mk, plus a higher fee for cars. For the best views, take a ferry from Galtby to Kökar, and then to mainland Åland to Långnäs. From Osnäs, take a ferry to northern Brändö, and another from the southern tip (20 km overland) to Kumlinge, and then to mainland Åland via Hummelvik.

Getting Around
Bus The five main buses depart from Mariehamn near the library, and go to Eckerö, Geta, Saltvik, Vårdö (Hummelvik) and Långnäs for fares ranging up to 30 mk.

Ferry There are three kinds of inter-island ferry. For short launches across straits, ferries ply nonstop and are always free. For longer routes, ferries run according to schedule. These ferries take cars, bicycles and pedestrians. There are also three bicycle ferries in summer, a ride is 25 to 40 mk per person. For timetables ask the tourist office or Ålandstrafiken at Strandgatan 25, Mariehamn.

Bicycle Cycling is a great way to tour the islands. Clearly marked routes cover the most scenic roads. Ro-No Rent has bicycles available at Mariehamn and Eckerö harbours (daily rental starts at 30 mk).

FINLAND

MARIEHAMN

Mariehamn's small port helped provide some impressive chapters in maritime history. It retains its village flavour despite the summer tourist rush. Torggatan is the colourful pedestrian street, and there are great museums.

Information

Åland postage stamps are available and money exchange is possible at the main post office in Torggatan from 9 am to 5 pm weekdays, and from 11 am to 2 pm on Saturday in summer. There is a poste restante service.

You'll find the police on the corner of Styrmansgatan and Servicegatan. The hospital (☎ 5355) is on Norragatan.

Luggage storage is for 24 hours only in the lockers at the ferry terminal, but Ålandstrafiken will store backpacks for 5 mk a day, or 10 mk for longer periods.

Things to See & Do

The stalwarts of Åland are mariners and the **Maritime Museum** at Västra Hamnen, a sort of folk museum of fishing and maritime commerce, is devoted to them. Admission costs 20 mk. Nearby the ship *Pommern* is moored and you can clamber through it for 15 mk, it's open from May to October.

Trade and crafts are covered by the **Köpmannagården** in Parkgatan (free, open weekdays from 1 to 3 pm in summer). Of more general interest is the fine **Ålands Museum** and **Art Museum** at the east end of Storagatan (15 mk, closed Monday from September to April).

The **Ålandsparken** amusement park, above the ferry terminal, is open in summer until 9 pm (entry costs 20 mk).

Places to Stay & Eat

Gröna Udden (☎ 190 41) is the main camping ground and charges 10 mk a head per night.

For the cheapest beds, the hotel boat *Botel Alida* (☎ 137 55) is moored at the north end of Östra Hamnen and charges from 70 mk per bed in a two-bunk cabin. There is also a nice café with snacks.

Gästhem Kronan (☎ 126 17) at Neptunigatan 52, charges singles/doubles 195/295 mk and is open from mid-May to mid-August. For small groups, *Hotel Adlon* at Hamngatan 7 has inexpensive rooms for up to six people.

Many cafés, including the one opposite the ferry terminal, serve Åland 'pancakes' for 15 mk. Ask for special lunch packages at *Tropical* or *Nikolaj* on Torggatan, or check the staggering variety of pizzas at *Rob's* at Strandgatan 12. The boat restaurant *FP Knorring* has costly but classy seafood meals, plus a pleasant beer terrace on the deck.

SUND

In the municipality of Sund, about 20 km north-east of Mariehamn (take bus No 4), is the medieval **Kastelholm** castle. The 20 mk tickets are also valid for the nearby **Jan Karlsgården**, a farm dating from last century open from May to September, and the jail museum.

Further east, the ruins of the Russian fortress at **Bomarsund** are always accessible, as are the nearby cemeteries of five religions on Prästö Island. The 13th-century **church** is open daily until 4 pm in summer.

Places to Stay

Not far from Bomarsund is *Puttes Camping* (☎ 44016), which also has huts from 110 mk. On the nearby Prästö Island, the *Prästö Stugor* rents similar huts near the main road.

ORRDALS KLINT

The highest point on Åland has the best views across the archipelago. You can stay overnight in the hut at the top free of charge. Carry all the water you need and try not to be too boisterous as locals often make early morning sojourns to the top and if they are put off by noisy tourists the hut may end up with a padlock on the door. There is a prehistoric trail nearby.

Getting There & Away

There is no public transport. Follow gravel roads and the signs *Långbergsöda* or

Orrdalsklint to the parking area. You can take your bicycle all the way to the stairway.

ECKERÖ
The westernmost municipality of Eckerö is linked by ferry to Sweden. The ferry terminal is at Storby and there is a bank, as well as shops and a tourist office at the harbour. Old postal routes are exhibited at **Postrote Museum** in the large post office building. The small-boat harbour with a **Hunting & Fishing Museum** (20 mk) is just to the north. Post offices are at Storby and Kyrkoby. Bus No 1 runs to Mariehamn.

The medieval **Eckerö Church**, open daily, in the middle of the island has beautiful interior paintings.

Places to Stay
Ängstorps Gästhem (☎ 38665) in Storby is one of the best places to stay on Åland, but it's often full. Rooms cost 250 mk. *Käringsund Camping* has four-bed huts from 150 mk not far from Storby.

NORTHERN ARCHIPELAGO ROUTE
You can visit Jurmo, Brändö, Lappo, Kumlinge and Enklinge islands on the northern archipelago route. As for other routes, these ferries are free for bicycles and pedestrians if you stop en route.

Getting There & Away
From Mariehamn, take bus No 4 to Hummelvik harbour on the Vårdö Island. From Turku, take a bus to Kustavi, and on to Vartsala Island to reach the harbour of Osnäs (Finnish: Vuosnainen). These buses can take a few bicycles. There are half a dozen connections from Osnäs to Brändö every day.

Brändö
This weird looking island group is your first leg on the northern ferry route. Ferries from Osnäs arrive at the northern pier of Åva, and the next one departs from the southern pier at Torsholma. There is a taxi service for the 20 km between these two harbours, or you can hitchhike. The top-end *Hotell Gullvivan* is halfway.

Kumlinge
This interesting island is the best place to break your journey (to qualify for free travel). The medieval **church** has unique 16th-century paintings, and is open from 9 am to 9 pm in summer. You can take a free ferry to the quiet **Seglinge Island**, south of Kumlinge.

Places to Stay The *Remmarina stugor* (☎ 55402), south of the Kumlinge village, has huts from 215 mk. Near the pier for the ferries to Seglinge, *Ledholm Camping* has cheap camping and cabins from 80 mk.

SOUTHERN ARCHIPELAGO ROUTE
You can visit Kökar, Husö, Sottunga and Föglö islands along the southern route between Finland and Åland.

Getting There & Away
From Mariehamn, take bus No 5 to the harbour of Långnäs. There are two to four departures daily. From mainland Finland, you will have to travel through Parainen, Nauvo and Korppoo (Swedish: Pargas, Nagu and Korpo, respectively), and take (free) ferries twice en route to reach the harbour of Galtby on Korppoo Island, 75 km from Turku. There are one or two departures daily. From Turku, take the Saaristotie bus to Galtby. From Helsinki, change buses at Kaarina near Turku.

Kökar
Kökar Island is distant from the main Åland group and its sleepy villages are more quaint. The main sight is **Hamnö Island** where there are ruins of a 14th-century abbey, and a 18th-century church. The fragile nature and prehistoric sites can be discovered by following marked trails.

A boat tour to the island of **Källskär** in summer reveals glimpses of eccentric island life and pristine nature.

Places to Stay Accommodation is scattered around the island and is available in summer only. The guesthouses *Kökar logi* and *Antons Gästhem*, and *Österlunds Camping* have mid-range rooms and cottages. The top-end *Hotell Brudhäll* is in the central township of Karlby.

Southern Finland

Nowhere in Finland are there so many historical monuments as on the southern coast between Turku and Hamina. This region, dotted with medieval churches, old manors, castles and other buildings, is strongly influenced by early Swedish settlers, and several Swedish dialects are still spoken in coastal communities.

TURKU
Turku, the oldest city in Finland and the former Swedish capital (Åbo), is now a large port and the third largest city of Finland (population 165,000). It is a likely entry point if you are coming from Sweden, and you could spend hours at the riverside between visits to museums and the medieval monuments.

Information
The main tourist office Kaupungin Matkailutoimisto, at Aurakatu 4 is open to 7.30 pm, and in summer at weekends from 10 am to 5 pm. The Tourist Association of South-west Finland, at Läntinen Rantakatu 13, is open from 8 am to 3.30 pm on weekdays and handles cottage bookings and tours. The Youth Travel Information Café, at Läntinen Rantakatu 47 is open Monday to Saturday from 9 am to 9 pm from July to August. You can store luggage free for a week or more. Also good is the Cultural Centre at Vanha Suurtori 3, with exhibitions, information on concerts and ticket sales for events throughout Finland.

Money Forex has an exchange booth near the market at Eerikinkatu 12 with better rates than banks. It is open daily. You can also exchange money on the ferries.

Post & Communications The main post office is at Eerikinkatu 21, open from Monday to Friday 9 am to 5 pm. Some public phones only accept a local phone card – others do accept the national Tele card.

The telephone code is ☎ 02.

Things to See & Do
The riverside remains the most attractive part of Turku. The small **Pharmacy Museum** at Läntinen Rantakatu 13 is actually the oldest wooden house in Turku, with attractive collections, open daily. Diagonally opposite, **Aboa Vetus & Ars Nova** is the newest museum and art gallery in Turku with archaeological exhibitions and a modern art collection. It is open daily from 8.30 am to 7 pm. Tickets are 50 mk for both wings, or 35 mk individually. Ask for discounts.

Luostarinmäki is the only surviving 18th-century area of this medieval town – Turku has been razed 30 times by fire – and here, artisans work inside the old wooden houses in summer. The area is open daily in summer from 10 am to 6 pm, entry is 15 mk. In winter, opening hours are 10 am to 3 pm daily except Monday.

The **cathedral**, dating from the 13th century, and its museum is open daily. The **Orthodox church**, facing Kauppatori, is open every day except Saturday to 3 pm. The three museum ships dominate the river banks. *Suomen Joutsen* and the minelayer *Keihässalmi* cost 15 mk and are open daily from 10 am to 6 pm from mid-May to mid-August. The *Sigyn* can be seen near the castle.

The **Sibelius Museum** at Piispankatu 17 collects musical instruments and exhibits memorabilia of the composer (15 mk, open daily except Monday to 3 pm, and from 6 to 8 pm Wednesday). On the other side of the street, **Ett Hem** is a museum of a 19th century residence.

The **Samppalinna windmill** marks the park sector next to the **Wäinö Aaltonen Museum** of sculpture. The city **Art Museum** with notable collections is at the head of Aurakatu.

Part of the **Turku Castle** is a museum of old Turku and the remains of the medieval

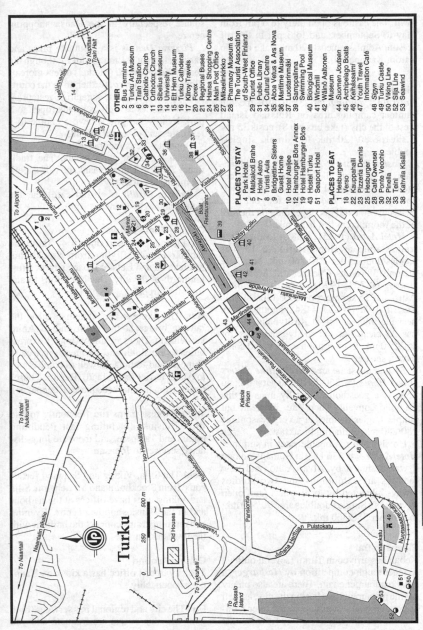

Turku

0   250   500 m

Old Houses

To Kupittaa
Train Halt

To Hotel
Nuukumatti

To Airport

To Hotel
Nuukumatti

To Naantali

Naantalin Pikatie

To Turkuhalli

To Ruissalo
Island

FINLAND

Kakola
Prison

OTHER
2   Bus Terminal
3   Turku Art Museum
6   Train Station
9   Catholic Church
11 Orthodox Church
13 Sibelius Museum
14 University
15 Ett Hem Museum
16 Turku Cathedral
17 Kilroy Travels
20 Forex
21 Regional Buses
24 Hansa Shopping Centre
26 Main Post Office
27 Mikaelinkirkko
28 Pharmacy Museum &
     The Tourist Association
     of South-West Finland
29 Tourist Office
31 Public Library
34 Cultural Centre
35 Aboa Vetus & Ars Nova
36 Maritime Museum
37 Luostarinmäki
39 Samppalinna
     Swimming Pool
40 Biological Museum
41 Windmill
42 Wäinö Aaltonen
     Museum
44 Suomen Joutsen
45 Archipelago Boats
46 Keihässalmi
47 Youth Travel
     Information Café
48 Sigyn
49 Turku Castle
50 Viking Line
52 Silja Line
53 Seawind

PLACES TO STAY
4   Park Hotel
5   Matkakoti Brahe
7   Hotel Astro
8   Turisti Aula
9   Bridgettine Sisters
     Guest Home
10 Hotel Ateljee
12 Hamburger Börs Annex
19 Hotel Hamburger Börs
43 Hostel Turku
51 Seaport Hotel

PLACES TO EAT
1   Hesburger
18 Verso
22 Kauppahalli
23 Pizzeria Dennis
25 Hesburger
28 Café Qwensel
30 Ponte Vecchio
32 Pinella
33 Teini
38 Kahvila Kisälli

town. The castle is open daily to 6 pm from May to September, and to 3 pm in the off season. Admission costs 20 mk (take bus No 1 from Kauppatori).

Places to Stay

Ruissalo Camping (☎ 258 9249), the big summer camping area on Ruissalo Island west of the city (take bus No 8), costs 35 mk a site or 80/120 mk for simple singles/doubles.

Hostel Turku (☎ 231 6578), at Linnankatu 39, is open all year round. Services include free use of the laundry, a well-equipped kitchen and lockers for your gear. Beds cost 40 to 60 mk depending on the size of the room, breakfast is 20 mk.

Hotel Astro (☎ 251 7838), closest to the train station at Humalistonkatu 18, has singles/doubles for 210/260 mk, but there are only 38 rooms. Cheaper still, *Matkakoti Brahe* (☎ 231 1973), directly opposite Astro, has 15 simple rooms for 130/180 mk. *Turisti Aula* (☎ 233 4484), another place near the train station at Käsityöläiskatu 11, has 23 clean but not-so-stylish rooms for 150/210 mk. Each room has a TV and some have a shower.

Also in the same area, *Bridgettine Sisters Guest Home* (☎ 250 1910), at Ursininkatu 15A, is a guesthouse kept by nuns at this Catholic convent. There are 30 clean but simple singles/doubles at a very reasonable 180/280 mk, including breakfast.

Hotels have reasonable rates in summer. *Hotel Ateljee* (☎ 336 111) at Humalistonkatu 7 was designed by Alvar Aalto, and now features art exhibitions and two studios always inhabited by local artists (and open to visitors). Singles/doubles are 390/500 mk; in summer 330/360 mk.

Places to Eat

Kebab has arrived in Turku (several outlets) to meet tough competition by *Hesburger*, a local hamburger chain. There are also plenty of fine restaurants and bars in the city, as well as popular boat restaurants on the river. Convenient are the eateries around the market

square, especially in the Hansa shopping centre.

Pizzeria Dennis is a reputable pizza and pasta restaurant at Linnankatu 17, though the nearby *Kauppahalli* (market) offers more of a local flavour. *Verso*, further on in the courtyard by the river, is a vegetarian restaurant with hot dishes as well as salads (open to 5 pm). Near Verso you'll have a choice of a few cafés and pizza restaurants.

Opposite the cathedral, *Pinella* is a nice wooden tea house with meals. The traditional *Teini*, at Uudenmaankatu 1, is superb for meals and drinks.

Kahvila Kisälli is an old café near the Luostarinmäki entrance.

Getting There & Away

Air Finnair is at Eerikinkatu 4. There are regular Finnair flights from Stockholm, Mariehamn and Helsinki to the airport a few km north of the city. Bus No 1 runs to and from the airport.

Bus The express bus station is near the railway bridge at the north end of Aninkaistenkatu. There are almost hourly express buses to Helsinki, and frequent services to Tampere and Rauma, as well as connections to Åland ferries (see Åland). Regional buses depart from the market square (Kauppatori).

Train Express trains run frequently to and from Helsinki (including fast Pendolino trains) and Tampere, and there are long-distance services to Joensuu.

Boat The Silja, Viking and Seawind ferries come from Stockholm and Mariehamn. Silja and Viking lines have offices at the harbour and in the Hansa shopping centre. Evening and morning trains connect the harbour with the town station.

Getting Around

The city transit office has a kiosk on Kauppatori open daily.

Bus The city and regional bus services (both gold and blue buses) are frequent and you pay 8 mk for a basic journey or 20 mk for a day tourist ticket. There is a Museum Line bus service in summer that accepts the 20 mk tourist ticket.

Bicycle The cheapest bicycle hire is at the Youth Travel Information Café for 10 mk per day, although you must leave a deposit.

Boat Archipelago cruises and the steamer to Naantali depart from Martinsilta bridge and waterbuses leave from Auransilta.

NAANTALI

Naantali, the most popular of Finnish seaside towns, 13 km from Turku, developed after the founding of a convent in the 1440s. The **church** (open daily in summer) is the main attraction today, although the entire old town with a quaint museum is also worth a stroll. Scandinavian families come for the Moomin World theme park (open in summer only, daily pass 75 mk), located on the island of Kailo and in a few old town villas.

Tourist information and regional tours are available at Naantalin Matkailu (☎ 850 850) at Kaivotori 2.

Places to Stay & Eat

Look for guesthouses on Mannerheiminkatu, but expect high prices. *Hotelli Unikeko* (☎ 436 2852), at Luostarinkatu 20, charges 270/320 mk. Cheaper are cottages at *Naantali Camping* 800 metres from the town centre.

Naantali has excellent restaurants. *Merisali* at the harbour has a good fish buffet for lunch and dinner. At the market square near the bus terminal, *Torin tupa* has inexpensive meals.

Getting There & Away

Take a bus from Turku, which terminates at the harbour. For a day trip take the steamer from Turku daily in summer (see Turku, Getting Around).

SEVEN CHURCHES ROAD

Nowhere else in Finland are there as many medieval churches as there are around Turku. To visit them all would take days (weeks with a bicycle), but combined with other plans (eg travelling to the Åland ferry pier), the best churches are certainly worth a visit.

Consult the map first, and make sure your visit will be between noon and 6 pm, from Tuesday to Sunday, when most churches are open.

North from Turku

On your way to the Osnäs ferry (see Åland), there are interesting churches at **Masku**, **Nousiainen**, **Lemu** and **Askainen** and also **Mynämäki**, the largest of them all. The road then passes to **Taivassalo**, which has extensive paintings, and on to **Kustavi** with a wooden church.

In Askainen there is the large **Louhisaari Manor** with an extensive museum. It is open daily from 11 am to 5 pm.

Further north, there are interesting paintings in the churches of **Kalanti** and **Laitila**.

South from Turku

From Naantali, the road to **Merimasku** (wooden 18th-century church) takes you south to the 14th-century vaulted and painted church at **Rymättylä**. Near the Turku town centre, there are the churches of **Kaarina** and **Maaria**. On your way to Galtby (see Åland) there are interesting churches at Parainen, Nauvo and Korppoo.

Places to Stay

The youth hostel *Päiväkulma* in Rymättylä (☎ 252 1894) has beds from 35 mk.

WESTERN KING'S ROAD

The old road on the south coast of Finland was initially an ordinary track but was established by Swedish kings as a mail route running from Oslo to St Petersburg via Stockholm, Turku and Helsinki. Strict regulations ensured boarding and lodging for travellers. Today King's Road has several route options between Turku and Helsinki, and you will need a car or a bicycle to cover the attractions.

Salo & Kemiö Island

The high-tech industrial town of Salo offers little in terms of attractions, but the bus station has half a dozen daily connections to places such as the trekking and fishing area of **Teijo**, or **Kemiö Island**, which has excellent possibilities for bicycle tours. The 18th-century churches and the museums of **Sagalund** and **Dalsbruk** are worth a visit, and there is access to the **Archipelago National Park** via the park centre in Kasnäs.

Places to Stay The Salo youth hostel *Laurin koulu* (☎ 308 4400) in a school building at Venemestarinkatu 37 has simple bunks for 28 mk. *Pensionat* (☎ 424 553) in the village of Dragsfjärd on Kemiö Island is a youth hostel with 55 mk beds (for HI members), and there are bicycles for rent, and a map available.

Getting There & Away All buses and trains between Helsinki and Turku stop at Salo. The bus station in the Anttila building is close to the train station.

Tammisaari & Around

Near the attractive wooden town of Tammisaari (Swedish: Ekenäs), there are castle ruins of **Raasepori**, and several medieval churches and old Swedish ironworks, such as **Fiskars** and **Billnäs**.

Inkoo & Siuntio

These small towns boast medieval churches. From the west, you should drive on road No 105 via **Fagervik**, an old ironworks area.

EASTERN KING'S ROAD

From Helsinki, the historical King's road leads east to Russia via Sipoo and several larger towns. There are frequent buses on this route.

Porvoo

This medieval town is a perfect day trip from Helsinki, some 50 km away (take a bus or a ferry in summer). The **cathedral** and several museums are main sights, but there are also nice cafés and one of the best *youth hostels*

(☎ 523 0012) in Finland, at Linnankoskenkatu 1-2. Beds cost from 50 mk.

Loviisa

Swedish is still spoken in this pleasant place which has 18th-century fortifications and old town quarters. The Laivasilta pier, south of the centre, has services in summer, including cruises to the renovated 18th-century Svartholm Fort. The best place to stay is *Resandehem M Helgas* at Sibeliuksenkatu 6, with rooms from 120/180 mk.

Ruotsinpyhtää

The quaint 18th-century ironworks area has a superb *youth hostel* (☎ 618 474) with beds from 110 mk.

Pyhtää

The 15th century-church, open daily in summer, has a six-metre medieval painting, the largest in Scandinavia. Boats to Kaunissaari island depart from opposite the church on Tuesday and Sunday.

Kotka

This industrial town (population 56,000) is one of the largest in Finland. At **Langinkoski rapids** there is a preserved tsarist 19th-century log house and a summer hotel. The town centre has a fine museum, an impressive cathedral and a superb seaside park. Boats to nearby fortresses and **Kaunissaari** (fishing village, museum and camping ground) and **Haapasaari** (fishing community and a church) depart from the Sapokka harbour. Kotka is served by express buses and a local train from Kouvola.

The tourist office (☎ 227 4424) is at Keskuskatu 7.

Hamina

Russians were largely responsible for the unusual architecture in this small town, not far from Kotka. *Anna* (☎ 344 7747) at Annankatu 1 is a summer hostel east of the centre.

Central Finland

TAMPERE

Tampere is Finland's second largest city (population 185,000) and is set between Näsijärvi and Pyhäjärvi lakes. Manufacturing industry found it an ideal site and factories clustered around the water's edge. Many factories have been converted into cultural centres, and there is plenty to see.

Orientation

The commercial centre is either side of the narrows of the Tammerkoski River and the industrial areas on its banks; many riverside buildings have been restored for community use. The sprawling parklands of Pyynikki front onto the water south of the centre and the Näsinneula tower dominates Särkänniemi and the northern shore.

Information

The city tourist office (☎ 212 6652) is at Verkatehtaankatu 2, and is open daily in summer. Check also http://www.tampere.fi/. The international youth centre Vuoltsu at Vuolteenkatu 13 provides information, cheap snacks and free luggage storage. It is open from late June to the end of August, from 4 to 10 pm daily. The main post office is at Rautatienkatu 21 and is open daily. Forex at Hämeenkatu 1 is open daily in summer.

The telephone code is ☎ 03.

Things to See

Around the old industrial centre are the restored **Verkaranta** (handicraft) and **Kehräsaari** buildings, which combine textile and gift sales with displays.

The city **library** gives an example of modern architecture and inside is the **Moominvalley** exhibition based on the children's books of Tove Jansson (15 mk). The **Häme Museum** is on Näsilinna in parklands (10 mk, closed Monday during the off season). The **Doll Museum** in the old Hatanpää Manor can be reached by bus No

21, and the authentic Amuri **Museum of Workers' Housing** (closed Monday) on Makasiininkatu is one of the highlights of Tampere.

The **Lenin Museum** is a tiny two-room museum with rather unique relics. It may be one of the last museums of its kind outside Russia.

The parklands and amusements of **Särkänniemi** will fill in any family day (a general pass costs 120 mk for an adult and 60 mk for a child). There is an **aquarium** (25 mk), a **planetarium** and the **Dolphinarium** (30 mk). A trip up the **Näsinneula Tower** costs 12 mk. The art museum, **Sara Hildén Taidemuseo**, concentrates on modern and Finnish art and sculpture (15 mk).

The **cathedral** built in National Romantic style features the weird interior frescos of Hugo Simberg and is open from 10 am to 6 pm daily. The small but ornate **Orthodox church** is open from May to August from 9.30 am to 3 pm weekdays.

Aleksanterin kirkko has interesting wooden interiors and the new **Kalevan kirkko** is an angular adventure in modern church architecture.

If you want views of both lakes forget the Näsinneula Tower and go to the top of the older **Pyynikki Tower** on the hill west of the centre where there is a café (take bus No 12 or 15).

Places to Stay

Tampere Camping (☎ 651 250) at Härmälä is five km south of the city centre (take bus No 1) and costs 70 mk a night, or from 120 mk in small cabins.

The clean *NNKY* hostel (☎ 223 5900 or 222 5446) opposite the cathedral costs from 55 to 70 mk a bed during summer.

The hostel *Uimahallin Maja* (☎ 222 9460), Pirkankatu 10, charges from 80 mk a bed. Its singles/doubles cost from 145/210 mk.

The youth hostel *Domus* (☎ 255 0000), east of the centre at Pellervonkatu 9, offers doubles for 120 mk from June to August.

There are plenty of fine hotels, such as *Arctia Hotel Tampere* (☎ 244 6111), opposite

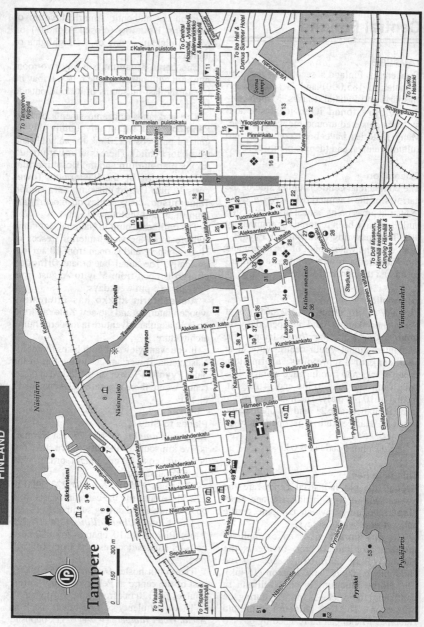

Tampere

FINLAND

Näsijärvi

Särkänniemi

To Vaasa & Lielahti
To Pispala & Lamminpää

To Tampereen Kylpylä

Kalevan puistotie

Salhojankatu

Tammelan puistokatu

Pinninkatu

Tammelan-
tori

Rautatienkatu

Tammela

Näsijärvenkatu

Näsinpuisto

Finlayson

Tammerkoski

Satakunnankatu

Puutarhakatu

Kortelahdenkatu

Amurinkatu

Marianikatu

Niemikatu

Sepänkatu

Paasikiventie

Pirkankatu

Itsenäisyydenkatu

Tammelankatu

Yliopistonkatu

Pinninkatu

Kalevantie

Ronganakatu

Kyttälänkatu

Tuomiokirkonkatu

Aleksanterinkatu

Hatanpään Valtatie

Hämeenkatu

Aleksis Kiven katu

Kauppakatu

Hämeen puisto

Mustanlahdenkatu

Kuninkaankatu

Näsilinnankatu

Hallituskatu

Laukon-
tori

Rahhan suvanto

Stadium

Tampereen valtatie

Viinikanlahti

Kaivokatu

Kaukajarvenkatu

Tillruukonkatu

Pyhäjärvenkatu

Eteläpuisto

Satamakatu

Pyynikintie

Vuolteenkatu

Näkötornintie

Pyynikki

Pyhäjärvi

To Central
Hospital, Jyväskylä,
Kaleva Church
& Messukylä

Jääkiekko

To Ice Hall &
Domus Summer Hotel

Sorsa
Lampi

Viinikankatu

To Turku
& Helsinki

Lempäälänlle

To Doll Museum,
Härmälä kesähotelli,
Camping Härmälä &
Pirkkala airport

0   150   300 m

PLACES TO STAY
9 NNKY Hostel
14 Rantasipi
16 Sokos Hotel Villa
20 Arctia Hotel Tampere
30 Sokos Hotel Ilves
48 Uimahallin Maja
52 Arctia Hotel Rosendahl

PLACES TO EAT
11 Salhojankadun pubi
15 Attila House
21 Salud
23 Donatello
24 Linkosuo
28 Silakka
33 Wanha Posti
37 McDonald's
38 Hesburger
39 Kauppahalli Market
41 Anttila
42 Ohranjyvä

OTHER
1 Amusement Park
2 Sara Hildén Art Museum
3 Aquarium & Planetarium
4 Näsinneula (Observation Tower)
5 Children's Zoo
6 Delfinaario
7 Passenger Wharf for Lake Näsijärvi
8 Näsinlinna (Häme Museum)
10 Tampere Cathedral
12 Tampere University
13 Tampere-talo (Concert Hall)
17 Train Station
18 Main Post Office
19 Forex
22 Orthodox Church
25 Akateeminen Bookshop
26 Bus Station
27 Vuoltsu
29 Koskikeskus Shopping Centre
31 Verkaranta
32 Tourist Office
34 Kehräsaari
35 Keskustori Square & Local Buses
36 Passenger Wharf for Lake Pyhäjärvi
40 Student House
43 Lenin Museum
44 Aleksanteri Church
45 Moominvalley Museum
46 Tampere City Library
47 Swimming Pool
49 Tampere Art Museum
50 Museum of Worker's Housing
51 Pyynikki Tower
53 Pyynikki Summer Theatre

the train station, and the landmark *Sokos Hotel Ilves* (☎ 262 6262) at Koskikeskus.

Places to Eat

There are plenty of places to eat kebab, hamburgers or snacks, and the main street, Hämeenkatu, has many pubs. The local speciality, mustamakkara, or black sausage, can be had at Laukontori market, or in the Kauppahalli indoor market.

Hesburger is on Hämeenkatu opposite the Kauppahalli. Across the bridge and closer to the train station, *Wanha Posti* serves beer from a local brewery, and *Linkosuo* at Hämeenkatu 9 is a traditional bakery with lunch packages.

Inside the large Koskikeskus shopping centre, *Silakka* has a fish buffet for lunch. Across the road at Aleksanterinkatu 37, *Donatello* serves cheap pasta and pizza, and the nearby *Salud* at Otavalankatu 10 is a local favourite for gourmet food.

The university's student restaurants are to be found inside the main building, and in the Attila House.

Getting There & Away

Air There are daily Finnair services from the Pirkkala airport (18 km to the south) to Helsinki and direct flights from Stockholm. The Finnair office has moved to Pirkkala.

Bus The main bus station is near the stadium. Express buses run from Helsinki and from Turku; there are also frequent services to Hämeenlinna and Jyväskylä.

Train Express trains run hourly during the day between Tampere and Helsinki. Intercity trains continue to Oulu and there are trains to Turku, Pori, Vaasa and Joensuu.

Boat Suomen Hopealinja (Silver Line) cruises from Hämeenlinna daily to Laukontori quay and from Mustalahti quay (near Särkänniemi) north to Ruovesi and Virrat (286 mk return).

Getting Around

The city transport and ticket office is at

FINLAND

Aleksis Kiven katu 11. The bus service is good and a basic journey costs 9 mk. A 'smart-card' tourist day-ticket is 25 mk.

PORI

The annual Pori Jazz Festival is one of the most appreciated summer events in Finland, with a wide variety of music available in July. The town itself, despite being one of the oldest in Finland, has little appeal, but the **Satakunnan museo** is one of the best regional museums in Finland, and the **mausoleum** at the Käppärä cemetery has frescos by the famous 19th-century painter Gallen-Kallela.

Places to Stay

Tekunkorpi (☎ 637 8400) at Korventie 52 is the only youth hostel in town. It has beds from 55 mk for HI members. Centrally located *Matkakoti Keskus*, at Itäpuisto 13, charges 150/200 mk.

Getting There & Away

There are five trains daily from Tampere, and several buses from Rauma and other nearby towns.

RAUMA

The 600 old wooden houses constitute the acclaimed UNESCO heritage area of Rauma, perfect with its **medieval church** (with frescos) and several **house museums** (joint ticket 10 mk). The old town is complemented by a nice seaside area at Poroholma. The tourist office (☎ 834 4551) is at Valtakatu 2.

Places to Stay & Eat

The seaside *Poroholma Youth Hostel* (☎ 822 4666), a long walk from the bus station, has 150 mk doubles and 45 mk dorm beds. They also have four-bed cottages at 170 mk at the camp site. Another hostel, *Kesähotelli Rauma* (☎ 824 0130) at Satamakatu 20, is only open in summer, and has singles/doubles for 170/240 mk.

Kalatorin majatalo (☎ 822 7111) is a pricey guesthouse offering excellent meals, and *La Bamba* near the market square has

huge pizzas, but locals prefer *Buena Vista* at Kanalinranta 5. *Kontion Leipomo* at Kuninkaankatu 9 is one of several pleasant cafés in town.

Getting There & Away

There are buses from Pori, Turku and other centres. If you prefer trains, take the Pori-bound train from Tampere, and get off at Kokemäki and continue by bus (all train tickets are valid).

HÄMEENLINNA

The historical town of Hämeenlinna (population 45,000) and its medieval **castle** are at the southern tip of the lake network and 100 km north-west of Helsinki. The castle has an extensive museum, is open daily and costs 14 mk to visit. The home of composer Jean Sibelius, at Hallituskatu 11, is open daily (5 mk). The art museum near the train station is also worth a look. The tourist office is at Sibeliuksenkatu 5.

Places to Stay & Eat

There is a small *youth hostel* (☎ 682 8560) near the large Aulanko park (beds are from 60 mk), take bus No 2, 13 or 17. *Vanaja* opposite the train station has singles/doubles at 120/ 190 mk.

Popino near the bus station serves large pizzas, and *Kaneli* has coffee and cakes. More style awaits at *Piparkakkutalo* behind the church.

Getting There & Away

Take an hourly Tampere train from Helsinki or one of the several daily express buses. The train station is one km outside the town centre, over the bridge. The bus station near the town centre has services to regional attractions. To Tampere you can take a Silver Line eight-hour cruise from June to mid-August for 170 mk one way.

JYVÄSKYLÄ

The capital (population 75,000) of the province of Central Finland *(lääni)* is known for its **Alvar Aalto Museum** and several architecturally interesting buildings, including the spacious university campus. There are several museums and a lively pedestrian area. The tourist office (☎ 624 903) is near the train station at Asemakatu 6, but check also http://www.jkl.fi/.

Places to Stay & Eat

Laajari (☎ 253 355) at Laajavuorentie 15 is a hostel with beds at 65 mk. *Tuomiojärvi Camping* (☎ 624 895) has four-bed cabins from 200 mk. Most hotels in the town centre are more expensive, but there are summer discounts. Try *Yöpuu* (☎ 333 900) at Yliopistonkatu 23 for style and class.

Most good restaurants are on Kauppakatu. In the campus, *Lozzi* is an Alvar Aalto-designed restaurant with student food at student prices.

Getting There & Away

There are regular trains from Tampere, Pieksämäki junction and Joensuu, and buses to nearby towns.

Pohjanmaa

The flat coastal area of Pohjanmaa (Swedish: Österbotten) facing the Gulf of Bothnia has some of the most interesting wooden towns in Finland, dating back to the heyday of the international tar trade, such as Kristiinan-kaupunki, Uusikaarlepyy and Raahe (Swedish: Kristinestad, Nykarleby and Brahestad, respectively). These towns can be visited via nearby train stations, or by bus.

SEINÄJOKI

This town is a railway junction. It is mostly known for the modern town centre designed by Alvar Aalto, the Finnish architect, and there is a large museum area at Törnävä (take bus No 1 or 5). The best time to visit is during large events, such as the Tango markkinat or Provinssi Rock.

The tourist office (☎ 414 3890) is at the Torikeskus shopping centre.

The telephone code is ☎ 06.

Places to Stay

There are large hotels near the train station. The most attractive location is available in summer at *Hostel Kortteeri* (☎ 420 4800) near the river at the end of Puskatie. Beds start from 85 mk. *Matkustajakatu Vuorela* at Kalevankatu 31, and *Perhehotelli Nur-mela* next door, offer singles/doubles from 160/250 mk.

VAASA

The bilingual town of Vaasa (Swedish: Wasa) is one of the most attractive towns in Finland. It was founded in 1606 near an earlier port which is now called Vanha Vaasa where ruins remain. In addition to several churches, museums and art collections, Vaasa can be used as a base for bicycle tours on narrow roads along the Kyrönjoki and Laihianjoki rivers, or to the artisan village of Stundars, 16 km away. The tourist office (☎ 325 1145) is at Hovioikeudenpuistikko 11.

Places to Stay & Eat

Tekla (☎ 327 6411) at Palosaarentie 58 is a youth hostel, open all year round, with beds from 100 mk. There are four-bed cottages at *Vaasa Camping* in Vaskiluoto (two km from the centre) for 170 mk. Near the train station, *Olo* at Asemakatu 12 charges 100/150 mk.

Most restaurants are around the central square, or check *Bacchus* at Rantakatu 4 for fine dining.

Getting There & Away

There are one to three daily ferries from the Swedish town of Umeå (Finnish: Uumaja); the trip takes 3½ hours. There are also ferries from Sundsvall. There is a bus from Vaasa (Kauppapuistikko 12) to the harbour 30 minutes before each departure. There are six daily trains from Seinäjoki to Vaasa, and a direct IC-train from Helsinki, 420 km away.

KOKKOLA

This coastal town (population 36,000) is one of the 17th-century ports which took part in the busy tar business. **Neristan** is an idyllic old town, with several museums (with free entry) on Pitkänsillankatu, open daily except Monday from noon.

The tourist office (☎ 831 1902) is at Mannerheiminaukio.

Places to Stay

The youth hostel and the camping ground share the area of *Camping Suntinsuu* (☎ 831 4006) at the seaside. Beds start at 70 mk. There are several hotels in town.

Getting There & Away

All trains between Helsinki and Oulu stop at Kokkola. There are buses which continue on to other coastal towns, such as Pietarsaari and Uusikaarlepyy.

PIETARSAARI

This delightful town (Swedish: Jakobstad) is one of the distinctively Swedish centres on the west coast.

Things to See

The old town, Skata, includes 18th-century houses on Hamngatan. The museums generally open at noon and close four or five hours later. **Jakobstads Museum** at Storagatan 2 is the finest, and the private collections at **MC Museum** and **Vapen Museum**, both at Alholmsgatan 8, exhibit motorcycles and guns, respectively. In the old harbour area at Gamla Hamn, see the *Jacobstad Wapen*, a newly constructed vessel according to a 17th century design. Don't miss the medieval **Pedersöre Church** next to the Bodgärdet summer hotel, with its 85-metre spire.

Places to Stay

Svanen (☎ 723 0660), the youth hostel and camping ground six km north of town, has dormitory beds for 30 mk. One km south of the town centre is *Bodgärdet*, a hostel on Sockenvägen. Beds in double rooms cost just 65 mk. It is only open from 1 June to 31 July. *Westerlund resandehem* (☎ 723 0440) in the old town at Norrmalmsgatan 8 charges 130/210 mk, including breakfast.

Getting There & Away

There are regular express and ordinary buses to Pietarsaari from Kokkola, Vaasa and other coastal towns. Bennäs (Finnish: Pännäinen), 11 km away, is the closest train station to Pietarsaari. A shuttle bus meets arriving trains.

Silja Line has ferry connections from Skellefteå and Umeå (in Sweden) to Pietarsaari in summer. The Pietarsaari harbour is six km north of the town centre, and there are buses.

OULU

Oulu (population 110,000), the technologically oriented industrial centre of north Finland, was founded in 1605 and rebuilt after a fire in 1822. It is a large town with several attractions, including a lively seaside market.

Information

The tourist office (☎ 314 1294) is at Torikatu 10, open daily in summer. VR has a travel bureau at the train station, and there are bicycles for rent. The post office is near the railway station.

The telephone code is ☎ 08.

Things to See & Do

Visiting the **Tietomaa**, a science and technology centre and extensive Uniform Gallery, could occupy a day. It's open daily all year round, but expensive at 75 mk (ask for discounts).

The **provincial museum** in the Ainola parkland charges 10 mk admission (closed Friday) and has extensive collections over four floors dealing with everything from seal hunting and old coins to Sami culture. The nearby **art gallery** has temporary exhibitions.

The imposing **cathedral** has Finland's oldest portrait (dating from 1611) in its vestry. The small square on Rotuaari pedestrian street (Kirkkokatu) is lively in summer, as is the market hall **Kauppahalli** near the quay, which is the produce centre. The modern **provincial library** is a refuge from rain and has international newspapers and periodicals in English as well as a café.

Turkansaari is a large open-air folk museum 13 km east of town and can be

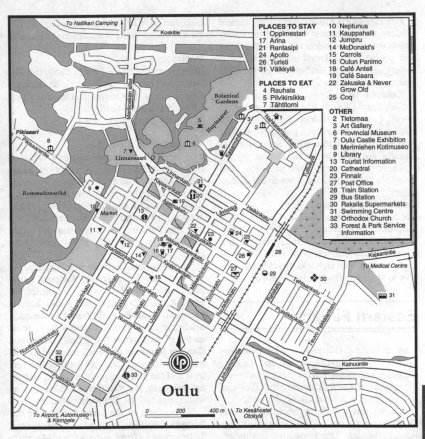

PLACES TO STAY
1 Oppimestari
17 Arina
21 Rantasipi
24 Apollo
26 Turisti
31 Välkkylä

PLACES TO EAT
4 Rauhala
5 Pilvikirsikka
7 Tähtitorni

10 Neptunus
11 Kauppahalli
12 Jumpru
14 McDonald's
15 Carrols
16 Oulun Panimo
18 Café Antell
19 Café Saara
22 Zakuska & Never
   Grow Old
25 Coq

OTHER
2 Tietomaa
3 Art Gallery
6 Provincial Museum
7 Oulu Castle Exhibition
8 Merimiehen Kotimuseo
9 Library
13 Tourist Information
20 Cathedral
23 Finnair
27 Post Office
28 Train Station
29 Bus Station
30 Raksila Supermarkets
31 Swimming Centre
32 Orthodox Church
33 Forest & Park Service
   Information

Oulu

0   200   400 m

reached by waterbus or bus No 3 or 4 in summer. It is open daily from 11 am to 8 pm in summer. Entry is 10 mk, with several discounts available.

Places to Stay

Nallikari Camping (☎ 554 1541) is open from May to October. The seaside camping ground, five km north-east of town, charges 65 mk for a site, for cabins you pay 140/200/280 a single/double/triple in summer. Take bus No 5.

Välkkylä (☎ 311 8060) is the central hostel at the rear of Kajaanintie 36 and is

open from June to August for 50 mk a bed. *Oppimestari* (☎ 313 0527) at Nahkatehtaankatu 3 opposite Tietomaa is a summer hostel, open in June and July only. Beds cost 100 mk, and there is a kitchen in all rooms.

Directly opposite the train station is the good budget hotel *Bed & Breakfast Hotelli Turisti* (☎ 377 233), with singles/doubles for 225/290 mk, including breakfast.

Places to Eat

There are local specialities in the indoor *Kauppahalli* and the outdoor market, open until 2 pm.

Pilvikirsikka is a nice café in the botanical gardens on Hupisaaret Island. The nearby *Tähtitorni* is a wooden tower with snacks and coffee. *Café Antell* is the traditional bakery in the centre, or check the newer *Café Saara* at Kirkkokatu 2.

Zakuska is a Russian restaurant at Hallituskatu 13 with fine cuisine at higher prices. *Coq*, at Asemakatu 39 near the train station, offers cheap lunch packages, as does *Pikantti* in the Citymarket Superstore at Raksila, not far from the bus station.

There are several bars in Oulu, and *Rauhala* at Mannenkatu 1 has live music.

Getting There & Away

Finnair has many direct flights from Helsinki. The airport is 15 km south of town (Finnair buses cost 20 mk). Trains and express buses connect with Oulu from all main centres. The Helsinki direct train takes five to six hours (longer via Kajaani).

Eastern Finland

Eastern Finland (Karelia) is a romantic region of lakes, rivers, locks and canals. Consider taking the ferries that ply between the inland ports or try canoeing the lakes and rapids. There is 50,000 km of shoreline.

Karelia has a culture which was once Orthodox and has close links over the Russian border. The museums, costumes, clothes and local foods are the traveller's proof of this. Runon ja Rajan tie (the Bard and Border Way), is a notable scenic road that hugs the border from Virolahti on the Gulf of Finland to Kuusamo near Lapland.

Further west, Savo is the main lakeland area in Finland, with a distinctive tradition, and Kainuu is a wilderness area.

LAPPEENRANTA

Lappeenranta (population 57,000) was a frontier garrison town until the building of the Saimaa canal made it an even more important port. Today it is an attractive harbour for summer cruises if you ignore the pulp factories in the background. The fortress is one of the best attractions in Finland.

Information

The city tourist office (☎ 415 6860) is in the bus station complex and there is an information booth at the harbour. The main post office is at Pormestarinkatu 1.

The telephone code is ☎ 05.

Things to See & Do

The central, wooden **Lappee Church** (Lappeen kirkko) has 18th-century paintings. The water tower east of the town centre offers a lake view for 5 mk, and there is a display of **old radios** and also a café. **Wolkoffin Talomuseo** at Kauppakatu 26 is a home museum of a Russian emigrant family. It is open daily in summer, entry costs 20 mk.

Above the main harbour a cultural reserve has been developed around **fortress ruins** and 15 mk will admit you to all museums. **Etelä Karjalan museo** (the South Karelia Museum), is linked with **Viipurin museo**, a celebration of Vyborg, where a large-scale model of the town is being built. There is a **Cavalry Museum** and uniformed riders still train (for summer tourists) between the fortress and the market square. There is also an **art museum**, the **Kristina Studios** and art workshops and the **Orthodox church**.

If you want to see **Lake Saimaa** or the **Saimaa Canal** more closely, consider the daily cruises (from June to mid-August) for 60 mk.

Places to Stay & Eat

Most cheap places are to the west of the centre, such as *Huhtiniemi* (☎ 451 5555), Kuusimäenkatu 18, which is open in summer and has beds for 40 mk in summer. *Finnhostel Lappeenranta* on the same site is open all year and has singles/doubles for 210/240 mk a night (take bus No 26). There are also cabins and tent sites. Just 300 metres west, *Karelia-Park* (☎ 675 211) the summer hotel in Korpraalinkuja beyond the camp site, charges 70 mk from June to August for clean rooms that may be noisy on weekends.

Eastern Finland

FINLAND

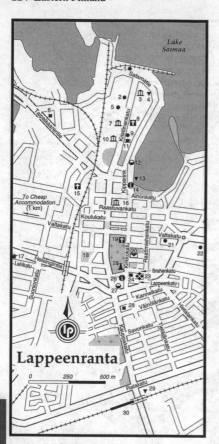

PLACES TO STAY
6   Hotelli Pallo
17 Kesä-LOAS
24 Sokos Hotel Lappee
28 Matkahovi

PLACES TO EAT
4   Majakka
11 Kahvila Majurska
13 Ship Restaurants
14 Martat & Other Stalls
29 McDonald's & Hansa Discounter

OTHER
1   Ceramics Studio
2   Art Exhibition
3   South Karelia Museum
5   Workshops
7   Art Museum
8   Orthodox Church
9   Handicraft Shops
10 Cavalry Museum
12 Passenger Quay
14 Tourist Information
15 Lappeenranta Church
16 Wolkoffin Talomuseo
18 Market Square & Indoor Market
19 Lappee Church
20 Post Office
21 Library
22 Water Tower
23 Shopping Centre
25 War Monument
26 Tourist Office
27 Bus Station
30 Train Station

Kesä-LOAS (☎ 453 0900) at Leirikatu 2F, also has hostel beds in summer.

Matkahovi (☎ 415 6705), not far from the train station at Kauppakatu 52, offers rooms at 160/200 mk. The entrance is at the back.

The novelty restaurant is *Prinsessa Armaada*, a ship at the head of the harbour, offering some mid-priced lunches.

Opposite the ship, and also at the market square, a number of stalls offer delicacies, such as waffles with jam and whipped cream. *Kahvila Majurska*, a charming tea room opposite the cavalry museum in the fortress area, is definitely a must.

Getting There & Away

There are flights to Lappeenranta. Take bus No 34 to the airport. Trains from Helsinki are frequent, as are the express buses.

SAVONLINNA

Savonlinna grew up between lakes near the stronghold of Olavinlinna castle in some of the prettiest of waterscapes. As a summer spot or opera venue it is unbeatable.

The tourist office (☎ 273 492) is at Puistokatu 1.

The telephone code is ☎ 015.

Things to See & Do

The lively market at Kauppatori is open from dawn Monday to Saturday all year. Sweet pastries such as *omena-lörtsy*, an apple turnover, are available at the market.

Several 1½-hour cruises leave from Kauppatori and the going rate is from 30 to 40 mk per adult.

The best preserved medieval castle in the northern countries is **Olavinlinna**. It was used by both Swedish and Russian overlords but today is best known for the international opera festival in July, with tickets from 300 mk. There is also two museums. You have to take the hourly guided tour for 20 mk.

Savonlinnan Maakuntamuseo is the provincial museum by the lake, near the castle. It features lake traffic, logging and hunting. There are also museum ships nearby that relate to the museum. Admission costs 15 mk. There are exhibits dealing with the threatened Saimaa ringed seals (of which less than 200 remain).

Places to Stay
The cheapest beds in summer are at the SS *Heinävesi* after the last cruise in the evenings.

You can camp at *Savonlinna Camping* (☎ 537 353), at Vuohimäki seven km from town, from 75 mk a site.

The two youth hostels in Savonlinna charge 95 mk per person. In July, go to *Malakias* (☎ 533 283), some two km outside town. Near the spa, *Vuorilinna* (☎ 739 5495) is open in June and August, and has student flats with balcony and kitchen, but you will need your own utensils.

The best place to stay in Savonlinna is the homely *Hospits* (☎ 515 661), at Linnankatu 20 near the castle. The quiet garden faces the beach. Singles start at 200 mk. Hospits is open all year round but it's often full in summer.

For grace and style, splurge on a stay at the summer hotel at *Rauhalinna* (☎ 523 119). It's a wooden villa 16 km from town or 40 minutes by boat. Doubles cost 380 mk (open from June to August).

Places to Eat
The boat *Hopeasalmi* is moored at the market square and serves mid-priced meals and salads. There is also an outdoor bar. Close to the castle at Linnankatu 10,

Linnakrouvi is merely a beer-drinking joint, but the setting is nice.

There are good restaurants in most of the hotels. The buffet at the Hospits is something to look forward to. You can also dine inside the castle.

Paviljonki, the restaurant school, on the left over the highway bridge, at the east end of town, is cheaper than average for meals.

Getting There & Away
Finnair flies from Helsinki. From Helsinki there are three express buses a day and trains via Parikkala. Connecting buses from the Pieksämäki junction accept train passes. The main station is a long walk from the town centre, so get off at the Kauppatori platform instead.

KERIMÄKI
The small town of Kerimäki on Lake Puruvesi, 25 km east of Savonlinna, is noted for its 1847 wooden parish **church**, which is claimed to be the world's biggest – it seats 3300 people. You'll also find a **fishing museum** in town.

Korkeamäki Hostel (☎ 442 186) is eight km south of Kerimäki and has beds from 50 mk.

PUNKAHARJU
The famous pine-covered sand esker (sand or gravel ridge), between Parikkala and Savonlinna, is one of the most unusual places to visit in Finland. The Finnish Forest Museum **Lusto** is a grandiose achievement and exhibits relate to forests and their products. Lusto is open daily from 10 am to 6 pm, and is complemented by a large research park (with tracks and all kinds of trees) and an information centre in an old railway station. Coming by train or bus, you can also get off at the weird underground art centre **Retretti**, with superb exhibitions in summer. Tickets cost from 55 to 60 mk. There is a two-hour summer cruise (one-way 80 mk, return 110 mk).

Tourist Centre in the village centre, near the bus station, has beds from 125 mk and rents bicycles and canoes.

FINLAND

LINNANSAARI NATIONAL PARK

To get a glimpse of the rare Saimaa ringed seal, you should take a regular boat to Linnansaari Island. The park consists of a number of uninhabited islands, but the main activity centres around the harbour of Sammakkoniemi on Linnansaari Island. You can rent a boat there, buy provisions at a canteen and stay at comfortable huts (☎ 049-659 475). Linnansaari has a small museum and marked trails. Before rushing to the park, visit the superb **Järviluonnonkeskus** (Lakeland Centre) in the village of Rantasalmi. There is a tourist office and other museums next door.

Getting There & Away

There are buses to Rantasalmi from Savonlinna and Pieksämäki (train passes are valid on most of these), and to the Mustalahti quay, a taxi service is available on request from the Lakeland Centre. MS *Linnansaari* has two daily launches from Mustalahti to Linnansaari; return tickets cost 75 mk.

MIKKELI

Mikkeli was the headquarters of the Finnish army during WWII, and some of its attractions relate to those years. **Päämajamuseo** was the command centre, and **Jalkaväkimuseo** is one of the largest military museums in Finland. **Kenkävero**, outside the centre, is a handicraft centre where you can create something for yourself. The oldest building in town, **Kivisakasti**, has a small church museum, and there is also a regional museum in Mikkeli.

The helpful tourist office (☎ 151 444) is at the lively market on Hallituskatu.

Places to Stay & Eat

There are several more expensive hotels in the town centre, but somewhat cheaper is *Nuoriso-opisto* (☎ 414 800) at Paukkulantie 22.

There are snacks at the market until the afternoon, and popular waffles at the Naisvuori Hill café (5 mk entry to the tower). The best buffet is available at the Kenkävero

centre. For lunch specials, enquire at restaurants on Maaherrankatu near the market.

For a splurge, the buffet of *Tertin kartano* (☎ 176 012) is worth every markka (and it will take lots of them) if you are driving. It is seven km from Mikkeli towards Kuopio; enquire at the tourist office.

Getting There & Away

There are five daily trains from Helsinki and a similar number of connections from the north. From other directions, change at Pieksämäki or Kouvola.

KUOPIO

One of the largest towns in Finland, Kuopio is surrounded by forests and lakes. There is a wide variety of things to see and do in this centre of the Savo region, on Lake Kallavesi.

Information

The main tourist office *Kuopio-Info* (☎ 182 585) is at Haapaniemenkatu 17. The office is open from June to mid-August from 9 am to 6 pm (closed Saturday after 2 pm). During the rest of the year it is open only to 5 pm weekdays. There is also information at the railway station, or check http://www.travel.fi/kuopio.

The International Meeting Point (☎ 182 675) at Kauppakatu 44 has a café, an inexpensive laundry, showers, and left luggage. It is open from July to mid-August on weekdays from 9 am to 9 pm (entry from the back yard).

The telephone code is ☎ 017.

Things to See & Do

The main attraction is **Puijo Hill**, and the spectacular lookout of **Puijo Tower** is a must (take bus No 6). There are also walking tracks and ski trails in the area.

There are several two-hour lake cruises costing 50 to 60 mk, recommended when the weather is fine, or a longer monastery cruise to Valamo Monastery.

Museums The most impressive museum is the **Ortodoksinen kirkkomuseo**, at Karjalankatu 1, the museum belonging to the

Orthodox archdiocese with monastic relics rescued from Russia. It is open daily all year round, closed Monday in summer. Note the castle-like **Kuopion museo**, at Kauppakatu 23, which is a regional and local museum, open daily from May to August and closed Saturday during other months. Not to be missed is **Korttelimuseo**, Kirkkokatu 22, covering three centuries of local history and architecture (open from mid-May to mid-September). Old photos and special exhibitions are featured at the top-class **VB Photographic Centre** at Kuninkaankatu 14.

Places to Stay & Eat

The camping area *Rauhalahti* (☎ 361 2244) by the water and off the highway, charges from 35 to 85 mk for tenting or 130 mk for two-bed cabins. The nearby *Hostelli Rauhalahti* (☎ 473 111) charges 135 mk per person (take bus No 6 or 19). Cheap guesthouses near the train station include *Puijo-Hovi* and *Souvari* on Vuorikatu, and the cheapest of them all, *Hospitsi* (☎ 261 4501) at Myllykatu 4, with singles/doubles from 90/180 mk.

There are indoor and outdoor markets in the main square where you can try 'kala-kukko', a local fish inside a rye loaf (eaten hot or cold), or fresh fruit, coffee and snacks. Most restaurants around the square, such as *Zorbas* at Puijonkatu 37, offer inexpensive lunch packages. *Sampo* at Kauppakatu 13 is the oldest restaurant in town, serving local muikku fish specialities. *Wanha Satama* at the harbour is a lively pub, and *Trube Torinkulma* at the Sokos building near the market has the best pastries and cakes. By far the most attractive gourmet restaurant is the vaulted *Musta Lammas* at Satamakatu 4, where some dishes are under 100 mk.

Getting There & Away

Finnair flies to the airport, 20 km north of town, several times daily from Helsinki. The airport bus departs from the market square.

Kuopio is easy to reach by train or bus from Helsinki or Kajaani. The express bus station is north of the railway station and local buses converge on the market square.

IISALMI

This North Savo town is the main centre of the region, with a large brewery which provides an excuse for the numerous beer terraces and an annual beer festival in early July. Oluthalli and Olutmestari, two restaurants at the harbour's edge, on opposite sides of the small bay, share the **brewery museum** which has free entry.

The main attraction is **Evakkokeskus** near the train station, an Orthodox heritage centre, which has the third largest collection of Karelian icons and cult items, saved from annexed churches in (Russian) Karelia. Enquire at the Artos Hotel in the same complex. There is also a local museum in Iisalmi. The tourist office (☎ 150 1223) is at Kauppakatu 22.

Places to Stay & Eat

There are three hotels in the town centre. *NNKY Youth Hostel* (☎ 23940), a bit north of town at Sarvikatu 4, has clean rooms with kitchen from 105 mk per person.

The train station canteen serves lunch at 28 mk, including salad and coffee. Savonkatu, just opposite the train station, is the main street and has many restaurants. At the harbour's edge, there are beer restaurants with good meals, and *Korkki*, the smallest restaurant in the world.

Getting There & Away

Trains connect Iisalmi with Kajaani, Ylivieska, and the south.

JOENSUU

Joensuu is the centre for North Karelia. It is a good place to learn something about the distinctive Karelian culture, although it isn't a very interesting town in itself. The markets, and summer events, such as the song festival and Ilosaari Rock, contribute much to the spirited Karelian atmosphere.

Information

The fine wooden building at Koskikatu 1 is the North Karelian tourist office (☎ 167

5300). The post office is at Rantakatu 6, and the modern library is at Koskikatu 25.

The telephone code is ☎ 013.

Things to See & Do

The main **park** and **market** are pleasant: big and lively from 7 am until mid-afternoon from Monday to Saturday. There is an outdoor stage for summer folk music and dance. Sample Karelian sweet pastries and *Karjalan piirakka*, a rice-filled pastry. Flea markets are active daily from 9 am to 6 pm near the market.

At the small **Pohjois-Karjalan museo**, the regional museum on Pielisjoki Island, admission costs only 5 mk (closed Monday). An extraordinary spectacle is the tropical butterfly and turtle garden **Perhospuutarha** at Avainkuja 2 north of town (open daily, 40 mk per adult). The university's **botanical gardens** at Heinäpurontie 70 have a tropical section (15 mk).

The best example of the wooden architecture of the older town is the Orthodox **St Nicholas Church** (open on summer weekdays) at the north end of Kirkkokatu. The **Lutheran church** at the other end of the street is equally impressive.

Places to Stay

The camp site *Linnunlahden leirintäalue* (☎ 126 272) by the lake costs 55 mk per person or 75 mk per family, and there are cabins from 160 mk a night.

The clean summer hostel *Elli* (☎ 225 927), Länsikatu 18, is big and charges from 55 mk for a bed. More modest is the scout-hall hostel *Partiotalo* (☎ 123 381), Vanamokatu 25, costing from 38 mk (open from June to August). The regional sports institute *Finnhostel Joensuu* (☎ 167 5076) at Kalevankatu 8, offers singles/doubles for 175/230 mk for HI members. Good value is *Hostel Aaro* (☎ 148 1051) at Kirkkokatu 20. This central hostel has clean rooms for 140/220 mk, and a good kitchen.

Places to Eat

Solid budget eating is available at the market or in the junk food outlets around the market.

The bus station has a *cafeteria*. *Teatteri-ravintola* is one of the fine restaurants situated in the imposing town hall. Ask for Karelian specialities, or check out the beer terrace in summer.

Café Helenna, Siltakatu 16, and *Trube* at Torikatu 23, have tempting cakes. Don't miss *Matelin Kahvikammari* at Niskakatu. It has heaps of handicrafts for sale.

Getting There & Away

Finnair flies to and from Helsinki six times a day. The 11-km trip on the airport bus costs 20 mk, the bus departs from Kirkkokatu 25.

Express and local buses arrive at the main bus station near the railway. The bus station ticket office has all timetables for northbound services.

Direct trains run from Turku, Jyväskylä, Nurmes and Helsinki, but from Savonlinna you have to change at Parikkala. The Nurmes Marina ferry runs to Koli on Saturday from June to August.

HEINÄVESI

The tiny town of Heinävesi on Lake Kermajärvi is a popular stop during lake cruises between Kuopio and Savonlinna. Enquire about off-the-beaten-track accommodation at the tourist office (☎ 578 1273) at Kermanrannantie 10. The tall **wooden church** seats 2000 people.

The friendly hostel *Pohjataipaleen kartano* is by the lake, about 13 km to the south of the station (served by trains from Jyväskylä, Joensuu and Pieksämäki). Call ahead (☎ 566 419) to be picked up by the staff, and be prepared for a prolonged sauna session. Beds cost only 50 mk.

UUSI-VALAMO

The monastery Uusi-Valamo, north of Heinävesi, is the centre of Finnish Orthodox culture and has traditions going back 800 years. The founders escaped from old Valamo and Soviet attentions in 1940; the newest church was consecrated in 1977. The monks organise tours for 20 mk and courses on their faith, art and lifestyle and you can attend some services. The monastery (☎ 570 111;

e-mail veli.jeremia@pcb.mpoli.fi) is four km north of road 23 to Joensuu and is open to visitors from 10 am to 6 pm..

You can stay in a single room for 175 mk or in hostel accommodation from 80 mk (9 pm curfew) and there is a restaurant. There is a bus direct from Helsinki.

ILOMANTSI
The eastern municipality of Ilomantsi is the most Orthodox region in Finland (as opposed to Lutheran), and has some of the best preserved nature in the country. The theme route, Runon ja rajan tie, follows the eastern border from Ilomantsi to Lieksa and further north. **Parppeinvaara** is the Karelian heritage centre near Ilomantsi township (15 mk, open daily in summer from 8 am to 8 pm). The tourist office (☎ 881 707) is at Mantsinkatu 8 in Ilomantsi.

Susitaival, the Path of the Wolf, runs 90 km from the **Petkeljärvi National Park** near Möhkö at the border about 20 km east of Ilomantsi (bus from Joensuu). There is accommodation from 60 mk at the Petkeljärvi park centre, and *Möhkön Lomakylä* offers camping, and two-bed cabins for 150 mk.

The trail ends at the **Patvinsuo National Park**, with 30 mk beds at the park centre. The birds, forests, and peatlands are protected, although in some parts berries and mushrooms may be picked. Observation towers are available for scanning the landscape. There are seven camp sites and more than 50 km of paths in the park.

VUONISLAHTI
The small train station south of Lieksa is the jumping-off point for the lakeside hostel *Herranniemi* (☎ 542 110) with beds for 45 mk and hot sauna baths. Rent a rowing boat for a three-km trip to Eva Ryynänen's **ateljee Paateri** (studio) with a private church and huge sculptures made from cedar and birch.

LIEKSA
The small centre of Lieksa, lying about 100 km from Joensuu on Lake Pielinen, will be important if you are hiking, paddling or sightseeing. It has transport links, accommodation and services.

Lieksa is also one of the areas to try the comfort of the traditional smoke sauna.

Information
Lieksan Matkailu Oy information office (☎ 520 2400) is at Pielisentie 7 and is open in summer until 6 pm weekdays and to 2 pm Saturday, and in July only to 3 pm Sunday. It has information on bookings, fishing, paddling, smoke saunas and national parks as well as local hiking maps.

Things to See & Do
The excellent **Pielisen museo** is a complex of almost a hundred Karelian buildings and open-air exhibits with an emphasis on the livelihood and life of the logging culture (open daily from mid-May to mid-August, 14 mk per adult) and an indoor museum of local war and folk history (open all year, but closed Monday).

Places to Stay & Eat
You can get a cabin at the river mouth at *Timitran Camping* (☎ 521 780), open from June to August. A two-bed cabin costs 170 mk, a four-bed one costs from 210 mk and there is space for tents and caravans.

The riverside *Hotelli Puustelli* (☎ 525 544) is a comfortable hotel charging 300/380 mk in summer, including breakfast and sauna. *Hotelli Kulma* (☎ 522 112), at Pielisentie 44, opposite the square, has a few simpler singles/doubles for 150/260 mk.

Getting There & Away
Lieksa is best reached by train from Helsinki or by train or bus from Joensuu. The scenic mode of transport is by Nurmes Marina boat from Joensuu (via Koli, 130 mk). The Koli car ferry runs from mid-May to mid-August twice a day for 80 mk return. Cars cost 30 mk extra.

RUUNAA
Ruunaa, 30 km east of Lieksa, is a great area for fishing, white-water rafting and easy hiking. The bus only goes as far as

FINLAND

Pankakoski, so you might consider hitchhiking from there, or ask Lieksan Matkailu Oy about transport and reservations.

There are six rapids, and several daily launches of wooden and rubber boats. There is an information centre (☎ 533 165) near the bridge over the Naarajoki River, which is where most boat trips end.

The walking trails cover the entire area, which is quite extensive and there are bridges, camp sites and free lean-to *(laavu)* shelters. In addition to accommodation and services at Naarajoki, **Ruunaan Retkeilykeskus** (☎ 533 170) has a café, camping and luxurious four to six-bed cabins from 400 mk. A wheelchair path goes a short distance from here to the rapids of Neitikoski where fishing is popular.

TREKS AROUND KARELIA

The best trekking routes in North Karelia were recently linked together to create **Karjalan Kierros**, an 800-km loop around Lake Pielinen. The highlight is the Bear Trail (Karhunpolku), a 133-km hiking trail of medium difficulty leading from the southern Patvinsuo National Park along the Russian border, but the route includes Hiidenportti and Koli national parks and other protected nature reserves. Lieksa is also a centre for horseback riding on Icelandic horses or husky tours along the Russian border. Enquire at Lieksan Matkailu.

Karelia has excellent canoeing routes, especially those running to/from Nurmijärvi, north-east from Lieksa. Equipment can be hired locally at Erästely Ky (☎ 546 550 or 546 551).

KOLI NATIONAL PARK

Finns regard the views from the heights of Koli overlooking Lake Pielinen as the best in the country. The national park offers good hiking routes with great scenery, and a free hut (one night only). Nurmes Marina has boat services from Lieksa (less than two hours), Nurmes and Joensuu (seven hours) on various days from June to mid-August. A bus goes from the quay to the hill top about 350 metres above the lake. There are two

slalom centres, each with six slopes, and cross-country possibilities.

Places to Stay & Eat

Hotelli Koli (☎ 672 221) at the top of Koli is a typical 1970s concrete box with summer doubles for 340 mk. Ask for keys at the hotel for the free four-bed *Ikolanaho* wilderness hut inside the park.

At *Loma Koli Camping* (☎ 673 211) there are four-bed cabins for 230 mk a night and camping for 55 mk a night per family.

The secluded hostel *Kolin retkeilymaja* (☎ 673 131) on a gravel road five km from the bus stop, has beds from 45 mk. *Kolin Loma-aitat* (☎ 672 257), which is on Merilänrannantie, has cheaper rooms from 80 to 140 mk.

NURMES

This small town is currently the terminus for the eastern railways. There are plenty of historical buildings on the esker near the train station, but most tourists go to **Bomba**, a Karelian heritage building some two km from the town centre. Bomba also arranges treks and other activities to the wilderness on request.

Places to Stay & Eat

Bomba (☎ 482 260) is also a top-end hotel with a Karelian smorgasbord, but most shoestring travellers head to *Hyvärilä* (☎ 481 770) near Bomba (four km from the train station). There are 40 mk beds and a variety of rooms and cottages. There is also a tourist information office there, and good meals.

Getting There & Away

There are two daily trains from Joensuu, and connecting trains between Nurmes and Kajaani.

KAJAANI

Kajaani is the centre of the Kainuu region. It was a vital stronghold in the 18th century (until its castle was ruined by the Russians) and an important station on the Kainuu tar transportation route. The **regional museum** near the train station is the best place to get acquainted with local history, including the epic *Kalevala* and its author, Elias Lönnrot who used Kajaani as a base for his travels. The museum is open daily except Monday.

The beautiful wooden **church** is a rare example of neogothic architecture. The **castle ruins**, at the bridge over the river, have little to offer, but the nearby **tar canal** has tar boat shows on Sunday at 7 pm; ask at the tourist office (☎ 155 555) at Pohjolankatu 16.

Places to Stay & Eat
Matkustajakoti, also known as Huone ja Aamiainen (☎ 622 254), at Pohjolankatu 4, near the station, has rooms for 130/170 mk for HI members. There are also several hotels in Kajaani.

Kauppakatu is the main street and has many restaurants. *Pikantti* at the Citymarket building has excellent lunch buffets on weekdays until 5 pm.

Getting There & Away
Kajaani can be reached by daily Finnair flights from Helsinki. Trains connect with Kuopio, Nurmes and Oulu, and there are buses to towns around Kainuu.

KUHMO
The lively wilderness centre of Kuhmo is known for the annual chamber music festival, which attracts some of the best musicians from around the world. The **concert hall** holds most of the concerts. The **Kalevala** theme park three km from the town is the main sight, with Karelian exhibitions and artisan displays. The tourist office (☎ 561 382) is open from Monday to Saturday in summer.

Places to Stay
Piilolan koulu (☎ 655 6245) is a school building near the main street that has beds for 55 mk in summer for HI members.

Getting There & Away
There are 12 daily buses from Kajaani, 102 km away. Hitchhiking is not difficult in the Kainuu region.

KUUSAMO
Kuusamo is a frontier town about 200 km north-east of Oulu. The tourist centre, Karhuntassu (☎ 850 2910), is at Torangintaival at the west end of the town and distributes an excellent free guide. There are many possibilities for hiking and fishing and many fast, rugged rapids on the **Kitkajoki River**.

The very popular **Ruka** skiing centre is about 25 km north of town. There are 25 slopes, and plenty of accommodation. There is also a monster toboggan slope.

Places to Stay
The tourist office publishes a free accommodation guide for the entire region. The local hostel *Kuusamon Kunsanopisto* (☎ 852 2132), at Kitkantie 35, is open only in summer and beds cost from 40 mk for HI members. *Hotel Martina* (☎ 852 2051), at Ouluntie 3, has rooms from 260 mk.

Getting There & Away
Finnair flies daily from Helsinki to the Kuusamo airport, which is seven km to the north-east of the town centre.

Buses run daily from Kajaani, Oulu and Kemijärvi as well as Ruka.

THE KARHUNKIERROS TRAIL
The circular Karhunkierros trail covers 75 km of rugged cliffs, gorges and suspension bridges from Rukatunturi, 25 km north of Kuusamo to the Oulanka National Park.

The hike to the information centre at Kiutaköngäs and further on to road No 951 (Kuusamo to Salla road) can take two days, but there are shelters and free overnight huts on the trail, and there is a holiday centre at Juuma. Juuma is another gateway to the region, with accessibility to some of the main sights, such as the **Myllykoski** and **Jyrävä** waterfalls. There is a hut in both places and fires are permitted only at established sites on the trail.

Rukatunturi-Oulanka map (1:40,000) is essential for trail and hut information.

FINLAND

Lapland

The Lapland region north of the Arctic Circle offers the spectacle of constant daylight (or darkness in winter) and the chance of seeing the Northern Lights (aurora borealis). The forests around Rovaniemi give way to tundra and fells to the north. Lake Inarijärvi is popular, winter and summer.

There are fewer than 5000 Sami people in Finnish Lapland and their living culture is best seen in the villages of Hetta, Inari or Utsjoki. Traditional dress can only be seen on festival days. Reindeer farming, fishing and forestry employ most people, although there is a tourist industry in handicrafts.

The snow disappears in May, but sometimes not before June in the very north. Summer is short but hectic and sometimes pleasantly warm. The *ruska* period from September produces exceptional autumn colours and in the far north *kaamos*, the season of eerie bluish light, begins late in October.

You can use Swedish and Norwegian currency at most shops in Finnish Lapland near the borders.

The telephone code for Lapland is ☎ 016.

Driving through Finnish Lapland

At times Lapland is the most international region in Finland, because of hassle-free border crossings to Sweden and Norway. The popular route to Nordkapp (see Norway) runs either via road No 4 from Rovaniemi to Sodankylä to Inari, and further to Karigasniemi, or along road No 21 near the Tornionjoki River valley to Kilpisjärvi (or via Enontekiö to Alta). Both routes are recommended, and can be done in either direction. All major townships have service stations and supermarkets, but on the road between them there is little in the way of help if you get into trouble.

Hitchhiking is a very natural way of transport in this large region with so few buses, but the waiting period is sometimes very long.

TORNIO

Tornio has a twin across the Tornionjoki River – the Swedish town of Haparanda. These towns share tourist brochures, and even a golf course. You can't really play golf at midnight anywhere else: if you start from the Finnish side at, say, 0.30 am you can hit the next ball in Sweden, yesterday! Tornio has a superb 17th-century **wooden church** with colourful paintings inside, and several museums, such as the **Aine Art Museum** and the extensive regional **Maakuntamuseo**. The tourist office (☎ 432 733) is at the Green Line building just at the border. Price comparisons between Finland and Sweden are essential for budget travellers!

Places to Stay

The best place to stay is the youth hostel *Suensaari* (☎ 481 682) at Kirkkokatu 1, which is open in June and July only. Beds cost from 65 mk. *Heta* at Saarenpäänkatu 39 charges 150/250 mk, including breakfast.

Getting There & Away

To get to Tornio from Sweden, just walk. The border post between Haparanda and Tornio is very relaxed. To get to Tornio from Kemi, take a bus from Kemi train station. From the north, drive, take a bus or hitchhike along road No 21.

KEMI

Kemi is an industrial town with huge pulp factories. The **Jalokivi Galleria** at Kauppakatu 29 has a collection of gemstones, copies of royal jewels and geological displays. It is open daily from 10 am to 8 pm and costs 25 mk per adult.

A four-hour cruise on the icebreaker *Sampo* – an eerie experience in the semi-twilight of January, costs 600 mk. Ask at the tourist office (☎ 199 469), Kauppakatu 22.

The 16th-century stone church at **Keminmaa**, north of Kemi opposite the power station on the Kemijoki River is something special. There is a unique mummified Lutheran clergyman, although there are also mummies in Sodankylä. There is another museum near the church.

Places to Stay
Turisti (☎ 250 876) at Valtakatu 39, has beds from 75 mk for HI members, and there are several hotels.

Getting There & Away
There are trains from Helsinki and Rovaniemi to Kemi. Buses from Tornio will take you to Kemi train station, and they are free with a train pass.

ROVANIEMI
The modern town of Rovaniemi is the gateway for tourists entering Lapland and its skiing makes it a year-round destination. The town has recently become an up-market destination for European bus groups, but this also means plenty of new activities such as white-water rafting and visits to reindeer farms.

Information
The city tourist office at the hotel Pohjanhovi at Koskikatu 1 (☎ 322 2279), is open until 7 pm daily in summer (to 4 pm weekdays from September to May). Lapland Travel Ltd next door, organises many tours for winter and summer. It is closed weekends.

The main post office is on Rovakatu 36, and there is a branch near the train station. The library is at Hallituskatu 9.

Things to See & Do
The glass-covered **Arktikum** at the riverside, combines an arctic and regional museum with a research centre; and with its modern construction featuring well laid out displays it is one of the best museums in Finland. Arktikum is open daily from 9 am to 7 pm in summer, at other times from 10 am to 6 pm Tuesday to Sunday. Entry costs 45 mk, but there are discounts.

Lapin metsämuseo, Metsämuseontie 7, is a comprehensive open-air forestry museum (take buses No 3 and 6 from Hallituskatu).

The **Ounasvaara** slalom centre is three km above the town. In summer you can bobsleigh for 16 mk.

Bus No 8 will take you to the Arctic Circle

marker, at **Napapiiri** with the Santa Claus post office. This is the busiest tourist trap in Finland (in fact, the only one of this magnitude), with computerised portraits with Santa Claus available while you wait! The **Etiäinen** at Napapiiri is the information centre for national parks and trekking regions, with essential information and maps available.

For tours of the **reindeer farm**, you must book with any of the operators that have offices near the main hotels. You can also book river cruises, white-water rafting, fishing or other tours ranging from 100 to 600 mk per person.

Places to Stay
Camping at *Ounasvaara* (☎ 369 039), Taljatie, costs 55 mk a site.

The hostel *Tervashonka* (☎ 344 644), Hallituskatu 16, is a popular place to stay overnight, with beds for 60 mk. *Matka Borealis* (☎ 342 0130), Asemamieskatu 1, opposite the train station, has singles/ doubles from 150/180 mk. The central *Outa* at Ukkoherrantie 16 is a small, strictly non-smoking guesthouse, with singles/doubles at 150/200 mk. There are several big hotels in Rovaniemi. *Hotelli Oppipoika* (☎ 338 8111) is one of the cheapest at Korkalonkatu 33.

Places to Eat
Rovaniemi has plenty of grillis and hamburger restaurants in the centre. Inexpensive lunches are available at the train station and at *Torikeidas* near the market. *Kisälli*, Korkalonkatu 35, is a restaurant school, with good deals available. The nearby *Sandwitz* is an art café on Koskikatu.

Getting There & Away
Air Finnair has several daily flights from Helsinki, Turku, Tampere and Oulu and there are connections to Ivalo, Sodankylä and Enontekiö (Ounas-Pallas National Park). The bus from the airport costs 15 mk.

Bus Eskelisen Lapin Linjat and Postilinjat run express buses to Muonio, Enontekiö and Kilpisjärvi in the west, to Sodankylä, Inari,

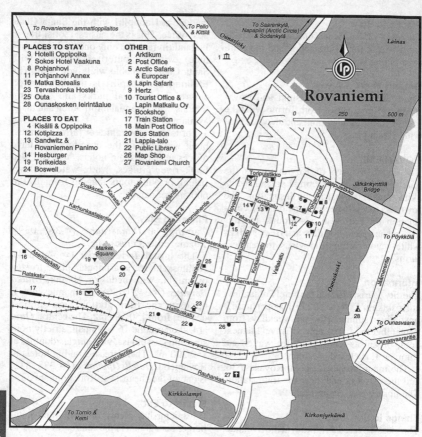

PLACES TO STAY
3   Hotelli Oppipoika
7   Sokos Hotel Vaakuna
8   Pohjanhovi
11 Pohjanhovi Annex
16 Matka Borealis
23 Tervashonka Hostel
25 Outa
28 Ounaskosken leirintäalue

PLACES TO EAT
4   Kisälli & Oppipoika
12 Kotipizza
13 Sandwitz &
    Rovaniemen Panimo
14 Hesburger
19 Torikeidas
24 Boswell

OTHER
1   Arktikum
2   Post Office
5   Arctic Safaris
    & Europcar
6   Lapin Safarit
9   Hertz
10 Tourist Office &
    Lapin Matkailu Oy
15 Bookshop
17 Train Station
18 Main Post Office
20 Bus Station
21 Lappia-talo
22 Public Library
26 Map Shop
27 Rovaniemi Church

Karigasniemi and Utsjoki in the east, and into Norway. Most buses are met with connections to places further north.

Train The train from Helsinki and Oulu usually terminates in Rovaniemi and you will probably take buses farther north or to Kemijärvi (there is only one train connection daily) – here your rail pass will be valid only as far as Kemijärvi.

SODANKYLÄ
The busy market town of Sodankylä is best known for the Midnight Sun International Film Festival in mid-June. Tickets and tourist information are available from Sodankylän Matkailu (☎ 613 474), Jäämerentie 9, 99600 Sodankylä. Don't miss the art exhibition upstairs, and the nearby 17th-century **wooden church**, one of the oldest and best preserved in Finland. The summer hostel *Lapin opisto* (☎ 612 181), across the river, has apartments, camping facilities, cabins and hostel bunks at 55 mk for a bed.

SAARISELKÄ & URHO KEKKONEN NATIONAL PARK
Saariselkä is a ski resort 30 km south of Ivalo

and hiking and cross-country trails lead into the Urho Kekkonen National Park. The village is a popular up-market destination. For more details of trekking routes see Lonely Planet's *Finland – travel survival kit*.

Just north of the Saariselkä region is Raja-Jooseppi, a border-crossing point to Russia, from where it's 250 km by road to Murmansk.

IVALO

Ivalo is the centre of the Inari district, where there is midnight sun from 23 May to 22 July and polar night from 3 December to 9 January. Most travellers consider Ivalo as a place for shopping rather than sightseeing.

The cheapest place to stay is *Matkakoti* (☎ 661 106), with rooms from 175 mk. *Hotelli Ivalo* (☎ 661 911), Ivalontie 34, is dearer but it's definitely top class.

Getting There & Away

Finnair flies to Ivalo airport from Helsinki, Oulu and Rovaniemi. Ivalo is best reached by express buses which run from Rovaniemi north to Norway and return.

INARI

The pleasant lakeside settlement of Inari is a place to see living Sami culture. The express bus runs from Rovaniemi through Inari into Norway two or three times daily. There are banks, a post office and a good tourist office.

Things to See & Do

Inari is probably the most interesting town anywhere in northern Lapland, although a full day is often enough to see the three main attractions. **Saamelaismuseo** (15 mk) covers the crafts, reindeer-farming and fishing traditions of these people. Not far from the museum, there is a marked seven-km walking track to the 18th-century **wilderness church**, with a hut and a sauna nearby. There is a warden there in summer.

In summer, boat trips leave for the prominent Ukko Island, an ancient cult site for the Inari Samis.

Visit the **Samekki** workshop on Lehtolantie to look at or buy handicrafts. These handicrafts are not inexpensive, but they are genuine traditional products.

Places to Stay

The popular hostel is closed, but you can stay free at the hut near the wilderness church or at the çamping ground three km towards Lemmenjoki. *Inarin Kultahovi* (☎ 671 221) has singles/doubles for 360/400 mk, but the wooden *Inari Keskus* (☎ 671 026) is cheaper at 145/200 mk. There are also inexpensive cottages to the south of Inari. Some of them almost touch the main road.

LEMMENJOKI NATIONAL PARK

The mountain stream Lemmenjoki runs 50 km from the heart of the big Lemmenjoki National Park through a deep valley into the lake above Inari. It is a natural hikers' challenge extending for over 70 km and indicated by orange markers. There are free wilderness huts and you'll have a chance to see gold-panning in the middle of the mighty nature reserve. Use the Lemmenjoki 1:100,000 map which is available in bookshops.

Getting There & Away

Take a regular post bus from Inari to Njurgulahti where there is accommodation. There are motorboats daily (50 mk one way) up the river to Kultala, or you can get off at any other hut along the river.

KAAMANEN

All northern buses (and most locals for that matter) stop at the hectic roadhouse *Kaamasen kievari* which has cheap lunch packages and huts at the riverside. There is also *Jokitörmä* (☎ 672 725) further south with HI discounted beds, and *Neljäntuulen tupa* further north. *Jouni Nuorgam*, five km north from the Kaamasen kievari, sells reindeer-horn powder, which is popular among Japanese males as an aphrodisiac. Finns regard the substance's reputation as something of a joke.

Getting There & Away

Road No 4 runs from Inari to Kaamanen and turns west to Karigasniemi and further to

Karasjok and Nordkapp in Norway. Road No 970 continues straight north to Utsjoki and further to Norway. Road No 971 runs via Sevettijärvi to Neiden and further to Kirkenes (both in Norway). There are buses on all these routes from Monday to Friday, and some connections on Saturday and Sunday.

KARIGASNIEMI

There are several guesthouses in this small Sami centre at the border. *Välimäki* is one of the cheapest, and cabins in other establishments cost from 150 mk. The river marks the border.

NORTH-WESTERN LAPLAND

As an alternative trans-Lapland route, the western road No 21 gives you the possibility of crossing the border into Sweden across the Tornionjoki and Muonionjoki rivers. Nowhere else is the border as easily crossed as here, and locals cross it almost daily. After the last border crossing at Karesuvanto, the scenery becomes even more barren until the snow-capped mountains reveal where Finland ends and Norway starts. This route is certainly more exciting than the more popular eastern route to Nordkapp.

Kolari

There is a *youth hostel* (☎ 561 086) not far from the village centre, with beds at 55 mk.

Muonio

This small town is the last significant township on road No 21, before the road continues on towards Kilpisjärvi. *Lomamaja Pekonen* (☎ 532 237) has attractive cottages from 115 mk for HI members.

Pallastunturi National Park

You can easily cover the 60-km trekking route by following the marked trail between the township of **Hetta** (also called Enontekiö) in the north and *Hotelli Pallastunturi* (☎ 532 441) in the south. All accommodation is in free wilderness huts, but they are occasionally packed with people. At the Hetta end of the route, you will have to employ a boat taxi across the lake for a small fee.

Getting There & Away There are buses from Muonio and Rovaniemi to the Hotel Pallastunturi. There are a few weekly flights from Helsinki, Oulu and Rovaniemi to Hetta, and two daily buses from Rovaniemi to Hetta, which is 26 km from Palojoensuu on road No 21.

Karesuvanto

The northernmost Swedish town of Karesuando has its twin on the Finnish side. *Ratkin* (☎ 522 101) has cottages from 180 mk, and there are other huts south of the bridge. Some 20 km north of Karesuvanto, near the main road, there is a German fortification area, **Sturmbock Stellung**, dating from 1944. It's always accessible for inspection, and some of the renovated bunkers give excellent shelter from the weather.

Kilpisjärvi

Some of the highest mountains in Finland are to be seen in this small tourist centre on the banks of Lake Kilpisjärvi. Most people climb the **Saana** (1029 metres), or walk (or take a boat taxi) to the **Malla Nature Park**, which has access to the joint border post of Sweden, Norway and Finland (you can visit three countries in a few seconds). Die-hard trekkers walk to the **Halti Fell**, which is the highest in Finland. There are wilderness huts en route (35 mk per night), but a map is essential.

Places to Stay Of the three choices, the best services to trekkers are provided by *Kilpisjärven retkeilykeskus* (☎ 537 771), with doubles at 220 mk.

Some 25 km south of Kilpisjrvi, *Peera* (☎ 532 659) is a very relaxing hostel to stay at, with beds from 75 mk. There are meals available. There are walks to nearby fells, or cross the river to the Swedish Sami village of Keinovuopio, with further walking tracks available inside Sweden.

Getting There & Away There are daily buses from Rovaniemi, 440 km away. In summer, the bus continues to Skibotn in Norway.

Iceland

Nowhere are the forces of nature more evident than in Iceland (Ísland), which offers glaciers, hot springs, geysers, active volcanoes, icecaps, tundra, snowcapped peaks, vast lava deserts, waterfalls, craters and even Mt Snæfell, Jules Verne's gateway to the centre of the Earth. On the high cliffs that characterise much of the coastline are some of the most densely populated sea-bird colonies in the world, and the lakes and marshes teem with waterfowl. The island is also a backdrop for the sagas, considered by literature enthusiasts to be the finest of all Western medieval works.

Facts about the Country

HISTORY

Irish monks were the first people to arrive on Iceland, in about the year 700 AD. Although they regarded Iceland as a hermitage until the early 9th century, the Age of Settlement is traditionally defined as the period between 874 and 930 when political strife on the Scandinavian mainland caused many Nordic people to flee westward.

The human history of Iceland was chronicled from the beginning. The *Íslendingabók* was written by the 12th-century scholar Ari Þorgilsson (Ari the Learned) about 250 years after the fact. He also compiled the more detailed *Landnámabók*, a comprehensive chronicle of that era. The *Íslendingabók* credits the first permanent settlement to Norwegian Ingólfur Arnarson who set up in 874 at a place he called Reykjavík (Smoky Bay) because of the steam from thermal springs there.

Early Icelanders decided against a Scandinavian-style monarchy in favour of the world's first democratic parliamentary system. In 930 Þingvellir (Parliament plains) near Reykjavík was designated the site of the national assembly or parliament, the Alþing.

Iceland was converted to Christianity in about 1000.

In the early 13th century, after 200 years of peace, violent feuds and raids by private armies ravaged the countryside and the chaos eventually led to the cession of control to Norway in 1380. In 1397 the Kalmar Union (of Norway, Sweden and Denmark) brought Iceland under Danish rule. During the disputes between Church and State caused by the Reformation of 1550, the Danes seized church property and imposed Lutheranism.

At the end of the 16th century Iceland was devastated by natural disasters. Four consecutive severe winters led to crop failure; 9000 Icelanders starved to death and thousands were uprooted from their homes.

In 1602 the Danish king imposed a trade monopoly whereby Swedish and Danish firms were given exclusive trading rights in Iceland. This resulted in large-scale extortion, importation of inferior goods and more suffering.

Over the next 200 years, natural disasters continued. In 1783 Lakagígar (Laki) erupted for 10 months and devastated much of southeast Iceland, spreading a poisonous haze that destroyed pastures and crops. Nearly 75% of Iceland's livestock and 20% of the human population perished in the resulting famine.

By the early 1800s, a growing sense of

ATLANTIC OCEAN

Arctic Circle

HORNSTRANDIR

Hornbjarg

Aðalvík

Jökulfirðir

Furufjörður

Bolungarvík

Suðureyri

Ísafjörður

Drangajökull

Unaðsdalur

Flateyri

Suðavík

Ísafjarðardjúp

Þingeyri

Reykjanes

Norðurfjörður

Djúpavík

Gláma

Westfjords Peninsula

Hólmavík

Húnaflói

Skagafjörður

Skagaströnd

Sauðárkrókur

Látrabjarg

Bíldudalur

Patreksfjörður

Breiðavík

Brjánslækur

Blönduós

Hóp

Hvammstangi

Flatey

Breiðafjörður

Stykkishólmur

Búðardalur

Brú

ARNARVATNSHEIÐI

Blanda

Hellissandur-Rif

Ólafsvík

Grundarfjörður

SNÆFELLSNES

Hveravellir

Eiríksjökull

KJÖLUR

Snæfellsjökull 1446 m

Búðir

Langjökull

Arnarstapi

Ok

Hvítárvatn

Borgarnes

Faxaflói

Þórisjökull

Akranes

ÞINGVELLIR NATIONAL PARK

Geysir

Gullfoss

REYKJAVÍK

Kópavogur

Þingvallavatn

Keflavík

Hafnarfjörður

Hvítá

Njarðvík

Hveragerði

Fjallabak Reserve

Blue Lagoon

Selfoss

Grindavík

Þorlákshöfn

Hella

Þjórsá

Tindfjallajökull

Hvolsvöllur

Fljótsdalur

ATLANTIC OCEAN

Eyjafjallajökull 1666 m

Þórsmörk

Skógar

Heimaey

Heimaey

Vestmannaeyjar

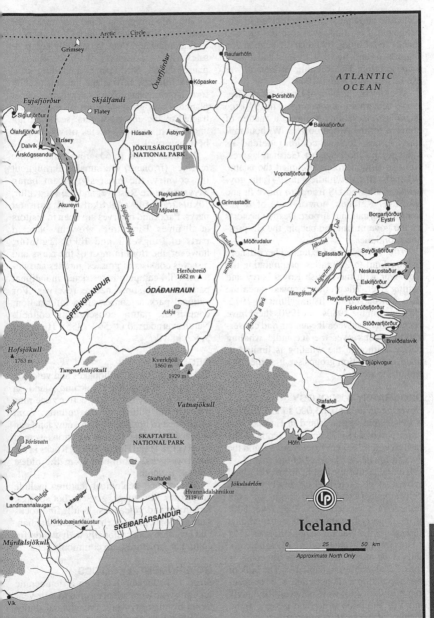

Iceland

0   25   50 km

Approximate North Only

Icelandic nationalism was perceived in Copenhagen. Free trade was restored in 1855 thanks to lobbying by Icelandic scholar Jón Sigurðsson and, by 1874, Iceland had drafted a constitution. The Republic of Iceland was established on 17 June 1944.

After the occupation of Denmark and Iceland's declaration of sovereignty in 1940, the island's vulnerability became a matter of concern for the Allied powers. Without military forces, Iceland couldn't defend its strategic position against German aggression, so British troops occupied the island. When the British withdrew in 1941, the government allowed US troops to move in and take over Keflavík, now the site of Reykjavík's international airport. Despite protests by the government and people, the US presence continues.

In the 1970s Iceland extended her offshore fishing limit to 200 miles, precipitating the Cod War with the British Royal Navy and fishing fleet. The trouble stopped when the British accepted the fishing limit in 1976. However, in the 1980s and 1990s there have been clashes between Icelanders and conservation groups over the Icelandic whaling policy. Although the whaling is limited in scale, conservation groups see it as the 'thin end of the wedge'.

GEOGRAPHY & ECOLOGY

Covering an area of 103,000 sq km, Iceland is the second-largest island in Europe. The south-east coast is 798 km from Scotland, the eastern end is 970 km from Norway, and the Westfjords lie 287 km east of Greenland.

Iceland, a juvenile among the world's land masses, is characterised by desert plateaus (52%); lava fields (11%); *sandur* or sand deltas (4%); and icecaps (12%). Over 50% of the country lies above 400 metres and its highest point, Hvannadalshnúkur, rises 2119 metres from beneath the glacier Öræfajökull. Only 21% of the land, all near the coast, is considered arable and habitable. The bulk of the population and agriculture is concentrated in the south-west between Reykjavík and Vík. Pollution in Iceland is very slight, because of the small population.

The only indigenous land mammal is the arctic fox. While Iceland lacks a diversity of land animals and flora, it certainly compensates with vast numbers of birds and a rich marine fauna. Bird species including kittiwakes, fulmars, puffins and gannets usually form large coastal colonies. Vast amounts of plankton and great varieties of fish are attracted to the coastal waters; seals are not uncommon, and 17 species of whale have been observed.

National parks (þjóðgarður) and nature reserves (friðland) are situated throughout the country, the most significant being Mývatn Nature Reserve, and the Þingvellir, Jökulsárgljufúr and Skaftafell national parks. Parks and reserves are open to visitors at all times. Birch trees grow in sheltered parts of Þingvellir and Jökulsárgljufúr; however, the flora in most of the parks and reserves consists of grasses, mosses and lichens. Wild camping is restricted in national parks and in some nature reserves. For national park or conservation information, contact the nature conservation council, Náttúruverndarráð (☎ 562 7855), Hlemmur 3, Reykjavík.

GEOLOGY

Iceland is prone to earthquakes and volcanic eruptions because it's a volcanic island on the mid-Atlantic ridge. The active zone runs through the middle of the country, from south-west to north-east; here, new land can appear at any time. Recent eruptions were at Krafla (1984) and Hekla (1991). Rocks in the north-west and south-east form the oldest parts of Iceland.

Active zone geological features include lava flows, lava tubes, geysers, hot springs, fumaroles and volcanoes. You'll find rocks such as basalt, pumice, rhyolite and obsidian. Old lava flows, occasionally with wonderful columnar structures, are commonly seen.

GOVERNMENT & POLITICS

Since 1944 Iceland has been a democratic republic with a president elected to four-year terms by majority vote. Presidential duties are similar to those of the monarch in a constitutional monarchy, and legislative powers rest with the Alþing. Executive functions are performed by the prime minister and a cabinet of ministers. Every citizen over 18 years of age has voting rights.

Vigdís Finnbogadóttir, the first woman elected to the presidency of a democratic country, held office from 1980 until standing down in 1996, when Ólafur Ragnar Grímsson was elected.

After the 1995 parliamentary election, there was little change in the distribution of support for the four main political parties, and the tradition of coalition government continues.

ECONOMY

Iceland's economy is dependent on fishing. A nationwide fleet of 940 vessels employs 5% of Iceland's work force and fish processing occupies another 5%. The total annual catch averages about 1.5 million tonnes, 97% of which is exported. This amounts to 20% of the total Gross National Product (GNP), representing about US$1300 million or the 15th largest fishing industry in the world.

Icelanders are also employed in agriculture, aluminium smelting, construction, tourism and transport, finance and government services.

In 1995 the unemployment rate was 5% and inflation was 2%. The GNP was US$6630 million in 1994.

POPULATION & PEOPLE

Most Icelanders are descended from the early Scandinavian and Celtic settlers. Nowadays immigration is strictly controlled, so foreigners living in the country are mainly temporary workers or spouses of citizens. The population of just over 266,000 is increasing by only about 1% annually and nearly 160,000 of these people live in Reykjavík and environs. Iceland has a literacy rate of 100% and its inhabitants have a life expectancy topped only by Japan's.

Icelanders' names are constructed from a combination of their Christian name and their father's (or mother's) Christian name.

Girls add the suffix *dóttir*, meaning daughter, to the patronymic and boys add *son*. Therefore, Jón, the son of Einar, would be Jón Einarsson. Guðrun, the daughter of Halldór, would be Guðrun Halldórsdóttir. Telephone directories are alphabetised by Christian name rather than patronymic, so the aforementioned Guðrun would be listed before Jón rather than the other way around.

ARTS
Literature

The traditions of Icelandic poetry mostly date from prior to the 14th century. Poetry divides neatly into two categories: Eddic poetry, actually more like free-metre prose, and Skaldic poetry, written by court poets employing a unique and well-defined syntax and vocabulary. Eddic poetry deals primarily with two themes, the heroic and the mythical. The heroic Eddas are based on Gothic legends and German folk tales, while the mythical Eddas are derived primarily from stories of Norse gods. It's assumed Skaldic poetry was composed by Norwegian court poets to celebrate the heroic deeds of Scandinavian kings.

The most popular early literary works were the sagas. They were written in Old Norse, which differed little from modern Icelandic. During the Saga Age (the late 12th and 13th centuries), epic tales of settlement, romance and dispute were recorded and sprinkled liberally with dramatic licence. For commoners, they provided entertainment and a sense of cultural heritage. One of the best known, *Egils Saga*, is a biography of the Skaldic poet Egill Skallagrímsson. Authorship is attributed to Snorri Sturluson, Iceland's greatest historian.

Some of the sagas are available in English. Since they're mainly anonymous works, they're found in catalogues and bookshops under the names of their translators, in most cases Magnús Magnússon, Hermann Pálsson or both. Available titles include *Hrafnkels Saga*; *Egils Saga*; *Laxdæla Saga*, the tragic account of a north-west Iceland family; *King Haralds Saga*; *Grettis Saga*,

ICELAND

about a superhuman outlaw; and *Njáls Saga*, perhaps the most popular of all.

Icelanders have also contributed to modern literature. In the late 1800s, Jón Sveinsson (Nonni), a priest from Akureyri, wrote a body of juvenile literature that was translated into 40 different languages. Jóhann Sigurjónsson wrote *Eyvind of the Hills*, a biography of the 18th-century outlaw Fjalla-Eyvindar. The best known modern Icelandic writer is Nobel Prize winning Halldór Laxness, whose work deals with daily life in Iceland. Much of his writing has been translated into English. *Independent People* describes the formerly harsh living conditions of Icelandic fishing and farming families. Other highly acclaimed novels of his include *The Fish Can Sing*, *Salka-Valka* and *The Atom Station*.

Music

The pop music world was astounded in 1986 when the Icelandic band the Sugarcubes arrived on the scene, having emerged from a plethora of local 'garage bands'. Their work may be sampled on their most successful compilation, *World Domination or Death*. The music scene continues to flourish as new bands appear; some of the more successful include Reptile, Bootlegs and Todmobile. Björk, the former lead singer of the Sugarcubes, is possibly the most notorious Icelandic rock star of the mid-1990s.

CULTURE

Icelanders are noted for being self-reliant, stoic and reserved, which gregarious visitors may find a little disconcerting. Objecting too vocally to whaling and bird hunting may upset locals, who are likely to be sensitive about these issues.

RELIGION

Before the year 1000 AD or so, the Icelandic Norse followed the pagan church of the day, which submitted to a pantheon of Norse deities: Þór, the main god; Óðinn, the god of war and poetry; and Freyr, the god of fertility and sensuous pleasure. The Norse belief system was simple and unburdened with the-

ology or dogma, with no salvation possible or necessary. Immortality came only to warriors who died in battle; they'd be gathered up by the Valkyries, the warrior-maids, and carried into Valhalla to indulge in mead, feasting and women until the gods themselves fell in battle.

Iceland officially converted to Christianity around 1000 AD but disputes between Church and State resulted in the Reformation of 1550. At this time, the Danish government seized church property and imposed Lutheranism, which still prevails today.

LANGUAGE

Icelandic is a Germanic language, in the same family as German, Dutch and all the Scandinavian languages except Finnish. Its closest 'living relative' is Faroese, which is also derived from Old Norse, with few changes.

The country is so protective of its linguistic heritage that it refuses to cannibalise foreign words for new technology, discoveries, or concepts. A committee in Reykjavík has responsibilities to invent new Icelandic words for these. The Icelandic word for 'computer', for example, is *tölva*, a combination of the words *tala* ('number') and *völva* ('prophet').

Icelandic is a highly inflected language, which means that words (usually endings) change according to their form. Nouns inflect in four cases (nominative, accusative, dative and genitive), with different endings for singular and plural. Most pronouns and adjectives are also inflected. Prepositions and certain verbs determine cases. Objects may be defined as any of three genders: masculine, feminine or neuter.

Icelandic has no indefinite article ('a/an' in English), only a definite article ('the' in English). The article changes according to gender: *hinn* (masculine), *hin* (feminine), and *hið* (neuter). It's normally attached to the end of a noun, when it drops the *h*: *maðurinn* (the man). The definite article also declines with the noun. Verbs are inflected in three persons, 1st, 2nd and 3rd, singular and plural.

Most Icelanders speak English, and some speak as many as three or four other languages, although, among themselves, they converse only in Icelandic. Your efforts to speak Icelandic will most certainly be met with great enthusiasm.

See the Language Guide at the back of the book for pronunciation guidelines and useful words and phrases.

Facts for the Visitor

PLANNING
Climate & When to Go
Warm Gulf Stream waters and prevailing south-westerly winds combine to give the southern and western coasts mild temperatures. However, this warm air meets cold polar seas and mountainous coastlines to form condensation and, alas, rain. In January, Reykjavík enjoys an average of three entirely sunny days and in July, only one. Fierce, wind-driven rains alternate with partial clearing, drizzle, gales and fog to create a miserable climate. Basically, it's a matter of 'if you don't like the weather now, wait five minutes – it will probably get worse'. May, June and July are the 'driest' months of the year.

Further north and east around Akureyri, Mývatn and Egilsstaðir, the situation improves. The interior deserts are also more prone to clear weather than coastal areas, but they may experience blizzards at any time of year, with icy winds whipping up grit and dust into opaque sandstorms.

Similar conditions occur on the sandur of the northern and southern coasts, a nasty experience if you're caught outdoors.

The weather forecast, in English, is available by dialling ☎ 902 0600 (extension 44).

The tourist season begins in early June, but some highland bus tours don't start operating until July because of snow.

Each year after mid-August, someone puts on the brakes and Icelandic tourism begins to wind down; many hotels close, hostels and camping grounds shut down and some buses stop running. By 30 September, the country has almost gone into hibernation, apart from Reykjavík.

From January to March, skiing, ice-fishing, snow-scooter trips and winter jeep safaris can be arranged from Reykjavík.

Books
There are several bookshops in Reykjavík and Akureyri. A complete bibliography of books on Iceland is available free from the Mál og Menning Bookshop (☎ 552 4240; fax 562 3523), 'Books on Iceland', Laugavegur 18, IS-101 Reykjavík, Iceland.

The following books may be of interest:

Iceland, Greenland & the Faroe Islands – travel survival kit by Deanna Swaney
Iceland Saga by Magnús Magnússon
Letters from High Latitudes by Lord Dufferin
Letters from Iceland by WH Auden & Louis MacNeice
Last Places – A Journey in the North by Lawrence Millman
Iceland Road Guide by Einar Guðjohnsen and Pétur Kidson Karlsson
Field Key to Flowering Plants of Iceland by Pat Wolseley
Hiking Trails in Iceland – The Western Fjords by Einar Guðjohnsen

See also Literature under Arts in the Facts about the Country section of this chapter.

Maps
Landmælingar Íslands (the Icelandic Geodetic Survey) offers three series of high-quality topographic sheets (1:25,000, 1:50,000 and 1:100,000) and a variety of thematic maps. Most travellers use the *Ferðakort 1:500,000* (touring map), the best general map of the country. Other useful maps are the 1:5000 map of Reykjavík, the 1:25,000 maps of Skaftafell and Þingvellir, the 1:50,000 maps of Hekla, Mývatn, and Vestmannaeyjar, and the 1:100,000 coverage of Hornstrandir and the trek from Landmannalaugar to Þórsmörk and Skógar.

For a catalogue and mail-order form contact Landmælingar Íslands (☎ 533 4000; fax 533 4011), Laugavegur 178, PO Box 5060, IS-125 Reykjavík, Iceland. Maps are also

ICELAND

available from the Mál og Menning bookshop at Laugavegur 18 in Reykjavík, and Dick Phillips (☎ 44-1434-381440), Whitehall House, Nenthead, Alston, Cumbria, CA9 3PS, England.

Online Services
Net-surfers can start their search with http://www.centrum.is/news.

What to Bring
Several efficient layers of warm dry clothing are of utmost importance. Even in summer you'll need wool or polypropylene socks and underwear, thick gloves, high protection sunglasses, sunscreen, a hat with ear protection, a warm pullover, T-shirts and thick cotton shirts, waterproofs (jacket and trousers), hiking boots or shoes, and a swimsuit for hot springs and heated pools.

Take a good sleeping bag, a torch, camera supplies, reading material and copies of medical and optical prescriptions.

Tents should be sturdy, waterproof, freestanding and easily assembled, with a porch for storage of wet clothing, boots and cooking implements. You'll also need a camping stove and aluminium fuel bottle (MSR mountain stoves or alcohol stoves are preferable to butane stoves), cooking implements, ground cover, a compass and relevant maps.

To transport that lot, you'll probably also need a vehicle!

SUGGESTED ITINERARIES
Depending on the length of your stay you might wish to see and do the following:

Two days
    The Golden Circle Tour, taking in Gullfoss, Geysir and Þingvellir in south-central Iceland
One week
    Visit urban Akureyri and explore the volcanic features and birdlife of Mývatn
Two weeks
    As above plus Vestmannaeyjar and Jökulsárgljúfúr
One month
    As above plus Skaftafell, Fjallabak and the Landmannalaugar to Þórsmörk and Skógar trek

Two months
    As above plus the Westfjords, Askja, Kverkfjöll, Lakagígar, Snæfellsnes, Vatnajökull and east Iceland

HIGHLIGHTS
Highlights for visitors are mostly natural. They include the geologically and biologically fascinating Mývatn and Krafla areas; Landmannalaugar and the beautiful Fjallabak reserve; Skaftafell, Þingvellir and Jökulsárgljúfur national parks; the green glacial valley of Þórsmörk; the volcanically active islands Vestmannaeyjar; the immense Askja caldera and the wild coast of Hornstrandir. The pleasant urban centre Akureyri is also well worth a visit.

TOURIST OFFICES
There are official information offices in Reykjavík as well as in cities and towns all over the country. They're very helpful and employees usually speak Scandinavian languages, English, German and French. Services are free but a charge may apply to telephone calls made on your behalf. National park brochures and commercial maps are sold at bookshop prices. In addition to providing information, the staff will book tours, sell bus passes and make hotel and transport reservations. Ask for *Around Iceland* and *Iceland: it's all there*, which are published annually and distributed free. For advance information, contact:

Tourist Information Centre
    Bankastræti 2, IS-101 Reykjavík, Iceland (☎ 562 3045; fax 562 3057)
Iceland Tourist Board
    655 Third Ave, New York, NY 10017, USA (☎ 212-949 2333)
Isländisches Fremdenverkehrsamt
    City Center, Carl-Ulrich-Strasse 11, D-63263 Neu-Isenburg 1, Germany (☎ 6102-254388)

VISAS & DOCUMENTS
Visas
Scandinavians only need proof of citizenship if entering Iceland from another Nordic country. Citizens of the USA and Commonwealth countries need a valid passport to enter as tourists. Stays of up to three months

during a nine-month period are usually granted with proof of sufficient funds for the declared length of stay. Officials are fairly liberal with this requirement but if they think you may run short of cash (eg less than US$20 per day), they may ask to see an onward ticket. Lengths of stay may be extended at police stations.

Documents

Hostelling International (HI) members pay discounted prices at Icelandic youth hostels. Holders of student cards will enjoy substantial discounts on flights and museum admissions. Students and Iceland bus-pass holders receive 10% discount on most camping fees, all sleeping-bag accommodation at Edda hotels, ferry fares and a few restaurants. These discounts aren't advertised so it often pays to ask.

Drivers of motor vehicles must present registration, proof of international insurance and a home driving licence. A free motor vehicle permit will be issued for the duration of your stay.

EMBASSIES
Icelandic Embassies Abroad

Australia & New Zealand
Icelandic Consulate General, 44 St George's Road, Toorak, Victoria 3142 (☎ 03-9827 7819)
Denmark
Islands Ambassade, Dantes Plads 3, DK-1556 Copenhagen V (☎ 33 15 96 04)
France
Ambassade d'Islande, 8 Avenue Kléber, F-75116 Paris (☎ 01 44 17 32 85)
Germany
Isländische Botschaft, Kronprinzenstrasse 6, D-53173 Bonn (☎ 228-364021)
UK
Embassy of Iceland, 1 Eaton Terrace, London SW1 8EY (☎ 0171-730 5131)
USA & Canada
Embassy of Iceland, 1156 15th Street NW, Suite 1200, Washington, DC 20005-1704 (☎ 202-265 6653)
Permanent Mission of Iceland to the UN, 800 Third Ave, 36th Floor, New York, NY 10022 (☎ 212-593 2700)

Foreign Embassies in Iceland

France
Túngata 22, Reykjavík (☎ 551 7621)
Germany
Laufásvegur 31, Reykjavík (☎ 551 9535)
Sweden
Lágmúli 7, Reykjavík (☎ 581 2022)
UK
Laufásvegur 31, Reykjavík (☎ 550 5100)
USA
Laufásvegur 21, Reykjavík (☎ 562 9100)

CUSTOMS

Visitors are permitted to import up to Ikr4000 worth of food provided it doesn't weigh more than three kg and doesn't include animal products. On payment of duties, you can import up to 10 kg of food. Those over 20 years of age may import duty-free a litre of spirits (less than 47% alcohol) and a litre of wine (less than 21%) or six litres of foreign beer (instead of wine or spirits). Those aged over 15 years may bring 200 cigarettes or 250g of other tobacco products.

Foreign vehicles cannot be sold in Iceland without payment of import duty. People employed in Iceland must pay duty regardless of length of stay.

MONEY
Currency

The Icelandic unit of currency is the króna (Ikr), which is equal to 100 aurar. Notes come in 500, 1000, 2000 and 5000-krónur denominations. Coins come in one, five, 10, 50 and 100-krónur denominations.

Exchange rates

Exchange rates at the time of publication were:

Australia	A$1 =	Ikr53.02
Canada	C$1 =	Ikr48.99
Denmark	Dkr1 =	Ikr11.47
Germany	DM1 =	Ikr44.05
Norway	1Nkr =	Ikr10.32
New Zealand	NZ$1 =	Ikr46.91
UK	UK£1 =	Ikr104.51
USA	US$1 =	Ikr66.95

ICELAND

Costs

The lowest price of a double hotel room in Reykjavík is about Ikr6000. If you stay in hostels, eat at snack bars and travel on bus passes, you can keep expenses to about Ikr3000 a day. Rock-bottom budget travel in Iceland is only possible with near total exposure to the difficult weather conditions. If you must get by on less than Ikr1000 a day, you'll have to camp, self-cater and hitchhike, cycle or walk.

If you can bring a camper van or caravan, you'll be able to travel in comfort on a reasonably low budget. High petrol costs (Ikr78 a litre) can be minimised by sharing expenses with travellers without vehicles.

Changing Money

Foreign-denomination travellers' cheques, postal cheques and banknotes may be exchanged for Icelandic currency at banks for a small commission. Beware of other exchange offices; a commission of 8.75% has been charged. Any leftover krónur may be exchanged for foreign currency before departure. Eurocheques are also accepted but they yield only about 75% of their face value and aren't recommended for travel in Iceland.

ATM, Debit & Credit Cards

Cash can be withdrawn from banks using a MasterCard, Visa or Cirrus ATM card. Maestro and Electron debit cards are widely accepted.

Major credit cards (MasterCard, Visa, Diners Club, American Express, Eurocard etc) will be accepted at most places. Icelanders use cards for buying groceries and other small purchases.

Tipping & Bargaining

Tipping isn't required in Iceland; restaurants automatically add service charges to the bill. If you want to tip for particularly good or friendly service, however, you won't be refused. Bargaining is not a standard practice in Iceland.

Consumer Taxes

The Icelandic VAT (*söluskattur*) is 24.5% and it's included in marked prices. When first introduced in 1990, such items as water, electricity, books and newspapers were exempt, but in 1993 the tax was extended to printed matter. In 1994 VAT was added to accommodation, transport and other tourism-related goods and services.

For foreign tourists, there's a scheme to take some of the sting out of shopping if you purchase more than Ikr5000 worth of goods at one time. Items bought in specially designated shops with the sign *'Iceland Tax-Free Shopping'* and exported within 30 days of purchase are eligible for a partial tax refund. In order to collect, fill in a refund voucher at the time of purchase, including your name, address and passport number.

Present all items purchased (except woollens, which can be packed in luggage) and your refund vouchers at the Keflavík international airport duty-free shop when you depart; refunds are in Icelandic krónur. If you leave on the Seyðisfjörður ferry, present the items to the customs official, who'll stamp your voucher. Post the voucher to the Icelandic address shown on it within 90 days, and you'll be refunded in US dollars.

POST & COMMUNICATIONS

The Icelandic postal system is reliable, efficient and has reasonable rates. To send an airmail letter or postcard to Europe costs Ikr35, beyond Europe it costs Ikr55. Poste restante is available in all cities and villages but Reykjavík is best set up to handle it. Mail should be addressed with your name to Poste Restante, Central Post Office, Reykjavík, Iceland.

Public telephone offices are affiliated with the postal system (known as Póstur og Símí) and both services often occupy the same buildings. Reverse-charge (collect) calls may be made to many countries.

Direct dialling is available via satellite to Europe, North America and elsewhere. After dialling the international access code (00 from Iceland), dial the country code, area or city code and the telephone number. Iceland's country code is ☎ 354; from outside Iceland, follow with the seven digit number. Within Iceland, just dial the seven digit number. For operator assistance, call ☎ 114. Directory assistance is ☎ 118.

Telefax services are available at the public telephone offices in Reykjavík and most post offices around the country. The public fax number in Reykjavík is ☎ 550 7579.

NEWSPAPERS & MAGAZINES

The only English-language newspaper is the monthly *News From Iceland*, published for Icelandic emigrants to Britain, the USA and Canada. This publisher also produces the informative quarterly magazine *Iceland Review*; the Internet address is http://www.centrum.is/icerev/. For subscription information, contact Iceland Review/News From Iceland, Höfdabakki 9, IS-112 Reykjavík (☎ 567 5700; fax 567 4066; e-mail iceland@icenews.is). The annual subscription rate for *News from Iceland* is US$28 to Europe and US$35 elsewhere; for *Iceland Review*, it's US$29.50 anywhere in the world.

German and English-language periodicals, including *Der Spiegel*, *Time* and *Newsweek* are available at Eymundsson's in Reykjavík and at Bókaverslunin Edda in Akureyri.

RADIO & TV

US military radio broadcasts in the Reykjavík area in English at AM 1485. Station FM 106.8 (Klassík FM) transmits news from the BBC six times a day. In June, July and August at 7.30 am daily, station FM 92.4/93.5 broadcasts news in English; a recorded version is available by phoning ☎ 515 3690. The state-run TV station operates during afternoon and evening hours; prime time is dominated by subtitled British and US programmes.

PHOTOGRAPHY & VIDEO

Crystal-clear air combined with long, red rays cast by a low sun create excellent effects on film but, because of glare from water, ice and snow, photographers should use a UV or skylight filter and a lens shade. Although photographic supplies (including regular and camera-size videotape) are available in Reykjavík and Akureyri, they are quite expensive, so it would be wise to bring a supply of film. Photographic equipment and camera repairs are also expensive. Specialised processing for Kodachrome isn't available locally.

TIME

From late October to late March or early April, Iceland is on the same time as London (GMT/UTC), five hours ahead of New York, eight hours ahead of Los Angeles and 11 hours behind Sydney, Australia. Iceland doesn't have daylight-saving time, so in summer it's one hour behind London, four hours ahead of New York, seven hours ahead of Los Angeles and 10 hours behind Sydney.

ELECTRICITY

Electricity is at 220V, 50 Hz. Plugs are typically Scandinavian, with two round pins.

WEIGHTS & MEASURES

Iceland uses the metric system exclusively.

LAUNDRY

Laundrettes *(þrottahús)* are thin on the ground. In Reykjavík, try Þvoið Sjálf at Barónsstígur 3. The camping grounds in both Reykjavík and Akureyri have machines for guests. Large hotels also offer laundry services.

HEALTH

Travellers will have to concern themselves with few health hazards. Tap water is safe and surface water is potable except in urban areas. Glacial river water may appear murky but, if necessary, it's drinkable in small quantities. It's a good idea to purify drinking water because most unpopulated lands in

Iceland serve as sheep pastures. Giardiasis does exist but it isn't a major problem.

Sunburn and windburn should be concerns on snow and ice. The sun will burn you even if you feel cold, and the wind will cause dehydration and chafing of skin. Use a good sunscreen and a moisturising cream on exposed skin, even on cloudy days. A hat is recommended, as is zinc oxide for your nose and lips. Reflection and glare from ice and snow can cause snow blindness, so high protection sunglasses are essential for glacier and ski trips.

Health centres and doctors can be found in all towns and some villages.

WOMEN TRAVELLERS

Women travelling alone in Iceland will have few problems.

GAY & LESBIAN TRAVELLERS

Icelanders generally have a fairly open attitude to gays and lesbians. There's an organisation called Samtökin '78 (☎ 552 8539; fax 552 7525), at the Reykjavík Gay Centre, Lindargata 49, IS-101 Reykjavík. The gay bar, 22, is in Reykjavík, at Laugavegur 22.

DISABLED TRAVELLERS

Many hotels, restaurants and large shops have facilities for people who are disabled. All airlines that fly internationally can take disabled passengers, as can two of the coastal ferries, the *Baldur* and the *Herjólfur*. Facilities aren't available on scheduled bus services, but tours on specially equipped buses can be arranged. For details, contact the tourist information centre in Reykjavik or *Sjálfsbjorg* (☎ 552 9133), Hátún 12, Reykjavík.

DANGERS & ANNOYANCES

Iceland has a low crime rate, so there are few dangers or annoyances for travellers. Police don't carry guns, and prisoners go home on public holidays.

When visiting geothermal areas avoid thin crusts of lighter coloured soil around fumaroles (vents for hot gases) and mudpots, snowfields that may overlie hidden fissures, loose sharp lava chunks, and slippery slopes of scoria (volcanic slag).

BUSINESS HOURS

Weekday shopping hours are from 9 am to 6 pm, although some shops open at 8 am and close at 4 pm or later. On Saturday, shops usually open at 9 or 10 am and close between 1 and 4 pm. Petrol stations, kiosks and some supermarkets are open daily from 9 am to between 10 and 11.30 pm. Post offices have variable opening hours, but most are open from 8.30 or 9 am to 4.30 or 5 pm on weekdays. Banking hours are from 9.15 am to 4 pm (weekdays).

PUBLIC HOLIDAYS & SPECIAL EVENTS

The following public holidays are observed in Iceland:

1 January, *New Year's Day*
Maundy Thursday, Good Friday, Easter Day, Easter Monday
April, *First Day of Summer*
1 May, *Labour Day*
May, *Ascension Day*
May, *Whit Sunday, Whit Monday*
17 June, *Independence Day*
First Monday in August, *Shop & Office Workers' Holiday*
24 December (afternoon), *Christmas Eve*
25 December, *Christmas Day*
26 December, *Boxing Day*
31 December (afternoon), *New Year's Eve*

The largest nationwide festival is Independence Day on 17 June, celebrating the day in 1944 on which Iceland gained independence from Denmark. Tradition has it that the sun is not supposed to shine on this day, perhaps a psychological concession to what normally happens, anyway!

The first day of summer, or Sumar dagurinn fyrsti, is celebrated in carnival style on the third Thursday in April, with the biggest bash staged in Reykjavík. The first day of winter, Fyrsti vetrardagur, occurs on the third Saturday of October but it is not, of course, an occasion that inspires much merriment.

Sjómannadagurinn, celebrated in the first week in June, is dedicated to seafarers. The

Seamen's Union sponsors a celebration in each coastal town, where it may be the greatest party of the year.

Midsummer is celebrated around 24 June in Iceland but with less fervour than on the Scandinavian mainland.

Another earth-shaking festival, Þjóðhátíð Vestmannaeyjar, takes place in early August in Vestmannaeyjar, commemorating the day in 1874 when foul weather prevented the islands from celebrating the establishment of Iceland's constitution. Elsewhere in Iceland Verslunarmannahelgi is held on the same weekend (or in some years on an adjacent weekend) with barbecues, horse competitions, campouts and family reunions.

During September in the highlands the *réttir* (autumn sheep roundup) is also a festive occasion.

ACTIVITIES
Hiking, Trekking & Mountaineering
Most visitors to Iceland agree that the best way to see the country is on foot, whether on an afternoon hike or a two-week wilderness trek. The weather is variable, and can be a nuisance: rain is common and snow may fall in any season at higher altitudes. The best months for walking in the highlands are July, August and September. Earlier or later, some routes will be impassable without complete winter gear. At any time of year, unbridged rivers may be difficult to cross. Negotiating lava fields may be unpleasant, but strong boots will help. Use caution when walking with children, especially in fissured areas such as Mývatn and Þingvellir where narrow cracks in the earth can be hundreds of metres deep.

You can hike or trek in many areas (especially in national parks and reserves), the most popular being Hornstrandir, Mývatn, Skaftafell and Landmannalaugar to Þórsmörk. With proper equipment and maps, you'll find many other trekking opportunities. Serious mountaineering routes include Hvannadalshnúkur, Iceland's highest peak at 2119 metres above sea level.

For information on hiking and mountaineering, contact Ferðafélag Íslands (☎ 568 2533; fax 568 2535), Mörkin 6, IS-108 Reykjavík, or Íslenski Alpaklúbburinn (☎ 581 1700), at the same address.

Iceland's main outdoor shops are Skátabúðin (☎ 561 2045) at Snorrabraut 60 and 66°N (☎ 552 7425) at Skúlagata 51, both in Reykjavík. To hire camping or skiing equipment, try Tjaldaleigan (☎ 551 9800), beside the BSÍ bus terminal in Reykjavík.

Whale-Watching
Boat trips to see whales and dolphins are popular with travellers. Regular sailings depart from Reykjavík, Húsavík, Höfn and Vestmannaeyjar.

Swimming
Thanks to an abundance of geothermal heat, every city and village has at least one public swimming hall (*sundlaug* or *sundhöll*), with pools and jacuzzis. A session, including shower and sauna, will usually cost about Ikr150. Alternatively, visit one of Iceland's many natural hot springs.

Skiing
Skiers who enjoy out-of-the-way slopes will find some pleasant no-frills skiing in Iceland. In winter, nordic skiing is possible throughout the country, and in highland areas it continues until early July. The greatest drawbacks are the lack of winter transport in rural areas and almost constant bitter winds. Both Reykjavík and Akureyri have winter resorts for downhill skiing, and a summer ski school operates at Kerlingarfjöll near Hofsjökull in central Iceland.

Horse Riding
The Icelandic horse (*Equus caballus scandinavicus*) has been prominent in the development of the country. It's small (about 133 cm high) and weighs between 390 and 400 kg, but it's a sturdy animal perfectly suited to the rough Icelandic terrain. These horses are also used recreationally. They're known for their smooth fifth gait, the *tölt*.

You can hire horses and organise riding expeditions through farmhouse accommodation, tour agencies and individual

ICELAND

farmers throughout the country. Icelandic horses are gentle, and novice riders should have no problems. Horse tours are expensive, costing about Ikr10,000 a day including tent or hut accommodation. Short-term rental costs about Ikr1400 an hour. In September, you can volunteer for the *réttir*, or sheep round-up; the job normally provides room and board as well as an interesting experience. Arrangements are made through tourist offices or some tour operators.

WORK

High-paying jobs on fishing boats are hard to come by and normally go to friends and relatives of boat owners. Most foreign workers in Iceland will probably find themselves slopping fish guts eight hours a day for wages only slightly higher than could be earned at similar jobs at home – and well below an average Icelandic salary. Some companies, however, include food and/or accommodation in the deal. Intending workers will first need a job offer while still outside Iceland, then apply for the necessary work permit. Icelandic embassies abroad keep lists of businesses hiring seasonal employees.

ACCOMMODATION
Camping

Camping provides the most effective relief from high accommodation prices. Bring only a stable, seam-sealed, well-constructed and durable tent; you probably can't imagine the forces meted out by North Atlantic storms!

Only a small amount of land in Iceland is privately owned. If you'd like to camp on a private farm, ask the owner's permission before setting up. Otherwise, apart from nature reserves, where camping is either forbidden or restricted to certain areas, you're free to camp anywhere you like. Take care to keep toilet activities away from streams and surface water and use biodegradable soaps for washing up.

Organised camping grounds are known as *tjaldstæði*. Amenities and charges vary, but usually you'll pay about Ikr400 to 500 per person.

Natural fuel shortages and Icelandic regulations will preclude campfires, so carry a stove and enough fuel for the duration of your trek. Butane cartridges are found in shops and petrol stations. Unleaded petrol *(blýlaust)* and white spirits *(hreinsað bensin)* are found at most petrol stations. Coleman fuel may be purchased at the Laugardalur camping ground and at the shop Skátabúðin (☎ 561 2045), Snorrabraut 60, Reykjavík. Kerosene *(steinólíu)* works in Peak II stoves and MSR mountain stoves (and, with difficulty, in Whisperlites); it's available at some petrol stations, Skátabúðin and ironmongers (hardware stores). Methylated spirits is expensive and it's sold only in chemists and State Monopoly stores. A similar but cheaper alternative is *rauðspritt*, available from Skátabúðin and the Laugardalur camping ground.

Emergency Huts

The Lifesaving Association and the Icelandic Automobile Association maintain orange emergency huts on high mountain passes, remote coastlines and other places subject to life-threatening conditions. They're stocked with food, fuel and blankets and must only be used in emergencies.

Mountain Huts

The Icelandic Touring Club, Ferðafélag Íslands, and smaller local clubs, maintain a system of *sæluhús* (mountain huts). Several of these, such as those at Landmannalaugar and Þórsmörk, are accessible by 4WD vehicle but most are in wilderness areas. Huts along the popular Landmannalaugar to Þórsmörk route must be reserved and paid for in advance through the club office or through wardens at the Þórsmörk or Landmannalaugar huts.

Some have cooking facilities but guests must carry food and sleeping bags.

The huts are open to anyone. In the more rudimentary ones, Touring Club members pay Ikr400 while nonmembers pay Ikr750. In posher places, members pay Ikr750 and nonmembers Ikr1150. For more information, contact Ferðafélag Íslands (☎ 568 2533; fax 568 2535), Mörkin 6, IS-108 Reykjavík.

A Reykjavík tour company, Útivist (☎ 561 4330; fax 561 4606), Hallveigarstígur 1, Reykjavík, operates huts at Goðaland and Fimmvörðuháls along the Þórsmörk to Skógar route.

Hostels

In Iceland, youth hostels are called *farfuglaheimili*, which translates into something like 'little home for migrating birds'. All hostels offer hot water, cooking facilities, luggage storage and opportunities to meet other travellers. There are curfews and, with a few notable exceptions (eg Reykjavík), sleeping bags are welcome, so guests won't have to provide or rent sleeping sheets. HI members pay Ikr1000 and others pay Ikr1250.

For information on hostels, contact Bandalag Íslenskra Farfugla (Icelandic Youth Hostel Association; ☎ 553 8110; fax 588 9201), Sundlaugavegur 34, IS-105 Reykjavík.

Farmhouse Accommodation

In Iceland some farms date back to Settlement times and are mentioned in the sagas. Farmhouse accommodation will allow you to become acquainted with everyday country life. Some offer meals and others just have cooking facilities. Horse hire and horse-riding tours are often available. It's advisable to book off-season (September to May) accommodation in advance. For a detailed listing, contact Icelandic Farm Holidays Ltd (☎ 562 3640; fax 562 3644; e-mail ifh@centrum.is), Hafnarstræti 1, IS-107 Reykjavík. Official prices (July and August) are:

breakfast – Ikr700
lunch – about Ikr950
dinner – about Ikr1400
sleeping-bag accommodation (per person) – Ikr1350

cottage (daily rate), four to six-person – Ikr4400 to 6100
cottage (weekly rate), four to six-person – Ikr19,000 to 39,000
child rate – half price
bed linen (daily per person) – Ikr600
horse hire (hourly) – Ikr1350

Guesthouses

There are several types of *gistiheimilið* (guesthouses), from private homes that let out rooms in order to bring in extra cash, to others that are quite elaborate. Hostel-style sleeping-bag accommodation may be available. In some cases, a continental breakfast is included. Sleeping-bag accommodation costs about Ikr1300; double rooms range from Ikr3000 to 6000; and self-contained units, between Ikr5000 and 9000. Rooms are always cheaper if booked through a travel agent abroad. Most guesthouses are only open seasonally.

Edda Hotels & Summer Hotels

Most Edda hotels, operated by the Iceland Tourist Bureau, and other summer hotels, are school dormitories that are used as hotels during summer holidays. Some offer sleeping-bag accommodation (just a dry spot to roll out a sleeping bag) or dormitory facilities as well as conventional lodging. Single/double rooms cost Ikr3700/4800. Sleeping-bag and dormitory accommodation range from Ikr900 to 1400 per person.

Hotels

Major towns have at least one up-market hotel that may seem sterile and characterless, but with all amenities: restaurant, pub, baths, telephones and TV. In Reykjavík you'll pay an average of Ikr10,000 to 11,000 for these creature comforts, including a continental breakfast.

FOOD

Traditionally, Icelanders showed little culinary imagination owing to a lack of ingredients. Nowadays, however, there are cafés and restaurants catering to most tastes.

Although traditional delicacies may remind foreigners of the nightmare feast in

Indiana Jones and the Temple of Doom, they aren't always as bad as they sound. The glaring exception is *hákarl*, putrefied shark meat that has been buried in sand and gravel for three to six months to ensure sufficient decomposition. It reeks of a cross between ammonia and old 'road kill' – few foreigners appreciate it.

Moving towards the less bizarre, Icelanders make a staple of *harðfiskur*, haddock that is cleaned and dried in the open air until it has become dehydrated and brittle. It's torn into strips and eaten with butter as a snack. Icelanders also eat broiled *lundi*, or puffin, which looks and tastes like calves' liver. Whale blubber, whale steaks and seal meat are also available, but you might resist for environmental or other reasons.

A unique Icelandic treat is *skyr*, a delicious yoghurt-like concoction made of pasteurised skimmed milk and bacteria culture. Surprisingly, this rich and decadent dessert is actually low in fat, but it's often mixed with sugar, fruit and milk to give it a creamy, pudding-like texture.

Snack Bars, Fast Food & Restaurants

Relatively inexpensive chips, hot dogs, sandwiches, doughnuts, ice cream and coffee are available at petrol stations and kiosks. For a light meal of chips, hot dog and trimmings you'll pay about Ikr300. In larger towns, you will find kiosks selling pizza, pastries and pre-packaged pop-it-in-the-microwave items.

There are two McDonald's in Reykjavík, and a couple of fried chicken outlets in Akureyri. Pizza restaurants have become quite popular.

In Reykjavík and Akureyri, a couple of good-value restaurants offer all the bread, soup and salad you can eat for about Ikr750. Reykjavík has several intimate pub-style cafes where you can drink beer, eat a meal or chat over coffee for hours without attracting comment. These places are great value, with light meals for about Ikr700.

The word 'restaurant' usually denotes an up-market establishment, often associated with expensive hotels. In Iceland, hotel restaurant quality varies from slightly dubious through to excellent. Breakfasts and lunches are often served buffet style.

Reykjavík has an increasing variety of ethnic restaurants, including Thai, Chinese, Italian, Indian and Mexican.

Self-Catering

Self-catering minimises food costs. Every town and village has at least one *kaupfélagið* (cooperative supermarket), your key to inexpensive dining in Iceland. The most economical chain is Bónus, followed by Hagkaup; good-value groceries include skyr, tinned fish and dried fruit.

Icelandic greenhouse produce is very good, but imported vegetables are often already past their peak when they hit the shelves.

DRINKS

Coffee is a national institution in Iceland. A 500g bag of good coffee costs about Ikr300, and a cup of filter coffee with at least one refill will cost about Ikr150.

The only nonalcoholic traditional drink (although it may be spiked with alcohol) is *jólaöl* or 'Christmas brew'. British travel writer Tony Moore disparagingly described the taste as 'de-alcoholised Guinness seasoned with Marmite'. Yuck.

Alcohol

Alcohol is another matter. Iceland is what is popularly referred to in European jargon as a 'nanny state', one in which high taxes are levied on alcohol in the hope that they will discourage excessive consumption. If you want to see how successful this has been, just look around Reykjavík on any Friday night! In fact, beer didn't become legal until 1989.

Beer, wine and spirits are available to people over 20 years of age from licensed bars, restaurants and *áfengisbúðar*, or State Monopoly stores. Inexpensive 2.2% beer sold in petrol stations and corner shops is Ikr90 per can.

Drinking in restaurants and pubs is definitely for the wealthy. A glass of house wine costs up to Ikr500, and the average price for beer is Ikr500 for 500 ml.

The traditional Icelandic alcoholic brew is *brennivín* (burnt wine), a sort of schnapps made from potatoes and caraway. Its nickname *svarti dauði*, or 'black death', may offer some clues about its character but it's actually quite good.

ENTERTAINMENT

Apart from some cinemas, there's not much entertainment outside Reykjavík and Akureyri. See these sections for details.

THINGS TO BUY

Every visitor to Iceland seems to end up with a *lopapaysa* (woolly pullover), although you can also buy hats and gloves. Pullovers come in many designs but the traditional ones, which are more expensive than the delicate pastel fashion sweaters, are thicker and have white and blue, violet or earth tones. For these you'll pay about Ikr6000. Reykjavík city tours stop at the Álafoss factory outlet in the suburb of Mossfellsveit, which is a bit cheaper than the tourist shops.

The Handknitting Association of Iceland has a shop at Skólavörðustígur 19 in Reykjavík with prices up to Ikr6700 for a traditional handknitted sweater. Rock-bottom prices (Ikr1500 to 3500) and inconsistent quality are found in street stalls on Austurstræti in Reykjavík.

Handmade ceramics, glassware and silver jewellery can be bought from various outlets on Austurstræti.

Getting There & Away

AIR

Icelandair, Iceland's national carrier, offers shorter stay 'cheap' tickets with only very limited possibilities for rescheduling. Air Atlanta offers the best deals but its once-weekly flights between London and Iceland are only in summer.

Icelandair serves Keflavík direct from many European airports including Amsterdam, Copenhagen, Frankfurt, Glasgow, Hamburg, London, Luxembourg, Oslo, Paris, Stockholm and Vágar (Faroe Islands). In the high season, the Hamburg-Copenhagen-Keflavík flight operates twice daily, while the London and Luxembourg nonstop flights operate once daily. Flights between Reykjavík and the Faroe Islands are twice weekly.

A return ticket from Luxembourg to Reykjavík costs US$665, and must be purchased at least seven days in advance. Flights from the UK to Iceland are cheaper, for example UK£353 return from London (at least seven days advance purchase, stay one Saturday night and a maximum of one month). Contact Icelandair for details of special fares on connecting bus and train services.

During the high season (31 March to 26 October), there are daily Icelandair flights from Keflavík to New York JFK and Baltimore/Washington. Flights to Boston and Halifax go several times weekly. The frequency of flights to Fort Lauderdale and Orlando varies, with more in winter. The Apex fare between New York and Luxembourg is US$828 return with seven-day advance purchase, and a maximum stay of three days in each direction. For the latest information, call within the USA toll-free ☎ 1-800-223 5500.

Other airlines serve Iceland, mainly in summer. Those with offices in Reykjavík include Greenland Air (☎ 565 8880; fax 565 8882), Scandinavian Airlines System (☎ 562 3222; fax 562 2281) and Air Atlanta (☎ 566 7700; fax 566 7766). Samvinn Travel (☎ 569 1010; fax 552 7796) at Austurstræti 12, IS-101 Reykjavík are the only agent for Air Atlanta. From Samvinn, a London-Keflavík return ticket (valid for stays of between three days and one month) costs only Ikr19,780.

Combined air/ferry tickets to Iceland are now available from the UK and from Scandinavia. Contact your travel agent for full details.

SEA
Ferry
You can travel from the European mainland by ferry. Although this takes longer than flying and isn't much cheaper, it allows you the option of taking a vehicle.

Smyril Line's *Norrøna* operates from early June to early September out of Esbjerg in Denmark. The *Norrøna* sails from Esbjerg on Saturday, arriving in Tórshavn in the Faroe Islands on Monday morning. All Iceland-bound passengers must disembark while the ship continues to Bergen, Norway. It returns to Tórshavn on Wednesday, gathers up Iceland passengers, and sails overnight to Seyðisfjörður. On the return journey, it sails back to Tórshavn on Thursday, arriving Friday morning, then returning to Esbjerg to begin another circuit.

Note that Iceland passengers cannot remain aboard while the ship sails to Norway; they must spend two nights in the Faroes en route. To stay longer in the Faroes, you'll have to break your journey there and pay for two sectors. The high-season deck fare between Esbjerg and Seyðisfjörður (which includes a couchette or sleeper) is Danish kroner (Dkr) 1980 each way. Esbjerg to Tórshavn is Dkr1260 and Tórshavn to Seyðisfjörður is Dkr1180, adding up to Dkr2440 for the broken trip. Discounts are available to holders of student cards.

Avoid changing money on the ship; exchange rates are poor and the commission is high.

To transport a vehicle up to five metres long between Esbjerg and Seyðisfjörður will cost Dkr1660. Motorcycles cost Dkr660 and bicycles, Dkr80. Above deck class, there are three classes of cabins and a luxury suite. For more information, contact Smyril Line (☎ 298-15900; fax 298-15707), J Broncksgøta 37, PO Box 370, FR-110 Tórshavn, Faroe Islands. In the UK, contact P&O Scottish Ferries (☎ 44-1224-572615; fax 44-1224-574411), PO Box 5, Jamieson's Quay, Aberdeen, AB9 8DL, Scotland.

Coming from the UK, you can take Strandfaraskip Landsins' ferry, the *Smyril*, which sails twice weekly between 14 June and 18 August (once weekly at other times) from Aberdeen, Scotland to Tórshavn. There, connect with the *Norrøna* to Iceland. For information contact Strandfaraskip Landsins (☎ 298-14550; fax 298-18140), Yviri við Strond 6, Postbox 88, FR-110 Tórshavn, Faroe Islands.

Cargo Ship
The Icelandic cargo-shippers, Eimskip, can take passengers on its vessel *Brúarfoss*. The ship sails every second Thursday from Reykjavík to the Faroe Islands and Hamburg, returning via Denmark, Sweden, Norway and the Faroes. The trip to Hamburg takes four days and costs Ikr27,400 per person, one way in a double cabin (full board). To transport a car shorter than five metres costs Ikr22,500. Contact the sales agent in Iceland: Úrval-Útsýn Travel (☎ 569 9300; fax 588 0202), Lágmúli 4, IS-108 Reykjavík.

The Samskip Line (☎ 44-1482-322399; fax 44-1482-229529) has its UK base at Silvester House, The Maltings, Silvester St, Hull, England. It is cheaper but facilities are considerably more basic.

LEAVING ICELAND
Iceland levies an airport departure tax of Ikr1340, payable when airline tickets are issued. There's no departure tax when leaving Iceland by ferry or cargo ship.

Getting Around

AIR
Iceland's domestic airline, Flugleiðir (☎ 505 0200; fax 505 0250), has daily flights in the summer between Reykjavík and Akureyri, Egilsstaðir, Höfn, Ísafjörður and Vestmannaeyjar. Smaller towns are served two to six times weekly. Some flights offer unadvertised discounted seats, so enquire before paying full fare. Since inclement weather can lead to postponed or cancelled flights, flexible travel plans are essential.

Gaps in Flugleiðir's schedule are filled by

Flugfélag Norðurlands (☎ 461 2100; fax 461 2106), based at Akureyri airport. A third domestic airline is Flugfélag Austurlands (☎ 471 1122; fax 471 2149), based at Egilsstaðir airport.

BUS

Although Iceland is small and has a well-established public transport system, there are no railways and the highway system is Europe's least developed. Parts of National Highway 1, the 'Ring Road', which was completed in 1971, remain unsurfaced.

Bifreiðastöð Íslands (BSÍ; ☎ 552 2300 or 562 3320), a collective organisation of Iceland's long-distance bus operators, covers the country with feasible connections. Many routes are straightforward but on some minor routes connections may take several days. Many buses stop running in September and don't resume until June. Interior routes rarely open before July, and in years of high snowfall, they may not open at all. Most are closed again by early to mid-September.

BSÍ offers two bus passes, the Hringmiði ('Ring Pass' or Full-Circle Pass) and the Tímamiði ('Time Pass' or Omnibuspass). The former allows a circuit of the Ring Road in either direction, stopping anywhere you like. It costs Ikr13,600 (Ikr19,900 with the Westfjords extension) – not much less than the normal fare – but you're entitled to 10% discount on ferries (if tickets are bought from BSÍ) and at some camping grounds and other accommodation. There's also 5% discount on some organised tours.

The Omnibuspass is good for one to four weeks and allows unrestricted travel on all but interior bus routes and some other special routes. On interior routes there are substantial discounts for Omnibuspass holders; on some bus tours, 5% discount is offered. The pass also offers ferry and accommodation discounts.

With the one and two-week passes, you'd have to do a lot of travelling to get your money's worth but three and four-week passes are good value. One week costs Ikr14,800; two weeks cost Ikr21,400; three weeks, Ikr28,000 and four weeks, Ikr31,300.

Ask for a free copy of the *Leiðabók* (bus timetable).

CAR & MOTORCYCLE
Private Vehicles

It's easy to bring a vehicle on the ferry from mainland Europe. Drivers must carry the vehicle's registration, proof of valid insurance and a driving licence. After the vehicle is inspected, a free temporary import permit will be issued if the driver isn't employed in Iceland. Diesel vehicles have to pay a tax on entry to the country (about Ikr3000 per week for vehicles under 1000 kg), but this may be replaced by a tax on the price of diesel (currently much cheaper than petrol).

Petrol costs about Ikr78 per litre; diesel is about Ikr30. Leaded petrol isn't available.

Travellers in the interior must have a 4WD vehicle. Bear in mind that petrol and diesel are available only at Versalir, Kerlingarfjöll and Hveravellir and there are no repair services on the F-numbered (interior) highway system. A suggested spares and repair kit includes extra oil, brake fluid, extra petrol, sealing compound for the radiator and petrol tank, a distributor cap, a rotor arm, a condenser, a fuel filter, a fan belt, at least two spare tyres and a puncture repair kit, spark plugs, insulated wire, fuses and headlights. You'll need the expertise to identify all this stuff and fix any mechanical problems!

Also required are large-scale maps, a compass, extra food rations, a shovel and some means of protecting your eyes and skin from wind-driven sand. Tool kits should include a tow rope, a crow bar, the relevant sockets and wrenches, a jack, a torch, batteries, flares and a fire extinguisher.

In the interior, it's best to travel with another vehicle. The greatest threats are posed by unbridged rivers and drifting sand (even 4WD vehicles get bogged in sand drifts). Glacial rivers change course and fords change nature. Warm days may cause heavy glacial melting and placid rivers can become torrents without warning. Tyre marks into the water don't mean a river can be crossed.

If possible, try to check the depth and

condition of the riverbed before driving in. Only cross where there are rocks or gravel, never sand. The narrowest fords are usually the deepest. Before entering the water, remove the fan belt, cover the distributor and ignition system with a woollen rag and switch off headlights. Don't stop in midstream unless you cannot continue and want to reverse out.

Most Icelandic highways aren't suitable for high-speed travel. Headlight and radiator protection from dust and flying rocks is advisable. For further information, contact the Icelandic Automobile Association, Félag Íslenskra Bifreiðaeigenda (☎ 562 9999; fax 552 9071), Borgartún 33, IS-105 Reykjavík.

Road Rules

In Iceland, you drive on the right. The use of seat belts (front and rear) is compulsory. The speed limit on unpaved roads is 80 km/h; unfortunately, it's universally ignored. In urban areas, the speed limit is 50 km/h.

Drink driving laws are very strict in Iceland and the legal limit is set at 0.05% blood alcohol content.

Car Rental

The Sultan of Brunei would think twice before renting a car in Iceland. The cheapest vehicles, such as the Nissan Micra, cost Ikr4500-5000 per day, with 100 km and 24.5% VAT included. After your 100 km, add Ikr25 to 30 per km, compulsory insurance and some very dear petrol to the price. Rental charges for 4WD vehicles are nearly double the above. However, there's now some real competition with Hasso-Ísland offering lower rates. You must be at least 20 years old to rent a car from most of the following agencies:

ALP
Skemmuvegur 20, IS-200 Kópavogur (☎ 567 0722). There's another office at the BSÍ terminal in Reykjavík (☎ 551 7570)

Hasso-Ísland
Hringbraut 62, IS-101 Reykjavík (☎ 555 3340; fax 555 3330)

Icelandair/Hertz
Reykjavík airport, IS-101 Reykjavík (☎ 505 0600). Other offices are in Keflavík (☎ 425 0221), Akureyri (☎ 461 1005), Egilsstaðir (☎ 471 1210), Höfn (☎ 478 1250) and Vestmannaeyjar (☎ 481 3300)

InterRent Europcar
Skeifan 9, IS-108 Reykjavík (☎ 568 6915). It also has offices throughout the country, including Tryggvabraut 12, Akureyri (☎ 461 3000)

RVS/Avis
Sigtún 5, IS-105 Reykjavík (☎ 562 4433). Avis also has offices in Akureyri (☎ 461 2428), Höfn (☎ 478 1260) and Keflavík (☎ 562 4423)

BICYCLE

In Iceland the wind, rough roads, gravel, river crossings, sandstorms, intimidating vehicles and horrid weather conspire against cyclists. Hard-core cyclists will find a challenge in Iceland but come prepared to pack up your bike and travel by bus when things become intolerable. The Kjölur route through the interior now has bridges over all major rivers, so it's accessible to cyclists.

In areas best suited to cycling, such as Mývatn or urban Reykjavík and Akureyri, bicycles can be hired for about Ikr1000 per day plus deposit. Domestic airlines usually accept bicycles as checked luggage and they may provide bike bags free. Bicycles may be carried on long-distance buses for Ikr500 if there's space available, but there are lots of cyclists in the summer, so don't count on it.

HITCHING

Summer hitching is possible but inconsistent. If there's traffic, you'll get a ride eventually, but long waits are common in most areas, especially the Westfjords. It's best not to hitch in groups of more than two people. See the Hitching section in the introductory Getting Around chapter.

BOAT

Major ferries operating in Iceland include the *Akraborg*, which connects Reykjavík and Akranes; the *Herjólfur* between Þorlákshöfn and Vestmannaeyjar; the *Baldur* between Stykkishólmur, Flatey, and Brjánslækur; the *Sævar* between Arskógssandur and Hrísey; the *Sæfari* between Akureyri, Hrísey, Dalvík and Grímsey; and the *Fagranes*, which operates around Ísafjarðardjúp and between Ísafjörður, Jökulfjörður and Hornstrandir. The first three are car ferries and only the *Fagranes* and *Sæfari* don't operate year-round.

Ferry schedules are designed to coincide with buses. They are outlined in detail in the *Leiðabók* timetable. Holders of bus passes (and sometimes, student identity cards) get 10% discount on fares.

LOCAL TRANSPORT

Reykjavík and Akureyri have good town bus and taxi services; the bus service in Ísafjörður is more limited. Taxis with an English or German-speaking driver are available in most towns. Sightseeing hires for up to five passengers typically cost Ikr2150 for one hour or Ikr6400 for three hours.

ORGANISED TOURS

Many of the nicest sights in Iceland are in remote locations where public transport isn't available. If you don't have a hardy vehicle and don't want to walk, endure difficult hitching conditions or attempt cycling, tours will provide the only access.

The least expensive and most loosely organised tours are offered by BSÍ, the consortium of long-distance bus companies, in association with small local operators. They run much like ordinary bus services, but stop at points of interest. Sometimes a guide is included. It's also possible to leave non-guided tours at any time and rejoin at a later specified date. Buy a 15-unit Highland Pass (Ikr18,800) from BSÍ; it will be cheaper than individual tickets. BSÍ also offers glacier tours and various boat trips, including whale-watching trips. Watch out for the 'Tour of the Week', which is discounted by up to 33%.

Several companies and groups operate hiking, trekking, horse-riding or photography tours. There are also up-market bus tours with accommodation in tents and mountain huts. Contact the following:

BSÍ Travel
Umferðarmiðstöðin, Vatnsmýrarvegur10, IS-101 Reykjavík (☎ 552 2300; fax 552 9973)
Ferðafélag Íslands
Mörkin 6, IS-108 Reykjavík (☎ 568 2533; fax 568 2535)
Guðmundur Jónasson
Borgartún 34, IS-105 Reykjavík (☎ 511 1515; fax 511 1511)
Reykjavík Excursions
Bankastræti 2, Reykjavík (☎ 562 1011; fax 552 3062)
Úrval-Útsyn
Lágmúli 4, IS-108 Reykjavík (☎ 569 9300; fax 588 0202)
Útivist
Hallveigarstígur 1, IS-101 Reykjavík (☎ 561 4330; fax 561 4606)

Reykjavík

Iceland's capital Reykjavík, home to 160,000 of the country's 266,000 people, is unlike any other European city. It's the world's most northerly capital city and also one of its smallest. By European standards, Reykjavík is historically and architecturally rather unexciting, but politically, socially, culturally, economically and psychologically, it dominates Iceland: in essence, everything that happens in the country happens in Reykjavík.

Reykjavík was the first place in Iceland to be intentionally settled. The original settler, Ingólfur Arnarson, tossed his high-seat pillars (a bit of pagan paraphernalia) overboard in 874 AD, and built his farm near where they washed ashore, between Tjörnin (the Pond) and the sea, where Aðalstræti now intersects with Suðurgata. He called the place Reykjavík (Smoky Bay) because of the steam rising from nearby geothermal features. Ingólfur claimed the entire south-west corner of the island, then set about planting his hayfields at Austurvöllur, the present town square.

Orientation

Reykjavík's heart is still between Tjörnin and the harbour, and many old buildings

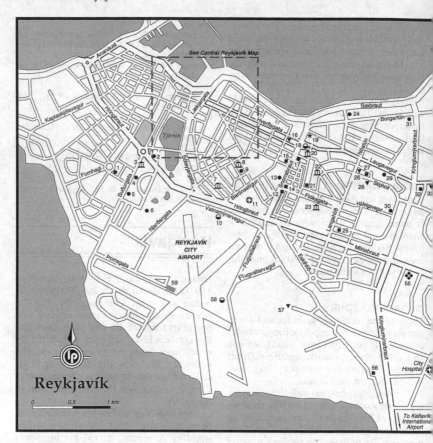

Reykjavík

remain. Nearly everything in the city lies within walking distance of the old settlement, and most meeting and lounging activity takes place around Lækjartorg and the adjacent pedestrian shopping street, Austurstræti. The shopping district extends east along Laugavegur from Lækjargata to the Hlemmur bus terminal.

Information

Tourist Offices The main tourist information centre (☎ 562 3045) (Upplýsingamiðstöð Ferðamála), is at Bankastræti 2 near Lækjargata. From 1 June to 31 August, it's

open daily from 8.30 am to 7 pm. You'll find a second branch at the new city hall (☎ 563 2005), open daily in summer from 10 am to 6 pm. There's another helpful desk at the BSÍ long-distance bus terminal. Pick up a copy of *Around Reykjavík*, published seasonally.

The Reykjavík Tourist Card, available at both tourist offices, gives you free entry to museums, swimming pools etc, and it includes a bus pass. It costs Ikr600/800/1000 for one/two/three days.

Money Banks can be found on Austurstræti and Bankastræti. After-hours banking is

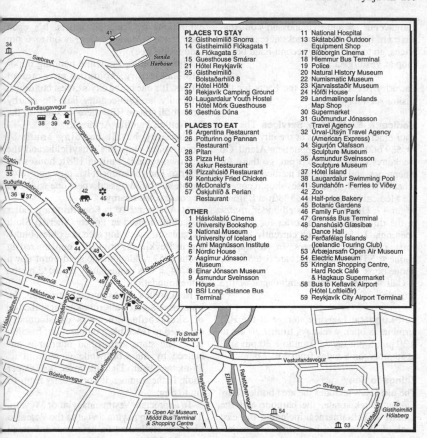

PLACES TO STAY
12 Gistiheimilið Snorra
14 Gistiheimilið Flókagata 1
   & Flókagata 5
15 Guesthouse Smárar
21 Hótel Reykjavík
25 Gistiheimilið
   Bolstaðarhlíð 8
27 Hótel Höfði
39 Rekjavík Camping Ground
40 Laugardalur Youth Hostel
51 Hótel Mörk Guesthouse
56 Gesthús Dúna

PLACES TO EAT
16 Argentina Restaurant
26 Potturinn og Pannan
   Restaurant
28 Píitan
33 Pizza Hut
36 Askur Restaurant
43 Pizzahúsið Restaurant
49 Kentucky Fried Chicken
50 McDonald's
57 Óskjuhlíð & Perlan
   Restaurant

OTHER
1 Háskólabíó Cinema
2 University Bookshop
3 National Museum
4 University of Iceland
5 Árni Magnússon Institute
6 Nordic House
7 Ásgímur Jónsson
   Museum
8 Einar Jónsson Museum
9 Ásmundur Sveinsson
   House
10 BSÍ Long-distance Bus
   Terminal
11 National Hospital
13 Skátabúðin Outdoor
   Equipment Shop
17 Bíóborgin Cinema
18 Hlemmur Bus Terminal
19 Police
20 Natural History Museum
22 Numismatic Museum
23 Kjarvalsstaðir Museum
24 Höfði House
29 Landmælingar Íslands
   Map Shop
30 Supermarket
31 Guðmundur Jónasson
   Travel Agency
32 Úrval-Útsýn Travel Agency
   (American Express)
34 Sigurjón Ólafsson
   Sculpture Museum
35 Ásmundur Sveinsson
   Sculpture Museum
37 Hótel Ísland
38 Laugardalur Swimming Pool
41 Sundahöfn - Ferries to Viðey
42 Zoo
44 Half-price Bakery
45 Botanic Gardens
46 Family Fun Park
47 Grensás Bus Terminal
48 Danshúsið Glæsibæ
   Dance Hall
52 Ferðafélag Íslands
   (Icelandic Touring Club)
53 Árbæjarsafn Open Air Museum
54 Electric Museum
55 Kringlan Shopping Centre,
   Hard Rock Café
   & Hagkaup Supermarket
58 Bus to Keflavík Airport
   (Hótel Loftleiðir)
59 Reykjavík City Airport Terminal

available at Keflavík international airport from Monday to Friday between 6 am and 6 pm (from 15 June to 15 August, also Friday to Sunday, 6 am to 2.30 am). The Change Group at Bankastræti 2 is open daily from 8.30 am to 8 pm (May to September), 9 am to 5.30 pm in winter (8.75% commission out of banking hours). During non-banking hours, hotels exchange foreign currency but charge a high commission.

ATMs at banks accept MasterCard, Visa and Cirrus.

Post & Communications Reliable poste restante is available at the main post office on Pósthússtræti, open weekdays only, 8.30 am to 4.30 pm. There's a substation in the BSÍ bus terminal. Faxes or calls may be sent or received from the telephone office, on Kirkjustræti, open weekdays only from 9 am to 6 pm. Public phones at the Lækjartorg bus terminal, on the corner of Hafnarstræti and Lækjargata, can be used from 6 am (7 am on Sunday) to 11 pm.

Bookshops The widest varieties of English-language books are at Mál og Menning (which also sells topographic maps) at

Laugavegur 18, and Eymundsson's on Austurstræti. For used paperbacks at reasonable prices, go to the friendly second-hand bookshop at Vesturgata 17.

Laundry See Laundry in the Facts for the Visitor section.

Medical & Emergency Services The 24-hour emergency ward is at the city hospital (☎ 569 6600), on Fossvogur near Áland. On weekdays from 8 am to 5 pm, go there for emergency and non-urgent medical help. At other times, non-urgent cases should consult the Medical Centre (☎ 552 1230) at Barónsstígur 47. Dispensaries, listed under *apótek* in the directory, have a roster for 24-hour openings. To learn which currently has the shift, check daily papers. In Reykjavík, phone ☎ 551 8888. Dentists are listed in the phone book.

Call ☎ 112 for police, ambulance or fire brigade.

Left-Luggage Luggage storage at the BSÍ terminal is open weekdays from 7.30 am to 9.30 pm, Saturday 7.30 am to 2.30 pm and, in summer, on Sunday from 5 to 7 pm.

Things to See

The **old town** includes the area bordered by Tjörnin, Lækjargata, the harbour and the suburb of Seltjarnarnes, including the east bank of Tjörnin and both sides of Lækjargata. The Lækjartorg area is the socialising centre of town.

The houses on the southern side of **Hafnarstræti** were used by Danish traders during the trade monopoly between 1602 and 1855. Today, tourist shops here sell woollens, pottery and souvenirs.

Old Reykjavík grew up around **Tjörnin**, the pleasant lake in the centre of town. The park at Tjörnin has jogging and bike trails, a fountain and colourful flower gardens. Reykjavík's new **Raðhus** (city hall), on the northern bank of Tjörnin, could be described as a sort of postmodern floating palace. The **National Gallery**, behind the church Fríkirkjan near Tjörnin, is worth visiting for

exhibitions by Icelandic artists. It's open daily, except Monday, from noon to 6 pm (admission free).

Stjórnarráðið, the white building opposite Lækjartorg, contains government offices. It's one of the city's oldest buildings, originally an 18th-century jail. On nearby **Árnarhóll** (Eagle Hill) there's a statue of the first settler, Ingólfur Arnarson.

The grey basalt building south of Austurvöllur (Ingólfur's hayfields and the old town square), built in 1881, houses the **Alþing**. The government has now outgrown the present building and a new one will soon be constructed nearby.

At Aðalstræti 10 is **Fógetinn**, a popular restaurant housed in Fógeti (Sheriff) Skúli Magnússon's weaving shed, the oldest building in Reykjavík, originally constructed in about 1752. Although the shed burnt down in 1764, it was immediately replaced on the same foundation.

Reykjavík's most imposing structure, the immense church **Hallgrímskirkja**, at the top of Skólavörðustígur, was unashamedly designed to resemble a mountain of basaltic lava. The stark, light-filled interior is enhanced by the worthwhile view from its 75-metre tower. The lift costs Ikr200 per adult. In the summer, it's open daily from 10 am to 6 pm.

To appreciate Vestmannaeyjar or Mývatn, it's well worth paying a visit to the **Volcano Show** at Hellusund 6a beforehand. Filmed by locals Vilhjálmur and Ósvaldur Knudsen, the show offers an insight into the volcanic spectre under which Icelanders live. The daily 2½-hour shows (in English) begin at 10 am, and 3 and 8 pm in summer. French and German programmes are shown at 12.30 pm and 5.30 pm, respectively. Admission is Ikr850.

The **National Museum** at Suðurgata 41 is obligatory for anyone interested in Norse culture and Icelandic history. The best exhibits include the Settlement Era religious and folk relics and tools; nautical and agricultural artefacts, fishing boats and the ingenious early farm implements. It's open daily except Monday from 11 am to 5 pm between 16 May and 14 September and for limited hours the rest of the year. Admission is Ikr200.

Jóhannes Kjarval, born in 1885, was Iceland's most popular artist. The surrealism that characterises his work was derived from the ethereal nature of the distinctive Icelandic landscape. **Kjarvalsstaðir**, the Kjarval Museum, is in Miklatún park on Flókagata. It's open from 10 am to 6 pm daily. Admission costs Ikr300.

Also known as the Open Air Museum, **Árbæjarsafn** is a 12.5-hectare historic farm set up as a museum in 1957. It also includes a collection of old homes and buildings moved from various places to illustrate life in early Iceland. In the summer, it's open daily except Monday from 10 am to 6 pm. Admission is Ikr300 per person. Take the museum bus, bus No 10 or 110, from the city centre.

Activities
At the Laugardalur pool, **swimming** costs Ikr150. It's conveniently situated near the youth hostel and camping ground (bus No 5). In summer it's open weekdays from 7 am to 9.30 pm, and on weekends from 8 am to 7.30 pm.

Places to Stay
In the summer, finding a place to stay may be difficult. Bring a tent or book accommodation in advance if you'd rather not risk being left out in the cold.

Camping The *Reykjavík Camping Ground* (☎ 568 6944), with cooking and laundry facilities, is 15 minutes on bus No 5 from Lækjartorg or a Ikr500 taxi ride from the BSÍ terminal. It's immense, but at the height of summer, you'll be lucky to find space for a tent. It's open from 15 May to 15 September and costs Ikr250 per person and Ikr250 per tent. From 15 June to 15 August, a free shuttle bus runs from the camping ground to the BSÍ terminal at 7 am.

Hostels Beside the camping ground, at Sundlaugavegur 34, is the clean *Laugardalur*

Youth Hostel (☎ 553 8110). Unfortunately, it gets crowded and noisy. HI members pay Ikr1000 per night and nonmembers, Ikr1250. In summer, it's wise to book well in advance. Otherwise, try in the evening and hope for a cancellation.

Guesthouses The cheapest guesthouse is the *Salvation Army Guest House* (☎ 561 3203; fax 561 3315) at Kirkjustræti 2. It offers single/double rooms for Ikr2200/3000 without bathroom, and sleeping-bag accommodation for Ikr1100/1300 without/with sheets.

There are plenty of other options. *Gistiheimilið Svala* (☎ 562 3544; fax 562 3650) at Skólavörðustígur 30 is an old house on a quiet central street. Single/double rooms cost Ikr4000/6000 (including breakfast); sleeping-bag accommodation is Ikr1500.

More basic is *Gistiheimilið Bólstaðarhlíð 8* (☎ 552 2822; fax 562 3535) at Bólstaðarhlíð 8, which offers sleeping-bag accommodation for Ikr1250 per person, including use of kitchen facilities. It's about 10 minutes walk from the BSÍ terminal. Another option is *Gistiskálinn* (☎ 568 3188) at Ármúli 17a, which costs Ikr1250 per person.

Guesthouse Smárar (☎ 562 3330; fax 562 3331) at Snorrabraut 52 charges Ikr1500 for sleeping-bag accommodation. Singles/doubles cost Ikr3500/4900. Nearby is *Gistiheimilið Flókagata 1* (☎ 552 1155; fax 562 0355), which charges Ikr3800/5500 and Ikr1300 for sleeping-bag accommodation. *Gistiheimilið Flókagata 5* (☎ 551 9828; fax 551 2448) charges Ikr3800/5500 for singles/doubles.

Gistiheimilið Snorra (☎ 552 0598; fax 551 8945), at Snorrabraut 61, has singles/doubles for Ikr4700/6400 and sleeping-bag accommodation in double rooms for Ikr1500. Kitchen facilities are available. *Gesthús Dúna* (☎ 588 2100; fax 588 2102), at Suðurhlíð 35d, has B&B (without private bath) for Ikr4500/6500 a single/double. Sleeping-bag accommodation costs Ikr1500.

At Mörkin 8 you'll find *Hótel Mörk Guesthouse* (☎ 568 3600; fax 568 3606),

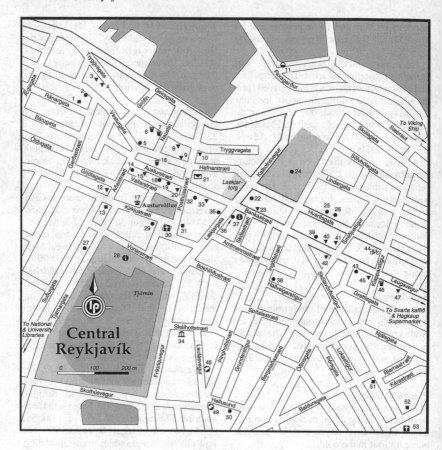

Central
Reykjavík

Tjörnin

To National
& University
Libraries

which has flats for two people for Ikr6500 and sleeping-bag accommodation for Ikr900.

Gistiheimilið Hólaberg (☎ 567 0980; fax 557 3620) is fairly far out at Hólaberg 80. However, there's free pick up from the city airport or the BSÍ bus terminal if you're booked in. Singles/doubles cost Ikr3770/5500, and sleeping-bag accommodation is Ikr1250.

Hotels One budget option is *Hótel City* (☎ 511 1155; fax 552 9040) at Ránargata 4a, which charges Ikr5100 for a small single

room with shared bathroom. Singles/doubles with shower cost Ikr6300/10,000. Avoid the restaurant. Cheaper still is *Hótel Höfði* (☎ 552 6210; fax 562 3986) at Skipholt 27. Single/double rooms start at Ikr4100/5900.

The stark *Hótel Reykjavík* (☎ 562 6250; fax 562 6350) at Rauðarárstígur 37 charges Ikr11,700 for single rooms with shower and Ikr15,900 for doubles with shower and breakfast. A relatively affordable option is *Hótel Leifur Eiríksson* (☎ 562 0800; fax 562 0804) at Skólavörðustígur 45. Rates are Ikr7500/10,200, including breakfast.

Right in the centre at Pósthússtræti 11 is

Hótel Borg (☎ 551 1440; fax 5511420), a pleasant older-style hotel with rooms for Ikr10,900/13,900 with bathroom and breakfast.

Places to Eat

Some up-market restaurants offer a Tilboðsréttir, a scaled-down menu for the budget-conscious (from Ikr800 to 1000 for lunch and Ikr1100 to 1700 for dinner). However, many less pretentious places serve better food for similar prices.

Restaurants *Potturinn og Pannan* (☎ 551 1690), at Brautarholt 22, has an all-day soup and salad buffet (Ikr790). In the evening it serves fish, lamb, and beef dishes for about Ikr1800. *Ítalía* (☎ 562 4630), Laugavegur 11, has pasta dishes for Ikr1000 to 1200 and pizzas for about Ikr1200. In the evening, there's an Italian buffet for Ikr1500.

Sjanghæ at Laugavegur 28 serves Westernised Mandarin Chinese dishes. Evening meals cost from Ikr1300 to 1800. For Chinese, Thai, Malaysian and Japanese options, there's *Asía* (☎ 562 6210) at Laugavegur 10. Lunch costs about Ikr450.

The excellent vegetarian restaurant, *Á nœstu grösum*, (☎ 552 8410), on the corner of Laugavegur and Klapparstígur, serves macrobiotic and standard vegetarian meals with coffee and cake for under Ikr1000. It's open for lunch and dinner, but it's closed on Saturday.

For good Mexican food, try *Amigo's* at Tryggvagata 8 (☎ 511 1333), open for lunch and dinner.

Acceptable pizzas are served at *Pizzahúsið*, Grensásvegur 10. The US chain *Pizza Hut* at the Hotel Esja offers a self-serve salad bar, pizzas, pasta, beer and wine. You'll spend about Ikr1500 for a meal including beer. *Pizza 67* at Tryggvagata 26 is a hippy-theme pizza-pub, where small pizzas cost about Ikr700.

Cafés There are several pub-style cafés serving inexpensive food. *Kaffi Austurstræti* at Austurstræti 6 has great value daily specials (soup and a main fish course) for Ikr700 to 800. The popular but stuffy *Café*

ICELAND

Paris is at Austurstræti 14; you'll get a cafetiere for Ikr180 and light continental lunches for Ikr400 to 600. A similar option is *Café au Lait* at Hafnarstræti 11. Alternatively, there's Iceland's only bohemian café (complete with art gallery), *Café Sólon Íslandus*, at Bankastræti 7.

For delicious Thai food, try *Thailandi* at Laugavegur 11 (the entrance is on Smiðjustígur), where you'll pay Ikr500 to 600 for mild to spicy set dishes.

Fast Food For a quick bite on the run, nothing beats the snack kiosks on Lækjartorg and the Austurstræti mall. At *Svarta Pannan*, Hafnarstræti 17, you'll pay Ikr400 to 700 for fried snacks and burgers. For a change, try the pita sandwiches at *Pítan*, Skipholt 50c.

There are two *McDonald's*, one on Austurstræti, and the other at Suðurlandsbraut and Skeiðarvogur. A quarterpounder, medium chips and soft drink costs Ikr599. Otherwise, try the *Kentucky Fried Chicken* at Faxafen 2.

Self-Catering *Hagkaup* supermarkets are located in the Kringlan Centre and on Laugavegur near Snorrabraut. Both have salad bars for Ikr198/299/499 for small/ medium/large serves, but they're only open during shopping hours. There's also a half-price bakery on Suðurlandsbraut (open daily).

Entertainment

Cinemas Reykjavík has five cinemas and there's another in nearby Breiðholt. Listings, times and addresses can be found in daily newspapers. All cinemas charge Ikr600 per film and screen films in their original language with Icelandic subtitles.

Discos For an unforgettable cultural experience, try a Friday night crawl with the beautiful youth through Reykjavík's most 'in' bars and discos. Discos aren't for the destitute; cover charges range from Ikr700 to 1000 and there are queues on weekend evenings. The most frantic is *Tunglið* at Lækjargata 2. Other popular spots include *Óðal* at

Austurstræti 12a (free admission), *Ingólfskaffi* at Hverfisgata 8-10 and *Hótel Ísland* at Ármúli 9. There's also a weekend gay disco on the 2nd floor of *22*, at Laugavegur 22

Theatre There are several theatre groups, an opera, a symphony orchestra and a dance company. Important box offices are: the National Theatre (☎ 551 1200) Hverfisgata 19, and Kaffileikhúsið (☎ 551 9055) Vesturgata 3. For other venues, check daily papers for information or contact the tourist information centre for details and tickets. In summer, the Viking-theme tourist show *Tjarnarbíó* (Light Nights) plays Monday to Saturday from 9 pm at Tjarnargata 10e.

Pubs Some of the best pubs include the enduring *Gaukur á Stöng* at Tryggvagata 22, the trendy *Glaumbar* at Tryggvagata 20, the wild *22* at Laugavegur 22, and the Irish-style *Dubliner* at Hafnarstræti 4, where you'll also get bar meals. The pub/cafe *Svarta kaffið* at Laugavegur 54 serves the cheapest beer in Reykjavík, daily between 6 and 9 pm (Ikr350 for half a litre).

Getting There & Away

Air Reykjavík city airport serves all domestic flights and flights to and from the Faroe Islands, Narsarsuaq and Kulusuk (both in Greenland). All other flights operate through Keflavík international airport. Icelandair (☎ 505 0300/0100; fax 505 0350) has an office at Laugavegur 7 in central Reykjavík.

Bus Long-distance buses use the BSÍ terminal (☎ 552 2300) at Vatnsmýrarvegur 10. In the summer, daily services ply between Reykjavík and Akureyri, Mývatn, Skaftafell, Höfn, Akranes, Borgarnes, Reykholt, Þorlákshöfn, Reykjanes and Snæfellsnes (connecting with services to Ísafjörður via the ferry from Stykkishólmur). Travellers between Reykjavík and Egilsstaðir must overnight in Akureyri, Mývatn or Höfn.

Boat The car and passenger ferry *Akraborg* (☎ 431 1095) does four trips daily between Reykjavík and Akranes (Ikr650 one way).

Take any bus numbered between No 1 and No 7 to the Lækjartorg bus terminal, then walk to Faxagarður. Ferries to Viðey (☎ 562 8000) depart several times daily from Sundahöfn harbour (☎ 852 0099; Ikr400 return). To get to the harbour take bus No 4 from Lækjartorg.

Getting Around

To/From the Airport The Flybus to Keflavík international airport leaves Hótel Loftleiðir 2½ hours prior to international departures The 50-minute journey costs Ikr600. From 15 June to 31 August, the bus leaves from the Laugardalur Youth Hostel daily at 4.45 am, then picks up at the Grand Hotel Reykjavík and Hótel Loftleiðir. Buses from Keflavík airport into town leave about 45 minutes after the arrival of an international flight.

Bus Reykjavík's excellent city bus system runs from 6.45 am to 1 am. Buses pick up and drop passengers only at designated stops which are marked with the letters SVR. For information call ☎ 551 2700. The two central terminals are at Hlemmur near the corner of Laugavegur and Rauðarárstígur, and on Lækjargata near Lækjartorg. The fare is Ikr120 (no change given), but *skiptimiði* (transfer tickets) are available. The Reykjavík Tourist Card includes a bus pass. The museum bus visits most museums, operating daily between 21 June and 31 August from 1 to 5 pm.

Taxi Reykjavík is small but taxis will be handy if you have a lot of luggage or you're catching an airport bus.

Since there's no tipping, taxi fares actually work out cheaper than in the USA or most of Europe.

There are five taxi companies: Hreyfill (☎ 558 5522), Bæjarleiðir (☎ 553 3500), BSR (☎ 561 0000), Borgarbíll (☎ 552 2440) and BSH (☎ 565 0666).

Bicycle Bicycles may be hired from Borgarhjól (☎ 551 6577), Hverfisgata 50, as well as from the youth hostel on Sundlaugavegur

and at the Laugardalur camping ground, all at Ikr1000 per day.

AROUND REYKJAVÍK

Blue Lagoon

The Blue Lagoon (Bláa Lónið) isn't a lagoon, but rather a pale blue 20°C pool of effluent from the Svartsengi power plant, 70 km south-west of Reykjavík. Its deposits of silica mud combined with an organic soup of dead algae have been known to relieve psoriasis.

A swim can be an ethereal experience with clouds of vapour rising and parting at times to reveal the stacks of the power plant and moss-covered lava in the background.

Bring enough shampoo for several rinses or your hair will be left a brick-like mass after swimming.

The bath house is open from 10 am to 10 pm daily in summer and shorter hours in winter. Admission is Ikr350.

Getting There & Away From BSÍ in Reykjavík, take one of three daily Grindavík buses. The one-way fare is Ikr500.

The South

THE GOLDEN TRIANGLE

The term 'Golden Triangle' refers to Gullfoss, Geysir and Þingvellir, the 'Big Three' destinations for Icelandair's stopover visitors.

Things to See

If Iceland has a star attraction, it's **Gullfoss**, where the river Hvitá drops 32 metres in two falls. Ten km down the road is Geysir, after which all the world's spouting hot springs are named. The **Great Geysir** died earlier this century, plugged by debris tossed in to encourage it to perform. Fortunately, it has a faithful stand-in, **Strokkur** (Butter Churn), which spouts approximately every three minutes.

Þingvellir has been the most significant historical site in Iceland since the Alþing was established here in 930. The site was selected for its topography, acoustics and proximity to population. In 1928 its history and wealth of natural attractions led to it being set apart as Iceland's first national park.

Most of the historical buildings are concentrated in a small area of the park and the remainder is left to nature. A maze of hiking trails crisscrosses the plain and leads through the woods to points of interest or simply through scenic areas. Of particular interest are **Almannagjá**, a large tectonic rift; **Lögberg** (Law Rock), which served as the podium for the Alþing from 930 to 1271; **Þingvallavatn**, Iceland's largest lake; and the clear blue wishing spring, **Peningagjá**.

Places to Stay & Eat

Þingvellir has the *Hótel Valhöll* (☎ 482 2622; fax 483 4775) near the church, with three dining rooms and fairly elegant accommodation for Ikr6800/8500 single/double occupancy. Nearby at Leirur is the main camping ground (☎ 482 2660) and a petrol station selling basic snacks. At Geysir is the summer hotel, *Hótel Geysir* (☎ 486 8915; fax 486 8715). Sleeping-bag accommodation costs Ikr600 (floor) or Ikr1200 (bed) and single/double rooms cost Ikr2200/3300. The souvenir shop/cafe sells burgers, chips etc. Camping costs Ikr350 per person.

Getting There & Away

The popular Golden Circle day tours offered by Reykjavík Excursions and BSÍ cost Ikr4600 per person without lunch. They leave Reykjavík daily in summer at 9 am and 8.45 am, respectively. Tours cover the standard route through the Eden souvenir shop in Hveragerði, the Kerið crater, the southern bishopric at Skálholt, Gullfoss, Geysir and Þingvellir.

BSÍ tours has a twice-daily scheduled bus service between Reykjavík, Gullfoss and Geysir, which depart daily at 9 and 11.30 am from the BSÍ terminal (tour price Ikr2420). Public buses travel between Reykjavík and Þingvellir twice daily in summer, departing BSÍ at 8.45 am (Ikr1600 return) and 1.30 pm (Ikr1000 return).

VESTMANNAEYJAR

The 16 Vestmannaeyjar islands were formed by submarine volcanoes between 10,000 and 5000 years ago and, in 1963, the world witnessed on film the birth of its newest island, Surtsey. Only Heimaey (the Home Island), with 5000 residents, supports a permanent population. Characterised by brightly coloured roofs, the town spreads across about a third of the island. Its spectacular setting is defined by the *klettur* (rock) escarpments that rise abruptly behind the well-sheltered harbour, the steaming red peak of Eldfell and the conical hill Helgafell.

Things to See

The **Vestmannaeyjar Natural History Museum** has an aquarium of bizarre Icelandic fish and a wonderful collection of polished agate and jasper slices, some of which form natural landscape paintings. It's open daily between 1 May and 15 September, from 11 am to 5 pm; admission is Ikr200. The worthwhile **folk museum** upstairs in the library also costs Ikr200. The **Volcano Show** in the cinema on Heiðarvegur costs Ikr500 admission.

Hiking

Hiking opportunities abound on the island, including the walk to Stórhöfði and climbs of Helgafell, Eldfell and Dalfjall.

Organised Tours

For sightseeing, sea-fishing and whale-watching from the boat *Lubba*, contact Ólafur Týr Guðjónsson (☎ 481 2333). Per person, trips cost Ikr1200 for the first hour and Ikr800 for each additional hour (minimum four people). Landings on some islands are possible. PH Tours (☎ 481 1515; fax 481 2007) at Hotel Bræðraborg use the large boat *Viking* (Ikr1600). Westmann Islands Hiking Tours (☎ 481 2269) charges just Ikr700 per person (minimum three people).

Places to Stay & Eat

The camping ground in Herjólfsdalur (☎ 481 2922) costs Ikr200 per tent and Ikr200 per

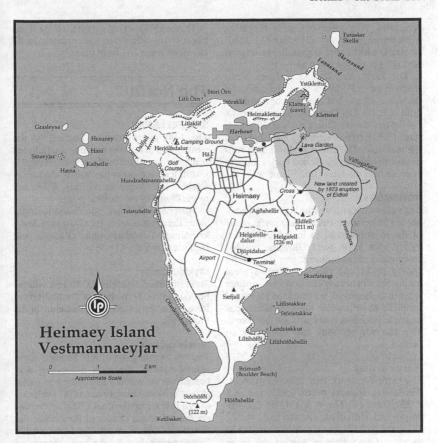

**Heimaey Island
Vestmannaeyjar**

0   1   2 km
Approximate Scale

person, including showers and use of laundry facilities. *Faxi Youth Hostel* (☎ 481 2915), at Faxastígur 38, is open from 1 June to 15 September. Be warned that it fills up quickly when the ferry arrives. Sleeping-bag accommodation costs Ikr1000 at *Brekastígur 26* (☎ 481 2269).

Gistiheimilið Heimir (☎ 481 1515; fax 481 2007), Herjólfsgata 4, offers sleeping-bag accommodation for Ikr1900 and single/double rooms for Ikr4300/6100. The expensive *Hótel Þórshamar* (☎ 481 2900; fax 481 1696) has a guesthouse, *Sunnuhöll*, with sleeping-bag accommodation for Ikr1250. The

popular *Gistiheimilið Hvíld* (☎ 481 1230), at Höfðavegur 16, costs Ikr1900 for a bed.

For Vestmannaeyjar delicacies, try the *HB* restaurant/pub at Heiðarvegur 3. More basic are *Pizza 67*, Heiðarvegur 5, and the fast food at the *Esso* petrol station at the top of the harbour. *Turninn*, at Bárustígur 1, serves snacks and coffee from 7 am. You'll find the peculiar-looking *Vöruval* supermarket on Vesturvegur.

Getting There & Away
Flugleiðir flies at least once daily to/from Reykjavík but poor weather can interrupt

schedules. A cheaper option is Flugfélag Vestmannaeyja (☎ 481 3255; fax 481 2652) in Hella, with charter flights for as little as Ikr1300 per person one way.

The ferry *Herjólfur* sails from Vestmannaeyjar to Þorlákshöfn on the mainland daily at 8.15 am and returns from Þorlákshöfn at noon. On Thursday (summer only), Friday and Sunday, there's a second departure at 3.30 pm from Heimaey and 7 pm from the mainland. The fare is Ikr1300. BSÍ runs buses between Reykjavík and Þorlákshöfn to connect with the ferry (Ikr550 one way).

ÞÓRSMÖRK

The valley of Þórsmörk (the Woods of Thor), about 130 km south-east of Reykjavík, is one of the most beautiful in Iceland, a glacial valley with scrub birch, flowers, braided rivers and clear streams surrounded by snowy peaks and glaciers. There's great hiking but it gets busy and noisy on summer weekends. Þórsmörk is a terminus for two of Iceland's most popular hikes, Landmannalaugar to Þórsmörk (see Fjallabak Reserve in The Interior section) and Þórsmörk to Skógar.

Places to Stay

The three Þórsmörk area huts – Þórsmörk (Ferðafélag Íslands, ☎ 568 2533; fax 568 2535), Básar (Útivist, ☎ 561 4330; fax 561 4606) and Húsadalur (Austurleið, ☎ 577 1717; fax 577 1718) – are often crowded in summer. Camp sites at any of the three centres cost Ikr400 per person.

There's also a cosy turf-roofed *youth hostel* (☎ 487 8499) at nearby Fljótsdalur.

Getting There & Away

In summer, buses leave BSÍ in Reykjavík daily at 8.30 am and Monday to Thursday at 5 pm, arriving at Húsadalur (over the hill from Þórsmörk) at around noon and 9 pm, respectively. Buses depart Húsadalur for Reykjavík at 8 am (Monday to Friday; three hours) and 3.30 pm (daily; 3½ hours). On Friday nights, there's a special weekenders' bus departing Reykjavík at 8 pm (three hours). The return fare is Ikr4300.

To reach Fljótsdalur, get off the Ring Road bus at Hvolsvöllur, then walk or hitch the 27 km along route 261 from there.

The North

SNÆFELLSNES

The 1446-metre volcano Snæfell, at the western end of the 100-km-long Snæfellsnes peninsula, is capped by the glacier Snæfellsjökull. It served as the gateway to the underworld in Jules Verne's adventure, *A Journey to the Centre of the Earth*.

Most of Snæfellsnes' population is strung along the north coast in the villages of Stykkishólmur, Grundarfjörður, Ólafsvík and Hellissandur-Rif.

Stykkishólmur

Stykkishólmur, Snæfellsnes' largest village, lies on the southern shore of Breiðafjörður; from there, ferries go to Brjánslækur in the Westfjords.

Snæfellsjökull

Visitors wanting to climb Snæfell have several options, the most interesting way being from the western end of the peninsula, along the Móðulækur stream (4WD vehicles can go four km up the track). This route goes via the red scoria craters of Rauðhólar, the waterfall Klukkufoss and the scenic valley Eysteinsdalur. It will take you a couple of days, so make sure you're fully equipped. You may need crampons and ice axes to reach the summit.

Tours are operated by Tryggvi Konráðsson/Ferðaþjónustan Snjófell (☎ 435 6783), Arnarstapi and Gistiheimilið Höfði (☎ 436 1650), Ólafsvík.

Places to Stay & Eat

Stykkishólmur has a youth hostel (☎ 438 1095), a camping ground and an up-market hotel. *Hótel Stykkishólmur* (☎ 438 1330; fax 438 1579), has singles/doubles for Ikr6400/8600, including breakfast. *Skjöldur* (☎ 438 1528) at Helgafellsveit, eight km south of Stykkishólmur, has sleeping-bag accommodation for only Ikr900.

In Ólafsvík, *Gistiheimilið Höfði* (☎ 436 1650; fax 436 1651) offers comfortable singles/doubles for Ikr3300/4600 and sleeping-bag space for Ikr1500. In the same building is *Grillskálinn*, which serves basic meals. The *camping ground* lies one km east of town.

Ferðaþjónustan Snjófell (☎ 435 6783; fax 435 6795) in Arnarstapi has singles/doubles for Ikr2100/3800 and sleeping-bag accommodation for Ikr1000 (floor) or Ikr1500 (bed). It also has a restaurant.

Getting There & Away
The daily bus journeys between Reykjavík and Stykkishólmur take three hours and costs Ikr2000. Buses between Reykjavík, Stykkishólmur and Ólafsvík meet at a remote intersection called Vegamót (meaning 'intersection') where passengers sort themselves out according to destination. Explanations are given only in Icelandic, so stay on your toes.

The buses leaving Reykjavík at 7 am on Monday, Wednesday, Friday and Saturday, and the Saturday service leaving at 1 pm, connect with the car ferry *Baldur* to the Westfjords.

THE WESTFJORDS
Extending claw-like towards Greenland, the Westfjords peninsula, attached to the mainland by a narrow isthmus, is the most rugged and remote corner of Iceland.

Ísafjörður
Ísafjörður, the Westfjords' commercial centre, is the region's largest settlement, with about 3500 people. The **Westfjords Maritime Museum**, one of Iceland's finest, has historical displays and lovely old photographs of the early settlement. It's out near the point of the spit at Neðstikaupstaður and is open daily from 1 to 5 pm (Ikr200 admission).

Places to Stay & Eat The summer hotel *Mentaskólinn Torfnes* (☎ 456 4485; fax 456 4767), west of town, has doubles without bath for Ikr6500; sleeping-bag accommodation starts at Ikr850.

There are two *camping grounds*, one in Tungudalur (☎ 456 4485; Ikr450 per person) four km from town and one behind the *Mentaskólinn Torfnes* (Ikr450 per person). *Hótel Ísafjörður* (☎ 456 4111; fax 456 4767) is a typically sterile Icelandic hotel, with doubles for Ikr9400.

There's also *Fönðurloftið* (☎ 456 3659 or 436 3970) at Mjallargata 5, with sleeping-bag accommodation and cooking facilities for Ikr1200.

Gallery Pizza (Mánagata 1), *Pizza 67* (Hafnarstræti 12) and *Tæ Væ* (Aðalstræti 22b), a Thai restaurant, are all centrally located.

Hornstrandir
The wildest corner of the Westfjords, the uninhabited Hornstrandir peninsula, offers excellent hiking and camping. It's accessible on the *Fagranes* ferry from Ísafjörður (Ikr3100 one way). Accommodation and food aren't available on Hornstrandir.

Látrabjarg
The cliffs of Látrabjarg have one of the greatest populations of birds in Iceland. Lying at the westernmost end of the Westfjords, the 12-km-long cliffs range from 40 to 511 metres high. Puffins and seals are usually the main attractions.

There's a guesthouse (☎ 456 1575) at Breiðavík 12 km away (sleeping-bag accommodation from Ikr850). On request, the Brjánslækur-Breiðavík bus will continue to Látrabjarg for Ikr170 per person (each way), stopping for up to three hours before returning to Breiðavík.

Getting There & Away
Air Flugfélag Norðurlands has daily (except Saturday) flights between Akureyri and Ísafjörður for Ikr6500/13,000 one way/ return. Between Reykjavík and Ísafjörður, Flugleiðir has one to three flights daily costing Ikr6100/7400.

Bus Buses between Reykjavík and Ísafjörður, requiring a change at Hólmavík, leave Reykjavík on Tuesday and Friday (and Sunday in summer) at 10 am. Alternatively, on Monday, Wednesday and Friday (and Saturday in mid-summer) at 7 am you can go from Reykjavík to Ísafjörður via the Stykkishólmur (Snæfellsnes) to Brjánslækur (Westfjords) ferry.

Travelling between Ísafjörður and Akureyri requires connections in both Hólmavík and Brú.

Boat The car and passenger ferry *Baldur* (Ikr 1300) operates between Stykkishólmur and Brjánslækur twice daily between 1 May and 31 August, connecting with buses as described above.

AKUREYRI

Akureyri (Meadow Sandspit), 250 km northeast of Reykjavík, is the best of urban Iceland, and sunny days are common in this small and tidy town beneath perpetually snow-capped peaks. Along the streets, in flower boxes and in private gardens, grow Iceland's most colourful blooms, and the summer air is filled with the fresh scent of sticky birch.

Things to See

The geological theme that pervades modern church architecture in Iceland has not been lost on **Akureyrarkirkja**. Less blatantly 'basalt' than Reykjavík's Hallgrímskirkja, Akureyrarkirkja is basalt, nonetheless. Notice the angel sculpture by renowned Danish sculptor Bertel Thorvaldsen. The church is open daily from 10 am to noon and 2 to 4 pm.

Most of Akureyri's **museums** are the homes of 'local boys made good'. Icelanders proudly commemorate their artists, poets and authors but unless you have a particular admiration for their work, some may be of limited interest. The best of them is **Nonnahús**, at Aðalstræti 45b, the childhood home of children's writer Reverend Jón Sveinsson (nicknamed 'Nonni') who lived from 1857 to 1944. This cosy old home, built in 1850, is a good example of an early village dwelling. It is open daily from 1 June to 31 August from 10 am to 5 pm; admission is Ikr200.

The **Minjasafn Akureyrar** (Akureyri Folk Museum), at Aðalstræti 58, houses artwork and historical household items. From 1 June to 15 September, it's open daily 11 am to 5 pm. Admission is Ikr250.

The **Lystigarður Akureyrar** (botanical gardens) were opened in 1912. They include every species native to Iceland and high-latitude and high-altitude plants from around the world. They're open from 1 June to 31 October from 8 am to 10 pm weekdays and 9 am to 10 pm on weekends.

Places to Stay

The spacious central *camping ground* costs Ikr400 per person. Laundry facilities cost Ikr500 for washing and drying.

Advance booking for the central *Akureyri Youth Hostel* (☎ 462 3657) at Stórholt 1 is advised. The *Lónsá Youth Hostel* (☎ 462 5037) is at Glæsibæjarhreppur, three km from Akureyri. Up until 5 pm, city buses stop within 300 metres; otherwise, phone ahead to be picked up.

All mid-range accommodation is guesthouse-style and prices are controlled by the municipality. The maximum for single/double rooms is Ikr2900/4200 in made-up beds and Ikr1500 for sleeping-bag accommodation.

A recommended guesthouse with both rooms and sleeping-bag accommodation is the central *Gistiheimilið Salka* (☎ 461 2340) at Skipagata 1. Even nicer is the *Ás Guesthouse* (☎ 461 2248), with two locations: Skipagata 4 and Hafnarstræti 77. Both have sleeping-bag accommodation and cooking facilities.

Perhaps the best deal in town is the *Sólgarður* (☎ 461 1133) at Brekkugata 6, which has single/double rooms for Ikr2500/3800 and sleeping-bag accommodation (with cooking facilities) for Ikr1250.

More sleeping-bag accommodation is found at *Bakki* (☎ 462 5774) at Bakkahlíð 18; *Brekkusel* (☎ 462 3961) at Hrafnagilsstræti 23; *Guesthouse Súlur* (☎ 461 1160)

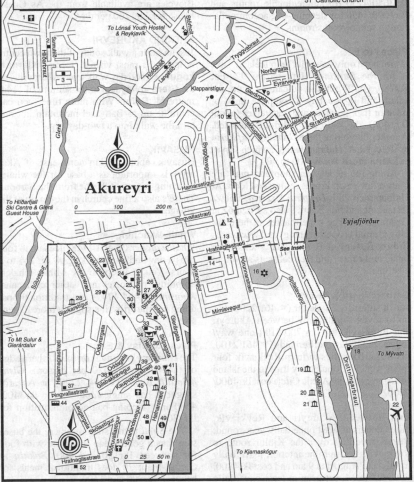

PLACES TO STAY
2 Sunnuhlíð 5
3 Bakki
4 Youth Hostel
5 Langahlíð 6
12 Camping Ground
14 Brekkusel
15 Guesthouse Súlur
23 Sólgarður
25 Hótel Norðurland & Pizza 67
26 Studió Íbúðir
32 Gistiheimilið Salka
33 Ás Skipagata
37 Gula Villan
38 Gilsbakkavegur 13
40 Hótel KEA & Súlnaberg Cafeteria
42 Hótel Harpa
48 Ás Hafnarstræti
50 Hótel Óðal
52 Edda Hotel

PLACES TO EAT
9 Greifinn Restaurant
31 Einars Bakery
35 Fiðlarinn
36 Dropinn Pizzeria & Pub
41 Bautinn Restaurant

OTHER
1 Glerá Church
6 Hagkaup Supermarket
7 Folda Factory Shop
8 View Disc & Helgi the Lean Statue
10 Police
11 Sports Stadium
13 KEA Supermarket
16 Botanical Gardens
17 Laxdalshús
18 Esso Petrol Station
19 Friðbjarnarhús Museum
20 Nonnahús Museum
21 Minjasafið á Akureyri (Akureyri Folk Museum)
22 Akureyri Airport
24 Cinema
27 Búnaðarbanki Bank
28 Davíðshús Museum
29 Town Library & District Archives
30 Landsbanki Íslands Bank
34 Post Office
39 Akureyri Art Museum
43 Stone Museum & Shop
44 Swimming Pool
45 Akureyrarkirkja
46 Natural History Museum
47 Matthías Jochumsson Memorial Museum (Sigurhæðir)
49 Tourist Office & Long-distance Bus Terminal
51 Catholic Church

ICELAND

at Þórunnarstræti 93; **Gula Villan** (☎ 461 2860) at Þingvallastræti 14; **Sunnuhlíð 5** (☎ 462 2236); and **Langahlíð 6** (☎ 462 3472). Of these, Brekkusel, Gula Villan and Langahlíð 6 lack cooking facilities.

The Bavarian-looking **Hótel Óðal** (☎ 461 1900; fax 461 1899), at Hafnarstræti 67 near the bus terminal, costs Ikr9300/11;400 a single/double. The **Edda Hotel** (☎ 461 1434; fax 461 1423) in the grammar school charges Ikr3650/4750 for single/double rooms and Ikr1000/1450 for sleeping-bag accommodation in schoolrooms/rooms.

Places to Eat

If you have only one splurge in Iceland, save it for the **Bautinn**, Hafnarstræti 92. For Ikr780, you'll get all-you-can-eat soup and salad, and if you buy a complete meal of meat or fish, potatoes and vegetables (about Ikr1400), the soup and salad are included. Another bargain is the **Súlnaberg Cafeteria** at Hótel KEA, Hafnarstræti 89, which serves cafeteria meals for Ikr500 to 900.

Along the pedestrian shopping mall are quite a few small kiosks selling fast food. At Hafnarstræti 98 is **Dropinn Pizzeria**, a pizza restaurant and bar. There's also a **Pizza 67** at Geislagata 7. The supermarket at the camping ground is open evenings and weekends. **Einars Bakery** at Brekkugata 7 sells fresh bread and cakes, and free coffee is served to customers.

Getting There & Away

Air In summer, Flugleiðir (☎ 461 2200) has up to seven flights daily between Akureyri and Reykjavík for Ikr6700/8100 one way/ return. Flugfélag Norðurlands (☎ 461 2100; fax 461 2106) flies to/from Reykjavík four times weekly. Popular day trips to the island of Grímsey on the Arctic Circle cost Ikr4600/ 9200.

Bus Between Akureyri and Reykjavík, buses depart at least once daily year-round. Buses travelling over the Kjölur route to Reykjavík, through the interior, leave daily in July and August at 9 am and cost Ikr4800.

Buses to Mývatn run at least once daily

between 20 May and 30 September. From 18 June to 31 August buses to Húsavík depart once or twice daily (except Sunday).

Boat The **Sæfari** sails to Grímsey Island on Monday and Thursday at 9 am, returning from Grímsey at 7 pm. The trip takes five hours each way and costs Ikr3200 return.

Getting Around

Bicycles are available from the Ás Guesthouse for Ikr1200 per day.

AROUND AKUREYRI

Just an hour's walk south of the town centre is Iceland's most visited 'forest', **Kjarnaskógur**. A good day walk from Akureyri is up the **Glerá valley** and to the summit of 1144-metre **Mt Sulur**. With more time, you can continue up to Baugasel mountain hut and turn the walk into a two-day trip.

HÚSAVÍK

Húsavík, about 50 km north-east of Akureyri, is important as a base for the whale-watching trips that depart from the harbour. There's also a fine church in the centre of the village.

Whale-Watching

Whalewatcher (☎ 464 1748) does up to four trips a day and charges Ikr2500 for 2½ to 3 hours. You're likely to see Minke whales, dolphins, porpoises and other cetaceans. **Knörinn** (☎ 464 1741) is a traditional boat doing similar trips; it's slightly more expensive.

Places to Stay & Eat

The **camping ground** is on the northern edge of the village (Ikr450 per person). **Gistiheimilið Árból** (☎ 464 2220) at Ásgarðsvegur 2 has singles/doubles for Ikr3400/ 4500 and sleeping-bag accommodation for Ikr1300.

The **Shell** petrol station (where the buses stop) has a good value snack bar with food for between Ikr150 and 400. **Bakkin** at Garðarsbraut 20 does traditional meals for between Ikr800 and 1500.

Getting There & Away

Buses to Akureyri depart at least once daily from 18 June to 31 August. During the same period, there are daily buses to Ásbyrgi. Buses to Reykjahlíð (Mývatn) depart up to three times daily in summer, otherwise only once on weekdays. The cost is Ikr880 and the trip takes from one to 2½ hours.

MÝVATN

The Mývatn basin sits on the spreading zone of the mid-Atlantic ridge and although most of the interesting sights are volcanic or geothermal features, the centrepiece of the reserve is the blue Lake Mývatn itself and its diverse waterfowl. Here, travellers can settle in and spend a week camping, sightseeing and relaxing. The main population and service centre, **Reykjahlíð**, was one of the area's Age of Settlement farms. Visit the tourist office for free entry to the **Mývatn Museum**.

Around the Lake

From the petrol station or camping grounds in Reykjahlíð you can hire a mountain bike for the 37-km trip around the lake (Ikr1000/1500 for six/12 hours).

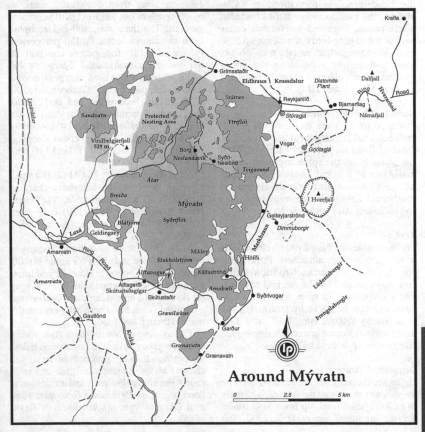

Around Mývatn

0   2.5   5 km

Several side trips will take you away from the main roads. The most interesting begins at **Stóragjá**, a rather scummy hot spring near the village. After a few minutes, the walk dead ends at a pipeline. There you should turn left and walk several hundred metres until the track turns southward. It crosses an overgrown lava field before reaching **Grjótagjá**, a hot spring in a cave, then continues to the prominent tephra crater, **Hverfjall**, and **Dimmuborgir**, a maze of oddly shaped lava pillars and crags created 2000 years ago.

Other sites of interest around the lake include the forested lava headland of **Höfði**; the *klasar* pinnacle formations at **Kálfaströnd**; the pseudocraters at **Skútustaðir**, where ponds, bogs and marshlands create havens for nesting birds; the climb up 529-metre **Vindbelgjarfjall**; and the high-density waterfowl nesting zone along the northwestern shore (off-road entry is restricted between 15 May and 20 July).

Námafjall & Hverarönd
Produced by a fissure eruption, the pastel-pink coloured Námafjall ridge lies south of the Ring Road six km east of Reykjahlíð. It sits squarely on the spreading zone of the mid-Atlantic rift and contains numerous steaming vents. At its foot is the Hverarönd geothermal field with numerous fumaroles and solfataras (sulphurous vents).

Krafla
The incredible steaming fissure **Leirhnjúkur** is Krafla's primary attraction. From there you can look out across **Kröfluöskjunni**, lava flows created by the original Mývatnseldar eruptions and from the 1975 eruptions, overlain in places by steaming 1984 lava. Nearby **Viti**, meaning 'hell', is a 320-metre-wide explosion crater containing a hot lake; it now appears to be inactive.

Organised Tours
Organised tours operate only in summer. The three-hour tour around the lake departs daily from Reykjahlíð (pick-up from Skútustaðir may be arranged) and costs Ikr2300. The

Grand Mývatn tour (Ikr3600) leaves Hotel Reynihlíð daily at 8.45 am, picking up again at Eldá (Gistiheimilið Bjarg, see Places to Stay & Eat). The morning segment is a 3½-hour version of the round-the-lake tour; in the afternoon, the tour visits Krafla. A Mývatn-Krafla tour operates from Akureyri. The excellent seven-hour Gjástykki Rift Zone volcano tour (Ikr3600) includes hiking. It starts from Eldá, between 15 July and 20 August, on Monday and Thursday at 8.45 am.

Places to Stay & Eat
Reykjahlíð Reserve regulations prohibit camping away from designated areas, so most travellers use the Reykjahlíð camping grounds. The main one, 300 metres uphill from the church, costs Ikr450 per person. Private cabins for four people cost Ikr1100 per person. *Gistiheimilið Bjarg* (☎ 464 4220), also known as Eldá, charges the same rates for camping by the lakeshore, Ikr3300/4350 for singles/doubles and Ikr1250 for sleeping-bag accommodation. Also in the village is *Gistiheimilið Vogar* (☎ 464 4399), with rooms for Ikr2250 per person, sleeping-bag accommodation for Ikr1350 and camping for Ikr400.

Hótel Reykjahlíð (☎ 464 4142) is a small 12-room hotel on the lakeshore charging Ikr5000/7500 a single/double. The larger *Hótel Reynihlíð* (☎ 464 4170) costs from Ikr4400/5400 single/double, including breakfast.

In the Hótel Reynihlíð dining room you can order coffee and chips for about Ikr400. *Gamli Bærinn*, opposite Hótel Reynihlíð, is a popular new restaurant with goulash soup for Ikr490. The only other place is *Hverinn*, a glorified snack bar where campers can dry out and munch fast food.

Try to sample *hverabrauð* (hot spring bread), a gooey cake-like concoction baked underground using geothermal heat. It's cheaper at the supermarket than at tourist shops. For smoked salmon and arctic char at good prices, try *Reykhúsið Geiteyjarströnd* near Dimmuborgir, six km south of Reykjahlíð.

Skútustaðir Skútustaðir at the southern end of the lake has a general store, cafeteria, and a snack bar at the petrol station. The school, *Skútustaðaskóli* (☎ 464 4279), charges Ikr2500/3800 single/double and Ikr1000 (floor) or 1300 (bed) for sleeping-bag accommodation. Sleeping-bag accommodation at the community centre *Skjólbrekka* (☎ 464 4202) costs Ikr1000. The *Skútustaðir Farm Guesthouse* (☎ 464 4212) has single/double rooms for Ikr3200/ 4400, sleeping-bag accommodation for Ikr1300 and camping for Ikr450 per person.

Getting There & Away
Air In summer, there are daily Mýflug (☎ 464 4107 at Reykjahlíð airfield) flights between Reykjavík and Mývatn for Ikr7600/ 14,000 one way/return.

Bus The main long-distance bus terminal is at Reykjahlíð, but buses between Mývatn and Akureyri also stop at Skútustaðir. In the summer, there's at least one bus daily doing the 1½-hour trip between Akureyri and Mývatn (Ikr1200). There are also buses from Mývatn to Egilsstaðir (daily in summer; Ikr2200) and Húsavík (not Sunday). Twice a week there are departures to/from Reykjavík via Sprengisandur (see Sprengisandur Route in The Interior section for details).

JÖKULSÁRGLJÚFUR NATIONAL PARK
The nearly unpronounceable name ('YEW-kl-sour-GLYU-fr') of this national park means 'glacial river canyon', but this belies the fact that it contains a myriad of other wonderful natural features. Sometimes known as 'Iceland's Grand Canyon', Jökul-sárgljúfur is also known for its sticky-birch forests, bizarre rock formations and **Ásbyrgi**, a canyon formed by a glacial burst 200 km away. The swirls, spirals, rosettes, honeycombs and columns at **Hljóðaklettar** (Echo Rocks) are unique in the world, and near the park's southern boundary is **Dettifoss**, Europe's most powerful waterfall.

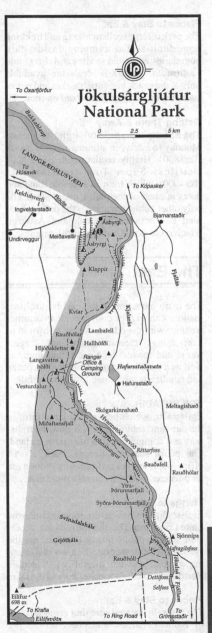

Jökulsárgljúfur National Park

Places to Stay & Eat

The park offers excellent hiking and trekking opportunities but camping inside park boundaries is limited to sites at *Ásbyrgi* and *Vesturdalur* (Ikr500). Meals are available only at the snack bar, supermarket and petrol station at the *Ásbyrgi farmstead* on route 85.

Getting There & Away

The BSÍ day tours to Jökulsárgljúfur operate Monday to Friday in summer from Húsavík (Ikr3800). Highly recommended is Eldá's Dettifoss Super Tour from Mývatn (Ikr4000), which follows a remote route and takes in most of the park's major sites. The only other public transport is the daily scheduled bus between Húsavík and Ásbyrgi, which costs Ikr800 and takes 50 minutes.

The East

The main attraction in the east is sunshine; visitors can expect cool but clear summer weather with the odd rainy day thrown in to keep things interesting. Iceland's largest forest and longest lake are found here, as well as a wealth of rugged and remote peaks and headlands, and some lovely waterfalls.

EGILSSTAÐIR

Egilsstaðir, which began as a large farm in the late nineteenth century, is now the transport and commercial hub of eastern Iceland. The petrol station, cafeteria, bank, tourist office, supermarket and camping ground are all clustered near the central crossroads.

Things to See

Egilsstaðir sits beside the long and narrow **Lake Lögurinn**. The main attractions, accessible by car, public bus or tour bus, are the **Hallormsstaður woods** with a wooded camping ground; and the magnificent waterfall, **Hengifoss**, on the opposite shore of the lake.

Places to Stay & Eat

The centrally located *camping ground* is one of Iceland's nicest and costs Ikr450 per person. There's also sleeping-bag accommodation for Ikr900 and an eight-bed hut with cooking facilities for Ikr1000 per person.

The *Hotel Valaskjálf* (☎ 471 1500; fax 471 1501) charges Ikr7500 for the cheapest double and also has a cinema.

For meals, there's the bland Hotel Valaskjálf dining room, the *Söluskáli* (Esso) cafeteria near the camping ground (great pizza for about Ikr700), the *Shell* petrol station and the *Ormurinn* restaurant/bar. The *supermarket* is well stocked with travellers' supplies. Ask locally whether the farm market has reopened. In Fellabær (across the bridge) there's a good *Pizza 67*.

Getting There & Away

Air Flugleiðir has several flights daily between Reykjavík and Egilsstaðir for Ikr8200/9900 one way/return.

Bus In summer, it's possible to travel between Akureyri and Höfn via Egilsstaðir in one day. The main terminal is at the camping ground.

Between 3 June and 1 September the Seyðisfjörður bus runs at least once daily, Monday to Friday (30 minutes, Ikr800). On Wednesday, it does two additional runs in either direction in order to accommodate passengers travelling on the ferry *Norröna* between Iceland and mainland Europe. Buses also run once a day in July on Saturday and Sunday.

SEYÐISFJÖRÐUR

Seyðisfjörður, the terminal for ferries from the European mainland, is a pleasant introduction to Iceland for many travellers. It's an architecturally interesting town surrounded on three sides by mountains and on the other by a deep, 16-km-long fjord.

The bank is 300 metres from the dock. The information desk in the Smyril Line office will book your onward accommodation; there's also a tourist office at Norðurgata 3.

A great introduction to walking in Iceland is the popular trip up the valley Vestdalur and around Mt Bjólfur to the Seyðisfjörður-Egilsstaðir road.

Places to Stay

The *camping ground* is beside the Shell petrol station in the town. Otherwise, the best deals are the *Hafaldan Youth Hostel* (☎ 472 1410; fax 472 1486) and the nearby *Þórsmörk* (☎ 472 1324) farmhouse, with sleeping-bag accommodation for Ikr850 (floor) or Ikr1300 (bed). The pleasant and well-located *Hotel Snæfell* (☎ 472 1460) costs Ikr5100/6500 for singles/doubles.

Places to Eat

The only fully fledged restaurant is at the *Hotel Snæfell* but it's expensive. Alternatively, try the cafeterias at the *Shell* and *Esso* petrol stations.

Getting There & Away

For bus information, see the Egilsstaðir section. Details of the ferry service from mainland Europe are described in the Getting There & Away section earlier.

STAFAFELL

Stafafell, about 100 km south of Egilsstaðir, is a great hiking area with an excellent location between the lagoon **Lón** and the colourful **Lónsöræfi** mountains.

Organised Tours

Jeep tours to Kollumúli, in the Lónsöræfi mountains, are highly recommended. They cost Ikr2700 with Lónsöræfaferðir (☎ 478 1717, or arrange at the youth hostel).

Places to Stay & Eat

There's a *youth hostel*, *guest house* (Ikr2500/3600 single/double), *camping ground* (Ikr300) and cabins. Meals are available if you're staying in the youth hostel or guest house; they must be reserved in advance.

Getting There & Away

There's one daily bus to Egilsstaðir (8.55 am; four to five hours; Ikr3000), and another to Höfn (6.30 pm; 30 minutes; Ikr400).

SKAFTAFELL NATIONAL PARK

Skaftafell National Park, beneath a breathtaking backdrop of peaks and glaciers, is ideal for day walks and longer wilderness hiking trips, but don't approach or climb the glaciers without proper equipment and training.

Hiking

One of the most popular walks is the easy one-hour return walk to **Skaftafellsjökull** glacier. The track begins at the service centre and leads to the glacier face where you'll experience evidence of glacial activity: bumps, groans and flowing water as well as the brilliant blue hues of the ice itself.

Skaftafell's most photographed feature is **Svartifoss**, a waterfall flanked by unusual overhanging basalt columns. A well-worn trail leads from the camping ground. If the weather is fine, follow the recommended loop walk around **Skaftafellsheiði**. The longer day walk from the camping ground to the glacial lagoon in **Morsárdalur** is tiring but enjoyable; plan on about seven hours for the return trip.

Places to Stay & Eat

The immense grassy *camping ground* (Ikr500 per person) is broken only by the odd windbreak hedge or barbecue spit. The service area has an information office, coffee shop, cafeteria, supermarket and shower and toilet block.

Another option is *Bölti* (☎ 478 1626), the farm on Skaftafellsheiði, which offers private rooms for Ikr3400/4900 and dormitory sleeping-bag accommodation for Ikr1300.

Getting There & Away

The daily buses (1 June to 15 September) between Reykjavík and Höfn stop at Skaftafell, passing at 2.45 pm eastbound and 11.15 am westbound. To/from Höfn (two to 2¾ hours) costs Ikr1300; to/from Reykjavík (five to 6¼ hours) costs Ikr3000. The more expensive Fjallabak bus (Ikr5100), which runs from 1 July to 8 September, follows the more scenic inland route through Landmannalaugar and Eldgjá rather than the coastal Ring Road.

ICELAND

Morsárjökull

Morsárdalur

Morsá

Svarthamragil

Kristinartindar
1126 m

Bratthálsar

Nyrðrihnaukur
706 m

979 m

Fremra-
Djúpagil

Fremrihnaukur
610 m

650 m

Gláma

Innriskriða

Skaftafellsjökull

Fremriskriða

To Bæjar-
staðarskógur

Kambgil

Skerhóll
526 m

Stórilækur

Lautirðartungur

Smiðgil

Hallshyrnugil

Skaðafoss

Kumbulgil

Skaftafellsheiði

Sjónarnípugil

Leynidalstorfugil

Eyjagil

Hrafnagil

Sjónarsker

Svartifoss

Skaftafell
National Park

Kolgráfargil

| 0 | 0.5 | 1 km |

Hæðir ●

Magnúsarfoss

Bölti ●

Heygötufoss

ⓘ Information, Service Area, Supermarket,
Restaurant, Camping Ground & Registration

Skeiðará

ICELAND

VATNAJÖKULL
The 8400-sq-km glacier Vatnajökull, which reaches a thickness of one km in places, is Iceland's greatest icecap. Scores of smaller valley glaciers flow down from Vatnajökull as crevasse-ridden rivers of sculptured ice.

Jökulsárlón
This 100-metre-deep lagoon near the Ring Road is more or less an obligatory stop between Skaftafell and Höfn. It's full of icebergs calved from the glacier Breiðamerkurjökull, which descends from the Vatnajökull icecap.

Organised Tours
Access to the icecap is by organised glacier tours that depart from the tourist office in Höfn from 1 June to 7 September daily at 9 am, or from Skaftafell from 1 July to 31 August at 9 am. The price of Ikr8700 per person includes equipment; a 1½-hour skidoo or glacier buggy excursion to 1128-metre Miðfellsegg and 1250-metre Birnudalstindar; and a cruise on Jökulsárlón. Tours may be booked in Höfn through the tourist office (☎ 478 1701; fax 478 1901) or places of accommodation (there's a *camping ground*, *youth hostel*, *hotel* and several *guesthouses*). For longer stays, sleeping-bag accommodation is available at *Jöklasel Hut* (☎ 478 1001) near the edge of the ice for Ikr1500 per night. You can rejoin the tour when you're ready to return to Höfn.

Warning Walkers are cautioned not to wander beyond the red poles planted about a km from the Jöklasel hut, beyond which there are lots of dangerous snow-bridged crevasses. If you see a narrow depression in the snow, steer clear and don't continue further.

The Interior

The vast, barren interior of Iceland comprises one of Europe's greatest wilderness areas. Gazing across the expanses, you could imagine yourself in Tibet, Mongolia or, as some have noted, on the moon. In fact, the Apollo astronauts held training exercises here in preparation for lunar landings. This is remote wilderness and there are practically no tourist facilities, no accommodation, no bridges and no guarantees should something go awry. For independent travellers, careful preparations are essential.

ROUTES OF CENTRAL ICELAND
Historically, the interior routes were used as summer short cuts between the northern and southern coasts. The harsh mountains, valleys and broad expanses were considered the haunt of *utilegumenn*, outlaws fleeing revenge. For commoners, the vast deserts were regarded as undesirable places of fear and tragedy.

Kjölur Route
The Kjölur (Keel) Route (F37) was named in reference to its topographic shape. Although it was greener, more interesting and geographically more inviting than its counterpart, the Sprengisandur, it was historically the less popular, probably due to legends of superhuman outlaws inhabiting its remote ranges.

Kjölur's main attraction for modern visitors is Hveravellir, a geothermal area of fumaroles and multicoloured hot pools at the northern end of the pass. This route is better suited to walking or cycling than other interior routes thanks to its smoother nature and lack of sand and lava flows.

Organised Tours Most travellers opt for the 10½-hour BSÍ tour, which departs daily at 9 am from Reykjavík and 9 am from Akureyri. The standard fare is Ikr4800 but Omnibuspass holders pay only Ikr1200. With the Hringmiði (Full-Circle Pass), you can opt to replace the Akureyri-to-Reykjavík section of the Ring Road with the Kjölur Route for Ikr1200.

Sprengisandur Route
The Sprengisandur Route (F28) may be the least interesting of the interior routes but it

Central Iceland

0   25   50 km

ATLANTIC OCEAN

Northern/eastern area:
Seyðisfjörður
Eskifjörður
94
96
92
Egilsstaðir
Lagarfljót
1
85
Snæfell Route
923
Snæfell
Snæfellsskáli
Þrándarjökull
Geldingafell
Egilssel
Hofsjökull
Múlaskáli
Kollumúli
Goðahnúkar
Staðarfell
Hólm
F68
F98
Óskjuleið Route
Þorsteinsskáli
Aldeyjarfoss
Bræðrafell
Herðubreið
848
ÓÐÁÐAHRAUN
New (Northern) Gæsavatnaleið Route
Dreki
Askja
F98
Kverkfjöll
F96
VATNAJÖKULL
Esjufjöll 1522 m
Jökulsel

842
F26
Bárðardalur Route
Old Gæsavatnaleið (Running Blind) Route
F98
Tungnafellsjökull
Grímsvötn 1719 m
SKAFTAFELL NATIONAL PARK

F82
AKUREYRI
Eyjafjörður Route
F82
Laugafell
F76
F72
Ingólfsskáli
F28
Nýidalur
New Sprengisandur Route
Old Sprengisandur Route
Jökulheimar
Laki
Laki Route
F206
1

F87
Skagafjörður Route
F72
Kjölur Route
Hofsjökull
Valdivötn
Fjallabak Route
F22
Fjallabak Reserve
Torfajökull

Stórisandur Route
Hveravellir
Hrútafell
Þjófadalir
Summer Ski School
Kerlingarfjöll
Hrútmúlar
Landmannalaugar
Fjallabak Route
Myrdalsjökull
68
Brú
Langjökull
Eiríksjökull
F35
Þórisjökull
Kaldidalur Route
52
Tindfjallajökull
Þórsmörk
Eyjafjallajökull
Vik

Búðardalur
60
1
Hella
Hvolsvöllur
Selfoss
REYKJAVÍK

ICELAND

offers great views of Vatnajökull, Tungna-fellsjökull and Hofsjökull glaciers as well as Askja and Herðubreið from the western perspective. You may want to break the journey at Nýidalur, where there's a *camp site* and two Ferðafélag Íslands' *huts*, which are staffed between 1 July and 31 August. From the huts, you can take leisurely hikes up the valley or a day hike to the pass, Vonarskarð, a colourful 1000-metre saddle between Tungnafellsjökull, the green Ógöngur hills and the Vatnajökull icecap.

Organised Tours There are a couple of variations on the Sprengisandur tour. From south to north, buses travel from Reykjavík to Akureyri on Monday and Thursday, departing at 8 am. On Wednesday and Saturday, they go via the magnificent waterfall Aldeyjarfoss (which is flanked with basalt columns) and terminate at Mývatn. From north to south, they operate only from Mývatn, departing from Hótel Reynihlíð on Thursday and Sunday at 8.30 am. One-way fares are Ikr7200 to Akureyri and Ikr7000 to Mývatn.

Öskjuleið Route
Herðubreið and Askja on the Öskjuleið Route are the most visited wonders of the Icelandic desert.

Herðubreið This oddly-shaped 1682-metre mountain has been said to resemble a birthday cake, a cooking pot and a lampshade, but the tourist industry calls it 'Queen of the Icelandic Desert'. The track around it makes a nice day hike from **Herðubreiðarlindir**, a grassy oasis created by springs flowing from beneath the lava. There's a tourist office, a *camp site* and Ferðafélag Íslands' *Þorsteins-skáli Hut* (open from June to August) with gas and coal stoves. It's an ideal overnight stop before continuing to Askja or returning to Mývatn.

Askja Askja is an immense 50-sq-km caldera (a volcano that has collapsed into its magma chamber) that sets one thinking about the power of nature. Part of this collapsed

magma chamber contains the sapphire blue (when it's liquid) **Lake Öskjuvatn**, Iceland's deepest at 217 metres. At its north-eastern corner is **Viti**, a hot lake in a tephra crater, which was formed in 1875 after a volcanic eruption. Nearby *Dreki Hut* at **Drekagil** (Dragon Ravine) accommodates 20 people but the cold is brutal, so be prepared with warm and hefty sleeping bags.

Organised Tours Tours depart from Reykjahlíð (Mývatn) between 20 June and 31 August at least three times weekly (between 15 July and 15 August departures are daily) – if the road is passable. It's a gruelling 12-hour return trip and many participants opt to stay at Herðubreiðarlindir or Drekagil and rejoin the tour later. The fare is Ikr5300.

FJALLABAK RESERVE
Fjallabak Reserve is a landscape of rainbow-coloured rhyolite peaks, rambling lava flows, blue lakes and soothing hot springs that can hold you captive for days.

Things to See
The star attractions around Landmannalaugar are the **Laugahraun** lava flow; the hot vents at colourful **Brennisteinsalda** (Burning Stones Crest); and the blue lake **Frostastaðavatn**, just over the rhyolite ridge north of Landmannalaugar. **Bláhnúkur** (Blue Peak), immediately south of Laugahraun, offers a scree scramble and fine views from the 943-metre top.

Landmannalaugar to Þórsmörk & Skógar Trek
The four-day trek from Landmannalaugar to Þórsmörk (or vice versa) is the premier walk in Iceland and can be completed by anyone in reasonable physical condition. Most people walk the track from north to south because of the net altitude loss. Some continue to Skógar, making it a six-day trip. Thanks to its popularity, those staying in the three huts along the track must pay hut fees and pick up keys from hut wardens in Landmannalaugar or Þórsmörk, or from Ferðafélag Íslands in

Landmannalaugar to
Þórsmörk & Skógar Trek

Reykjavík. Wardens can also answer questions and provide information on trail conditions. Due to at least two substantial river crossings, this route may not be suitable for children.

Places to Stay
The Ferðafélag Íslands' *hut* at Landmanna-laugar accommodates 115 people on a first-come-first-served basis. In July and August, it's usually booked out by tour groups and club members. Others will probably have to use the *camping ground* (Ikr400 per person), which shares facilities with the hut.

Getting There & Away
The only public transport over the Fjallabak Route is the BSÍ mountain bus, which operates daily between Reykjavík and Skaftafell from 1 July to 8 September, snow and river conditions permitting.

From either direction, it stops at Land-mannalaugar from 1 to 2.30 pm. Buses to/from Skaftafell stop at Eldgjá (Fire Gorge) allowing an hour for a walk to the nearby waterfall, Ófærufoss. The fare from Reykjavík to Landmannalaugar is Ikr2250; buspass holders get a 50% discount.

Kaliningrad Region

A disconnected wedge of Russia too strategic to have been left in anyone else's hands, the 21,000 sq km of the Kaliningrad Region (population one million) lies between Lithuania, Poland and the Baltic Sea. From the 13th century until 1945, Kaliningrad was German, part of the core territory of the Teutonic Knights and their successors the dukes and kings of Prussia. Its capital, now named Kaliningrad, was the famous German city Königsberg.

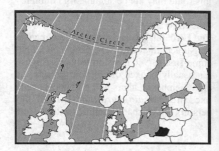

After WWI, East Prussia (the northern half of which the Kaliningrad Region approximates) was separated from the rest of Germany. Hitler's desire to reunite it was one of the sparks that lit WWII. The three-month campaign by which the Red Army took it in 1945 was one of the fiercest of the war, with hundreds of thousands of casualties on both sides.

Until 1991 the Kaliningrad Region was closed to Western tourists. Today it is home to the Russian naval base at Baltiysk (Russia's only ice-free port since the loss of the Baltic states) and as such, is still a strongly-militarised area. The number of military personnel remains a state secret and estimates range from 40,000 to 200,000.

Group travel is favoured here – simply because of the huge numbers of German 'nostalgia tourists' who flooded in to Kaliningrad when the area opened up to trace their ancestry. With the rapid decline of this 'niche market' however – the estimated 50,000 tourists in 1991 plummeted to less

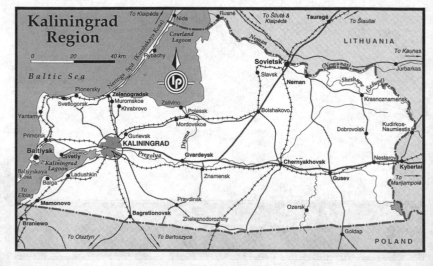

than 5,000 in 1995 – the tourism industry has yet to adapt to the demands set by the few independent travellers who make their way here.

The Kaliningrad *oblast* (region) is one region where Soviet-era street names remain firmly intact (unlike elsewhere in Russia where street names are being changed back to their former pre-communist names). There is no talk of restoring the city's German name, Königsberg.

Facts about the Region

GOVERNMENT & ECONOMY
The Kaliningrad Region is one of several dozen *oblasty* (regions) into which Russia is divided. Like other oblasty, it has its own *soviet* (local assembly) with powers over some of its affairs, but it is answerable to Moscow. For the past few years local authorities have attempted to set up economic incentives for local companies in a bid to boost Kaliningrad's bankrupt economy. And after a lot of bungling in Moscow – Kaliningrad was actually made a free economic zone in 1992, which was then abrogated by mistake in March 1995, leading to massive compensation payouts – the Kaliningrad Region finally became a free economic zone in January 1996. Various local companies are exempt from import and export duty.

So far the effects of this are not evident and the economy remains reliant on heavy federal subsidies from Moscow. Inflation stood at 110% in 1995 and foreign investment is minimal (US$5 million in 1995). In Moscow the fear of Kaliningrad becoming economically self-sufficient and going for the fourth 'Baltic State' option still lurks.

Living standards are slightly higher than the rest of Russia and, with lower prices than either St Petersburg or Moscow, Kaliningrad is an attractive option for travellers who want to 'do' something of Russia quickly and on the cheap.

POPULATION & PEOPLE
People living in the Kaliningrad Region generally think of themselves as Kaliningraders first and Russian second. Kaliningrad Region's population is 78% Russian, 10% Belarusian, 6% Ukrainian, 4% Lithuanian and 0.8% of German origin. Just over 42% of the total population live in the city of Kaliningrad.

RELIGION
In recent years the Russian Orthodox Church has enjoyed a massive revival, so much so that Moscow has given the go ahead for a new Orthodox Cathedral to be built in the small park behind Lenin's statue in the centre of Kaliningrad.

LANGUAGE
To get by in the Kaliningrad Region and St Petersburg, it is essential that even if you don't speak any Russian (the official language) you can at least decipher Cyrillic script. If you cannot read Cyrillic then you can't make sense of street names, bus destination placards or railway timetables; Lonely Planet's *Russian Phrasebook* will prove invaluable. In Kaliningrad it is rare to find anyone who can speak any other language, except those people involved in the tourist industry who will most likely speak a little German only. In St Petersburg English-speakers are more common.

See the Language Guide at the back of the book for the Russian alphabet chart, as well as pronunciation guidelines and useful words and phrases.

Facts for the Visitor

VISAS & DOCUMENTS
You need a Russian visa to go to the Kaliningrad Region. A Russian visa is a separate document, not a stamp in your passport or an attached piece of paper. It can be time-consuming to obtain and it is preferable to get one from the Russian embassy in your own country before you leave.

An overland trip between the Kaliningrad Region and anywhere else in Russia, eg St Petersburg, means you must be in possession of a double or multiple-entry visa, as the trip will involve crossing on to foreign territory before re-entering Russia.

Visas

There are six types of Russian visas available to foreign visitors: tourist, business, student, transit, 'private' and 'on-the-spot' visas.

A tourist visa requires written confirmation of hotel reservations; business visas require a letter of invitation from a Russian company guaranteeing to put you up for your stay; student visas are flexible, extendible and require proof of enrolment at an accredited Russian school or university. A transit visa, valid for 48 hours, is for 'passing through' and does not require proof of accommodation; private visas are supported by a personal invitation. 'On-the-spot' are basically fast-track business visas issued at airports by Intourist. To get one of these you have to be met at the airport by a representative of a Russian company who will 'invite' you to Russia. Apart from this visas cannot be obtained at borders.

Applying for a Visa The Russian embassies in the three Baltic capitals (see Embassies below) are painfully bureaucratic. If however you speak loudly in English and flash your Western passport from the minute you line up outside the embassy with the tens of Baltic nationals also attempting to be let in by the completely unhelpful staff, you should have no problem. At embassies and consulates in other major capitals (see list following) the process is less taxing though usually quite slow. If there's any kind of travel agency involved in planning your trip then it's easiest to let them handle your visa application although it will cost more.

To apply yourself, you need your passport (valid for at least a month beyond your return), two or three passport photos, a completed application form including entry/exit dates (available at the embassy), the relevant invitation or proof of accommodation

depending on the type of visa you are applying for (see above), and a handling fee. This varies by nationality but is typically around US$30. Most embassies also offer a 'quick visa', issued within two or three days, but costing double.

Obtaining the necessary invitation or proof of confirmed accommodation from establishments in the Kaliningrad Region can be tough. One way around this is to plan a trip that includes St Petersburg or another destination in Russia, which requires your applying for a multiple-entry visa. The visa can usually be issued on the strength of a St Petersburg booking – but remember when you fill in your application form to mention Kaliningrad as a destination: if the destination on your visa reads only St Petersburg then you will not be permitted entry to the Kaliningrad Region.

For visa support in Kaliningrad try the Ministry of Foreign Affairs (☎ 211 668) at ulitsa Kirova 17 or Baltma Tours (see Kaliningrad – Information).

Registration The company or organisation that invited you to Russia is responsible for your registration. When you check in to a hotel, you will have to surrender your passport and visa so the hotel can register you with OVIR. If you are travelling on your own, you must remember that *all* Russian visas must be registered with OVIR within three working days of your arrival in Russia.

In Kaliningrad the main OVIR office (☎ 228 274) is at Sovietsky prospekt 13, room 9.

Documents

Taking photocopies of your passport and visa is particularly recommended. Upon entering Russia you will also have to fill out a customs declaration form (*deklaratsia*) listing valuables and money you bring in to the country. If you don't have it when you leave, customs could theoretically confiscate your foreign cash. When you leave the country you give the stamped form back to them and also fill in a second one, declaring what goodies you are taking out.

For driving documents see Estonia, Facts for the Visitor.

EMBASSIES
Russian Embassies Abroad
Australia
  78 Canberra Ave, Griffith, ACT 2603 (☎ 06-295 9033, 295 9474)
Canada
  285 Charlotte Street, Ottawa, Ontario K1N 8L5 (☎ 613-235 4341, 235 5376)
Denmark
  Kristianiagade 5, DK-2100 Copenhagen (☎ 31 38 23 70, 31 42 55 85)
Estonia
  Hobusepea 3, EE0200 Tallinn (☎ 2-443 014)
Finland
  Tehtaankatu 1b, FIN-00140 Helsinki (☎ 09-66 14 49, 66 18 76/77)
Germany
  Waldstrasse 42, D-53177 Bonn (☎ 0228-31 20 85/6/7)
Latvia
  Atonijas iela 2, Rīga (☎ 2-7220 693, 7332 151)
Lithuania
  Latvių 53/54, Vilnius (☎ 2-721 763, 723 893)
Poland
  Ulitsa Belwederska 49, PL-00761 Warsaw (☎ 022-213 453)
  Consulate: ulica Batorego 15, PL-80251 Gdańsk (☎ 058-414 200)
Sweden
  Gjoerwellsgatan 31, S-11260 Stockholm (☎ 08-130 441, 533 732)
UK
  5 Kensington Palace Gardens, London W8 4QS (☎ 0171-229 8027)
USA
  1825 Phelps Place NW, Washington, DC 20008 (☎ 202-939 8907)

CUSTOMS
Entering Russia, you can take in a litre of hard liquor or wine, up to 250 cigarettes plus modest amounts of other items except weapons or illegal drugs.

When leaving, all art works including antiquarian books (those published before 1975), coins, jewellery, musical instruments etc have to be assessed by the Ministry of Culture who will issue a receipt for tax paid (usually 100% of the purchase price – take your sales receipt). In Kaliningrad take the object to the Customs office (☎ 499 245, 443 450) at Prichalnaja 4a, building 1.

Exporting works of art dating from before the 1917 revolution is prohibited.

MONEY
As part of Russia, the Kaliningrad Region uses the Russian rouble, which is the only legal tender. Transactions in other currencies are forbidden – even though some hotels may give their rates in Deutschmarks, you pay in roubles. The best currencies to take into the Kaliningrad Region are Deutschmarks or US dollars. Credit cards and travellers' cheques are useless in Kaliningrad; even major hotels and restaurants do not accept them. Only one bank we know of gives cash advance on Visa/Eurocard: Investbank (see Kaliningrad, Information for details).

Exchange Rates

Australia	A$1	=	R4279
Canada	C$1	=	R3954
France	1FF	=	R1051
Germany	DM1	=	R3555
Japan	¥100	=	R4900
New Zealand	NZ$1	=	R3786
UK	UK£1	=	R8434
USA	US$1	=	R5406

POST & COMMUNICATIONS
Post & Telephone
Mail service out of the Kaliningrad Region is slow. Expect letters to take from a week to 10 days to reach Western Europe and longer still to Australia and the US. Postal rates for letters weighing up to 20g are R850 within Russia and R3750 to Western Europe. If you want postcards to reach their destination you should put them in an envelope.

International phone calls can be made from all private phones as well as card-operated public phone booths. Cards are available from post offices, kiosks and most major hotels. To make an international call dial ☎ 8, wait for the tone, then dial ☎ 10 followed by the country code, area code and telephone number. To make long distance calls dial ☎ 8-tone followed by the area code. Area codes from Kaliningrad phones include Sovietsk ☎ 261, Neman ☎ 262, Baltiysk ☎ 245,

St Petersburg ☎ 812, Moscow ☎ 095. Only local calls can be made from the old token-operated public phones.

To call Kaliningrad from the West dial ☎ 7-0112; from the CIS ☎ 8-0112.

Fax & E-mail

Faxes and electronic mail can be sent and received from the International Information Centre (☎ 451 515) inside the Hotel Kaliningrad (see Places to Stay).

TIME

Kaliningrad does not share Moscow time. It is in the Eastern European time zone, which is GMT/UTC plus two hours from the last Sunday in September to the last Saturday in March; GMT/UTC plus three hours for the rest of the year.

ELECTRICITY

Standard voltage is 220V, 50 cycles AC, although a few places still have old 127V system. Sockets require a continental or European plug with two round pins, although you might find that some sockets stubbornly refuse to accept anything other than the slighter, thinner two-pinned Russian plugs. You may be able to buy an adapter for this problem locally.

WEIGHTS & MEASURES

Russia operates on the metric system. Restaurant menus often list the weight of food and drink servings in grams, and in particular you order drinks by weight; a tea-glass is about 200g, a shot-glass about 50g. The unit of items sold by the piece, such as eggs, is *shtuka* or *sht.*, which literally means 'thing' or 'piece'.

HEALTH

It's risky to drink Kaliningrad water; instead drink bottled water and avoid fruits and vegetables that have come into contact with tap water. Likewise, be careful when you buy food sold in the streets; make sure that it's freshly cooked.

WOMEN TRAVELLERS

Bring sanitary towels or tampons. You may find tampons but you can't count on it. You're unlikely to experience sexual harassment on the streets in most parts of the country, though sexual stereotyping remains strong. Anywhere in the country, revealing clothing will probably attract unwanted attention. Any young or youngish woman alone in or near flashy bars frequented by foreigners risks being mistaken for a prostitute.

DISABLED TRAVELLERS

Inaccessible transport, lack of ramps and lifts and no centralised policy for people with physical limitations make the Kaliningrad Region a challenging destination for wheelchair-bound travellers.

In Kaliningrad, Hotel Kaliningrad and the Italian Café are wheel chair accessible.

BUSINESS HOURS & HOLIDAYS

Government offices open Monday to Friday from 9 or 10 am to 5 or 6 pm. Most shops open Monday to Saturday for the same hours with an hour or two break at some point in the day. Once a month almost all establishments – shops, museums, restaurants – without any warning, shut down for a one-day *sanitarnyy den* (sanitary day).

Russian national holidays include:

1 January, *New Year's Day*
7 January, *Russian Orthodox Christmas Day*
8 March, *International Women's Day*
1 & 2 May, *Labour Day Holiday*
9 May, *Victory Day* (commemorating victory in WWII)

BOOKS

If you can read German, try to get hold of the excellent guide *Königsberg Kaliningrad* by Henning Sietz (Edition Temmen, Bremen, 1992). Otherwise, the only thing available in English is a coffee-table album, *Leben Danach/Life After* (published in Finland, 1994), containing some highly evocative photos of the region taken between 1988 and 1992. However, you're likely to have more success finding the book in neighbouring Lithuania, or in Estonia or Finland, than you are in the Kaliningrad Region itself.

ACCOMMODATION

The accommodation scene in the developed specifically to suit the needs – or rather the wallets – of elderly, affluent Germans revisiting their 'homeland'. Those looking for something cheaper will have to track down the few shoddy hotels used by visiting Russians from out of town, for which you pay the foreigners price (at least four times the rate for locals).

If you do not already have a reservation at a hotel, it is difficult to find one that is prepared to give you a room for a night. When checking in at a hotel your passport will be held by reception staff and they may well also ask to see your visa.

FOOD & DRINKS

Food is unlikely to be the highlight of your visit to the Kaliningrad Region although new, Western-style eating places are slowly crawling out of the woodwork. Otherwise, dishes tend to be of the bland meat and potato mix with menus in many establishments in Russian only. Drinks on the menu are usually imported and expensive. Bread is served with every meal – for an extra charge! Unless you explicitly state you do not want it (a sure way to immediately upset the waiter), you will automatically get it and be expected to pay for it. The moment you take the last slice from the plate, the waiter will immediately bring you more which you will also be expected to pay for.

Getting There & Away

AIR

SAS (Kaliningrad airport office, ☎ 459 453, 459 580) has four weekly flights from Kaliningrad to Copenhagen, from where there are connecting flights to over 100 destinations. Kaliningrad Airlines (airport office, ☎ 441 463) has three flights daily to

Moscow, three flights weekly to Copenhagen, twice-weekly flights to Kiev and six flights weekly to St Petersburg. It also has flights to a whole host of other cities in Russia and the CIS.

LAND
Bus

There are cheap daily buses from Vilnius (US$7), Kaunas and Šiauliai to Kaliningrad, and several buses daily from Smiltynė both via Sovietsk and along the picturesque Neringa Spit and via Zelenogradsk. There is also an overnight service from Tallinn via Rīga (departing daily at 7.45 pm, arriving at around 11 am the next day for US$20).

There are a number of bus services between north-eastern Poland and Kaliningrad, operated jointly by König Auto of Kaliningrad (☎ 430 480) and various Polish companies. The starting points in Poland include Olsztyn, Białystok, Elblag and Gdańsk.

Train

The *Königsberg Express* runs directly from Berlin to Kaliningrad. Bookings in Germany can be made through Rail Tours Mochel Reisen (☎ 7821-430 37; fax 7821-429 98). There are also one or two trains daily between Kaliningrad and Braniewo in northeast Poland. Between Braniewo and Warsaw, a trip of five or six hours, you need to change trains at Olsztyn. There are numerous trains from Kaunas and Vilnius, originating from St Petersburg or Moscow.

Car & Motorcycle

From the south it is possible to enter Kaliningrad from Poland although the Lithuanian borders at Kybartai or on the Neringa Spitare are more promising. Petrol is widely available.

SEA

Anjuta (☎ 210 742; fax 228 998) runs a hydrofoil service twice-daily between Kaliningrad and Elblag in Poland, one-way tickets costing around US$10.

Getting Around

BUS
Long-distance buses serve all towns and are a comfortable way of getting around. Tickets, however, should be bought as far in advance as possible as, especially during summer, the buses become full very quickly.

TRAIN
There are frequent services to almost all towns in the Kaliningrad Region. Trains tend to be a better bet than the buses simply because you're always going to get on them; the suburban services have no numbered seats so just climb aboard anywhere. The trains running out to the coast, particularly to Zelenogradsk and Svetlogorsk, do become crowded though and if you're slow boarding you can end up standing for the entire journey.

CAR & MOTORCYCLE
The wide and well-kept roads (a rare beneficial spin-off of the region's heavy military presence) make private transport an ideal way to get around the Kaliningrad Region, especially since most restricted areas can be entered by tourists. On some roads you may encounter tri-lingual Russian-German-English signs telling you that you need special permission to enter that territory; although this is the official story, you're unlikely to be stopped. Be aware that some of these areas are under military control. In border areas you will come across blue Russian-only signs stating that you need documents to proceed further. Your passport, visa, vehicle registration and driving licence should be sufficient.

Kaliningrad

Founded as a Teutonic Order fort in 1255, Königsberg joined the Hanseatic League in 1340 and from 1457 to 1618 was the residence of the grand masters of the Teutonic order and their successors the dukes of Prussia. The first king of Prussia was crowned here in 1701. The city was nearly flattened by British air raids in 1944 and the Red Army assault from 6 to 9 April 1945. Many of the surviving Germans were sent to Siberia – the last 25,000 were deported to Germany in 1947-48. The city was renamed (after Mikhail Kalinin, one of Lenin's henchmen who also found favour with Stalin), rebuilt and re-peopled mostly by Russians. Today it has 419,000 residents and a lot of drab Soviet architecture enhanced by a fair amount of green open space and some tree-lined avenues.

Orientation
Leninsky prospekt, a broad north-south avenue, is Kaliningrad's main artery, running three km from the bus station and main train station, the Yuzhny Vokzal (South Station), to the suburban Severny Vokzal (North Station). About halfway it crosses the Pregolya River and passes Kaliningrad's cathedral, the town's major landmark. Just north of the river, Leninsky prospekt passes through Tsentralnaya ploshchad, with the Kaliningrad hotel and the unmistakable House of the Soviets.

Information
You can change money Monday to Friday from 9 am to 6 pm at branches of Investbank at Leninsky prospekt 28, or at ulitsa Shevchenko 11, where you can also get cash advance on Visa and Eurocard. Most hotels can also change money. The exchange bureau at the Kaliningrad hotel is particularly useful, although the banks and non-hotel exchange bureaus offer better rates (the best rate is at the bureau next to the Sailor's Hostel and Flagman Restaurant). If you are planning to go elsewhere in Russia it is worth changing extra money here, as the rates are far better in Kaliningrad than either St Petersburg or Moscow.

The main post office is out of the way at Kosmonavta Leonova 22, about 700 metres north of prospekt Mira. For express mail try

UPS (☎ 434 684, 474 354) at Chernyakhovskogo 66. The Kaliningrad hotel has a handy fax, telex and e-mail office and an international information centre which has a fair amount of information and some useful English-language brochures. For a complete guide to the region pick up a copy of the bi-lingual city guide *Kaliningrad In Your Pocket*, published annually in English and German and available from most major hotels for the equivalent of US$1.

Staff at Baltma Tours (☎ 211 880; fax 22 88 40) at Mir 19 speak English, are extremely helpful and can arrange wild boar hunting, fishing and other 'un-right-on' specialist tours which are a big hit with some tourists.

The Kaliningrad city telephone code is ☎ 22 if you're dialling from within the Kaliningrad Region or ☎ 0112 from elsewhere.

Things to See

The outstanding German remnant is the red brick Gothic **Dom**, or cathedral, founded in 1333 and recently rebuilt. The **tomb of Immanuel Kant**, the 18th-century philosopher who was born in, studied in and taught in Königsberg, is on the outer north side. The fine but run-down blue Renaissance-style building just across the river to the south of the cathedral is the old **Stock Exchange** built in the 1870s, now a 'Sailors' Culture Palace'.

At the east end of wide Tsentralnaya ploshchad, on the site of the 1255 castle (whose ruins were dynamited in 1965), stands the upright-H-shaped **House of the Soviets** (Dom Sovietov), one of the ugliest Soviet architectural creations ever (no mean achievement). It has stood empty ever since they ran out of money to complete it in 1961. Just north of Tsentralnaya ploshchad, on ulitsa Universitetskaya near the university, is the justly popular **Bunker Museum** (Muzey Blindazh), the German command post in 1945 (open daily from 10 am to 6 pm).

North of the House of Soviets stretches the **Lower Pond** (Prud Nizhny), in German times the Schlossteich, a favourite recreation and relaxation spot. Kaliningrad's **History &**

Art Museum is housed in a reconstructed 1912 concert hall on the east bank. It's open daily except Monday from 11 am to 6 pm. Ulitsa Chernyakhovskogo separates the pond's north end from the larger **Upper Pond** (Prud Verkhny). At its south-east corner are the fat red-brick **Dohna Tower** (Bashya Dona), a bastion of the city's old defensive ring now housing the **Amber Museum**, open daily except Monday, from 10 am to 6 pm, and the **Rossgarten Gate**, one of the old German city gates. Another bastion (now in Soviet military use) the rotund **Wrangel Tower**, stands near the south-west corner of the pond. From here ulitsa Profesora Baranova heads west to ploshchad Pobedy, passing the **central market** on ulitsa Chernyakhovskogo just to the south.

About 300 metres west along prospekt Mira is the 1927 **Kaliningrad Drama Theatre**, restored in 1980. Another half a km further on is the splendid **Cosmonaut Monument**, a real gem of Soviet iconography. Immediately after the monument is **Kalinin Park**, a favourite Königsberg park.

The **Museum of the World Ocean**, ceremonially opened to mark the 300th anniversary of the Russian naval fleet in 1996, is moored along the Pregolya between the two floating hotels. It is open from Wednesday to Sunday from 11 am to 6 pm.

Places to Stay

There are no hostels although at the time of writing there was talk of transforming the extremely seedy *Moskva Hotel* (☎ 272 089) at Mira 19 into a youth hostel. Singles/doubles cost US$4/6 although these prices are known to fluctuate depending on the day/staff/your face. It is owned by the same team who run the town's principal hotel, *Kaliningrad* (☎ 432 591; fax 469 590), handily placed on Tsentralnaya ploshchad at Leninsky prospekt 81 but filled with staff who apparently work 24 hour shifts (which explains their surly manner). Singles/doubles are expensive at US$40/72.

The cheapest option is the *Patriot Hotel* (☎ 275 017), three km north of the city at Ozernaya 25A: take tram No 6 or 10 north

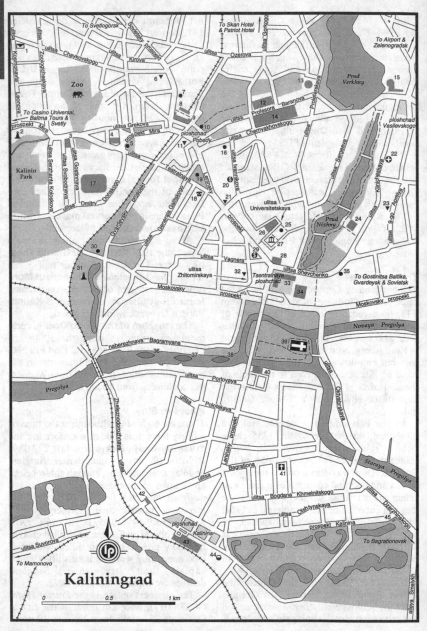

Kaliningrad

up ulitsa Gorkogo from the central market. Singles/doubles are US$14/23.

One of the few hotels prepared to let guests stay without an invitation is the more expensive *Skan Hotel* (☎ 465 461; fax 451 823), at Alexandra Nevskovo 53, which claims to be a 'Königsberg hotel with a Euro-

pean accent'. It has a 24-hour currency exchange; singles/doubles are US$40/60.

The more expensive options include the two cruise ships moored to the north bank of the Pregolya, just west of the Leninsky prospekt bridge. The *Hotelschiff Hansa* (☎ 433 737; fax 433 806) is fairly shabby from the outside and smells somewhat damp and stuffy inside. Singles/doubles cost US$49/91. Second in line is the *Hotelschiff Baltcompany A* (☎ & fax 461 604), definitely more swanky (to the point of being tacky) with singles/doubles for US$33/56. On the top deck is a casino.

Places to Eat

Cheap and cheerful and definitely one of the most Western places in town is the *Italian Café* at Leninsky prospekt 27, serving veal in red wine sauce, crêpes with black caviar and the like for around US$5. Pizza is only served from 6 pm and it closes daily at 2 am.

A more old-time Soviet experience can be had at the *Belarus* at Zhitomirskaya 14, which serves quite palatable dishes to the blare of German MTV for around US$5. It is open daily from noon to 11 pm.

Along Sovietsky prospekt is Kaliningrad's first English pub, the *Francis Drake*, which serves toasted sandwiches, soups (including 'Golden Hinde', which is actually the broth seljanka), Welsh-style baked fish and other dishes purporting to be 'typically British' for around US$6. British lagers and bitters are on tap for US$2 a pint.

The *Chorny tiulpan* (Black Tulip), at 9-go Aprelya 60a, specialises in Armenian food. The menu is a book of photographs, which is extremely handy if you can't speak Russian.

Within the kiosk village opposite the Kaliningrad hotel there are a couple of great little places. *Oleg's* at Kiosk No 52 is glam and glitzy but serves reasonable Uzbek cuisine at reasonable prices. *Karolina's Bar* is at Kiosk No 2 and is the best place for cocktails. Nothing can beat the smell of freshly-ground coffee beans inside the Western-style coffee shop inside Kiosk No 63 (maybe that is why the management have banned smoking inside). It's open daily from 11 am to 10 pm and serves the best coffee and cakes in town.

If you're after recognisable western European fare, you'll have to go to a more expensive restaurant. Try *Valencia* at ploshchad Pobedy 1 for exotic and delicious Spanish dishes (open daily 1 pm to midnight) or *Casino Universal* at Mira prospekt 43. The extensive menu includes 40 starters, 33 desserts and tantalising main dishes such as fried frogs paws for US$12. It is open daily from noon to 6 am. The *Flagman* restaurant beneath the sailors' hostel is open from noon to 2 am and also gets good reports.

Getting There & Away
See the earlier Kaliningrad Region Getting There & Away section for information about train and bus services.

Bus The bus station is on ploshchad Kalinina at the southern end of Leninsky prospekt.

Train Kaliningrad has two train stations: Severny Vokzal (North Station) just off ploshchad Pobed and Yuzhny Vokzal (South Station). All long-distance and many of the local trains go from Yuzhny Vokzal, passing through (but not always stopping at) Severny Vokzal.

Getting Around
Local Transport Trams, trolleybuses and buses use the usual ticket-punching system (see Estonia, Getting Around for an explanation); tickets are sold in strips of 10 for 5,000 roubles from kiosks around town. A life-saving tram and trolleybus scheme is included in *Kaliningrad In Your Pocket*.

Taxis Taxis are cheap but difficult to find. Private drivers are also often prepared to use their cars as makeshift taxis if they're going in your general direction. A trip across the centre (about one or two km) should cost no more than US$3.

Other Destinations

The 15,100 sq km of the Kaliningrad Region are mostly low-lying and gently rolling, with a lot of farmland, about 20% woodland and some marshes. The attractive coast includes the popular seaside resort of Svetlogorsk where amber is washed up on to the shores during Spring and Autumn storms. The highlight of this region is the small village of Yantarny, home to the world's largest amber mine.

SVETLOGORSK
Svetlogorsk (formerly the German Rauschen) is a pleasant green coastal town, 35 km north-west of Kaliningrad. The narrow beach is backed by high, steep sandy slopes and the small town is dotted with wooden houses, some of which were used in the Soviet era as sanatoriums for workers and officials. Svetlogorsk is an easy day visit from Kaliningrad but could also be a pleasant base from which to make forays to the city.

Orientation & Information
Svetlogorsk has two train stations: Svetlogorsk I and II. The station you should get off at is Svetlogorsk II, which is where the train terminates. Immediately south of the station, ulitsa Lenina runs roughly east-west, parallel to the tracks. The town's market, post office and telephone and telegraph office are east of the station, 450 metres along ulitsa Lenina then south down ulitsa Oktyabrskaya. There is also a small *univermag* (department store) at the end of ulitsa Oktyabrskaya.

The local telephone code for Svetlogorsk is ☎ 2533. To call Svetlogorsk from abroad dial ☎ 7-011533.

Things to See & Do
The **beach** lies 200 metres north of the Svetlogorsk II station and can be reached by the neighbouring chair lift. On ulitsa Oktyabrskaya are the 25-metre **water tower**

and the curious red-tile-domed Jugendstil (Art Nouveau) **bathhouse**. About 200 metres east along ulitsa Lenina from the ulitsa Oktyabrskaya corner, there's another small crossroad where a left (north) turn takes you to the main steps down to the beach. Near the bottom of these steps is a very large, colourful **sundial**, believed to be the largest in Europe.

At Lenina 5 there is a **Commemorative Chapel**, opened in 1994 on the former site of a kindergarten. It is a memorial to the 34 people (23 of which were children aged between three and seven) who died after an A-26 Soviet military transport plane on a low-flying training mission above the Baltic Sea crashed into the building. The tragedy was hushed up for almost 20 years and only came to light when the Russian Orthodox Church decided to build the chapel in 1991.

Places to Stay & Eat

The best hotel is the *Volna* (☎ 3733) at Kaliningradsky prospekt 68b. Singles/ doubles cost around US$20/28. There's also a casino here and a bar serving over 100 cocktails. From Svetlogorsk II station, go east along ulitsa Lenina (that's left if your back is to the tracks) and take the first street on your right, ulitsa Karla Marxa. At the end of ulitsa Karla Marxa turn right onto Kaliningradsky prospekt. There's also a small, very basic-looking *Gostinitsa* at the other end of Kaliningradsky prospekt, just past the east end of the lake.

By far the best place to eat, drink and be merry in Svetlogorsk is *The Lame Horse* at Oktyabryskaya 23. The spicy Mexican-style food here is far from lame. The bar stools with real saddles are truly a sight to behold. It's open daily from noon to 3 am.

Getting There & Away

There are about 20 to 25 trains a day from Kaliningrad to Svetlogorsk. Direct trains take about one hour; those going via Zelenogradsk take about 1½ hours.

YANTARNY

Yantarny(formerly Palmnicken), 50 km west of Kaliningrad and formerly a closed village, is now open to tourists. This little-known village, literally called 'made of amber,' is a place that just should not be missed.

The Russky Yantar amber mine, around which the entire village revolves, produces almost 90% of the world's amber, its annual yield of the fossilised resin estimated to total 600 tonnes. There is still no public access to the workings, but it is possible to call in advance and arrange a visit to the small **amber museum** (☎ 2533-450 458; fax 2533-466 729) inside the mine. Exhibits include an impressive amber rock weighing 2.86 kg and portraits of Lenin made from amber beads. At the northern end of the main street, ulitsa Sovietskaya, there is a **factory outlet** selling fine pieces of jewellery made from Yantarny amber. It is open Monday to Friday from 8 am to 12.30 pm and from 1.30 pm to 5 pm.

On the beach, several hundred metres west of ulitsa Sovietskaya, there is a waste water pipe outside the barbed wire surrounding the mine. Here, tens of men and women, dressed in the full fisherman's gear, fish for amber in the black waste water that shoots from the pipe. Some catch up to half a kilo in just four hours and are happy to sell you the small unpolished pieces. When we were there the going rate was US$140 for 200g of small pieces or US$1 a gram for larger pieces.

Getting There & Away

Trains to Pokrovskoe, Primorsk and Baltiysk from Svetlogorsk I station stop at Yantarny six times a day; many of these services start in Kaliningrad. The journey takes around one hour. Around six buses run daily from Kaliningrad, taking 1½ hours and costing about US$0.50.

MUROMSKOE

This small village 30 km north-west of Kaliningrad has been the 'Klondike of Kaliningrad' since 1993 when a tractor driver uncovered a huge piece of amber in a

KALININGRAD

nearby field. The lucrative find sparked off a massive amber rush in the area. In summer 1995 a 12 year old boy was buried alive and died after the hole he was digging fell in around him. Despite police imposing stiff fines in early 1996 for anyone caught digging for amber, the 'rush' continues. The field is covered with countless holes, some up to five metres deep, and still attracts hundreds of amber seekers every year.

To reach the amber field from the centre of town, take the first right turn off the Muromskoe-Zelenogradsk road and continue for 2.5 km through a wooded area until you reach a cluster of trees where the road veers left.

Muromskoe is between Kaliningrad and the jaded seaside resort of Zelenogradsk. There is no train station so you can only get there by car.

Latvia

Latvia (Latvija), lacking Estonia's close proximity to a Western country (Finland) or the fame Lithuania achieved on its path to independence, used to be the least known of the Baltic states. With the dramatic influx of tourists and foreign investors in recent years, this is no longer the case.

Rīga remains Latvia's chief tourist magnet as it is the largest and most cosmopolitan city in the Baltic states. Several attractive destinations lie within day-trip distance of it, among them the coastal resort Jūrmala, Sigulda Castle overlooking the scenic Gauja River valley, and the Rastrelli-designed palace at Rundāle.

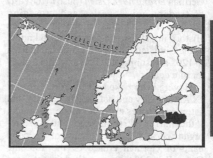

Facts about the Country

HISTORY

The idea of Latvia being a discrete political entity inhabited by speakers of Latvian did not become current until the late 19th century. For centuries, under various rulers, most of what's now Latvia had fallen into either Courland, the area west of Rīga, or Livonia, the eastern half of Latvia and the southern half of Estonia.

German Rule

Peoples arriving in the south-eastern Baltic region from the south around 2000 BC introduced settled agriculture to Latvia and

297

eventually grouped into what are called the 'Baltic' tribes, which were dragged into recorded history in the 12th century by the German *Drang nach Osten* (push to the east) of traders, missionaries and crusading knights. The Knights of the Sword (see History in the Estonia chapter), also known as the Livonian Order, were founded in Rīga in 1202 and subjugated Latvia within a quarter of a century.

Having been ticked off by Pope Gregory IX for brutality and defeated by Latvian and Lithuanian tribes at Saulė (modern Šiauliai, Lithuania) in 1236, these knights were reorganised in 1237 as a branch of a second band of German crusaders, the Teutonic Order. By 1290 they controlled the seaboard from modern Poland to Estonia, plus inland Latvia. The existing inhabitants became serfs to a German nobility which dominated until the early 20th century.

Polish, Swedish & Russian Rule
In 1561 Latvia came under Polish control after the Livonian Order appealed to Poland-Lithuania for protection against Russia's Ivan the Terrible. In the 1620s Sweden took all of Latvia except Courland, where the dukes of Jelgava, descended from the last Livonian Grand Master, maintained allegiance to Poland. Russia's Peter the Great destroyed Swedish power in the Great Northern War (1700-21), and most of Latvia became part of the Russian empire, the remainder following in the Partitions of Poland (see History in the Lithuania chapter) towards the end of the 18th century.

Latvia experienced an awakening of national consciousness in the 19th century. Serfs were freed and native (non-German, non-Russian) interests were promoted.

WWI & Independence
After WWI fighting between Latvian nationalists (who had declared independence in November 1918), Bolsheviks trying to incorporate Latvia into Soviet Russia, and lingering German occupation forces went on until 1921, when Moscow signed a peace treaty with the independent Latvian parliamentary republic. By this stage Latvia had lost about 40% of its population through death or emigration. Factories had been 'evacuated' to Russia, and trade through Rīga in 1926 was only a tenth of what it had been in 1913. From 1934 authoritarian leader Kārlis Ulmanis headed a non-parliamentary government of unity.

WWII & Soviet Rule
Between 1939 and 1941 events in Latvia followed a similar path to those in Estonia – the Molotov-Ribbentrop Pact (a 'mutual assistance pact' with the USSR), occupation by Soviet troops, a Communist 'election' victory, incorporation into the USSR, nationalisation, purges, about 35,000 deportations, and killings. Latvia was occupied partly or wholly by Nazi Germany from 1941 to 1945. Some Latvians collaborated in the murders of up to 90,000 Jews at the Salaspils concentration camp near Rīga and Latvia's Jewish population was virtually wiped out.

Reconquest by the Red Army was followed by farm collectivisation and further nationalisation. An estimated 175,000 Latvians were killed or deported. There was some armed resistance until 1952. With postwar industrialisation, Latvia received an influx of migrant workers from all over the Soviet Union, which increased local resentment towards Soviet rule.

New Independence
The first significant public protest in the glasnost era was on 14 June 1987 when about 5000 people rallied at the Freedom Monument in Rīga to commemorate the 1941 Siberia deportations. Several large rallies on environmental, national and other issues were held in 1988. On 23 August 1989 about two million Latvians, Lithuanians and Estonians formed a 650-km human chain stretching from Vilnius, through Rīga, to Tallinn, in protest at the 50th anniversary of the Molotov-Ribbentrop Pact. A reformist, pro-independence Latvian Popular Front was formed which included the new Latvian Communist Party leadership. By 1989 the Latvian Popular Front had over 200,000

members. After its supporters won a big majority in the March 1990 elections to Latvia's Supreme Soviet (or parliament), the pre-WWII constitution was reinstated and the words 'Soviet Socialist' dropped from the republic's name. A transition period was envisaged for independence to be negotiated, but prospects for this faded as hardliners regained the ascendancy in Moscow in the winter of 1990-91. On 20 January 1991 Soviet troops, trying to destabilise the Baltics, stormed the Interior Ministry building in Rīga, killing four people.

The August 1991 coup attempt in Moscow turned the tables and Latvia declared full independence on 21 August. It was recognised first by the West then, on 6 September, by the USSR. Latvia's first democratic elections were held in June 1993, with citizenship a contentious issue. All citizens of the pre-1940 Latvian Republic and their descendants automatically became citizens of modern Latvia, but this left roughly 30% of the population as noncitizens, who weren't allowed to vote. This has been a stick that Moscow has occasionally used to beat Latvia and it's also been cause for concern in the West. The Latvian worry was that automatic citizenship for all would mean that the country had a predominantly nonethnic-Latvian, Russian-speaking electorate.

As of July 1994, disenfranchised noncitizens can apply to become citizens of Latvia, having to pass tough language and history tests in order to be naturalised. As of June 1996, 2133 out of 3685 applicants had been granted citizenship.

GEOGRAPHY & ECOLOGY

Green and rolling, Latvia covers an area of 64,600 sq km, which is a little smaller than Lithuania. Over half of this area is less than 100 metres above sea level. The four regions of Latvia are: Kurzeme in the west; fertile and low-lying Zemgale, which is south and south-west of Rīga; Vidzeme, east of Rīga, with an upland of mixed farmland and forest that includes Gaiziņkalns (311 metres), the country's highest point; and Latgale in the south-east, with more upland and over 40% of Latvia's several thousand lakes.

The Daugava, flowing from Belarus to the sea at Rīga, is the most voluminous of Latvia's rivers. The Gauja, flowing down from the north-east, is the longest at 440 km. Pollution of rivers and the Gulf of Riga has reached serious proportions owing mainly to agricultural run-off and waste from the city of Rīga, which lacks a modern sewerage system.

Woodland still covers 40% of Latvia, half of it pine. Northern Kurzeme and northern Vidzeme are the most forested areas.

GOVERNMENT & POLITICS

The second parliamentary elections since the restoration of independence were held on 1 October 1995. None of the nine political parties gained a clear majority of the 100 seats to form a government however, leaving Latvia without a government for almost three months. This crisis was resolved on 21 December 1996 when the president invited nonpartisan 37-year-old businessman Andris Šķēle to head a large coalition government comprising the outgoing ruling party Latvijas Celš (Latvian Way), the National Independence Party (LNNK), the Fatherland and Freedom party, the leftist Unity Party and the left-leaning Saimnieks Party. On 18 June 1996, President Guntis Ulmanis, the great nephew of pre-WWII leader Kārlis Ulmanis, was re-elected president of Latvia.

ECONOMY

Following a shaky couple of years where the collapse of the Soviet economy led to price rises, the disruption of fuel and other supplies from Russia, falling output, and the loss of established markets, the Latvian economy stabilised and enjoyed steady growth. Latvia introduced its own national currency, the *lats* (plural: *lati)*, in April 1993, replacing the transitional Latvian rouble that had been in existence since early 1992.

However, in June 1995 the country's largest commercial bank, Banka Baltija, collapsed and sparked a major banking crisis which left thousands of people devastated as their life savings literally vanished overnight.

With the government encouraging foreign investment and credit, the private sector is growing rapidly, with many new joint ventures being registered with foreign partners. Some large multinational companies such as Kellogs favour Rīga for its geographical location at the centre of the Baltic states. However, the high cost of living and equally high corruption in Rīga compared to the other two Baltic countries coupled, with Latvia's lack of important population centres outside the capital, remain a disincentive for many.

Latvia's major trading partner remains Russia (accounting for 21.6% of exports and 25.3% of imports) but Germany, Finland, Sweden and Lithuania are also significant markets. The UK and USA are the largest foreign investors in Latvia. In mid-1996, inflation in Latvia stood at 20%.

POPULATION & PEOPLE

Latvia's population is a little less than 2.5 million, over 70% of which live in towns or cities. Only 56.6% is ethnic Latvian, and Latvians are a minority in all seven of the country's major cities including the capital. Russians account for 30.3%, Belarusians 4.3% and Ukrainians 2.7%. Since 1987 the natural growth rate of the population in Latvia has decreased: amongst the Russian-speaking population this is due to emigration but amongst the ethnic Latvians it's because the death rate now exceeds the birth rate.

Latvians and Lithuanians are the only surviving members of the Baltic ethnic family, an Indo-European but non-Slavic group whose third branch – the old Prussians – was exterminated by the Teutonic Knights.

ARTS

The earliest features of Latvian culture are the 1.4 million *dainas* (folk songs) identified and collected by Krišjānis Barons (1835-1923). Latvia only made the transition from a peasant, folkloric-based culture to a modern urban culture in the mid to late 19th century. The cornerstone of the new culture was the epic *Lāčplēsis* (The Bear Slayer), formed from traditional folk tales by Andrējs Pumpurs in 1888. Pumpurs' work has remained a source of inspiration for successive generations of writers and artists – the beginnings of the nationalist movement in 1988 were accompanied by a rock-opera *Lāčplēsis*.

A play based on the Lāčplēsis theme, *Uguns un nakts* (Fire and Night), was written by the most celebrated figure in Latvian literature, Jānis Rainis (1865-1929), who Latvians claim might have had a reputation to match Shakespeare or Goethe if he had written in a less obscure language. His leading works were written in the first quarter of the 20th century and their criticism of social and political oppression forced him to live much of his life in exile in Siberia and Switzerland.

Latvia also has a strong film-making tradition. Sergei Eisenstein was born in Rīga (his father was an architect responsible for some of the city's most fabulous apartment houses), as was the documentary maker Jūris Podnieks, who died young in 1992 but not before he produced some outstanding, haunting documentaries of life in the late Soviet era including *Is it Easy to be Young?*, *Hello Do You Hear Us?* and *Homeland*.

CULTURE

It is difficult to define the Latvian character without reference to their neighbours: they're more emotional and romantic than the Estonians but less so than the Lithuanians; they're warmer and less cautious than the Estonians but again not to the degree of the Lithuanians, and so on. One reason for this difficulty in pinning down the Latvians may be the fact that their roots are so entangled, having at one time or another come under the domain of Lutheran Germans and Swedes, Catholic Poles and Orthodox Russians. All these elements are combined in Rīga, the giant amongst Baltic cities, and itself a force in the shaping of national character.

RELIGION

Lutheranism is the predominant faith among Latvians but there's a significant Roman Catholic community too, especially in Latgale, the south-eastern region. Amongst the Russians, Russian Orthodoxy holds sway, though there are also another 46 registered denominations in Latvia.

LANGUAGE

Latvians speak Latvian, one of the two languages of the Baltic branch of the Indo-European language family (the other is Lithuanian). Even more than Estonians, Latvians regard their language as an endangered species: just over half the people in the country, and just over a third of the people in Rīga speak it as their first language. English is widely spoken in Rīga.

See the Language Guide at the back of the book for pronunciation guidelines and useful words and phrases.

Facts for the Visitor

PLANNING
Climate & When to Go

Latvia has a damp climate, with over 600 mm of precipitation a year. July is the warmest month and also the wettest; temperatures reach 22°C but there are also persistent showers. Late June is noted for thunderstorms. From May to August and September is usually the most comfortable time. Winter starts in November and lasts until late March, with temperatures rarely above 4°C, and snow from January to March in coastal regions. The east is usually 1°C warmer than the coast in summer and 4°C colder in winter.

Books & Maps

See Facts for the Visitor in the Estonia chapter for some titles which cover the Baltic states. Latvia is adequately covered by many of the large-scale Baltic states maps available in the West, also listed under Facts for the Visitor in the Estonia chapter.

What to Bring

See the Facts for the Visitor section in the Estonia chapter.

SUGGESTED ITINERARIES

The following are a couple of possibilities:

Two days
    Rīga with a day trip out to Jūrmala
One week
    Rīga; Jūrmala; maybe Kurzeme or Latgale; Sigulda, Līgatne and Cēsis

HIGHLIGHTS

Apart from the obvious destination of Rīga, the other highly recommended spot in Latvia is the Gauja valley. For the most adventurous, the ideal way to experience the scenery is to take a canoe trip down the Gauja River from Valmeria (see the Activities section later), but for those pushed for time a day's hiking from Sigulda is a pleasant alternative.

TOURIST OFFICES

Latvia has no tourist information offices abroad but its embassies and consulates, as well as Baltic specialist travel agencies (see Getting There & Away in the Estonia chapter) may have information. There are a handful of tourist information offices in Latvia itself as well as many private organisations which can help.

VISAS & DOCUMENTS

A valid passport is the only requirement for citizens of the Czech Republic, Estonia, Hungary, Ireland, Lithuania, Poland, the Slovak Republic, the UK and the USA.

To extend a visa once you're in Latvia contact the visa office (☎ 7219 118, 7219 834) in the Department of Immigration & Citizenship at Raiņa bulvāris 5 in Rīga. Single-entry visas can also be upgraded to multiple-entry here.

Visas are generally not issued at land borders although Western travellers can sometimes purchase a nonextendable two-day transit visa here. If you arrive at Rīga airport or ferry port you can obtain a 10-day visa without any problems.

LATVIA

For further information on visas and details of other documents you may need, see the Facts for the Visitor section in the Estonia chapter.

EMBASSIES
Latvian Embassies Abroad

Australia
Consulate-General, 38 Longstaff St, Ivanhoe East, Victoria 3073 (☎ 03-9499 6920)

Canada
112 Kent Street, Place de Ville, Tower B, Suite 208, Ottawa, Ontario K1P 5P2 (☎ 613-238 6014)

Denmark
17 Rosbaeksvej, 2100 Copenhagen (39 27 60 00)

Estonia
Tönismägi 10, Tallinn (☎ 2-646 1313)

Finland
Armfeltintie 10, 00150 Helsinki (☎ 09-4764 720)

Germany
Bertha-von-Suttner-Platz 1-7, 5300 Bonn 1 (☎ 228-658 276)

Lithuania
Čiurlionio 76, 2009 Vilnius (☎ 2-231 260, 231 125)

Poland
Reteana 15-19, 02516 Warsaw (☎ 22-481 946, 485 706)

Russia
ulitsa Chaplygina 3, Moscow 103062 (☎ 095-925 2707)

Sweden
Odengatan 5, Box 19167, 10432 Stockholm (☎ 8-700 6300)

UK
45 Nottingham Place, London W1M 3FE (☎ 0171-312 0040)

USA
4325 17th Street NW, Washington DC 20011 (☎ 202-726 6757, 726 8213)

Foreign Embassies in Latvia

Belarus
Elizabetes iela 2, Rīga (☎ 7322 550)

Canada
Doma laukums 4, Rīga (☎ 7830 141)

Estonia
Skolas iela 13, Rīga (☎ 7820 460)

Finland
Teātra iela 9, Rīga (☎ 7216 040)

Germany
Basteja bulvāris 14, Rīga (☎ 7229 096); to move to Raiņa bulvāri 13 in October 1997

Lithuania
Rūpniecibas iela 22, Rīga (☎ 7321 519)

Poland
Elizabetes iela 2, Rīga (☎ 7321 617)

Russia
Antonijas iela 2, Rīga (☎ 7220 693)

Sweden
Lāčplēša iela 13, Rīga (☎ 7286 276)

UK
Alunāna iela 5, Rīga (☎ 7338 126)

USA
Raiņa bulvāris 7, Rīga (☎ 7210 005)

CUSTOMS
See the Facts for the Visitor section in the Estonia chapter.

MONEY
See Facts for the Visitor in the Estonia chapter for general information on money in the Baltic states.

Currency
The lats (plural lati) is the country's only legal tender and comes in five, 10, 20, 50, 100 and 500-lati denomination notes. One lats is divided into 100 santīmi, and there are one, two, five, 10, 20 and 50-santīmi coins and also one and two lati coins.

Exchange Rates
The following currencies convert at the approximate rates:

Australia	A$1	=	0.43 lati
Canada	C$1	=	0.40 lati
Finland	1FmK	=	0.12 lati
Germany	DM1	=	0.37 lati
Sweden	1SKr	=	0.08 lati
UK	UK£1	=	0.85 lati
USA	US$1	=	0.54 lati

POST & COMMUNICATIONS
Post
Expect air-mail letters or cards to take about 10 days to/from North America and about five days to/from Western Europe. Letters/postcards weighing up to 20g cost 0.16/0.13 lati to Europe and 0.24/0.20 lati to the USA. Stamps can only be bought from post offices or hotels. The poste restante desk, which keeps mail to be collected for one month, is at the large post office at Stacijas laukums 1

(☎ 7213 297), next to Rīga train station. Address letters to Poste Restante, Rīga 50, LV-1050, Latvia.

Telephone

Public card phones accept *telekartes*, worth one, five or 10 lati which can be bought from kiosks, shops and post offices. Coin-operated phones, accepting everything from a one santīmi to two lati coin, can be found at train and bus stations. To call other cities in Latvia simply dial the area code followed by the telephone number. Area codes from Latvian phones include Rīga ☎ 2, Bauska ☎ 39, Cēsis ☎ 41, Daugavpils ☎ 54, Jelgava ☎ 30, Liepāja ☎ 34, Valmiera ☎ 42, Ventspils ☎ 36.

All international calls (including the ex-USSR) require the international access code 00, followed by the country code, area code and telephone number. Charges are 0.23 lati per minute to the Baltic states, 0.93 lati to Europe, and 1.70 lati to the USA. The country code for calling Latvia from abroad is ☎ 371. You do not need an area code when calling to Latvia from abroad, except if you are calling a six-digit, analogue number (see below).

Analogue Phones The old Soviet analogue system, requiring users to book long-distance and internationals calls through an operator, can still be found in some rural areas and one or two outermost suburbs in Rīga. Analogue numbers have only six digits. To call a digital number from an analogue phone dial ☎ 1, wait for the tone, then dial the number. To dial an analogue number from a digital phone dial ☎ 2 before the six-digit number. To call other cities in Latvia, dial ☎ 8-tone, then dial ☎ 2 followed by the area code. To call cities in the former Soviet Union dial ☎ 8-tone followed by the area code. These include: Vilnius ☎ 0122, Kaunas ☎ 0127, Tallinn ☎ 014, St Petersburg ☎ 812 and Moscow ☎ 095. International calls still have to be booked through an operator (☎ 1-tone-115). Calls take between 10 minutes and one hour to come through.

If you're unlucky you might stumble upon token-operated, analogue phone boxes in some remote areas. These Soviet monstrosities, which accept *žetonis* (costing 0.4 santīmi from some kiosks and post offices), are hotly pursued worldwide by phonebox collectors who have been known to install the entire Doctor Who set-up in their homes.

Fax, Telegraph & E-mail

Faxes can be sent from most main post offices in Latvia. Costs are: to Europe 1.71 to 1.78 lati per page; to the USA 1.85 lati per page; and to Australia 1.99 lati per page.

International telegrams, inbound or outbound, usually arrive the same or next day. They can be sent from any telegraph *(telegrāfs)* office (often part of the post office).

For Internet access in Latvia contact LvNet-Teleport (☎ 7551 133; e-mail info@lvnet.lv) at Brīvības iela 204. If you subscribe to SprintNet, CompuServe or MCIMail you can access your account in Rīga (☎ 7223 816). You can set up a temporary e-mail account at Bimini Ņam-Ņam in Rīga (see Post & Communications in the Rīga section).

NEWSPAPERS & MAGAZINES

The weekly *Baltic Times*, the offspring of a merger between the ailing Rīga-based *Baltic Observer* and the equally ailing Tallinn-based *Baltic Independent*, is published in Rīga every Thursday and enjoys moderate success as the only English-language newspaper to cover the three Baltic states. It's sold for 0.30 lati at bookstalls and hotels. Distributed for free in some hotels and travel agencies is *Rīga This Week*, a supposedly bimonthly tourist guide with a lot of ads, a bunch of official propaganda and not much else. The top-quality city guide *Rīga In Your Pocket* covers everything you need to know (as well as a collection of bizarre facts you'd be proud to know). Western newspapers and magazines of the day can be found at some cafés and major hotels in Rīga.

RADIO & TV

The BBC World Service can be picked up 24 hours a day on 100.5 FM. Latvian State Radio, Latvijas radio I, transmits daily short-wave broadcasts at 5935 kHz in English from 8 to 8.30 pm, and in Swedish from 9.30 to 10 pm. The classical music programme, broadcast by Amadeus on 89.2 FM, is also worth tuning in to between 7 pm and 7 am. A number of pubs, bars and hotels show CNN and Eurosports on cable TV.

PHOTOGRAPHY & VIDEO
See the Facts for the Visitor section in the Estonia chapter.

TIME
See the Facts for the Visitor section in the Estonia chapter.

ELECTRICITY
See the Facts for the Visitor section in the Estonia chapter.

WEIGHTS & MEASURES
See the Facts for the Visitor section in the Estonia chapter.

LAUNDRY
Rīga has two good laundrettes. See that section for details.

TOILETS
See the Facts for the Visitor section in the Estonia chapter.

HEALTH
See Facts for the Visitor in the Estonia chapter for general information on health in the Baltics.

Drinking unboiled tap water is not advisable in Rīga, although a couple of glasses won't kill you, Most residents boil water.

Between May and September there's a risk of tick-borne encephalitis in parks in Rīga and in Jūrmala's wooded areas backing on to the beach. Consider immunisation with a vaccine or specific tick-borne encephalitis immunoglobulin, readily available in Europe. To avoid tick-bites cover bare skin or use an insect repellent. If you're bitten smother the tick with alcohol or oil and then pull the head out.

Swimming anywhere on Latvia's coast is risky owing to pollution. People still swim though.

WOMEN TRAVELLERS
See the Facts for the Visitor section in the Estonia chapter.

GAY & LESBIAN TRAVELLERS
Rīga is the most gay-friendly of the Baltic capitals although public expressions of affection are treated with contempt by some. The extremely active Latvian Association for Sexual Equality (☎ 7223 293; e-mail lasv@com.latnet.lv) at Puškina iela 1a publishes *The Gay Guide to Rīga* which lists some bars, clubs and cruising parks.

DISABLED TRAVELLERS
For information contact the Baltic Association of Rehabilitation of Disabled Persons at Vaivari Children's Rehabilitation Centre (☎ 766 211; fax 766 124), Asaru 61, Jūrmala LV 2008.

DANGERS & ANNOYANCES
See the Facts for the Visitor section in the Estonia chapter.

BUSINESS HOURS
Shop, office, café and restaurant hours are similar to those in Estonia (see Facts for the Visitor in the Estonia chapter).

PUBLIC HOLIDAYS & SPECIAL EVENTS
Latvia's national holidays are:

1 January, *New Year's Day*
Good Friday
Second Sunday in May, *Mother's Day*
23 June, *Ligo* (Midsummer Festival)
24 June, *Jāni* (St John's Day)
18 November, *Day of Proclamation of Latvian Republic, 1918*
26 December, *Boxing Day*
31 December, *New Year's Eve*

Latvia shares a number of regular cultural events with Estonia and Lithuania, the most important of these being the national song festival (held every five years with the next in 1999 in Estonia, the Baltika International

Folk Festival (next in Rīga in 1997) and midsummer celebrations.

Smaller annual festivals include: the Folklore Fair at the (open-air) Latvian Ethnography Museum the first weekend of June; the International Festival of Organ Music at the end of June; Rīga Summer – a festival of symphonic and chamber music – in July; every even year, the Jūrmala Pop Festival; and in Rīga every year, Rīga Rock Summer, a three-day rock festival which attracts international names. Every July an Opera Music Festival takes place in Sigulda, and a Festival of Ancient Music takes place amid the ruins of Bauska Castle. In mid-September every even year is Arsenāls, an international film festival in Rīga.

ACTIVITIES
Cycling
It is possible to hire bicycles in Rīga from the bicycle tourism Gandrs (☎ 614 775), at Kalnciema iela 28/30, for eight lati a day. It also organises tours as does Rīga Tourist Information Bureau (☎ 7221 731, 7221 113), Skārņu iela 22, which arranges individual cycling and canoeing tours of Vidzeme, Latgale and Kurzeme for 6 to 20 lati a day. It can also arrange yachting on the Gulf of Riga and ballooning. The cheapest bikes can be rented from Ruķis (☎ 426 020) at Skolas iela 161. It charges 1 lats a day and requires a 30 lati deposit.

Canoeing
The Gauja, Salaca and Abava rivers and the Latgale lakes region all offer uninterrupted routes of several days – the Gauja and Latgale being the prime choices. The Makars Tourism Agency (☎ 973 724; fax 972 006), at Peldu iela 1 in Sigulda, also organises one, two and three-day boating trips from Sigulda to Līgatne, Cēsis, Rāmnieki and Valmiera for 8 to 44 lati. Rafting on the Gauja costs 3 lati per person per hour.

The Latvian University Tourist Club (LUTK; ☎ 7223 114) at Raiņa bulvāris 19 apparently arranges canoeing tours but can be difficult to contact.

Winter Sports
The Gauja valley is the winter sports centre with a 1200-metre-long bobsleigh run at Šveices iela 13 (☎ 973 813) in Sigulda. The European luge championships are held here in January each year and in summer you can take an exhilarating trip down the bobsleigh run in a wheel-bob every Saturday and Sunday for 3 lati. In Valmiera there is a ski run and also an artificial slope. The Makars Tourism Agency in Sigulda (see Canoeing above) also arranges skiing.

WORK
See the Facts for the Visitor section in the Estonia chapter.

ACCOMMODATION
Camping
Latvia has some camping grounds (kempings). Motorists can try asking at farms and homesteads for permission to camp. Don't even attempt to spend the night in a city park where the police can fine you 5 lati just for walking on the grass.

Hostels & Colleges
Latvia lacks a wide youth hostel network, although places in college hostels can be found in Rīga.

Private Homes & Flats
There are one or two enterprises offering apartment or cottage rental in Rīga and Jūrmala. You can also organise homestays in any of the Baltic states through organisations in the West (see Facts for the Visitor in the Estonia chapter for details).

Hotels
In Rīga there are plenty of bottom-end accommodation possibilities but it is vital that you try to book in advance. Rooms are available all year round at Rīga's top-end hotels. It is cheaper to book hotel rooms through travel agencies such as Latvia Tours (☎ 7213 652; fax 7820 020; e-mail lt@mail.bkc.lv) at Kaļķu iela 8, Rīga. Sometimes they can get you a room even when the hotel claims to be full.

LATVIA

Often room prices will vary within an establishment, depending on the degree of refurbishment that has taken place. The more 'Western' the management thinks a room is, the more you will be charged for it.

FOOD

See Facts for the Visitor in the Estonia chapter for general information on the food and restaurant scene in the Baltic states.

The Latvian diet leans heavily on dairy products, grains and fish, though you'll find meat in restaurants. *Šprotes* (sprats) crop up as a starter in many places. If they're *ar sīpoliem*, they'll be with onions. You may also find *siļe* (herring), *līdaka* (pike) and *lasis* (salmon). If fish or meat is *cepts* it's fried; if *kūpīnats*, it's smoked. Soups and sausage *(desa)* are popular. In summer and autumn good use is made of many types of berry. Throughout Latvia you will find a mouth-watering choice of freshly baked cakes, breads and pastries for as little as 0.06 lati a piece. A few food words in Latvian are:

bread	maize
starters	uzkoda
salad	salāti
soup	zupa
potatoes	kartupeli
fish	zivs
chicken	vista
meat or main dishes	gaļas ēdieni
vegetables	saknes
fruit	augļi
cheese	siers
ice cream	saldējums
cake	kūkas
bill	rēķinu
tea	tēja
coffee	kafija

DRINKS

Beer is *alus* in Latvian and the best beer is produced by the Aldaris brewery. A 330 ml bottle of Aldaris Zelta cost 0.30 lati. A wide range of cheaper, cloudy beers is available from other breweries, all named after Latvian regions or towns (Baltija, Rīga etc). A Latvian speciality is Black Balsam *(Melnais Balzāms)*, a thick, dark, vaguely noxious liquid with supposedly medicinal properties. It's often drunk 50/50 with vodka or mixed in coffee.

Take care with tap water (see Health earlier in this section).

ENTERTAINMENT

See the Facts for the Visitor section in the Estonia chapter.

Getting There & Away

Several options for reaching Latvia directly are listed here. See also the Estonia and Lithuania chapters for other ways of reaching the Baltic region.

TRAVEL AGENCIES

See the Getting There & Away section of the Estonia chapter for Baltic states specialist travel agencies in Western countries.

AIR

Routes

Rīga has scheduled flights to/from Copenhagen and Stockholm daily with SAS; Helsinki six times weekly with Finnair; Frankfurt daily with Lufthansa; Hamburg and Berlin Tempelhof six times weekly with Hamburg Airlines; Prague four times weekly with ČSA; and Vienna three times weekly with Austrian Airlines. These six airlines offer a wealth of worldwide connections via their home bases.

Air Baltic, the Latvian state airline supported by SAS, flies daily to Copenhagen, Frankfurt, Geneva, Stockholm; six times weekly to Helsinki and London; three times weekly to Kiev, Minsk and Warsaw; and five times weekly to Tallinn and Vilnius. Riair (Rīga Airlines) flies five times weekly to London; twice weekly to Paris; and daily to Moscow.

Fares

The cheapest tickets may not be offered by the airlines themselves but by their 'general sales agents' such as Regent Holidays of 15 John Street, Bristol, England (☎ 0117-921 1711; fax 0117-925 4866), which in 1996 had London-Rīga open-jaw returns with SAS and Lufthansa for UK£265. SAS offers similar fares from Manchester, Newcastle, Glasgow and Edinburgh.

The Baltic home-grown airlines offer some good deals. In mid-1996 Riair (in the UK ☎ 01293-535 727) had a US$350 round Rīga-London-Rīga fare with no restrictions. Air Baltic (in London ☎ 0171-828 4223, in Frankfurt ☎ 69-6655 8111) had a US$380 round Rīga-London-Rīga fare, the only restrictions being a minimum seven-day stay and purchasing the ticket a week in advance. Their return fares to Germany start at US$390.

In mid-1996 Finnair was offering returns to/from New York for US$795, undercutting most other airlines by about US$300. Return fares from Helsinki and Stockholm generally start at around US$250, the only restriction being you stay over a weekend.

See Getting There & Away in the Estonia chapter for information on charter flights.

LAND

For any travel through Russia, Belarus or Kaliningrad, look into the visa situation well ahead of departure. Some information on Belarusian visas is given in Lithuania, Facts for the Visitor.

Bus

Eurolines (☎ 7211 158) at Aspazijas bulvāris 26, Rīga, runs daily buses to Berlin, twice-weekly buses to Munich and Stuttgart, and weekly buses to Bremen and Cologne. Nordeka (☎ 7213 502) at Rīga bus station runs daily buses to Warsaw and Kiel.

Train

From Warsaw the *Baltic Express*, which goes direct to Tallinn in Estonia, stops at Rīga (see Getting There & Away in the Estonia chapter).

Car & Motorcycle

See the Getting Around chapter at the begin-ning of this book for information on driving and riding in the Baltic states.

SEA

Sweden

At present there are twice-weekly overnight sailings to Rīga from Slite on the eastern coast of Gotland, Sweden, by Transline Baltic Tours (☎ 329 903) at Eksporta 1a, Rīga. The fare starts at US$35 one-way plus US$60 for a car. At the time of writing no ferry operated between Stockholm and Rīga.

Germany

Transline Baltic Tours operates a weekly crossing between Travemünde in Germany and Rīga. Sailing time is 31 hours and fares start at DM150.

ORGANISED TOURS

See the Getting There & Away section of the Estonia chapter.

LEAVING LATVIA

There are no departure taxes to be paid and no other formalities to be completed before leaving.

GETTING AROUND

See the Getting Around section of the Estonia chapter for information on getting around the Baltic states.

Rīga

Rīga has always been the Baltic states' major metropolis. With just over 800,000 people it has a big-city feel. During the 1930s the city was the West's major post for listening into 'the Russian bear' to the east, and the city was a thrumming mix of diplomats, traders and intrigues – earning it the accolade of 'the Paris of the east'. Today, like its neighbouring Baltic capitals, Rīga has a well-preserved historic old quarter, which isn't as picture-postcard pretty as Tallinn's or Vilnius', but neither is it as provincial.

Rīga is a fascinating mix of Latvian,

LATVIA

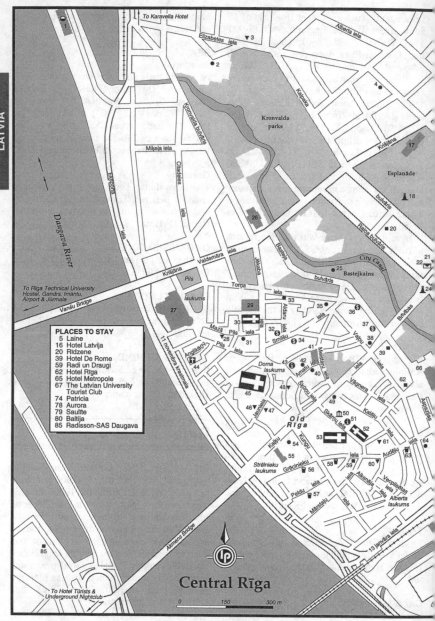

To Karavella Hotel

Elizabetes iela ▼3

Alberta iela

● 2

Kronvalda bulvāris

● 4

Kalpaka

Kronvalda
parks

Mikela iela

Kristiāna

● 17

Citadeles iela

Esplanāde

🔱 18

Raina bulvāris

Eksporta iela

26

■ 20

City Canal

22

Daugava River

Kronvalda bulvāris

Krišjāna

Pils

Valdemāra iela

Bastejas

Bastejkalns

25

Basteja bulvāris

21

Torņa

iela

24

To Rīga Technical University
Hostel, Gandrs, Imantu,
Airport & Jūrmala

laukums

Brīvības

Vanšu Bridge

27

29

33

35

36

11 novembra krastmala

30

32

Smilšu iela

34

37

38

39

Mazā Pils iela

31

41

66

28

Pils iela

42

Anglikāņu

44

43

Amatu iela

40

Meistaru iela

Skārņu iela

62

PLACES TO STAY
5 Laine
16 Hotel Latvija
20 Rīdzene
39 Hotel De Rome
59 Radi un Draugi
62 Hotel Rīga
65 Hotel Metropole
67 The Latvian University
    Tourist Club
74 Patricia
78 Aurora
79 Saulite
80 Baltija
85 Radisson-SAS Daugava

Doma
laukums

45

48▼

46▼ ▼47

Vāgnera iela

49

Jauniela

50

51

Old
Rīga

Skapu iela

52

Kaļķu iela

53

Aldaru

▼61

64

54

Kungu

iela

63

55

Atgrēži

Strēlnieku
laukums

Grēcinieku

56

58

iela

59

60

Vecpilsētas iela

Peldu

iela

Alberta
laukums

🛏 57

Mārstaļu

iela

Akmens Bridge

13 janvāra iela

To Hotel Tūrists &
Underground Nightclub

Central Rīga

0   150   300 m

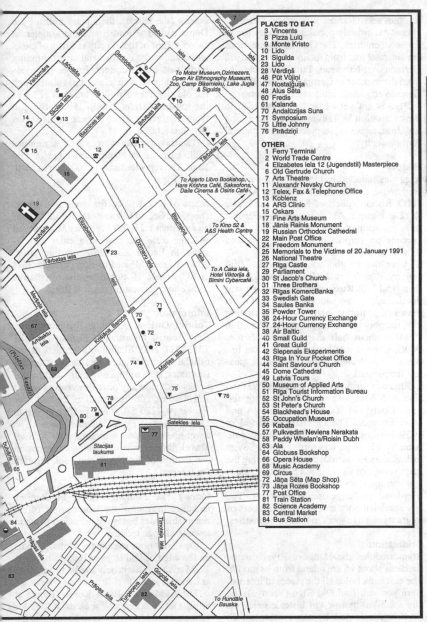

LATVIA

PLACES TO EAT
3 Vincents
8 Pizza Lulū
9 Monte Kristo
10 Lido
21 Sigulda
23 Lido
28 Vērdiņš
46 Pūt Vējiņi
47 Nostaļģija
48 Alus Sēta
60 Fredis
61 Kalanda
70 Andalūzijas Suns
71 Symposium
75 Little Johnny
76 Pīrādziņi

OTHER
1 Ferry Terminal
2 World Trade Centre
4 Elizabetes iela 12 (Jugendstil) Masterpiece
6 Old Gertrude Church
7 Arts Theatre
11 Alexandr Nevsky Church
12 Telex, Fax & Telephone Office
13 Koblenz
14 ARS Clinic
15 Oskars
17 Fine Arts Museum
18 Jānis Rainis Monument
19 Russian Orthodox Cathedral
22 Main Post Office
24 Freedom Monument
25 Memorials to the Victims of 20 January 1991
26 National Theatre
27 Rīga Castle
29 Parliament
30 St Jacob's Church
31 Three Brothers
32 Rīgas KomercBanka
33 Swedish Gate
34 Saules Banka
35 Powder Tower
36 24-Hour Currency Exchange
37 24-Hour Currency Exchange
38 Air Baltic
40 Small Guild
41 Great Guild
42 Slepenais Eksperiments
43 Rīga In Your Pocket Office
44 Saint Saviour's Church
45 Dome Cathedral
49 Latvia Tours
50 Museum of Applied Arts
51 Rīga Tourist Information Bureau
52 St John's Church
53 St Peter's Church
54 Blackhead's House
55 Occupation Museum
56 Kabata
57 Pulkvedim Neviens Neraksta
58 Paddy Whelan's/Roisin Dubh
63 Ala
64 Globuss Bookshop
66 Opera House
68 Music Academy
69 Circus
72 Jāņa Sēta (Map Shop)
73 Jāņa Rozes Bookshop
77 Post Office
81 Train Station
82 Science Academy
83 Central Market
84 Bus Station

To Motor Museum, Dzimezers,
Open Air Ethnography Museum,
Zoo, Camp Bikernieku, Lake Jugla
& Sigulda

To Aperto Libro Bookshop,
Hare Krishna Café, Saksofons,
Daile Cinema & Osiris Café

To Kino 52 &
A&S Health Centre

To A Čaka iela,
Hotel Viktorija &
Bimini Cybercafé

To Rundāle
Bauska

Russian and German influences. Germans almost exclusively populated the city for its first six centuries. The German connections are clear not just from its fine old *Jugendstil*, German Art-Nouveau, buildings but also from the number of German visitors, and the German economic interest evident here.

Rīga is not yet as far down the road to Westernisation as Tallinn and is still a long way from regaining its place as an influential European city.

History

Rīga was founded in 1158 as a river-mouth storehouse for Bremen merchants. Around 1200, Bishop Albert of Buxhoevden chose Rīga as his seat. At his instigation, German knights soon conquered Livonia. Rīga became an important fortified port and joined the Hanseatic League in 1282.

After the knights' decline in the 16th century, Rīga fell under Polish, Swedish and then (in 1710) Russian control, though still dominated by the old German nobility. It grew into an important industrial and trading city, the population jumping from 28,000 in 1794 to about half a million just before WWI, when it was Russia's third most important industrial city and the world's greatest timber port.

Rīga was seriously damaged in WWI (and also in WWII), and was left with a population of only 181,000 after evacuations and other ravages. The Germans departed in 1939 heeding Hitler's 'come home' call. After WWII, Rīga was turned into a Soviet technical and industrial centre, becoming the main source of the USSR's railway engines and carriages, and a big supplier of radios, telephone exchanges and computers. The city sprawled outwards as large numbers of migrants came to work in the new industries.

Orientation

Rīga straddles the Daugava River on the flatlands about 15 km inland from its mouth. The east bank holds all the places of interest. Here you will find Old Rīga (Vecrīga), the city's 1.5-km-by-one-km historic heart, its skyline dominated by three steeples: St

Peter's (the tallest), the square bulk of the Dome cathedral tower, and the simpler St Jacob's. East of the old city is a ring of parks and boulevards. Rīga's axial street, running north-east from Akmens Bridge (Akmens tilts), is called Kaļķu iela as it passes through the old city, then Brīvības bulvāris as far as the towering Hotel Latvija, about two km from the river, from where it becomes Brīvības iela.

The train and bus stations are five minutes walk apart on the south-east edge of Old Rīga. The ferry terminal is 500 metres north of Old Rīga.

Maps The best place for maps is the map shop Jāņa Sēta at Elizabetes iela 83/85. It has an excellent 1:25,000 *Rīga City Map* as well as large-scale maps of most cities and regions in Latvia. Latvian-Australian artist, Aldis Tīlens of Pilot Projekts (☎ 7225 337) at Šķūņu iela 19 publishes the alternative 'bird's-eye panoramic map' of Rīga.

Information

Tourist Offices Although privately run, Rīga Tourist Information Bureau (☎ 7221 731, 7221 113), Skārņu iela 22, acts as the official tourist office. Open daily, it organises tours, sells top-quality maps and guidebooks and generally provides visitors with a wealth of valuable information. *Rīga In Your Pocket* (☎ 7220 580) has an office at Šķūņu 19 (entrance on Doma laukums), as well as a web site (http://www.omnitel.net/OurSite/Travel/rihome.htm) containing information and listings of hotels you can book through the Internet.

Money The exchange office at Stacijas laukums, in front of the train station, offers acceptable rates but is not the safest place in town to change money.

Rīga's 24-hour exchanges include Ahāts on the edge of Old Rīga at Basteja bulvāris 12, Marika at Basteja bulvāris 14 and another at Brīvības iela 90.

The ATM inside Rīgas KomercBanka at Smilšu iela 6 accepts Visa cards. ATMs for Eurocard and MasterCard can be found at the airport, the central post office, Saules Banka at Smilšu iela 16, the World Trade Centre at Elizabetes iela 2, the Hotel Metropole at Aspazijas bulvāris 36/38, Hotel Latvija, and at Statoil at Krasta 101. Most major banks give cash advances on Visa, MasterCard and Eurocard.

Latvia Tours (☎ 7213 652) at Kaļķu iela 8 is the agent for American Express. It cannot cash travellers' cheques, but will issue them and replace any lost American Express cheques and cards. All the banks listed above change travellers' cheques and Eurocheques, although Saules Banka charges the lowest handling fee (1% of total sum).

Post & Communications Rīga's central post office at Brīvības bulvāris 19 (☎ 7333 285) is open 24 hours, and also has telephone services. The post office (☎ 7213 297) at Stacijas laukums, immediately on your right as you come out of the train station (open weekdays from 8 am to 8 pm, Saturday from 8 am to 4 pm and on Sunday from 10 am to 4 pm) is the best place from which to send large parcels as they will wrap them for you. Express Mail Service (☎ 7211 226) is in the hall to your right as you enter.

There is a telex, fax and telephone office (☎ 7217 293) on Dzirnavu iela immediately behind the Hotel Latvija, open Monday to Saturday from 9 am to 8 pm and Sunday from 9 am to 7 pm.

E-mail messages can be sent and received from the Bimini Ņam-Ņam cybercafé (☎ 290 610; e-mail bimini@mailbox.riga.lv) at Čaka 67/69, where you can log on for 2.5 lati an hour and set up your own e-mail account for 5 lati a year.

Travel Agencies Latvia Tours (☎ 7213 652; fax 7820 020; e-mail lt@mail.bkc.lv) at Kaļķu iela 8 arranges short tours of the city as well as day trips to Sigulda, Kurzeme, Cēsis, Jūrmala and Rundāle. The Travel Agency Satellite (TAS; ☎ 7216 216; fax 7820 285) at Kaļķu iela 20 organises tailor-made tours of the Baltics and Russia, amongst other services.

Bookshops Aperto Libro at Barona iela 31 stocks a good range of textbooks, contemporary fiction, travel and guidebooks. Globuss at Vaļņu iela 26 opens weekdays from 10 am to 7 pm and Saturday from 10 am to 5 pm. Dictionaries and Penguin Classics are its speciality. The biggest, Jāņa Rozes at Elizabetes iela 85a (open weekdays from 10 am to 7 pm and Saturday from 10 am to 4 pm) stocks the best range of children's books and encyclopaedias, as well as top postcards and posters.

Laundry There is an excellent laundrette, Miele (☎ 7217 696) at Elizabetes iela 85a, close to the train station. It is open 24 hours and offers service washes for around five lati. Tīrītava (☎ 7276 108) at Gertrūdes iela 37 does dry cleaning (open weekdays from 8 am to 8 pm and on Saturday from 9 am to 4 pm).

Left Luggage There is a 24-hour left-luggage room (rokas bagāžas glabātuve) downstairs in the long-distance section of the train station. Small bags can be left here for 0.50 lati a day and large bags for 1 lati. The locker room (open 24 hours) is on the right as you walk towards the tracks. It costs 0.60 lati per locker. Put your bags in, and turn the keys on the inside of the door to any combination of one Cyrillic letter and three numbers. Next close the door and turn the knobs on the outside of the door to something other than your combination and put the tokens (žetonis) you were given by the assistant in the slot. To open the locker, turn the outside knobs to your combination and put a second token in the slot. At the bus station the left-luggage room is to the left as you enter the main hall (open daily 5 am to 11 pm). At the airport it is behind the staircase to your left as you enter the arrival hall.

Medical & Emergency Services ARS Clinic (☎ 201 001, 201 007) at Skolas iela 5 offers a 24 hour, English-speaking service as well as an emergency home service (☎ 201 003). There is an emergency dental service at the A & S Health Centre (☎ 7289 516) on

Lāčplēša 60. The Aids Centre (☎ 529 895) is at Pilsoņu iela 13 and the Centre for Sexual Diseases (☎ 272 198) is at Blieķu iela 2. Pharmacies stocking Western drugs include Koblenz at Dzirnavu iela 57 (open Monday to Saturday from 10 am to 9 pm and on Sunday from 10 am to 7 pm), Drogas at Tērbatas 52 (open Monday to Saturday from 10 am to 9 pm) and Kamēlijas aptieka on Brīvības iela 74 (open daily from 8 am to 8 pm). For 24-hour service, ring the bell at Kamēlijas aptieka.

Dangers & Annoyances As a foreigner, the mobile-phone, shell-suited Mafia types will leave you well alone. Street kids and beggars, however, pleading for a few santīmi will harass you almost everywhere.

Things to See

Old Rīga The Old Town retains whole squares or rows of German buildings that have stood since the 17th century or earlier. It's a protected, mainly pedestrian zone, made prettier by restoration, and motorists have to pay 5 lati to enter. Walking its streets is one of the chief pleasures of Rīga but don't forget to keep looking up so as not to miss the playful statuettes and carvings that adorn many of the buildings.

Kaļķu iela neatly divides the old city in half, each half focusing on a towering church: the Dome cathedral in the north, St Peter's church in the south.

The brick cathedral, **Rīgas Doms** (from the German: *Dom*, cathedral), founded in 1211 for the Rīga bishop, is now an all-in-one church, museum and organ concert hall. It opens Tuesday to Friday from 1 to 5 pm and Saturday from 10 am to 2 pm, admission 1 lati. There are services at noon on Sunday.

The cathedral is a 13th to 18th-century blend of architecture: the east end (the oldest) has Romanesque features, the 18th-century tower is baroque, and much of the remainder is 15th-century Gothic.

The floor and walls are dotted with old stone tombs: a 1709 cholera and typhoid outbreak, which killed a third of Rīga's pop-

ulation, was blamed on a flood that inundated these.

The huge 1880s organ with 6768 pipes is reckoned to be the world's fourth largest. A cloister next to the Dome at Palasta iela 4 contains the **Museum of the History of Rīga & Navigation**, open daily except Monday and Tuesday, from 11 am to 5 pm.

Parts of **Rīga Castle** at Pils laukums 3 date from 1330, when it was built for the German knights. Now, painted bright canary yellow, it is home to Latvia's president and also houses an unexciting **Museum of Foreign Art**, which is open daily except Monday from 11 am to 5 pm.

Nearby at Mazā Pils iela, Nos 17, 19 and 21 is a quaint row of houses known as the **Three Brothers**. No 17 is a 15th-century house, which makes it the oldest in Latvia. **St Saviour's Church** at Anglikāņu 2a was built in 1857 by a small group of British traders on 30 feet of British soil brought over as ballast in the ships transporting the building material. English services are at 10 am every Sunday. At the end of Mazā Pils iela is Jēkaba iela and the 13th-century **St Jacob's Church**, the seat of Rīga's Roman Catholic archbishop. Next door, at Jēkaba iela 11, is Latvia's **parliament** building.

The picturesque **Swedish Gate** at the junction of Torņa iela and Aldaru iela was built onto the city walls in 1698. The round, peaked 14th-century **Powder Tower** (Pulvertornis) at the end of Torņa iela has been a gunpowder store, prison, torture chamber, Soviet Revolution Museum and students' party venue.

South of Kaļķu iela, the red-brick Gothic bulk of **St Peter's Church** (Pētera Baznīca) dates mainly from the 15th century, though the pink-stone western façade is 17th century. Its famed 72-metre spire has been built three times in the same baroque form: originally in the 1660s, again in the 18th century after being hit by lightning, and most recently after its destruction during WWII. The rest of the church was also badly damaged and much restoration has taken place. St Peter's is now used as an exhibition hall, open daily except Monday from 10 am to 7 pm. There's a lift to the second gallery of the spire for a marvellous panoramic view of Old Rīga (admission 1 lats). The **Occupation Museum** on Strēlnieku laukums, close to St Peter's, is an impressive account of the Soviet and Nazi occupations of Latvia between 1940 and 1964, although the exhibition has been criticised as having a strong nationalist bias. Either way it is informative, disturbing in parts and probably Rīga's most interesting museum. It's open daily from 11 am to 5 pm.

Between the museum and St Peter's on Strēlnieku laukums is the construction site of the **Blackhead's House**, a 14th-century architectural gem built in 1344, destroyed in 1941 and currently being rebuilt.

A row of particularly pretty restored buildings faces St Peter's on Skārņu iela. No 10/16, originally a 13th-century chapel for the Knights of the Sword, is the **Museum of Applied Arts** (Dekoratīvi Lietišķās Mākslas Muzejs), full of outstanding Latvian work, open daily except Monday from 10 am to 6 pm.

Parks & Boulevards East of Old Rīga's jumbled streets, the city's old defensive moat, the **City Canal** (Pilsētas kanāls), snakes through parks laid between wide 19th-century boulevards. On Brīvības bulvāris near the junction with Raiņa bulvāris stands the central landmark of the park ring, the **Freedom Monument** (Brīvības piemineklis), topped by a bronze Liberty holding aloft three stars. Erected in 1935, this monument was out of bounds in the Soviet years, when a statue of Lenin, facing the other way down Brīvības iela, was put up two blocks east (Lenin has now been removed). In the late 1980s and early 90s the Freedom Monument became a hub of the Latvian independence movement, starting on 14 June 1987 when 5000 people rallied illegally there to commemorate the victims of Stalin's deportations. It would be possible to climb inside 'Milda', as the bronze statue is called, and walk to the top for a breathtaking view of Rīga from the small window cut

in her chest, if the authorities were prepared to open her up to the public.

In Bastejkalns, west of the monument, five red stone slabs lie as **Memorials to the Victims of 20 January 1991**, killed here when Soviet troops stormed the nearby Interior Ministry. Two of those commemorated are Andris Slapinš and Gvido Zvaigzne, members of Jūris Podnieks' film crew, whose dying footage was included in the documentary *Homeland*.

Opposite the Interior Ministry, across Brīvības bulvāris, is the domed 19th-century **Russian Orthodox cathedral**, returned to church use after years of use as a Soviet planetarium. The **Fine Arts Museum** at Krišjāna Valdemāra iela 10A, on the northern corner of the Esplanāde park, houses what is probably the best art collection in the Baltics. It has permanent collections of Russian and Latvian work plus some interesting temporary exhibitions. It's open daily except Tuesday from 11 am to 5 pm.

New Rīga The commercial soul of the city lies beyond the ring of Elizabetes iela in a grid of broad, six-storey streets. It is in this part of town that Rīga really starts to feel like a major city. Along the boulevards are many impressive and flamboyant 19th and early 20th-century buildings in Rīga's characteristic *Jugendstil* style. One of the best examples, designed by Mikhail Eisenstein, father of the renowned film maker, is at Elizabetes iela 10b, just north of the Arts Museum. Around the corner, on nearby **Alberta iela**, the buildings become even more fantastical, looking as though they were designed as an all-purpose backdrop for productions of Anthony and Cleopatra, Montezuma and the Count of Monte Cristo.

Suburbs Rīga's **Motor Museum** (Motormuzejs) is a long way out at Eizenšteina iela 6, eight km east of the old city, but it's worth the trip for the cars that once belonged to Stalin and Brezhnev, complete with wax images of the former Soviet leaders. The museum is open daily except Monday from 10 am to 7 pm. Bus No 21 from the Russian

Orthodox cathedral goes to the Pansionāts stop on Šmerļa iela, within half a km of the museum.

The open-air **Latvian Ethnography Museum** beside Lake Jugla on the eastern edge of the city, is a collection of over 900 buildings from rural Latvia, mostly wooden, and from the 18th and 19th centuries, assembled on a one-sq-km site. It's open from 10 am to 5 pm, daily from mid-May to mid-October, except the last day of the month. Take bus No 1 from opposite the Russian Orthodox cathedral.

Places to Stay

Camping In the suburbs there are some places to pitch your tent. *Dzirnezers* (☎ 951 415), 14 km north of Rīga on the road to Tallinn offers magnificent views of Lake Dzirnezers from the small summerhouses it rents out, but there's no hot water. Campervans, tents and caravans cost 4 lati; beds in a summerhouse 7 to 9 lati. To get there follow signs for Lake Dzirnezers on the road to Tallinn. Electricity, hot water and showers are provided at *Camp Biķernieku* (☎ 7552 322, 7530 920), in a forest on the north-east edge of the city limits, at Eizenšteina iela 2. Pitching a tent costs 3 lati. Take trolleybus No 7 from the centre and get off at the Biķernieku stop.

Hostels & Colleges The Latvian University Tourist Club or *LUTK* (Latvijas Universitātes Tūristu Klubs; ☎ 7223 114), in the university building at Raiņa bulvāris 19, has single, double and triple rooms in the university youth hostel at Basteja bulvāris 10 (☎ 7220 703). It is best to book in advance as this place is always packed in the summer. A bed in a double room with communal showers and toilet costs 6 lati. A bed in a double with private wash facilities costs 12 lati.

Alternative student accommodation includes *Rīga Technical University Hostel* (☎ 201 491, 203 395) on the other side of the river at Āzenes iela 22a. Rooms here tend to be cleaner as they are not in such demand. A bed for one night costs 3 lati. Take trolleybus

No 7 from the centre and get off one stop after Akmens Bridge. *Imantu*, (☎ 413 847) in Rīga's major sleeping region (ie nothing but sky-high housing blocks) at Zolitūdes 30, has beds in dormitories for 2.36 lati per person. Take the Jūrmala train to the Imanta stop.

Private Homes & Flats *Patricia* (☎ 7284 868) at Elizabetes iela 22-6 offers rooms in private flats all over Latvia, including one next door to the office, which is a five-minute walk from the train station. Rooms cost 7.50 lati without breakfast or 10 lati with breakfast. Rīga Tourist Information Bureau (☎ 7221 731, 7223 113); see Information) can find rooms in private flats in the old town for 7.50 lati per person per night. It also has four luxury rooms overlooking St Peter's for 15 to 25 lati. Lauku Ceļotājs (☎ 617 600) at Kuģu iela 11 organises rooms for the night in farmhouses in the country.

Hotels – bottom end There are a handful of cheap options right by the train station. The best of the worst is *Aurora* (☎ 7224 479), opposite the station at Marijas iela 5. Rooms are small and tend to be very noisy. Singles/doubles/triples cost 3.40/5.80/6.30 lati. *Saulīte* (☎ 7224 546), just round the corner at Merķeļa iela 12, is one of the few cheap hotels in which rooms have actually been repainted in recent years. Singles/ doubles cost 5/7 lati. Luxury rooms (which lack the garish colour schemes of the others) cost 15 to 20 lati depending on the degree of refurbishment. *Viktorija* (☎ 272 305), one km north-east from the station at Čaka iela 55, is in the locally known 'red light district' but offers fairly decent rooms with shared toilets and showers at 8/16 lati. *Baltija* (☎ 722 7461) at Raiņa bulvāris 33 is only for the absolutely desperate; singles/doubles cost 3.90/5.20 lati.

Laine (☎ 7288 816), centrally located at Skolas iela 11, on the 3rd and 4th floors of a run-down old building, has singles/doubles with communal bathroom for 12/24 lati and singles/doubles with private bathroom for 22/35 lati.

Hotels – middle & top end Probably the best value for money is *Radi un Draugi* (☎ 7220 372) at Mārstaļu iela 1. Owned by British-Latvians, it is clean and particularly popular with Brits. Singles/doubles cost 23.60/35.40 lati.

Elias (☎ 518 117), close to Lake Ķīšezers, slightly out of town at Hamburgas iela 14, has seven large rooms costing 16 lati. Take bus No 9 from the central bus station or tram No 11 from Barona iela. *Karavella* (☎ 7324 597) at Katrīnas Dambis 27, by the docks in the Seamen's Centre, has a bowling alley and singles/doubles for 30/50 lati. The former Intourist Hotel, *Tūrists* (☎ 7615 455), on the other side of the river at Slokas iela 1, is grey, grotty and best suited for those into the 'Soviet experience'. Singles/doubles cost from 14/20 lati.

The ex-Intourist *Hotel Latvija* (☎ 7229 020) at Elizabetes iela 55 is the cheapest – and ugliest – of Rīga's more expensive hotels. Locally, the mere sight of it still sends shivers down the spines of many who for years were not even allowed to set foot inside the 27-floor monstrosity. Singles/doubles start at 42/52 lati, with the better rooms costing 61/65 lati. Also ex-Intourist is the *Hotel Rīga* (☎ 7216 107) at Aspazijas bulvāris 22, although today this is hard to believe. Rooms are bright and modern with singles/doubles costing 55/132 lati. *Hotel Metropole* (☎ 7820 065), further down the street towards the station at Aspazijas bulvāris 36/38 was a centre of diplomatic intrigue and espionage in the 1930s. Singles/doubles cost from 39/44 lati and range up to 48/58 lati. The *Rīdzene* (☎ 7324 433) at Reimersa iela 1 was run exclusively for Communist Party officials and other Soviet top dogs when it opened in 1984. Singles/doubles cost 77/85 lati.

Hotel De Rome (☎ 7820 050) in the heart of the Old Town at Kaļķu iela 28 has been considered the top hotel since 1991 when it opened. Today it remains the mainstay for foreign business people. Singles/doubles cost 91/100 lati, luxury suites 125 lati and a suite fit for a president, 500 lati. Equally expensive but on the 'wrong' side of the river is the *Radisson-SAS Daugava* (☎ 7061 111) at Kuģu 24.

Places to Eat
Dining out in Rīga is substantially more expensive than Vilnius or Tallinn. If you have the cash however, the choice of where to dine is quite dizzying. Cheap and cheerful bars and cafés serving palatable dishes from plates other than plastic ones are slowly starting to sprout in Rīga though, with at least two new places cropping up every month.

Restaurants *Pūt Vējiņ* at Jauniela iela 18/22 is very much a trendy restaurant, bar and café all rolled into one, offering a quick carrot and orange soup for 0.80 lati or a more lavish souvlaki for 2.90 lati. Before independence, the cellar was strictly reserved for government officials. At Jāņa iela 8/10 is *Kalanda*, a quiet restaurant serving traditional Latvian fare for no more than 5 lati a head (open daily from 11 am to 11 pm).

Around Doma laukums there are two good options. The Latvian beer bar *Alus Sēta* at Tirgoņu iela 6 (open daily from noon to 1 am) dishes out mammoth portions of ribs, shaslik and other hunks of meat for around 5 lati a head. A minute's walk away at Mazā Pils iela 11 is *Vērdiņš*, a French-style restaurant boasting one of the best courtyards in Rīga and favoured as the best crêperie in the Baltics. An excellent bean and watermelon salad costs 2.75 lati; sweet and savoury crêpes cost 2 to 3 lati.

The best of Rīga's expensive restaurants is *Symposium*, a light and airy 'French' bistro in a restored shopping mall at Dzirnavu iela 84/1. Home-made pasta starts at 5 lati and main dishes at 7 lati. They play classical music and stock a constant supply of English and German dailies. Equally popular is *Vincents* at Elizabetes iela 19 which claims to have the best chef in town cooking up similar French-style dishes such as grilled chevre. More off-beat is the Salvador Dali inspired *Andalūzijas Suns* at Elizabetes iela 81/85. The food is lavish, the décor almost industrial, and at weekends Charlie Chaplin films are screened while you eat.

LATVIA

Cafés At the trendy breakfast and lunch spot, *Osiris* at Barona iela 31 (open weekdays from 8 am to 1 am and on weekends from 10 am to 1 am) you can sit for hours reading Western newspapers and listening to classical music.

Favoured for its exotic range of coffee and cakes is *Monte Kristo* at Gertrūdes iela 27 (open Monday to Saturday from 9 am to 9 pm and on Sunday from noon to 9 pm). Ice cream and milkshake lovers should try *Ice Queen* a few doors down at No 20 (open daily from 11 am to 11 pm).

A must for anyone who misses the Soviet Union is the Baltic's first purpose-built Soviet café *Nostaļģija* at Krāmu iela 4 (open daily from 10 am to 11 pm). Stale buns, plastic cups, drab walls and vodka at rock-bottom prices are all part of the deal. Dishes are even more dirt cheap at the Hare Krishna Rāma & Svāmīdži's Space Station on Barona iela 56 (open daily from 8 am to 8.30 pm). Between noon and 6 pm an entire soup and porridge meal costs just 0.40 lati. *Shalom* at Brīvības iela 158 is the main hang-out for Rīga's Jewish community.

Fast Food Plumping for the fast-food option no longer means steeling your stomach against cardboard fries and gritty burgers. *Lido* at Gertrūdes iela 54, however, remains as popular as ever despite the grease. A second outlet is close to Hotel Latvija on the corner of Elizabetes and Tērbatas iela. Both open 24 hours daily. Of equal standing is *Sigulda* on Brīvības bulvāris 21, where a quick lunch of pizza bread topped with a blob of tomato sauce and sprinkling of cheese can be had standing up for less than 1 lati. *Little Johnny's*, close to the train station at Elizabetes iela 91/93 (open daily from 8 am to 2 am) also serves reasonable pizza slices.

The best bet for pizza is *Pizza Lulū* at Gertrūdes iela 27 and Valdemāra iela 143/145 (open daily from 8 am to midnight). Run by a Canadian-Latvian team, Lulūs serves up giant-sized pizza slices for 0.69 to 0.85 lati. *Fredis* (☎ 7213 731) at Audēju iela 5, open daily from 9 am to midnight, is favoured for

its US-style sub sandwiches and spicy salads, which you can eat in or take out for 1 lat. *Pīrādziņi*, close to the train station at Birznieka-Upīša iela 10, specialises in traditional Latvian buns, pīrādziņi, ranging in price from 0.07 lati for a potato one to 0.13 lati for meat-filled ones (open weekdays from 8 am to 9 pm, weekends from 9 am to 8 pm).

Self-Catering Rīga's colourful central market is housed in five great zeppelin hangars on Prāgas iela behind the bus station (open Tuesday to Saturday from 7 am to 6 pm and on Sunday and Monday from 7 am to 4 pm). Visiting the fresh meat hangar is not a particularly savoury experience however. The Interpegro grocery store opposite the train station is open 24 hours.

Entertainment

Rīga has a lively cultural life: the *Baltic Times* and *Rīga In Your Pocket* list upcoming events.

Bars & Clubs Rīga's hot spot is *Paddy Whelan's* at Grēcinieku iela 4, Rīga's first Irish pub serving pints of Aldaris at a cheap 0.60 lati to appease the boisterous crowd (open daily 8 am to 1 am). Upstairs from Paddy's is the *Roisin Dubh*. Run by the same management, the same beer is sold for 0.90 lati to ensure the riff-raff stays downstairs. Just round the corner at Peldu iela 26/28 is most drinkers' second port-of-call, *Pulkvedim Neviens Neraksta*, an off-beat bar with a football table and packed dance floor (open Sunday to Thursday from noon to 3 am, and on Friday and Saturday from noon to 5 am).

Rīga's first Western-style nightclub, *Underground*, at Slokas iela 1 next door to Hotel Tūrists (open nightly from 9 pm to 6 am), is definitely for techno enthusiasts. The local art scene tends to gather at the industrial-designed *Slepenais Eksperiments* at Šķūņu iela 15 (open daily from 5 pm to 5 am). The entrance is around the corner on Amatu iela. For a flashback to life under communism, try *Groks Stacija* at Kaļķu iela 12. This nightclub, decked out as a Soviet train complete with the cloakroom in a re-created train compartment and the DJ in the driver's cabin, is open daily from noon to 6 am.

For live rock, pop and jazz try *Ala* (☎ 7223 957) at Audēju iela 11 where local bands often play at weekends (open daily 10 am to 4 am). Other alternative cellar bars where wild dancing is freely permitted include *Kabata* (☎ 7225 334) at Peldu iela 19 (open daily from noon to 5 am); *Karakums* (☎ 7282 287) on Lāčplēša iela 18 which closes daily at 3 am; and the more bohemian *Saksofons* (☎ 296 678) at Stabu iela 43, where you can listen to great jazz in a smoke-filled cellar.

Classical Music, Opera & Cinema The Dome cathedral's acoustics, as well as its huge organ, are spectacular, and the frequent organ and other concerts are well worth attending. The ticket office is opposite the west door and schedules are listed there. The highly regarded *Latvia Philharmonia* has its concert hall at Amatu iela 6 in the Great Guild, a 1330 merchants' meeting hall.

On 29 September 1995, Rīga's 1860 *Opera House* was reopened for the first time since independence, and a night at the opera, if only to admire the massive renovation job, is a must. Tickets can be bought from the box office inside the opera house at Aspazijas bulvāris 3 or from the box office at Teātra iela 10/12.

The *Daile Cinema* on Barona iela 31, *Oskars* at Skolas iela 2 and *Kino-52* at Lāčplēša iela 52/54 all show films in English with Latvian or Russian subtitles. An English-speaking telephone information line (☎ 367 777) can tell you what's on where. The film studio inside the *Andalūzijas Suns* at Elizabetes iela 81/85 screens a colourful variety of old back-and-white and contemporary art films.

Rīga has the only permanent *circus* in the Baltics, at Merķeļa iela 4, and it's worth visiting for the bizarre nature of some of the acts (performing pigs and stubbornly non-performing domestic cats); however, the circus goes on holiday from June to September. *Rīga Zoo* (☎ 518 409) is at Meža prospekts

1. Take tram No 11 from the centre to the Zoo darzs stop.

Getting There & Away

Air International connections to/from Rīga are covered in the Getting There & Away section earlier in this chapter. Connections with Estonia and Lithuania are covered in Estonia, Getting There & Away, Travel Between the Baltics. Airline offices in Rīga include:

Air Baltic
    Kaļķu iela 15 (☎ 722 9 166, 7226 355)
Austrian Airlines
    Kaļķu iela 8 (☎ 7216 309)
Finnair
    Airport (☎ 7207 010); Barona iela 36 (☎ 7243 008)
Hamburg Airlines
    Mārstaļu iela 12 (☎ 7227 638)
LOT
    Māza Pils iela (☎ 7227 234, 7227 263)
Lufthansa
    Airport (☎ 7207 183, 7207 381)
Riair
    Airport (☎ 7207 325, 7207 725); Mellužu iela 1 (☎ 424 283)
SAS
    Kaļķu iela 15 (☎ 7216 139)

Bus National and international buses use Rīga's main bus station (*autoosta*; ☎ 7213 611) at Prāgas iela 1, behind the railway embankment just beyond the south edge of the Old City. Handwritten timetables are posted up, with services listed under their final destination and the platform they depart from. Services include:

Destination	Distance	Time (hrs)	Frequency
Bauska	65 km	1½	24 buses daily
Cēsis	90 km	2	14 buses daily
Daugavpils	230 km	4	two buses daily
Jelgava	40 km	1	66 buses daily
Liepāja	220 km	4	five buses daily
Rēzekne	245 km	4½	two buses daily
Sigulda	55 km	1	14 buses daily
Valmiera	120 km	2½	12 buses daily
Ventspils	200 km	4	10 buses daily

Train Rīga station (centrālā stacija; ☎ 23 30 95) on Stacijas laukums is split into two parts: one for long-distance trains (the bigger block, on the left as you face the station) and one for slow 'suburban' trains which travel to destinations up to 150 km away from Rīga. A huge wall chart shows the stations on each suburban line.

The timetable for departures *(atiešanas laiks)* listing the final destination, platform number, name of train and departure time is on the right as you enter the main hall. Arrivals *(pienakšanas laiks)* are posted up on the opposite side.

To buy a ticket 24 hours or more before departure, go to the advance-booking hall *(iepriekšpārdošanas kases)* reached through the suburban hall. You can also call in advance and have your train ticket delivered to your home for a 1 lati fee (☎ 7216 664). Train fares within Latvia are usually 1 santīmi per km.

Car & Motorcycle Neste, Shell, Statoil and Texaco operate 24-hour petrol stations selling all types of Western-grade petrol including unleaded and diesel all around Rīga and at strategic places around the country. Most Western car dealers have showrooms and repair workshops in Rīga. For a full listing see *Rīga In Your Pocket*.

Car Rental Avis (☎ 7207 535), Europcar (☎ 7207 825), Hertz (☎ 7207 980) and Lasto (☎ 7207 091) all have offices at the airport. Avis city centre office (☎ 7225 876) is at Teātra 12. Hertz (☎ 201 241) is at Kaļķu 15 in the city, and Europcar (☎ 7212 652), at Basteja bulvāris, is open 24 hours. Hertz offers the cheapest rates at US$61 to US$83 a day.

Getting Around

To/From the Airport Rīga airport (Lidosta Rīga) is at Skulte, 8 km west of the city centre. Bus No 22 runs there every 20 minutes from the 13th janvāra stop opposite the bus station. The airport information booth (☎ 7207 009, 7207 136) in the departure hall also sells bus tickets. You will be lucky to get a taxi driver to take you to the city centre for anything less than 7 lati.

Local Transport All the routes of buses, trolleybuses and trams are clearly marked on the *Rīga City Map*. All use the usual ticket-punching system, but buses use different tickets to trams/trolleybuses. Both types of ticket cost 0.14 lati and are sold at most news kiosks and from the driver. City transport runs daily from 5.30 am to 12.30 am.

AROUND RĪGA

The places in this section are easy day trips from Rīga – though Jūrmala is also a place you may wish to stay longer, especially during the better days in summer.

Salaspils

Between 1941 and 1944 an estimated 45,000 Jews from Rīga and about 55,000 other people, including Jews from other Nazi-occupied countries and prisoners of war, were murdered in the concentration camp at Salaspils, 15 km south-east of Rīga, along the Daugava. Giant, gaunt sculptures stand on the site as a memorial, and there's also a museum. The inscription on the huge concrete barrier at the entrance translates as 'Behind this gate the earth groans'.

Getting There & Away From Rīga take a suburban train on the Ogre-Krustpils line to Dārziņi (not Salaspils) station. A path leads from the station to the memorial *(piemine-klis)* – about a 15-minute walk.

Jūrmala

Jūrmala (Seashore) is the combined name for a string of small towns and resorts stretching for 30 km west along the coast from Rīga. Jūrmala's long sandy beaches are backed by dunes and pine woods, and its shady streets are lined with low-rise wooden houses. Holiday-makers have been coming here since the 19th century and in Soviet times 300,000 visitors a year from all over the USSR flooded in to boarding houses, holiday homes and sanatoriums owned by trade unions and other institutions. Today it is pitifully quiet. Be wary of ticks.

Orientation & Information Jūrmala lies

between the coast, which faces north, and the Lielupe River which runs parallel to it, a km or so inland. The Jūrmala townships are, from the east (Rīga) end: Lielupe, Bulduri, Dzintari, Majori, Dubulti, Jaundubulti, Pumpuri, Melluži, Asari, Vaivari, Kauguri (on the coast), Sloka (two km inland), Jaunķemeri (on the coast) and Ķemeri (six km inland).

All except Kauguri and Jaunķemeri have train stations. The hub is the four or five km between Bulduri and Dubulti, centred on Majori and Dzintari. Majori's main street is the one-km pedestrians-only Jomas iela, across the road from Majori train station, then to the right. Streets and paths lead through the woods on the left to the beach.

The tourist information centre (☎ 7-64 276) at Jomas 42 is open weekdays only, from 9 am to 5 pm. Drop the hyphenated digit from the numbers given here if calling from within Jūrmala.

Things to See To walk along the beach, over the dunes, and through the woods is reason enough to visit Jūrmala. The highest **dunes** are at Lielupe. In Majori, at Pliekšāna iela 7 between Jomas iela and the beach, was the poet Jānis Rainis' country cottage, where he died in 1929, now a **museum**.

Places to Stay *Eila* (☎ 7-63 978) at Rīga 50/52 in Dzintari is the place to camp. You can pitch a tent (6 lati) or rent a wooden cabin (18 lati). *Zinātnes nams* (☎ 7-51 205) at Vikingu 3, five minutes walk from Lielupe station, offers singles/doubles for 12.50/20 lati. *Hotel Majori* (☎ 7-61 380) at Jomas 29 is a minute's walk from the seashore and one of the more attractive of Jūrmala's concrete-jungle style rest homes. Singles/doubles cost 11/12.50 lati.

Places to Eat Every second building on Jomas iela offers some eating option. More refined places include the Latin-American *Habanas* at Jomas 66, which serves not-very-authentic tacos and burritos for around 3 lati. In the summer it hosts open-air concerts on the terrace. Just around the corner on Jauna iela is *Barbara*, a cosy, candle-lit bistro which claims to be Spanish. The menu touts paella and tortilla for around 3.50 lati, but that is as far as the Spanish connection goes. The Middle-Eastern *Orients*, which has an outlet either end of Majori at Jomas 86 and 33, is the most authentic of the lot and worth the wait for a table. *Sicilia* at Jomas 77 serves pizza daily from 10 am to 10 pm.

Getting There & Away About three trains an hour go from Rīga to Jūrmala along the Ķemeri-Tukums line. They all stop at Majori but not every other station.

Vidzeme

Vidzeme is the northern half of Latvia, east of Rīga, and is the country's most scenically varied and attractive region. Its highlight is the Gauja River valley, part of which is a national park, dotted with castles. There are three main towns within the park: Sigulda, which is known as the Switzerland of Latvia, Cēsis and Valmiera. Sigulda is the closest to Rīga and the most accessible. Cēsis, 30 km further north-east, is older and more attractive, and Valmiera, a further 30 km north, is less historic than either of the former but is a good base for canoeing and bicycling (contact the Sporta Bāze Baiļi, ☎ 42-21861, on the eastern outskirts of town, or via the LUTK – see Facts for the Visitor, Canoeing).

Also in the region are the Vidzeme Upland (Latvia's highest region) and a long stretch of fairly unspoilt coast along the Gulf of Rīga.

SIGULDA
One of the best trips from Rīga is to Sigulda, 53 km east on the southern lip of the picturesque, steep-sided, wooded Gauja valley. It's close enough to visit in a day but there's plenty to justify a longer stay, including long walks, canoeing and interesting places nearby such as Līgatne and Cēsis.

LATVIA

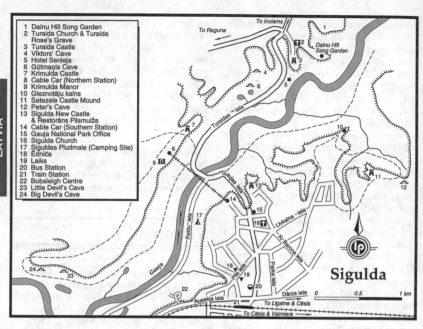

1 Dainu Hill Song Garden
2 Turaida Church & Turaida Rose's Grave
3 Turaida Castle
4 Viktors' Cave
5 Hotel Senleja
6 Gūtmaņis Cave
7 Krimulda Castle
8 Cable Car (Northern Station)
9 Krimulda Manor
10 Gleznotāju kalns
11 Satezele Castle Mound
12 Peter's Cave
13 Sigulda New Castle & Restorāns Pilsmuiža
14 Cable Car (Southern Station)
15 Gauja National Park Office
16 Sigulda Church
17 Siguldas Pludmale (Camping Site)
18 Ēdnīca
19 Laiks
20 Bus Station
21 Train Station
22 Bobsleigh Centre
23 Little Devil's Cave
24 Big Devil's Cave

History

Finno-Ugric Liv tribes inhabited the area as far back as 2000 BC, and by the 12th century they had built several wooden, hilltop strongholds. But they were unable to prevent the German conquest in the early 13th century. The Gauja later became the boundary between the lands of the Knights of the Sword to the south, and the archbishop of Rīga who held the north side. Both built castles in the area. Sigulda started to develop as a country resort with the building of the Pskov-Rīga railway in 1889.

Orientation & Information

Sigulda is the main gateway to the 920-sq-km Gauja National Park which stretches north-east as far as Valmiera. The park is down the hill from town and across the river. The national park office (☎ 971 345) is at Raiņa iela 15 (open weekdays from 8.30 am to 5 pm and on weekends from 10 am to 5 pm).

The telephone area code is the same as for Rīga, ☎ 2.

Things to See

Sigulda Castle Little remains of the knights' stronghold built between 1207 and 1226, but its ruins *(pilsdrups)* are perhaps all the more evocative for this. There's a great view through the trees to the reconstructed Turaida Castle on the far side of the valley. On the way to the ruins from the town you pass the 1225 **Sigulda Church**, rebuilt in the 18th century, and the 19th-century New Sigulda Castle, the former residence of Prince Kropotkin. To the west of Raiņa iela is a cable car, which runs every 15 minutes between 7.25 am and 6.25 pm across to Krimulda Castle, on the way affording splendid views of the valley (0.5 lati one way). To get a different perspective on the whole matter, try a 43-metre bungee jump from the cable car for 10 lati. Jumps take place every Saturday and Sunday at 6 pm (☎ 926 482).

The Bungee Jumping Cub of Latvia in Rīga can also organise jumps in Sigulda from a hot air balloon (☎ 7326 155).

Krimulda Castle & the Gauja Valley There is little left of Krimulda Castle, built in 1255-73, save some stone walls in a grassy glade. Below the viewing tower, immediately to the left of the castle as you face it are some steep wooden steps. Walk down all 410 steps to the bottom and follow the wooden riverside path leading to **Gūtmaņis Cave** (Gūtmaņa ala). The water from the stream flowing out from the cave is supposed to remove facial wrinkles and the spring inside is meant to represent the tears of this Liv chieftain's wife.

Turaida Castle The red-brick archbishop's castle, founded in 1214 on the site of a Liv stronghold, was blown up when lightning struck its gunpowder store in the 18th century. The restored structure is none too pretty and better viewed from afar, but the museum (☎ 971 402) inside the 42-metre tower offers a detailed account of the Livonian state from 1319 to 1561. It's open daily from 10 am to 5 pm and admission 0.5 lati. The castle is in Turaida's **Dainu Hill Song Garden**. The 23 sculptures in the park are dedicated to different figures within Latvian folklore.

On the path between the tower and road, near the small wooden-spired **Turaida Church** (Turaidas Baznīcas), two lime trees shade the grave of the 'Turaida Rose' – a legendary beauty who met an untimely death in Gutmānis' Cave, after events which tour guides are delighted to relate at great length. Services take place in the church on the first Sunday of every month at 11 am.

Places to Stay
At *Siguldas Pludmale* (☎ 973 724) at Peldu 1 you can pitch a tent for 1 lats a night plus a further 1 lats for each person who sleeps in it. It can also provide B&B in private homes around Sigulda for 5 to 12 lati per person and it rents out boats, canoes and rafts.

Hotel Senleja (☎ 972 162), in the valley below Turaida Castle at Turaidas iela 4, has clean, basic singles/doubles for 10/17 lati. The hotel nightclub opens Friday to Sunday from 9 pm until the last guest leaves.

Places to Eat
For dirt cheap food try the Soviet-style *canteen* (ēdnīca) next to the department store at Paegles iela 3. *Laiks* at Pils iela 8 (☎ 971 450) serves cheap meals daily from 8 am to 2 am in a trendy bar kitted out with a pool table, darts, one-armed bandits and air hockey.

Restorāns Pilsmuiža (☎ 971 395), inside Sigulda New Castle at Pils iela 16, overlooks the ruins of the old castle and is open daily noon to 2 am. Ask the waiter for the key to the castle tower which dates back to 1937 and offers panoramic views of the Gauja valley.

Getting There & Away
Trains and buses run from Rīga to Sigulda. Trains, running every half hour on the Rīga-Cēsis-Valmiera line, take 1¼ hours and cost 0.53 lati. There are 14 buses a day between Rīga and Sigulda, a handful of which are express buses and take about 1½ hours.

Zemgale

Zemgale is the region of central Latvia west of the Daugava River, between Rīga and the Lithuanian border. It is low-lying (below sea level in parts) and drained by dozens of rivers. Most places in Zemgale can be reached on day trips, if quite lengthy ones, from Rīga.

RUNDĀLE
The 18th-century **Rundāle Palace** (Rundāles Pils) is the architectural highlight of provincial Latvia and makes a popular day trip from Rīga. It was designed by Bartolomeo Rastrelli, the baroque genius from Italy who created many of St Petersburg's finest buildings including the Winter Palace, and was built in two phases – the first in the 1730s, the latter in the 1760s.

The 138-room palace and pitifully overgrown park open Wednesday to Sunday from 11 am to 6 pm (5 pm October to April).

Getting There & Away

Unless you have your own transport, the best way to reach Rundāle, 77 km south of Rīga, is to go to Bauska (see below) and take a bus for Rundāles Pils (not Rundāle which is 2.5 km further west).

There are also several buses a day between Rundāles Pils and Jelgava, 33 km north-west.

BAUSKA

Bauska, 65 km south of Rīga on the main Rīga-Vilnius road, is worth a stop in its own right if only to see the imposing **Bauska Castle** (Bauskas Pilsdrupas). The castle was built between 1443 and 1456 for the Livonian Knights, blown up during the Great Northern War in 1706, but recently rebuilt.

The castle is a km from the town centre on a hillock between the Mēmele and Mūsa rivers, on the western edge of town. From the bus station, walk towards the centre along Zalē iela then branch left along Uzvaras iela beside the park at the top of Kalna iela.

Getting There & Away

There are no trains to Bauska so you have to rely on buses. Normal Rīga-Bauska buses run 24 times daily, starting at 6 am, and take a tedious 1½ hours. Several express buses run during the week.

JELGAVA

Jelgava (population 75,000), 42 km south-west of Rīga, is the biggest town in Zemgale. It was once the capital of the Dukes of Courland – one of whom, Duke Jacob (1642-82), had his own navy, counted Tobago and an island in the mouth of the Gambia River amongst his possessions and laid plans to colonise Australia.

Unfortunately, a lot of old Jelgava was destroyed in the two world wars and it's no longer such an interesting place. However, the duke's 18th-century riverside **baroque palace** still stands beside the Rīga road in the north-east of town, bearing the unmistakable touch of Rastrelli, architect of nearby Rundāle. It has been rebuilt twice this century and is now in use as an agricultural college.

Getting There & Away

More than 50 buses daily make the trip to/ from Rīga for a fare of no more than one lati. There are also two or three suburban trains to/from Rīga every hour for a fare of 0.41 lati.

Kurzeme

Kurzeme, the western region of Latvia, is known in English as Courland and in German as Kurland. It's one of Latvia's least densely settled regions, and the northern part is still heavily forested.

Kuldīga, 165 km west of Rīga on the Venta River, is the most picturesque small town in the region with numerous 16th to 18th-century buildings, a fortress and a pleasant waterfall. It was briefly, from 1561 to 1573, the first capital of the Duchy of Courland. The *Hotel Kursa* (☎ 233-22 430) at Pilsētas laukums 6 is the only hotel.

There's not a great deal to do there but **Talsi**, 50 km north-east of Kuldīga, is quite pretty, lying as it does between two lakes in the bottom of a shallow valley. The *Viesnīca Talsi* (☎ 232-22 689) at Kareivju iela 16 is the only hotel. Between Talsi and the northern tip of Kurzeme, **Cape Kolka**, where there are remains of an old lighthouse, is a 13th-century castle at **Dundaga**. At **Vidale**, the road north-east from Dundaga descends the Slītere precipice, a 35-metre cliff which is 15 km long.

On the Gulf of Riga coast there are a number of small fishing villages between **Mērsrags** and Jūrmala. On the Baltic coast, **Liepāja** (population 115,000) is Latvia's second port. **Ventspils** further north suffers bad industrial pollution.

Latgale

Latgale is south-east Latvia and the main bastion of Roman Catholicism in Latvia, having been under Polish control from 1561 to 1772. The Latgale Upland, in the far south-east corner, is a scenic lake district with **Rēzekne** prominent among the medium-sized towns around its fringes. Some of the best scenery is around **Lake Rāzna** (Rāznas ezers). The church at **Aglona** is a Roman Catholic centre and large crowds descend on it for the Festival of the Assumption on 15 August. **Daugavpils**, to the south-west, with only 10 to 15% of Latvians in its 128,000 population, is Latvia's second largest city owing to industrial development since WWII. There are hotels in Rēzekne and Daugavpils.

LATVIA

Lithuania

The southernmost Baltic state is in many ways the most vibrant, as it showed the world by its daring, emotional drive for independence. Lithuania (Lietuva) owes much to the rich cultural currents of central Europe. With neighbouring Poland it once shared an empire stretching to the Black Sea, and still shares the Roman Catholicism which sets it apart from its Baltic neighbours.

Vilnius, the historic, lively capital, is the obvious base for visitors. But Lithuania has other sizeable cities such as Kaunas, briefly its capital this century, and the seaport Klaipėda, formerly the German town Memel. Other intriguing places include Neringa (the Kuršių Spit on the coast), the strange Hill of Crosses near Šiauliai, and the forests and castles of the south.

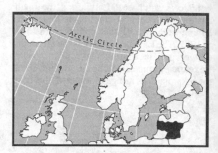

Facts about the Country

HISTORY
Beginnings
By the 10th century AD the south-eastern Baltic was occupied by three related groups of tribes: the Livs in present-day Latvia, the Prussians in the present Kaliningrad region of Russia, and modern north-east Poland and the Lithuanians in between.

German Invasion & Lithuanian Expansion
In the 1220s the German crusading Teutonic Order was invited into Mazovia in northern Poland to protect it against the marauding Prussians.

By 1290 the order had exterminated most of the Prussians, settling Germans in their place, and ruled the eastern Baltic from around modern Gdańsk in Poland to southern Estonia. But the Lithuanians, protected by forests, restricted them to a coastal strip.

Gediminas, leader of a united Lithuania from 1316 to 1341, profited from the decline of the early Russian state based in Kiev. He pushed Lithuania's borders south and east, but found his own willingness to accept Christianity opposed by pagan kin. After his death his son Algirdas, based in Vilnius, pushed the borders past Kiev, while another son Kestutis, at Trakai, fought off the Teutonic Knights.

Union with Poland
In 1386 Algirdas' son and successor Jogaila married Jadwiga, Queen of Poland, becoming Wladyslaw II of Poland and a Christian, forging an alliance against the knights and initiating a 400-year bond between the two states. Together they won control of a huge swathe of land from the Baltic to the Black Sea by the turn of the 16th century. But Lithuania ended up the junior partner, its gentry adopting Polish culture and language, its peasants becoming serfs.

In 1410 Jogaila, and Kestutis' son Vytautas, who governed Lithuania, decisively defeated the Teutonic Order at the battle of Grünwald (also called Tannenberg or algiris) in modern Poland. Kazimieras IV of Poland (1447-92), also Grand Duke of Lithuania, reduced the knights' realm to a small area, itself under ultimate Polish control.

The Reformation sent a wave of Protestantism across Lithuania and Poland but it petered out by the 1570s and the country

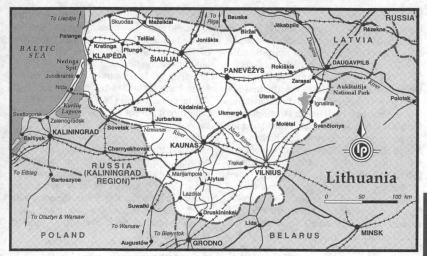

remains predominantly Roman Catholic to this day.

Russian Control

Polish and Lithuanian forces briefly took Moscow in 1610, but in 1654 Russia invaded and took significant territory. In the 18th century, divisions in the Polish-Lithuanian state, with factions calling in Russian help from time to time, so weakened it that it finally vanished from the map when Russia, Austria and Prussia (successor to the Teutonic Order) carved it up in the Partitions of Poland (1772, 1793 and 1795-96). Most of Lithuania went to Russia.

In the 19th century, while Vilnius became a bastion of Polish culture and a focus of uprisings against Russian rule, there was a growth of Lithuanian national consciousness in the countryside, encouraged by the abolition of serfdom in 1861.

Independence

With the collapse of the old order in Eastern Europe in 1917-18, Lithuanian nationalists declared independence on 16 February 1918 and managed to fend off an attempted Soviet takeover in the next two years. Independent

Lithuania's capital was Kaunas, since it had been Polish troops who took Vilnius from the Red Army in 1919. Vilnius was a constant source of Lithuanian-Polish tension.

The new democracies in the war-damaged Baltic states couldn't withstand the world slump and the rise of fascism. Lithuania suffered a military coup in 1926 and from 1929 was ruled along similar lines to Mussolini's Italy.

Soviet Rule & WWII

In 1940, following the Molotov-Ribbentrop Pact and subsequent events (see History in the Estonia chapter), Lithuania found itself part of the USSR. Within a year around 40,000 Lithuanians were killed or deported. A further 150,000 to 300,000-plus, mostly Jews, died in concentration camps and ghettos during the 1941-44 Nazi occupation.

Between 1945 and 1952, with Soviet control re-established, an estimated 200,000-plus people were killed or deported. The Lithuanian forests were the centre of armed resistance to Soviet rule, which may have involved tens of thousands of people, but resistance was crushed by 1952.

New Independence

In the late 1980s Lithuania came to lead the Baltic push for independence after candidates supporting its popular front, Sajūdis, won 30 seats in the March 1989 elections for the USSR Congress of People's Deputies. In December 1989 Lithuania was the first Soviet republic to legalise noncommunist parties. In February 1990 Sajūdis was elected to form a majority in Lithuania's new Supreme Soviet (now 'parliament'), which on 11 March declared Lithuania independent and stated that its 1918 constitution had never lost its validity.

Moscow shunted troop convoys around Vilnius and cut off Lithuania's fuel supplies. The heat was finally taken off after 2½ months, when Lithuania's music-professor-turned-president, the Sajūdis leader Vytautas Landsbergis, agreed to a 100-day moratorium on the 11 March declaration in exchange for independence talks with the USSR.

The independence momentum flagged as the Baltic republics' economic reliance on the USSR became clear and Lithuania's talks with Moscow bogged down. Then in January 1991 Soviet troops and paramilitary police stormed key buildings in Vilnius, apparently to pave the way for a communist coup and Soviet crackdown. Thirteen people were killed in the storming of the Vilnius TV tower and many more hurt. Lithuanians barricaded their parliament, the violence drew heavy condemnation from the West, and the threat subsided.

Lithuania and the other Baltic states were finally brought real independence by the failed coup in Moscow in August 1991, which resulted in Western and then, on 6 September, Soviet recognition of Lithuanian independence. The country became the first Baltic state to be completely free of any Soviet presence when the last troops based on Lithuanian soil departed for Russia on 31 August 1993.

GEOGRAPHY & ECOLOGY

Lithuania, covering an area of 65,200 sq km, is the biggest of the three Baltic states. Retreating glaciers formed a rolling landscape with higher areas in the north-west (the Žemaičių upland), across the south-east (the Baltic highlands), and in the east (stretches of the Lithuanian-Belarusian uplands including the country's highest hill, 294-metre Juozapinės). The central lowland, a north-south band up to 100 km wide, is the most fertile region. Forest (38% pine, 21% spruce, 21% birch) covers a little over a quarter of the country as a whole, but about half of the south.

Half Lithuania's short coastline is on Neringa, a spit stretching 90 km north from near Kaliningrad with high dunes and pine forests. The Nemunas River, which drains most of Lithuania, flows into the semi-salt Kuršių Lagoon behind the spit. Inland Lithuania is dotted with over 4000 mostly shallow lakes.

GOVERNMENT & POLITICS

Lithuania's first democratic elections, held over two rounds in October and November 1992, produced what to the rest of the world was an astonishing turn-around when the ex-communist LDDP (Lithuanian Democratic Labour Party) won an overall majority of seats (74) in the 141-seat *Seimas*, the Lithuanian parliament.

In presidential elections in February 1993, Algirdas Brazauskas, a former Communist Party first secretary and the leader of the LDDP, won with 60% of the votes.

While the president is head of state, actual power resides with the prime minister, nominated by the president and approved by the Seimas. In March 1993, Brazauskas-nominee Adolfas Šleževičius, an LDDP member, was approved for the post. However, following Lithuania's banking crisis in December 1995 (see Economy below), during which it emerged that Šleževičius had withdrawn substantial amounts of his private deposits from a major bank just two days before the bank's activities were suspended, President Brazauskas called for his prime minister's resignation. On 8 February 1996 the Minister for Government Reforms, Laurynas Mindaugas Stankevičius, was appointed prime minister.

Lithuania was expected to hold general elections on 20 October 1996.

ECONOMY

Lithuania was industrialised after WWII, but privatisation of the giant state-run industries has yet to begin and there continues to be state support for industries such as machine building, textiles and food processing.

Lithuania continues to rely on Russia for imported fuel. Other major trading partners include Germany, Belarus, Latvia, Ukraine, Netherlands and Poland. Since the introduction in July 1993 of the litas, inflation has been brought under control, in mid-1996 standing at 35%.

In December 1995 Lithuania witnessed the shock collapse of two of its largest banks and depositors lost almost 400 million litai (US$100 million). Rather than follow the successful Latvian or Estonian example of a painful but brief shake-out, the government decided to recapitalise the failed banks at a cost of US$325 million – much to the disapproval of the IMF and World Bank.

POPULATION & PEOPLE

Lithuania's population in 1995 was 3.71 million. Lithuanians form 81% of the population, meaning Lithuanians had nothing to fear when they introduced a citizenship law in 1991 granting automatic citizen status to all those resident in the country before 3 November 1989. The main minority groups in Lithuania are Russians (8.5%) and Poles (7%). Nearly all the Poles live in the two south-eastern districts of Vilnius and Šalčininkai.

The Lithuanian diaspora is by far the biggest of any of the peoples of the Baltic states, with an estimated 800,000 Lithuanians in the USA alone (the main concentration is in Chicago) and other sizeable communities in Canada, South America and Australia.

ARTS

After early beginnings – most notably the poem *Metai* (The Seasons) by Kristijonas Donelaitis published in the late 18th century – Lithuanian literature suffered from harsh persecution by the Tsarist authorities, who banned the Latin alphabet. As in Estonia and Latvia, there was a national awakening in the late 19th century, which in Lithuania's case gave rise to the publication of the first native-language academic journal, the influential *Aušra* (Dawn). Extensive cultural interchanges, both east (with St Petersburg) and west (with Germany and France) followed.

The favourable intellectual climate produced figures such as Maironis, the poet of the National Revival, whose romantic *Pavasario balsai* (Voices of Spring) heralded the start of modern Lithuanian poetry.

Lithuania's intimate relations with Poland down the centuries give it a share of credit for some of the best of Polish literature, too. Adam Mickiewicz, inspiration of the 19th-century Polish nationalists, began his great poem *Pan Tadeusz* ('Lithuania, my fatherland ...'). Czesław Miłosz, poet, essayist and winner of the 1980 Nobel Prize, wrote about the Soviet occupation of the Baltic states in the last chapter of his book *The Captive Mind*.

The extensive Lithuanian diaspora has also produced major cultural figures, such as the poet Tomas Venclova and novelist Antanas Škėma, whose *A White Shroud*, which concerns an emigrés reflections on his homeland, has been compared to the work of James Joyce.

However, for Lithuanians the pre-eminent national artist will always be Mikalojus Konstantinas Čiurlionis (1875-1911), a depressive genius who was also a major com- poser of symphonic poems and piano pieces.

CULTURE

With their romanticism, garrulousness and occasional obstinacy, the Lithuanians could be described as the Italians of the Baltic region. A memory of the time when the Grand Duchy of Lithuania stretched from the Baltic to the Black Sea, combined with the fairly irrelevant fact that the geographical centre of Europe lies just to the north of Vilnius, lends Lithuanians a great confidence in their national identity.

LITHUANIA

Lithuanians are far more likely than Estonians or Latvians to strike up a casual conversation with strangers or to invite visitors into their homes and then do their utmost to make their guests feel welcome.

RELIGION
Like their southern neighbours the Poles, Lithuanians are predominantly Roman Catholic, and much more enthusiastic about their creed than the Lutherans to the north. The Catholic Church is a conservative element in Lithuanian society but played an important organisational role in the drive to independence.

Lithuania was one of the last parts of Europe to be Christianised and strong elements of early paganism still exist. The characteristic Lithuanian portrayal of Christ is *Rupintojelis* (The Thinker), a mournful figure, generally with his head in his hands, who far predates the coming of Christianity. Travelling through Lithuania you will constantly come across large, carved, wooden Rupintojelis and crosses beside the road, forbidden during the Soviet era but now being replaced as symbols of Lithuanian faith – though not necessarily faith in Catholicism so much as faith in Lithuanian traditions.

LANGUAGE
Lithuanian is one of only two surviving languages of the Baltic branch of the Indo-European language family (the other is Latvian). See the Estonia Language section for information on the use of English, Russian and other languages in the Baltic states.

See the Language Guide at the back of the book for pronunciation guidelines and useful words and phrases.

Facts for the Visitor

PLANNING
Climate & When to Go
Lithuania's climate is similar to Latvia's with the warmest period, late June to early August

(maximum temperature 22°C), also being the wettest. In winter, temperatures may not rise above freezing from mid-November to mid-March.

Winter lasts about six weeks longer in the inland east of the country than the coastal west. Annual precipitation ranges from 540 mm in the central lowland to 930 mm in parts of the Žemaičių upland. Winter is foggy.

Books & Maps
See Facts for the Visitor in the Estonia chapter for titles covering the three Baltic states.

Lithuania is adequately covered by large-scale Baltic states maps available in the West (again see the Estonia chapter).

Online Services
Two top web sites on Lithuania include *Lithuania* (http://www.soften.ktu.lt/imbras/lithuania.html) which provides links to most Lithuanian web sites, and the on-line versions of the unbeatable city guides, *Vilnius*, *Klaipėda* and *Kaunas In Your Pocket* which contain up-to-date information about these cities (http://www.omnitel.net/OurSite/Travel/viyp).

What to Bring
See the Facts for the Visitor section in the Estonia chapter.

SUGGESTED ITINERARIES
Here are some ideas to consider:

Two days
    Vilnius with a trip to Trakai
One week
    Two days in Vilnius including a trip to Trakai, Klaipėda and an excursion down the Neringa Spit to Nida or Juodkrantė
Two weeks
    Several days exploring Vilnius including a trip to Trakai, Klaipėda and an excursion down the Neringa Spit, a couple of days in Kaunas with a visit to the Hill of Crosses near Šiauliai

HIGHLIGHTS
The Old Town of Vilnius, a chocolate box of three-storey baroque and classical buildings, is the definite highlight. No less enchanting

is the coastal region of Neringa, a magnificent silent world of windswept sand dunes and pine trees. Difficult to reach, but the perfect representation of the Lithuanian spirit, is the Hill of Crosses near Šiauliai.

TOURIST OFFICES

Possible tourist information sources include Lithuanian embassies and specialist travel agencies in other countries (see Getting There & Away in the Estonia chapter), and hotels and travel agencies in Lithuania.

There are a number of user-friendly privately run tourist offices in Vilnius (see the Vilnius section).

VISAS & DOCUMENTS

A valid passport is the only entry requirement for citizens of Australia, Bulgaria, Cyprus, the Czech Republic, Denmark, Estonia, Hungary, Iceland, Ireland, Italy, Japan, Latvia, Liechtenstein, Malta, Norway, Poland, Slovakia, Slovenia, Switzerland, the UK and the USA.

To extend your Lithuanian visa contact the immigration department *(imigracijos tarnyba)* at Saltoniškių 19 (☎ 725 864, 725 853, 659 847) or at Verkių 3 (☎ 756 453) in Vilnius.

For further details on visas and information on other documents you might need, see Facts for the Visitor in the Estonia chapter.

EMBASSIES

Lithuanian Embassies Abroad

Australia
   Consulate, 40B Fiddens Wharf Rd, Killara, NSW 2071 (☎ 02-9498 2571)
Canada
   130 Albert Street, Suite 204, Ottawa, Ontario K1P 564 (☎ 613-567 5458)
Estonia
   Uus tn 15, EE0100 Tallinn (☎ 2-631 4030)
Finland
   Raohankatu 13a, Helsinki 20180 (☎ 09-608 210)
Germany
   Argelander strasse 108a, 5300 Bonn 1 (☎ 228-914 910, 914 9113)
Latvia
   Rūpniecibas iela 22, Rīga 226010 (☎ 2-7321 519)
Poland
   aleje Szucha 5, Warsaw (☎ 2-625 3368)

Russia
   Borisoglebsky pereulok 10, Moscow 121069 (☎ 095-291 2643)
Sweden
   Strandvagen 53, 11523 Stockholm (☎ 8-667 1134)
UK
   17 Essex Villas, London W8 7BP (☎ 0171-938 2481)
USA
   2622 16th St NW, Washington, DC 20009 (☎ 202-234 5860)

Foreign Embassies in Lithuania

Belarus
   Muitinės gatvė 41, Vilnius (☎ 263 828)
Canada
   Didžioji gatvė 8-5, Vilnius (☎ 220 898)
Estonia
   Tilto 29, Vilnius (☎ 220 486, 622 030)
Finland
   Klaipėdos gatvė 6, Vilnius (☎ 221 621)
Germany
   Sierakausko gatvė 24, Vilnius (☎ 650 272, 263 627)
Latvia
   Čiurlionio gatvė 76, Vilnius (☎ 231 260)
Poland
   Smėlio gatvė 20a, Vilnius (☎ 709 001)
Russia
   Latvių 53/54, Vilnius (☎ 721 763)
Sweden
   Jogailos gatvė 10, Vilnius (☎ 226 467)
UK
   Antakalnio gatvė 2, Vilnius (☎ 222 070)
USA
   Akmenų gatvė 6, Vilnius (☎ 223 031)

CUSTOMS

Lithuania limits amber exports but a few necklaces as souvenirs or gifts should be OK providing their value doesn't exceed US $250. You're supposed to get a Culture Ministry permit, and pay 10% to 20% duty, to export artworks over 50 years old. For further information enquire at the Committee of Cultural Heritage (☎ 724 005) at Šnipiškių 3, Vilnius.

MONEY

See the Facts for the Visitor section of the Estonia chapter for general information.

Currency

Lithuania introduced its national currency, the litas, on 25 June 1993, replacing the transitional 'talonas'. The litas (plural litai, abbreviated to Lts) is Lithuania's only legal tender. It's a fully convertible currency that has managed to hold to the rate of 4 Lts to US$1 that it was pegged at when introduced.

The litas comes in one, two, five, 10, 20, 50 and 100 Lts denomination notes. One litas is broken down into 100 centų (abbreviated to ct), and there are one, two, five, 10, 20 and 50 centų coins.

Exchange Rates
The following currencies convert at these approximate rates:

Australia	A$1	=	3.16 Lts
Canada	C$1	=	2.92 Lts
Finland	1 Fmk	=	0.89 Lts
Germany	DM1	=	2.69 Lts
Sweden	1 SKr	=	0.60 Lts
UK	UK£1	=	6.24 Lts
USA	US$1	=	4.00 Lts

POST & COMMUNICATIONS
Post
Mail from the USA takes 10 to 14 days; letters from Europe arrive in about week. Things go faster the other way. Letters/postcards weighing under 20g cost 1 Lts/0.70 Lts air mail or 0.70/0.50 Lts surface mail. Stamps can be bought from post offices or hotels.

Telephone
To call other cities in Lithuania or in the former Soviet Union, simply dial ☎ 8, wait for the tone, then dial the area code and telephone number. Area codes from Lithuanian phones include Klaipėda ☎ 26, Kaunas ☎ 27, Vilnius ☎ 22, Palanga ☎ 236, Šiauliai ☎ 21, Neringa ☎ 259, Rīga ☎ 013, Kaliningrad ☎ 0112 and Tallinn ☎ 014. If the number you are calling in Rīga/Tallinn is analogue the area code is ☎ 0132/0142.

To make an international call dial ☎ 8-tone-10 followed by the country code, area code and telephone number. Tariffs per minute are: to Poland 3.57 Lts, the rest of Europe 5.80 Lts, the USA and Australia 10.50 Lts.

The country code for calling Lithuania from abroad is ☎ 370 (followed by the international area code which you can work out by dropping the first 2 from the area code used from Lithuania phones, ie Kaunas ☎ 7).

Public Phones Most public phones accept magnetic strip cards (tear the perforated corner off to use) costing 3.45 to 28.32 Lts and available from news kiosks and post offices. In some rural areas and parts of Kaunas and Vilnius, some Soviet public phone booths still exist. Only local calls can be made from these phones which are either free or require tokens which are practically impossible to find (except in Kaunas at the time of writing).

Fax, Telegraph & E-mail
Official post office fax rates are: Europe, 23.77 Lts per A4 page; USA and Australia 42.65 Lts. International telegrams (incoming or outbound) arrive the same or next day and can be sent from most post offices. Rates per word are: Europe 0.59 Lts, the USA 0.83 Lts, and Australia 0.84 Lts.

In every major city noncommercial electronic mail (e-mail) can be sent and received free of charge. If you subscribe to CompuServe, MCIMail and SprintNet you can access your account in Vilnius (☎ 22 41 80), Kaunas (☎ 20 63 73) and Klaipėda (☎ 31 06 90). Lithuania's main Internet provider is Omnitel (☎ 221 712) at Ševčenkos 25 in Vilnius.

NEWSPAPERS & MAGAZINES
The pan-Baltic *Baltic Times* is sold at news kiosks for 4 Lts. Sparkling features can be found in *Lithuania In The World*, a superb glossy which is, in fact, Lithuanian Airlines' in-flight magazine but available in most bookshops and kiosks. The Lithuanian business biweekly *Verslo Žinios* has brief news summaries in English and good information on its excellent web site (http://www.omnitel .net/OurSite/Business and Economy/vz).

Western newspapers, just a day or two old, are widely available in Vilnius but not in Kaunas or Klaipėda.

RADIO & TV

The Lithuanian Baltic TV channel screens CNN news in English daily at midnight, and World Net every day at 1 pm. The 24-hour radio station Voice of America (VOA) can be picked up at 105.6 FM, and Radio France International (RFI) at 100.1 FM. M1, with its heady mix of rock and pop, is Lithuania's most popular commercial channel.

PHOTOGRAPHY & VIDEO

See the Facts for the Visitor section in the Estonia chapter.

TIME

See the Facts for the Visitor section in the Estonia chapter.

ELECTRICITY

See the Facts for the Visitor section in the Estonia chapter.

WEIGHTS & MEASURES

See the Facts for the Visitor section in the Estonia chapter.

TOILETS

See the Facts for the Visitor section in the Estonia chapter.

HEALTH

See Facts for the Visitor in the Estonia chapter for general information. Drinking unboiled tap water is not advisable in Vilnius. Swimming in the Baltic Sea and in some rivers is risky owing to pollution, although people do still swim.

WOMEN TRAVELLERS

See the Facts for the Visitor section in the Estonia chapter.

GAY & LESBIAN TRAVELLERS

Lithuania is the least tolerant of the three Baltics and 'gay-bashing' incidents do occur. The Lithuanian Gay League (☎ 23 92 82, 65 59 40) arranges accommodation for gay and lesbian travellers and also organises parties every Saturday at a location which it does not publicise.

DISABLED TRAVELLERS

The Disability Information and Consultation Bureau (☎ & fax 731 425), at Vytauto gatvė 15 in Vilnius, has a registry of services available for the disabled visiting Lithuania.

DANGERS & ANNOYANCES

See the Facts for the Visitor section in the Estonia chapter.

BUSINESS HOURS

Shop, office, café and restaurant hours are similar to Latvia and Estonia (see Facts for the Visitor in the Estonia chapter).

PUBLIC HOLIDAYS & SPECIAL EVENTS

Lithuania's national holidays are:

1 January, *New Year's Day*
16 February, *Day of Restoration of Lithuanian State* (anniversary of 1918 independence declaration)
Good Friday and *Easter Monday*
1st Sunday in May, *Mother's Day*
6 July, *State Holiday* (commemoration of coronation of Grand Duke Mindaugas, 13th century)
25 December, *Christmas Day*
26 December, *Boxing Day*

The next Lithuanian Song Festival will take place in the year 2000. The Baltika international folk festival is due in Vilnius in mid-July 1999. Other annual festivals include the Kaunas International Jazz Festival in April, the week-long Life Theatre Festival in Vilnius in May, Vilnius Summer Music Festival in July, the Vilnius International Street Festival in August, and in November, the Vilnius International Jazz Festival. For more information contact the Lithuanian Folk Culture Centre in Vilnius at B Radvilaitės (☎ 612 594; e-mail pjurkus @ktl.mii.lt).

WORK

See the Facts for the Visitor section in the Estonia chapter.

ACCOMMODATION

Accommodation can be heavily booked, especially in summer, and it's worth booking ahead. In smaller provincial places the few options might occasionally be booked out.

LITHUANIA

Camping

There are camping grounds at holiday towns such as Palanga, Trakai and Druskininkai. Your best bet is to contact the local tourist centre for information: Palanga Tourism Centre (236-539 27) at Vytauto 106, Druskininkai Tourist Information Centre (☎ 233-517 77) at Vasario 16/5 or the tourism information office in Trakai (☎ 238-519 34). Most camping grounds also have small unheated cabins for hire.

Hostels & Colleges

It is possible to stay in fairly cheap hostels or student accommodation in Vilnius and throughout Lithuania.

Private Homes & Flats

A number of agents offer accommodation in private flats in Vilnius. You can also organise homestays through organisations in the West. See Estonia, Facts for the Visitor and Getting There & Away for more details.

Hotels

Hotels in Lithuania are fairly user-friendly and, in general, more than meet the demands set by the most discerning Western traveller and backpacker. In recent years most older hotels have undergone extensive renovation, often resulting in a range of room prices in the one establishment that are based on the degree of renovation in individual rooms. Many hotels are still under such *remontas*.

FOOD

See Facts for the Visitor in the Estonia chapter for general information on food and res-taurants in the Baltic states.

Common Lithuanian starters include herring *(silkė)* and mushrooms *(grybai)*; also salads and sprats *(šprotai)*. Most traditional meals are based on potato and one that must be tried – even if only once – is *cepelinai* (named after Herr Zeppelin's dirigibles) a fist-sized parcel of potato dough stuffed with cheese, meat or mushrooms. Another staple is *bulvinai blynai*, pancakes made of grated potato. Cold beet soup *(šaltibarščiai)* is also popular and traditionally comes with boiled

potatoes. Dairy products such as cottage cheese *(varške)* and sour milk *(rūgusis pienas)* are also among the mainstays of the ordinary diet, though meat and other vegetables are standard in restaurants. Another good standby is *koldūninė*, small ravioli-style dumplings stuffed with cheese, mushrooms or meat.

bread	*duona*
salad	*salatos, mišrainė*
soup	*sriuba*
fried pork	*karbonadas*
fried meat	*kepsnys*
chicken	*vištiena*
fish	*zuvis*
vegetables	*daržovės*
fruit	*vaisiai*
cake	*pyragas, tortas*
ice cream	*ledai*
bill	*sąskaita*

DRINKS

Beer is *alus* in Lithuanian and the best local brands such as Utenos and Kalnapilis are served in most restaurants and bars. 'Utenos porteris' is a good, hard-hitting dark ale. Lithuanians also drink mead *(midus)*, such as Salgiris and Suktinis which are as much as 60% proof, and *gira*, made from fermented grains or fruit. The more sober-minded should look out for *stakliskes*, a honey liqueur. The Lithuanian for wine is *vynas*.

Tea in Lithuanian is *arbata*, coffee *kava*, mineral water *mineralinis vanduo*.

ENTERTAINMENT

See the Facts for the Visitor section in the Estonia chapter.

Getting There & Away

Lithuania has cheap air, bus and rail links with Warsaw, which in turn has flights, trains and cheap buses to/from many Western European cities. In Polish, Vilnius is Wilno; in Lithuanian Warsaw is Varšuva. You can also easily reach Lithuania overland through Latvia (see Travel Between the Baltics in the Getting There & Away section of the Estonia chapter), by air or sea from Germany, or by air from Scandinavia.

TRAVEL AGENCIES

See Estonia, Getting There & Away for Baltic states specialist travel agencies in Western countries.

AIR

Routes

Lithuanian Airlines (LAL, Lietuvos Avialinijos) was the first independent Baltic-state airline to take wing (in December 1991). Flights in and out of Vilnius include: Amsterdam four times a week with LAL; Berlin three times a week with LAL and three times weekly en route to Hamburg with Hamburg Airlines; Copenhagen four times a week with LAL and daily with SAS; Frankfurt daily with LAL and Lufthansa; Helsinki twice weekly with Finnair; London five times a week with LAL; Rome and Dubai via Larnaca twice weekly with LAL; Istanbul and Paris three times a week with LAL; Vienna three times a week with Austrian Airlines; Warsaw five times a week with LOT and four times a week with LAL; and Moscow four times a week with LAL and three times weekly with Aeroflot.

The Latvian state airlines, Air Baltic, flies from Vilnius to Rīga five times a week. Estonian Air flies to Tallinn daily.

Fares

Regent Holidays (☎ 0117 921 1711; fax 0117 925 4866) 15 John St, Bristol BS1 2HR, UK, has open-jaw London-Vilnius returns for UK£226 with Lufthansa, and UK£250 with SAS, which also offers similar fares from Manchester, Newcastle, Glasgow and Edinburgh. It also offers a standard London-Vilnius return for UK£225 with Lithuanian Airlines. Regent Holidays also organises city breaks to the three Baltic capitals, hotel accommodation for individuals and 12-day group tours to the three Baltic States for UK£995.

Other airline 'general sales agents' (travel agents appointed to sell reduced-price tickets) such as Trailfinders in London may offer the best deals from other countries too, so it's worth pressing airline reservations departments about them.

A Warsaw-Vilnius-Warsaw APEX return (fixed dates, advance payment, valid for one month) with LAL is US$110. Apex returns on the LAL Vilnius-Berlin Schönefeld route in mid-1996 were about US$300 starting from either end. Returns to/from Frankfurt or Hamburg are generally US$425.

LAND

Bus

Poland & the West Four buses daily run between Vilnius and Warsaw (11 hours), departing from Vilnius bus station. An additional service is available Monday to Thursday and on Sunday. The fare in mid-1996 was about US$14 one way or US$28 return from Warsaw. In Vilnius, tickets can be bought from the bus station and cost 10 Lts more after 6 pm.

Daily buses also run between Vilnius and Białystok (US$15 from Vilnius) and Gdańsk (overnight, US$18). The Varita bus company (☎ 733 793), at Ukmergės 12a in Vilnius, runs a bus every Sunday from Vilnius to Paris, via Dresden, Eisenach, Frankfurt, Mannheim, Ludwigshafen, Kaiserslauten, Hamburg and Saarbrücken. A return ticket to Paris is US$161.

Train

Germany & Poland At 2.32 pm each day there's a train from Warsaw central train station to Šeštokai in Lithuania, arriving at 10.05 pm. There it connects with the *Baltic Express* service that runs direct to Tallinn, stopping at Kaunas (11.55 pm). It's possible to change at Kaunas for Vilnius.

Kaliningrad, Russia & Ukraine Vilnius is linked by *greit* (fast) trains with Kaliningrad (seven hours) four times daily and a fifth service on odd days only; St Petersburg (15 to 17 hours) four times daily; and Moscow

(18 hours) four times with an extra service on odd days.

Car & Motorcycle

See the Getting Around chapter at the beginning of this book for general comments on driving and riding in the Baltic states. The wait for private motorists on the Lithuanian-Polish borders at Kalvarija and Lazdijai can be anything from 10 minutes to 10 hours. The Lithuanian-Belarusian borders are equally notorious with motorists facing long and unpredictable waits.

SEA

Ferries sail between Klaipėda and Kiel in Germany six times a week (26 hours), between Klaipėda and Mukran in Germany daily (18 hours), and between Klaipėda and Åhus in Sweden twice weekly (18 hours). For tickets contact Krantas Shipping (☎ 26-365 444) at Perkėlos 10 in Klaipėda. Cargo ferries offering limited cabin space for passengers also sail between Klaipėda and Fredericia in Denmark (34 hours) twice weekly and between Klaipėda and Copenhagen in Denmark (22 hours) four times weekly. Tickets are handled by DFDS Baltic Line (☎ 310 598, 510 597) at Graičiūno 34 in Vilnius.

LEAVING LITHUANIA

There are no departure taxes. If you are travelling on to, or via, Poland check whether your bus or train passes through Belarus: if it does you need a Belarusian transit visa, which costs US$30.

GETTING AROUND

See the Getting Around section of the Estonia chapter for information on getting around the Baltic states.

Vilnius

The greenest and prettiest of the Baltic capitals, Vilnius (population 574,000) lies 250 km inland on the Neris River. The winding streets of Old Vilnius – a chocolate box of three-storey baroque and classical buildings – are a pleasure to explore, and there are many reminders of the city's pivotal role in the campaign for Baltic independence. Vilnius' historical links with Poland perhaps contribute to a less austere atmosphere than in Rīga or Tallinn. Evidence of the Polish connection can be seen in the many Catholic churches and the array of central European architectural styles from past centuries.

History

According to tradition Vilnius was founded in the 1320s by Duke Gediminas. But it may well have already been a political and trade centre, with river access to both the Baltic and Black seas. Fourteenth-century Vilnius was on the slopes of Gediminas Hill, with upper and lower castles and the townspeople's houses all protected by a moat and walls. The Teutonic Knights attacked at least six times between 1365 and 1402 but their defeat in 1410 at Grünwald launched Vilnius into an era of prosperity.

Many Gothic buildings went up and merchant and artisan guilds were formed. Following Tatar attacks, a 2.4-km stone wall was built between 1503 and 1522 around the new part of the town south of Gediminas Hill. Sixteenth-century Vilnius was one of the biggest cities in eastern Europe, with 25,000 to 30,000 people. It blossomed with buildings in late-Gothic and Renaissance styles as the Lithuanians Žygimantas I and II occupied the Polish-Lithuanian throne. The university was founded in 1579.

In the 17th and early 18th centuries Vilnius suffered fires, war, famine and plague, and shrank in population and importance, but in the 19th century it grew again as industry developed, and the town became a refuge for dispossessed Polish-Lithuanian gentry, and thus a Polish cultural centre. It was devastated, however, in WWI when the Germans occupied it for 3½ years, and by the subsequent Soviet/Polish/Lithuanian fighting.

When the shooting died down, Vilnius found itself in Poland, where it remained till

1939. By now its population was one-third Jewish (between 60,000 and 80,000 people) and it developed into one of the world's three major centres of Yiddish culture (the others being Warsaw and New York), earning it the nickname 'Jerusalem of Lithuania'. WWII saw another three-year German occupation and nearly all the Vilnius Jews were killed in its ghetto or the Paneriai death camp. Much of the city was wrecked in the six-day battle in which the Red Army recaptured it towards the end of the war.

New residential and industrial suburbs sprang up all around the city after WWII. The population today includes up to 100,000 Poles and 110,000 Russians.

Orientation

Central Vilnius is on the south side of the Neris River and its heart is Katedros aikštė, the cathedral square with Gediminas Hill rising behind it. South of Katedros aikštė are the streets of the Old Town; to the west Gedimino prospektas is the axis of the newer part of the centre. The train and bus stations are just beyond the south edge of the old city, 1.5 km from Katedros aikštė.

Maps Top quality road maps, city maps and atlases published by Briedis (☎ 220 970) at Bokšto gatvė 10-9 can be found in most bookshops or at the *Vilnius In Your Pocket* tourist information centre (☎ 260 875; e-mail viyp@post.omnitel.net) at Vilnius airport (open daily 11 am to 4 pm).

Information

Tourist Offices The official State Tourism Information Centre (☎ 620 7620; fax 616 622) is at Vilniaus 25-306. It provides little practical information however, and your best bet is to turn to the private travel agencies (see below). The friendly Lithuanian Youth Hostel Association staff run a budget travel information office (☎ 262 660; fax 725 453; e-mail root@jnakv.vno.soros.lt) from their head office at Kauno gatvė 1a, room 407.

Money Vilnius' best 24-hour exchange is on your left as you exit the train station at

Geležinkelio gatvė 6 (☎ 630 763). Another is inside the Hotel Lietuva, on the north-edge of town at Ukmergės gatvė 20. In the Old Town there is an exchange inside the Gintarine sala travel agency (see Travel Agencies below) which is open office hours.

The central post office (see Post & Communications) is one of the few places to cash travellers' cheques and Eurocheques. Vilniaus Bankas at Gedimino prospektas 12 (open Monday to Thursday from 9 am to 4.30 pm and on Friday from 9 am to 4 pm) accepts travellers' cheques and offers cash advances on Visa. It has a branch at the airport which has an ATM accepting Visa and MasterCard.

Post & Communications The central post office (☎ 616 759) at Gedimino prospektas 7 (open weekdays from 8 am to 8 pm and on weekends from 11 am to 7 pm) has telephone and telegraph facilities too. The Hotel Lietuva has a fax service which is open 24 hours a day but it tends to be expensive. The best service is said to be at the telegraph centre at Universiteto gatvė 14, open daily 24 hours.

Express mail can be sent with the state Express Mail Service (EMS) at Vokiečių gatvė 7, open weekdays from 8.30 am to 5.30 pm.

Travel Agencies Several travel agencies in Vilnius also offer help in booking accommodation, tickets and other services within Lithuania and the Baltics. West Express (☎ 222 500; fax 619 436) at Stulginskio gatvė 5 has a home delivery ticket service; Viliota (☎ 652 238) at Basanavičiaus gatvė 15 sells invitations for US$4 to Belarus in support of visa application; the Booking Centre (☎ 727 921; fax 721 815) at Šeimyniškių gatvė 12 offers a worldwide booking system; Lithuanian Student and Youth Travel (☎ 220 220; fax 222 196) at Basanavičiaus gatvė 30, room 13, offers cheap fares for ISC holders; and Gintarine sala (☎ 223 223; fax 223 213) at Vokiečių gatvė 8 arranges guided tours.

LITHUANIA

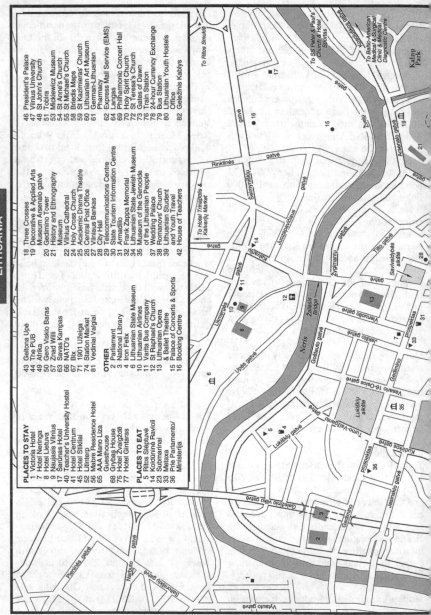

PLACES TO STAY
1 Victoria Hotel
7 Hotel Neringa
8 Hotel Lietuva
9 Naujasis Vilnius
17 Sardinas Hotel
40 Teacher's University Hostel
41 Hotel Sentrum
51 Hotel Stikliai
52 Litinterp
56 Mabre Residence Hotel
65 AAA Mano Liza
   Guesthouse
68 Grybas House
75 Hotel Žvaigždė
77 Hotel Gintaras

PLACES TO EAT
5 Ritos Slėptuvė
14 Koldūninė Ravioli
23 Submarinal
33 Metaxa
36 Prie Parlamento/
   Ministerija

43 Geltona Upė
44 The PUB
49 Afrika
50 Gero Viskio Baras
57 Znad Wilii
63 Savas Kampas
66 NATO's
67 Bix
71 901 Užeiga
74 Station Market
81 Vedinai Valgiai

OTHER
2 Parliament
3 National Library
4 Iron Felix
6 Lithuanian State Museum
10 Lithuanian Airlines
11 Varta Bus Company
12 St Raphael's Church
13 Lithuanian Opera
   & Ballet Theatre
15 Palace of Concerts & Sports
16 Booking Centre

18 Three Crosses
19 Decorative & Applied Arts
   Museum Arsenalo gatvė
20 Gedimino Tower
21 History and Ethnography
   Museum
22 Vilnius Cathedral
24 Holy Cross Church
25 Academic Drama Theatre
26 Lithuanian Art Museum
27 Central Post Office
   Vilnius Bankas
28 City Hall
29 Telecommunications Centre
30 State Tourism Information Centre
31 Armadillo
32 Frank Zappa Memorial
34 Lithuanian State Jewish Museum
35 Museum of the Genocide
   of the Lithuanian People
37 Wedding Palace
38 Romanovs' Church
39 Lithuanian Student
   and Youth Travel
42 House of Teachers

46 President's Palace
47 Vilnius University
48 St John's Church
51 Tobira
53 Mickiewicz Museum
54 St Anne's Church
55 St Michael's Church
58 Skiedis Maps
59 St Kazimieras' Church
60 Lithuanian Art Museum
61 German-Lithuanian
   Pharmacy
62 Express Mail Service (EMS)
64 Lanpas
69 Philharmonic Concert Hall
70 Holy Spirit Church
72 St Teresa's Church
73 Gates of Dawn
76 Train Station
78 24-hour Currency Exchange
79 Bus Station
80 Lithuanian Youth Hostels
   Office
82 Geležinis Kablys

Central Vilnius

LITHUANIA

Bookshops Penki Kontinentai at Stulginskio 5 stocks a good range of English-language textbooks and dictionaries. The university bookshop, Litera, at Šv Jono 12 (open Monday to Thursday from 10 am to 6 pm and Friday from 10 am to 5 pm) has a large selection of foreign-language books as well as great postcards. Rūtos Knygos at Daukanto aikštė 2, room 13, offers a two-for-one book exchange (open weekdays from 11 am to 7 pm and on Saturday from 10 am to 5 pm).

Laundry Vilnius has good laundries which are not too expensive. Baltoji Kojinė at Saulėtekio gatvė 33 is open daily from 10 am to 7 pm. Palūstrė at Savanorių prospektas 11a accepts washing daily from 7 to 11 am and home delivers between 3 and 7 pm. Dry cleaning is possible at Virkštis (☎ 456 654) at Vairo gatvė 18.

Left Luggage There is no baggage room at the bus station. Walk across to the train station instead where there is a left-luggage office with lockers in the basement. It is open 24 hours.

Medical & Emergency Services Two private clinics offer an English-speaking, Western service. The Baltic-American Medical and Surgical Clinic (☎ 742 020) inside Vilnius University Antakalnio hospital at Antakalnio gatvė 124 is open weekdays from 9 am to 5 pm, but also offers a 24-hour emergency service. Cheaper is the Medical Diagnostic Centre (☎ 709 120, 709 121) at Grybo gatvė 32 (open weekdays from 8.30 am to 8.30 pm). A recommended dental service is AS Klinika (☎ 225 919) at Sėlių gatvė 18a. The German-Lithuanian pharmacy at Didžioji gatvė 13, open weekdays from 9 am to 7 pm and on Saturday from 10 am to 5 pm, stocks the best range of Western medicines. Gedimino Vaistinė (☎ 624 930) at Gedimino prospektas 27 offers 24-hour emergency service.

Things to See
Katedros aikštė & Around The **Gedimino Tower**, on top of the 48-metre **Gediminas Hill** (Gedimino kalnas) behind the cathedral, is a good starting point. Walk up the path from Katedros aikštė. The red-brick tower was part of the upper castle. Inside is a museum (open daily from 11 am to 6 pm, except Monday and Tuesday) featuring old Vilnius, and on top there's an observation platform.

Katedros aikštė, scene of most of the mass gatherings during Lithuania's independence campaign, is dominated by **Vilnius Cathedral**, reconsecrated in 1989 after being used as a picture gallery during the Soviet era. The cathedral originally stood within the old lower castle, and its tall belfry, standing separately, was once part of the castle's defences.

The site was originally one of pagan worship and a pagan altar is said to still stand beneath the foundations. The first wooden cathedral was built here in the 13th or 14th century, then rebuilt in the 15th century in a Gothic style. That too has vanished beneath successive rebuildings – the major one being from 1783 to 1801, when the outside was completely redone in today's classical form. The five-metre **bronze statues** of St Helene (the cross she's wielding is nine metres long), St Stanislav and St Casimir on top of the cathedral, were levelled in 1956 but at the time of writing were expected to be resurrected any day following years of restoration work. The façade statues on the south side facing the square are of Lithuanian dukes, those on the north are saints. The interior retains more of its original aspect. The showpiece is the **Chapel of St Kazimieras** at the east end of the south aisle, created in 1623-36 with a baroque cupola, with coloured marble and granite and white stucco sculptures.

The **Decorative & Applied Arts Museum** (Taikomosios Dailės Muziejus), a little further along at Arsenalo gatvė 3, is testament to the skills of Lithuania's artisans since the 15th century. The furniture, tapestries, jewellery and ceramics are all marvellous. It's open daily except Monday and Tuesday from noon to 6 pm.

East of Gediminas Hill The white **Three Crosses** (Trys Kryžiai) overlooking the city from Three Crosses Hill are old Vilnius landmarks said to have stood here since the 17th century in memory of three monks who were crucified on this spot. The current crosses, erected in 1989, are replicas of the three knocked down and buried by the Soviet authorities. You can walk up to them from Kosciuškos gatvė.

Inside **St Peter & St Paul's Church** (Šv Petro ir Povilo Bažnyčias) at the far end of Kosciuškos gatvė is a sea of sparkling white stucco sculptures of real and mythical people, animals and plants, broken here and there by touches of gilt, paintings or coloured statues. Most of the decoration was done by Italian sculptors between 1675 and 1704. The tomb of the Lithuanian noble who founded the church, Mykolas Kazimieras Pacas, is on the right of the porch as you enter. If you don't want to walk, trolleybus No 2, 3 or 4 will take you there from the Gedimino stop on Vrublevskio gatvė near the cathedral.

Old Town – Pilies gatvė & around The area stretching a km or so south from Katedros aikštė was built up in the 15th and 16th centuries and the area is well worth repeated visits. The focal streets are Pilies gatvė and its southward continuations, Didžioji gatvė and Aušros Vartų gatvė.

The central buildings of **Vilnius University** occupy most of the block between Pilies gatvė and Universiteto gatvė. The university, founded in 1579, was one of the greatest centres of Polish learning and produced many notable scholars in the 17th and early 19th centuries, before being closed by the Russians in 1832. It was reopened in 1919 and today it has about 14,000 students.

The 12 linked courtyards can be entered by several passages and gates: the southern gate on Šv Jono gatvė brings you into the Didysis or Skarga Courtyard, with three sides of galleries in the early 17th-century Mannerist style, and **St John's Church** (Šv Jono Bažnyčia) which has an outstanding 18th-century baroque main façade.

The arch through the 16th-century building opposite St John's leads to a two-domed **observatory** whose late 18th-century façade

is adorned with reliefs of the zodiac. The other main courtyard, reached from the north side of the Didysis Courtyard, is the Sarbievijus Courtyard.

East of Pilies gatvė, the old rooms of the Polish Romantic poet Adam Mickiewicz (1798-1855) at Bernardinų gatvė 11 are now the **Mickiewicz museum**, open Friday from 2 to 6 pm and Saturday from 10 am to 2 pm. Mickiewicz grew up near Vilnius and studied at its university from 1815 to 1819 before being exiled for anti-Russian activities. Much of his work, which inspired the 19th-century Polish nationalists, is set in the Vilnius region.

Across Maironio gatvė is the fine 1581 brick façade of **St Anne's Church** (Šv Onos Bažnyčia), a high point of Lithuanian Gothic architecture with its sweeping curves and delicate pinnacles. The austere church behind it was part of the city's defensive wall.

Old Town – Didžioji gatvė & around Southern Didžioji gatvė widens into a plaza which was long one of the centres of Vilnius life, with markets from the 15th century.

The large **St Kazimieras' Church** (Šv Kazimiero Bažnyčios) at Didžioji 43 is Vilnius' oldest baroque church, built by the Jesuits between 1604 and 1615. Under Soviet rule it spent two decades as a museum of atheism.

Pretty Aušros Vartų gatvė was once the start of the Moscow road. On the east side of the street, just above a 16th-century house, is the big, pink, domed 17th-century **Holy Spirit Church**, Lithuania's chief Russian Orthodox church. The amazingly preserved bodies of three 14th-century martyrs lie in a chamber in front of the altar. The Catholic **St Teresa's Church** (Šv Teresės Bažnyčios), above the Church of the Holy Spirit, is early baroque (1635-50) outside and more elaborate late baroque inside.

At the southern end of Aušros vartų gatvė are the **Gates of Dawn** (Aušros Vartai) – in fact just a single gate tower, the only one of the original nine in the town wall that's still intact. Just before the gate, a door on the left opens on to a staircase up to a little 18th-century chapel directly over the gate arch.

LITHUANIA

This houses a supposedly miracle-working **icon of the Virgin** reputed to have been souvenired from the Crimea by Grand Duke Algirdas in 1363. The chapel is particularly revered by the Poles and is one of Eastern Europe's leading pilgrimage destinations.

New Town The main street of modern Vilnius, laid out in 1852, is **Gedimino prospektas**, which runs west from Katedros aikštė to the river. Its 1.75-km length is dotted with shops, restaurants, banks and offices. Lukiškių aikštė, which is the square at roughly the mid-point on Gedimino prospektas, used to be named Lenin Square with a statue of the man at its centre. **Lenin**, who was levelled in 1991, now lies, along with his Communist mate Stalin, outside the Dailės Studija at Dariaus ir Girėno gatvė 25. The large building facing the square, at Gedimino prospektas 4, used to be the Vilnius KGB headquarters and prison and is now the **Museum of the Genocide of the Lithuanian People**. The museum guides are all former inmates and will show you round the cells where they were tormented (open Tuesday to Sunday from 10 am to 5 pm). Immediately north of Gedimino prospektas before it crosses the river is the **parliament building** where a few concrete slabs remain as reminders of the barricades erected there in January 1991 to halt a feared attack by Soviet tanks and troops. As it happened the attack never came but the barricades stayed in place until December 1992.

Close by at Pamėnkalnio gatvė 12 is the **Lithuanian State Jewish Museum**, open Monday to Thursday from 9 am to 5 pm and on Friday from 9 am to 4 pm.

Beyond the Hotel Lietuva on Ukmergės gatvė is the **Lithuanian State Museum** (Lietuvos Vaklstybės Muziejus), open daily except Monday and Tuesday.

At Kalinuasko gatvė 1, outside a medical clinic, stands a 4.2-metre-high memorial to the American rock 'n' roll legend **Frank Zappa**, who died from cancer in 1993 when he was in his mid-50s. The bust, said to be the first of its kind in the world, was erected by the Lithuanian Frank Zappa fan club in 1995 after a long dispute with various authorities who found the whole idea totally preposterous.

Just over a km south-west of parliament, at the west end of Čiurlionio gatvė, is Vilnius' biggest city park, the pleasant **Vingis parkas**, whose huge stage is the usual setting for the Lithuanian Song Festival. The 326-metre **TV tower** (where Soviet tanks and troops killed 12 people and injured many more as they fought through the crowd encircling it on 13 January 1991) is in the suburb of Karoliniškes, across the river from Vingis parkas. Carved wooden crosses stand as memorials to the victims. Trolleybus No 7 from the train station to Justiniškės goes within a couple of minutes walk of the tower. More crosses stand outside the **TV & Radio Centre**, also stormed by Soviet troops that night, on the corner of Konarskio gatvė and Pietario gatvė, 2.5 km west of the city centre.

Places to Stay

Camping The nearest camp site is 25 km east of Vilnius on the road to Minsk, at Rukainiai. At *Rytų Kempingas* (☎ 651 195) you can stay in small wooden summerhouses by the river as well as pitch a tent. Doubles/triples cost 40/50 Lts and luxury rooms cost 105/135 Lts.

Hostels & Colleges *Lithuanian Youth Hostels* (Lietuvos Jaunimo Nakvynės Namai; ☎ 262 660; fax 725 453) in room 407, Kauno gatvė 1A, 400 metres from the train and bus stations, runs the *Filaretų Hostel* (☎ 696 627) at Filaretų gatvė 17 in the Užupis area, one km east of the Old Town. It has 15 rooms with two to 10 beds in each: beds in a double room cost 32 Lts with linen and breakfast. Beds in other rooms cost 24 Lts.

Vilnius University Student Representation (VUSA; ☎ 614 414; ☎ & fax 617 920), in the courtyard of the main university building at Universiteto gatvė 3, offers rooms in student blocks about a 20-minute trolleybus ride from the centre. Rooms with a shared shower and toilet cost 16/20 Lts for Lithuanians/other nationalities. Book and pay in advance at the VUSA office.

The ***Teacher's University Hostel*** (☎ 230 704; fax 262 291), on the west edge of the Old Town at Vivulskio 36, has singles/doubles costing 50/56 Lts. A very cheap alternative worth considering is ***Vilnius train station*** where you can sleep in a standing carriage overnight for 15 Lts including linen. The 'reception' (☎ 692 472), marked 'Budinti', is on your right as you enter the main ticket hall.

Private Homes & Flats *Litinterp* (☎ 223 850; fax 223 559) at Bernardinų gatvė 7-2 can arrange B&B accommodation in the Old Town for 60 Lts a single or 100 Lts for a double. It also arranges accommodation in Klaipėda, Nida, Palanga and Kaunas.

Also providing private accommodation but at more expensive rates are ***Vilniaus Kalvos*** (☎ 220 894) at Ašmenos gatvė 10 (singles/doubles cost 80/120 Lts) and ***Trečjasis aukštas*** (☎ 220 918, 222 973; fax 222 963) at Gedimino prospektas 41-3. ***Lobis*** (☎ 737 162) at Mečetės gatvė 4 can find apartments for short stays from 120 Lts a night, as can ***Vingriai*** (☎ 222 950) at Vingrių gatvė 19.

Hotels Recommended travel agencies in Vilnius that have the best chance of getting you into some of the better hotels at short notice include Baltic Travel Service (☎ 220 151, 220 220) at Subačiaus gatvė 2, and the Booking Centre (☎ 727 921, 722 363) Šeimyniškių gatvė 12. For cheaper accommodation go through the *Vilnius In Your Pocket* tourist information centre (☎ 260 875) at Vilnius airport.

Hotels – bottom end A convenient place to stay close to the train and bus station is ***Hotel Žvaigždė*** (☎ 619 626) at Pylimo gatvė 63, although the staff only speak Russian. Doubles/triples cost 18/15 Lts per person and a room with four/five beds costs 13 Lts per person. ***Hotel Gintaras*** (☎ 634 496), at Sodų gatvė 14 in front of the train station, has brightened up its appearance in recent months but only the unrenovated rooms remain cheap. Singles/doubles start at 39/59

Lts and rise to 100/160 Lts, depending on how much has been renovated. As with everything in close range of the station, security is not the best here.

Five km north of centre in the Žirmūnai district, near the river at Verkių gatvė 66, is ***Hotel Trinapolis*** (☎ 778 913; fax 762 605). It's not the best location, but its single rooms for 40 Lts a night with a bathroom or 20 Lts a night without are popular among hardened travellers. To get here take trolleybus No 5 from the train station.

Two km north-east of the cathedral is the ***Hotel Sportas*** (☎ 748 953) at Bistryčios gatvė 13, a large decaying Soviet hotel where you can get basic singles/doubles/triples for 47/61/60 Lts per person. Take trolleybus No 2, 3 or 4 from the Gedimino stop near the cathedral, five stops to the Minskas stop on Antakalnio gatvė; walk east along Tramvajų gatvė and turn left along Grybo gatvė at the end; Bistryčios is then the first on the right.

At the airport try ***Hotel Skrydis*** (☎ 262 223) which offers a 25% discount if you stay for more than five days. The normal rate for basic singles and doubles is 70 Lts and for triples, 75 Lts.

Hotels – middle & top end Good value are the cheaper rooms in the attic of ***Hotel Centrum*** (☎ 232 770; fax 232 760) at Vytenio gatvė 9/25. A 10-minute walk from the Old Town, this sparkling hotel located within a business centre is becoming increasingly popular with Western business people and tourists. Singles/doubles start at 180/260 Lts and the larger rooms go for 320/440 Lts.

The Swedish-run ***Victoria Hotel*** (☎ 724 013), Saltoniškių gatvė 56, also offers good value for money (singles/doubles 168/238 Lts), as does ***Naujasis Vilnius*** (☎ 726 756) in a shopping precinct at Ukmergės gatvė 14. Doubles/luxury rooms start at 180/330 Lts.

If you're into basketball stay at the ***Šarūnas Hotel*** (☎ 723 888) at Raitininkų gatvė 4 built by Lithuanian basketball god Šarūnas Marčiulionis. Singles/doubles cost 280/329 Lts.

For a Soviet blast-from-the-past try the central ***Hotel Neringa*** (☎ 610 516) at

LITHUANIA

Gedimino prospektas 23 (singles/doubles at 240/300 Lts) or the *Hotel Lietuva* (☎ 726 090; e-mail lietuva@aiva.lt) at Ukmergės gatvė 20, the largest and ugliest hotel in Vilnius with all the facilities. A few Soviet-era hangovers also remain at the *Draugystė* (☎ 236 711; e-mail hotel draugyste@post .omnitel.net), Čiurlionio gatvė 84, formerly the top hotel for Party officials. The glass elevator and rooftop bar offer brilliant views of Vingis parkas. Singles/doubles start at 200/220 Lts.

Vilnius' most exclusive hotels include the *AAA Mano Liza Guest House* (☎ 222 225) in the Old Town at Ligoninės gatvė 5 (suites 320 to 640 Lt), and *Grybas House* (☎ 619 695) in a courtyard close by on Aušros Vartų 3a (suites 440 to 560 Lts). The *Mabre Residence Hotel* (☎ 222 087) at Maironio gatvė 13 is in a former Orthodox monastery converted into 23 rooms. Singles/doubles cost 300/340 Lts.

Tucked down a pretty cobbled street in the heart of the Old Town, *Hotel Stikliai* (☎ 627 971; e-mail stikliai@mail.tipas.lt) at Gaono gatvė 7 outstrips them all. Singles/doubles cost 560/640 Lts.

Places to Eat

Eating out in Vilnius is substantially cheaper than Rīga or Tallinn. The Lithuanian capital also offers the greatest choice of places to eat with new cafés, bars and restaurants springing up every month.

Restaurants For a cheap and cheerful meal guaranteed to fill there are two obvious options. Both are British-run and have been packed since they revolutionised the dining scene in 1995. *The PUB*, in the Old Town at Dominikonų gatvė 9, dishes up shepherd's pie, lasagne, Lithuanian black garlic bread, shaslik, and a whole host of other mammoth-sized meals for around 10 Lts (open daily from 8 am to 2 am). More up-market is *Prie Parlamento* at Gedimino prospektas 46 whose specialities include steaks for around 18 Lts as well as yummy chocolate brownies and crumbles for 9 Lts.

Offsetting these is a host of colourful off-beat eating places, each of which compete to be the most outrageous. *Savas Kampas* near The PUB at Vokiečių gatvė 4 sports the most daring colour scheme, serving delicious salads for 7 to 12 Lts and great mozzarella-stuffed pancakes topped with a spicy tomato sauce for 11 Lts (open daily noon to 3 am).

Metaxa at Gedimino prospektas 32a (open weekdays from 10 am to midnight and on weekends from noon to midnight) and *Gero Viskio Baras* at Pilies gatvė 28 (open daily 10 am to midnight), are run by the same Lithuanian team, are equally fun and serve the best salads and stuffed chicken (with pears, ham or cheese) in town.

Bix at Etmonų gatvė 6 was formed by the Lithuanian hard-rock band Bix. At the time, its avant-garde, industrial-style décor was almost as shocking as its menu: chicken with promise to fly, chew chew pig and ecstasy are just some of their delights.

The most hard-hitting of them all is the military-inspired *NATO's* at Pasažo skg 2 (open daily noon to 3 am). 'When muses and arms are silent, it is NATO's that inspires' it claims. The black interior with various military memorabilia splattered over the walls certainly inspired NATO's secretary-general to pop in during an official visit to Vilnius in spring 1996.

For authentic Lithuanian cuisine try *Ritos Smuklė* at Žirmūnų gatvė 68. The owner, Rita Dapkute, is an American-Lithuanian who worked for Vytautas Landsbergis in the pre-independence period and 'freelanced' for the KGB with the approval of the CIA. Her restaurant serves strictly Lithuanian fodder made from strictly Lithuanian produce, meaning that Coca-Cola, Marlboro cigarettes and Soviet-introduced champagne are completely banned. Wild folk bands play every weekend (open daily 11 am to 2 pm).

The first fun place to open in Vilnius, *Ritos Sleptuvė*, also run by Rita at Goštauto gatvė 8, retains the same glorious retro-US-meets-USSR style but is no longer as hot as it used to be.

Fans of the dynamic Stikliai team's first cooperative café in the former Soviet Union (it's now closed) can opt for Chinese at

Stikliai's **Geltona Upė** at Stiklių gatvė 18 or French at the **Hotel Stikliai** at Gaono gatvė 7, among others. Each is lavishly furnished, costs at least 100 Lts a head and is open daily from noon to midnight.

Cafés & Fast Food *Afrika*, located halfway between the cathedral and the Gates of Dawn at Pilies gatvė 28, is bright, cheerful and popular with the local arts scene. Its sliced meat cooked on a spit (gyros) is particularly good (open daily from 9 am to 8 pm). **Kavinė F**, further up Pilies gatvė at Aušros vartų 5, has some of the best cakes and pastries in town.

For traditional Lithuanian 'cold noses' served in a could-be-Portugal courtyard try **1901 Užeiga**, close to the Gates of Dawn at Aušros Vartų 11. For Lithuanian cuisine at dirt-cheap prices try **Koldūninė Ravioli**, close to the Kalvarijų market at Kalvarijų 13, where you can sample meat or cheese stuffed ravioli cushions (koldūnai) for around 7 Lts. The Hare Krishna canteen, **Vediniai Valgiai**, close to the train station at Kauno gatvė 2/21 serves great vegetarian food for around 7 Lts (open weekdays from 10.30 am to 6 pm).

For a touch of Polish Vilnius, try **Znad Willi**, inside a Polish art gallery at Išganytojo gatvė 2/4 (open daily from 11 am to 6 pm).

On Gedimino heading towards the Cathedral is *McDonald's*, which also has a drive-through opposite the train station at Seinų gatvė 3 (open 8 am to midnight).

Submarinai, a kiosk on the corner of Gedimino prospektas opposite the cathedral does great takeaway hot chicken-filled submarine sandwiches for 10 Lts.

Self-Catering Šviežia Duona at Savanorių 6 is the best place for traditional Lithuanian rye bread (bočių). Fresh milk straight from the cow's udder, home-made honey and smoked eels are just some of the culinary delights to be found at the farmers' market at Kalvarijų gatvė 6 (open daily except Monday from 7 am to noon). French-owned Iki supermarkets stocking every importable product imaginable as well as Lithuanian fare have outlets on Žirmūnų gatvė 68 and Architektų gatvė 43/31, among others.

Entertainment
See *Vilnius In Your Pocket*, the weekly *Baltic Times* or the local daily *Lietuvos Rytas* for information about what's on.

Bars & Clubs For live jazz and rock try **Langas** at Ašmenos gatvė 8 where concerts kick off most evenings at 8 pm. Less hectic are the Sunday afternoon jazz sessions from 2 to 4 pm at the ever-popular nightclub **Ministerija** in the basement of Prie Parlamento restaurant at Gedimino prospektas 46. Some of the best live music can be heard at **Geležinis Kablys**, known locally as the Hook House, close to the train station at Kauno gatvė 5 (open Wednesday to Sunday from 10 pm to 6 am).

Strictly house and techno is played in Vilnius' Western-style nightclubs, all of which are in large, grey Soviet blocks a few km from the city centre. **Nasa** at Laisvės gatvė 58 is open Thursday to Sunday from 9 pm to 6 am, and **Max Dance World** at Justiniškių gatvė 64, is open Wednesday to Sunday from 9 pm to 3 am.

One to watch out for is the more central **Iron Felix** (Geležinis Felix) at Lukiškių 3. Named after the Vilnius-born Cheka founder, Feliksas Dzerzinski, this is Vilnius' first purpose-built Soviet club and attempts to recapture the whole Soviet experience down to newspaper squares for toilet-paper (as a compromise it offers real toilet paper too).

Bars worth visiting include the Tex-Mex pool hall, **Armadillo**, at Gedimino prospektas 26 (open daily from 5 pm to 5 am) and the Japanese karaoke bar **Tobira** at Mykolo gatvė 4. The PUB, Prie Parlamento and Bix (see Places to Eat) are all unbeatable options.

Classical Music, Opera & Ballet The State Symphony and Lithuania Chamber Orchestras have high reputations, as does the Lithuanian Philharmonia. Concert halls include the **Philharmonic** at Didžioji gatvė 45. The **Lithuanian Opera & Ballet Theatre**, a modern building with poor acoustics at Vienuolio gatvė 1, stages several mainly classical productions in repertoire.

LITHUANIA

Getting There & Away
See the Getting There & Away section earlier in this chapter for international connections to/from Vilnius. For connections with Latvia and Estonia, see Travel between the Baltics in the Getting There & Away section of the Estonia chapter.

Air If you're buying an international ticket, it's worth trying a travel agent (see the Information section earlier) to see if they can do anything cheaper than the airlines themselves.

Airline offices in Vilnius include:

Air Baltic
    Airport (☎ 236 000, 233 202)
Air Lithuania
    Tilto 2 (☎ 227 013)
Austrian Airlines, SAS
    Airport (☎ 236 000, 233 202)
Finnair
    Rūdininkų 18/2 (☎ 619 339)
Hamburg Airlines
    Airport (☎ 262 251)
Lithuanian Airlines (LAL)
    Ukmergės gatvė 12 (☎ 752 588, 753 212)
LOT
    Room 104, Hotel Skrydis at the airport
    (☎ 260 819, 632 772)
Lufthansa
    Airport (☎ 636 049, 262 222)

Bus The long-distance bus station (*Autobusų stotis*; ☎ 262 482, 262 483) is just south of the old town at Sodų gatvė 22 near the train station. The ticket hall on the right as you enter is for same-day departures; the one on the left is for advance bookings. With buses to nearby destinations (on the left side of the platform) you can pay on board. For the longer-distance buses you need a ticket unless the bus is in transit, in which case you may have to scrum for a seat when it gets in.

Within Lithuania, buses are usually more frequent, quicker and definitely cheaper (around four Lts per hour of travelling) than trains. Timetable information is clearly displayed in the ticket halls (green letters indicate a microbus), and on the platform. Domestic departures from Vilnius include:

Destination	Distance	Time (Hrs)	Frequency
Druskininkai	125 km	2½	six buses daily
Kaunas	100 km	2	40+ buses daily
Klaipėda	310 km	5-6½	13 buses daily
Palanga	340 km	7	seven buses daily
Šiauliai	225 km	4½	six buses daily
Trakai	30 km	¾	30+ buses daily

Train The train station (*geležinkelio stotis*; ☎ 630 088, 630 086) lies slightly to the left behind the bus station at Geležinkelio 16. Timetables are displayed in English. There is a handful of daily trains to Kaunas (two to three hours), Klaipėda (five hours), Šiauliai (four hours) and Trakai (1½ hours).

Car & Motorcycle Numerous 24-hour petrol stations run by Statoil, Neste, Shell and Texaco, selling Western-grade fuel including unleaded petrol and diesel, are dotted at strategic points all over the city. Most Western car manufacturers are represented in Vilnius and sport showrooms and repair services.

Car Rental Litinterp (☎ 223 850, 223 291) at Bernardinų gatvė 7-2 rents out chauffeured, self-drive cars and minibuses in Vilnius, Kaunas and Klaipėda for 190 to 300 Lts a day. Equally good value is Rimas (☎ 77 62 13) which offers an excellent chauffeur service and also has the cheapest self-drive cars to rent. Europcar (☎ 222 739) has an outlet at the airport and also at Vilniaus gatvė 2/15. Avis (☎ 733 226, 733 005) is inside Hotel Naujasis Vilnius at Ukmergės gatvė 14. Close by is Hertz (☎ 726 940) at Ukmergės gatvė 2, which also rents out limousines.

Getting Around
To/From the Airport Vilnius airport (*aerouostas*) is 5 km south of the city at Rodūnės kelias 2 in the Kirtimai suburb. Bus No 2 runs between the airport and the northwestern suburb of Šeškinė via the city centre and the Hotel Lietuva. Bus No 1 runs between the airport and the train station

A taxi from the airport to the city centre should cost no more than 15 Lts.

Local Transport Trolleybuses run daily

from 5.30 am to 12.30 am. Bus and trolley-bus tickets cost 0.60 Lts each and are sold at most kiosks. If you buy a ticket directly from the driver it costs 0.75 Lts. Tickets have to be punched inside the carriage. Unpunched tickets warrant a 20 Lts on-the-spot fine. Trolleybus and autobus routes are in *Vilnius In Your Pocket*.

Taxis Former state taxis (all pale blue or yellow Volgas) are the best as they have meters which the drivers can be persuaded to use. The official charge per km should be 1.20 Lts but its rare you'll get that. Two useful taxi ranks are on Katedros aikšte and in front of the Old Town Hall on Didžioji gatvė. The cheapest type of taxis are those that you call by telephone (☎ 228 888).

AROUND VILNIUS
Paneriai
Between July 1941 and July 1944, about 100,000 people were killed in the Nazi death camp at Paneriai 10 km south-west of central Vilnius. The entrance to the wooded site is marked by a memorial, the **Panerių Memorialas**, which now states that 70,000 of the victims here were Jewish – in the past the victims were referred to simply as 'Soviet citizens'. A path leads down to the small **Paneriai Museum**, open from 11 am to 6 pm daily except Tuesday. From here paths lead to a number of grassed-over pits where the Nazis burnt the exhumed bodies of their victims in order to hide the evidence of their crimes.

Getting There & Away Bus No 8 from Vilnius train station runs to Aukštieji Paneriai about every 15 minutes. Get off near the footbridge over the Paneriai marshalling yards, cross the bridge and turn right along the street at the far side of the tracks, Agrastų gatvė, which leads straight to the site 900 metres away.

Trakai
Gediminas reputedly made Trakai, 27 km west of Vilnius, his capital in 1321. Its two lakeside castles were built within the next 100 years to fend off the German knights. Today it's a small, quiet town on a north-pointing peninsula between two vast lakes, making it a popular spot for a day out or weekend break from Vilnius. From the train station in Trakai, follow Vytauto gatvė north to the central square, where you'll find the bus station, then continue north to Karaimų gatvė and the main points of interest.

The Trakai National Park information bureau (☎ 8-238-528 33) is at Kęstučio gatvė 1, close to the ruins of the Peninsula Castle, and the tourism information centre (☎ 8-238-519 34) is at Vytauto gatvė 69 (open weekdays from 9 am to 6 pm).

The local telephone code is ☎ 238.

Karaites Among the wooden cottages along Karaimų gatvė, at No 30, is an early 19th-century Kenessa (prayer house) of the Karaites, or Karaimai, a Judaist sect originating in Baghdad and adhering only to the Law of Moses. Some Karaites were brought to Trakai from the Crimea by Vytautas around 1400 to serve as bodyguards. Some 150 Karaites still live in Trakai.

Castles The remains of Trakai's Peninsula Castle are towards the north end of town, in a park close to the shore of Lake Luka. The castle is thought to have been built between 1362 and 1382 by Vytautas' father, Kestutis. The painstakingly restored Gothic red-brick Island Castle (open daily from 10 am to 7 pm) probably dates from around 1400 when Vytautas found he needed stronger defences. It stands east of the north end of the peninsula, linked to the shore by footbridges. The moated main tower has a cavernous central court and a range of galleries, halls and rooms, some housing the Trakai History Museum (admission 4 Lts).

Places to Stay *Kempingas Slėnyje* (☎ 513 87) is a top camping ground with limited hostel accommodation 4 km north of Trakai on the road to Vievis. It costs 7 Lts a night to pitch a tent and from the fourth night onwards campers get 10% discount. Beds in the hostel cost 16 Lts.

LITHUANIA

Getting There & Away More than 30 buses daily run from 6.55 am to 9.53 pm from Vilnius bus station to Trakai, leaving every 15 minutes between 9 am and noon. The 40-minute journey costs 1 to 3 Lts. Trains to Trakai run approximately every hour from 5.18 am to 7.53 pm, the journey also 40 minutes.

Central Lithuania

KAUNAS

Lithuania's second city is 100 km west of Vilnius at the confluence of the Nemunas and Neris rivers. Kaunas' 423,900 population is about 90% ethnic Lithuanian which means that the city is often considered more 'Lithuanian' than the capital. Founded in the 11th century, it's said to have been reduced to ashes 13 times before WWII, in which it received yet another battering. It was an important river-trade town in the 15th and 16th centuries, and Lithuania's capital between WWI and WWII, when Vilnius was taken over by Poland. Today it's still a river port as well as Lithuania's chief industrial city and entrepreneurial centre. The city is a cultural bastion with a big student population and some fine architecture, museums and galleries.

Orientation

Kaunas' historic heart, Rotušės aikštė (City Hall Square), is on the point of land between the two rivers at the west end of the city centre. The new town, the modern-day heart of Kaunas, is centred on the mostly pedestrianised Laisvės alėja, further east (public smoking is banned on this street). Around here you'll find most of the main shops, hotels, restaurants, galleries and museums. The bus and train stations are around a km south of the east end of Laisvės alėja, down Vytauto prospektas. Kaunas is big (the biggest noncapital city in the Baltic states) and it takes the best part of an hour to walk from the train station to Rotušės aikštė.

Information

There are numerous currency exchanges along Laisvės alėja, with 24-hour exchanges inside the Dali supermarket at Partizanų gatvė 22a and inside Elivija at Savanorių prospektas 170. Vilniaus Bankas at Donelaičio gatvė 62 (open weekdays from 9 am to 4 pm with a break from 12.30 to 2 pm) gives cash advances on Visa and changes travellers' cheques. The central post, telegraph and telephone office is at Laisvės alėja 102, open weekdays from 8 am to 8 pm and Saturday from 8 am to 3 pm, and for phone calls 24 hours a day.

Most shops open at 10 am; galleries and museums open from noon except Monday when they are closed. *Kaunas In Your Pocket* is useful for city maps and information.

The telephone code is ☎ 27.

Things to See

Rotušės Aikštė Many 15th and 16th-century German **merchants' houses** around this pretty square have been restored, some now contain cafés or shops. The fine, white baroque former **city hall** is late 18th century. It's now a Palace of Weddings – a role for which its 'wedding cake' architecture seems far better suited.

In the square's south-west corner stands a **statue of Maironis**, or Jonas Maculevičiaus, the Kaunas priest and writer whose works were banned by Stalin but who is now Lithuania's national poet. The **Lithuanian Literary Museum** is in the house behind, where Maironis lived from 1910 to 1932. The south side of the square is dominated by an 18th-century twin-towered Jesuit church, now back in religious use after years as a school.

At Aleksotas gatvė 6, just off the south-east corner of the square, is the curious 16th-century brick **House of Perkūnas**, built as offices on the site of a former temple to the old Lithuanian thunder god Perkūnas. Just beyond, backing onto the river, is **Vytautas Church**, the biggest in Lithuania, built by Vytautas about 1400.

The single-towered **Kaunas Cathedral**, on the north-east corner of the square, owes

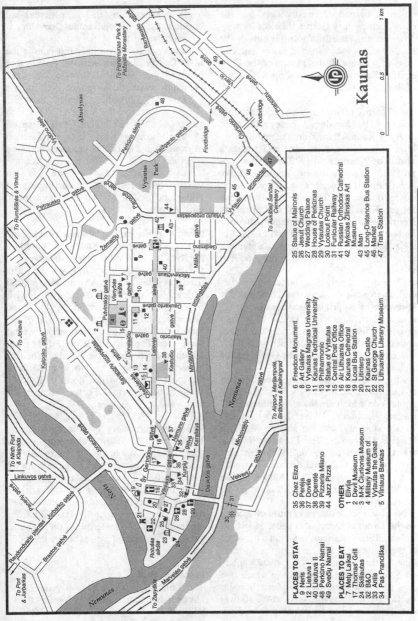

Kaunas

LITHUANIA

1 km

0.5

0

PLACES TO STAY
9 Neris
12 Lietuva I
40 Lietuva II
48 Perkūno Namai
49 Svečių Namai

PLACES TO EAT
17 Metų Laikai
19 Thomas Grill
24 Skliautas
32 B&O
33 Antis
34 Pas Pranciška
35 Chez Eliza
36 Perėja
37 Dovilė
38 Operetė
39 Pizzeria Milano
44 Jazz Pizza

OTHER
1 Eilvija
2 Devil Museum
3 M K Čiurlionis Museum
4 Military Museum of
   Vytautas the Great
5 Vilniaus Bankas
6 Freedom Monument
8 Art Gallery
10 Vytautas Magnas University
11 Kaunas Technical University
13 Philharmonic
14 Statue of Vytautas
15 Central Post Office
16 Air Lithuania Office
18 Kaunas Cathedral
19 Local Bus Station
20 Litinterp
21 Kaunas Castle
22 St George Church
23 Lithuanian Literary Museum
25 Statue of Maironis
26 Jesuit Church
28 Wedding Palace
29 House of Perkūnas
29 Vytautas Church
30 Lookout Point
31 Funicular Railway
41 Russian Orthodox Cathedral
42 Mykolas Žilinskas Art
   Museum
43 Man
45 Long-Distance Bus Station
46 Market
47 Train Station

much to baroque reconstruction, but the early 15th-century Gothic shape of its windows remain. **Maironis' tomb** is outside the south wall. A reconstructed tower and sections of wall are all that remain of the 11th-century **Kaunas Castle**, a short walk north of Rotušės aikštė.

New Town The two-km-long pedestrianised Laisvės alėja (Freedom Avenue) is the main artery of Kaunas though architecturally it's a little dull. Towards its west end stands a **statue of Vytautas**. In 1972, in the park opposite the statue, a student, Romas Kalanta, burnt himself to death as a protest against Soviet occupation. The blue neo-Byzantine former **Russian Orthodox cathedral** on Nepriklausomybės aikštė (Independence Square), dominates the east end of Laisvės alėja. For many years it housed a stained-glass museum but now it's reopened to worshippers.

Directly to the right as you face the cathedral, in front of the **Mykolas Žilinskas Art Museum** at Nepriklausomybės aikštė 12, stands **Man**, a glorious statue of a man revealing his manhood which, when it was commissioned by the municipality in 1987, was intended to symbolise the Greek god of victory, Nike.

Straddling Donelaičio gatvė, a block north of Laisvės alėja, is Vienybės aikštė (Unity Square) on which are the main buildings of Kaunas Technical University, which has 14,000 students, and the smaller Vytautas Magnus University. The **Freedom Monument** Vienybes aikšte, dated 16 February 1918 (the day Lithuania declared independence), was erected in 1928, hidden during the Stalin era, and put back in place on 16 February 1989.

Nearby is the **Military Museum of Vytautas the Great** at Donelaičio gatvė 64, which isn't a military museum at all but a museum of the history of Lithuania from prehistoric times to the present day. Of particular interest is the wreck of the aircraft in which two of Lithuania's greatest modern heroes, Darius and Girėnas (pictured on the 10 litas note), attempted to fly nonstop from New York to Kaunas in 1933. The heroes are buried in the **Aukštieji Šančiai Cemetery** at Ašmenos gatvė 1.

Next door to the military museum is the **M-K Čiurlionis Museum** at Putvinskio gatvė 55, with an extensive collection of the Romantic symbolic paintings of Čiurlionis (1875-1911), Lithuania's greatest artist and composer. Across the street at Putvinskio gatvė 64 is the fascinating **Devil Museum** (Velnių Muziejus) with a bizarre collection of more than 1700 devil statuettes gathered together by the landscape artist Antanas Žmuidzinavičius (1876-1966). Worth looking out for are the satanic figures of Hitler and Stalin, formed from tree roots, dancing over Lithuania.

Ninth Fort Built in the late 19th century, the fort, on the outskirts of Kaunas, was used by the Russians in WWI to defend their western frontier against Germany. In WWII the Nazis used it as a death camp. An estimated 80,000 people, including most of Kaunas' Jewish population, were murdered here. One of the prison buildings remains and the site of the mass grave is marked by stark, monumental sculptures. The museum is open daily from 10 am to 6 pm, closed on Tuesday. The fort is reached by taking bus No 35 or 23 from the local bus station just north of Rotušės aikštė to the bus stop IX Fortas, seven km out of town.

Pažaislis Monastery This fine example of 17th-century Baroque architecture stands about nine km east of the city centre near the Kaunas Sea (Kauno marios), a large artificial lake and itself a popular day trip. The highlight is the monastery church with a 50-metre-high cupola and a sumptuous interior. To get there, take trolleybus No 5 from the train station to its terminus on Masiulio gatvė, a few hundred metres before the monastery.

Places to Stay
The Lithuanian Youth Hostel Association has three-bed rooms at *Svečiu Namai* (☎ 748 972) at Pranūzų gatvė 59, about a 1.25 km

walk east of the train station, for 40 Lts. From the train station walk east along Čiurlionio gatvė and take the second bridge over the train line, climb the steps on the far side and then bear left.

For bed and breakfast get in touch with *Litinterp* (☎ 228 718) at Kumelių gatvė 15-4. Singles/doubles cost 60/100 Lts. It rents bicycles too.

Pieno Centras (☎ 202 763) at Kaunakiemo gatvė 1 has doubles, and rooms with four beds. Rooms for one person/shared rooms cost 40/30 Lts per person. The reception is open from 9 am to 6 pm. Equally acceptable is the *Preksta* at Pramonės 16 which still has a three-tier pricing system for Lithuanians, CIS residents and foreigners. Doubles and luxury suites for foreigners cost from 150 Lts a night.

Former Intourist options include the *Neris* (☎ 203 863) at Donelaičio gatvė 27 which offers singles/doubles for 100/160 Lts; *Lieutuva II* (☎ 221 791) at Laisvės alėja 35, with rooms for 80/120 Lts; and the slightly more up-market *Lietuva I* (☎ 205 992) at Daukanto gatvė 21 which is as Soviet as the rest of them but has made some attempts at refurbishment. Singles/doubles/triples cost 160/240/300 Lts.

Top hotels include *Perkūno Namai* (☎ 209 386), on a hill overlooking the city at Perkūno gatvė 61, which has singles/doubles for 260/320 Lts, and *Minotel* (☎ 229 981) down a cobbled street in the Old Town at Kuzmos gatvė 8. Singles/doubles cost 380/400 Lts but are worth it.

Places to Eat

Thomas' Grill, in the Old Town at Mapų gatvė 2 (open weekdays from 10 am to 8 pm and on Saturday from 11 am to 8 pm), serves great gyros. Equally quick is Kaunas' first pizza chain, *Jazz Pizza*. Outlets at Kęstučio gatvė 6, Gričiupio gatvė 9 and Perkūno gatvė 3 offer you a colourful choice of pizza for around 14 Lts. All three open weekdays from 11 am to 11 pm and on weekends from noon to midnight. The Italian-run *Pizzeria Milano* at Mickevičiaus gatvė 10 serves the best

pizza in town for 7 to 12 Lts daily from 8 am to 1 am.

Pas Pranciška at Zamenhofo gatvė 11 serves delicious home-made soups and other cheap Lithuanian dishes for 2 to 10 Lts. *Metų Laikai* at Mickevičiaus gatvė 40b is surprisingly popular.

More expensive but great for a treat is the classy Italian *Operetė 21* at Kęstučio gatvė 58 or *Antis*, an off-beat cellar-bar and bistro in the Old Town at Vilniaus 21. Both open daily noon to midnight. Top of the league is the French-inspired *Chez Eliza*, a few doors down at Vilniaus gatvė 30. Vegetarians or those counting the calories should head for the ultra-trendy, almost clinical, *Dovilė* above Benetton at Vilniaus gatvė 56.

Cool hang-outs include the hard-rock *B & O* just off Rotušės aikštė at Muitinės 9 (open Monday to Saturday from noon to 11 pm) and *Skiliautas* in a tiny courtyard at Rotušės aikštė 26 where local artists meet to play chess (open daily 11 am to 11 pm). *Perėja* at Birštono gatvė 20 (open daily from 8 am to midnight) is a must for anyone wanting an early breakfast, a laid-back lunch or a glimpse of the cream of Kaunas' art scene.

Getting There & Away

Some international bus and rail connections are mentioned in the Lithuania Getting There & Away section.

Air Kaunas airport (☎ 541 309) is 10 km from the centre at Karmėlava. The privately owned Air Lithuania (Aviakompanija Lietuva; ☎ 229 706) flies to/from Palanga six times a week and also to Budapest, Hamburg, Helsinki, Kristianstad, Prague and Zurich. Its office is at Gertrūdos gatvė 7.

Bus Kaunas long-distance bus station (☎ 224 192) is at Vytauto prospektas 24. There is a bus to Kaliningrad every day except Monday (six hours); three buses daily to/from Klaipėda (four hours); a daily bus to/from Rīga and Tallinn; hourly buses to Vilnius (two hours) and three buses daily to Minsk (five hours). A Eurolines bus runs daily to Berlin, Frankfurt and Munich, leaving Kaunas at 4.35 pm and arriving in Kaunas at 12.25 pm on the return journey.

Train Kaunas train station (☎ 221 093) is at Čiurlionio gatvė 16, at the south end of Vytauto prospektas. There's an advance booking office (☎ 292 455) near the Old Town at Šv Gertrūdos gatvė 7, open daily from 9 am to 7 pm except Sunday. About 15 local and nine or 10 long-distance trains make the trip to/from Vilnius daily. The two types are shown on separate timetables.

The *Baltic Express*, travelling between Tallinn and Warsaw, passes through Kaunas, as does the Vilnius-Šeštokai train. To/from Klaipėda there's one train nightly each way, taking eight hours; to/from Rīga there's one train nightly taking 5½ hours; and to/from Kaliningrad there are two trains daily taking 3½ to 4½ hours.

Boat Between June and August the *Raketa* speed boat sails daily except Monday from Kaunas pier *(prieplauka)* on the east edge of the city at Raudondvario plentas 107 to Nida (four hours) and, upon request, to Klaipėda (4½ hours). See Getting There & Away in the Klaipėda section.

ŠIAULIAI

Šiauliai (population 147,000), 140 km north of Kaunas and 80 km west of Panevėžys, is Lithuania's fourth biggest city. Most of the town dates from after 1872 when it was burned down in a great fire. The real magnet of the Šiauliai area is the strange Hill of Crosses, which is within a day's drive from any of the Lithuanian cities and Rīga. However, if you're travelling by public transport you may need to spend a night in Šiauliai unless you're coming to/from Rīga.

Orientation & Information

The main north-south street is Tilžės gatvė, with the bus station towards its south end and the tall St Peter & Paul's Church towards its north end, almost a km away. To the south Tilžės gatvė becomes the road to Kaliningrad, to the north the road to Rīga. The main east-west axis is Vilniaus gatvė which

crosses Tilžės gatvė 300 metres south of the church.

The tourist information centre (☎ 8-214-430 795) is at Vilniaus gatvė 88. There are currency exchange offices at the bus station (open 10 am to 7 pm) and at the Lietuvos Bankas, half a block west of the post office. The main post office is at Aušros alėja 42, two blocks west of St Peter & Paul's Church.

The telephone code is ☎ 214.

Hill of Crosses

About 10 km north of Šiauliai, two km east off the road to Joniškis and Rīga, the strange Hill of Crosses (Kryžių kalnas) is a place of national pilgrimage. It's a two-hump hillock covered in a forest of thousands upon thousands of crosses. Some are devotional, others are memorials (many for people deported to Siberia) and some are finely carved folk-art masterpieces.

The hillock is said to have originally been a fortification and it's thought that the tradition of planting crosses may have begun in the 14th century. At least three times in the Soviet era the crosses were bulldozed, only to spring up again.

You can get there from Šiauliai by taxi or bus. Buses to Meškuičiai, Joniškis and Rīga pass the beginning of the two-km tree-lined road to the hill.

Places to Stay

The *Viešbutis Šiauliai* (☎ 437 333) at Draugystės gatvė 25 has decent rooms with private bathroom for around 70 Lts. A second choice might be the *Viešbutis Salduvė* (☎ 56 230) at Donelaičio gatvė 70.

Getting There & Away

Bus Services include to Kaliningrad, four buses daily (five hours); Kaunas, 10 buses daily (three hours); Klaipėda, up to 15 buses daily (2½ hours); Rīga, 12 buses daily (2½ to three hours); Tallinn, two buses daily (8½ hours); and Vilnius, six buses daily (four hours or more).

Train Šiauliai is on the main Kaunas-Rīga line so it has a fairly good train service. The station is at Dubijos gatvė 44, about 700 metres east of the bus station. Up to nine trains a day go to/from Rīga (two to 2½ hours) and Vilnius (four hours or six via Kaunas).

Western Lithuania

Lithuania has a short (under 100 km), but attractive, coastline. Palanga is the main seaside resort while Klaipėda is Lithuania's historic third city and major port. The Baltic states' most unusual feature, the **Kuršių Spit** (known as Neringa to Lithuanians) stretches south of Klaipėda. This is a thin finger of sand (98 km long but in places only 400 metres wide, and nowhere wider than five km) dividing the Baltic Sea from the Kuršių Lagoon. The landscape is a mix of pine forest and sand dunes, sometimes up to 66 metres high. The northern half is Lithuanian while the southern part belongs to the Russian oblast of Kaliningrad. A well-maintained road runs down its length from Smiltynė, the northern tip opposite Klaipėda, to Zeleno-gradsk in Kaliningrad.

PALANGA
The seaside resort of Palanga is 30 km north of Klaipėda on a 10-km sandy beach backed by dunes and pine woods. Although the town's permanent population is only 20,000, it's swollen greatly in summer when Palanga becomes the Lithuanian resort of choice.

Orientation & Information
Vytauto gatvė, the main street, runs parallel to the coast about one km inland. The Catholic church at Vytauto gatvė 51 is roughly the middle of town. The bus station is a few steps east of it on Kretingos gatvė (☎ 8-236-53 333), with the post office opposite at Vytauto gatvė 53. The tourist information office (☎ 8-236-539 27) is at Vytauto gatvė 56.

The telephone code is ☎ 236.

Things to See & Do
Besides the obvious attractions of the beach and the pretty older parts of town, there's a large landscaped **botanical park** at the south end of Vytauto gatvė which contains an excellent **amber museum** in the former palace of the Polish noble Tyszkiewicz family.

Places to Stay & Eat
The camping ground *Palanga* (☎ 251 676), two km out of Palanga on the Klaipėda-Palanga highway, has good facilities including a shop selling basic provisions. *Nemirseta Camp Site*, five km before Palanga on the same road, has excellent wash facilities.

A private *youth hostel* (☎ 57 076) is run at Nėries gatvė 24, west of the Catholic church and 300 metres from the sea. A bed for the night is 20 Lts. At the time of writing a second youth hostel was expected to open in the centre.

For bed and breakfast try the ever-efficient *Litinterp* (☎ 216 962) in Klaipėda, which can find you a single/double room in Palanga for 60/100 Lts. The cheapest hotels in town are run by *Baltija* (☎ 538 41) at Ganyklų gatvė 39, which can arrange accommodation in any of its seven rest homes for 25 to 135 Lts a night. *Hotel Dilkas* (☎ 575 19), in the city centre at Gintaro gatvė 25, is probably a more friendly bet. Singles/doubles cost 60/120 Lts.

Monika is in a wooden cabin on the road leading to the beach at Basanavičiaus gatvė 12 and offers traditional Lithuanian dishes (open daily noon to midnight). Also recommended is the *Club Rivjera* at Vytauto gatvė 98a where you can bop until you drop – or eat (open daily 10 am to 2 am). *Mextaxa*, close to the beach, is another must.

Getting There & Away
Air Lithuania flies to/from Kaunas five times a week and Kristianstad in Sweden twice a week. Its office (☎ 10 665) is at Daukanto gatvė 23-2.

The nearest train station is at Kretinga 10 km away but there are regular daily buses to Kaunas, Klaipėda, Rīga, Šiauliai and Vilnius.

LITHUANIA

KLAIPĖDA

The port of Klaipėda, the third biggest city in Lithuania with 204,600 people, and a centre of amber-ornament production, is 315 km west of Vilnius, at the mouth of the Kuršių Lagoon. Before the Soviet era Klaipėda was a German-populated town called Memel. In 1923 Lithuania seized it from the Western allies who had been administering it pending a decision on its post-WWI fate. Hitler annexed it in 1939 and it was wrecked towards the end of WWII when the Red Army took it.

Orientation & Information

The Danės River flows westward across the city centre to enter the Kuršių Lagoon four km from the open Baltic Sea. The main street, running roughly north-south, is Manto gatvė which becomes Tiltų gatvė south of the river. The old town is centred on Tiltų gatvė. Most hotels and restaurants and the train and bus stations are north of the river. The central post office is at Liepų gatvė 16 (open weekdays from 9 am to 7 pm and on weekends from 9 am to 5 pm), and the central telephone centre is at Liepų gatvė 1 (open daily from 8 am to 11 pm).

Klaipėda In Your Pocket is available at most hotels and news kiosks.

The local telephone code is ☎ 26.

Things to See

An important landmark, on Teatro aikštė (Theatre Square) off Turgaus gatvė, south of the river, is the 1820 **Klaipėda Theatre**. Hitler stood on the balcony of this theatre in 1939 to proclaim the connection of Memel to Germany. Here too stands Klaipėda's much-loved statue of Ännchen von Tharau, unveiled in 1989 in dedication to the 17th-century German poet Simon Dach.

North of the river, there's a **riverside park** immediately east of the H Manto gatvė bridge. Klaipėda's **art gallery** and sculpture park (which was formerly a cemetery!) are at Liepų gatvė 33 (open Wednesday to Sunday from noon to 6 pm). At Liepų gatvė 12 there's a **Clock & Watch Museum** open Tuesday to Sunday from noon to 5.30 pm.

The nearby **post office** is worth a visit for its beautiful painted wood interior.

Smiltynė The narrow north end of Neringa Spit is Klaipėda's playground with beaches, high dunes and, set in a large 19th-century German fort, the **Sea Museum & Aquarium** with performing seals, penguins and sea-lions. Dolphin shows run from May to September at noon, 2 and 4 pm (open 11 am to 7 pm daily except Monday). Ferries run every half hour from the old castle port (cost 0.80 Lts).

Places to Stay

Litinterp (☎ 216 962) at Šimkaus gatvė 21-8 offers B&B for 60/100 Lts for singles/doubles. It also rents out bicycles. The central *Hotel Viktorija* (☎ 213 670) at Šimkaus gatvė 28 has spartan but clean singles/doubles/triples with shared bathrooms for 35/55/65 Lts and excellent-value rooms with five beds for 100 Lts.

Others include *Hotel Jūra* (☎ 299 857), close to the port at Malūnininkų gatvė 3 (singles/doubles cost 100/110 Lts), and the former Intourist *Hotel Klaipėda* (☎ 217 324) at Naujoji Sodo gatvė 1 which serves the only early breakfast in town (7 to 11 am). Singles/doubles cost 160/240 Lts.

Outstripping them all in price and prestige is *Svečių Namai* (☎ 310 900) at Janonio 11 which has luxurious apartments for 200 to 400 Lts. One of Kalipėda's few remaining hammer & sickle is carved on the top of the building opposite.

Places to Eat

The top place to eat in Klaipėda is also one of the best bars in the Baltics. Decked out with swings suspended from the ceiling and a public phone installed in an old black car parked inside, *Skandalas* at Kanto 44 is a place you cannot miss. One trip here and you'll be dreaming of its giant-sized American steaks served with creamed, fried, jacket or boiled potatoes every time you eat somewhere else (open daily noon to 3 am).

The other eating-joint Klaipėda is famed for (in Lithuania at least) is *Bambola Pizzeria*, a two-minute walk from the train station

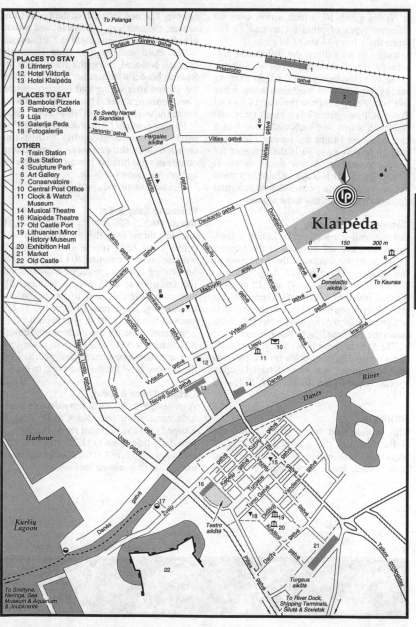

PLACES TO STAY
8 Litinterp
12 Hotel Viktorija
13 Hotel Klaipėda

PLACES TO EAT
3 Bambola Pizzeria
5 Flamingo Café
9 Lūja
15 Galerija Peda
18 Fotogalerija

OTHER
1 Train Station
2 Bus Station
4 Sculpture Park
6 Art Gallery
7 Conservatoire
10 Central Post Office
11 Clock & Watch Museum
14 Musical Theatre
16 Klaipėda Theatre
17 Old Castle Port
19 Lithuanian Minor History Museum
20 Exhibition Hall
21 Market
22 Old Castle

Klaipėda

0   150   300 m

To Palanga

Dariaus ir Girėno gatvė

Priestočio gatvė

To Svečių Namai & Skandalas

Pergalės aikštė

Vilties gatvė

Janonio gatvė

Daukanto gatvė

To Kaunas

Donelaičio aikštė

Vytauto gatvė

Danė River

Danės

Harbour

Kuršių Lagoon

Teatro aikštė

To Smiltynė, Neringa, Sea Museum & Aquarium & Joubkrantė

Turgaus aikštė

To River Dock, Shipping Terminals, Šilutė & Sovietsk

LITHUANIA

at Nėries gatvė 10, which serves over 40 different types of pizza for around 13 Lts (open daily from 11 am to 10 pm).

Inside an art gallery, the stylish and reasonably priced *Galerija Peda* at Turgaus gatvė 10 is the best place for light evening snacks, especially at weekends when it has live jazz. *Fotogalerija* in the heart of the Old Town at Tomo gatvė 7 is a touch more offbeat with soups and karbonadas for 4 to 8 Lts, while the bright and breezy *Flamingo* café on Manto gatvė 38 is the best spot for people-watching. A few doors down at Manto gatvė 20 is *Lūja*, Klaipėda's most expensive restaurant which demands formal dress and offers a show most nights.

Getting There & Away

International connections including a ferry from Germany are covered in the Getting There & Away section at the beginning of this chapter. There are 13 daily buses to Vilnius (five to 6½ hours) and 12 or so to Kaunas (three to 3½ hours). There are also three daily buses to Rīga (six or seven hours) and from Smiltynė two daily buses travelling down the Neringa Spit to Kaliningrad.

The *Raketa* speed boat sails at 3 pm daily except Monday from Nida on the Neringa Spit to Kaunas, and from Klaipėda upon special request (☎ 8-26-212 224, 8-27-227 218).

NERINGA

This wonderland sandy spit between the Baltic Sea and the Kuršių Lagoon is an attractive combination of sand dunes and pine woods, much of it being a national reserve. The northern half of the spit is Lithuanian, the southern is Russian, and a road runs the whole 90-km length to Kaliningrad.

The main settlement is **Nida** (formerly German Nidden), a popular resort near the Russian border where amber is washed up on the shores after spring and autumn storms. The German writer Thomas Mann had a house (now a museum) in Nida in the 1930s.

Further north of Nida is **Juodkrantė** (formerly German Schwarzort) with a fine stretch of elk-inhabited forest. German tour companies use holiday homes at both places and private homes at Nida.

The telephone code is ☎ 259.

Places to Stay & Eat

Rasytė (☎ 525 92) in Nida at Lotmiškio 11, a stone's throw from the magnificent dunes, offers cosy little rooms in a traditional wooden house for around 40 Lts a night. The best eating options are either downstairs in the guesthouse café or the wonderfully authentic *Seklyčia*, next to the beach and overlooking the dunes at Lotmiškio 1. The smoked fish just melts in your mouth.

In Juodkrantė try the modern guesthouse *Ažuolynas* (☎ 531 74) at Liudviko Rėzos 54. The in-house restaurant *Kopos*, overlooking the lagoon, is by far the best place to eat.

Getting There & Away

A passenger and vehicle ferry departs every half hour from the Old Castle Port in Klaipėda for the northern tip of Neringa. It runs daily from 6 am to 11.30 pm and tickets one way cost 0.80/8 Lts for a deck passenger/ car for the five-minute journey.

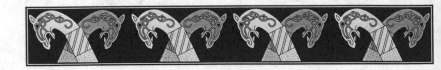

Norway

Norway (Norge) is a ruggedly beautiful country of high mountains, deep fjords and icy blue glaciers. It stretches 2000 km from beach towns in the south to treeless arctic tundra in the north. Norway offers incredible wilderness hiking, year-round skiing and some of the most scenic ferry, bus and train rides imaginable. Summer days are delightfully long, and in the northernmost part of the country the sun doesn't set for weeks on end.

In addition to the lure of the spectacular western fjords, Norway has pleasantly low-key cities, unspoiled fishing villages and rich historic sites that include Viking ships and medieval stave churches.

Norway retains something of a frontier character, with even its biggest cities surrounded by forested green belts. Wilderness camping is one of the best ways to see the country up close and a good way to beat some of Norway's high costs.

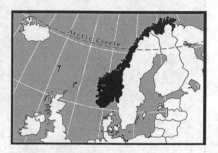

Facts about the Country

HISTORY

The first settlers to Norway arrived more than 10,000 years ago with the end of the Ice Age. As the glaciers retreated north, these early hunters and gatherers followed, pursuing migrating reindeer herds.

Norway's greatest impact on history was during the Viking Age, a period usually dated from the plundering of England's Lindisfarne monastery by Nordic pirates in 793 AD. Over the next century, the Vikings made raids throughout Europe and established settlements in the Shetland, Orkney and Hebrides islands, the Dublin area and Normandy, the latter named for the 'North men'. Viking leader Harald Fairhair unified Norway around 900 and King Olaf, adopting the religion of the lands he had conquered, converted Norway's people to Christianity a century later.

With their sleek seaworthy ships, the Vikings became the first to cross the Atlantic Ocean, beginning with Erik the Red's visit to Iceland and Greenland. Shortly after, in the year 1001 according to the sagas, Leif Eriksson, the son of Erik the Red, explored the coast of North America, which he called Vinland the Good.

The Viking Age ended in 1066 with the defeat of the Norwegian king Harald Hardrada at the Battle of Stamford Bridge in England.

In the 13th century Oslo emerged as a centre of power and a period of prosperity and growth followed until the mid-14th century when the bubonic plague swept the country, wiping out nearly two-thirds of the population. In 1380 Norway was absorbed into a union with Denmark that lasted over 400 years.

Denmark's ill-fated alliance with France in the Napoleonic Wars resulted in its ceding of Norway to Sweden in January 1814 under the Treaty of Kiel. Tired of forced unions, on 17 May 1814 a defiant Norway adopted its own constitution, though its struggle for independence was quickly quelled by a Swedish invasion. In the end the Norwegians were allowed to keep their new constitution but were forced to accept the Swedish king.

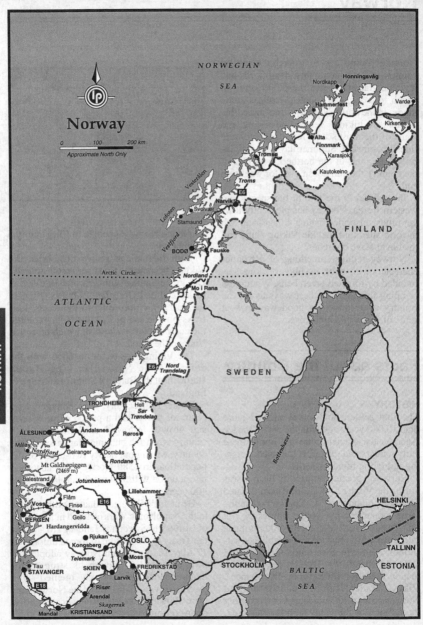

In 1884 a parliamentary government was introduced in Norway and a growing nationalist movement eventually led to a peaceful secession from Sweden in 1905. By referendum Norwegians voted in favour of a monarchy over a republic. Having no royalty of their own, Norway's parliament selected Prince Carl of Denmark to be king. Upon acceptance, he took the title Håkon VII and named his infant son Olav, both prominent names from Norway's Viking past.

Norway stayed neutral during WWI. Although it restated its neutrality at the start of WWII, Norway was attacked by the Nazis on 9 April 1940 and, after a two-month struggle, fell to the Germans. King Håkon set up a government in exile in England and placed most of Norway's huge merchant fleet under the command of the Allies. Although Norway remained occupied until the end of the war, it had an active Resistance movement.

In one of the most renowned sabotage efforts of WWII, Norwegian Resistance fighters parachuted into the German heavy-water plant at Rjukan, in southern Norway, and blew the plant sky-high, shattering Germany's efforts to develop an atomic bomb. During their retreat at the end of the war, the Nazis torched and levelled nearly every town and village in northern Norway.

The royal family returned to Norway in June 1945. King Håkon died in 1957 and was succeeded by his son, Olav V, a popular king who reigned until his death in January 1991. Crown Prince Harald, Olav's son, was crowned king of Norway (Harald V) in June 1991.

Norway joined the European Free Trade Association (EFTA) in 1960 but has been reluctant to forge closer bonds with other European nations, in part due to concerns about its ability to preserve small-scale farming and fishing. In 1972 Norwegians voted against joining the European Community (EC) amidst a divisive national debate. It took two decades for membership to once again become a forefront issue. In 1994 a second national referendum was held, this time on joining the EC's successor, the European Union (EU), and voters rejected that as well.

GEOGRAPHY & ECOLOGY

Norway, occupying the western part of the Scandinavian peninsula, has a land area of 323,878 sq km and shares borders with Sweden, Finland and Russia. The country is long and narrow, with a coastline deeply cut by fjords – long, narrow inlets of the sea bordered by high, steep cliffs. Mountains, some capped with Europe's largest glaciers, cover more than half of the land mass. Only 3% of Norway is arable.

'The Land of the Midnight Sun' is more than just a promotional slogan, as nearly a third of Norway lies north of the Arctic Circle, the point at which there is at least one full day when the sun never sets and one day when it never rises.

In 1993 Norway resumed commercial whaling of minke whales in defiance of an international whaling ban. While Norway supports the protection of other threatened species, the government contends that minke whales, which have an estimated North Atlantic stock of 75,000, can sustain a limited harvest. Greenpeace has spearheaded a campaign to challenge the whaling, placing its boats in front of the harpoons and waging other protests. However, overall the world's response has been quite limited. In 1993 Norwegian hunters harpooned 157 minke whales; the quota has since risen to twice that number.

GOVERNMENT & POLITICS

Although officially a monarchy, Norway is a constitutional democracy with a parliamentary form of government. General elections are held every four years for the 165 seats in parliament (Storting). Gro Harlem Brundtland has been Norway's prime minister since 1986. The first woman to hold this office, she is a member of the labour party, the largest of the six major parties represented in parliament.

Norway's politics has few extremes. The major conservative party is quite moderate by European standards, the communist

NORWAY

parties have only minuscule membership, and there is no right-wing neofascist movement. The labour party is social-democratic in orientation, promoting extensive social programmes supported by high taxation.

ECONOMY

North Sea oil fields, discovered on the Norwegian continental shelf in the 1960s, have brought prosperity to Norway, which has one of the world's highest per capita incomes.

Fishing, shipbuilding and shipping are mainstays of the economy and abundant hydroelectric power provides the basis for a number of industries including aluminium, steel and paper production. Norway has a comprehensive cradle-to-grave social welfare system. All citizens are entitled to free university education, free hospital treatment and a guaranteed pension.

POPULATION & PEOPLE

Norway has 4,348,000 people and the lowest population density in Europe. The largest cities are Oslo with 483,000 residents, Bergen with 223,000, Trondheim with 143,000 and Stavanger with 104,000.

Most Norwegians are of Nordic, Alpine and Baltic origin. In addition, there are about 30,000 Lapps (called Sami in Norway), many of whom still live a traditional nomadic life herding reindeer in the far north.

ARTS

Norway's best known artists include painter Edvard Munch, composer Edvard Grieg, sculptor Gustav Vigeland and playwright Henrik Ibsen, whose works include the classic *A Doll's House*.

Norwegians Sigrid Undset and Knud Hamsun have both won the Nobel Prize for Literature. Undset is best known internationally for *Kristin Lavransdatter*, a trilogy that portrays the struggles and earthy lifestyle of a 13th-century Norwegian family. Hamsun won the Nobel Prize for his 1917 novel *The Growth of the Soil*; other works of his such as *Hunger* and *Mysteries* delve into the more troubled aspects of the human character. To many Norwegians it is not Hamsun's accom-

plishments for which he is most remembered but rather his collaborative relationship with the Nazis during WWII and his subsequent imprisonment as a traitor.

As for architecture, Norway's unique stave churches are some of the oldest wooden buildings on earth, having one foot in the Viking Age and the other in the 11th-century early Christian era. The churches, named for their vertical supporting posts, are distinguished by dragon-headed gables that resemble the ornately carved prows of Viking ships and by their unique pagoda-like shape.

CULTURE

Norwegians tend to be independent and outdoor-oriented people. On summer weekends hiking, fishing and boating are popular, while in winter, Norwegians head for the ski runs. 'No trespassing' signs are virtually unknown and public access to wilderness areas is guaranteed.

Norway holds onto many of its cultural traditions. The wearing of elaborate regional folk costumes is still commonplace at weddings and other festive events. Traditional folk dancing and singing is enjoying a resurgence in popularity and visitors can enjoy these activities at festivals around the country.

Storytelling is another centuries-old tradition. Trolls are an essential element in Norwegian folklore, born from a custom of fireside storytelling that helped pass the dark winter months. Trolls are especially associated with mountainous areas. While some trolls could be befriended, others were pesky creatures who lived in the ground under houses and barns, and were a convenient source of blame for all of life's woes. Trolls live on in Norway's place names, as mascots, as carved figurines and in scores of folk tales.

Most Norwegians are straightforward and easy-going, and nothing out of the ordinary is expected of visitors. One simple rule of etiquette: as a guest in a Norwegian home, you shouldn't touch your drink before your host makes the toast *'skål'*, which you should answer in return.

RELIGION

More than 90% of all Norwegians belong to the Church of Norway, an Evangelical Lutheran denomination.

LANGUAGE

Norway has two official languages. They are quite alike, and every Norwegian learns both at school. Bokmål, literally 'Book-language', referred to in the Language Guide at the back of this book as BM (or indicated within brackets), is the urban-Norwegian variety of Danish, the language of the former rulers. BM, also called Dano-Norwegian, it is used by more than 80% of the population. It is the predominant language in all Norwegian cities, the primary language of education for most Norwegian school children and the language most frequently used on TV and in newspapers.

The other language is Nynorsk, or 'New Norwegian' – as opposed to Old Norwegian, the language in Norway before 1500, before Danish rule. Nynorsk, referred to in the Language Guide as NN, is a kind of common denominator of everyday speech in all its dialects. Nynorsk has a rural base and is the predominant language in the western fjord area and the central mountain districts. Growing urbanisation since the end of WWII has led to a marked decrease in the use of Nynorsk: nearly one-third of all school children used it as their primary language 50 years ago, but only about 15 % do today.

In speech the distinction between BM and NN is no problem, since Norwegians understand both of them. Both are used in the media, although BM is predominant in the daily papers. A striking feature of both written languages is that many words have two or more officially authorised forms of spelling.

English is widely understood and spoken in Norway, especially in the urban areas and in most tourist destinations. In the rural (and therefore mostly NN) areas you may come across people who will speak very little English. If you show an effort to speak their tongue, it will help a great deal to establish contact.

See the Language Guide at the back of the book for pronunciation guidelines and useful words and phrases.

Facts for the Visitor

PLANNING
Climate & When to Go

Due to the warming effects of the Gulf Stream, which flows north along the Norwegian coastline, Norway's coastal areas have a surprisingly temperate climate. In Bergen the average monthly temperature in winter never drops below 0°C and in Vardø in the far north the average December temperature is only -4°C. The mountainous inland areas see a more extreme range of temperatures with colder winter weather.

Norway is at its best and brightest from May to September. Late spring is a particularly pleasant time – fruit trees are in bloom, daylight hours are long, and most hostels and sights are open but uncrowded.

Unless you're heavily into winter skiing or searching for the Aurora Borealis of the polar nights, Norway's cold dark winters are not the prime time to visit.

Midnight-sun days, when the sun never drops below the horizon, extend from 13 May to 29 July at Nordkapp and from 28 May to 14 July in the Lofoten islands. Even southern Norway has daylight from 4 am to 11 pm in midsummer.

Books

These books provide useful background information:

Mountain Hiking in Norway, by Erling Welle-Strand, has wilderness trail information including hiking itineraries, sketch maps and details on trail huts.
Motoring in Norway, by Erling Welle-Strand, is a concise book describing scenic motor routes.
A Brief History of Norway, by John Midgaard, covers Norwegian history from prehistoric to modern times.
The Viking World, by James Graham-Campbell, traces the history of the Vikings by detailing excavated Viking sites and artefacts.

NORWAY

Maps

For drivers, the best road maps are the Cappelens series, available in Norwegian bookshops. Most local tourist offices have simple town maps that they distribute for free. Topographical hiking maps can be purchased from DNT, which has offices throughout Norway (see Hiking under Activities).

Online Services

Both general and tourism-related information about Norway can be accessed on the Internet at http://www.norway.org.

What to Bring

Norwegians are quite casual and most travellers are unlikely to need dressy clothing. As the weather can change quickly it's best to bring layers of clothing that can be added and taken off as needed.

Even in summer you won't regret having a jacket, or at least an anorak (windbreaker), for windy fjord cruises and the high country. Good walking shoes are important. You should bring hiking boots if you plan to do wilderness hiking, a warm sleeping bag and appropriate gear if you're camping. Consider bringing snacks such as trail mix, peanut butter and instant coffee to save a few bucks. Hostellers will save money by bringing their own sheets as hiring linen sets adds from 30 to 40 kr to the bill.

SUGGESTED ITINERARIES

Depending on the length of your stay you might like to see and do the following:

Two days
    Visit Bergen, then rail to Flåm and take a combination boat/bus trip back to Bergen allowing you to see some of the fjords
One week
    Spend two days in Oslo, two days in Bergen and go on a three-day jaunt through the western fjords
Two weeks
    As above, plus continue north through Åndalsnes, Trondheim and the Lofoten islands
One month
    As above, plus a coastal steamer cruise breaking at Tromsø and Nordkapp

Two months
    Explore the country thoroughly – spend some time skiing and hiking in the Jotunheimen and Hardangervidda areas

HIGHLIGHTS

Train Rides

The 470-km trip on the Oslo-Bergen railway is Norway's finest: a scenic journey through snow-capped mountains and the windswept Hardanger plateau. Don't miss the side trip on the Flåm line, which hairpins its way down the Flåm valley, stopping at a thundering waterfall midroute. Another special train trip is the Rauma line from Dombås to Åndalsnes, which passes waterfalls galore.

Museums & Churches

Oslo's Bygdøy peninsula holds a fascinating collection of explorers' ships: the polar *Fram*, the *Kon-Tiki* raft and three ships built by Vikings a millennium ago. Be sure to visit one of the 29 remaining stave churches, which date to medieval times and incorporate Viking influences. In the 19th century many of the surviving stave churches were moved to open-air folk museums, along with other historic timber buildings. Bygdøy has Norway's largest folk museum, but the one in Lillehammer is the most evocatively presented.

Top Fjord Sights

Nothing typifies Norway more than its glacier-carved fjords, and ferrying along these inland waterways is Norway's top sightseeing activity. The Geirangerfjord has the most spectacular waterfalls, whereas the Nærøyfjord provides the most stunning scenery in the Bergen region.

Although the fjords are scenic from the water, often the most majestic angle is found on the surrounding mountainsides. Many fjord-side villages have hiking trails that lead up to lookouts with picturesque views. In addition, the road from Gudvangen to Voss, and the Trollstigen and Eagle roads between Åndalsnes and Geiranger, have high vantages with breathtaking fjord scenery.

TOURIST OFFICES

There are tourist offices in nearly every town of any size in Norway, usually near the train station, dock or town centre. In smaller towns they may be open only during peak summer months, while in cities they're open all year round.

Tourist Offices Abroad

Australia
Royal Norwegian Embassy, 17 Hunter St, Yarralumla, ACT 2600 (☎ 06-273 3444)

Denmark
Norges Turistkontor, Trondhjems Plads 4, 2100 Copenhagen Ø (☎ 31 38 41 17)

Germany
Norwegisches Fremdenverkehrsamt, Mundsburger Damm 45, 22087 Hamburg (☎ 040-22 71 0810)

Sweden
Norska Turistbyrån, Sven Rydellsgata 3, 3 tr, 401 251 Gothenburg (☎ 31 18 80 80)

UK
Norwegian Tourist Board, Charles House, 5 Lower Regent St, London SW1Y 4LR (☎ 0171-839 6255)

USA & Canada
Norwegian Tourist Board, 655 Third Ave, New York, NY 10017 (☎ 212-949 2333)

VISAS & DOCUMENTS
Visas

Citizens of the USA, Canada, the UK, Australia and New Zealand need a valid passport to visit Norway, but do not need a visa for stays of less than three months.

Documents

Taking along a hostel association card will save on hostel rates, and students who bring their student identity card will get discounts at many museums and on some buses and ferries.

EMBASSIES
Norwegian Embassies Abroad

Australia
17 Hunter St, Yarralumla, ACT 2600 (☎ 06-273 3444)

Canada
Royal Bank Centre, 90 Sparks St, Suite 532, Ottawa, Ontario K1P 5B4 (☎ 613-238 6571)

Denmark
Trondhjems Plads 4, 2100 Copenhagen Ø (☎ 31 38 89 85)

Finland
Rehbinderintie 17, 00150 Helsinki (☎ 09-171 234)

Germany
Mittelstrasse 43, 53175 Bonn (☎ 228-819 970)

Sweden
Strandvägen 113, Stockholm (☎ 08-665 6340)

UK
25 Belgrave Square, London SW1X 8QD (☎ 0171-235 7151)

USA
2720 34th St NW, Washington DC 20008 (☎ 202-333 6000)

Foreign Embassies in Norway

Australia & New Zealand
Contact the British embassy.

Canada
Oscars gate 20, Oslo (☎ 22 46 69 55)

Denmark
Olav Kyrres gate 7, Oslo (☎ 22 54 08 00)

Finland
Thomas Heftyes gate 1, Oslo (☎ 22 43 04 00)

Germany
Oscars gate 45, Oslo (☎ 22 55 20 10)

Russia
Inkognitogaten 24B, Oslo (☎ 22 44 91 77)

Sweden
Nobels gate 16A, Oslo (☎ 22 44 38 15)

UK
Thomas Heftyes gate 8, Oslo (☎ 22 55 24 00)

USA
Drammensveien 18, Oslo (☎ 22 44 85 50)

CUSTOMS

Alcohol is expensive in Norway, so you might want to bring in your duty-free allotment: one litre of spirits and one litre of wine (or two litres of wine), plus two litres of beer. You're also allowed to bring in 400 cigarettes duty free, 200 if you're a European resident.

MONEY

Post offices and banks exchange major foreign currencies and accept all travellers' cheques. Travellers' cheques command a better exchange rate than cash by about 1%.

Post offices charge a service fee of 10 kr per travellers' cheque or 20 kr for any size cash transaction. Some banks, including Kreditkassen and Den Norske Bank, match those rates, but others charge a steep 20 kr per travellers' cheque. Because of these per-cheque fees, you'll save money by bringing travellers' cheques in higher denominations.

Those with plastic can get cash any time at ATMs found adjacent to many banks and at busy public places such as shopping centres; the ubiquitous Kreditkassen ATMs accept major credit cards and Cirrus and Plus bank cards.

Visa, Eurocard, MasterCard, American Express and Diners Club cards are widely accepted throughout Norway and generally you'll be better off using a credit card as you avoid the aforementioned transaction fees. Credit cards can be used to buy train tickets but not most domestic ferry tickets other than those for the coastal steamer.

Currency

The Norwegian krone is most often written NOK in international money markets, Nkr in northern Europe and kr within Norway.

One Norwegian krone equals 100 øre. There are 50-øre and one, five, 10 and 20-kroner coins, while bills are in 50, 100, 200, 500 and 1000-kroner denominations.

Exchange Rates

The following currencies convert at these approximate rates:

Australia	A$1	=	5.14 Nkr
Canada	C$1	=	4.76 Nkr
Denmark	1Dkr	=	1.11 Nkr
Finland	1Fmk	=	1.43 Nkr
France	1FF	=	1.26 Nkr
Germany	DM1	=	4.26 Nkr
Japan	¥100	=	6.03 Nkr
New Zealand	NZ$1	=	4.55 Nkr
Sweden	1Skr	=	0.98 Nkr
UK	UK£1	=	10.14 Nkr
USA	US$1	=	6.50 Nkr

Costs

Norway can be very expensive, but if you tighten your belt there are ways to take some of the sting out of this.

If you use only camping grounds and prepare your own meals you might squeak

by for 175 kr a day. If you stay at hostels, breakfast at a bakery, lunch at an inexpensive restaurant and shop at a grocery store for dinner, you should be able to get by for 275 kr a day. If you stay at 'cheap' hotels that include a buffet breakfast, have one meal at a moderately priced restaurant and eat a snack for the other meal, expect to spend 400 kr a day if you're doubling up, 500 kr if you're travelling alone. This is still pretty bare-bones – entertainment, alcohol, even a couple of Cokes are going to cost extra.

To this you need to add transport costs. If you've got a rail pass and stick mainly to train routes these costs will be low. Trying to cover the whole country can be quite expensive – not because the per-km rate is particularly high, but because the distances are great.

Happily, admission to museums is sometimes free, seldom more than 30 kr – and students who flash a student ID will frequently get a discount.

Tipping & Bargaining

Service charges and tips are included in restaurant bills and taxi fares with no additional tip expected. Bargaining is not a common practice in Norway.

Consumer Taxes

The 20% value-added tax (VAT), which is written 'mva' but pronounced 'moms', is already included in the price you pay for goods and services, including hotel rooms. One exception is car rentals, where you may be quoted rates with or without the tax.

If you buy goods exceeding 308 kr from a store with a 'Tax Free for Tourists' sign, you're entitled to a refund of the VAT, minus a service charge, which comes to between 10% and 17% of the purchase price. Ask the store for a 'Tax-Free Shopping Cheque', which you present along with your purchases at your departure point from Norway to get the refund.

POST & COMMUNICATIONS

Norway has an efficient postal service. Postcards and letters weighing up to 20g cost 4

NORWAY

kr to mail to Nordic countries, 4.50 kr to the rest of Europe and 5.50 kr elsewhere. Mail can be received c/o poste restante at any post office in Norway.

Norway has no telephone area codes; when making any domestic call all eight digits must be dialled.

Most pay phones accept one, five and 10-kr coins and will return unused coins but won't give change, so it's best to use coins in small denominations. Domestic calls cost a minimum of 2 kr. You get three times as much calling time per krone between 5 pm and 8 am, and on weekends for local calls, twice as much time for regional calls. You can get directory assistance by dialling ☎ 180 but the cost is 8 kr per minute.

Card phones, which can be convenient if you have a lot of calls to make, are generally found side by side with coin phones. Phonecards (telekort) are sold in 35, 98 and 210 kr denominations and work out a bit cheaper than using coins. The cards can be purchased at Narvesen newspaper kiosks.

The country code for calling Norway from abroad is ☎ 47. To make international calls from Norway dial 00 and then the country code for the country you're calling.

Faxes can be sent from your hotel, and telegrams can be sent by calling ☎ 138; both can also be sent from public telephone offices.

NEWSPAPERS & MAGAZINES
Domestic newspapers are in Norwegian only but the International Herald-Tribune, British newspapers and English-language magazines such as Time can be found at major transport terminals and large city kiosks.

RADIO & TV
Most TV broadcasts are in Norwegian, though US and British programmes are presented in English with Norwegian subtitles. Hotels with cable TV often have CNN and English-language sports channels. Norwegian Radio broadcasts the news in English weekdays at 9 am and 9 pm on 88.7 or 93 FM in Oslo, 89.1 FM in Bergen. The BBC World Service broadcasts on 9410 kHz.

PHOTOGRAPHY & VIDEO
Although both print and slide film are readily available in major cities, prices are high. A 24-exposure roll of Kodacolor Gold 100 will cost about 55 kr to buy, 120 kr to develop and print.

If you purchase videos in Norway, make sure they're compatible with your home system. Norway uses PAL, which is incompatible with the North American NTSC system.

TIME
Time in Norway is one hour ahead of GMT/UTC, the same as Sweden, Denmark and most of Western Europe. When it's noon in Norway, it's 11 am in London, 1 pm in Finland, 6 am in New York and Toronto, 3 am in San Francisco, 9 pm in Sydney and 11 pm in Auckland.

Norway observes daylight-saving time, with clocks set ahead one hour in late March and back an hour at the end of October. Timetables and business hours are posted according to the 24-hour clock.

ELECTRICITY
The electric current is 220V, from 50 to 60 Hz, and plugs have two round pins.

WEIGHTS & MEASURES
Norway uses the metric system. At delis, the price shown is commonly followed by pr/hg (ie per 100 grams). Fruit and other single items are commonly sold by the piece (stykke), which is abbreviated 'stk'.

LAUNDRY
Coin laundries (mynt-vaskeri) are expensive and surprisingly rare, though washers and dryers can often be found at hostels and camping grounds. It's a good idea to bring a little laundry soap and plan on doing some hand washing.

TOILETS
Toilets are western style and not too hard to find, though some places, such as train stations, charge a small fee.

NORWAY

HEALTH

Norway is a very healthy place and no special precautions are necessary when visiting. For a medical emergency dial ☎ 113; for non-emergency medical and dental needs your hotel or the nearest pharmacy can make a referral. More health information is in the introductory Facts for the Visitor chapter of this book.

WOMEN TRAVELLERS

The main Norwegian feminist organisation is Kvinnefronten (☎ 22 37 60 54), literally 'Women's Front', at Holsts gate 1, 0473 Oslo. Women who have been attacked or abused can call the Krisesenter (☎ 22 37 47 00) in Oslo or dial ☎ 112 nationwide.

GAY & LESBIAN TRAVELLERS

Norwegians are generally tolerant of different lifestyles, but public displays of affection (regardless of sexual preference) are not common practice. Gay and lesbian travellers can find gay entertainment spots in the larger cities. For gay issues, contact Landsforeningen for Lesbisk og Homofil Frig- jøring, or LLH (☎ 22 36 19 48), St Olavs plass 2, 0165 Oslo.

DISABLED TRAVELLERS

Norway can be a challenging destination for disabled travellers, and those with special needs should plan ahead. The Norwegian Tourist Board can provide a list of hotels and hostels that are wheelchair accessible. Some, but not all, trains have coaches designed for wheelchair users.

SENIOR TRAVELLERS

Seniors are often entitled to discounts on museum admissions, air tickets and other transport. A few hotels, including the SAS chain, also have discount senior schemes – so enquire whenever you make a reservation.

DANGERS & ANNOYANCES

Norway is a very safe country and travelling presents no unusual dangers or annoyances.

BUSINESS HOURS

Business hours are generally from 9 am to 4 pm Monday to Friday, though stores often stay open to 7 pm on Thursday and to 2 pm on Saturday.

Be aware that many museums have short hours (from 11 am to 3 pm is quite common) which can make things tight for sightseeing. On Sunday most stores are closed, including bakeries, grocers and many restaurants.

PUBLIC HOLIDAYS & SPECIAL EVENTS

Public holidays are:

1 January, *New Year's Day*
Maundy Thursday
Good Friday
Easter Monday
1 May, *Labour Day*
17 May, *Constitution Day*
The 40th day after Easter, *Ascension Day*
The eighth Monday after Easter, *Whit Monday*
25 December, *Christmas Day*
26 December, *Boxing Day*

Constitution Day, 17 May, is Norway's biggest holiday, with many Norwegians taking to the street in traditional folk costumes. There are events throughout the country. The biggest celebration is in Oslo, where marching bands and thousands of schoolchildren parade down Karl Johans gate to the Royal Palace to be greeted by the king.

Midsummer's Eve, which is celebrated by bonfires on the beach, is generally observed on 23 June, Saint Hans day. The Sami people (Lapps) hold their most colourful celebrations at Easter in Karasjok and Kautokeino, with reindeer races, *joik* (traditional chanting) concerts and other festivities.

ACTIVITIES

Much of Norway is wilderness. Åndalsnes and the Lofoten islands are centres for mountain climbing; Nigardsbreen near Sogndal has guided glacier hikes; and bird-watchers can see flocks of sea birds in Runde and in the Lofoten islands of Røst and Værøy.

Hiking

Norway has some of Europe's best hiking, ranging from easy trails in the green zones around cities to long treks through national forests. Much of it, however, is seasonal; in the high snow country, hiking is often limited to the period of June to September. The most popular wilderness hiking areas are the Jotunheimen and Rondane mountains and the Hardanger plateau.

The Norwegian Mountain Touring Association, or DNT, maintains a network of mountain huts a day's hike apart throughout much of Norway's wilderness. These range from unstaffed huts with two beds to large staffed lodges with more than 100 beds. At unstaffed huts, keys must be picked up in advance at DNT offices in nearby towns, while at staffed huts hikers simply show up – no-one is turned away, even if there's only floor space left. Nightly fees average about 150 kr. Contact the DNT head office, Den Norske Turistforening (☎ 22 82 28 00), Postboks 7 Sentrum, 0101 Oslo, for more information on trails and lodging.

Skiing

'Ski' is a Norwegian word and Norwegians make a credible claim to having invented the sport. It's no exaggeration to say it's the national pastime in winter and no matter where you are in the country you're seldom far from a ski run.

Norway has thousands of km of maintained cross-country ski trails and scores of resorts with downhill runs. The Holmenkollen area near Oslo, Geilo on the Oslo-Bergen railway line, and Lillehammer and the surrounding Gudbrandsdalen region are just a few of the more popular spots. If you're a summer skier, head for the glaciers near Finse, Stryn or the Jotunheimen mountains. DNT is a good source for information on skiing throughout Norway.

Fishing

Norway's salmon runs are legendary – Finnmark in June and July is tops. The 175-page book *Angling in Norway*, available from tourist offices for 130 kr, has details on the best salmon and trout-fishing areas, fees and regulations.

For saltwater fishing, no licence is required. In freshwater, a national licence (which is available from post offices for 90 to 180 kr) is mandatory and often a local licence (available from sporting shops) will be required as well.

WORK

Unemployment is high in Norway and work is difficult to get. However, as a member of the European Economic Area (EEA), Norway grants citizens of the other EEA countries (essentially EU and Scandinavian countries) the right to look for work for a three-month period without obtaining permits; those who find work have a right to remain in Norway.

Other foreigners intending to work must apply for work permits through the Norwegian embassy or consulate in their home country before entering Norway. However restrictions on the issuing of work permits are currently in effect, with exceptions granted only in cases where highly skilled workers are in demand in a specialised occupation.

ACCOMMODATION
Camping & Cabins

Norway has nearly 1000 camping grounds. Tent space generally costs from 80 to 120 kr and many camping grounds also rent simple cabins from about 250 kr a day. The cabins often have cooking facilities though linen and blankets are rarely provided, so you'll need your own sleeping bag.

In addition Norway has an 'everyman's right' rule dating back 1000 years. This allows you to pitch a tent anywhere in the wilderness for two nights, as long as you camp at least 150 metres from the nearest house or cottage and leave no trace of your stay. From 15 April to 15 September lighting a fire in the proximity of woodlands is strictly forbidden.

Den Norske Hytteformidling (☎ 22 35 67 10), Postboks 3404 Bjølsen, 0406 Oslo, can send you an English-language photo catalogue describing hundreds of self-catering cabins and cottages in the western fjord area. Prices for a week's rental start from around 1300 kr for a simple place in the off season to about 5500 kr for something more elaborate in midsummer. Most cabins hold at least four people, some as many as 12.

Hostels

There are 100 HI hostels *(vandrerhjem)* in Norway. Some are quite comfortable lodge-style facilities open all year round, while others operate out of school dorms in summer only. Most have two to six beds to a room. The cost for a dorm bed varies from 70 to 175 kr a person, with breakfast generally included at the higher priced hostels. Many hostels also have single, double and family rooms at higher prices. During the summer it's best to call ahead and make reservations, particularly for popular destinations where hostels often fill to capacity.

Prices given throughout the Norway chapter are for hostel members; if you're not a member you'll have to pay 25 kr more for each night's stay.

Hostels that don't provide breakfast in their rate offer a buffet-style breakfast for an additional 40 to 60 kr. Some also offer dinner for about 80 kr and nearly all hostels have kitchens that guests can use to cook their own meals.

You can pick up a brochure in English listing all hostels from tourist offices, or get the detailed 156-page *Vandrerhjem i Norge* free at hostels. Note that the word *lukket* next to a hostel listing simply means 'closed' and not 'lock-out' and refers to the hours (usually from 11 am to 4 pm) when the reception office is closed and the phone is not answered.

The head office of the national hostel organisation is Norske Vandrerhjem (☎ 22 42 14 10), Dronningens gate 26, 0154 Oslo.

Rooms in Private Homes

Next to camping and hostels, the cheapest places to sleep are in private rooms booked through tourist offices, which average about 150/250 kr for singles/doubles. Many towns have pensions and guesthouses in the 250 to 400 kr range.

Hotels

Although normal hotel prices are high, some hotels substantially cut their rates on weekends and in the summer season, which are slow periods for business travel. Nationwide chains that offer good summer and weekend deals include the Rainbow Hotels, Rica Hotels and the missionary-affiliated Havly Hotels, all of which have pleasant good-value rooms.

One important consideration in this land of sky-high food prices is that hotels usually include an all-you-can-eat buffet breakfast, while most pensions do not.

The Norwegian Tourist Board's annually updated accommodation brochure lists many of the country's hotels and explains various hotel discount schemes; overseas tourist bureaus will send you one on request.

FOOD

Food prices can be a shock. To keep within a budget, expect to frequent grocery stores and bakeries. Some grocery stores have reasonably priced delis where you can pick up salads sold by weight or a baked chicken for about 40 kr.

Common throughout Norway is the *konditori*, which is a bakery with a few tables where you can sit and eat pastries and inexpensive sandwiches. Other relatively cheap eats are found at *gatekjøkken* (food wagons and streetside kiosks), which generally have hot dogs for about 20 kr and hamburgers for 40 kr. Only marginally more expensive, but with more nutritionally balanced food, are *kafeterias*, which have simple meals from about 50 kr. Meals at moderately priced restaurants often cost from 90 to 120 kr, though many places feature a daily special *(dagens rett)* for about 75 kr.

Norwegian specialities include grilled or smoked salmon *(laks)*, boiled shrimp *(reker)*, cod *(torsk)* and other seafood. Expect to see sweet brown goat cheese called *geitost*, *flatbrød* and pickled herring alongside the breads and cereals included in the breakfast buffet. *Lutefisk*, dried cod made almost gelatinous by soaking in lye, is popular at Christmas time but it's definitely an acquired taste.

DRINKS

The legal drinking age is 18 years for beer and wine, 20 for spirits.

Beer can be purchased in supermarkets, but wine and spirits can only be purchased at government liquor stores called *vinmonopolet*. These shops are generally open to 5 pm on weekdays and to 1 pm on Saturday. Wine is the most reasonably priced alcoholic beverage, costing from 60 kr a bottle.

Some local communities in rural areas have restrictions on alcohol sales and a few have virtual prohibition.

ENTERTAINMENT

Although Norway is not known for having a riveting entertainment scene, you can find reasonable nightlife in the bigger cities. Entertainment tends to be pricey. A movie ticket or the cover charge for a music club averages 50 kr, while a glass of beer *(øl)* will set you back a good 30 kr.

THINGS TO BUY

Norway has high-quality products at high prices. Specialities include attractive wool sweaters and other hand-knitted clothing, pewterware, silver jewellery, Sami sheath knives, reindeer-leather products, troll figurines, wooden toys and woodwork with rosemaling (painted or carved) decoration.

Getting There & Away

AIR

SAS, British Airways, KLM, Air France, Lufthansa, Sabena, Swissair, Alitalia, Finnair and Icelandair link Oslo with major European and North American cities. Bergen, Stavanger and Trondheim also have direct international flights.

LAND
Denmark

Trains run three times daily (including a 10.40 pm night train) from Oslo to Copenhagen via Helsingborg, Sweden, where the train boards a rail ferry across the Øresund to Helsingør, Denmark. The journey takes 9½ hours and costs 602 kr, or 450 kr for those under 26.

Finland

The E8 highway runs from Tornio, Finland, to Tromsø and there are secondary highways connecting Finland with the northern Sami towns of Karasjok and Kautokeino. All three routes have bus services.

Russia

Russia has a short arctic border with northern Norway and there are both bus and boat services; see the Kirkenes section for more details.

Sweden

Bus Nor-Way Bussekspress runs express buses three to four times daily between Oslo and Gothenburg (five hours, 290 kr) and at 8 am on weekdays from Oslo to Stockholm (nine hours, 310 kr).

Train There are daily trains to Stockholm from Oslo (seven hours, 504 kr), from Trondheim (11 hours, 700 kr) and from Narvik (22 hours, 1010 kr). Trains also run daily from Oslo to Helsingborg (7½ hours, 549 kr) via Gothenburg.

Car & Motorcycle The main highways between Sweden and Norway are the E6 from Gothenburg to Oslo, the E18 from Stockholm to Oslo, the E14 from Sundsvall to Trondheim and the E12 from Umeå to Mo i Rana. Many secondary roads also cross the border.

SEA
Denmark

DFDS Scandinavian Seaways (☎ 22 41 90 90) runs daily overnight ferries from Oslo to Copenhagen, with the cheapest cabin fare costing from 415 kr (Sunday to Wednesday in the off season) to 715 kr (on summer weekends). Car fares range from 225 to 330 kr. The cabins in all categories are quite pleasant and there's an excellent dinner buffet that you can splurge on en route. The departure in either direction is at 5 pm, with arrival at 9 am.

The Color Line (☎ 22 94 44 00) runs three to four ferries daily between Kristiansand and Hirtshals, the shortest connection (four hours) between Norway and Denmark. Fares vary from 140 kr in winter to 360 kr on summer weekends for a passenger, from 180 to 500 kr for a car. There's also a daily 7.30 pm ferry crossing from Oslo to Hirtshals (no Sunday service in the off season), which costs from 150 to 200 kr per person, 280 to 470 kr for a car.

The Stena Line (☎ 22 33 50 00) operates ferries from Oslo to Frederikshavn daily in summer, slightly less frequently the rest of the year. Boats leave Oslo at 8 pm, take 12 hours and cost from 300 to 550 kr for a passenger, 370 to 700 kr for a car.

The Fjord Line (☎ 55 32 37 70) sails from Bergen to Hanstholm on Monday, Wednesday and Friday afternoons, stopping en route in Egersund. The Bergen-Hanstholm fare ranges from 250 kr on winter weekdays to 640 kr on summer weekends. Cars cost from 310 to 515 kr.

The Larvik Line (☎ 22 52 55 00) has a daily ferry from Larvik (via Moss) to Frederikshavn. It takes six hours and costs from 240 to 380 kr for passengers, 300 to 510 kr for a car. The Larvik Line also operates a daily catamaran service between Larvik and Skagen for the same fares; it takes just three hours.

Germany

The Color Line (☎ 22 94 44 00) has a daily ferry between Oslo and Kiel. It takes 19 hours. Departures in both directions are in the afternoon, but the exact times vary with the day of the week. The cheapest cabin costs 540 kr, cars cost from 250 to 500 kr.

Iceland & the Faroe Islands

The Smyril Line (☎ 55 32 09 70) runs weekly in summer between Bergen and Seyðisfjörður (Iceland), via the Faroe Islands. One-way fares from Bergen begin at 450/650 kr to Tórshavn in the Faroe Islands and 1160/1660 kr to Iceland. These fares are for a couchette, with the lower fares for the first three sailings in June and the last four sailings in August, and the higher fares for midsummer travel. The boat leaves Bergen at 3 pm on Tuesday.

Sweden

DFDS Scandinavian Seaways (☎ 22 41 90 90) runs daily overnight ferries between Oslo and Helsingborg, with fares varying according to the season and day of the week, but usually beginning at about 500 kr. The boats leave Oslo at 5 pm southbound and Helsingborg at 7 pm northbound.

The Scandi Line (☎ 33 46 08 00) runs ferries a few times daily between Sandefjord (Norway) and Strømstad (Sweden). It takes 2½ hours and in summer costs 125 kr for a passenger, 165 kr for a car. In addition, there's a summertime passenger ferry from Strømstad to Fredrikstad.

UK

The Color Line (☎ 55 54 86 60) sails from Bergen to Newcastle, via Stavanger, twice weekly in winter and thrice weekly in summer. Summer sailings are on Tuesday, Friday and Sunday from Bergen and on Monday, Wednesday and Saturday from Newcastle. The trip takes 21 hours. The cheapest fare, which is for a reclining chair, ranges from 160 kr in midwinter to 980 kr on summer weekends. The fare to transport a small car is 500 kr, a motorcycle 200 kr.

P&O Scottish Ferries (☎ 55 31 15 80) sails from Bergen to Aberdeen (Scotland) via Lerwick (Shetland Islands) once weekly from the first week in June to late August. The boat leaves Bergen at 2 am on Sunday, arriving in Lerwick at 2 pm and in Aberdeen at 8 am the next day. Going to Bergen, the boat leaves Aberdeen at 6 pm on Friday. The cheapest passenger fare is for a reclining chair: 605 kr to Lerwick, 990 kr to Aberdeen. A motorcycle/car costs 220/550 kr to Lerwick, 440/880 kr to Aberdeen.

LEAVING NORWAY

There are no departure taxes leaving Norway.

Getting Around

Public transport in Norway is quite efficient, with trains, buses and ferries often timed to coordinate with one another. The handy *NSB Togruter*, available free at train stations, has rail schedules and information on linking buses. Boat and bus departures vary with the season and the day (services on Saturday are particularly sketchy), so pick up the latest timetables *(ruteplan)* from regional tourist offices.

AIR

Norway has nearly 50 airports with scheduled commercial flights, from Kirkenes in the north to Kristiansand in the south. Because of the great distances, air travel in Norway may be worth considering even by budget travellers.

Norway's main domestic airlines are SAS, Braathens SAFE and Widerøe. Typical one-way fares from Oslo are 1075 kr to Trondheim and 2070 kr to Tromsø, but a variety of discounts can make air travel competitive. Standard 'minipris' return tickets only cost about 15% more than full-fare one-way tickets and there are sometimes promotional fares that make return tickets even cheaper than one-way tickets. There are 50% discounts on return fares for accompanying family members, including spouses, and for senior citizens over 67 years of age. Travellers aged under 25 years can fly stand-by at substantial discounts; with Braathens SAFE and SAS, youth stand-by fares are 400 kr for short flights, 800 kr for long flights.

In addition, there are some good-value passes. Widerøe has a 410 kr summer ticket (valid from 1 June to 31 August) for flights within any one of four sectors, which are divided at Trondheim, Bodø and Tromsø. For example, flights from Oslo to Stavanger or Trondheim cost 410 kr, and multisector flights from Oslo cost 820 kr to Bodø, 1230 kr to the Lofoten islands and 1640 kr to Nordkapp.

Braathens SAFE's Visit Norway Pass divides Norway into northern and southern sectors at Trondheim. Flights between any two points in one sector cost the equivalent of US$85. Tickets can now be purchased directly from Braathens SAFE after you arrive in Norway but it's still best to make advance reservations as seats are limited.

In addition to these domestic discount fares, SAS offers its international passengers advance-purchase tickets for US$80 to US$110, which allow travel on direct flights between any two Scandinavian cities it serves, including a number of Norwegian cities (see the introductory Getting Around chapter).

To all fares you'll need to add on a newly imposed 65 kr commuter tax if you're flying between any two cities (except Bodø) that are also served by trains.

BUS

Norway has an extensive bus network and long-distance buses are quite comfortable. Tickets are sold on the buses, with fares based on distance, averaging 112 kr per 100 km. Many bus companies have student, senior and family discounts of 25% to 50% – always ask.

Nor-Way Bussekspress (☎ 23 00 24 40) operates the largest network of express buses in Norway, with routes connecting every main city and extending north all the way to Nordkapp and Kirkenes.

TRAIN

Norway has a good, though somewhat limited, national rail system. All railway lines are operated by the Norwegian State Railways (Norges Statsbaner or NSB). From Oslo, the main lines go to Stavanger, Bergen, Åndalsnes, Bodø and Sweden.

Second-class travel, particularly on long-distance trains, is generally comfortable, with reclining seats, footrests and the like – 1st-class travel, which costs 50% more, simply isn't worth the extra money.

NORWAY

The Norway Rail Pass, which allows unlimited travel within the country, can be purchased after you arrive in Norway. High-season prices for 2nd-class travel are 1260/1700 kr for 7/14 consecutive days of travel or 900 kr for three days of travel within a one-month period. Prices are 20% lower from October to April. Details on ScanRail, Eurail and other international passes valid in Norway are in the introductory Getting Around chapter.

If you're not travelling with a rail pass, there's a 'minipris' ticket available for travel on long-distance trains. You must buy the ticket at least one day in advance. The minipris covers many, but not all, departures; those that are eligible are marked by green dots in the *NSB Togruter* schedule.

Regular/minipris fares from Oslo are 510/390 kr to Bergen, 500/320 kr to Åndalsnes and 580/390 kr to Trondheim. For the maximum minipris fare of 490 kr, you can even go all the way from Stavanger to Bodø, the greatest rail distance in the country.

There's a 50% discount on train travel for people aged 67 and older and for children under 16.

To be assured of a seat you can always make reservations for an additional 20 kr, and on many long-distance trains, including all those between Oslo and Bergen, reservations are mandatory.

Second-class sleepers offer a good way to get a cheap sleep: a bed in a three-berth cabin costs 100 kr; two-berth cabins cost 200 kr a person in old carriages and 250 kr in new carriages.

Booking and schedule information is available by dialling ☎ 81 50 08 88. Train stations almost invariably have luggage lockers for 10 to 20 kr and many also have a baggage storage room.

CAR & MOTORCYCLE

If you plan to drive through mountainous areas in winter or spring, check first to make sure the passes are open, as many are closed until May or June. However main highways, such as route 11 from Oslo to Bergen and the entire E6 from Oslo to Kirkenes are kept open all year round. Drivers who expect to drive in snow-covered areas should have studded tyres or carry chains. The Road User Information Centre (☎ 22 65 40 40) can tell you about the latest road conditions throughout the country.

If you plan to travel along Norway's west coast, keep in mind that it is not only mountainous but deeply cut by fjords. While it's a spectacular route, travelling along the coast requires numerous ferry crossings, which can be time consuming and rather costly. For a complete list of ferry schedules, fares and reservation phone numbers, consider investing in the latest copy of *Rutebok for Norge*, a phone-book-size transport guide (210 kr) available in bookshops and at larger Narvesen kiosks.

Fuel costs average 8.4 kr for a litre of unleaded petrol, 9 kr for super petrol and 7.3 kr for diesel.

The national automobile club, Norges Automobilforbund (NAF), has its main office (☎ 22 34 14 00) at Storgata 2, 0155 Oslo.

Road Rules

In Norway, you drive on the right side of the road. All vehicles, including motorcycles, must have dipped headlights on at all times. The use of seat belts is obligatory, and children under the age of four must have their own seat or safety restraint. On motorways and other main roads the maximum speed is generally 90 km/h, while speed limits on through roads in built-up areas are generally 50 km/h unless otherwise posted.

Drink driving laws are strict in Norway: the maximum permissible blood alcohol concentration is 0.05% and violators are subject to severe fines. Driving with a blood alcohol level of 0.08% or greater warrants a 21-day prison sentence.

You are required to carry a red warning triangle in your car to use in the event of a breakdown. Third party auto insurance is compulsory and carrying a Green Card is recommended.

NORWAY

Motorcycles are not allowed to be parked on the pavement and must follow the same parking regulations as cars.

The speed limit for caravans (cars pulling trailers) is usually 10 km/h less than for cars. There are a few mountain roads where caravans are forbidden and numerous other roads that are only advisable for experienced drivers, as backing up may be necessary to allow approaching traffic to pass. For a map outlining these roads, and caravan rules, write to Vegdirektoratet, Postboks 8142 Dep, 0033 Oslo.

Car Rental

Major car-rental companies, such as Hertz, Avis and Europcar, have offices at airports and in city centres. Car rentals are expensive. The walk-in rate for a compact car with unlimited km is about 800 kr a day (including VAT and insurance), although car-rental companies sometimes advertise a 'hotel' rate for about 600 kr, which is geared for tourists. Generally you'll get much better deals by booking with an international agency before you arrive in Norway.

One relatively good deal readily available in Norway is the weekend rate offered by major car-rental companies, which allows you to pick up a car after noon on Friday and keep it until 10 am on Monday, for about 1000 kr. Be sure the rate includes unlimited km as not all the plans do.

BICYCLE

Given its great distances, hilly terrain and narrow roads, Norway is not ideally suited for extensive touring by bicycle. There are a number of places good for cycling on a regional basis, however, and bikes can be rented at some tourist offices, hostels and camping grounds.

For information on long-distance cycling routes, contact Syklistenes Landsforening (☎ 22 41 50 80), Storgata 23C, 0184 Oslo.

HITCHING

Hitching is not terribly common in Norway and traffic to many places is very light. Still, with a bit of luck and a lot of patience, some people do manage to get rides; expect long waits and uneven results. One good approach is to ask for rides from truck drivers at ferry terminals and petrol stations.

BOAT

An extensive network of ferries and express boats links Norway's offshore islands, coastal towns and fjord districts. See specific destinations for details.

Coastal Steamer

For more than a century Norway's legendary coastal steamer, *Hurtigruten*, has been the lifeline linking the tiny fishing villages scattered along the north coast. One ship heads north from Bergen every night of the year, pulling into 33 ports on its six-day journey to Kirkenes, where it then turns around and heads back south. If the weather's agreeable, the fjord and mountain scenery along the way is nothing short of spectacular.

The ships are accommodating to deck-class travellers, offering free sleeping lounges, baggage rooms, a shower room, a 24-hour cafeteria and a cheap coin laundry. Deck passengers can also rent cabins on a space-available basis from about 160/390 kr in winter/summer. Sample deck fares from Bergen are 1125 kr to Trondheim, 1916 kr to Stamsund, 2306 kr to Tromsø, 2907 kr to Honningsvåg and 3578 kr to Kirkenes. One en route stopover is allowed on these fares. Accompanying spouses and children, and all senior citizens over the age of 67, receive a 50% discount off the above fares.

There are some great off-season deals. From 1 September to 30 April, all passengers are entitled to a 40% discount off the basic fare for voyages beginning any day other than Tuesday. If you're aged between 16 and 26 and are travelling between 1 September and 30 April you can get a coastal pass for 1750 kr that allows unlimited travel for 21 days; this gives you plenty of time to make the return trip from Bergen to Kirkenes and still do quite a bit of exploring along the way.

The coastal steamer can also be booked as an all-inclusive cruise (see the Organised Tours section that follows).

NORWAY

LOCAL TRANSPORT

Cities and towns in Norway are served by public bus. As a general rule, the local bus terminal is adjacent to the train station or ferry depot. For more details, see the relevant destination sections.

Taxi

Taxis are readily available at train stations; prices average 24 kr at flagfall and 12 kr per km.

ORGANISED TOURS

Norway's most popular tour is the *Hurti-gruten* coastal steamer cruise from Bergen to Kirkenes. The one-way, six-day journey, including meals and cabin, starts at about US$750 in winter and US$1200 in summer. These rates are for the newer ships, which have cruise ship comforts; the older, traditional ships – which are gradually being replaced – have somewhat cheaper cabin options. Shore excursions, including one to a glacier and another to Nordkapp, are available at reasonable rates.

Reservations are made through the Bergen Line (☎ 212-319 1300) in the USA & Canada, Norwegian Coastal Voyages (☎ 0171-371 4011) in the UK, and Bentours (☎ 02-9241 1353) in Australia.

Oslo

Founded by Harald Hardrada in 1050, Oslo is the oldest of the Scandinavian capitals. After being levelled by fire in 1624, the city was rebuilt in brick and stone by King Christian IV who renamed it Christiania, a name that stuck until 1925 when Oslo took back its original name.

Despite being Norway's largest city, Oslo has barely 500,000 residents and for a European capital it is remarkably low-key, casual and manageable. The city centre is a pleasant jumble of old and new architecture.

Oslo sits at the head of the Oslofjord, an inlet of the Skagerrak. Its northern border is the Nordmarka, a forested green belt crossed by hiking and skiing trails. The city has good museums, plenty of parks and an abundance of statues. The Nobel Peace Prize is awarded in Oslo each year in December.

Orientation

Oslo's central train station (Oslo Sentral-stasjon or Oslo S) is at the east side of the city centre. From there Karl Johans gate, the main street, leads through the heart of the city to the Royal Palace.

Oslo is easy to get around. Most central city sights, including the harbourfront and Akershus Fortress, are within a 15-minute walk of Karl Johans gate, as are the majority of Oslo's hotels and pensions. Many of the sights outside Oslo centre, including Vige-land Park and the Munch Museum, are a short bus ride away, and even Bygdøy peninsula is a mere 10-minute ferry ride across the harbour. The trails and lakes of the Nordmarka wilderness are also easily reached by public transport.

Information

Tourist Offices The main tourist office (☎ 22 83 00 50), Vestbaneplassen 1, 0250 Oslo, is west of Rådhus, near the harbour. It's open daily from 9 am to 8 pm in July and August; daily from 9 am to 6 pm in June; and from Monday to Saturday from 9 am to 6 pm in May and September and 9 am to 4 pm the rest of the year. Be sure to pick up the useful *Oslo Guide* there or at the Oslo S tourist-information window, which is open from 8 am to 11 pm daily. Only the main tourist office has brochures for destinations throughout Norway.

Use It (☎ 22 41 51 32), the youth information office at Møllergata 3, is open from 7.30 am to 6 pm Monday to Friday and 9 am to 2 pm on Saturday between mid-June and early August, and from 11 am to 5 pm weekdays the rest of the year. The staff can give you the lowdown on what's happening around Oslo and provide advice on everything from cheap accommodation to hitching.

Oslo Card If you plan on doing a lot of sightseeing, consider buying an Oslo Card which provides free entry to most museums and attractions and free travel on all Oslo public transport. It costs 130/200/240 kr for one/two/three days (50/80/110 kr for children aged from four to 15 years) and is sold at the tourist office, post offices and some hotels. Students and senior citizens, who get half-price entry at many sights, may do better buying a public transport pass and paying separate museum admissions.

Money Fornebu airport has a bank open from 8 am to 8 pm, with slightly shorter weekend hours. The post office at Oslo S changes money from 7 am to 6 pm weekdays and from 9 am to 3 pm on Saturday. Oslo S has a 24-hour automatic exchange machine, near the rail information desk, which changes foreign currency notes into Norwegian kroner. Full-service banks can be found opposite Oslo S along Karl Johans gate.

You'll generally get the best deal at American Express, which changes all types of travellers' cheques without transaction fees. Its main office, north of Rådhus at Fridtjof Nansens plass 6, is open in summer from 8.30 am to 9 pm weekdays, 10 am to 7 pm on Saturday and 1 to 7 pm on Sunday; the rest of the year it closes at 6 pm weekdays, 3 pm on Saturday. There's another American Express at Karl Johans gate 33.

Outside banking hours the tourist office exchanges money at a disadvantageous rate.

Post & Communications The main post office, at Dronningens gate 15, is open from 8 am to 6 pm weekdays, to 3 pm on Saturday. To receive mail, have it sent to poste restante, Oslo Sentrum Postkontor, Dronningens gate 15, 0101 Oslo. There are convenient branch post offices at Oslo S and on Karl Johans gate opposite Stortinget.

You can send telegrams or faxes and make long-distance calls from 9 am to 5 pm weekdays at the telephone office at Kongens gate 21.

You can check your e-mail at Børsen, an Internet café at Nedre Vollgate 19.

Travel Agencies Kilroy Travels (☎ 22 42 01

20), Nedre Slottsgate 23, specialises in student and youth travel. For other travel needs, you'll find a handful of travel agencies near Rådhus, including the American Express office.

Bookshops Tanum Libris at Karl Johans gate 43 and Norli, around the corner on Universitetsgata, are large bookshops with comprehensive selections of English-language books, maps and travel guides.

Laundry Majorstua Myntvaskeri at Vibes gate 15, about a km north of the Royal Palace, is open to 8 pm weekdays, 5 pm on Saturday.

Medical & Emergency Services Dial ☎ 112 for police and ☎ 113 for an ambulance. Jernbanetorgets Apotek, opposite Oslo S, is a 24-hour pharmacy. Oslo Kommunale Legevakt (☎ 22 11 70 70), Storgata 40, is a medical clinic with 24-hour emergency services.

Things to See
Oslo's highlights include the Bygdøy peninsula with its folk museum and Viking ships, Vigeland Park with the sculptures of Gustav Vigeland, and Akershus Fortress with its castle and harbour views.

Walking Tour Many of Oslo's city sights can be combined in a half-day walking tour. Starting at Oslo S, head north-west down Karl Johans gate, Oslo's main pedestrian street, which is lined with shops and pavement cafés and is a popular haunt for street musicians.

After walking a couple of blocks you'll reach **Oslo Domkirke**, the city cathedral, which was built in 1697 and has an elaborately painted ceiling. It's open from 10 am to 4 pm and admission is free.

Midway along Karl Johans gate is **Stortinget**, the yellow-brick parliament building, which has free tours during the summer recess. Also architecturally notable is the stately **Grand Hotel** across the street, built in the 1870s, a decade after Stortinget.

NORWAY

NORWAY

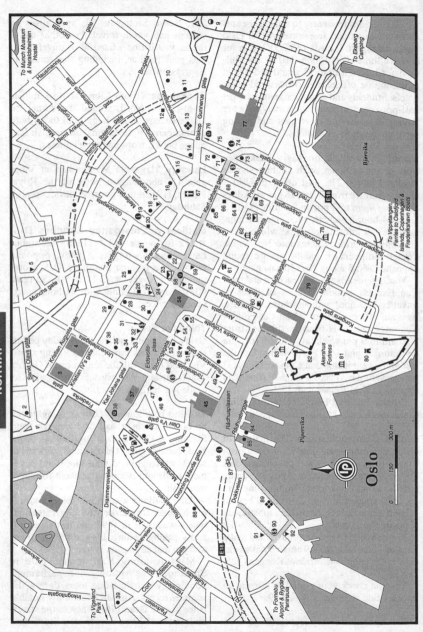

Oslo

0   150   300 m

To Munch Museum
& Haraldsheimen
Hostel

To Blæberg
Camping

Bjørvika

To Vippetangen
Ferries to Oslofjord
Islands, Copenhagen &
Frederikshavn Boats

Akersgata

Munchs gate

Sankt Olavs gate

To Vigeland
Park

Akershus
Fortress

Pipervika

To Fornebu
Airport & Bygdøy
Peninsula

Drammensveien

Parkveien

Inkognitogata

PLACES TO STAY		3	Historic Museum	56	Stortinget (Parliament)
12	Hotel Terminus	4	National Gallery	58	Stortinget T-bane
20	KFUM Sleep In	6	Library		Station
25	Norrøna Hotell	7	Rockefeller Music Hall	61	Telephone Office
26	Rica Travel Hotel	8	Oslo Kommunale	62	Post Museum
29	Hotel Bristol		Legevakt (Medical	63	Main Post Office
30	Grand Hotel		Clinic)	65	Enka (Nightspot)
51	Rica Victoria Hotel	9	Bus Station	67	Oslo Domkirke
53	Cecil Hotel	10	Oslo Spektrum		(Cathedral)
64	Fønix Hotel	11	Budget Car Rental	68	Norsk Vandrerhjem
66	Hotell Astoria	13	Oslo City Shopping		(Hostel
69	City Hotel		Centre		Organisation)
		14	Oslo Sweater Shop	70	Bank
PLACES TO EAT		15	NAF (Norges	72	Pharmacy
5	Thai Orchid		Automobilforbund)	73	Stena Line
17	Rema 1000 Grocery	16	DNT Office	74	Trafikanten (Transport
	Store	18	Husfliden		Information)
24	7-Eleven	19	Use It	75	Jerbanetorget
27	Pizza Hut	21	So What (Nightspot)	76	T-Bane Subway
32	Oluf Lorentzen Grocery	22	Kilroy Travels	77	Oslo S (Central Train
	Store	23	Post Office		Station)
33	Egon/Paleet Complex	28	Heimen Husflid	78	Astrup Fearnley Museet
36	Helios Health Food	31	American Express	79	National Museum of
41	Vegeta Vertshus	34	Tanum Libris Bookshop		Contemporary Art
47	Baker Hansen Bakery	35	Norli Bookshop	80	Akershus Castle
49	Bakery	37	National Theatre	81	Norway's Resistance
52	Mr Hong	38	T-Bane Subway		Museum
54	Peppe's Pizza	39	Barbeint (Nightspot)	82	Fortress Entrance
57	Samson's Bakery	40	Petrol Station	83	Christiania Bymodel
59	Tacoland	42	Belleville (Nightspot)	84	Sightseeing Boats
60	Kafé Celsius	43	Saga Cinema	85	Bygdøy Boats
71	Peppe's Pizza	44	Braathens SAFE	86	Main Tourist Office
91	Smør-Petersen Deli	45	Rådhus	87	Den Rustne Eike (Bike
92	La Piazza	46	Vinmonopolet (Liquor		Rental)
			Store)	88	Avis Car Rental
OTHER		48	American Express	89	Aker Brygge
1	Royal Palace	50	Smuget (Nightspot)	90	24-Hour Money
2	Hertz Car Rental	55	Børsen		Exchange Machine

NORWAY

Eidsvollsplass, a city square filled with fountains and statues, stretches between Stortinget and the **National Theatre**. The theatre, which has a lavish rococo hall, was built a century ago to stage Henrik Ibsen's plays.

Across Karl Johans gate is the University of Oslo's law and medical campus and one block to the north is the university's **Historic Museum** and the **National Gallery**. Karl Johans gate ends at the **Royal Palace**, which is surrounded by a large public park.

Heading down from the National Theatre, Olav V's gate leads to the **Rådhus** and the bustling harbourfront. For a hill-top view of it all, walk down Rådhusgata and turn right on Akersgata to **Akershus Fortress**, where

you could easily spend a couple of hours exploring the castle and museums inside.

Rådhus Oslo's twin-towered red-brick city hall, opposite the harbour, has wooden reliefs depicting scenes from Norse mythology lining its outside entrance and splashy wall murals decorating the interior halls and chambers.

You can view the main hall from the front corridor or, for 15 kr (free in winter), walk through it all. In summer it's open from 9 am to 5 pm Monday to Saturday, from noon to 5 pm on Sunday; in winter it closes at 4 pm.

National Gallery The Nasjonalgalleriet, Universitetsgata 13, has the nation's largest collection of Norwegian art. Some of Munch's best known works are on display, including the *Scream*, which created quite a stir when it was brazenly stolen (and later recovered) in 1994. There's also a respectable collection of other European art including works by Gauguin, Monet and Picasso. The museum is open from 10 am to 4 pm on Monday, Wednesday, Friday and Saturday; 10 am to 8 pm on Thursday; and 11 am to 3 pm on Sunday. Hours are slightly longer in summer. Admission is free.

Historic Museum The Historisk Museum of the University of Oslo, Frederiks gate 2, is three museums under a single roof. Most interesting is the ground floor **antiquities collection** with its exceptional displays of Viking-era coins, jewellery and ornaments, and its medieval church art section, which includes the richly painted ceiling of a 13th-century stave church. The 2nd floor has an Arctic exhibit and a **numismatic collection** of coins dating to 995 AD. The top floor holds the **Ethnographical Museum** with changing displays on Asia and Africa. Hours are from 11 am (noon in winter) to 3 pm daily except Monday. Admission is free.

Royal Palace The Royal Palace, on a hill at the end of Karl Johans gate, is the official residence of the king of Norway. The palace building itself is not open to visitors but the rest of the grounds are a public park. If you happen to be around at 1.30 pm you can catch the changing of the guard, but it's not worth rushing across town to see.

Akershus Fortress Strategically located on the eastern side of the harbour, this medieval fortress and castle was built by King Håkon V around 1300. The park-like grounds, which offer excellent views of the city and Oslofjord, are the venue for a host of concerts, dances and theatrical productions during summer.

Entry into the fortress (free) is either through a gate at the end of Akersgata or over a drawbridge spanning Kongens gate, which is reached from the southern end of Kirkegata. The fortress grounds are open to 9 pm; after 6 pm use the Kirkegata entrance. The information centre just inside the main gate has a brief history display and distributes a handy map of the grounds.

In the 17th century, Christian IV renovated **Akershus Castle** into a Renaissance palace, though the front is still decidedly medieval. In its dungeons you'll find dark little cubbyholes where outcast nobles were kept under lock and key, while the upper floors have banquet halls and staterooms.

The chapel is still used for royal events and the crypts of King Håkon VII and Olav V lie beneath it. Tours led by university students in period dress provide a good anecdotal history (at 11 am, 1 and 3 pm) and are included in the 20 kr admission fee, or you can wander through on your own. From May to mid-September the castle is open from 10 am to 4 pm Monday to Saturday, from 12.30 to 4 pm on Sunday. In late April and from mid-September to the end of October it's open on Sunday afternoons only.

During WWII the Nazis used Akershus as a prison and execution grounds, and today it's the site of **Norway's Resistance Museum**, which gives a vivid account of German occupation and the Norwegian struggle against it. It's open daily all year round, from 10 am (Sunday from 11 am) to 5 pm in summer, to 3 pm in winter. Admission is 15 kr.

Of interest mainly to history buffs, the **Christiania Bymodell**, just outside the northern wall of the fortress, features a model of the old city and a multimedia display of its history. It's open from 10 am to 4 pm (closed Monday) from June to mid-September. Admission is 20 kr.

Modern Art Museums The **National Museum of Contemporary Art** at Bankplassen 4, in a classic Art-Nouveau building formerly housing the Central Bank of Norway, features Scandinavian modern art. It's open from 10 am to 5 pm Tuesday to Friday (to 8 pm Thursday), from 11 am to 4 pm on weekends. Admission is free.

A block to the east is the **Astrup Fearnley Museet**, which has quality changing exhibits of Norwegian and foreign modern art. It's open from noon to 4 pm Tuesday to Sunday. Admission is 30 kr.

Munch Museum Dedicated to the life work of Norway's most renowned artist, Edvard Munch (1863-1944), this museum, at Tøyengata 53, contains more than 5000 drawings and paintings that Munch bequeathed to the city of Oslo. Despite the artist's tendency towards tormented visions, all is not grey – *The Sick Child* and *The Maiden & Death* are exhibited here but so are other works with lighter themes, such as *The Sun* and *Spring Ploughing*.

The museum is open from 10 am to 6 pm daily from 1 June to mid-September, with shorter winter hours. Admission is 40 kr. Take the T-bane to Tøyen, from where it's a five-minute signposted walk.

Botanical Garden & Museums Next door to the Munch Museum is the university's **Zoological Museum** with well-presented displays of stuffed creatures, and the **Mineralogical-Palaeontological Museum** with rocks, gemstones and a few dinosaur bones. The museums, inside a fragrant botanical garden, are open from 11 am to 4 pm Tuesday to Sunday and entry is free.

Vigeland Park Frognerparken, or Vigeland Park, is a wonderful city park with expansive green spaces, duck ponds and rows of shady trees – a fine place for leisurely strolls and picnics on the lawn. Its central walkway is lined with life-sized statues by Gustav Vigeland. In nearly 200 works in granite and bronze, Vigeland presents the human form in a range of emotions from screaming pot-bellied babies and entwined lovers to tranquil elderly couples.

The most impressive piece is the monolith of writhing bodies, said to be the world's largest granite sculpture. The circle of steps beneath the monolith is lined with voluptuous stone figures and provides a popular spot for sitting and contemplating it all. The park is free and always open, making this a good place to come in the evening when

other sights have closed. To get there take tram No 12 or 15.

Vigeland Museum For a more in-depth look at the development of Gustav Vigeland's work, visit Vigeland Museum at Nobels gate 32, across from Vigeland Park. The museum was built by the city as a home and workshop for Vigeland in exchange for the bulk of his life's work and contains his early statuary, huge plaster moulds, woodblock prints and sketches.

It's open from 10 am to 6 pm (noon to 7 pm Sunday) in summer, from noon to 4 pm in winter. It's closed on Monday. Admission is 20 kr.

Holmenkollen The Holmenkollen **ski jump**, perched on a hillside above Oslo, draws the world's top jumpers in a ski festival each March and doubles as a concert site in summer. From the top of the ski jump there's a bird's-eye view of the steep ramp, as well as a panoramic view of Oslo city and fjord – a lift goes part of the way up and then you climb 114 steps on your own. The 50 kr admission fee includes a ski museum with a collection of skis and sleds dating back as far as 600 AD.

From Oslo, take T-bane line 1 for the 25-minute ride to Holmenkollen station, from where it's a 15-minute walk up to the jump. It's open daily from 9 am to at least 8 pm in summer, from 10 am to 5 pm in May and September, and until about 4 pm in winter. If you intend to also visit Tryvann-stårnet, get the combination ticket, which is only 10 kr more.

Tryvannstårnet North of the ski jump, this observation tower offers superb views of the Nordmarka wilderness, as well as snow-capped Mt Gausta to the west, the Oslofjord to the south and the forests of Sweden to the east. For 30 kr, a lift zips you up to the top. The opening hours parallel those at Holmenkollen.

To get to Tryvannstårnet from Holmenkollen, get back on the T-bane for a scenic ride to Frognerseteren, where the tram line

NORWAY

ends in the woods. A signposted trail above the stop leads to the tower, and takes about 20 minutes.

Bygdøy Bygdøy peninsula holds some of Oslo's top attractions: an open-air folk museum; excavated Viking ships; Thor Heyerdahl's raft, the *Kon-Tiki*; and the *Fram* polar exploration ship. You can rush around all the sights in half a day, but allotting a few extra hours will be more enjoyable.

Although only minutes from central Oslo, Bygdøy (roughly pronounced 'big day') has a rural character and a couple of good **beaches**. The royal family maintains a summer home on the peninsula, as do many of Oslo's other well-to-do residents.

Ferries operate from mid-April to late September, making the 10-minute run to Bygdøy (18 kr) every 40 minutes, starting at 7.45 am (9.05 am on weekends). The last crossing returns from Bygdøy at 6 pm in April and September, 9.20 pm in summer. The ferries leave from Rådhusbrygge 3 (opposite Rådhus) and stop first at Dronningen, from where it's a 10-minute walk up to the folk museum. The ferry continues to Bygdøynes, where the *Kon-Tiki*, *Fram* and maritime museums are clustered. You can also take bus No 30 to the folk museum from Jernbanetorget, a bus-stop area fronting Oslo S. From the folk museum it's a five-minute walk to the Viking ships and 15 minutes more to Bygdøynes. The route is signposted and makes a pleasant walk.

There's a fruit stand opposite the entrance to the folk museum and simple restaurants at the folk and maritime museums.

Norwegian Folk Museum More than 140 buildings, mostly from the 17th and 18th centuries, have been gathered from around the country and are clustered according to region in Norway's largest open-air museum. Dirt paths wind past old barns, storehouses on stilts (*stabbur*) and rough-timbered farmhouses with sod roofs that sprout wildflowers.

One highlight is the restored **stave church**, built around 1200 in Gol and brought to Bygdøy in 1885. There are also two worthwhile **museums** just inside the main entrance, one with interesting displays of Sami culture and the other with folk costumes and historical exhibits.

The folk museum is open daily from 9 am to 6 pm June to August, 10 am to 5 pm in May and September and 11 am to 3 pm the rest of the year. Sunday is a good day to visit, as there's usually folk music and dancing. Admission, which includes entry to all sights, is 50 kr (children 10 kr).

Viking Ship Museum This captivating museum houses three Viking ships that were excavated from the Oslofjord region. The ships had been drawn ashore and used as tombs for nobility, who were buried with all they expected to need in the hereafter: jewels, furniture, food and servants. Built of oak in the 9th century, these Viking ships were buried in blue clay, which preserved them amazingly well.

The impressive **Oseberg ship**, which has elaborate dragon and serpent carvings, is 22 metres long and took 30 people to row. It was excavated with a burial chamber containing the largest collection of Viking Age artefacts ever found in Scandinavia. A second ship, the 24-metre-long **Gokstad**, is the world's finest example of a longship.

The museum is open daily, from 9 am to 6 pm May to August, from 11 am to at least 3 pm the rest of the year. Admission is 30 kr.

Kon-Tiki Museum This museum displays the *Kon-Tiki* balsa raft, which Norwegian explorer Thor Heyerdahl sailed from Peru to Polynesia in 1947 to prove that Polynesia's first settlers could have come from South America.

Also on display is the papyrus reed boat *Ra II* in which Heyerdahl crossed the Atlantic in 1970. The museum is open daily from 9.30 am to 5.45 pm from June to August, from 10.30 am to 4 or 5 pm the rest of the year. Admission is 25 kr.

Polarship Fram This museum, opposite the Kon-Tiki Museum, holds Fridtjof Nansen's

39-metre rigged schooner *Fram*, which was launched in 1892 and used for polar expeditions, including the 1911 discovery of the South Pole by Roald Amundsen. You can clamber around inside the boat, go down to the hold where the sled dogs were kept and view fascinating photo displays of the *Fram* trapped in the polar ice. Opening hours are from 9 am to 5.45 pm daily from mid-May to 31 August, with shorter off-season hours. Admission is 20 kr.

Norwegian Maritime Museum This museum has small fishing boats, displays of dried cod and an abundance of model ships. The balcony on the top floor of the larger wing has a good view of the Oslofjord islands. It's open daily from 10 am to 7 pm from mid-May to 30 September, with shorter off-season hours. Admission costs 30 kr.

Islands & Beaches Ferries to half a dozen islands in the Oslofjord leave from Vippetangen, south-east of Akershus Fortress. **Hovedøya**, the closest island, has a rocky coastline but its south-west side is a popular sunbathing area. There are walking paths around the perimeter, some old cannons and the ruins of a 12th-century monastery.

Further south, the undeveloped island of **Langøyene** offers far better swimming. It has both sandy and rocky beaches, including one on the south-east side designated for nude bathing. Boats to Hovedøya leave about twice an hour between 6.45 am and midnight from late May to mid-August, with much shorter hours the rest of the year.

Boats to the other islands are somewhat less frequent. There's a once-hourly boat to Langøyene but it runs only in summer, with the first service leaving at 10 am and the last returning at 7.20 pm.

The Bygdøy peninsula also has two popular beaches, **Huk** and **Paradisbukta**, which can be reached by taking bus No 30 from Jernbanetorget to its last stop. Huk, which is right at the bus stop, is separated into two beaches by a small cove, with the beach on the north-west side a nude bathing area.

While there are some sandy patches, most of Huk is comprised of grassy lawns and large smooth rocks, which are ideal for sunbathing. If the crowds are too large, a 10-minute walk through the woods north from the bus stop leads to the more secluded Paradisbukta.

For freshwater swimming, try the east side of **Sognsvann** lake at the end of T-bane line 3, about six km north of central Oslo.

Other Sights Oslo's oldest building is **Gamle Aker Kirke**, a medieval stone church built in 1080 and still used for services. It's open from noon to 2 pm Monday to Saturday; admission is free. Take bus No 37 from Jernbanetorget, get off at Akersbakken and walk up past the cemetery.

The **Post Museum** is worth a visit if you're at the main post office – the entrance is at the opposite end of the block. Exhibits include a reindeer sledge once used for mail delivery and Norway's largest stamp collection. It's open from 10 am to 3 pm weekdays; admission is free.

The area's newest attraction is **Vikinglandet**, a Viking-era theme park with reconstructed houses, costumed interpreters and craft demonstrations; admission is 90 kr. It's about 10 km south of Oslo, adjacent to its sister operation, the TusenFyrd amusement park. There are free buses from Oslo S in summer.

Oslo also has a number of more esoteric museums, including ones dedicated to architecture, ice skating, transport, children's art, customs and tolls, the armed forces, theatre, and playwright Henrik Ibsen. For more details see the *Oslo Guide*.

Activities

Hiking A network of trails leads off into the Nordmarka from Frognerseteren, at the end of T-bane line 1. One good hardy walk is from Frognerseteren over to Lake Sognsvann, where you can take T-bane line 3 back to the city. If you're interested in wilderness hiking, contact the DNT office (☎ 22 82 28 00) at Storgata 3.

Cycling Den Rustne Eike (☎ 22 83 72 31), near the harbour by the tourist office, rents seven-speed bicycles for 95 kr for 24 hours, mountain bikes for 170 kr. It has information on bike paths and organises cycling tours. Hours are from 10 am to 6.30 pm daily May to October, to 3.30 pm weekdays in winter.

One popular outing is to take the weekend bike train (*sykkeltoget*) to Stryken, 40 km north of Oslo, and cycle back through the Nordmarka. The train leaves Oslo S at 9.15 am on Saturday and Sunday from May to October. For a shorter ride, there's also a bike train that runs from Majorstuen to Frognerseteren on summer weekends at 11 am, noon and 1 pm.

Skiing Oslo's ski season is roughly from December to March. There are over 1000 km of ski trails in the Nordmarka area north of Oslo, many of them floodlit. Easy-access tracks begin right at the end of T-bane lines 1 and 3. Tomm Murstad Skiservice (☎ 22 14 41 24) at the Voksenkollen station, one T-bane stop before Frognerseteren, has skis for hire. The Ski Society (Skiforeningen; ☎ 22 92 32 00), Kongeveien 5, 0390 Oslo, can provide more information on skiing.

Organised Tours

Oslo is so easy to get around that there's little need for organised tours. However, if time is tight, Båtservice Sightseeing (☎ 22 20 07 15) does a tidy full-day tour of the Bygdøy sites, Vigeland Park and Holmenkollen ski jump plus a cruise of the Oslofjord for a reasonable 320 kr, or a three-hour version minus the cruise for 190 kr. Båtservice's frequent hour-long 'mini-cruise' of the Oslofjord makes a nice orientation to the city; it costs 70 kr, or is free with the Oslo Card.

Places to Stay

Staff at the tourist office window at Oslo S books rooms in private homes (two nights' minimum stay) for 170/300 kr singles/doubles. They also book unfilled hotel rooms at slightly discounted rates, which are worth pursuing during the week but are roughly the equivalent of rates that you can book directly from hotels on weekends. There's a 20 kr fee for all bookings.

Use It (☎ 22 41 51 32), at Møllergata 3, books rooms in private homes for 100 kr a person if you have your own sleeping bag, 125 kr with bedding included. There's no minimum stay and no booking fee.

Camping Oslo has two large camping grounds with full facilities. Both charge 110 kr for two people with a tent. *Ekeberg Camping* (☎ 22 19 85 68), at Ekebergveien 65 on a knoll south-east and overlooking the city, is open from 1 June to 31 August. Take bus No 24 from Jernbanetorget to the Ekeberg stop, a 10-minute ride. The lakeside *Bogstad Camping* (☎ 22 50 76 80), at Ankerveien 117 up in Holmenkollen, is open all year round. Take bus No 32 from Jernbanetorget to the Bogstad Camping stop, a 30-minute ride.

A good summer alternative is the more primitive *camping ground* (☎ 22 36 37 98) on the Oslofjord island of Langøyene, which charges two people 50/250 kr a day/week to pitch a tent. There are showers and a kiosk selling simple food items.

Possibilities for camping rough include taking T-bane line 1 to Frognerseteren at the edge of the Nordmarka or taking line 3 to Sognsvann. Camping is not permitted at Lake Sognsvann itself, so you'll need to walk a km or two beyond it.

Hostels Oslo has two HI-affiliated hostels. The year-round *Haraldsheim Hostel* (☎ 22 15 50 43), Haraldsheimveien 4, has 270 beds, mostly in four-bed rooms. Rates, breakfast included, are 145 or 165 kr in a dorm, 260 or 330 kr for a single room and 370 or 450 kr for a double room. The higher rates are for rooms with private baths. There are kitchen and laundry facilities. It's a busy place so make advance reservations. The hostel is four km from the city centre; take tram No 10 or 11 to Sinsenkrysset, from where it's a five-minute walk.

Holtekilen Hostel (☎ 67 53 38 53) at Michelets vei 55, Stabekk, nine km south of Oslo, near Fornebu airport, is a summer hostel open from late May to mid-August. A bed in a room with three to four people costs 145 kr, while singles/doubles cost 240/390 kr, breakfast included. To get there catch a local train to Stabekk station and then take the footbridge over the E18.

KFUM Sleep In (☎ 22 20 83 79), a YMCA summer hostel at Møllergata 1 (enter from Grubbegata), has beds at 100 kr and a great central location only 10 minutes walk from Oslo S. There's no bedding so you'll need a sleeping bag; kitchen facilities are available. It's open from early July to mid-August and often fills early. Reception hours are from 8 to 11 am and 5 pm to midnight.

If Sleep In is full, there's *Oslo Vineyard* (☎ 22 15 20 99), Lillogata 5, a church-run hostel with a similar setup, season and reception hours. The cost is 85 kr, breakfast included. It's three km north of the centre via tram 12 or 17 to Grefsenveien.

Pensions *Ellingsen's Pensjonat* (☎ 22 60 03 59) at Holtegata 25, in a neighbourhood of older homes five blocks north of the Royal Palace, is the best-value pension. It has 20 small but adequate rooms, each with a desk, chair and sink; toilets and showers are accessed from the hall. Singles/doubles cost 230/360 kr. During the summer it's wise to call ahead for reservations. To get there take bus No 1 (towards Majorstuen) from Jernbanetorget and get off at Uranienborgveien.

Somewhat pricey but closer to the centre is *Cochs Pensjonat* (☎ 22 60 48 36) at Parkveien 25, just north of the Royal Palace. The 65 rooms are a bit spartan, though not uncomfortable, and cost 300/400 kr for singles/doubles with shared bath, 380/510 kr for rooms with a private bath and cooking facilities.

Bella Vista (☎ 22 65 45 88), Årrundveien 11B, is a 16-bed pension six km north of the city centre by bus No 31. Rooms with shared baths cost 230/350 kr and there's a double room with private bath for 400 kr. Guests have kitchen privileges.

Hotels The *Fønix Hotel* (☎ 22 42 59 57), Dronningens gate 19, just a couple of blocks from Oslo S, is rundown and not recommended but it does have the lowest standard hotel rates: 325/500 kr for singles/doubles with shared bath.

City Hotel (☎ 22 41 36 10), Skippergata 19, is an older hotel with a bit of character, including a front parlour with Victorian furniture. The rooms, which are quite straightforward, cost 380/550 kr with shared bath, 495/680 kr with private bath. Those sensitive to traffic noise should be sure to ask for a courtyard room.

Rica Travel Hotel (☎ 22 00 33 00), Arbeidergaten 4, is a good-value business hotel. Rooms are compact, yet pleasant and modern, and have private baths, TVs, phones and minibars. Standard rates are 650/750 kr on weekdays, 550/650 kr on weekends.

Norrøna Hotell (☎ 22 42 64 00), Grensen 19, is a mission-run hotel with comfortable rooms on a par with those in many of Oslo's better hotels. All rooms have private baths, TVs and phones. Rates are 465/625 kr on weekends from autumn to spring, 600/700 kr daily from late June to early August, 725/850 kr at other times.

The following three hotels are members of the Rainbow chain, which offers good weekend and summer rates. The *Cecil Hotel* (☎ 22 42 70 00), Stortingsgata 8, has a great location a stone's throw from parliament. Rooms are modern and quiet with private baths, TVs, minibars and the like and there's an excellent breakfast buffet. Rates are 460/680 kr on weekends and throughout July, 775/995 kr at other times. There's also a cheaper 'combi' double, but it's claustrophobically small and the second bed is an uncomfortable fold-out couch.

The *Hotell Astoria* (☎ 22 42 00 10), Dronningens gate 21, just west of Oslo S, is not as spiffy as the Cecil, but the amenities are similar and the rates cheaper at 395/520 kr on weekends (and during July), 585/685 kr on weekdays. Rainbow's best summer value is the new *Hotel Terminus*, Stenersgata 10, 200 metres north of Oslo S. The rooms are comfortable with full amenities, nonsmoking rooms are available, the breakfast is above average, and complimentary tea and fruit are available throughout the day. The rate is 410/560 kr from late May through August and on weekends year-round, 610/810 kr at other times.

The best value of the city's classic hotels is the Inter Nor *Hotel Bristol* (☎ 22 82 60 00), Kristian IV's gate 7. Rooms are pleasant with cable TV, minibars and bathtubs, and the halls and lobby are filled with antiques, chandeliers and old-world charm. The standard rate for singles/doubles is 1295/1595 kr, but there's a weekend price of 620/850 kr and a summer rate of 895/1050 kr.

Another hotel laden with period character is the regal *Grand Hotel* (☎ 22 42 93 90), Karl Johans gate 31, which has weekday rates of 1475/1875 kr and weekend rates of 775/990 kr.

Places to Eat

Eating can be an expensive proposition in Oslo. One way to save money is to frequent bakeries, many of which have reasonably priced sandwiches as well as pastries and hearty wholegrain breads. *Baker Hansen* and *Samson's* are two good chains with numerous shops around Oslo.

Oslo S & Around The main section of Oslo S has a *Caroline Café* with fairly good cafeteria fare at average prices, a small food mart open to 11 pm daily, hot-dog stands, a sandwich shop and a *Burger King*. The south wing, Østbanehallen, has *McDonald's* and *Tacoland* fast food; *Rooster Coffee*, a good espresso bar; *Baker Nordby*, with pastries, sandwiches and ice cream; and a grocery store with fruit and a deli. Fruit stalls set up daily except Sunday in front of Oslo S.

Oslo City, a shopping complex opposite the north side of Oslo S, also has numerous eateries, mostly of the fast-food variety. There are bakeries, a hamburger joint, a pizzeria, and Chinese and Mexican restaurants. Oslo City is open to 8 pm weekdays, 6 pm on Saturday, closed on Sunday. The bus station has a couple of small stores with fruit and snacks, and a bakery that opens weekdays at 6.30 am.

Aker Brygge Aker Brygge, the shopping complex along the west side of the harbour, has a food court with various eateries including *Chopsticks*, with Chinese dishes for about 60 kr; *Bakeriteater*, with good pastries and hearty baguette sandwiches; and a *McDonald's*, a baked-potato stall and hot-dog and ice-cream stands.

At the rear of Aker Brygge, just inside the entrance of the *Rema 1000* supermarket, is the *Smør-Petersen* deli, which sells delicious salmon quiche, good salads and other quality deli foods. You can order takeaway, which works out a bit cheaper, or eat inside at one of the café tables. Just south of Rema 1000 is *La Piazza*, a popular Italian restaurant with pizza and pasta dishes for about 100 kr.

Elsewhere in Oslo *Oluf Lorentzen*, a grocery store at Karl Johans gate 33, has roasted chickens for 40 kr and other takeaway deli foods; it's open to 8 pm on weekdays, 6 pm on Saturday. The *7-Eleven* on Lille Grensen is open 24 hours every day and sells yoghurt, light beer, 5 kr coffee, hot dogs and other snack food. *Helios*, a small health-food store at Universitetsgata 22, has organic produce.

The fast-food *Tacoland*, at Nedre Slottsgate 15, is a good alternative to the nearby McDonald's and has reasonable tacos, burritos and fajitas for 20 kr.

Egon, in the Paleet complex at Karl Johans gate 37, has good pizza, burgers and kebab sandwiches; the best deal is the 65 kr pizza buffet served with a simple salad bar from 10 am to 6 pm daily (to 11 pm on Monday and Sunday). In the same complex are a couple of moderately priced ethnic restaurants, including the Greek *Hellas* and the Indian *Ma'raja*.

Pizzerias include the Norwegian chain *Peppe's Pizza* and the American chain *Pizza Hut*; both have several branches in the city centre.

Vegeta Vertshus, at Munkedamsveien 3B near the National Theatre, has a single-serving vegetarian buffet that includes wholegrain pizza, casseroles and salads. It costs 69 kr for all you can stack on a small plate, 79 kr for a bigger dinner plate. Hours are from 11 am to 11 pm daily.

If you eat meat, a better deal is the 79 kr all-you-can-eat lunch buffet in the solarium at the *Rica Victoria Hotel*, Rosenkrantz gate 13. It includes fresh salads, cold cuts, a couple of hot dishes and simple desserts and is available Monday to Saturday from noon to 2.30 pm.

Mr Hong, next to the Cecil Hotel on Rosenkrantz gate, has a good all-you-can-eat 105 kr dinner buffet with fresh salad and a 'Mongolian grill' of meat, seafood and vegetables that you select to be stir fried. Weekdays from 11 am to 3 pm, there are 49 kr lunches that include a Chinese main course, rice and coffee.

A popular place with local art students is *Kafé Celsius*, at Radhusgata 19, a low-key café with a pleasant courtyard beer garden, and Greek salads and pastas for about 85 kr. It's open from 11.30 am (1 pm on Sunday) to 1 am, closed on Monday.

Kafé Sesam, in the National Museum of Contemporary Art, has cheap Chinese food, including a hearty Peking soup with bread for 29 kr and a dozen filling Chinese dishes with rice and salad for 49 kr. It's open during museum hours.

The *Grand Café* at the Grand Hotel on Karl Johans gate has been serving Oslo's cognoscenti for more than a century – as a reminder, a wall mural depicts the restaurant in the 1890s bustling with the likes of Munch and Ibsen. Some of the more affordable dishes are from the light '*småretter*' menu averaging 100 kr, and the 98 kr daily special that features a traditional dish and is served weekdays from 3 to 6 pm.

Thai Orchid, a dinner restaurant at Peder Claussøns gate 4, has good Thai food in a fine-dining atmosphere, with dishes averaging 100 kr.

In the Nordmarka area, the *Holmenkollen Restaurant*, a few minutes walk from the Holmenkollen tram station, has a good daily *koldtbord* lunch buffet of traditional Norwegian cold and hot dishes for 180 kr – or you can enjoy the same broad view of Oslofjord from the adjacent cafeteria for a fraction of that.

Entertainment

The tourist office's monthly *What's on in Oslo* brochure lists current concerts, theatre and special events, while the free *Natt & Dag* entertainment newspaper covers the club scene.

Smuget, Rosenkrantz gate 22, is a reliable hot spot with a disco and live jazz, rock and blues. The trendy new *Belleville* on Munkedamsveien features world music and attracts an international crowd. Just a stone's throw from Sleep In is *So What*, Grensen 9, a café and club with alternative music. *Barbeint*, Drammensveien 20, is a hip music bar with funk, rock and late hours. The popular gay bar *Enka*, Karl Johans gate 10, has a disco and drag shows.

The city's largest concert halls, *Oslo Spektrum*, near Oslo S, and *Rockefeller Music Hall*, Torggata 16, host international musicians such as Red Hot Chili Peppers and Tina Turner. The six-screen *Saga cinema* on Olav V's gate shows first-run movies in their original language.

Or take advantage of summer's long daylight hours and spend evenings outdoors – go down to the harbour and enjoy live jazz wafting off the floating restaurants, have a beer at one of the outdoor cafés at Vigeland Park, or take a ferry out to the islands in the Oslofjord.

Things to Buy

Traditional Norwegian sweaters are popular purchases; for good prices and selections, check the Oslo Sweater Shop on Skippergata near Oslo S, and Unique Design at Rosenkrantz gate 13. Husfliden, at Møllergata 4, and Heimen Husflid, at Rosenkrantz gate 8, are larger shops selling quality Norwegian clothing and crafts, with items ranging from carved wooden trolls to elaborate folk costumes.

NORWAY

Getting There & Away

Air Oslo's main airport currently is at Fornebu, eight km south-west of the city centre. Gardermoen airport, 50 km north of Oslo, is scheduled to replace Fornebu in October 1998 after the completion of a new fast-rail system linking it to Oslo.

The SAS ticket office (☎ 22 17 00 20) is in the Oslo City shopping centre. Braathens SAFE (☎ 22 83 44 70) has an office at Håkon VII's gate 2.

Bus Long-distance buses arrive and depart from Galleri Oslo, east of Oslo S. The train and bus stations are linked via an overhead walkway.

Train All trains arrive and depart from Oslo S in the city centre. The reservation windows are open from 6 am (international from 6.30 am) to 11 pm daily. There's also an information desk where you can get details on travel schedules throughout Norway.

Oslo S has backpack-sized lockers for 20 kr. The left-luggage window, open from 7 am to 11 pm daily, charges 20 kr a bag. The station also has a summertime Inter-Rail Centre where travellers with rail passes can shower and wait for their next train.

Car & Motorcycle The main highways into the city are the E6 from the north and south, and the E18 from the east and west. You'll have to pass through one of 19 toll stations and pay 12 kr each time you enter Oslo. Be aware that if you use one of the lanes for vehicles with passes and get stopped, there's a 250 kr fine. Motorcycles aren't subject to the tolls.

Car Rental All major car rental companies have booths at the airport. The following also have offices in the city centre:

Avis
  Munkedamsveien 27 (☎ 22 83 58 00)
Budget
  Oslo Spektrum, near Oslo S (☎ 22 17 10 50)
Hertz
  SAS Hotel, Holbergs gate 30 (☎ 22 20 01 21)

Hitching When leaving Oslo it's generally best to take a train to the outskirts of the city in whatever direction you're heading and start hitching from there. The ride board at Use It is worth checking, though there are usually far more people seeking rides than offering them.

Boat Boats to and from Copenhagen and Frederikshavn (Denmark) use the docks off Skippergata, near Vippetangen. Bus No 29 brings you to within a couple of minutes walk of the terminal.

Boats from Hirtshals (Denmark) and Kiel (Germany) dock at Hjortneskaia, west of the central harbour, from where there are connecting buses to Oslo S.

The summer boat to Arendal, Risør and Kragerø docks at Rådhusbrygge, opposite the Rådhus.

Getting Around

Oslo has an efficient public-transport system with an extensive network of buses, trams, subways and ferries. A one-way ticket on any of these services costs 18 kr and includes a free transfer within an hour of purchase. A day ticket *(dagskort)* good for unlimited 24-hour travel (40 kr) and one-week cards (120 kr) are sold at Trafikanten, Narvesen kiosks and staffed underground stations. In addition, all city transport is free if you have an Oslo Card.

Bicycles can be brought on Oslo's trams and trains for an additional 18 kr. Note that while it may seem easy to board the underground and trams without a ticket, if confronted by an inspector you'll receive an automatic 450 kr fine.

Trafikanten, situated below the tower at the front entrance of Oslo S, has schedules and a free public-transport map, *Sporveiskart Oslo*. The office is open from 7 am to 8 pm weekdays, 8 am to 6 pm on weekends. Dial ☎ 177 daily to 11 pm for schedule information.

To/From the Airport SAS airport buses, Flybussen, run between Fornebu airport and Oslo S every 15 minutes (35 kr). The less frequent public bus No 31 (18 kr) runs from in front of the airport to Oslo S. Taxis from Fornebu to the city centre cost about 120 kr.

Bus & Tram Bus and tram lines crisscross the city and extend into the suburbs. There's no central station but most converge at Jernbanetorget in front of Oslo S. Most westbound buses, including those to Bygdøy and Vigeland Park, also stop at the south side of the National Theatre.

Underground T-bane, which in the city centre is an underground system, is faster and goes further outside the city centre than most bus lines. All lines can be boarded at the National Theatre, Stortinget and Jernbanetorget stations.

Taxi Taxis charge 24 kr (30 kr after 7 pm and on weekends) at flagfall and about 12 kr per km. There are taxi stands at the train station, shopping centres and city squares. Taxis with lit signs can be flagged down, or call ☎ 22 38 80 90 (the meter starts at the dispatch point). Oslo taxis accept major credit cards.

Car & Motorcycle Oslo has its fair share of one-way streets, which can complicate city driving a bit, but otherwise traffic is not terribly hard to deal with. Still, the best way to explore central sights is to walk or take local transport, though a car can be quite convenient for exploring outlying areas such as Holmenkollen.

Metered street parking, identified by a solid blue sign with a white letter 'P', can be found throughout the city. Hours written under the sign indicate the period in which the meters are in effect, which is usually from 8 am to 5 pm, with Saturday hours written in parentheses. Unless otherwise posted, parking is free outside of that time and on Sunday. Parking at most meters costs from 5 to 20 kr an hour – busy spots, such as those around post offices, have the highest rates. There are a dozen multistorey car parks in the city centre, including ones at major shopping centres such as Oslo City and Aker

Brygge. If you buy an Oslo Card, it includes free parking at municipal car parks.

Boat Ferries to Bygdøy leave from Rådhusbrygge, while ferries to the islands in the Oslofjord leave from Vippetangen.

AROUND OSLO
The **Østfold** region, on the eastern side of Oslofjord, is a mixture of farmland and small industrial towns based on the timber trade.

Trains leave every couple of hours from Oslo to the border town of Halden (just south of Frederikstad), where four trains a day continue on to Sweden. **Halden** has an imposing 17th-century fortified hill-top castle that was the site of many battles between Norway and Sweden. There's a *camping ground* on the castle grounds and a *hostel* in town.

The most interesting excursion into the Østfold region from Oslo is to Fredrikstad, which takes 1¼ hours and costs 120 kr each way by train.

The city of **Fredrikstad** has an old enclosed fortress town complete with moats, gates and a drawbridge, built in 1567 as protection against a belligerent Sweden. You can walk around the perimeter of the fortress walls, which were once ringed by 200 cannons, and through narrow, cobbled streets lined with still-lived-in historic buildings, most dating from the 17th century. The fort's long arsenal and infantry barracks are also still in use. The central square has a bank, a café and a statue of King Frederik II who founded the town.

From Fredrikstad station it's a five-minute walk down to the waterfront, where a ferry (two minutes, 5 kr) shuttles across the river Glomma to the fortress' main gate.

After exploring the fortress you can cross the moat and walk 15 minutes down Kongens gate to the intact Kongens Fort, which sits on a bluff above a city park. It all makes for pleasant strolling and there are no admission fees. There's a *camping ground* near Kongens Fort.

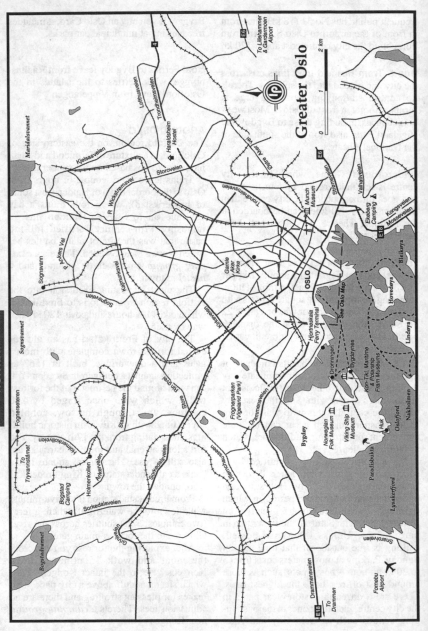

Greater Oslo

NORWAY

Southern Norway

Sørlandet, the curving south coast, is magnetic for Norwegians when the weather turns warm. The coast is largely rocky with a heavy scattering of low stone islands, and Sørlandet's numerous coves and bays are ideal for the many Norwegian holiday-makers who have their own boats. The attraction is generally not as great for foreign travellers, the majority of whom have just arrived from places with warmer water and better beaches.

The Sørland train line, which runs 586 km from Stavanger to Oslo via Kristiansand, stays inland most of the way, though buses that connect with the train go to several south coast towns. The E18, the main highway and bus route, runs inland from Stavanger to Mandal; eastward from there it passes through a number of coastal towns.

STAVANGER

Stavanger, Norway's fourth largest city, was a bustling fishing centre at the turn of the century and in its heyday had more than 50 sardine canneries. By the 1960s the depletion of fish stocks had brought an end to the industry, but the discovery of North Sea oil spared Stavanger from hard times. The city now holds the title of 'Oil Capital of Norway' – perhaps no greater tourist attraction than pickled herring, but it has brought prosperity and a cosmopolitan community that includes nearly 3000 British and US oil people.

Most visitors to Stavanger arrive on the ferry from England and make a beeline for Bergen or Oslo. If your time is limited, that's not a bad idea. Otherwise, it's worth spending a day in Stavanger – it has an historic harbour area, a medieval cathedral and a few local museums.

Orientation & Information

The adjacent bus and train stations are a 10-minute walk from the harbour. The modern Kulturhus, a town centre of sorts, holds the public library, a cinema, an art gallery and a couple of places to eat. On sunny days the pedestrian streets behind Kulturhus are alive with students, street musicians and pavement vendors.

The main tourist office (☎ 51 89 66 00), at the east side of Kulturhus (Postboks 11, 4001 Stavanger), is open from 9 am to 5 pm Monday to Friday, and to 2 pm on Saturday. In summer there's also a tourist booth at the inner harbour, open daily from 10 am to 8 pm. Most of Stavanger's sights are within easy walking distance of the harbour.

The Norwegian Emigration Centre (☎ 51 50 12 67), which helps foreigners of Norwegian descent trace their roots, is at Bergjelandsgata 30 and is open from 9 am to 3 pm Monday to Friday.

Things to See & Do

A nice quarter to stroll through is **Gamle Stavanger**, on the west side of the harbour, where cobblestone walkways lead through rows of early 18th-century whitewashed wooden houses. With more than 150 homes, it's said to be northern Europe's best preserved wooden-house settlement.

Stavanger Domkirke, on the south end of Kirkegata, is an impressive medieval stone cathedral dating back to the 12th century. It's open daily from 9 am to 6 pm (Sunday from 1 pm) from 15 May to 15 September, from 9 am to 2 pm Monday to Saturday the rest of the year. An atmospheric time to visit is at 11.15 am on Thursday, when an organ recital takes place.

You can get a good view of the city and the harbour oil rigs from the top of **Valbergtårnet**, a tower at the end of Valberggata.

The **Stavanger Museum** at Muségata 16 has the standard collection of stuffed animals in one wing and period furnishings in another. More interesting are the **Maritime Museum**, in a restored seaside warehouse at Nedre Strandgate 17, which gives a good glimpse into Stavanger's maritime history, and the **Canning Museum**, in an old sardine canning factory at Øvre Strandgate 88A. Other museums include two 19th-century manor houses built by wealthy ship owners, one of which, **Ledaal**, serves as the residence

NORWAY

Stavanger

PLACES TO STAY
3 Melands Gjestgiveri
6 Commandør Hotel
7 Havly Hotel

PLACES TO EAT
4 India Tandoori Restaurant
11 China House
15 Finns Konditori
16 Ponti's Pizza
17 McDonald's
18 Dickens

OTHER
1 International Ferries
2 Canning Museum
5 Bergen Express Boat
8 Tau Ferry
9 Clipper Sightseeing Boat
10 Valbergtårnet tower
12 Maritime Museum
13 Kulturhus
14 Main Tourist Office
19 Fish Market
20 Summer Tourist Office
21 Torget (Market)
22 Post Office
23 Stavanger Domkirke
24 Laundrette
25 Norwegian Emigration Centre
26 Train Station
27 Bus Station
28 Stavanger Museum

for visiting members of the royal family. In summer, the museums are open daily from 11 am to 4 pm; a 30 kr one-day ticket includes entrance to all.

Pulpit Rock The most popular outing from Stavanger is the two-hour hike to the top of the awesomely sheer Pulpit Rock (Preikestolen). You can inch up to the edge of its flat top and peer 600 metres straight down to the Lysefjord. From Stavanger take the 8.30 am ferry to Tau (40 minutes, 25 kr) from where there's a connecting bus (38 kr) to the trail-head; allow a full day. The bus operates from late June to early September.

If you'd rather look up at Pulpit Rock from the bottom, the *Clipper* sightseeing boat (☎ 51 89 52 70) leaves Stavanger daily to cruise the steep-walled Lysefjord. Tickets (190 to 275 kr) can be purchased at the tourist office.

A good outing to consider if you have your own car, is to take the local ferry from Stavanger all the way to Lysebotn, at the head of the Lysefjord. From there, drive up the mountain pass to Sirdal along a narrow road that climbs 1000 metres with 27 hairpin turns for a scenic ride back to Stavanger. The ferry takes four hours, leaves daily at 8.30 am from mid-June to mid-August and costs 197 kr for a car with driver plus 88 kr for each additional adult, 44 kr for children. Car reservations (☎ 51 89 32 12) should be made in advance.

Places to Stay
The lakeside *Mosvangen Hostel* (☎ 51 87 09 77), three km from the city centre (bus No 130, 15 kr), charges 100 kr for a dorm bed, 250 kr for a single or double. The hostel is open from late May to 1 September. A *camping ground* (☎ 51 53 29 71) is next door. There's also a *summer hostel* (☎ 94 53 11 11) within walking distance of Pulpit Rock.

Melands Gjestgiveri (☎ 51 89 55 85), near the harbour at Nedre Holmegate 2, is a friendly guesthouse with 19 adequate rooms costing 330/450 kr for singles/doubles.

The *Havly Hotel* (☎ 51 89 67 00) at Valberggata 1 and the *Commandør Hotel* (☎ 51 89 53 00) at Valberggata 9 both offer comfortable rooms with private baths for about 400/550 kr in summer and on weekends.

Places to Eat
There's a moderately priced *Caroline Café* at the train station and a takeaway sandwich shop at the bus station. In the centre, *Ponti's Pizza*, opposite the Kulturhus, has good pizza at good prices. Nearby *Finns Konditori* has tempting pastries and sandwiches.

Dickens, at Skagenkaien 6, has a nice pub atmosphere, with good salads and lunch specials for about 85 kr. *China House*, at Salvågergata 3, has a 56 kr lunch special with coffee that's served until 5 pm daily except Sunday. *India Tandoori Restaurant* at Valberggata 14 has authentic Indian dishes priced around 100 kr.

Getting There & Away
For information on the boat from England see the introductory Getting There & Away section to this chapter.

Flaggruten's (☎ 51 89 50 90) express passenger catamaran to Bergen leaves from Stavanger harbour, takes four hours and costs 450 kr. Spouses and hostel members get a 25% discount, ScanRail holders 50%. There are four sailings each way on weekdays, two on weekends, including a daily sailing in each direction at 12.30 pm.

Stavanger's only train line runs to Oslo (eight hours, 580 kr), via Kristiansand and Bø, a few times a day. On weekdays there's also an overnight train, which leaves Stavanger at 10 pm. All trains require reservations. A daily express bus to Oslo (10 hours, 490 kr) leaves Stavanger at 8.45 am.

The main south coast highway, the E18, terminates in Stavanger, where it turns into Motorveien; turn south on Madlaveien to get to the city centre.

Getting Around
The city centre is a combination of narrow streets and pedestrian walkways that are best explored on foot. There are car parks next to the post office and at the south side of the bus station.

KRISTIANSAND
Kristiansand, the closest port to Denmark, offers the first glimpse of Norway for many travellers. The capital of Sørlandet, Kristiansand has a grid pattern of wide streets laid out by King Christian IV, who founded the city in 1641. It's a busy seaside holiday resort for Norwegians but of less interest to foreign visitors who generally pile off the ferries and onto the next train.

Orientation & Information
The train, bus and ferry terminals are together on the west side of the city centre. There's parking in this area and along most city streets. Markens gate, a pedestrian street a block inland, is the central shopping and restaurant area.

The tourist office (☎ 38 12 13 14) is at Dronningens gate 2, six blocks down Vestre Strand gate from the train station. Change money at the post office at Markens gate 19 or in the bank at the ferry terminal.

Things to See & Do
For a quick look around, walk south-east

PLACES TO STAY
5 Hotel Bondeheimen
17 Hotel Norge
23 Kristiansand Hostel
24 Roligheden Camping

PLACES TO EAT
3 Rimi Grocery Store
7 Peppe's Pizza
8 China Palace
9 Mega Grocery Store
   & Cafeteria
14 Bakery
20 Sjøhuset

OTHER
1 Vest-Agder Folk Museum
2 Oddernes Kirke
4 Town Square
6 Domkirke (Cathedral)
10 Train Station
11 Bus Station
12 Ferry Terminal
13 Libris Bookstore
15 Post Office
16 MS *Maarten* Excursion Boat
18 Tourist Office
19 Fønix Movie Theatre
21 Yacht Harbour
22 Christiansholm Fortress

Kristiansand

along Vestre Strand gate to its end and then along Strandepromenaden and the yacht harbour to **Christiansholm Fortress** (circa 1674), where there's a coastal view from the cannon-ringed wall. From there walk inland along the tree-lined Festningsgata and turn left onto Gyldenløves gate, passing the **town square** and **cathedral** on the way back to the transport terminals.

Ravnedalen, a park with lakes and trails, is just north of the city centre. If you want to explore further, a **zoo**, the **Vest-Agder folk museum** and the 11th-century **Oddernes kirke** are on the outskirts of town.

In summer the MS *Maarten* (☎ 38 12 13 15) cruises to the offshore islands. Tour time ranges from one to 3½ hours, prices from 40 to 140 kr.

Places to Stay
Roligheden Camping (☎ 38 09 67 22), at a popular beach three km east of town, can be reached by bus No 15. The new *Kristiansand Hostel* (☎ 38 02 83 10) at Skansen 8, about a 10-minute walk east of the fortress, is open year-round with dorm beds for 150 kr, singles/doubles for 310/350 kr.

The *Hotel Bondeheimen* (☎ 38 02 44 40)

is central at Kirkegata 15, and has summer rates of 330/560 kr for singles/doubles. More up-market is the *Hotel Norge* (☎ 38 02 00 00) at Dronningens gate 5, which has a summer rate of 700 kr for doubles.

Places to Eat

Mega grocery store, opposite the train station, has a cheap cafeteria. *Peppe's Pizza* at Gyldenløves gate 7 has good pizzas from 114 kr that are large enough to feed two people. *China Palace*, nearby on Markens gate, has cheap lunch specials. There's a good bakery on Rådhus gate near the post office.

For more of a splurge, join the crowd at the harbourside *Sjøhuset*, Østre Strandgate 12A. This seafood restaurant has high prices, but the setting and food are good.

Getting There & Away

Express buses head north at 9 am daily to Voss (11 hours, 460 kr) and Bergen (12 hours, 520 kr) via Odda. There are daily trains to Oslo (five hours, 385 kr) and Stavanger (3¼ hours, 275 kr), as well as express buses.

Regional buses depart a few times daily for towns along the south coast. It takes 1¾ hours to Arendal (76 kr) and three hours to Risør (128 kr) – catch the early bus and you can break your journey and still reach Oslo the same day. Fares are half-price for students and spouses.

The E18 runs along the north side of the city centre and is reached via Vestre Strand gate. For information on ferries to Denmark see Norway, Getting There & Away.

ARENDAL

Arendal is the administrative centre of Aust-Agder county. Just a few minutes walk south of the bus station brings you into the old harbourside area of Tyholmen, with its restored 19th-century wooden buildings and town hall. For a tasty snack, stop at the waterfront fish market, which sells good inexpensive fish cakes.

Getting There & Away

Arendal is connected with the main rail system by a trunk line that runs from Nelaug, and is a stop for express buses between Kristiansand and Oslo.

In summer, the Sørlandscruise ferry (☎ 38 32 13 00) leaves Oslo at 9 am daily except Friday and Saturday, arrives in Arendal at 3.45 pm, and makes the return journey 30 minutes later. En route (both directions) it stops in Risør and Kragerø. The Oslo-Arendal fare is 360 kr; there's a 50% student discount and a 10% discount on return tickets.

RISØR

Risør, with its cluster of historic white houses built up around a busy little fishing harbour, is one of the most picturesque villages on the south coast. It's a haunt for artists, and many well-to-do yachties make it their summer hang-out.

Next to wandering around the harbour, one of the most popular activities is to visit the offshore islands, which can be reached by inexpensive water taxis. The most frequented island, **Stangholmen**, has an old lighthouse with a restaurant and bar; boats leave every hour from 10 am and cost 20 kr. In summer, there's a tourist office (☎ 37 15 85 60) at the harbourfront.

Places to Stay & Eat

Most visitors to Risør stay on their boats; rooms at the only in-town hotel, the *Risør Hotel* (☎ 37 15 07 00), start at a pricey 690 kr. You could consider camping – roughing it on one of the offshore islands, which is allowed for up to two nights.

There are a couple of moderately priced pavement cafés at the harbour. Ice-cream shops abound, there's fresh fruit at the harbourside market and a bakery one block west on Kragsgate.

Getting There & Away

Buses to and from Risør connect with the train at Gjerstad a few times a day. Buses between Kristiansand and Oslo stop en route

NORWAY

in Risør. The summer ferry from Oslo costs 330 kr.

OTHER SOUTH COAST TOWNS

Forty-five km west of Kristiansand is **Mandal**, the southernmost town in Norway, with nice sandy beaches and numerous nearshore skerries. The nearby **Lindesnes** lighthouse marks Norway's southernmost point.

Between Kristiansand and Arendal you'll pass **Lillesand**, which has an unspoiled village centre of old whitewashed houses befitting the 'white town' image that so many other south coast towns claim, and **Grimstad**, where the house that Henrik Ibsen lived in has been incorporated into a museum.

If you want to stay the night, both Mandal and Lillesand have *hostels*.

TELEMARK

Most of the Telemark region (which lends its name to a type of ski turn) is sparsely populated and rural, with steep mountains, deep valleys, high plateaus and a myriad of lakes.

Unfortunately, travel around Telemark is geared primarily to the automobile. Train lines run only through the south-eastern part of Telemark and buses are infrequent. Telemark's westernmost train station is at Bø; from there, the train connects with buses that lead west to Dalen, Amot and on to Odda in Hardanger.

Telemark's most visited attraction is the impressive **Heddal stave church** (circa 1242), the largest stave church in Norway. It's on route 11 five km west of **Notodden**, the closest rail stop.

For tourist information on all of Telemark, contact Telemarkreiser (☎ 35 53 03 00), Postboks 2813 Kjørbekk, 3702 Skien.

Telemark Canal

The Telemark canal system, 105 km of waterways with 18 locks, runs from the industrialised city of **Skien** to the small town of **Dalen**. From mid-May to early September two turn-of-the-century sightseeing boats (☎ 35 53 03 00) make the unhurried, if not sluggish, 10-hour journey for 250 kr one way. At the height of summer, the boats operate daily in both directions.

Places to Stay Dalen has a *camping ground* (☎ 35 07 75 87) with hostel-style rooms for 130 kr and cabins for 300 kr. Skien has a year-round *hostel* (☎ 35 59 95 51) at Moflatvien 65 and a relatively cheap hotel, *Nye Herkules* (☎ 35 59 63 11), nearby at Moflatvien 59.

Rjukan

The long, narrow industrial town of Rjukan is squeezed into the deep Vestfjord valley at the base of the 1883-metre **Mt Gausta**, Telemark's highest peak. A trail to the mountain top starts at Lake Hedder, 16 km from town.

The **Vemork Industrial Workers Museum**, seven km west of Rjukan, has an exhibit of the Norwegian Resistance's daring sabotage of the heavy-water plant that was built here by the Nazis during WWII.

From Rjukan it's a nine-hour walk north to the Kalhovd mountain hut and a network of trails that stretches north and west across the expansive moors of **Hardangervidda**, a popular wilderness hiking area that boasts Norway's largest wild reindeer herd.

There's a year-round *hostel* (☎ 35 09 05 27) in Rjukan. A daily express bus connects Rjukan to Oslo (3¾ hours, 210 kr) via Kongsberg.

Kragerø

A popular seaside resort with narrow streets and whitewashed houses, Kragerø has long been a retreat for Norwegian artists. Kragerø's summer *hostel* (☎ 35 98 33 33), at Lovisenbergveien 20, has dorm beds/ doubles for 195/390 kr including breakfast.

The simplest approach is by rail from Oslo or Kristiansand to Neslandsvatn, where most of the trains meet a connecting bus to Kragerø. There's also a summer ferry from Oslo (see Arendal).

Kongsberg

The settlement of Kongsberg was founded in 1624 following the discovery of one of the world's purest silver deposits in the nearby Numedal Valley. Kongsberg briefly became the largest town in Norway as a result of the ensuing silver rush. The national mint is still located in town, but the last mine, no longer able to turn a profit, closed in 1957. The tourist office (☎ 32 73 50 00), Storgata 35, is south of the train station.

Things to See The **Norwegian Mining Museum** (40 kr), Hyttegata 3, just over the bridge in an 1844 smelting building, has exhibits of mining, minting and skiing. The **Lågdal folk museum** (20 kr), which has a collection of period farmhouses and an indoor museum with recreated 19th-century workshops, is 10 minutes south of the train station: turn left on Bekkedokk, take the walkway parallel to the tracks and follow the signs.

In summer there are daily tours of the old **silver mines** at Saggrenda, eight km from Kongsberg, which include a train ride through cool subterranean shafts (50 kr) – bring a sweater! Weekday buses to the mines (get off at Søvverket) leave from Kongsberg station on the hour.

Places to Stay & Eat The *Kongsberg Hostel* (☎ 32 73 20 24) is two km from the train station; walk south on Storgata, cross the bridge, turn right at the post office and take the pedestrian walkway over route 40. Dorm beds cost from 165 kr, doubles 396 kr, including breakfast.

Of Kongberg's two hotels the *Gyldenløve Hotel* (☎ 32 73 17 44) offers the cheapest rates at 645/795 kr for singles/ doubles.

Gamle Kongsberg Kro, on the south side of the river, has good food, a varied menu and moderate prices. There's a bakery at the Rimi grocery store west of the train station, and another at Storgata 19.

Getting There & Away Kongsberg is a 1½-hour (105 kr) train ride from Oslo. Daily express buses connect Kongsberg with Rjukan (two hours, 123 kr), Notodden (35 minutes, 40 kr) and Oslo (1½ hours, 95 kr).

Central Norway

The central part of Norway, stretching west from Oslo to the historic city of Bergen and north to the mountaineering town of Åndalsnes, takes in Norway's highest mountains, largest glacier and most spectacular fjords. Not surprisingly, this region is the top destination for travellers to Norway.

FROM OSLO TO BERGEN
The Oslo-Bergen railway line is Norway's most scenic, a seven-hour journey past forests, alpine villages and the starkly beautiful Hardangervidda plateau.

Midway between Oslo and Bergen is **Geilo**, a ski centre where you can practically walk off the train and onto a lift. Geilo has a *hostel* (☎ 32 09 03 00) near the train station and there is good summer hiking in the mountains above town.

From Geilo the train climbs 600 metres through a tundra-like landscape of high lakes and snow-capped mountains to the tiny village of **Finse**, near the glacier Hardangerjøkulen. Finse has year-round skiing and is in the midst of a network of summer hiking trails. One of Norway's most frequently trodden trails winds from the Finse train station down to the fjord town of Aurland, a four to five-day trek. There's breathtaking mountain scenery along the way as well as a series of DNT mountain huts a day's walk apart – the nearest is the Finsehytte, 200 metres from the Finse station. There's also a bike route from Finse to Flåm on the century-old railway construction road.

Myrdal, the next train stop, is the connecting point for the spectacularly steep Flåm railway, which twists its way 20 splendid km down to **Flåm** village on the Aurlandsfjord, an arm of the Sognefjord.

Many people go down to Flåm, have lunch and take the train back up to Myrdal where they catch the next Oslo-Bergen train. A better option is to take the ferry from Flåm up the waterfall-laden Nærøyfjord to Gudvangen where there's a connecting bus that

NORWAY

climbs a steep valley on the dramatically scenic ride to Voss. From Voss, trains to Bergen run nearly hourly. To include a cruise of the Nærøyfjord in a day trip from Oslo to Bergen, you'll need to take the 7.42 am train from Oslo, which connects with the afternoon ferry from Flåm. For details on Flåm see the Sognefjord section.

Voss

Voss is another winter-sports centre with attractive surroundings. Buses stop at the train station. The tourist office (☎ 56 51 00 51) is on Utrågata, a 10-minute walk east from the station; turn right at the 13th-century stone church.

Places to Stay & Eat There's a lakeside camping ground 300 metres south of the tourist office and several moderately priced pensions around town. The modern *Voss Hostel* (☎ 56 51 20 17) has a nice lakeside location, a km west of the train station, but it's pricey, starting at 149 kr for dorm beds, 400 kr for doubles, a simple breakfast included. There's no guest kitchen. Bicycles and rowing boats can be hired and there's a free sauna.

There's a grocery store and bakery on the north side of the church and a number of moderately priced restaurants in the town centre.

BERGEN

Bergen was the capital of Norway during the 12th and 13th centuries and in the early 17th century had the distinction of being Scandinavia's largest city – with a population of 15,000.

Set on a peninsula surrounded by seven mountains, Bergen's history is closely tied to the sea. It became one of the central ports of the Hanseatic League of merchants, which dominated trade in northern Europe during the late Middle Ages. The Hanseatic influence is still visible in the sharply gabled row of houses that line Bergen's picturesque harbour front.

Even though it's Norway's second-largest city, Bergen (population 223,000) has a pleasant, slow pace. A university town and the cultural centre of western Norway, it has theatres, good museums and a noted philharmonic orchestra.

Odds are that you'll see rain, as it falls 275 days a year. Still, that's not as dismal as it sounds – the rain keeps the city green and flowery, and the low skyline of red-tiled roofs manages to look cheery even on damp, drizzly days.

Bergen is the main jumping-off point for journeys into the western fjords: numerous buses, trains, passenger ferries and express boats set off daily.

Orientation

Bergen is a fairly compact city and easy to get around, albeit hilly. The bus and train stations are a block apart on Strømgaten, a 10-minute walk from the city centre. Much of the city is built up around the waterfront and many of the sights, restaurants and hotels are within a few blocks of Vågen, the inner harbour.

Information

Tourist Office The tourist office (☎ 55 32 14 80) on Bryggen (Postboks 4055 Dreggen, 5023 Bergen) has brochures on destinations throughout Norway. Be sure to pick up the detailed *Bergen Guide*. Hours are from 8.30 am to 9 pm daily from May to September, 9 am to 4 pm Monday to Saturday the rest of the year. From late May to late August there's a branch at the train station that's open from 7.15 am to 11 pm daily.

Bergen Card The Bergen Card allows free transport on local buses, free parking, funicular rides and admission to many museums and historic sights. The Schøtstuene and the Hanseatic Museum are not covered. A 24-hour card costs 120 kr, a 48-hour card 190 kr, half-price for children. It's sold at the tourist offices, hotels and the bus terminal.

Money Money can be changed at the Kreditkassen bank on Christies gate or the nearby post office. The tourist offices will

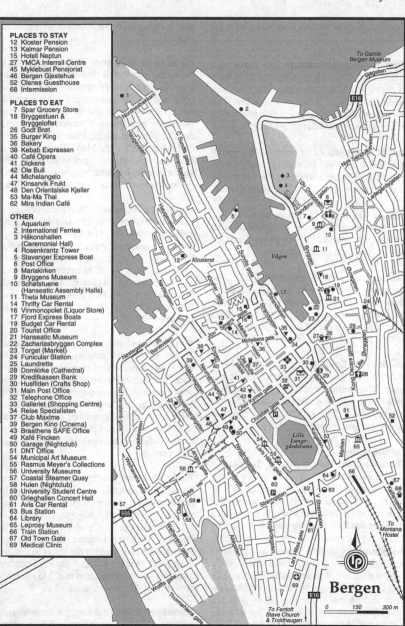

PLACES TO STAY
12 Kloster Pension
13 Kalmar Pension
15 Hotell Neptun
27 YMCA Interrail Centre
45 Myklebust Pensjonat
46 Bergen Gjestehus
52 Olsnes Guesthouse
68 Intermission

PLACES TO EAT
7 Spar Grocery Store
18 Bryggestuen &
   Bryggeloftet
26 Godt Brød
35 Burger King
36 Bakery
38 Kebab Expressen
40 Café Opera
41 Dickens
42 Ole Bull
44 Michelangelo
47 Kinsarvik Frukt
48 Den Orientalske Kjeller
53 Ma-Ma Thai
62 Mira Indian Café

OTHER
1 Aquarium
2 International Ferries
3 Håkonshallen
   (Ceremonial Hall)
4 Rosenkrantz Tower
5 Stavanger Express Boat
6 Post Office
8 Mariakirken
9 Bryggens Museum
10 Schøtstuene
   (Hanseatic Assembly Halls)
11 Theta Museum
14 Thrifty Car Rental
16 Vinmonopolet (Liquor Store)
19 Fjord Express Boats
20 Budget Car Rental
21 Hanseatic Museum
22 Zachariasbryggen Complex
23 Torget (Market)
24 Funicular Station
25 Laundrette
28 Domkirke (Cathedral)
29 Kreditkassen Bank
30 Husfliden (Crafts Shop)
31 Main Post Office
32 Telephone Office
33 Galleriet (Shopping Centre)
34 Reise Specialisten
37 Club Maxime
39 Bergen Kino (Cinema)
43 Braathens SAFE Office
49 Kafé Fincken
50 Garage (Nightclub)
51 DNT Office
54 Municipal Art Museum
55 Rasmus Meyer's Collections
56 University Museums
58 Coastal Steamer Quay
59 Hulen (Nightclub)
59 University Student Centre
60 Grieghallen Concert Hall
61 Avis Car Rental
63 Bus Station
64 Library
65 Leprosy Museum
66 Train Station
67 Old Town Gate
69 Medical Clinic

NORWAY

To Gamle
Bergen Museum

Vågen

Klosteret

To Montana
Hostel

Bergen

0   150   300 m

To Fantoft
Stave Church
& Troldhaugen

change money at 4% less than banks but with no fees.

Post & Communications The main post office, on Småstrandgaten, is open from 8 am to 5 pm weekdays (to 6 pm Thursday and Friday), 9 am to 3 pm on Saturday. The telephone office, at the south side of the post office, is open weekdays from 9 am to 4 pm.

Travel Agencies Reise Specialisten, opposite the Galleriet, handles general travel bookings. Kilroy Travels in the university student centre specialises in student tickets.

Library The public library, between the bus and train stations, has a good selection of foreign newspapers. It's open to 7 pm on weekdays, 2 pm on Saturday.

Laundry At Jarlens Vaskoteque, 17 Lille Øvregate, it costs 60 kr to wash a load of clothes, or for 85 kr you can leave them with the manager and pick them up two hours later. It's open from 10 am to 6 pm on weekdays, 9 am to 3 pm on Saturday.

Medical & Emergency Services Dial ☎ 112 for police and ☎ 113 for an ambulance. The medical clinic (☎ 55 32 11 20) at Lars Hilles gate 30 is open 24 hours a day for emergencies. The pharmacy at the bus station is open to midnight daily.

Things to See
The waterfront **fish market** at Torget is a good starting point for an exploration of the city's historic district. Bergen has lots of quaint cobblestone streets lined with older homes; one particularly picturesque area good for strolls is near the funicular station.

Bryggen Bryggen, the site of the old medieval quarter, is a compact area that's easily explored on foot. The streetside of Bryggen's long timber buildings hold museums, restaurants and shops, while the alleys that run along their less-restored sides offer an intriguing look at the stacked-stone foundations

and rough-plank construction of centuries past.

Hanseatic Museum This worthwhile museum, in a rough-timber building dating from the 16th century, retains its period character and furnishings and offers a glimpse of the austere working and living conditions of Hanseatic merchants. It's open daily from 9 am to 5 pm in summer, from 11 am to 2 pm daily September to May. Tours given in English (at noon and 3 pm in summer) provide a nice background but you can also walk through on your own. Admission costs 35 kr.

Bryggens Museum This archaeological museum was built at the site of Bergen's earliest settlement. The 800-year-old foundations unearthed during the construction have been incorporated into the museum's exhibits along with excavated medieval tools, pottery and skeletons. It's open daily from 10 am to 5 pm May to August, and from 11 am to 3 pm September to April. Admission costs 20 kr.

Schøtstuene Schøtstuene, at Øvregaten 50, houses one of the original assembly halls where the fraternity of Hanseatic merchants once met for their business meetings and beer guzzling. It's open from 10 am to 4 pm daily in summer, and from 11 am to 2 pm daily in May and September and on Sunday in the off season. Schøtstuene's 35 kr ticket is also valid for the Hanseatic Museum (and vice versa).

Theta Museum This clandestine one-room Resistance headquarters, uncovered by the Nazis in 1942, is now Norway's tiniest museum. Appropriately enough, finding it is still a challenge – it's at the back of the building with the unicorn figurehead; go through the alley and up the stairs to the 3rd floor. It's open from 2 to 4 pm on Tuesday, Saturday and Sunday from mid-May to mid-September. Admission costs 15 kr.

Mariakirken This Romanesque stone church with twin towers dates from the 12th century and is Bergen's oldest building. The interior has 15th-century frescos and a splendid baroque pulpit donated by Hanseatic merchants in 1676. It's open from 11 am to 4 pm weekdays from mid-May to mid-September and from noon to 1.30 pm Tuesday to Friday the rest of the year. Admission is 10 kr.

Rosenkrantz Tower Opposite the harbour is the Rosenkrantz tower, built in the 1560s by Bergen's governor as a residence and defence post. The tower incorporates parts of an earlier building that dates back to 1260. You can climb up spiral staircases past halls and sentry posts to the lookout on top. The tower is open from 10 am to 4 pm daily from mid-May to mid-September, but only from noon to 3 pm on Sunday in the off season. Admission costs 15 kr.

Håkonshallen This large ceremonial hall, adjacent to the Rosenkrantz Tower, was built by King Håkon Håkonsson in 1261 for his son's wedding. The roof was blown off in 1944 when a German ammunition boat exploded in the harbour; the building has since been extensively restored. It's open daily from 10 am to 4 pm from mid-May to mid-September, from noon to 3 pm (3 to 6 pm on Thursday) the rest of the year. Entry costs 15 kr.

Other City Sights The university, at the end of Christies gate, has a **Maritime Museum** with models of Viking ships, a **Natural History Museum** full of stuffed creatures and mineral displays, and of greater interest, an **Historical Museum** with Viking weaponry, medieval altars, folk art and period furnishings. The museums are open daily in summer from 10 am to 3 pm. A combination 20 kr ticket covers the latter two museums; there's a separate 20 kr admission to the Maritime Museum.

The **Municipal Art Museum** and the **Rasmus Meyer's Collections**, on Rasmus Meyers Allé opposite the lake fountain, exhibit a superb collection of Norwegian art from the 18th and 19th centuries, including many works by Munch and JC Dahl, as well as contemporary works by Picasso, Klee and others. Both are open daily from 11 am to 4 pm (Sunday from noon to 3 pm) from 15 May to 15 September; winter hours are shorter. There's a combined entrance fee of 35 kr, 20 kr for students.

The **Bergen Aquarium** has a big outdoor tank with seals and penguins as well as indoor fish tanks. It's near the northern tip of the peninsula, reached by bus No 4 or a 15-minute walk from the city centre. Opening hours are daily from 9 am to 8 pm May to September, 10 am to 6 pm the rest of the year. Admission is 45 kr. The **public park** just beyond the aquarium is a pleasant place with shaded lawns, sunbathing areas and an outdoor heated swimming pool.

Bergen Environs The open-air museum **Gamle Bergen,** which has about 35 buildings from the 18th and 19th centuries, is north of the city centre and is reached by bus No 1 or 9. Guided tours begin on the hour from 11 am to 5 pm in summer (30 kr).

The **Fantoft stave church** was built in Sognefjord in the 12th century and moved to the southern outskirts of Bergen in 1884. Unfortunately, an arsonist burned it down in 1992, but since then it's been painstakingly reconstructed. From Bergen take any bus leaving from platforms 19 to 21, get off at Fantoft and walk uphill for 10 minutes. It's open (20 kr) from 10.30 am to 5.30 pm daily mid-May to mid-September.

If you want to continue on to the former lakeside home and workshop of composer Edvard Grieg, get back on the bus until the Hopsbroen stop and follow the signs to **Troldhaugen,** a 20-minute walk. If you're not a big Grieg fan, however, you might not find this low-key museum (40 kr) worth the effort. It's open from 9 am to 5.30 pm daily in summer.

Activities
Cable Cars & Hiking For an unbeatable city view, take the **funicular** to the top of 320-metre Mt Fløyen. If you also want to do some hiking, well-marked trails lead into the forest from the hill-top station. Trail 3 makes a

NORWAY

1.3-km loop around a lake, and trails 1 and 2 each make five-km loops through hilly woodlands. For a delightful 40-minute walk back to the city, take trail 4 and connect with trail 6. The funicular runs from 7.30 am to 11 pm (midnight in summer) on the hour and half-hour and costs 15 kr one way.

The **Ulriksbanen cable car** to the top of 642-metre Mt Ulriken offers a panoramic view of the city and surrounding fjord and mountains. There's a 70 kr ticket that includes the cable car and a return bus from the tourist office in Bergen. It's also possible to take the cable car one way (25 kr) and walk across to the funicular station at Mt Fløyen along a well-beaten trail that takes about three hours.

For information on wilderness hiking and hut rentals, contact the DNT office (☎ 55 32 22 30), Tverrgaten 4.

Norway in a Nutshell The railway sells a packaged ticket combining a morning train from Bergen to Flåm, a ferry up the spectacular Nærøyfjord to Gudvangen, a bus to Voss and a train back to Bergen in time for a late dinner. It makes for a very scenic day trip at 450 kr.

Special Events
The Bergen International Festival (☎ 55 31 21 70), held for 12 days at the end of May, is the big cultural event of the year with quality dance, music and folklore events taking place throughout the city.

Places to Stay
Camping The closest camping ground is *Bergenshallen Camping* (☎ 55 27 01 80) in Landås, 10 minutes from the city centre by bus No 3.

Hostels The 150-bed *YMCA Interrail Centre* (☎ 55 31 72 52), Nedre Korskirkealmenning 4, is a good central place to crash. Open from 15 June to 1 September, the centre has friendly staff, kitchen access and a reception that's open from 7.30 am to 1 am. You can choose between same-sex or coed

dorms; the cost is 100 kr. There's a grocery store and a good bakery just metres away.

The other in-town option is *Intermission* (☎ 55 31 32 75), in a period home at Kalfarveien 5, where the hospitable Christian Student Fellowship provides dorm space for 95 kr. It's open from late June to mid-August. A kitchen, laundry facilities and 20 kr breakfasts are available.

The 230-bed HI-affiliated *Montana Hostel* (☎ 55 29 29 00), at Johan Blytts vei 30, five km from the city centre by bus No 4, is open from 6 January to 20 December. Dorm beds cost 150 kr, breakfast included, and doubles cost from 400 kr.

Private Rooms & Pensions The tourist office books rooms in private homes from 160/270 kr for singles/doubles, plus a 15/20 kr booking fee.

Olsnes Guesthouse (☎ 55 31 20 44), Skivebakken 24, is in a quiet neighbourhood of older homes, a five-minute walk from the train station (turn uphill opposite the Leprosy Museum). It has 10 adequate rooms, a shared kitchen and a nice mix of Norwegian and foreign travellers. Rooms cost 180/270 kr for singles/doubles with shared bath, 310 kr for a double with private bath.

Kloster Pension (☎ 55 90 21 58), Strangehagen 2, is a popular lodge-style guesthouse which has 18 clean, simple rooms from 300/450 kr including a continental breakfast.

Myklebust Pensjonat (☎ 55 90 16 70), Rosenbergsgaten 19, has six delightfully comfortable rooms with natural wood floors and tasteful décor from 350/450 kr. An optional continental (20 kr) or full (50 kr) breakfast is available.

Hotels *Kalmar Pension* (☎ 55 23 18 60), Jon Smørs gate 11, is at a busy central intersection. Though the size and style of the 45 rooms vary, overall they're adequate for the price, which begins at 300/450 kr singles/doubles with shared bath and kitchen privileges. Breakfast is available for 49 kr.

Bergen Gjestehus (☎ 55 31 96 66), Vestre Torggate 20A, is a 23-room hotel with commodious rooms, simple but not cheerless, most with kitchenettes, TV, phone and private baths. Rates are 450/650 kr in summer, 350/450 kr in winter.

A good top-end hotel is *Hotell Neptun* (☎ 55 90 10 00), Valkendorfsgate 8, which has well-appointed rooms decorated with original artwork. The regular rate is 1095/1350 kr, but there are weekend and summer discounts available with various hotel passes, such as the Bonuspass.

Places to Eat

The bus station is a mecca of cheap-food stalls serving inexpensive sandwiches and pizza, a fruit stand, a grocery store, and the Sol Brød bakery with oversized pastries for 7 kr.

The family-run *Mira Indian Café*, opposite the bus station on Vestre Strømkaien, has vegetarian dishes for 50 kr and meat dishes with rice and nan for 79 kr. It's open from 3 to 11 pm daily.

Ma-Ma Thai, Kaigaten 20, is a cosy Oriental restaurant that attracts university students with its good-value specials, including a selection of 55 kr 'lunches' that can be ordered all day long.

Café Opera, Engen 24, is a trendy place for artists and students, with good, reasonably priced food. Pastas, salads and vegetarian or beef burritos average 50 to 60 kr.

Den Orientalske Kjeller, a basement restaurant at Olav Kyrres gate 28, has a dozen lunch specials (43 to 55 kr) that are served from 1 to 6 pm; otherwise most dishes are about 100 kr.

For a splurge, *Ole Bull* at the Hotel Norge has a pleasant 2nd-floor park view and a tempting buffet that includes cold salmon and shrimp, a few hot dishes, salads and good desserts. The price is 169 kr from noon to 4 pm and 198 kr from 7 to 10 pm.

The popular *Dickens* has a sunny dining room overlooking Ole Bulls plass. A lunch special, often steak and potatoes, costs about 80 kr, as do a variety of salads and light dishes that are served any time. *Michelangelo*, a dinner restaurant at Neumannsgate 25, has authentic Italian food at moderate prices.

Bryggestuen & Bryggeloftet, a two-storey restaurant in the midst of the historic district at Bryggen 11, has a pleasant atmosphere with traditional Norwegian food. At all times except midsummer there's a generous daily special for 69 kr; dishes otherwise begin at about 120 kr. It's open from 11 am to 11.30 pm, on Sunday from 1 pm.

The waterfront Zachariasbryggen, at the inner harbour, houses several pubs and eateries including *Kina Kina*, which offers nine Chinese lunch specials until 6 pm weekdays for 48 kr, the *Baker Brun* konditori with good pastries and sandwiches, a *Peppe's Pizza* and an ice-cream shop.

The *fish market* at Torget is the place to buy fruit and seafood, including tasty open-faced salmon rolls for 10 kr – or pick up a half-kg bag of boiled shrimp or crab legs for 40 kr and munch away down at the harbour. It's open Monday to Saturday from about 8 am to 3 pm.

Grocery stores abound in Bergen. The *Mekka* chain, which has a branch at the bus station, has cheaper prices and longer hours than most. The *Spar* grocery store, opposite the Bryggens Museum, has a takeaway deli with whole grilled chickens for 30 kr. *Kinsarvik Frukt* on Olav Kyrres gate is a small grocery store with a health-food section. The central *Godt Brød*, Nedre Korskirkealmenning 17, has delicious organic breads and pastries, a couple of café tables and long opening hours. Other bakeries are numerous in the centre and many offer reasonably priced sandwiches. Bergen brews its own beer under the Hansa label.

Entertainment

The central *Club Maxime* at Ole Bulls plass has a disco, an English-style pub and a cellar wine bar with live music. *Garage*, Christies gate 14, is Bergen's top rock music venue, and *Hulen*, behind the student centre at Olaf Ryes vei 47, also attracts a university crowd. *Bergen Kino* on Neumannsgate has 13 cinema screens and first-run movies. *Kafé Fincken*, Nygårdsgaten 2A, is a gay meeting place.

Things to Buy

The broadest selection of handicrafts, wooden toys and traditional clothing can be found

NORWAY

at Husfliden, Vågsalmenning 3. The Galleriet shopping centre, north-west of the post office, has boutiques, camera shops, a grocery store and a good bookshop, Melvær Libris. The bus station contains another large shopping centre.

Getting There & Away
Air The airport is in Flesland, 19 km south-east of central Bergen. The SAS Flybussen (40 kr) runs a couple times an hour between the airport and Bergen, stopping at the Braathens SAFE office on Olav Kyrres gate and the SAS Hotel beside the Bryggens Museum.

Bus Daily express buses run to Odda in Hardanger (four hours, 195 kr) and to the western fjord region. From Bergen it costs 315 kr (seven hours) to Stryn, 445 kr (10½ hours) to Ålesund and 715 kr (14½ hours) to Trondheim. There's a bus from Bergen to Stavanger (5¾ hours, 340 kr) at least twice daily.

Train Trains to Oslo (seven hours, 490 kr) depart several times a day; seat reservations are required. In addition, local trains run regularly between Bergen and Voss (1¼ hours, 105 kr). The train station has 10 kr-lockers.

Car The main highway into Bergen is the E16. There's a 5 kr toll for vehicles entering the city on weekdays from 6 am to 10 pm.

Car Rental These companies have offices in Bergen centre:

Avis
    Lars Hilles gate 20 (☎ 55 32 01 30)
Budget
    Lodin Leppsgate 1 (☎ 55 90 26 15)
Thrifty
    Jon Smørs gate 8 (☎ 55 90 22 50)

Boat There's a daily Sognefjord express boat to Balestrand and Flåm, a northbound express boat to Måløy and a southbound express boat to Stavanger. All leave from the west side of Vågen.

The coastal steamer, *Hurtigruten*, leaves from the quay south of the university at 10.30 pm daily. Details are in the introductory Getting Around section to this chapter.

Boats to Newcastle, Iceland, Scotland and Denmark dock north of Rosenkrantz tower; for details see this chapter's introductory Getting There & Away section.

Getting Around
The bus fare within the city boundaries is 13 kr per ride. A free bus runs between the post office and the bus station. Taxis line up along Ole Bulls plass or you can call ☎ 55 99 70 00.

If you have a car, it's best to park it and explore the city centre on foot. Except in spots where there are parking meters, street parking is reserved for residents with special zone-parking stickers; if you see a 'P' for parking but the sign has 'sone' on it, it's a reserved area. Metered parking has a 30-minute limit in the busiest spots, two hours elsewhere including lots on the west side of the Grieghallen concert hall and the north side of Lille Lungegårdsvann. Less restricted are the indoor car parks; the largest one (open 24 hours a day) is Bygarasjen at the bus station.

During the summer, Bergen Kommune rents bicycles at the kiosk on the square near Husfliden, opposite the post office.

SOGNEFJORD
The Sognefjord is Norway's longest (200 km) and deepest (1300 metres) fjord – a wide slash across the map of western Norway. In some places sheer lofty walls rise more than 1000 metres straight up from the water, while in others there is a far gentler shoreline with farms, orchards and small towns sloping up the mountainsides.

The Sognefjord's broad main waterway is impressive, but it's by cruising into the fjord's narrower arms that you get closest to the steep rock faces and cascading waterfalls. The loveliest branch is the deeply cut Nærøyfjord, Norway's narrowest fjord.

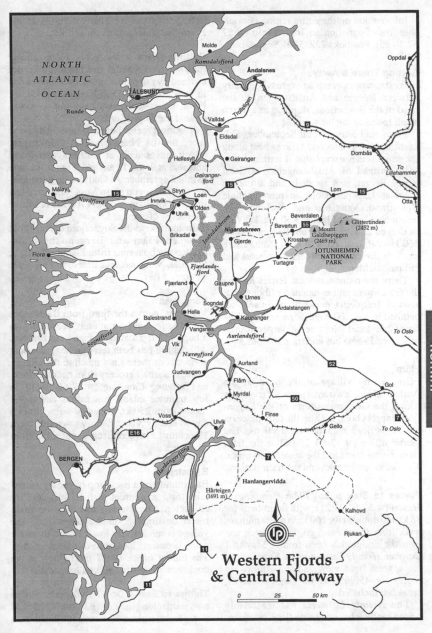

Western Fjords & Central Norway

0   25   50 km

Information on the entire region is available from Sognefjorden Tourist Info (☎ 57 67 30 83), Postboks 222, 5801 Sogndal.

Getting There & Away

Fylkesbaatane operates an express boat daily between Bergen and Årdalstangen, at the head of the Sognefjord, stopping at a dozen small towns along the way.

From mid-May to mid-September, Fylkesbaatane runs a second express boat along the same route, except that it terminates in Flåm instead of Årdalstangen. This boat leaves Bergen at 8 am daily and arrives in Flåm at 1.25 pm; stops en route include Balestrand, Vangsnes and Aurland. The return boat leaves Flåm at 3.30 pm, arriving in Bergen at 8.45 pm. From Bergen it costs 360 kr to Balestrand, 430 kr to Flåm. There are 50% discounts for students, spouses and rail pass holders.

There are numerous local ferries linking the fjord towns and an extensive (though not always frequent) network of buses, all detailed in the 200-page *Sogn og Fjordane* timetable available free at larger tourist offices and some bus and train stations.

Flåm

Flåm, a tiny village at the head of the Aurlandsfjord, is a transit point for travellers taking the Gudvangen ferry or the Sognefjord express boat. It's also the only place on the Sognefjord with rail connections. The tourist office (☎ 57 63 21 06) at the train station rents bikes and the hostel rents boats. The docks are just beyond the train station.

Places to Stay & Eat *Flåm Camping & Hostel* (☎ 57 63 21 21), with dorm beds for 85 kr and doubles for 260 kr, is a few minutes walk from the station; go up the track and over the bridge. It's open from 1 May to 1 October. *Heimly Pensjonat* (☎ 57 63 23 00) has a great fjord view and straightforward rooms for 450/650 kr for singles/doubles, breakfast included.

The *Heimly Cafeteria* has reasonably priced sandwiches and a fine fjord-side location, and there are also cafeterias at the *Fretheim Hotel* and the boat dock.

Getting There & Away The Flåm railway runs between Myrdal and Flåm (50 kr, not covered by rail passes) numerous times a day in sync with the Oslo-Bergen service. At Flåm, buses and boats head out to towns around the Sognefjord.

The most scenic boat ride from Flåm is the ferry up the Nærøyfjord to Gudvangen, which leaves daily at 2.30 pm year-round and also at 9 am, 11 am and 2 pm from June to mid-September. At Gudvangen a connecting bus takes you on to Voss. The ferry-bus ticket from Flåm to Voss (162 kr) is sold at the tourist office.

In addition to the Sognefjord express boat between Flåm and Bergen, the Flåm-ekspressen boat runs from Flåm to Aurland, Sogndal, Vangsnes and Balestrand a couple of times a day.

Vangsnes

Vangsnes, across the fjord from Balestrand, is a little farming community crowned with a huge hill-top statue of saga hero Fridtjof. Although it has both ferry and express boat connections there's not much to the village. There is a small grocery store near the dock, and *Solvang Camping* (☎ 57 69 66 20), a few minutes inland, has cabins and motel rooms from 250 kr. Buses go a few times a day to nearby Vik, a factory town that has a 12-century **stave church** about a km from its centre.

Balestrand

Balestrand has a backdrop of snowy mountains and a genteel British hill-country character. Considering that it's the main resort destination on the Sognefjord, the village is remarkably low-key and there are some pleasant, inexpensive places to stay. The tourist office (☎ 57 69 12 55), at the dock, rents bikes for 50 kr a half day.

Things to See & Do The village road that runs south along the fjord has little traffic and is a pleasant place to stroll. It's lined with apple orchards, ornate older homes and gardens, a 19th-century English church and Viking burial mounds. One mound is topped by a statue of the legendary King Bele, erected by Germany's Kaiser Wilhelm II who spent his holidays here regularly until WWI.

For a longer hike take the small ferry (10 kr) across the Esefjord to the Dragsvik side, where an abandoned country road is the first leg of an eight-km walk back to Balestrand.

Places to Stay & Eat At *Sjøtun Camping* (☎ 57 69 12 23), a 15-minute walk south along the fjord, you can pitch a tent amidst apple trees or rent a rustic four-bunk cabin for 175 kr.

Balestrand Hostel (☎ 57 69 13 03), in the lodge-style Kringsjå Hotel, has dorm beds/ doubles for 145/420 kr, breakfast included; it's open from mid-June to mid-August. The Victorian *Bøyum Pensjonat* (☎ 57 69 11 14), open in summer only, has singles/ doubles for 200/300 kr. Both places are minutes from the dock.

Midtnes Pensjonat (☎ 57 69 11 33), next to the English church, is popular with returning British holiday-makers, and costs from 475/590 kr with breakfast.

There's a fast-food café opposite the dock, the hostel restaurant serves dinner for 95 kr and there's an up-market restaurant at the fjordside *Kvikne's Hotel*.

Getting There & Away In addition to the Sognefjord express boat, local boats run daily to Flåm, Hella and Fjærland.

Buses, some of which must be picked up across the fjord in Vangsnes, go to Sogndal (68 kr) and Bergen (200 kr). Taking the bus to Bergen is not only cheaper than the express boat, but also more scenic, as the road passes Vik's Hopperstad stave church and climbs through the impressive Vika mountains on the way to Voss.

Fjærland

Fjærland is a farming village at the head of scenic Fjærlandsfjord and near two arms of the massive glacier **Jostedalsbreen**, an inviting location for day-trippers.

Things to See & Do From Balestrand you can take the 8.30 am ferry to Fjærland and a connecting bus (90 kr) to the glacier. En route the bus stops at the **Norwegian Glacier Centre** (65 kr), which has educational displays and a film on Jostedalsbreen. The bus visits two arms of the glacier: the **Supphellebreen**, where you can walk up to the edge and touch the ice; and the creaking blue-iced **Bøyabreen**, where it's not uncommon to witness small breaks dropping into the meltwater beneath the glacier. Alternatively, a taxi from the Fjærland dock to the glacier, with waiting time, costs about 200 kr return.

Getting There & Away Ferries run a few times daily between Fjærland and Balestrand (1¼ hours, 35 kr), stopping in Hella en route. Buses connect Fjærland and Sogndal (35 minutes, 43 kr). There are also daily bus departures from Fjærland to Stryn (two hours, 115 kr), including a weekday 9.45 am bus that has onward connections to Hellesylt and Geiranger.

Sogndal

Sogndal is a modern regional centre of little note but it's a starting point for day trips in the surrounding area. Of most interest is the glacier Nigardsbreen 70 km to the north, followed by Norway's oldest **stave church** (circa 1130) in Urnes across the Lustrafjord, and the **Sogn Folk Museum** near Kaupanger. The tourist office (☎ 57 67 30 83) is at Kulturhus on Gravensteinsgata, about a five-minute walk east of the bus station.

Places to Stay & Eat The tourist office books rooms in private homes from about 100 kr per person. There's a summer *hostel* (☎ 57 67 20 33) 15 minutes east of the bus station that costs 90 kr for a dorm room, 160/ 210 kr for singles/doubles.

Good places for cheap eats are the cafeterias in the adjacent *Domus* and *K-Sentret* supermarkets on Gravensteinsgata.

Getting There & Away Buses run from Sogndal to Kaupanger (20 kr) and Hella (43 kr), sites of the nearest boat connections.

NORWAY

Daily buses go north-east to Lom (3½ hours, 112 kr) and on to Otta (4¼ hours, 158 kr), a hiking centre between the Jotunheimen and Rondane mountains on the Dovre railway line. Sogndal has Sognefjord's only airport.

Nigardsbreen

Nigardsbreen, the most attractive arm of the Jostedalsbreen glacier, is a popular summer destination, with guided hikes across the glacier's rippled blue ice. Outings include easy 1½-hour family walks (80 kr); hardy four-hour blue-ice treks (250 kr) that cross deep crevices and require hiking boots and warm clothing; and a couple of day-long options. More information on glacier walks is available from Jostedal Breheimsenteret (☎ 57 68 32 50), 5827 Jostedal, or at nearby tourist offices.

A bus leaves Sogndal at 8.50 am for the glacier, and a return bus leaves Nigardsbreen at 5 pm. The fare is 73 kr each way. Although this will give you time to do a short hike, if you're doing a longer hike you might want to stay in rural Gjerde, five km from Nigardsbreen, where there are pensions and camping grounds.

NORDFJORD

For most travellers the 100-km-long Nordfjord is but a stepping stone between the Sognefjord and the Geirangerfjord. The latter two fjords are linked by a road that winds around the head of the Nordfjord past the villages of Utvik, Innvik, Olden and Loen to the larger town of Stryn.

If you want to break your journey there are fjord-side lodging and camping grounds en route and a *hostel* at Stryn (☎ 57 87 11 06) open from mid-May to mid-September.

The chief Nordfjord attraction is **Briksdal glacier**, one of Jostedal's icy arms. Although a barrage of package-tour buses make the drive up Olden valley to Briksdal, there's only one public bus. It leaves Stryn (10 am, 49 kr) and Olden (10.15 am, 30 kr) daily from mid-June to mid-August, arriving at Briksdal at 11 am.

From there it's a three-km hike to the glacier – give yourself about two hours re-

turn. Briksdal has a lodge, *Briksdalsbre Fjellstove* (☎ 57 87 38 11), charging 250 kr a person, and there's also a camping ground, a café, souvenir shops and pony cart rides to the glacier for those who don't want to walk. The return bus leaves Briksdal at 1.45 pm.

Getting There & Away

There are about four daily buses (only one on Saturday) between Stryn and Fjærland (two hours, 115 kr), including a southbound one daily at 8.45 am.

Afternoon buses run in both directions between Stryn and Hellesylt (one hour, 58 kr), connecting with the Geiranger ferry.

Måløy, a fishing town at the mouth of the Nordfjord, can be reached by daily buses from Stryn (two hours, 109 kr), the express boat from Bergen (4½ hours, 445 kr) and the coastal steamer.

JOTUNHEIMEN NATIONAL PARK

The road between Sogndal and Lom passes the north-west perimeter of Jotunheimen National Park, Norway's most popular wilderness destination. Hiking trails lead to the park's 60 glaciers, up to the top of Norway's loftiest peaks (2469-metre Mt Galdhøpiggen and 2452-metre Glittertinden) and along ravine-like valleys with deep lakes and plunging waterfalls. There are DNT huts and private lodges along many of the routes.

From **Turtagrø**, a rock-climbing centre midway between Sogndal and Lom, there's a three-hour hike to Fannaråkhytte, Jotunheimen's highest (2069 metres) DNT hut, which offers great panoramic views. **Krossbu** is in the midst of a network of trails, including a short one to the Smørstabbreen glacier.

The 75-bed *Krossbu Turiststasjon* (☎ 61 21 29 22) has singles/doubles for 135/270 kr with your own sleeping bag. The town of **Bøverdalen**, 18 km south of Lom, has a *hostel* (☎ 61 21 20 64), which is open from late May to 30 September and has dorm beds/doubles for 75/190 kr.

ÅNDALSNES

Åndalsnes, at the edge of the Romsdalsfjord, is the northern gateway to the western fjords.

Most visitors arrive on the train from Dombås, a scenic route that descends through a deeply cut valley with dramatic waterfalls. Just before reaching Åndalsnes the train passes **Trollveggen**, whose jagged and often cloud-shrouded summit is considered the ultimate challenge among Norwegian mountain climbers. The road (route 9) between Dombås and Åndalsnes runs parallel to the railway line and is equally spectacular.

The town of Åndalsnes is rather nondescript, but the scenery is top notch. Camping grounds are plentiful and it has one of the finest hostels in Norway. The tourist office (☎ 71 22 16 22) is at the train station.

Things to See & Do
The **Norsk Tindemuseum**, 2½ km from the centre on the road to Åndalsnes Camping, has exhibits on the climbing expeditions of renowned mountaineer Arne Randers Heen.

The mountains and valleys surrounding Åndalsnes offer excellent **hiking**. One good trail, which goes to the top of Mt Nesaksla, starts right in town 50 metres south of the Esso petrol station, and makes a fine half-day outing. While the path is quite steep, at the top you'll be rewarded with a terrific view of the surrounding fjords and mountains. In summer the ascent can be hot in the midday sun, so get an early start and be sure to take water.

Serious mountain climbers will want to contact the **Aak Fjellsportsenter** (☎ 71 22 64 44), Postboks 238, 6301 Åndalsnes, which is four km from Åndalsnes on the way to Dombås. The centre offers mountaineering courses, sells topographic maps, rents skis and mountain-climbing equipment, and has a few rooms for rent.

Places to Stay & Eat
Åndalsnes Camping (☎ 71 22 16 29), three km from the centre on the south-east side of the Rauma River, has heated cabins from 210 kr. It rents canoes for 40 kr an hour, mountain bikes for 90 kr a day and cars for 550 kr a day.

The best place to stay in Åndalsnes is the sod-roofed *Setnes Hostel* (☎ 71 22 13 82),

two km from the train station on route 9. Open from 15 May to 15 September, the hostel has pleasant rooms with singles/doubles for 200/275 kr and dorm beds for 100 kr. Don't miss the famous pancakes-to-fried-fish breakfast (55 kr). If you don't want to walk, catch the Ålesund bus, which meets the train and goes past the hostel.

If the hostel is full, the nearby *Romsdal Gjestegård* (☎ 71 22 13 83) has straightforward rooms for 320/490 kr with breakfast and pleasantly rustic two-bedroom cabins with kitchens for 500 kr.

The train station sells fruit and sandwiches and there are a couple of grocery stores and cafeteria-style restaurants nearby in the centre. The nearest cafeteria to the hostel is *Vertshuset Rauma* on the E69 at the west side of the river.

Getting There & Away
The train from Dombås runs three times daily (1½ hours, 135 kr), in sync with Oslo-Trondheim trains. Buses to Ålesund, an attractive coast town, and Molde, noted for its summer jazz festival, meet the trains. Buses to Geiranger (three hours, 111 kr) via the Trollstigen highway operate from 15 June to 31 August, leaving Åndalsnes at 6.45 am and 5.05 pm. If you have your own car, the mountain pass is cleared and open by at least 1 June every year, and early in the season it's an awesome drive through deep walls of snow.

FROM ÅNDALSNES TO GEIRANGER
The **Trollstigen** (Troll's Path) winding south from Åndalsnes is a thriller of a road with hairpin bends, a 1:12 gradient and, to add a daredevil element, it's practically one lane all the way. The bus makes photo stops at the thundering 180-metre **Stigfossen waterfall** on its way up to the mountain pass. At the top it usually stops long enough for you to walk to a lookout with a dizzying view back down the valley.

There are waterfalls galore smoking down the mountains as you descend to **Valldal**. You could break your journey in Valldal – there are camping grounds, cabins and a hostel – though most travellers continue on, taking the short ferry ride across to **Eidsdal**. From there a waiting bus continues along the Ørneveien (Eagle's Highway), ending with a magnificent bird's-eye view of the Geirangerfjord before descending into Geiranger village.

GEIRANGERFJORD

The 16-km Geirangerfjord is narrow and winding with towering rock faces, a scattering of abandoned farms clinging to the cliffsides, and breathtakingly high waterfalls with names such as Seven Sisters, Suitor and Bridal Veil.

The villages of Geiranger and Hellesylt, at either end of the fjord, are connected by ferry. The cruise down the Geirangerfjord is Norway's most stunning and shouldn't be missed.

Geiranger

Geiranger, at the head of the Geirangerfjord, is surrounded by high mountains with cascading waterfalls. Although the village has only 300 residents, it's one of Norway's most visited spots. Nevertheless, it's reasonably serene in the evening when the cruise ships and tour buses have gone.

There's great hiking all around Geiranger to abandoned farmsteads, waterfalls and some beautiful vista points. One special walk is to **Storseter waterfall**, a 45-minute hike that actually takes you between the rock face and the cascading falls. The tourist office (☎ 70 26 30 99), at the pier next to the post office, has an album detailing trails.

Places to Stay & Eat Hotels in Geiranger can be quickly booked out by package tourists, but cabins and camping spots are plentiful. A dozen camping grounds skirt the fjord and hillsides, including *Geiranger Camping* (☎ 70 26 31 20), right in town at the head of the fjord.

The *Grande Fjord Hotell* (☎ 70 26 30 90), on the fjord two km north-east of the village, has cabins, tent space and moderately priced motel rooms. You can find *husrom* signs around the village advertising

rooms for rent, or for 20 kr the tourist office will book one for you. Either way they average 200/300 kr for singles/doubles.

Naustkroa, near the pier in the town centre, has pizza and other inexpensive fare, and the nearby *Olebuda* has good seafood dishes and salads at moderate prices. You can pick up groceries at a couple of small stores in town.

Getting There & Away In summer there are daily buses to Åndalsnes leaving Geiranger at 1 and 6.10 pm, as well as buses to Ålesund and Molde. The Geiranger-Hellesylt ferry (70 minutes, passengers 30 kr, cars 95 kr) cruises the fjord four to 10 times a day from 1 May to 29 September.

Hellesylt

Although this end of the fjord is not as spectacular as at Geiranger, the village of Hellesylt does have a dockside tourist office (☎ 70 26 50 52) that rents rowing boats and fishing rods. There's also a fine summer *hostel* (☎ 70 26 51 28) perched just above town with dorms (100 kr) and a row of cabins (280 kr) with fjord views. Buses heading south to Stryn (one hour, 56 kr) leave from the pier where the ferry pulls in.

ÅLESUND

Ålesund is an agreeable coastal town with central streets lined with turn-of-the-century Art Nouveau buildings erected after a sweeping fire in 1904. Compact and easy to explore, much of the town can be seen during the three-hour coastal steamer stop. There's a local history museum (20 kr), but the most popular thing to do is to walk the 418 steps up Mount Aksla for a splendid view of Ålesund and the surrounding islands. Take Lihauggata from the pedestrian shopping street Kongensgade to begin the 15-minute walk to the top of the hill. The helpful tourist office (☎ 70 12 12 02) is in the town hall, opposite the bus station.

Ålesund could also make a good base for touring the region. Not only is it a jumping-off point for the island of Runde, but on summer weekdays it's possible to make a scenic bus-ferry day trip (275 kr) that includes a cruise down the Geirangerfjord, three hours in Geiranger and a return to Ålesund via the Eagle's Highway.

Places to Stay & Eat
Prinsen Camping (☎ 70 15 52 04), east of town, has tent space and cabins (bus No 14; 13 kr). The new *Ålesund Hostel* (☎ 70 12 04 25), in the centre of town at Parkgata 14, has 125 kr dorm beds and cooking and laundry facilities. The *Atlantic Hotel* (☎ 70 12 91 00), beside the bus station, has modern rooms and a summer rate of 490/580 kr for singles/doubles.

There's a pleasant, reasonably priced cafeteria in the Atlantic Hotel. *Café Hoffmann*, Kongensgate 11, has a fine harbour view and simple food such as fish soup with bread for about 35 kr; there's a bakery in the same shopping centre.

Getting There & Away
There are daily buses to Hellesylt (2½ hours, 112 kr), Åndalsnes (2½ hours, 134 kr) and other major coastal and fjord towns. The northbound coastal steamer arrives at noon and departs at 3 pm.

RUNDE
The island of Runde, 67 km south-west of Ålesund, has just 160 inhabitants but plays host to half a million sea birds, including migrating puffins that arrive in May and stay until late July. Most birding sites are best seen by sea; half-day bird-watching boat tours cost about 150 kr.

The harbourside *Runde Hostel & Camping* (☎ 70 08 59 16) has dorm beds (80 kr), cabins (220 kr) and tent space. Use the guest kitchen or eat at the café.

Runde is connected by bridge to the mainland. A catamaran-bus combination departs from Ålesund (2½ hours, 96 kr) daily in summer; on weekdays it's possible to do it as a day trip, leaving Ålesund at 8.30 am.

LILLEHAMMER
Lillehammer, population 23,000, has long been a popular ski resort for Norwegians,

and since hosting the 1994 Winter Olympics it has attracted foreign visitors as well.

Orientation & Information
Lillehammer centre is small and easy to explore. Storgata, the main pedestrian walkway, is two short blocks east of the adjacent bus and train stations. The main tourist office (☎ 61 25 92 99) is at Elvegata 19; there's a branch office at the train station. The DNT office, Storgata 82, sells hiking and skiing maps and has information on trail huts.

Things to See & Do
Until interest wanes, it's possible to tour the Winter Olympic sites, including Håkons Hall (the hockey venue), the ski jump and the bobsleigh areas; the main tourist brochure lists opening times and admission fees.

At Hunderfossen, 15 km north of town, speed fanatics can ride a bobsleigh down the actual Olympic run – in summer, when there's no ice, a 'wheeled bob' is used. This popular ride costs 120 kr; reservations (☎ 61 27 75 50) are advised.

For in-town activities, there's a downhill ski and bobsleigh simulator ride (35 kr) near Håkons Hall. The Olympiasenteret, Elvegata 19, features Olympic exhibits, is open from 10 am to 5 pm (to 8 pm in summer) and costs 50 kr.

The Olympics aside, Lillehammer's main attraction is the exceptional **Maihaugen folk museum**, a collection of historic farm buildings and a stave church in a traditional village setting. There are guided tours in English and workshop demonstrations by interpreters in period costumes. It's open from 10 am to 5 pm in May and September, 9 am to 7 pm June to August, and costs 60 kr. Maihaugen is a 20-minute walk from the train station; go up Jernbanegata, right on Anders Sandvigs gate and left up Maihaugvegen.

Lillehammer also has an **automobile museum**, an **art museum** and the **Kulturhuset Banken**, a century-old bank restored as a cultural centre.

Lillehammer is at the northern end of **Mjøsa**, Norway's largest lake, which is

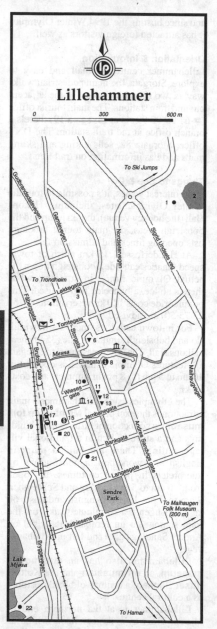

Lillehammer

0   300   600 m

To Ski Jumps

To Trondheim

Gudbrandsdalsvegen

Gamlevegen

Nordsetervegen

Sigrid Undsets veg

Lekkegata

Tomtegata

Storgata

Fåberggata

Brudos gate

Mesna

Elvegata

Wieses gate

Jernbanegata

Bankgata

Andnes Sandvigs gate

Mathisensvegen

Langesgate

Søndre Park

Mathiesens gate

Brygevegen

Lake Mjøsa

To Maihaugen Folk Museum (200 m)

To Hamar

edged with farms, forests and small towns. From mid-June to mid-August the *Skibladner* (☎ 62 52 70 85), the world's oldest operating **paddle steamer**, cruises from one end to the other. On Tuesday, Thursday and Saturday the boat sails at 11 am from Hamar to Lillehammer (3¾ hours, 135 kr), leaving Lillehammer at 3 pm for the return trip to Hamar.

Places to Stay & Eat

The *Lillehammer Hostel* (☎ 61 26 25 66), upstairs at the bus station, has 32 rooms each with four beds, shower and toilet. Beds cost 165 kr, singles/doubles 320/450 kr, breakfast included.

A fine budget option is the friendly *Gjeste Bu* (☎ 61 25 43 21), Gamleveien 10, a guest-house with dorm beds for 60 kr and singles/doubles from 175/250 kr. Rooms are simple, bathrooms are shared and sheets rent for 40 kr if you don't have your own. There's a group kitchen, free coffee and a TV room. Reception is open from 9 am to 11 pm; breakfast is available for 30 kr at a nearby bakery.

PLACES TO STAY
3   Gjeste Bu
17 Lillehammer Hostel
20 Best Western Breiseth Hotel

PLACES TO EAT
4   Bakery
6   M-Burger
11 Peppe's Pizza
12 Bakery
13 Caroline Café
16 Café Fønix

OTHER
1   Ski & Bobsleigh Simulator
2   Håkons Hall
5   Post Office
7   Automobile Museum
8   Tourist Office & Olympiasenteret
9   Grocery Store
10 DNT Office & Bookstore
14 Art Museum
15 Kreditkassen Bank
18 Bus Station
19 Train Station
21 Kulturhuset Banken (Cultural Centre)
22 Skibladner Dock

NORWAY

The cheapest central hotel is the *Best Western Breiseth Hotell* (☎ 61 26 95 00), opposite the train station, which has rooms in summer from 495/700 kr.

Café Fønix, adjacent to the hostel, has reasonably priced cafeteria fare. Storgata is lined with numerous shops, bakeries and restaurants, including a *Peppe's Pizza* and an inexpensive *Caroline Café*. *M-Burger*, a pavement stand, up Lysgårdsvegen from Storgata, has the best burgers in town.

Getting There & Away

Lillehammer is on the Dovre railway line between Oslo (three hours, 220 kr) and Trondheim (five hours, 395 kr). There are four daily trains from Trondheim and seven from Oslo.

Northern Norway

The counties of Sør Trøndelag, Nord Trøndelag, Nordland, Troms and Finnmark comprise a vast and varied area stretching over 1500 km, mostly north of the Arctic Circle. The terrain ranges from majestic coastal mountains that rise above tiny fishing villages and scattered farms to the barren treeless arctic plateau in the far north.

Trains run as far north as Bodø and from there it's all buses and boats. Because distances are long, bus travel costs can pile up, though Inter-Rail and Scanrail holders get a 50% discount on express buses between Bodø and Kirkenes. A fine alternative to land travel is the *Hurtigruten* coastal steamer, which pulls into every sizeable port between Bergen and Kirkenes, passing some of Europe's best coastal scenery along the way.

RØROS

Røros is an old copper-mining town with a well-preserved historic district that's on UNESCO's World Heritage list. The first mine opened in 1644 and the last one closed in 1986. The town makes for delightful strolling and everything's within easy walking distance. The tourist office (☎ 72 41 00

00) is on Peder Hiortsgata 2, a two-minute walk north-east of the train station.

Things to See & Do

Røros' main attractions are turf-roofed **miners' cottages** and other centuries-old timber buildings, a prominent 1784 **church** with a baroque interior, **slag heaps**, and the old smelting works, which is now a **mining museum**. The museum (35 kr) features intricate scale models of life in the mines and is open daily year-round; summer hours are from 10.30 am to 6 pm on weekdays, to 4 pm on weekends.

You can also visit the defunct **Olav copper mine** (35 kr), 12 km north-east of town. In summer, subterranean tours into the mine (5°C – bring a sweater!) are given six times daily between 10.30 am and 6 pm. In July and early August, a special bus to the mine departs from the train station (60 kr return) at 1 pm (10 am on Saturday).

Places to Stay & Eat

Idrettsparken Hostel (☎ 72 41 10 89), Øra 25, at the edge of a sports stadium one km from the train station, has camping, dorm beds (160 kr), private rooms (260/360 kr for singles/doubles) and cabins (330 kr). To get there, walk east from the train station, cross the tracks opposite Bergstadens Hotel and follow the signs.

Ertzscheidergården (☎ 72 41 11 94), a 15-room guesthouse at Spell Olaveien 6, is but a stone's throw from the church and mining museum. Singles/doubles cost from 350/580 kr, breakfast included.

Within a block of the tourist office there are a couple of bakeries and a *Domus supermarket* with an inexpensive cafeteria. *Soloppgangen Helse & Miljø*, a health-food store, is at Kjerkgata 6. *Rammkjellarn*, in an historic building at Kjerkgata 34, has a nice atmosphere and a varied menu.

Getting There & Away

Røros is 46 km west of the Swedish border, via route 31. It's also a stop on the eastern railway line between Oslo (six hours, 430 kr) and Trondheim (2½ hours, 200 kr). Røros has the highest altitude of any town in Norway – both the railway line and the parallel route 30 between Røros and Trondheim pass snow-capped mountains, rushing streams and small farms.

TRONDHEIM

Trondheim, Norway's third-largest city and its first capital, is a lively university town with a rich medieval history. Founded at the estuary of the winding Nidelva River in 997 by the Viking king Olaf Tryggvason, the city is currently celebrating its millennium. After a fire razed most of the city in 1681, Trondheim was redesigned by General Caspar de Cicignon with wide streets and a Renaissance flair. Today, the steeple of the medieval Nidaros cathedral is still the highest point in town.

Orientation & Information

The central part of town is on a triangular peninsula that's easy to explore on foot. The train station and coastal steamer quay are across the canal, a few minutes north of the centre.

Torvet, the central square, has a fruit market, a head-on view of the cathedral, a statue of King Olaf and a 12th-century stone church.

The tourist office (☎ 73 92 93 94) at Torvet (Postboks 2102, 7001 Trondheim) is open from 8.30 am (10 am Sunday) to 8 pm from mid-May to late August, weekdays 9 am to 4 pm the rest of the year.

The library, open weekdays to 4 pm and Saturday to 2 pm, has a fine collection of international newspapers.

Things to See

Nidaros Domkirke The grand Nidaros Cathedral is the city's most dominant landmark and Scandinavia's largest medieval building. The first church on this site was built in 1070 over the grave of St Olaf, the Viking king who replaced the worship of Nordic gods with Christianity. The oldest wing of the current building dates back to the 12th century.

One of the most spectacular parts of the cathedral is the ornately embellished exterior west wall, which is lined with statues of biblical characters and Norwegian bishops and kings.

The interior of the cathedral is open daily. Weekday hours are from 9 am to 5.30 pm from mid-June to mid-August, until 3 pm in spring and early autumn, and noon to 2.30 pm the rest of the year. It always closes at 2 pm on Saturday and is open from 1 to 4 pm (to 3 pm in winter) on Sunday. Admission is 12 kr, which includes entrance to the adjacent 12th-century **Archbishop's Palace**, the oldest secular building in Norway.

The cathedral, which is the site of Norwegian coronations, also displays the crown jewels in summer from 9.30 am to 12.30 pm weekdays and 1 to 4 pm on Sunday, the rest of the year from noon to 2 pm on Friday only. From mid-June to mid-August visitors can climb the cathedral tower (5 kr) for a rooftop view of the city.

If old swords, armour and cannons sound interesting, visit the **Rustkammeret military museum** (5 kr) out the back.

Museums The eclectic **Museum of Applied Art**, Munkegata 5, has a fine collection of contemporary arts and crafts ranging from Japanese pottery by Shoji Hamada to tapestries by Hannah Ryggen, Scandinavia's most acclaimed tapestry artist. It's open from 10 am to 5 pm weekdays and from noon to 5 pm on Sunday from 20 June to 20 August, with earlier closing times the rest of the year. Admission is 25 kr.

Trondhjems Kunstforening, an art museum (20 kr) at Bispegata 7, has a hallway of Munch lithographs. Trondheim also has a small **maritime museum** (20 kr) and the **University Museum of Natural History & Archaeology** (25 kr).

The **Ringve Museum** at Lade Allé 60, four km north-east of the city centre (bus No 4), is a fascinating music history museum in a period estate. Music students from the university give tours, demonstrating the antique instruments on display. Tours in English are given daily at 11 am, 12.30 and 2.30 pm in

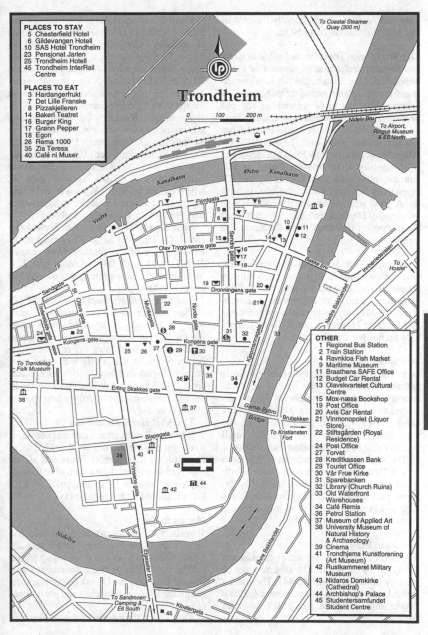

PLACES TO STAY
5 Chesterfield Hotel
6 Gildevangen Hotell
10 SAS Hotel Trondheim
23 Pensjonat Jarlen
25 Trondheim Hotell
45 Trondheim InterRail Centre

PLACES TO EAT
3 Hardangerfrukt
7 Det Lille Franske
8 Pizzakjelleren
14 Bakeri Teatret
16 Burger King
17 Grønn Pepper
18 Egon
26 Rema 1000
35 Zia Teresa
40 Café ni Muser

Trondheim

To Coastal Steamer Quay (300 m)

Nidelv Bru

To Airport, Ringve Museum & E6 North

0   100   200 m

Kanalhavn

Østre Kanalhavn

Vestre

Fjordgata

Olav Tryggvasons gate

Sandre gate

Bakke bru

Innherredsveien

To Hostel

Dronningens gate

Sandgate

St Olavs gate

Tordenskidds gate

Munkegata

Norde gate

Kjøpmannsgata

Nedre Bakklandet

Kongens gate

Kongens. gate

To Trøndelag Folk Museum

Erling Skakkes gate

Gamle Bybro Bridge

Brubakken

To Kristiansten Fort

Bispegata

Prinsens gate

Øvre Bakklandet

Elgeseter bru

Nidelva

To Sandmoen Camping & E6 South

Klostergata

OTHER
1 Regional Bus Station
2 Train Station
4 Ravnkloa Fish Market
9 Maritime Museum
11 Braathens SAFE Office
12 Budget Car Rental
13 Olavskvartelet Cultural Centre
15 Mox-næss Bookshop
19 Post Office
20 Avis Car Rental
21 Vinmonopolet (Liquor Store)
22 Stiftsgården (Royal Residence)
24 Post Office
27 Torvet
28 Kreditkassen Bank
29 Tourist Office
30 Vår Frue Kirke
31 Sparebanken
32 Library (Church Ruins)
33 Old Waterfront Warehouses
34 Café Remis
36 Petrol Station
37 Museum of Applied Art
38 University Museum of Natural History & Archaeology
39 Cinema
41 Trondhjems Kunstforening (Art Museum)
42 Rustkammeret Military Museum
43 Nidaros Domkirke (Cathedral)
44 Archbishop's Palace
45 Studentersamfundet Student Centre

NORWAY

July and August, less frequently the rest of the year. Admission costs 50 kr.

Old Trondheim The excavated **ruins of early medieval churches** can be viewed free in the basement of the Sparebanken at Søndre gate 4 and inside the entrance of the public library nearby. Also not to be missed are the old **waterfront warehouses** resembling Bergen's Bryggen which are best viewed from Gamle Bybro (the Old Town Bridge). There's a good city view from the top of the 17th-century **Kristiansten Fort**, a 10-minute uphill walk from Gamle Bybro. It's open daily in summer to 3 pm, admission 3 kr. A good strolling area is the cobblestone west end of Dronningens gate, which is lined with wooden buildings from the mid-19th century.

Trøndelag Folk Museum At Sverresborg, this open-air folk museum has good hill-top views of the city and 60 period buildings including a small 12th-century stave church. From 20 May to 31 August it's open daily (40 kr) from 11 am to 6 pm. It's a 10-minute ride on bus No 8 or 9.

Activities
A popular place to sunbathe and picnic is **Munkholmen** island, the site of an 11th-century Benedictine monastery later converted to a prison fortress. From mid-May through August, boats (28 kr) leave on the hour from 10 am to 6 pm from the small harbour east of the **Ravnkloa fish market**.

The west side of Trondheim is bordered by the **Bymarka**, a green area crossed with good skiing and wilderness trails. To get there, take the tram (15 kr) from St Olavs gate to Lian, which has good city views, a bathing lake and hiking paths.

Places to Stay
The nearest camping ground is *Sandmoen Camping* (☎ 72 88 61 35), 10 km south of the city on the E6 (bus No 44). The tourist office books rooms in private homes for 200/300 kr singles/doubles, plus a 20 kr booking fee.

From 1 July to 20 August, university students operate an informal crash pad called *Trondheim InterRail Centre* (☎ 73 89 95 38) at Elgesetergate 1, a five-minute walk south of the cathedral. A night's sleep costs 90 kr, breakfast included. This friendly operation is free of curfews and has a café with inexpensive food and beer.

Trondheim Hostel (☎ 73 53 04 90), two km east of the train station at Weidemannsvei 44 (bus No 63), open from 5 January to 22 December, has dorm beds for 150 kr, breakfast included. More central is *Pensjonat Jarlen* (☎ 73 51 32 18), Kongens gate 40, which has rooms with TV, shower and kitchenette and charges 150 kr for a hostel-style bed, 300/400 kr for singles/doubles.

Two Rainbow hotels – the *Trondheim Hotell* (☎ 73 50 50 50) at Kongens gate 15 and the turn-of-the-century *Gildevangen Hotell* (☎ 73 51 01 00) at Søndre gate 22 – have summer and weekend rates of 410/510 kr for singles/doubles.

The *Chesterfield Hotel* (☎ 73 50 37 50) on Søndre gate 26 has commodious rooms with private baths. A few rooms have cooking facilities at no extra cost. If you want to bask in the midnight sun, ask for one of the corner rooms on the 7th floor as these have huge skylights and broad city views. Rates are 625/725 kr on weekdays and 450/550 kr on weekends, except in July when they're 500/600 kr daily.

The *SAS Hotel Trondheim* (☎ 73 53 53 10), at the Olavskvartalet cultural centre, is a fine 1st-class hotel in a good central location. Rooms have marble baths and all the expected amenities. From mid-May to mid-September there's a *'sommerpris'* of 620/780 kr, about half the regular rate.

Places to Eat
Travellers stumbling off the night train can head to *Det Lille Franske*, Søndre gate 25, which opens at 8 am on weekdays and has coffee, good pastries and a pavement table. *Bakeri Teatret* in the Olavskvartalet cultural centre has hearty sandwiches and pizza slices (25 kr).

Kafé Gjest Baardsen in the library is a

gathering place for international students and has inexpensive cakes, salads and simple eats. *Café ni Muser*, in a period house at Bispegata 9, is a casual spot with inexpensive light meals and an arty crowd – it's busiest on sunny afternoons when the outdoor terrace doubles as a beer garden.

Zia Teresa, a cosy Italian bistro on Vår Frue Strete, offers a good lunch special from noon to 3 pm weekdays, which includes a pasta dish and salad bar for 65 kr. At other times, main dishes start at about 75 kr. *Grønn Pepper*, a Mexican restaurant at Søndre gate 17, has a lunch special of four tacos with rice and salad for 55 kr until 4 pm Monday to Saturday. The adjacent *Egon* has a good 65 kr pizza-and-salad buffet served until 6 pm daily, while *Pizzakjelleren*, Fjordgata 7, has a simple 54 kr pizza buffet from noon to midnight.

For a thoroughly Norwegian experience, *Tavern* (☎ 73 52 09 32) in Sverresborg, an 18th-century inn near the folk museum, serves traditional Norwegian meals for about 100 kr.

There's a small health-food store, *Hardangerfrukt*, at Fjordgata 62. For more standard fare *Rema 1000* at Torvet has good prices on groceries and bakery items – or munch out on inexpensive fish cakes from the Ravnkloa fish market.

Entertainment
Studentersamfundet, at Elgesetergate 1, is a student centre with a pub, cinema, lounges and some good alternative music, though most of the activities gear down in the summer. During the school year, Friday's the main party night.

Olavshallen, at the Olavskvartalet cultural centre, is the city's main concert hall, hosting performers that range from the Trondheim Symphony Orchestra to international rock musicians.

Café Remis, Kjøpmannsgata 12, is a meeting place for gay men and lesbians.

Getting There & Away
Air The airport is in Vaernes, 32 km east of Trondheim. Airport buses (45 kr) leave from the Braathens SAFE office, Kjøpmannsgata 73, in conjunction with SAS and Braathens SAFE flights.

Train There are half a dozen trains to Oslo daily (560 kr) and two to Bodø (650 kr). If you're in a hurry to get north, consider taking the overnight train from Oslo, tossing your gear into a locker at the station and spending the day exploring Trondheim before continuing on an overnight train to Bodø – which, incidentally, goes through Hell just before midnight.

There are also trains from Trondheim to Storlien in Sweden (two hours, 125 kr) at 7.50 am and 3.49 pm daily, with onward connections to Stockholm.

Car & Motorcycle The E6, the main north-south motorway, passes through the heart of the city. There's an 11 kr toll on vehicles entering the city weekdays from 6 am to 5 pm.

For car rentals, Avis (☎ 73 52 69 15) is at Kjøpmannsgata 34 and Budget (☎ 73 51 89 00) is at Kjøpmannsgata 73.

Boat On its northbound journey, the coastal steamer arrives in Trondheim at 6 am and departs at noon; southbound, it arrives at 6.30 am and departs at 10 am.

Getting Around
The central transit point for city buses is the intersection of Munkegata and Dronningens gate. The bus fare is 14 kr, or buy a 24-hour ticket for 35 kr, both paid to the driver, exact change only. The tourist office rents bicycles for 80 kr a day.

If you have a car, it's easy to drive between sights on the outskirts of town, but best to explore the centre on foot. There's metered parking along many streets, at zones marked *P Mot avgift* or *P Avgift*. Look for green meters, which cost 3 kr an hour, and avoid red meters, which cost 5 kr for 15 minutes and have a 30-minute maximum.

BODØ
Besides being the terminus for the northern railway line, Bodø is Nordland's biggest

town and a jumping-off point for the Lofoten islands. As the town was levelled during WWII air raids and completely rebuilt in the 1950s, Bodø itself is rather ordinary in appearance but it does have a lovely mountain backdrop.

The tourist office (☎ 75 52 60 00), at Sjøgata 21, and an adjacent Kreditkassen bank are near the waterfront in the city centre. From the tourist office, the bus station is a five-minute walk west along Sjøgata, and the train station is five minutes to the east.

Things to See & Do
There's not much to see in the centre other than a small museum of Nordland history (15 kr) and a modern cathedral with limited viewing hours, both two blocks uphill from Glasshuset. There's also an aviation museum (65 kr) on the outskirts of town that's reached by the Sentrums bus (10 kr). The tourist office rents bikes for 60 kr a day.

Places to Stay & Eat
The nearest camping ground is *Bodøsjøen Camping* (☎ 75 56 36 80), three km from town via bus No 12. The 25-room *Bodø Hostel* (☎ 75 52 11 22), conveniently located on the top floor of the train station and open year-round, squeezes in about 90 guests in summer, half that in winter. Dorm beds cost 140 kr, doubles 280 kr. The tourist office books private rooms from 150 kr a person.

The friendly *Norrøna Hotel* (☎ 75 52 55 50), opposite the bus station at Storgata 4, has comfortable rooms with private bath and a summer price of 340/550 kr for singles/ doubles.

For inexpensive food, head to *Glasshuset*, an indoor shopping centre midway between the tourist office and bus station, which has a grocery store, a cafeteria, a pizzeria and the *Aga-mat* konditori with good sandwiches and discounted day-old bread. For more traditional Norwegian fare and prices, the nearby *Central Hotel* has reindeer or fresh fish for 110 kr.

Getting There & Away
Trondheim trains arrive in Bodø at 9.50 am

and 6.30 pm. If you're continuing north by bus, be sure to get off one stop before Bodø at Fauske, where the two daily express buses to Narvik (262 kr) and Alta (823 kr) connect with the train. Southbound trains leave Bodø at 11.25 am and 9 pm daily.

The northbound coastal steamer arrives in Bodø at 12.30 pm and departs at 3 pm; southbound, it's in port from 1 to 4 am. The coastal steamer and Lofoten car ferry docks are a five-minute walk north of the train station, while express catamaran boats dock beside the bus station. Information on Lofoten boats is in the Lofoten islands section.

AROUND BODØ
The 19th-century trading station **Kjerringøy**, on a sleepy island 40 km north of Bodø, has been preserved as an open-air museum. Guided tours cost 40 kr. On summer weekdays bus No 810 (1½ hours, 50 kr) leaves Bodø at 1.10 pm and returns at 5.10 pm. Or you could stay nearby at the old rectory, which is now the *Kjerringøy Prestegård* guesthouse (☎ 75 58 34 60), with hostel-style beds for 100 kr.

There are also buses (No 819) going 33 km south from Bodø (50 minutes, 39 kr) to **Saltstraumen**, the world's largest maelstrom, where at high tide an immense volume of water swirls and churns its way through a three-km strait that links two fjords. Unfortunately, although it may pack a lot of power, there isn't all that much to see and it's really not a very exciting tourist attraction.

NARVIK
Narvik was established a century ago as an ice-free port for iron-ore mines in Swedish Lapland. The city is bisected by a monstrous transshipment facility where the ore is offloaded from rail cars onto ships bound for Germany and Japan.

The tourist office (☎ 76 94 33 09) and bus station are at Kongens gate 66 and the train station is a five-minute walk to the east. The Lofoten express boat and the hostel are on Havnegata, two km south down Kongens gate.

Things to See & Do
Narvik is basically a transit point for travellers, though if you've got time on your hands there's a **war museum** (25 kr) on the town square that commemorates the fierce battles fought here in WWII. Behind the town, from 10 am to 1 am in summer, a cable car (60 kr) runs 650 metres up **Fagernesfjellet** for views of the midnight sun.

Places to Stay & Eat
The nearest camping ground is *Narvik Camping* (☎ 76 94 58 10), two km north-east of town on the E6. *Narvik Hostel* (☎ 76 94 25 98), Havnegata 3, has dorm beds for 140 kr, singles/doubles for 240/360 kr, breakfast included. More central is *Breidablikk Gjestgiveri* (☎ 76 94 14 18), a pleasant pension at Tore Hunds gate 41, with a hillside fjord view and singles/doubles for 285/365 kr (optional breakfast 50 kr).

The train station has a *Café Caroline* and there are places to eat within walking distance of the bus station, including *Astrup Kjelleren*, three blocks south at Kinobakken 1, which has pizza, daily specials and late hours. The *Domus* supermarket at Frydenlundsgata 15, just over the bridge from the town square, has a cheap cafeteria. The hostel cooks up a filling dinner for 70 kr.

Getting There & Away
Some express buses between Fauske and the far north make an overnight break in Narvik. A couple of trains run daily to Kiruna in Sweden with connections to Stockholm. Information on the express boat to Svolvær is in the Lofoten islands section.

LOFOTEN ISLANDS
The spectacular Lofoten islands are peaks of glacier-carved mountains that shoot straight up out of the sea. From a distance they appear as an unbroken line, known as the Lofoten Wall, and are separated from the mainland by the Vestfjord.

The Lofoten islands are Norway's prime winter-fishing grounds. The warming effects of the Gulf Stream draw spawning arctic cod from the Barents Sea south to the Lofoten waters each winter, followed by migrating north coast farmers who for centuries have drawn most of their income from the seasonal fishing. Although fish stocks have dwindled greatly in recent years, fishing continues to be the Lofoten islands' largest industry and the cod is still hung outside on wooden racks to dry through early summer.

Fishermen's winter shanties (*rorbu*) and dorm-style beachhouses (*sjøhus*) double as summer tourist lodges, providing some of Norway's most atmospheric accommodation.

The main islands of Austvågøy, Vestvågøy, Flakstad and Moskenes are all ruggedly beautiful. Artists are attracted by Austvågøy's light and there are art galleries in Svolvær, Kabelvåg and the busy fishing village of Henningsvær. Vestvågøy has Lofoten's richest farmland, and Flakstad and Moskenes islands have sheltered bays, sheep pastures, and sheer coastal mountains that loom above strikingly picturesque fishing villages.

The four main islands are all linked by bridge or tunnel, with buses running the entire Lofoten road (E10) from Fiskebøl in the north to Å at road's end in the south-west. Bus fares are half-price for Inter-Rail and ScanRail pass holders.

Svolvær
By Lofoten standards the main port town of Svolvær on the island of Austvågøy is busy and modern. On the square facing the harbour, you'll find a couple of banks, a taxi stand and the helpful regional tourist office, Destination Lofoten (☎ 76 07 30 00; Postboks 210, 8301 Svolvær), which has information on all the Lofoten islands.

Things to See & Do Daredevils like to scale **The Goat**, a distinctive two-pronged peak visible from the harbour, and then jump from one horn to the other – the graveyard at the bottom awaits those who miss!

Excursion boats from Svolvær run daily in summer to the Trollfjord, which is just two km long but spectacularly steep and narrow. The coastal steamer also makes a jaunt into

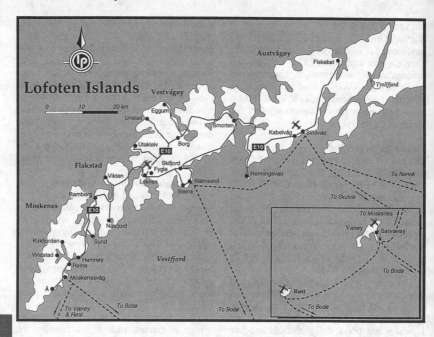

the Trollfjord, the huge ship practically kissing the rock walls at the innermost point where it makes a 180° turn.

Places to Stay & Eat The *Svolvær Sjøhus* (☎ 76 07 03 36) is a rustic dockside beachhouse with beds from 120 kr and doubles for 300 kr; turn right on the first road past the library, five minutes east of the harbour. *Havna Hotel* (☎ 76 07 10 55), near the tourist office, has comfortable rooms with private bath and a summer rate of 550/650 kr for singles/doubles.

The café at the *Havna Hotel* has pizza for 55 kr and a daily special for 75 kr. There's a pub-style restaurant, a bakery and a couple of other eateries on the square and a *Rimi* grocery store a block inland on Torggata.

Getting There & Away Flights from Bodø to Svolvær (or Leknes) cost 630 kr one way, 755 kr return. Buses to Leknes leave Svolvær (two hours, 79 kr) at 6.50 am, 9.45 am and

3.40 pm weekdays, at 6.30 pm daily, and at 10 pm daily except Saturday. A car ferry runs between Svolvær and the mainland town of Skutvik (two hours, 50 kr for a passenger, 174 kr for a car) a few times a day. The coastal steamer leaves Bodø at 3 pm daily, arriving in Svolvær (263 kr) at 9 pm. Express boats leave Bodø for Svolvær at 5.15 pm weekdays, 8.30 pm on Sunday (3½ hours, 213 kr) and leave Narvik for Svolvær (3½ hours, 249 kr) at 3.15 pm weekdays, noon on Sunday. There are no express boats on Saturday in either direction and there's no Monday sailing from Svolvær to Narvik.

Kabelvåg

The road into the quiet hamlet of Kabelvåg passes a **wooden church** that's one of Norway's largest. Built a century ago to minister to the influx of seasonal fisherfolk, the 1200 seats far surpass the village's current population.

Kabelvåg's small square has a market,

café and post office. From Svolvær you can walk the five km to Kabelvåg or catch one of the hourly buses (14 kr).

Things to See & Do Behind the old prison a trail leads uphill to the **statue of King Øystein** who in 1120 ordered the first rorbu to be built to house fishermen who had been sleeping in their overturned rowing boats – it was more than a touch of kindness, as the tax on the exported dried fish was the main source of the king's revenue.

Excavations of those original **rorbu** have recently taken place just beyond the **Lofoten Museum**, a regional history museum (30 kr). Nearby there's an **aquarium** (50 kr) with an outdoor tank containing harbour seals.

Borg

Norway's largest Viking building, an 83-metre-long chieftain's house, has been excavated in Borg, near the centre of Vestvågøy island. The site's new **Lofotr Viking-museum** (80 kr) offers a look at life in Viking times, complete with a full-scale reconstruction of the building, costumed interpreters and a Viking-style ship. Borg is a stop on the Svolvær-Leknes bus route.

Leknes

Other than to change buses or catch a flight, there's little reason to visit Leknes, the island of Vestvågøy's modern municipal centre. There's a moderately priced restaurant at the bus station and a bakery across the street. The town hall, next to the station, has a tourist office, post office and taxi stand.

Stamsund

The traditional fishing village of Stamsund makes a fine destination largely because of its dockside hostel, a magnet for travellers who sometimes stay for weeks on end.

A bakery with good pastries, a grocery store, post office and bus stop are a couple of minutes uphill from the hostel.

Places to Stay At *Justad Hostel/Rorbuer* (☎ 76 08 93 34), bunks in the old beachhouse cost 75 kr, double rooms from 190 kr, and

pleasant four-person cabins are available from 390 kr. Manager Roar Justad lends rowing boats for free (catch and cook your own dinner!), rents bicycles and knows all the hiking trails. The hostel is open from mid-December to mid-October; laundry facilities are available.

Getting There & Away The coastal steamer stops en route (7.30 pm northbound, 9.15 pm southbound) between Bodø (245 kr) and Svolvær (87 kr). Buses run every hour or two from Leknes to Stamsund (25 minutes, 25 kr).

Reine

The delightful village of Reine, on the island of Moskenes, is on a calm bay backed by lofty mountains and has an almost fairy-tale setting.

All buses from Leknes to Å stop in Reine; there's a bus stop near the post office.

Things to See & Do In summer, ferries run from Reine to **Vindstad** (40 minutes, 21 kr) through the scenic Reinefjord. From Vindstad you can make a one-hour hike over a ridge to the abandoned beachside settlement of **Bunes** on the other side of the island. If you take the morning ferry from Reine you can catch the afternoon ferry back.

Places to Stay & Eat At the road's end the rustic *Gammelbua* is a nice place to try cod tongues (135 kr), a Lofoten speciality, and they make a delicious fish soup for 58 kr. There's a small market opposite Gammelbua. *Reine Rorbuer* (☎ 76 09 22 22) at Gammelbua has seaside rorbu from 600 kr in summer, 300 kr in the off season. There are *'sjøhus'* signs along the road advertising cheaper private rooms.

Å

Å is a special place – a preserved fishing village with a shoreline of red rorbu, cod drying on racks everywhere and picture-postcard scenes at almost every turn.

Things to See Many of Å's 19th-century buildings have been set aside as the **Norwegian Fishing Village Museum**, complete

NORWAY

with old boats and boathouses, a period bakery, storehouses and so on. There are guided tours in summer for 35 kr. A second period museum, the **Lofoten Stockfish Museum** (25 kr), details the history of cod fishing.

The camping ground at the end of the village has a hillside view of Værøy island, which lies on the other side of the **Moskenesstraumen**, a maelstrom with a mighty whirlpool that has inspired tales by Jules Verne and Edgar Allen Poe.

Places to Stay & Eat *Moskenesstraumen Camping* (☎ 76 09 11 48) has simple cabins for 300 kr. *Å Hostel* (☎ 76 09 11 21), open year-round, offers accommodation in some of the museum's historic buildings for 95 kr a person. Best is *Sjøhus Salteriet*, a restored 1920s waterfront warehouse with comfortable rooms, mostly doubles, complete with the sound of lapping waves. *Å-Hamna Rorbuer* (☎ 76 09 12 11), also at the museum, has pleasant rooms in a restored 1860s home for 80 kr a person.

Food choices are limited – the best bet is to use the kitchen where you're staying. You can buy fresh fish from local fishers and pick up other supplies at the small grocery store behind the hostel office.

Getting There & Away Daily there's a bus at 8 pm from Leknes to Å (two hours, 74 kr) and a bus from Å to Leknes at 4 pm; on most days there are also a couple of earlier buses in each direction.

Ofotens og Vesteraalens Dampskibsselskab (☎ 76 15 14 22) runs car ferries from Bodø to Moskenes, five km north of Å, some of which continue on to Værøy and Røst. It takes 4¼ hours, costs 102 kr for a passenger, 375 kr for a car, and in summer operates about four times daily.

Værøy & Røst

Lofoten's southern islands of Værøy and Røst have some of the finest bird-watching in Norway, with large colonies of razorbills, guillemots, kittiwakes and terns. There are puffins as well, but the population has dropped by more than 50% in the past decade as a result of dwindling stocks of herring, the main food source for puffin chicks.

Craggy Værøy has only a thousand people, but hundreds of thousands of sea birds. Hiking trails take in some of the more spectacular sea-bird rookeries. The main trail goes along the north coast, beginning a few hundred metres past the airport and continuing all the way to the deserted fishing village of Mostad. This 10-km hike makes for a full day's outing, but is not terribly strenuous. Other birding outings, including boat tours, can be arranged through the hostel.

Røst, south of Værøy, enjoys one of the mildest climates in Norway, thanks to its location in the midst of the Gulf Stream. Access to the best bird-watching requires a boat, as the largest rookeries are on offshore islands. The Røst hostel arranges an all-day boat trip (110 kr) that cruises by the major sea-bird colonies and then drops you off for a few hours on an island where a trail up a mountain provides a good view of Røst. En route it's common to see seals and there are occasional spottings of killer whales as well. Røst itself is flat and other than the boat trip there's not much to do, so when planning your trip check the ferry timetable carefully as there can be a couple of days wait between boats.

Places to Stay The *Røst Hostel* (☎ 76 09 61 09) charges 100 kr, is open from 1 May to 30 August and has a café on site. There's a sauna available and rowing boats for rent. The *Værøy Hostel* (☎ 76 09 53 52), which provides accommodation in an old seaside sjøhus and rorbu, is open from 15 May to 15 September and charges 80 kr a bed, 240 kr for a private room. There's a nearby café. Both hostels have guest kitchens.

Getting There & Away There are scheduled flights to Røst from Bodø and Leknes on Widerøe airlines, but only private flights to Værøy.

In summer, there's at least one ferry daily between Bodø and Værøy (six hours, 94 kr) and there's also daily service between

Moskenes and Værøy (1¾ hours, 41 kr). There's boat service five days a week from Værøy to Røst (two hours, 50 kr) and from Røst to Bodø (4½ hours, 112 kr). Sailing times given are for direct ferries, but not every boat is direct. You can also purchase a return ticket routed Bodø-Værøy-Røst-Bodø for 170 kr. Detailed schedules are available at boat terminals and local tourist offices.

TROMSØ

Tromsø (population 57,000) is the world's northernmost university town and the capital of Troms county. In contrast to some of the more sober communities dotting the north coast of Norway, Tromsø is a spirited town with street music, cultural happenings and more pubs per capita than any other place in Norway – it even has its own brewery.

Snow-capped mountains provide a scenic backdrop for the city and good skiing in winter. Many polar expeditions have departed from Tromsø, earning the city the nickname 'Gateway to the Arctic'. A statue of explorer Roald Amundsen, who headed some of the expeditions, stands in a little square down by harbour.

Orientation & Information

Tromsø's city centre and airport are on the island of Tromsøya, which is linked by a bridge to the mainland where the city's eastern outskirts spill over. The tourist office (☎ 77 61 00 00), at Storgata 61, is open from 8.30 am to 6 pm weekdays and 10 am to 5 pm weekends from June to 15 August, and from 8.30 am to 4 pm weekdays in the off season.

Things to See & Do

The city centre has many period buildings, including the old cathedral, **Tromsø Domkirke**, one of Norway's largest wooden churches, and a **Catholic church**, both built in 1861. However, Tromsø's most striking church is the **Arctic Cathedral** (open in summer from 10 am to 8 pm, 10 kr) on the mainland just over the bridge. This modernist building bears a resemblance to Aus-

tralia's Sydney Opera House, though it looks best from a distance.

The **Tromsø Museum**, at the southern end of Tromsøya, is northern Norway's largest museum, and has well-presented displays on arctic birds, Sami culture and regional history. It's open daily year-round, in summer from 9 am to 9 pm. Admission costs 10 kr. Take bus No 22 or 27 from Bananas, opposite the Domkirke.

The harbourside **Polar Museum** has frontier exhibits on the Arctic, some interesting and others – such as the display on clubbing and gutting baby seals – of more questionable taste. It's open daily, from 11 am to at least 6 pm in summer, and to 3 pm the rest of the year. Admission costs 30 kr.

The city also has a regional art museum, the **Nordnorsk Kunstmuseum** (free) on Muségata 2 and a **planetarium** dedicated to the northern lights (50 kr) on the outskirts of town (bus No 37).

You can get a fine city view by taking the **cable car** 420 metres up Mt Storsteinen. It runs from 10 am to 5 pm daily April to September, and until 1 am on clear nights June to August when the midnight sun is in view. The ride costs 50 kr return. Take bus No 28 from Stortorget harbour.

Places to Stay

The closest tent space and cabins are at *Tromsdalen Camping* (☎ 77 63 80 37) on the mainland, two km east of the Arctic Cathedral; take bus No 36.

Tromsø Hostel (☎ 77 68 53 19) is in Elverhøy at Gitta Jønsonsvei 4, two km west of the city centre via bus No 24. It's open from 20 June to 19 August and costs 95 kr for dorms, 195/240 kr for singles/doubles. Reception is closed from 11 am to 5 pm. The tourist office books rooms in private homes from 150 kr per person plus a 25 kr booking fee.

Two guesthouses on the hillside a few minutes walk from the centre are *Kongsbakken Gjestehus* (☎ 77 68 22 08) at Skolegata 24 (ask for a front room – they have great city views) and *Hotell Nord* (☎ 77 68 31 59) at Parkgata 4. Both charge 370/480 kr

NORWAY

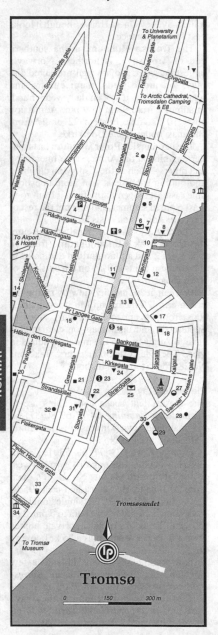

NORWAY

for singles/doubles with shared bath and have comparable rooms that are straightforward but clean, each with TV, phone and a sink; rates include breakfast. The cheapest rooms with private bath (450/550 kr) are at Kongsbakken Gjestehus.

Polar Hotel (☎ 77 68 64 80), at Grønnegate 45, has modern guestrooms, a cheery breakfast room with a city view and weekend rates of 475/650 kr; summer (July to mid-August) rates are 575/750 kr. Rates are 675/850 kr at other times.

Places to Eat

Buy fresh boiled shrimp from fishing boats at Stortorget harbour and a loaf of bread at the nearby bakery and you've got yourself a meal – there are even dockside picnic tables. The harbourside *Domus* grocery store has a cheap 2nd-floor cafeteria and a water view.

Pizzahuset, near the bridge at Skippergata 44, has good pizza and is a popular student hang-out that's open from 3 pm (from 1 pm on weekends) to at least midnight daily.

Two trendy places in the city centre are *Paletten Kafé*, which has 30 kr sandwiches, meals from 85 kr and live music, and *Le Mirage*, a casual café which has 25 kr sandwiches and tacos, omelettes, and spaghetti for about 70 kr. Both are near the intersection of Storgata and Strandskillet.

Fast-food choices include a *Burger King* on Storgata and a food kiosk at the express boat dock. *Prelaten*, a pleasant basement pub at Sjøgata 12, has Mack on tap and occasionally offers a simple 50 kr meal.

Getting There & Away

Tromsø is the main airport hub for the northern region, with direct flights to Oslo, Bergen, Bodø, Trondheim, Honningsvåg and Kirkenes. There are a few daily express buses to Narvik (five hours, 263 kr) and an afternoon bus to Alta (seven hours, 298 kr). Both services pass through beautiful scenery as they leave Tromsø.

The coastal steamer arrives at 3.15 pm and departs at 6.30 pm northbound and arrives at 11.45 pm and departs at 1.30 am southbound. The fare is 758 kr to Bodø, 522 kr to Hammerfest. In summer there's a twice-weekly boat between Tromsø and Hammerfest (4½ hours, 560 kr); call ☎ 78 41 10 00 for the schedule, as it varies each year.

Getting Around

The airport bus (25 kr) can be picked up at the SAS Hotel, and a taxi to the airport costs about 75 kr. Thoroughly exploring Tromsø can take time, as the city is split up and many of the sights are outside the centre. Most rides on city buses cost 15 kr; you can buy a 24-hour pass on the bus for 50 kr.

If you have your own car, you'll find it quite convenient for getting around. Tromsø has numerous parking areas spread around the city and a huge underground car park along Vestregata due east of the harbour.

FINNMARK

Finnmark's curving north coast is cut by fjords and dotted with fishing villages. The interior is populated by nomadic Sami people who for centuries have herded their reindeer across the vast mountain plateau Finnmarksvidda, a stark wilderness with only two major settlements, Karasjok and Kautokeino.

Virtually every town in Finnmark was razed to the ground at the end of WWII by retreating Nazis whose scorched-earth policy was meant to delay the advancing Soviet troops. The rebuilt towns look altogether of a kind, with most buildings constructed in a plain box-like style.

You can get information on the entire region from the Finnmark Travel Association (☎ 78 43 54 44), Postboks 1223, 9501 Alta.

ALTA

Alta is a sprawling town with fishing and quarrying industries. The town's two main centres, Sentrum and Bossekop, are two km apart. The Alta tourist office (☎ 78 43 77 70) is by the bus stop in Bossekop, as are a bank and post office.

Things to See & Do

Alta's main sight is the **prehistoric rock art** at Hjemmeluft on the E6, a couple km south of Bossekop. A five-km-long network of boardwalks leads past many of the 3000 rock carvings of hunting scenes, fertility symbols and reindeer that date back as far as 4000 BC. The 40 kr admission fee includes the adjacent **Alta Museum**, which has notable regional exhibits and is open until 11 pm daily in midsummer.

Alta is also renowned for its salmon run; several local companies provide fishing tours.

Places to Stay & Eat

Skogly Camping (☎ 78 43 56 03) is off the E6 near the rock carvings. The *Alta Hostel*

(☎ 78 43 44 09), Midtbakken 52, a short walk from the Sentrum bus stop, costs 110 kr. It's open from 20 June to 20 August; reception is closed from noon to 5 pm. *Alta Gjestestue* in Bossekop and *Café Eden* at the SAS Alta Hotell in Sentrum have moderately priced food.

Getting There & Away

Many express buses between Bodø and the far north stop in Alta at night and depart in the morning, requiring an overnight stay. Buses for Hammerfest, Olderfjord, Kirkenes and Karasjok leave Alta at 7.15 am daily except Sunday, and at 3.35 pm daily.

HAMMERFEST

Hammerfest has a population of 10,000, an economy based on fishing and a claim to being the 'northernmost town in the world' – perhaps a matter of semantics as Honningsvåg 'village' is farther north!

Most visitors arrive on the coastal steamer and have two hours to look around. The tourist office (☎ 78 41 21 85) is a few minutes walk from the dock, on Strandgata near the bank. Nearby in the town hall the **Royal & Ancient Polar Bear Society** has arctic hunting displays; entry is free.

A five-minute walk west on Kirkegata leads to Hammerfest's contemporary **church**, where there's a fair chance you'll find reindeer grazing in the graveyard. For lovely views of the town, coast and mountains, climb the 86-metre **Salen Hill**; the 10-minute trail begins behind the small park directly up from town hall.

Places to Stay & Eat

NAF Camping Storvannet (☎ 78 41 10 10), two km east of the town centre, is open from 1 June to 15 September and has inexpensive cabins. The cheapest central hotel rooms are at *Håja Hotell* (☎ 78 41 18 22), Storgata 9, where doubles with shared bath cost 550 kr. The *Domus* supermarket on Strandgata, a few minutes east of the town hall, has an inexpensive cafeteria.

Getting There & Away

The coastal steamer stops daily at 5.30 am northbound and 11.45 am southbound. The Express 2000 bus leaves Hammerfest for Oslo (1600 kr) via Sweden at noon on Wednesday and Saturday, arriving at 5.30 pm the next day.

FFR (☎ 78 41 10 00) runs an express boat to Honningsvåg (two hours, 260 kr) from mid-June to mid-August. The boat leaves Hammerfest daily at 7 pm; the return boat leaves Honningsvåg at 1.30 am. You can also get a return ticket that includes a bus to Nordkapp to see the midnight sun.

HONNINGSVÅG

Honningsvåg, the only sizeable settlement on the island of Magerøy, has a little museum and a 19th-century church, but the centre of attention is at Nordkapp, 34 km away. The tourist office (☎ 78 47 25 99), Postboks 34, midway between the bus station and quay, covers the Nordkapp area and arranges winter snowscooter safaris to Nordkapp.

Places to Stay & Eat

Nordkapp Camping & Hostel (☎ 78 47 33 77), open from mid-May to mid-September, is in a scenic fjordside locale eight km north of Honningsvåg on the road to Nordkapp (15 kr by bus). Dorms cost 100 kr, doubles 400 kr and cabins 440 kr. Honningsvåg's in-town hotels are expensive; the cheapest, the *Hotel Havly* (☎ 78 47 29 66), charges 550/830 kr for singles/doubles.

There's a grocery store on Storgata up from the coastal steamer quay. The reasonably priced *Kafé Corner*, open until midnight (2 am on weekends when it doubles as a disco), is behind the tourist office.

Getting There & Away

From early June to mid-August an express bus leaves Alta daily at 7.15 am, arriving at Nordkapp at 12.50 pm (242 kr).

The road approach from E6 is via Olderfjord, from where you take route 69 north-west to Kåfjord. Car ferries (☎ 78 41 10 00) cross from Kåfjord to Honningsvåg every couple of hours (45 minutes; passenger

34 kr, car 107 kr). In 1998 a new tunnel will eliminate the need for the ferry.

The coastal steamer stops at Honningsvåg at 1 pm northbound and 6.45 am southbound. The northbound stop is 4½ hours, long enough to make the trip up to Nordkapp (the coastal steamer offers its passengers a moderately priced Nordkapp tour). See the Hammerfest section for information on the express boat from that town.

NORDKAPP

Nordkapp (North Cape), a high rugged coastal plateau at 71°10'21", is Europe's northernmost point and the main destination for most travellers to the far north. The sun never drops below the horizon from mid-May to the end of July. To many visitors Nordkapp, with its steep cliffs and stark scenery, emanates a certain spiritual aura – indeed, long before other Europeans took an interest in the area, Nordkapp was considered a power centre by the Sami people.

It was Richard Chancellor, the English explorer who drifted this way in 1553 on a search for the Northeast Passage, who gave it the name North Cape. Following a much-publicised visit by King Oscar II in 1873, Nordkapp became a pilgrimage spot of sorts.

Nowadays there's a 150 kr entrance fee and a touristy complex with exhibits, eateries, souvenir shops and a post office. The 180° theatre runs a good short movie but to really appreciate Nordkapp take a walk out along the cliffs. If the weather is fair you can perch yourself on the edge of the continent and watch the polar mist roll in.

Getting There & Away

An asphalt road winds across a rocky plateau and past herds of grazing reindeer up to Nordkapp. Depending on the snow, it's usually open from May to mid-October; the National Road User Information Center (☎ 22 65 40 40) gives opening dates.

From mid-May to the end of August, buses run four times a day from Honningsvåg to Nordkapp (one hour, 42 kr), the first at 11.50 am and the last at 10.55 pm. The last bus returns from Nordkapp at 1.10 am.

VARDØ

Vardø, Norway's easternmost village, is on an island linked to the mainland by a three-km tunnel under the Barents Sea. It's a coastal steamer stop, but is otherwise out of the way for all but the most die-hard travellers. The only sight of interest is the small 1737 star-shaped **fort** with cannons and sod-roof buildings, a five-minute walk directly up from the coastal steamer quay.

KIRKENES

Kirkenes, a mining town beneath a smoke-belching factory, was Norway's most bombed village during WWII. The town is not a major tourist destination, but it does get some visitors as it's the end of the line for the coastal steamer and a jumping-off point into Russia.

Things to See & Do

Kirkenes' biggest attractions are a **statue** dedicated to the Soviet soldiers who liberated the town, an **underground cave** formerly used as an air-raid shelter and an anti-climactic ride (300 kr return by taxi) to the Russian **border-crossing** point of Storskog. The Kirkenes Tourist Office (☎ 78 99 25 01) is at Storgata 10, in the centre.

Tour to Russia A sightseeing package to Murmansk, Russia, is offered by Finnmark Fylkesrederi og Ruteselskap (FFR), which runs a high-speed catamaran between Kirkenes and Murmansk from late June to the end of July. The boat leaves Kirkenes at 8 am every day except Wednesday and Sunday, returning around midnight. Tour passengers do not need visas, but must bring their passports. Bookings (☎ 78 41 10 00) must be made at least 24 hours in advance. The cost of 1190 kr includes a sightseeing tour and dinner in Murmansk.

Cheaper day tours to Murmansk by bus (800 kr, including lunch and sightseeing) can be arranged through Sovjetreiser (☎ 78 99 19 81), but unlike the FFR tours, Russian visas must be obtained in advance.

NORWAY

Places to Stay & Eat

The nearest *hostel* (☎ 78 99 88 11) and nearest *camping ground* (☎ 78 99 80 28) are six km west of town off the E6 in Hesseng; both are open in summer only. The in-town *Rica Arctic Hotel* (☎ 78 99 29 29), Kongensgata 1, has a summer rate of 580/860 kr for singles/doubles. You'll find grocery stores, a pizzeria and a few cafés near the town square.

Getting There & Away

The airport is a 20-minute drive from town. A bus leaves Kirkenes daily at 9.15 am, arriving in Karasjok at 2.45 pm (331 kr), Olderfjord at 5.35 pm (474 kr) and Alta at 8 pm (584 kr). The coastal steamer departs southbound at 1.45 pm on Sunday, Tuesday and Thursday and at 11.30 am other days, after a two-hour layover in port.

Travellers to Russia, other than those on FFR's day tour, must be in possession of a Russian visa, which can be obtained in Oslo. The FFR summer catamaran costs 550 kr one way to Murmansk. A bus to Murmansk (five hours, 350 kr) leaves Kirkenes at 3 pm on Wednesday, Friday and Sunday.

KARASJOK

Karasjok is the most accessible Sami town and the site of the newly established **Sami Parliament**. It has Finnmark's oldest **church**

(1807), the only building left standing in Karasjok after WWII.

The tourist office (☎ 78 46 73 60), in the **Samiland Centre** at the junction of E6 and route 92, can book wintertime sleigh rides and arrange gold panning, riverboat trips and other summer activities. In addition to the displays at the Samiland Centre, there's an interesting **Sami museum** (25 kr); from the tourist office walk up the E6 and turn right on Museumsgata.

Places to Stay & Eat

Karasjok Camping (☎ 78 46 61 35), one km south of Samiland Centre on Kautokeinoveien, has hostel beds for 115 kr and cabins from 220 kr. *Anne's Overnatting* (☎ 78 46 64 32), Tanaveien 40, charges 300/395 kr for singles/doubles, or 100 kr less if you use your own sleeping bag. The café at the Samiland Centre and *Lailas Kafé*, over the bridge on Markangeaidnu 1, have moderately priced meals. *Gammen Restaurant*, north of Samiland Centre, has traditional Sami food and atmosphere.

Getting There & Away

Buses leave Karasjok at 6.30 am and 3 pm daily for Hammerfest (4¾ hours, 234 kr) and Alta (five hours, 265 kr). Buses to Kirkenes leave Karasjok at 2.10 pm on Sunday and Friday, at 12.25 pm other days.

St Petersburg

If Moscow is Europe's most Asiatic capital, St Petersburg, with a population of 5.5 million, is Russia's most European city. Created by Peter the Great as his 'window on the West' at the only point where traditional Russian territory meets a seaway to Northern Europe, it was built with 18th and 19th-century European pomp and orderliness by mainly European architects. The result is a city that remains one of Europe's most beautiful: where Moscow intimidates, St Petersburg enchants. Its beauty, happily little harmed by Stalinist reconstruction, is of a brand all its own.

Today St Petersburg is a cosmopolitan city with a lively artistic and entertainment scene equal to Moscow's. It is Russia's biggest port and a huge industrial centre. Small, Russian-owned businesses are popping up every where and Western businesses are following suit.

Planet's *St Petersburg – city guide* or *Russia, Ukraine & Belarus – travel survival kit*.

Online Services
The Internet site of the HI St Petersburg Hostel is excellent, and has lots of practical information and useful links (http://www.arcom.spb.su/users/ryh/).

Facts for the Visitor

PLANNING
Climate & When to Go
St Petersburg's latitude – level with Seward, Alaska and Cape Farewell, Greenland – gives it nearly 24-hour daylight in midsummer but long, grey winters. From June to August temperatures reach 20°C. Winter usually sees the Neva freeze over with January temperatures averaging -8°C; it can get very slushy so bring along good waterproof boots or rubbers.

Hotels and tourist attractions are less crowded between October and February when there is a twinkling magic to the dark winter sky. During the white nights of the last 10 days in June, the city is packed.

Books
If you plan to hit St Petersburg for more than a couple of days, pick up a copy of Lonely

HIGHLIGHTS & SUGGESTED ITINERARIES
For art-lovers, the Hermitage and the Russian museum are must-sees. The splendour of such architecture as the Winter Palace; a night at the ballet; a cruise around the city's lively bars and clubs; or a trip to the magnificent tsarist parks and palaces outside the city can be equally breathtaking.

St Petersburg offers a huge number of attractions, but you can still see a fair bit on a short visit.

Two days
    A walking tour of Nevsky prospekt and the surrounding sights, including some or all of the Winter Palace and Hermitage, the Admiralty, St Isaac's Cathedral, Kazan Cathedral, the Church of the Resurrection of Christ and the Summer Garden & Palace; visits to the Hermitage and/or Russian Museum, and to SS Peter & Paul Fortress, Tauride Gardens and Smolny Cathedral. If you're there in the season, try to catch a ballet.

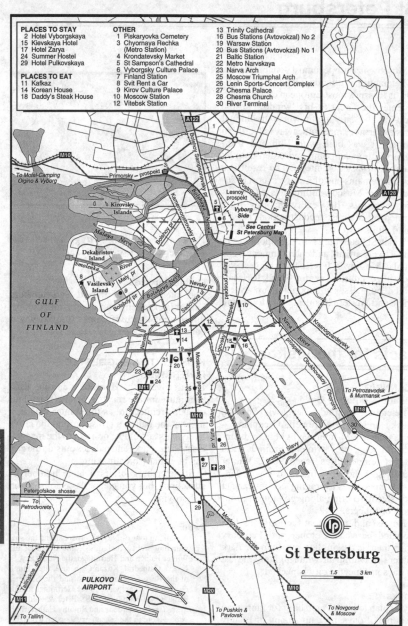

PLACES TO STAY
2   Hotel Vyborgskaya
15 Kievskaya Hotel
17 Hotel Zarya
24 Summer Hostel
29 Hotel Pulkovskaya

PLACES TO EAT
11 Kafkaz
14 Korean House
18 Daddy's Steak House

OTHER
1   Piskaryovka Cemetery
3   Chyornaya Rechka
    (Metro Station)
4   Krondatevsky Market
5   St Sampson's Cathedral
6   Vyborgsky Culture Palace
7   Finland Station
8   Svit Rent a Car
9   Kirov Culture Palace
10 Moscow Station
12 Vitebsk Station

13 Trinity Cathedral
16 Bus Stations (Avtovokzal) No 2
19 Warsaw Station
20 Bus Stations (Avtovokzal) No 1
21 Baltic Station
22 Metro Narvskaya
23 Narva Arch
25 Moscow Triumphal Arch
26 Lenin Sports-Concert Complex
27 Chesma Palace
28 Chesma Church
30 River Terminal

ST PETERSBURG

GULF
OF
FINLAND

Kirovsky
Islands

Malaya Neva

Dekabristov
Island

Smolenka River

Vasilevsky
Island

Bolshaya Neva

Nevsky pr

Sadovaya ul

Vyborg
Side

See Central
St Petersburg Map

Lesnoy
prospekt

Primorsky – prospekt

To Motel-Camping
Olgino & Vyborg

Liteyny prospekt

Nevy River

Krasnogvardeysky pr

Obukhovskoy Oborony

To Petrozavodsk
& Murmansk

Moskovsky prospekt

pr Stachek

pr Yunia Gagarina

prospekt Slavy

Petergofskoe shosse

To
Petrodvorets

Tallinskoe shosse

To Tallinn

PULKOVO
AIRPORT

To Pushkin &
Pavlovsk

Moskovskoe shosse

To Novgorod
& Moscow

St Petersburg

0   1.5   3 km

Three days

As above, with more time at the Hermitage and Russian Museum, or with the addition of a day-trip to Petrodvorets.

One week

As above, with more time at the Hermitage and Russian Museum; and depending on your interests, select from shopping at Gostiny Dvor and Passazh, exploration of Petrograd Side, Vyborg Side and Vasilevsky Island, visits to other museums and palaces, more walking tours (see *St Petersburg – city guide* for suggestions), trips to Petrodvorets, Pushkin and Pavlovsk.

VISAS & CONSULATES

See the Facts for the Visitor section in the Kaliningrad chapter for general information and a listing of Russian embassies abroad. In St Petersburg organisations that can provide you with visa support for Kaliningrad as well as other parts of Russia for a moderate fee include HI St Petersburg Hostel (☎ 812-329 80 18; fax 812-329 80 18; e-mail ryh@ryh.spb.su) and Peter TIPS (☎ 812-279 00 37).

Visa Registration Office

The main OVIR office is at Saltykova-Shchedrina ulitsa 4 (☎ 278 24 81, 273 90 38), open Monday to Friday from 9.30 am to 5.30 pm.

Foreign Consulates

Consulates in St Petersburg include:

Canada
    Malodetskoselsky prospekt 32 (☎ 325 84 48; fax 325 83 93)
Estonia
    Bolshaya Monetnaya ulitsa 14 (☎ 233 55 48)
Finland
    ulitsa Chaykovskogo 71 (☎ 273 73 21, 116 06 52)
Latvia
    Galernaya ulitsa 69 (☎ 315 17 74)
Sweden
    10-ya linia No 11, Vasilevsky Island (☎ 213 41 91)
UK
    ploshchad Proletarskoy Diktatury 5 (☎ 325 60 36, 325 61 66)
USA
    ulitsa Furshtadtskaya 15 (☎ 274 86 89, 274 85 68).

CUSTOMS

See the Facts for the Visitor section in the Kaliningrad chapter for general information. To have art works assessed for customs, go to the Ministry of Culture (☎ 812-314 8234) at Naberezhnaya Kanala Griboedova 107.

MONEY

St Petersburg is not as cheap as the Baltic States or Kaliningrad. The Russian currency unit is the rouble (see the Facts for the Visitor section in the Kaliningrad chapter). Prices are often listed in US dollars (the most accepted foreign currency) but you have to pay in roubles. Travellers' cheques are useful, but outside of St Petersburg hard to change. Credit cards are accepted at many restaurants, hotels and shops, and cash advances against Visa and MasterCard are a simple matter.

Promstroy Bank at Nevsky prospekt 38 offers cash advances on Visa/Master Card/Eurocard. Most major hotels change money, give cash advance on credit cards and organise travellers' cheques, but the banks offer the best rates.

POST & COMMUNICATIONS

If you're travelling on to Scandinavia, you might consider saving mail and phone calls for then.

Post

St Petersburg's central post office *(glav-pochtamt)* is at ulitsa Pochtamtskaya 9. Expect letters or cards to take about two to three weeks to Europe and three to four weeks to the US and Australia. Postcards have more chance of arriving if you put them in an envelope. Incoming mail is a hit-or-miss affair.

For a quicker service try Westpost (☎ 275 07 84; e-mail wp@sas.spb.su) at Nevsky prospekt 86 which mails letters/postcard via Finland for a small fee.

Telephone

To make an international call dial ☎ 8, wait for the tone, then dial ☎ 10 followed by the country code, area code and telephone

number. To make a call within the CIS dial
☎ 8-tone followed by the area code and telephone number.

The State-run long-distance telephone
office is at ulitsa Bolshaya Morskaya (formerly ulitsa Gertsena) 3/5 where you can
pre-pay the operator to connect you or call
direct from the international card-operated
phones inside. Cards for these phones, which
can also be found at strategic points in the
city, can be bought from telephone offices,
Peter TIPS and major hotels.

To make a local call from the older, token-
operated pay phones, put a metro token in the
slot on top, dial the number and wait for the
token to drop. Long-distance calls within
Russia and the CIS can only be made from
pay phones marked междугородный *(mezh-
dugorodny)*. These accept wrinkled-metal
tokens which are available from kiosks and
newsstands. When the person you are calling
answers, make sure you push the Ответ
(otvet) button on the front of the phone.

Private telephone companies offering
direct country service from St Petersburg
include MCI (dial ☎ 8, wait for the tone, dial
☎ 10-800-497 72 22) and AT & T USA
Direct (☎ 325 50 42).

St Petersburg's telephone code is ☎ 812.

Fax & E-Mail

Faxes can be sent and received at the central
post office. Electronic mail messages can be
sent for a small fee from the HI St Petersburg
Hostel, or at Sovam Teleport (☎ 311 84 12),
Nevsky prospekt 30.

TIME

St Petersburg time is GMT/UTC plus three
hours except from the last Sunday in March
to the last Sunday in September when it's
'summer time' and GMT/UTC plus four hours.

ELECTRICITY

See the Facts for the Visitor section in the
Kaliningrad chapter.

WEIGHTS & MEASURES

See the Facts for the Visitor section in the
Kaliningrad chapter.

TOILETS

Smelly toilets are free or inexpensive and
generally a place only for the absolutely
desperate. They're also hard to find outside
of bus and train stations. Women's toilets are
marked Ж and men's with an M. Your best
bet is to walk into a restaurant or hotel and
plead nicely.

HEALTH

Don't drink St Petersburg tap water – it
harbours *Giardia lamblia*, an intestinal parasite which can cause diarrhoea, stomach
cramps and nausea. Stick to bottled water,
which is readily available at supermarkets
and hotels; avoid ice and, ideally, raw fruit
and vegetables that may have come into
contact with tap water.

Dive-bombing mosquitoes are rife in
summer and it is advisable to bring mosquito
repellent, coils or a net.

WOMEN TRAVELLERS

See the Facts for the Visitor section in the
Kaliningrad chapter.

GAY & LESBIAN TRAVELLERS

The gay and lesbian scene in St Petersburg
is still in its infancy. For details of what's on
where try calling the Chaykovsky Fund
(☎ 311 09 37), a gay resource centre; Krilya
(☎ 312 31 80), an action group which lobbies
for gay and lesbian rights; or Olga Kauze's
Independent Women's Club (☎ 511 91 16)
which acts as a lesbian information centre.

DISABLED TRAVELLERS

Like most of Russia, St Petersburg is not
wheelchair friendly; some venues that do
make provision are the Grand Hotel Europe
and the Nevskij Palace Hotel and their
accompanying restaurants.

DANGERS & ANNOYANCES

Petty theft, pick-pocketing and purse-
snatching is as rife in St Petersburg as it is in
any other major city. Black marketeers and
prostitutes are equally rife. Just make it clear
that you are not interested in any 'business'.
Nothing can be more annoying, however,

than St Petersburg's thriving mosquito population (bring a good repellent with you).

BUSINESS HOURS & HOLIDAYS

See the Facts for the Visitor section in the Kaliningrad chapter.

LANGUAGE

See the Language Guide at the back of the book for the Russian alphabet chart, as well as pronunciation guidelines and useful words and phrases.

The City

History

Alexandr of Novgorod defeated the Swedes near the mouth of the Neva in 1240. Sweden took control of the region in the 17th century. In the Great Northern War (1700-21) Peter the Great captured the Swedish outposts on the Neva, and in 1703 founded the Peter & Paul Fortress on the Neva. In 1709 he named the city Sankt Pieter Burkh and three years later made it his capital. By the time of Peter's death in 1725, Sankt Pieter Burkh had a population of 40,000 and 90% of Russia's foreign trade passed through it. Between 1741 and 1825 under Empress Elizabeth, Catherine the Great and Alexander I it became a cosmopolitan city with a royal court of famed splendour.

St Petersburg was the hub of the 1905 revolution, started on 'Bloody Sunday' (9 January 1905) when strikers marching to petition the tsar in the Winter Palace were fired on by troops. In a wave of patriotism at the start of WWI the city's name was changed to the Russian-style Petrograd. The city was again the cradle of revolution in 1917 when, following workers' protests leading to the end of the monarchy in March, Lenin came back here from exile to drive his Bolshevik Party to power on 25 October.

In March 1918, the Bolshevik Party was renamed the Communist Party and moved to Moscow. Three years of civil war saw Petrograd's population drop to about 700,000. The

Union of Soviet Socialist Republics (USSR) was established in 1922 and in 1924, following Lenin's death in January, Petrograd was renamed Leningrad.

During the 1930s the city was a hub of Stalin's industrialisation programme. When the Germans attacked in June 1941 it took Hitler's troops just two-and-a-half months to reach Leningrad. During the '900 Days' siege (actually 872), between 500,000 and a million people died. After the war, Leningrad was reconstructed and reborn, though it took until 1960 for its population to exceed pre-WWII levels.

During the 1991 putsch which led to the demise of Mikhail Gorbachev and the rise of Boris Yeltsin, the army, in true Leningrad style, refused to aid Moscow's coup leaders. As hundreds of thousands of Leningraders filled Palace Square, Sobchak appeared on local TV denouncing the coup. Almost as soon as Dzerzhinsky's statue hit the asphalt in Moscow, the Leningrad city council was proposing to change the city's name back to St Petersburg, a measure that was instantly approved.

Population & People

St Petersburg is estimated to have 4,829,000 residents, the majority of whom are ethnic Russian. Minorities include Jews, Ukrainians, Belarusians and other nationalities from within the former Soviet Union.

Arts & Culture

St Petersburg was the birthplace of Russian ballet in 1738. At the turn of the 20th century – the heyday of Russian ballet – the St Petersburg Imperial School of Ballet rose to world prominence; the Kirov premiered Tchaikovsky's *Sleeping Beauty* and *Nutcracker*, and nurtured Nijinsky, Anna Pavlova, Nureyev, Makarova and Baryshnikov.

It was also the birthplace of Russian opera: Mikhail Glinka's opera *A Life For The Tsar*, which merged traditional and Western influence, was performed on 9 December 1836. The 19th-century flowering of other Russian musical forms was also centred in St Petersburg. Nijinsky, Rimsky-Korsakov and

Borodin, to name but a few, spent important periods here. Peter Tchaikovsky, a student of the St Petersburg Conservatory, who embraced both Russian folklore and music as well as the disciplines of the Western European composers in his work, is widely regarded as the father of Russian national composers.

St Petersburg's status as cultural centre of Russia has a lot to do with the writers and poets associated with it. The list is a veritable 'Who's Who' of literary figures: Pushkin, who was educated in, exiled from, readmitted to and killed in St Petersburg; Dostoevsky, who set *Crime and Punishment* here; Lermontov, whose *Death of a Poet* accused the government of plotting Pushkin's death; and Anna Akhmatova, the long suffering poet whose work contains bittersweet depictions of the city she so loved.

Orientation

St Petersburg sprawls across and around the delta of the Neva River, at the end of the easternmost arm of the Baltic Sea, known as the Gulf of Finland.

The heart of St Petersburg spreads south and east from the Winter Palace and the Admiralty on the Neva's south bank, its skyline dominated by the golden dome of St Isaac's Cathedral. Nevsky prospekt, stretching east-south-east from the Admiralty, is the main street, with many of the city's sights, shops and restaurants.

The north side of the city has three main areas. The westernmost is Vasilevsky Island, at whose east end – the Strelka – many of the city's fine early buildings still stand. The middle area is Petrograd Side, a cluster of delta islands whose south end is marked by the tall gold spire of the SS Peter & Paul Cathedral. The third, eastern, area is Vyborg Side, divided from Petrograd Side by the Bolshaya Nevka channel and stretching east along the north bank of the Neva.

Information

Tourist Offices The privately-run tourist information centre, Peter TIPS (☎ 279 0037) at Nevsky prospekt 86, in Dom Aktyor, offers free hotel booking services, arranges

city tours and also sells tickets to all the city's cultural outlets at the Russian price plus a 10% mark-up.

Not a tourist office but equally helpful and certainly more smiling is the HI St Petersburg Hostel (☎ 329 80 18) at 3-ya Sovietskaya ulitsa 28. There's also a budget travel agency downstairs, Sindbad Travel (see Travel Agencies).

Post & Communications See the earlier Facts for the Visitor section.

Travel Agencies Sindbad Travel (☎ 327 83 84; fax 329 80 19; e-mail sindbad@ryh.spb .su; http://www.spb.su/ryh) at the HI St Petersburg Hostel, 3-ya Sovietskaya ulitsa 28 is a genuine Western-style student and discount air-ticket office, specialising in one-way and short or no-advance purchase tickets.

American Express (at the Grand Hotel Europe) does discounted return tickets to European and American destinations.

Newspapers & Magazines The bi-weekly *St Petersburg Times* (http://www.spb.su/) published every Tuesday and Friday is packed with practical information and listings of clubs, pubs, restaurants, museums, theatres etc; as is *Pulse*, a slick colour monthly. Both are available free in outlets all over the city. Western newspapers, three to four days old, can be picked up at a price in most major hotels.

Medical & Emergency Services Western-quality treatment at a price is available at the American Medical Center (AMC; ☎ 325 61 01; fax 325 61 20) at naberezhnaya reki Fontanki 77 which also offers 24-hour emergency care. Apteka Petrofarm at the corner of Nevsky and Bolshaya Konyushennaya is an all-night pharmacy packed with Western everything.

The state-run ambulance service is still free; Russian-speakers can get help by dialling ☎ 03. Private ambulance service is available through the AMC.

Things to See & Do

Museum hours change like quicksilver as do their weekly days off. Most are open from 11 am to 6 pm (exceptions are noted) and seem to close either Monday or Tuesday, but it's best to check by ringing the museum beforehand.

Walking is a good way to see the main architectural sights.

The Historic Heart From Gostiny Dvor or Nevsky prospekt metro, a 15-minute walk along Nevsky prospekt brings you to **Dvortsovaya ploshchad** (Palace Square), where the stunning green, white and gold **Winter Palace** (Zimny dvorets) appears like a mirage. The baroque/rococo palace, commissioned from Rastrelli in 1754 by Empress Elizabeth and boasting 1057 rooms and 117 staircases, houses part of the **Hermitage** (☎ 311 34 65), one of the world's great art museums. The remainder of the Hermitage is housed in four more linked buildings – the Little Hermitage, the Old and New Hermitages and the Hermitage Theatre – running west to east from the palace. The main ticket hall is inside the main entrance on the river side of the Winter Palace. The Hermitage is open from 10.30 am to 5.30 or 6 pm Tuesday to Sunday, closed Monday. Entry costs non-Russians about US$7.50.

The 47.5-metre **Alexander Column** in Dvortsovaya ploshchad commemorates the 1812 victory over Napoleon. Across the road from Dvortsovaya ploshchad is the gilded spire of the old **Admiralty**, the former headquarters of the Russian navy from 1711 to 1917 . West of the Admiralty is **ploshchad Dekabristov** (Decembrists' Square), named after the Decembrists' Uprising of 14 December 1825. The most famous statue of Peter the Great, the **Bronze Horseman**, stands at the river end of the square.

The golden dome of bulky **St Isaac's Cathedral**, built between 1818 and 1858, looms just south of ploshchad Dekabristov.

Several hundred steps lead up to the colonnade (*kolonnada*) around the drum of the dome from where sublime city views can be enjoyed. About 600 metres west of plo-shchad Dekabristov, at naberezhnaya Krasnogo Flota 44, is the **St Petersburg History Museum** which has good information on the 1941-44 siege. It's open 11 am to 5 or 6 pm, closed Wednesday.

Nevsky Prospekt Russia's most famous street runs four km from the Admiralty to the Alexandr Nevsky Monastery, from which it takes its name. The inner 2.5 km to Moscow Station is St Petersburg's main shopping centre. Tchaikovsky died at Malaya Morskaya ulitsa 13 (formerly ulitsa Gogolya). Across the Moyka river, Rastrelli's green **Stroganov Palace** (1752-54) has kept most of its original appearance. A block beyond are the great colonnaded arms of the **Kazan Cathedral**, which reach out towards the north side of the avenue. Inside is the **Museum of the History of Religion**, in the north transept of which is the grave of Field Marshal Kutuzov, the Russian commander against Napoleon in 1812. The popular department stores **Gostiny Dvor** and **Passazh** stand opposite each other a few blocks further east, and provide a good experience of shopping Russian style.

Nevsky prospekt crosses the Fontanka on the **Anichkov Bridge**, with its famous 1840s statues of rearing horses at its four corners. From here, the red 1840s **Beloselsky-Belozersky Palace** provides a photogenic baroque backdrop. At the end of Nevsky prospekt is the working **Alexandr Nevsky Monastery**, founded by Peter the Great in 1713. The **Tikhvin Cemetery** within, is where some of Russia's most famous artistic figures, including Tchaikovsky, are buried. You can wander most of the grounds free, but it costs US$0.75/0.35 for full/concession entry to Tikhvin.

Between Nevsky & Neva Just a block north of Nevsky prospekt metro is **ploshchad Iskusstv** (Arts Square), home to the **Large Hall** of the St Petersburg Philharmonia and the **Russian Museum** which houses one of the country's two finest collections of Russian art.

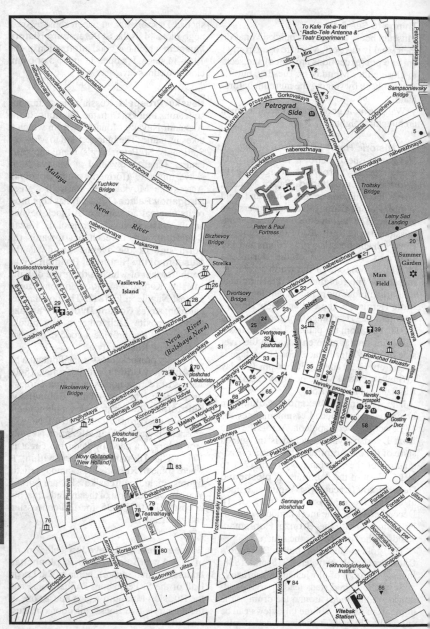

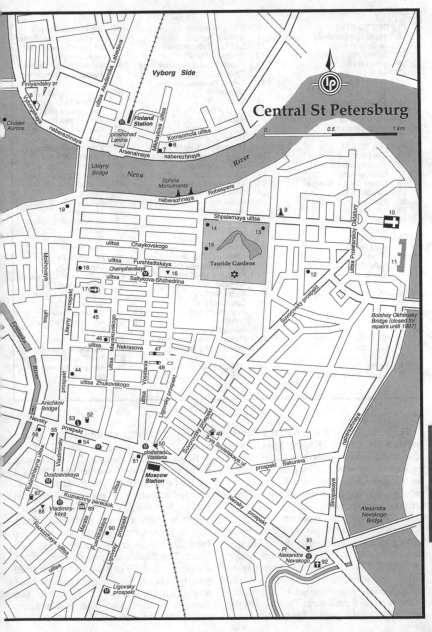

Central St Petersburg

Vyborg Side

Finlyandsky pr

Cruiser Aurora

Finland Station

ploshchad Lenina

ulitsa Akademika Lebedeva

Mikhaylova ulitsa

Komsomola ulitsa

Arsenalnaya naberezhnaya

Liteyny Bridge

Neva River

Sphinx Monuments

naberezhnaya

Robespera

Shpalernaya ulitsa

Tauride Gardens

ulitsa Chaykovskogo

ulitsa Furshtadtskaya

Chernyshevskaya

ulitsa Saltykova-Shchedrina

ulitsa Nekrasova

ulitsa Zhukovskogo

Mokhovaya ulitsa

Liteyny prospekt

Mayakovskogo ulitsa

Vosstania ulitsa

Anichkov Bridge

Nevsky prospekt

Vladimirsky

Rubinshteyna ulitsa

Dostoevskaya

Kuznechny pereulok

Vladimir-skaya

Marata ulitsa

Pushkinskaya

Razezzhaya ulitsa

ulitsa

Ligovsky prospekt

Moscow Station

ploshchad Vosstania

Suvorovsky prospekt

Ligovsky prospekt

3-ya Sovietskaya ul

prospekt Bakunina

Nevsky prospekt

Sinopskaya naberezhnaya

Suvorovsky prospekt

ulitsa Proletarskoy Diktatury

Bolshoy Okhtinsky Bridge (closed for repairs until 1997)

Alexandra Nevskogo Bridge

Pl Alexandra Nevskogo

Fontanka River

0   0.5   1 km

ST PETERSBURG

The multi-domed **Church of the Resurrection of Christ** (Khram Voskresenia Khristova) on the Griboedova Canal just off ploshchad Iskusstv was built in 1887-1907 on the spot where Alexander II, despite his reforms, was blown up by the People's Will terrorist group in 1881.

The **Pushkin Flat-Museum** (☎ 312 19 62), naberezhnaya reki Moyki 12, was home to the poet for the last year of his life. He died here after a duel in 1837 with a French soldier of fortune, d'Anthes, who had been paying public and insulting court to his beautiful wife, Natalia. The museum is open daily from 11 am to 5 pm except Tuesday and the last Friday of the month. Entry costs about

US$1.40 for foreigners and US$0.45 concession.

Between Mars Field and the Fontanka River is the lovely **Summer Garden**, laid out for Peter the Great with fountains, pavilions and a geometrical plan to resemble the park at Versailles. The modest, two-storey **Summer Palace** in the north-east corner was St Petersburg's first palace, built for Peter in 1704-14, and it remains pretty well intact. The garden is open all year, except during April, daily at 8 am and closes at 10 pm from May to August, 8 pm in September and 7 pm from October to March. The Summer Palace is also open as a museum during the summer.

Smolny The **Cathedral** at Smolny, three km east of the Summer Garden, is one of the most fabulous of all Rastrelli's buildings. Today the convent houses the city administration's offices while the cathedral is a concert hall, usually open only for performances. The **Smolny Institute**, built by Quarenghi in 1806-08 as a school for aristocratic girls, had fame thrust upon it in 1917 when Trotsky and Lenin directed the October Revolution from the headquarters of the Bolshevik Central Committee and the Petrograd Soviet which had been set up here.

South & West of Nevsky Prospekt At naberezhnaya reki Moyki 94 is the old **Yusupov Palace**, where the notorious Grigory Rasputin was murdered (open to visitors for a small fee). The baroque spires and domes of **St Nicholas' Cathedral** (1753-62), rising among the trees at the bottom of ulitsa Glinki, shelter many 18th-century icons and a fine carved wooden iconostasis. Just west of Sennaya ploshchad and across the Griboedova Canal, at ulitsa Kaznacheyskaya 7, is the flat where Dostoevsky wrote *Crime and Punishment*. Further east at Kuznechny pereulok 5 is the **Dostoevsky Museum**, where the writer died in 1881. The museum is open 11 am to 5 pm daily except Monday and the last Wednesday of every month. Admission is US$2 or US$1 concession.

Vasilevsky Island Here you can stand on the Strelka (Tongue of Land), where Peter the Great wanted his new city's administrative and intellectual centre, and admire one of the best views in the city. The **Central Naval Museum** (Tsentralny Voenno-Morskoy muzey) is full of maps, excellent modelships, flags and the *Botik*, Peter's first boat – a pre-turn-of-the-century submarine. It's open from 10.30 am to 5.30 pm (last entry is 4.45 pm), closed Monday, Tuesday, and the last Thursday of the month. Admission for non-Russians is US$1. Just south is the **Museum of Zoology** (Zoologichesky muzey), said to be one of the biggest and best in the world. Among the dioramas and the

tens of thousands of mounted beasties is a complete woolly mammoth thawed out of the Siberian ice in 1902. The museum is open daily (last entry 5 pm) except Friday; entry costs US$0.20/0.05 for full/concession tickets.

Peter's own personal collection of 'curiosities' is housed in the blue and white building with the steeple, the **Museum of Anthropology & Ethnography**, founded by Peter himself in 1714. It's open daily except Thursday and costs US$1.70.

Petrograd Side Petrograd Side (Petrogradskaya storona) is a cluster of delta islands between the Malaya Neva and Bolshaya Nevka channels. Founded in 1703, the **Peter & Paul Fortress** (Petropavlovskaya krepost) is the oldest building in St Petersburg. Its main use up to 1917 was as a political prison; one of its first inmates was Peter's own son Alexey, whose torture Peter is said to have overseen personally inside the **Trubetskoy Bastion**. Other famous residents were Dostoevsky, Gorky, Trotsky and Lenin's older brother, Alexandr. In the south wall is **Nevsky Gate**, a later addition, where prisoners were loaded on boats for execution elsewhere. At noon every day a cannon is fired from the **Naryshkin Bastion**, scaring the daylights out of the tourists. Most spectacular of all is the **Cathedral of SS Peter & Paul**, with its landmark needle-thin spire and magnificent baroque interior. Entry to the fort is free. It's open from 11 am to 6 pm (to 4 pm Tuesday), closed Wednesday and the last Tuesday of the month.

East of Kamennoostrovsky prospekt at ulitsa Kuybysheva 4 is the Ksheshinskaya Palace containing the Museum of Political History in Russia (☎ 233 71 13). It's open 10 am to 6 pm every day except Wednesday and costs US$1.50. The Bolsheviks made their headquarters here and Lenin often gave speeches, from the balcony of this elegant Art Nouveau palace that once belonged to Matilda Kshesinskaya, famous ballet dancer and one-time lover of Tsar Nicholas II.

East of the fortress at Petrovskaya naberezhnaya 6 is St Petersburg's first residence,

Peter's Cabin (Domik Petra) where Peter lived in 1703 while supervising the construction of the fortress and city. At the northern end of Petrograd side is the **Leningrad Radio-Tele Broadcasting Centre's antenna** which is open for excursions by arrangement with Peter TIPS (see Tourist Offices). The 50,000-watt transmitter tower stands 310 metres, giving excellent views over the city, and was the first of its kind in the Soviet Union when it was constructed in 1963.

Organised Tours

Practically every travel agency and hotel organises tours (see Travel Agencies). Eighty-minute 'City on the Neva' cruises, up the river and back from Hermitage No 2 landing, leave every 40 minutes and cost US$0.75. Excursion boats also leave the Anichkov Bridge landing on the Fontanka River just off Nevsky prospekt every 15 minutes from 10.45 am to 8 pm for a 75-minute sail. The HI St Petersburg Hostel organises unbeatable walking tours.

Special Events

The last 10 days of June, during St Petersburg white nights, is one massive celebration which includes the *White Nights Dance Festival*. The *Russian Winter* (25 December to 5 January) and *Goodbye Russian Winter* (late February to early March) festivities centre outside the city, with troika rides, folk shows and performing bears. The week before Christmas is the classical music festival, the *Christmas Musical Meetings in Northern Palmyra*. The *St Petersburg Music Spring*, an international classical music festival, is held in April or May, and the mid-November international jazz festival, *Osenie Ritmy* (Autumn Rhythms), is built around St Petersburg's jazz clubs.

Places to Stay

Hostels The *HI St Petersburg Hostel* (☎ 329 80 18; fax 329 80 19; e-mail ryh@ryh .spb.su to book) could not have a better location, five-minutes walk north-east of Moscow Station and ploshchad Vosstania.

Beds cost US$15 a night (US$17 for non-members), including breakfast, in rooms with two to six beds.

The *Holiday Hostel* (☎ 542 73 64; fax 325 85 59; e-mail postmaster@hosteling.spb.su) at ulitsa Mikhailova 1, Vyborg Side, just south of Finland Station and next door to the noisy Kresty Prison, has beds for US$17 a night. Its rooftop café offers the classic panorama of Peter & Paul Fortress against the backdrop of raised drawbridges. The code for the front door is 1648.

The *Summer Hostel* (☎ 252 75 63; fax 252 40 19) at ulitsa Baltiyskaya 26 (metro Narvskaya) is not well located but it's the cheapest in town.

Hotels – bottom end The crumbling *Oktyabrskaya* (☎ 277 63 30) at Ligovsky prospekt 10 opposite Moscow Station has comfortable, but well-worn, singles/doubles for US $30/40.

The *Hotel Rus* (☎ 273 46 83, 272 66 54) at ulitsa Artilleryskaya 1 (metro Chernyshevskaya) is a large, modern and popular place not far from the city centre and a good bet at US$28/40 for singles/doubles.

Near metro Chyornaya Rechka, is the *Hotel Vyborgskaya* (☎ 246 91 41, 246 23 19) at Torzhkovskaya ulitsa 3, Vyborg Side. Its three buildings have singles/doubles from US$28/48, some with attached bath, some communal.

South of the centre is the dumpy but cheerful *Kievskaya Hotel* (☎ 166 04 56), Dnepropetrovskaya ulitsa 49, and the *Hotel Zarya* (☎ 166 83 98), a block away at Kurskaya ulitsa 40, both of which charge a reasonable US$22/44.

Hotels – middle *Hotel St Petersburg* (☎ 542 90 31, 542 94 11) opposite the Cruiser *Aurora* at Vyborgskaya naberezhnaya 5/2, Vyborg Side (metro Ploshchad Lenina) has singles/doubles for US$75/95 – not a bad deal.

The *Hotel Moskva* (☎ 274 30 01, 274 20 51) opposite the Alexander Nevsky Monastery and popular with package tours has singles/doubles for US$65/72.

About three km north of the airport and eight km south of the city centre at ploshchad Pobedy 1 is the Intourist *Pulkovskaya Hotel* (☎ 264 51 22). Singles/doubles cost US $120/140 including breakfast.

Hotels – top end Luxurious to the point of being decadent with price tags to match include the *Hotel Astoria* (☎ 210 57 57; fax 315 96 68) in front of St Isaac's Cathedral at ulitsa Bolshaya Morskaya (ulitsa Gertsena) 39; the *Nevskij Palace Hotel* (☎ 275 20 01) at Nevsky prospekt 57; and the much-admired *Grand Hotel Europe* (☎ 325 60 00; fax 325 60 01), considered the finest property in town, at Mikhailovskaya ulitsa 1/7.

Places to Eat

To sum up this city's dining scene in a nutshell, whatever you want, you've got; from Uzbek to Arabian, Chinese to Italian, Western European cuisine to good ol' Russian cooking, it's here and in abundance. For self-caterers (definitely a cheaper option), chain stores such as Babylon and Holiday have a number of well-stocked, 24-hour outlets open all over the city.

Restaurants The *Korean House* at Izmaylovsky prospekt 2 serves up some of the best Korean food in Eastern Europe with a decidedly heavy hand on the garlic and spices. Main courses range from US$3 to US$5.

For Georgian food look no further than the excellent *Kafkaz* immediately on your left after crossing Alexandra Nevskogo Bridge. If you stick to a selection of appetisers you can eat to full capacity for no more than US$15.

Tandoor (☎ 312 38 86), Voznesensky prospekt 2, just off Isaakievskaya ploshchad, is *the* Indian place in town, with a full traditional Indian menu for about US$9 for a main dish. If you like things spicy, insist on *spicy* (open daily from noon to 11 pm).

Bistro le Francais (☎ 210 96 22) at Galernaya ulitsa 20 is just that – the genuine French chef greets guests with a jaunty *'Bonjour'* – but *sans* surly maître d' who pretends not to speak English. It has very nice, very rich specialities from US$8 to US$20.

For Russian cuisine try *Staraya Derevnaya*, a family-run traditional Russian restaurant north of the centre at Savushkina ulitsa 72 (nearest metro is Chyornaya Rechka, then take tram No 2, 31 or 37).

Daddy's Steak Room is a bit out of the way, south of the city centre at Moskovsky prospekt 73 (just next to metro Frunzenskaya), but the trip is worth it. St Petersburg's first Western-style steak house, this Finnish-run godsend serves great slabs of beef at very reasonable prices – for about US$10.

Cafés At the Admiralty end of Nevsky prospekt, the *Kafe Druzhba*, at No 15, has good chicken and bliny from US$1.50 to US$3 (open from 11 am to 11 pm). Close by at Nevsky prospekt 3 is one of our favourite ice-cream cafés, *Kafe Morozhenoe*, open daily from 10 am to 9 pm.

North and east of Nevsky prospekt there is *Bagdad Kafe* at ulitsa Furshtadtskaya 27 which is cooler than ever, serving excellent huge and tasty manty dumplings for around US$2.40 and plov for US$1.90. It's open from noon to 11 pm.

Springtime Shwarma Bistro at ulitsa Radishcheva 20 is our favourite Middle-Eastern place in town because it's so darn cheap and good. You can get a gyro or felafel for under US$1 and it has a large selection of other Middle-Eastern specialities, especially vegetarian ones (open daily from 11 am to 11 pm).

The best place to sample Russian cuisine is *Staroye Café* at naberezhnaya reki Fontanki 108, a small and cosy joint furnished in turn-of-the-century style (open daily noon to 11 pm).

On Petrograd Side, the *Grand Café Antwerpen* (☎ 233 97 46) at Kronverksky prospekt 13/2 is a bit of a flash place with fantastic stuffed mushrooms, scrumptious cakes and darn good Belgian beer. It's open from noon to midnight.

Not far north from here, at ulitsa Malaya Posadskaya 2, is *Troitsky Most* (aka the *Hare Krishna Kafe*), which specialises in excellent vegetarian dishes and herbal teas for under US$2. It's open from 11 am to 8 pm (break from 3 to 4 pm). In contrast, *Kafe Tet-a-Tet*, at Bolshoy prospekt 65, Petrograd Side, only has tables for two, and you can listen to a pianist tinkling away while you dine (open from 1 to 5 pm and 7 pm to midnight).

Fast Food Practically every street in the city centre has several places where you can grab a bite of something. In addition, the standard Russian blinnayi, bistros, kafe morozhenoe, kafeterii, stolovayi and bufety are all over the place.

Centrally located is *Pizza Hut*, at 71/76 naberezhnaya reki Moyki, dishing out a variety of pizza for US$5 to US$11. South of the city centre, *Pizza House* near metro Tekhnologichesky Institut at ulitsa Podolskaya 23 serves Finnish-style pizzas for US$8 to US$ 10 as well as decent Italian food. A third good pizza place, *Pizza Pronto*, is at Zagorodny 8.

Next to the Chayka bar at naberezhnaya kanala Griboedova 14 is the *Laima Bistro*, open 24 hours and serving the best freshly-squeezed juice in town as well as chicken, gyros and various salads for around US$3.

Burgers are available at *Carrols* at ulitsa Vosstania 5, Nevsky prospekt 45 and Kamennoostrovsky prospekt 31. It is a Finnish-run place doing fast-food set meals for under US$5. It opens daily from 9 am to 11 pm.

For a healthier option try the largest *Minutka* sandwich shop in the world at Nevsky prospekt 20. It is a life-saver (open from 10 am to 10 pm daily).

Equally fantastic is *Gril Diez* at Kamennoostrovsky prospekt 16, Petrograd Side, which dishes up whole spit-roast chicken (though on some days they can be a tad scrawny) for about US$2 (open from 10 am to 8 pm).

Entertainment

Check the *St Petersburg Times* and *Pulse* for listings of what's on.

Ballet, Opera, Theatre & Classical Music

September to early summer is the main performing season. Most theatres and concert halls are closed on Monday.

The Kirov Ballet and Opera are at the Mariinsky Theatre at Teatralnaya ploshchad 1. Your best bet for tickets (which cost around US$4) is through the Teatralnaya Kassa (☎ 314 93 85) at Nevsky prospekt 42.

The St Petersburg Philharmonic performs at the Bolshoy Zal (Large Hall; ☎ 311 74 89) on ploshchad Iskusstv, and the Maly Zal imeni MI Glinki (Small Hall) nearby at Nevsky prospekt 30.

The premier drama theatre is the Pushkin at ploshchad Ostrovskogo 2. Other top theatres include the Lensoviet Theatre at Vladimirsky prospekt 12, and the Gorky Bolshoy Dramatic Theatre at naberezhnaya reki Fontanki 65. Teatr Experiment at the corner of Kamennoostrovsky and Bolshoy prospekt (Petrograd Side), hosts alternative performances and is a gay and lesbian nightclub at the weekend.

Bars, Clubs & Discos

The Tribunal bar opposite the Bronze Horseman on the Embankment is lively; it's the kind of place where it's difficult to decide which women don't charge for their services, but fun nonetheless. It's open daily from 11 am to 3 am. Pints start at US$4. Other top bars include *Mollies Irish Bar* at ulitsa Rubinshteyna 36 (open daily from 11 am to 3 am); another Irish one, the *Shamrock* at ulitsa Dekabristov 27, and the *Rose Pub* at Liteyny prospekt 14. *The Beer Garden*, opposite the Nevskij Palace Hotel is a great summer spot.

Mainstream clubs worth frequenting are *Domenico's* at Nevsky prospekt 70, a class-act disco and nightclub popular with expatriates and Russians alike; *XL*, at Bolshaya Konyushennaya 1 and the ultra-hip *Pyramid* on the corner of Dumskaya ulitsa and Lomonosova ulitsa. More alternative and definitely cheaper is *Fish Fabric* at Pushkinskaya 10. Jazz fans should try the *Jazz Philharmonic Hall* at Zagorodny prospekt, a 10-minute walk to the south-west from metro Dostoevskaya.

Circus The St Petersburg State Circus
(☎ 210 46 49) at naberezhnaya reki Fontanki
3, half a km south of the Summer Garden has
nightly shows at 7.30 pm, plus afternoon and
lunch-time performances at weekends.
Tickets bought here cost up to US$2.

Getting There & Away

Air St Petersburg has direct air links with
most major European capitals and airlines,
many offering several connections each
week (Lufthansa offers six flights a week
to/from Frankfurt).

You can also fly just about anywhere you
want within Russia, but only a few times a
week in some cases. There are daily flights
to Moscow, Kiev, Minsk, Murmansk,
Odessa, Petrozavodsk, Pskov and Tbilisi.
Tickets can be purchased at Aeroflot offices
(☎ 104 38 22), Nevsky prospekt 7, and
travel agencies such as Sindbad Travel.

Bus St Petersburg has two long-distance bus
stations: Avtovokzal 1 at naberezhnaya
Obvodnogo kanala 118 (near metro Baltiyskaya) serves northern destinations such as
Vyborg and Karelia; Avtovokzal 2 at
naberezhnaya Obvodnogo kanala 36 (10
minutes from metro Ligovsky prospekt)
serves Baltic countries and destinations to
the south and east including Moscow and
beyond.

Three bus companies offer a daily service
between Helsinki and St Petersburg: St
Petersburg Express, which leaves from the
Hotel Astoria; Finnord (☎ 314 89 51) at
ulitsa Italyanskaya 37; and Sovtransavto
Express Bus (☎ 264 51 25). The journey
takes seven hours and costs around US$40.

Train St Petersburg has four major long-
distance train stations: Finland Station
(Finlyandsky vokzal) on ploshchad Lenina,
Vyborg Side, serves trains on the Helsinki
railway line; Moscow Station (Moskovsky
vokzal), at ploshchad Vosstania on Nevsky
prospekt, handles trains to/from Moscow,
the far north, Crimea, the Caucasus, Georgia
and Central Asia; Vitebsk Station (Vitebsky
vokzal), at Zagorodny prospekt 52, deals

with Smolensk, Belarus, Kiev, Odessa and
Moldova; and Warsaw Station (Varshavsky
vokzal), at naberezhnaya Obvodnogo kanala
118, covers the Baltic states and Eastern
Europe. Baltic Station (Baltiysky vokzal),
just along the road from the Warsaw Station,
is mainly for suburban trains.

Domestic and international train informa-
tion and tickets are available from the
Intourist counter (No 13) at the Central Train
Ticket Centre at naberezhnaya kanala
Griboedova 24. Sindbad Travel at the HI St
Petersburg Hostel also has a ticket-buying
service, adding US$5 on to the ticket price.
Foreigners have to pay about a third more
than Russians for tickets.

Two day-trains to Helsinki depart from St
Petersburg daily. The journey takes around
six hours and a one-way ticket costs US$65
at the train station, or around US$50 at
Sindbad Travel. Between St Petersburg and
Tallinn there is one overnight train, leaving
St Petersburg at 10.57 pm and arriving in
Tallinn the next day at 10 am. A Rīga-bound
overnight train leaves St Petersburg daily at
9.37 pm, arriving in Rīga the next day at
11.20 am. There are several trains a day to
Vilnius, taking around 12 hours and costing
US$30 one way.

Car & Motorcycle The cheapest car rental
companies include Astoria Rent A Car
(☎ 210 58 58) inside the Astoria Hotel and
Svit (☎ 356 93 29) inside the Prebaltiyskaya
Hotel.

Getting Around

To/From the Airport St Petersburg's airport
is at Pulkovo, about 17 km south of the city
centre. From Moskovskaya metro, bus No 39
runs to Pulkovo-1, the domestic terminal,
and No 13 to Pulkovo-2, the international
terminal. Taxis to/from the airport cost from
US$6 to at least US$20.

Local Transport A handy, pocket-sized
metro map is printed on the reverse of the
Traveller's Yellow Pages City Map, sold in
most book stores and at Peter TIPS (see
Tourist Offices). Metro tokens *(zhetony)*,

which you drop in a slot at the entry gates, cost US$0.25 and can be bought from booths in the station. The metro runs from 5.30 am to around 12.30 am. Tram, trolleybus and bus all use the usual ticket-punching system. Tickets, valid for all three, are available in kiosks or directly from the driver.

Taxi There are few official, metered taxis in St Petersburg. The average price for a ride across the centre of town in a private car is about US$2. Calling to order a taxi is the most reliable way: City Taxi Service (☎ 265 13 33). Water taxis start at US$30.

Around St Petersburg

Outside of St Petersburg lie a handful of splendid old tsarist palaces – Petrodvorets on the coast with its famous flowing fountains, Pavlovsk with its magnificent park and Pushkin, the most glorious palace of all. They can all be visited in a day from the city.

The 13th-century city of Vyborg filled with old buildings and cobblestone streets near the Finnish border, is a good stop en route between St Petersburg and Helsinki.

PETRODVORETS

Petrodvorets, an estate built by Peter the Great 29 km west of St Petersburg, was destroyed by the Germans in WWII and is largely a reconstruction. The centrepiece of the grounds is the **Grand Cascade & Water Avenue**, a symphony of over 140 fountains and canals. Between the cascade and the formal **Upper Garden** is the **Grand Palace** (closed Monday and the last Tuesday of the month). The finest room in this vast museum of lavish rooms and galleries is Peter's study, apparently the only room to survive the Germans. The estate also features other buildings of interest — **Monplaisir**, Peter's villa, the **Hermitage**, and **Marly** – and other parks and pavilions. To the east an old Orangery houses the **Historical Museum of Wax Figures**, containing 49 figures of big-wigged Russians from the 18th and 19th centuries.

The grounds are open from 9 am to 10 pm daily, with museums opening 11 am to 8 pm from the end of May to the end of September.

Getting There & Away

Trains take 40 minutes from St Petersburg's Baltic Station to Novy Petrodvorets, departing every 30 to 60 minutes until early evening. From Novy Petrodvorets Station, take any bus but No 357 to the fifth stop (the fourth is a church); one-way tickets cost about US$1.

From May to September the hydrofoil departs from the jetty in front of St Petersburg's Hermitage every 20 to 30 minutes until at least 7 pm. Sailing time is 30 minutes, and one-way tickets cost about US$5.

PUSHKIN & PAVLOVSK

The centrepiece of Pushkin's palaces and parks, 25 km south of St Petersburg, is the Rastrelli baroque **Catherine Palace** (designed by Rastrelli and built in 1752-56), also destroyed in WWII. The exterior and 20-odd rooms have since been restored. The ticket office is in the middle of the courtyard side.

Around Catherine Palace extends **Catherine Park**. In the outer section of the park is the **Great Pond**, surrounded by an intriguing array of structures including the **Pyramid** where Catherine the Great buried her favourite dogs.

Pavlovsk's park, 29 km south of St Petersburg and designed by Charles Cameron between 1781 and 1786, is one of the most exquisite in Russia. Pavlovsk's **Great Palace** was a royal residence until 1917, burnt down in WWII but fully restored by 1970. Park highlights include the **Treble Lime Alley** stretching north-east from the palace, the two **Great Circles** just to its north with their statues of Justice and Peace, and the **Classical Temple of Friendship** down by the Slavyanka River (by Cameron, 1782).

Entry to either main palace costs foreigners US$7.25, and they are open daily from 11 am to 6 pm (5 pm in winter) (except

Tuesday and the last Monday of the month for Catherine Palace, and Friday and the first Monday of the month for the Great Palace).

Getting There & Away

Trains depart from St Petersburg's Vitebsk Station from platforms No 1, 2 or 3 to the Detskoe selo Station (zone 3 ticket) for Pushkin and from the same platforms to Pavlovsk Station (zone 4). The journey takes about half an hour. A five-minute ride on bus No 370, 371, or 378 from outside Detskoe selo Station takes you to within two minutes walk of Pushkin's Catherine Palace. From Pavlovsk Station, you can reach the Great Palace either by bus No 370, 383, 383A or 493 (five to 10 minutes); or by entering the park opposite the station, and walking 1.5 to two km to the palace. Bus No 370 also runs between Pushkin and Pavlovsk.

VYBORG

Vyborg, 160 km from St Petersburg, is one of the oldest cities in Europe. Its central feature is the medieval **Vyborg Castle**, built by the Swedes in 1293. Close by is the 16th century **Round Tower**, **Peter & Paul Cathedral** and **Cathedral of the Transfiguration**. Across the bridge is the **Anna Fortress**, built in the 18th century as protection against the Swedes.

Places to Stay & Eat

The *Hotel Druzhba* (☎ 278-2 57 44), close to the train station at ulitsa Zheleznodorozhnaya 5, has comfortable singles/doubles for US$45/60. If you don't fancy eating in the hotel's more than adequate restaurant, try the surprisingly good Chinese restaurant, *Samira* at Storozhevoy Bashni ulitsa 10, near to the watch tower of the cathedral.

Getting There & Away

From St Petersburg, all buses to Helsinki stop at Vyborg. Trains leave every hour from St Petersburg's Finland Station, taking 2½ hours.

ST PETERSBURG

Sweden

Sweden has everything: Danish castles in the south, thousands of lakes and saunas and even a few minor fjords. The north has Samis and reindeer, the midnight sun shines all night long and the royal castles around Stockholm don't just look French, they *are* French. Only one thing's missing: the tourists.

You could blame the tourism officials or say that Sweden doesn't have anything very unique, but that's not the case.

The last time Swedes fought a war was in 1809 when they lost Finland to Russia. In this country unravaged by war, society has been able to flourish. Perhaps no other nation has been so international for such a long time. Today Swedes are everywhere: helping the poor in Africa, selling Volvos in Bangkok, backpacking in Australia or modelling in California (or drinking in Torremolinos). Swedes tend to think of themselves as observers rather than the ones to be observed: they visit other countries, they've accepted more foreigners per capita than almost any other country and they enjoy ethnic cuisines with the best French wines. Somewhere along the way they forgot about their own country.

Yet, the statistics are astounding: Sweden has more than 25,000 protected Iron Age graveyards or burial mound areas, 1140 prehistoric fortresses, 2500 open-air rune stones, 3000 churches (almost one third of them medieval), thousands of protected nature reserves and more than 10,000 km of trekking and bicycle paths. All these attractions can be visited free of charge but doing so could take a lifetime. Add 10 royal castles in the Stockholm area alone, hundreds of superb museums, and more Top 40 hits (since Abba) than any other continental European country has produced. It would be difficult to imagine more starkly beautiful landscapes than those found in northern Sweden, one of the last remaining wilderness areas in Europe. The coastal archipelago

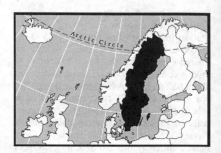

(skärgård) around Stockholm has 24,000 islands, served by one of the largest fleets of century-old steamers anywhere.

There are so many free things in Sweden, but when you pay, you pay dearly. Yet the quality is invariably high. Beware: after you've seen one attraction, you may want to see them all!

Facts about the Country

HISTORY
Written records survive only from late in the Middle Ages. But the number and variety of fortifications, assembly places, votive sites and graves is impressive. Of these the highest concentrations are around the Mälaren valley, in Uppland (the ancient region centred on Uppsala) and on the Baltic islands Gotland and Öland.

Humankind and metallurgy made late appearances and only in the Bronze Age, after the arrival of Indo-Europeans, was there rich trade. But the early cultural life is still eloquently expressed by the *hällristningar* (rock paintings) that survive in many parts of Sweden. They depict ritual or mythological events using familiar symbols of the warrior, the boat, the sun and the beasts of the hunt. Stone Age dolmens and chambered

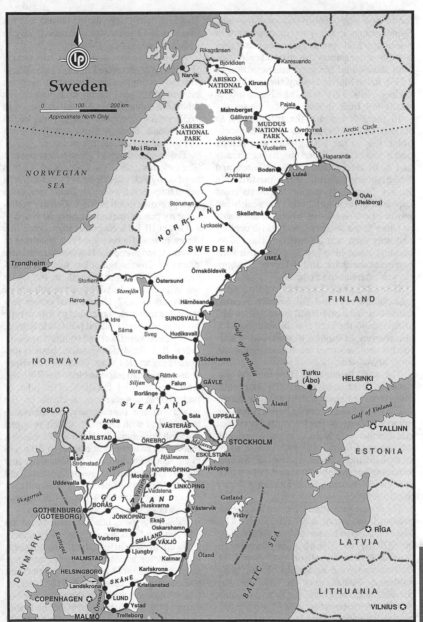

tombs gave way to cairns and small mounds. Stone settings in the shape of ships were in use by the Iron Age as graves or cenotaphs of this warrior society that still had chieftains (and slaves until the great emancipation of 1335). In the Mälaren valley, the first known trading posts were established and monuments with runic inscriptions can be seen.

In the 9th century the missionary St Ansgar visited Birka near modern Stockholm, just as the Viking Age was getting under way. Gotland and the Svear already had links throughout the Baltic area and Swedish adventurers have meddled in Russia. Roman, Byzantine and Arab coins appeared in huge numbers. The wealth and power of the Svear overwhelmed the Gauts or *Götar* to the south before the 11th century and only then was a Christian, Olof Skötkonung, made king just as a Swedish state began to take shape. In 1164 an archbishopric was established in Uppsala.

King Magnus Ladulås instigated a national law code in 1350. Sweden avoided feudalism, but a privileged aristocracy owed allegiance to the king and the wealth of the church grew. St Birgitta, the fascinating spiritualist and reformer of Rome, began an order at Vadstena.

The south belonged to Denmark and was strongly influenced by it. The Hanseatic League established walled trading towns such as Visby and a strong German presence in early Stockholm. But Denmark interceded and together with Norway joined Sweden in the Union of Kalmar in 1397. Danish monarchs held the Swedish throne for awhile, tolerating an assembly of four estates which was the forerunner of the modern *Riksdag* (parliament).

The regent Sten Sture loosened the Danish hold with the sword at Stockholm in 1471. The execution of his son and namesake there in 1520 by the Danish king Christian II caused further rebellion that began in Dalarna under the leadership of the young nobleman Gustaf Vasa. In 1523 he was crowned as Gustaf I and set about introducing the Reformation and a powerful, centralised nation-state. In mainly Catholic Småland, Nils Dacke defied Gustaf, but his death in 1543 left a strong throne firmly in control of a Lutheran Sweden.

A period of expansion began under Gustaf II Adolf, who interfered in the Thirty Years' War to champion the Protestant German princes and remove the imperial threat to his ambitions in the Baltic. He fell at Lützen in 1632, yet Sweden was to gain territory on the Baltic coast. Sweden then controlled much of Finland and the Baltic countries.

The so-called age of great power passed. The megalomania of the young Karl XII was crushed by Peter the Great at Poltava. Karl's adventures cost Sweden its Baltic territories and the crown much prestige. Greater parliamentary power marked the next 50 years.

Gustaf III led a coup that interrupted this development. He brought French culture to his court, and introduced a Swedish academy of culture. His foreign policy was less auspicious and he was murdered, at the opera while in fancy dress, by a conspiracy of aristocrats in 1792. Unrestricted power vested in the monarch was ended by aristocratic revolt in 1809 and Finland was lost to Russia.

The same year Sweden produced a constitution that divided legislative powers between king and Riksdag. The king's advisory council was also responsible to the Riksdag, which controlled taxation. The post of ombudsman appeared as a check on the powers of the bureaucracy. Sweden also made a deal with Denmark which swapped Swedish Pomerania for Norway. Napoleon's marshal Bernadotte was chosen to fill a gap in the succession and, as Karl Johan, became regent. Thus began the rise of liberalism and Sweden's policy of neutrality. The military enforcement of the 1814 union with Norway was Sweden's last involvement in war.

Industry arrived late but was based on efficient steel making and the safety match, a Swedish invention. Iron-ore mining, important for at least 300 years, and then steel manufacture, began to expand and produce a middle class. But the 1827 statute, which scattered the agricultural villages of much of the Swedish countryside, had more immediate and far-reaching effects – the old social fabric disappeared. Potatoes had become the staple crop, producing amongst other things *brännvin*, sometimes called schnapps or Swedish vodka.

In 1866 a very limited franchise was introduced for a new and bicameral Riksdag. Many farmers preferred to migrate and endure hardship in the USA, but when US corn began to penetrate the Swedish market, tariffs became the great issue. This led to tensions with free-trading Norway and ultimately to the end of the union in 1905.

By 1900 almost one in four Swedes lived in cities and industry (based on timber, precision machinery and hardware) was on the upswing. In this environment the working class was radicalised.

Conscription was first introduced as a measure against Russian power in 1901 and men aged over 24 years received the vote in 1907. Moves to cut wages caused 300,000 people to strike two years later, which was a setback for the labour movement. Temperance movements profoundly influenced the labour movement and alcohol restrictions became state policy.

Sweden declared itself neutral at the outbreak of WWI and was governed bilaterally until 1917. But food shortages caused unrest and consensus was no longer possible: for the first time a social democratic government, a coalition, took control. Reforms followed quickly and suffrage for all adults aged over 23 years was introduced, as well as the eight-hour working day.

The social democrats dominated politics after 1932 and the liberal tendencies of the 1920s *statsminister*, Hjalmar Branting, joined with economic intervention (under Per Albin Hansson) and measures to introduce a welfare state.

These trends were scarcely interrupted by Sweden's studied and ambiguous approach to WWII. The social democrats sponsored models for industrial bargaining and full employment which attracted imitators and allowed the economy to blossom in harmony under Tage Erlander. The economic pressures of the 1970s began to cloud Sweden's social goals and it was under Olof Palme that support for social democracy first wavered. Palme's murky assassination in 1986 and subsequent government scandals shook national confidence and, in 1991, a right-of-centre coalition under the Moderates won power.

Sweden's move towards the EU was begun through its membership in the European Free Trade Agreement. Sweden joined on 1 January 1995, but higher food prices and unemployment figures, if not the planned reforms aimed at dismantling the welfare state, caused the Union's popularity to plummet.

GEOGRAPHY & ECOLOGY

Sweden covers an area of 450,000 sq km and its maximum north-south extent is over 1500 km. This size allows for a little diversity, but the dominant characteristics of the landscape go back to the time of the glaciations. The flatness and openness of Skåne is like Denmark but the forests, mainly conifer but sprinkled with birch and hardwoods, thicken further north into Småland.

Geographical divisions in Sweden are complicated. The two kingdoms that were united in the 11th century form the southern half of the country: Götaland in the south and Svealand in lower central Sweden. Anything north of Svealand is called Norrland. The 25 historical regions (based on common dialect), or *landskap* remain as denominators for people's identity and a basis for regional tourist promotion. Modern administration is based on 24 provinces, or *län*, that also run regional traffic *(länstrafik)* and regional museums *(länsmuseums)*.

The rocky south-west coast is most notable for its fjords and skerries, although the Göta älv scarcely compares with the barrage of rocky archipelago that shields Stockholm. (Fjords, shaped mainly by glaciers, are much shallower at the mouth than at the centre.) There are approximately 100,000 lakes in Sweden. The islands of Öland and Gotland consist of flat limestone and sand.

Lake Mälaren is the heart of Sweden, although of the south and central lakes,

Vänern is by far the biggest. In Norrland there is a nearly uniform expanse of forest cut by river and rapid. Only in Lappland and Norrbotten do the trees seem to thin out and the low mountains of the far north-west assert themselves. The Norwegian spine provides a natural frontier in the west.

It is no surprise that Sweden led Europe in setting up national parks and that the biggest and best of these are in Lapland. Rules that govern the parks vary locally, but the principle is that responsible and careful people may have access to open areas (see Activities in the Facts for the Visitor section). Beaches are also protected and there are secondary areas maintained at a local level throughout Sweden. The level of ecological consciousness is high and reflected in concern for native animals, clean water and renewable resources.

GOVERNMENT & POLITICS

Sweden has maintained its monarch as head of state under the constitution, but the *statsminister* is chosen by the speaker of the Riksdag (parliament). Since 1971 there has been only one chamber in the parliament. From it come the cabinet ministers, who then lose their parliamentary vote. After several constitutional reforms in the 1970s, cabinet was confirmed as the ultimate decision-making power. The Riksdag, which has about 350 members, is elected every third September, but representatives of union, business and cooperative movements also sit and serve on its commissions.

The councils of the 24 *län* are convened by cabinet appointees, can levy taxes and are responsible for the administration of regional services such as public transport and health. At municipal level, more than 280 *kommuner* provide housing, roads and water.

ECONOMY

While Sweden is still one of the wealthiest and most regulated countries in the world, many economic indicators have nose-dived in the 1990s.

One of the most socialised countries in the world (the public sector constitutes some 65% of the domestic economy, the highest percentage in the world), Sweden is also one of the strongest industrial nations in Europe – demonstrated by such names as Volvo, Ericsson, SAAB or ABB. Until recently, there was nearly full employment. The unemployment rate is now about 8%, and the krona has been volatile. Tax rates rank among the highest in the world.

Even the social democrats (who built the system) admit that the era of the *folkhemmet* (the Swedish welfare state) is over. Yet, the idea of cradle-to-grave welfare is deeply entrenched in the Swedish psyche.

Timber and ore are vital to industry. About half the country is forested and half of this is in the hands of government or forestry companies. The iron mines of Kiruna and Gällivare in the Arctic north are of greatest importance. Only 10% of Sweden is farmland and most of this is in the south.

POPULATION & PEOPLE

There are 8.9 million people, which makes Sweden the most populous country in this book. The density is just over 20 people per sq km.

There are two native minorities: the 15,000 Sami or Lapps and about 30,000 Finns who live in the north-east. The Sami can be considered the 'original' inhabitants of the north. Today they keep reindeer or are engaged in tourism and forestry.

Birth and mortality rates in Sweden are low, but there has been a net immigration since WWII. Over one million residents are foreigners (either foreign nationals or people born outside Sweden), including nearly 50,000 Africans, a similar amount of South Americans, over 200,000 Asians and more than 200,000 Finns.

Greater Stockholm has 1.5 million inhabitants, Gothenburg is home to more than 700,000 and Malmö and Lund together have up to 500,000. Apart from a sprinkling of towns up the Bothnian coast there is only sparse settlement in Norrland – Umeå has over 100,000 inhabitants.

ARTS

The best known members of Sweden's artistic community have been writers: chiefly the influential dramatist and author August Strindberg and the widely translated children's writer Astrid Lindgren. But to the Swedish soul the Gustavian balladry of Carl Michael Bellman is perhaps dearest. Sweden lacks its own Grieg or Sibelius but its modern music industry is one of the strongest in continental Europe. Vilhelm Moberg, a representative of 20th-century proletarian literature, won international acclaim with *The Immigrants* and *The Emigrants*. Movie director Ingmar Bergman remains foremost among the great directors of all time.

The most important figure from Swedish culture, however, has been the scientist Carl von Linné, who classified plant species under Latin names in the 18th century and made pioneering field studies. Still better known is Alfred Nobel, first patron of the Nobel Institute and the international prizes.

CULTURE

Swedes are decent and serious people, who use their historical superpower status to boost their self-esteem – the 10th-century Vikings and the 17th-century expansionist kings are good role models. Elk (moose), the stubborn wild animal, is another symbol of Sweden. Vikings are remembered in boisterous drinking sessions, especially when Swedes travel to countries where booze is cheaper. Yet, another addictive substance is more closely associated with Swedes, *snus*, ground snuff-like tobacco that males (and a few females) keep under their stiff upper lips. Considering how strict Sweden is about other drugs, it's strange that so many bus drivers work mildly stoned!

Sweden's reputation as a social reformer, albeit sometimes misunderstood, is justified. After having sold (as a neutral country) weapons of destruction to the rest of the world during WWII, Sweden decided to save the world from all other evils, including capitalism. This institutionalised niceness saved oppressed refugees in the Third World, built the most comprehensive welfare state in the world, established equality among workers (90% are union members), liberated women and made life easier for the old and disabled. Just when other nations started to tire of this perfect 'watchdog of the world', the policy came to an abrupt end with the assassination of Olof Palme in 1986 – in the new unpredictable Sweden some neo-Nazis have been known to assault a person because of race or national origin.

Although the strong rural traditions have not been forgotten (the summer cottage by the water is a cliché – there are 600,000 second homes) modern Sweden is becoming increasingly urban. Nowhere else are Volvos and mobile phones so common. Since Abba stunned the world in the 1970s, the Swedish music industry has created new hits like there was no tomorrow (although I am not sure whether we should mention Ace of Base under this heading). The tall, good-looking sporty Swede complements this dynamic image perfectly.

Still today, Sweden regulates, and both taxes and subsidises, every step from cradle to grave. As a tourist you have to take a number and wait until it comes up on a digital display, and even then you may only book a seat! But this is all just *lagom* (satisfactorily acceptable) to Swedes who have created one of the most comfortable and stylish societies – a perfect destination for travellers, if you only can afford it!

Other Scandinavians resent Sweden's success – if Sweden meets, say Italy in a sports event, Norwegians and Finns will applaud when Italy scores.

RELIGION

Sweden has a Lutheran state church, which all citizens in principle join (in fact about 95% of citizens are members). The state, however, guarantees religious freedom. All but conscientious objectors pay a flat-rate church tax. Members also have rights of baptism and marriage in the home parish. The church synod is elected through delegates by members 18 years or over. Women may be ordained. Some half million foreigners are non-Christians.

LANGUAGE

Swedish is a Germanic language, belonging to the Nordic branch, and is spoken throughout Sweden and in parts of Finland. Swedes, Danes and Norwegians can, however, make themselves mutually understood since their languages are similar. Most Swedes speak English as a second language.

Since they share common roots, and the Old Norse language left sprinklings of words in Anglo-Saxon, you will find many similarities between English and Swedish. The pronunciations alter, however, and there are sounds in Swedish that are not found in English. There are, for instance, three more letters at the end of the Swedish alphabet: **å**, **ä** and **ö**.

One suggestion is to try to learn the common phrases for politeness, as your attempts will be greatly appreciated by the Swedes, who are not used to foreigners speaking Swedish.

Sami dialects (there are three main groups) are Uralic (hence not Indo-European) and ancestrally related to Finnish.

See the Language Guide at the back of the book for pronunciation guidelines and useful words and phrases.

Facts for the Visitor

PLANNING

Climate & When to Go

If you want sunshine, visit between late May and late July, bearing in mind that August can be wet. Monthly average temperatures in Stockholm and Malmö are highest in July at about 17°C. At this time the average in the northern mountains is about 11°C and there is usually plenty of sun in August. Humidity is generally low.

Light refraction in the northern latitudes increases the length of the day in the far north by 15 minutes before dawn and after sunset. Malmö in the south gets 17½ hours of light in midsummer, Sundsvall has constant light during the second half of June, and Kiruna has 45 days of continuous light. Stockholm has an average of about nine hours of sunshine daily from May to July, but Luleå leads the country in July with more than 10 hours. At 69° north, there is an average 'day' of only four twilight hours in December. There can be occasional minus temperatures and snowfalls in the mountains and the north even in summer: the range of temperatures north of the Gulf of Bothnia is almost 30°C.

Annual rainfall is greatest around Gothenburg at well over 700 mm, although this city's annual average temperature is amongst the warmest at just under 8°C. About a third of the precipitation in Lapland is snow, which lies on the ground for anything between 150 and 200 days a year.

Many youth hostels, camping grounds and attractions open only in summer, from late June to mid-August. Summer in Sweden can be hot, sunny and beautiful but travel in winter should be better planned and restricted. Big cities are in full swing all year round.

Books & Maps

There is a good range of general books, with an emphasis on art and literature, at the Sweden Bookshop (see Information in the Stockholm section). Some useful titles are:

Nature in Sweden, P Hanneberg/Swedish Institute (softback)
Swedish History in Outline, J Weibull (hardback)
A Concise History of Sweden, A Åberg (softback)
Swedish Politics During the 20th Century, S Hadenius (softback)
Gustavus Adolphus: A History of Sweden 1611-1632 Vol I-II, M Roberts (hardback)
Nordic Folk Art M Nodermann (hardback)
Manor Houses and Royal Castles in Sweden, B Söderberg (hardback)
Traditional Festivities in Sweden, I Liman, Swedish Institute (booklet)
A Small Treasury of Swedish Food, Federation of Swedish Farmers (booklet)
Gamla Stan, B & G Glase (softback)
Museer i Sverige/Museums of Sweden (softback)

Free maps are available in Swedish tourist offices abroad and around Sweden. The recommended maps are Lantmäteriverket's survey series coded in blue (1:100,000, 85 kr) and red (1:250,000, 110 kr). The *Fjällkartan* series is for the mountains (1:100,000, 99 kr); the more detailed green series is in a scale of 1:50,000 costs 69 kr each. Sailing maps (scales vary) cost 139 kr each. Motorists should compare the half a dozen Sweden atlases, such as the soft-cover *KAK Bilatlas* for 275 kr or the hard-cover *ICA Vägatlas* for 272 kr.

What to Bring
Raincoat and jumper (sweater) are necessary luggage at all times of year, because sudden changes can spoil summer weather quite quickly. From at least November to March only scarf and mittens and anorak or overcoat will suffice. In the more temperate months, use layers of thinner clothing that will dry more quickly. Other useful items include a hostel sleeping sheet (saves US$5 per day) and a tent and sleeping bag for cyclists. See also the What to Bring section in the Facts for the Visitor chapter.

SUGGESTED ITINERARIES
Depending on the length of your stay you might like to see and do the following:

Two days
    Visit Stockholm
One week
    Visit Stockholm and Gothenburg, and stop briefly at many small towns en route, including Uppsala
Two weeks
    Visit Stockholm, Gothenburg and Uppsala, and tour the Dalarna and Skåne regions
One month
    You can explore the country pretty thoroughly, including a few days visit to Abisko national park
Two months
    Visit all places mentioned in this chapter, or see Gotland or Dalarna in more detail and cut some of the towns

HIGHLIGHTS
National Parks
There are about 20 national parks in all kinds of landscape, but the best places to admire the mountains are the giant Sarek and the tiny Abisko in Lapland. Different again is the forest at Tiveden at the north end of Lake Vättern.

Islands
The Baltic islands Gotland and Öland have a different character to the mainland and this is reflected in the rare *raukar* rock forms and the flora. The islands are also summer centres and cabin holidays are popular. Some 24,000 islands off Stockholm and many more around the long coastline provide endless opportunities for exploration.

Historic Towns
When Gothenburg was founded in the early 1500s, Sweden already had 80 towns. Hailing from a mute antiquity is Birka, a Viking town on an island near Stockholm, and the rebuilt Eketorp fortified village on Öland is special. Lund is the oldest remaining town in Sweden, and Visby is the only walled medieval town remaining. Other fine examples include Sigtuna, Kalmar, Ystad, Stockholm, Linköping and Eksjö.

Museums
There are hundreds of colourful museums in Sweden, and especially the 50-odd museums of Stockholm exhibit world-class treasures. Regional museums *(länsmuseum)* and museum villages *(hembygsmuseum)* are very popular in Sweden and are better presented than most of those in Europe. Skansen in Stockholm combines folk-life, wildlife and livestock. Kulturen in Lund, Jamtli in Östersund and Malmöhus castle in Malmö are among the best. *Museer i Sverige* is a national guide in Swedish and English (80 kr).

Castles
Sweden has hundreds of castles, royal palaces and castle-like manor houses. Skåne has some very fine Danish castles from a bygone era, and the Royal Family in Stockholm still overlooks some 10 castles in and around Stockholm. Castles in Sweden can be palaces with gardens such as Drottningholm near Stockholm, lakeside residences such as Skokloster slott by Lake Mälaren and Vadstena slott, formidable fortresses such as Kalmar and Örebro castles and impressive ruins such as those at Borgholm on Öland.

SWEDEN

Uppsala slott and Malmöhus also function as museums.

Churches

Sweden has 3000 churches, built during the last 900 years. There are 100 medieval churches in Gotland, 240 in Skåne and more than 130 in the Stockholm-Uppsala region. Wooden medieval churches number 14 in Sweden. Entry to churches is free, except for the Riddarholmskyrkan burial church in Stockholm. There are all styles of cathedrals; the *domkyrkor* of Lund (Romanesque), Uppsala (Gothic) and Kalmar (baroque) are fine examples of each style. The wooden Särna gammelkyrka in upper Dalarna is also worthy of a visit.

TOURIST OFFICES

Sweden has about 350 local tourist information offices. Most are open long hours in summer and short hours (or not at all) in winter; others exhibit nomadic tendencies. Many of the offices in big towns stock brochures from all around Sweden.

Svenska Turistföreningen or STF, a national club, provides services to its members and general information and books. It also coordinates the *vandrarhem* (hostels) and mountain huts. Paying annual membership (adults 215 kr, juniors 65 kr, families 65 kr a member) attracts the same discounts as an HI card as well as discounts on books. The services, discounts and opportunities might make a year's membership worthwhile. Write to: Svenska Turistföreningen, Box 25, 10120 Stockholm. Its offices are at Kungsgatan 2, Stockholm; Östra Skeppsbron 1, Malmö; and Larmgatan 15-21, Gothenburg.

Tourist Offices Abroad

These offices can assist with tourist promotional material and enquiries:

Australia
    Scandinavian Airlines System (SAS), 5th floor, 350 Kent St, Sydney, NSW 2000 (☎ 02-9299 6688)
Denmark
    Sveriges Rejse og Turistråd, Skindergade 38, 1159 Copenhagen K (☎ 33 93 90 49)

Finland
    Ruotsin Matkailuneuvosto, Meritullintori 3a, 00170 Helsinki (☎ 09-669 313)
Germany
    Schweden-Werbung für Reisen und Touristik, Lilienstrasse 19, 20095 Hamburg (☎ 040-33 82 12)
Norway
    Sveriges Reise og Turistråd, Klingenbergsgate 5, 0120 Oslo 1 (☎ 22 83 34 15)
UK
    Swedish Travel & Tourism Council, 11 Montague Place, London W1H 2Al (☎ 0171-724 5868; fax 0171-724 5872)
USA
    Swedish Travel & Tourism Council, 655 Third Ave, New York, NY 10017-5617 (☎ 212-949 2333; fax 212-697 0835)

VISAS & DOCUMENTS

Visas

Temporary residency visas *(uppehållstillstånd)* are generally required only for stays of more than three months in Sweden and are issued free for specified periods. But citizens of South Africa, Hong Kong residents with Chinese passports and citizens of many African, Asian and Eastern European countries require special tourist visas for entry, which are valid for 90 days. Permits *(arbetstillstånd)* are necessary if you are working (see Work later in Facts for the Visitor). You cannot collect a visa inside Sweden and cannot normally extend your stay. You will probably wait two months before receiving your visa.

Guest students need special student residency permits and are allowed to take only summer jobs between mid-May and mid-September. These permits are not normally available to those wishing to attend folk high schools or local adult education centres.

Documents

Statens invandrarverk, the immigration authority, handles all applications for visas and work permits lodged at overseas diplomatic posts. This means that a minimum of six weeks (allow eight) is needed to process applications, which are examined by the police. You may have to post away your passport to have it stamped inside. Work permits can be renewed by Statens invandrarverk

(☎ 011-15 60 00), Vikboplan 5, Box 6113, 60006 Norrköping.

Citizens of the EU, Norway or Iceland do not need passports to travel to Sweden or permits to work. Identification must be carried but we recommend you always bring a passport.

To be eligible for discounts, you should be prepared to apply for a number of discount cards or passes. An international HI card will give discounts at STF-affiliated hostels. Most cards are available in Sweden only, including a national camping card, a Telia phonecard, the Reslust card for train discounts, some regional transport passes and discount cards for big cities.

EMBASSIES
Swedish Embassies Abroad
These legations handle visa applications abroad:

Australia
    5 Turrana St, Yarralumla ACT 2600 (☎ 06-273 3033)
Canada
    377 Dalhousie St, Ottawa K1N 9N8 (☎ 613-241 8553)
Denmark
    Sankt Annæ Plads 15A, 1250 Copenhagen K (☎ 33 14 22 42)
Finland
    Pohjoisesplanadi 7B, 00170 Helsinki (☎ 09-651 255)
Norway
    Nobelsgate 16, 0244 Oslo 2 (☎ 22 44 38 15)
UK
    11 Montague Place, London W1H 2RL (☎ 0171-417 6400)
USA
    Consulates-General, 1 Dag Hammarskjold Plaza, New York, NY 12201 (☎ 212-751 5900)
    19990 Wilshire Blvd, Los Angeles, CA 90024 (☎ 310-441 9233)

Foreign Embassies in Sweden
These embassies and legations are in Stockholm, although some neighbouring countries have consulates in Gothenburg, Malmö and Helsingborg:

Australia
    Block 5, Sergels Torg 12 (☎ 08-613 29 00)
Canada
    7th floor, Tegelbacken 4 (☎ 08-453 30 00)
Denmark
    Jakobs Torg 1 (☎ 08-406 75 00)
Finland
    Jakobsgatan 6 (☎ 08-676 67 00)
Germany
    Skarpögatan 9 (☎ 08-670 15 00)
New Zealand
    Consulate-General, Arsenalsgatan 8C (☎ 08-611 68 24)
Norway
    Strandvägen 113 (☎ 08-665 63 40)
Poland
    Consulate-General, Prästgårdsgatan 5, Sundbyberg (☎ 08-764 48 00)
UK
    Skarpögatan 6-8 (☎ 08-671 90 00)
USA
    Secretariat, Strandvägen 101 (☎ 08-783 53 00)

CUSTOMS
Sweden is a member of the EU, and going through customs rarely involve hassles. However, while Denmark is relatively liberal about drugs, Sweden is extremely strict. Sometimes it seems the good old Iron Curtain has been transferred to southern Sweden! Alcohol imports are more liberal than before: 15 litres of beer, five litres of wine and one litre of strong alcohol. Changes in allowances are likely in the near future.

MONEY
You should encounter few problems if you carry cash in any convertible currency or travellers' cheques of international brands. The safest form of money these days is your personal ATM card carrying a Visa, Plus, EC, Cirrus, Eurocard or MasterCard symbol. All these cards are accepted by the national Bankomat network of ATMs, provided by most Swedish banks.

Forex is one of the cheapest and easiest places to exchange money, found in the biggest cities and some ferry terminals. Forex charges 20 kr when you buy kronor (banks charge 35 kr). Forex has worse rates for travellers' cheques, however, and charges 15 kr per cheque (banks charge 50 kr per transaction but have better rates than Forex). You can buy foreign notes at no cost at Forex.

SWEDEN

Xchange Valutaspecialisten is another company with good deals.

Currency

The Swedish krona (plural kronor) is usually called 'crown' by Swedes speaking English. There are four coins: the 50 öre and the one, five and 10 kronor pieces. Prices are rounded off to the nearest 50 öre. The notes are 20, 100, 150, 500 and 1000 kronor.

Exchange Rates

The following currencies convert at these approximate rates:

Australia	A$1 =	5.24 Skr
Canada	C$1 =	4.86 Skr
Denmark	1 Dkr =	1.13 Skr
Finland	1 Fmk =	1.45 Skr
France	1FF =	1.29 Skr
Germany	DM1 =	4.34 Skr
Japan	¥100 =	5.97 Skr
New Zealand	NZ$1 =	4.63 Skr
Norway	1 Nkr =	1.02 Skr
UK	UK£1 =	10.35 Skr
USA	US$1 =	6.62 Skr

Costs

You can't have it all in Sweden. If you don't store your luggage but carry it around instead, you save US$4 in some cities. If you brew your own coffee at hostels, each cup saves you at least US$2.

But Sweden can be cheap too. Bring a tent and you can sleep for free in forests. Bring sheets and a HI membership card, and you pay 75 to 145 kr per night in each of the 400 hostels. Big towns offer excellent hotel packages which come with free entry to all attractions and public transport. Don't just buy a one-way bus ticket – ask about daily or weekly passes instead.

Stuff yourself at the breakfast buffet for about 40 kr (included in the price in most hotels), or at the special lunch package at around 50 kr, instead of dining á la carte in the evening.

Intoxicate yourself in merry central Europe and in Sweden opt for the cheap *lättöl* (light beer) instead.

Avoid the overpriced tourist traps and look for any of the free 30,000-odd historical or natural attractions.

The base prices for petrol are high (around 8 kr per litre for super in the south; expect the prices to be about 20 öre per litre higher in the far north). You can sometimes save 10 öre per litre by looking around or by visiting a self-service pump that uses 100 kronor notes *(sedlar)*.

Tipping

Tipping is not necessary in restaurants where there is a provision for service in the bill, but adding a few kronor is still quite common. In taxis round up the meter tariff if you can manage it, particularly if there is luggage. Cloakrooms often cost about 15 kr.

Bargaining

This is not customary: a price is generally a price. If you want bargains look for the signs *rea* (sale) and *lågpris*, *extrapris* or *rabatt* (discounts).

Consumer Taxes

The main extra cost for the traveller is *mervärdeskatt* or *moms*, the value-added tax on goods and services, included in the marked price. This varies but adds up to as much as 25% on some goods. Examples are: bus and train tickets 12%, hotels 12%, groceries 18%, phonecards 20%, restaurants and fast food 21%, pleasure cruises 21%.

Foreigners buying souvenirs and gifts can avoid tax or be reimbursed if the goods leave the country within seven days. By showing your passport in business premises with the blue-and-yellow 'tax-free for tourists' sign, you can get a certificate for the tax paid (at a small charge and valid for a month unless you specify longer) which you take with the item to the refund desk (if there is one) when you leave the country. The goods will be sealed at the shop, or you can sometimes arrange to have them posted home. To make shopping easier, get the *Shopping in Sweden* tax-free guide at shops and tourist offices.

POST & COMMUNICATIONS
Postal Rates
Sending postcards is expensive. Any item under 50g carries the minimum charge so write thick letters instead! Letters to other parts of Sweden and the Nordic countries will cost 3.85 kr and 6 kr, respectively. Basic letters or postcards sent by air mail to Europe are 6 kr. Letters beyond Europe cost 7.5 kr. Not all classes of mail may be available from Sweden to your home country, so ask at the post office.

A package weighing two kg costs 200 kr by air mail outside Europe, but there may be a limit of 500g or one kg on parcels to your country. If this or the quoted rate worry you, ask about the 20% savings of *ekonomibrev* (surface post that can take a month or more).

Sending Mail
Main city post offices are open from 8.30 am to 6 or 6.30 pm weekdays and sometimes until 1 pm Saturday (others don't open until 10 am). Stamps can be bought at Pressbyrån newspaper sellers. You may have to be stubborn at some windows if you know a certain price-weight combination is possible. Air mail will take a week to reach most parts of North America, perhaps a little longer to Australia and New Zealand. Specify the mode or else air mail may be assumed.

Receiving Mail
Poste-restante services are available at the main post offices in large cities such as Gothenburg and Malmö during normal opening hours (from 10 am in Gothenburg). For smaller places you will need to specially arrange to have mail held for collection at the local post office, for which you will need the correct postcode.

Telephone
To make a phone call in Sweden, you will usually need a Telia phonecard. These cards cost 35, 60 or 100 kr (giving 30, 60 or 120 credits, respectively). Telia booths also accept most credit cards. Extra charges are added to most calls made from hotel rooms.

For overseas telephone calls, buy a Telia phonecard with 120 credits (100 kr). Dial ☎ 009 and the country code and wait for the tone before proceeding. You can also dial your home operator for a collect call with these numbers:

Australia: ☎ 020-79 90 61
New Zealand: ☎ 020-79 90 64
UK: British Telecom ☎ 020-79 51 44, Mercury ☎ 020-79 90 44
USA: AT&T ☎ 020-79 56 11, MCI ☎ 020-79 59 22, Sprint ☎ 020-79 90 11

Using the 100-kr Telia phonecard, calls to Norway, Denmark and Finland cost 3.60 kr per minute, to the UK 5.75 kr, to North America 8.65 kr and to Australia 14.45 kr.

In addition to the typical yellow pages, Swedish phone books include green (for community services) and blue pages (for regional services). The toll-free general emergency number is ☎ 112.

Fax & E-mail
For faxes the Telia's rates are cheapest at just over 30 kr a page. Most public libraries have computers with Internet access, and they can be used free of charge.

NEWSPAPERS & MAGAZINES
You will not lack news in English. Pressbyrån in cities display international news magazines and you can usually find a copy of the *International Herald-Tribune*, the *Times*, the *Guardian* or the *Wall Street Journal* at the main railway stations.

RADIO & TV
Bring a walkman with a radio if you use a bicycle: national radio stations are on FM frequencies throughout the country and there is often 'more music, less talk' on many stations. Radio Sweden, the overseas network, broadcasts a few programmes in English (1179 kHz nationally or FM 89.6 in Stockholm), though you can tune to the BBC's European frequencies.

Sweden has half a dozen TV channels (some on cable networks only) and satellites bring more English programmes within reach. Subtitled English films and series are common.

PHOTOGRAPHY & VIDEO

The only problem with buying film in Sweden is the cost. For your snaps sort through the bargain bins for 24-shot rolls for under 30 kr at photo stores, but for 36-shot slide films you will commonly pay 100 or 120 kr. Processing need cost only 36 kr plus mounting, so shop around.

Do not risk photographing the military unless they are on parade. Photography is forbidden in certain militarily restricted areas in the north of Gotland around Fårö and off the north Bothnian coast.

TIME

Sweden is one hour ahead of GMT/UTC, but summer time (from the end of March to the end of September) is another hour ahead. Otherwise, at noon in Sweden, it is 11 am in London, 6 pm in New York and Toronto, 3 pm in San Francisco, 9 pm in Sydney, 11 pm in Auckland, noon in Oslo, Copenhagen and Berlin and 1 pm in Helsinki. The 24-hour clock is used.

ELECTRICITY

The electric current in Sweden is 220V AC, 50 Hz, plugs have two round pins and often clip in. Some hotels have 110V-sockets or suitable adapters.

WEIGHTS & MEASURES

The metric system applies in Sweden, but note the term *mil*, which is simply 10 km, is often used in conversation or for long distances. Decimals are indicated by commas and thousands by points.

LAUNDRY

The coin laundrette is not widespread in Sweden and a 'quick wash', where you leave clothes for laundering, is not available everywhere and can actually take a week or more. Many hostels and camping grounds have laundry facilities (look for small symbols in listings) and some hotels can offer a wash service. Swedish-made washing machines and dryers are thorough but slow, so select short cycles if you can. It is best to have portable tube soap or soap powder in your luggage for doing your washing in basins.

TOILETS

A public toilet at stations generally costs 1 or 2 kr, but most restaurants and cafés have a good toilet free of charge.

HEALTH

No vaccinations are required for visitors. The national pharmacist, Apoteket, provides prescription and nonprescription medicines (the maximum charge is 130 kr) and advice on how to deal with everyday ailments and conditions. The *nattapotek* are open 24 hours.

For emergencies and casualty services, local medical centres *(vårdcentraler)* or hospitals *(sjukhus* or *lasarett)* are the best places to go (you must show your passport). This is the public health system and duty doctors *(distriktsläkare* or *jourhavande läkare)* are standing by. Ordinary casualty visits cost 200 kr. There are centres in all districts and main towns. They are listed in the blue pages of local telephone books (don't forget they are indexed by area under the *kommun)*. The general emergency telephone number, including the ambulance, is ☎ 112.

The early summer crowds will face mosquitoes. These annoying creatures are worst in the northern lowlands near water or marsh and in some forests. Take a trusted repellent because a few proven local preparations are being banned from sale in Sweden. For guidance go to Apoteket.

Winter travellers should note that there are long cold stretches. If you are out of doors in the far north or during winter, exposure is a threat best avoided by common sense. Complicated health treatment in Sweden can cost foreigners a great deal and travel insurers recommend top levels of coverage. Private doctors *(läkare)* are also listed in telephone books, but check that they are affiliated with the national health scheme in Sweden (UK citizens enjoy reciprocity). Dentists *(tandläkare)* can be expensive: travellers will pay almost 700 kr for an hour's treatment.

WOMEN TRAVELLERS

Equality of the sexes is emphasised in Sweden and there should be no question of discrimination. Kvinnojouren is the national organisation that deals with violence against women; its Stockholm office is at Kvinnohus, Blekingegatan 67B, and the telephone service (☎ 08-644 09 25) is available from noon to 2 pm Monday to Friday. Local centres are listed in the green pages of telephone directories. Pregnant women with health emergencies should contact the nearest *mödravårdcentral* in the blue pages of the local telephone directory under the municipality.

Ask for a women-only compartment if you do not want male company in a 2nd-class rail sleeping section. A few Stockholm taxi concerns offer cut rates for women at night.

GAY & LESBIAN TRAVELLERS

Sweden is a liberal country, and gay marriages are legal. The organisation concerned with equality for lesbians and gays is Riksförbundet för Sexuellt Likaberättigande (☎ 08-736 02 12), based at Stockholm's Gayhus, Sveavägen 57, Stockholm.

DISABLED TRAVELLERS

Sweden is perhaps the easiest country to travel in a wheelchair. De Handikappades Riksförbund is the national organisation for people with disabilities. For information you can write to Informationsavdelning, De Handikappades Riksförbund (☎ 08-18 91 00; fax 08-645 65 41), Katrinebergsvägen 6, 11743 Stockholm.

TRAVEL WITH CHILDREN

Swedes treat children very well, and services range from children's carriages in trains to children's 'activity rooms' in major museums.

DANGERS & ANNOYANCES

Sweden is one of the safest countries imaginable and crimes perpetrated against travellers are fairly rare. Neo-Nazis, crimes associated with illegal drugs and the few trouble spots of big cities are the main concerns. Lack of service, inflated prices or locked doors at hostels are annoyances that can be avoided by careful planning and self-sufficiency. Note also that mosquitoes can be a nuisance (see Health earlier).

BUSINESS HOURS

Businesses and government offices are open from 8.30 or 9 am to 5 pm, although they can close after 3 pm in summer. Banks usually open at 9.30 am and close at 3 pm, but some open from 9 am to 5 or 6 pm in cities.

Normal shopping hours are from 9.30 am to 6 pm weekdays and 9.30 am to 2 or 3 pm on Saturday, but department stores are open longer and sometimes on Sunday. Some supermarkets will be open until 7 or 9 pm in big towns. Lunch often begins at 11 am and is over by 2 pm in restaurants. Stockholm has many 24-hour shops.

PUBLIC HOLIDAYS & SPECIAL EVENTS

There is a concentration of public holidays in spring and early summer, and Midsummer in particular brings life almost to a halt for three days. Transport and other services are reduced, even on Midsummer's Eve, so read your timetables carefully. Some food stores are open and many tourist offices, but not all attractions. Some hotels are closed from Christmas to New Year and it is not uncommon for restaurants to close during July and early August. Public holidays, which often see attractions close (some businesses will close early the day before and all day after) are:

1 January, *New Year's Day*
6 January, *Epiphany*
Good Friday
Easter Monday
1 May, *Labour Day*
late May, *Ascension Day*
late May or early June, *Whit Monday*
Saturday, late June, *Midsummer's Day*
Saturday, late October or early November, *All Saints' Day*
26 December, *Boxing Day*

In Sweden, New Year's Eve is not a big event in itself, but is a busy time for eating and entertainment: in some places there are fire-works. Walpurgis Valborgsmässoafton (30 April) is popular with students, who are easy to spot in Uppsala and Lund. Bonfires and fireworks are lit and some museums may close early.

May Day (1 May) is observed by marches and labour movement events, which stop the traffic in the name of the red rose. Flag Day, the national day, is 6 June.

Midsummer is the festival of the year. Maypole dancing is a traditional activity on Midsummer's Eve and everyone who can goes to the country, perhaps to the old family home or the summer cabin. For the folk touch, Dalarna is a good place to celebrate, but music, dancing and drinking are normal no matter where you are, so enjoy it: not much will be open.

The crayfish season begins on the second Wednesday in August, ushered in by feasting on the first catch (or a frozen batch from abroad). In the north, where crayfish are even rarer, they substitute the sour Baltic herring and hold a similar festival on the Thursday of the following week.

In just 60 years the Lucia festival on 13 December has become very popular. Oddly, it seems to merge the folk tradition of the longest night and the story of St Lucia of Syracuse. A choir in white, led by Lucia, who wears a crown of candles, leads the singing, and *glögg*, a hot alcoholic fruit punch, is drunk. Christmas Eve is the main day of celebration during this season: the night of the *smörgåsbord* and the arrival of *jultomten*, the Christmas gnome with the sack of gifts.

ACTIVITIES

Outdoor pastimes are precious to Swedes, who are active on bicycles, forest jogging tracks, rivers and lakes, mountain trails and the snow and ice.

Right of Public Access

By law, you are allowed to walk, travel on water, ski or swim anywhere outside private property (which means the immediate vicinity of a house and its garden and all fenced areas and cultivated land). You are allowed to camp more than one night at one spot, and you may pick berries and mushrooms.

You may not leave any rubbish nor take living wood, bark, leaves, bushes or nuts. Fires may be set where safe (not on bare rocks) with fallen wood. Use a bucketful of water to douse a camp fire even if you think the fire is out. Cars may not be driven across open land or on private roads. Close all gates. Do not disturb reindeer.

If you have a bicycle and want free camping opportunities, look for unsealed forest tracks from secondary country roads. Make sure your spot is at least 50 metres from the track and not visible from any house or building or a sealed road. Dry pine forests are your best bet. Bring drinking water and some food, although flowing water from creeks can normally be used for washing, and even for drinking.

Skating

There is skating in winter wherever the ice is thick enough. Stockholm's lake and canal system is exploited by the local children and enthusiasts seeking the longest possible 'run'. In Stockholm you can hire cheap skates, but if conditions are not good, go and watch a wild crowd of ice-hockey spectators.

Skiing

Cross-country (nordic) skiing opportunities vary depending on the snow and temperatures, but the north-west usually has plenty of snow. Practically all town areas (except the very south) have marked, often illuminated skiing tracks.

Do not leave marked cross-country routes without a good map, local advice, and proper equipment including plastic sheet and ropes. Wind-chill temperatures of -30°C are possible, so you should know the daily forecasts. Police and tourist offices have information on local warnings. In the mountains there is the risk of avalanche *(lavin)* and susceptible areas are marked by yellow multilingual signs and buried-skier symbols. The national SLAO insurance covers all injuries on marked slopes and lifts run by the national

SLAO slalom organisation, and can be purchased for less than 100 kr per season.

Hiking

Hiking is popular everywhere, and the mountain challenge of the northern national parks is most compelling. But these parks are rarely snow-free and the jewel, Sarek, is only for experienced hikers. For information on organised group walks, write to or visit STF or, better still, pay a year's membership. Good waterproof jackets, pants and boots are important equipment.

Easy walking trails are common. Most regions maintain a representative route that runs via the best natural attractions. Many *kommuner* (municipalities) have their own wilderness tracks. Many of these off-the-beaten-track routes offer bunks in huts, or rain shelters at no cost.

The STF mountain huts (about 90 of them are maintained by Naturvårdsverket) are placed at intervals averaging about 20 km. You may stay the night (or camp nearby and pay 30 kr to use the facilities) for a fee which is slightly higher than youth hostel rates. The eight STF mountain stations have shops, showers and restaurants.

A special card is available to those aged under 26 and allows hut accommodation for 10 nights (370 kr). Visit STF or buy a card at a mountain station, where up-to-date maps are also available. Conditions are self-service, similar to those in STF hostels, and you must bring sheets (for huts, sleeping bags). The *STF Fjällhandbok* (89 kr) is written in Swedish but maps show all huts and facilities.

Canoeing

There are 80 approved canoeing centres and excellent areas on lowland and mountain lakes as well as river rapids in the north. You can hire canoes from 300 to 700 kr a week. The national body, Svenska kanotförbundet (fax 08-605 60 00), produces the annual guide *Kanotvåg* and maps of 800 routes all over the country. Write to Storforsplan 44, 12387 Farsta. According to the right of common access there is the right to boat,

paddle or moor temporarily. The brochure *Important Information for You Who Paddle* is recommended and is available from Naturvårdsverket (☎ 08-698 10 00; fax 08-29 23 82), Blekholmsterrassen 36, 10405 Stockholm.

Fishing

There are national fishing ordinances, but local restrictions on inland waters may also apply, especially concerning salmon, salmon trout and eel, so check with tourist offices or the county authority before dropping a line. You generally need the owner's permission (in the case of government authorities this is covered by local permits), but open areas include parts of Vänern, Vättern, Mälaren, Hjälmaren and Storsjön lakes and most of the coastline (except for fishing the Baltic salmon off Norrland and in some protected areas). Local permits (for the waters of a *kommun*) can be bought from sports or camping shops (or ask at a tourist office) and typically cost 50 kr a day, 300 kr per month.

Three authorities maintaining fishing waters should be noted: Kronofiske, with its centres of farmed stocks and developed facilities; Domänfiske, which administers 1500 charted lakes and rivers; and Vattenfall, which has salmon farms in south and central Norrland. Domänfiske annual cards are cheap for 200 kr a year and will cover a family. For brochures write to Domänfiske, 72185 Västerås.

Boating & Sailing

The lake and canal routes offer pleasant sailing in spring and summer (the canals are mostly open for limited seasons) but the lock fees can be high. Some simpler harbours are free, but one with good facilities can cost 75 kr a night.

The dotted skärgård (archipelago) areas, particularly around Stockholm, are a different if demanding setting for sailing or motor boats. A useful guide is STF's annual *Båtturist* book, with details of 460 guest harbours and facilities, prices and services and radio details. For charts go to Kartcentrum, Vasagatan 16, Stockholm.

SWEDEN

WORK

A job, if you can get one, requires a permit. For this you need an application form from a Swedish diplomatic post and you must apply for a temporary-residency visa at the same time. The basis for application is a letter from the potential employer confirming a job offer and some idea of proposed accommodation.

Students enrolled in Sweden can take summer jobs and get leads from student services, but these jobs are not offered to travelling students. To ask about prospects in particular fields, write to Arbetsmarknadsstyrelsen, 17199 Solna, which can send you the brochure *Applying for Work in Sweden* (see also Visas & Embassies and Documents earlier).

EU citizens will be able to work in the common labour market and will not require permits, though they will still be at a disadvantage compared to citizens of Nordic countries. Aside from that, jobs are tight; knowing Swedish helps. Go to the local branch of Arbetsförmedlingen, the employment office, which may be able to help; they have some literature in English. Prospects may lie in technical manufacturing areas. No-one is looking for builders or people with social services or care skills. Service work opportunities are tight.

ACCOMMODATION
Camping

Sweden has some 700 camping grounds and a free guide with maps is available. Some camping grounds are open in winter and offer comforts, but the best time for camping is from May to August. Prices vary with facilities: from 70 to 150 kr a site plus electricity. Most camping grounds have kitchens and laundry facilities.

You must have the Svenskt Camping Kort to be able to stay at Swedish camping grounds. For the free card, apply at least one month before your journey at Sveriges Campingvärdars Riksförbund, Box 255, 45117 Uddevalla. If this is not possible, you will be given a temporary card on arrival. The annual stamp on your card costs 49 kr and is obtainable at the first camping ground you visit.

See Activities earlier for information on free camping in Sweden. Primus and Sievert are the common gas products available at service stations.

Hostels

Sweden has more than 400 hostels, including 305 'official' hostels that are affiliated with Svenska Turistföreningen (STF), which produces a detailed guide for 99 kr. Holders of Hostelling International cards get a 35 kr discount each night and can stay for the budget rates of 70 to 100 kr. Guest cards for non-members can be bought at most hostels. Almost 80 private hostels are members of the Sveriges Vandrarhem i Förening (SVIF). No membership is required and rates range from 90 to 145 kr. Ask around for the free guide. Several unaffiliated hostels are popping up so ask around.

Youth hostels in Sweden have a problem that few other countries know of: they are difficult to get into. Most of the day (and much of the winter) they have firmly locked doors. The secret is a telephone reservation during specific telephone hours (which vary). As a rule, try to call between 5 and 6 pm. Write down the four-digit door code and ask where the key will be when you arrive. Theoretically, you could stay overnight without seeing another person, except in the morning when you pay. Typical for Sweden, written reservations are recommended but they carry the threat of a 50 kr cancellation penalty! Breakfast is often available for 40 kr but has to be arranged the night before. Always carry sheets as this will save you money. Many hostels have kitchens, but you sometimes need your own utensils.

Be careful in December: check that each hostel you intend to stay at is really open at Christmas and New Year. In June, July and August you can expect longer reception hours but a reservation is recommended because many hostels are full. The principle is that you should clean up after yourself, but some hostels push optional 'cleaning fees' of up to 200 kr.

Mountain huts and stations are also affiliated with STF, and cost money, unlike in Finland.

Cabins

Daily rates for cabins at camping grounds offer good value for small groups and families. Regional tourist offices and some national agencies rent cabins and cottages by the week – there are detailed listings.

Hotels

There are absolutely no cheap hotels in Sweden. Budget travellers may find weekend and summer (June to mid-August) rates reasonable, often below 500 kr for a double. Again, Sweden offers some attractive packages that are good value if you plan ahead. Stockholm, Gothenburg and Malmö offer discounted hotel rooms which include free entry to local transport and all attractions and even a discounted return train ticket. Most tourist offices and travel agents will give details.

Sometimes prices are expressed as 'per person in a two-bed room', so be careful. There are discount vouchers: some are Scandinavia-wide and run by the big chains, others such as the Pro Skandinavia or Biltur Logi packages are available through travel agents.

FOOD

Budget travellers stuff themselves at the breakfast buffet, look for lunch packages, and visit discount food stores for self-catering dinners. Stylish restaurants are numerous and offer a real splurge with dinner and drinks for around 150 kr.

Solid, meat-based, cafeteria-style meals, usually with a big helping of potatoes, can come in at 40 kr. The *husmanskost* specials are often meatballs; they usually include potato and are high in cholesterol, but if this suits, you will pay as little as 35 kr. The *sallad* is often simply coleslaw and rolls at the buffet.

Lunch can be most reasonable: look for *dagens rätt* (today's special) which will generally include bread, salad, coffee and a drink. Lunch usually starts at 11 am and is over at 2 pm, and will cost 40 to 50 kr.

Chinese restaurants are less likely to be a cheap option in Sweden, but Middle Eastern fare down to takeaway kebabs and many pizzas are budget alternatives. *Fullständiga rättigheter* means fully licensed. It might pay to eat lightly at dinner.

Pure vegetarian restaurants exist but are usually closed at weekends. Salads and vegetarian pizzas are common in many places, sometimes costing less than 40 kr.

In cafés, getting a coffee of any size for less than 10 kr is rare, although often there is *påtår*, a practice that gives you a free refill.

Self-Catering

Shopping is easy enough in supermarkets and worth it if you are hostelling. In supermarkets note the item price and comparative price per kg, which have to be shown by law. Plastic carry-bags will usually cost 1 or 2 kr at the checkout.

Bread and milk prices are kept low at around 12 kr per 450g loaf and 7 kr per litre. To some people, the selection of fresh vegetables and fruit will seem limited. At produce markets prices are not always displayed, but the selection is better. Low-fat milk is *lättmjölk* and *filmjölk* is the processed sour milk that Swedes like with breakfast cereals. *Mellanmjölk* is all-purpose with reduced fats.

The Svensk Lantmat network of small fresh-food producers publishes regional guides available at tourist offices. You can visit local strawberry patches (sometimes you can pick your own), dairy farms or market gardens and buy on-site from the growers – some of the more exotic places, such as fish-smoking houses, are outings in themselves.

DRINKS

Bring some of your own from other, cheaper countries as strong alcohol is expensive in Sweden. Lighter supermarket beer *lättöl* and *klass II* are good value – only if you drink them chilled. Strong beer, wines and spirits are sold by the state monopoly Systembolaget at outlets in the cities and towns, which are open weekdays to 5 pm. Alcohol prices are kept high as a matter of policy, but drinkable wines can be bought for less than 60 kr a bottle.

Soft drinks are relative expensive. If you visit in summer, or bring a bicycle, carry a plastic bottle and fill it from taps. Aluminium cans are recycled – supermarket disposal machines give 0.50 kr per can.

ENTERTAINMENT

Discos and nightclubs admit no-one aged under 20, although the minimum age limit for men is usually 23 and sometimes 25. Drinking at these places is the most expensive of options, but the strength of the brews might restrict your outlay. Cloakroom charges average 10 kr. Pubs and restaurants can charge 30 kr or less for the standard *storstark*, 450 ml of klass III, although the cheaper 375 ml bottle is common in pubs.

Theatre tickets cost around 200 kr or more if there is no subsidy, and for the cinema it's anything from 50 to 70 kr. Going to the cinema is a good option as many subtitled features in English are shown.

THINGS TO BUY

Souvenirs, handicrafts or quality Swedish products in glass, wood or pewter are relatively expensive (see Glasriket for discount shops). Typically Swedish is the Dalarna painted wooden horse and, if you want a good handmade one, go to the workshops in Dalarna (see Mora).

On Sami handicrafts, which are quite expensive, look for the *'Duodji'* label (a round coloured token of authenticity) on knives, textiles and trinkets, although the fakes are dear enough. Handicrafts carrying the round token *'Svensk slöjd'*, or the craftsperson's hammer and shuttle, are endorsed by the national handicrafts organisation Svenska hemslöjdsföreningarnas riksförbund, whose symbol is found on affiliated handicraft shops.

Getting There & Away

AIR

Although you may not find a cheap direct flight to Sweden from outside Europe, there are plenty of European companies that will sell an inexpensive flight to Stockholm via their hub. Note that the Copenhagen airport is just 45 minutes from Sweden by a hovercraft ferry – ask for cheaper flights to Copenhagen. It makes sense to start your Sweden excursion from the south, especially if the Copenhagen flight is cheaper than the Stockholm flight.

Although SAS is actually based in Copenhagen, there are plenty of international direct flights to Stockholm. Transwede has direct flights to Stockholm from London. From Asia a standard European fare on European carriers is a good deal, although SAS flights are available from Delhi, Tokyo, Hong Kong and Bangkok.

Stockholm has an interesting flight market if you shop around (in the south, go to Copenhagen). Sometimes there are very cheap last-minute charter flights to distant shores.

LAND

Scandinavia is essentially an enormous island, and there is land access to Sweden only via Norway or Finland. However, trains and buses will go directly to ferries and if you sleep, you won't even notice the sea journey! Just include ferry fares and the waiting time in your budget if you're driving. Your national driving licence is sufficient documentation to drive in Sweden.

The Continent

Bus Eurolines' services run from several European cities, including London to Stockholm (1065 kr) and Gothenburg (895 kr): there are at least three services per week and the Stockholm service takes 36 hours. Gothenburg to Berlin costs 675 kr (once weekly), while to Brussells it costs 840 kr (twice weekly).

Eurolines has its main offices at City-terminalen in Stockholm (☎ 08-23 71 90) and Kyrkogatan 40 in Gothenburg (☎ 031-10 02 40) and you can buy tickets at travel agents.

Swebus runs the Continentbus services throughout Europe to Swedish cities (for timetables write to Swebus Continent AB, Gullbergs Strandgata 34, 41104 Göteborg).

Train Direct trains from Berlin run twice daily to Malmö, via Sassnitz and Trelleborg. The journey takes nine hours.

Denmark
Bus The Kustlinjen bus No 998 from Halmstad and Helsingborg crosses to Copenhagen and Kastrup airport by ferry (100 kr). Bus No 999 runs a Lund-Malmö-Copenhagen service (60 kr). The Copenhagen Eurolines service runs five times a week to/from Stockholm (390 kr) and Gothenburg (210 kr).

Train Kustpilen trains run three times daily between Copenhagen and Hässleholm. Rail passes apply, and the ferry price is included. There are also two direct trains daily between Stockholm and Copenhagen, and a train that runs twice daily between Copenhagen and Oslo, via Helsingborg and Gothenburg.

Finland
Bus There are six crossings across the rivers that mark the border. See the Finland chapter for details. Bus services from Luleå or Boden to Haparanda, Övertorneå and Pajala on the Swedish side are operated by Länstrafik i Norrbotten buses and some long-distance buses run from Stockholm or Sundsvall.

Train Train passengers will reach Boden or Luleå in Sweden and Kemi in Finland on rails. Bus connections between these towns are free for those who carry train passes. The connecting buses depart from outside the Boden train station, from the Luleå bus station, from outside the Kemi train station, from the Tornio bus station and from the Haparanda bus station. The buses in Boden wait no more than 10 minutes for delayed

trains – and not even one minute when the train comes from Kiruna!

Norway
There are more than 20 crossing points between the countries, and formalities range from nonexistent to hardly noticeable.

Bus There are direct services, such as bus No 820 from Gothenburg to Oslo (280 kr) and the weekend bus No 879 from Stockholm to Oslo via Karlstad. Bus Nos 802 and 870 (at weekends) cross the border near Sälen and terminate at the village of Trysil. In Norrbotten bus No 95 runs daily from Kiruna across the border to Bjerkvik.

More exciting are the Swedish *länstrafik* services that will take you near the border, from where you can test hitchhiking prospects in the mountains. On some routes there are connecting Norwegian buses – the Umeå to Mo i Rana service has a connecting bus waiting at Tärnaby.

Train The main railway links are those from Stockholm to Oslo via Hallsberg, from Gothenburg to Oslo, from Östersund to Storlien (Swedish trains) and further to Trondheim (Norwegian trains) and from Luleå to Kiruna and Narvik.

SEA
Denmark
There are about 200 launches daily either way between Denmark and Sweden. The quickest and most frequent services are between Helsingør and Helsingborg (21 kr, free with train passes). If you have a train pass, head for Helsingør. If not, the heavy competition on the Copenhagen to Malmö route will be a pleasant surprise – boats in Copenhagen depart from the Havnegade/Nyhavn area, and in Malmö from just near the train station. The Direkten service between Copenhagen (Havnegade) and Landskrona runs five times daily (50 kr, bicycles 30 kr).

Passenger cars up to six metres may carry five people: the Helsingør to Helsingborg ferry charges 330 kr one way (495 kr return).

The Copenhagen to Malmö route is dearer – 465 kr (695 kr return) and runs between Limhamn and Dragør.

There are services between Jutland and Sweden. Stena Line cruises between Gothenburg and Frederikshavn up to 10 times daily and takes just over three hours, although the SeaCat covers the journey in half that time. Lion Ferries from Grenå, travel four hours to reach Varberg and Halmstad.

Bornholmstrafikken runs daily services from Ystad to Rønne (three hours). Quicker is the boat from Simrishamn to Allinge (110 kr) that travels three times daily in one hour to Bornholm.

Finland

Daily services throughout the year are available on Stockholm to Turku and Stockholm to Helsinki routes but other options are numerous in summer. There are inexpensive connections to Åland from Kapellskär and Grisslehamn, both accessible via Norrtälje, north of Stockholm. Further north, there are connections from Umeå and Skellefteå. The Sundsvall to Vaasa route may see a catamaran service in the near future. See appropriate towns and Finland for further details.

Norway

There are enough bus and train services between the two countries, but if you get stuck in Strömstad, there are frequent ferries to Fredrikstad (passengers only) and Sandefjord. See Strömstad for further details.

Germany

Trelleborg is the main gateway – there are more than a dozen ferries arriving daily from Travemünde, Rostock and Sassnitz. Stena Line cruises between Gothenburg and Kiel daily, taking 10 hours. From Malmö, Nordö-Link sails to Travemünde.

Poland

There are daily services from Świnoujście to Ystad and Malmö, from Gdynia to Karlskrona and slightly less frequent services from Gdańsk to Oxelösund (about 18 hours).

The Baltic States & Russia

At the time of writing there were direct services to Estonia only – from the Värtan harbour in Stockholm to Tallinn (Estline) and from Gamla Stan in Stockholm to Saaremaa, which Swedes call Ösel (Ånedin Linjen). It is safer and perhaps cheaper to travel via Finland to the Baltic States and Russia.

The UK

Scandinavian Seaways sails from Gothenburg to Harwich (all year round) and from Gothenburg to Newcastle (June to early September). Both trips will take 23 hours or more. Single fares from either British port cost UK£90.

LEAVING SWEDEN

To collect tax refunds on gifts and souvenirs when leaving Sweden you must go to the tax-free collection counters at airport halls and ferry terminals with documents and the items. At Arlanda airport, counters are in halls A and B and there is a check desk in the departure hall. An airport tax of 14 kr is included in ticket prices.

Getting Around

One of the largest countries in Europe, Sweden takes time and money to travel through. Public transport is well organised, and relies regionally and locally on provincial traffic systems (länstrafik). Heavily subsidised, the regional networks are some of the best bargains in Sweden. Unfortunately, there are 24 different systems. National air, train and bus networks have several discount schemes available.

The general confusion of different systems is partly solved by the Tågplus system whereby you buy just one ticket which will be valid on trains and on any länstrafik. But Tågplus is only warranted if you're not using any other discount scheme.

People with disabilities will find special

services and adapted facilities of a generally high standard, ranging from trains to taxis.

AIR

Sweden has more than 10 domestic airlines, most of them using Arlanda as a hub. SAS (SK) daily domestic flights serve the country from Malmö in the south to Kiruna in the north. Skyways (JZ) runs an even larger network.

Most airlines cooperate with SAS, notable exceptions being Transwede (TQ, from Terminal 2 at Arlanda to Halmstad, Jönköping, Luleå, Sundsvall and Umeå) and Malmö Aviation (6E, from Bromma airport west of Stockholm to Gothenburg, Malmö and Visby).

Flying in Sweden is expensive, but substantial discounts are available, such as return tickets booked at least seven days in advance or low-price tickets for accompanying family members and for pensioners. Young people under 25 years of age should go to the airport just in case: standby one-way tickets cost as little as 280 kr on SAS flights, certainly good value for flights to Lapland.

BUS

You can travel by bus in Sweden either on national long-distance routes, or using any of the 24 regional länstrafik networks. In Sweden, each bus line has a route number.

Regional Traffic

Länstrafik is usually complemented by regional trains, and one ticket is valid on any bus, local or regional. Rules vary but transfers are usually free within one to four hours. Most provinces are divided into zones. Travel within one zone will cost from 10 to 16 kr. Every time you enter a new zone, the price is increased. Each system usually has a maximum price, allowing you to travel as long as you can within the network and the time limit.

There are thick timetables for each province, or dozens of thin local timetables – they are free or almost free. Study them carefully, including the various discount schemes.

Daily or weekly passes are always good value, and there are 30-day passes for longer stays. Value cards are also good: you pay 200 kr but your travelling is worth over 250 kr. Always ask how the regional discount pass works: you may have to run the ticket through a machine, press buttons, tell the driver where you want to go, get your ticket stamped or something else.

Express Buses

Long-distance buses are either extended regional services (prices vary) or truly national networks. The largest is Swebus, and there are Svenska Buss (weekend buses in the southern half of the country only), Linjebuss (from Sundsvall) and the post-buses of Postens Diligenstrafik that operate around Norrland. Svenska Buss (☎ 020-67 67 67) requires advance seat reservations, and Swebus fares are 5% cheaper if you book at a Swebus office or travel agent, although you can buy from Swebus drivers.

Pensioners qualify for discounts of up to 50% on some express buses, and holders of the European Youth Card can travel on Swebus weekend services for half-fare.

TRAIN

Sweden has an extensive railway network, and trains are certainly the quickest way to explore the country. Surprisingly, there are almost 50 train operators in Sweden, although the national network of SJ covers all the main lines. The flag carriers are the futuristic X2000 fast train services at speeds of up to 200 km/h, with services from Stockholm to Gothenburg, Malmö, Karlstad, Mora, Växjö, Jönköping, Sundsvall and Härnösand. Several provinces run regional train networks, and there is the touristy *Inlandsbanan*, one of the great rail journeys in Scandinavia.

The Swedish rail system was rearranged in 1996, and although the system was simplified, learning the discount options takes time.

SJ covers mostly main lines and some feeder services on secondary lines. Individual 2nd-class tickets are expensive, but there are discounts. Swedish trains have no surcharges – all train journeys include a seat reservation, night trains include a sleeper or a seat. If you have no discount pass, then you must travel less than 150 km to get a 30 kr discount – but there is no seat reservation. The national discount scheme is the annual discount pass Reslust card which costs 150 kr. The one card is valid for two people. The card offers a 25% discount in 2nd class on Tuesday, Wednesday, Thursday and Saturday. There are also 50% discounts for Reslust card holders on *röda avgångar* ('red departures', see SJ timetables) on most lines. All X2000 trains and night trains have a few Reslust seats/sleepers. Just one Reslust journey may save you more than 150 kr if you get a Reslust seat. Reserve as early as possible. If a Reslust seat is not available, ask which departure has one. Two children under 15 years old can travel free with an adult and passengers aged 19 to 25 years will be eligible for discounts.

The international passes Inter-Rail, Eurail, Scanrail and Rail Europ S cards (50% discounts) are accepted on SJ services and all regional trains (except local *pendeltåg* trains around Stockholm). Inlandsbanan gives 50% discounts. Many SJ trains require a supplement: InterCity and InterRegio, 30 kr for a seat reservation; and X2000, 100 kr. Budget-conscious pass holders should avoid X2000 trains altogether. For other SJ trains, supplements are waived when the train journey is less than 150 km. Pass holders never pay a supplement on regional trains and often not even on IC trains. Rail passes are also accepted on all SJ-run buses, and on buses between Boden/Luleå and Haparanda.

There are some 25 individual regional train services (länstrafik) run by provinces, but often with close cooperation with SJ. International train passes are valid on regional trains. Regional train services are subsidised, and are good value. You can bring a bicycle on many länstrafik trains without prior announcement, unlike on SJ trains.

In summer, almost 25 different tourist trains offer unusual train experiences. The most notable is Inlandsbanan – 1000 km from Mora to Gällivare costs 600 kr (700 kr high season) a single, but a special card allows two weeks' unlimited travel on the route for 995 kr (including regional bus connections and discounts from Gällivare to Narvik). Service on this line is slow – 14 hours direct from Östersund to Gällivare.

Station luggage lockers cost between 15 and 25 kr for 24 hours. Check that the station building will be open when you want to collect: some places close just after the last arrival.

CAR & MOTORCYCLE

The good road network and the excellent E-class motorways are far from crowded except in the south at the height of summer. You need only a recognised full licence to drive in Sweden: an international licence is unnecessary unless you want to rent a car.

If your vehicle breaks down, telephone the local number of the Larmtjänst 24-hour towing service. Insurance Green Cards are not necessary but will give you peace of mind.

Automatic ticket parking on the street is common and small signs point you to the nearest P-automat *(parkeringsautomat)*, the ticket machine. This sort of parking will typically cost 8 kr per hour during the day, but may well be free evenings and at weekends. There are car parks (parking houses) in all cities of any size.

In the far north, reindeer and elk (moose) are road hazards around dawn and dusk. They wander near roads and car horns will rarely shift them; signs warn of the worst areas. Reindeer should be considered as property and elk as protected animals. If there's an accident ask for help at the nearest house. Report incidents to police; you have no charge to fear but you can be charged if you fail to report an accident. Sandboxes on many roads may be a help in mud or snow.

The national motoring association is Motormännens Riksförbund, Box 23142, 10435 Stockholm.

Road Rules

In Sweden you drive on the right and give way to the right. Headlights should be dipped but must be on at all times when travelling on the roads. Seat belts must be worn in all seats, and children under seven years old should be in appropriate harnesses or in child seats, if fitted.

You cannot afford to drink and drive as the blood-alcohol limit is stringent at 0.02%. The normal maximum speed on the motorway is 110 km/h. Speeds on other roads are 50 (in built-up areas) to 90 km/h. The general speed limit for cars towing caravans is 70 km/h.

Most road signs match international standards. On many highways broken lines define wide-paved edges, and the vehicle being overtaken is expected to ease into this area to allow faster traffic to pass comfortably.

According to law, you must, in event of an accident, exchange names and details with other drivers or the property owners involved. Injuries and serious accidents should be reported to police (on no account move any car before the police arrive).

Car & Motorcycle Rental

Car rental with the international chains is expensive (climbing to 800 kr a day for medium-sized sedans for short rental periods), although railway and airline packages can bring some savings. Weekend and summer packages are also offered at discount rates which can be better but are not always available at airport branches.

Basic small cars cost from 200 kr per day (plus about 1.80 kr per km), although the national chain Happy Rental charges as little as 99 kr a day and offers low rates per km for the smallest model car and some small operators offer similar rates.

To rent a car it is commonly required that you be at least 19 years of age (or older to rent a large model) and you often need to show an international licence.

MC-huset (☎ 040-21 04 35), at Jägershillsgatan 6, 20121 Malmö, will rent out 650 cc motorcycles from 1895 kr per week (with 2500 kr deposit) plus 45 öre per km. Motor-cycles can be rented in many places, but you will pay large deposits and may need both a credit card and an international licence.

Purchase

The used-car columns of *Dagens Nyheter* are best for car-hunting, although anything under 15,000 kr will be at least 10 years old and well used. If you think you have been ripped off, ask Konsumentverket (☎ 08-759 83 00), Sorterargatan 26, Box 503, 16215 Vällingby, about your rights.

BICYCLE

The cycling season in Sweden is from May to September in the south, and July and August in the north. Beware of distances! Gotland is the top destination for cyclists, and Småland, Skåne and the Stockholm-Uppsala region are equally exciting. Avoid all highways (bicycles are forbidden on the motorways) and look for quiet secondary roads. Use your own initiative or ask for bicycle maps at tourist offices.

Cycling is an excellent way to look for prehistoric sites, parish churches and some free services, such as quiet spots to pitch your tent. In towns, follow the marked bicycle paths, or signs for long-distance bicycle routes to leave the urban area. You must turn on lamps after dusk.

There are over 20 off-road and signposted national routes, and if you want an epic challenge follow the green signs along Sverigeleden, the national circuit, linking up over 6000 km of tracks. For suggestions on bicycle routes, write to Svenska Cykelförbundet (☎ 08-592 529 36), Drakslingan 1, 19340 Sigtuna.

Taking a bicycle on public transport is easy on länstrafik, including some trains and most regional buses. The fee ranges from free to 30 kr per ride. SJ trains are more difficult: you have to book three days ahead, and the service costs 125 kr! Dismantled bicycles, however, can be taken with other luggage into your compartment. For a fee, you can take bicycles on ferries but on long-distance buses it is usually impossible.

Hire generally costs about 70 kr a day for

geared bicycles or from 250 kr a week. If you want to buy second-hand, try the bicycle workshops in university towns first.

HITCHING

Hitching is not so popular in Sweden, where the consensus is that you have less luck getting lifts than in other countries. Short-distance trips should be no problem outside the main highways – Norrland is not bad.

BOAT

The national road authority, Vägvärket runs about 90 ferries across straits or rivers. They are part of the road network and usually free.

An extensive boat network opens up the attractive Stockholm archipelago, and boat services on Lake Mälaren, west of Stockholm, are busy in summer. Gotland is served by regular ferries from Nynäshamn and Oskarshamn, and there are summer services for islands off the coast.

There are one-week or two-week passes available for the Stockholm archipelago, but the quaint fishing villages off the west coast can normally be reached by boats that accept a regional transport pass – enquire in Gothenburg or Strömstad.

The canals provide cross-country routes linking the main lakes. The longest cruise is on the Göta canal from near Stockholm across to Gothenburg. It runs from May to mid-September, takes four days and includes the lakes in-between at fares of more than 4500 kr a bed (more for single cabins). Rederiaktiebolaget Göta Kanal (☎ 031-80 63 15) operates over the whole distance, but day trips or sections are also available.

LOCAL TRANSPORT

In Sweden, local transport is always linked with the regional länstrafik – rules and prices for city buses may differ slightly from long-distance transport, but a regional pass is valid both in the city and on the rural routes.

Stockholm has an extensive underground metro system, and Gothenburg and Norr-köping run delightful tram networks. Gothenburg also has a city boat service.

ORGANISED TOURS

Apart from many boat tours around the islands of Stockholm, most 'tours' are actu-ally packages, offered by big towns or SAS, SJ or STF. Instead of travelling with dozens of Swedish grandmothers in a glass house on wheels, you will travel quite independently but with a discount.

Stockholm

Stockholm is no doubt one of the most beau-tiful national capitals in the world (if you see the Old Town in summer), although the fringe is industrialised and some suburbs were inspired by Kafka and Stalinist baroque.

Stockholm is a royal capital that has always been ideally situated for trade and maritime connections. The 24,000 islands and islets of the *skärgården* (archipelago) protect the urban islands from the open seas. Some 1.5 million people live in Greater Stockholm, and over 15% of them are for-eigners. This lively, international city has suburban schools where over 100 different languages are spoken, and areas where kebab is more common a word than *köttbullar* (meatballs).

The city is best seen from the water but you'll also enjoy seeing the parklands of Djurgården or the alleys of Gamla Stan on foot. Many of the 50-plus museums contain world-class treasures. The 10 royal castles include the largest palace in the world still in use, and the World Heritage-listed Drott-ningholm. Stockholm has the best selection of budget accommodation in Scandinavia, and although it isn't really cheap, it's all clean and comfortable.

Orientation

Stockholm is built on islands, except for the modern centre (Norrmalm), whose focus is on the ugly Sergels Torg. This is the business and shopping hub and is linked by a network of subways to the central train station and the gardens of Kungsträdgården, popular and packed in summer. The subways link with the metro (*tunnelbana* or T) stations.

The triangular island Stadsholmen and its appendages accommodate the old town, Gamla Stan, separated from Norrmalm by the narrow channels of Norrström around the royal palace but connected to it by several bridges. To the west of this is Lake Mälaren.

On the south side the main bridge Centralbron and the Slussen interchange connect the southern part of the city, Södermalm, and its spine Götgatan. From its top end the giant golf ball of the stadium Globen is the southern landmark, although you will cross water again at Skanstull before reaching it.

To the east of Gamla Stan is the small island Skeppsholmen, and further down Strandvägen and past the berths you cross to Djurgården, topped by Skansen.

Information

You will find pretty much everything at the central train station complex. Another major spot for tourist information is Sweden House (Sverigehuset) in Kungsträdgården on Hamngatan.

The best overall guide is the monthly *Stockholm This Week*, available free at tourist offices, which includes events and a shopping, restaurant and accommodation guide.

The free papers *Nöjesguiden* and *Citynytt* concentrate on contemporary music, theatre, film and pubs. *D&N* is a free paper in English that gives a run-down of the pub, music and entertainment scene. Also check http://www.stoinfo.se.

Tourist Offices The main tourist office of Stockholm Information Service (☎ 789 24 95, weekends ☎ 789 24 90) is on the ground floor of Sweden House in Kungsträdgården. You can also book special tickets and packages for such things as boat trips to the archipelago. The Finnish province of Åland has its tourist information office here, too. The office is open in summer from 8 am to 6 pm Monday to Friday and from 9 am to 5 pm at weekends (to 3 pm in winter). Upstairs you'll find the Sweden Bookshop and information in English about Swedish life and

culture provided by the Swedish Institute. You can park nearby on Regeringsgatan.

Perhaps more convenient for arriving travellers is the Hotellcentralen information office at the central train station, open from 7 am to 9 pm from June to August, from 8 am to 7 pm in May and September and from 9 am to 6 pm from October to April. In addition to tourist information, you may reserve hotel rooms and youth hostel beds, buy the Stockholm Package, the Stockholm Card or the Tourist Card, book sightseeing tours and buy maps, books and souvenirs.

Gotland City Resebutik on the corner of Kungsgatan and Klara Norra Kyrkogatan sells Gotland packages and distributes free brochures and timetables. The Klarakyrkan church, opposite the central train station, houses the church tourist information booth in summer.

Stockholm Card This will cover all transport and sightseeing needs for an adult and two children aged under 18. Cards cost 185/350/470 kr for one/two/three days – for best value buy two cards in three days, and rest between the two 24-hour periods.

With the card you travel free on buses, metro and local trains (not airport buses), and can take advantage of trips on the Katarinahissen lift and free parking in public areas.

Most of the attractions mentioned in the following Things to See section, including Skansen and the palace museums, will admit card-holders free. Note the opening hours – Skansen remains open until late, whereas royal palaces are only open until 3 or 4 pm.

The Stockholm Card is available at tourist offices and you present it for validation at the first venue.

Money Forex dominates at the central train station with four counters; the one in the main hall is open daily from 7 am to 9 pm. If you have several travellers' cheques to cash, or a Visa card, go to the post office in the main hall for better rates and the 50 kr fee. Between these two booths are the ATMs which accept many international bank cards.

You can also exchange money at the banks

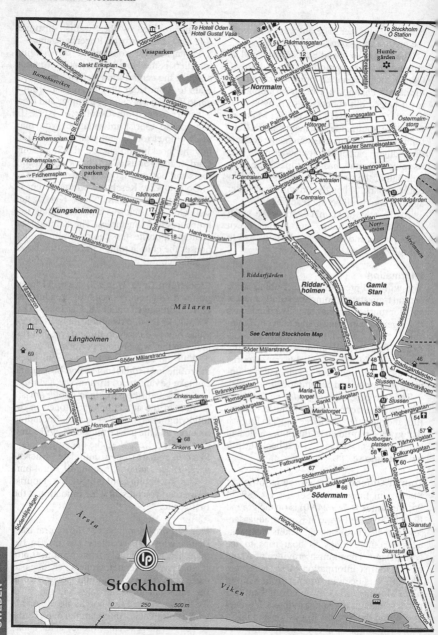

Stockholm

0   250   500 m

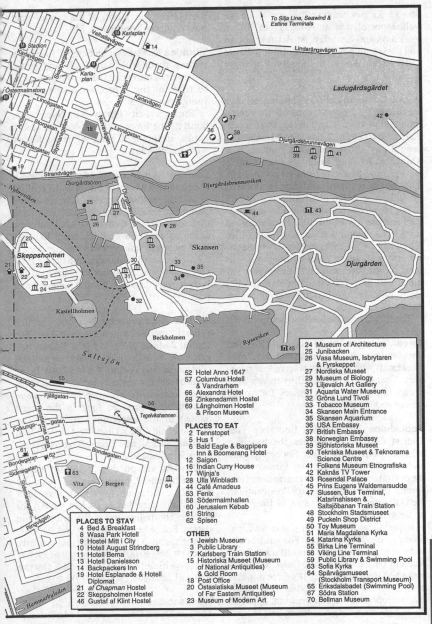

To Silja Line, Seawind &
Estline Terminals

Lindarängsvägen

Ladugårdsgärdet

Djurgårdsbrunnsvägen

Djurgårdsbrunnsviken

Skansen

Djurgården

Skeppsholmen

Kastellholmen

Beckholmen

Ryssviken

Saltsjön

Fjällgatan

Tegelvikshamnen

Bondegatan

Vita Bergen

Hammarbyleden

24 Museum of Architecture
25 Junibacken
26 Vasa Museum, Isbrytaren
   & Fyrskeppet
27 Nordiska Museet
29 Museum of Biology
30 Liljevalch Art Gallery
31 Aquaria Water Museum
32 Gröna Lund Tivoli
33 Tobacco Museum
34 Skansen Main Entrance
35 Skansen Aquarium
36 USA Embassy
37 British Embassy
38 Norwegian Embassy
39 Sjöhistoriska Museet
40 Tekniska Museet & Teknorama
   Science Centre
41 Folkens Museum Etnografiska
42 Kaknäs TV Tower
43 Rosendal Palace
45 Prins Eugens Waldemarsudde
47 Slussen, Bus Terminal,
   Katarinahissen &
   Saltsjöbanan Train Station
48 Stockholm Stadsmuseet
49 Puckeln Shop District
50 Toy Museum
52 Maria Magdalena Kyrka
54 Katarina Kyrka
55 Birka Line Terminal
56 Viking Line Terminal
63 Public Library & Swimming Pool
63 Sofia Kyrka
64 Spårvägsmuseet
   (Stockholm Transport Museum)
65 Eriksdalsbadet (Swimming Pool)
67 Södra Station
70 Bellman Museum

52 Hotel Anno 1647
57 Columbus Hotell
   & Vandrarhem
66 Alexandra Hotel
68 Zinkensdamm Hostel
69 Långholmen Hostel
   & Prison Museum

PLACES TO EAT
2 Tennstopet
5 Hus 1
6 Bald Eagle & Bagpipers
   Inn & Boomerang Hotel
12 Saigon
16 Indian Curry House
17 Wijnja's
28 Ulla Winbladh
44 Café Amadeus
53 Fenix
58 Södermalmshallen
60 Jerusalem Kebab
61 String
62 Spisen

OTHER
1 Jewish Museum
3 Public Library
7 Karlsberg Train Station
15 Historiska Museet (Museum
   of National Antiquities)
18 Post Office
20 Östasiatiska Museet (Museum
   of Far Eastern Antiquities)
23 Museum of Modern Art

PLACES TO STAY
4 Bed & Breakfast
8 Wasa Park Hotell
9 Hostel Mitt i City
10 Hotell August Strindberg
11 Hotell Bema
13 Hotell Danielsson
14 Backpackers Inn
19 Hotel Esplanade & Hotell
   Diplomat
21 af Chapman Hostel
22 Skeppsholmen Hostel
46 Gustaf af Klint Hostel

SWEDEN

for 35 kr per transaction, or Xchange Valutaspecialisten at Kungsgatan 30 on weekdays and Saturday. At Arlanda airport you can change money daily from 6.30 am to 10.30 pm. American Express is at Birger Jarlsgatan 1.

Post & Communications The longest hours are offered by the postal centre at the central train station, open from 7 am to 10 pm weekdays and 10 am to 7 pm at weekends. The central post office and poste restante is at Vasagatan 28, open weekdays from 8 am to 6.30 pm and Saturday from 10 am to 2 pm. The poste-restante address is Postens huvudkontor, 10110 Stockholm.

For all telephone calls, buy a Telia phonecard and use any of the Telia booths around town. The central train station Telia office (open from 8 am to 9 pm Monday to Saturday, from 10 am to 7 pm on Sunday), sells them, sends faxes and rents an Internet terminal (20 kr per 10 minutes) but charges more for its booths than use of a phonecard costs.

The telephone code for Stockholm is ☎ 08.

Travel Agencies The STF central office and travel bureau is at Kungsgatan 2 (closed weekends) where you can reserve tour packages. Next door at No 4, Kilroy travels sells cheap flights and train passes for young people and students.

Bookshops The Sweden Bookshop (see Tourist Offices above) has the broadest selection of thematic books. For newspapers and paperbacks in English try Pressbyrån at the central train station. For international and special-interest magazines, try Presscenter in the Gallerian shopping centre, or Interpress on Sergels Torg.

Imported books are expensive in Sweden, owing to the 25% sales tax. For guidebooks and a good map selection go to Akademibokhandeln on the corner of Mäster Samuelsgatan and Regeringsgatan. It's three minutes walk from the Sweden House. The widest map selections are at Kartcentrum, opposite the central train station at Vasagatan 16, and Kartbutiken, just north of the central train station area at Kungsgatan 74.

Libraries Kulturhuset on Sergels Torg has a reading room with periodicals and newspapers from many parts of the world that can be read for free. There are also books in various languages.

The largest city library is on Sveavägen, north of the town centre. It has zillions of books, including a good reference library with guidebooks.

Laundry Laundry options are limited and it is best to find a hotel or hostel with facilities or a fast washing service. The so-called *snabbtvätt* washing services in the telephone directory are not all that fast, taking a week or longer: the price is usually about 40 kr per kg. One small laundrette in the city area is Tvättomat at Västmannagatan 61 (metro: T-Odenplan), which charges 58 kr per load and is open weekdays to 6 pm and Saturday to 2 pm.

Medical & Emergency Services The free general emergency number is ☎ 112. The central 24-hour pharmacy is at Klarabergsgatan 64. At night, in medical emergencies, contact the duty doctor (☎ 644 92 00). In the suburbs seek the nearest *vårdcentral* medical centre listed in the blue pages (for *kommun* or municipal services look in the green pages) of the telephone directory. The private clinic City Akuten (☎ 411 71 77) at Holländargatan 3 near Hötorget receives casualties from around the city.

Dentists are on duty at Sankt Eriks, Fleminggatan 22, from 8 am to 7 pm daily (for acute cases up to 9 pm). Overnight contact the duty dentist (☎ 644 92 00) for advice. The police are at the central train station. Police headquarters (☎ 769 30 00) is at Agnegatan 33. The police lost-property office (☎ 769 30 00) is at Bergsgatan 39. For motor-vehicle breakdowns and towing contact Larmtjänst (☎ 020-91 00 40).

Things to See
The Stockholm Card gives free admission to

most of the 50-odd museums. Many of Stockholm's sights are closed on Monday. Children under 16 are generally admitted for half-price to attractions (especially museums) and small children can usually enter free if accompanied by a paying adult. Almost all major museums have a special children's room with toys or other activities, free lockers, clean toilets and coffee automates or cafés. Not all museums offer students discount admission.

Gamla Stan The oldest part of Stockholm is also its most attractive, containing old houses, vaulted cellar restaurants and the Royal Palace. You should allow a day to explore Gamla Stan: do walk along the touristy Västerlånggatan but don't miss the narrow parallel alleys or the quiet squares.

The city emerged here in the 13th century and took on the newer pursuits of trade and, partly, the accents of its German Hanseatic guests. It grew with Sweden's power until the 17th century, when the castle of Tre Kronor, symbol of that power, was burned to the ground.

The 'new' **Royal Palace** is a highlight. With 608 rooms, it's the largest royal castle in the world still in its original use. Many visitors find the **Royal Apartments** the most interesting, two floors of royal pomp and portraits of the pale princes. The **Royal Armoury** has a large collection of royal memorabilia, including five colourful horse carriages. Crowns are displayed at the **Royal Treasury**, near the **Palace Church**. **Gustav III Museum of Antiquities** displays Mediterranean treasures that were acquired by the eccentric Gustav III. The **Royal Coin Cabinet** is opposite the palace, next to the small **Finnish Church**. The Royal Palace attractions are open daily from 10 am to 4 pm in summer (30 to 45 kr each, free with the Stockholm Card).

Near the palace, **Storkyrkan** is the Royal Cathedral of Sweden, but charges 10 kr for admission. The most notable attraction is the 1494 **St George & the Dragon** sculpture.

The excellent **Post Museum** at Lilla Nygatan 6 (open daily except Monday) is free and well worth a visit.

The island of Riddarholmen has some of the oldest buildings in Stockholm, such as **Riddarholmskyrkan**, no longer a church but the royal necropolis and armorial glory of the Serafim knightly order. See the sarcophagus of Gustav II Adolf, Sweden's mightiest monarch, and the massed wall-plates displaying the arms of the knights. Admission is 20 kr and the church is open daily to 4 pm from May to August, on Wednesday and at weekends in September. **Riddarhuset** (House of Nobility) is open only around noon (20 kr), and displays over 2300 coats of arms.

The **Museum of Medieval Stockholm** on Strömparterren is a relatively recent addition. The location had been allocated as a parking space for representatives of the nearby **Riksdagen** (parliament, free guided tours in summer). Today you may see why the underground space became a museum instead.

The streets of the eastern half of Gamla Stan are medieval enough, still winding along their 14th-century lines and linked by a fantasy of lanes, arches and stairways. Also worth a look is the lavishly decorated **German Church** on Tyska brinken.

Central Stockholm Few people seem to like the central **Sergels Torg** but it's the centre of activity much of the year. **Kulturhuset** has many art venues at any given time plus a library and a café.

Stadshuset, the Town Hall, looks like a church but features the mosaic-lined Gyllene salen, Prins Eugen's own fresco re-creation of the lake view from the gallery, and the hall where the Nobel Prize banquet is held. The daily tours, in English (30 kr, 10 am to 2 pm), are interrupted from time to time by the preparations for special events. Climb the tower (15 kr) for a good view of the Old Town.

Klara kyrka is just opposite the central train station, and provides information on Stockholm's other churches. Also worth a visit is **Jakobs kyrka** in Kungsträdgården.

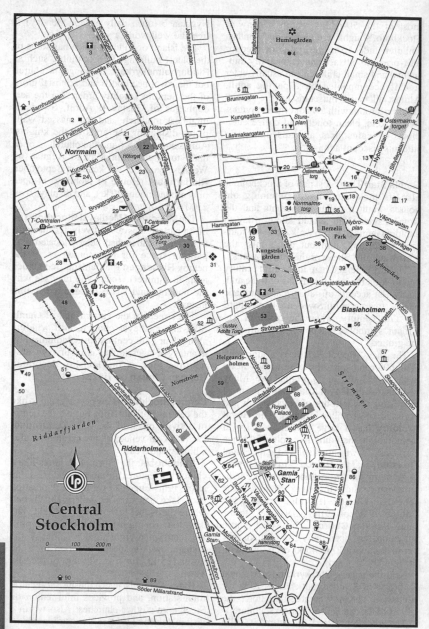

Central
Stockholm

0   100   200 m

PLACES TO STAY		79	Skitiga Duken	38	Strömma Kanalbolaget
1	City Backpackers	81	Café Art		Boats
	Vandrarhem & Dance	82	Michelangelo	41	Jakob Kyrka
	Museum	83	Kristina	42	Denmark Embassy
2	Queen's Hotel	84	Engelen & Kolingen	43	Finland Embassy &
28	SAS Radisson Royal	85	Den Gyldene Freden		Hambuger Börs
	Viking Hotel	87	Tullhus 2	44	Presscenter
56	Grand Hotel	88	Zum Franziskaner	45	Klara Kyrka & Church
65	Lady Hamilton Hotel				Information
89	Mälaren den Röda Båten	**OTHER**		46	Kartcentrum & Forex
90	MS *Rygerfjord*	3	Adolf Fredriks Kyrka	47	Viking Line
		4	Royal Library	48	Central Train Station &
PLACES TO EAT		5	Puppet Theatre Museum		Travel Centre
6	Glenn Miller Café	8	Finnish Tourist Board &	50	Stadshuset
7	Golden Hits		Kilroy Travels	51	Lake Mälaren Boats
10	StureCompagniet &	9	Silja Line & STF	52	Museum of
	Sturegallerian & Spa		(Svenska		Mediterranean
11	East		Turistföreningen)		Antiquities
13	Capri	12	Östermalms Market Hall	54	Stockholm
14	Sturekatten		& Örtagården		Sightseeing
15	Collage	17	Musikmuseet	55	Waxholmsbolaget
16	Pampas	22	Konserthuset		Information & Boat
18	Riche	23	Hötorgshallen & Clock &		Tickets
19	KB		Filmstaden	57	National Museum
20	Gröna Linjen	25	Gotland City Resebutik	58	Museum of Medieval
21	Kungshallen		(Tourist Information)		Stockholm
24	Vetekatten	26	Main Post Office	59	Riksdagen (Parliament)
33	Aqvarium	27	Cityterminalen & Airport	60	Riddarhuset (House of
36	Berns' & Berns' Hotel		Buses & World Trade		Nobility)
39	Wedholms fisk		Center	61	Riddarholmskyrkan
40	Café Söderberg	29	Post Office	66	Storkyrkan (Cathedral)
49	Eken & Stadshuskällaren	30	Kulturhuset & Library	67	Royal Apartments
53	Operakällaren, Café	31	Gallerian Shopping		Entrance
	Opera & Operabaren		Centre	68	Gustav III Museum of
62	Leijontornet & Victory	32	Sweden House &		Antiquities
	Hotel		Bookshop, Tourist	69	Royal Armoury
63	Stampen		Office & Forex	70	Royal Treasury & Palace
64	Hermans Hermitage	34	Finnair & Hotel		Church
73	Fem Små Hus		Stockholm	71	Royal Coin Cabinet
74	Eriks	35	Hallwyl Collection &	72	Finnish Church
75	Diana		American Express	78	Post Museum
76	Stortorgskällaren	37	Stockholm Sightseeing	80	German Church
77	Siam Restaurant		& Djurgården Boats	86	Ånedin Linjen

The Mediterranean collections in the **Museum of Mediterranean Antiquities**, at Fredsgatan 2 near Gustav Adolfs Torg (30 kr, students 20 kr, closed Monday) includes items from Egypt. The delightful **Hallwyl Collection** at Hamngatan 4 is a private palace from 1895 and is shown hourly (50 kr), once daily in English.

The **National Museum** on Blasieholmskajen has the main national collection of painting and sculpture but hosts other exhibitions on a variety of themes including design, so it is worth checking even if mainstream art is not your province (40 kr, closed Monday). There is also an excellent museum shop.

Across the bridge on Skeppsholmen, **Östasiatiska museet** (Museum of Far Eastern Antiquities), displays old and contemporary ceramics and crafts. The cost is 30 kr (students 15 kr): on Wednesday admission is free, on Monday the museum is closed. The **Museum of Modern Art** (due to open 1998) and the **Museum of Architecture** with its temporary exhibitions on Swedish architecture, are also on Skeppsholmen.

SWEDEN

In Vasastaden north of the centre, the wine-and-liquor museum **Vin och sprithistoriska museet**, at Dalagatan 100, sounds eccentric but might make sense of the weird story behind *brännvin* (schnapps) and the birth of a conservative Swedish alcohol policy (25 kr, closed Monday and Friday). To get there go to metro T-Odenplan or take bus No 58. The small **Jewish Museum** at Häslingegatan 2 opens from Sunday to Thursday only, admission 30 kr.

The dance museum **Dansmuseet**, Barnhusgatan 12, claims to be unique and covers all aspects of staging and costume. Admission costs 30 kr (children free) and the museum is closed on Monday. The **Puppet Theatre Museum** at Brunnsgatan 6 is closed in June and July but offers living theatre at selected times.

Musikmuseet, Sibyllegatan 2, is the best presented of the small collections and you can handle some of the instruments (from all periods) – they're the ones specially marked in green (admission 20 kr, closed Monday).

The main national historical collection is at **Historiska museet** at Narvavägen 13. It covers archaeology and culture, particularly from the Viking age, and also features coins. Don't miss the incredible **Gold Room** with rare golden treasures, many discovered by ordinary Swedes. Entry is 55 kr (students 30 kr) and the museum is closed on Monday (T-Karlaplan).

Djurgården No serious traveller should miss the royal park and its attractions.

Skansen was the world's first open-air museum, and the ambitious Stockholmites never stop developing it further. You could spend all day here: choose between the **zoo**, the **handicraft precinct**, the **open-air museum** or any of the daily events on Skansen's stages. The point to Skansen is that it gathers its exhibits from all over Sweden, so if you see only one open-air museum, let this be it. The **aquarium** is also a must – before the fish, you walk amongst the lemurs and witness the smallest monkeys in the world. The hilltop location is part of Skansen's attraction and the lazy can take the mini-railway to the top and make their own way down and around the exhibits.

Admission is 50 kr in tourist seasons, 30 kr from September to April. Folk-dancing is demonstrated during summer and a more modern touch is the ecologically oriented **forestry pavilion**. The history of smoking is at **Tobacco Museum**, also a part of Skansen and included in the entry price.

Skansen is surrounded by other museums. **Nordiska museet** was founded by Artur Hazelius (who also started Skansen), and the enormous Danish-style castle houses notable temporary exhibitions and endless Swedish collections.

Vasamuseet, behind the Nordic museum on the western shore of Djurgården, allows you simultaneously to look into the lives of 17th-century sailors and to appreciate a brilliant achievement in marine archaeology. The flagship *Wasa* went almost straight to the bottom when launched without a shot having been fired and the literature or tour guides will explain the extraordinary and controversial 300-year story of its death and resurrection (45 kr, open daily). The bookshop is also interesting enough to be a trap. Behind, at the moorings, is the rather later *Isbrytaren* (icebreaker) and the *Fyrskeppet* (beacon ship) both of which are open for inspection (15 kr, open daily).

Junibacken re-creates some of Astrid Lindgren's children's books into life. A train journey will require some fantasy but children who are familiar with the characters may like it here. Admission is 75 kr (open daily in summer).

Minor museums include the **Museum of Biology, Liljevalch Art Gallery** and the perhaps overpriced **Aquaria Water Museum** that is essentially another aquarium.

Gröna Lund Tivoli is almost a cliché – technically perfect and usually crowded and noisy. There are often good concerts there, but if you want just thrills, buy the 170 kr *åkbandet* that allows unlimited rides (or waiting time!). Gröna Lund has free admission on many tourist passes, or 40 kr without.

Beyond Djurgården's big and famous tourist traps are plenty of little gems. **Prins**

Eugens Waldemarsudde was a private palace of the prince who preferred art to royal pleasures. The buildings, art galleries and the old windmill are open daily except Monday to 5 pm but the park is accessible even later. **Rosendal Palace** further north was used by Karl XIV Johan in the 1820s, and is shown hourly from noon to 3 pm daily except Monday (40 kr). At the east end of Djurgården is **Thielska Galleriet** with a notable collection of Nordic art (40 kr, open daily). Take bus No 69 from the central train station.

Cycling is the best way to get around Djurgården but if you have just come for the attractions, take bus No 47 from the central train station or the summer Djurgården ferry services from Nybroplan or Slussen. Parking is limited during the week and prohibited on summer weekends, when Djurgårdsvägen is closed to traffic.

Ladugårdsgärdet North of Djurgården is an open paddock for the royal sheep, but more interesting are the good museums (open daily).

Sjöhistoriska museet exhibits maritime memorabilia, open daily from 10 am to 5 pm, 30 kr. **Tekniska museet & Teknorama Science Centre** covers exhaustively Swedish inventions and their applications, and the **Telecommunications Museum** has everything you ever wanted to know about LM Ericsson. **Folkens Museum Etnografiska** brings the entire world under one roof (closed Monday). Not far is the **Kaknäs TV Tower**, the tallest building in town. There's an observation deck and a restaurant on top (20 kr, open daily until 10 pm).

Take bus No 69 for these attractions.

Södermalm Mostly residential, Södermalm is also a suburb with more character than other parts of Stockholm. For evening walks, head to the northern cliffs for good views and old houses. Especially fine neighbourhoods are around the **Katarina kyrka**, in the park near the **Sofia kyrka**, around the 'Puckeln Shop District' on Hornsgatan, and on Lotsgatan and Fjällgatan, not far from the Viking Line terminal.

Still better are the views from **Katarina-hissen**, an old lift that takes you to the heights from Slussen.

Stockholm Stadsmuseet exhibits the streets and houses of Stockholm, and is worthwhile once you have developed a romantic attachment to Stockholm. The **Toy Museum** (30 kr, open daily except Monday) on Mariatorget, behind the **Maria Magdalena kyrka**, is an oversized fantasy nursery full of everything you probably wanted as a child – children will enjoy themselves in the playing room. The **Spårvägsmuseet** (Stockholm Transport Museum: 20 kr, free on SL tourist card, open daily) on Tegelviksgatan in the Söderhallen transport depot, near the Viking Line terminal, has a large collection of vintage trams and buses.

Långholmen This wild and mysterious island once housed a prison. The **Prison Museum** remains in one of the cells in the building that today is a hotel and a STF hostel. The tiny **Bellman Museum**, commemorating the 18th-century composer of daring drinking songs, is mostly of local interest.

Northern Suburbs Amongst the popular attractions is **Millesgården**, at Carl Milles väg 2, Lidingö, an outdoor sculpture collection by Carl Milles (50 kr, open daily in summer). Take the metro to Ropsten and bus Nos 201 to 206.

The **Natural History Museum** at Frescativägen 40 is extensive and includes the Omnimax theatre **Cosmonova**. Entry costs 40 kr (65 kr extra to Cosmonova) and the museum is open daily (T-Universitetet).

The large parks, spanning from Djurgården in the south, form the **National City Park**, the first such protected city area in the world. The **Haga Park** is pleasant for walks and bicycle tours, and attractions include the royal **Gustav III Pavilion** and a **Butterfly House**. Further north is the royal **Ulriksdals Castle** which has an **Orangery** housing Swedish sculpture, and the **stables** of Queen Kristina.

Activities

Stockholm offers a great variety of activities for its taxpayers, and prices are subsidised. In summer, many people head to beaches on the capital's shores, or organise picnics in the great parks. Eriksdalsbadet is an open-air pool in the far south of Södermalm. Before and after summer, an indoor pool is open on Medborgarplatsen, also on Södermalm.

Organised Tours

Stockholm Sightseeing runs interesting hourly cruises from mid-April to mid-December around the central bridges and canals from Strömkajen (near the Grand Hotel), Nybroplan or Klara Mälarstrand, near Stadshusbron (80 kr, one hour; 130 kr, two hours). Daily city coach tours last three hours and cost 230 kr.

Special Events

There are many festivals, concerts and other happenings on Sergels Torg and Kungsträdgården throughout the summer, and the major museums exhibit temporary exhibitions on a grand scale. *Stockholm This Week* lists daily events.

The biggest annual event is the **Stockholm Water Festival**, which runs for 10 days in early August and involves all manner of concerts, exhibitions and cultural events as well as boat sports, regattas and fireworks competitions. A special pass is required for most concerts and events, but the enormous festival area is open to all.

Places to Stay

Camping *Bredäng Camping* (☎ 97 70 71), on Stora Sällskapets väg in Bredäng 10 km south of Stockholm (T-Bredäng), is open all year with sites for 80 kr a night, or 165 kr with a vehicle.

Hostels Stockholm has more than a dozen hostels, both HI-affiliated STF hostels (where a membership card yields a 35 kr discount) and independent hostels (no cards required). The choice includes four boat hostels, one in an old prison and some central options. Most hostels will fill up during the late afternoon in summer so arrive early or book in advance. Tourist offices in the city centre usually will assist in getting a bed for a fee – or buy a Telia phonecard and start dialling.

Open only from late June to 10 August, *Backpackers Inn* (☎ 660 75 15) in a school building at Banérgatan 21 (T-Karlaplan) has 300 beds and charges 85 kr for HI members.

Most travellers head first to Skeppsholmen (take bus No 65 from the central train station or do like everyone else – walk). The popular STF boat hostel *af Chapman* (☎ 679 50 15), has done plenty of travelling of its own but is now a big hostel rolling gently in sight of the centre of the city. Bunks down in the basement cost 100 kr, including the ambience. Beside the boat hostel on dry land is the even bigger hostel *Skeppsholmen* (☎ 679 50 17). Beds in four-bed rooms cost 100 kr. There is no kitchen or laundry; breakfast is 45 kr.

Even nearer the central train station is *City Backpackers* (☎ 20 69 20) at Barnhusgatan 16, with dorms (145 kr) in what is one of the cleanest and best equipped hostels in Stockholm. There's a kitchen, sauna and laundry. In the same area, a bit north, *Hostel Mitt i City* (☎ 21 76 30) at Västmannagatan 13 occupies the entire 5th floor, and has beds from 145 kr. It's open 24 hours all year round but is not the cleanest in town. Further north in the Vasastaden district, *Brygghuset* (☎ 31 24 24) at Norrtullsgatan 12N (T-Odenplan) is an ex-brewery building that is open from June to August as a summer hostel. Beds in quiet 5th-floor dorms cost 125 kr, and there is a café and laundry machines. Also north from the centre, *Bed & Breakfast* (☎ 15 28 38) at Rehnsgatan 21 (T-Rådmansgatan) is an informal basement hostel with big beds in large dormitories (125 kr), a sauna and a kitchen. Yet another hostel in the northern suburbs, *Solna Sleep-In* (☎ 34 46 80) is just outside the Stockholm City area beside the E4 motorway. It was previously a SAS bus terminal (and looks like a petrol station). It has beds in large dormitories (85 kr), a café and information available. The location is good for excursions to the royal castles in the nearby parks.

There are many hostels in and around Södermalm, many within walking distance from the Viking Line boats and even from the central train station. The boat *Gustaf af Klint* (☎ 640 40 77) has beds for 120 kr in four-bed cabins and you can arrange to arrive any time. It is open all year round, and in summer there are beds in large dorms for 100 kr. Unfortunately the restaurant tends to be noisy prior to ferry departures. West of the railway lines, *Mälaren den Röda Båten* (☎ 644 43 85) at Kajplats 6 is a red boat and easily the cosiest of all boat hostels in Stockholm, thanks to the fine restaurant. Bunks in clean cabins cost 160 kr, including sheets. Breakfast is 45 kr. A bit further west is MS *Rygerfjord* (☎ 84 08 30) at Kajplats 12. There are 48 cabins, with a few bunks for 150 kr, as well as singles/doubles for 350/450 kr (including sheets and breakfast).

The private *Columbus Hotell & Vandrarhem* (☎ 644 17 17) is in a quiet location in Södermalm at Tjärhovsgatan 11 (T-Medborgarplatsen). There are 120 beds for 125 kr, a kitchen, laundry and a restaurant. Hotel rooms are very clean and cost 395/500 kr. In the west end of Södermalm, *STF Vandrarhem Zinkensdamm* (☎ 616 81 18) at Zinkens väg 20 (T-Zinkendamm) is a large complex in a quiet location near a park. There are beds in clean four-bed rooms from 100 to 125 kr. The other side has pricey hotel rooms. Off the north-western corner of Södermalm, the small island of Långholmen includes hostel cells at *Långholmen* (☎ 668 05 10), formerly a prison. There are both dorm beds for 125 kr (booking is essential) and typically expensive hotel rooms.

If things get desperate, there are more than 20 hostels in the province that can be reached by SL buses or trains or archipelago boats within an hour or so. Some options are mentioned in the Around Stockholm section.

Private Rooms The main source of private rooms is Hotelltjänst (☎ 10 44 37) at Vasagatan 15, which can arrange single/double rooms at 250/350 kr per night (a minimum of two). The office is open from 9 am to 5 pm only.

Hotels The central hotel booking office is Hotellcentralen (☎ 24 08 80), with branches at the central train station (open weekdays from 9 am to 5 pm), and in Sweden House (see Tourist Offices above). You can book hotels for a fee of 40 kr the same day (for hostels it's 15 kr). In summer hotels tend to be cheaper, and this is also the time to ask about Stockholmspaket: a package of an inexpensive hotel room and the Stockholm Card, whereby you pay half the rate of the room and get a complimentary public transport and entrance pass to all attractions for 24 hours. Travel agents in other Scandinavian capitals or major Swedish cities should help with arrangements.

In the middle of the city is the pleasant *Queen's Hotel* (☎ 24 94 60) above the shopping street at Drottninggatan 71a – a mild splurge on weekends and in summer with singles/doubles from 420/520 kr. Another place for a splurge is *Hotel Oden* (☎ 34 93 40) at Karlsbergsvägen 24 (T-Odenplan). At weekends and in summer there are singles/doubles for 560/660 kr, at other times singles start at 825 kr.

Hotell Gustav Vasa (☎ 34 38 01) is a little way uptown at Västmannagatan 61 and has reasonably priced rooms for 350/450 kr in summer. *Hotell Bema* (☎ 23 26 75), at Upplandsgatan 13, discounts rates to 430/500 kr during summer. Nearby, *Hotell August Strindberg* (☎ 32 50 06) at Tegnérgatan 38 is a quiet little hotel with rooms for 475/575 kr in summer. Also in this area, *Hotell Danielsson* (☎ 411 10 65) at Wallingatan 31 has a few rooms in summer for 250/350 kr.

The simplest rooms of the historical *Hotel Anno 1647* (☎ 644 04 80), just off Slussen at Mariagränd 3, are a bargain at 395/495 kr in summer. Also in Södermalm, *Alexandra Hotel* (☎ 84 03 20), Magnus Ladulåsgatan 42, has summer deals from 315/495 kr.

Wasa Park Hotell (☎ 34 02 85), at Sankt Eriksplan 1, is just north-west of the business district (T-Sankt Eriksplan) and has rooms from 350/450 kr all year round.

Hotels that are attractions in themselves include all the small hotels in Gamla Stan, and the best of them all is the *Grand Hotel*. Singles/doubles start at 930/1400 kr in summer, 1490/2470 kr in winter. Between the two Art Nouveau hotels at Strandvägen 7, *Hotel Esplanade* at 695/1095 kr (summer) and 995/1300 kr (winter) is cheaper than *Hotell Diplomat* at 895/1295 kr and 1395/1995 kr.

The big hotels on the outskirts of Stockholm are especially useful for their lower rates and free parking. Look for ads along the main arteries.

Places to Eat

Stockholm has thousands of restaurants and eateries, including inexpensive lunch cafeterias and some of the finest dining halls in Scandinavia. The cheapest snacks are to be found in the numerous *gatukök* outlets that serve greasy sausages, including the tasty Argentinian chorizos. Hamburger restaurants include *Burger King* and *Clock*, and the 24-hour *McDonald's* outside the central train station. There are also several 24-hour 7-Eleven shops that serve coffee and sandwiches.

Market Halls Excellent places to sample local and exotic tastes are the colourful market halls. *Hötorgshallen* on Hötorget has many Mediterranean eateries and good specialist shops. *Östermalms Market Hall* includes some very fine fish restaurants, and upstairs you'll find *Örtagården* that serves very good vegetarian food. *Söderhallarna* at T-Medborgarplatsen is more modern but has the atmosphere of a food centre.

Gamla Stan Tourists love Gamla Stan, and many dine on Västerlånggatan, in stylish places like *Michelangelo* or *Kristina*, or drink their coffee in the vaulted *Café Art*. Equally popular are the places on Stortorget, including the large *Stortorgskällaren* and many fine cafés. Many locals, however, prefer other streets and places like *Siam Restaurant*, Stora Nygatan 25 (inexpensive Thai food) or *Skitiga Duken*, Stora Nygatan 35 (Italian). *Stampen*, Stora Nygatan 5, has live jazz music, and *Hermans Hermitage*, Stora Nygatan 11, is popular among vegetarians.

For fine restaurants, go to Österlånggatan, where you'll find *Fem Små Hus*, *Eriks*, *Diana* (Brunnsgränd 2) and *Den Gyldene Freden*. *Zum Franziskaner* nearby at Skeppsbron 44 serves German sausages and is the oldest restaurant in town. Across the street, *Tullhus 2* is one of the newest, and has its own brewery. *Leijontornet*, adjacent to Victory Hotel at Lilla Nygatan 5 is also very fine.

Engelen & Kolingen at Kornhamnstorg 59, street-level and basement locations, respectively, are popular in the evening – come at 5 pm for special 'after work' meals.

City *Kungshallen* on Hötorget is a genuine food centre with some inexpensive sandwiches and more stylish outlets. Nearby at Kungsgatan 55, *Vetekatten* is one of the traditional cafés in town. Similar but perhaps even more attractive is *Sturekatten* at Riddargatan 4 just east of the centre. This is a good place to look for very stylish places, some of which open in the evening. *Collage* at Smålandsgatan 2 is the best bargain in town with its 25 kr buffet available every evening from 6.30 to 9.30 pm. *Pampas*, on Riddargatan is only worthy if you're prepared to pay for a good beef steak.

Birger Jarlsgatan has many good places, and *Riche* at No 4 should be seen for its décor alone. The evening smorgasbord is pricey at 220 kr. Nearby at Smålandsgatan 7, *KB* is a traditional restaurant with Swedish meals available, and has catered to many local artists.

Further north on Stureplan, *East* is a large Asian restaurant. Across the street, *Sture Compagniet* is more known for its nightlife but it also has good eating prospects – the place is huge. The nearby Sturegallerian shopping centre is another landmark and has a few places to eat and drink.

Some of the best music pubs in Stockholm are near Stureplan. *Glenn Miller Café* at Brunnsgatan 21 plays jazz from CDs, but for tunes from the 1950s, go to *Golden Hits* at Kungsgatan 29.

Good pizzas are served at *Capri* at Nybrogatan 15. *Gröna Linjen* at Mäster Samuelsgatan 10, 2nd floor, serves a vegetarian buffet. Surprisingly reasonable meals are available during lunch hours at *Eken*, within the Town Hall near the central train station. Don't confuse Eken with the vaulted *Stadshuskällaren* which is very chic but worth a look anyway.

Aqvarium on Kungsträdgården is where anybody who is anybody will want to be seen. *Café Söderberg* at the other end of the park is a regular café but has the finest toilets in town. The trendiest places within the Opera House include the century-old *Operakällaren*, lively *Café Opera* with lunch specials and a nightly disco, and the intimate *Operabaren* with Art Nouveau décor.

Nearby on Berzelii Park, *Berns'* is mostly known for evening entertainment and brilliant shows, and the inconspicuous *Wedholms fisk* at Nybrokajen 17 serves the most expensive fish in town.

Neighbourhood Restaurants A typical place to eat and drink in the evenings is the *kvarterskrog* or neighbourhood pub that combines excellent cuisine with a fully licensed bar. The typical krog is open from 5 pm to 4 am or so. On Kungsholm, the popular evening restaurants are around Scheelegatan, including the reasonably cheap *Indian Curry House* and *Wijnja's*, a stylish deli.

In Södermalm, there are many places on Götgatan, such as *Fenix* at No 44, with many beer varieties and meals. *Jerusalem Kebab*, a regular fast food outlet at Götgatan 92, announces that it's 'open 24 hours' in more languages than most of us would know. Another trendy area is around Bondegatan. *String* at Nytorgsgatan 38 looks like an antique shop and everything is for sale. *Spisen* at Bondegatan 54 is another popular evening restaurant.

North of the city, *Saigon* at Tegnérgatan 19 recalls the years of the Vietnam War, but check the surrounding area for more places. Around Rörstandsgatan there are many pubs, such as *Bald Eagle* (American), *Bag-*

pipers Inn (British) and *Boomerang Hotel* (Australian).

Djurgården There are so many places on this touristy island that you won't go hungry. Very special (and very expensive) is the old *Ulla Winbladh* villa along the northern loop road. Further east is *Café Amadeus* that enables an alfresco coffee break.

Entertainment

Pubs & Clubs Early Stockholm nightlife centres around neighbourhoods that offer several krogs conveniently within walking distance. In Södermalm check Götgatan and the Skånegatan area. In Kungsholmen, try Scheelegatan, and in the northern centre (Vasastaden) try the Tegnérgatan and the Rörstrandsgatan areas.

Stockholm is a theatre city with great musicals from time to time. Tickets are not cheap, but are often sold out, especially for Saturday shows. *Hamburger Börs* at Jakobsgatan 6 has popular variety shows (some in English) for about 300 kr.

Hus 1, in the Gay-Hus at Sveavägen 57, is open from Wednesday to Saturday only.

Getting There & Away

Air Arlanda airport is just over half an hour from the city centre by Flygbuss (see the Getting Around section for details).

The air services to Copenhagen, Oslo, Helsinki, Tampere and Turku are run by SAS (☎ 020-91 01 50) and Finnair (☎ 679 93 30). British Airways (☎ 679 78 00), KLM (☎ 593 624 30) and Lufthansa (☎ 611 22 88) also have regular European services. Finnair and Lufthansa are at Norrmalmstorg 1. British Airways is at Hamngatan 11.

Bus Long-distance buses arrive at and depart from Cityterminalen at Klarabergsviadukten, adjacent to the central train station. The Busscenter ticket office is open from 9 am to 6 pm Monday to Friday, and from 9 am to 3 pm on Saturday, and represents the big concerns such as Swebus, Eurolines and Svenska buss and many of the direct buses to the north.

Train Stockholm is the hub for SJ's national services, and there are direct services to Copenhagen, Oslo, Storlien (for Trondheim) and Narvik. All these services arrive and depart from the central train station (Stockholm C), as do the SL pendeltåg commuter services that run to/from Nynäshamn, Södertälje and Märsta. See the Getting Around section for hints on travelling by train in Sweden.

Lockers cost 15, 20 or 25 kr and showers (next to the tunnel-level toilets) 25 kr.

Boat The Silja Line ferries (☎ 22 21 40) to Finland depart from Värta Hamnen (walk from T-Gärdet or take a bus from T-Ropsten). Viking Line ferries (☎ 714 56 00) to Turku and Helsinki depart from the terminal at Tegelvikshamn (bus from central train station or walk from T-Slussen). Viking Line has an office in the central train station. Birka Line's ferries depart from Stadsgårds-terminalen (T-Slussen). Ånedin-linjen is by the water at Tullhus 1 on Skeppsbron. Stena Line (☎ 14 14 75) is at Kungsgatan 14.

See Grisslehamn, Kapellskär, Vaxholm and Nynäshamn in the Around Stockholm section for other boat connections.

Getting Around

The Storstockholms Lokaltrafik (SL) runs all *tunnelbana* (T) metro trains, local trains and buses within the entire Stockholm province. The SL Centre in the basement level of the central train station gives out all timetables and sells SL Tourist Cards and the general Stockholm Card. The counter is open from 6.30 am to 11.30 pm Monday to Saturday, from 7 am to 11.30 pm on Sunday. Information is also available at Sergels Torg, Slussen and other locations.

A Stockholm Card for one day (see Stockholm, Information) covers travel on all SL trains and buses in greater Stockholm. There is also a SL Tourist Card that is valid for 24 hours (56 kr) or three days (107 kr), which is cheaper per day than the Stockholm Card and also gives free entry to some attractions. This ticket is especially good value if you use the third afternoon for transport to either end

of the province – you can reach the ferry terminals in Grisslehamn, Kapellskär or Nynäshamn, as well as all the archipelago harbours with this card. The train to Gnesta will exit you at Sörmlands province. If you want to explore the province in more detail, bring a passport photo and get yourself a monthly pass (355 kr, valid for each calendar month).

Rail passes are not valid on the SL trains. Individual tickets are not cheap (from 13 kr which includes two coupons). You can buy a 20-coupon discount ticket for 85 kr, and each new zone costs another coupon (maximum four zones which takes five coupons). The ticket will last one hour and must be stamped at the start of the journey.

To/From the Airport Flygbuss services between Arlanda airport and Cityterminalen leave every 10 or 15 minutes for the 30-minute journey. There are also services to suburbs (60 kr).

The Flygbuss desk is in the international arrivals terminal at the airport. A taxi to/from the city centre will cost up to 800 kr.

If you're using the Bromma airport for domestic flights, the bus from City-terminalen costs 40 kr.

Metro The most useful mode of transport in Stockholm is the tunnelbana (abbreviated T), which converges on T-Centralen, a tunnel walk from the main hall of the central train station. There are three main through lines with branches. Off-peak services vary but no trip from the city centre will take longer than 40 minutes. The 'blue line' has the most comprehensive collection of modern art decorating the underground stations, well worth a look if you have a travel pass and time to kill.

Bus Although bus timetables and route maps are complicated, studying them is no waste of time. City buses can be replaced by metro or walking but there are useful connections to rural attractions. The inner-city buses radiate from Sergels Torg, Odenplan, Fridhemsplan west of the city and Slussen.

Bus No 47 runs from Sergels Torg to Djurgården, bus No 69 runs to North Djurgården's museums and Kaknästornet.

Check where the regional bus hub is for different outlying areas. Islands of the Ekerö municipality (including the superb Drottningholm castle) are served by bus Nos 301 to 323 from T-Brommaplan. Buses to Vaxholm, Norrköping and the Åland ferries depart from T-Tekniska Högskolan.

Train Local pendeltåg trains are useful for connections to Nynäshamn (for ferries to Gotland), to Märsta (for buses to Sigtuna and even the airport) and Södertälje. There are also services to Nockeby (from T-Alvik), to Lidingö (from T-Ropsten), to Kårsta, Österskär and Näsbypark (from T-Tekniska Högskolan) and to Saltsjöbaden (from T-Slussen).

Tram The historical No 7 tram runs to/from Norrmalmstorg and passes most of the attractions on Djurgården. Separate fees apply – tourist cards are not valid.

Taxi There are absolutely no cheap taxis in Stockholm, but it is usually no problem finding one. When ordering at night, women should ask about *tjejtaxa*, a discount rate offered by some operators.

Car & Motorcycle If you are driving, note that Djurgårdsvägen is closed near Skansen at night, on summer weekends and some holidays. Parking houses are marked on all city maps and evening rates can be as low as 10 kr.

Bicycle Stockholm has a wide network of bicycle paths, and in summer you will never regret bringing a bicycle with you. There are maps for sale but they are not necessary. The Top Five day trips are Djurgården, a loop from Gamla Stan to Södermalm to Långholmen to Kungsholmen (on lakeside paths), Drottningholm (return by steamer), Haga Park and the adjoining Ulriksdal Park. Some long-distance routes are marked all the way from central Stockholm: Nynäsleden to

Nynäshamn joins Sommarleden near Västerhaninge and swings west to Södertälje. Roslagsleden leads to Norrtälje (linking with Blåleden to Vaxholm). Upplandsleden leads to Märsta north of Stockholm and you can ride to Uppsala via Sigtuna. Sörmlandsleden leads to Södertälje, south of Stockholm.

Bicycles can be carried free on SL local trains, except on weekdays between 6 and 9 am and 3 and 6 pm, or to/from the central train station. They are forbidden on the metro, although you will see some daring souls from time to time.

Around Stockholm

The good thing about Stockholm is the SL tourist card (or monthly ticket) that allows unlimited travel on all buses and local trains. Free timetables are available at the central train station, in Slussen and in various location around Stockholm.

VAXHOLM
Vaxholm is the gateway to Stockholm's archipelago and has a collection of quaint summerhouses that were fashionable in the last century. The 16th-century **Vaxholm castle** on a small island is now a museum, open daily in summer (30 kr).

Take bus No 670 from the metro station T-Tekniska Högskolan or any of the Waxholmsbolaget boats from Strömkajen (45 minutes).

NYNÄSHAMN
The Nynäshamn ferry terminal is the main gateway to Gotland but ferry services to Russia are yet to resume. There are also boats to Ålö on the island of Utö (see the following Stockholm Archipelago section). The STF hostel *Nickstagården* (☎ 08-520 208 34) west of the town centre at Nickstabadsvägen 17 is open all year but from September to May you have to book. Beds cost 70 or 95 kr, and there's a good kitchen. A regular local train runs from Stockholm to Nynäshamn,

Around
Stockholm

To Gävle

To Grisslehamn

Älmsta

Edsbro

Uppsala

Erken

Norrtälje

Skokloster

Knivsta

To Kapellskär

Rimbo

E18

Arlanda
Airport

Märsta

Bergshamra

Sigtuna

To
Västerås

Vallentuna

Bålsta

E18

Brunna

Åkersberga

Ljusterö

Bro

Upplands
Väsby

Täby
Church

E18

Kungsängen

Sollentuna

Täby

Munsö
Church

Jakobsberg

Ulriksdal Park
Haga Park

Vaxholm

Grinda

Färingsö

Bromma
Airport

Lidingö

Vindö

Stenhamra

Lövön

Boo

Gustavsberg

Värmdö

Adelsön

Drottningholm

Djurö

Birka

Ekerön

Nacka

Starsnäs

Ekerö

Alta

Mariefred

Botkyrka

STOCKHOLM

Saltsjöbaden

Ingarö

Huddinge

Tyresö

Nämdö

Södertälje

E20

Tumba

Vårsta

Jordbro

Järna

E4

Västerhaninge

Dalarö

Örnö

Gnesta

Årsta

Himmerfjärden

Ösmo

Muskö

Vagnhärad

Rånö

Utö

To Nyköping
& Norrköping

Trosa

Nynäshamn

Ålö

Nattarö

0   10   20 km

and takes bicycles and SL tickets but *not* international train passes.

STOCKHOLM ARCHIPELAGO

Depending on which source you read, the archipelago around Stockholm has anything between 14,000 and 100,000 islands – a matter of definition. A summer cottage on a rocky islet is popular among wealthy Stockholmites, and regular boats offer options for outings.

The biggest operator is Waxholmsbolaget; timetables and information are available outside the Grand Hotel on Strömkajen and in Vaxholm. *Båtluffarkortet* (250 kr) is valid for 16 days and gives unlimited rides plus a handy island map and free bicycle hire. The ferries wind through the archipelago to Ljusterö, Ingmarsö, Möja, Sandhamn, Nämdö, Ornö, Utö and many more. Bicycles can be taken for 17 kr per trip.

Before you make up your mind go to Nybrokajen and check what Strömma Kanalbolaget has to offer. The seven-day *Skärgårdskortet* for 450 kr offers unlimited rides on Strömma and Cinderella boats to many of the most interesting islands.

Each island has its own character. **Sandhamn** is popular among wealthy sailors and best on a day trip (90 minutes from Vaxholm). **Finnhamn** is quieter, and you must book in advance to stay at the *STF Hostel* (☎ 08-542 462 12). **Utö** is more popular among cyclists, and the *STF Hostel* (☎ 08-501 576 60) in Gruvbyn is open daily. Beds cost 100 kr but the reception is at Utö Värdshus.

GRISSLEHAMN

The quickest and cheapest ferry to Finland departs from this small settlement in the north end of Stockholms *län* – SL tickets apply on bus No 637 which runs four to six times daily from Norrtälje. If you have time to kill, the home museum and the isolated studio of the artist Albert Engström are worth a look.

The Eckerö Linjen ferries depart five times daily (three times in the low season) from Grisslehamn and arrive two hours later at Eckerö on Åland. Return tickets cost just 60 kr, a car is 40 kr and bicycles are free. Eckerö Linjen runs a direct bus from Stockholm Cityterminalen.

KAPELLSKÄR

The Viking Line ferry shuttles four times daily between Mariehamn (Åland) and the tiny village of Kapellskär. The *STF Hostel* (☎ 0176-441 69), about two km from the ferry terminal, has beds for 100 kr from 1 June to 20 August.

The direct bus from Stockholmn Cityterminalen costs 35 kr, but if you have a SL pass, take bus No 640 or 644 from T-Tekniska Högskolan to Norrtälje and change there to No 631 which runs every two hours or so.

EKERÖ

Surprisingly rural, Ekerö consists of several large islands on Lake Mälaren, three UNESCO World Heritage-listed sites and a dozen medieval churches.

If you're too busy to cycle, or the weather doesn't permit it, take the metro to Brommaplan and change to bus Nos 301 to 323.

Drottningholm

The royal residence and parks of Drottningholm on Lövön are among the best tourist attractions of Stockholm. The main Renaissance-inspired **palace** surrounded by geometric baroque gardens was built about the same time as Versailles, late in the 17th century. The highlights of the chambers inside are the **Karl X Gustav Gallery**, in baroque style, and the painted ceilings of the **State Hall**. The palace is open daily from May to September (40 kr). The court theatre **Slottsteater** has a museum (40 kr) but more unique are the original 18th-century surroundings. Ask about shows in summer.

At the far end of the gardens is the 18th-century **Kina slott**, a lavishly decorated 'Chinese palace' that was given by the king as a gift to queen Lovisa Ulrika.

Adelsö

The World Heritage site on Adelsö is around the medieval **church** and includes burial mounds that are associated with nearby Birka.

SL bus No 312 runs to the Adelsö church from Brommaplan via the medieval Ekerö and Munsö churches. Bus No 311 takes you to the ferry only, but you can walk on the other side to the STF hostel *Adelsögården* (☎ 08-560 514 00), just south of the ferry pier and open from 15 June to 31 August. Beds cost 85 kr. There are a kitchen and a restaurant, and bicycles can be hired. A walking trail from the hostel leads via some prehistoric sites to the church.

Birka
Summer cruises to the Viking-age trading centre of Birka (a UNESCO World Heritage site), on Björkö in Lake Mälaren, have increased in popularity as archaeologists have unearthed more of the town and its cemetery, harbour and fortress. You can cruise there and back (185 kr) in summer on the *Victoria* from Stadshusbron, Stockholm, and there are tours in English (included in the cruise price) of the remains of the trading town and fortifications at noon on Friday and at weekends in July and August. The outing takes most of the day. The tiny museum is open daily in summer to 5 pm. In summer (early May to mid-September), there are also connecting boats between Adelsö and Birka.

SIGTUNA
The most pleasant town around Stockholm, Sigtuna is also one of the oldest in Sweden. Stora Gatan is probably Sweden's oldest main street and ruins of the churches of St Per, St Olof and St Lars remain. **Maria-kyrkan** has restored medieval paintings. Among the museums, see **Lundströmska gården** and the big **Sigtuna Museum**.

The tourist office is at the Drakegården house, Stora Gatan, and the STF Hostel *Kyrkans utbildningcentrum* (☎ 08-592 583 84), at Manfred Björkquists allé 12, has beds from mid-June to mid-August for 100 kr.

Getting to Sigtuna is easy: take a train to Märsta and change to bus No 570 or 575 just outside the Märsta train station. In summer there are cruises from Stockholm and

Uppsala (going via the baroque castle in Skokloster.)

Skåne

The ancient province of Skåne, sometimes called Scania by English-speakers, was Danish until the middle of the 17th century: this is easily detected in the strong dialect and in the architecture.

Bicycle tours are popular in Skåne – there are more hostels than in any other region in Sweden, and numerous attractions are scattered around the gently rolling landscape.

MALMÖ
Malmö is a lively and personal city, perhaps due to the influence of Copenhagen across the Öresund. The dense boat traffic means you can shuttle to and fro by ferry in less than an hour one way (Europe's longest bridge, planned to span the water, will shorten that).

Orientation
Stortorget square is the focus of the city and the central train station is near the ferry port, just outside the city's encircling canals. Malmöhus castle guards the west end in its park setting and the Limhamn ferry terminal lies beyond.

Information
Tourist Offices The tourist office (☎ 040-30 01 50) is inside the central train station building. STF has an office inside the main post office building at Skeppsbron 1 (open weekdays only).

The free booklet *Malmö this Month* is a useful general guide. The discount card *Malmökortet* allows free parking in the city, free entry to several museums, and free sightseeing tours. The card costs 75 kr for a day, 100 kr for two days and 125 kr for three.

Money Forex is at Skeppsbron 2 (open from 8 am) and opposite the tourist office within the train station. An exchange counter is open daily at the hydrofoil terminal on

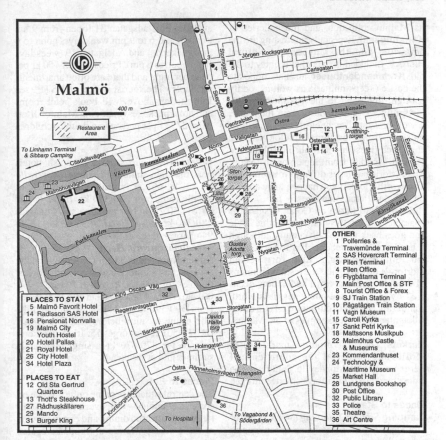

Malmö

0   200   400 m

Restaurant
Area

To Limhamn Terminal
& Sibbarp Camping

Citadellsvägen

Västra

Malmöhusvägen

Parkkanalen

hamnkanalen

Stortorget

Gustav
Adolfs
torg

King Oscars Väg

Regementsgatan

Banérsgatan

Kronborgsvägen

Östra Rönneholmsvägen Triangeln

To Hospital

Jörgen Kocksgatan
Carlsgatan

Stromgatan

Skeppsbron

Centralplan

Vallgatan

Norra

Adelgatan

Östra

hamnkanalen

Drottning-
torget

Östergatan

Rundelsgatan

Kalendegatan

Baltzarsgatan

Stora Nygatan

Nygatan

Lilla

Storgatan

Davids
Halls
torg

Holmgatan

To Vagabond &
Södergården

Stora Tvärgatan

Rörsjökanal

Drottninggatan

PLACES TO STAY
5 Malmö Favorit Hotel
14 Radisson SAS Hotel
19 Pensionat Norrvalla
19 Malmö City
   Youth Hostel
20 Hotell Pallas
21 Royal Hotel
26 City Hotell
34 Hotel Plaza

PLACES TO EAT
12 Old Sta Gertrud
   Quarters
13 Thott's Steakhouse
27 Rådhuskällaren
29 Mando
31 Burger King

OTHER
1 Polferries &
   Travemünde Terminal
2 SAS Hovercraft Terminal
3 Pilen Terminal
4 Pilen Office
6 Flygbåtarna Terminal
7 Main Post Office & STF
8 Tourist Office & Forex
9 SJ Train Station
10 Pågatågen Train Station
11 Vagn Museum
16 Caroli Kyrka
17 Sankt Petri Kyrka
18 Mattssons Musikpub
22 Malmöhus Castle
   & Museums
23 Kommendanthuset
24 Technology &
   Maritime Museum
25 Market Hall
28 Lundgrens Bookshop
30 Post Office
32 Public Library
33 Police
35 Theatre
36 Art Centre

Skeppsbron and you can exchange Swedish currency for Danish currency free at the main post office on weekdays from 8 am to 6 pm, Saturday from 9.30 am to 1 pm.

Post & Communications The central post office is at Skeppsbron 1 and there is a branch at Stora Nygatan 31a.

The telephone code is ☎ 040.

Bookshops The best place for general books and guidebooks is Lundgrens at Södergatan 3. For newspapers and international magazines go to Press Stop at Södergatan 20.

Medical & Emergency Services The duty pharmacy is at Bergsgatan 48. The medical centre is at the Allmänna Sjukhus at Södra Förstadsgatan 101. An emergency doctor (☎ 33 35 00, at night ☎ 33 10 00) and dentist (☎ 33 10 00) are on duty. The police centre is on Storgatan at Davidshallstorg.

Things to See
The combined museums of Malmö are based at the moated **Malmöhus castle**. For combined entry you pay 30 kr to walk through the **royal apartments** with their interiors and portrait collections, **Stadsmuseet** with

its Malmö collection, and the galleries of **Konstmuseet**. Especially interesting are the **aquarium** and the **Museum of Natural History**. Included in the ticket is entry to the old **Kommendanthuset** arsenal, opposite the castle (keeps militaria as well as, oddly enough, toys) and to the **Teknik och Sjöfartsmuseet**, at Turbinbron near the castle, a well-presented technology and maritime museum displaying aircraft, motor vehicles, steam engines and a walk-in submarine (closed Monday from September to May). The historic carriages of **Vagn museum** are also worth a look if you happen to be around on a Friday (admission free).

Sankt Petri kyrka on Göran Olsgatan is characteristic of the northern Gothic style and goes back to the 14th century, although it has been much rebuilt. The focal point is the 18th-century organ. **Lilla Torg** behind Stortorget on the right is the restored remains of the late medieval town and is now occupied by galleries and boutiques. It is worth wandering around Drottningtorget and down Adelgatan for more examples of old Malmö.

Markets The best produce market is at Möllevångstorget at the south end of Bergsgatan from Monday to Saturday. The indoor market is at Lilla Torg behind Stortorget.

Places to Stay
Camping *Sibbarp Camping* (☎ 15 51 65) at Strandgatan 101 in Limhamn accepts caravans only but is open all year. Take bus No 12B or G from Gustav Adolfs torg.

Hostels *Malmö City Youth Hostel* (☎ 23 56 40), Västergatan 9, has simple beds for 100 kr in big rooms, or better beds in smaller rooms for 125 kr. Laundry costs just 20 kr, and there's a kitchen. The STF hostel *Södergården* (☎ 822 20) on Backavägen beside the E6 is big and well equipped, offering beds for 100 kr and breakfast at 38 kr (take bus No 21 from Centralplan in front of the train station).

Private Rooms Rooms are available through *Takvåningen Triangeln* (☎ 795 94)

at Södra Förstadsgatan 31 (open from 9 am to noon and 6 to 9 pm weekdays, noon to 6 pm weekends) and Adelgatan 19 (weekdays from noon to 6 pm). Prices start at 150 kr per head per night and there are often apartments available. The tourist office and STF (see Information above) will book hotel rooms and hotel packages (including Malmökortet) from 275 kr per person in a double (children free).

Hotels There are several cheapish hotels near the train station. *Pensionat Norrvalla* (☎ 12 48 66) at Norra Vallgatan 32 has simple rooms for 250/350 kr. *Hotel Pallas* (☎ 611 50 77) at Norra Vallgatan 74 charges 280/380 kr. *Royal Hotel* (☎ 97 63 03) at No 94 charges 450/575 kr.

Malmö Favorit Hotel (☎ 10 18 00), at Jörgen Kocksgatan 3 near the ferries and the station, has summer and weekend singles/doubles for 400/530 kr. *Hotel Plaza* (☎ 771 00) at Södra Förstadsgatan 30 has rooms from 390/590 kr at weekends and in July. The prime location belongs to *City Hotell* (☎ 714 50) at Stortorget 15. It's a good city splurge for 470/670 kr a single/double in summer and at weekends.

Places to Eat
The central squares become quite a scene on summer evenings – well over a dozen restaurants offer alfresco dining and drinking. One of these places, *Mando* at Skomakaregatan 4, is purely a steakhouse with specialities, a little over mid-priced. *Rådhuskällaren* below the town hall at Stortorget is ideal for a splurge. *Vagabond* is a pub-diner near the STF hostel on Backavägen, which also makes it a natural watering hole.

If you're looking for old houses around the Sta Gertrud quarters, there are also a few renovated restaurants. Entrance to *Thott's Steakhouse* is via Radisson SAS Hotel. Hamburger restaurants are on Gustav Adolfs torg.

Entertainment
The disco and club *Étage* at Stortorget 6 boasts a mobile glass roof and is a mildly expensive splurge (the lower age limit is 23

for women and 25 for men). **Mattssons Musikpub** on Göran Olsgatan has jazz and big bands, but closes during July.

Getting There & Away

For a round tour of the Öresund or a visit to Copenhagen you can buy the Öresund Runt card for 149 kr, which gives free travel on ferries and the local trains for two days. The cards can be bought at the Pågatågen train station in Malmö, the tourist office or some branches of Pressbyrån.

A three-day card that covers Länstrafiken Malmöhus buses and Pågatågen costs 165 kr, and a weekly card costs 280 kr.

Air Sturup airport is 31 km south-east of the city. SAS has many nonstop flights to Stockholm daily and the hovercraft service to Copenhagen airport allows SAS flight connections.

Bus The länstrafik operates in zones (60 kr from Malmö to Helsingborg). The airport bus No 110 runs from Malmö to Sturup (60 kr). The intercity bus No 999 from Lund connects with Dragør ferries at Limhamn, stopping at Mälarbron on Norra Vallgatan and continuing to Copenhagen (40 kr). Regional buses stop there and at Slussplan. No 109 runs to/from Copenhagen airport (85 kr), stopping at Centralplan.

Train The Pågatågen local trains run to Helsingborg (60 kr), Lund (25 kr), Ystad and other destinations in Skåne (bicycles may be accepted, ask first). The platform is at the end of the central train station and you buy tickets from the machine. International rail passes are accepted.

SJ runs regularly to/from Helsingborg (65 kr) and Gothenburg via Lund. Direct trains run between Stockholm and Malmö – beware of the expensive X2000 departures.

At the station you can shower for 20 kr and rest rooms cost 15 kr per hour.

Boat Malmö can be reached from Copenhagen, Germany or Poland – there are three terminals for Copenhagen boats and the new

Polferries terminal near the train station. Flygbåtarna catamarans (95 kr) and Pilen (from 30 kr off peak to 50 kr) and Shopping Linjen ferries (45 kr) run Copenhagen services from the harbour on Skeppsbron. Pilen carries bicycles for 20 kr.

The bus stop outside the train station serves buses to Copenhagen via Linhamn, some five km from Malmö.

Getting Around

Malmö Lokaltrafik offices are at Gustav Adolfs torg and Värnhemstorget. The excellent free bus map at the tourist office should sort out any confusion. The card Malmökortet includes bus and ferry travel and discounts on Pågatågen trains. Local tickets are 12 kr for one hour's travel. The bus hubs are Centralplan (in front of the train station), Gustav Adolfs torg, Värnhemstorget and Triangeln.

LUND

The oldest town in Sweden, Lund was Danish in the 12th century and the archiepiscopal centre of the northern countries. Much of the medieval town can still be seen. The university was founded in the 1660s after Sweden took over Skåne. Today Lund retains its quiet yet airy campus feel and has a youthful population.

Information

The tourist office (☎ 046-35 50 40) is at Kyrkogatan 11 opposite the cathedral. The student union is on the 3rd floor of Akademiska Föreningen on Sandgatan (open from 10 am to 3 pm weekdays, closed for lunch). The excellent Gleerups bookshop is on Stortorget. The library at St Petri kyrkogatan 6 opens at 11 am. The main post office is at Knut den Stores torg 2.

The telephone code is ☎ 046.

Things to See

The magnificence of Lund's Romanesque **cathedral** is well known but for a real surprise, visit at noon or 3 pm (1 pm on Sunday and holidays) when the astronomical clock strikes up *In Dulci Jubilo* and the figures of

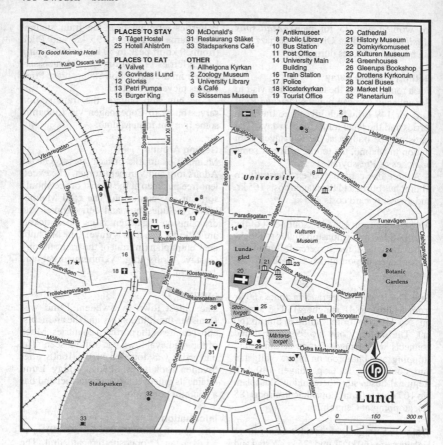

PLACES TO STAY	30	McDonald's	7	Antikmuseet	20	Cathedral
9 Tåget Hostel	31	Restaurang Stäket	8	Public Library	21	History Museum
25 Hotell Ahlström	33	Stadsparkens Café	10	Bus Station	22	Domkyrkomuseet
			11	Post Office	23	Kulturen Museum
PLACES TO EAT	OTHER		14	University Main	24	Greenhouses
4 Valvet	1	Allhelgona Kyrkan		Building	26	Gleerups Bookshop
5 Govindas i Lund	2	Zoology Museum	16	Train Station	27	Drottens Kyrkoruin
12 Glorias	3	University Library	17	Police	28	Local Buses
13 Petri Pumpa		& Café	18	Klosterkyrkan	29	Market Hall
15 Burger King	6	Skissernas Museum	19	Tourist Office	32	Planetarium

the three kings begin their journey to the child Jesus. The main **university** building, which faces Sandgatan, is worth a glance inside and Scanian **rune stones** are arranged in the park nearby.

There's a good **planetarium** at Svanegatan 9 which has two shows every Tuesday evening for 30 kr. The **Botanic Gardens** with tropical **greenhouses** (free, open daily from noon to 3 pm) east of the town centre are open daily.

Museums As far as Swedish museums go, you can't find many that are better than

Kulturen (30 kr, open daily from 11 am to 5 pm, to 9 pm on Thursday). The collections fill two blocks and include period houses and Swedish china. Entrance is from Tegnérsplatsen. There are guided tours in English on Sunday in summer.

Also worth a visit is the **History Museum** in the university quarter, and its annexe **Domkyrkomuseet** (Cathedral Museum). The two museums are open only from 11 am to 1 pm Tuesday to Friday; the 10 kr ticket is valid for both museums.

The medieval museum of **Drottens kyrkoruin** (open from 10.30 am to 12.30 pm

Monday to Thursday and at weekends, admission free) is on Kattesund. The ruins of the church are visible from the street, but the underground museum has models and exhibits that fill in the details of Lund's past.

The **Skissarnas Museum** at Finngatan 2 is part of the art museum (10 kr, closed Monday) and has a collection of sketches and designs of public decorative art in Sweden and abroad. The tiny **Antikmuseet** nearby is a university department (as is the Zoology Museum) but can be seen free of charge during office hours.

Places to Stay

You could keep Lund as a base and take trains to nearby towns, if you stay at the central STF hostel *Tåget* (☎ 14 28 20). The carriages are old sleeping stock with three bunks to a room – quiet yet tiny and perhaps too familiar to weary train travellers. Beds cost 100 kr, and breakfast is 40 kr. The erratic showers need a one-kr coin or two.

The SVIF hostel *La Strada* (☎ 32 32 51), at Brunnshögsvägen 3 north-east of the city centre, charges 125 kr for beds.

Private rooms can be booked at the tourist office (☎ 15 50 40) at rates between 130 and 200 kr a person plus a 50 kr fee. *Hotell Ahlström* (☎ 11 01 74) at Skomakaregatan 3 has singles/doubles for 375/575 kr weekdays and weekend discounts, but is closed in late June and in July.

Places to Eat

Lund has plenty of eating possibilities ranging from hamburger restaurants and library cafés to popular evening hang-outs. *Valvet* on Allhelgona kyrkogata near the arch has a fine mid-priced lunch. The vaulted *Restaurang Stäket* in the historic building at Stora Södergatan 6 is for lashing out.

Petri pumpa opposite the library has lunch specials. *Govindas i Lund* at Bredgatan 23 is the vegetarian option (open to 5 pm Monday to Thursday, to 3 pm Friday and Saturday).

American Cajun fare is served at *Glorias* on Sankt Petri Kyrkogatan. *Stadsparkens café* is an open lunch area in the city park where you can hire a chessboard or backgammon. Free live rock is common on summer weekends in the park nearby.

Getting There & Away

Lund is just 10 minutes or so from Malmö by train and there are frequent departures, both SJ and Pågatågen trains. All long-distance trains from Stockholm stop in Lund.

Buses leave outside the train station.

TRELLEBORG

Trelleborg's few medieval remnants around Gamla Torg were recently complemented by a recreation of a Viking fortress, **Trelleborgen** off Bryggaregatan (free).

The medieval **church** looks very Danish. **Trelleborgs Museum** is open on afternoons daily except Monday in summer.

The tourist office (☎ 0410-533 22, open daily from early June to mid-August) and the post office are both on Hamngatan opposite the Hansa ferry terminal. Forex is opposite the TT-Line terminal at Norra Kajgatan 20.

Night Stop (☎ 0410-410 70) opposite the museum at Östergatan 59 offers singles/doubles with shared facilities at 190/290 kr all year (breakfast 30 kr).

Getting There & Away

Train & Bus There are just two or three trains a day from nearby Malmö, but the express bus No X146 runs every 30 to 60 minutes from Malmö (35 kr) to the bus station, some 500 metres from the ferry terminals. See Ystad for further information.

Boat There are two terminals. The international Stockholm to Berlin trains use the Hansa terminal on the eastern side of the harbour; Hansa Ferries (☎ 0410-103 90) connects Trelleborg to Sassnitz (five times a day) and Rostock (three times a day). The western terminal is used by the TT-Line (☎ 0410-562 00) ferries and catamarans that shuttle between Trelleborg and Travemünde three to five times a day, and between Trelleborg and Rostock up to six times daily.

YSTAD

Rambling cobbled streets and half-timbered houses remain in this medieval town that is visited by daily ferries from Bornholm and Poland – change money at the terminal. The friendly tourist office (☎ 0411-776 81), just opposite the train station, is open daily and provides a good town map. Next door is the large **Art Museum** (30 kr, open daily). Don't miss the 16th-century **Sankt Maria kyrka** at Stortorget or the historical **Ystadbygdens Museum** in the old monastery church of Gråbrådraklostret (20 kr, open daily).

East of Ystad right at the Baltic coast is **Ales Stenar**, a mysterious stone formation built by the Vikings. The stones form an oval with a diameter of 67 metres but half the fun is the walk to the site.

Places to Stay & Eat

Those with their own wheels can choose between B&B and cabin options along the scenic coastal roads. Just two km east of Ystad, the *STF hostel* (☎ 0411-109 13) has beds for 100 kr, a kitchen and laundry facilities. Ystad has a few inexpensive guesthouses to choose from, not far from the train station. *Ljungs rumshotell* at Stickgatan 17 charges 285/385 kr, or check the nearby *Bäckagården* at Dammgatan 36.

Most budget eateries are on Stora Östergatan, the main pedestrian street.

Getting There & Away

The Unity Line ferry from Swinoujście runs daily to the terminal, which is within walking distance from the train station (more if you drive). The same terminal is used by the frequent ferries to/from Bornholm (see the Denmark chapter).

Pågatågen trains arrive hourly from Malmö (fewer trains on weekends), and some continue to Simrishamn. The buses depart from outside the train station. To get to Trelleborg by bus (45 kr), take first bus No 303 to Skateholm and transfer to bus No 183.

SMYGEHUK

The most southerly point in Sweden has become something of a tourist centre with shops and camping facilities. The *STF hostel* (☎ 0410-245 83) has beds for 100 kr all year round but you should book beforehand in winter. The southern coast is very scenic and has prolific bird life. The Ystad to Trelleborg bus service will take you to Smygehuk.

HELSINGBORG

The busy port of Helsingborg is perched on the coastline of the Öresund and often experiences big winds. There is a summer boulevard atmosphere in Stortorget and the older buildings in the winding streets blend well with the newer shops. The seaside character is enhanced by the pastiche styles of the high beachfront houses. Denmark is only 25 minutes away by ferry.

Information

Practically all travel-related needs have their solution inside the vast Knutpunkten complex just at the seafront, where you will find the tourist office (☎ 042-12 03 10) and Forex. The large public library is at Stadsparken near Knutpunkten.

Stortorget has a good bookshop, and the central post office is at Norra Storgatan 17 by Stortorget.

The telephone code is ☎ 042.

Things to See

Too many travellers leave Helsingborg without seeing more than the black wall of the underground train station.

The square, medieval tower **Kärnan** dates back to the defences of the 1300s and looked out over the Öresund to the Danish heartland and upon struggles that delivered the fortress finally to Swedish hands. Entry to the castle museum is 15 kr (open daily except Sunday to 4 pm and in summer daily until 7 pm).

Other museums in the town centre include the **Art Museum** in the park, the small **Idrottsmuseum** (Sports Museum) nearby, and **Skolmuseum** and **Medicinhistoriska Museet** (Museum of Medical History) on Bergaliden just west of the Kärnan.

More imposing is the 18th-century manor

PLACES TO STAY
6 Hotell Viking
11 Vandrarhem Hostel
23 Hotel Marina Plaza
27 Hotel Linnea
28 Cityhotellet

PLACES TO EAT
4 Kebab-house
5 Cleopatra
8 Telegrafen

14 Fahlmans Café
16 Källarkrogen
17 Restaurang Porten
20 Möllebackens Våffelbruk

OTHER
1 Art Museum
2 Theatre
3 Concert Hall
7 Idrottsmuseum
(Sports Museum)

9 Kärnan
10 School Museum
12 Museum of Medical
History
13 Post Office
15 Rådhuset
18 Bookshop
19 Mariakyrkan
21 Sundsbussarna
Boat Terminal
22 Boats to Ven

24 Scandlines Terminal
25 Tourist Office
& Forex
26 Train Station
29 Bus Terminal
30 Public Library
31 Sunds Terminal
32 Car Ferry Passenger
Ticket Booths
33 Police Station

Helsingborg

at **Fredriksdals Museum**, a park and museum village on Oscar Trapps väg immediately east of the city (admission 20 kr). In summer, highlights are performances in the open-air theatre. Wildflowers of the area are grown in the gardens.

The historic **Mariakyrkan** on Mariatorget is worth a visit for its medieval features and choral and organ concerts.

North of the town, the Pålsjö area contains a fine park, including the historical (but closed) **Pålsjö Castle**, and nearer the town centre, the quaint **windmill** at the north end of Strandvägen. The interiors are on display

for a few hours on afternoons from May to August.

Places to Stay
The tourist office can book private rooms, and will also help find a hotel room.

Camping *Råå Vallar Camping* (☎ 10 76 80) on Kustgatan about five km south of the city centre is open from mid-May to August and charges 130 kr a site. Take bus No 1B from Rådhuset or No 41 from Söderport. *Stenbrogårdens Camping* on Rausvägen eight km

SWEDEN

south-east of the city (via Landskronavägen) is open all year for 100 kr a site.

Hostels The only hostel in the town centre is *Vandrarhem* (☎ 14 78 81) at Östravalla-gatan 11 in a building that certainly isn't the prettiest in town. It's open all year round and charges 150/280 kr for singles/doubles. In summer there are also *Sommarhotell* prices at 250/380 kr, including breakfast.

The hostel *Villa Thalassa* (☎ 11 03 84), 3.5 km from the town centre, is reached by the path from the bus No 7 (or 43) terminus at Pålsjöbaden. The villa and gardens are beautiful but you stay in huts and pay 100 kr. About three km further north is the summer hostel *Nyckelbo* (☎ 920 05), near the royal Sofiero castle.

Hotels Two good budget hotels in the city are *Hotell Linnea* (☎ 11 46 60) at Prästgatan 4 with singles/doubles from 450/550 kr and *Cityhotellet* (☎ 13 64 35) at Trädgårdsgatan 19, from 395/495 kr. More expensive hotels on Stortorget or near the harbour discount heavily at weekends or in summer and *Hotell Viking* (☎ 14 44 20) at Fågelsångsgatan 1 reduces its rates to 500/630 kr.

Places to Eat
The quickest snacks are to be found upstairs in the Knutpunkten complex but you'll miss the town centre.

Fahlmans Café on Stortorget is the most traditional of the town's cafés although older traditions await you at *Möllebackens våffelbruk* up the stairs from Södra Storgatan. This 'waffle factory' serves hot waffles with whipped cream and jam for 20 kr. A good licensed restaurant is *Telegrafen* on Norra Storgatan.

The friendliest surroundings for dinner are at the waterfront tavern *Källarkrogen* opposite the station at Kungsgatan 4. You can have more of a splurge at *Restaurang Porten* at Drottninggatan 1, where there are reasonably priced specials.

Cleopatra is a late-opening pizzeria on Roskildegatan that charges 35 kr for all pizzas. The best of the budget food bars is

Kebab-house at Kullagatan 55, which offers a lunch special with drink for 37 kr (closed Sunday).

Getting There & Away
The main transport centre is Knutpunkten on Järnvägsgatan. The underground train platforms serve both SJ and Pågatågen trains that depart from here to Stockholm, Copenhagen, Oslo and to nearby towns. Above ground and a bit south, but still inside the same complex, is the bus terminal where the regional Länstrafiken Malmöhus buses dominate.

Boat Knutpunkten is the terminal for Scandlines ferries to Helsingør – there are frequent departures (21 kr, free on most train passes). Across the inner harbour, Sunds-bussarna boats have a terminal with boats to Helsingør every 15 to 20 minutes in summer. The boats to Ven depart near the Sunds-bussarna terminal. For Scandinavian Seaways ferries, use the Sunds terminal.

Götaland

The medieval kingdom of Götaland joined Svealand and Norrland, to become Sweden, 1000 years ago, but was strongly influenced by Denmark. Soon after Gothenburg was founded by Gustav II Adolf, in 1619, Sweden conquered the rest of the region.

Pricey but unforgettable is the long journey along the Göta Canal – from the rolling country of Östergötland, north of Linköping, into the great Lake Vättern, before continuing into the province of Västergötland on the other side and further to Gothenburg.

Culturally unique Skåne and Småland are part of Götaland but in this chapter have been given separate sections.

GOTHENBURG
The sunny west coast is almost as island-studded as the east. Gothenburg (Swedish: Göteborg, which sounds rather different) has

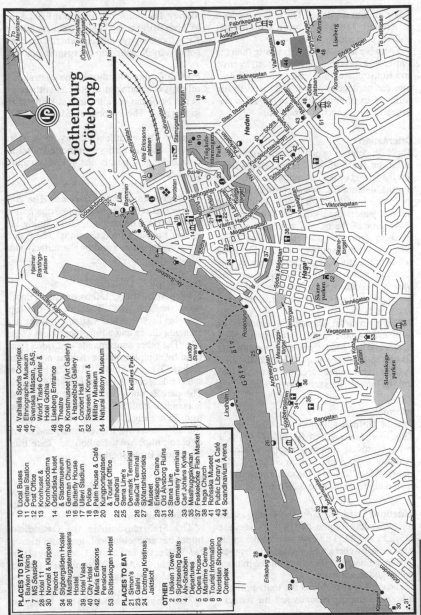

half a million residents. The city is wedded to its port and has a more Continental outlook than Stockholm.

There is a lot more to Gothenburg than the showpiece boulevard Kungsportsavenyn and Konstmuseet, not least its heavy industries and heritage as a port. The Liseberg fun park and its prominent 'space tower' is statistically Sweden's top attraction.

Orientation

The 17th-century expansion and militarism of Gustaf II Adolf and his successors have left the kernel of the city within the remains of canal defences, which are now well suited to sightseeing (the city's Dutch planners laid out many more canals that are now gone).

An arm of the canals snakes its way to Liseberg (you can take the *Paddan* canal boat from near the railway station). From the centre of the city, Kungsportsavenyn crosses the canal and leads up to Götaplatsen. The 'Avenyn' is the heart of the city with boutiques, restaurants, galleries, theatres and street cafés.

The shipyards, showing symptoms of decline, are on the island of **Hisingen**, which is reached by road from the monumental bridge Älvsborgs bron south-west of the city, by Götaälvbron near the central train station, and the tunnel Tingstadstunneln.

Information

Tourist Offices City tourist offices are at Kungsportsplatsen 2 (☎ 031-10 07 40) and in the Nordstan shopping complex (closed Saturday from 3 pm and on Sunday). The main office of STF is at Östra Larmgatan 15, open daily from 9 am to 5.30 pm.

Göteborg Card The *Göteborgkortet*, available separately for one, two or three days for 125, 225 and 275 kr, admits the holder to all museums, Liseberg and sightseeing by bus and canal boat, free travel within the municipality and much more.

The card is available at the tourist office, at hotels, camping grounds and the numerous Pressbyrån.

Money The Forex offices (open from 8 am to 9 pm daily) at the central train station, on Kungsportsavenyn and elsewhere face competition by Xchange on Kungsportsplatsen.

Post & Communications The central post office is at Drottningtorget 6, and others are in the Nordstan complex and at Kungsportsavenyn 12. The telephone code is ☎ 031.

Library The excellent library is at Göta Platsen, and has plenty of imported newspapers and magazines, books in English and a good café.

Medical & Emergency Services The duty pharmacist is in Nordstan (press the button after hours). The hospital, Östra Sjukhuset, is near the No 1 tram terminus. The police are at Skånegatan 5 and on the railway side of Nordstan.

Liseberg

Spaceport Liseberg, 150 metres high, dominates this fun park. The ride to the top, attended by sound and vision, climaxes in a spinning dance and a breathless view of the city. The other amusements and rides seem tame by comparison but there is no lack of variety. You can ride all day for 185 kr or select rides for between eight and 24 kr each. The park is open daily from mid-April to September until 11 pm. Admission costs from 35 kr early in the season to 40 kr in July (for all visitors aged seven years and over), or check http://www.liseberg.se. Take tram No 5 from Brunnsparken.

Museums

After Liseberg the museums are the strongest attractions, and if several take your fancy use the Göteborg Card.

The Stadsmuseum in the **Östindiska huset** has archaeological, local and historical collections (closed Monday from September to April). **Kronhuset** (30 kr, closed Monday) has changing art exhibitions.

The handicraft boutiques **Kronhusbodarna** are nearby in the square between

Postgatan and Kronhusgatan. The workshops deal in pottery, glass, textiles and works of art and sell their wares.

Art Museums The main collections are at **Konstmuseet** on Götaplatsen. This museum has impressive collections of Nordic and European masters and is notable for works by Rubens, Van Gogh, Rembrandt and Picasso. The sculpture section is behind the main hall. Entry is 35 kr (closed Monday from September to April). **Röhsska museet**, Vasagatan 37, is mostly devoted to Swedish handcrafted work but contains also classical and Oriental items. Entry is 35 kr (closed Monday from September to April).

Maritime Museums The **Göteborgs Maritima Centrum** (45 kr) claims to be the largest in the world and displays historical ships and is based around the submarine *Nordkaparen* and a frigate. The main museum of maritime history is **Sjöfartshistoriska museet** at Karl Johansgatan 1, near Stigbergstorget (35 kr, take tram No 3 or 4). The interesting **aquarium** is attached. A museum depicting past waterfront life is the **Klippan precinct**, comprising 18th-century sailor's cottages (take bus No 64 from Brunnsparken or the Älv-Snabben). Klippan is on Götaleden about 400 metres east of Älvsborgs bron.

Other Museums The **Natural History Museum** (35 kr) in Slottsparken has at least 10 million animals and provides a useful guide in English. **Skansen Kronan** is the last of the city towers in any state of repair, sitting on Skansberget to the south-east of the business district with, naturally, fine views. Uniforms and firearms dating back to the 17th century are exhibited in the military museum here (20 kr, open noon to 2 or 3 pm only, take tram No 1). **Etnografiska museet**, with exhibits from many cultures, is at Åvägen 24 (35 kr, take tram No 5 to Liseberg).

Teaterhistoriska museet, on Berzeliigatan off Kungsportsavenyn, is devoted to the development of presentation in the dramatic arts (10 kr, open from noon to 4 pm weekdays).

Churches Gothenburg's churches are not very old but they reflect Swedish architecture more than Stockholm's Italian imitations. In addition to central churches, such as the Cathedral and the Haga Church, don't miss the superb view from Masthuggskyrkan.

Parks The City Park, or **Trädgårdsföreningen** on Nya Allén charges 10 kr. The butterfly house and the Palm Houses also charge an admission fee. **Slottsparken** is the 'lungs' of the city, where you can stroll or visit the **botanical gardens** nearby. From the heights of **Ramberget** on Hisingen is the best city view, but unless you take the city bus tour you are in for a climb. Bus No 31 from Hjalmar Brantingsplatsen takes you to the foot of Ramberget.

Activities

A day or week in Gothenburg doesn't necessarily have to mean museums and crowds only. The municipality offers an enormous range of facilities for its taxpayers, and travellers are welcome to participate for the often nominal fee.

The Göteborg Card gives free admission to a few swimming pools, including the vast Valhalla sports complex. Walking, jogging and people-watching are popular in the Slottsskogen Park and in the nearby Botanical Gardens.

Perhaps the most popular way to pass time in Gothenburg is to take a boat cruise on the Göta Älv, or further afield to the sea. The *Paddan* boats run on sunny days along the canals, and are free if you have your Göteborg Card.

Daily cruises to the fortress jail of **Nya Elfsborg** near the river mouth are popular, but cheaper are the Älv-Snabben regular departures – free with the Göteborg Card, or 16 kr without. For serious island hopping, take tram No 4 to Saltholmen and you'll have at least 15 different islands to explore.

Book a free bus tour (1½ hours) at the

Kungsportsplatsen's tourist office if you have the Göteborg Card.

Places to Stay

Gothenburg offers several good hostels near the city centre, and even hotel prices seem reasonable considering prices in other Swedish towns.

Hostels For a little novelty consider the moored and renovated *MS Seaside* (☎ 10 10 35) at Packhuskajen, charging 100 kr for last-minute beds, but if you book the charge is 175 kr per person in two to four-bed cabins, 250 kr for a private cabin (breakfast 45 kr).

In what is perhaps the biggest and ugliest building in town, *Masthuggsterrassens Vandrarhem* (☎ 42 48 20) at Masthuggsterrassen 8 is very clean and quiet as far as European hostels go, and its rooms have good views. Rooms have two or four beds, each costing 125 kr. Facilities include a satellite TV and a kitchen. Take tram No 3, 4 or 9 to Masthuggstorget and follow the signs.

Nearby is the STF hostel *Stigbergsliden* (☎ 24 16 20) in an old but renovated house at Stigbergsliden 10. Beds cost 100 kr, breakfast is 40 kr, and there is a good kitchen, laundry (20 kr) and a TV room. Take tram No 3 or 9 to Stigbergstorget.

Another clean hostel in an ugly building is the STF hostel *Slottsskogen* (☎ 42 65 20) at Vegagatan 21. Beds cost 100 kr. The kitchen and the TV room are excellent. Take tram No 1 or 2 to Olivedalsgatan.

The enormous STF hostel *Ostkupan* (☎ 40 10 50) at Mejerigatan 2, three km south-east of Liseberg, is only open in summer and may even be closed in the near future. Call ahead! Take bus No 64 from Brunnsparken.

Kärralund (☎ 25 27 61) on Olbergsgatan, also three km south-east of Liseberg, is open as a hostel all year and has beds for 100 kr. There are also camping sites for 115 and 145 kr and four-bed cabins. Take tram No 5 to Welandergatan.

Hotels & Pensions The large boat hotel *Barken Viking* (☎ 63 58 00) is moored outside Lilla Bommen and has singles/doubles for 295/425 kr in summer. *Hotel Vasa* (☎ 17 36 30), at Viktoriagatan 6, has singles/doubles starting at 480/580 kr; there are even cheaper rooms lacking only a shower. *City Hotel* (☎ 18 00 25), at Lorensbergsgatan 6 in a fine location behind Kungsportsavenyn, has singles/doubles for 320/420 kr.

Maria Erikssons Pensionat (☎ 20 70 30) at Chalmersgatan 27a offers rooms in apartment buildings. Singles/doubles start from 295/395 kr.

Places to Eat

Kungsportsavenyn is the Champs-Élysées of Gothenburg, and is lined with all kinds of restaurants, including, as its counterpart in Paris, many hamburger restaurants. Alfresco dining is popular as soon as the rain stops. Similar but less known is Linnégatan (take tram No 1) with quite a few popular places. If you need something quick, the enormous Nordstan shopping arcade houses many fast food outlets, including a *McDonald's*, which is open 24 hours.

Cafés are numerous and invariably of high quality in Gothenburg. *Simon's*, a café at Korsgatan 11 near Kyrkogatan, makes very reasonably priced gourmet sandwiches and baguettes. *Galini* at Kungsgatan 20 is open for dinner every night and charges mid-range prices.

Nya Andrum, at Östra Hamngatan 19a, is an interesting vegetarian restaurant with meals under 50 kr (closed Sunday). *Drottning Kristinas Jaktslott*, up the ramp on Otterhällegatan, is a novelty café in a restored 18th-century building (open to 4 pm).

There's also a café inside City Park.

Entertainment

Facing each other near the Art Museum are the City Theatre and the Concert Hall. The New Opera is also worth a visit. Gothenburghers are keen on following sports events, and there are outdoor stadiums such as the old and new Ullevi, and the indoor Scandinavium.

Getting There & Away

Air Landvetter airport is 25 km east of the city and the airport bus from the central train station costs 50 kr. There are regular services to Stockholm every day, daily direct flights to Helsinki, several daily flights to Oslo, daily flights (except on Saturday) to Stavanger and flights most days to Amsterdam, Hamburg and Frankfurt. You can also fly to/from London daily with British Airways or SAS (see also the Sweden, Getting There & Away section).

Bus The bus station is outside the train station. There are regional buses within the Göteborg and Bohuslän provinces, and the 'GL-Bohus-kort' (1040 kr, valid for 30 days) gives access to all länstrafik buses, trains and boats. The frequent Swebus buses to all major towns also depart from the bus station. Swebus and Eurolines have an office in the central train station.

Train The central train station serves SJ and regional trains: there are direct trains to Copenhagen, Malmö, Oslo, Stockholm and even trains to the north. Direct trains to Stockholm depart almost every hour, but budget travellers should avoid the expensive X2000s.

Boat Gothenburg is a major entry point for ferries, but there are several terminals. Transport to/from them is rather complicated and few terminals have exchange facilities.

Nearest to the town centre, the Stena Line Denmark terminal near Masthuggstorget (take tram No 3, 4 or 9) serves up to 10 departures a day in summer. Slow car ferries to Frederikshavn are free for Göteborg Card holders, and there are discounts for train pass holders. The catamarans cross in two hours and are dearer.

The Sea Cat catamarans depart from opposite the Maritime Museum four times a day for Frederikshavn in summer and charge

80 kr per adult, and 50 kr a cycle. Take tram No 3 or 9 to Stigbergstorget.

Further west is the Stena Line terminal for the car ferry to Kiel. Take tram No 3 or 9 to Chapmans Torg.

Scandinavian Seaways sails to Newcastle and Harwich from Skandiahamnen on Hisingen (take bus No 28).

Getting Around

Local buses, trams and boats are run by Göteborgsregionens Lokaltrafik (GL). Free bus and tram travel goes with the Göteborg Card. An individual ticket costs 16 kr. Cheaper and easy-to-use magnetic cards cost 100 kr. A day card for the city costs 35 kr.

Boat The Älv-Snabben boats between Lilla Bommen and Klippan run every 30 minutes or so and are part of the transit system. The Göteborg Card gives free travel, and individual tickets cost 16 kr.

Tram The easiest way to cover lengthy distances in Gothenburg is by tram. There are nine lines, all converging somewhere near Brunnsparken.

MARSTRAND

The seaside village Marstrand, with its wooden buildings, conveys the essence of Bohuslän and its fishing villages. Marstrand is a popular weekend recreation and boating spot. The **Carlsten Fästning** fortress (open from June to August) reflects a martial and penal history. You can get here by bus No 312 from Gothenburg and a ferry.

Båtellet (☎ 0303-600 10) is a tourist hotel with multi-bed rooms, charging from 140 kr in winter and 200 kr in summer. Tourist information is dispensed here in summer.

TANUMSHEDE & UDDEVALLA

The *hällristningar* pictures from Sweden's Bronze Age are well represented in Bohuslän. The most famous pictures are the UNESCO World Heritage-listed ones at **Vitlycke**, two km south of Tanumshede. Near the site is a museum (30 kr, open daily) showing the pictures' origins and types. The tourist office (☎ 0525-204 00) is at Apoteksvägen 5. If you get off at the Tanumshede train station, you have to catch a connecting bus to the village and walk two km south. Swebus No 820 runs via Tanumshede between Gothenburg (136 kr, two hours) and Oslo.

Another noteworthy stop is **Uddevalla**, a pleasant seaside town halfway between Gothenburg and Tanumshede. Don't miss the regional museum (free) near the bus station. The *STF Hostel* (☎ 0522-152 00) at the old spa of Gustafsberg, four km from the centre, can be reached by a regular boat that departs from the jetty opposite the museum across the river. Beds cost 100 kr.

STRÖMSTAD

The northern terminus of the Bohuståg train system, Strömstad is an attractive seaside resort. There are no real tourist attractions to visit but many boats trips on offer to nearby islands and to Norway. Get the latest information from the tourist office between the two harbours.

The *STF hostel* (☎ 0526-101 93) at Norra Kyrkogatan 12 fills early in summer – call before 7 pm. Beds cost 100 kr.

Getting There & Away

There are regular trains from Gothenburg until late, and connecting buses depart from near the train station.

Boats to nearby islands, including the Koster islands, depart from the small-boat or 'visitor' harbour. Koster islands are the most westerly in Sweden, and popular for cycling.

Scandi Line ferries to the Norwegian town of Sandefjord leave five times a day in summer (last departure at 11 pm). One-way tickets cost 125 kr (Scanrail pass gives 50% discount). There are also boat services to the historic Norwegian town of Fredrikstad, but these do not take vehicles.

HALMSTAD

Founded along the Nissen River, Halmstad was Danish until the 17th century. Medieval attractions include the 15th-century **church** and the **Tre Hjärtan** building that also houses

a café. Along the river is a Danish castle (not open to visitors), an old boat, *Najaden* (free, open only occasionally), and **Tropichuset** in the old customs house. North of the town centre, **Hallands Museum** at Tollsgatan is open daily but the nearby open-air annexe **Hallandsgården** is closed in winter.

Halmstadspasset costs 50 kr and gives discounts to the town's attractions and bus services, and is available at the tourist office (☎ 035-10 93 45) at Österskans.

Vandrarhem (☎ 035-12 05 00) at Skepparegatan 23 is the central hostel that charges 125 kr per bed but is open from mid-June to mid-August only.

Getting There & Away

Regular trains between Gothenburg and Malmö stop in Halmstad but the ferry terminal for launches from Grenå is about three km from the town centre (see Varberg).

VARBERG

The medieval fortress with its superb museums is the main attraction in this pleasant coastal town, but you should brave the Nordic weather and swim in the **Kallhusbadet** (a sauna bath costs 27 kr), built above the sea on stilts in Moorish style.

Places to Stay & Eat

The *hostel* (☎ 0340-887 88) is one of the most thrilling in Sweden – inside the fortress, it offers singles for 120 kr in old prison cells or larger rooms in other buildings. Breakfast is available for 40 kr.

Most cheap restaurants are along the pedestrianised Kungsgatan, but the fortress café offers by far the best sea views in town.

Getting There & Away

The ferries from the Danish town of Grenå dock near the town centre, making Varberg more friendly for travellers than Halmstad. SJ trains between Gothenburg and Malmö stop at the train station and don't require supplements. Buses depart from outside the train station.

NORRKÖPING

Industries grew alongside the rapids in Norrköping, and today the architecture that surrounds the fast-flowing blackish water and several waterfalls creates one of the most awesome urban sights in Sweden. Norrköping is a large town with good services, although the principal attraction is the animal park at Kolmården, 30 km north-east.

Information

The tourist office (☎ 011-15 15 00) is at Drottninggatan 11 and is open daily (except weekends in the low season). Families with children should ask about discount passes that allow entry to Kolmården. The central post office is at Drottninggatan 20.

The local telephone code is ☎ 011.

Things to See & Do

There are walking tracks and bridges that allow good views to the breathtaking riverside. The industrial past is exhibited at the city museum, **Stadsmuseum** (free admission, closed Monday) at Västgötegatan 19. More general is Sweden's only museum of work, **Arbetets Museum** (free, open daily), which is just across the bridge from Stadsmuseum.

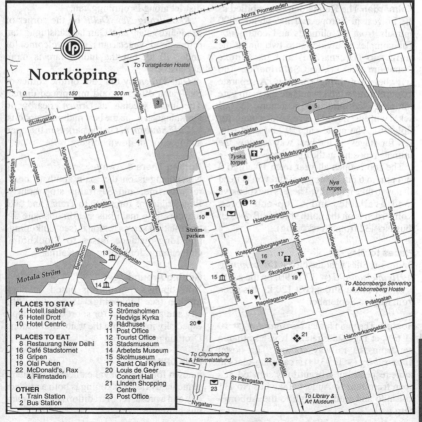

Norrköping

0   150   300 m

PLACES TO STAY
4   Hotell Isabell
6   Hotell Drott
10 Hotel Centric

PLACES TO EAT
8   Restaurang New Delhi
16 Café Stadstornet
18 Gripen
19 Olai Puben
22 McDonald's, Rax & Filmstaden

OTHER
1   Train Station
2   Bus Station
3   Theatre
5   Strömsholmen
7   Hedvigs Kyrka
9   Rådhuset
11 Post Office
12 Tourist Office
13 Stadsmuseum
14 Arbetets Museum
15 Skolmuseum
17 Sankt Olai Kyrka
20 Louis de Geer Concert Hall
21 Linden Shopping Centre
23 Post Office

To Turistgården Hostel
To Abborrebergs Servering & Abborreberg Hostel
To Citycamping & Himmelstalund
To Library & Art Museum

Motala Ström

A modern addition to the riverside scenery is the **Louis de Geer** Concert Hall.

Admission to the large art museum **Norrköpings konstmuseum**, south of the centre at Kristinaplatsen, is 25 kr (closed Monday in summer). The most important works are from early this century. For a view of the city and out on to Bråviken climb the **Rådhuset** tower (10 kr, open on summer weekdays). **Sankt Olai kyrka** in the park at the centre of town is one of the few noteworthy baroque churches in Sweden.

The tiny vintage tram No 1 runs twice daily from Rådhuset during summer afternoons and evenings (25 kr).

Kolmården The Kolmården zoo is billed as the biggest in Europe and has about 1000 animals from all climates and continents. The complex is divided into two areas: the main **zoo** (Djurparken) and its annexe **Oceanum** (160 kr), and **Safariparken** (60 kr) where you bring your car. A separate **tropical house** (50 kr) outside the main gate completes the attraction. A general 'Maxi' ticket will cost 200 kr (there are discounts for children). The cable car (50 kr round trip, less for stages) is the best way to view the animals reposing in the open areas.

The zoo is open all year from 10 am to 3 or 4 pm (to 6 pm in summer) and you'll need all day to take it in fully. There is inexpensive food available, and a top-end hotel. Kolmården is on the north shore of Bråviken (bus No 432 from Norrköping).

Places to Stay

Camping Sites near the city at *Citycamping & Himmelstalund* (☎ 17 11 90) on the south bank of Motala Ström cost 120 kr. It's open from May to September.

Hostels The main hostel *Turistgården* (☎ 10 11 60), at Ingelstadsgatan 31, is less than a km from the railway station. The hostel *Abborreberg* (☎ 11 93 44) is camping-class in some respects but is beautifully situated. It's open from June to August. Take bus No 111 to Lindö and walk through to the Abborreberg park.

Hotels *Hotel Centric* (☎ 12 90 30) at Gamla Rådstugugatan 18 is a good city hotel at the bottom of this price list, with weekend and summer singles/doubles at 320/440 kr. If you are seeking bigger savings, the tourist office can book private rooms from 120 kr a night, but asks a 60 kr fee.

Hotell Drott (☎ 18 00 60), at Tunnbindaregatan 19, has summer singles/doubles from 330/430 kr. *Hotell Isabell* (☎ 16 90 82), at Vattengränden 7, is a bit more expensive but holds prices steady all year. It's small and has shared amenities.

Places to Eat

There are plenty of eateries in the shopping district along Drottninggatan.

Restaurang New Delhi on the corner of Trädgårdsgatan and Gamla Rådstugugatan offers food vegetarians will welcome for under 70 kr, but the Indian fare is more expensive.

Olai Puben by the park on the corner of Skolgatan offers a good mid-priced dinner. The lunch specials at *Gripen*, nearby on Drottninggatan, are the best mid-price options.

Café Stadstornet in the park is in the open and fine for sit-down burgers.

Getting There & Away

Norrköping is on the main south to north railway line, and SJ trains stop hourly. Regional trains run south to Tranås and take bicycles. The main bus station opposite the train station serves regional (see Linköping) and long-distance buses to Stockholm, Gothenburg, Jönköping and Kalmar.

Getting Around

Norrköping's transport is based on länstrafiken (see Linköping). Trams cover the city and are quickest for short or long hops, especially to and from the train station along Drottninggatan.

LINKÖPING

Known for its medieval cathedral and aeroplane industries, Linköping is both a modern city and a preserver of traditions in its numerous museums.

Information

The tourist office (☎ 013-20 68 35) is in the imposing Konsert & Kongress building (Congress Centre) near the museum. In the evenings, Hotel Ekoxen distributes tourist pamphlets. The central post office is at Kungsgatan 20. The large library near the cathedral is worth spending some time in.

The telephone code is ☎ 013.

Things to See

The enormous **cathedral** with its 107-metre spire is the landmark of Linköping and one of Sweden's oldest and biggest churches.

There are numerous gravestones and other medieval treasures, and the cathedral is open daily all year round. The surrounding parks contain old houses (there is no admission to the castle).

Just north of the cathedral, **Östergötlands länsmuseum** (Provincial Museum) has a big collection by a variety of European painters, including Cranach's view of Eden, *Original Sin*, and Swedish art reaching back to the Middle Ages. The prehistoric collection is well organised. Entry is 20 kr, and the museum opens at noon daily except Monday.

The concrete floor of **Sankt Lars kyrka**

Linköping

0   100   200 m

PLACES TO STAY
3 Frimurarhotellet
10 Hotel Stånga City
11 Hotel Östergyllen
14 Stora Hotellet
15 Good Evening Hotel
25 Linköpings Vandrarhem

PLACES TO EAT
16 Överste Mörner
20 Shalom
21 Siesta Café
24 McDonald's

OTHER
1 Regional Bus Terminal
2 Train Station & Swebus Tickets
4 Theatre
5 Provincial Museum
6 Congress Centre
7 Tourist Office
8 Klostret
9 Post Office
12 Tullbron Jetty
13 St Lars Kyrka
17 Cathedral
18 Public Library
19 Castle
22 Book Shop
23 Press Stop

SWEDEN

on Storgatan was built above the medieval church ruins. Downstairs, you can see 11th-century gravestones and skeletons. The church is open from 11 am to late afternoon daily except Sunday, and serves an inexpensive lunch at noon.

The best attractions are just outside the centre. Some two km west of the city is **Gamla Linköping**, one of the biggest living-museum villages in Sweden. Amongst the 60 quaint houses there are a dozen theme museums, many shops and a small chocolate factory. You can wander among the 19th-century buildings at will, and many buildings are open daily all year round. There is no general admission charge. *Wärdshus* serves an inexpensive lunch, and there are tempting cafeterias in the precinct. Take bus Nos 204 to 207.

Just 300 metres from Gamla Linköping across the forest, **Valla Fritidsområde** has domestic animals, museums and more. Between the 'colony garden' area and the children's playground are Mjellerumsgården (meals and hostel reception), Järnvägsmuséet (railway museum), Westmanska vagnmuséet (old carriages), Odalmannens Museum (farming items) and many old houses. The museums are open daily in summer from 1 to 4 pm, and on weekends at other times.

Outside the centre, you may visit impressive manor houses, or drive seven km west to see the exhibits in the **Flygvapenmuseum** with exhibits on air-force history and local industries. The museum is on Carl Cederströms gata, Malmslätt (10 kr, bus No 551).

Kinda Kanal

Any visitor to Sweden should know about the engineering marvel of the Göta kanal, but Linköping boasts its own canal system, the 90-km Kinda kanal. There are 15 locks, including the deepest one in Sweden. Cruises run from mid-May to August down the canal to Rimforsa. The trip, on MF *Kind*, departs from the Tullbron jetty on Wednesday, Friday and Sunday at 10 am and costs 235 kr (return trip by bus or train included).

Places to Stay

The STF-associated *Linköpings Vandrarhem* at Klostergatan 52a (☎ 14 90 90), open all year, has beds at 100 kr. There are also a few single and double rooms from 200 to 300 kr. In the centre of the Valla area (see Things to See), *Mjellerumsgårdens Vandrarhem* (☎ 12 27 30) is a hostel with 110 kr beds and a kitchen. There are 28 beds and it's open all year round – ask at the restaurant.

The tourist office books rooms costing from 120 to 185 kr a night. *Hotell Östergyllen* (☎ 10 20 75) at Hamngatan 2b has singles/doubles from 250/330 kr in summer and at weekends (up to 300/485 kr with shower and toilet). *Hotel Stångå City* (☎ 11 12 75) is next door and offers rooms at 350/440 kr at weekends and in summer. *Good Evening Hotel* (☎ 12 90 00) at Stora Torget 9 has summer and weekend rates of 345/430 kr and 495/595 kr other times.

Places to Eat

Most eateries are on the main square or nearby streets, especially Ågatan and St Larsgatan. Around the Stora Torget, *Siesta Café* has sandwiches and *Överste Mörner* is one of the Irish-style pub-cum-restaurants in town. *Shalom* on Torggatan offers the pick of the budget pizzas, kebabs and salads.

Getting There & Away

Linköping is on the main south to north railway line, and SJ trains stop almost hourly. Regional and local buses have their terminal and platforms adjacent to the train station (Centralstationen). Long-distance buses depart 500 metres north of the railway station, but go to the railway office for Swebus tickets and timetables.

Regional (and local) traffic is run by Östgöta Trafiken. All trains and buses depart from Centralstationen, and free route maps are available. Ask for the 24-hour *dygnskort* (90 kr) that is valid on all buses and local trains within the province, including some services to towns outside the province (trains to Tranås will take you to Jönköpings län, and you can bring a bicycle).

VADSTENA

Beautiful Vadstena on Lake Vättern is a legacy of both church and state power. The dominant figure was St Birgitta, who established her order here in the 1380s. The abbey and the castle compete for the visitor's interest. The atmosphere in the old town and by the lake make it perhaps the most pleasant spot in Sweden, if you don't meet up with one of the many local ghosts.

Information

The main tourist office (☎ 0143-151 25) is in a historic house at Rådhustorget and another office operates inside the castle.

The telephone code is ☎ 0143.

Things to See

The Renaissance castle **Vadstena slott** looks straight over the harbour and lake beyond. It is a mighty family project of the early Vasa kings and in the upper apartments are some items of period furniture and paintings. The castle and chapel are open daily from early in May to September. Admission costs 35 kr.

The odd 15th-century **klosterkyrkan** or abbey (free admission) is a combination of Gothic and some Renaissance features. Inside are the accumulated **relics of St Birgitta** and late-medieval sculpture, including the saint depicted during revelation. **Bjälboättens palats** was the old convent and once also a royal residence (open from June to early September, sometimes only to daily tours). The **Rådhus** on the square and **Rödtornet** on Sånggatan also remain from late medieval times.

Rökstenen

Sweden has many historical regions but the area around Vadstena is certainly one that deserves a closer look. Cycling is an option as the scenic flatlands around Vättern lend themselves to the pedal. A whole series of ancient legends is connected with Rökstenen, Sweden's biggest and most famous rune stone, at the church at Rök. It is just off the E4 on the road to Heda and Alvastra. In ancient and intricate verse, the sections we understand refer to the Ostrogothic hero-king Theodoric, who conquered depleted Rome in the 6th century, but the stone is dated to the 9th century. There is a small tourist centre on the site.

Places to Stay & Eat

A good camping ground is **Vätterviksbadet** (☎ 127 30) on the lake two km north of the town, open from May to mid-September. Camp sites cost 110 kr.

The STF hostel **Vandrarhem Vadstena** (☎ 103 20) is open all year, but by booking only (☎ 104 04) from mid-August to mid-June. It is at Skänningegatan 20 near the fire station, and beds cost 70 or 100 kr. You can also stay, expensively, at the **Klosterhotell** (☎ 315 30) in the convent grounds (doubles 860 kr, 980 kr with a view). However, if you drop in latish at the tourist office, empty rooms will go for 625 kr. The office charges 50 kr for hotel bookings.

Rådhuskällaren under the old town hall has a pleasant stone-and-timbered atmosphere and has mid-priced courses. **Hamnpaviljongen** in the park in front of the castle is an open-air café.

Getting There & Away

See Linköping for regional transport information. Only buses run to Vadstena – take bus No 65 from Linköping Centralstationen, or express bus No 840 from Jönköping (95 kr) or Örebro. Bus No 610 runs from Motala.

Småland

The forested province of Småland has become famous for the glass production of its numerous factories, many of which you can visit, and was the homeland of many immigrants to the USA last century.

JÖNKÖPING

Located dramatically at the southern end of Lake Vättern, Jönköping is a popular summer spot and the home of the safety match. It is the main centre of an urban strip

Jönköping

PLACES TO STAY
1 Kulturhusets Vandrarhem
5 Prize Hotel City
20 Grand Hotel

PLACES TO EAT
4 Mäster Gudmunds Källare
10 Burger King
13 Bernards Konditori
14 Café Louice
17 Krogen Amadeus

OTHER
2 Radio Museum
3 Tändsticksmuseet
6 Train Station
7 Bus Station
8 Tourist Office
9 Bookshop
11 Sofiekyrkan
12 Main Post Office
15 Post Office
16 Gamla Rådhuset
18 Kristine Kyrka
19 Göta Hovrätt
21 Länsmuseum
22 Public Library

that stretches east around the shore to Huskvarna, which is known for its sewing machines and motorcycles.

Information
The main tourist office (☎ 036-10 50 50) is in the Djurläkartorget complex above the railway station, or e-mail to turist@jonk oping .se. The central post office is at Barnarpsgatan 17. The large public library is in the museum building.

The telephone code for the area (including Huskvarna) is ☎ 036.

Things to See
A museum on the history of matches, **Tändsticksmuseet**, is west of the train station. A good brochure explains the development of a Swedish innovation much taken for granted. Admission is 25 kr and the museum is open daily in summer (closed Monday from September to early June). Nearby is the **Radio Museum** with a collection of all manner of radio and TV sets and memorabilia – a playground for technical buffs (20 kr, closed Monday).

In the old town square of Hovrättstorget are the 17th-century buildings of **Göta**

Hovrätt and the red **Gamla Rådhuset**, which has displays on the history and practice of Swedish justice (10 kr). The neoclassical **Kristine kyrka** on Östra Storgatan is the centre of a restored part of the old town.

The **Länsmuseum** collections (15 kr, open daily) on Dag Hammarskjölds plats cover local history and contemporary culture: no-one should miss the childish yet strangely haunting fantasy works of John Bauer.

Above the town to the west is the expanse of **Stadsparken** and its curiosities, which include the 1400 mounted ornithological taxidermic masterpieces of **Fågelmuseet** (10 kr, open daily from May to September), and the little baroque **Bäckaby kyrka**. The **bell tower** dominates a fine lookout over Lake Vättern (take bus No 1C up the hill). A few km south-east of the centre of Jönköping at the A6 centre is **Tropikhuset**, full of snakes, primates and tropical birds (40 kr, open daily).

In Huskvarna the **Husqvarna fabriksmuseum** covers the manufacturing and technical history of the area, which has produced famous sewing machines and motorcycles (20 kr, open daily from mid-March to mid-September, otherwise weekends only).

Places to Stay

Rosenlunds Stugby & Camping (☎ 12 28 63) on the lake off Huskvarnavägen east of the town centre asks 110 kr per site. As well as some cabins, there are some guest rooms for 250 kr per person.

Close to the train station, *Kulturhusets Vandrarhem* (☎ 19 05 85) is open from mid-June to mid-August. Dorm beds cost 60 kr without breakfast, and bicycles 20 kr a day.

There are several hotels in the town centre. *Grand Hotel* (☎ 71 96 00) on Hövrättstorget and *Prize Hotel City* (☎ 71 92 80) at Västra Storgatan 25 are the cheapest in summer.

The STF hostel *Huskvarna Vandrarhem* (☎ 14 88 70) is at Odengatan 10 in Huskvarna (take bus No 4 from Djurläkartorget to Linnégatan). Beds cost 100 kr, and there is breakfast available.

Places to Eat

Most cheap eateries are on the pedestrian streets in the eastern part of the town centre, but *Burger King* is near the tourist office. *Bernards konditori* on the corner of Skolgatan and Kyrkogatan opened in the 1910s, and still serves tasty cakes and good coffee. Almost as old is *Mäster Gudmunds Källare* at Kapellgatan 2. There are special lunch packages in this cellar restaurant.

Café Louice in the surrounds of Hamnparken is open late in summer and you can eat in the open. *Krogen Amadeus* at Östra Storgatan 39 has affordable lunch specials and a very Swedish atmosphere.

Getting There & Away

The central train station serves SJ and regional trains and most buses. Most SJ trains run hourly to connect the main lines (in Nässjö and Falköping), and require no seat reservation nor supplement for train pass holders. Only the expensive X2000 trains go direct to/from Stockholm. Swebus services include Nos 830 and 831 to Gothenburg, No 831 to Stockholm and No 833 to Malmö.

All regional and local traffic is run by Länstrafiken, including Länstågen train services and the ferry to Visingsö. Each ticket costs 11 to 77 kr (depending on distance and allowing transfers within a four-hour period) but there are 30-day passes or two-month passes (20 travel days) for 600 kr. Perhaps the best deal is *Värdekortet* for 200 kr which gives a 45% discount outside peak hours. These 'smart card' tickets are not personal so you can resell to someone else.

Getting Around

Catch a local bus at Djurläkartorget. Bus No 4 runs regularly to Huskvarna.

EKSJÖ

Perhaps the best preserved wooden town in Sweden, Eksjö was built in the 16th century, and many of the wooden buildings and part of the medieval street plan have been preserved.

Finding the youth hostel is simplicity itself – just walk directly from the train station, five minutes along Österlånggatan. Reception for the *STF hostel* (☎ 0381-361 80) is in the tourist office at Österlånggatan 31. Beds cost 100 kr, and this may mean a single room if you're alone. Three museums are within the same precinct (10 to 20 kr admission to each).

The rural Smålandic surroundings of Eksjö deserve visiting – hire a bicycle (from 40 kr a day) at the tourist office and tour the historic villages and the Skurugata cliff, or just trek along the Höglandsleden track.

Getting There & Away

Catch the tiny *länståg* train from Nässjö – all train passes are accepted. The bus station is just outside the Eksjö train station.

VÄXJÖ

Millions of Americans have their roots in Sweden, and quite a few of them in Småland. Those who 'return' to Sweden should not miss **Utvandrarhuset**, which has archives, information and historical exhibitions on the beckoning America. This 'Emigrant House' is just behind the central train and bus station, and conveniently close to **Smålands Museum** which has an excellent collection of glass from Glasriket.

Växjö was one of the Catholic centres in medieval Sweden. There was a wooden church already in 1050 AD in the place where the imposing **Cathdedral** from the 15th century now stands. Ravaged by fire many times, the edifice with two spires was renovated in 1995 but houses a fine 15th-century altar.

The manageable business centre is next to the central train station, and has a good range of services, including the top-end *Hotel Statt* and the slightly cheaper *Cardinal Hotel*. The *STF hostel* (☎ 0470-630 70) is six km north of the centre, and charges 100 kr.

Getting There & Away

Växjö is between Alvesta and Kalmar and is served by SJ trains that run almost hourly. Kronobergs Länstrafik runs the regional bus network. Each ticket costs 12 to 54 kr, and there are 30-day passes for 440 kr (700 kr when trains are included). Long-distance buses also depart from the train station.

GLASRIKET

This area with dense forests and quaint red houses is popular among tourists – it's the most visited area in Sweden outside Stockholm and Gothenburg. The 'Kingdom of Crystal' has at least 16 glass factories (look for signs that say *glasbruk*) scattered around the wilderness, and its roots go way back: Kosta was founded in 1742, and 100 years ago 10 factories were in full swing. Factory outlets have big discounts on seconds but don't just come for glass and crystal: there are ceramics, wood, leather and handicrafts for sale. Not everything is cheap but you pay for the quality and design. The immense popularity is not only shared by bus loads of northern Europeans. Lots of Americans tour the country looking for their roots – emigration was popular 100 years ago because locals were not given enough work by the factories. Just outside the busy parking areas, the image of isolation remains.

Bicycle tours are excellent if you follow the narrow roads – there are plenty of hostels, and you can camp almost anywhere *except* near the military area on the Kosta to Orrefors road.

Nybro

The centre of the eastern part of Glasriket boasts two glass factories: only Pukeberg is worth a look for its quaint setting and higher quality. The business centre offers services including the top-end *Stora Hotellet* and the tourist information office on Stadshusplan (don't miss the fresco, reputedly the largest in Scandinavia). A few km west from the centre is the 200-metre-long *kyrkstallarna* building, an old stable that now houses the excellent Madesjö Hembydgsmuseum (20 kr, open daily in summer).

The *STF hostel* (☎ 0481-109 32) south of the centre near Pukeberg is a very clean building with a kitchen on each floor. Beds cost 100 kr, and you should call or arrive between 5 and 7 pm.

SJ trains between Alvesta and Kalmar stop here almost hourly, and you can catch a regional bus from Kalmar.

Boda

The factory here was founded in 1864 and is now part of the Kosta Boda company. This is a quaint little village with a large factory outlet and many other shops, including the modern Nova Boda shop. There are plenty of places to eat, and the *STF hostel* (☎ 0481-242 30) in an old school building behind the factory has beds for 100 kr.

Unless you proceed to Nybro or Orrefors, you should visit the 19th-century factory areas in nearby **Johansfors**, **Åfors** and **Skruf**, with glass shops and museums open daily in summer.

Orrefors

Perhaps the most famous of all Swedish glass factories, Orrefors is very busy in summer and has a museum, glass blowing shows and a shipping service in the shop. Orrefors was founded in 1898 and some old houses remain. In the evening it's a boring little place where only the petrol station sells food.

You can camp two km west of Orrefors at a lakeside camping ground. The informal *STF hostel* (☎ 0481-300 20) is conveniently located near the factory area. Beds are 100 kr, and there are kitchens but no breakfast is served. You can dine at the *Värdshuset*.

Hälleberga & Målerås
Hälleberga, a tiny village five km north-west from Orrefors, includes the dilapidated Gullaskruf glass factory and leather outlets. At the south end of the village, *Pensionat Hällegården* (☎ 0481-320 21) has accommodation ranging from hostel-style singles/doubles for 130/160 kr to hotel rooms for 320/560 kr. Plenty of old houses have been preserved around the nearby modern church.

Målerås, 10 km north-west, has a large factory which is only worth a visit if you're specifically looking for engraved glass.

Kosta
This is where Glasriket started in 1742. At times it looks like the biggest tourist trap in southern Sweden but will be appreciated if you only concentrate on the finesse and quality of the local craftsmanship. Spend time at the two museums and admire the glass blowing and the old factory quarters, although there are also plenty of discount shops here.

The town itself spans two km, and includes a range of services. Opposite the factory, *Kosta värdshus* has double rooms for 500 kr and serves inexpensive lunches. At the south end of Kosta, *Björkängen* has rooms. Across the highway towards Lessebo, another glass factory, SEA, has a café and a shop.

Kosta is served by bus from Växjö via Lessebo.

Strömbergshyttan & Bergdala
A branch of Kosta Boda, this roadside studio between Lessebo and Hovmanstorp was founded in 1987. Now it's a major stop on any tour with a glass-painting studio and a doll museum.

A detour to Bergdala will take you to another glass factory plus *Bergdala Härbärge* (☎ 0478-180 30) with hostel-style accommodation.

Hovmanstorp
This large town has a train station and thus provides travellers with good connections to regional buses to Kosta and Strömbergshyttan. The town itself has less appeal but the old Sandvik factory produces Orrefors glass.

Klavreström
The good *STF hostel* (☎ 0474-409 44) has beds for 100 kr in this town that includes the Rosdala glass factory. There are quite a few historical attractions in the region, including medieval churches in Granhult and Dädesjö.

OSKARSHAMN
Vital for boat connections and useful for travel-related services, Oskarshamn is not an immensely interesting town. Look for the town maps in several locations for orientation: Stora Torget is the main square, and includes the fine *Hotell Post*. Hantverksgatan is one of the main streets, and has a post office and the bus station. At Hantverksgatan 18 you'll find a good library, the tourist office (open Monday to Friday until 2 pm) and a museum (open daily except Monday, 25 kr) exhibiting maritime items and famous wood-carvings by Döderhultan. The church is worth a look, but is closed on Monday.

The pleasant *STF hostel* (☎ 0491-881 98) is a few hundred metres from the train station at Åsavägen 8. Beds cost 70 or 100 kr and there is a kitchen. The hostel is signposted, as is the seaside camping ground at Gunnarsö, several km away.

The **Jungfru National Park**, a granite island rising 86 metres above sea level, was long known as the 'Mountain of Witches' by sailors, and a stone labyrinth remains. There are boat launches in summer from the jetty near the bridge that leads to Badholmen.

Getting There & Away
There are länstrafik trains from Linköping and Nässjö (train passes are valid, no supplement

payments). Regional bus services are part of the Länstrafik system (see Kalmar). The bus station has clear timetables which include long-distance services. Boats to Öland (Byxelkrok) run only from mid-June to mid-August, and cost 120 kr one way. Bicycles cost 40 kr. Boats to Gotland depart from near the train station daily most of the year (except Saturday in winter) and twice a day in summer.

OSKARSHAMN TO KALMAR

When the ferry to Öland doesn't run, the mainland route is a good option for cyclists. Study the map first: you can follow quiet rural roads and see glimpses of the real Småland culture. Small places worth a stop include Timmernabben (ceramics factory and ferries to Bornholm in summer), Strömsrum (look for the privately owned large wooden manor house) and Pataholm, an old trading village.

KALMAR

The port of Kalmar was long the key to Baltic power and its castle became the site of the short-lived Scandinavian union agreement of 1397 – an event to be celebrated in 1997. It was vital to Swedish interests until the 17th century and its streets and impressive edifices retain much of the historical flavour.

Information

The tourist office (☎ 0480-153 50) is at Larmgatan 6. The post office is on the corner of Fiskaregatan and Västra Sjögatan. Storgatan is the main street and has a good bookshop but the public library is outside the city grid on Unionsgatan.

The telephone code is ☎ 0480.

Things to See

The once powerful Renaissance castle **Kalmar slott**, on the water south of the railway, was the key to Sweden before lands to the south were claimed from Denmark. The imprisonment of women here was common in crueller times and a punishment museum has been set up inside. The panelled **King Erik chamber** is the interior highlight.

Admission costs 40 kr and the castle is open daily from April to October, weekends only from November to March. There is an **art museum** near **Gamla Stan** (the old town).

Kalmar länsmuseum is in the old steam mill by the harbour on Skeppsbrogatan and the highlight is the exhibition of the flagship *Kronan*, which went to the bottom controversially off Öland – a disaster to match the *Wasa*'s sinking. The museum is open daily and admission is 30 kr (students 15 kr). Aft and slightly to port is **Kalmar Sjöfartsmuseum**, a delightfully eccentric little maritime museum at Södra Långgatan 81 (20 kr, open daily in summer, on Sunday only from mid-August to mid-June).

The landmark baroque **cathedral** on Stortorget was designed by Tessin who was the leading 16th-century architect working for the Swedish king.

Places to Stay

The STF hostel *Vandrarhem Svanen* (☎ 129 28) is attached to *Kalmar Lågprishotell* (☎ 255 60) at Rappegatan 1c, across the bridge almost one km from town off Ängöleden. Beds cost 100 kr, and rooms from 275/395 kr for singles/doubles. There is a kitchen, and the breakfast buffet is good value at 40 kr.

There are plenty of hotels in the city centre, *Frimurarhotellet* (☎ 152 30) at Larmtorget offers some good summer deals, and *Slottshotellet* (☎ 882 60) at Slottsvägen may offer some last-minute discounts.

Places to Eat

There are plenty of restaurants around the market square although *McDonald's* is at the Baronen Shopping Centre. *Restaurang Eurasia* on the corner of Södra Långatan and Larmgatan has European meals. *Holmgrens Konditori* is a traditional café on Kaggensgatan, and the nearby *Källaren Kronan* is a stylish and expensive cellar restaurant. *Slottsparken* gives an excellent view of the castle. The *Golden Horn*, near the library, serves inexpensive lunches.

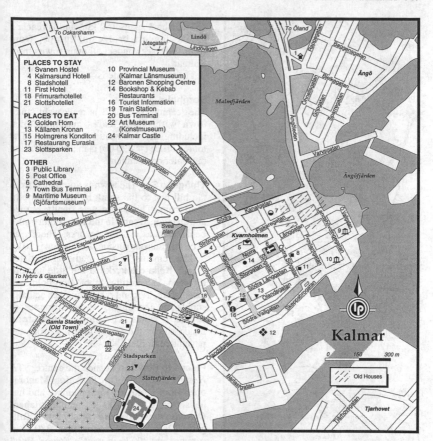

PLACES TO STAY
1 Svanen Hostel
4 Kalmarsund Hotell
8 Stadshotell
11 First Hotel
18 Frimurarhotellet
21 Slottshotellet

PLACES TO EAT
2 Golden Horn
13 Källaren Kronan
15 Holmgrens Konditori
17 Restaurang Eurasia
23 Slottsparken

OTHER
3 Public Library
5 Post Office
6 Cathedral
7 Town Bus Terminal
9 Maritime Museum
  (Sjöfartsmuseum)
10 Provincial Museum
  (Kalmar Länsmuseum)
12 Baronen Shopping Centre
14 Bookshop & Kebab
  Restaurants
16 Tourist Information
19 Train Station
20 Bus Terminal
22 Art Museum
  (Konstmuseum)
24 Kalmar Castle

Kalmar

Getting There & Away

There are SJ trains nearly every hour between Kalmar and Alvesta (with connections to the main SJ lines) and Gothenburg.

All regional traffic is run by Kalmar Läns Trafik and includes the Rasken long-distance services. The province covers a large area and includes Öland. A one-way ticket will cost from 13 to 90 kr within the province, but there are no useful discount passes. For those who just can't get enough, *Sommarkort* is valid from 15 June to 14 August on all buses and trains within the province and costs 740 kr. Consider the prepaid value card *betalkort* for 200 kr that gives a 10 to 17% discount on each trip. All regional and long-distance buses depart from the train station. Local town buses have their own terminal.

ÖLAND

More windmills than Holland? There are 400 on Öland today, some lived in. Most are the characteristic wooden huts, on a rotating base. Also prominent are the lighthouses at the north and south tips of the island. Youth hostels and camp sites are indicated on the map.

The island spans 150 km, and is reached by the longest bridge in Europe, from Kalmar. Buses connect all main towns from Kalmar.

The telephone code is ☎ 0485.

Borgholm

The 'capital' of Öland is a pleasant small town with shops, cafés and museums, including the enormous castle ruins. The tourist office (☎ 890 00) is in the park facing the water on Hamnen.

Things to See The town is dominated from the hill just to the south by the **Borgholm slottsruin**. This castle was finally burned and abandoned early in the 18th century after being used as a dyeing works. There's an excellent museum inside. Admission is 20 kr.

The remains of the medieval fortified church **Källa odekyrka** at the little harbour off road 136 north-east of Borgholm are fascinating, as it and other churches actually supplanted the mighty stone fortresses as defensive works. The broken **rune stone** inside shows the Cross growing from the pagan tree of life.

Places to Stay Just outside the centre, *STF Hostel* (☎ 107 56) in the Rosenfors Manor is open from 1 May to 15 September and has beds for 70 and 100 kr, and a kitchen. *Olssons rumsuthyrning* (☎ 119 39) at Tullgatan 12a has double rooms from 380 kr in summer and 300 kr in winter. *Strand Hotel* (☎ 888 88) on the beach fills last-minute vacancies for 575 kr a room. The camping ground just north of the bus terminal is complemented by a choice of several seaside camping grounds north of Borgholm.

Northern Öland

Sandvik, on the west coast of Öland about 30 km north of Borgholm, is where you'll find the more familiar 'Dutch' type of windmill. In summer, you can climb the eight storeys for a view back to the mainland. There is also a restaurant.

Byxelkrok in the very north has a ferry connection to Oskarshamn in summer. The natural attractions in the nearby **Trollskogen** are worth a visit.

Places to Stay Northern Öland has plenty of camping grounds, and the *STF Hostel Mellböda* (☎ 220 38) near Böda is open from 1 April to 1 September and has 100 kr beds, a kitchen and laundry facilities.

Färjestaden & Around
The 'Ferry Town' has a prebridge name, but the old jetty area is still the centre of summer activities. From Kalmar, the six-km bridge Ölandsbron lands you on the island just north of Färjestaden, where there is a tourist office (☎ 390 00) at the Träffpunkt Öland centre beside the road.

Things to See & Do Färjestaden itself has nothing of interest, but north of the bridge is **Ölands djurpark**, which is a zoo and amusement park. The park can keep you busy all day (if you are so inclined) for 125 kr (105 kr from mid-September to early in summer) and is open daily. Adjacent to the tourist office, south of the bridge, **Historium** is worth a visit if you are touring the island's ancient sites, but not all the exhibits are meant to be taken seriously. Admission is 40 kr.

The **Ismantorp** fortress, with its house remains and nine mysterious gates, is five km west of the Himmelsberga museum (see below). It is the most 'faithful' of the fortress ruins, showing clearly how the village and its tiny huts were encircled by the outer wall (Eketorp, described in the following Southern Öland section, is an imaginative reconstruction of similar remains). The area, just south of the Ekerum-Långlöt road, can be freely visited all year.

On the middle of the east coast at Långlöt, **Himmelsberga** is a farm village of the single-road type from a bygone age. This is not the only one on Öland, but here the quaint cottages have been fully re-equipped as a **museum**, open daily in summer. They've been furnished and their painted interiors have been restored.

The biggest Iron-Age ring fort on the island, **Gråborg**, has a diameter of 200 metres, and was used comparatively recently for purely defensive work, for which much of the internal stone walls were plundered. Nearby is the ruin of a medieval chapel. The complex is on the Norra Mockleby road about 10 km east of Färjestaden, a walk of a few km from the windmills, and bus Nos 103 and 413 stop east of Färjestaden or bus Nos 101 and 411 at Algutsrum.

Karlevistenen, the rune stone in the paddock near Karlevi, looks over the water from a small mound six km south of Färjestaden (off the coast road to Mörbylånga). It was raised in the 10th century (when the land was considered Danish) for a Viking chieftain, Sibbe, who is eulogised in the verse inscription. Some buses on route No 103 run past the site, but check before boarding.

Places to Stay The tourist office in Färjestaden will book rooms (doubles from 150 to 350 kr) or available cabin accommodation for a 25 kr fee.

Southern Öland
The southern half of the island is chiefly a haven for nature and the relics of humankind's settlements and conflicts, attested to by the Iron-Age fortresses and graveyards of all periods.

Things to See & Do The unusual limestone-based plain, **Stora Alvaret**, interests all manner of naturalists, but mostly those keen on bird life, insects and flora. The expanse takes up most of the inland southern half of Öland and can be crossed by road from Mörbylånga or Degerhamn. The mid-summer traffic is probably too annoying for observation, particularly if you are bird-watching, but late April, May and early June are usually good for venturing out by bicycle.

The ancient grave fields of **Mysinge** and **Gettlinge**, stretching out several km on the ridge along the main Mörbylånga-Degerhamn road, include burials and standing stones from the Stone Age to the late Iron Age, but the biggest single monument is the mound

Mysinge hög, 15 km south of Färjestaden (take bus No 112 to/from Mörbylånga).

The most southerly of the big ring forts, **Eketorp**, three km south of Gräsgård, has been partly reconstructed as a museum to show what the fortified villages, which went in and out of use over the centuries, must have been like in medieval times. The fort can be viewed at any time and the museum building is open daily in summer, but only at weekends during other times of year. The admission fee to the museum is 40 kr (open from May to mid-September) and daily tours in English are from mid-June to the end of August. Take bus No 112 from Mörbylånga.

Places to Stay *Mörby Vandrarhem & Lågprishotel* (☎ 493 93) is one km east of the Mörbylånga town centre near the sugar factory and offers hostel-standard dorm beds from 100 kr (breakfast 40 kr) and singles/doubles at 250/400 kr.

Gotland

Gotland, the largest of the Baltic islands, is also one of the most historical regions in Sweden – there are more than 100 medieval churches and an untold number of prehistoric sites. But Swedes come for the beaches and the culture; for them Gotland is like a foreign country, halfway between mainland Sweden and Latvia. Other attractions include the odd limestone formations *(raukar)*, the remains of 400 million-year-old coral reefs, and the walled medieval trading post of Visby. A week is minimum for seeing the highlights.

Gotland is also the main budget travel destination in Scandinavia – bicycle travel is by far the best option, camping in forests is easy and legal, most attractions are absolutely free and there are more than 20 hostels around the island.

The telephone code for the island is ☎ 0498.

Churches

Nowhere else in northern Europe are there so many medieval churches in such a small area. There are 92 of them outside Visby, and over 70 of them have either medieval frescos or (very rare) medieval glass paintings, or both. In addition, Visby has a dozen church ruins and a magnificent cathedral. Each village had a church built between the early 12th and the mid-13th century until wars ended the tradition. Each church is still in use, and all those medieval villages still exist as entities. Most churches are open from 15 May (or 1 June) to 31 August daily from 9 am to 6 pm. Some churches have the old key in the door even before 15 May, or sometimes the key is hidden above the door. Or a note says the key is kept 'in the third house on your right after the sports field' – in Swedish only! The free *Nyckel till alla Gotlands kyrkor* is a useful leaflet in Swedish.

Prehistoric Sites

There are hundreds, perhaps thousands of sites around the island, many of them signposted. They range from remains of hilltop fortresses to burial mounds, but few deserve to be mentioned. Keep your eyes open for signboards or information boards along all roads. You can visit these sites, as well as the numerous nature reserves any time, free of charge.

Getting There & Away

Air You can choose between SAS or Skyways flights from Stockholm/Arlanda, Malmö Aviation flights from Stockholm/Bromma or Helsinki (Finland) and Air Express flights from Norrköping. Book early for discounts, and young people should look for standby fares. The airfield is four km north of Visby, and there are buses.

Boat Gotlandslinjen has a monopoly on Gotland launches until 1 January 1998 when Gotlandsbolaget takes over in cooperation with Silja Line. Currently, there are daily car ferries in winter from Nynäshamn and Oskarshamn, and two daily departures in summer. The new catamaran service from

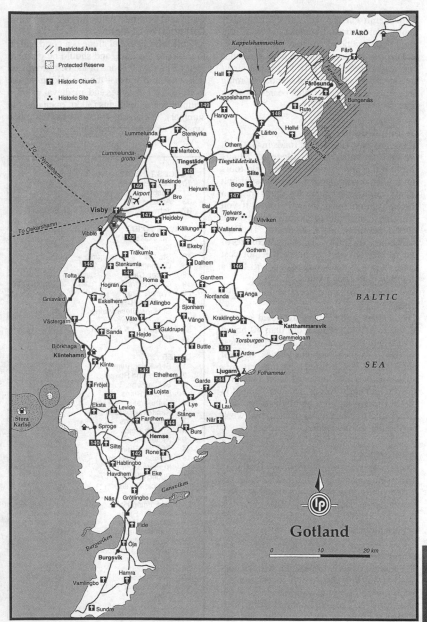

Gotland

0   10   20 km

Nynäshamn carries cars (anything smaller than a Volvo station wagon), takes a little more than two hours to cross and shuttles to and fro up to three times a day. A regular one-way ticket is 135/210 kr for the ferry/catamaran, but weekend and Monday morning departures in summer are 50% dearer. Bicycles cost 35/50 kr, cars 196/295 kr.

Getting Around

There are over 1200 km of roads in Gotland, typically running from village to village through the pretty landscape. Bicycle tours are highly recommended. The forested belt (study maps in advance for roads that run through uninhabited areas) is useful if you bring a tent and want to take advantage of the liberal camping laws. Kollektiv Trafiken runs buses via most villages to all corners of the island. A one-way ticket will not cost more than 41 kr, but enthusiasts will find a monthly ticket good value.

VISBY

The walled and cobbled medieval port of Visby is a living relic: more than 40 proud towers and the ruins of great churches attest to Visby's former Hanseatic glories. Today it is a World Heritage-listed town that certainly leaves no tourist disappointed or even hungry! In July and early August cars are banned in the old town, and the highlight is the costumes and re-enactments of medieval week during the second week of August.

Information

There are two tourist offices. Gotlands Turistförening (☎ 21 09 82) is at Strandgatan 9, open daily, and the municipal tourist information is at Donnersplats. The library is good for imported magazines and the Internet (one hour rule applies).

Things to See

The town itself is a noble sight, with its wall of 40 towers breached in only two places. Set aside enough time to walk or cycle on the narrow roads. The contemporary **ruins** of 10 medieval churches are all within the town

walls and contrast with the old but sound **Cathedral of St Maria**.

Gotlands Fornsal alone is a good reason to travel to Gotland, and should be given at least half a day. It is one of the best provincial museums in Sweden – the pre-Viking picture stones, silver treasures and medieval wooden sculptures are highlights (30 kr, open daily in summer). The nearby **Naturmuséet** is much smaller, as is the art museum.

PLACES TO STAY
10   Lindgården
31   Wisby Hotel
33   Ambassador
37   Jernvägshotellet & Hotel Villa Borgen

PLACES TO EAT
11   Gutekällaren
12   Nunnan
13   Sta Carins Rosengård
15   Clematis
18   Rosas Café
19   Café Regnbågen
20   Wallers Krog
25   Skafferiet Café
28   St Hans Uteservering
34   Kaffestugan
35   Magasin 3 & Saluhall
39   Effes

OTHER
1   St Nikolai Ruins
2   Helge And Ruins
3   St Clemens Ruins
4   St Olof Ruins
5   Cathedral
6   Kapitelhusgården
7   Drotten Ruins
8   St Lars Ruins
9   Kruttornet
14   St Carin Ruins
16   Fornsal Museum
17   Konstmuseum
21   Public Library
22   Bicycle Rental
23   Pharmacy
24   Swimming Hall
26   St Peter Ruins
27   St Hans Ruins
29   Naturmuseet
30   Tourist Office
32   Gotlands Turistförening
36   Bicycle Rentals
38   Book Shop
40   Bus Station
41   Water Tower
42   Post Office

SWEDEN

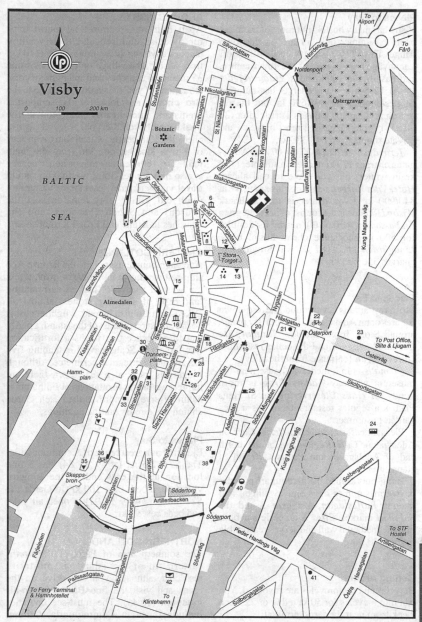

Visby

0   100   200 km

BALTIC

SEA

To
Airport

To
Fårö

Nordervåg

Nordenport

Östergravar

Silverhättan

Studentallén

St Nikolaigränd

St Nikolaigatan

Tranhusgatan

Smedjegatan

Botanic
Gardens

1

2

3

4

Sankt
Olofsgatan

9

Biskopsgatan

Norra Kyrkogatan

Nygatan

Norra Murgatan

6

5

Sankt Drottensgatan

Sankt Hansgatan

Mellangatan

7

8

12

Strandgatan

10

11

Stora
Torget

14   13

15

Almedalen

16   17

Sankt Hansgatan

Donnersgatan

Kaserngatan

Cramérgatan

Hamnplan

Strandgatan

29

Donners-
plats

30

32

31

33

34

35

36

Skepps-
bron

18

Mellangatan

28

27   26

Hästgatan

20

21

19

Österport

22

23

To Post Office,
Slite & Ljugam

Östervåg

Skolportsgatan

24

Kung Magnus våg

Sankt Hansgatan

Slottsbacken

Björngränd

Bredgatan

Väcklockegatan

Adelsgatan

Södra Murgatan

25

37

38

39   40

Södertorg

Artilleribacken

Söderport

Peder Hardings Våg

To STF
Hostel

Artilleri gatan

Solbergagatan

41

Skepparegatan

Visborgsgatan

Söderväg

Solbergsgatan

Palissadgatan

Färjeleden

To Ferry Terminal
& Hamnhotellet

42

To
Klintehamn

Östra Hansegatan

SWEDEN

Places to Stay

Visby has many hostels but most of them are open in summer only, or are on the town fringe. The *STF Hostel* (☎ 26 98 42) is off Lännavägen south-east of the town centre, and has 70 and 100 kr beds. *Hamnhotellet* (☎ 20 12 50) at Färjeleden 3 has summer singles/doubles for 495/690 kr, but the off season is cheaper. Gotlands Turistcenter (27 90 95) behind Magasin 3 rents bicycles and private rooms from 240/380 kr.

Jernvägshotellet (☎ 27 17 07) on Adelsgatan charges 170 kr per bed in summer (150 kr in winter) but you have to call ahead. *Hotel Villa Borgen* next door is expensive at 840/990 kr. Even dearer is the landmark *Wisby Hotel* near the tourist office, but go to *Ambassador* (☎ 20 60 00) nearby for doubles for 500 kr and some cheap hostel beds. *Lindgården* (☎ 21 87 00) on Strandgatan charges 550/690 kr.

Places to Eat

Most restaurants are around the old town squares or on Adelsgatan. The touristy places around Stora Torget include *Nunnan*, *Sta Carins Rosengård* and the cellar restaurant *Gutekällaren* (entrance from the alley).

Clematis is in a medieval house near the museum, whereas *Wallers Krog* is more trendy. *St Hans Uteservering* on St Hans Plan is a regular restaurant but has a nice garden in summer.

Pleasant cafés include *Skafferiet Café* on Adelsgatan, *Café Regnbågen* at the north end of Adelsgatan and *Rosas Café* on St Hansgatan.

Hang-outs around the harbour are popular on warm summer days and evenings, and include *Kaffestugan*, *Magasin 3* and the *Saluhall* market. *Effes* is an eerie bar built into the medieval wall and serves reasonable pizzas.

Getting Around

Bicycles and motorcycles are favoured. You can hire bicycles for 50 kr a day or 225 kr a week from near the ferry terminal.

AROUND VISBY

Apart from some commercial tourist traps for Swedish children and their wealthy parents, anything interesting is at least 10 km from Visby. The village belt includes some 35 medieval churches and many prehistoric attractions. If you're heading north, go to the **Bro church** and look for the signposted prehistoric sites nearby, and stop at the **Väskinde church**. On your way to Ljugarn, check the 12th-century Cistercian monastery of **Roma kloster**, one km from the main road. The 18th-century manor house nearby is also impressive. Going south, you should travel via Stenkumla, Eskelhem, Västergarn (with old Viking port remains near the church) and Sanda churches, and the churches in Klinte and Fröjel further south.

EASTERN GOTLAND

Ancient monuments include the Bronze Age ship-setting known as **Tjelvars grav**, a few km west of road 146, and its surrounding landscape of standing stones, almost all linked with Gutnish legend. Mightier still is **Torsburgen** on the east of the island, a partly walled eminence that forms a fortification (the largest in Scandinavia) extending five km around its irregular perimeter. Although Ljugarn is more of a sea resort, there are impressive raukar formations at Folhammar nature reserve just north of the beach. Garde church has rare Byzantine paintings.

Places to Stay

Ljugarn has a great range of accommodation. The *STF Hostel* (☎ 49 31 84) has a fine location at the east end of the Ljugarn village, and beds cost 100 kr. In Garde the *STF Hostel* (☎ 49 13 91) is open all year, and beds cost 95 kr.

NORTHERN GOTLAND

The southern area of Fårö, at the north-eastern tip of the island, is militarily restricted, although you can drive on the roads and visit the fine **Bunge open-air museum** (30 kr). The must-see churches include those in Lummelunda, Othem,

Lärbro and Bunge, although there are a dozen more to see.

The grotto south of Lummelunda is the largest in Gotland and is open for a fee from May to September.

Places to Stay
There are *STF hostels* in Fårö (☎ 22 36 39) 17 km north of the ferry, and in Lärbro (☎ 22 57 86) at Gutegården.

SOUTHERN GOTLAND
Hemse is the commercial centre with good services and a medieval church worth a look. Klintehamn on the west coast boasts a similar range of services. You can also catch a boat to one of the two Karlsö islands from Klintehamn. Öja church is the highlight among medieval buildings, although there are more than 30 others. Lye church has more medieval glass paintings than any other church in Scandinavia. Churches in Fardhem, Rone and Stånga are also worth a look. Lojsta has the deepest lakes in Gotland, remains of a medieval fortress and a very fine church.

Places to Stay
In Klintehamn, the *STF Hostel* (☎ 24 00 10) has beds from 70 kr, and assists in arranging a hostel and boat trip reservations to Stora Karlsö. Beds at the simple STF hostel *St Karlsö* (☎ 24 05 00) cost 100 kr – boats depart from Klintehamn at 9 am (170 kr return).

In summer, there are also *STF hostels* in Näs and Sproge, and a *SVIF hostel* in Vamlingbo, seven km south of Burgsvik.

Svealand

This is where Sweden was born: Viking Age rune stones and forts are reminders of the time when Lake Mälaren offered safe harbours and sea connections to the Baltic Sea and Russia. The kingdom of the Svear became synonymous with the entire country, that the Swedes call Sverige, or Svea Rike.

Further west, amidst some breathtaking

lake and forest scenery, lies Dalarna (Dalecarlia), a province of rich folk culture and beautiful landscapes centred around the smaller Lake Siljan and the twin branches of the Dalälven River. This region has become popular for travel and winter sports.

UPPSALA
Uppsala is the fourth largest city in Sweden, and one of its oldest. Gamla (Old) Uppsala flourished as early as the 6th century. The cathedral was consecrated in 1435 after 150 years of building and the castle was first built in the 1540s, although today's appearance belongs to the 18th century. The town focus is the sprawling university, Scandinavia's oldest.

Information
A tourist office of Uppsala Turist och Kongress (☎ 018-27 48 00) at Fyris torg 8 is open from 10 am to 6 pm weekdays (and to 2 pm Saturday from late August to late June). Forex is next door. Students in search of information can go to the student union on the corner of Åsgränd and Övre Slottsgatan. The public library on the corner of Sankt Olofsgatan and Svartbäcksgatan opens at noon in summer.

The main post office is in the shopping arcade on the corner of Bredgränd and Dragarbrunnsgatan. One of the best bookshops in Sweden, Akademibokhandeln Lundeqvistska is on the corner of Östra Ågatan and Drottninggatan.

The telephone code is ☎ 018.

Medical & Emergency Services The police are at Salagatan 18. There is a pharmacy at Svartbäcksgatan 8 and for emergency treatment go to the university medical centre (☎ 16 60 00); enter from Sjukhusvägen. The pharmacy there (at entrance No 70) is open until 9 pm. A duty doctor is available to 11.30 pm on the corner of Bangårdsgatan and Kungsgatan.

Things to See
The Gothic **cathedral** dominates the city just as some of the dead who rest there dominated

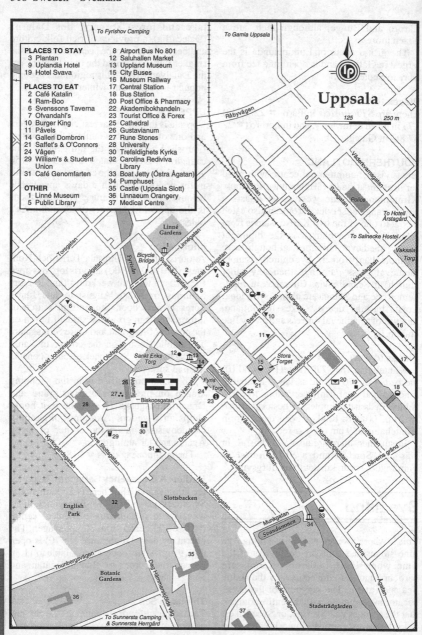

To Fyrishov Camping

To Gamla Uppsala

Uppsala

0   125   250 m

PLACES TO STAY
3 Plantan
9 Uplandia Hotel
19 Hotel Svava

PLACES TO EAT
2 Café Katalin
4 Ram-Boo
6 Svenssons Taverna
7 Ofvandahl's
10 Burger King
11 Påvels
14 Galleri Dombron
21 Saffet's & O'Connors
24 Vågen
29 William's & Student
   Union
31 Café Genomfarten

OTHER
1 Linné Museum
5 Public Library

8 Airport Bus No 801
12 Saluhallen Market
13 Uppland Museum
15 City Buses
16 Museum Railway
17 Central Station
18 Bus Station
20 Post Office & Pharmacy
22 Akademibokhandeln
23 Tourist Office & Forex
25 Cathedral
26 Gustavianum
27 Rune Stones
28 University
30 Trefaldighets Kyrka
32 Carolina Rediviva
   Library
33 Boat Jetty (Östra Ågatan)
34 Pumphuset
35 Castle (Uppsala Slott)
36 Linnaeum Orangery
37 Medical Centre

To Hotell
Årstagård

To Salnecke Hostel

Police

Linné
Gardens

Bicycle
Bridge

Sankt Eriks
Torg

Stora
Torget

Fyris
Torg

Linnégatan

English
Park

Slottsbacken

Botanic
Gardens

To Sunnersta Camping
& Sunnersta Herrgård

Stadsträdgården

SWEDEN

their country: St Erik, Gustaf Vasa, Johan III, and Carl von Linné who established the binomial system of scientific names for species. The **Archiepiscopal Museum** is in the north tower (10 kr, closed weekdays from September to May). The nearby **Trefaldighets kyrka** is not outwardly as impressive, but has beautiful painted ceilings.

The old **Gustavianum** building (open daily from 11 am to 5 pm, 10 kr) features an 'anatomical theatre' and is worth a look. The **Uppland Museum**, in the old mill at Sankt Eriks gränd 6, houses interesting county collections from the Middle Ages and onwards as well as natural-history exhibits (free entry, open daily from noon).

Carolina Rediviva, the old university library, has a display hall with maps and historical and scientific literature, the pride of which is the surviving half of the 6th-century Codex Argentus, written on purple vellum in the extinct Gothic language (admission free).

The **Linnaeum Orangery** and the **Botanic Gardens** and greenhouse are below the castle hill and are not to be confused with the **Linné Museum** and its gardens at Svartbäcksgatan 27, open from June to September (10 kr). The museum, which keeps memorabilia of von Linné's work in Uppsala, is closed on Monday. The garden, with more than 1000 herbs, has been designed according to an 18th-century plan.

Take sandwiches and sit by the main **Uppsala University** building (which is imposing enough to demand a glance inside) and absorb the ambience of a historic university (first opened in 1477). On the lawn in front are nine typical Uppland **rune stones**. On 30 April the students gather dressed in white to celebrate the Walpurgis festival in procession and song.

Uppsala Slott The castle is open daily from mid-April to 1 September and entry is 40 kr. The castle features the genuinely death-stained dungeons, the state hall and the so-called **Vasa vignettes**: dioramas showing the colour and treachery of the castle's past. The bell tower **Gunillaklockan** and cannon

look out over the old town from the courtyard. Allow two hours so you can take everything in.

Gamla Uppsala Uppsala began at the three great **grave mounds** at Gamla Uppsala, three km north of the modern city. The mounds, said to be the graves of legendary pre-Viking kings, mark a cemetery of about 200 small mounds. It has also been suggested that it was a great heathen temple site. Christianity came in the 12th century and with it the bishops: from 1164 the archbishop had his seat in a cathedral on the site of the present **church**, which, by the 15th century, was enlarged and painted with frescos.

Next to the flat-topped mound **Tingshögen** is the **Odinsborg Inn**, known for its horns of mead, although daintier refreshments are offered on site in summer. The **Disagården** museum village, quite a walk from the church is open daily from June to August (free). The old **train station** is also a museum piece: take bus No 20, 24 or 54 from Uppsala.

Markets The indoor produce market, Saluhallen, is at Sankt Eriks torg between the cathedral and the river (open on weekdays and Saturday), and an open six-day market is at Vaksala torg, behind the train station.

Activities
You can ride the steam train *Lennakatten* on the narrow-gauge museum railway into the Uppland countryside (on Sunday, from mid-June to early in September for 60 kr return). The two tours depart from the Uppsala Östra museum station behind the main station.

The old steamers depart from Östra Ågatan to the baroque castle in Skokloster, and there are connecting boats to Stockholm.

Places to Stay
Fyrishov Camping (☎ 27 49 60), by the river at Fyrisfädern, north of the city, offers powered sites for 110 kr in summer. There are four-bed cabins with cooking facilities for 390 kr; take bus No 24 or 54.

Plantan (☎ 10 43 00) at Dragarbrunnsgatan

18, is a modern student apartment building with beds in six-bed rooms from 125 kr all year round – even in summer beds are not hard to get. Each room has a kitchen and a bath tub.

Sunnersta herrgård (☎ 32 42 20), a hostel in the manor house at Sunnerstavägen 24, is open all year and charges 100 kr. Take bus No 20 or 50 six km to the south.

Not far from the city is *Hotell Årstagård*, (☎ 25 35 00) Jordgubbsgatan 14 (bus No 7 or 56), where singles/doubles cost 350/475 kr, but the place also rent rooms at *Salnecke Hostel* at Vaksalagatan 55, for 215/300 kr. *Hotel Svava* (☎ 13 00 30), Bangårdsgatan 24, charges 600/700 kr all year round. *Uplandia Hotel* (☎ 10 21 60) at Dragarbrunnsgatan 32 has rooms in summer for 500/675 kr.

Places to Eat

There are several eateries on the pedestrian mall and Stora Torget, although most of the hamburger restaurants are on Dragarbrunnsgatan. *Saffet's* on Stora Torget offers a great variety in fast food, including salads. Upstairs, *O'Connors* is an Irish pub.

Vägen on Fyris torg has kebabs and is open long after midnight. *Ram-Boo* at Sankt Olofsgatan 15 has pizza and fast food with some style and class.

Ofvandahl's at Sysslomansgatan 3-5 is the oldest and most stylish café in town, but if you like small vaulted rooms and an unusual outdoor spot at the rapids, go to *Galleri Dombron* next to the Uppland Museum. *Café Genomfarten* at Drottninggatan 13 is run by the church and has the cheapest coffee in town.

In the evenings, local students converge at the popular krog restaurants, including *Svenssons taverna* at Sysslomansgatan 14, *Påvels* at Påvel Snickares gränd and *Café Katalin* on Svartbäcksgatan, which offers meals and live music. *William's*, in the university quarter at Övre Slottsgatan 7, is an English pub.

Getting There & Away

There are frequent SJ trains from Stockholm but choose wisely – some trains require a supplement. All SJ services to/from Gävle, Östersund and Mora also stop in Uppsala. SL coupons take you (and your bicycle) only as far as Märsta from Stockholm.

The bus station is outside the train station. Bus No 810 departs at least twice an hour from Uplandia Hotel and the bus station for the nearby Arlanda airport (75 kr).

Getting Around

A local bus ticket costs 16 kr and is valid for 1½ hours – just enough for a visit to Gamla Uppsala. Catch a city bus from Stora Torget or at Uplandia Hotel. Upplands Lokaltrafik runs regional traffic within the province – tickets cost from 12 kr, or buy a *rabattkort* (300 kr, allows 375 kr worth of travel) or a *flerzonskort* for 420 kr (22 trips in 15 days). Regional timetables cost 5 kr.

You can hire a bicycle at Cykel & Skidstället, Svartbäcksgatan 20, for 70 kr a day and 260 kr a week. Regional buses of Upplands Lokaltrafik take bicycles for 20 kr but local trains don't.

VÄSTERÅS

Both an old and a modern city, Västerås is a centre of Asea Brown Boweri (ABB) industrial technology. Ignore the sprawling suburbs and head for the old town centre and wooden buildings along the Svartån River, or Lake Mälaren's shores.

Västerås is the seventh largest city in Sweden and has an international feel – over 7% of its 125,000 inhabitants are foreigners.

Information

The tourist office (☎ 021-10 37 00) at Stora Gatan 40 is open daily (except Sunday in winter). The main post office is at Sturegatan 18, and there's a Forex exchange office at Stora Gatan 18. The public library is next to the cathedral on the corner of Vasagatan and Biskopsgatan.

The telephone code is ☎ 021.

Things to See

The castle housing the **Västmanlands länsmuseum**, Västerås slott, has a strong general historical collection but diverts into peculiarities such as Swedish porcelain. Admission is free, and the museum is open daily except Monday. The neighbouring turbine house **Turbinhuset** is part of the complex. Admission is free (closed Monday).

The nearby art museum **Konstmuseum**, at Fiskartorget, has temporary exhibitions of Swedish painters (free, closed Monday). The fine **cathedral** (open daily) and its **museum** (5 kr) reflect 700 years of episcopal activity.

The **Vallby friluftsmuseum**, off Vallby-leden near the E18 interchange north-west of the city, is an open-air collection assembled by the regional museum. The area is open for free daily from June to August. Among the 40-odd buildings, the highlight is the **Vikingagården**, a reconstructed 11th-century farm. Take bus No 12 or 92 from Munkgatan.

The city is surrounded by ancient cult sites and the most interesting and extensive is **Anundshög**, six km north-east of the city along Tortunavägen. It has a full complement of prehistoric curiosities such as mounds, stone ship-settings and a big rune stone. The row of stones beside the modern road is presumably the ancient royal ceremonial road **Eriksgata**. Bus No 12 or 92 will only get you within two km of the site: walk east.

Places to Stay

Västerås is no paradise for budget travellers – you could visit the sights in half a day and catch a train somewhere else for the night. There are camping grounds aplenty around Lake Mälaren's shores, but only *Johannisbergs camping* (☎ 14 02 79), six km south of the city, is close (take bus No 25). Nearby, but still over five km from the town centre, is the STF hostel *Lövudden* (☎ 18 52 30), off Johannisbergsvägen. Beds cost 100 kr, and there are singles/doubles without breakfast for 325/450 kr.

Cheap hotels are also far from the centre: *Aabrin Lågprishotell* (☎ 14 39 80), at Kopparbergsvägen 47 by the E18, comes down to 250/325 kr in summer, and *Raka vägen* (☎ 30 04 00), at Hallsta Gårdsgata 1 about five km from the city centre, to 390/450 kr.

Places to Eat

Many of the cheapest restaurants are on Vasagatan, including *Piazza di Spagna* at No 26, a mid-priced and good lunch alternative. *Bill & Bobs Krog* and *Stadskällaren* on Stora Torget are the pick of the restaurants, for mid-priced and splurge dinners, respectively. For more affordable fare, the *City Grill*, at Smedjegatan 2, an informal kebab and burger bar, is usually open and *Kebabhuset* on the corner of Köpmangatan and Stora Torget is similar.

Getting There & Away

Västerås is now more accessible by train with the new tracks from Stockholm and around Lake Mälaren. Trains to Sala, Uppsala and Örebro are also frequent.

The regional buses and trains are run by Västmanlands Lokaltrafik (VL). Each ticket costs at least 10 kr; Västerås to Sala costs 44 kr. *Turistkortet* for 100 kr is valid for three consecutive days, and is valid on all buses and trains within the province. Bicycles are not accepted on regional trains but buses take them for 30 kr. The bus terminal is next to the train station, but you can catch most buses also on Munkgatan.

SALA

The sleepy town of Sala, 120 km from Stockholm, is worth at least a day's visit. The silver mine was considered the treasury of Sweden in the 16th and 17th centuries and its importance changed the face of the town: the channels and pondages that weave through and around it were the source of power for the mines. The little wooden bridges that cross them are the town's signature features.

Information

The tourist office (☎ 0224-131 45) is on Drottning Christina väg. Though the town is small, the sketched map is useful if you want to use the walking paths.

The telephone code is ☎ 0224.

Things to See & Do

A stroll along the **Gröna gången** path takes you south-east through the parks and to the

Mellandammen pondage at Sofielund. Further on the path takes you to **Sala gruvbyn**, the old silver mine area (off the Västerås road, or take bus No 61) which was worked from the 1400s. You can take tours down to 60 metres in the shafts (80 kr including entry to the **museum**) or walk through the museum village. You can look at the displays in the information centre, including a superb working **model mine**, and films in the **Hjulhuset** theatre (30 kr). The centrepiece is the **Drottning Christinas schakt** minehead. The village is open daily in summer, otherwise weekends only: take bus No 69 from the railway station.

In town by the main park area of **Ekeby dammar** is **Väsby kungsgård**, a farm where Gustaf II Adolf and his mistress used to rendezvous. Excitement for the traveller is limited to the beautiful preserved interiors and the comprehensive **weapons** collection of the sort wielded by the mighty Swedish armies of the 17th century. The vaulted cellars and wine benches have been restored. There is a small **textile museum** attached (10 kr inclusive, open weekday afternoons and daily from May to August).

The rebuilt 17th-century **Kristina kyrka** on Gruvgatan is impressive enough today, but once had an 83-metre-high spire!

Older is **Sala sockenkyrka** off Hyttvägen, with the remains of frescos by the esteemed Albertus Pictor from the 15th century.

Places to Stay

The tourist office will book rooms from 120 kr a night, but there are other budget options. The pleasant STF hostel *Sofielund* (☎ 136 59, winter ☎ 127 30, beds 100 kr), and *Sofielunds Familjecamping* (☎ 127 30) are by the pondage south-east of the town centre: walk about 25 minutes along Gröna gången from Kvarngatan. You can also take bus No 69 from the train station to the water tower. The basic camping ground is open from mid-May to September and charges from 60 kr (40 kr per tent). The place has a pleasant summer *café*.

Hotell Svea (☎ 105 10), Väsbygatan 19,

discounts singles/doubles to 380/480 kr at weekends and in summer. There are also some hostel-type beds at 150 kr each (without breakfast).

Getting There & Away

The regional train or bus No 69 from Västerås (44 kr) is convenient and the regional bus network will take you to/from Uppsala (62 kr) or Gävle. Sala is on the main Stockholm to Mora line, and there are several trains daily.

ÖREBRO

Perhaps the most photogenic castle in Sweden stands by the water at the centre of Örebro. It is a pretty town, another pleasant place to spend a day or two when the weather is fine. The wealth of Örebro was built on a prosperous textile industry.

Information

The main tourist office (☎ 019-21 21 21) is in the castle (closed weekends from autumn to spring). The library is south of the town centre on Näbbtorgsgatan.

The telephone code is ☎ 019.

Things to See & Do

The once powerful **Örebro slott** has been restored. You can choose between a castle tour (50 kr) or the museum (25 kr) on the 3rd floor, or both (60 kr), but the small exhibition (entrance B) is free. The summer tours are in English at 2 pm daily. Outside the castle is **Konstmuseet**, the art museum (25 kr).

Walk east of the castle along the river to Stadsparken. The pleasant **Stadsträdgården** greenhouse precinct has a café. Further east is the **Wadköping** museum village, which has craft workshops, a bakery and period buildings, something not to miss; entry is free.

The commercial centre and some of the monumental buildings are around Stortorget, including the 13th-century **St Nicolai Church**.

You can see Lake Hjälmaren from the **Svampen** water tower on Dalbygatan north of the town centre. Built in 1957, it was the first of Sweden's modern 'mushroom' water towers, which now earns small change as a lookout; there is a café and restaurant open all day until 9 pm in summer.

Activities include bicycle tours along the river – Å-kartan is a free map that shows the routes and attractions. Boat cruises depart near the castle, MS *Gustaf Lagerbjelke* sails once a week to Stockholm and back.

Places to Stay
The *STF hostel* (☎ 31 02 40) at Fanjunkare-vägen 5, one km north-east from the train station, has beds for 100 kr. *Hotell Linden* (☎ 611 87 11), just off the main square at Köpmangatan 5, has singles/ doubles from 195/275 kr in summer. *Hotell Storgården* (☎ 12 02 00) close to the train station charges 340/440 kr in summer.

Getting There & Away
There are few direct trains from Stockholm – change at Hallsberg or catch a train from Västerås. The main train station Örebro C is a little way out from the town centre.

The regional bus station is opposite the train station (access via a tunnel) at Kloster-gatan 37. Swebus Nos 844 and 879 run to/from Karlstad, and No 840 runs to/from Jönköping. You can also catch direct buses from Stockholm or Oslo.

KARLSTAD
The port of Karlstad is on Vänern, Sweden's biggest lake, and is the gateway to outdoor experiences in the province of Värmland. Värmlands Turistbyrå (☎ 054-14 90 55) at Carlstads Conference Center on Tage Erlandergatan has details on both.

Things to See & Do
The **Mariebergsskogen** leisure park by the water on Långövägen combines amuse-ments with an open-air **museum** and animal park; see the example of a mill-saw. **Skogens mini-zoo** is open daily, but the amusements are open only from May to the end of August. The 18th-century stone bridge **Östra Bron** is the longest such bridge in Sweden and is the best place to admire the

lower reaches of the Klarälven River. Cruises on Vänern on *Sola Båten* leave from Inre Hamnen Monday to Friday at 2 and 4 pm (60 kr).

Places to Stay
The STF hostel *Ulleberg* (☎ 054-56 68 40) is off the E18, three km south-west of the town (take bus No 11 or 21). Beds cost 100 kr, and there's a kitchen and breakfast is served.

Getting There & Away
Stockholm to Oslo trains pass through Karlstad and several daily services also run from Gothenburg. Express bus No 844 runs to/from Örebro (100 kr), No 839 to/from Jönköping (185 kr) and No 879 to/from Oslo (150 kr) and Stockholm (160 kr, via Örebro). You will find the Swebus terminal at Drottninggatan 43.

Värmlandstrafik AB runs regional buses, and there are value cards and discount passes available; bicycles are transported in buses.

FALUN
Falun, traditionally the main centre of Dalarna, is synonymous with mining and with Stora, perhaps the world's oldest public company. The Falun Folkmusik festival, which has an international flavour as well as airing regional traditions, is held over four days in mid-July.

Information
The tourist office (☎ 023-836 37) is on Stora Torget, and the library is around the corner on Kristinegatan.

The telephone code is ☎ 023.

Things to See & Do
The **Falu koppargruva** copper mine was the world's most important by the 17th century and drove many of Sweden's international aspirations during that period. The mine also provided, as a by-product, the red coatings that became the characteristic house paint of the age. The minerals and vitriol in this paint protect wood and the *falurött* paint is still practical and popular today. There are many

exhibits in the **Stora museum** describing the miners' wretched life and work, and the shocking tale of Fett-Matts, the lad plucked, in a perfect state of preservation, from rubble two generations after the mine took his life. The museum (open daily) is above the town at the top end of Gruvgatan in front of the present open-cut mine. Museum admission costs 10 kr, but to enter the bowels of the disused mines for a once-only experience will cost 55 kr (take bus No 709 from Falugatan). Restored homes from the mines' heyday are grouped around Östanfors, Gamla Herrgården and Elsborg.

There is more folk culture at **Dalarnas museum**, by the bridge on Stigaregatan (admission 20 kr, open daily). The feature of this fine museum is the stories and sounds of the famous minstrels of Dalarna. The baroque interiors of **Kristine kyrka** on Stora Torget show some of the riches that came into the town but don't miss **Stora Kopparbergs kyrka**, a bit north of the centre, the oldest building in town.

Falun is a winter-sports centre with plenty of ski runs, nordic courses and toboggan runs. The Lugnet area includes the **sports museum** (open daily except Sunday, 10 kr).

Places to Stay

The *Lugnet Camping* camping ground (☎ 835 63), in the ski area two km from the centre, has camping sites for 130 kr and some two-bed cabins at 150 kr. The big STF hostel *Hälsinggården* (☎ 105 60) is at Hälsinggårdsvägen 7, three km east of the town and a 10-minute walk from the bus stop (take bus No 701 from Vasagatan). Beds cost 100 kr.

Hotel Falun (☎ 291 80) at Trotzgatan 16 has comfortable singles/doubles with shower access from 390/560 kr, reduced to 310/425 kr in summer. *Hotel Bergmästaren* (☎ 636 00), at Bergskolegränd 7, reduces its luxury doubles to 595 kr in summer.

Places to Eat

There are quite a few eateries on the main square and the adjoining pedestrian mall, Holmgatan, including *Oscar's Café*, at Holmgatan 15, a lively music bar serving food and drinks. The little lunch restaurant and café *Kopparhatten* at Dalarnas museum serves some traditional folk-cuisine lunches for around 50 kr (closed Sunday). *Mariannes Café* near the museum at Stigaregatan 1 has cheap lunches.

Getting There & Away

Falun is not on the main railway lines – change at Borlänge when coming from Stockholm or Mora. There are direct trains from Gävle. If you're in a hurry to get to Rättvik, catch the regional bus No 70, this one-hour journey costs 43 kr.

Regional traffic is run by Dalatrafik and covers all corners of the 28,000-sq-km province. Tickets cost 13 kr for trips within a zone, and 15 kr extra for each new zone. A *periodkort* for 31 days costs 600 kr, and includes some trips beyond the province. This pass is not personal and can be resold. Timetables cost 1 kr.

RÄTTVIK

Rättvik is a popular skiing centre on Lake Siljan but the lake view in summer is not less interesting. There is a regional information office (☎ 0248-702 00) at the train station.

The telephone code is ☎ 0248.

Things to See & Do

Best preserved is the area around the medieval **church** and its 100-odd **church stables**. The pseudo-rune **memorial** beside the church by the lake commemorates the rising of Gustaf Vasa's band against the Danes in the 1520s, the rebellion that created modern Sweden. Further north is **Gammelgården**, the open-air museum that keeps old peasant traditions alive by preparing and selling Dalarna food.

The library, the **Art Museum** and **Naturmuseum** are located at the Kulturhuset near the Enån River, open daily from 11 am.

Views from surrounding hills and the **ski slopes** (there are four lifts) are excellent, and don't miss the longest pier in the world, the 628-metre **Långbryggan**.

The lakeshore is natural cycling country and you can follow **Siljansleden** with a hired bike from Cykel & Motor at Torget for 75 kr a day, 225 kr a week: maps are available at the tourist office. Or try the **rodel run**, a sort of summer luge that's lots of fun.

Dalhalla, an old open-cut mine several km north of Rättvik is used as an open-air concert venue in summer – the acoustics are incredible.

Places to Stay

Rättvik is a good place to stay for a few days; the cheapest places are good value. The tourist office will book all types of accommodation.

The best value is the mission-run *Jöns-Andersgården* (☎ 507 35), at Bygatan 4 on the hill (the view is superb). Bunks in traditional huts are 60 kr but you will probably be offered a single room for 90 or 100 kr. Tent sites are available at 50 kr, and breakfast for 35 kr. The other places on the hill are more expensive. *Siljansbadets Camping* (☎ 516 91), on the lakeshore near the train station, has four-bed cabins all year from 360 kr (280 kr in spring and autumn). *Rättviksparken* (☎ 516 10), by the river off Centralgatan one km from the train station, is even larger. There are a few doubles for 175 kr, and plenty of cottages for 330 kr. The nearby *STF hostel* (☎ 105 66) is one of the best in the country, and has beds for 100 kr and a good kitchen in the main building. *Stiftsgården Rättvik* (☎ 510 20) by the lake near the church is an affordable hotel in summer, from 300/380 kr.

Places to Eat

The cheapest places are opposite the train station: *Fricks Bageri* has cakes and coffee, and *Kebab Pizza* offers some cheap deals. A proof of the strong local culture awaits you at *Rättviks Rasten* next to the Statoil petrol station on the main highway. The place serves typical fast food but has quite incredible décor.

Getting There & Away

Direct trains from Stockholm stop at Rättvik's train station by the lake. Dalatrafik's buses depart from outside the train station: bus No 70 runs from Falun and further to Mora (both trips 43 kr). See Falun for information on regional traffic. MS *Gustaf Wasa* shuttles between Rättvik, Leksand and Mora in summer.

MORA

The legend is that Gustaf Vasa took off alone in high dudgeon to take on the Danes in 1521. The good yeomen of Dalarna, after due consideration, chose to brave the winter and follow. Vasaloppet, the ski race which ends at the entrance to Mora, commemorates Gustaf's sally and involves 90 km of gruelling nordic skiing. It is entered by thousands of people each March.

The tourist office (☎ 0250-265 50) is by Lake Siljan on Ångbåtskajen, not far from the prominent church and the race's finish line.

The telephone code is ☎ 0250.

Things to See & Do

The landmark **Mora kyrka** (open daily to 7 pm) is an example of local style and has notable portraits within. Go then to **Zornmuseet**, which celebrates the works and private collections of the Mora painter Anders Zorn, who was one of the wealthiest Swedes until his death in 1920. Aside from the characteristic portraits and nudes are collections of art including the odd traditional *dalmålningar* paintings. Admission costs 25 kr (students 20 kr) and the museum is open daily all year. Zorn family estate **Zorngården** (25 kr, open daily) is between the church and the museum, and is an excellent example of a wealthy artist's house, reflecting his National Romantic aspirations.

Zorns Gammelgård (20 kr, open daily in summer), Zorn's collection of local building traditions and textiles, is one km south of the town centre.

Vasaloppsmuseet tells about the largest skiing event in the world, and has a section on the US sister town of Mora, Minnesota. The museum is open daily, 30 kr.

The most reputable of the painted Dalecarlian **wooden horses** *(dalahästar)* are produced by Nils Olsson Hemslöjd at

Nusnäs, 10 km south of Mora, just off Nusnäs bygata. You can inspect the workshops daily (except on Sunday from September to May).

Siljansleden extends for more than 300 km around Siljan and has excellent walking and cycling paths for which maps are available at local tourist offices.

Places to Stay

The very central *STF Hostel* (☎ 381 95) at Fredsgatan 6 has beds for 100 kr, laundry facilities, a sauna and a kitchen. Some of the beds are at Vasagatan 19. In this building is *Målkull Ann's Pensionat* with singles/doubles for 390/490 kr, and the hostel reception in winter.

Mora Camping (☎ 153 52), on the river north of the town centre, has tent sites for 65 kr as well as two-bed cabins for 230 kr and four-bed cabins for 325 kr. *Hotell Kung Gösta* (☎ 150 70), opposite the main station on Kristinebergsgatan, has doubles in its summer annexe for 460 kr.

Places to Eat

There are several restaurants and good cafés on Kyrkogatan, including *Restaurang Lilla Björn* at No 5. *Strand Restaurang* by the tourist office offers cheap pizzas, but the tables with a view are in the pricey restaurant section. The summer café *Korsnäsgården* opposite the tourist office is overpriced, but the garden and interiors are very pleasant.

Getting There & Away

Air Airborne (ZF) and Highland Air (HS) fly direct to the airfield (south-west of town on the Malung road) from Stockholm/Arlanda.

Bus & Train The Dalatrafik buses from Rättvik and Falun (No 70) use the bus station at Moragatan 23. Bus No 170 continues to Särna (124 km), Idre (156 km) and Grövelsjön (196 km).

Mora is the SJ terminus and the southern extent of Inlandsbanan proper: the main train station is about one km around the lake from town. Mora strand is a platform in the town but is not used by all trains.

Going to Östersund, you may choose between Inlandsbanan (50% discount for rail pass holders) or bus No 245.

Car The desire to see other delights around Siljan or Upper Dalarna might make you decide to hire a car at Mora – for small budget models try Happy Rental (☎ 109 84).

SÄRNA & AROUND

The village of Särna is the start of some of the most beautiful upland wilderness for hikers. The tourist office (☎ 0253-102 05) at Särnavägen 6 is open from June to August.

The telephone code is ☎ 0253.

Things to See & Do

The wooden 17th-century **Särna gammelkyrka** (open daily in summer) is reminiscent of Norwegian wooden churches and attests to the period when Särna belonged to Norway. Next to the church is the **gammelgård**, consisting of buildings from the same period. The forestry museum **Lomkällan** is three km west of the town on road 70 and will help explain the town's past.

For one of the best views in Sweden, drive up or climb to the peak of **Mickeltemplet** two km above the village. There, from an altitude of 625 metres, you can see much of upper Dalarna and the singular **Städjan** peak (not a volcano). There is a lift and two simple runs (up to 350 metres) and 20 km of nordic trails. For lessons or ski hire book at Halvarssons Alpin (☎ 106 00).

The hills around the mountain of Fulufjället, west of Särna, feed **Njupeskär**, Sweden's tallest waterfall at 97 metres. You can take road 1056 from Särna towards the Norwegian border through rugged and beautiful country. The road leading south from the junction at Mörkret, 30 km from Särna, turns into a mountain trail (you can park near Stormorsvallen) and leads about two km to the falls at the beginning of the ancient forests of the **nature reserve**. Maps are available at the tourist office in Särna.

Further north-west is **Idre**, a ski centre with 32 downhill runs (lift cards cost 175 kr per day), a bank, post office and a small supermarket. For bookings and details call Idre Fjäll (☎ 400 00). Bus No 170 runs as far as **Grövelsjön**, the STF mountain station at the border.

Places to Stay

The two small STF hostels at Särna, *Turistgården* (☎ 104 37) at Sjukstugvägen 4, and *Björkhagen* (☎ 103 08) nearby, are open all year – beds cost 100 kr. You could also try *Knappgården* (☎ 180 60) at Särnaheden for budget doubles and dorm beds.

Getting There & Away

Dalatrafik bus No 170 runs from Mora to Särna (88 kr, two hours) and further to Idre and Grövelsjön. There are two to four services a day (one only on Saturday).

Norrland

The northern half of Sweden, Norrland, has always been considered separate from the rest of the country. It is associated with forest and dale and the pioneers' struggle to produce the timber and iron ore necessary in the construction of the railways that opened up the region. The development of the Swedish working class here was decisive.

The timber remains, but most heavy mining moved north to Kiruna and Malmberget. The Arctic wilderness attracts walkers, skiers and paddlers.

Inlandsbanan, the railway from Mora to Gällivare via Östersund, Storuman and Arvidsjaur, can be covered today by a combination of railcar and steam train. Getting to the far north from Gävle by train is a night exercise only; when necessary, you can change trains in some comfort at Ånge (open 24 hours a day), but expect two hours wait. Bräcke is the usual change for Östersund. Bus alternatives are limited.

GÄVLE

Gävle is the gateway to Norrland and probably the most pleasant of the northern cities to walk in because of its architecture and

parks; note the contrast between the wooden residences of Villastaden and Gamla Gefle. The pace steps up during the City Fest three-day street festival in mid-August.

Information

The helpful tourist office (☎ 026-14 74 30) is through the courtyard of the Berggrenska gården quarter off Kyrkogatan. The duty pharmacy at Nygatan 31 is not open at night; go to the hospital/medical centre off Västra Vägen. The library is near the castle. The central post office is at Drottninggatan 16 off Stortorget.

The telephone code is ☎ 026.

Things to See & Do

The wooden old town of **Gamla Gefle** south of the city centre shows what Gävle was like before it burned last century. One of the houses, **Joe Hill-gården**, was the birthplace of the US union organiser who was executed on a murder charge in Utah in 1915. Some of Hill's poetry is part of the memorial.

The regional **Länsmuseum** on Södra Strandgatan has an excellent art collection and interesting historical exhibitions (admission 20 kr, students free, closed Monday).

The **Silvanum** forestry museum (free, closed Monday), by the river, features aspects of forestry and conservation and there is a practical demonstration around the parks of **Boulognerskogen** over the footbridge (used for open-air music and summer theatre) and at **Valls Hage** further west.

The oldest of the churches in Gävle is the **Heliga Trefaldighets kyrka** at the west end of Drottninggatan, which has an 11th-century **rune stone** inside. The buildings of the **castle** on the south bank of Gävleån are now in administrative use.

Daily summer boat tours (30 kr one way) to the island of **Limön** can be booked at the tourist office. Limön, part of an archipelago, has a **nature trail** and a mass grave and **memorial** to the sailors of a ship which was lost early last century. The boat departs from Södra Skeppsbron.

Railway buffs or children will not be able to resist the preserved steam locomotives of

Järnvägsmuseet, the national rail museum, two km south of the town centre on Rälsgatan off Österbågen (admission 30 kr, open to 4 pm daily except Monday).

The leisure park and zoo **Furuvik**, about 12 km south-east of Gävle, aims to provide a little of everything; you can behave like a monkey on the loops and minitrains and then see the real thing at the **Gibbon House**. The park is open daily from early May to mid-August to 5 or 6 pm. Check also http://www. furuvik.se. Admission is 85 kr (children 55 kr) in summer and a day token for all rides costs 95 kr.

Places to Stay

The central STF *Gävle hostel* (☎ 62 17 45), at Södra Rådmansgatan 1, is clean and quiet. Beds cost 100 kr, and there's a good kitchen. It is open all year round. The hostel *Engeltofta* (☎ 961 60) is at Bönavägen 118 about six km north-east of the city and open from May to August. Take bus No 15.

The cheapest hotel is *Nya Järnvägshotellet* (☎ 12 09 90) opposite the train station; singles/doubles cost 300/450 kr in summer. *Hotell Gävle* (☎ 11 54 70), at Staketgatan 44, has singles/doubles for 375/575 kr at week-

ends and in summer. *Hotell Boulogne* (☎ 12 63 52) at Byggmästargatan 1 has singles/ doubles at 320/ 450 kr in summer and at weekends.

Hotel Winn (☎ 17 70 00) at Norra Slottsgatan 9 charges 495/700 kr in summer.

Places to Eat

Good lunch packages are available at *Flanör* and *Café Blance* (until 7 pm), diagonally opposite each other on Stortorget. *Café Artist*, in Hotel Winn at Norra Slottsgatan 9, is elegant, more expensive and more subdued. *Kungshallen*, at Norra Kungsgatan 17, is a budget meal option at any time. *Centralcafé* opposite the train station is reasonably priced for solid meals, has a bar and an animated clientele.

Getting There & Away

There are IC or X2000 trains from Stockholm every two hours, via Uppsala. All north-bound trains from Stockholm go via Gävle. There are also useful direct trains from Gävle to Falun and Örebro.

The bus station behind the train station serves big cities. The regional traffic, including Xtåget regional trains, is run by Xtrafik.

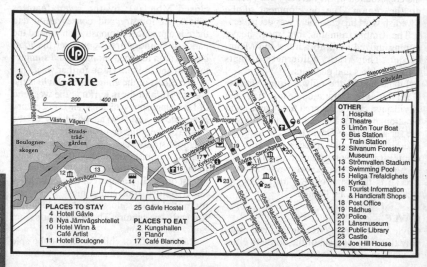

Gävle

OTHER
1 Hospital
3 Theatre
5 Limón Tour Boat
6 Bus Station
7 Train Station
12 Silvanum Forestry Museum
13 Strömvallen Stadium
14 Swimming Pool
15 Heliga Trefaldighets Kyrka
16 Tourist Information & Handicraft Shops
18 Post Office
19 Rådhus
20 Police
21 Länsmuseum
22 Public Library
23 Castle
24 Joe Hill House

PLACES TO STAY
4 Hotell Gävle
8 Nya Järnvägshotellet
10 Hotel Winn & Café Artist
11 Hotell Boulogne
25 Gävle Hostel

PLACES TO EAT
2 Kungshallen
9 Flanör
17 Café Blanche

SWEDEN

Individual tickets cost 13 to 100 kr depending on the distance, daily passes are available for 100 kr.

Getting Around
Bus No 550, or Turistlinjen, runs in summer between some hotels and tourist attractions, including Furuvik. Each ticket costs 13 kr (20 kr to Furuvik).

ÖSTERSUND
This pleasant town on Lake Storsjön is worth a visit for a couple of days and has good budget accommodation. Many of its attractions lie on the adjacent Fröson Island, where there is a winter-sports centre.

The area around Lake Storsjön attracts campers and summer and winter-sports enthusiasts. This area used to be Norwegian and many of the locals maintain an independent spirit. Most importantly, there is a monster in the lake.

Information
The regional tourist office (☎ 063-14 40 01) is opposite the town hall. The budget card *Storsjökortet*, valid for nine days, gives discounts or free entry to activities in the area (100 kr). The post office is at Storgatan 38 and handles currency exchanges until 5 pm. The large public library is opposite the bus station and opens at noon in summer.

The telephone code is ☎ 063.

Things to See & Do
Don't miss **Jamtli**, one km north of the town centre. This museum is the highlight in Östersund, combining lively exhibitions of the regional museum and a large museum village with staff wearing period clothing (60 kr, open daily). The regional museum exhibits the curious **Överhogdal tapestry**, a Viking-age relic that is perhaps the oldest of its kind in Europe.

The city museum **Stadsmuseum** next to the tourist office opens at noon, and the nearby **old church** serves coffee in summer.

Frösön This island is reached by road or footbridge from the middle of Östersund. The island features the animals at **Frösöns djurpark** (open from mid-May to August, 80 kr) and the old **Frösöns kyrka** with its characteristic separate **bell tower**. For skiers there are slalom and nordic runs on the island at Östberget (lift cards cost 200 kr a day). Lake cruises on an old steamship from Östersund cost from 55 to 75 kr (50% off with the Storsjökortet).

Places to Stay & Eat
The cheapest place to stay is the clean and central *STF hostel* (☎ 13 91 00) at Södra Gröngatan 34. Beds in triples cost 100 kr, and there's a kitchen but no utensils or breakfast. Most rooms have a TV.

Also near the centre is *Vandrarhemmet Hjortronet* (☎ 51 24 95) at Köpmangatan 51B with singles/doubles for 200/260 kr. More quaint is *Vandrarhemmet Jamtli* (☎ 10 23 43) in the Jamtli museum precinct, with beds for 160 kr.

Also inexpensive are places like *Nya Pensionatet* (☎ 51 24 98) at Prästgatan 65 or *Pensionat Svea* (☎ 51 29 01) at Storgatan 49.

Most restaurants are on Prästgatan, the main street for pedestrians, including *Volos* at No 38, with daily pizza lunches for 55 kr, and *Lilla Cafét* at No 44, good for sandwich lunches with a drink for 37 kr. The bus station on Gustav III Torg also serves inexpensive meals. The countercultural *Café Tingshuset* on the corner of Rådhusgatan and Samuel Permans Gata is closed in summer.

Getting There & Away
The train station is a short walk from the town centre, but the main regional bus station is central on Gustav III Torg. Trains run direct from Stockholm through Gävle, and some continue to Storlien. Bus No 45 to/from Arvidsjaur stops at both stations, or catch the Inlandsbanan train in summer. The regional Mittlinjen trains shuttle from Sundsvall and Ånge – rail passes apply.

Länstrafiken i Jämtlands län AB runs regional buses and offers some excellent alternatives. A two-day pass costs 180 kr.

From early June to late July, the 30-day *länskort* costs just 360 kr (normal price 520 kr). Bicycles are transported for 30 kr.

Getting Around

Local buses run to the train station and past the main bus station: bus Nos 3 and 4 go to Frösön. Cycling on Frösön is popular.

ÅRE

Downhill skiing tracks six km long await you in this alpine village, and the area's 42 ski lifts offer superb possibilities for winter sports.

Åre has a reputation for being Sweden's top skiing destination, but there are also attractions in summer, including the medieval **church** (open daily) and the popular **Åre kabinbana** that shuttles to the top of Åreskjutan (1274 metres) daily until 4 pm (75 kr).

The tourist office (☎ 0647-177 20) is at the central square.

Places to Stay & Eat

In winter, book accommodation in advance via Årefjällen Resor (☎ 0647-177 00). Ask for budget accommodation in places like *Diplomat Ski Lodge* just opposite the train station. In summer, look for summer bargains, such as *Åre Fjällby* with apartments for 995 kr a week, or *Café Villan* with beds for 165 kr. The nearest *STF hostel* (☎ 0647-301 38) is eight km east of Åre, near Undersåker.

Typical Swedish junk food is available at *Åre Kiosk & Grill* at the central square, but nearby places like *Labands krog* or *Bubblan* have more style. For evening beer, check *Torvtaket* near the tourist office.

Getting There & Away

Regular trains between Stockholm and Storlien, via Östersund, stop at the Åre station. Regional bus No 157 runs from Östersund, and connects Åre to the nearby winter-sports centre of Duved.

STORLIEN & AROUND

The area west of Åre is popular among fell walkers. There is a network of *STF wilderness huts* that charge 130 to 170 kr for HI members (50 kr extra for nonmembers), but reservations are not possible. The main track forms a loop around the mountain range of **Sylarna**.

Trains stop at all stations, including **Ånn** that has a *STF hostel* (☎ 0647-710 70) just opposite the train station, with beds for 100 kr, and a café.

Storlien is the frontier town with a fairly popular downhill skiing station. In summer, beds and rooms are discounted starting from below 100 kr. Storlien is also the terminus for SJ trains – change here for the Norwegian train to Hell and Trondheim.

UMEÅ

Umeå has a large university and a port with ferry connections to Finland. It is the fastest growing town in Sweden, and has a large student population. The tourist information (☎ 090-16 16 16) is at Renmarkstorget 15.

Things to See & Do

Gammlia consist of several museums and should not be missed. The area, one km north-east from the town centre, includes the regional **Västerbottens museum**, the art museum **Bildmuseet**, the **Maritime Museum** and the **Friluftsmuseet** with old houses, and staff wearing period clothes. The museums are open daily in summer (closed Monday in winter), and admission is free to all museums.

Places to Stay

The clean *STF Hostel* (☎ 090-77 16 50) is central at Västra Esplanaden 10. The hostel has a kitchen, and beds cost 100 kr. Hotels are expensive. *Strand Hotel* (☎ 090-12 90 20) at Västra Strandgatan 11 is the cheapest and charges 300/500 kr in summer.

Getting There & Away

Bus The bus station is near the train station. Umeå is the main centre for Länstrafiken Västerbotten, the regional bus network that covers over 55,000 sq km. There are also direct buses to the Norwegian border, with connecting buses to Mo i Rana. There are monthly travel cards available.

Train Only one train daily departs from Umeå. Vännäs is the nearest train station on the main south to north line. All connecting SJ buses (see the timetable at the station) between Umeå and Vännäs accept all train passes.

Boat Ferries to Vasa depart from the harbour at Holmslund – the bus costs 30 kr. There are up to four daily departures in July, one or two at other times.

SKELLEFTEÅ
One of the most pleasant coastal towns in northern Sweden, Skellefteå also has ferry connections to Finland in summer.

The tourist office (☎ 0910-73 60 20) is at Kanalgatan 56. In summer go to the market square for tourist information. The post office and the library are also on Kanalgatan.

The telephone code is ☎ 0910.

Things to See
All attractions are in the parks along the river, west of the town centre. The pleasant walk takes you to the Nordanå park that includes the **Skellefteå museum** (free) and several old houses, some of which contain handicraft shops. West of Nordanå is **Bonnstan**, a unique housing precinct with 400 grey, preserved 17th-century houses – many of them are still inhabited in summer. Further west is the old church and the small island of Kyrkholmen. Cross the river on the **Lejonströmsbron,** Sweden's longest wooden bridge, built in 1737.

Places to Stay & Eat
The *STF Hostel* (☎ 372 83) is two km from the bus station, across the river at Elevhemsgatan 13. The hostel is only open from mid-June to mid-August, and beds cost 100 kr. *Stiftsgården* (☎ 257 00) behind the old church on Brännavägen has an even shorter season in summer, and rooms cost from

155/260 kr – bring your own sheets. *Hotell Stensborg* (☎ 105 51) is central on Vinkelgränd and has rooms from 300/450 kr in summer.

The café at the Åhléns department store has good lunch deals, or check *Spisbaren* near the bus station at Järnvägsgatan 50. The café on the Kyrkholmen island serves waffles.

Getting There & Away
Buses to/from Umeå run almost hourly (every two hours on weekends) and cost 95 kr. The nearest train station is Bastuträsk, and there are three to four connecting buses daily between 6.50 am and 9.30 pm.

Silja Line ferries to the Finnish town of Pietarsaari (Swedish: Jakobstad) depart from the harbour of Skelleftehamn – buses depart from the Skellefteå bus station one hour prior to departure and cost 24 kr. In summer, one-way tickets to Finland cost 150 kr.

LULEÅ
Sweden's fourth busiest airport lies just outside Luleå, the capital of Lappland with over 70,000 inhabitants. The regional **museum** on Köpmangatan is worth a visit just for the Sami section (free, open daily). The 1893 **Cathedral** has mostly modern religious art. Other attractions are outside the centre. **Teknikens Hus** within the technical high school is a hands-on exhibition on technological phenomena (free, open daily except Monday). The most famous sight in Luleå is **Gammelstad**, or the 'Old Town' – catch bus No 32. This was the medieval centre of Lappland; the 15th-century stone church and 425 old church stables remain. This is the biggest of the restored 'church villages' that housed the pioneers on their weekend pilgrimages. The open-air museum **Hägnan** and a nature reserve are nearby.

Storgatan is the main pedestrian mall in Luleå – the tourist office (☎ 0920-29 35 00) is at Storgatan 43B. SAS is opposite the bus station on the corner of Storgatan and Hermelinsgatan.

The telephone code is ☎ 0920.

Places to Stay & Eat

The *STF Hostel* (☎ 523 25) is several km west of Luleå at Örnviksvägen 87, catch bus No 6 and walk 400 metres. Beds cost 100 kr, and there is a kitchen and a restaurant. The cheapest hotel in town is *Park Hotell* (☎ 21 11 49), Kungsgatan 10. *Pensionat Vänggåvan* (☎ 22 92 00) at Älvgatan 3 charges 300/450 kr.

Getting There & Away

Air People under 25 years of age should enquire about casual standby tickets from Stockholm/Arlanda for less than 300 kr – there are buses from Luleå to the airport.

Bus Länstrafiken i Norrbotten AB runs buses in the largest of Sweden's *län* – almost 100,000 sq km or one-fourth of Sweden. Individual tickets cost from 13 to 230 kr, and 30-day tickets cost 1210 kr. Bicycles are transported for a fee of 30 kr. Bus No 60 from Luleå (or No 50 from Boden) to Haparanda (129 km) accepts train passes but the 'E4 train' (a connecting bus service between Luleå and Härnösand train stations) doesn't. The express bus to Skellefteå runs four times daily and costs 103 kr. Bus No 501 to Boden (37 km) runs at least hourly and costs 34 kr. Bus No 354 from Luleå to Arvidsjaur (155 km) is 109 kr.

Train Direct trains from Stockholm and Gothenburg are invariably night trains, or catch an early morning train from Vännäs near Umeå. Most trains from Narvik and Kiruna terminate at Luleå.

HAPARANDA

Haparanda was founded in 1821 as a trading town to replace Sweden's loss of Tornio (see the Finland chapter) to Russia. There are no attractions although the **church** looks exactly like a grain silo in Saskatchewan.

You can walk from Haparanda to the Finnish town of Tornio – compare prices in both towns and shuttle between the two to find the best bargains! Haparanda's helpful tourist office (☎ 0922-615 85) is at the bus station near the customs house. If you're going to Finland, the last chance to withdraw money from a Swedish ATM is at Storgatan 76, the only Bankomat in town.

The telephone code is ☎ 0922.

Places to Stay & Eat

The STF Hostel *Torneälven* (☎ 617 84) at Strandgatan 26 is close to the border post and, unlike the hostel in Tornio, open all year. Beds cost 100 kr, and there is a kitchen and meals.

Nearby, *Resandehem* (☎ 120 68) at Storgatan 65B is a simple guesthouse, with singles/doubles for 150/250 kr. The finest hotel in the region, *Stadshotell* (☎ 614 90), on the market, has doubles from 390 kr.

If you don't fancy grills, *Leilani* at Köpmansgatan 15 serves Chinese food, and *El Paso* at Storgatan 71 has pizza and kebabs. The large Prix supermarket near the bus station also has an eatery, and competitive prices on some foodstuffs.

Getting There & Away

Haparanda has no train services but buses to Boden/Luleå and to Tornio (Finland) are free for train pass holders. See Luleå for price information. Bus No 052 runs along the border to Övertorneå and Pajala via the Kukkolaforsen rapids.

ARVIDSJAUR

Welcome to Lapland. The small settlement of Arvidsjaur on Inlandsbanan was an early Sami market. The **Lappstaden** museum village and Sita Sameland are run by the Sami community and there are almost 100 buildings as well as forestry and reindeer-breeding concerns to visit. Tours of the village cost 25 kr (by request in English, summer only).

The tourist office (☎ 0960-175 00) at Garvaregatan 4 will help you book accommodation.

Lappugglans Turistviste (☎ 0960-124 13) is a private hostel a few minutes from the station (beds 100 kr).

The Gällivare to Östersund bus (No 45) stops at Arvidsjaur. Arvidsjaur is the end station for the Vildmarkståget section of

Inlandsbanan and the railcars take you to Gällivare (full price 175 kr). The steam locomotive-operated *Ångloket* train costs 250 kr in July.

JOKKMOKK

The village of Jokkmokk, reached by Inlandsbanan, is just north of the Arctic Circle and started as a Sami market and mission. The Sami winter fair still takes place early in February, when you can shop seriously for handicrafts *(sámi duodji)*.

Information

The tourist office (☎ 0971-121 40) at Stortorget is open daily from 8 am to 4 pm (to 9 pm in June, July and August). It also has information you need for braving the snows or mountainous interior, although you should see the mountain information room at the Ájtte museum.

The police are on the corner of Storgatan and Klockarvägen. The medical centre (☎ 0971-444 00, after hours ☎ 0971-444 44) is at Lappstavägen 9.

The telephone code is ☎ 0971.

Things to See & Do

The Sami and mountain museum **Ájtte** at Kyrkogatan 3 has authentic handicrafts for sale (they are not cheap) and a restaurant where you can try some local fish or a sandwich with reindeer meat. The information on the wilderness parks is excellent and includes a full set of mountain maps, slides, wildlife information and Sami cultural background (25 kr, open daily in summer, closed Monday from October to April).

A day's research visit is highly recommended if you are planning adventures. A plantation and exhibition on mountain trees is being developed nearby.

The beautiful **wooden church** on Storgatan nearby should be seen; the 'old' church on Hantverkargatan has been rebuilt, as the original was burned in the 18th century.

Places to Stay & Eat

The tourist office will book private rooms in the town from 100 kr. The STF hostel *Åsgården* (☎ 119 77, 010-664 22 99) at Åsgatan 20 is open all year. Beds cost 100 kr, and there's a kitchen. At *Jokkmokks Turistcenter* (☎ 123 70), three km south-east of town, two-bed cabins start at 280 kr, tent sites 60 kr.

The liveliest restaurant is *Restaurang Milano* on Berggatan.

Getting There & Away

Bus No 102 runs to/from Gällivare (74 kr) and connects with SJ trains, No 45 runs to/from Arvidsjaur daily (109 kr). Buses stop at the Klockarvägen bus station and near the museum. The train station is only for railcars using the Inlandsbanan: to meet SJ trains take the bus to Gällivare or the cheaper route, No 254 to Murjek via Vuollerim (two to four times daily).

GÄLLIVARE

The town of Gällivare and its northern twin Malmberget are surrounded by northern wilderness and dwarfed by the bald Dundret hill. Gällivare offers excellent facilities, including inexpensive accommodation and a good library. The region is important for mining and winter sports. The well-equipped tourist office (☎ 0970-166 60) is near the church at Storgatan 16 and is most helpful in organising tours to national parks. Bicycles can be hired for 50 kr a day.

The telephone code is ☎ 0970.

Things to See & Do

Hembygdsmuseum has a cute collection of local artefacts above the tourist office (free, open weekdays). Also located in the tourist office, **Sportfiskemuseum** is a private collection of fishing equipment, open daily in summer (20 kr).

The 1882 **church** is open daily in summer. The **old church** near the train station is from 1755.

The **hembygdsområde** by the camping ground collects pioneer and Sami huts in a small open-air museum.

The top of **Dundret** is a nature reserve and the view is reputed to encompass one-twelfth of Sweden: the midnight sun is from early in

June to mid-July. Ski-gear hire starts at 150 kr a day for downhill; day lift tickets are 130 kr. There are 10 runs of varying difficulty and four nordic courses. Hire of nordic gear is 100 kr a day. Halfway to the top, **Vägvisaren** exhibits Sami traditions, and has reindeer (open daily from late June to late August).

In Malmberget, a few km north of Gällivare, the **Kåkstan** is a historical 'Ghost Town' museum village, open daily from mid-June to mid-August. Also of interest is **Gruvmuseum**, covering 250 years of mining. Local buses to Malmberget depart from opposite the Gällivare church.

Places to Stay & Eat

Gällivare has some of the best budget accommodation in Sweden – just bring your own sheets. You can camp near the Vassara älv at *Gällivare Camping* (☎ 165 45) from June to August (tents 75 kr, cabins from 380 kr).

The *STF hostel* (☎ 143 80) is across the footbridges from the railway station and is open all year. Beds cost just 70 kr in large dorms, or 100 kr in smaller ones. There is a sauna, and breakfast is served for 45 kr. South of the hostel near the railway line is *Lapphärbärget* (☎ 125 34), with dorm beds for 100 kr, a kitchen and a pleasant TV room.

For other cheap accommodation, go to the museum (☎ 153 75) above the tourist office to book: *Lokstallarna* near the train station has dorm beds from 80 kr and doubles for 300 kr, and the *hembygdsområde* (see Things to See) has doubles/quads from 250/350 kr, and plain Sami *kåta* hut bunks are a steal at 40 kr each. *Hotell Dundret* (☎ 550 40), on the corner of Per Högströmsgatan and Tingshusgatan, has weekend and summer singles/doubles for 250/330 kr.

MD:s Grill near the tourist office is the place for solid, cheap fare, but for atmosphere and cake go to *Centralskolans café* under the tourist office or *Strandcaféet* (summer only) near the camping ground.

Getting There & Away

Skyways (JZ) flies direct to the airport (seven km from the town) from Stockholm.

Länstrafik i Norrbotten regional buses depart from the train station: No 45 runs daily to/from Östersund, No 103 serves Ritsem (see Abisko & Kungsleden) and No 101 Kiruna (both twice daily) and No 102 Jokkmokk (68 kr, five times a day on weekdays and once a day on weekends).

SJ trains come from Luleå and from Stockholm (sometimes changing at Boden), and from Narvik in Norway. More exotic is the Inlandsbanan which terminates at Gällivare: Rälsbussen from Arvidsjaur costs 175 kr, the steam train is 250 kr – train passes give 50% discount.

KIRUNA

The windy hilltop Kiruna must be the ugliest town in Sweden unless you like the view of black mountains of mining residue.

Kiruna is the northernmost town in Sweden, and at 19,446 sq km, the largest kommun in the country. The area includes Sweden's highest peak, Kebnekaise (2111 metres), and several fine national parks and trekking routes. This makes Kiruna an excellent base for wilderness tours. The midnight sun lasts from the end of May to mid-July and there is a bluish darkness throughout December and New Year. Many people speak Finnish; Samis are a small minority.

The tourist information centre (☎ 0980-188 80) is next to the landmark Scandic Hotel at Lars Janssonsgatan 17. The library is behind the bus station.

The telephone code is ☎ 0980.

Things to See & Do

The highlight is the bus tour to the bowels of the **LKAB iron ore mine**, 350 metres underground. These tours depart from the tourist office daily in summer from 10 am to 4 pm and cost 90 kr. The **Kiruna church** in the town centre looks like a Norwegian stave church. It's particularly pretty against a snowy backdrop.

The space base **Esrange**, almost 40 km away (tours from Monday to Friday, 120 kr), researches **northern lights** (*norrsken*), a greenish midwinter heavenly light show caused by particle collisions in the atmosphere. If you miss the lights there is an all-year slide show in the tourist centre (20 kr).

Places to Stay & Eat

The **STF hostel** (☎ 171 95) at Skyttegatan 16a, open from mid-June to mid-August, charges 100 kr per bed in small rooms that can't really be darkened. The budget hotel **Kiruna** (☎ 137 50) at Bergmästaregatan 7, and its annexe **Yellow House** at Hantverkaregatan 25, has dorm beds costing 150 kr and doubles from 300 kr.

A special place to stay is **Samegården** (☎ 170 29) at Brytaregatan 14, a Sami cultural centre that includes a small museum. Spotless rooms cost 285/410 kr, but come before 4 pm.

Svarta Björn, the popular eatery at the bus station on Hjalmar Lundbohmsvägen opposite the town hall, opens early in the morning. Most restaurants in the town centre offer good-value lunch deals but ordinary menu prices are more expensive.

Getting There & Away

There are daily, nonstop SAS flights from Luleå and Stockholm to the airfield about 10 km east of the town. Regular trains connect Kiruna with Luleå, Stockholm and Narvik (Norway).

Regional buses serve all major settlements around Norrbotten, including bus No 002 to Karesuando (bridge to Finland) and No 004 to Nikkaluokta for Kebnekaise treks. If you don't fancy the scenic train ride, bus Nos 001 and 95 run to Riksgränsen.

JUKKASJÄRVI

Every winter, a real igloo by the name Arctic Hall opens as a hotel, theatre and pub in this small town, seven km from the main road just south-east of Kiruna. There are regular buses from Kiruna.

ABISKO & KUNGSLEDEN

The 75-sq-km Abisko National Park is on the southern shore of the scenic Lake Torneträsk and is well served by trains, buses and a mountain highway between Kiruna to Narvik. It is the soft option of the northern

parks; less rugged and more accessible. The popular trail follows the Abiskojåkka valley and day trips of 10 or 20 km are no problem from Abisko. Information and free film shows are available at the **Naturum**, next to the provisions shop (both open daily). For 50 kr, the **Linbana** chair lift takes you to the top of Njulla fell (1169 metres), that has a café open until 3 pm.

The 500-km Kungsleden trekking route leads south from Abisko and offers diversions to the summit of **Kebnekaise** or the magical national park of **Sarek** (no huts and few bridges). Waterproof boots are essential at any time of the year: the thaw is in May and June. July, August and September are recommended months for hiking although in July there is some boggy ground, which attracts the mosquitoes. It can still be cold, despite the midnight sun. Winter escapades are too risky for the uninitiated because of the threat of avalanche.

A good alternative to the Kungsleden trail is a trek to **Sjangeli** which was an unsuccessful mine in the 17th century. These days it's a wilderness centre run by Samis, south-west from Abisko. Sjangeli can be reached from either Abisko or Riksgränsen, and a loop between these two stations is 70 km.

Good information is available at the tourist offices. Fill out the sheets and books (*färdmeddelande*) provided at mountain huts with your details as you go. The range of 1:100,000 *Fjällkartor* maps usually costs 79 kr each. Tours are organised by STF, which maintains huts and several big mountain stations with excellent facilities and services. Various types of phones are installed in or near mountain huts and hikers are urged to use them to check weather trail conditions.

Places to Stay

Abisko Fjällstation (☎ 0980-402 00), open from mid-February to mid-September, offers beds from 220 kr (170 kr for HI members) and singles/doubles for 350/580 kr. Trekking gear can be hired here, and there are lunches for 65 kr.

Huts along Kungsleden are spread at 10 to

20 km intervals between Abisko and Kvikk-jokk, and charge 130 to 170 kr for HI members (50 kr extra for nonmembers), but reservations are not possible. An entry charge during daytime is 20 kr. You need a sleeping bag only as there are blankets and gas inside. The 100-km trek from Abisko to Nikkaluokta runs via the mountain hostel **Kebnekaise Fjällstation** (beds from 220 kr). It's 130 km from Abisko to the Vakkotavare wilderness hut, or a little over 200 km to **Kvikkjokks Fjällstation**, which has beds from 195 kr.

Getting There & Away

Apart from SJ trains (get off at Abisko Turiststation) there are bus Nos 001 and 95 from Kiruna. Nikkaluokta is served twice daily by bus 004 from Kiruna. Bus No 103 runs between Gällivare and Ritsem via Saltoluokta Fjällstation and the Vakkotavare hut twice daily. Kvikkjokk is served by bus No 253 that runs twice daily from the Murjek SJ train station via Jokkmokk. You can send on extra luggage with bus drivers to an agreed destination for 50 kr.

RIKSGRÄNSEN

The best midnight (or daytime) skiing in June in Scandinavia awaits you at this rugged frontier area (Riksgränsen translates as 'National Border'). You can briefly visit Norway at full speed on downhill skis! Daily rental of slalom gear costs 205 kr per day, and a full-day lift pass is 190 kr, less for a half-day. Don't miss the mountain photographs by Sven Hörnell in his gallery (free, daily slide show costs 40 kr).

Accommodation at **Riksgränsen** (☎ 0980-400 80) is expensive at 590 kr per person (or 900 kr for triples) but summer prices (from late June) start from 390 kr per person.

Getting There & Away

Riksgränsen is the last train station in Sweden before the train rushes through tunnels and mountain scenery back to sea level at Narvik in Norway. Two bus lines and two to three daily trains connect Riksgränsen to Kiruna.

The historical 'Navvy Trail' follows the railroad line and will take you back to Abisko.

Appendix I – Alternative Place Names

The following abbreviations are used:

(D) Danish
(E) English
(Est) Estonian
(F) Finnish
(Far) Faroese
(G) German
(Lat) Latvian
(Lit) Lithuanian
(N) Norwegian
(P) Polish
(R) Russian
(S) Swedish

DENMARK
Danmark

Copenhagen (E) – København (D), Kööpenhamina (F), Köpenhamn (S)
Helsingør (D) – Elsinore (E)
Jutland (E) – Jylland (D)
Funen (E) – Fyn (D)
Zealand (E) – Sjælland (D), occasionally Sealand (E)

ESTONIA
Eesti

Tallinn (Est) – Talinas (Lit), formerly Reval or Revel
Tartu (Est) – Tartto (F)
Saaremaa (Est) – Ösel (S)

FAROE ISLANDS
Færoe Islands (E), Færøerne (D), Føroyar (Far)

FINLAND
Suomi

Åland (S) – Ahvenanmaa (F), formerly Åbo (S)
Hämeenlinna (F) – Tavastehus (S)
Haparanta (F) – Haparanda (S)
Helsinki (F) – Helsingfors (S)
Kokkola (F) – Karleby (S)
Lappeenranta (F) – Villmanstrand (S)
Lapland (E) – Lappi (F), Lappland (S)
Naantali (F) – Nådendal (S)
Oulu (F) – Uleåborg (S)
Pietarsaari (F) – Jakobstad (S)
Tampere (F) – Tammerfors (S)
Tornio (F) – Torneå (S)
Tornionjoki (F) – Tornealv (S)
Turku (F) – Åbo (S)
Vaasa (F) – Vasa (S)

ICELAND
Ísland

LATVIA
Latvija

Cesis (Lat) – formerly Wenden (G)
Kurzeme (Lat) – formerly Courland (E), Kurland (G)
Riga (E) – Rīga (Lat), Riika (F)
Sigulda (Lat) – formerly Segewold (G)

LITHUANIA
Lietuva

Kaunas (Lat) – Kowno (P)
Klaipėda (Lit) – formerly Memel (G)
Juodkrante (Lit) – formerly Schwarzort (G)
Nida (Lit) – formerly Nidden (G)
Vilnius – Wilno (P)

NORWAY
Norge

Kirkenes (N) – Kirkkoniemi (F)
Lofoten (N) – Lofootit (F)
North Cape (E) – Nordkapp (N)
Tromsø (N) – Tromsö (S), Tromssa (F)
Vardø (N) – Vuoreija (F)

RUSSIA
Rossiya

Belorussia (E) – Belarus (R)
Kaliningrad (R) – formerly Königsberg (G)
Kiev – Kijevas (Lit)
Moscow (E) – Moskva (R,S), Moskova (F)
St Petersburg – Pietari (F), formerly Leningrad (R)
Vyborg (R) – Viipuri (F)
Zelenogradsk (R) – Cranz (G)

SWEDEN
Sverige

Gothenburg (E) – Göteberg (S)
Haparanda (S) – Haaparanta (F)
Stockholm (S) – Tukholma (F)

MISCELLANEOUS
Lübeck (G) – Lyypekki (F)
Warsaw (E) – Varsova (F)

Appendix II – European Organisations

	Council of Europe	EU	EFTA	NATO	Nordic Council	OECD	WEU
Albania	✓	–	–	–	–	–	–
Andorra	✓	–	–	–	–	–	–
Austria	✓	✓	–	–	–	✓	–
Belgium	✓	✓	–	✓	–	✓	✓
Bulgaria	✓	–	–	–	–	–	–
Croatia	•	–	–	–	–	–	–
Cyprus	✓	–	–	–	–	–	–
Czech Republic	✓	–	–	–	–	✓	–
Denmark	✓	✓	–	✓	✓	✓	–
Estonia	✓	–	–	–	–	–	–
Finland	✓	✓	–	–	✓	✓	–
France	✓	✓	–	✓	–	✓	–
Germany	✓	✓	–	✓	–	✓	✓
Greece	✓	✓	–	✓	–	✓	✓
Hungary	✓	–	–	–	–	✓	–
Iceland	✓	–	✓	✓	✓	✓	–
Ireland	✓	✓	–	–	–	✓	–
Italy	✓	✓	–	✓	–	✓	✓
Latvia	✓	–	–	–	–	–	–
Lithuania	✓	–	–	–	–	–	–
Luxembourg	✓	✓	–	✓	–	✓	✓
Macedonia	✓	–	–	–	–	–	–
Malta	✓	–	–	–	–	–	–
Netherlands	✓	✓	–	✓	–	✓	✓
Norway	✓	–	✓	✓	✓	✓	–
Poland	✓	–	–	–	–	–	–
Portugal	✓	✓	–	✓	–	✓	✓
Romania	✓	–	–	–	–	–	–
Slovakia	✓	–	–	–	–	–	–
Slovenia	✓	–	–	–	–	–	–
Spain	✓	✓	–	✓	–	✓	✓
Sweden	✓	✓	–	–	✓	✓	–
Switerland	✓	–	✓	–	–	✓	–
Turkey	✓	–	–	✓	–	✓	–
UK	✓	✓	–	✓	–	✓	✓
Yugoslavia	–	–	–	–	–	✓	–

✓ – full memeber
• – special guest status

Council of Europe

Established in 1949, the Council of Europe is the oldest of Europe's political institutions. It aims to promote European unity, protect human rights, and assist in the cultural, social and economic development of its member states, but its powers are purely advisory. Founding states were Belgium, Denmark, France, Ireland, Italy, Luxembourg, the Netherlands, Norway, Sweden and the UK. Its headquarters are in Strasbourg.

European Union (EU)

Founded by the Treaty of Rome in 1957, the European Economic Community, or Common Market as it used to be known, broadened its scope far beyond economic measures as it developed into the European Community and finally the European Union. Its original aims were to develop and expand the economies of its member states by abolishing customs tariffs, coordinating transportation systems and general economic policies, establishing a common economic policy towards nonmember states, and promoting the free movement of labour and capital within its borders. Further measures included the abolishment of border controls and the linking of currency exchange rates. Since the Maastricht treaty of December 1991, the EU is committed to establishing a common foreign and security policy, close cooperation in home affairs and the judiciary, and a single European currency to be called the euro. The EEC's founding states were Belgium, France, West Germany, Italy, Luxembourg and the Netherlands – the Treaty of Rome was an extension of the European Coal and Steel Community (ECSC) founded by these six states in 1952. Denmark, Ireland and the UK joined in 1973, Greece in 1981, Spain and Portugal in 1986 and Austria, Finland and Sweden in 1995. The main EU organisations are the European Parliament (elected by direct universal suffrage, with growing powers), the European Commission (the daily 'government'), the Council of Ministers (ministers of member states who make the important decisions) and the Court of Justice. The European Parliament meets in Strasbourg; Luxembourg is home to the Court of Justice. Other EU organisations are based in Brussels.

European Free Trade Association (EFTA)

Established in 1960 as a response to the creation of the European Economic Community, EFTA aims to eliminate trade tariffs on industrial products between member states, though each member retains the right to its own commercial policy towards nonmembers. Most members cooperate with the EU through the European Economic Area agreement. Denmark and the UK left EFTA to join the EU in 1973 and others have since followed suit, leaving EFTA's future in doubt. Its headquarters are in Geneva.

North Atlantic Treaty Organisation (NATO)

The document creating this defence alliance was signed in 1949 by the USA, Canada and 10 European countries to safeguard their common political, social and economic systems against external threats (read: against the powerful Soviet military presence in Europe after WW II). An attack against any member state would be considered an attack against them all. Greece and Turkey joined in 1952, West Germany in 1955, and Spain in 1982; France withdrew from NATO's integrated military command in 1966 and Greece did likewise in 1974, though both remain members. NATO's Soviet counterpart, the Warsaw Pact founded in 1955, collapsed with the democratic revolutions of 1989 and the subsequent disintegration of the Soviet Union; most of its former members are now NATO associates in the 'Partnership for Peace' programme. NATO's headquarters are in Brussels.

Nordic Council

Established in Copenhagen in 1953, the Nordic Council aims to promote economic, social and cultural cooperation among its member states (Denmark, Finland, Iceland, Norway and Sweden). Since 1971, the Council has acted as an advisory body to the Nordic Council of Ministers, a meeting of ministers from the member states responsible for the subject under discussion. Decisions taken by the Council of Ministers are usually binding, though member states retain full sovereignty. Environmental, tariff, labour and immigration policies are often coordinated.

Organisation for Economic Cooperation and Development (OECD)

The OECD was set up in 1961 to supersede the Organisation for European Economic Cooperation, which allocated US aid under the Marshall Plan and coordinated the reconstruction of postwar Europe. Sometimes seen as the club of the world's rich countries, the OECD aims to encourage economic growth and world trade. Its member states include most of Europe, as well as Australia, Canada, Japan, Mexico, New Zealand and the USA. Its headquarters are in Paris.

Western European Union (WEU)

Set up in 1955, the WEU was designed to coordinate the military defences between member states, to promote economic, social and cultural cooperation, and to encourage European integration. Social and cultural tasks were transferred to the Council of Europe in 1960, and these days the WEU is sometimes touted as a future, more 'European', alternative to NATO. Its headquarters are in Brussels.

Appendix III – Telephones

Dial Direct

You can dial directly from public telephone boxes from almost anywhere in Europe to almost anywhere in the world. This is usually cheaper than going through the operator. In much of Europe, public telephones accepting phonecards are becoming the norm and in some countries coin-operated phones are increasingly difficult to find.

To call abroad you simply dial the international access code (IAC) for the country you are calling from (most commonly 00 in Europe but see the following table), the country code (CC) for the country you are calling, the local area code (usually dropping the leading zero if there is one) and then the number. If, for example, you are in Italy (international access code 00) and want to make a call to the USA (country code 1), San Francisco (area code 212), number ☎ 123 4567, then you dial ☎ 00-1-212-123 4567. To call from the UK (00) to Australia (61), Sydney (02), number ☎ 123 4567, you dial ☎ 00-61-2-123 4567.

Home Direct

If you would rather have somebody else pay for the call, you can, from many countries, dial directly to your home country operator and then reverse charges; you can also charge the call to a phone company credit card. To do this, simply dial the relevant 'home direct' number to be connected to your own operator. For the USA there's a choice of AT&T, MCI or Sprint Global One home direct services. Home direct numbers vary from country to country – check with your telephone company before you leave, or with the international operator in the country you're ringing from. Remember that from phone boxes in some countries you may need a coin or local phonecard to be connected with the relevant home direct operator.

In some places (particularly airports), you may find dedicated home direct phones where you simply press the button labelled USA, Australia, Hong Kong or whatever for direct connection to the operator. Note that the home direct service does not operate to and from all countries, and that the call could be charged at operator rates, which makes it quite expensive for the person who's paying. In general placing a call on your phone credit card is much more expensive than paying the local tariff.

Dialling Tones

In some countries (eg France, Hungary), after you've dialled the international access code, you have to wait for a second dial tone before proceeding with the code for your target country and the number. Often the same applies when you ring from one city to another within these countries: wait for a dialling tone after you've dialled the area code for your target city. If you're not sure what to do, simply wait three or four seconds after dialling a code – if nothing happens, you can probably keep dialling.

Phonecards

In major locations you may find phones which accept credit cards: simply swipe your card through the slot and the call is charged to the card, though rates can be very high. Phone company credit cards can be used to charge calls via your home country operator.

Stored-value phonecards are now almost standard all over Europe. You usually buy a card from a post office, telephone centre, newsstand or retail outlet and simply insert the card into the phone each time you make a call. The card solves the problem of finding the correct coins for calls (or lots of correct coins for international calls) and generally gives you a small discount.

Call Costs

Avoid ringing from a hotel room unless you really don't care what it's going to cost. The cost of making an international call varies widely from one country to another. A US$10 call from Britain could cost you US$30 from Spain. Choosing where you call from can make a big difference to your budget. The countries in the table are rated from * (cheap) to *** (expensive). Reduced rates are available at certain times (usually from mid-evening to early morning), though these vary from country to country and should make little difference to relative costs – check the local phone book or ask the operator.

Telephone Codes

	CC	cost (see text)	IAC	IO
Albania	355			
Andorra	376	***	00	821111
Austria	43	**	00	09
Belgium	32	***	00	1224 (private phone)
				1223 (public phone)
Belarus	375		8(w)10	
Bulgaria	359	**	00	
Croatia	385	***	99	901
Cyprus	357	***	00	
Cyprus (Turkish)	905		00	
Czech Republic	42	***	00	0131
Denmark	45	**	00	141
Estonia	372	***	8(w)00	007
Finland	358	*	990	020222
France	33	**	00(w)	12
Germany	49	**	00	00118
Gibraltar	350	***	00	100
Greece	30	*	00	161
Hungary	36	*	00(w)	09
Iceland	354		90	09
Ireland	353	*	00	114
Italy	39	***	00	15
Latvia	371	***	00	115
Liechtenstein	41 75	***	00	114
Lithuania	370	***	8(w)10 8(w)	194/195
Luxembourg	352	**	00	0010
Macedonia	389		99	
Malta	356	**	00	194
Morocco	212	***	00(w)	12
Netherlands	31	***	00	060410
Norway	47	*	095	181
Poland	48	**	0(w)0	901
Portugal	351	**	00	099
Romania			40	071
Russia	7		8(w)10	
Slovakia	42	**	00	0131
Slovenia	386	**	00	901
Spain	34	***	07(w)	91389
Sweden	46	**	009(w)	0018
Switzerland	41	***	00	114
Tunisia	216	***	00	
Turkey	90	**	00	115
UK	44	*	00	155
Yugoslavia	381	**	99	901

CC – Country Code (to call *into* that country)
IAC – International Access Code (to call abroad *from* that country)
IO – International Operator (to make enquiries)
(w) – wait for dialling tone
Other country codes include: Australia 61, Canada 1, Hong Kong 852, India 91, Indonesia 62, Israel 972, Japan 81, Macau 853, Malaysia 60, New Zealand 64, Singapore 65, South Africa 27, Thailand 66, USA 1

Appendix IV – International Country Abbreviations

The following is a list of official country (and other) abbreviations that you may encounter on motor vehicles in Europe. Other abbreviations are likely to be unofficial ones, often referring to a particular region, province or even city. A vehicle entering a foreign country must carry a sticker identifying its country of registration, though this rule is not always enforced.

A	–	Austria
AL	–	Albania
AND	–	Andorra
AUS	–	Australia
B	–	Belgium
BG	–	Bulgaria
BIH	–	Bosnia-Hercegovina
BY	–	Belarus
CC	–	Consular Corps
CD	–	Diplomatic Corps
CDN	–	Canada
CH	–	Switzerland
CY	–	Cyprus
CZ	–	Czech Republic
D	–	Germany
DK	–	Denmark
DZ	–	Algeria
E	–	Spain
EST	–	Estonia
ET	–	Egypt
F	–	France
FIN	–	Finland
FL	–	Liechtenstein
FR	–	Faroe Islands
GB	–	Great Britain
GBA	–	Alderney
GBG	–	Guernsey
GBJ	–	Jersey
GBM	–	Isle of Man
GBZ	–	Gibraltar
GE	–	Georgia
GR	–	Greece
H	–	Hungary
HKJ	–	Jordan
HR	–	Croatia
I	–	Italy
IL	–	Israel
IRL	–	Ireland
IS	–	Iceland
L	–	Luxembourg
LAR	–	Libya
LT	–	Lithuania
LV	–	Latvia
M	–	Malta
MA	–	Morocco
MC	–	Monaco
MD	–	Moldavia
MK	–	Macedonia
N	–	Norway
NL	–	Netherlands
NZ	–	New Zealand
P	–	Portugal
PL	–	Poland
RL	–	Lebanon
RO	–	Romania
RSM	–	San Marino
RUS	–	Russia
S	–	Sweden
SK	–	Slovakia
SLO	–	Slovenia
SYR	–	Syria
TN	–	Tunisia
TR	–	Turkey
UA	–	Ukraine
USA	–	United States of America
V	–	Vatican City
WAN	–	Nigeria
YU	–	Yugoslavia
ZA	–	South Africa

Appendix V – Climate Charts

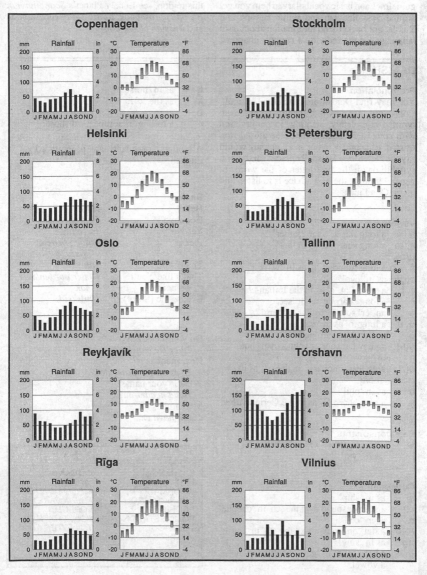

Language Guide

This Language Guide contains pronunciation guidelines and basic vocabulary to help you get around Scandinavian and Baltic Europe and Russia. For background information about each language see the individual country chapters.

For a more detailed treatment of languages in this region, see Lonely Planet's *Scandinavian Europe phrasebook*, *Baltic States phrasebook* and *Russian phrasebook*.

DANISH

Pronunciation

You may find Danish pronunciation difficult. Consonants are drawled, swallowed and even omitted completely, creating, in conjunction with vowels, the peculiarity of the glottal stop or *stød*. Its sound is rather as a Cockney would say 'bottle'. Stress is usually placed on the first syllable or on the first letter of the word. In general though, the best advice is to listen and learn. Good luck.

Vowels

a	a long flat 'a' as in 'father'
a, æ	a long sharp 'a' as in 'act'
u(n),	
å & o	a long rounded 'a' as in 'walk'
e(g)	as in 'eye'
e, i	a short flat 'e' as in the Italian *che*
i	a long sharp 'e' as in 'see'
ø	an 'er' sound similar to 'fern'
o, u	a long 'o' as in 'zoo'
o	a short 'o' as in 'pot'
o(v)	somewhat shorter sound than 'out' or 'vow'
o(r)	with less emphasis on the 'r', as in 'more'
u	as in 'pull'
y	a long sharp 'u' as in the German *über*

Semiconsonants

w	similar to the 'wh' in 'what'
j	as in 'yet'

Consonants

sj	as in 'ship'
ch	a sharper sound than the 'ch' in 'cheque'
c	as in 'cell'
(o)d	a flat 'dh' sound, like the 'th' in 'these'
ng	as in 'sing'
g	a hard 'g' as in 'get', if followed by a vowel
h	as in 'horse'
k	as the 'c' in 'cat'
b	as in 'box'
r	a rolling 'r' abruptly cut short

All other consonants are pronounced as in English.

Basics

Hello	*Hallo*
Goodbye	*Farvel*
Yes/No	*Ja/Nej*
Please	*Må jeg bede* or *Værsgo*
Thank you	*Tak*
That's fine/You're welcome	*Det er i orden/Selv tak*
Excuse me (Sorry)	*Undskyld*

Do you speak English?
 Taler De engelsk?
How much is it?
 Hvor meget koster det?
What is your name?
 Hvad hedder du?
My name is ...
 Mit navn er...

Signs

ENTRANCE	*INDGANG*
EXIT	*UDGANG*
INFORMATION	*INFORMATION*
OPEN/CLOSED	*ÅBEN/LUKKET*
PROHIBITED	*FORBUDT*
POLICE STATION	*POLITISTATION*
TOILETS	*TOILETTER*
(MEN'S/WOMEN'S)	*(HERRER/ DAMER)*

Getting Around

What time does ... leave/arrive?
Hvornår går/ankommer...?

the boat	*båden*
the bus (city)	*bussen*
the bus (intercity)	*rutebilen*
the tram	*sporvognen*
the train	*toget*

Where can I hire a car/bicycle?
Hvor kan jeg leje en bil/cykel?
I would like ...
Jeg vil gerne have ...

a one-way ticket	*en enkeltbillet*
a return ticket	*en tur-retur billet*
1st class/2nd class	*første klasse/ anden klasse*
left luggage office	*reisegodsoppbevar in gen*
timetable	*køreplan*
bus/tram stop	*bus/sporvogn hold- eplads*
train station/ ferry terminal	*jernbanestation (banegård)/ ferjeleiet*

Where is...? *Hvor er...?*
far/near *fjern/nær*
Go straight ahead. *Gå ligefrem.*
Turn left/right. *Drej venstre/til højre.*

Around Town

bank	*bank*
...embassy	*...ambassade*
my hotel	*mit hotel*
post office	*postkontoret*
market	*markedet*
chemist/pharmacy	*apotek*
newsagency	*aviskiosk*
telephone centre	*telefoncentralen*
tourist office	*turistinformatione*

What time does it open/close?
Hvornår åbner/lukker det?

Accommodation

hotel	*hotel*
guesthouse	*gæstgiveri*
hostel	*vandrerhjem*
camping ground	*campingplads*

Do you have any rooms available?
Har I ledige værelser?

I would like...
Jeg ønsker...

a single room	*et enkeltværelse*
a double room	*et dobbeltværelse*
one day/two days	*en nat/to nætter*

How much is it per night/per person?
Hvor meget koster det per nat/per person?
Does it include breakfast?
Er morgenmad inkluderet?

Time, Days & Numbers

What time is it?
Hvad er klokken?

today	*i dag*
tomorrow	*i morgen*
yesterday	*i går*
morning/afternoon	*morgenen/efter- middagen*

Monday	*mandag*
Tuesday	*tirsdag*
Wednesday	*onsdag*
Thursday	*torsdag*
Friday	*fredag*
Saturday	*lørdag*
Sunday	*søndag*

0	*nul*
1	*en*
2	*to*
3	*tre*
4	*fire*
5	*fem*
6	*seks*
7	*syv*
8	*otte*
9	*ni*
10	*ti*
100	*hundrede*
1000	*tusind*
one million	*en million*

Emergencies

Help!	*Hjælp!*
Call a doctor!	*Ring efter en læge!*
Call the police!	*Ring efter politiet!*
Go away!	*Forsvind!*
I'm lost.	*Jeg har gået vild.*

ESTONIAN

Pronunciation

Estonian follows a phonetic alphabet where each letter has only one distinct unmodifiable sound. The following sounds are specific to Estonian:

ä	like the 'a' in 'cat'
õ	like the 'oo' in 'cook'
ö	like the 'u' in 'fur' but with rounded lips
ü	like the 'u' as in the French 'tu'
j	like the 'y' in 'yes'

When a vowel is doubled its sound is lengthened, for example *pit* or *pod* would have the same pronunciations as in English but *piit* would be pronounced as the English peat and *pood* would rhyme with 'toad'.

Basics

Hello	*Tere*
Goodbye	*Nägemist*
Yes/No	*Ja/Ei*
Please	*Palun*
Thank you	*Tänan* or *Aitäh*
You're welcome	*Palun*
Excuse me (Sorry)	*Vabandage*

Do you speak English?
Kas te räägite inglise keelt?
How much does it cost?
Kui palju see maksab?
What is your name?
Kas ma tohin küsida teie nime?
My name is ...
Minu nimi on ...

Signs

ENTRANCE	*SISSEPÄÄS*
EXIT	*VÄLJAPÄÄS*
FULL/NO VACANCIES	*KOHAD KINI*
INFORMATION	*INFORMATSIOON*
OPEN/CLOSED	*AVATUD/SULETUD*
POLICE STATION	*POLITSEI-JAOSKOND*
ROOMS AVAILABLE	*ON VABU KOHTI*
TOILETS (MEN'S/WOMEN'S)	*TUALETT (WC) (MEESTELE/NAISTELE)*

Getting Around

What time does the ... leave/arrive?
Mis kell lähels/saabub ...?

the boat	*paat*
the bus	*buss*
the tram	*tramm*
the train	*rong*

Where can I hire a car/bicycle?
Kust ma saan laenutada auto/jalgratas?
Please (give me a) one-way/return ticket.
Palun üks/edasi-tagasi pilet.

left luggage	*pagasi hoiuruum*
timetable	*sõiduplaan*
bus station	*bussijaam*
train station/ ferry terminal	*rongijaam/ sadam*

Where is the ...?	*Kus on ...?*
Is it far/near?	*Kas see on kaugel/lähedal?*
Go straight ahead.	*Otse.*
Go left/right.	*Vasakule./Paremale.*

Around Town

bank	*pank*
... embassy	*... saatkond*
my hotel	*minu hotell*
post office	*postkontor*
market	*turg*
chemist/pharmacy	*apteek*
public telephone	*telefon*
the tourist office	*turismibüroo*

What time does it open/close?
Mis kell see avatakse/suletakse?

Accommodation

hotel	*hotelli*
youth hostel	*noorte hotell*
camping ground	*telkimis plats*

Do you have any rooms available?
Kas teil kohti on?
I would like a ...
Ma tahaksin ... tuba.

single room	*ühe voodiga*
double room	*kahe voodiga*
one/two days	*üheks/kaheks päevaks*

How much is it per night/person?
Kui palju maksab ööpäev/voodikoht?
Does it include breakfast?
Kas hommikusöök on hinna sees?

Time, Days & Numbers
What time is it?
Mis kell on?

today	*täna*
tomorrow	*homme*
yesterday	*eile*
morning/evening	*hommikul/õhtul*

Monday	*esmaspäev*
Tuesday	*teisipäev*
Wednesday	*kolmapäev*
Thursday	*neljapäev*
Friday	*reede*
Saturday	*laupäev*
Sunday	*pühapäev*

1	*üks*
2	*kaks*
3	*kolm*
4	*neli*
5	*viis*
6	*kuus*
7	*seitse*
8	*kaheksa*
9	*üheksa*
10	*kümme*
100	*sada*
1000	*tuhat*
one million	*üks miljon*

Emergencies

Help!	*Appi!*
Call a doctor!	*Kutsuge arst!*
Call the police!	*Helistage politseile!*
Go away!	*Minge ära!*
I'm lost.	*Ma olen eksinud.*

FAROESE

Pronunciation
In most cases, Faroese words are stressed on the first syllable. Grammar is very similar to that of Icelandic, but pronunciation is quite different due to a mix of Icelandic, Danish, and even Gaelic influences; eg the name of Eiði village is inexplicably pronounced 'OY-yeh'. The nearby village of Gjógv is referred to as 'Jagv'. The capital, Tórshavn, gets the more or less Danish pronunciation, 'TORSH-hown'.

Everyone speaks Danish, can handle Norwegian and Swedish, and some speak English.

Basics

Hello	*Hey, Hallo, Góðan dag*
Goodbye	*Farvæl*
Please	*Ger so vael*
Thank you	*Takk fyri*
Excuse me (Sorry)	*Orsaka*

Do you speak English?
Tosar tú enskt?

Some Useful Words

youth hostel	*ferðamannaheim*
bird cliffs	*fuglaberg*
coast	*strond*
harbour	*havn*
island	*oy* or *oyggj*
bread	*breyð*
milk	*mjólk*
sugar	*sukur*
fish	*fiskur*

Time, Days & Numbers
What time is it?
Hvat er klokkan?

Monday	*mánadagur*
Tuesday	*týsdagur*
Wednesday	*mikudagur*
Thursday	*hósdagur*
Friday	*fríggjadagur*
Saturday	*leygardagur*
Sunday	*sunnudagur*

1	*eitt*
2	*tvey*
3	*trý*
4	*fýra*
5	*fimm*
6	*seks*
7	*sjey*
8	*átta*
9	*níggju*
10	*tíggju*
20	*tjúgu*
100	*hundrað*
1000	*túsund*

FINNISH

Pronunciation

Finnish has eight vowels, **a, e, i, o, u, y, ä** and **ö**. The alphabet also includes Swedish **å**. The final letters of the alphabet are **Å, ä** and **ö** (important to know when looking for something in a telephone directory).

Vowels

y	is like the German 'ü'
ä	is pronounced as the 'a' in 'act'
ö	is like the 'e' in 'summer'

Consonants

Consonant sounds which differ from English are listed here.

z	which can be written and is pronounced as 'ts'
v & w	which Finns consider as more or less the same letter
h	is a weak sound, except at the end of a 'closed' syllable, when it is almost as strong as German 'ch' in 'ich'
j	like the 'y' in 'yellow'
r	which is rolled

Double consonants like **kk** in *viikko* or **mm** in *summa* are held longer.

Basics

Hello	*Hei, Terve (Moi)*
Goodbye	*Näkemiin (Moi)*
Yes	*Kyllä* or *Joo*
No	*Ei* (pronounced 'ay')
Please	*Kiitos*
Thank you	*Kiitos*
That's fine/You're welcome	*Ole hyvä (Eipä kestä)*
Excuse me (Sorry)	*Anteeksi*

Do you speak English?
Puhutko englantia?
How much is it?
Paljonko se makasaa?
What is your name?
Mikä Teidän nimenne on?
Mikä sun nimi on? (informal)
My name is ...
Minun nimeni on ...
Mun nimi on ... (informal)

Getting Around

What time does ... leave/arrive?
Mihin aikaan ... lähtee/saapuu?

the boat	*laiva*
the bus (city)	*bussi*
the bus (intercity)	*bussi, linja-auto*
the tram	*raitiovaunu (raitsikka)*
the train	*juna*

Where can I hire a car/bicycle?
Mistä mina voisin/voin vuokrata polkupyörän?
I would like a one-way/return ticket.
Saanko menolipun/menopaluulipun.

1st class/2nd class	*ensimmäinen luokka/ toinen luokka*
left luggage	*säilytys*
timetable	*aikataulu*
bus/tram stop	*pysäkki*
train station/ ferry terminal	*rautatieasema/ satamaterminaali*

Where is ... ?	*Missä on ... ?*
far/near	*kaukana/lähellä*
Go straight ahead.	*Kulje suoraan.*
Turn left/right.	*Käänny vasempaan/ oikeaa.*

Around Town

bank	*pankkia*
... embassy	*...-n suurlähetystöä*
my hotel	*minun hotellia*
post office	*postia*
market	*toria*
chemist/pharmacy	*apteekkia*

newsagency/	*lehtikioski/*
stationers	*paperika uppa*
	vessa
telephone centre	*puhelinta/puhelin*
tourist office	*matkailutoimistoa/*
	matkailutoimisto

What time does it open/close?
Milloin se aukeaa/suljetaan?

Accommodation
hotel	*hotelli*
guesthouse	*matkakoti*
youth hostel	*retkeilymaja*
camping ground	*leirintäalue*

Do you have any rooms available?
Onko teillä vapaata huonetta?

I would like ...
Haluaisin ...
a single room	*yhden hengen*
	huoneen
a double room	*kahden hengen*
	huoneen

one day/two days
yhden päirän/kaksi päivää
How much is it per night/per person?
Paljonko se on yöltä/hengeltä?
Does it include breakfast?
Kuuluko aamiainen hintaan?

Time, Days & Numbers
What time is it?
Paljonko kello on?

today	*tänään*
tomorrow	*huomenna*
yesterday	*eilen*
morning	*aamulla*
afternoon	*iltapäivällä*

Monday	*maanantai*
Tuesday	*tiistai*
Wednesday	*keskiviikko*
Thursday	*torstai*
Friday	*perjantai*
Saturday	*lauantai*
Sunday	*sunnuntai*

0	*nolla*
1	*yksi*
2	*kaksi*
3	*kolme*
4	*neljä*
5	*viisi*
6	*kuusi*
7	*seitsemän*
8	*kahdeksan*
9	*yhdeksän*
10	*kymmenen*
100	*sata*
1000	*tuhat*
one million	*miljoona*

Emergencies
Help!	*Apua!*
Call a doctor!	*Kutsukaa lääkäri!*
Call the police!	*Soittakaa poliisi!*
Go away!	*Mene pois! (Häivy!)*
I am lost.	*Minä olen eksyksissä.*

ICELANDIC

Pronunciation
Stress is generally on the first syllable. Double consonants are pronounced as such.

Vowels
a	as the 'a' in 'father'
a	as in 'at'
e	as in 'fear'
e	as in 'get', 'bet'
i, y	as the 'e' in 'pretty'
í, ý	as the 'e' in 'see', 'evil'
o	as in 'pot'

u	there is no equivalent sound in English. It sounds a bit like the vowel sound in the French word *peut*.
ú	as the 'o' in 'moon', 'woman'
ö	as in 'fern', 'turn', but without a trace of 'r'

Diphthongs
á	as in 'out'
ei, ey	as in 'paid', 'day'
ó	as in 'note'
æ	as in 'eye', 'dive'
au	as in French, *oeil*

Semiconsonants
é   as in 'yet', 'yes'

Consonants
ð   as in 'lather'
f   as in English. When between vowels or at the end of a word it is pronounced as 'v'. When followed by **l** or **n** it is pronounced as 'b'.
g   as in 'good'. When between vowels or before **r** or **ð**, *(sagt* 'said'), it has a guttural sound as in 'loch'.
h   as in English, except when followed by 'v', when it is pronounced as 'k'
j   as in 'yes', 'yellow'
l   as in English, except when double 'l' occurs, when it is pronounced as 'dl' *(kalla* 'call')
n   as in English, except when double 'n' forms an end to a word, when it is pronounced as 'dn', 'einn' (one), but never when double 'n' forms part of the article 'hinn'.
p   as in English, except when before 's' or 't', when it is pronounced as 'f' *(skipta* 'exchange')
r   always trilled
þ   as in 'thin', 'three'

Basics
Hello	*Halló*
Goodbye	*Bless*
Yes/No	*Já/Nei*
Please	*Gjörðu svo vel*
Thank you	*Takk fyrir*
That's fine/You're welcome	*Allt í lagi/Ekkert að þakka.*
Excuse me (Sorry)	*Afsakið*

Do you speak English?
   Talar þú ensku?
How much is it?
   Hvað kostar það
What is your name?
   Hvað heitir þú?
My name is ...
   yehgh hay-ti ...

Getting Around
What time does... leave/arrive?
   Hvenær fer/kemur...?

the boat	*báturinn*
the bus	*vagninn (city bus)*
the tram	*sporvagninn*

I'd like to hire a car/bicycle.
   Ég vil leigia bíl/reiðhjól
I would like...
   Gæti ég fengid...

a one-way ticket	*miða, aðra leiðina*
a return ticket	*miða, báðar leiðir*
1st class/2nd class	*fyrsta farrými/ annaq farrými*
timetable	*tímaáætlun*
bus stop	*biðstöð*
ferry terminal	*ferjuhöfn*

Where is...?	*Hvar er...?*
far/near	*langt í burtu/nálægt*
Go straight ahead.	*Farðu beint af augum.*
Turn left/right	*Beygðu til vinstri/hægri*

Around Town
bank	*banka*
... embassy	*... sendiráðinu*
my hotel	*hótelinu mi'nu*
post office	*pósthúsinu*
market	*markaðnum*
chemist/pharmacy	*apótek*
newsagency/stationer	*blaðasala/bókabúð*
telephone centre	*símstöðinni*
tourist office	*upplýsingaþjónustu fyrir ferðafólk*

Accommodation
hotel	*hótel*
guesthouse	*gistiheimili*

| youth hostel | *farfuglaheimili* |
| camping ground | *tjaldstæði* |

Do you have any rooms available?
Eru herbergi laus?

I would like...	*Gæti ég fengid...*
a single room	*einstakling-*
	sherbergi
a double room	*tveggjaman-*
	naherbergi
one day/two days	*einn dag/tvo daga*

How much is it per night/per person?
Hvað kostar nóttin fyirir manninn?
Does it include breakfast?
Er morgunmatur innifalinn?

Time, Days & Numbers
What time is it?
Hvað er klukkan?

today	*í dag*
tomorrow	*á morgun*
yesterday	*í gær*
in the morning	*að morgni*
in the afternoon	*eftir hádegi*

| Monday | *mánudagur* |

Tuesday	*þriðjudagur*
Wednesday	*miðvikudagur*
Thursday	*fimmtudagur*
Friday	*föstudagur*
Saturday	*laugardagur*
Sunday	*sunnudagur*

0	*núll*
1	*einn*
2	*tveir*
3	*þrír*
4	*fjórir*
5	*fimm*
6	*sex*
7	*sjö*
8	*átta*
9	*níü*
10	*tíu*
20	*tuttugu*
100	*eitt hundrað*
1000	*eitt þúsund*
one million	*ein milljón*

Emergencies
Help!	*Hjálp*
Call a doctor!	*Náid í lækni.*
Call the police!	*Náid í lögregluna!*
Go away!	*Farðu!*
I'm lost	*Ég er villtur*

LATVIAN

Pronunciation
Here are some sounds specific to Latvian, followed by some useful words and phrases:

c	is pronounced as 'ts'
č, š, ž	as 'ch', 'sh' and the 's' in 'pleasure'
ģ	as the 'j' in 'jet'
j	as the y in 'yes'
ā, ē,	like the vowel sounds in 'bar', 'bare',
ī & ū	'he' and 'too'
ie, o	like the vowel sounds in 'ear' and 'four'
ķ	as 'ch'
ļ	like the 'lli' in 'billiards'
ņ	as the 'ni' in 'onion'

Basics
Hello	*Sveiki*
Goodbye (casual)	*Atā*
Goodbye (formal)	*Uzredzēšanos*
Yes/No	*Jā/Nē*

Please	*Lūdzu*
Thank you	*Paldies*
That's fine/you're	*Paldies/laipne*
welcome	*lūdzam*
Excuse me (Sorry)	*Atvainojiet*

Do you speak English?
Vai jūs runājiet angliski?
How much is it?
Cik maksā?
What is your name?
Kā jūs sauc?
My name is ...
Mani sauc ...

Getting Around
What time is the next .... to ...?
Cikos attiet nākamis ... uz ...?
| the boat | *kugis* |
| the bus | *buss/autobuss* |

the tram	*tramvajs*
the train	*vilciens*

Where can I hire a car/bicycle?
Kur es varu noīrēt mašīnu/velosipēds?
I want to buy a one-way/return ticket.
Es vēlos nopirkt vienvirziena/turp-atpakaļ biļete.

1st class/2nd class	*pirmā/otrē klase*
left luggage	*bagāžas glabātuve*
timetable	*vilcienu saraksts*
tram/trolleybus stop	*tramvaja/ trolejbusa pietura*
train station/ ferry terminal	*vilcienu stacija/osta*

Where is the ...?	*Kur atrodas ...?*
Is it far from here?	*Vai tas atrodas tālu?*
Go straight ahead.	*Uz priekšu.*
Turn left/right.	*Pa kreisi/labi*

Around Town

bank	*banka*
... embassy	*... vēstniecība*
my hotel	*mana viesnīca*
post office	*pasts*
market	*tirgus*
chemist/pharmacy	*aptieka*
newsagency/stationer	*rakstampiederumu veikals*
public telephone	*telefons*
tourist office	*tūrisma aģentūgra*

What time does it open/close?
Cikos ciet/atvērts?

Accommodation

hotel	*viesnīca*
guesthouse	*viesu māja*
youth hostel	*jauniešu kopmītne*
camping ground	*kempings*

Do you have any rooms available?
Vai Jums ir brīvas istabas?
I would like a ...
Es vēlos

single room	*istabu vienai personai*
double room	*istabu divām personām*
one night/two nights	*vienu nakti/divas naktis*

How much is it per night?
Cik maksā pa nakti?
Does it include breakfast?
Vai brokastis ir ieskaitītas?

Time, Days & Numbers

What time is it?
Cik ir pulkstenis?

today	*šodien*
tomorrow	*ritdien*
yesterday	*vakar*
morning/afternoon	*rīts/pēcpusdiena*

Monday	*pirmdiena*
Tuesday	*otrdiena*
Wednesday	*trešdiena*
Thursday	*ceturtdiena*
Friday	*piektdiena*
Saturday	*sestdiena*
Sunday	*svētdiena*

1	*viens*
2	*divi*
3	*trīs*
4	*četri*
5	*pieci*
6	*seši*
7	*septiņi*
8	*astoņi*
9	*deviņi*
10	*desmit*
100	*simts*
1000	*tūkstotis*
one million	*viens miljons*

Signs

ENTRANCE	*IEEJA*
EXIT	*IZEJA*
FULL, NO VACANCIES	*VIETU NAV*
INFORMATION	*INFORMĀCIJA*
OPEN/CLOSED	*ATVĒRTS/SIĒGTS*
PROHIBITED	*AIZLIEGTA*
POLICE STATION	*POLICIJAS IECIRKNIS*
ROOMS AVAILABLE	*BRĪVAS ISTABAS*
TOILETS (MEN'S/WOMEN'S)	*TUALETES (VĪIEŠU/ SIEVIEŠU)*

Emergencies

Help!	*Palīga*
Call a doctor!	*Izsauciet ārstu!*
Call the police!	*Izsauciet policiju!*

Go away!	*Ejiet projam!*
I'm lost.	*Es esmu apmald-ījusies*(f)/ *apmaldījies*(m).

LITHUANIAN

Pronunciation

The letters are generally pronounced as in English except:

y	like the 'ea' in 'heat'
ie	like the 'ea' in 'hear'
ui	like 'wi' in 'win'
c	as 'ts'
č	as 'ch'
š	as 'sh'
ž	as the 's' in 'pleasure'
j	as the 'y' in 'yes'

Diacritical marks have the effect of lengthening the vowel:

ą	as the 'a' in 'father'
ę	as the 'ai' in 'air'
į	like the 'ee' in 'feet'
ū & ų	like the 'oo' in 'boot'
ė	like the 'a' in 'late'

Basics

Hello	*Laba diena*
Goodbye	*Viso gero*
Yes/No	*Taip/Ne*
Please	*Prašau*
Thank you	*Ačiū*
You're welcome	*Sveiki atvykę*
Excuse me (Sorry)	*Atsiprašau*

Do you speak English?
Ar kalbate angliškai?
How much is it?
Kiek kainuoja?

What is your name?
Koks jūsų vardas?
My name is ...
Mano vardas yra ...

Signs

ENTRANCE	*ĮĖJIMAS*
EXIT	*IŠĖJIMAS*
FULL, NO VACANCIES	*VIETŲ NĖRA*
INFORMATION	*INFORMACIJA*
OPEN/CLOSED	*ATIDARYTAS/ UŽDARYTAS*
HOTEL	*VIEŠBUTIS*
POLICE	*POLICIJA*
ROOMS AVAILABLE	*VIETŲ YRA*
TOILETS (MEN'S/WOMEN'S)	*TUALETAI (VYRŲ/ MOTERŲVIETŲ)*

Getting Around

What time does the next ... leave/arrive?
Kada atvyksta/išvyksta sekantis?

the boat	*laivas*
the bus	*autobusas*
the tram	*tramvajus*
the train	*traukinys*

Where can I hire a car/bicycle?
Kur aš galėčiau išsinuomuoti mašiną/ dviratį?
I would like a one-way/return ticket.
Aš norėčiau bilietą į vieną/abi puses.

1st class/2nd class	*pirmos klasės/antros klasės*
left luggage	*bagažo saugykla*
timetable	*tvarkaraštis*
bus stop	*autobusų stotelė*
train station	*geležinkelio stotis*

Where is the ...?	*Kur yra ...?*
far/near	*toli/arti*
straight ahead	*tiesiai*
Turn left/right.	*Pasukti į kairę/dešinę.*

Around Town

bank	*bankas*
.... embassy	*ambasada*
my hotel	*mano viešbutis*

post office	*paštas*
market	*turgus*
chemist/	*vaistinė*
pharmacy	
newsagency/	*spaudos kioskas*
stationer	
public telephone	*telefonas*
tourist office	*turizmo informacijos*
	centras

Accommodation

hotel	*viešbutis*
guesthouse	*svečių namai*
youth hostel	*jaunimo viešbutis*
camp site	*stovyklavietės*

Do you have any rooms available?
  Ar turite laisvų kambarių?
I would like a ...
  Aš norėčiau ...
  single room   *vienviečio*
                  kambario
  double room   *dviviečio*
                  kambario
one day/two days *vieną dieną/dvi*
                  dienas
How much is it per night, per person?
  Kiek kainuoja nakvynė nakčiai asmeniui?
Does it include breakfast?
  Ar į kainą įeina pusryčiai?

Time, Days & Numbers

What time is it?
  Kiek dabar valandų?

today	*šiandien*
tomorrow	*rytoj*
yesterday	*vakar*
morning/afternoon	*rytas/popietė*
Monday	*pirmadienis*
Tuesday	*antradienis*
Wednesday	*trečiadienis*
Thursday	*ketvirtadienis*
Friday	*penktadienis*
Saturday	*šeštadienis*
Sunday	*sekmadienis*

1	*vienas*
2	*du*
3	*trys*
4	*keturi*
5	*penki*
6	*šeši*
7	*septyni*
8	*aštuoni*
9	*devyni*
10	*dešimt*
100	*šimtas*
1000	*tūkstantis*
one million	*vienas milijonas*

Emergencies ·

Help!	*Gelbėkite!*
Call a doctor!	*Iškvieskite gydytoją!*
Call the police!	*Iškvieskite policiją!*
Go away!	*Atstok!*
I'm lost.	*Aš pasiklydau.*

NORWEGIAN

Norway has two official languages. Bokmål (indicated here as BM within parentheses) and Nynorsk (NN). For a more detailed description of these languages and their usage see Language in the Facts about the Country section of the Norway chapter.

Pronunciation

The length of vowels is a very important feature in the pronunciation of Norwegian. Every vowel has a (very) long and a (very) short counterpart, when appearing in a stressed syllable. Generally, it is short when followed by one consonant, and long when followed by two or more consonants.

Vowels

a	as in 'cut'
a	long as in 'father'
å	as in British English 'pot'
å	long as in British English 'lord'
æ	has the same pronunciation as the first four varieties of **e**
e	before **r**, as in British 'bat'
e	before **r**, as in British 'bad'
e	as in 'bet'
e	long as in posh British 'day'; close to German *sehen*
e	as the 'u' in 'lettuce', always unstressed
i	like 'beat', but very short, as the French *si, il*
i	long as in 'seethe'

o	as in British 'pot'
o	long like the American 'zoo', but more like the German *u* in *Suchen*
o	as the 'u' in put
o	long as in 'lord'
ø	as in German *zwölf*, or French *boeuf*
ø	long as in British 'fern'
u	as in French *sud*
u	long like British 'soon', but more like German *süss*
u	as in 'put'
y	between French *sud* and *si*
y	between 'seethe' and German *süss*

Diphthongs
ai	similar to 'dive'
ei	similar to Australian English 'day'
au	similar to Australian English 'mown'
øy	as the French *eui* in *fauteuil*

Consonants & Semivowels
d	at the end of a word, or between two vowels, it is often silent
g	as the 'g' in 'get', but before the letters or combinations **ei, i, j, øy,** and **y** it is, in most cases pronounced like the 'y' in 'yard'. The combination **gn** is pronounced as the 'ng' of 'sing', followed by an 'n'.
h	like the 'h' in 'her', but before **v** and **j** it is silent
j	always like the 'y' in 'yard'
k	a hard sound as in 'kin', but before the letters or combinations **ei, i, j, øy,** and **y**, it is, in most words, pronounced as the 'ch' in 'chin'. In many areas though, these combinations are pronounced like the 'h' in 'huge', or like the German *ch* in the word *ich.*
l	pronounced thinly, as in 'list', except after the phonetic 'ah', 'aa', 'o' and 'or' sounds, when it becomes the 'l' sound of 'all'
ng	in most areas, like the 'ng' sound in 'sing'
r	trilled, as in Spanish. In south-west Norway, however, the **r** is pronounced gutturally, as in French. The combinations **rd, rl, rn, rt** sound a bit like American 'weird', 'earl', 'earn' and 'start', but with a much weaker 'r'. The combination **rs** is pronounced 'sh'as in 'fish'.
s	always voiceless, like the 's' in 'us'.

The combination **sk** followed by **ei, i, j,** and **y** is pronounced as 'sh': so the Norwegian word *ski* sounds like the English 'she'.

t	like the English 't', except in two cases where it is silent: in the Norwegian word *det* (meaning 'it, that'), roughly pronounced like British English 'dare'; and in the definite singular ending *-et* of Norwegian neutral nouns
v	is nearly always pronounced like the English 'w' but without rounding the lips – rather like a German speaker would pronounce a 'w'

Basics
Hello	*Goddag*
Goodbye	*Morna*
Yes/No	*Ja/Nei*
Please	*Ver (Vær) så snill*
Thank you	*Takk*
That's fine	*Inga årsak* (NN)
You're welcome	*Ingen årsak* (BM)
Excuse me (Sorry)	*Unnskyld*

Do you speak English?
  Snakkar du engelsk? (NN)
  Snakker du engelsk? (BM)
How much is it?
  Kor mykje kostar det?(NN)
  Hvor mye koster det? (BM)
What is your name?
  Kva heiter du? (NN)
  Hva heter du? (BM)
My name is ...
  Eg heiter .... (NN)
  Jeg heter .... (BM)

Getting Around
What time does...leave/arrive?
  Kva tid går/kjem? (NN)
  Når går/kommer...? (BM)
the boat	*båten*
the bus (city)	*bussen (bybussen)*
the bus (intercity)	*bussen (linjebussen)*
the tram	*trikken*
the train	*toget*

Where can I rent a car/bicycle?
  Kor kan eg leige ein bil? (NN)
  Hvor kan jeg leie en bil? (BM)

I would like...
Eg (Jeg) vil gjerne ha...

a one-way ticket	*enkeltbillett*
a return ticket	*tur-retur*
1st class/2nd class	*første klasse/*
	andre klasse (NN)
	annen klasse (BM)
left luggage	*reisegods*
timetable	*ruteplan*
bus/tram stop	*buss/trikkhaldeplass*
	buss/trikkholdeplass
train station/ferry	*jernbanestasjon/*
terminal	*ferjeleiet*

Where is...?
Kor er...? (NN)
Hvor er árr...? (BM)

far/near	*langt/nær*
Go straight ahead.	*Det er rett fram.*
Turn left.	*Ta til venstre.*
Turn right.	*Ta til høgre.* (NN)
	Ta til høyre. (BM)

Around Town

bank	*banken*
... embassy	*... ambassade*
my hotel	*hotellet mitt*
post office	*postkontoret*
market	*torget*
chemist/pharmacy	*apotek*
newsagency/stationer	*kiosk*
telephone centre	*televerket*
tourist office	*turistinformasjon*

Accommodation

hotel	*hotell*
guesthouse	*gjestgiveri/*
	pensionat
youth hostel	*vandrerhjem*
camping ground	*kamping/leirplass*

Do you have any rooms available?
Har du ledige rom?
I would like...
Eg (Jeg) vil gjerne...

a single room	*ha eit enkeltrom*
a double room	*ha eit dobbeltrom*
one day/two days	*ein dag/to dager*

How much is it per night/per person?
Kor mykje er det pr dag/pr person? (NN)
Vor mye er det pr dag/pr person? (BM)

Does it include breakfast?
Frukosten medrekna? (NN)
Inklusive frokosten? (BM)

Signs

ENTRANCE	*INNGANG*
EXIT	*UTGANG*
INFORMATION	*OPPLYSNINGAR* (NN)
	OPPLYSNINGER (BM)
OPEN/CLOSED	*OPEN/STENGD* (NN)
	ÅPEN/STENGT (BM)
PROHIBITED	*FORBODE* (NN)
	FORBUDT (BM)
POLICE STATION	*POLITISTASJON*
TOILETS	*TOALETTAR* (NN)
(MEN'S/WOMEN'S)	*(HERRER/ DAMER)*
	TOALETTER (BM)

Time, Days & Numbers

What time is it?
Kva (Hva) er klokka?

today	*i dag*
tomorrow	*i morgon* (NN)
	i morgen (BM)
yesterday	*i går*
in the morning	*om formiddagen*
in the afternoon	*om ettermiddagen*

Monday	*måndag* (NN)
	mandag (BM)
Tuesday	*tysdag* (NN)
	tirsdag (BM)
Wednesday	*onsdag*
Thursday	*torsdag*
Friday	*fredag*
Saturday	*laurdag* (NN)
	lørdag (BM)
Sunday	*sundag*
	søndag (NN)

0	*null*
1	*ein* (NN), *en* (BM)
2	*to*
3	*tre*
4	*fire*
5	*fem*

6	*seks*		
7	*sju* (NN), *syv* (BM)		
8	*åtte*		
9	*ni*		
10	*ti*		
100	*hundre*		
1000	*tusen*		
one million	*ein million* (NN)		
	en million (BM)		

Emergencies

Help!	*Hjelp!*
Call a doctor!	*Ring ein lege!*
Call the police!	*Ring politiet!*
Go away!	*Forsvinn!*
I'm lost.	*Eg har gått meg vill.* (NN)
	Jeg har gått meg vill. (BM)

RUSSIAN

Cyrillic Alphabet
The Cyrillic alphabet resembles Greek with some extra characters. Each language that uses Cyrillic has a slightly different variant. The alphabet chart shows the letters used in Russian with their Roman-letter equivalents and common pronunciations.

Pronunciation The sounds of a, o, e and я are 'weaker' when the stress in the word does not fall on them – eg in вода (*voda*, water) the stress falls on the second syllable, so it's pronounced '*va-DA*', with the unstressed pronunciation for o and the stressed pronunciation for a. The vowel й only follows other vowels in so-called diphthongs, eg ой '*oy*', ей '*ey, yey*'. Russians usually print ё without the dots, a source of confusion in pronunciation.

The 'voiced' consonants б, в, г, д, ж and з are not voiced at the end of words (eg хлеб, bread, is pronounced '*khlyep*') or before voiceless consonants. The г in the common adjective endings -ero and -oro is pronounced '*v*'.

Two letters have no sound but only modify others. A consonant followed by the 'soft sign' ь is spoken with the tongue flat against the palate, as if followed by the faint beginnings of a '*y*'. The rare 'hard sign' ъ after a consonant inserts a slight pause before the next vowel.

Grammar
This drives even serious students crackers. Nouns have gender and six possible endings; verbs also decline, as in Latin. One result is that things named after people have odd endings – Lenin Ave is prospekt Lenina, Tchaikovsky Square is ploshchad Chaykovskogo and so on.

For a beginner the best way around this is to ignore it; you can pick up the meanings of printed words without worrying much about endings.

There are simplifications, too. Russian has no 'a' or 'the'. The verb 'to be' commonly drops out of simple sentences – eg 'I am an American' (male) is я американец *('ya uh-mi-ri-KAHN-yits')*. Russians also don't normally use the verb 'to have'. Instead they use the preposition у, which means 'at' or 'by', and the third person singular of the verb 'to be': eg 'I have' is у меня есть *('u min-YA yest')*, literally 'by me (is)'.

Questions The easiest way to turn a statement into a question is just to say it with a rising tone and a questioning look, or follow it with a quizzical *da?* – eg 'is this Moscow?', это Москва, да? *('EH-ta mahsk-VA, da?')*.

Basics

Hello	*ZDRAST-viytye* Здравствуйте
Goodbye	*Dasvid-AN-ya* До свидания
Yes/No	*Da/Nyet* да, нет
Please	*Pa-ZHAL-sta* Пожалуйста
Thank you	*Spa-SEE-ba* Спасибо
Excuse me.	*Izvi-NItye, paz-HAL-sta* Простите, пожалуйста

Do you speak English?
Vih ga-var-EE-tyeh pa-an-GLEE-ski?
Вы говорите по-английски?

The Cyrillic Alphabet

Russian is spoken by nearly everyone in the Baltic states, though as a second language by Estonians, Latvians and Lithuanians themselves. The chart shows printed letters, transliterations (Latin-letter equivalents) and common pronunciations.

Letter	Transliteration	Pronunciation
А, а	*A, a*	like the 'a' in 'father' (stressed)
		like the 'a' in 'about' (unstressed)
Б, б	*B, b*	like the 'b' in 'but'
В, в	*V, v*	like the 'v' in 'van'
Г, г	*G, g*	like the 'g' in 'god'
Д, д	*D, d*	like the 'd' in 'dog'
Е, е	*Ye, e*	like the 'ye' in 'yet' (stressed)
		like the 'ye' in 'yeast' (unstressed)
Ё, ё	*Yo, yo*	like the 'yo' in 'yore'
Ж, ж	*Zh, zh*	like the 's' in 'measure'
З, з	*Z, z*	like the 'z' in 'zoo'
И, и	*I, i*	like the 'ee' in 'meet'
Й, й	*Y, y*	like the 'y' in 'boy'
К, к	*K, k*	like the 'k' in 'kind'
Л, л	*L, l*	like the 'l' in 'lamp'
М, м	*M, m*	like the 'm' in 'mad'
Н, н	*N, n*	like the 'n' in 'not'
О, о	*O, o*	like the 'o' in 'more' (stressed)
		like the 'a' in 'about' (unstressed)
П, п	*P, p*	like the 'p' in 'pig'
Р, р	*R, r*	like the 'r' in 'rub' (but rolled)
С, с	*S, s*	like the 's' in 'sing'
Т, т	*T, t*	like the 't' in 'ten'
У, у	*U, u*	like the 'oo' in 'fool'
Ф, ф	*F, f*	like the 'f' in 'fan'
Х, х	*Kh, kh*	like the 'ch' in 'Bach'
Ц, ц	*Ts, ts*	like the 'ts' in 'bits'
Ч, ч	*Ch, ch*	like the 'ch' in 'chin'
Ш, ш	*Sh, sh*	like the 'sh' in 'shop'
Щ, щ	*Shch, shch*	like the 'shch' in 'fresh chips'
ъ		('hard sign')
Ы, ы	*Y, y*	like the 'i' in 'ill'
ь		('soft sign')
Э, э	*E, e*	like the 'e' in 'end'
Ю, ю	*Yu, yu*	like 'you'
Я, я	*Ya, ya*	like the 'ya' in 'yard'

How much is it?
SKOL-ka STO-eet
Сколько стоит?
What is your name?
kahk vahs za-VOOT?
Как вас зовут?
My name is...
min-YA za-VOOT...
Меня зовут...

Getting Around

When does it leave?
kug-DA aht-li-TA-yit?
Когда отлетает?

bus	*uf-TOH-boos* автобус
trolleybus	*trahl-YEY-boos* троллейбус
tram	*trum-VAI* трамвай
fixed-route minibus	*marsh-ROOT-na-yuh tahk-SEE* маршрутное такси
train	*PO-yest* поезд
bicycle	*vyelasi-PYET* велосипед
soft or 1st-class (compartment)	*MYAKH-ki* мягкий
hard or 2nd-class (compartment)	*ku-PYEY-ni* купейный
reserved-place or 3rd-class (carriage)	*plahts-KART-ni* плацкартный
timetable	*raspi-SA-niye* расписание

bus stop	*ah-sta-NOV-kuh* остановка
railway station	*zhi-LYEZ-nuh-da-ROHZH-ni vahg-ZAHL* железнодорожный (ж. д.) вокзал
pier/quay	*pri-CHAHL* or *pri-STAHN* причал ог пристань

Where is...?
gdyeh...?
Где...?

Is it near/far?
BLIS-ka/dayle-KO?
Близко/далеко?

straight on	*PRYAH-ma* прямо
to (on) the left	*nuh-LYEH-va* налево
to (on) the right	*nuh-PRAH-va* направо

Around Town

bank	*bahnk* банк
post office	*pohch-TAH* почта
market	*RIH-nuk* рынок
chemist/pharmacy	*up-TYEK-a* аптека
telephone	*ti-li-FOHN* телефон
tourist office	*byu-RO tu-RIZ-ma* бюро туризма

Signs

ENTRANCE, EXIT	*fkhot, VIH-khut*	ВХОД, ВЫХОД
NO VACANCY	*myest nyet*	МЕСТ НЕТ
INFORMATION	*SPRAHV-ki*	СПРАВКИ
OPEN, CLOSED	*aht-KRIT, zuh-KRIT*	ОТКРЫТ, ЗАКРЫТ
CASHIER/ TICKET OFFICE	*KAHS-suh*	КАССАб
HOSPITAL	*BOHL-nit-suh*	бОЛЬНИЦА
POLICE	*mi-LEET-si-yuh*	МИЛИЦИЯ
TOILET (MEN'S/WOMEN'S)	*tu-al-YET* *MOOZH-skoy/* *ZHEN-ski tu-al-YET*	ТУАЛЕТ МУЖСКОЙ (М)/ ЖЕНСКИЙ (Ж)

Accommodation

hotel	*gus-TEE-nit-suh*	гостиница
room	*KOM-nata*	комната

How much does it cost (per day/week)?
SKOL-ka STO-eet (f-SUT-ki/v nye-DYEL-yu)?
Сколько стоит (в сутки/в неделю)?

breakfast	*ZAHF-truk*	завтрак

Time, Days & Numbers

What time is it?
ka-TOR-i chahs
Который час?

today	*si-VOHD-nyuh*	сегодня
tomorrow	*ZAHF-truh*	завтра
yesterday	*fchi-RA*	вчера
in the morning	*oo-TRA*	утра
in the afternoon	*dnya*	дня
Monday	*pa-ni-DEL-nik*	понедельник
Tuesday	*FTOR-nik*	вторник
Wednesday	*sri-DA*	среда
Thursday	*chit-VERK*	четверг
Friday	*PYAT-nit-suh*	пятница
Saturday	*su-BOHT-uh*	суббота
Sunday	*vas-kri-SEN-yuh*	воскресенье

1	*ah-DYIN*	один
2	*dva*	два
3	*tree*	три
4	*chi-TIR-yeh*	четыре
5	*pyaht*	пять
6	*shest*	шесть
7	*syem*	семь
8	*VO-syim*	восемь
9	*DYEV-yut*	девять
10	*DYES-yut*	десять
100	*stoh*	сто
1000	*TIH-suh-chuh*	тысяча
one million	*ah-DYIN mi-li-OHN*	один миллион

Emergencies

Help!	*na POH-mushch!* or *pa-ma-GEET-yeh!*	На помощь! or Помогите!
I need a doctor.	*mnyeh NU-zhin vrahch*	Мне нужен врач.
Police!	*mi-LEET-si-yuh*	милиция
I'm lost.	*ya patye-RYA-las'.* (m) *ya patye-RYA-lsa.* (f)	Я потерялась. (m) Я потерялся. (f)

SWEDISH

Swedish grammar follows the pattern of the Germanic languages. Verbs are the same regardless of person or number: 'I am, you are' etc are, in Swedish, *Jag är, du är* and so on. Definite articles in Swedish ('the' in English) are determined by the ending of a noun: *-en* and *-et* for singular nouns and *-na* and *-n* for plural. To determine if it is *-en* or *-et* as an ending can be difficult and has to be learnt word by word.

Pronunciation

Sweden is a large country, and there is a great variety of dialects. There are sounds in Swedish which do not exist in English, so we have tried to give as close approximations as possible.

Vowels

The vowels are pronounced as short sounds if there is a double consonant afterwards, otherwise they are long sounds. Sometimes the **o** in Swedish sounds like the **å**, and **e** as the **ä**. There are, however, not as many exceptions to the rules as there are in English.

Vowel	Long	Short
a	as the 'a' in 'father'	as in 'cut' or the French *ami*
o	as in 'zoo'	as in 'pot'
u	as in 'ooze'	as in 'pull'
i	as in 'see'	as in 'in'
e	as in 'fear'	as in 'bet'
å	as in 'poor'	almost like the 'o' in 'pot'
ä	as in 'act '	as in the French *et*
ö	similar to 'fern' or the German *schön*	as in the French *deux*
y	as in the German *über*	as in the French *tu*

Consonants

The consonants are pronounced almost the same as in English. The following letter combinations and sounds are specific to Swedish:

c	as the 's' in 'sit'
ck	like a double 'k' which gives the vowel before it a short sound
tj, rs	a 'sh' sound, as in 'ship'
sj, ch	a 'kh' sound, as in the Scottish *loch*, or German *ich*
g, lj	a 'y' sound, as in 'onion'. Sometimes the g is pronounced this way, before certain vowels and after 'r'

Basics

Hello	*Hej/Hej då*
Goodbye	*Adjö*
Yes/No	*Ja/Nej*
Please	*Snälla, vänligen*
Thank you	*Tack*
That's fine/You're welcome	*Det är bra/Varsågod.*
Excuse me (Sorry)	*Ursäkta mig/Förlåt*

Do you speak English?
Talar du engelska?
How much is it?
Hur mycket kostar den?
What is your name?
Vad heter du?
My name is ...
Jag heter ...

Getting Around

What time does... leave/arrive?
När avgår/kommer... ?

the boat	*båten*
the bus (city)	*stadsbussen*
the bus (intercity)	*landsortsbussen*
the tram	*spårvagnen*
the train	*tåget*

Where can I hire a car/bicycle?
Var kan jag hyra en bil/cykel
I would like...
Jag skulle vilja ha...

a one-way ticket	*en enkelbiljett*
a return ticket	*en returbiljett*
1st class/2nd class	*första klass/andra klass*
left luggage	*effektförvaring*
timetable	*tidtabell*
bus stop	*busshållplats*
train station	*tågstation*

Where is... ?	*Var är... ?*
far/near	*långt/nära*
Go straight ahead.	*Gå rakt fram.*
Turn left/right.	*Sväng till vänster/höger.*

Signs

ENTRANCE	*INGÅNG*
EXIT	*UTGÅNG*
FULL, NO VACANCIES	*FULLT*
INFORMATION	*INFORMATION*
OPEN/CLOSED	*ÖPPEN/STÄNGD*
PROHIBITED	*FÖRBJUDEN*
POLICE STATION	*POLISSTATION*
ROOMS AVAILABLE	*LEDIGA RUM*
TOILETS (MEN/ WOMEN)	*TOALETT (HERRER/ DAMER)*

Around Town

bank	*bank*
... embassy	*... ambassaden*
my hotel	*mitt hotell*
post office	*postkontoret*
market	*marknaden*
chemist/pharmacy	*apotek*
newsagency/ statiners	*nyhetsbyrå/pappers handel*
a public telephone	*en offentlig telefon*
tourist office	*turistinformation*

What time does it open/close?
När öppnar/stänger de?

Accommodation

hotel	*hotell*
guesthouse	*gästhus*
youth hostel	*vandrarhem*
camping ground	*campingplats*

Do you have any rooms available?
Finns det några lediga rum?

I would like...
Jag skulle vilja ha...

a single room	*ett enkelrum*
a double room	*ett dubbelrum*
for one/two nights	*en natt/två nätter*

How much is it per night/per person?
Hur mycket kostar det per natt/per person?
Does it include breakfast?
Inkluderas frukost?

Time, Days & Numbers

What time is it?
Vad är klockan?

today	*idag*
tomorrow	*imorgon*
yesterday	*igår*
morning/afternoon	*morgonen/efter middagen*

Monday	*måndag*
Tuesday	*tisdag*
Wednesday	*onsdag*
Thursday	*torsdag*
Friday	*fredag*
Saturday	*lördag*
Sunday	*söndag*

0	*noll*
1	*ett*
2	*två*
3	*tre*
4	*fyra*
5	*fem*
6	*sex*
7	*sju*
8	*åtta*
9	*nio*
10	*tio*
100	*ett hundra*
1000	*ett tusen*
one million	*en miljon*

Emergencies

Help!	*Hjälp!*
Call a doctor!	*Ring efter en doktor!*
Call the police!	*Ring polisen!*
Go away!	*Försvinn!*
I'm lost.	*Jag är vilse.*

Index

Note that the letters å, ä, æ, ø, þ and ö fall at the end of the alphabet.

ABBREVIATIONS

MAPS

TEXT

LONELY PLANET PHRASEBOOKS

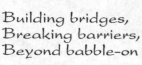

Building bridges,
Breaking barriers,
Beyond babble-on

Listen for the gems

Speak your own words

Ask your own
questions

Master of
your
own
image

- handy pocket-sized books
- easy to understand Pronunciation chapter
- clear and comprehensive Grammar chapter
- romanisation alongside script to allow ease of pronunciation
- script throughout so users can point to phrases
- extensive vocabulary sections, words and phrases for every situations
- full of cultural information and tips for the traveller

'...vital for a real DIY spirit and attitude in language learning' – **Backpacker**

'the phrasebooks have good cultural backgrounders and offer solid advice for challenging situations in remote locations' – **San Francisco Examiner**

'...they are unbeatable for their coverage of the world's more obscure languages' – **The Geographical Magazine**

Arabic (Egyptian)
Arabic (Moroccan)
Australia
  Australian English, Aboriginal and Torres Strait languages
Baltic States
  Estonian, Latvian, Lithuanian
Bengali
Burmese
Brazilian
Cantonese
Central Europe
  Czech, French, German, Hungarian, Italian and Slovak
Eastern Europe
  Bulgarian, Czech, Hungarian, Polish, Romanian and Slovak
Egyptian Arabic
Ethiopian (Amharic)
Fijian
French
German
Greek

Hindi/Urdu
Indonesian
Italian
Japanese
Korean
Lao
Latin American Spanish
Malay
Mandarin
Mediterranean Europe
  Albanian, Croatian, Greek, Italian, Macedonian, Maltese, Serbian, Slovene
Mongolian
Moroccan Arabic
Nepali
Papua New Guinea
Pilipino (Tagalog)
Quechua
Russian
Scandinavian Europe
  Danish, Finnish, Icelandic, Norwegian and Swedish

South-East Asia
  Burmese, Indonesian, Khmer, Lao, Malay, Tagalog (Pilipino), Thai and Vietnamese
Spanish
Sri Lanka
Swahili
Thai
Thai Hill Tribes
Tibetan
Turkish
Ukrainian
USA
  US English, Vernacular Talk, Native American languages and Hawaiian
Vietnamese
Western Europe
  Basque, Catalan, Dutch, French, German, Irish, Italian, Portuguese, Scottish Gaelic, Spanish (Castilian) and Welsh

---

LONELY PLANET JOURNEYS

JOURNEYS is a unique collection of travel writing – published by the company that understands travel better than anyone else. It is a series for anyone who has ever experienced – or dreamed of – the magical moment when they encountered a strange culture or saw a place for the first time. They are tales to read while you're planning a trip, while you're on the road or while you're in an armchair, in front of a fire.

JOURNEYS books catch the spirit of a place, illuminate a culture, recount a crazy adventure, or introduce a fascinating way of life. They always entertain, and always enrich the experience of travel.

THE GATES OF DAMASCUS
Lieve Joris
Translated by Sam Garrett

This best-selling book is a beautifully drawn portrait of day-to-day life in modern Syria. Through her intimate contact with local people, Lieve Joris draws us into the fascinating world that lies behind the gates of Damascus. Hala's husband is a political prisoner, jailed for his opposition to the Assad regime; through the author's friendship with Hala we see how Syrian politics impacts on the lives of ordinary people.

Lieve Joris, who was born in Belgium, is one of Europe's leading travel writers. In addition to an award-winning book on Hungary, she has published widely acclaimed accounts of her journeys to the Middle East and Africa. *The Gates of Damascus* is her fifth book.

'Expands the boundaries of travel writing' – Times Literary Supplement

KINGDOM OF THE FILM STARS
Journey into Jordan
Annie Caulfield

Kingdom of the Film Stars is a travel book and a love story. With honesty and humour, Annie Caulfield writes of travelling in Jordan and falling in love with a Bedouin. Her book offers fascinating insights into the country – from the traditional tent life of nomadic tribes to the first woman MP's battle with fundamentalist colleagues. *Kingdom of the Film Stars* unpicks some of the tight-woven Western myths about the Arab world, presenting cultural and political issues within the intimate framework of a compelling love story.

Annie Caulfield, who was born in Ireland and currently lives in London, is an award-winning playwright and journalist. She has travelled widely in the Middle East.

'Annie Caulfield is a remarkable traveller. Her story is fresh, courageous, moving, witty and sexy!' – Dawn French

LONELY PLANET TRAVEL ATLASES

Lonely Planet has long been famous for the number and quality of its guidebook maps. Now we've gone one step further and in conjunction with Steinhart Katzir Publishers produced a handy companion series: Lonely Planet travel atlases – maps of a country produced in book form.

Unlike other maps, which look good but lead travellers astray, our travel atlases have been researched on the road by Lonely Planet's experienced team of writers. All details are carefully checked to ensure the atlas corresponds with the equivalent Lonely Planet guidebook.

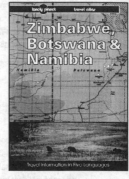

The handy atlas format means no holes, wrinkles, torn sections or constant folding and unfolding. These atlases can survive long periods on the road, unlike cumbersome fold-out maps. The comprehensive index ensures easy reference.

- full-colour throughout
- maps researched and checked by Lonely Planet authors
- place names correspond with Lonely Planet guidebooks
  – no confusing spelling differences
- legend and travelling information in English, French, German, Japanese and Spanish
- size: 230 x 160 mm

Available now:
Chile & Easter Island • Egypt • India & Bangladesh • Israel & the Palestinian Territories •Jordan, Syria & Lebanon • Kenya • Laos • Portugal • South Africa, Lesotho & Swaziland • Thailand • Turkey • Vietnam • Zimbabwe, Botswana & Namibia

---

LONELY PLANET TV SERIES & VIDEOS

Lonely Planet travel guides have been brought to life on television screens around the world. Like our guides, the programmes are based on the joy of independent travel, and look honestly at some of the most exciting, picturesque and frustrating places in the world. Each show is presented by one of three travellers from Australia, England or the USA and combines an innovative mixture of video, Super-8 film, atmospheric soundscapes and original music.

Videos of each episode – containing additional footage not shown on television – are available from good book and video shops, but the availability of individual videos varies with regional screening schedules.

Video destinations include: Alaska • American Rockies • Australia – The South-East • Baja California & the Copper Canyon • Brazil • Central Asia • Chile & Easter Island • Corsica, Sicily & Sardinia – The Mediterranean Islands • East Africa (Tanzania & Zanzibar) • Ecuador & the Galapagos Islands • Greenland & Iceland • Indonesia • Israel & the Sinai Desert • Jamaica • Japan • La Ruta Maya • Morocco • New York • North India • Pacific Islands (Fiji, Solomon Islands & Vanuatu) • South India • South West China • Turkey • Vietnam • West Africa • Zimbabwe, Botswana & Namibia

The Lonely Planet TV series is produced by:
Pilot Productions
The Old Studio
18 Middle Row
London W10 5AT UK

For video availability and ordering information contact your nearest Lonely Planet office.

Music from the TV series is available on CD & cassette.

PLANET TALK

Lonely Planet's FREE quarterly newsletter

We love hearing from you and think you'd like to hear from us.

When...is the right time to see reindeer in Finland?
Where...can you hear the best palm-wine music in Ghana?
How...do you get from Asunción to Areguá by steam train?
What...is the best way to see India?

For the answer to these and many other questions read PLANET TALK.

Every issue is packed with up-to-date travel news and advice including:

- a letter from Lonely Planet co-founders Tony and Maureen Wheeler
- go behind the scenes on the road with a Lonely Planet author
- feature article on an important and topical travel issue
- a selection of recent letters from travellers
- details on forthcoming Lonely Planet promotions
- complete list of Lonely Planet products

To join our mailing list contact any Lonely Planet office.

Also available: Lonely Planet T-shirts. 100% heavyweight cotton.

LONELY PLANET ONLINE

Get the latest travel information before you leave or while you're on the road

Whether you've just begun planning your next trip, or you're chasing down specific info on currency regulations or visa requirements, check out Lonely Planet Online for up-to-the minute travel information.

As well as travel profiles of your favourite destinations (including maps and photos), you'll find current reports from our researchers and other travellers, updates on health and visas, travel advisories, and discussion of the ecological and political issues you need to be aware of as you travel.

There's also an online travellers' forum where you can share your experience of life on the road, meet travel companions and ask other travellers for their recommendations and advice. We also have plenty of links to other online sites useful to independent travellers.

And of course we have a complete and up-to-date list of all Lonely Planet travel products including guides, phrasebooks, atlases, Journeys and videos and a simple online ordering facility if you can't find the book you want elsewhere.

www.lonelyplanet.com
or
AOL keyword: lp

LONELY PLANET PRODUCTS

Lonely Planet is known worldwide for publishing practical, reliable and no-nonsense travel information in our guides and on our web site. The Lonely Planet list covers just about every accessible part of the world. Currently there are eight series: *travel guides, shoestring guides, walking guides, city guides, phrasebooks, audio packs, travel atlases* and *Journeys* – a unique collection of travel writing.

EUROPE

Amsterdam • Austria • Baltic States phrasebook • Britain • Central Europe on a shoestring • Central Europe phrasebook • Czech & Slovak Republics • Denmark • Dublin • Eastern Europe on a shoestring • Eastern Europe phrasebook • Estonia, Latvia & Lithuania • Finland • France • French phrasebook • German phrasebook • Greece • Greek phrasebook • Hungary • Iceland, Greenland & the Faroe Islands • Ireland • Italian phrasebook • Italy • Mediterranean Europe on a shoestring • Mediterranean Europe phrasebook • Paris • Poland • Portugal • Portugal travel atlas • Prague • Russia, Ukraine & Belarus • Russian phrasebook • Scandinavian & Baltic Europe on a shoestring • Scandinavian Europe phrasebook • Slovenia • Spain • Spanish phrasebook • St Petersburg • Switzerland • Trekking in Greece • Trekking in Spain • Ukrainian phrasebook • Vienna • Walking in Britain • Walking in Switzerland • Western Europe on a shoestring • Western Europe phrasebook

Travel Literature: The Olive Grove: Travels in Greece

NORTH AMERICA

Alaska • Backpacking in Alaska • Baja California • California & Nevada • Canada • Florida • Hawaii • Honolulu • Los Angeles • Mexico • Miami • New England • New Orleans • New York City • New York, New Jersey & Pennsylvania • Pacific Northwest USA • Rocky Mountain States • San Francisco • Southwest USA • USA phrasebook • Washington, DC & the Capital Region

CENTRAL AMERICA & THE CARIBBEAN

Bermuda • Central America on a shoestring • Costa Rica • Cuba • Eastern Caribbean • Guatemala, Belize & Yucatán: La Ruta Maya • Jamaica

SOUTH AMERICA

Argentina, Uruguay & Paraguay • Bolivia • Brazil • Brazilian phrasebook • Buenos Aires • Chile & Easter Island • Chile & Easter Island travel atlas • Colombia • Ecuador & the Galápagos Islands • Latin American Spanish phrasebook • Peru • Quechua phrasebook • Rio de Janeiro • South America on a shoestring • Trekking in the Patagonian Andes • Venezuela

Travel Literature: Full Circle: A South American Journey

ANTARCTICA

Antarctica

ISLANDS OF THE INDIAN OCEAN

Madagascar & Comoros • Maldives • Mauritius, Réunion & Seychelles

AFRICA

Africa - the South • Africa on a shoestring • Arabic (Moroccan) phrasebook • Cape Town • Central Africa • East Africa • Egypt • Egypt travel atlas • Ethiopian (Amharic) phrasebook • Kenya • Kenya travel atlas • Malawi, Mozambique & Zambia • Morocco • North Africa • South Africa, Lesotho & Swaziland • South Africa, Lesotho & Swaziland travel atlas • Swahili phrasebook • Trekking in East Africa • West Africa • Zimbabwe, Botswana & Namibia • Zimbabwe, Botswana & Namibia travel atlas

Travel Literature: The Rainbird: A Central African Journey • Songs to an African Sunset: A Zimbabwean Story

MAIL ORDER

Lonely Planet products are distributed worldwide. They are also available by mail order from Lonely Planet, so if you have difficulty finding a title please write to us. North American and South American residents should write to Embarcadero West, 155 Filbert St, Suite 251, Oakland CA 94607, USA; European and African residents should write to 10 Barley Mow Passage, Chiswick, London W4 4PH; and residents of other countries to PO Box 617, Hawthorn, Victoria 3122, Australia.

NORTH-EAST ASIA

Beijing • Cantonese phrasebook • China • Hong Kong • Hong Kong, Macau & Guangzhou • Japan • Japanese phrasebook • Japanese audio pack • Korea • Korean phrasebook • Mandarin phrasebook • Mongolia • Mongolian phrasebook • North-East Asia on a shoestring • Seoul • Taiwan • Tibet • Tibet phrasebook • Tokyo

Travel Literature: Lost Japan

INDIAN SUBCONTINENT

Bangladesh • Bengali phrasebook • Delhi • Hindi/Urdu phrasebook • India • India & Bangladesh travel atlas • Indian Himalaya • Karakoram Highway • Nepal • Nepali phrasebook • Pakistan • Rajasthan • Sri Lanka • Sri Lanka phrasebook • Trekking in the Indian Himalaya • Trekking in the Karakoram & Hindukush • Trekking in the Nepal Himalaya

Travel Literature: In Rajasthan • Shopping for Buddhas

SOUTH-EAST ASIA

Bali & Lombok • Bangkok • Burmese phrasebook • Cambodia • Ho Chi Minh City • Indonesia • Indonesian phrasebook • Indonesian audio pack • Jakarta • Java • Laos • Lao phrasebook • Laos travel atlas • Malay phrasebook • Malaysia, Singapore & Brunei • Myanmar (Burma) • Philippines • Pilipino phrasebook • Singapore • South-East Asia on a shoestring • South-East Asia phrasebook • Thailand • Thailand travel atlas • Thai phrasebook • Thai audio pack • Thai Hill Tribes phrasebook • Vietnam • Vietnamese phrasebook • Vietnam travel atlas

MIDDLE EAST & CENTRAL ASIA

Arab Gulf States • Arabic (Egyptian) phrasebook • Central Asia • Iran • Israel & the Palestinian Territories • Israel & the Palestinian Territories travel atlas • Istanbul • Jerusalem • Jordan & Syria • Jordan, Syria & Lebanon travel atlas • Middle East • Turkey • Turkish phrasebook • Turkey travel atlas • Yemen

Travel Literature: The Gates of Damascus • Kingdom of the Film Stars: Journey into Jordan

ALSO AVAILABLE:

Travel with Children • Traveller's Tales

AUSTRALIA & THE PACIFIC

Australia • Australian phrasebook • Bushwalking in Australia • Bushwalking in Papua New Guinea • Fiji • Fijian phrasebook • Islands of Australia's Great Barrier Reef • Melbourne • Micronesia • New Caledonia • New South Wales & the ACT • New Zealand • Northern Territory • Outback Australia • Papua New Guinea • Papua New Guinea phrasebook • Queensland • Rarotonga & the Cook Islands • Samoa • Solomon Islands • South Australia • Sydney • Tahiti & French Polynesia • Tasmania • Tonga • Tramping in New Zealand • Vanuatu • Victoria • Western Australia

Travel Literature: Islands in the Clouds • Sean & David's Long Drive

THE LONELY PLANET STORY

Lonely Planet published its first book in 1973 in response to the numerous 'How did you do it?' questions Maureen a Tony Wheeler were asked after driving, bussing, hitching, sailing and railing their way from England to Australia.

Written at a kitchen table and hand collated, trimmed and stapled, *Across Asia on the Cheap* became an instant lo bestseller, inspiring thoughts of another book.

Eighteen months in South-East Asia resulted in their second guide, *South-East Asia on a shoestring*, which they put togeth in a backstreet Chinese hotel in Singapore in 1975. The 'yellow bible', as it quickly became known to backpackers arou the world, soon became *the* guide to the region. It has sold well over half a million copies and is now in its 9th edition, s retaining its familiar yellow cover.

Today there are over 240 titles, including travel guides, walking guides, language kits & phrasebooks, travel atlases and tra literature. The company is the largest independent travel publisher in the world. Although Lonely Planet initially specialise guides to Asia, today there are few corners of the globe that have not been covered.

The emphasis continues to be on travel for independent travellers. Tony and Maureen still travel for several months of ea year and play an active part in the writing, updating and quality control of Lonely Planet's guides.

They have been joined by over 70 authors and 170 staff at our offices in Melbourne (Australia), Oakland (USA), Lond (UK) and Paris (France). Travellers themselves also make a valuable contribution to the guides through the feedback receive in thousands of letters each year and on our web site.

The people at Lonely Planet strongly believe that travellers can make a positive contribution to the countries they visit, b through their appreciation of the countries' culture, wildlife and natural features, and through the money they spend addition, the company makes a direct contribution to the countries and regions it covers. Since 1986 a percentage of income from each book has been donated to ventures such as famine relief in Africa; aid projects in India; agricult projects in Central America; Greenpeace's efforts to halt French nuclear testing in the Pacific; and Amnesty Internatior

'I hope we send people out with the right attitude about travel. You realise when you travel that there are so m different perspectives about the world, so we hope these books will make people more interested in what they s Guidebooks can't really guide people. All you can do is point them in the right direction.'

– Tony Whe

LONELY PLANET PUBLICATIONS

Australia
PO Box 617, Hawthorn 3122, Victoria
tel: (03) 9819 1877 fax: (03) 9819 6459
e-mail: talk2us@lonelyplanet.com.au

USA
Embarcadero West, 155 Filbert St, Suite 251,
Oakland, CA 94607
tel: (510) 893 8555 TOLL FREE: 800 275-8555
fax: (510) 893 8563
e-mail: info@lonelyplanet.com

UK
10 Barley Mow Passage, Chiswick,
London W4 4PH
tel: (0181) 742 3161 fax: (0181) 742 2772
e-mail: lonelyplanetuk@compuserve.com

France:
71 bis rue du Cardinal Lemoine, 75005 Paris
tel: 1 44 32 06 20 fax: 1 46 34 72 55
e-mail: 100560.415@compuserve.com

World Wide Web: http://www.lonelyplanet.com
or *AOL keyword: lp*